IRISH LAND LAW

IRISH LAND LAW

by

J.C.W. WYLIE
LL.M. (Harvard), LL.D (Belfast)
Professor of Law and Head of the
Department of Law, University College, Cardiff

CONSULTANT EDITOR FOR THE
REPUBLIC OF IRELAND

The Hon. Mr. Justice Kenny
M.A., LL.B. (N.U.I.), HON. LL.D. (Dublin)
Former Judge of the Supreme Court of the
Republic of Ireland

SECOND EDITION

PROFESSIONAL BOOKS LIMITED
1986

First Edition	1975
Second Impression	1979
Third Impression	1980
Supp. (1975–80)	1981
Fourth Impression	1982
Fifth Impression	1983
Sixth Impression	1984
Second Edition	1986

Published in 1986 by
Professional Books Limited,
Milton Trading Estate, Abingdon, Oxon.
Typeset by WBC Print Ltd., Bristol
Printed and bound in Great Britain by
William Clowes Limited, Beccles and London

ISBN: Hardback: 0 86205 217 3
Paperback: 0 86205 218 1

PREFACE

Some ten years have elapsed since publication of the first edition of this book. After such a lapse of time the temptation existed to start afresh but, at the urging of several people, I have in general resisted that temptation. The fact is that the book in its present form has come to be accepted, for better or worse, by practitioners and students in both parts of Ireland, not to mention law teachers and the courts.

I have, therefore, concentrated my efforts on bringing everything up to date and attempting to incorporate a vast quantity of new material without damaging the basic structure. I am afraid that most statistics bore me and so I have not kept a count of the new cases and pieces of legislation which have had to be incorporated, but no doubt they are to be counted by the dozens, if not the hundreds in the case of the former. Periodical literature and, what I regard as the most welcome development of all since the early seventies when the first edition of this book was being written, the spate of new textbooks on Irish law have not been ignored, I hope. Otherwise the aims of the book remain as set out in the Preface to the first edition, which is reproduced hereinafter.

One significant development which readers will note is that this new edition incorporates cross-references to my other publications on Irish law, *viz. Irish Conveyancing Law* (1978) and the two casebooks, *A Casebook on Irish Land Law* (1984) and *A Casebook on Equity and Trusts in Ireland* (1985). This fulfils the aim of those later works which was to provide a comprehensive land lawyer's library, in which the various parts are closely interlinked. Thus readers will be able to tell at a glance whether the full report of a case referred to in the present text or its footnotes can be found in one of the casebooks, which will usually be so where it is a leading case.

Finally, I must point out that Mr. Justice Kenny's continuing poor health prevented him from playing any part in the preparation of this new edition, so that the sole responsibility for it is mine. However, since much of the first edition remains, and so much of that was subject to his scrutiny and benefited from his wisdom, his name rightly remains on the title page.

J.C.W. WYLIE
1st January, 1986

v

PREFACE TO THE FIRST EDITION

In 1970 the Incorporated Law Society of Ireland decided to promote the writing and publication of a new textbook on Irish land law. As a result of discussions which took place during 1970–71, this book was commissioned by the Society and sponsored by the Arthur Cox Foundation. The chairman of the Foundation, Mr. Justice Kenny, agreed to act as Consultant Editor for the law of the Republic of Ireland.

The need for a new textbook on the subject was clear. The last (3rd) edition of Strahan and Baxter's book on property law was published in 1926 and has long been out of print. Yet Irish land law in the second half of the twentieth century remains different in many respects from the law on the other side of the Irish Sea. There is no legislation in either part of Ireland corresponding to much of the English 1925 property legislation, e.g., the Law of Property and Settled Land Acts, 1925. The law in both parts of Ireland has been greatly influenced by Irish history and can be understood only by constant reference to that history. For this reason English textbooks must be used with extreme caution, though frequently students and practitioners have had to turn to them for want of anything better. Even if it does nothing else, it is hoped that this book will help Irish lawyers to meet the strictures of Kennedy C.J. given in the Irish Supreme Court in the case of R. (Moore) v. O'Hanrahan [1927] 1 I.R. 406 at 422: "Only too frequently one observes with regret even in this Court that diligence in the search for Irish precedent and authority is numbed by the facility of reference to English text-books."

As the Contents pages indicate, the book has a rather wider scope than the title might suggest. It seeks to cover not only land law as traditionally defined by law school curricula but also equity, trusts and succession. The book may even have a use as an introduction to conveyancing. These subjects are, of course, all closely connected, historically and conceptually, and their splitting up into separate compartments for the convenience of teaching should not be allowed to disguise this. It is also fair to point out that some of the concepts discussed in the book (e.g., trusts) relate also to property other than land. The primary purpose of the book remains, however, to deal with the law relating to land. The title "Land Law" had been preferred to what was the more common title, "Real Property," because the former is a more accurate title. The subject includes all interests in land and is not confined to real property only. Land law is also, perhaps, the title becoming more commonly used in law school curricula.

Publication of the book has coincided with a time of rapid increase in printing and publication costs. This, apart from any other factor, has meant that space was not unlimited and discussion has had to be kept within reasonable bounds. In making choices in this matter I have taken into account the existence of other books. This is particularly relevant with respect to chapters 17 and 18, which deal with landlord and tenant law. This topic has been the subject of numerous books even down to comparatively modern times, e.g., the late Judge (as he then was)

Deale's *Law of Landlord and Tenant in the Republic of Ireland* was published as recently as 1968. Because of this the opportunity was taken to reduce the discussion in chapters 17 and 18 from what would otherwise have been a much fuller treatment.

The absence of any other modern book on Irish law in general has inevitably influenced the writing of this one. The emphasis is on a statement of the law as it *is* rather than as it *ought* to be. However, my academic training has often prevented me from resisting the temptation to suggest that all is not well with some of the law as it is and references have been made throughout to the *Survey of the Land Law of Northern Ireland* (1971), of which I was a co-author. This contains numerous recommendations for reform, many of which are equally applicable to the Republic. In a sense this book aims partly at forming the basis of any further discussion of reform, a prerequisite of which must be a comprehensive knowledge of the law as it exists and operates in practice. It is also my firm belief that this book should be regarded as a beginning only. Much remains to be written on the subject and, in particular, a comprehensive book on conveyancing law and practice is needed. Apart from that, textbooks on related subjects, such as planning and housing law, compulsory purchase and compensation and taxation, would be extremely useful. These subjects could be alluded to only in this book, though some more extensive reference may be given in future Supplements. This is especially so with respect to taxation. The radical changes in the tax systems on both sides of the Irish Sea, such as the replacement of estate duty, made it impracticable to deal with taxation in detail in, *e.g.*, the chapters on trusts. The new legislation in both parts of Ireland will require lengthy study before its full effect can be stated accurately. It is hoped that the relevance of this legislation to chapters such as the ones relating to trusts can be dealt with in a future Supplement to this book.

The book has been written with both practitioners and students in mind. There is, of course, something of a conflict here. The practitioner is more concerned with having a convenient reference work whereas the student is more concerned with explanations. Every effort has been made to produce an acceptable compromise. So far as the practitioner is concerned, it is hoped that he will find it easy to look up the point in question, and then will find a reasonably clear statement of the law and a comprehensive citation of the authorities. The emphasis is, of course, on the Irish authorities and one of the "discoveries" of the research for this book has been the existence of an abundance of Irish material, much of which seems to have been largely forgotten in recent decades. The opportunity has also been taken to include references to several recent unreported decisions. Mr. Justice Kenny very kindly made available to me the transcripts of recent decisions in the Republic. Unreported decisions in Northern Ireland are digested regularly in the *Northern Ireland Legal Quarterly* and reference has been made to these. There is also considerable reference to English authorities, especially where Westminster legislation remains in force in Ireland (*e.g.*, the Settled Land Acts, 1882–90), and partly for comparative purposes.

So far as the student is concerned, every effort has been made to explain the law in as straightforward a manner as possible. To some extent the apparent conflict between the needs of the practitioner and the student can be reconciled because often the best explanation is one indicating how the law operates in practice. The gap between law in theory and law in practice is, perhaps, not as great in land law as it is in other subjects. The student will also find fairly extensive reference to periodical literature, from which further guidance may be sought.

The law of both the Republic of Ireland and Northern Ireland is covered. This, of course, has meant that in some chapters separate treatment has had to be given to the two jurisdictions. However, this has proved to be the exception rather than the rule and integrated discussion occurs wherever possible. Unless the contrary is expressly indicated, it can be taken that the law stated applies to both jurisdictions.

One other important point should be noted. Paragraph numbers (usually corresponding to paragraphs of the text) have been inserted throughout the book, on a chapter by chapter basis. Thus the third and one hundred and third paragraphs of chapter 17 are designated: 17.003 and 17.103. All cross-references in the footnotes and references in the Tables of Statutes and Cases and in the Index are to these paragraph numbers, so that the reader can tell at a glance the chapter to which he should turn. Cross-references in future Supplements to the book will also be to these paragraph numbers. The references in the Contents pages are, of course, to page numbers.

At this point, perhaps, a few remarks may be made about the precise contents of the book. Chapter 1 contains what is probably a rather more extensive historical introduction than is usual in textbooks nowadays. This is essential, however, for the student of Irish land law. Much of the history of the island has revolved around the ownership of the land and the law's development has inevitably reflected this. Chapters 2 and 3, on tenure and equity, reiterate this principle and chapter 3 also emphasises the influence of equity on the development of land law. The student must appreciate this from the outset and chapter 3 seeks to give him an overall picture of the extent of the influence. Though Part II deals with various estates and interests which make up ownership of land, it should be noted that some other interests are dealt with in a later Part. Part VIII deals with covenants and licences (and similar interests) because these interests are more easily understood *after* study of landlord and tenant law, which forms the subject-matter of Part VII.

Many people have given me help in the writing of this book, but three in particular must be mentioned. As I have already indicated, Mr. Justice Kenny acted as Consultant Editor for the law of the Republic of Ireland and he has very kindly undertaken to accept joint responsibility for statements of the law of the Republic. Together we have gone through the entire manuscript at regular intervals over the past two years. It has been a fascinating experience for an academic to work so closely with a judge of his knowledge and experience of Irish chancery practice. Numerous amendments and additions have been suggested by him and, indeed, parts of two chapters were substantially re-drafted by him. I must record my deepest appreciation for all his help in the project. I would also like to thank his wife and family for their very kind hospitality during my frequent visits to Dublin.

Two other people have seen drafts of the entire manuscript. Professor L. A. Sheridan first introduced me to Irish land law when I was a student at Belfast and most of my academic career has been spent in close association with him. As some of his comments on the manuscript indicated, he is still teaching me! Mr. John F. Buckley, Solicitor and sometime lecturer in Land Law and Conveyancing for the Incorporated Law Society of Ireland, has also saved me from many a slip or error. I must, however, emphasise that neither Professor Sheridan nor Mr. Buckley can be held in any way responsible for statements in the book.

Finally, most grateful thanks are due to my mother, who has spent much of her free time in the past four years typing various drafts of the manuscript. It has often been a wretched job, but she has never complained. Nor has my wife, who has had to put up with much during the past two years.

The publishers and printers must also be congratulated for an excellent job done with the utmost speed. Every effort has been made to ensure that the book states the law as on May 1, 1975.

J.C.W. WYLIE.

University College,
Cardiff.

Most Irish lawyers are not, I think, aware of their rich heritage of Irish case law on chancery and property matters. Decisions given before 1924 are rarely cited in court though the judgments of Chatterton, Holmes, Fitzgibbon and Walker are as learned and well-written as those of their contemporaries in the judiciary in England. As Mr. Wylie and I worked on this book during (to use one of Arthur Cox's favourite expressions) what other people call the vacations, my admiration for his industry in searching the Irish Reports and Digests for authorities grew. I hope that this book will lead to the more frequent citation of Irish authorities in court and that it will induce those practising and studying the law in the Republic of Ireland and in Northern Ireland to take pride in our joint inheritance.

JOHN KENNY.

The High Court,
Dublin.

THE ARTHUR COX FOUNDATION

Arthur Cox, classical scholar, senator and former President of the Incorporated Law Society of Ireland, was associated both as director of and solicitor to many industries which have become great enterprises. He was a specialist in company law and was Chairman of the Company Law Reform Committee. He made many outstanding contributions to our community. When he decided to retire from practice, a number of his clients, professional colleagues and other friends thought that the most appropriate tribute to him would be a fund to subsidise the publication of legal textbooks. The market in Ireland for these is so small that very few of them have been written and their absence is a severe handicap to lawyers and law students. There was a generous response to our appeal.

After his retirement he was ordained a priest and went to Zambia to do missionary work. He died there as a result of a motor car accident.

He often spoke to me about the importance of having textbooks on Irish law and their vital role in the education of students and in the practice of the law. So I was happy to accept Mr. Wylie's invitation to act as Consultant Editor for this book. The Trustees of the Foundation (Mr. C. Russell Murphy, F.C.A., The Incorporated Law Society and I) are glad to have been able to subsidise the publication of Mr. Wylie's book. It is appropriate that those who use it (and we hope that there will be many) will be reminded of Arthur Cox. He would have been glad to think that his name would be remembered, in part at least, by its association with a legal textbook.

The High Court,   JOHN KENNY.
    Dublin.

May, 1975.

CONTENTS

PART X—EXTINGUISHMENT OF INTERESTS

CHAPTER 23

CHAPTER 24

PART XI—DISABILITIES

CHAPTER 25

TABLE OF STATUTES

[*N.B.* References in this Table are to *paragraph* numbers.]

1. STATUTES OF THE PARLIAMENT OF IRELAND

2. Statutes of the Parliaments of England, Great Britain and the United Kingdom

3. STATUTES OF SAORSTÁT ÉIREANN AND OF THE OIREACHTAS

4. STATUTES OF THE PARLIAMENT OF NORTHERN IRELAND

[Note: Orders in Council made under the U.K. Northern Ireland (Temporary Provisions) Act, 1972, have, by virtue of section 1 (3) of that Act, effect as Acts of the Parliament of Northern Ireland.]

5. OTHER STATUTES

TABLE OF STATUTORY INSTRUMENTS, RULES AND ORDERS

[*N.B.* References in this Table are to *paragraph* numbers.]

1. REPUBLIC OF IRELAND STATUTORY INSTRUMENTS

2. NORTHERN IRELAND STATUTORY RULES AND ORDERS

3. UNITED KINGDOM STATUTORY RULES AND ORDERS

TABLE OF ARTICLES OF
IRISH CONSTITUTION

[*N.B.* References in this Table are to *paragraph* numbers.]

TABLE OF CASES

[*N.B.* References in this Table are to *paragraph* numbers.]

liv

TABLE OF ABBREVIATIONS

Irish Reports

Alc. & Nap.	Alcock and Napier, King's Bench Reports, 1831–3.
Alc.Reg.Cas.	Alcock, Registry Cases, 1832–41.
Arm.Mac. & Og.	Armstrong, Macartney and Ogle, *Nisi Prius* Reports, 1840–2.
Ba. & B.	Ball and Beatty, Chancery Reports, 1802–9.
Batty	Batty, King's Bench Reports, 1825–6.
Beat.	Beatty, Chancery Reports, 1813–30.
Bl.D. & O.	Blackham, Dundas and Osborne, *Nisi Prius* Reports. 1846–8.
Con. & L.	Connor and Lawson, Chancery Reports, 1841–3.
Cr. & Dix	Crawford and Dix, Cases on the Circuits, 1839–46.
Cr. & Dix, Abr.Cas.	Crawford and Dix, Abridged Notes of Cases, 1837–8.
Dav.	Davies, King's Bench Reports, 1604–12.
Dru. *temp.* Nap.	Drury, Select Cases during the time of Lord Napier, 1858–9.
Dru. *temp.* Sug.	Drury, Report of Cases during the time of Chancellor Sugden, 1843–4.
Dr. & Wal.	Drury and Walsh, Chancery Reports during the time of Lord Plunket, 1837–40.
Dr. & War.	Drury and Warren, Chancery Reports during the time of Lord Sugden, 1841–3.
Fl. & K.	Flanagan and Kelly, Chancery (Rolls) Reports, 1840–2.
Fox & Sm.	Fox and Smith, King's Bench Reports, 1822–4.
Glasc.	Glascock, King's Bench, Common Pleas and Exchequer Reports, 1831–2.
Hayes	Hayes, Exchequer Reports, 1830–2.
Hay. & Jon.	Hayes and Jones, Exchequer Reports, 1832–4.
Hud. & Br.	Hudson and Brook, King's Bench and Exchequer Reports, 1827–31.
Ir.Ch.R.	Irish Chancery Reports, 1850–66.
Ir.Cir.Rep.	Irish Circuit Reports (Cases on the Six Circuits), 1841–3.
I.C.L.R.	Irish Common Law Reports, 1849–66.
Ir.Eq.R.	Irish Equity Reports, 1838–51.
Ir.Jur.(o.s.)	Irish Jurist Reports (Old Series), 1849–55.
Ir.Jur.(n.s.)	Irish Jurist Reports (New Series), 1855–66.
Ir.Jur.Rep.	Irish Jurist Reports, 1935–65.
Ir.L.R.	Irish Law Reports, Common Law, 1838–50.
I.L.R.M.	Irish Law Reports Monthly, 1980–(current)
I.L.T.R.	Irish Law Times Reports, 1867–(current). (*Note*: notes or digests only of cases in the Irish Law Times and Solicitors' Journal are signified by the reference "I.L.T." or "I.L.T.S.J.")
I.R.	Irish Reports, 1894–(current).
I.R.C.L.	Irish Reports, Common Law, 1867–77.
I.R.Eq.	Irish Reports, Equity, 1866–77.
Ir.Term Rep.	Irish Term Reports (Ridgeway, Lapp and Schoales), 1793–5.
Ir.W.L.R.	Irish Weekly Law Reports, 1895–1902.
Jebb. & B.	Jebb and Bourke, Queen's Bench Reports, 1841–2.
Jebb & Sym.	Jebb and Symes, Queen's Bench Reports, 1838–41.
Jo. & Lat.	Jones and Latouche, Chancery Reports, 1844–6.
Jon.	Jones, Exchequer Reports, 1834–8.
Jon. & Car.	Jones and Carey, Exchequer Reports, 1838–9.
L.J.Ir.	Law Journal, Irish Supplement, 1931–4.
L.Rec(o.s.)	Law Recorder (Old Series), 1827–31.
L.Rec(n.s.)	Law Recorder (New Series), 1833–8.
L.R.Ir.	Law Reports (Ireland), 1878–93.
Leg.Rep.	Legal Reporter, 1840–3.
Ll. & G. *temp.* Plunk.	Lloyd and Goold, Chancery Cases during the time of Lord Plunket, 1834–9.
Ll. & G. *temp.* Sug.	Lloyd and Goold, Chancery Cases during the time of Lord Sugden, 1835.
Long. & Town.	Longfield and Townsend, Exchequer Reports, 1841–2.
Mol.	Molloy, Chancery Reports, 1827–31.
N.I.J.R.	New Irish Jurist Reports, 1900–5.
N.I.	Northern Ireland Law Reports, 1925–(current).
Ridgw.P.C.	Ridgeway, Parliamentary Reports, 1784–96.
Rowe	Rowe, Interesting Cases, 1798–1823.
S. & Sc.	Sausse and Scully, Chancery (Rolls) Reports, 1837–40.

Sch. & Lef.	Schoales and Lefroy, Chancery Reports, 1802–6.
Sm. & Bat.	Smith and Batty, King's Bench Reports, 1824–5.
Vern. & Scriv.	Vernon and Scriven, Irish Reports, 1786–8.

Periodicals

A.J.C.L.	American Journal of Comparative Law.
Alberta L.Rev.	Alberta Law Review.
A.L.R.	University of Western Australia, Annual Law Review.
B.T.R.	British Tax Review.
Cambrian L.Rev.	Cambrian Law Review.
C.B.R.	Canadian Bar Review.
C.L.J.	Cambridge Law Journal.
C.L.P.	Current Legal Problems.
Col.L.Rev.	Columbia Law Review.
Conv.	Conveyancer and Property Lawyer (New Series).
De Paul L.Rev.	De Paul Law Review
D.U.L.J.(n.s.)	Dublin University Law Journal (New Series).
E.H.R.	English Historical Review.
Ér.	Ériu.
Gaz.I.L.S.I.	Gazette of the Incorporated Law Society of Ireland.
Hast.L.J.	Hastings Law Journal.
Hist.Stud.	Historical Studies.
H.L.R.	Harvard Law Review.
I.C.L.Q.	International and Comparative Law Quarterly.
I.E.R. (4th Series)	Irish Ecclesiastical Record (4th series, 1903–12).
I.H.S.	Irish Historical Studies.
I.L.T.S.J.	Irish Law Times and Solicitors' Journal.
Ir.Ecc.Rec.	Irish Ecclesiastical Record (5th series, 1913–current).
Ir.Jur.	Irish Jurist.
Ir.Jur.(N.S.)	Irish Jurist (New Series).
J.D.S.S.	Journal of the Dublin Statistical Society.
J.I.B.I.	Journal of the Institute of Bankers in Ireland.
Jo.R.S.A.I.	Journal of the Royal Society of Antiquaries of Ireland.
J.S.S.I.S.I.	Journal of the Statistical and Social Inquiry Society of Ireland.
L. & Cont.Prob.	Law and Contemporary Problems.
Louis.L.Rev.	Louisiana Law Review.
L.Q.R.	Law Quarterly Review.
L.Soc.Gaz.	Law Society Gazette (England).
M.L.R.	Modern Law Review.
Mich.L.Rev.	Michigan Law Review.
M.U.L.R.	University of Malaya Law Review.
New L.J.	New Law Journal.
N.I.L.Q.	Northern Ireland Legal Quarterly.
N.Y.U.L.R.	New York University Law Review.
Proc.Brit.Acad.	Proceedings of the British Academy.
Proc.I.C.H.C.	Proceedings of the Irish Catholic Historical Committee.
Proc.R.I.A.	Proceedings of the Royal Irish Academy.
Pub.Admin.Ir.	Public Administration in Ireland.
Rev.Pol.	Review of Politics.
S.A.L.J.	South African Law Journal.
Sol.Jo.	Solicitors' Journal.
Stud. Hib.	Studia Hibernica.
Sydney L.Rev.	Sydney Law Review.
U.Brit. Col.L.Rev.	University of British Columbia Law Review.
U.Penn.L.Rev.	University of Pennsylvania Law Review.
U.Q.L.J.	University of Queensland Law Journal.
U.Toronto L.J.	University of Toronto Law Journal.
Vand.L.Rev.	Vanderbilt Law Review.
Y.L.J.	Yale Law Journal.

PART I

INTRODUCTION

CHAPTER 1

INTRODUCTION

I. NATURE OF LAND LAW

1.01. Land law, or the law of real property as it is frequently called,[1] is concerned with rights and liabilities which arise under our law in respect of land.[2] "Land" in this context includes things attached to land, such as buildings and other permanent structures.[3] It therefore includes flats situated in tower blocks, where each flat may be separately owned despite the fact that only the basement flats touch the ground.[4] But the law is more concerned with defining the wide variety of rights and interests in or over land which may be said to make up "ownership." These rights and interests may be enjoyed in respect of one's own land or they may be enjoyed in respect of land more generally owned by others. Mostly these rights and interests are created by the action of private parties but increasingly in recent decades more and more rights and liabilities in respect of land have been imposed on private parties by the state through legislation.[5] Having defined the rights and interests of the parties, the law then goes on to say how those parties may deal with their rights and interests. It must always be borne in mind that land was until the Industrial Revolution the main source of wealth, that it is still an important source of wealth and it is as much, if not more, a commercial commodity today as in past eras. This is where land law merges into its closely associated

---

[1] The standard English textbooks are: Cheshire and Burn, *The Modern Law of Real Property* (13th ed., 1982); Megarry, *Manual of the Law of Real Property* (6th ed. by Hayton, 1982); Megarry and Wade, *The Law of Real Property* (5th ed., 1984). See also Gray and Symes, *Real Property and Real People* (1981).

[2] See Pearce, *Land Law* (1985). Also Lawson and Rudden, *The Law of Real Property* (2nd ed., 1982); Riddall, *Introduction to Land Law* (3rd ed., 1983).

[3] Denman, *Origins of Ownership* (1959); Lightwood, *Possession of Land* (1894); Noyes, *Institution of Property* (1936); Garner, "Meaning of 'Land' in Administrative Statutes" (1957) 21 Conv. 141; Kiralfy, "The Meaning of 'Land' in Property Legislation" (1956) 20 Conv. 10. For the purpose of statutes passed before 25th October 1922, the word "land" in the Republic of Ireland has the definition given to it by the Interpretation Act, 1889, s. 3, while in those passed since the establishment of the Irish Free State, it is given an "including" definition by the Interpretation Act, 1937. Ss. 4 and 12 of, and the Sched. to, the 1937 Act provide that, in every Act of the Oireachtas, the word "land" includes "messuages, tenements and hereditaments, houses and buildings of any tenure." The Interpretation Act (N.I.), 1954, s. 45 (1) *(a)* defines "land" in Northern Ireland statutes as including "(i) messuages, tenements and hereditaments of any tenure; (ii) land covered by water; (iii) any estate in land or water; and (iv) houses or other buildings or structures whatsoever." See also Challis, *Law of Real Property* (3rd ed., 1911), ch. VII.

[4] Leyser, "Ownership of Flats: Comparative Study" (1958) 7 I.C.L.Q. 31; Richardson, "Private Property Rights in Air Space" (1953) 31 C.B.R. 117; Scamell, "Legal Aspects of Flat Schemes" (1961) 14 C.L.P. 161; Tolson, " 'Land' without Earth: Freehold Flats in English Law" (1950) 14 Conv. 350. See the discussion in Wylie, *Irish Conveyancing Law* (1978), para. 17. 11 *et seq.* See also George and George, *The Sale of Flats* (5th ed., 1984).

[5] Potter, "New Land Law under the Town and Country Planning Bill' (1947) 11 Conv. 147; Reich, "The New Property" (1964) Y.L.J. 733; Gray and Symes, *Real Property and Real People* (1981), ch. 1. See paras. 1.63–80, *post.*

subject—conveyancing.[6] These preliminary remarks may become clearer if a typical land transaction is given by way of illustration of the nature of land law.

1.02. P is contemplating the purchase of a large house in one of the residential areas of Dublin (or Belfast). He is considering converting the house into a small hotel, with a public restaurant and bar. At present the house is occupied by V and his family, and V has expressed a willingness to sell the house to P. At first sight this may seem to be a simple, straightforward trans-action. Yet to a conveyancer the statement of facts just given raises a myriad of problems. Here are some of the immediate questions that would spring to his mind:

1. What estate or interest in the house does V have, which gives him the right to sell it to P? The point here is that V's occupation of the house by no means indicates necessarily that he has the right to sell it, *i.e.*, so as to give P rights of ownership sufficient for his purposes. V may be in any one of a number of positions ranging from a pure squatter with no rights to the property at all[7] to a freeholder, holding it subject to the minimum of restrictions.[8] He may be a tenant of the property, holding under a landlord who has superior rights,[9] or he may be one of several co-owners who have equal interests in the property.[10] He may be a beneficiary holding under a trust, where the house is part of the property held by the trustees,[11] or be the life tenant occupying under an old family settlement.[12] In each case his ability to transfer sufficient rights of ownership in the house to P for his purposes will vary, and much of the discussion in the ensuing chapters is taken up with explaining why this is so.

2. Even supposing V has some substantial rights in the property to sell to P, there are very likely to be many restrictions of a private nature which P ought to take into account. As is explained later in this book, most urban land in Ireland is held on very complicated titles, which have resulted from centuries of confiscations, resettlements and sub-divisions of the land.[13] The consequence is that many parcels of urban land are subject to rights over them owned by other people, whether or not those other people own or occupy neighbouring land. Thus it is quite possible that V's house and the land upon which it is situated are subject to restrictive covenants, prohibiting use of the property for certain purposes (*e.g.*, use other than residential or for sale of intoxicating liquor).[14] The owners of these covenants might be able to enforce them against P and thereby thwart his development of the property. Other or the same people might own equally burdensome rights from P's point of view: some might own easements, like rights of way or rights to light which would affect or be affected by P's conversion of the property into an hotel; some might even own apparently useless rights like shooting, fishing, mining and quarrying rights.[15] They may appear useless now because the neighbourhood has

---

[6] See generally, Wylie, *Irish Conveyancing Law* (1978).
[7] Ch. 23, *post.*
[8] Ch. 4, *post.*
[9] Ch. 17, *post.*
[10] Ch. 7, *post.*
[11] Ch. 9, *post.*
[12] Ch. 8, *post.*
[13] Paras. 1.27–34, *infra.*
[14] Ch. 19, *post.*
[15] Ch. 6, *post.*

changed so much since their original creation. but in the eyes of the law they do still exist, though there may be difficulties in their enforcement. P will have to come to some arrangement with the owners of these rights if he is going to be able to develop without the fear of future actions by the owners. Obtaining an indemnity from V in respect of them will probably not provide sufficient protection; it rarely does in the case of a developer engaging in substantial building works on the premises.[16] And Ireland, like Britain, until recently, has never adopted the system of title insurance (to cover risks taken by developers of property with complicated titles) so prevalent in some countries, notably the United States of America.[17] If V's interest in the property is held under a lease, he may not be able to dispose of it without getting the consent of his landlord.[18] The question will also arise whether V has mortgaged or charged his interest.[19] If he has, P may be liable for the amount secured by the mortgage or charge unless this is paid out of the purchase money. P has thus to have the title investigated and this will involve searches in registries, *e.g.*, the Land Registry or Registry of Deeds.[20]

3. In addition to these questions, modern statute law, with its emphasis on public control of land use, has imposed many new restrictions. For example, development such as that proposed by P would be subject to the town and country planning legislation, and he will have to obtain planning permission from the relevant planning authority. The actual conversion operations relating to the hotel will probably be subject to control by the building bye-laws of the relevant local authority. He will need a licence under the Licensing Acts for the bar, and since the premises are for use by the general public he will find that he has to comply with a wide variety of regulations governing public health, fire, safety and car parking facilities. Care will have to be taken to see that no public authority has already made plans with respect to the property, which may involve the exercise of powers of compulsory purchase. P would not wish to go to the trouble of developing the property if in a few years' time a new road is going to pass through it or if it is going to be razed to the ground as part of a major clearance and redevelopment scheme for that area.

4. Other obvious factors to be taken into account by P are the time and expense involved in completing the formalities of the sale. The title complications mentioned above will obviously affect these matters. Another question that could affect them is whether the title to the property is registered or not. The fact that the title is registered could save the conveyancers much time and trouble in checking the title for P; unfortunately, since this is urban land it is quite likely that the title is not registered.[21]

5. Finally there is the question of whether P has to raise money for the purchase and redevelopment of the property. If he does have to seek loans he will usually have to provide security for repayment to the lenders, be they

[16] See para. 19.22, *post.*
[17] See Wylie, *Irish Conveyancing Law* (1978), paras. 1.54–56.
[18] Ch. 17, *post.*
[19] Ch. 12, *post.*
[20] Chs. 21 and 22, *post.*
[21] Ch. 21, *post.*

bankers, building societies, insurance companies or any other loan-financing agency. The most common method of providing security is to create a mortgage on the property itself. So P will need advice both as to the types of lenders he he can approach and as to the types of mortgages that can be created.[22] In matters of this nature considerations relating to taxation will become important.

1.03. Land law is, therefore, concerned with the wide variety of rights and interests which may exist in land, and with the various methods of dealing with them. It is very rare for one person only to be the absolute owner of a particular piece of land. Usually the various rights and interests that have been created have been split up among several people, the so-called "fragmentation of ownership" has occurred. This splitting up of the ownership and enjoyment of rights and interests in land can be achieved in many ways and for different reasons. Thus rights may be enjoyed concurrently; this can take the form of co-ownership of rights of equal value or ownership of rights of unequal value. Rights may be enjoyed successively, with the ownership of the land "settled" for decades ahead. The land may be used primarily as a family asset, where the ownership and enjoyment of rights, concurrently or successively, are confined to people within a particular family group. On the other hand, the land may be used as a purely commercial asset; it may be regarded as a capital asset to be invested to produce income or as a valuable piece of security for a loan. Each of these aspects of land law will be examined in the ensuing chapters of this book.

1.04. The foregoing discussion should help to explain why transactions relating to land often create many difficulties. It is because titles to land can be so complex that the conveyancing process can take so long to complete. No doubt this is often frustrating for the layman; it is certainly often frustrating for his lawyer who is trying to ensure that his client gets what he wants. It may be questioned whether the system need be like this, but the truth of the matter lies largely in the principle that, if the public wish to do complicated things with their land, they will have to reconcile themselve to a complicated system of law designed to facilitate their desires.

II. IRISH LAND LAW

1.05. Irish lawyers commonly assert the view that of all the branches of the law, land law has resisted most over the centuries the influence of English common law and has retained its particularly "Irish" characteristics.[23] Ireland may have

---

[22] Ch. 12, *post*. See also Wylie, *Irish Conveyancing Law* (1978), ch. 4.

[23] On the subject generally, see Pearce, *Land Law* (1985). See also Challis's *Real Property* (3rd ed., 1911), *Irish Supplement* (1956, Sheridan); De Moleyns, *Landowners' and Agents' Practical Guide* (8th ed., 1899); Donaldson, *Some Comparative Aspects of Irish Law* (1957), ch. 6; Ferguson and Vance, *Tenure and Improvement of Land in Ireland* (1851); Leet and McCutcheon, *A Sketch of the Law of Property in Land in Ireland* (1937); Strahan and Baxter, *Law of Real Property* (3rd ed., 1926); Boyd, "Law of Property in Land in Ireland" (1958) 60 J.I.B.I. 98, 184 and 263; Delany, "English and Irish Land Law—Some Contrasts" (1956) 5 A.J.C.L. 471; Lawson, "Land Law in Northern Ireland and the Republic of Ireland" (1958) 7 I.C.L.Q. 148; Sheridan, "Irish Private Law and the English Lawyer" (1952) 1 I.C.L.Q. 196.

been the venue of the "first adventure of the common law,"[24] but the subsequent social and political history of the country has decreed that its development on this side of the Irish Sea has frequently not been in accord with its development in its birthplace. Most of the remaining pages of this chapter will be taken up with explaining this historical background, a knowledge of which is essential to the understanding of Irish land law. But first something must be said about the composition of Irish land law in general.

1.06. In the latter half of the twentieth century, Irish land law is a mixture of four basic elements: (1) *English common law,* in the sense of principles grounded in the feudal system introduced into England by the Normans, and developed over the centuries by conveyancers and judges[25]; (2) *English statute law,* which includes statutes passed at Westminster for both England and Ireland and statutes passed exclusively for Ireland; (3) *Irish statute law,* that is, statutes passed in Ireland for the whole of Ireland; or one of its two presently separate jurisdictions, the Republic of Ireland and Northern Ireland; (4) *Irish common law,* in the sense of principles fashioned by Irish conveyancers and judges exclusively for Ireland.

1.07. There are three major points to be borne in mind in this context, for they affect in a crucial manner the remainder of the discussion in this book. The first is that the legislation which makes up such an important part of the land law is derived in Ireland from several sources.[26] There are seven main sources: (a) statutes of the Parliament of Ireland passed during the years 1310–1800, in which year the Act of Union[27] amalgamated the Parliaments of Ireland and Great Britain; (b) statutes of the Parliaments of England and Great Britain from 1226–1800[28]; (c) statutes of the Parliament of the United Kingdom of Great Britain and Ireland from 1801–1922 and, for Northern Ireland, from 1922 to date[29]; (d) statutes of the Parliament of what is now the Republic of Ireland, the Oireachtas, from 1922 to date; (e) statutes of the Parliament of Northern Ireland, from 1921–72; (f) Orders in Council made under the Northern Ireland (Temporary Provisions) Act, 1972 (which prorogued the Northern Ireland Parliament, until it was abolished by the Northern Ireland Constitution Act, 1973), from 1972–73 and from 1974 to date under the Northern Ireland Act, 1974; (g) Measures of the Northern Ireland Assembly, established under the Northern Ireland Assembly Act, 1973, made under the Northern Ireland Constitution Act, 1973, during 1973–74 until the Assembly was prorogued in the Spring of 1974. Apart from the obvious complexity which arises from such a

---

[24] Johnston, 'The First Adventure of the Common Law" (1920) 36 L.Q.R. 9; Maitland, "The Introduction of English Law into Ireland" (1889) IV E.H.R. 516; Moran, "The Migration of the Common Law: 7: The Republic of Ireland" (1960) 76 L.Q.R. 69.

[25] Simpson, *A History of Land Law* (2nd ed., 1985).

[26] Much learning on this subject is contained in A. G. Donaldson's unpublished Ph.D. thesis, 1952, Queen's University of Belfast, entitled "The Application in Ireland of English and British Legislation made before 1801."

[27] Which came into force on Jan. 1, 1801.

[28] The Parliament of England operating in the period 1226–1707, the Parliament of Great Britain in the period 1707–1800.

[29] Statutes of the Parliament of the United Kingdom of Great Britain and, since 1920, Northern Ireland may be extended to Northern Ireland and, indeed, much important law, especially in the public law field, is contained in such statutes.

multiplicity of sources, the further difficulty has arisen sometimes that duplicative provisions come into force which are not always easily reconciled.[30]

1.08. The second point to be made is an even more obvious one. It is, of course, that Irish land law nowadays means the land law of two independent jurisdictions, the Republic of Ireland and Northern Ireland. They do have very much in common in the field of land law because of their common history prior to 1920, but there is no denying that legislative developments since 1920 have resulted in considerable divergencies. Furthermore, since land law belongs generally to the field of private law delegated to the Northern Ireland Parliament by the Government of Ireland Act, 1920, there have been equally considerable divergencies between the land law of Northern Ireland and that of the rest of the United Kingdom, particularly England and Wales. It is still the case that land law in Northern Ireland is much closer to that in the Republic of Ireland, close enough to permit integrated treatment in a book such as the present. However, it should be pointed out that the divergencies between the law of the Republic and that of Northern Ireland are such that separate discussion is from time to time introduced in some of the ensuing chapters. It is hoped that this will clarify the statement of the law applicable in each jurisdiction.

1.09. The third point is all important. Land law can only be understood if its essentially historical and evolving nature is always remembered. A knowledge of legal history is often essential for its understanding. The answer to a question on modern land law may lie in some eighteenth-century Act of Parliament or decision. This makes the subject difficult to master.

III. HISTORICAL BACKGROUND

1.10. The history of Irish land law may be divided into five main eras: (1) prior to the twelfth century, the period of ancient Irish law; (2) the twelfth to seventeenth centuries, the period of the introduction of English common or feudal law by the Normans and its eventual displacement of the old Irish law; (3) the seventeenth to eighteenth centuries, the period of confiscation and resettlement of Irish land by the English, and sowing of the seeds of what came to be called universally "the Irish land problem"; (4) the nineteenth century, the period of increased legislative activity at Westminster, the beginning of the resolution of the land problem and the passing of fundamental reforms at the end of the century; (5) the twentieth century, the carrying through of the reforms begun at the end of the previous century and the rapid growth of state intervention in, and public control over, the use of land and the rights of owners and occupiers to do what they like with it.

---

[30] See para. 17.071, *post.*

A. ANCIENT IRISH LAW: PRE-TWELFTH CENTURY

1.11 As an introduction, some words written in 1966 by a distinguished Irish scholar, Professor D. A. Binchy, should be remembered:

> "The study of native Irish law is still in its infancy. A considerable proportion of the sources has not even been published, and the extremely difficult language in which they are written, full of archaisms and obscure technical terms, raises problems of translation and interpretation so formidable as to scare away the average Celtic scholar. Yet until all sources have been properly edited and translated the jurist who attempts to work on them does so at his peril unless he is prepared to acquire expert knowledge of the original language."[31]

The sources of which Professor Binchy was speaking were the ancient Irish law tracts written down during the seventh and eighth centuries A.D.[32] The custodians of these laws, which were by no means universal in their application or observance by the various tribes throughout Ireland, were a professional class of jurists, the "brehons," thought to be descendants ultimately of the druids. The extreme conservatism of the brehons led to "canonisation" of the laws, and from the ninth century onwards there were produced many commentaries and glosses on the original tracts. The result has been that historians seeking information from the tracts which have survived are faced not only with the problems of transcription and translation, but with the task of distinguishing the later gloss from the original text. Sadly many scholars have failed to meet this test, including Sir Henry Maine,[33] and have thereby invoked the wrath of later scholars.[34] The British Royal Commission[35] appointed in 1852 to supervise the transcription and translation of the ancient law tracts eventually produced woefully inaccurate English versions.[36] Later scholars have pointed out that this was hardly unexpected; the Commission simply was not equipped to do the job, though they did employ the two leading Irish scholars of the day, John O'Donovan and Eugene O'Curry.[37] It has only been in the past few decades that scholars like Thurneysen, MacNeill and Binchy have undertaken the painstaking, and still incomplete, transcription of the materials which have survived, from which accurate translation can be made.

---

[31] "Ancient Irish Law" (1966) 1 Ir.Jur.(N.S.) 84; see also his earlier article, "The Linguistic and Historical Value of the Irish Law Tracts" (1943) XXIX Proc. Brit-Acad. 195 and later one, "Irish History and Irish Law" (1975) 15 Stud. Hib. 7, (1976) 16 Stud. Hib. 7. *Cf.* Gavan Duffy P. in *Foyle and Bann Fisheries Ltd. v. Att.-Gen.* (1949) 83 I.L.T.R. 29 at 41.

[32] On this subject generally, see Coghlan, *Ancient Land Tenures of Ireland* (1933); Ginnell, *The Brehon Laws* (1924); Macauliffe, *Gaelic Law* (1924); MacNeill, *Phases of Irish History* (1919), *Early Irish Laws and Institutions* (1935); Thurneysen (and others), *Studies in Early Irish Law* (1936). See also Ronayne, "Seandlithe na nGael: An Annotated Bibliography of the Ancient Laws of Ireland" (1982) 17 Ir.Jur. (N.S.) 131; McLeod, "Ronayne's 'Seandlithe na nGael': A Supplement" (1983) 18 Ir.Jur. (N.S.) 360.

[33] *Early History of Institutions* (1875).

[34] See especially MacNeill, *op. cit.*, and Coghlan, *op. cit.* See Tierney, *Eoin MacNeill: Scholar and Man of Action 1867–1945* (ed. Martin; 1981).

[35] Its members included Francis Blackburne, Lord Chancellor of Ireland, Richard Pigot, Lord Chief Baron of the Court of Exchequer and Joseph Napier, Attorney-General for Ireland.

[36] *Ancient Laws and Institutions of Ireland*, 6 volumes, published from 1865–1901.

[37] Unfortunately, they were both dead when the first volume of the Commission's work was published in 1865 and were unable to correct the translations made from their transcriptions from the old Irish of the tracts.

1.12. In the meantime, modern scholars have been increasing our knowledge of the brehon law and early Irish society, some of which is of interest to the student of land law.[38] The ancient Irish law continued to exert influence until the seventeenth century and it is useful to compare some of its salient features with those of the feudal system introduced by the Normans in the twelfth century.

1.13. Ancient Irish society was essentially decentralised[39]; it knew nothing of the Norman theory of centralisation through a system of land tenure emanating from one chief lord or king.[40] The key unit in the system was the clan or tribe (the *tuath*), of which there were over a hundred. Each tribe was ruled over by a tribal king or lord, and the tribes themselves were often grouped together under the lordship of some royal overlord such as the King of Leinster or Connaught. The society was a hierarchical structure, under which a man's status was closely connected with the obvious sources of wealth in those times, the land and farm stock.[41] There were free and unfree classes within the society. The free class included property owners, higher craftsmen (like house or boat builders) and, of course, learned scholars like the brehons. The unfree class included lower craftsmen and those who did not own any land or have other possessions. The hierarchical structure with respect to the land, which is our main concern here, consisted of freemen of the landed class at the top (subject, of course, to the chief of the *tuath*) who usually granted their surplus stock and land to a class of clients (*céli*). There were two classes of client, free and unfree. The free client received capital from his patron, probably in the form of livestock, and was obliged to repay the patron by rent or interest and to make some personal attendance on the patron. The unfree client in addition received his "honour price," *i.e.,* payment equal to the valuation of his freedom, thereby ensuring that his patron would enjoy the fruits of that franchise so long as their relationship lasted. The *céle* was under an obligation to perform certain "services" for his patron, *e.g.,* to render an annual food-service (supply of farm produce) or to supply agricultural labourers to farm the patron's land. At first sight this looks like the Norman feudal system of services and incidents of tenure held between the feudal lord and tenant. But the similarities are superficial only. The ancient Irish patron-client relationship was terminable at will and was based on *contract*, not upon *tenure,* a distinction that was to crop up again in Irish land law, many centuries later.[42]

1.14. A class lower than the *céli* were *bothach*[43] and *fuidir,* who were essentially tenants at will bound to provide uncertain services to their lord. They were not bound to the soil, as it were, and so were free to move, until nine

---

[38] See Hand, *English Law in Ireland, 1290–1324* (1967); Otway-Ruthven, *A History of Medieval Ireland* (1968). See also Mac Niocaill, *Ireland Before the Vikings* (1972); O'Corráin, *Ireland Before the Normans* (1972).

[39] See MacNeill, *Phases of Irish History* (1919), *Early Irish Laws and Institutions* (1935); Dillon (ed.) *Early Irish Society;* Thurneysen (and others), *Studies in Early Irish Law* (1936).

[40] See para. 1.16, *infra.*

[41] Much information can be gleaned from the Brehon Tract *Críth Gablach* re-edited by Binchy in 1941.

[42] See para. 17.005 *post.* This patron-client relationship was also similar to the relationship adopted by some native Irish towards their Norman overlords after the twelfth century, see para. 1.22, *infra.*

[43] Which seems to have been the derivation of the word later used to describe a certain class in the Norman times, the *betagh,* see para. 1.21, *infra.*

generations had lived on the same land. When that happened they sank to the lowest class, that of the *sen-cléithe*, an unfree serf or villein bound to the soil. The *sen-cléithe* was simply regarded as part of the land, passing along with any transfer of the land itself.

1.15. There remain to be mentioned two further features of the native system, which were to give rise to much discussion centuries later.[44] The first was the law of succession to chieftaincies, commonly referred to as *tanistry* (though some have queried this use of the word).[45] This law of succession decreed that the chieftaincy, or seignory, and all lands and other property connected with it, would pass to the tanist, *i.e.*, to the eldest and worthiest male kinsman of the present chief. This person was chosen in the lifetime of the present chief, thereby purporting to settle the succession in advance. This law of succession may be compared with the feudal law of primogeniture[46]; the two laws were destined later to come into direct conflict.[47] Primogeniture was also at the same time to come into conflict with another Irish law of succession, often known by its English name, *gavelkind,* under which a chief could divide land owned by a member of one of the inferior classes among the males of the clan, on that member's death. Under this system of succession, it seems illegitimate persons were given portions along with legitimate persons, wives were given no dower and daughters could not inherit even if there were no male issue of the deceased owner. Gavelkind, in its Irish sense, should not be confused with the system of succession of the same name formerly known in parts of England, especially Kent.[48] Such a system of frequent redistribution of the land has survived down to recent times in Ireland in the shape of the "rundale" system prevalent in the Western counties. Under this system, rights of pasturage continue to be owned in common by many landowners, while rights to arable land are periodically redistributed amongst the farmers of particular neighbourhoods.[49] It should also be noted that rights of pasturage in respect of mountain land seem to have been enjoyed in common by several landowners in many areas of the country and some such rights still exist.[50]

---

[44] See para. 1.28, *infra.*

[45] See Binchy, (1943) xxix Proc. Brit-Acad. 195; *cf.* Newark, "The Case of Tanistry" (1952) 9 N.I.L.Q. 215; Butler, *Gleanings from Irish History* (1925), pp. 80–91. MacNeill's view that the institution originated more than a century after the Norman invasion in the twelfth century (see his *Early Irish Laws and Institutions,* p. 148) is now known to be wrong; the *tanist* is referred to in an eighth-century law tract (see Binchy, *Críth Gablach,* p. 108). See also Mac Niocaill, "The 'Heir Designate' in Early Medieval Ireland" (1968) 3 Ir.Jur. (N.S.) 326.

[46] Maine's suggestion that tanistry may have been the "parent" of primogeniture is not as fanciful as may appear (see his *Early History of Institutions,* p. 208 and *Early Law and Custom,* pp. 138 and 249); see Binchy, (1943) xxix Proc.Brit.Acad. 195.

[47] See para. 1.28, *infra.*

[48] See Challis, *Real Property* (3rd ed.), 14–17, 373–4; Megarry and Wade, *Law of Real Property* (5th ed., 1984), pp. 19–20; *The Case of Gavelkind* (1605) Dav. 49.

[49] For accounts of the practice in the early nineteenth century, see Wakefield, *An Account of Ireland, Statistical and Political* (1812); Mason, *Statistical Accounts or Parochial Survey of Ireland* (1816), vol. 2; Hill, *Facts from Gweedore* (1846); Connell, *The Population of Ireland 1750–1845* (1950), pp. 77–9. S.27 (1) (*c*) of the Republic's Land Act, 1950, enables the Irish Land Commission to purchase land where it requires it "to facilitate re-arrangement of lands held in rundale or intermixed plots."

[50] See the Irish Land Commissioners' *Annual Report 1971–1972,* pp. 6–9 (R.I.).

B. The Introduction of English Common Law:
Twelfth-Seventeenth Centuries

1.16. It is some 800 years since Henry II and his Norman kinsmen brought English common law to Ireland.[51] The Norman Conquest, which really got under way with the visit of Henry during late 1171 to early 1172, meant the introduction to Ireland of the feudal system of land tenure, under which all land was held ultimately from the King, as chief lord superior to all other landowners.[52] The feudal system was more than a system of land tenure, it was a system of government designed to centralise the administration of the country under the power of the King.[53] As such it came into conflict with the native Irish system which militated against such centralisation, and for the next four centuries there was constant tension between the two systems.[54] Prior to the seventeenth century the feudal system never covered the whole of Ireland and, indeed, after the comparative success of the Norman conquest during the thirteenth century, its influence waned during the numerous wars and Irish risings in the fourteenth and fifteenth centuries. There came a time when the system could be said to be operating effectively only around Dublin and a strip of land along the East coast of Ireland that came to be called "the Pale."[55] Judge Longfield, one of the most knowledgeable of Irish land lawyers and a judge of the Landed Estates Court in Ireland during the nineteenth century, wrote the following oft-quoted words about the feudal system in Ireland and England:

> "In both countries the law is based upon the feudal system, which gave the landlord a certain superiority over his tenants. But the feudal relation, with its reciprocal rights and duties, never existed in Ireland. Here the landlord never led his tenants to battle; if they fought in the same field, it was on different sides. They had no traditions of common victories or common defeats. The relations that existed between them were hostile. According to the old feudal law, the lordship could not be transferred without the consent of the tenant, lest an enemy might be made his feudal superior; but in a great part of Ireland a sudden and violent transfer of the lordship was made to persons whom the tenants only knew as their victorious enemies."[56]

---

[51] Hand, "English Law in Ireland, 1172–1351" (1972) 23 N.I.L.Q. 393; Johnston, "The First adventure of the Common Law" (1920) 36 L.Q.R. 9; Maitland, "The Introduction of English Law into Ireland" (1889) IV E.H.R. 516; Moran, "The Migration of the Common Law: 7: The Republic of Ireland" (1960) 76 L.Q.R. 69; Newark, "The Bringing of English Law to Ireland" (1972) 23 N.I.L.Q. 3.

[52] On this subject generally, see Curtis, *Medieval Ireland* (2nd ed., 1938); Dolley, *Anglo-Norman Ireland* (1972); Hand, *English Law in Ireland, 1290–1324* (1967); Lydon, *Ireland in the Later Middle Ages* (1973); Orpen, *Ireland under the Normans* (1911–20), 4 vols.; Otway-Ruthven, *History of Medieval Ireland* (1968); Richardson and Sayles, *The Irish Parliament in the Middle Ages* (1952) and *The Administration of Ireland, 1172–1377* (1963).

[53] See Holdsworth, *Historical Introduction to Land Law* (1935); Milsom, *Historical Foundations of the Common Law* (1969), chs. 5–9; Pocock, *The Ancient Constitution and the Feudal Law* (1957); Simpson, *A History of Land Law* (2nd ed., 1985); Stenton, *First Century of English Feudalism*. Also ch. 2, *post*.

[54] Mac Niocaill, "The Contract of Irish and Common Law" (1972) 23 N.I.L.Q. 16.

[55] Otway-Ruthven, *History of Medieval Ireland* (1968), ch. VIII.

[56] "The Tenure of Land in Ireland" in *Systems of Land Tenure* (ed. Probyn, 1881), 1; *cf.* Nutt, *Land Tenure in Ireland* (3rd ed., 1866); Fisher, *History of Landholding in Ireland* (1877); Gibbs, *English Law and Irish Tenure* (1870); Montgomery, *History of Land Tenure in Ireland* (1889); Richey, *Irish Land Laws* (2nd ed., 1880).

1.17. Care must be taken in reading these sentences if a totally misleading picture is not to be acquired. It must be remembered that they were written at the height of the political storms at Westminster, and the social and economic upheavals in Ireland, centering around the land problem in the latter half of the nineteenth century.[57] By that time the feudal relationship of lord and tenant had been displaced in significance by the more modern relationship of landlord and tenant.[58] These are two distinct systems of tenure[59] and Judge Longfield to some extent may seem to be confusing them in his remarks. Land law in Ireland is still, it is true to say, based on the feudal system, as is land law in England, but it is not true to say that the feudal relationship never existed in Ireland. In fact, as we shall discuss in a moment, it did exist to a considerable extent in medieval times, and there are still vestiges remaining in Ireland today, some of which are of practical importance.[60] Judge Longfield's comments are more accurate when applied to the relationship of landlord and tenant as it developed in Ireland from the seventeenth century onwards, culminating in the extensive legislative reforms of the late nineteenth and twentieth centuries.[61] χ

1.18 The Norman conquest really began to take effect with the appointment by Henry II of Hugh de Lacy as justiciar of Ireland in 1172.[62] As one learned scholar has said with respect to the Normans' development of the structure of central and local government in Ireland, "its basis was the occupation of the land, and this was provided for on the standard lines of Norman feudalism."[63] As had been done in the case of the conquest of England a century earlier, Henry granted large parts of Ireland to his henchmen, to be held by them as tenants in chief. Thus Meath was granted to Hugh de Lacy to be held by the service of fifty knights; Leinster was granted to Strongbow to be held by the service of one hundred knights. The difference from the conquest of England was that Ireland was never completely subdued so that some of the early grants had little practical significance—the condition precedent of *physical* conquest of the area granted had still to be performed. However, fairly complete subinfeudation of Leinster was achieved within the first few decades of Henry's coming to Ireland. The areas of Meath, Kildare and across the centre of Ireland to the River Shannon, and down the east coast from Drogheda to South of Cork, were to follow before the end of the twelfth century. But most of the West and North-West of Ireland, Connaught and parts of Ulster, remained in the hands of the Irish chiefs and relatively unaffected by the feudal system.

---

[57] See paras. 1.38–60, *infra*.
[58] See ch. 17, *post*.
[59] See para. 2.55, *post*.
[60] See ch. 2, *post*.
[61] See paras. 1.44–68, *post*.
[62] See Orpen, *Ireland under the Normans* (1911–1920), esp. vol. 3; Otway-Ruthven, *History of Medieval Ireland* (1968), chs. II and III.
[63] Otway-Ruthven, *op. cit.*, pp. 102.

1.19. The state of continuous warfare in Ireland decreed the institution of military tenure, grants and sub-grants of the land to be held by knight-service.[64] With the extensive subinfeudation of the land into smaller and smaller portions, the concept of *scutage, i.e.,* a money payment in substitution for performance of the services, was introduced from the earliest stages of the development of the feudal system. One writer has described that development in these terms:

"All these military tenancies were held by exactly the same rules of law as applied in England . . . even where a military tenant was of native Irish descent, as a few were, the ordinary legal rules of Norman feudalism as developed in England applied. The tenant, though he had that absolute right of inheritance which had by this time been established,[65] paid a relief on his succession, the recognition of the lord's original right to regrant the fee as he pleased on the death of a tenant; at his death, his minor heir and lands were in the wardship of the lord,[66] who, subject only to the obligation of maintaining the heir and other children, and to the rules as to waste laid down in the Great Charter and subsequent legislation, might enjoy the profits, including the marriage of the heir, himself, or grant them away as he pleased. As in England the king enjoyed the right of prerogative wardship[67]; that is, he had the wardship of all the lands of a tenant-in-chief, even though some of them were held immediately of other lords . . . If the tenant died without heirs, or if he committed a felony, his land would escheat to the lord[68]: in the case of a felony the king had the right of year, day and waste, might, that is, enter on the land and extract every possible profit from it, regardless of any rules as to waste, for a year and a day, after which it was handed over to the immediate lord. The tenant's widow, who had a right to be dowered with a third of her husband's lands for life,[69] must obtain the lord's leave for her marriage, since her new husband would be the tenant of the dower lands.[70] A widower, on the other hand, provided that a living child had been born to them (the formal proof required was that it should have been heard to cry within the four walls), continued, by the custom known as the courtesy of England, to hold all his wife's lands for life, to the exclusion of her heirs. Finally . . . though the tenant's eldest son was the sole heir to his lands to the exclusion of all others,[71] should he leave no son but several daughters his lands must be divided equally between the daughters."[72]

[64] See, generally, Brooks, *Knights' Fees in Counties Wexford, Carlow and Kilkenny* (1950); Dolley, *Anglo-Norman Ireland* (1972); Frame, *The Lordship of Ireland 1318–1361* (1982); Mac Niocaill, "The Contact of Irish and Common Law" (1972) 23 N.I.L.Q. 16; Mills, "Norman Settlement in Leinster; the Cantreds near Dublin" (1894) xxiv Jo.R.S.A.I. 160, "Tenants and Agriculture near Dublin in the Fourteenth Century" (1890) xx Jo.R.S.A.I. 54; Otway-Ruthven, "Anglo-Irish Shire Government in the Thirteenth Century" (1946) v I.H.S. 1, "Knight Service in Ireland" (1959) Lxxxix Jo.R.S.A.I. 1, "Knights' Fees in Kildare, Leix and Offaly" (1961) xci Jo.R.S.A.I. 163, "The Character of Norman Settlement in Ireland" (1965) v Hist.Stud. 75, "The Partition of the de Verdon Lands in Ireland in 1332" (1967) Lxvic Proc. R.I.A. 22.

[65] See para. 2.19, *post.*   [66] *Ibid.*
[67] *Ibid.*   [68] Para. 2.24, *post.*
[69] Para. 4.157, *post.*   [70] Ch. 15, *post.*
[71] Para. 7.40, *post.*
[72] Otway-Ruthven, *History of Medieval Ireland* (1968), pp. 105–6.

1.20. In those parts of Ireland so subjected to feudalism manors were developed, which contained the central residences of the tenants in chief suitably fortified with motes and stockades. Each manor had its quota of tenants owing service to the lord of the manor. In passing, it should be noted that the use of the word "tenant" can create difficulties for students in the twentieth century. In feudal times anyone who held land from another, whether as a freeholder or leaseholder, might be referred to as a "tenant." This should be borne in mind when reading the ensuing paragraphs for the word may not be confined to its twentieth century meaning for the layman, *i.e.*, a leasehold tenant.

1.21. During the thirteenth and fourteenth centuries six classes of tenants seem to have been found on Norman-Irish manors.[73] The most important class were the *free tenants,* those holding by military tenure and liable to all the incidents of that tenure and also, it seems, a class holding in fee-farm who owed money rent rather than personal service (or scutage in lieu of it).[74] All free tenants would owe suit at the lord's court. Then came a class known as *farmers,* generally holding land for a term of years but often owing labour service in addition to rent and owing suit of court. Next came *gavillers,* who were really tenants-at-will rather like the English copyholders, but, unlike them, they seem to have been personally free. They owed both labour service and money rent, plus suit of court. Similar in position to gavillers were *cottiers,* the main distinction being that cottiers held only their cottages and crofts.[75] Then there were the *betaghs,* a class which has given rise to much discussion recently.[76] It seems clear that they were unfree tenants, drawn from the native Irish population, who owed labour services rather than rent and were bound to the soil. There has been some suggestion that the word *betagh* might be derived from the Irish word *bothach,* meaning a tenant-at-will who might become bound to the soil by his family's occupation of it for nine generations.[77] But this has been disputed and the better view now seems to be that the word is derived from the Irish word *bíatach,* meaning "food-provider."[78] The betagh's position seems to have been similar to that of the villein under the feudal system in England.[79] Finally, there were the *burgesses,* who seem to have been a special class of urban tenants not owing suit to the court of the manor, but to the "hundred," a court composed of their fellow burgesses.[80]

---

[73] Otway-Ruthven, "The Organisation of Anglo-Irish Agriculture in the Middle Ages" (1951) LXXXI Jo.R.S.A.I. 1. See also Mills, "Notices of the Manor of St. Sepulchre" (1879). IX Jo.R.S.A.I. 35.

[74] Fee farm grants have played an important part in the development of Irish land law, but it is doubtful if any of those referred to in the text survive, see ch. 4, *post.*

[75] For the more modern meaning of cottier, see para. 17.102, *post.*

[76] Curtis, "Rental of the Manor of Lisronagh, 1333, and Notes on 'Betagh' Tenure in Medieval Ireland" (1944) XLIIIC Proc.R.I.A. 41; Hand, "The Status of the Native Irish in the Lordship of Ireland, 1272–1331" (1966) 1 Ir.Jur. (N.S.) 93; Mac Niocaill, "The Origins of the *Betagh*" (1966) 1 Ir.Jur. (N.S.) 292; Murphy, "The Status of the Native Irish after 1331" (1967) 2 Ir.Jur. (N.S.) 116; Price, The Origin of the Word *Betagius*" (1966) XX *Eriu* 185.

[77] See para. 1.14, *ante.*

[78] See Hand, *English Law in Ireland, 1290–1324* (1967), pp. 195 and 213.

[79] See Megarry and Wade, *The Law of Real Property* (5th ed., 1984), pp. 23–27.

[80] Otway-Ruthven, *History of Medieval Ireland,* pp. 112–3. See also on "burgage" tenure in Limerick, *Lyons* v. *Fitzgerald* (1825) Sm. & Bat. 405.

1.22 It seems clear that the majority of the superior tenants under this system were in fact settlers from England and Wales. But some native Irish could become free tenants.[81] For example, there was a system of "avowries" whereby native Irish could pay sums of money to English lords to come under their protection.[82] It seems that Irishmen who were free under the native system might continue free when they became tenants of the manor of an English lord. And many of the Irish chiefs, even though often only nominally subject to English overlords, undertook to pay the dues they had previously paid to their Irish overlords.

1.23. In view of this development of the feudal system, extensive in some parts of Ireland, it is not surprising to find that most of the early English legislation on land law was imported into Ireland.[83] Prior to 1495, such statutes were made applicable in one of three ways: by being originally enacted as applicable (which was rare), by becoming applicable later through transmission to Ireland with a royal writ for their observance and by extension through subsequent legislation. In 1495 the famous Poynings' Law, an Act of the Irish Parliament,[84] provided that "all estatutes, late made within England, concerning or belonging to the common and publique weal of the same, from henceforth be deemed good and effectuall in the law, and over that be acceptyd, used, and executed within Ireland in all points at all times requisite according to the tenor and effect of the same. . . . " It was, however, also the case prior to 1495 that certain statutes were observed and enforced by the courts in Ireland without any evidence of their being made applicable formally.[85]

1.24. It is clear that the following major English statutes relating to land law were made applicable or were observed in Ireland: Magna Carta, 1215[86]; the Statute of Merton, 1235[87]; the Statute of Marlborough, 1267[88]; the Statute of Westminster I, 1275[89]; the Statute of Gloucester, 1278[90]; the Statute of Mortmain, 1279[91]; the Statute of Westminster II, 1285 (c. 1, *De Donis*

---

[81] Mills, "Tenants and Agriculture near Dublin in the Fourteenth Century" (1890) xx Jo.R.S.A.I.54.

[82] *Cf.* the clients (*céli*) under the native Irish system of tenure, para. 1.13, *ante*.

[83] On this subject, see Donaldson, *Some Comparative Aspects of Irish Law* (1957), ch. 2; Hand, *English Law in Ireland, 1290–1324* (1967), ch. VIII; Richardson and Sayles, *Irish Parliament in the Middle Ages* (1952). See also, *Statutes and Ordinances and Acts of the Parliament of Ireland, King John to Henry V* (ed. Berry, 1907).

[84] "Poynings' Law" is also often taken to refer to the statute 10 Hen. 7, c. 4 (Ir.), which declared that no Parliament was to be held in Ireland without leave under the Great Seal of England. See Newark, *Notes on Irish Legal History* (1960), p. 30. Poynings' Law was also amended in 1556, see 3 & 4 Phil & Mar., c. 4 (Ir.). Edwards and Moody, "The History of Poyning's Law: Pt. I, 1494–1615" (1941) VIII I.H.S. 324.

[85] The Statute of Mortmain 1279 seems to come into this category, see Hand, *op. cit.*, pp. 164–5.

[86] See also Magna Carta 1217, and para. 2.40, *post*. For judicial discussion of the applicability of Magna Carta in the twentieth century, see *R. (Moore)* v. *O'Hanrahan* [1927] I. R. 406; *Moore* v. *Att.-Gen.* [1934] I.R. 44 (see *A Casebook on Irish Land Law* (1984), p.5); *Little* v. *Cooper* [1937] I.R. 1; *Foyle and Bann Fisheries Ltd.* v. *Att.-Gen.* (1949) 83 I.L.T.R. 29.

[87] Confirmed by an Irish Statute of 1320, 13 Edw. 2, c. 2 (Ir.). See para. 2.20, *post*.

[88] Also confirmed by 13 Edw. 2, c. 2 (Ir.). See para. 17.057, *post*.

[89] Confirmed by 13 Edw. 2, c. 2 (Ir.); it was also extended by writ in 1285. See para. 2.22, *post*.

[90] Extended by writ in 1285; confirmed by 13 Edw. 2, c. 2 (Ir.). See Hand. *op. cit.*, pp. 163–4.

[91] For discussion as to its applicability prior to Poyning's Law, see Hand, *op. cit.*, pp. 164–5. See also para. 2.41, *post*.

Conditionalibus)[92] and the Statute of Westminster III, 1290 (especially cc. 1 and 2, *Quia Emptores*).[93]

1.25. Finally, there remains to be mentioned the position of the native Irish under the common law so introduced by the Normans. The fact is that during the first few centuries after the conquest, the native Irish were in an extremely underprivileged position as far as the common law and the King's courts were concerned. As Professor Hand has recently written:

> "If they lived where a native chief still held sway, they were perforce left to their own law; if they lived within the effective influence of the governors of the lordships, they were treated as members of an unfree class not entitled to use the king's courts. For the classes already unfree at native law the change of master cannot have mattered greatly. But the formerly free Irish caught up in the spread of Anglo-Norman power, by being treated unfree, endured many disabilities."[94]

1.26. These formerly free Irish, *hibernici, nativi* or *betagii*,[95] as they were variously called, could sue in the royal courts only through their lord and failure to sue in this way was a complete defence to the action. The killing of an Irishman was not a felony. However, some Irishmen did have the privilege of enjoyment of English law. The Irish bishops and prelates seem to have had it to some extent, as did those of the "five bloods," the royal families of O'Neill of Ulster, O'Melaghlin of Meath, O'Connor of Connaught, O'Brien of Thomond and MacMurrough of Leinster. Further, there was a practice of making royal charters granting the benefit of English law to some native Irish. There were various moves towards more general extensions of English law to the Irish during the fourteenth century,[96] but much of the demand was by then declining simply because the sphere of Anglo-Norman influence in Ireland was declining and was to continue to decline during the fifteenth and early sixteenth centuries. And, indeed, so many of the former conquerors were becoming *hibernis ipsis hiberniores* that it was considered necessary in 1366 to pass the Statute of Kilkenny expressly forbidding the English in the colony of Ireland from using the native brehon law themselves.[97]

---

[92] Extended by writ in the same year; confirmed by 13 Edw. 2, c. 2 (Ir.). See paras. 4.114 and 15.04, *post*, and Hand, *op. cit.*, pp. 166–71.

[93] See paras. 2.42–47, *post*, and Hand, *op. cit.*, p. 162.

[94] *English Law in Ireland, 1290–1324* (1967), p. 188. See also Otway-Ruthven, *History of Medieval Ireland*, pp. 125, 188–90; Davies, *Discoverie of the True Causes Why Ireland was never Entirely Subdued* (1612); and the Irish Chiefs' *Remonstrance* to Pope John xxii in 1317 (see Curtis and McDowell, *Irish Historical Documents* (1943), pp. 38–46 and Hand, *op. cit.*, pp. 198–205). See also Frame, *English Lordship in Ireland 1318–1361* (1982); Lydon, *The Lordship of Ireland in the Middle Ages* (1972).

[95] Use of this word is particularly ambiguous since it had a narrower meaning, more equivalent to the English word *villeins*, see para. 1.21, *ante*.

[96] An ordinance of 1331 provided the same law to be made for the Irish as for the English, except the service of betaghs (in the narrow sense, presumably) in the power of their lords. See *Statutes and Ordinances and Acts of the Parliament of Ireland, King John to Henry V* (ed. Berry), p. 324; Gwynn, "Edward I and the Proposed Purchase of English law for the Irish, c. 1276–80" (1960) x R.Hist.Soc.Trans. (5th series), p. 111; Otway-Ruthven, "The Request of the Irish for English Law, 1277–8" (1949) vi I.H.S. 261, "The Native Irish and English Law in Medieval Ireland" (1950) vii I.H.S. 1.

[97] Hand, "The Forgotten Statutes of Kilkenny—A Brief Survey" (1966) 1 Ir.Jur. (N.S.) 299.

C. CONFISCATION AND RESETTLEMENT OF IRISH LAND: SEVENTEENTH-EIGHTEENTH CENTURIES

1.27. The seventeenth century saw the completion of the conquest of Ireland begun by Henry II some five centuries earlier. This meant the completion of the imposition of English common law and the displacement of the ancient Irish law. It was a century marked by bitter and bloody wars fought over the length and breadth of Ireland, wars which to this day vitally affect social and political thought in both parts of the country. A central factor in these struggles was the ownership of the land, which provided the main source of economic wealth and, indeed, the very sustenance of life itself.[98]

1.28. The century began with the determination by the judges of the King's Bench in Dublin that neither *tanistry* nor *gavelkind,* the ancient Irish customary modes of succession, could be recognised or enforced in the King's courts. In the *Case of Tanistry*,[99] as reported by James I's Attorney General for Ireland, Sir John Davies,[1] the judges passed a resolution criticising the custom of tanistry[2] and determining that the custom, as detailed to the judges, failed to meet the criteria for recognition at common law.[3] The judges had taken the same line with respect to the Irish custom of gavelkind[4] in the *Case of Gavelkind*[5] a couple of years earlier. From then on, the English feudal concept of succession to land, *primogeniture,* governed the land of Ireland and continued so to do until very recent times.[6] Though dealing only with specific aspects of the ancient Irish system of land law, these two cases were universally regarded as establishing the complete dominance of the English feudal system of land tenure in Ireland. As things have developed, only in comparatively modern times has reference been made in Irish courts back to the *brehon* system, *e.g.,* in an attempt to solve difficult questions relating to fisheries.[7]

1.29. The early seventeenth century also saw the beginning of the comprehensive confiscation of Irish land and resettlement of that land amongst outsiders that was to have such a momentous effect on the country and, as a direct consequence, on its land law.[8] The process of confiscation and resettlement was not new to Ireland then. Henry VIII, who had been declared "King" of Ireland, in place of the title "lord," by the Crown of Ireland Act, 1542,[9] had pursued a policy of "surrender and re-grant" during the mid-

---

[98] See, generally, Bagwell, *Ireland under the Stuarts* (1909–16), 3 vols.; Beckett, *The Making of Modern Ireland 1603–1923* (1966); MacCurtain, *Tudor and Stuart Ireland* (1972); Moody, Martin and Byrne (eds.), *A New History of Ireland;* Vol. III: *Early Modern Ireland 1534–1691* (1976); O'Brien, *Economic History of Ireland in the Seventeenth Century* (1919); Morley (ed.), *Ireland under Elizabeth and James First* (1890).

[99] (1607) Dav. 28 (see *A Casebook on Irish Land Law* (1984), p. 1); Newark, (1952) 9 N.I.L.Q. 215.

[1] Solicitor-General, 1603–6; Attorney-General, 1606–19. His major writings are contained in Morley, fn. 98, *supra.*

[2] See para. 1.15, *ante.*

[3] See para. 6.044, *post.*

[4] See para. 1.15, *ante.*

[5] (1605) Dav. 49.

[6] Para. 15.05, *post.*

[7] Para. 6.042, *post.*

[8] See, generally, Delany, "Irish and Scottish Land Resettlement Legislation" (1959) 8 I.C.L.Q. 299.

[9] 33 Hen. 8, c. 1. (Ir.). See *Northern Bank Ltd.* v. *Barrington* [1979] N.I. 161.

sixteenth century. Under this scheme the Irish chief landowners were induced to enter into a formal agreement with the Crown, whereby they submitted to English feudal law, surrendered their lands and obtained in return a re-grant of that land to be held of the King in accordance with feudal principles.[10] Henry had also applied his reformation policy to Ireland, resulting in the dissolution of monastries and the redistribution of church lands.[11] During this period various inquisitions had been held to determine the ownership of individual parcels of land, and in the reign of Mary Tudor larger scale resettlement of the land had been attempted in, for example, Offaly and Leix, which were renamed King's County and Queen's County.[12] Land was continually becoming available for resettlement when various Acts of Attainder were passed against rebellious Irish landowners,[13] who forfeited their lands for treason so that by English feudal law it then escheated to the Crown.

1.30. This process accelerated rapidly after the "Flight of the Earls" in 1607, following the failure of a rebellion against the Crown by the Irish leaders from the North (until then never completely conquered), O'Neill, the Earl of Tyrone and O'Donnell, Earl of Tyrconnell (Donegal). They were indicted for treason, Acts of Attainder were duly passed[14] and their lands escheated to the Crown. There then began the famous "plantation of Ulster,"[15] under which a large part of the land in that province was granted to English and Scottish settlers, English livery companies and the Irish Society.[16] These grants were usually made by creation of feudal tenure, with a perpetual rent payable to the Crown, a subject which will be discussed in greater detail later.[17] Though some grants were made to the native Irish inhabitants, the great majority were given to the settlers from across the Irish Sea, leaving the Irish to become tenants of these settlers. This resettlement of Ulster land was by far the most successful imposed on Ireland by the British and that success has been a major factor in the history of Ireland ever since.

1.31. Apart from the North, the rest of Ireland in the early seventeenth century suffered from continuing disturbances and rebellions, often

---

[10] See the 1542 Statute, 33 Hen. 8, sess. 2, c. 4 (Ir.) (Crown grants of land).

[11] See the 1537 statutes, 28 Hen. 8, c. 5 (Ir.). (King Supreme Head of the Church), c. 6 (Ir.) (Appeals to Rome), c. 16 (Ir.) (Suppression of Abbeys), c. 21 (Ir.) (Penal Laws).

[12] Butler, *Confiscation in Irish History* (1918); Bagwell, *Ireland under the Tudors* (1885–90).

[13] *E.g.*, 28 Hen. 8, c. 1 (Ir.) (1537) (Attainder of the Earl of Kildare and others); c. 9 (Forfeiture of Sir Walter Delahyde's estate); 2 Eliz. 1, c. 8 (Ir.) (1560) (Attainder of Sir Oswald Massingberde); 11 Eliz. 1, sess. 3, c. 1 (Ir.) (1569) (Shane O'Neill and others); c. 3 (Thomas Fitzgerald); 12 Eliz. 1, sess. 2, c. 1 (Ir.) (1570) (Thomas Queverford); 13 Eliz. 1, c. 3 (Ir.) (1571) (John Fitzgerald); 27 Eliz. 1, c. 1 (Ir.) (1585) (James Eustace, Lord Baltinglas); 22 Eliz. 1, c. 7 (Ir.) (1586) (Earl of Desmond and others). The last Act related to lands in the province of Munster and a comprehensive scheme for its "plantation" was drawn up in which Sir Walter Raleigh (who had devised a scheme for Virginia in America) and Sir Humphrey Gilbert participated.

[14] 11, 12 & 13 Jas. 1, c. 4 (Ir.) (1613–15).

[15] See Moody, *The Londonderry Plantation, 1609–41* (1939); also Hill, *Historical Account of the Plantation in Ulster at the Commencement of the Seventeenth Century, 1608–20* (1877). See *Toome Eel Fishery (N.I.) Ltd. v. Cardwell* [1966] N.I. 1.

[16] The "Society of the Governors and Assistants, London, of the New Plantation in Ulster within the Realm of Ireland" undertook the plantation of the Derry and Coleraine areas, renaming the former Londonderry and giving the county the same name.

[17] Ch. 4, *post.* See also *Stewart v. Marquis of Conyngham* (1850) 1 Ir.Ch.R. 534.

accompanying abortive attempts at resettlements of the land in other provinces. A series of statutes passed in 1634[18] purported to confirm many of the grants made under the Ulster Plantation and authorised the establishment of the Commission for Defective Titles, which did more harm than good as far as the Irish were concerned.[19] Despite another Act of 1639,[20] a rebellion in 1641 shook much of Ireland. Inevitably the lands of the rebels were forfeited, in this instance by a series of Acts of the English Parliament passed in 1642.[21] Under these the lands could be granted to "adventurers" prepared to comply with the terms of the statutes. Worse was to follow from the Irish point of view. In 1649 Cromwell, with an army of "Ironsides," undertook a campaign which was to end in 1652 with the conquest of Ireland and a new settlement of the land.[22] It was a bitter and bloody affair highlighted by the sacking of Drogheda in September 1649 and the massacre of its garrison and many of its inhabitants. The Irish have never forgotten the campaign and the large-scale confiscations and resettlement of lands which followed contributed to this attitude.

1.32. The 1642 settlement had not been executed because of the continuing state of war in Ireland and the English Parliament in 1652 took further steps to satisfy the adventurers who had subscribed under the 1642 legislation, and to meet arrears of pay owed to Cromwell's soldiers. Those who had taken part in the rebellion in Ireland against the Commonwealth forfeited large proportions of their lands and were to receive lands elsewhere in Ireland equivalent in value to what they were allowed to retain, generally in the West, across the river Shannon. Hence the notorious "transplantation to Connaught," which was completed by about 1658.[23] This resulted in another comprehensive change of ownership of Irish land, a record of which was noted down on maps (the "Down survey"[24]).

1.33. The restoration of Charles II in 1660 brought renewed claims by the Irish for return of their forfeited lands, and a new scheme of settlement was declared on November 30 that year. This was adopted by the Irish Parliament in an Act of Settlement in 1662,[25] which provided for the establishment of a

---

[18] Settlement of Ireland Acts, 10 Chas. 1, c. 3 (Ir.), 10 Chas. 1, sess. 3, c. 2 and c. 3 (Ir.). The Irish Parliament, sitting in 1634 under the guidance of Charles I's strong lord deputy, Thomas, Viscount Wentworth, indulged in a frenzied bout of legislative activity on the subject of land law never to be repeated in Ireland, see para. 1.34, *infra*.

[19] Another grievance was the activity of the Irish "Court of Star Chamber" (the Court of Castle Chamber) which seems to have begun operations around 1571 and to have withered away by the beginning of the eighteenth century (no statute seems to have abolished it expressly). Wood, "The Court of Castle Chamber or Star Chamber" (1913) xxxii Proc. R.I.A. 152.

[20] Settlement of Ireland Act, 16 Chas. 1, sess. 2, c. 6 (Ir.).

[21] 16 Chas. 1, cc. 33–35, 37.

[22] Barnard, *Cromwellian Ireland* (1975); Dunlop, *Ireland under the Commonwealth* (1913); Simington (ed.), *Civil Survey, 1654–56* (10 vols., 1931–61), *Books of Survey and Distribution* (3 vols., 1949–62).

[23] Prendergast, *The Cromwellian Settlement in Ireland* (2nd ed., 1870); Gardiner, "The Transplantation to Connaught" (1909) xiv E.H.R. 700.

[24] So-called because the scheme involved, at the suggestion of William Petty (physician-general to the army), the noting down on maps of the results of the survey of titles to the forfeited lands, as opposed to the alternative scheme suggested by Benjamin Worsley (surveyor-general) which involved preparations of a descriptive list of forfeited lands. See *Tisdall* v. *Parnell* (1863) 14 I.C.L.R. 1; *Poole* v. *Griffith* (1863) 15 I.C.L.R. 239; *Foyle and Bann Fisheries Ltd.* v. *Att. Gen.* (1949) 83 I.L.T.R. 29 at 38.

[25] 14 & 15 Chas. 2, sess. 4, c. 2 (Ir.).

Court of Claims (consisting of seven commissioners) to carry out the scheme. The Act confirmed grants made to adventurers and soldiers from 1652–58, but provided for restoration of lands to those who could prove claims of "innocency." If the court was satisfied about such claims, it could restore the original owners and compensate any Cromwellian occupant with land of equal value elsewhere in Ireland. The activities of the Court of Claims not surprisingly led to great tension between the Cromwellian settlers and the Irish claimants of innocence. Eventually an amending Act of "Explanation" was passed by the Irish Parliament in 1665 as a compromise.[26] It confirmed decrees of innocency already issued but prohibited further claims. Named persons were to be given back all or part of their lands, which was made possible by surrender by the adventurers and soldiers of one-third of the lands they had already obtained. Like most compromises it satisfied neither side; the Irish Catholics still felt particularly aggrieved—prior to the 1641 rebellion they had owned about three-fifths of the land in Ireland, whereas after 1665 this was reduced to about one-fifth. When James II held the "Patriot Parliament" in Dublin in 1689, the largely Catholic Assembly purported to repeal the 1662 Act of Settlement and 1665 Act of Explanation; an Act of Attainder was to lead to forfeiture of most land occupied by Protestants.[27] But the defeat of James and his followers during 1690–91 by William III and his commanders swept these measures away,[28] and the Treaty of Limerick 1691,[29] which marked the end of William's campaign, envisaged further confiscations of lands owned by Jacobites.[30] It has been estimated that as a result of the Williamite settlement the proportion of land in Ireland owned by the Catholics dropped to about one-seventh.[31]

1.34. At this point it may be useful to reflect briefly upon the effect this history of confiscation and resettlement of Irish land in the seventeenth century had on the development of land law.[32] It was clearly significant and remains so in the mid-twentieth century. The following points may be emphasised:

(1) The seventeenth century, which, at its beginning, saw the first triumph of English feudal law over Irish brehon law,[33] also saw the rapid decline of the feudal system of landholding as such. The same development had been taking place in England. The complex scheme of tenures, with their wide variety of services and incidents, had fallen into disuse—the services had been commuted into money payments and the incidents were increasingly being avoided by settling the land to *uses*.[34]

---

[26] 17 & 18 Chas. 2, c. 2 (Ir.).

[27] Gavan Duffy, *The Patriot Parliament of 1689* (1893).

[28] An Act of the Irish Parliament in 1695 declared the Patriot Parliament to be "an unlawful and rebellious assembly" and all its acts and proceedings to be "null and void." See 7 Will. 3, c. 3 (Ir.). This followed the English Act, 1 Will. & Mar., sess. 2, c. 9.

[29] Confirmed by the Irish Parliament in 1697, 9 Will. 3, c. 2 (Ir.).

[30] See also the English statute relating to Crown grants and forfeited estates of 1698, 11 Will. 3, c. 2.

[31] Simms, *The Williamite Confiscation in Ireland, 1690–1703* (1956).

[32] *Cf.* Butler, *Confiscation in Irish History* (2nd ed., 1918); Pomfret, *The Struggle for the Land in Ireland* (1930); Davitt, *The Fall of Feudalism in Ireland* (1904).

[33] See para. 1.28, *ante*.

[34] Para. 3.008, *post*.

Henry VIII had tried to halt this process because of its effects on his revenues as Lord paramount of all the land in the Kingdom, by obtaining passage of the Statute of Uses, 1535 in England.[35] This statute did not extend to Ireland and no equivalent was passed until the Statute of Uses (Ireland), 1634.[36] By that date it was clear in England that this sort of legislation could easily be defeated in its purposes by the ingenuity of conveyancers, ably supported by the Chancery judges. So it is doubtful if the Irish statute had any effect at all *in this regard*.[37] The recognition by both Parliaments of the decline of the feudal system of tenure came later in the century with the passage of the Tenures Abolition Act, 1660[38] and the Tenures Abolition Act (Ireland), 1662.[39] These abolished all the various forms of feudal tenure (with many of their incidents) so as to leave one single form, free or common socage (to become known by its popular name "freehold"). The other main form of landholding to survive these Acts, copyhold, probably did not exist to any great extent in Ireland, though it continued to be common in England down to the present century.[40]

(2) From the ashes of the system of feudal or freehold tenure there arose in Ireland (much more so than in England) a system of leasehold "tenure".[41] A direct factor was the confiscation and resettlement of Irish land during the seventeenth century. It is true that the original Crown grants created feudal tenure, because invariably the freehold was granted subject to a rent, called in Ireland a Crown or quit rent.[42] These grants, given in letters patent, in turn entitled the grantees to sub-infeudate *non obstante Quia Emptores*.[43] Subinfeudation was the process by which a person to whom lands had been granted made a grant of those lands or part of them to another person in return for feudal services or a money rent. It was not a transfer of the lands but a further or sub-grant of them. This gave rise to the creation of one type of fee farm grant which is unique to Ireland.[44] The grantees, or their agents, also embarked upon a process of leasing and sub-leasing the land into sub-divided parts, in an effort to extract as much income from it as possible. The result was a rapid growth in Ireland of leasehold tenure to an extent never experienced in England, a generalisation that remains true to this day in respect of urban land.[45] Finally, it has also been suggested that the terms and conditions of the letters patent given to the seventeenth-century settlers, especially in Ulster, may have been responsible for the

---

[35] 27 Hen. 8. c. 10.
[36] 10 Chas. 1, sess. 2, c. 1 (Ir.).
[37] On this subject generally, see paras. 3.015–19, *post*.
[38] 12 Chas. 2, c. 24.
[39] 14 & 15 Chas. 2, sess. 4, c. 19 (Ir.).
[40] See generally, paras. 2.30–33, *post*.
[41] On the subject of "tenure", see ch. 2, *post*.
[42] Para. 6.008, *post*.
[43] Para. 4.059, *post*.
[44] Ch. 4, *post*.
[45] Chs. 4 and 17, *post*.

introduction of special kinds of leases in Ireland, such as the lease for lives renewable for ever.[46]

(3) This growth of the modern relationship of landlord and tenant must, however, be considered against its social, political and economic background. It had been established on a policy of confiscation and resettlement that was likely to be a source of hatred and bitterness. So it proved. As we shall see, the next two centuries in Ireland were dominated by the battles, political and physical, revolving around landlord and tenant relations. The ultimate consequence was drastic legislative reforms introduced by the Westminster Parliament in the latter half of the nineteenth century.[47] And in passing, it may be noted that one of the main issues in these struggles was a custom known as Ulster tenant-right, whose origin lay directly in the Ulster plantation beginning early in the seventeenth century.[48]

(4) It is, perhaps, not surprising that a century of such upheavals should also mark the beginning of the legislation of modern land law. The Statute of Uses (Ireland), 1634 has already been mentioned; most of it is still in force in both parts of Ireland.[49] That year also saw the passing of the first legislation in Ireland permitting wills to be made with respect to land, the Statute of Wills (Ireland).[50] There was also passed in 1634 legislation relating to fraudulent conveyances,[51] reversions,[52] arrears of rent,[53] limitation of actions,[54] fines and recoveries,[55] and administration of estates.[56] Another year of considerable legislative activity was 1695, when the Irish Parliament passed the Statute of Frauds (Ireland), which is still a vital feature of modern conveyancing,[57] the Statute of Distributions (Ireland)[58] and the Life Estates Act (Ireland).[59] At the turn of the century, the registration of deeds system was introduced into Ireland by the Registration of Deeds Act (Ireland), 1707.[60] This system is still today a central part of land law practice in Ireland, a development which never occurred in England.[61]

1.35. We come now to the eighteenth century, a period when developments in land law were a natural progression from the events of the previous

[46] Para. 4.168, *post*.
[47] Paras. 1.44–55, *infra*.
[48] Para. 1.44, *infra*.
[49] Para. 3.015, *post*.
[50] 10 Chas. 1, sess. 2, c. 2 (Ir.). This was not the first Irish statute relating to wills generally, see the Probate Act (Ir.) 1537, 28 Hen. 8, c. 18 (Ir.).
[51] Conveyancing Act (Ir.) 1634, 10 Chas. 1, sess. 2, c. 3 (Ir.), para. 9.076, *post*.
[52] Grantees of Reversions Act (Ir.) 1634, 10 Chas. 1, sess. 2, c. 4 (Ir.), para. 17.070, *post*.
[53] 10 Chas. 1, sess. 2, c. 5 (Ir.).
[54] Limitation Act (Ir.) 1634, 10 Chas. 1, sess. 2, c. 6 (Ir.). See ch. 23, *post*.
[55] 10 Chas. 1, sess. 2. cc. 8–10 (Ir.), 10 Chas. 1, sess. 3, cc. 11 and 20 (Ir.), ch. 4, *post*.
[56] Administration of Estates Act (Ir.) 1634, 10 Chas. 1, sess. 3, c. 10 (Ir.). See ch. 16, *post*.
[57] 7 Will. 3, c. 12 (Ir.), paras. 9.021–5 and 17.012, *post*.
[58] 7 Will. 3, c. 6 (Ir.), para. 15.03, *post*.
[59] 7 Will. 3, c. 8 (Ir.), para. 1.35, *infra*.
[60] 6 Ann., c. 2 (Ir.).
[61] See, generally, ch. 22, *post*.

century.[62] Many English landowners may have acquired grants of large areas of Irish land, but the disturbances in Ireland did little to entice them to spend much time in occupation there. They preferred to remain "absentee landlords" and to turn the running of their Irish estates over to agents, "middlemen" as they came to be called.[63] These middlemen had one abiding aim: to make as much profit out of the land by every means possible (so long as it appeared legal). The amount of commission they earned depended upon this. The result was a widespread subdivision of the large estates by means of grants and sub-grants conferring estates and interests in the land less than freehold. Leasehold conveyancing, with its characteristic recurrent rents and other profits issuing out of the land, was the order of the day.[64] And true to their largely mercenary attitudes, the middlemen and their conveyancing advisers soon devised special types of leaseholds which would produce the most profit. Long leases became very common and, in Ireland, "long" indicated a term of years running well into the hundreds; 999 years was, perhaps, the most common. Then there were perpetually renewable leases, which usually meant a lease for three lives renewable for ever.[65] This had the advantage from the middleman's point of view that a sum of money (a "fine") could be charged every time one of the lives was renewed. And in this the middleman had the aid of the Life Estates Act (Ireland), 1695 which specified that if persons for whose lives estates were granted should remain "beyond the seas, or elsewhere absent themselves in this realm" for seven years, and no proof existed that they were alive, they should be presumed dead. Leases for lives perpetually renewable also held the advantage that they gave the lessee a freehold estate and so the right to vote in parliamentary elections. As voting was in public until 1872,[66] this was a considerable advantage to landlords and made it possible to have "pocket boroughs."

1.36. The proliferation of various types of lease from the eighteenth century onwards was also encouraged by legislation. Thus the eighteenth century was marked by the rapid growth of the "penal" laws, which were statutes imposing disabilities on Catholics.[67] An Irish statute of 1703,[68] for example, debarred Catholics from purchasing land and limited the length of lease they could

---

[62] See, generally, on the period, Johnston, *Ireland in the 18th Century* (1974); Lecky, *A History of Ireland in the Eighteenth Century* (1892); McDowell, *Irish Public Opinion, 1750–1800* (1944); McDowell, *Ireland in the Age of Imperialism and Revolution* (1979); O'Brien, *Economic History of Ireland in the Eighteenth Century* (1919).

[63] See Hussey, *Reminiscences of an Irish Land Agent* (1904).

[64] Which is still so in respect of urban land in Ireland, ch. 17, *post.*

[65] Para. 4.167, *post.*

[66] See Ballot Act, 1872.

[67] Burns, "The Irish Popery Laws: A Study of Eighteenth Century Legislation and Behaviour" (1962) 24 Rev.Pol. 485; Creighton, "The Penal Laws in Ireland, and the Documents in the Archives of Propaganda" (1961) Proc. I. C.H.C. 5; Kelly, "Catholic Disabilities" (1902) 11 I.E.R. (4th ser.) 545; Simms, "Irish Catholics and the Parliamentary Franchise 1692–1728" (1960) 12 I.H.S. 28; Wall, *The Penal Laws 1691–1760* (1976).

[68] 2 Ann., c. 6 (Ir.). Even so apparently neutral legislation as the Registration of Deeds Act (Ireland), 1707 (see para. 1.34, *supra*, and ch. 22, *post*), was stated in its preamble to have been passed for "securing Purchasers, preventing forgeries and fraudulent gifts and conveyances of lands, tenements and hereditaments which have been frequently practised in this kingdom especially by Papists, to the great prejudice of the Protestant interest thereof. . . ." But, in recognition of its place in modern conveyancing practice, the registration of deeds legislation was not repealed by the late eighteenth- and early nineteenth-century legislation which advanced Catholic emancipation and repealed the penal laws.

obtain to 31 years; this statute has been said to have been a factor in the creation of leases for twenty to thirty years (sometimes longer) determinable on the expiration of three lives (which were once common in Ireland).[69] "Bishop's leases," which also became common, resulted from legislation prohibiting bishops from selling lands belonging to their sees, but which permitted them to grant leases for up to 21 years.[70] The practice developed of allowing these leases to be renewed, almost perpetually.[71] The same sort of development occurred in respect of "College leases," granted under powers conferred upon Trinity College, Dublin by the same legislation.[72] Tenants in tail were given powers of leasing for three lives or 41 years by a statute of Charles I;[73] other leasing powers were conferred by special legislation to encourage public works, such as building places of worship,[74] schools,[75] corn mills,[76] prisons,[77] for mining purposes[78] and bog reclamation.[79]

1.37. To match this increase in leasing powers there was an increase in the remedies provided by the law for landlords against their tenants. In particular, most of the old technicalities surrounding the action of ejectment for non-payment of rent were swept away by a series of statutes beginning in the eighteenth century and ending with consolidation in the mid-nineteenth century.[80] As the larger estates became more and more subdivided, the lot of the small tenant-farmer worsened. Usually he held under a very short lease, or a periodic tenancy such as from year to year; his acreage was so small that it barely supported him and his family—starvation was never far away and would have been often a pressing fact of life were it not for suitability of the land for growing what became the staple diet of the Irish peasant, the potato.[81] His position was made even more precarious by the fact that his rent was usually paid six months in arrear, the notorious "hanging gale,"[82] which enabled the landlord to hold the threat of ejectment constantly over him. His income from his few miserable acres also had to meet the expense of the tithe owed to the established Church of Ireland[83]—a Church to which he did not even belong. If

---

[69] Known as the Shelburne lease, see De Moleyns, *Landowner's and Agent's Practical Guide* (8th ed., 1899); Donaldson, *Some Comparative Aspects of Irish Law* (1957), p. 238.

[70] The first statute was 10 & 11 Chas. 1, c. 3 (Ir.), 1634. See also 14 & 15 Chas. 2, sess. 4, c. 2 (Ir.), 1662; 17 & 18 Chas. 2, c. 2 (Ir.), 1665; 35 Geo. 3, c. 23 (Ir.), 1795.

[71] Ch. 4, *post.*

[72] See fn. 70, *supra*, and para. 4.080, *post.*

[73] 10 Chas. 1, sess, 3, c. 6 (Ir.), 1634. See also Fines and Recoveries (Ir.) Act, 1834, s. 19. These statutes were replaced by the nineteenth-century settled land legislation, ch. 8, *post.*

[74] 2 Ann., c. 11 (Ir.), 1703; 12 Geo. 1, c. 9 (Ir.), 1725; 1 Geo. 2, c. 19 (Ir.), 1727; 32 Geo. 3, c. 28 (Ir.), 1792.

[75] 12 Geo. 1, c. 9 (Ir.), 1725. See also the leasing powers given to school governors by the Leases by Schools Acts (Ireland), 1781 (21 & 22 Geo. 3, c. 27) and 1785 (25 Geo. 3, c. 55).

[76] 25 Geo. 3, c. 62 (Ir.), 1785.   [77] 7 Geo. 4, c. 74, 1826.

[78] 10 Geo. 1, c. 5 (Ir.), 1723; 15 Geo. 2, c. 10 (Ir.), 1741; 23 Geo. 2, c. 9 (Ir.), 1749.

[79] 11 & 12 Geo. 3, c. 21 (Ir.), 1771.

[80] These statutes also contained provisions relating to that other important landlord's remedy, distress for rent. See 11 Ann., c. 2 (Ir.), 1712; 4 Geo. 1, c. 5 (Ir.), 1717; 8 Geo. 1, c. 2 (Ir.), 1721; 25 Geo. 2, c. 13 (Ir.), 1751; 15 & 16 Geo. 3, c. 27 (Ir.), 1775; 36 Geo. 3, c. 38 (Ir.), 1796; 56 Geo. 3, c. 88, 1816; 58 Geo. 3, c. 39, 1818; 1 Geo. 4, cc. 41 and 87, 1820; 6 Geo. 4, c. 43, 1825; 7 & 8 Geo. 4, c. 69, 1827; 9 & 10 Vict., c. 111, 1846; 23 & 24 Vict., c. 154, 1860. See generally, ch. 17, *post.*

[81] This dependence on the potato led to disaster in the nineteenth century, para. 1.40, *infra.* Connell, *The Population of Ireland, 1750–1845* (1950), ch. v; Lyons, *Ireland Since the Famine* (2nd ed., 1985).

[82] For meaning of the Irish word "gale" in this context, see para. 17.023, *post.*

[83] On the subject of tithes generally, see ch. 6, *post.*

his income was meagre, his capital was non-existent; and there was no incentive to invest anything on improving his land, for the landlord would claim it on determination of the tenancy or use it as a reason for demanding even higher rents. Any attempts to increase the size of farms were usually made through conacre and agistment "lettings," perhaps the cheapest form of farming, yet certainly one of the most destructive in the long term.[84] The result of these social and economic conditions, imposed on a population systematically deprived for a century of political rights, was inevitable—agrarian disturbances which ranged over Ireland in the latter half of the eighteenth century. Bands of men roamed the countryside, committing arson and destruction and threatening anyone co-operating with the large landowners and landlords' agents.[85] The Irish Parliament was forced to pass legislation to suppress groups like the Whiteboys,[86] the Hearts of Steel[87] and the Hearts of Oak.[88]

At this point we enter the nineteenth century, a century which saw the greatest developments of all in Irish land law.

D. NINETEENTH CENTURY REFORMS

1.38. Great controversy raged in Ireland over the Union with Great Britain effected by the Act of Union, 1800.[89] Few of the Irish population saw in it much hope for improvement of their conditions of life. One could hardly blame them when one recalls that the landlords under whom they suffered so much were the direct descendents of the British Crown grantees of the seventeenth century. But the Union of Ireland with Great Britain did mean one important thing—direct representation of the Irish people at Westminster. In Parliament there the struggle for improved conditions in Ireland took on a renewed force, driven on by the leader of some of the Irish members at Westminster, Daniel O'Connell.[90] However, the issue which first drew O'Connell's attention was not the land problem, but the completion of full Catholic emancipation. Something had already been achieved for this cause towards the end of the eighteenth century. In 1783 Westminster had renounced its claim to legislate for Ireland,[91] and, given this degree of independence, the Irish Parliament,

[84] Such lettings are still common in Ireland, para. 20.25, *post*.

[85] Wall, *The Penal Laws, 1691–1760* (1976); see also Jacob, *The Rise of the United Irishmen, 1791–4* (1937); Johnston, *Great Britain and Ireland, 1760–1800* (1963); Rogers, *The Volunteer and Catholic Emancipation, 1778–93* (1934). Cf. Broeker, *Rural Disorder and Police Reform in Ireland, 1812–26*.

[86] So-called because they wore white shirts over their clothes. See the Whiteboy Statutes, 15 & 16 Geo. 3, c. 21 (Ir.), 1775, 17 & 18 Geo. 3, c. 36 (Ir.), 1777; 27 Geo. 3, c. 15 (Ir.), 1787; Tumultuous Risings (Ir.) Act 1831. *R*. v. *Whelan* (1832) 1 Cr. & Dix 180; *Cotter's Case* (1842) Ir.Cir.Rep. 565.

[87] Formed in the North-east of Ireland after the Marquis of Donegall in 1771 evicted several tenants who refused to pay increased fines for renewal of their leases.

[88] Formed in the North of Ireland.

[89] Identical Acts were passed at Dublin and Westminster—40 Geo. 3, c. 38 (Ir.) and 39 & 40 Geo. 3, c. 67. Lyons and Hawkins (eds.), *Ireland under the Union* (1980); McDowell, *Irish Public Opinion, 1750–1800* (1944) and *Public Opinion and Government Policy in Ireland, 1801–1846* (1952); see also Locker-Lampson, *State of Ireland in the 19th century* (1907); Mansergh, *Ireland in the Age of Reform and Revolution* (1940). See also Montgomery, *History of Land Tenure in Ireland* (1889); Richey, *Irish Land Laws* (1880).

[90] For a very readable biography, see O'Faolain, *King of the Beggars* (1938). Also Macintyre, *The Liberator: Daniel O'Connell and the Irish Party, 1830–47* (1965); McCaffrey, *Daniel O'Connell and the Repeal Year* (1966).

[91] 23 Geo. 3, c. 28.

prompted by Henry Grattan[92] and under strong pressure from the English Government, some ten years later gave Catholics the right to admission as freemen in boroughs (and therefore the vote) and the franchise in counties.[93] O'Connell succeeded in his first aim with the passing at Westminster of the Roman Catholic Relief Act, 1829.[94]

1.39. Two issues from now on dominated the activities of the Irish members of Parliament at Westminster—resolution of the land problem in Ireland and Home Rule for Ireland, with repeal of the Act of Union. By the end of the century, the leadership of Irishmen like O'Connell, Isaac Butt[95] and Charles Stewart Parnell[96] and the support of one Englishman in particular, William Gladstone,[97] was to go far towards achieving both aims, particularly the former. And it is with the land problem that we are concerned here.

1.40. The years 1817 to 1851 were a disaster period for Ireland in the sphere of agriculture and the economy generally.[98] Economic distress hit many parts of Europe hard after the Napoleonic Wars, but it hit Ireland probably harder than most. The deplorable conditions of small tenant-farmers were exhibited by the famines which struck the country regularly, *e.g.,* in 1817 and 1822. Various British Government committees held enquiries into the state of Ireland,[99] but the enormous decrease in population through mass emigration (especially to America) continued. The greatest disaster of all was the Great Famine caused by the failure of the potato crop, upon which so much of the population depended for its very survival, in the successive years 1845–47.[1] By the second half of the century it had been estimated that the population of Ireland had been halved, dropping from eight to four million.[2]

1.41. Agitation for land law reform continued and eventually a Royal

---

[92] Dunlop, *Henry Grattan* (1889); Gwynn, *Henry Grattan and his Times* (1939).

[93] 33 Geo. 3, c. 21 (Ir.), 1793; See also 33 Geo. 3, c. 41 (Ir.), 1793, disqualifying holders of certain Crown offices from sitting in the Irish House of Commons. The conferment of the franchise on forty-shilling freeholders in 1793 was a factor in the creation towards the end of the century of numerous leases for a life or lives, which created a freehold interest rather than a leasehold term of years. In this way the large landlords could create a body of dependent voters who could be expected to vote according to their landlord's instructions. The conveyancers soon devised a mechanism whereby the best of both worlds could be obtained—dependent voters holding in practice for a term of years of certain duration, see paras. 1.35, *ante* and 4.177 *post.*

[94] 10 Geo. 4, c. 7. See Gwynn, *The Struggle for Catholic Emancipation* (1928).

[95] For a biography, see de Vere White, *The Road of Excess* (1946); Thornley, *Issac Butt and Home Rule* (1964).

[96] O'Brien (R. B.), *Life of C. S. Parnell* (3rd ed., 1899); O'Brien (C. C.), *Parnell and his Party, 1880–90* (1957); Lyons, *The Fall of Parnell, 1890–91* (1960).

[97] Morley, *Life of Gladstone* (1903); Eversley, *Gladstone and Ireland, 1850–94* (1912); Hammond, *Gladstone and the Irish Nation* (1938).

[98] See Johnston, *Irish Agriculture in Transition* (1951); see also Connell, *The Population of Ireland, 1750–1845* (1950); Freeman, *Pre-Famine Ireland* (1956); Goldstrom and Clarkson, *Irish Population, Economy and Society* (1982); O'Tuathaigh, *Ireland Before the Famine* (1972).

[99] See, *e.g., First and Second Reports of the Selected Committee on the State of Disease and Condition of the Labouring Poor in Ireland* (1819); *Report of the Selected Committee on the State of Ireland* (1825); *Report of the Select Committee on the State of the Poor in Ireland* (1830); *Reports of the Commissioners for Inquiring into the Condition of the Poorer Classes in Ireland* (1836).

[1] See Woodham-Smith, *The Great Hunger* (1962); also Edwards and Williams, *The Great Famine, Studies in Irish History 1845–52* (1956); Salaman, *The Influence of the Potato on the Course of Irish History* (1943) and *The History and Social Influence of the Potato* (1949).

[2] In the 3 years of the 1845–7 Famine, some 500,000 persons died of disease and starvation. Between 1831 and 1841 some 214,000 emigrated and between 1851 and 1861 this increased to nearly 1,150,000. Schrier, *Ireland and the American Emigration, 1850–1900* (1966).

Commission of Inquiry into the State of the Law and Practice in Relation to the Occupation of Land in Ireland, under the chairmanship of the Earl of Devon, was appointed and toured Ireland collecting evidence. It reported in 1847,[3] but little resulted from it.[4] Indeed, ironically the first major piece of legislation passed at Westminster was essentially a consolidation Act, bringing together much of the legislation passed in the previous century to favour the landlords at the expense of the tenants. This was the Landlord and Tenant Law Amendment Act, (Ireland), 1860, ever since known in Ireland as "Deasy's Act,"[5] after sergeant Deasy, then Attorney-General for Ireland, who piloted the Act through Parliament. To the extent that it added something of substance to the law, it was its introduction of the notion of contract as the basis of the relationship of landlord and tenant.[6] The latter half of the nineteenth century was the era when the principle of *laissez-faire* held paramount sway in economic thought.[7] This, of course, could only plunge the scales down even more in favour of the party to the "contract" in the superior bargaining position, the landlord, yet Deasy's Act remains the foundation of the law of landlord and tenant in both parts of Ireland.

1.42. Even the landlords did not escape the effects of the economic conditions of the age. In fact, most landlords in Ireland found it very difficult to make ends meet: their estates had been badly run down for decades; they were heavily mortgaged and creditors were pressing; the current owners had little incentive to make improvements because at most they had limited interests only, life or entailed estates held under some complex family settlement (tying up the succession to the property for generations[8]). Numerous Acts had been passed to bring some relief, mostly for particular cases.[9] Then, in 1849, a Court of Commissioners for the Sale of Incumbered Estates in Ireland was established,[10] charged with the function of authorising sales of land so as to discharge any incumbrances upon that land and to ensure the purchaser got a clean title. In 1858, this jurisdiction was transferred to a new court, the Landed Estates Court,[11] which became part of the Chancery Division of the High Court under the Judicature (Ireland) Act, 1877.[12] These courts supervised the sales and break-up of many large estates in Ireland in the second half of the

---

[3] *Report and Digest of Evidence,* 2 vols. (1847–8).

[4] In 1851 two members of the Irish Bar, William Dwyer Ferguson and Andrew Vance, attempted "to exhibit the present actual state and social results of the law of landlord and tenant in Ireland, to contrast it with the law of England and Scotland, to state its defects, and suggest measures for its consolidation and amendment." See *Tenure and Improvement of Land in Ireland* (1851).

[5] See, generally, chs. 4 and 17, *post.*   [6] Para. 17.006, *post.*

[7] Black, *Economic Thought and the Irish Question* (1960); Goldstrom and Clarkson (eds.), *Irish Population, Economy and Society* (1982); O'Brien, *Economic History of Ireland in the Nineteenth Century* (1919).

[8] Ch. 8, *post.*

[9] *E.g.,* Mines Act (Ir.), 1723; Mining Leases Act (Ir.), 1749; Bog Reclamation Act (Ir.), 1771; Leases for Lives Act (Ir.), 1777; Leasing Powers for Promoting Linen Manufacture Act (Ir.), 1787; Landlord and Tenant (Planting of Trees) Act (Ir.), 1788; Leases for Cotton Manufacture Act (Ir.), 1800; Mines (Ir.) Act 1806; Fines and Recoveries (Ir.) Act, 1834. See para. 8.008, *post.*

[10] 12 & 13 Vict., c. 77. Lyons, *Act to Further Facilitate Sale of Incumbered Estates in Ireland* (1850); MacNevin, *Practice of the Incumbered Estates Court in Ireland* (1859); O'Dowd, *Sale and Transfer of Encumbered Estates in Ireland* (1849); *Report of the Commissioners on the Incumbered Estates Court* (1855).

[11] Landed Estates Court (Ir.) Act, 1858 (21 & 22 Vict., c. 72). Madden, *Landed Estates Court Act* (1870).

[12] S. 3.

nineteenth century.[13] To some extent, however, their jurisdiction was made redundant by other later legislation increasing the powers of limited owners of land, especially their powers of disposition and general management. This legislation culminated in the Settled Land Acts, 1882–90, which applied to both England and Ireland (where they still apply).[14] Of even greater impact was the legislation introducing the famous land purchase scheme for Irish tenants. To this we now turn.

1.43. The first half of the nineteenth century was marked by the increasing bitterness which entered the relations between the British landlords and their Irish tenants. Agriculture was the mainstay of the economy, but it could not support the rapid growth in population that had occurred since the end of the eighteenth century. The population rose from about two million in 1784 to four million in 1800 and to eight million in 1841,[15] after which the Famine and emigration brought about an equally dramatic fall in population.[16] Some five-sixths of the population were living in rural areas, which had an average density of 217 persons per square mile. A frantic scramble for land took place, rents soared, much land was "canted" (let by public auction to the highest bidder) and the absentee landlords and their middlemen, faced with the mounting prospect of bankruptcy, put even harder pressure on the tenants. Wholesale "clearances" of estates took place if there was the slightest sign of trouble from the tenants, and while some areas of the country experienced for the first time considerable consolidation of holdings, other areas, especially in the less fertile Western parts of the country, suffered much rural congestion.[17] Fresh outbreaks of agrarian disturbances occurred and with Catholic emancipation achieved the Irish politicians gave more attention to the land problem.

1.44. By the mid-nineteenth century, it had become clear that the tenants in Ulster were far better off than their brethren elsewhere in Ireland. This was largely due to the fact that a custom, known as the Ulster tenant-right custom, had grown up among the descendants of the plantation settlers of the seventeenth century. The Devon Commission Report had produced much evidence of its existence and form.[18] The details of its operation varied in different parts of

[13] Up to 1870, some 10,655 estates were sold. But the depressed economic conditions did not make it easy to sell estates—in 1894, some 1,500 estates were left in the hands of the Landed Estates Court without a purchaser and had to be dealt with under the land purchase scheme, see para. 1.50, *infra*.   [14] See, generally, ch. 8, *post*.

[15] Connell, *The Population of Ireland, 1750–1845* (1950); see also Adams, *Ireland and Irish Emigration to the New World from 1815 to the Famine* (1932).

[16] See fn. 2, para. 1.40, *supra*.

[17] On this subject generally, see Dardis, *The Occupation of Land in Ireland in the First Half of the Nineteenth Century* (1920); Hooker, *Readjustments of Agricultural Tenure in Ireland* (1938); O'Brien, *Economic History of Ireland from the Union to the Famine* (1921); O'Tuathaigh, *Ireland Before the Famine* (1972); Pomfret, *The Struggle for Land in Ireland, 1800–1923* (1930); Devon Commission Report *Digest of Evidence* (1847); Brady, "English law and Irish Land in the Nineteenth Century" (1972) 23 N.I.L.Q. 24; Delany, "Irish and Scottish Land Resettlement Legislation" (1959) 8 I.C.L.Q. 299.

[18] See also Donnell, *Leaseholders Claim to Tenant-Right and Other Tenant-Right Questions* (1873); Ferguson and Vance, *Tenure and Improvement of Land in Ireland* (1851), Pt. II; Hooker, *op. cit.*; O'Brien, *Parliamentary History of Irish Land Question from 1829–69* (1880); Longfield, "The Tenure of Land in Ireland" in *Systems of Land Tenure* (ed. Probyn, 1881), pp. 34–43.

Ulster but the basic elements were threefold[19]; (1) the right of the tenant to
remain in possession so long as he paid his rent and performed his obligations,
reasonable limits being put on increases in rent for improvements made by the
tenant; (2) the right of the tenant to sell his interest without having to get the
consent of the landlord or wait for his recognition of the new tenant; (3) the
right of the tenant to compensation on eviction or determination of his tenancy.
A Tenant Right League was formed in 1847 to have this custom given legislative recognition and soon the campaign, led by Ulsterman Sharman Crawford,
was calling for its extension throughout the country.[20] But some 20 years went
by before substantive reforms were to be introduced. It was then that William
Gladstone began his task of solving the Irish land problem.[21] His first attempt
was the passing of the Landlord and Tenant (Ireland) Act, 1870.[22] Section 1 of
that Act declared:

> "The usages prevalent in the province of Ulster, which are known
> as, and in this Act included under, the denomination of the Ulster
> tenant-right custom, are hereby declared to be legal, and shall, in the case
> of any holding in the province of Ulster proved to be subject thereto, be
> enforced in the manner provided by this Act."

The Act also "legalised" similar customs in other parts of the country, and
several cases came before the courts in subsequent years.[23] However, for the
most part the law therein contained has passed into legal history, having been
superseded by subsequent nineteenth century legislation. Though it should be
noted that until recently the 1870 Act remained for the most part in force in
both parts of Ireland, apparently a permanent trap for the unwary conveyancer.[24]

1.45. Further amelioration of the position of tenants in Ireland was provided
by the 1870 Act in two forms: compensation for improvements to the land
made by the tenant[25] and compensation for disturbance on his giving up the
land.[26] In the case of improvements, generally compensation was to be paid
(after deductions for any rent due and depreciation of the holding) to a tenant
on leaving his holding for the unexhausted value of any improvements he had

---

[19] Bailey, "Ulster Tenant-Right Custom: Its Origin, Characteristics and Position under the Land Acts" (1894)
10 J.S.S.I.S.I. 12 and 28 I.L.T.S.J. 76, 85; Donnell, "The Ulster Tenant-Right Custom" (1880) 14 I.L.T.S.J. 346;
Ross, "Tenant-Right of Ulster" (1861) 3 J.D.S.S. 390.

[20] Crawford had played a large part in the establishment of the Devon Commission, para. 1.41, *supra*; he had
also introduced bills at Westminster in 1835 and 1836 to provide tenants with compensation for improvements to
the land.

[21] O'Brien, *Parliamentary History of the Irish Land Question from 1829–69* (1880); Hammond, *Gladstone and
the Irish Nation* (1964). See also Lyons, *Ireland Since the Famine* (2nd ed., 1985).

[22] Brooke, *Landlord and Tenant (Ireland) Act 1870* (1870); Hutton, *Handybook of Farm Tenure and Purchase
under the Landlord and Tenant (Ireland) Act 1870* (3rd ed., 1872); Mecredy, *Irish Land Act 1870* (1870); Morris,
Irish Land Act (1870).

[23] *E.g., Coleman* v. *Fry* (1873) I.R. 7 C.L. 247; *Lendrum* v. *Deazley* (1879) 4 L.R.Ir. 635; *McElroy* v. *Brooke*
(1885) 16 L.R.Ir. 46; *Upton* v. *Dufferin* (1898) 32 I.L.T.R. 118.

[24] Leitch, "Present-Day Agricultural Tenancies in Northern Ireland" (1965) 16 N.I.L.Q. 491. The position in
the Republic has changed dramatically as a result of the new legislation designed to encourage leasing of
agricultural land, the Land Act, 1984, as to which see para. 18.03, *post*.

[25] 1870 Act, s. 4. Butt, *New Law of Compensation to Tenants in Ireland* (1871).

[26] 1870 Act, s. 3.

made, at his own expense, with the consent of the landlord.[27] With respect to disturbance, a tenant not holding subject to the benefits of Ulster tenant-right or a similar custom could claim compensation on termination of his tenancy by the landlord, based on the assessment made by the court of the loss he suffered thereby.[28]

1.46. The 1870 Act was admirable so far as it went. It suffered, however, from one fundamental weakness; it did not give Irish tenants the basic security of tenure they sought. They did not want compensation after the eviction; they wanted protection from eviction itself. From their point of view the Act failed to provide an adequate solution to the land problem and the landlords were quick to exploit the weakness. They increased the rents so much that many tenants quickly fell into arrears and then, on their eviction, the landlords claimed the improvements to be used to pay off the arrears. And the acute shortage of land at the time meant that there were always plenty of other prospective tenants willing to pay the higher rents to obtain a piece of land.[29]

1.47. Renewed campaigns for reform were begun. In 1879 Michael Davitt formed the famous Land League in Co. Mayo, which soon became a national movement, with Parnell himself as President.[30] It campaigned in Ireland and at Westminster for the reduction of rents and the introduction of what the Irish tenants wanted above all else, the right to purchase the freehold of their land. Part of the campaign, aimed at disruption of the activities of landlords and their agents, was the ostracisation of any tenants co-operating with them, particularly in taking over holdings from which other tenants had been evicted. One of the first estates to be so affected was managed by one Captain Boycott, hence the word now common in the English language.[31] In the North of Ireland, a campaign grew advocating legislation to introduce the "Three F's"— Fair Rent, Free Sale and Fixity of Tenure.[32]

1.48. The standard reaction of the British Government occurred—another Committee was set up in 1880, under the chairmanship of the Earl of Bess-borough.[33] His Committee reported generally in favour of the Irish demands[34]

---

[27] And the tenant was aided in his claim by the presumption that improvements had been made by him, 1870 Act, s. 5.

[28] The Act laid down that this loss could not exceed an amount adjusted to the annual valuation of the holding, which ranged from seven years' rent (annual valuation not exceeding £10) to one year's rent (£100 or over). And in no case was the compensation to exceed £250, 1870 Act, ss. 16–9.

[29] See the *Report of the Select Committee of the House of Lords on the Landlord and Tenant (Ireland) Act 1870* (1877); *Reports from the Select Committee on the Working and Operation of the 44th, 45th and 47th Clauses of the Irish Land Act, 1870* (1877 and 1878).

[30] Davitt, *Fall of Feudalism in Ireland* (1912); Sheehy Skeffington, *Michael Davitt* (1908); Palmer, *Irish Land League Crisis* (1940); O'Hara, *Chief and Tribune: Parnell and Davitt* (1919); Bew, *Land and the National Question in Ireland 1858–1882* (1979). See also Moody, *Davitt and Irish Revolution 1846–82* (1982).

[31] Boycott was agent on the estate of the Earl of Erne on the shore of Lough Mask, Co. Mayo. See Palmer, *op. cit.*, ch. x.

[32] Butt, *Fixity of Tenure* (1866) and *Land Tenure in Ireland* (3rd ed., 1866); Gavin Duffy, *The League of North and South* (1886).

[33] Other members being Richard Dowse, Baron of the Irish Court of Exchequer, and Irish landlords Arthur Kavanagh and The O'Conor Don.

[34] *Report of H.M. Commissioners on the Working of the Landlord and Tenant (Ireland) Act 1870* (1881 Cd. 2779), 3 vols.

and Gladstone, now back in power, pushed through Parliament his second
attempt at solving the land problem. This was the Land Law (Ireland) Act,
1881, which among other things gave statutory recognition to the "Three
F's".[35]

1.49. The Act established a new tribunal, the Irish Land Commission which
was to be presided over by a High Court Judge.[36] Landlords and tenants were
given the right to apply to the county courts or the Commission[37] (organised
through sub-commissions sitting throughout the country) to have a "fair rent"
fixed.[38] If the landlord and tenant could agree on a fair rent, this would become
legally binding under the Act if filed in court.[39] The Act also granted tenants a
"judicial tenancy," in effect a statutory term of 15 years, renewable every 15
years with a revision of the rent at that time.[40] Tenants were also given the right
of free sale of their interests, subject to the landlord's right to buy out the
holding for himself or to make objections to the sale, the reasonableness of
which objections was to be determined judicially.[41] .

1.50. The 1881 Act was a success initially. About three-quarters of the
qualifying tenants[42] took advantage of it and the first general adjustment of
rents after the Act reduced rents on average by about 20·7 per cent.[43] The
second and third 15-yearly adjustments brought further average reductions of
19·3 per cent, and 9·1 per cent.[44] But the cost and time consumed in the
exercise were enormous. Some 383,145 cases in all Ireland were dealt with on
the first readjustment of rent, 144.133 on the second and 6,123 on the third.[45]
The writing was on the wall and the system of fixing fair rents was to be overtaken by an even more radical reform of the relationship of landlord and
tenant.[46] This was the very destruction of the relationship itself in respect of
agricultural land in Ireland by the land purchase scheme. The Irish could not
forget that the soil in respect of which they now held such minor interests once
belonged exclusively to them. The assumption of ownership by the British by
conquest, confiscation and resettlement may have occurred several generations previously, but the nationalistic spirit sweeping Ireland in the nineteenth

---

[35] Healy, *Land Law (Ireland) Act 1881* (1882); Johnson, *Land Law (Ireland) Act* (1881); Kisby, *Land Law
(Ireland) Act 1881* (1881).

[36] 1881 Act, Pt. VI.

[37] Ss. 41–9.

[38] Pts. II and VI.

[39] S. 8 (6).

[40] Pts. II and III.

[41] S. 1.

[42] Ss. 57 and 58.

[43] Hooker, *Readjustments of Agricultural Tenure in Ireland* (1938), Table 12 (p. 224); *Reports of the Lords
Committee on the Working of the Land Laws in Ireland* (1882–3); Irish Land Commission, *Report, 1920–21*, pp.
24–6; *Report of the Select Committee on the Land Acts (Ireland)* (1894).

[44] Hooker, *op. cit.*

[45] The Land Law (Ireland) Act, 1887 extended the 1881 Act to leaseholders by allowing them to get their rents
fixed before waiting for their leases to determine; the Land Law (Ireland) Act, 1896 provided for a uniform basis
of rent-fixing, according to the determination of the rental value of holdings and the deduction of improvements
allowances. Hooker, *op. cit.*, pp. 48–50 and Appendix A, Table 12.

[46] The right to have a fair rent fixed was abolished in the Republic of Ireland by the Land Act, 1923, s. 64, and
in Northern Ireland by the Northern Ireland Land Act, 1925, s. 23 (1).

century would never permit acquiescence in the *status quo*. The "winds of change" were reaching gale force.

1.51 The idea of land purchase, *i.e.* the purchase by the tenant of the landlord's estate in the holding so as to give the tenant the freehold, had been introduced some decades before in Ireland. Indeed, the first of the Land Purchase Acts,[47] as opposed to the Land Law Acts[48] we have been discussing so far, was the Irish Church Act, 1869.[49] This was the Act which effected the disestablishment of the Church of Ireland.[50] Part of this exercise entailed the vesting of much church property in Ireland, which was then considerable, in the Church Temporalities Commissioners. These Commissioners were empowered by the Act to sell the land to the church tenants,[51] who were aided by an advance of three-quarters of the purchase price, repayable by way of mortgage over 32 years.[52] This scheme, the idea of English economist John Bright,[53] was, of course, confined to church tenants, then about 7,000 landholders.[54] But when Gladstone introduced his 1870 Landlord and Tenant Act, Bright saw the opportunity for a wider extension of his idea of land purchase by tenants through state aid. In fact, the 1870 Act had contained some provisions, known as the "Bright Clauses."[55] Under these provisions, sales to tenants could be made in the Landed Estates Court, two-thirds of the purchase price coming from the Board of Public Works of Ireland.[56] This loan was to be repaid by a 5 per cent. annuity charged on the land, repayable over 35 years.[57] Then under Gladstone's 1881 Act, the Irish Land Commission took over the functions of the Board of Public Works and the proportion of the purchase price to be advanced was increased to three-quarters.[58] Further, if a proportion of tenants on a particular estate were willing to buy their holdings, the Land Commission was given power to purchase the whole of that estate with a view to selling off parts to the tenants.[59] Despite the apparent generosity of these provisions

---

[47] The leading work is Cherry, *Irish Land Law and Land Purchase Acts 1860–1901* (1903), Supps. (1906 and 1910). See also on land purchase, Acason, *Land Purchase Handbook* (1891); Bowen, *Statutory Land Purchase in Ireland* (1928); Campbell, *Irish Land Purchase* (1904); Fottrell, *Guide to the Land Purchase Acts* (1897); Johnson, *Land Purchase in Ireland* (1903); Maxwell, *Outlines of Law of Landlord and Tenant and Land Purchase in Ireland* (1909); O'Connell, *Landlords' and Tenants' Handy Guide to Land Purchase* (1904); Walker, *Law Relating to Land Purchase in Ireland* (1906, supp. 1907).

[48] Nolan and Kane, *Statutes Relating to the Law of Landlord and Tenant* (4th ed., 1894). See also McDermot, *Land Law (Ireland) Act, 1881 and Landlord and Tenant (Ireland) Act, 1870* (1881); McDavitt, *Irish Land Acts of 1870 and 1881* (1881); Richey, *Irish Land Laws* (1880).

[49] Atkins, *Irish Church Act, 1869* (1869); Bernard, *Irish Church Acts, 1869 and 1872* (1897); Brooke, *Irish Church Act, 1869* (1870); Todd, *Irish Church Act, 1869* (1869). See also Marshall, "Compulsory Registration and the Irish Church Act, 1869" (1983) Gaz. I.L.S.I. 5.

[50] See *The Report of the Commissioners of Church Temporalities in Ireland, for the Period 1869–80* (1881; C. 2773).

[51] Certain church tenants, *i.e.,* holders of Bishop's leases (para. 1.36, *ante*), had been given statutory relief some 30 years before by the Church Temporalities Act, 1833. They were given the right to purchase a fee farm grant (the fee simple subject to a perpetual rent) in place of their leases. Lyne, *Statute Law of Ecclesiastical Leases in Ireland and Purchases under the Church Temporalities Acts* (1838), and see para. 4.079, *post*.

[52] 1869 Act, ss. 34–7, 52 and 54.

[53] Trevelyan, *Life of John Bright* (1913).

[54] Hooker, *Readjustments of Agricultural Tenure in Ireland* (1938), pp. 53–5.

[55] 1870 Act, Pt. II; *Report of the Committee on the Purchase Clauses of the Landlord and Tenant (Ireland) Act, 1870* (1877–8).

[56] 1870 Act, Pt. II.

[57] S. 48.

[58] S. 24.

[59] S. 26.

there was still not enough inducement to the tenants to purchase voluntarily, so as to solve the land problem. Only tenants of some 1,500 holdings invoked the procedures of the 1870 and 1881 Acts.[60]

1.52. The first major step forward towards land purchase on a comprehensive scale was the passing of a Bill sponsored by the then Irish Lord Chancellor, Lord Ashbourne.[61] This was the Purchase of Land (Ireland) Act, 1885.[62] Under this the sum of £5 million was provided to the Land Commission to secure purchase of land by agreement.[63] The Commission could advance the whole of the purchase price to the tenant, though it had to retain a "guarantee-deposit" of one-fifth, which would not be paid to the landlord until the annuities repaid by the tenant amounted to the same sum of money.[64] The repayment period for annuities was extended from 35 years to 49 years, the rate of interest charged on the annuities being fixed at 4 per cent.[65] Instead of the previous method of executing the sale by way of an ordinary conveyance, sales now were to be by a vesting order made by the Land Commission.[66] And the Commission was given power to buy estates in the hands of the Landed Estates Court,[67] with a view to reselling them to the tenants.[68] It was a measure of the relative success of this Act, as amended in 1887[69] and 1888,[70] that tenants of some 25,000 holdings acquired the freehold of their holdings under it.[71]

1.53. The second major step involved the introduction of a new system of financing for the land purchase scheme. This was done by the "Balfour Acts,"[72] the Purchase of Land (Ireland) Act, 1891,[73] and the Land Law (Ireland) Act, 1896,[74] for the Conservatives had now become supporters of the idea of land purchase. Under the 1891 Act the landlord was to be paid in future, not in cash, but in a specially created Guaranteed Land Stock, equal in nominal value to the purchase price.[75] Repayment of the annuities was to be ensured by varying the amount of interest charged and by providing for additional payments.[76] And a further £30 million were voted to help finance the scheme. But the new administrative measures were not a success. The landlords objected to the issue

---

[60] Hooker, *op. cit.,* Appendix A, Table 13.

[61] It was proposed by a new Conservative Government and introduced near the end of the first session of the new Parliament; there was little debate and few amendments were proposed.

[62] Patton, *Purchase of Land (Ireland) Act 1885* (1885).

[63] S. 24.

[64] Ss. 2–3 and 5.

[65] S. 4.

[66] S. 8.

[67] See para. 1.42, *ante.*

[68] S. 10.

[69] Land Law (Ireland) Act, 1887; Healy, *Key to the Land Law (Ireland) Act 1887* (1887); Patton, *Land Law (Ireland) Act 1887* (1887); Sandford, *Land Law (Ireland) Act 1887* (1887).

[70] Purchase of Land (Ireland) Amendment Act 1888. Under the 1887 and 1888 Acts, a further £5 million were provided to the Land Commission to finance the land purchase scheme.

[71] Hooker, *op. cit.,* Appendix A, Table 13.

[72] Named after two Chief Secretaries for Ireland, Arthur Balfour and his brother Gerald; Arthur Balfour later became Prime Minister of Great Britain and Ireland.

[73] *Report of the Select Committee on the Land Law (Ireland) Acts* (1894).

[74] Barton and Cherry, *Land Law (Ireland) Act 1896* (1897); Stritch and Kenny, *Section 40 of the Land Law (Ireland) Act 1896* (1896).

[75] S. 1.

[76] Ss. 7–8.

of stock which had a fluctuating value in the market; the tenants found that the new provisions with respect to their repayments meant that it was difficult to work out at the outset the precise commitments each year.[77] The 1896 Act was introduced to remove some of these difficulties; it increased the repayment period to 73 years, reducing the amount of the annuity at the end of each of the first three decades of repayment.[78] That it satisfied most people is shown by the fact that sales doubled and tenants of some 46,000 holdings bought the freehold under the 1891 and 1896 Acts.[79]

1.54. Before leaving these Acts, an additional set of provisions in the 1891 Act should be mentioned, for they were the beginning of a scheme which was to assume great importance, which it still has, in the Republic of Ireland. The 1891 Act established what was called the Congested Districts Board;[80] certain counties in Ireland were designated "congested," according to criteria based on their population and rateable value.[81] These were the counties along the West coast of Ireland, stretching from Donegal in the North down to Cork and Kerry in the South, counties where it was estimated the population could not be adequately supported on the arable land available.[82] The Congested Districts Board was given £1½ million[83] (left out of the funds from disestablishment of the Church of Ireland under the 1869 Act[84]), to be used to develop agriculture and industry, assist with emigration and deal with small holdings generally.[85] Its powers included the right to purchase estates and sell them to tenants under the land purchase scheme (*i.e.*, financed by advances from, and annuities repaid to, the Land Commission).[86] As we shall see later, these activities are still being carried on in the Republic.[87]

1.55. The third major step in the land purchase scheme was the passing of the Irish Land Act, 1903,[88] sponsored by George Wyndham, then Secretary of State for Ireland.[89] A fillip to the scheme was urgently needed, largely because the price of government stock had fallen by some 20 per cent. since 1896 and landlords were unwilling to exchange their landed income for such stock. So the 1903 Act reintroduced the payment in cash system to replace the issue of stock system introduced by the 1891 Act[90]; further incentive to the landlords to

---

[77] Hooker, *op. cit.*, pp. 68–9.
[78] Part III.
[79] Hooker, *op. cit.*, Appendix A, Table 13. See also *Report of the Irish Land Commission* (1898).
[80] See Micks, *History of the Congested Districts Board* (1925).
[81] Part II.
[82] S. 36.
[83] S. 35.
[84] See para. 1.51, *supra*.
[85] Ss. 37–9.
[86] S. 37.
[87] Note that S. 7 of the Republic's Land Act, 1984, provides for the dissolution of the Irish Church Temporalities Fund and dispersal of funds standing to its credit, see para. 1.66, *post*.
[88] Collis, *Irish Land Act 1903* (1903); Fottrell and Fottrell, *Irish Land Act, 1903, Explained* (1904); Greer, *Irish Land Act* (1903); Quill, Hamilton and Longworth, *Irish Land Acts 1903 and 1904* (1904); Sanders, *Practical Guide to Irish Land Act 1903* (1904); Sullivan, *Irish Land Acts 1903 and 1904* (1906); Turnbull, *Land Purchase Tables under Irish Land Act* (2nd ed., 1905).
[89] Mackail and Wyndham, *Life and Letters of George Wyndham* (1925).
[90] S. 27.

sell was given by abolition of the guaranteed deposit requirement[91] and by payment of a 12 per cent. bonus on the purchase price.[92] A new system of sales was introduced, namely, sales by *estates* as opposed to sales of *holdings*.[93] Whole estates were to be sold to the tenants on the estates, under the supervision of the Land Commission's agents, the Estate Commissioners, established by the Act.[94] The tenants on the estate and their landlord were to agree amongst themselves the terms of the sale, draw up the necessary agreements and execute the appropriate documents, which were then to be lodged with the Commissioners, together with maps, documents of title and so on.[95] After the necessary checking of these, the Commissioners, if satisfied, paid the purchase price in cash and vested the holdings in the various tenants in fee simple, subject to payment of the annual annuities.[96] The purchase price was to be fixed according to whether or not the tenancies had had fair rents fixed judicially under the Land Law Acts.[97] If they had, the price was fixed within "zone" limits laid down by the 1903 Act; in effect, the purchase annuities were to be calculated on the basis of reductions of between 20 and 40 per cent. on first-term judicial rents and 10 and 30 per cent. on second-term judicial rents.[98] If the rents had not been fixed judicially, the purchase price agreed between the landlord and his tenants had to be approved by the Estate Commissioners.[99] The annuities, with interest charges of $3\frac{1}{4}$ per cent., were to be repayable over $68\frac{1}{2}$ years,[1] and the whole 1903 scheme was to be financed by £150 million, raised by a government issue of $2\frac{3}{4}$ per cent. stock.[2]

1.56. The 1903 Act was a spectacular success.[3] Some 220,000 holdings were bought by tenants under it.[4] Later Acts increased its success. Under the Evicted Tenants (Ireland) Act, 1907, the Estate Commissioners were given power to acquire land compulsorily for reinstatement of tenants who had been evicted, or their sons.[5] The Irish Land Act, 1909, known as "Birrell's Act" after the then Chief Secretary of Ireland, which extended the category of congested districts, about which it was largely concerned, authorised compulsory purchase of land in such districts and of congested estates elsewhere in Ireland.[6] For this scheme the Act reintroduced payment of the landlords in

---

[91] S. 11.
[92] S. 48. An interesting point about this bonus was that the "tenant for life" under a settlement (see ch. 8, *post*) could keep it for himself, despite his limited interest in the freehold (now replaced by capital money). And the fact is that many of the landlords at that time were only tenants for life holding under complicated family settlements, the vogue of the landed gentry of that period (ch. 8, *post*). Furthermore, under the 1903 Act, the landlord-tenant for life could sell the principal mansion house and demesne lands (para. 8.084, *post*) to the Land Commission and repurchase it subject to an annuity, *but* free from all prior encumbrances.
[93] S. 1.
[94] S. 23.
[95] Ss. 16–17.
[96] *Ibid.*
[97] See para. 1.49, *ante.*
[98] Ss. 1–5.
[99] S. 5.
[1] S. 45.
[2] S. 28.
[3] See fn. 92, *supra*, for some of the incentives introduced for landlords.
[4] Hooker, *op. cit.*, p. 82; *Reports of the Land Commission Estate Commissioners, 1903–11* and *1918–19.*
[5] S. 1. See *Report of the Royal Commission on Evicted Tenants in Ireland* (1893–4).
[6] S. 20. See *Report of the Royal Commission on Congestion in Ireland* (1906–8; Cd. 4097).

stock, this time 3 per cent. stock, and increased the rate of interest charged on tenants' repayment annuities to 3½ per cent., reducing the repayment period to 65½ years.[7] A sugar coating was put on the pill for the landlords by introduction of a new bonus on a graduated scale, to replace the old flat-rate 12 per cent. bonus.[8] The scheme worked well and some further 50,000 holdings were sold in the congested districts.[9] So much for the nineteenth-century land purchase scheme.

1.57. Before continuing further with developments in the twentieth century, it is time to pause and consider some other changes in land law which occurred in the nineteenth century. Some of these were extremely important and fundamental, though they could not of necessity have had the revolutionary effect that the land purchase scheme had. Some of them have already been mentioned, such as the consolidation of much of the statutory law relating to landlord and tenant relationships in Deasy's Act, 1860.[10] This Act is still in force in both parts of Ireland and provides the basic framework of the law, in so far as it is left generally to the parties to arrange their affairs privately.[11] As we shall see in a moment, that privilege of private arrangement of their legal rights and liabilities has been progressively whittled away by the state in the twentieth century.[12]

1.58. The nineteenth century also saw the passing of many statutory reforms which formed the very basis of modern land law and conveyancing practice. Most of this legislation applied to England and Wales as well and to a large extent the famous Birkenhead reforms in England and Wales of 1925,[13] which did not apply to Ireland,[14] were simply carrying through the nineteenth-century reforms to their logical conclusion.[15] For the most part these reforms were designed to get rid of anachronisms and restrictions on dealing with land and to introduce more simple, speedy and efficient methods of conveyancing. Thus the power of a tenant in tail (holding under a family settlement) to sell the property was facilitated by introduction of a much more straightforward method of conveyancing by the Fines and Recoveries (Ireland) Act, 1834.[16] Thereby an absurdly complicated, though extremely ingenious, conveyancing practice was displaced. A similar and much more far-reaching reform of conveyancing practice was effected by the Real Property Act, 1845, which intro-

---

[7] Ss. 1–3.

[8] S. 6.

[9] Hooker, *op. cit.*, p. 90.

[10] Para. 1.41, *ante.*

[11] Ch. 17, *post.*

[12] See also ch. 18, *post.*

[13] Grove, "Conveyancing and Property Acts of 1925" (1961) 24 M.L.R. 123; Hargreaves, "Modern Real Property" (1956) 19 M.L.R. 14; Holdsworth, "Reform of Land Law" (1926) 42 L.Q.R. 158; Johnson, "Bibliography of New Property Acts" (1926) 42 L.Q.R. 67; Johnson, "Reform of Real Property Law in England" (1925) 25 C.L.R. 609; Withers, "Twenty Years of the 1925 Legislation" (1946) 62 L.Q.R. 167.

[14] Para. 1.81, *post.*

[15] Megarry, "Change But Not Decay: A Century of the English Law of Real Property" (1960) 35 N.Y.U.L.R. 1331; Underhill, "Property 1885–1935" (1935) 51 L.Q.R. 221.

[16] Para. 4.123, *post.*

duced the modern device of a deed of conveyance which soon replaced the previous much more complicated methods, such as the lease and release and bargain and sale.[17] A more efficient law of easements and profits was introduced by the Prescription Act, 1832, which was extended to Ireland by the Prescription (Ireland) Act, 1858.[18] To a large extent, the modern statute law relating to limitation of actions for the recovery of land stems from the Real Property Limitation Act, 1833.[19] The Wills Act, 1837, consolidated much of the law relating to wills; it is still a basic statute in Northern Ireland and was only replaced in the Republic of Ireland by the Succession Act, 1965.[20] Rights to certain tithes and compositions for tithes were abolished, with savings for Crown rights, by the Tithe Rentcharge (Ireland) Act, 1838, which also commuted certain tithe compositions into annual rentcharges equal in value to three-quarters of the annual amount of the tithe.[21] The foundation of modern statutory provisions relating to trusts in Ireland was laid down in nineteenth-century legislation culminating in the Trustee Act, 1893.[22] There were also reforms introduced exclusively for Ireland. Thus the Renewable Leasehold Conversion Act, 1849, facilitated the conversion of leases for lives renewable for ever, so common in Ireland, into fee farm grants, with automatic conversion of all purported creations of such leases after the Act.[23]

1.59. The second half of the nineteenth century saw even more fundamental reforms. The Conveyancing Acts, 1881–1911, introduced many detailed changes in land law, relating to conveyances in general, leases[24] and mortgages.[25] The Married Woman's Property Act, 1882, brought several changes in the position of married women with respect to ownership of and rights of dealing with land.[26] The Settled Land Acts, 1882–90, following on from earlier legislation like the Settled Estates Act, 1877, revolutionised the law relating to land tied up in family settlements.[27] The nineteenth century was very much the era of the family settlement, when the primary objective of the landed gentry and large landowners in the British Isles was to preserve their estates intact for the enjoyment and prosperity of successive generations of the family. A large proportion of the family's wealth was attached to these estates—the commercial commodities of the modern business world, like stocks and shares, were still in the infancy of their development. The law tried to restrict the growth of these settlements of land by various rules governing the powers of settlors, but the ingenuity of conveyancers, as was so often the case in the history of land law, proved to be more than a match for the general common

---

[17] Para. 3.026, *post.*
[18] Ch. 6, *post.*
[19] Ch. 23, *post.*
[20] Ch. 14, *post.*
[21] Para. 6.123, *post*
[22] Ch. 10, *post.* The 1893 Act is still in force in the Republic of Ireland.
[23] Ch. 4, *post.*
[24] Ch. 17, *post.*
[25] Ch. 13, *post.*
[26] Ch. 25, *post.*
[27] Ch. 8, *post.*

law. The Settled Land Acts ensured the more efficient management of the large estates and paved the way for their eventual break-up and liquidation into more convenient, commercial capital assets. This process was to be further advanced, with considerable acceleration, by the introduction of taxation on land, in the form of death duties, replaced later in Northern Ireland by the single form of tax levied on death, estate duty.[28]

1.60. Then there was a vitally significant adjunct of the land purchase scheme discussed earlier. This was the introduction into Ireland of another type of registration system, additional to the registration of deeds system introduced at the beginning of the previous century.[29] The new system was a system of registration of the title to land, a version of the famous Torrens system devised in the Antipodes.[30] This system purported to enter on a public register the ownership of the land, in terms of the various estates and interests making up that ownership, as opposed to simply noting on a register the various transactions relating to a particular parcel of land without any indication of the effect of those transactions on the title or, indeed, of their validity. Registration of title involved the concept of a state-guaranteed title entered on a public register. The concept in company law that the share register should show the ownership of shares was then introduced into land law and there is evidence that this was the example which inspired the idea of registration of title to land.[31] The implications for conveyancing procedures were immense, and these were increased when the scheme introduced by the Local Registration of Title (Ireland) Act, 1891, included provisions requiring the *compulsory* registration of all the freehold titles bought out by the tenant-farmers under the land purchase scheme. Since the latter scheme eventually covered most agricultural land in Ireland, the effect of the 1891 Act has been to bring simplicity to transactions relating to agricultural land in Ireland—in marked contrast, as we shall see, to urban land.[32]

1.61. Finally, the nineteenth century saw the beginning of a new kind of land law, the public control of land by the state, imposed under the political philosophy which decreed that in certain circumstances the greater good of all required the overriding of the private rights of the individual landowner. This change of emphasis in the attitude of the state towards land ownership really only became dominant in the twentieth century and finds expression in the 1937 Constitution of the Republic of Ireland.[33] But the trend had clearly begun in the legislation of the nineteenth century. That legislation exhibited two primary ends being sought by the state: (1) control of the *use* of their land by private owners, particularly in environments where thoughtless or selfish

---

[28] Replaced in the Republic by the gift tax and inheritance tax introduced by the Capital Acquisitions Tax Act, 1976 and in Northern Ireland by the capital transfer tax introduced by the Finance Act, 1975 (U.K.). See Wylie, *Irish Conveyancing Law* (1978), paras. 1.27–8, 14. 42–3 and 17.70.

[29] Para. 1.34, *ante*. Leech, *Registration of Title* v. *Registration of Assurances* (1891).

[30] Ch. 21, *post*.

[31] See Ruoff and Roper, *Law and Practice of Registered Conveyancing* (4th ed., 1979).

[32] Ch. 21, *post*.

[33] See Art. 43, para. 1.77, fn. 92, *infra*.

claims to private rights could harm large numbers of other individuals; (2) provision by the state, through central or local governmental agencies, of what came to be regarded as *standard amenities* required by a civilised and rapidly developing industrial society, coupled with the preservation of *minimum standards and conditions* to be enjoyed by certain sections of the population in respect of land and buildings used and occupied by them. For the most part, this legislation related to the urban areas of the country, areas which were developing with the Industrial Revolution, though its effects were not felt so much in Ireland which was destined to remain a predominantly agricultural country. This was so even in the North which had more development of industrial enterprises.

1.62. The new type of legislation fell into four main categories. First, there was *public works* legislation passed to ensure the acquisition of land (compulsorily through state powers, if necessary) for the building of works necessary for the expanding and developing society—canals,[34] bridges,[35] roads[36] and railways[37] had to be provided in increasing numbers. Legislation had to confer on the appropriate public bodies the necessary powers of compulsory acquisition of land from private owners and had to lay down provisions relating to any compensation to be paid to the landowner for loss of his land. Much of this legislation was consolidated in 1845.[38] Secondly, *town government* legislation covered the provision of many of the basic services in urban areas which nowadays are taken so much for granted—paving, draining, cleansing and lighting streets, provision of sewers and a water supply, regulation of nuisances, removal of dangerous buildings and obstructions, and so forth.[39] Thirdly, *public health* legislation imposed a wide range of statutory duties relating to public health and sanitary conditions of buildings and public places, to be carried out by public authorities through extensive bye-law regulations.[40] Fourthly, *housing* legislation sought to further the tripartite goal of building *new* houses for those classes and groups within society unable to obtain accommodation for themselves; maintaining, preserving and, where possible,

---

[34] Inland Navigation Act (Ireland), 1800; Canals (Ireland) Act, 1816; Canal Carriers Act, 1845; Railway and Canal Traffic Act, 1854; Railway and Canal Traffic Act, 1888.

[35] Bridges (Ireland) Act, 1813; Bridges (Ireland) Act, 1834; Bridges (Ireland) Act, 1867; Bridges (Ireland) Act, 1875.

[36] Grand Jury (Ireland) Act, 1836; Grand Jury (Ireland) Act, 1856; Grand Jury (Ireland) Act, 1873.

[37] Railway Clauses Consolidation Act, 1845; Railways (Ireland) Act, 1851; Railways (Ireland) Act, 1860; Railways Clauses Act, 1863; Railways (Ireland) Act, 1864.

[38] Companies Clauses Consolidation Act, 1845; Lands Clauses Consolidation Act, 1845; Railway Clauses Consolidation Act, 1845. For these, and the importance in this area of the Railways (Ireland) Acts, see Suffern, *Law Relating to Compulsory Purchase and Sale of Lands in Ireland* (1882). Also Trimble, "Procedure Governing Compulsory Acquisition of Land in Northern Ireland" (1973) 24 N.I.L.Q. 466.

[39] Towns Improvement Clauses Act, 1847; Town Police Clauses Act, 1847; Towns Improvement (Ireland) Act, 1854; Municipal Corporations Act, 1882; Town Police Clauses Act, 1889. Vanston, *Law Relating to Local Government in Ireland* (1899–1905), 2 vols. (2nd ed., vol. 1, 1915; supp., vol. 2, 1919) and *Law Relating to Municipal Towns under the Towns Improvement (Ireland) Act, 1854* (1907).

[40] Public Health (Ireland) Act, 1878; Public Health Acts Amendment Act, 1890; Public Health Act, 1896; Public Health (Ireland) Act, 1896; Public Health Act 1904; Public Health Acts Amendment Act, 1907. Clery and McWalter, *Public Health Acts Amendment Act, 1907* (1908); Cotton, *Irish Public Health Acts, 1878–90* (1891) and *Public Health (Ireland) Act, 1896* (1896); McDonnell, *Manual of Sanitary Law* (1945); Vanston, *Law Relating to Public Health in Ireland* (1913); Wodsworth, *Public Health (Ireland) Act, 1878* (1878). See also Hadden, "Public Health and Housing Legislation—Towards an Integrated Code" (1976) 27 N.I.L.Q. 245.

converting and improving *existing* houses; removing *old* houses, especially those a danger to public health and safety, often as part of an extensive slum clearance and redevelopment scheme.[41] All four of these categories of legislation have developed extensively in the twentieth century.

E. Twentieth Century

1.63. To a great extent the twentieth century saw the continued development in Ireland of reforms begun in the nineteenth century. Thus the discussion above of the land purchase scheme carried over the history of that scheme to the 1903 Wyndham Act and the period before 1920, when Ireland was partitioned into two separate jurisdictions, the Republic of Ireland which became a country independent of Britain and, eventually, of the Commonwealth, and Northern Ireland which has remained an integral part of the United Kingdom. So it may be convenient first to continue the story of the land purchase scheme after 1920.

1.64. Prior to 1920, the land purchase scheme had been a purely *voluntary* one, in the sense that it was based upon agreement between the landlords and tenants, with aid from state bodies in carrying out that agreement and in finance. Some 316,000 holdings, comprising an area of about 11,000,000 acres of land, had been bought at a total price of some £100 million. Further, another 750,000 acres of "untenanted" land had been distributed among about 35,000 allottees, 600,000 of these acres being in the congested districts.[42] This was part of the scheme adopted by the Congested Districts Board for enlargement of uneconomic holdings and creation of new holdings. But in the early twentieth century there was some political movement for introduction of a *compulsory* scheme of purchase, to complete the programme as quickly as possible. Some 110,000 holdings, comprising over 3,000,000 acres, remained to be purchased in the Republic and it was calculated that about 2,000,000 acres would have to be acquired to relieve congestion. In the North about 39,000 holdings, comprising nearly 1,000,000 acres, still had to be bought out by the tenants.[43] The principle of compulsory purchase was in fact contained in a Bill introduced at Westminster in 1913, but it was lost during the Home Rule Crisis at that time. The all-party Irish Convention of 1918 reported in favour of automatic compulsory acquisition of all agricultural land still tenanted,[44] but a Bill introduced in 1920 suffered the same fate as the 1913 one. It was left to the two parts of Ireland to take action on their own after the 1921–22 constitutional changes.

[41] Housing of the Working Classes Act, 1890; Housing of the Working Classes (Ireland) Act, 1908; Housing (Ireland) Act, 1919. Bolton, *Labourers (Ireland) Acts, 1883–1906* (1908), *Housing of the Working Classes (Ireland) Acts, 1890–1908* (1914); Cotton, *Housing of the Working Classes Act, 1890* (1890); Fottrell, *Labourers (Ireland) Act, 1883* (1888); Johnson, *Labourers Act* (1907); O'Sullivan, *Key to the Labourers (Ireland) Acts* (1907). See also Hadden and Trimble, *Housing Law in Northern Ireland* (1985).

[42] Hooker, *Readjustments of Agricultural Tenure in Ireland* (1938), Chs. VII and VIII.

[43] *Ibid.*, pp. 101 an 103, Appendix A, Table 14.

[44] See the "Report of the Sub-Committee on Land Purchase" in the *Report of the Proceedings of the Irish Convention* (1918, Cd. 9019).

1.65. In the Republic of Ireland, legislation was introduced in 1923. The Land Law (Commission) Act, 1923. reconstituted the Irish Land Commission, which took over the powers of the old Estate Commissioners and the Congested Districts Board.[45] It consists of a Judicial Commissioner (a juge of the High Court)[46] and three lay Commissioners.[47] It is under the general control of the Minister for Agriculture (previously for Lands),[48] but in respect of land purchase and resettlement matters relating to particular cases, the Commissioners have unfettered jurisdiction, subject only to appeal to the Judicial Commissioner and thence to the Supreme Court (mainly on matters of law). The Commissioners have sole power to determine matters like the persons from whom the land is to be acquired, the lands to be acquired, the price to be paid and to whom the lands are to be allotted.[49]

1.66. The Land Act, 1923, was passed to further two principal objectives: (1) compulsory and automatic transfer of ownership to tenants of agricultural land, through a "vesting" system; (2) acquisition of land to relieve congestion and to secure economic holdings. The problem of congestion did not really exist in Northern Ireland and this is the main reason why the scheme in the Republic has moved much more slowly and, indeed, is still going on in the 1980s.[50] The 1923 Act specified that all tenanted[51] agricultural or pastoral land and all untenanted land in any congested district was to vest automatically in the Land Commission on an appointed day, to be used by the Commission in furtherance of its statutory duties relating to land purchase, congestion and resettlement. In addition, any untenanted land which the Land Commission declared to be required for the purpose of relieving congestion or facilitating the resale of tenanted land was to vest in the Commission. The Commission thereby became "interim" landlord, but tenants were deemed under the 1923 Act to have entered into a "purchase agreement" with the Commission on the appointed day.[52] After investigation of the title, the land was to be transferred to the tenant by a vesting order of the Commission[53] and the title registered in the Land Registry[54]; in the interim, the rents ceased but the tenants were to pay a sum in lieu of rents.[55] The Act provided for automatic fixing of the purchase price to be paid to the landlord in the form of 4½ per cent. Land Bonds, and to be repaid by the tenant by way of annuities over 66½ years.[56] With respect to

---

[45] Ss. 5–11.

[46] S. 3. See also the Land Act, 1923, s. 11; Land Act, 1933, s. 9; Courts of Justice Act, 1936, s. 7.

[47] Land Law (Commission) Act, 1923, s. 4; Land Act, 1933, ss. 2, 7; Land Act, 1950, ss. 13–18.

[48] Land Law (Commission) Act, 1923, s. 12; Land Act, 1950, s. 12.

[49] Land Law (Commission) Act, 1923, ss. 2–11. See *Corrigan* v. *Irish Land Commission* [1977] I.R. 317.

[50] See O'Sheil, "The Work of the Land Commission" (1949) II Pub. Admin.Ir. 73 and "The Changes Effected in Recent Land Commission Legislation" (1954) III Pub.Admin.Ir. 299. Also Irish Land Commissioners' *Annual Report 1982*.

[51] Defined (s. 24) to include land held under a contract of tenancy with less than 60 years to run, and excluding a fee farm grant, lease for lives renewable for ever, or letting in conacre or agistment, or other temporary letting.

[52] Land Acts, 1923, s. 28; 1927, ss. 9 and 17; 1931, s. 9; 1936, ss. 37 and 40; 1950, ss. 22 and 23; 1953, ss. 4 and 10 and Sched.

[53] Land Acts, 1927, ss. 17 and 53; 1931, Pt. II ; 1933, s. 54; 1936, ss. 10, 11 and 31; 1939, ss. 10 and 18; 1953, s. 8 and Sched.; 1965, ss. 21 and 45.

[54] Land Act, 1923, ss. 57, 61–2; Registration of Title Act, 1964, ss. 23 and 26.

[55] Land Act, 1933, ss. 14 and 15.

[56] The annuities were halved by the Land Act, 1933 (see ss. 12–13, 19–22).

holdings bought before 1923, there is a statutory prohibition of sub-division or sub-letting without the consent of the Land Commission, until the purchase advance has been paid off by the tenant; with respect to holdings bought after 1923, the prohibition remains whether or not the annuities have been paid off by the tenant.[57] The Commission may also "resume" (*i.e.*, take over) tenancies as part of its amalgamation schemes to produce more economic holdings, for relief of congestion and so on.[58] It may compulsorily acquire untenanted land for allotment and relief of congestion, though efficient farmers may successfully resist or, at least, obtain alternative holdings.[59] As a result of these provisions in the Republic of Ireland, since 1923 some 155,000 holdings, comprising over 1,800,000 hectares, have been sold to tenants under the land purchase scheme.[60] Under the congested districts scheme, some 760,000 hectares of untenanted land have been distributed to allottees.[61] But there are still some uneconomic holdings in the "congested counties" along the Western seaboard.[62] Some of these are strip holdings, held under the system of "rundale" tenure,[63] which has caused so much sub-division of the land in the West of Ireland. Frequently relatively small areas of land have been split up into numerous plots and parcels, with various tenants farming plots widely scattered over the whole area. Some consolidation and resettlement still has to be completed if such holdings are to become viable economic units and agriculture generally is to become efficient.

1.67. We turn now to Northern Ireland, where the story of the land purchase scheme since 1920 is much more simple. As a matter of constitutional law, land purchase remained under the Government of Ireland Act, 1920, a "reserved service,"[64] within the jurisdiction of Westminster. A Northern Ireland Land Purchase Commission was set up by Order in Council in 1923,[65] and the Northern Ireland Land Act, 1925, put the land purchase scheme on a compulsory basis, just as the 1923 Act had done in the Republic. The 1925 Act automatically vested tenanted land in the Commission through an "appointed day" system.[66] Once the Commission had identified the land so vested in it, that land was to be transferred to the tenants by a vesting order.[67] As in the

---

[57] Any purported sub-letting or sub-division being void and the Land Commission having the option of vesting the land in them: Land Acts, 1923, s. 65; 1927, ss. 3 and 4; 1936, s. 44; 1939, s. 30; 1946, ss. 3 and 6; 1965, ss. 12 and 13. See the discussion in Wylie, *Irish Conveyancing Law* (1978), ch. 8.

[58] Land Acts, 1923, s. 29; 1939, s. 39; 1965, s. 42.

[59] Land Acts, 1923, s. 24; 1926, s. 2; 1933, s. 29; 1936, ss. 21 and 40; 1953, s. 4 and Sched. See *Clarke* v. *Irish Land Commission* [1976] I.R. 375; *Keane* v. *Irish Land Commission* [1979] I.R. 321; *Nolan* v. *Irish Land Commission* [1981] I.R. 23; *Dreher* v. *Irish Land Commission* [1984] I.L.R.M. 95. Note the various detailed changes introduced by the Land Act, 1984, including dissolution of the Purchase Annuities Fund (s.5) and Irish Church Temporalities Fund (s.7) and provisions designed to simplify registration of title in cases of compulsorily acquired estates (ss. 8, 10 and 11).

[60] Up to Dec. 31, 1982, Irish Land Commissioners' *Annual Report, 1982*, p.15.

[61] *Ibid.*, p.12.

[62] *Ibid.*, p.5.

[63] See para. 1.15, *ante*. See also on "commonages," Irish Land Commissioners' *Annual Report, 1982*, p.7.

[64] S. 9 (3). Some legislative competence was later transferred to the Northern Ireland Parliament, see Northern Ireland Land Act, 1925, s. 27 (3); Northern Ireland Land Purchase (Winding Up) Act, 1935, ss. 1 (3), 14, 15 (2)–(4) and Sched. 2; Northern Ireland Act, 1962, s. 22 (1); Finance Act, 1963, s. 73 and Sched. 14.

[65] See S.R. & O. (N.I.) 1923, No. 615 for adaptation of earlier Land Purchase Acts to Northern Ireland.

[66] S. 8.

[67] Ss. 12 and 17.

Republic, the tenants were deemed by the statute to have entered into an agreement on the appointed day to purchase from the Commission.[68] The purchase price and annuities were fixed by the statute by reference to the rent the tenant had been paying,[69] the period of payment of the annuity being 65½ years.[70]

1.68. The scheme moved ahead rapidly and was completed by 1937, when the Commission ceased operation.[71] Thereafter all that remained to be done was collection of the annuities, presently carried out by the Northern Ireland Department of Finance and Personnel.[72] Some 39,000 holdings were sold under the 1925 Act, and the result of the land purchase scheme in Northern Ireland was that 90 per cent of the agricultural land (80 per cent. of the total area of the Province) was vested in the tenants who thereby became freeholders, holding under a title registered in the Land Registry and guaranteed by the state. Agricultural tenancies are still almost unheard of in Northern Ireland today, though, as we shall see, "lettings" of a special kind (*e.g.*, agistment and conacre) are common and the picture may change as more and more land is freed from payment of the annuities and thereby released from restrictions on sub-division and subletting.[73]

1.69. If the carrying through of the land purchase scheme was the first major development in Irish land law in the twentieth century, a development, of course, not shared with England and Wales, the second major development was the growth of state control over the private contractual arrangements of landlords and tenants of urban land. This development has been common throughout the British Isles and is an exclusively twentieth century development. There are several types of situation that arise, and in each case the state has intervened to provide statutory protection for tenants of urban property, on the ground that the economics of the situation favoured the landlord and facilitated unfair bargaining.

1.70 The first half of the twentieth century had been marked by the scarcity of housing accommodation. The phenomenon first became a serious problem in the British Isles during the First World War and it has never been solved. The immediate result was the passing at Westminster during that War of the first of a long line of Rent Restriction Acts, the Increase of Rent and Mortgage Interest (War Restrictions) Act, 1915. These early Acts, consolidated in the Increase of Rent and Mortgage Interest (Restrictions) Act, 1920, applied to the whole of Ireland.[74] They were regarded as purely temporary measures, designed to ensure that landlords should not take advantage of the housing shortage by

---

[68] S. 12 (1).
[69] S. 9 and Third Schedule.
[70] S. 1 (1) (a).
[71] Northern Ireland Land Purchase (Winding Up) Act, 1935. See Quekett, "The Completion of Land Purchase in Northern Ireland" (1940) 4 N.I.L.Q.26.
[72] 1935 Act, s. 3.
[73] See chs. 18 and 20, *post.* Also Leitch, "Present-day Agricultural Tenancies in Northern Ireland" (1965) 16 N.I.L.Q. 491. *Cf.* the provisions of the Republic's Land Act, 1984, see para. 18.03, *post.*
[74] 1920 Act, s. 18 (2).

charging exorbitant rents to those who were tenants or to those searching for accommodation for themselves and their families. They did this in two ways: (1) by restricting the level of rents that could be charged by landlords for accommodation (generally dwelling-houses with a low rateable value), a statutory formula being provided to fix the amount of rent; (2) by giving the tenant and his family security of tenure, in providing that the landlord could recover possession only by order of court, the statutes laying the precise grounds upon which only could a court make such an order. The pattern of the housing situation since 1920 has, however, decreed that in Ireland, as elsewhere in the British Isles, the rent restriction legislation has become a permanent feature of our land law.

1.71. In the Republic of Ireland,[75] the pre-1920 British system of control was adopted by the Increase of Rent and Mortgage Interest (Restrictions) Act, 1923.[76] This system was continued in operation by further legislation until the Second World War. After that War, a new system of control, arising out of the recommendations of the Black Tribunal,[77] was introduced by the Rent Restrictions Act, 1946. Local authority houses and most furnished accommodation were generally excluded from control. A new administrative procedure was introduced for speedy review and adjustment of rents paid by tenants of small premises (not exceeding £10 rateable value in Dublin, Dun Laoghaire, Cork, Limerick and Waterford). The system was again overhauled by the Rent Restrictions Act, 1960, as amended by the Rent Restrictions Act, 1968.[78] These Acts decontrolled a considerable amount of property, houses and self-contained flats (particularly all lettings after June 8, 1966, and all houses whose rateable value exceeded £40 in Dublin and Dun Laoghaire, £30 elsewhere), though sitting tenants were given rights to new leases under the Landlord and Tenant Act, 1931. The Acts laid down procedures for fixing rents of controlled property, by reference to the "basic rent" (gross rent on June 8, 1966, less rates, or the rent considered reasonable by the court) plus lawful additions in respect of rates, repairs and improvements. However Parts II and IV of the 1960 Act were declared unconstitutional by the Supreme Court in *Blake and Others* v *Attorney-General* and *Madigan* v *Attorney-General*,[79] with an immediate prospect of loss of protection by tenants. The Oireachtas responded at once by enacting the Rent Restrictions (Temporary Provisions) Act, 1981, which temporarily prohibited eviction of tenants of controlled dwellings and enforcement of rent increases notified on or after the date of the High Court decision in the

---

[75] Coffey, *Digest of Cases under Rent Acts* (1938); Coghlan, *Law of Rent Restriction in Ireland* (3rd ed., 1979); Walsh and Cosgrave, *Rent Restrictions Guide* (1943).

[76] Hughes, *Increase of Rent and Mortgage Interest (Restrictions) Act, 1923* (1923). The 1923 Act did, however, extend to business premises, see s. 17.

[77] *Agreed Report of the Town Tenants (Occupational Tenancies) Tribunal* (1941).

[78] Rents and Leaseholds Commission, *Report on Rent Control* (Pr. 1340; 1952); Rynne, "The Protection Racket or Observations on Section 54 of the Rent Restrictions Act, 1960" (1964) 30 Ir.Jur. 39; Keane, "Recent Landlord and Tenant Legislation" (1967) 2 Ir.Jur.(N.S.) 292. See also, ch. 18, *post*.

[79] Both appeals are reported at [1982] I.R. 117; [1981] I.L.R.M. 34 (see *A Casebook on Irish Land Law* (1984), p.55). See further on the constitutional law aspects of these cases, para. 1.83, *post*. See also *Reid* v. *Limerick Corporation* [1984] I.L.R.M. 366. And see Keane, "Land Use, Compensation and the Community" (1983) 18 Ir.Jur. (N.S.) 23.

cases in question, pending introduction of new legislation.[80] The first attempt
to introduce new legislation proved abortive, when the new Bill[81] passed by the
Oireachtas was referred by the President to the Supreme Court, which held
that its provisions for rebates in respect of rents were unconstitutional.[82]
Ultimately the Housing (Private Rented Dwellings) Act, 1982, came into force
on July 26, 1982,[83] providing security of tenure to tenants of dwellings
controlled by the 1960 and 1967 Acts.[84] It also provided for the fixing of the
terms of tenancies, e.g., the rent payable, by the District Court, but substantial
amendments were introduced by the Housing (Private Rented Dwellings)
(Amendment) Act, 1983, which came into force on August 2, 1983.[85] Under
the 1983 Act, a new body, the Rent Tribunal, was established to fix the terms of
controlled dwellings and this is now in operation.[86]

1.72. In Northern Ireland, a somewhat similar development has taken
place, though, until recently, rather more along the lines of what was the
position in England and Wales prior to 1957.[87] The "old" control system
operating under the "Principal Act," the Westminster 1920 Act, had been
continued in force by various Northern Ireland statutes passed from 1923–67
and functioned alongside the "new" control system introduced with the advent
of the Second World War by the Rent and Mortgage Interest (Restrictions) Act
(N.I.), 1940. Decontrol occurred during 1925–32 and after 1956, on the basis of
vacancy and resumption of possession by the landlord and by changing the
valuation limits governing control. Rent tribunals for fixing rents were
established during the Second World War but they ceased operation at the end
of the 1950s. The Rent and Mortgage Interest (Restrictions) Acts (N.I.),
1920–67, were the subject of the *Report of the Committee on Rent Restriction
Law of Northern Ireland* (published in 1975 by the then Department of
Housing, Local Government and Planning), and have now been repealed by
the Rent (N.I.) Order, 1978. This Order contains a comprehensive set of new
provisions which are discussed in a later chapter.[88]

1.73. Statutory control of landlord and tenant relations in urban areas since
1920 was extended by giving certain tenants a right to a grant of a new tenancy
on expiry of the existing tenancy. Legislation dealing with business premises

---

[80] The 1981 Act's operation was extended by the Rest Restrictions (Temporary Provisions) Continuance Acts, 1981 and 1982.

[81] Housing (Private Rented Dwellings) Bill, 1981.

[82] *Re Reference under Article 26 of the Constitution of the Housing (Private Rented Dwellings) Bill 1981* [1983] I.L.R.M. 246.

[83] See Housing (Private Rented Dwellings) Act, 1982 (Commencement) Order, 1982 (S.I. No. 216 of 1982). See on the new legislation, de Blácam, *The Control of Private Rented Dwellings* (1984) and ch. 18, *post*.

[84] See further para. 18.33, *post*.

[85] See Housing (Private Rented Dwellings) Act, 1983 (Commencement) Order, 1983 (S.I. No. 221 of 1983).

[86] See Rent Tribunal, *Annual Report and Accounts 1983/84*. Note that the 1983 Act empowers the Minister for the Environment to provide for the initial fixing of terms of tenancies by rent officers appointed by local housing authorities, with appeals from rent officer decisions lying to the Rent Tribunal. See para. 18.31, *post*.

[87] Frazer and Wylie, "The Rent Restriction Law of Northern Ireland" (1971) 22 N.I.L.Q. 99. See also Conaghan, "A Commentary on the Rent Restriction (Defective Tenancies) Act (Northern Ireland)" (1944) 6 N.I.L.Q. 125; Fetherstone, "The Rent Restriction Acts" (1946) 7 N.I.L.Q. 103; Getty, "Rent and Mortgage Restriction Acts: Their Present Application" (1936) 1 N.I.L.Q. 86; Anon., "The Rent Restriction Law (Amendment) Act (N.I.) 1951" (1951) 9 N.I.L.Q. 119.

[88] See para. 18.36 *et seq*.

came early in the century, with the Town Tenants (Ireland) Act, 1906.[89] This Act gave tenants of premises used wholly or partly for business purposes the right to compensation for improvements on quitting the premises, and for disturbance, loss of goodwill and expenses of removal, if the landlord had no good or sufficient cause.[90] The Act was little used for a variety of reasons,[91] though it seems to have been a precedent used by draftsmen of the English Landlord and Tenant Act, 1927.[92] In the Republic of Ireland, the 1906 Act was replaced by the Landlord and Tenant Act, 1931, as amended by the Landlord and Tenant (Amendment) Act, 1943.[93] The 1931 Act laid down a statutory procedure whereby a tenant could claim compensation for improvements on quitting his premises, and occupational tenants of business premises were given the right to claim a new tenancy at a rent fixed by the Circuit Court in default of agreement. The 1931 Act has since been replaced, with various amendments, by the Landlord and Tenant (Amendment) Act, 1980, which is also discussed later.[94] In Northern Ireland, the 1906 legislation was largely superseded by the Business Tenancies Act (N.I.), 1964.[95] This Act provides for compensation to tenants for improvements and gives tenants the right to new tenancies, if necessary by application to the Northern Ireland Lands Tribunal.

1.74. The question of tenants occupying residential property under moderately (by Irish standards) long leases had been under discussion since the latter half of the nineteenth century.[96] The problem was the plight of such tenants who held under a building lease, usually granted originally for 99 years,[97] under which the original tenant had covenanted to build dwelling-houses on the land, which were subsequently sold by assignment or sub-lease. At common law on expiration of the original lease, land *plus* buildings reverted to the ground landlord leaving the present tenants with no right to compensation for losing the houses they or their predecessors had bought and no guarantee of any renewal or extension of their leases at all or, if any, on terms

---

[89] Black and O'Leary, *Town Tenants (Ireland) Act, 1906* (4th ed., 1907); Brown, *Town Tenants and Landlords* (1906); Clery, Kennedy and Dawson, *Town Tenants (Ireland) Act, 1906* (1907, supp. 1913); Lehane and Coles, *Town Tenants (Ireland) Act, 1906* (1907); Muldoon and McSweeney, *Town Tenants Act* (1907); Quill, Hamilton and Longsworth, *Town Tenants (Ireland) Act, 1906* (1907). See also, *Report of the Select Committee on Town Holdings* (1884).

[90] *Byrnes* v. *Rohan* (1909) 43 I.L.T.R. 229; *Haughton* v. *Ross* (1915) 49 I.L.T.R. 72; *Bloomer* v. *O'Hara* (1917) 51 I.L.T.R. 71; *Herron* v. *O'Donnell* (1908) 42 I.L.T.R. 227.

[91] Landlord and Tenant Commission, *Report on Occupational Tenancies under the Landlord and Tenant Act, 1931* (Pr. 9685; 1967), para. 21. Para. 18.04, *post.*

[92] *Report of the Departmental Committee on the Law of Landlord and Tenant* (N.I.) (Cmd. 96; 1929), paras. 14–16.

[93] Deale, *Landlord and Tenant Acts, 1931 and 1943* (1953); Hughes and Dixon, *Landlord and Tenant Act, 1931* (1932); Moore and Odell, *Landlord and Tenant Act, 1931* (1932). Meredith Commission (R.I.), *Report of the Town Tenants Commission* (1928). Paras. 18.05–12, *post.*

[94] The 1980 Act has since been amended by the Landlord and Tenant (Amendment) Act, 1984, enacted largely to deal with problems created by the Supreme Court decision in *Gilsenay* v. *Foundary House Investments Ltd*, unreported (79/80). See ch.18, *post.*

[95] Which put on a permanent footing a series of temporary Acts beginning in 1952. (1965) 16 N.I.L.Q. 313. Paras. 18.13–18, *post.*

[96] See the historical background provided by the Republic's Ground Rents Commission, *Report on Ground Rents* (Pr. 7783; 1964).

[97] One factor in the standardisation of this period was that 99 years was the maximum limit on leases granted by tenants for life under the Settled Land Acts, 1882–90, see para. 8.071, *post.*

that were fair or reasonable.[98]

1.75. In the Republic of Ireland a considerable amount of legislation has been passed to deal with this problem. Under the Landlord and Tenant Act, 1931, as amended by the Landlord and Tenant Act, 1943, tenants in occupation of dwellings where a "long family equity" had been established became entitled to new tenancies at rents fixed by the Circuit Court, in default of agreement. That Act also entitled building lessees and proprietary lessees (sub-lessees of building lessees) to reversionary leases on termination of their building or proprietary leases. The latter provisions were replaced by the Landlord and Tenant (Reversionary Leases) Act, 1958, which reduced the maximum rents ground landlords could charge under reversionary leases.[99] The next step, echoing the land purchase scheme for agricultural tenants, came with the enactment of the Landlord and Tenant (Ground Rents) Act, 1967, which gave building and proprietary lessees the right to purchase the freehold of their properties.[1] The main distinctions from the land purchase scheme were that purchase under the 1967 Act required use of the usual conveyancing procedures (there was no vesting order system operated by a state body) and no state aid at all was given to help finance tenants. The provisions of the Landlord and Tenant Acts, 1931 and 1971, Landlord and Tenant (Reversionary Leases) Act, 1958, and Landlord and Tenant (Ground Rents) Act, 1967, have been substantially amended and to a large extent replaced by those contained in the Landlord and Tenant (Ground Rents) (No.2) Act, 1978, and the Landlord and Tenant (Amendment) Act, 1980.[2] Finally, a major step towards a permanent solution of the problem discussed here was taken in the Republic of Ireland by enactment of the Landlord and Tenant (Ground Rents) Act, 1978. This Act prohibits the creation of future ground rents in respect of "dwellings", i.e., permanent buildings constructed for use wholly or principally as dwellings. Any future lease purporting to create such a ground rent is void, unless it operates as a renewal of an existing ground lease. The prohibition extends to local housing authorities, but does not apply to separate and self-contained flats in premises divided into two or more such flats.

1.76. In Northern Ireland, legislation has been passed more recently, in the form of the Leasehold (Enlargement and Extension) Act (N.I.), 1971.[3] This Act follows fairly closely the Republic's 1967 Act and enables long lessees of residential property either to obtain a once-for-all extension of their leases for a

---

[98] Ground Rents Commission, *Report on Ground Rents* (Pr. 7783; 1964); *Report of the Committee on Long Leases* (N.I.) (Cmd. 509; 1967).

[99] Rents and Leaseholds Commission (R.I.), *Report on Reversionary Leases under the Landlord and Tenant Acts* (Pr. 2532; 1954); Landlord and Tenant Commission (R.I.), *Report on Occupational Tenancies under the Landlord and Tenant Act, 1931* (Pr. 9685; 1967).

[1] See Landlord and Tenant Commission (R.I.), *Report on Certain Questions arising under the Landlord and Tenants Acts, 1958 and 1967* (Prl. 59; 1968). See also Landlord and Tenant (Amendment) Act, 1971.

[2] The special five-year ground rents purchase scheme administered by the Land Registry under the (No. 2) 1978 Act was extended for 12 months by the Landlord and Tenant (Ground Rents) (Amendment) Act, 1983 and then for a further three years by the Landlord and Tenant (Ground Rents) (Amendment) Act, 1984. See para. 18.19 *et seq.*

[3] Wylie, "Leasehold (Enlargement and Extension) Act (N.I.) 1971—A Critique" (1971) 22 N.I.L.Q. 389. See also the Leasehold (Enlargement and Extension) (Amendment) (N.I.) Order, 1981. Para 18.40, *post.*

term of up to 50 years, or to buy out the freehold of their property.

1.77. We turn now to another form of state control over landowners, which has assumed great importance in the twentieth century. This is control over the use of land by town and country planning legislation. The central principle of this legislation is that the future development of the country as a whole, in terms of amenity, the environment and, indeed, the general economy, requires careful control and planning of the use of land. It has, therefore, a positive and negative aspect. It entails the concept that the government, centrally and locally, must plan how our towns, cities and countryside develop—which areas should be reserved for residential property, which for major industries, which for smaller commerce and where the roads, railways and airports should go. It equally entails the concept that existing landowners should be prevented from developing and using their land in a manner inconsistent with such plans and the general public interest. To achieve this, a basic principle of such legislation is that a landowner should not develop his property, whether by changing the nature of its user or putting buildings on it or making structural alterations to existing buildings, without first getting permission from the appropriate planning authority. The reconciliation of the claims of individual landowners to use their property as they please with the public interest is often an agonising one for government lawyers and planners alike. And a cynic might well comment that just as the Irish were on the brink of acquiring full ownership of their "castles," their governments reversed the process to make sure that they joined their former conquerors in finding that their homes were not their castles after all.[4] Views vary amongst theorists as to whether planning law is an entirely new breed of land law.[5] But the generally accepted view now is that it is simply a natural progression from the type of public control begun in the nineteenth century with the town government, public health and housing legislation.[6] This view was accepted by the House of Lords in a case on appeal from Northern Ireland.[7] The case arose over the provision in the Government of Ireland Act, 1920, prohibiting, like the famous Fifth Amendment to the American Constitution, the taking of property without compensation.[8] Town

---

[4] Thus Art. 43 of the Republic's 1937 Constitution prohibits the state from passing any law "attempting to abolish the right of private ownership or the general right to transfer, bequeath and inherit private property" and then goes on to qualify this by stating that the exercise of such private rights "ought, in civil society, to be regulated by the principles of social justice." To ensure this, the state is given power to delimit by law the exercise of such private rights "with a view to reconciling their exercise with the exigencies of the common good." On Art. 43, see the discussion in Kelly, *The Irish Constitution* (2nd ed., 1984), p.644 *et seq.*

[5] For one distinguished property lawyer's reaction to the English legislation, see Potter, "New Land Law under the Town and Country Planning Bill" (1947) 11 Conv. 147.

[6] Discussed at paras. 1.61–2, *ante*.

[7] *O.D. Cars Ltd.* v. *Belfast Corporation* [1960] N.I. 60. See also *McCann* v. *Attorney-General for Northern Ireland* [1961] N.I. 102 (H.L.).

[8] 1920 Act, s. 5. See Donaldson, "Taking Property without Compensation" (1960) 38 C.B.R. 114; Montrose, "Taking Property without Compensation" (1956) 11 N.I.L.Q. 278: Newark, "The Taking of Property without Compensation" (1941) 4 N.I.L.Q. 168, "Judicial Review of Confiscatory Legislation under the Northern Ireland Constitution" (1954) A.J.C.L. 552, "The O.D. Cars Case" (1960) 13 N.I.L.Q. 125 and "Taking Property" (1960) 23 M.L.R. 302; Sawer, "More on O.D. Cars" (1961) 14 N.I.L.Q. 483; Sheridan, "Taking Property without Compensation" (1954) 17 M.L.R. 249, "Nationalisation and Secion 5: Meaning of . . . Take any Property without Compensation" (1954) 10 N.I.L.Q. 183. *Cf.* The Republic's 1937 Constitution, Art 43, fn. 4, *supra*, and the discussion in the *Report of the Committee on the Price of Building Land* (1973; Prl.3632), ch. VIII. See Keane, "Land Use, Compensation and the Community" (1983) 18 Ir.Jur. (N.S.) 23.

and country planning, as we know it today, would become prohibitively expensive if this requirement were applied to it, and the House of Lords, as the American courts had done decades before,[9] rejected the argument that planning control involved a taking of property. All the same, that provision in the 1920 Act was promptly repealed by Westminster soon after the case was decided by the Lords, to remove any remaining doubt so far as Northern Ireland was concerned.[10]

1.78. In the Republic of Ireland, town and country planning legislation was introduced by the Town and Regional Planning Acts, 1934 and 1939,[11] under which the Minister for Local Government was responsible for considering planning schemes made by local authorities,[12] for holding local inquiries into objections to schemes and for giving final approval or disapproval. The Oireachtas was given power to annul schemes approved, and right of appeal to the High Court was given to persons whose property was affected. This legislation was replaced in 1963 by much more comprehensive legislation, modelled on the English legislation which had begun with the Town and Country Planning Acts, 1944 and 1947. The new Act was the Local Government (Planning and Development) Act, 1963, which imposed on planning authorities statutory duties to make development plans for their areas of jurisdiction (plans have to be revised every five years), to control development of land and take planning decisions in accordance with their plans, to keep registers of planning decisions, to create areas of special amenity and to enforce building regulations. Landowners have a direct statutory duty to seek planning permission from the appropriate planning authority before development of their property and development is defined in the widest terms. Breach of the statute in this regard is a criminal offence. The 1963 Act was amended substantially by the Local Government (Planning and Development) Act, 1976,[13] and provisions relating to pollution were contained in the Local Government (Water Pollution) Act, 1977.

1.79. In Northern Ireland, legislation in this area has not gone so far as in the Republic in some respects, though, perhaps, farther in other respects. As regards provision of the central core of planning legislation like that of England and Wales and, since 1963, the Republic of Ireland, Northern Ireland did not have this until the Planning Order, 1972, was made at Westminster.[14] Previously several undertakings in this regard had been given by government spokesmen, especially since the strictures on the subject delivered by Sir

---

[9] *Village of Euclid* v. *Ambler Realty Co.* (1926) 272 U.S. 365. See generally, Haar, *Land Use Planning* (1959).

[10] Northern Ireland Act, 1962, s. 14.

[11] Miley and King, *Town and Regional Planning Law in Ireland* (1951).

[12] *Re Application of O'Dea* (1957) 92 I.L.T.R. 34; *The State (Modern Homes (Ireland) Ltd.)* v. *Dublin Corporation* [1953] I.R. 202.

[13] See also Local Government (Planning and Development) Act, 1983. For a detailed discussion of the Republic's planning legislation, see Nowlan, *A Guide to the Planning Acts* (1978); Walsh, *Planning and Development Law* (2nd ed. by Keane, 1984); Wylie, *Irish Conveyancing Law* (1978), ch. 7. See also Keane, *The Law of Local Government in the Republic of Ireland* (1982), ch.7.

[14] S.I. No. 1634, made under the Northern Ireland (Temporary Provisions) Act, 1972, For a detailed discussion of the 1972 Order's operation, see Wylie, *Irish Conveyancing Law* (1978), para. 7.052 *et seq.*

Robert Matthew in 1963.[15] At that time there was no statutory duty to make plans imposed on local planning authorities and none had ever been made, and planning control had been exercised simply through a system of "interim development" control.[16] This system had been backed up by an indirect sanction—there was no positive statutory duty on landowners to obtain planning permission, but, if they did not do so, they might be deprived of the development without compensation if the planning authority sometime in the future adopted a planning scheme inconsistent with that development.[17] Several other pieces of planning legislation have been enacted since the Matthew Report. The Land Development Values (Compensation) Act (N.I.), 1965,[18] was passed to freeze future compensation claims to 1963 values, unless a certificate of development value was obtained for the particular site in question from the then Ministry of Development and registered in the Statutory Charges Register. This Act was regarded as an essential preliminary to the passing of the new comprehensive planning legislation, enforcement of which was thought otherwise to be too expensive. Also in 1965, there was passed the New Towns Act (N.I.), which was amended to cover existing towns and cities (like Londonderry) by the New Towns (Amendment) Act (N.I.), 1968. This Act provided for the establishment of new town development commissions charged with the duty of planning and developing in a comprehensive manner new towns, whether from scratch on new sites or by amalgamation of existing towns and villages. Since the Act, commissions have been established to develop a new city called Craigavon (sited between Lurgan and Portadown in Co. Armagh), an existing city, Londonderry, and to amalgamate and develop as one urban complex, Antrim and Ballymena (in Co, Antrim).[19] Then again in 1965, there was passed the Amenity Lands Act (N.I.),[20] which provides for the establishment and development of National Parks, nature reserves, areas of outstanding natural beauty and of scientific interest. The Act governs planning administration of such areas and the acquisition of land for such purposes. In 1971 legislation was passed to provide for compensation to be paid to owners of property suffering from "planning blight" as a result of planning decisions, as opposed to loss by direct acquisition as part of public authority development.[21] Then various amendments to Northern Ireland planning law were introduced by the Planning (Amendment) (N.I.) Order, 1978. Article 3 excludes compensation in certain cases where

[15] *Belfast Regional Survey and Plan* (Cmd. 451; 1963).

[16] The basic legislation was the Planning and Housing Act (N.I.), 1931 and the Planning (Interim Development) Act (N.I.), 1944. See *Belfast Corporation* v. *Goldring* [1954] N.I. 107; *Holland and Others* v. *Antrim C.C.* [1953] N.I. 1.

[17] *Shillington* v. *Belfast Corporation* [1960] N.I. 107; *R. (Antrim C.C.)* v *Ministry of Health* [1960] N.I. 1; *R. (Hanna)* v. *Ministry of Health and Local Government* [1966] N.I. 52; *R. (Antrim C.C.)* v. *Antrim Justices* [1967] N.I. 111; *R. (Bryson)* v. *Ministry of Development* [1966] N.I. 52.

[18] Hill, "Land Development Values (Compensation) Act (N.I.) 1965" (1967) 18 N.I.L.Q. 476.

[19] The housing functions of these commissions have since been taken over by the Northern Ireland Housing Executive under the Housing Executive Act (N.I.), 1971. As regards public housing generally, see the consolidating Housing (N.I.) Order, 1981.

[20] Lewis-Crosby, "Amenity Lands Act (N.I.) 1965" (1965) 16 N.I.L.Q. 562.

[21] Planning and Land Compensation Act (N.I.), 1971, Pt. I, replaced by the consolidating Planning Blight (Compensation) (N.I.) Order 1981.

planning permission is revoked. Article 4 prohibits demolition of buildings (other than those already subject to restrictions, such as listed buildings and historic monuments) in conservation areas, and article 5 authorises the making of grants or loans for specified expenditure in such areas. There are various other provisions amending the law relating to traffic signs, enforcement notices, stop notices, planning blight and blight and purchase notices. Comprehensive provisions relating to pollution are contained in the Pollution Control and Local Government (N.I.) Order, 1978. These include provisions for waste disposal, control of noise and prevention of pollution of the atmosphere. Finally, to aid the settling of disputes arising out of this sort of law, and related law like the law of rating, compensation, and questions arising under the Business Tenancies Act (N.I.), 1964, there was established in Northern Ireland a Lands Tribunal under the Lands Tribunal and Compensation Act (N.I.), 1964.[22]

1.80. One further aspect of the state control over landowners in the twentieth century which may be mentioned is registration. The Registry of Deeds and Land Registry (registration of title) systems have already been noted. The latter grew in importance as more and more agricultural land was compulsorily registered under the Local Registration of Title (Ireland) Act, 1891, so that by the 1970s the great bulk of non-urban land in Ireland is governed by the system. This means that conveyancing transactions must be carried out in accordance with the procedures and regulations of the Land Registry.[23] In urban areas, however, the Registry of Deeds has had a more important influence because registration of title is not compulsory, and voluntary registration is rare because of the complexities of urban titles in Ireland.[24] But recent developments should change this in the future. The machinery for extension of compulsory registration of title, so as to cover eventually all land in Ireland and thereby render the Registry of Deeds redundant, has been established in both the Republic of Ireland[25] and Northern Ireland.[26] But it will be a long and slow process and the Registry of Deeds will continue to be a vital factor in urban conveyancing for some decades to come.[27] With respect to Northern Ireland, it should also be noted that a separate registry was established by the Statutory Charges Register Act (N.I.), 1951 (though it is, in fact, housed in, and administered by the officials of, the Land Registry in Belfast).[28] This system is analogous to the English system of registration of local land charges established by the Land Charges Act, 1925

---

[22] Tenenbaum, "Lands Tribunal and Compensation Act (N.I.), 1964" (1965) 16 N.I.L.Q. See now the consolidating Land Compensation (N.I.) Order, 1982.

[23] Ch. 21, *post.*

[24] Ch. 22, *post.*

[25] Registration of Title Act, 1964, especially s. 24.

[26] Land Registration Act (N.I.), 1970, especially s. 25.

[27] Paras. 21.27–28, *post.*

[28] Murray, "Statutory Charges Registration Act (Northern Ireland) 1951" (1952) 9 N.I.L.Q. 90. See now Land Registration Act (N.I.), 1970, Pt. x. Paras. 21.57–9, *post.* See also the discussion in Wylie, *Irish Conveyancing Law* (1978), para. 7.097 *et seq.*

(now governed by the Local Land Charges Act, 1975[29]), and it covers registration of matters like local authority charges under public health and housing legislation, statutory conditions attached to houses under housing legislation, drainage charges, preservation orders and certificates of development value.

1.81. Finally, lest a misleading picture be obtained from the above discussion, it should be understood that there have also been major developments in the private law side of land law this century. It is true that neither the Republic of Ireland nor Northern Ireland has enacted the wide changes in the law made in England and Wales under the Birkenhead legislation of 1925.[30] But the fact that six major Acts were passed in the same year then has tended to obscure developments in Ireland since 1925. And it is the case that both parts of Ireland have been catching up, if rather belatedly. The six Birkenhead Acts were the Settled Land Act, Trustee Act, Law of Property Act, Land Registration Act, Land Charges Act and Administration of Estates Act. As regards the Land Charges Act, 1925 (since replaced by the Land Charges Act, 1972), Ireland had already in 1925 a universal Registry of Deeds system which England did not have.[31] Introduction of a third registry would have been of doubtful value, even if administrative staff had been available to run it. It is true that Northern Ireland introduced the Statutory Charges Register in 1951, but this has a much more limited scope than the English Land Charges Register.[32] As regards the Land Registration Act, 1925, it has already been mentioned that both parts of Ireland have recently introduced comprehensive legislation on registration of title, which envisages eventual extension of compulsory registration throughout Ireland, similar to what has been developing in recent years in England.[33] Northern Ireland's Trustee Act, 1958, as amended by the Trustee (Amendment) Act (N.I.), 1962, is the equivalent of the English 1925 Act and later Acts like the Variation of Trusts Act, 1958.[34] It is true that the Republic of Ireland still has the 1925 Act's forerunner, the Trustee Act, 1893, as its basic text, but various amendments have been passed to bring it up to date, *e.g.,* the Trustee Act, 1931, and the Trustee (Authorised Investments) Act, 1958. A comprehensive statute on charities was enacted for England and Wales in 1960, and this has been followed by the Republic's Charities Acts, 1961 and 1973, and the Charities Act (N.I.), 1964.[35] As regards administration of estates, the Republic of Ireland has enacted the Succession Act, 1965, which radically alters the law relating to the devolution and administration of estates, testamentary disposition, intestate distribution and disinheritance.[36] Northern Ireland has enacted the Administration of Estates

---

[29] See Adams, "Local Land Charges Act 1975" (1976) 40 Conv. 106.

[30] See, however, the proposals for N.I. in the *Survey of the Land Law of Northern Ireland* (1971), as modified by the Land Law Working Group's *Discussion Documents*, Nos. 1 (*Ground Rents and Other Periodic Payments*) (1980), 2 (*Estates and Interests and Family Dealings in Land*) (1981), 3 (*Landlord and Tenant*) (1982) and 4 (*Conveyancing and Miscellaneous Matters*) (1983) and their Interim Report (*Ground Rents and Other Periodic Payments*) (1983).

[31] Ch. 22, *post.*

[32] Para. 21.61, *post.*

[33] Ch. 21, *post.*

[34] Ch. 10, *post.*

[35] Ch. 9, *post.*

[36] Chs. 14–6, *post.*

Act (N.I.), 1955,[37] the Inheritance (Family Provision) Act (N.I.), 1960, and the Family Provision Act (N.I.), 1969, since replaced by the Inheritance (Provision for Family and Dependants) (N.I.) Order, 1979.[38] In the Republic of Ireland, a major new development was the enactment of the Family Home Protection Act, 1976, the detailed operation of which has been considered elsewhere.[39]

1.82. Thus only the Law of Propety Act, 1925, and the Settled Land Act, 1925, have not been followed. This is not surprising, for these two Acts may be said to form the core of the "revolution" effected in 1925. It is questionable how far it is desirable that they should be followed; the Settled Land Act has, in particular, proved to be controversial and it is extremely doubtful if it improved on the earlier Settled Land Acts, 1882–90, which still apply in both parts of Ireland. A full scale survey of this subject was completed for the Director of Law Reform of Northern Ireland in 1974,[40] and it remains to be seen what reforms in the North result from it.[41]

1.83. Finally, it should be noted that the 1937 Constitution of the Republic of Ireland contains an Article (Article 43) dealing with private property and any legislation which is repugnant to the principles stated in the Article, whether it is legislation passed before or after enactment of the Constitution, is void in so far as it is repugnant. This Article provides that the State acknowledges that man in virtue of his rational being has the natural right to the private ownership of external goods (this includes land) and that the State accordingly guarantees that it will not pass any law attempting to abolish the right of private ownership or the general right to transfer, bequeath or inherit property. It then provides that the exercise of property rights ought in civil society to be regulated by the principles of social justice and that the State may accordingly, as the occasion requires, delimit by law the exercise of these rights with a view to reconciling their exercise with the exigencies of the common good. A full discussion of this Article and of the cases decided on it is outside the scope of this book. The importance of the Article lies in the constitutional recognition of the right to private property,[42] and it was mentioned earlier how significant this has become in recent times in respect of property legislation, such as the rent restriction legislation.[43]

---

[37] Important changes in the law of succession were made by the Family Law Reform (N.I.) Order, 1977, and Administration of Estates (N.I.) Order, 1979, see *ibid*.

[38] *Ibid*.

[39] Wylie, *Irish Conveyancing Law* (1978), para. 6. 31 *et seq*. See also Shatter, *Family Law in the Republic of Ireland* (2nd ed., 1981), p. 317 *et seq*.

[40] *Survey of the Land Law of Northern Ireland* (H.M.S.O.; 1971). See Powers of Attorney Act (N.I.), 1971 and Commission on Sales of Land Act (N.I.), 1972 (Kerr, (1973) 24 N.I.L.Q. 1).

[41] Apart from the two Acts mentioned in fn. 40, see also the Property (N.I.) Order, 1978, as to which see further para. 19. 46, *post*. Note also the work being carried on now by the Land Law Working Group, see para. 1.81, fn. 30, *ante*.

[42] See the discussion in the *Report of the Committee on the Price of Building Land* (1973; Prl. 3632), ch. VIII.

[43] See para. 1.71, *ante*. For detailed treatment of Article 43, see Kelly, *The Irish Constitution* (2nd ed., 1984), p. 644 *et seq*. See also on constitutional law generally, Doolan, *Constitutional Law and Constitutional Rights in Ireland* (1984); Morgan, *Constitutional Law in Ireland* (1985); O'Reilly and Redmond, *Cases and Materials on the Irish Constitution* (1980).

CHAPTER 2

TENURE

I. INTRODUCTION

A. THE FEUDAL SYSTEM

2.01. The concept of *tenure*[1] was fundamental to the feudal system of land-holding introduced into Ireland in the twelfth century by Henry II and his Norman followers.[2] When William I had conquered England a century earlier, he had imposed a system of landholding under which all land in the kingdom belonged ultimately to the King. All other ownership of the land could be derived from the Crown only. The King was chief lord of all the land and all other landowners held their land from him, directly or indirectly. There was no such thing as absolute ownership (*allodial* tenure as opposed to feudal tenure), and with this system of derivative title to the land the early conquerors were able to exert controls over the more powerful in their kingdoms. The feudal system became not only a form of landholding, but also a system of government and provision of revenue.[3]

2.02. Henry II and his successors purported to apply these principles to Ireland.[4] There was, however, one major drawback. The conquest of Ireland was not like William's conquest of England. The conquest of Ireland was a long-drawn-out affair which took several centuries. The feudal system which was introduced in the twelfth century was not imposed over the whole of the country until the seventeenth century. During this period the system under-went many changes in both England and Ireland, and it is probably true that its final victory in Ireland in the early seventeenth century was a somewhat hollow one.[5]

2.03. Nevertheless the basic principles of the feudal system are still of con-siderable importance in the land laws on both sides of the Irish Sea. In Ireland their importance has two aspects. The first is in the survival of the notion that no land is allodial. In Northern Ireland, as in England and Wales, all land is still held under the Crown as ultimate successor to it. In the Republic of Ireland the position is the same except that the State now occupies the position of the

---

[1] Taken from the latin verb *tenere,* meaning "to hold."
[2] See Butt, *Land Tenure in Ireland* (3rd ed., 1866); Montgomery, *History of Land Tenure in Ireland* (1889); Probyn (ed.), *Systems of Land Tenure in Various Countries* (1881); Hogg, "Effect of Tenure on Real Property Law" (1909) 25 L.Q.R. 178; Norwood, "The Law of Land Tenure in Ireland" (1924) 10 Conv. 4.
[3] Challis, *Law of Real Property* (3rd ed., 1911; Irish Supp., 1956); Digby, *History of Law of Real Property* (5th ed., 1897); Coke, *Upon Littleton* (19th ed., 1832); Holdsworth, *Historical Introduction to Land Law* (1935); Simpson, *A History of Land Law* (2nd ed., 1985); Williams, *Principles of the Law of Real Property* (23rd ed., 1920).
[4] Paras. 1.16–9, *ante.* Lynch, *View of Legal Institutions, Honorary Hereditory Offices and Feudal Baronies Established in Ireland During the Reign of Henry II* (1830).
[5] Para. 2.44, *infra.*

Crown.[6] The second aspect is the fact that so much of our modern land law is derived from the old feudal rules and cannot be adequately explained without reference back to the feudal system. Thus in subsequent chapters in this book, especially those dealing with estates in land[7] and future interests,[8] constant reference will have to be made to the feudal system.

B. TENURE AND ESTATES

2.04. *Tenure,* as we have seen, involves the notion of one person holding land from or under another person. Under the feudal system there were several kinds of tenures and we shall discuss some of them later in this chapter.[9] In more modern times this notion of holding land from or under another has been applied to arrangements outside the purview of the feudal system. These will also be discussed later[10] and in more detail in the chapter on the law of landlord and tenant.[11] The distinction between the various types of tenure lies in the rights and obligations of the parties holding the land. In other words, tenure relates to the terms upon which the landowner holds his land, *i.e., how* he holds it.

2.05. The other central concept of the feudal system was that relating to *estates* in land.|Tenure governs the terms upon which the landowner holds his land; the doctrine of estates determines for how long he can so hold the land‖In this sense no one owns land; he owns an estate in the land. The landowner holds his land for an estate in accordance with the terms appropriate to the form of tenure under which he holds. As in the case of tenure, the doctrine of estates has also been applied to arrangements not recognised by the feudal system.[12]

C. TENURE

2.06. Under the feudal system imported into England and Wales, and thence to Ireland, the King granted large areas of land to his closest followers and supporters. This land was to be held by each grantee under the King subject to the terms and conditions specified (thereby fixing the type of tenure) and for the period of time specified (thereby fixing the type of estate). That grantee would probably in turn make sub-grants of part of his land to his followers, again on specified terms and conditions and for a set period of time. That sub-grantee might subsequently make sub-sub-grants, and so the process of sub-division of the land originally granted by the King might continue. Much of the land throughout the kingdom became subject to ownership by numerous individuals, all bound together by the links of tenure. The result was the construction of what is often called the feudal "pyramid of interests."

[6] Para. 2.52, *infra.*
[7] Ch. 4, *post.*
[8] Ch. 5, *post.*
[9] Paras. 2.13–33, *infra.*
[10] Para. 2.55, *infra.*
[11] Ch. 17, *post.*
[13] Ch. 4, *post.*

2.07. Because of the fundamental principle that all ownership was derived from the King on the basis of tenure, the process of grants and sub-grants inevitably created an hierarchical structure of ownership. At the top of the structure, the apex of the pyramid, was the King. Then in descending order came his immediate grantees, known as *tenants in chief* (*in capite*).[13] After them came the *mesne tenants,* so called because they occupied the intermediate tiers of the pyramid of ownership. There might be several such tiers sandwiched between the tenants in chief, one tier below the King, and the sub-grantees at the base of the pyramid. Those in occupation at the base of the pyramid were known as *tenants in demesne.*[14] The following rather simplified diagram should help to illustrate why the pyramid metaphor is so often used in this context.

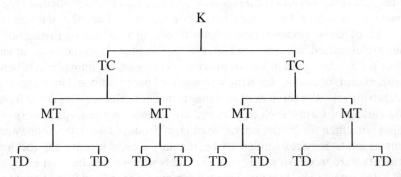

Key: K—the King; TC—tenants in chief; MT—mesne tenants; TD—tenants in demesne.

2.08. This diagram is over-simplified because it shows only that part of the pyramid structure relating to the land occupied together by the eight tenants in demesne. In theory all land in the kingdom was held under one enormous pyramid structure emanating from the King. And each tenant in chief could make numerous sub-grants from which could emanate even more numerous sub-sub-grants. All of these grants and sub-grants added both to the number of tiers in the pyramid structure and to the number of grantees on that tier, thereby constantly widening the base of the pyramid, until it covered all land in the Kingdom.

2.09. For reasons which we shall discuss later in this chapter, complex feudal pyramids of interests such as that outlined above no longer exist in Ireland any more than they exist in England.[15] Yet complex pyramids of interests of a different kind are very common in Ireland today, much more so than in England. Indeed the irony developed that the century when English common law finally gained universal recognition in Ireland, to the exclusion of the native

---

[13] See *County Palatine of Wexford Case* (1611) Dav. 159.

[14] The terms could still be applied today, but they have long fallen out of use because of the reduction in the practical significance of the feudal system of tenure, see para. 2.53, *infra*.

[15] Para. 2.44, *infra*.

brehon law,[16] was the century that also saw the crumbling of the feudal system. Yet from the ashes of that system there emerged in Ireland a hierarchical system of landowning just as complex, which survives undiminished in the urban areas of both parts of the country. This sytem is constructed of grants and sub-grants by way of fee farm and of leases and sub-leases for very long terms of years. This system is described in detail in a later chapter[17] and may be compared with the feudal system just described.[18]

D. Services and Incidents

2.10. It has already been stated that the concept of tenure involved the notion of holding land subject to certain terms and conditions. These terms and conditions were the *services* that had to be performed by the tenant (grantee) for his lord (grantor) and the *incidents* which attached to the particular type of tenure under which the tenant held. For the most part the services and incidents of tenure became standardized according to the tenure in question.[19] They are discussed in more detail later in this chapter. The landowner at each tier of the feudal pyramid had to provide services for his immediate superior (lord), except, of course, the King who was lord paramount and in the position of receiving only the services of his tenants in chief. The services could have a wide variety of forms, such as personal attendance on the lord, provision of armed horsemen for battle, provision of farm produce and, later, money payment as rent. Services tended to be regular, steady income for the lord. Incidents were more irregular, periodic rights which could be claimed by the lord with respect to his tenants. They were more standardised than services and some applied to nearly every form of tenure. The most common incidents were the lord's right to manage the land of an infant heir of one of his tenants (wardship), to select the spouse for any tenant in his wardship (marriage) and the incident of escheat, whereby the land reverted to the lord on death of his tenant without leaving any heirs to succeed to the land.

II.TENURES

2.11. There were many different types of tenure recognised by English feudal law.[20] But not all of these were imported into Ireland. The reasons for this have already been alluded to in the previous chapter.[21] The major underlying reason would seem to be the fact that the extent of the influence of English law in the first few centuries after Henry II's visit fluctuated greatly. Large areas of the country remained subject to the native brehon law until the seventeenth century, by which time, as we shall discuss in a moment, the feudal system was on the wane anyway. And the caveat must also be entered at this point that our knowledge of Irish legal history, especially of the period following medieval

---

[16] See para. 1.28, *ante.*
[17] Ch. 4, *post.*
[18] See also para. 2.55, *infra.*
[19] Paras. 2.13–33, *infra.*
[20] For modern discussion, see Megarry and Wade, *The Law of Real Property* (5th ed., 1984), ch. 2.
[21] See especially paras. 1.16–9, *ante.*

times, is somewhat sketchy.[22] It is dangerous to be too dogmatic on the subject of Irish land law in the fifteenth to the seventeenth centuries. Those were exceedingly turbulent times and the area of influence of English feudal law decreased rather than increased during the period.

2.12. The ensuing discussion concentrates on the English feudal law (as it was extended to Ireland) simply because it was the tenures of this system which were established as the sole method of landholding from the seventeenth century onwards. The native brehon system, to the extent that it coud be said to involve a concept of tenure,[23] ceased thereafter to have any practical significance—apart from a few isolated cases. And in passing it should be noted that the brehon concepts of *tanistry* and *gavelkind,* denied recognition by the Irish courts at the beginning of the seventeenth century, were not, technically speaking, systems of tenure. Rather they were customary modes of descent—incidents of tenures rather than tenures themselves.[24]

A. CLASSIFICATION

2.13. A basic distinction in various tenures recognised by English feudal law was between those under which the landholder, the tenant, was *free* and those under which the tenant was *unfree,* so far as his tenure was concerned. The concept of freedom in this context, however, is an elusive one. It could be applied both to the *tenure* under which the tenant held his land and to the *status* of the tenant generally in the eyes of the law. The question of freedom of tenure would affect matters like how far the services to be performed by the tenant were fixed and certain as to quantity and quality; or how far the feudal system would recognise the tenant's occupation of the land, so as to protect him, for example, from ejectment. The question of freedom of status under the general law affected matters like the tenant's ability to bring actions in the King's courts. This question has already been mentioned in connection with the subject of the status of the native Irish under English law in medieval times.[25] And it is not clear that under the feudal system the concepts did not become mixed. All tenants personally unfree necessarily held under unfree tenure; but in the early days it seems that not all tenants personally free held under a free tenure. This at least seems to have been the situation in England.[26]

2.14. As far as Ireland was concerned it may be questioned whether such distinctions were strictly observed. Again our knowledge of the subject is limited, but it seems to have been the case that as far as tenure, as opposed to status, was concerned, most feudal tenures were of the free kind in Ireland.[27]

---

[22] Mac Niocaill, "The Contact of Irish and Common Law" (1972) 23 N.I.L.Q. 16. See also Green, "Irish Land in the Sixteenth Century" (1907) 3 Er. 174; Dolley, *Anglo-Norman Ireland* (1972); Frame, *English Lordship in Ireland 1318–1361* (1982); Moody, Martin and Byrne (eds.), *A New History of Ireland*; vol. iii, *Early Modern Ireland 1534–1691* (1976).

[23] Paras. 1.12–5, *ante.*

[24] Para. 1.15, *ante.*

[25] Para. 1.22, *ante.*

[26] Megarry and Wade, *op. cit.,* p. 23.

[27] See, generally, Otway-Ruthven, *A History of Medieval Ireland* (1968) and the other authorities cited in fn. 64, para. 1.19, *ante.*

B. Free Tenures

The two major categories of free tenures were tenures in chivalry (more commonly known as military tenures) and tenures in socage. There were also some rather more specialised tenures, such as those applying to ecclesiastical land.

1. Military Tenures

2.15 There were two main types of military tenure, *grand sergeanty* and *knight-service*. Grand sergeanty was a very special tenure, being confined to the King's closest followers and servants. It usually involved service personal to the King[28] and became limited to tenants in chief. These limitations probably meant that little land, if any, in Ireland was held by such tenure. Purely practical difficulties, including those of travel in those days, would prevent holders of Irish land from rendering personal service to the King in England. And the Kings of England spent as little time as possible in their kingdom on the other side of the Irish Sea.

2.16. Knight-service, however, was much more common. It was an essential feature of the Norman conquerors' programme of settlement in both England and Ireland. Originally, the King granted the land to his tenants in chief subject to service by way of provision of a fixed number of knights or armed horsemen at certain periods of each year. In this way the King provided himself with the closest thing to a standing army owing loyalty to himself. But this form of tenure was not confined to tenants in chief; indeed, these tenants in turn often imposed the same tenure on their sub-grantees, so that several tiers in the feudal pyramid of interests might be occupied by tenants holding by knight-service. In those parts of Ireland which became subject to the feudal system prior to the seventeenth century, knight-service was the standard tenure.[29]

2.17. Early in the conquest of England, the obligation of the tenant to provide armed horsemen began to be commuted for a money payment to the lord, known as *scutage*.[30] And it seems that this was generally the position in Ireland from the thirteenth century onwards.[31] However, the main source of the lord's income from the lands he granted away came not so much from the services owed by the tenants as from the incidents of the tenure. The incidents attaching to knight-service were extremely important, for they continued to play a major part in the development of both English and Irish land law long after the break-up of the feudal system itself. The following were the main incidents of tenure:

---

[28] *E.g.*, service as part of the royal household, or carrying the King's colours in battle or on travel.

[29] See Otway-Ruthven, "Knight Service in Ireland" (1959) LXXXIX Jo.R.S.A.I. 1, "Knight's Fees in Kildare, Leix and Offaly" (1961) XCI Jo.R.S.A.I. 163 and "The Character of Norman Settlement in Ireland" (1965) v Hist.Stud. 75. Also para. 1.18, *ante*, And see *County Palatine of Wexford Case* (1611) Dav. 159 and the terms of the Crown patent in *Boyd* v. *Magee* (1848) 11 Ir.L.R. 166, (1849) 13 Ir.L.R. 435.

[30] See, generally, Stenton, *The First Century of English Feudalism.*

[31] Otway-Ruthven, *A History of Medieval Ireland* (1968), pp. 103–5.

(i) Homage

2.18. The tenant was obliged to pay homage to his lord. He had to swear to be his lord's man, and connected with this idea was the notion of fealty, an oath by the tenant to abide by his feudal obligations faithfully. He was also obliged to pay suit of court, *i.e.,* attend the lord's court and participate in its deliberations.[32]

(ii) Wardship

2.19. This arose wherever a tenant died leaving an infant heir only. In those days there was no right to make wills of land[33] and succession under the feudal system was based on the rules of *primogeniture*.[34] Under these rules, the eldest surviving male child was the heir of the tenant, females only succeeding in the absence of any male survivors. But the feudal times were exceedingly turbulent and the question arose as to what was the position if the heir was an infant (under twenty-one for males, fourteen for females).Such an heir would find it very difficult to perform the requisite services to the lord, and the concept of wardship was the feudal system's answer to the problem. Wardship gave the lord the right to manage the land until the heir came of age. The lord could, and usually did, manage the land for his own profit, subject to a general duty to keep and maintain the infant heir, and not commit waste on the land.[35] Originally, the lord had additional surrender rights at the end of the period of wardship—half a year's profits as the price of his surrender of the land to the heir. But this practice was prohibited for all except the King by Magna Carta in 1215.[36]

(iii) Marriage

2.20. This right arose also in the case of an infant heir. It was the right of the lord to choose a spouse for any tenant in his wardship. If the tenant declined to marry the lord's choice, or married without the lord's consent, the lord could fine him.[37]

(iv) Relief

2.21. This related to succession by an heir of full age. The lord was entitled to a payment by the heir as the price of his right to succeed as tenant. The usual price seems to have been an amount equivalent to one year's profits of the land. In the case of a tenant in chief holding directly under the King, it seems that the King had an additional right in this regard, known as *primer seisin*. This was a

---

[32] This did not mean that the tenant could not appeal to the independent King's courts. Military tenants were at the top of the feudal hierarchy and were all personally free in the eyes of the general law, enjoying rights of audience in the King's courts.

[33] This right was not granted by statute until the seventeenth century in Ireland, see para. 14.02, *post*, though the same result could be achieved prior to that by a "use".

[34] See para. 15.05, *post*.

[35] Magna Carta, 1215, cc. 4 and 5, imposing the penalty of loss of wardship rights. See Hand, *English Law in Ireland, 1290–1324* (1967), pp. 163–4.

[36] C. 3.

[37] Statute of Merton, 1235; Statute of Westminster 1, 1275, c. 22. Hand, *op. cit.*, p. 245.

prerogative right of the King to take possession of the land until the appropriate homage and relief were rendered to him. And no doubt the King helped himself to the profits of the land during his possession.

(v) Aid

2.22. The lord could demand payments from his tenants on certain specified occasions. These occasions were eventually fixed by statute,[38] such as when the lord's eldest son was knighted or his eldest daughter married. Aid could also be demanded to pay ransom for the lord should he be captured by enemies.

(vi) Forfeiture

2.23. It is questionable whether this right, which belonged to the King only, is properly described as an incident of tenure. It was essentially a prerogative right of the Crown to seize the land of any subject convicted or attainted by Act of Parliament of high treason. We have already seen that this was a right destined to assume enormous significance in Irish history, with consequent effects on the development of Irish land law.[39] This Crown right, which could be exercised against any landholder in the feudal pyramid, whether or not he held directly under the King, should not be confused with a right of forfeiture which an ordinary lord might claim against his immediate tenant. A lord could reserve, and frequently did, an express right of forfeiture if his tenant failed to perform any of his feudal services. Then the Statute of Gloucester, 1278,[40] conferred on the lord a right of action for forfeiture if services were two years in arrears and there were no distrainable goods on the land.[41] The Statute of Westminster II, 1285, extended the right of action for forfeiture to one enforceable against third parties who might acquire the land in question.[42]

(vii) Escheat

2.24. This was an extremely valuable right in an age when landowners could not make a will decreeing the succession to their land. Under the feudal system, if a tenant died without heirs, his land escheated to his immediate lord, *i.e.*, reverted back to the lord to be disposed of as the lord pleased.[43] Another form of escheat to the immediate lord occurred if the tenant was attainted (convicted and sentenced to death) for felony.[44] Though in this case the escheat was subject to the Crown's right to "year, day and waste."[45] This form of escheat to the immediate lord should not be confused with forfeiture to the Crown (whether or not the immediate lord) on attainder for high treason.

2. *Tenures in Socage*

2.25. These tenures were the second main category under which the tenant was free. Free and common socage[46] became the most prevalent tenure, so

---

[38] *E.g.*, Magna Carta, 1215, cc. 12 and 15; Statute of Westminster I, 1275, c. 36.

[39] Paras. 1.29–33, *ante*. See the *Report of the Commissioners' Inquiry into Irish Forfeiture* (1700).

[40] C. 4. See Hand, *op. cit.*, p. 167.

[41] As to the remedy of distress, see ch. 17, *post*.   [42] C. 21. Hand, *op. cit.*, p. 167.

[43] *Fawcett* v. *Hall* (1833) Alc. & Nap. 248 at 253 (*per* Burton J.) and see note at pp. 259–60; *Tisdall* v. *Tisdall* (1839) 2 Ir.L.R. 41.

[44] *Re Tracy* (1828) 2 L.Rec.(o.s.) 37

[45] *I.e.*, to hold the land for a year and a day and to commit waste on it, such as cutting timber.

[46] There has been some dispute as to the derivation of the word "socage." Some thought it came from the

much so that a presumption arose that a free tenure was socage unless proved to be some other form of tenure. For the most part the services usually attached to these tenures related to agriculture, such as ploughing so many days each year. Later these services were commuted into money payments by way of rent.[47]

2.26. In England there were special kinds of socage tenures which probably did not apply to Ireland. First there was petty sergeanty, which involved some immediate service to the King of a less personal nature than that owed under grand sergeanty.[48] For the same reasons given above,[49] it is unlikely that any Irish landowners were subject to such services. Then there were some customary variations on the tenure, particularly in relation to succession to the land. The two most famous customs in England were *Gavelkind*, which related to land in Kent, and *Borough English*, which related to land in Sussex and Surrey, and some other parts of England.[50] These customs did not, of course, apply to Ireland, though we have already seen that customary modes of succession did exist in Ireland during these times. But these Irish customs had nothing to do with the feudal system of tenure; indeed, they were not really forms of tenure at all.[51] They were the customs of *tanistry* and *gavelkind* (in its Irish sense[52]), which belonged to the ancient Irish brehon law and which were to vie with the feudal principle of primogeniture for recognition during the four centuries prior to the seventeenth century.[53]

    2.27. To come back to free and common socage, the distinguishing features of this form of tenure as opposed to military tenures lay, first, in the different nature of the services (agricultural as opposed to military) and, second, in the incidents. The general theory seems to have been that socage tenants were not subject to the same number of incidents as military tenants. In particular, they were not supposed to owe homage, nor be subject to wardship or marriage.[54] But it seems that in Ireland it was claimed as part of the "custom of the land of Ireland" that the lord of a socage tenant did have the rights of wardship and marriage. This custom seems to have been based on the rule that these rights accrued where homage was paid by the tenant, as seems to have been often the case in Ireland. Whatever the reasons for the Irish custom, it seems clear that Irish lords were determined in their efforts to ensure its observance in the

---

French "soc," meaning a plough-share, which would accord with the fact that such tenures usually attached to agricultural land. The more modern view seems to be that the word was derived from the Canon word "soc," meaning "seek"; the socage tenant had to seek his lord's "soke" or court. *Cf.* Holdsworth, *History of English Law*, vol. 3, p. 51; Pollock and Maitland, *History of English Law* (2nd ed., 1898), vol. 1, pp. 293–4.

[47] In England, these money payments were known as "quit rents," *i.e.*, rent paid by the tenant so that he might be quit of his services. But the expression "quit rent" has a rather more narrow meaning in Ireland, see para. 6.009, *post*.

[48] *E.g.*, supplying arms for the King's soldiers or providing him with minor servants.

[49] Para. 215, *supra*.

[50] For details, see Megarry and Wade, *The Law of Real Property* (5th ed., 1984), pp. 19–21.

[51] See paras. 1.15 and 2.12, *ante*.

[52] It had some similarity to the Kentish custom in that the eldest male heir did not succeed as he would under primogeniture. Division amongst males occurred in both cases.

[53] Para. 1.28, *ante*. For an early example, see Hand, *English Law in Ireland 1290–1324* (1967), p. 173.

[54] There was supposed to be a system of guardianship for infant heirs, but, and this is the significant point, the lord had no claim to the guardianship. See Holdsworth, *op. cit.*, p. 397; Pollock and Maitland, *op. cit.* vol. 2, pp. 436–47.

thirteenth and fourteenth centuries. Professor Hand has recently traced the long and tangled course of litigation in the late thirteenth century, revolving around the rights of wardship and marriage to the land of one John Comyn, tenant of the Manor of Kinsaley, in County Dublin. The actual case resulted in a judgment of the court *coram rege* in 1285 against the Irish custom, on the ground that there ought to be one and the same law in the two parts of the Kingdom. The judgment was, however, later declared null, because the wrong procedure had been used to start the action, and the Irish custom seems to have continued its somewhat shaky existence.[55]

3. *Religious Tenures*

2.28. The third category of free tenures were those relating to ecclesiastical land, such as land held by monasteries or persons connected with religion, such as a bishop. One common type was *Frankalmoign*, meaning "free alms." In this case no fealty was owed and the only service necessary was the tenant's obligation to pray for the lord's soul. As far as Ireland was concerned, it seems that many religious bodies, particularly those that had been in existence since prior to the Norman invasion, held in frankalmoign.[56] Though the Archbishops of Armagh and Dublin acquired land to be held by knight-service instead.[57]

C. UNFREE TENURES

2.29. We come now to those tenures which were unfree under the feudal system. In terms of social status the distinction was between those tenants regarded as landed proprietors and those who were simply common labourers with no independent claims to the land. As far as the law was concerned, the unfree tenant suffered from several disabilities. First, he had no *seisin* in the land. This is a difficult concept to define, and we shall discuss it in more detail later,[58] but its practical significance in the present context was clear. The King's courts would protect only the tenants seised on the land, because the more important incidents of tenure attached to those tenants only. If a tenant was unfree the seisin was in his lord, so that any dispute arising out of an unfree tenant's tenure could be referred only to his lord's court. He had no access to the King's courts. One of the privileges of a feudal landowner was to hold a court for determination of disputes as between his tenants. The way in which the King's courts gradually took away this jurisdiction is a matter of legal history outside the scope of this book. Secondly, while a free tenant's services were fixed both as a quantity and quality, an unfree tenant's were not fixed as a quality. He might know exactly how many days a year he had to work for his lord, but he did not know at what he would be working. In this sense his lord

---

[55] See Hand, *op.cit.*, pp. 178–86.
[56] Hand, "The Church and English Law in Medieval Ireland" in *Proceedings of the Irish Catholic Historical Committee* (1959), pp. 10–18.
[57] Richardson and Sayles, *The Irish Parliament in the Middle Ages* (1952), pp. 18, 120–1.
[58] Ch. 4, *post*.

had a discretion to determine how onerous the performance of services of an unfree tenant could be. Thirdly, many unfree tenants were also personally unfree, *i.e.,* of servile status. The unfree tenant could be bought and sold; frequently he was regarded as a part of the land and would pass along with the land if it were sold to a third party.

2.30. In England the main category of unfree tenure was that known as *villeinage,* or *copyhold* as it came to be called.[59] This was the tenure closely associated with an institution central to Norman feudal theory, the manor. The manor was a unit of landholding consisting of the lord's immediate demesne, *i.e.,* his manor house and the land attached to it which the lord cultivated himself. Each manor had its own tenants closely associated with it, and it would usually include a limited amount of land cultivated by these tenants. The manor had its own courts to settle disputes between the tenants attached to that manor. Villein tenants in the early days seem to have held their land at the will of the lord, but eventually a customary law developed to protect them, which was enforced in the manor court. They had no access to the independent King's courts. They were subject to mainly agricultural and labouring services and the incidents of their tenure included fealty, relief, escheat and forfeiture. There were also incidents not usually attached to free tenures, such as heriots, *i.e.,* the lord's right to take the tenant's best beast or chattel on his death.[60] Villeins were not permitted to alienate their land without the lord's consent, which, if granted, would be conditional upon payment of a fine.

2.31. In later centuries the customary law of the manor acquired in England much greater significance until the end of the fifteenth century, when the King's courts began to recognise and enforce it.[61] During this period the tenure assumed the title of copyhold, "tenure by copy of the court roll" to give it its full title. This was derived from the practice which had emerged of having tenants' transactions with the land executed by the lord's steward or bailiff and then recorded on the manor rolls. The tenant engaging in the transaction was given a copy of the appropriate entry to prove his title in any future transaction, rather like the modern day land certificate when a title is registered in the Land Registry.[62] The law relating to copyhold developed in England and remained of great significance down to the present century. We must, however, pause at this point to consider the position in Ireland in relation to copyhold.

2.32. The first point to emphasise is that our knowledge of this subject is very limited. Secondly, to the extent that the Normans introduced the concept of manors into Ireland, and it seems clear that they did in the early days, the numerous wars and uprisings in the centuries following the Normans' invasion

[59] See Megarry and Wade, *The Law of Real Property* (5th ed., 1984), pp. 22–8; Scriven, *A Treatise on the Law of Copyholds* (7th ed., 1896).

[60] For an Irish example, see *Earl of Inchiquin* v. *Burnell* (1795) 3 Ridgw. P.C. 376, 426.

[61] Holdsworth, *History of English Law,* vol. 2, pp. 324–6; Pollock and Maitland, *History of English Law* (2nd ed., 1898), vol. 1, pp. 585–94.

[62] Ch. 21, *post.*

were totally inimical to any sort of orderly development of a landholding
system according to its principles. And these were the centuries when the
principles of copyhold tenure were being evolved in England. In Ireland,
tenure of the land in any form fluctuated rapidly and during the fourteenth to
the sixteenth centuries the influence of the feudal system generally waned.
Having said that, there is no doubt that in the early medieval period there
existed in Ireland a class of tenant very like the English villein. In particular,
there were the native unfree Irish tenants known as *betaghs*, about whom
considerable controversy has arisen of late. This subject has been mentioned
earlier.[63] In the early years of the conquest, the grantees of land did build
manor houses to which were attached unfree tenants, whether native Irish
unfree betaghs bound to the soil or free Irishmen admitted to the protection or
avowry of the lord of the manor.[64]

2.33. Because of the turbulent history of Ireland it is unlikely that any
extensive system of copyhold could develop and there is little evidence that one
did.[65] The comprehensive recurrent confiscation and resettlement of the land
during the course of the seventeenth century would have destroyed much of
any system that did develop, because that resettlement was executed very
much along the lines of modern landlord and tenant law rather than feudal lord
and tenant law.[66] Some remnants may have survived in the form of local
customs, and there are quite a few references in later law to manors, manor
courts and related matters,[67] but these would all have been swept away by the
land purchase scheme in the nineteenth and twentieth centuries.[68] Support for
this view may be found in nineteenth century legislation. Thus the Manor
Courts (Ireland) Acts, 1826 and 1827, which extended earlier Acts of the Irish
Parliament,[69] dealt with various matters relating to the operation of manor
courts in Ireland and the activities of their stewards or seneschals. But these
courts were abolished by the Manor Courts Abolition (Ireland) Act, 1859,
which transferred their jurisdiction to petty sessions courts.[70] The English

---

[63] Para. 1.21, *ante*.

[64] See Hand, *English Law in Ireland 1290–1324* (1967), pp. 187–201; Otway-Ruthven, *A History of Medieval Ireland* (1968), pp. 108–19.

[65] Paras. 1.27–33, *ante*.

[66] Note, however, *Earl of Inchiquin* v. *Burnell* (1795) 3 Ridgw.P.C. 376. *Cf. Martin* v. *Cotter* (1846) 9 Ir.Eq.R. 351.

[67] *E.g.*, 10 & 11 Chas. 1, c. 18 (Ir.), 1634 (relating to heriots); 27 Geo. 3, c. 22 (Ir.), 1787 (recovery of small debts in manor courts). The Tenures Abolition Act (Ir.), 1662, s. 11, expressly saved tenure by copyhold from its provisions (see para. 2.48, *infra*), but this Act was largely a copy of the English 1660 Act. See *Anon* (1843) Ir.Cir.Rep. 825; *cf. Martin* v. *Cotter* (1846) 9 Ir.Eq.R. 351 at 356.

[68] Paras. 1.51–6, *ante*. See O'Brien, "An Account of the Manor of Kilmoon, and the Copyhold Tenure existing there" (1876) 7 J.S.S.I.S.I. 232; Hamilton, *Records of Court Leet for Manor of Dunluce in Co. Antrim, held 1798–1847* (1934).

[69] 25 Geo. 3, c. 44 (Ir.), 1785; 27 Geo. 3, c. 22 (Ir.), 1787. Both statutes were later repealed by the Statute Law Revision (Ir.) Act, 1879. See *Reports on Manor Courts in Ireland* (1837–8); also *Costelloe* v. *Hooks* (1848) 11 Ir.L.R. 294; *Caulfield* v. *Hutchinson* (1851) 3 Ir.Jur.(o.s.) 371; *Herbert* v. *MacLean* (1860) 12 Ir.Ch.R. 84. For further instances of litigation before manor courts, see *Robinson* v. *Hughes* (1840) 1 Cr. & Dix 405; *Henderson* v. *Pool* (1841) 2 Cr. & Dix 114; *White* v. *McConnell* (1841) 2 Cr. & Dix 115; *King* v. *Gibbons* (1842) Ir.Cir.Rep. 488; *Eken* v. *Doherty* (1843) Ir.Cir.Rep. 751; *Miller* v. *Turner* (1843) 3 Cr. & Dix 169; *Pidgeon* v. *McEvoy* (1845) 3 Cr. & Dix 386.

[70] Though s. 1 of the 1859 Act did save franchises and other rights attaching to existing manors, such as rights to "head money, leet money, or leet silver." Willes J. commented on the position of copyholds of Ireland: "We are not aware that these base tenures exist in Ireland. In them the freehold is always and immediately in the lord

legislation of the nineteenth century,[71] which provided for commutation of manorial rights and enfranchisement of tenants holding under copyhold or customary tenure, was expressed to apply to Ireland,[72] but when these statutes were consolidated in the Copyhold Act, 1894, that Act did not apply to Ireland.[73] By then, of course, the land purchase scheme for Ireland was well under way. None of the later English legislation[74] applied to Ireland nor was any equivalent enacted in either part of Ireland. The expression "manor" is still, of course, commonly used in Ireland, but one must remember to draw a distinction. The word as used in a conveyance, or for that matter in an auctioneer's or estate agent's brochure or advertisement, may simply be part of the description of the geographical location of the land.[75] It should not of itself be taken as indicating the tenure by which the land is held.

III. STATUTORY REFORMS

2.34. Any layman, even with a limited knowledge only of the methods of holding land in Ireland today, realises that little of the complex system of tenure outlined above survives. We must now discuss why that is so. For the historian, sociologist or economist the answer lies in the changing patterns of social and economic life in the country since the days of the Norman invasion. For the lawyer much of the answer lies in certain important statutes, which were passed no doubt to take account of those changing patterns. These statutes brought about a considerable simplification in the tenures recognised by the feudal system, and eventually a reduction in their number. This does not mean that we do not have a complicated system of tenure in Ireland today; indeed, nothing could be further from the truth, as we shall see in a moment.[76] The point here is, however, that the modern system is not the feudal system nor even a direct descendant of it.

Before discussing the various statutes, an initial distinction must be drawn. It is a distinction which was basic to the methods in the early days of conveying land held subject to feudal tenure. And it is a distinction which is just as valid in modern conveyancing.[77]

A. SUBINFEUDATION AND SUBSTITUTION

2.35. *Subinfeudation* was the process of making grants, followed by sub-grants and sub-sub-grants, out of the same piece of land. To refer back to the

---

only, though the usufruct is in the tenant." *Delacherois* v. *Delacherois* (1864) 11 H.L.C. 62, 83. Lord St. Leonards in the same case doubted if the "Manor of Donaghadee" was a manor retaining its old manorial customs, such as its own court, *ibid.*, p. 99. *Cf. Duke of Devonshire* v. *Neill* (1883) 8 App.Cas. 135; *Lord Midleton* v. *Power* (1886) 19 L.R.Ir. 1.

[71] Copyhold Acts, 1841, 1843, 1844, 1852, 1858 and 1887.

[72] 1841 Act, s. 100. The later Acts were to be deemed and construed as part of the 1841 Act.

[73] S.99.

[74] Law of Property Act, 1922, especially s. 128 and Scheds. 12 and 13; Law of Property Amendment Acts, 1924, Sched. 2 and 1926, Sched.; Administration of Estates Act, 1925, Sched. 2.

[75] *E.g.*, "the manor of Donaghadee in the baronies of Clandeboye and Ards in the County of Down." See *Delacherois* v. *Delacherois* (1864) 11 H.L.C. 62.

[76] Para. 2.55, *infra*.

[77] *Cf.* assigning and subletting under modern landlord and tenant law, ch. 17, *post*.

discussion of feudal pyramids of interests,[78] it was the process of adding new tiers to the pyramid in order descending from the King at the apex. Taking by way of illustration the diagram given earlier,[79] subinfeudation occurred each time a TC made a grant to an MT and each time an MT made a grant to a TD. Each of these parties then held the land comprised in the grant subject to the services specified in it, and the incidents appropriate to the form of tenure it created—each party, that is, except K, the King, because he enjoyed only the benefits of the feudal system, none of the burdens. He did not hold under anyone and so owed no services and was subject to no incidents. And herein lies the key to some of the early statutory reforms.

2.36. As we have stated before, the feudal system was not just a system of landholding; it had equally important governmental and financial significance. In medieval times land was the greatest source of wealth, quite apart from being the main source of subsistence for the bulk of the population. In those days there was nothing of the trappings of the modern stock market, based on industrial and commercial enterprise. The feudal system of landholding was the primary method of generating wealth, with its concepts of services and incidents. The King and his government depended upon the continued remission and enjoyment of these throughout the pyramid structure. This is where the process of subinfeudation could cause difficulties, particularly as regards the incidents of tenure which, though periodic in enjoyment, produced infinitely more income in the long run than services.

2.37. The problem was that the value of the incidents depended entirely upon the agreement of the grantor and grantee at each tier of the pyramid. The vice from superior grantors' point of view was that they had no control over this agreement. Let us take again the diagram given earlier as an illustration. Suppose K granted land to one of the TCs to hold by knight-service, but that TC, when sub-granting to an MT, imposed on MT the condition simply that he hold the land at a rent of one acre of corn a year. If TC died leaving an infant heir, K was entitled to wardship; if TC died leaving no heir, the land (*i.e.*, the interest retained by TC) escheated to K. But because of the terms of TC's grant to MT, this was worth very little, particularly when compared with the value of the land itself originally granted to TC by K. K would enjoy only wardship of TC's right to one acre of corn per year, or would get back only this right by escheat; he would have no right to possession of the land itself because this had been granted to MT. Additional problems could arise if TC subinfeudated all the land comprised in his grant from K; no longer retaining a part to be occupied by himself and his family, he might move to live elsewhere in the country or travel around. The result could be that K might find it difficult to discover when TC died, which was the crucial date determining K's rights to wardship and escheat. Of course, these problems did not only affect the King. They affected all grantors in the feudal structure; TC could have exactly the same problems

---

[78] Para. 2.07, *supra.*
[79] Para. 2.07, *supra.*

when MT sub-granted to TD and so on. The point is, however, that the King, being ultimate owner of all land in the country, suffered more than anyone else. And it is not surprising that early legislation was passed to deal with the matter. This brings us to the other form of conveyancing used in feudal times, *substitution*.

2.38. As its name implies, substitution was a method of granting land whereby the grantee, instead of holding under the grantor, was substituted for the grantor in the feudal structure. In other words, instead of adding a new tier to the pyramid, the existing tiers remained unchanged except that a new occupant was inserted for the old one, who disappeared from the scene. Taking our earlier diagram, TC instead of sub-granting to an MT could simply transfer his interest in the land to a new TC, who would from then on hold under K in exactly the same way, subject to exactly the same services and incidents.

2.39. This form of conveyancing did not suffer from the defects that sub-infeudation had for the King and other superior lords. But there were some drawbacks. One was that some lords objected to substitution by their tenants without their consent. They took the line that the smooth functioning of the relationship of lord and tenant to some extent was dependent upon personal characteristics. A lord would try to choose a hardworking, reliable and conscientious tenant, whatever form of tenure was imposed. Substitution without the lord's consent exposed the lord to the risk of being saddled with a completely untrustworthy tenant, with all the problems that that would involve. A related problem was the danger of the tenant sub-dividing his land and trying to substitute several tenants for himself. The lord would then find that he would have to deal with several people when questions arose about services to be provided, a matter obviously less convenient than dealing with only one tenant solely responsible for everything owed to the lord. Much controversy raged about these aspects of substitution in the early days of the feudal system, and again legislation was passed to deal with the matter. And it is to the legislation on feudal tenure that we now turn.

B. MAGNA CARTA, 1217

2.40. The Great Charter of 1217[80] had attempted to meet some of the lords' objections to alienation without consent. It purported to prohibit tenants from alienating so much of their land that the part retained would not be sufficient to yield the services owed to their lords. This was designed to prevent excessive fragmentation and sub-division of the land, which would rapidly decrease the lord's security for the services owed to him out of the land by his original tenant.

2.41. The Charter also forbade the conveyance of land in "mortmain," *i.e.*,

---

[80] 18 John, c. 39; for a later version, see 9 Hen. 3, c. 32. For the applicability of the various versions of Magna Carta to Ireland, see the cases cited in fn. 86, para. 1.24, *ante*. Also Richardson, "Magna Carta Hiberniae" (1942) 3 I.H.S. 31; Samuels, "Magna Carta as Living Law" (1969) 20 N.I.L.Q. 49.

into the dead hand of corporations or religious bodies like monasteries.[81] The reason was that this meant the loss of those feudal incidents which arose on the death of the tenant. An institution or corporation could not "die" like a human being, so in such a case the lords lost incidents like wardship, marriage and escheat.

C. QUIA EMPTORES, 1290

2.42. This statute[82] was a much more forthright attempt to meet the demands of the feudal lords.[83] In contained four main propositions:

(1) subinfeudation was prohibited[84];
(2) all free tenants were given the right to alienate the whole or part of their land by way of substitution, *without* the lord's consent[85];
(3) where there was alienation by substitution of parts only of the tenant's land, the services were to be apportioned between the various parts[86];
(4) the earlier legislation prohibiting alienation to mortmain was reiterated.[87]

2.43. The Act was expressly limited to grants of land to be held for an estate in fee simple,[88] so that it did not prohibit grants of lesser estates, such as a fee tail[89] or life estate,[90] by way of subinfeudation. It did not mention the Crown, expressly or by necessary implication, so the usual rule of construction in such circumstances applied, namely that the Crown was not bound by it.[91] The result was that tenants in chief were prohibited from subinfeudating, but were not given the right of free alienation without consent.[92] They were not given this right by statute until 1327, and then only on condition of payment of a

---

[81] C. 43. See also the Statute of Mortmain. 1279 (7 Edw. St. 2).

[82] To give it its fuller title, the Statute of Westminster III, cc. 1–3 (18 Edw. 1). Its terms are set out fully in *A Casebook on Irish Land Law* (1984), p.40. For very early citation of the statute in an Irish court (in 1302), see *Calendar of Justiciar Rolls of Ireland, 1295–1303*, pp. 383–5. See also (1966) 17 N.I.L.Q. 513.

[83] C. 1 contains a preamble stating some of the problems: "Forasmuch as puchasers of lands and tenements . . . have many times heretofore entered into their fees . . . to be holden in fee of their feoffors, and not of the chief lord of the fees, whereby the same chief lords have many times lost their escheats, marriages, and wardships of lands and tenements belonging to their fees. . . ." For the technical meaning of "feoffors" in this context, see para. 3.023, *post*; for the moment "grantors" may be substituted.

[84] C. 1. "From henceforth it shall be lawful to every freeman to sell at his own pleasure his lands and tenements, or part of them; so that the feoffee shall hold the same lands or tenements of the chief lord of the same fee, by such service and customs as his feoffor held before." Note that the apparently permissive nature of the wording at the beginning of this passage has always been interpreted as meaning that, if a tenant chooses to sell, he must do so by substitution.

[85] *Ibid.* As the passage quoted in the previous footnote indicates, the substituted tenant was to hold by the same services as the previous tenant.

[86] C. 2. The apportionment was to be made "according to the quantity of the land or tenement sold."

[87] C. 3. See fn. 81, *supra; Report and Evidence of Select Committee on Mortmain* (1845); *Incorporated Society v. Richards* (1841) 4 Ir.Eq.R. 177. See para. 25.21, *post*.

[88] *Ibid.* See para. 4.021, *post*.

[89] Para. 4.112, *post*.

[90] Para. 4.143, *post*.

[91] This point was to have particular relevance in Ireland, see para. 4.059, *post*. Also *Fowler* v. *Fowler* (1865) 16 Ir.Ch.R. 507.

[92] They had been forbidden to alienate without royal licence by an Ordinance of 1256. Though it may be noted that Irish tenants in chief were given the right to subinfeudate in marchlands in 1293, to ensure the better defence of such land, see *Statutes of the Parliament of Ireland, King John to Henry V* (ed. Berry 1907), p. 192.

reasonable fine to the Crown.[93] Payment of such fines was not abolished until the passing of the Tenures Abolition (Ireland) Act, 1662.[94] The Crown was to exercise its right to subinfeudate extensively in Ireland, particularly after the seventeenth century confiscations. We shall return to this matter in a moment. It may be useful first to pause and consider the implications of *Quia Emptores*, for they have had a lasting effect on the development of our land law.

2.44. First, it may be said that the statute contributed to the break-up of the feudal system of tenure. By prohibiting subinfeudation, albeit within the limits just mentioned, it ensured that the feudal pyramid of interests was more likely to contract in later centuries. After the 1290 restrictions, it was unlikely that the feudal pyramid would get bigger and so long as tenants were not allowed to make wills of their lands,[95] the doctrines of escheat and forfeiture meant it would get smaller with the passage of time. It led to the gradual disappearance of all mesne tenants, until most land was held directly under the Crown. This was certainly the case in England and probably in Ireland. The slight reservation is entered for two reasons. One is that the break-up of the system in Ireland was probably more attributable to the fact that the common law generally lost influence in the fourteenth to the sixteenth centuries.[96] The common law did not really reassert itself in Ireland until the seventeenth century, and that was the period of a revolution in land law which swept away many of the remaining concepts of the feudal system. Most of the land in the country during this period was subjected to successive confiscations and re-settlements,[97] which brings us to the other reason for the reservation.

2.45. When the Crown was making resettlements of land in Ireland during the seventeenth century, this was usually done through grants by letters patent.[98] These grants usually reserved a rent to the Crown, known as a quit rent,[99] and created feudal tenure between the Crown and the grantees. Since the Tenures Abolition Act (Ireland), 1662, the tenure would have to have been free and common socage.[1] We have already seen that the Crown could do this since, as a matter of construction, it was not bound by the statute *Quia Emptores*. But the Crown often in these grants of Irish land went further; the letters patent frequently contained a "non obstante" clause, authorising the grantee, the tenant in chief, to subinfeudate *non obstante Quia Emptores*.[2] Whether the Crown had the right to grant this dispensation to those who were clearly themselves otherwise bound by the Statute may be questioned,[3] but

---

[93] 1 Edw. 3, St. 2, cc. 12 and 13.
[94] S. 2. See para. 2.48, *infra*.
[95] See ch. 14, *post*.
[96] Para. 1.26, *ante*.
[97] Para. 1.27–33, *ante*.
[98] Para. 4.059, *post*.
[99] Para. 6.009, *post*.
[1] Ss. 4 and 5. See para. 2.49, *post*.
[2] See, *e.g.*, the terms of the grants discussed in *Tuthill* v. *Rogers* (1844) 6 Ir.Eq.R. 429; *Verschoyle* v. *Perkins* (1847) 13 Ir.Eq.R. 72; *Corporation of Dublin* v. *Herbert* (1860) 12 I.C.L.R. 502; *Delacherois* v. *Delacherois* (1864) 11 H.L.C. 62; *Re Maxwell's Estate* (1891) 28 L.R.Ir. 356; *Moore* v. *Att.-Gen* [1934] I.R. 44 (see *A Casebook on Irish Land Law* (1984), p. 5).
[3] As it was, without deciding the matter, in *Chute* v. *Busteed* (1862) 14 I.C.L.R. 115, (1865) 16 I.C.L.R. 222;

there is no doubt that most grantees exercised their powers. The result was the creation of grants in Ireland having no equivalent elsewhere in the common law world (apart from Scotland), namely, grants by way of sub-infeudation of the fee simple *since* 1290, creating the feudal relationship of lord and tenant between the parties. Some of these grants survive to this day in the urban areas of Ireland, and they make up one category of the species of fee farm grants so prevalent in the island.[4]

2.46. The second most important aspect of *Quia Emptores* was that it established the foundations of one of the basic principles of English and Irish land law, the rule against inalienability.[5] The statute laid down the general rule that the holder of a fee simple estate in land had a right of free alienation of that estate. This principle was developed into a rule that any attempt to put restrictions on such a holder, which had the effect of rendering his estate in the land inalienable, was void. And, as we shall see, this principle came to be enforced in respect of several kinds of property.[6] Yet once again reservations must be entered. It was the case that later statutes were to breach this principle even with respect to the fee simple estate. Thus it seems that the Conveyancing Act, 1881, which applied to both England and Ireland, may have permitted the continuance of restrictions on alienation (which are standard in leases[7]) when a long lease is enlarged into a fee simple under its provisions.[8] The point is still unsettled, probably because those provisions have been rarely used in England or Ireland. And they were unlikely to be used in Ireland where long leases rather than freeholds have been created as a matter of conveyancing practice for centuries. We shall discuss the matter in a later chapter.[9] Another clearer breach of the principle occurred in Ireland with the passing of the Renewable Leasehold Conversion Act, 1849.[10] This statute enabled lessees of leases for lives renewable for ever to convert them into fee farm grants (fees simple subject to perpetual rents), and automatically converted all such leases executed after the passing of the Act into fee farm grants. Section 1 of the Act stated that the new fee simple was to be subject to all the covenants and conditions contained in the original renewable lease.[11] This raised the question whether the provision included covenants unenforceable at common law in the

---

Corporation of Dublin v. *Herbert* (1860) 12 I.C.L.R. 502; *Fowler* v. *Fowler* (1865) 16 Ir.Ch.R. 507. See also *Stevelly* v. *Murphy* (1840) 2 Ir.Eq.R. 448; *Brady* v. *Fitzgerald* (1847) 11 Ir.Eq.R. 55, (1848) 12 Ir.Eq.R. 273; *Verschoyle* v. *Perkins* (1852) 13 Ir.Eq.R. 72. The question is now of largely academic interest for two reasons. First, most of these Crown grants were confirmed by the Irish Parliament, see the Settlement of Ireland Acts, 1634 (10 Chas. 1, c. 3; 10 Chas. 1, sess. 3, cc. 2 and 3), 1639 (15 Chas. 1, sess. 2, c. 6), 1665 (17 & 18 Chas. 2, c. 2) and 1695 (7 Will. 3, c. 3), see the discussion in *Moore* v. *Att.-Gen.* [1934] I.R. 44 (see *A Casebook on Irish Land Law* (1984), p. 5); also frequently the grantees were subsequently given the right to make fee farm grants by private Acts of Parliament, see, *e.g.*, *Re Costello* (1899) 33 I.L.T.R. 73. Secondly, these grants have been acted upon by all concerned for centuries and it is too late now to question the titles as a matter of conveyancing practice, see para. 4.059, *post*.

4 Fee farm grants are discussed in detail later, para. 4.057, *post*.
5 This rule is discussed in more detail later, para. 5.033, *post*.
6 Paras. 5.033–41, *post*.
7 See para. 17.035, *post*.
8 S. 65 and see also the Conveyancing Act, 1882, s. 11.
9 Ch. 19, *post*.
10 Discussed in detail, para. 4.081 *et seq.*, *post*.
11 See also s. 10, relating to running of covenants with the fee simple.

case of a fee simple, such as a restriction on alienation. The question has never really been authoritatively decided, but the general judicial opinion in Ireland seems to have been to the effect that the 1849 Act should be read as so modifying the common law position, even where that position was based on earlier statutes like *Quia Emptores*. Thus FitzGibbon L.J. in *Re McNaul's Estate*[12] stated:

> "We hold, in general, that the doctrine of repugnancy applicable at common law to an estate in fee is modified, in the case of fee-farm grants founded on renewable leases, by whatever obligations are lawfully inserted in the grants. The object of the Act was to give a perpetual estate, which was not a common law estate in fee, but was an estate created under the statute, which was to remain subject to all covenants and conditions which had bound the previous leasehold estate, save so far as they were got rid of in the manner provided by the Act."[13]

2.47. This view may not have been so surprising as it was given at the beginning of this century. By that time the law relating to fee farm grants in general was fairly clear and most grants created the full relationship of landlord and tenant between the parties. Indeed, for all practical purposes, the law applicable was the law relating to leases and leasehold estates, rather than the law relating to fees simple and freehold estates.[14]

D. TENURES ABOLITION ACT (IRELAND), 1662

2.48. By the seventeenth century the feudal system of landholding had greatly changed in England, though that country had not suffered in the previous centuries from the degree of internal strife experienced in Ireland. In particular, the idea of the private raising of revenue, or the raising of revenue by the King without the sanction or control of Parliament, was becoming politically unacceptable. In 1646 the Long Parliament passed a resolution to the effect that most forms of feudal tenure should be abolished, together with their incidents. This resolution was given force by the passing of the Tenures Abolition Act, 1660, and two years later the Irish Parliament followed suit and passed the Tenures Abolition Act (Ireland), 1662.

2.49. The 1662 Act abolished most forms of tenure prevalent in Ireland, in particular all tenures by homage, by knight-service (of the King or any other person) and by socage *in capite* (of the King).[15] All existing tenures were converted into free and common socage, and were to be deemed to be so converted from 1641.[16] The Act then went on to abolish most of the incidents attaching to the tenures, such as aids, wardships, marriages and fines for

---

[12] [1902] 1 I.R. 114 (see *A Casebook on Irish Land Law* (1984), p. 41). *Cf. Re Lunham's Estate* (1871) I.R. 5 Eq. 170; *Billing* v. *Welch* (1871) I.R. 6 C.L. 88; *Ex parte Raymond* (1874) I.R. 8 Eq. 231.
[13] *Ibid.*, pp. 124–5.
[14] See ch. 4, *post.*
[15] Ss. 2 and 3. The more significant sections are set out in *A Casebook on Irish Land Law* (1984), p. 50 *et seq.*
[16] For the meaning of free and common socage, see paras. 2.25–7, *ante.*

alienation.[17] Any future tenures to be created by the King could only be in free and common socage, subject only to incidents appropriate to such tenure.[18] Preserved, however, were certain fixed incidents, such as heriots and rents.[19] The Act also saved tenures like copyhold and frankalmoign.[20]

2.50. The result of this statute was that in Ireland feudal tenure eventually became confined to one category, free and common socage or freehold, as it came to be called. That one form of tenure remained subject to a limited number of incidents, such as escheat and forfeiture.[21] To the extent that services survived, these in future would be confined mainly to money payments by way of rent.

E. ADMINISTRATION OF ESTATES ACT (N.I.), 1955

2.51. As part of its general scheme for assimilation of real property with personal property for the purposes of devolution on intestacy, section 1 (5) of this Act abolished the doctrine of escheat to the Crown or to a mesne lord.[22] Escheat was replaced by section 16 with a right of the Crown to take the land as *bona vacantia*, where the owner died intestate, leaving no intestate successors. This was the rule in respect of personal property, and was the rule which had in fact been adopted some sixty years before for most land in Ireland. Under section 85 (1) of the Local Registration of Title (Ireland) Act, 1891,[23] all agricultural land bought out under the land purchase scheme and compulsorily registered under the 1891 Act was to continue to devolve as personalty. The reason for this was that most of such land was held as leasehold before the land purchase scheme, and so would descend as "personal" estate and not as "real" estate.[24] The 1891 Act was simply saying that conversion of estates under the land purchase scheme into freehold estates was not to affect their devolution on intestacy.

F. SUCCESSION ACT, 1965

2.52. The Republic of Ireland took the same step as Northern Ireland with respect to escheat in 1965. Section 11 (3) of the Succession Act, 1965,[25] abolished escheat to the State[26] and to a mesne lord. Unlike the Northern 1955 Act,

---

[17] Ss. 1, 2 and 5. See *Earl of Inchiquin* v. *Burnell* (1795) 3 Ridgw. P.C. 376 at 426 (*per* Yelverton C.B.). Also abolished was the Court of Wards and Liveries, by which the Crown enforced the incidents against tenants *in capite*. See Kearney, "The Court of Wards and Liveries in Ireland, 1622–41" (1954) 57 Proc. R.I.A. 29; Treadwell, "The Irish Court of Wards under James I" (1960) 12 I.H.S. 1.

[18] Ss. 8 and 9. Obviously examples in Ireland were resettlements by way of fee farm grants *non obstante Quia Emptores*, para. 2.45, *ante*.

[19] S. 9.

[20] S. 11. Paras. 2.28–33, *ante*.

[21] Forfeiture for high treason was abolished in England and Ireland by the Forfeiture Act, 1870, s. 1, with a saving for judgment of outlawry. Outlawry was abolished in Northern Ireland by the Criminal Procedure Act (N.I.), 1951, s. 2 and Sched., Pt. I.

[22] As regards estates of persons dying intestate (*i.e.*, without making a will) from Jan. 1 1956 onwards. On the Act generally, see chs. 15–16, *post*.

[23] See, generally, ch. 21, *post*.

[24] See paras. 15.03–6, *post*.

[25] See, generally, chs. 14–16, *post*.

[26] Replacing the Crown in this respect, see the Intestates' Estates Act, 1954, s. 6; State Property Act, 1954, Pt. III. See *In b. Doherty* [1961] I.R. 219 (see *A Casebook on Irish Land Law* (1984), p. 52).

however, the Republic's 1965 Act also replaced the notion of *bona vacantia*. Section 73 (1) of the 1965 Act simply provides: "In default of any person taking the estate of an intestate, whether under this Part or otherwise, the State shall take the estate as ultimate intestate successor." This change was made on the ground that a foreign court might not recognise the concept of *bona vacantia*.

IV. CONCLUSION

2.53. In both parts of Ireland the system of feudal tenure introduced by the Normans some eight hundred years ago has now been greatly simplified. There is only one form of feudal tenure, known as freehold, to which there are attached few incidents of practical significance. The basic theory of tenure may appear to hold good in Northern Ireland, in that all land is still held ultimately from the Crown. It may still revert to the Crown on intestacy, but now as *bona vacantia*, which is the same position in respect of personalty which is *not* held of the Crown. In other words, the Crown's right to succeed now rests more on statute law. In the Republic of Ireland, the theory of tenure has even less application now, since the State is specified as ultimate intestate successor by statute.

2.54. Land held subject to feudal tenure may, however, still be subject to services, in particular money rents in the form of State or Crown rents[27] or fee farm rents issuing out of fee farm grants made *non obstante Quia Emptores*.[28] But this does not apply to the great bulk of land in the country, namely agricultural land bought out under the land purchase scheme.[29] Under that scheme a freehold title was given to the tenant-purchaser, subject only to a terminable land purchase annuity. Any rents or other services issuing out of the land were redeemed as part of the purchase scheme.

✱ **2.55.** As regards urban land in Ireland, however, tenure of a different kind, but with very similar characteristics, has assumed great importance. This is leasehold tenure as opposed to freehold tenure. It is a system of landholding which developed independently of the feudal system and it will be dealt with in detail in later chapters.[30] Suffice it to say here that this area of land law has developed in Ireland along lines not to be seen in England. And the result has been the growth of pyramid titles in urban land in Ireland just as complex as the old feudal pyramid titles. Indeed, in some cases, the pyramid may be constructed of a combination of relationships between the grantors and grantees, some strictly feudal in their nature, others involving modern landlord and tenant law.[31] However, in the Republic the growth of leasehold tenure was stunted by the enactment of the Landlord and Tenant (Ground Rents) Act,

---

[27] Para. 6.008, *post*.
[28] Para. 2.45, *ante*.
[29] Paras. 1.51–6, *ante*.
[30] Chs. 17 and 18, *post*. Note that there will be a limited growth of leasehold tenure in agricultural land in the Republic as a result of the Land Act, 1984, see para. 18.03, *post*.
[31] Ch. 4, *post*, and *cf*. the example of a modern pyramid title given in paras. 4.179–82, *post*.

1978, which prohibited the future creation of ground rents in respect of "dwellings,"[32] and a similar switch from leasehold tenure to freehold tenure has been proposed for Northern Ireland.[33]

CHAPTER 3

Equity

I. GENERAL

3.001. One of the most striking features of our land law has been the extent to which it has been influenced by principles of equity. In this context the meaning of "equity" can only be understood by reference to the historical development of English common law,[1] as applied in Ireland since the twelfth century.[2] Generally it means that branch of the law over which the Court of Chancery had jurisdiction before the Judicature (Ireland) Act, 1877, and which was not recognised by the common law courts, like the Courts of King's Bench or of Common Pleas. From this jurisdiction grew a set of rules or principles, a body of law which we now call equity but which, since the "fusion" of common law and equity by the Judicature Act, may be applied in any of the superior courts of justice in either part of the country. So far as land law is concerned, equity has played a major, often the dominant, role in developing rights and interests which are now regarded as commonplace. It has certainly been responsible for much of the variety and complexity of these rights and interests.

Before discussing in some more detail the nature of equity's contribution to our land law, we must first explain the historical background to equity itself.[3]

II. HISTORICAL BACKGROUND

3.002. Equity developed as an independent body of law because the common law was regarded as defective. Two defects in particular became apparent. One was the fact that an action could not be brought in a common law court without an appropriate "writ" and in the early stages of development of the common law writs would only be issued to cover very narrow grounds of complaint.[4] Actions were often dismissed by the common law courts on the ground that the plaintiff's writ did not disclose any action or claim recognised by the common law. The other defect lay in the remedies provided by the common law courts. Even if the plaintiff succeeded in his action, he usually found that the only

---

[1] The standard English textbooks are Hanbury and Maudsley, *Modern Equity* (12th ed. by Martin, 1985); Keeton and Sheridan, *Equity* (3rd ed. 1985); Pettit, *Equity and the Law of Trusts* (5th ed., 1984); Snell, *Principles of Equity* (28th ed. by Baker and Langan, 1982). See also Maitland, *Equity* (2nd ed. by Brunyate, 1936).

[2] As to which see Kiely, *The Principles of Equity as Applied in Ireland* (1936); Hand, "A Note on the Early Irish Chancery" (1970) 5 Ir.Jur. (N.S.) 291. Also Ball, *The Judges in Ireland, 1221–1921* (1927); O'Flanagan, *Lives of the Lord Chancellors of Ireland* (1870).

[3] See Simpson, *A History of Land Law* (2nd ed., 1985); also Milsom, *Historical Foundations of the Common Law* (1969).

[4] The form of the writ was fixed and unless a plaintiff could bring his action within one of the forms, he had no remedy. It may be difficult for a student in the twentieth century to appreciate the effect of this, because today the plaintiff decides what will appear on the writ or summons. In the early days of the common law, the contents of the writ were fixed by the recognised forms and not by the plaintiff. Maitland, *Forms of Action at Common Law* (eds. Chaytor and Whittaker, 1936). The English register of writs was, it seems, transmitted to Ireland by Henry III in 1227, with instructions that the same forms of action be used by litigants here. See Maitland, *Collected Papers* (ed. by Fisher, 1911), vol. II, pp.81–3.

remedy available was damages. In many cases this was an unsatisfactory remedy. For example, if a landowner wished to stop trespassers coming on to his land, he wanted a remedy that would stop them trespassing. He may also have wanted an award of damages to cover any loss he had suffered, but his main aim was to stop the trespass. Similarly, if someone had contracted to buy a piece of land he wanted very much, an award of damages against the vendor if he failed to go through with the sale was a poor remedy. What the prospective purchaser wanted was a remedy that would force the vendor to complete his part of the bargain on the terms agreed.

A. Chancery Jurisdiction

3.003. In medieval times the only way round these defects in the common law was to appeal to the King as the fountain of all justice. After all, the common law courts were the King's courts and exercised their jurisdiction in his name and derived their powers from him. He could, and often did, temper the rulings of his courts in order to do justice between individual litigants. It was not long before this jurisdiction was turned over to one of his principal secretaries of state, the Lord Chancellor, who became head of the Chancery, the office from which writs issued. In the early days, the Chancellor was usually a high church dignitary and so ecclesiastical law, itself considerably influenced by Roman law, formed one of the main foundations of equity. In Ireland, this jurisdiction was exercised by the Lord Chancellor of Ireland, who followed the procedures of his English counterpart.[5] Like all high royal officials in Ireland, the Chancellor was English and was, therefore, inclined to adopt the same principles as his equivalent across the Irish Sea. This jurisdiction in later centuries was taken over by the Court of Chancery, which became an established court like the Court of King's Bench and the Court of Common Pleas.[6] During the Middle Ages, however, considerable equitable jurisdiction seems to have been exercised by the Irish Parliament.[7] The development of equity jurisdiction in the Irish Chancery also seems to have been delayed by the extent of equity jurisdiction claimed by the third main common law court, the Exchequer. The Irish Exchequer was claimed to be the *placea equitatis* during argument in a case litigated in 1299,[8] and it seems that the equity side of the Court of Exchequer in Ireland assumed greater importance than in England.[9] Until the early seventeenth century, the Court of Chancery's jurisdiction was limited as to geographical area, like all the royal courts, by the fact that until then much of the North and West of Ireland remained unconquered.[10]

3.004. The guiding principle governing the jurisdiction of the Chancellor,

---

[5] The first Irish Chancellor seems to have been Ralph Neville, appointed in 1232, see Hand, (1970) 5 Ir.Jur. (N.S.) 291.
[6] Newark, *Notes on Irish Legal History* (1960).
[7] Richardson and Sayles, *The Irish Parliament in the Middle Ages* (1952), pp. 217–20.
[8] Sayles, *Introduction to Select Cases in the Court of King's Bench, Edward I* (1938), vol. II, p. lix.
[9] Hand, *English Law in Ireland 1290–1324* (1967), pp. 99–103.
[10] Para. 1.16, *ante*. See also Davies, "A Discoverie of the True Causes Why Ireland was never entirely Subdued" in Morley (ed.), *Ireland under Elizabeth and James I* (1890), pp. 213–342.

and later of the Court of Chancery, was the doing of justice between the parties regardless of the technicalities of the law. In the early stages of the development of the common law the Chancellor might be able to help parties by devising new writs to enable them to bring actions in the royal courts. This was because the Chancery had the exclusive jurisdiction to issue these writs.[11] The issue of writs, however, did not guarantee the success of the action before the Courts of Common Law. The writ did obtain for the party a hearing before the court, but it might still dismiss the action on the ground that the writ did not disclose a claim recognised by the common law. In other words, the issue of a *writ* by the Chancery did not mean automatically that a *form of action* recognised by the common law existed. The only solution to this problem was for the party to come back to the Chancery to see if he could have his complaint dealt with there—hence the separate development of the Court of Chancery.

3.005. The procedure was that the plaintiff presented a *petition* or *bill* (in equity) to the Chancery raising his complaint. If the Chancery thought there was a case to answer, it would issue a writ (a *subpoena*[12]) ordering the defendant to appear and answer the complaint. In the common law courts the parties to an action were not allowed to give evidence, while in the Court of Chancery the defendant was "examined" by the Chancellor. In the early days, the Lord Chancellors seem to have exercised extremely wide-ranging jurisdiction, so that it was said that, while the common law was subject to well-defined rules and regulations, the only standard for the measure of equity was "a Chancellor's foot."[13] However, as we shall see, equity too became a fairly well-defined system of law, though it has never become as rigid as the common law. Even from the earliest days, it was subject to one abiding limitation. The Courts of Common Law were also royal courts deriving their authority from the King. They could not be overruled directly by the Chancellor, or later the Court of Chancery, without causing the most fundamental of constitutional crises. Regard had to be given to the judgments of these courts, otherwise the whole system of administration of law in the country would collapse. The Chancellor, like everyone else in the land, had to recognise the law as laid down by these courts; the most he could do was to try to temper their rulings in individual cases. The primary method of doing this was by issuing a remedy known as an *injunction*.

3.006. If the defendant claimed that his rights were recognised at common law, and this was supported by the common law courts, the Court of Chancery could not deny the defendant's legal rights. It could, however, try to ensure that the defendant did not exercise them so as to prejudice the plaintiff in equity, if this would be unfair. An injunction was an order restraining the defendant from exercising his strict legal rights, or restraining the plaintiff from enforcing his rights

---

[11] During the thirteenth century there was something of a struggle between the Irish and English Chanceries over matters such as the issue of writs in Ireland, but in the early fourteenth century it seems to have been established that the Irish Chancery ought to have sole jurisdiction in Ireland. See generally Hand, *English Law in Ireland 1290–1324*, pp. 26–9.

[12] So called because the defendant was ordered to appear "upon pain" of forfeiture of a sum of money if he failed to appear.

[13] Pollock (ed.), *Table Talk to John Selden* (1927), p. 43.

under a common law judgment.[14] If it were ignored the defendant was in contempt of the Court of Chancery and the penalty for that was imprisonment. Thus, while the Chancery in theory recognised the common law as the primary source of law in the country, in practice its issue of remedies like the injunction could curtail the operation of the common law quite considerably, and the injunction to restrain a plaintiff from executing a common law judgment curtailed the jurisdiction of the common law courts. A conflict between the courts was almost inevitable and it came to a head in the early seventeenth century in England. The Chief Justice of England, Edward Coke, disputed the jurisdiction of the Court of Chancery to restrain actions at common law and held in a number of cases that imprisonment for disobeying injunctions was unlawful.[15] The Lord Chancellor at the time, Lord Ellesmere, rejected the argument and claimed he was simply controlling the way legal rights (which he *ex hypothesi* recognised) were exercised in the interests of justice in individual cases. James I referred the matter to his legal advisers, in particular his Attorney-General, Francis Bacon, and they sided with Ellesmere, thereby ensuring the continued development of equity as a system of law alongside the common law.[16] At this same time in Ireland, English law (common law and equity) was finally extended to the whole of Ireland and the native system of *brehon* law ceased to have much practical significance.[17]

B. USES AND TRUSTS

3.007. Perhaps the best illustration of the effect of equity on the common law in relation to land law was the development of the *use*.[18] In the early stages of development of the common law it became the practice to convey land to one person, A, to be held by him to the use (*i.e.,* for the benefit) of another person, B. At common law such a conveyance gave A the ownership of the land, the legal title, which he could dispose of as he pleased. B had no claim at all to the land, yet it was clearly unconscionable that his claim to the benefit of the property, which the grantor intended he should have, should be disregarded. This was where equity intervened. It recognised A's claim to the legal title, but required him to exercise his legal ownership as intended, *i.e.,* for the benefit of B. Thus B came to be regarded as the owner of the property in equity and to this day this division of ownership of property (real and personal[19]), between legal ownership and equitable ownership, remains a vital element in our legal system. The whole law of land settlements is based upon it as we shall discuss in a later chapter.[20]

---

[14] See paras. 3.127–41, *post.*

[15] *E.g.,* *Heath* v. *Rydley* (1614) Cro.Jac. 335; *Bromage* v. *Genning* (1617) 1 Rolle 368.

[16] *Earl of Oxford's Case* (1615) 1 Ch.Rep. 1. Baker, "The Common Lawyers and the Chancery: 1616" (1969) 4 Ir.Jur. (N.S.) 368.

[17] Para. 1.28, *ante.*

[18] Derived from the latin word "opus," from "ad opus" (on his behalf), and from the early French "al ues" (to the use of). See Maitland, *Equity* (rev. ed., 1936), p. 24. On the subject of uses generally, see Gilbert, *Uses and Trusts* (3rd ed., 1811); Sanders, *Uses and Trusts* (5th ed., 1844); Maitland, "The Origin of Uses" (1894) 8 H.L.R. 127; Sweet, "Song of Uses: Some Reflections" (1919) 35 H.L.R. 127.

[19] Uses were created in respect of land but modern trusts, which developed from uses, may apply to any kind of property, see ch. 9, *post.*

[20] Ch. 8, *post.*

1. *Origin*

There were many reasons for the popularity of uses. The following were the main reasons.

(i) Feudal Dues

3.008. One of the primary purposes of uses was one which has survived with just as much intensity to the present day, *i.e.*, tax avoidance.[21] The taxes of the Middle Ages were, of course, the feudal dues payable under the feudal system of tenure, like reliefs, wardship and marriage. These dues, however, were payable only by the person seised of the land; in our example given above, A was liable, not B.[22] Landowners were not long in seeing the potential of a device which so split up the ownership of the land. Thus dues payable on the death of a tenant seised of the land, such as relief, marriage and wardship,[23] could be avoided by the tenant conveying the land before his death to adult friends to the use of his heirs. On his death, there was no succession by inheritance and so no relief payable, no infant heirs and so no marriage or wardship to be claimed by the lord. It is true that the adult holders of the legal title might die but the possibility of inheritance by their successors was avoided by conveying the land to several persons to hold it in use and specifying that their number should never fall below two. These persons held as joint tenants, so that on the death of one his share passed to the others by right of survivorship and *not* by inheritance.[24] The consequences of forfeiture for treason or escheat[25] could similarly be avoided by conveying the land to others to be held for one's own use. By the same token a landowner might try to put his land out of the reach of his creditors by conveying it to uses.

(ii) Family Settlements

3.009. At common law a man could not convey his land to himself nor, since the rule was that a man and wife were one person for the purposes of the law,[26] to his wife. This made it difficult for a man to make a settlement of his land on his family. The problem, however, was easily solved by conveying the land to third parties to be held by them to the use of the various members of the family as the settlor determined. Such a settlement might have been necessary because the landowner was going abroad for a substantial period of time, *e.g.*, to fight in the crusades.

(iii) Wills

3.010. It was not possible to make a will of land in Ireland until the passing of

---

[21] See in respect of the modern trust, ch. 9, *post.*
[22] Para. 3.007, *supra.*
[23] Paras. 2.18–24, *ante.*
[24] On joint tenants, see ch. 7, *post.*
[25] Paras. 2.23–4, *ante.*
[26] This is no longer the position in either part of Ireland, see ch. 25, *post.*

the Statute of Wills (Ireland), 1634.[27] Yet there was nothing to stop a land-owner achieving substantially the same result as a will by conveying the land to third parties before his death to be held by them to the uses declared by him on his death in a will.

(iv) Mortmain

3.011. The early Statutes of Mortmain prohibited the conveyance of land to corporations or religious bodies without licence of the Crown.[28] Such corporate bodies never died, could not commit treason or felony or leave infant heirs, and so the Crown and other lords were deprived of feudal revenue. This legislation could be avoided by conveying the land to other persons to the use of such religious bodies, until this avoidance was prohibited by later mortmain legislation.[29]

(v) Curtesy and Dower

3.012. A wife's prospective right to dower in any legal estate of inheritance held by her husband during the marriage[30] could be avoided by her husband ensuring that he acquired, whether by purchase or gift, only an equitable interest held under a use. Equity considered that the widow's claim to dower on her husband's death, which could not be defeated by dispositions made by her husband before his death, unduly restricted his ability to deal freely with his land and so refused to allow any claim to dower out of equitable interests held by her husband. The necessity for this device was removed by the Dower Act, 1833, which provided that dower could not be claimed out of land disposed of by the husband during his life or by his will.[31] In the early days curtesy could also be avoided by conveyances to uses, but these became ineffective when equity followed the law and allowed curtesy out of equitable interests.[32]

(vi) Powers of Revocation and Appointment

3.013. It was impossible at common law to make dispositions of land reserving to the grantor a power to revoke the disposition or settlement, or a power to appoint the land, or shares in it, to certain persons at a future date.[33] The grantor could, however, achieve this by conveying his land to others to be held to such uses as he should appoint or to specified uses, but reserving the right to revoke them and select new uses.

(vii) Executory Interests

3.014. Uses were employed by conveyancers to get round the rigidity of the

---

[27]   Para. 3.020, *infra*.
[28]   Para. 2.42, *ante*.
[29]   15 Ric. 2, c. 5 (1391), extending the prohibition to cover conveyances to the use of municipal corporations. The prohibition was further extended in England in 1531 to cover unincorporated bodies, 23 Hen. 8, c. 10. See now, para. 25.21, *post*.
[30]   Paras. 4.157–9, *post*.
[31]   *Ibid*.
[32]   Para. 4.158, *post*.
[33]   This subject is discussed in detail later, ch. 11, *post*.

common law rules relating to the creation of future interests. This matter is discussed in detail in a later chapter.[34]

2. *Statute of Uses (Ireland), 1634*

3.015. The English Statute of Uses was passed a century earlier than the Irish one, in 1535. The primary reason for its passing seems to have been that Henry VIII was concerned about the loss of royal revenue he, as chief lord in the feudal system of tenure, was suffering by the extent to which conveyances to uses were being employed in England.[35] The Statute purported to put a stop to this by reversing the effect of these conveyances and causing the legal title and the seisin to be placed in the person in whose favour the uses were created, the *cestui que use* as he was called.[36] The Irish Statute of 1634 is in the same terms as the English 1535 Statute,[37] but it can hardly be said to have the same primary object. By 1634 the significance of feudal dues had been greatly reduced[38] and, indeed, some 30 years later the Tenures Abolition Act (Ireland), 1662,[39] destroyed what little significance they had earlier in the seventeenth century. The real reason for the passing of the Irish Statute of Uses probably lies in the desire of the Irish Parliament at the time to produce greater parity with England in the field of legislation. The early seventeenth century had seen the final steps taken towards the English conquest of the whole of Ireland,[40] and the next few decades saw a considerable amount of legislative activity by the Irish Parliament, spurred on by the Chief Secretary, Thomas Wentworth. The year 1634 saw the passing of numerous statutes on land law, bringing Irish law into line with English law in most respects.[41]

(i) Its Provisions

3.016. Section 1 of the Statute is usually summarised as follows:

> "Where any person or persons are seised of any lands or other heredita-ments to the use, confidence or trust of any other person or persons or any body politic, the latter person or persons or body politic shall be deemed and adjudged in lawful seisin, estate and possession of the hereditaments for the like estates as they had in the use, confidence or trust."[42]

The effect of this section on a conveyance to uses was said to be that the uses were "executed," *i.e.*, perfected or completed.[43] Prior to the Statute, a

---

[34] Ch. 5, *post.*
[35] See Holdsworth, "Political Causes which Shaped the Statute of Uses" (1912) 26 H.L.R. 108
[36] *I.e.,* B in the example given in para. 3.007, *supra.* The person who held the property to the use of the *cestui que use* was known as the *feoffee to use* (A in the example). For the meaning of feoffment, see para. 3.023, *infra.*
[37] Thus the preamble to the Irish Statute contains a catalogue of the evils of uses similar to that in the English statute, including references to how "the lords lost their wards, marriages, reliefs, herriots, escheats . . . the Kings Highnesse hath lost the profits and advantages of the lands of persons attainted, and the lands craftily put in feoffment to the uses of aliens borne . . . "
[38] Para. 2.44, *ante.*
[39] Para. 2.48, *ante.*
[40] Para. 1.28, *ante.*
[41] Para. 1.34, *ante.*
[42] Megarry and Wade, *The Law of Real Property* (5th ed., 1984), p. 1166.
[43] See discussion in *King* v. *Jones* (1836) Jones 635. For further on the meaning "executed" and "executory," see paras. 5.018–9, *post.*

conveyance "to A and his heirs to the use of B and his heirs" gave A the legal fee simple and B the equitable fee simple. After the Statute, B had a legal fee simple; the use was executed and A was left with nothing. This rule applied to uses created before or after the Statute. It should be noted, however, that the Statute did not enlarge the estate of the *cestui que use,* it only converted his equitable estate into a legal estate. If the conveyance were "to A and his heirs to the use of B for life," the Statute transformed B's equitable life estate into a legal life estate. It did not transfer the fee simple estate conveyed to A. On the other hand, if the conveyance were "to A for life to the use of B for life," the Statute transformed B's equitable life estate into a legal estate *pur autre vie,* the *vie* being the life of A. The reason was that the *cestui que use* could not obtain under the Statute an estate larger than the one conveyed to the feoffee to uses (A). In our example, A's estate was limited in duration to his own life and so B's estate after execution of the use must be similarly so limited, thereby creating an estate *pur autre vie.* [44]

3.017. An interesting question arose under the early law as to what was the effect of a conveyance by a fee simple owner, O, "to A and his heirs to the use of B for life." Prior to the Statute, clearly O had disposed of the whole of his legal estate, his fee simple, to A but only part of the equitable estate, a life estate. Under the ordinary law of future interests, [45] an equitable fee simple reversion remained vested in O by way of *resulting use.* [46] What, then, was the effect of the Statute on such a conveyance? The answer was that A took nothing because the use was executed, B took a legal life estate and O's resulting use was executed by the Statute to give him a legal fee simple in reversion.

3.018. A resulting use also arose in one special case. If the owner of a fee simple in land conveyed it by a voluntary conveyance, *i.e.,* for no consideration, to a stranger and no use was expressed, equity took the view that it was unlikely that such a stranger was meant to enjoy the property beneficially. To give effect to this presumption, equity raised a resulting use in favour of the grantor and required the grantee to hold the legal fee simple to the grantor's use. This sort of resulting use was also executed by the Statute so that the parties to the conveyance would be put back to their original position. The grantor had his legal fee simple returned to him and the grantee was left with nothing. The conveyance, in other words, was rendered ineffective, a point conveyancers in Ireland still have to bear in mind.

(ii) Limitations

3.019. It is clear from the wording of the Statute that it only operates in certain circumstances. The following are the main points to be borne in mind.

---

[44] Sanders, *Uses and Trusts* (5th ed., 1844), vol. 1, p. 107; Gilbert, *Uses and Trusts* (3rd ed., 1811), pp. 127 and 430.

[45] See generally ch. 5, *post.*

[46] See discussion in *Lynch* v. *Clarkin* [1900] 1 I.R. 178 at 195–7 (uses declared upon a recovery by a tenant in tail not exhausting the fee simple and, therefore, leaving a resulting use in fee in the recoverer).

(a) *Seisin*

The Statute applied only in the case where a person was seised of land to be held to uses. Thus it did not apply if the estate to be held to uses was anything other than a freehold estate. Thus it had no application to leasehold estates or pure personalty. The Statute would execute the use if the conveyance were "to A and his heirs to the use of B for 99 years." It would not execute the use if the conveyance were "to A for 99 years to the use of B."

A problem arose under the Statute about incorporeal hereditaments, such as easements and profits, created for the first time in the conveyance to uses.[47] If these interests did not exist up to the time of execution of the conveyance, the feoffee to uses under the conveyance could not be seised of them to the use of someone else. It was otherwise, of course, if the interests already existed prior to the conveyance because then the seisin could be vested in the feoffee to uses and uses declared which would be executed by the Statute, so as to pass the legal estates in the incorporeal hereditaments. This point had to be dealt with later in the Conveyancing Act, 1881.[48] The point only affected interests like easements and profits. The Statute of Uses expressly dealt with the other main type of incorporeal hereditament, rentcharges. Section 4 provided that rentcharges could be created by uses and annexed the advantage that the *cestui que use* of the rent would be deemed to be seised of it immediately upon execution of the conveyance. The section also annexed a statutory right of distress which would otherwise have had to have been expressly reserved.[49]

(b) *Corporations*

The Statute did not apply where a corporation was seised of the land to be held to uses. The Statute in section 1 clearly distinguished between "persons" and "bodies politic" in this respect. The latter could be *cestuis que use* only. If they are named as feoffees to use the Statute did not apply.

(c) *Own Use*

The Statute applied only where a person was seised to the use of another person. In fact, this construction was really a matter of convenience, because at common law such a conveyance had the same effect as an executed use under the Statute.[50] Prior to the Statute, a conveyance "to A and his heirs to the use of A and his heirs" gave A a legal fee simple. The declaration of uses was really unnecessary and served only to make clear that A also enjoyed the beneficial ownership. This was presumed in a straight conveyance "to A and his heirs" anyway, unless it was a voluntary conveyance to a stranger raising the contrary presumption of a resulting use.[51]

(d) *Active Uses*

It was settled that the Statute would not operate if the feoffee to uses had any

---

[47] Sanders, *op. cit.*, pp. 105–7.
[48] S. 62, and see para. 6.057, *post*.
[49] Para. 6.141, *post*.
[50] Challis, *The Law of Real Property* (3rd ed.), p. 390; *Gorman* v. *Byrne* (1857) 8 I.C.L.R. 394.
[51] Para. 3.018, *supra*.

active duties to perform in respect of the property. The reason was simple. The feoffee would be unable to carry out his duties if the Statute executed the use and left him with no interest at all in the property.[52] Active duties would be matters like having to collect the rents and profits from the land and pay them to the *cestui que use,* or having to convey or sell the land and pay the proceeds to the *cestui que use.* The modern trust usually involves such active duties and is not affected by the Statute of Uses.

(e) *Use upon a Use*

Prior to the Statute of Uses, the question arose as to the effect of a conveyance in the form "to A and his heirs to the use of B and his heirs to the use of C and his heirs." The disposition to C was difficult to reconcile with the disposition of the equitable estate to B and so the courts eventually held that the gift to C was void.[53] Then the question arose as to what the effect of the Statute of Uses was on such a conveyance. Some twenty years after the English 1535 Statute, it was held in *Jane Tyrrel's Case*[54] that the old law should be applied. The Statute executed the use in favour of B, giving him the legal and equitable estate. A was left with nothing, and C's use was not enforced because, it was argued, there was no use recognised by law in his favour which would also be executed by the Statute or left to stand as a use binding B.[55] This ruling, however, was gradually questioned by the Court of Chancery, until by the mid-seventeenth century it became settled that the use upon a use would be recognised and enforced in equity, thereby creating the foundations of the modern trust. This story will be continued later in this chapter.[56]

(iii) Consequences

3.020. The Statute of Uses was one of the foundations of our modern land law, ranking in importance with statutes like *Quia Emptores,*[57] *De Donis*[58] and the Statute of Frauds.[59] However, the consequences of the Irish Statute, coming as it did a century after the English Statute, were not as striking as its English counterpart. The main consequences and their significance for Irish law may be summarised as follows.

(a) *Feudal Dues*

It has already been mentioned that the Irish Statute of 1634 came too late to have much effect on revenue raised in the form of feudal dues. By then the feudal system was on its last legs and the extensive resettlement of Irish land during the seventeenth century, largely through a leasehold tenure system,

---

[52] Sanders, *op. cit.,* pp. 253–4, 258–75; *Lysaght* v. *Scully* (1854) 6 Ir.Jur.(O.S.) 194.
[53] *Dillam* v. *Frain* (1595) 1 And. 309 at 313; *Corbet's Case* (1600) 2 And. 134 at 136.
[54] (1557) Dyer 155a. See further, para. 3.024, *infra.*
[55] Ames, *Lectures on Legal History,* pp. 242–7; Gilbert, *op. cit.,* pp. 348–9.
[56] Para. 3.170, *post.*
[57] Para. 2.42, *ante.*
[58] Para. 4.114, *post.*
[59] Para. 9.021, *post.*

meant that there was little land to which it could have applied effectively.[60] Apart from this, we have already seen that the Statute could be easily avoided by creating active uses or uses upon a use or uses attached to leaseholds, so that tax avoidance could still be achieved by careful draftsmanship.

(b) *Wills*

The English Statute was clearly intended to prohibit wills of land being achieved by uses. Its preamble makes this clear and, indeed, the preamble to the Irish Statute contains the same wording.[61] However such a storm was caused by the English Statute in this respect across the Irish Sea that the English Parliament had to pass a few years later the Statute of Wills, 1540, giving a general power to devise land by will for the first time.[62] In Ireland, however, the equivalent, the Statute of Wills (Ireland), 1634, was passed in the same year as the Statute of Uses, so that the effect of the latter on the power to devise was precisely nil, despite the wording of its preamble.

(c) *Family Settlements*

The Irish Statute, like its English counterpart, did facilitate conveyances by a grantor to himself or to his wife by executing a conveyance to uses and thereby passing the legal title. Similarly, a tenant in tail was enabled to disentail in his own favour, by declaring a use to himself on a fine or recovery.[63] The need of such conveyancing devices in respect of land remained until the Conveyancing Act, 1881, permitted a person to convey land to himself jointly with another person by an ordinary conveyance.[64]

---

[60] Para. 1.34, *ante*.

[61] " . . . by wills and testaments . . . by the most part made by such persons as be visited with sickness in their extreme agonies and pains, or at such time as they have had scantly any good memory or remembrance, at which times they being provoked by greedy and covetous persons lying in wait about them, do many times dispose indiscreetly and inadvisedly, their lands and hereditaments. . . . For the extirping and extinguishment of all such subtill practised feoffment, fines, recoveries, abuses and errours heretofore used and accustomed in this realm, to the subversion of the good and ancient lawes of the same, and to the intent that the Kings Highness, or any other his subjects of this realme, shall not in any wise hereafter, by any means or inventions, be deceived, damaged or hurted by reason of such trusts, uses, or confidences." See Megarry, "The Statute of Uses and Power to Devise" (1941) 7 C.L.J. 359.

[62] To be precise, the Statute gave a testator freedom to devise all land held by him in socage and two-thirds of land held by knight-service. See also the Irish Statute of Wills, 1634.

[63] Para. 4.117, *post*. Similarly with a disentailing assurance after the Fines and Recoveries (Ireland) Act, 1834, para. 4.123, *post*.

[64] S. 50. This power was conferred in respect of leaseholds (and other personalty) by the Law of Property Amendment Act, 1859, s. 21. Section 21 of the Law of Property Amendment Act, 1859, and section 50 of the Conveyancing Act, 1881, were repealed in Northern Ireland by the Property (N. I.) Order, 1978 (see art. 16 (2) and Sched. 2, Part I). Article 10(1) of the Order provides that a person may convey property to himself jointly with another person and thus replaces the earlier provisions (but omits the reference in section 50 of the 1881 Act to conveyances between husband and wife, as this became unnecessary with the enactment of the Married Woman's Property Act, 1882). Article 10(2) makes it clear that this provision does not apply to a lease or fee farm grant made by a person with himself. This is designed to avoid the difficulties which have arisen in England in respect of section 72 (3) of the Law of Property Act, 1925, to which attention was drawn in the *Survey of the Land Law of Northern Ireland* (1971) (see para. 179). It was pointed out in *Rye* v. *Rye* [1962] A.C. 496 (especially by Lord Denning at p. 513) that covenants (which are, of course, common in leases and fee farm grants) made by a person with himself are invalid, since a person cannot enforce contractual obligations against himself. And this rule is expressly recognised by article 10(4) (but this is without prejudice to the provisions of article 11, which govern covenants entered into by a person with himself *and others*). Article 10(3) makes it clear that two or more persons may convey property vested in them to any one or more of themselves in like manner as they could

(d) Powers of Revocation and Appointment

Prior to the Statute uses were used to create such powers and the effect of the Statute was to render these powers legal as opposed to equitable, so that the donee could exercise them in respect of the legal estate. For example, a conveyance "to A and his heirs to the use of B for life, remainder to such uses as B should appoint" gave B a legal power of appointment. If B appointed "to C and his heirs" to take effect after his death, C took a legal fee simple on B's death.

(e) Legal Executory Interests

This complex area of the law of future interests is discussed fully in a later chapter.[65] For the moment it is sufficient to say that the Statute revolutionised the law by enabling conveyancers to get round common law restrictions on the type of future interests that could be validly created. The restrictions, closely tied to the concept of seisin and grounded upon feudal notions, could be avoided by conveyances to uses, though these could create equitable estates only. The revolution that the Statute produced was that, by executing these uses in certain cases, it enabled the conveyancers to draft their dispositions in such a way as not only to avoid the common law restrictions but, at the same time, to create new legal estates, or legal executory interests as they were called. It was this freedom and the use made of it by conveyancers which forced the courts to devise new restrictions on future interests and led to new rules like the rule against perpetuities.[66]

There is one other major consequence of the Statute of Uses and that is that it brought about new forms of conveyances for the disposition of land. These were the standard forms used until the modern deed of conveyance was introduced as an alternative by the Real Property Act, 1845.[67] This is a difficult subject and it is dealt with in a later section of this chapter.

(iv) Subsequent History of the Use and the Trust

3.021. The decision in *Tyrrel's Case*, which established that the Statute of

convey it to a third person. This overcomes the difficulty (mentioned in *Napier* v. *Williams* (1911) 104 T.L.R. 380 at 381-2) that section 50 of the 1881 Act contained no reference to a lease by two or more persons to one of themselves alone. However, paragraph (3) also states expressly that this provision does not validate a conveyance which the persons in question, by reason of a fiduciary relationship or otherwise, are precluded from making. Thus a conveyance made by trustees in breach of trust is still liable to be set aside. Article 11 of the Order, again following recommendations made in the 1971 *Survey* (see para. 185), complements the provisions of article 10 by rendering enforceable covenants or agreements entered into in a conveyance validated by article 10. This corresponds to section 82 of the English Law of Property Act, 1925, but, of course, as mentioned above, the provision does not apply to covenants in leases or fee farm grants. With respect to covenants entered into by a person with himself and others, it simply renders the covenants enforceable against those *others*, but *not* against *himself*. Article 12 provides that where a covenant is entered into by more than one person on either side, it is enforceable separately by each person to whom it is given against all the persons giving it or against each individual one of them. This complements section 60 of the Conveyancing Act, 1881 (relating to the benefit of a covenant with two or more jointly passing to survivors) and, as was pointed out in the 1971 *Survey* (see para. 186), renders it unnecessary, when preparing a covenant with several persons, to have a separate covenant with each of them. This new provision applies only to covenants entered into after it came into force and is subject to any contrary intention expressed in the covenant, article 12(2).

[65] Ch. 5, *post*.
[66] Discussed in detail paras. 5.056–149, *post*.
[67] S. 2 (in fact replacing the Transfer of Property Act, 1844, ss. 2 and 13), para. 3.026, *post*.

Uses did not execute a use upon a use, and later the Chancery's determination to enforce a use upon a use, made it possible to create equitable interests as freely as before the Statute was passed. Before the Statute, as we have seen, if it was desired to vest the legal estate in A for the benefit of B the form adopted was "to A and his heirs to the use of B and his heirs." After the middle of the seventeenth century, this form became "to A and his heirs to the use of B and his heirs in trust for C and his heirs," for a grantee to uses (A) had to be inserted in order to exhaust the effect of the Statute of Uses.

In this new formula, the word used to describe C's interest was "trust" instead of "use." The Statute applied to "uses, confidences or trusts." What preserved the equitable interest was the use in favour of B. It became the practice of conveyancers to use a word which indicated that the person whose name followed had a mere equitable interest, so that in practice "use" was reserved for uses executed by the Statute and "trust" for interests which remained equitable. In law the two terms had the same meaning.

3.022. As time went by, the formula used was "unto B and his heirs to the use of B and his heirs in trust for C and his heirs" and this was shortened to "unto and to the use of B and his heirs in trust for C and his heirs." When the formula "unto B and his heirs to the use of B and his heirs in trust for C and his heirs" was used, B was seised to his own use and so the Statute did not execute the first use and B was seised at common law. Despite this, the trust in favour of C was not executed by the Statute for it was a use upon a use. A use upon a use did not mean a use upon a use executed by the Statute but a use upon a use *declared* by the instrument. Therefore trusts could be created as easily as uses had been before the passing of the Statute. All that was required was that, instead of conveying the land to the trustee, it should be conveyed "unto and to the use of" the trustee or more shortly "to the use" of the trustee. As a result of this construction, it was said by Lord Hardwicke that the Statute of Uses had no other effect than to add at most three words to a conveyance. The "three words" were in fact five ("and to the use of") and the Statute had many other consequences which we have described. The construction put upon the Statute and the ingenuity of lawyers thus meant that in Maitland's famous phrase "the modern trust developed from the ancient use."

3. *Forms of Conveyance*

In order to understand fully the effect of the Statute of Uses (Ireland), 1634 on the forms of conveyance it is necessary to consider the forms used prior to its passing.

(i) Prior to 1634

3.023. Apart from forms of conveyance used in special situations, such as fines and recoveries, there were two main standard forms of conveyance for real property.

(a) Feoffment with Livery of Seisin

This was, perhaps, the most common form used, certainly in the early stages of development of the common law. This form involved ceremonial action by the parties to the conveyance; they had to enter physically upon the land to be conveyed and the grantor (feoffor) had to deliver (hence "livery") the seisin to the grantee by some symbolic act, such as handing over to him a sod of earth, in front of witnesses. Sometimes this symbolic act would be accompanied by utterance of an appropriate verbal formula indicating the tranfer of the seisin, and sometimes these words would be in substitution for the symbolic act. Such a conveyance was usually evidenced by execution of a charter or deed of feoffment, though this did not become obligatory until the Statute of Frauds (Ireland), 1695, which required evidence in writing.[68]

This form of conveyance was considered to have several defects. First, it was often grossly inconvenient for the parties concerned to have to attend the ceremony on the property itself, especially in an age lacking modern communication systems. Secondly, it was much too public a transaction for many people, especially if they wished to preserve any degree of secrecy about the transaction. Thirdly, it smacked too much of medieval formalism and appeared to involve unnecessary rigmarole in a society becoming increasingly more sophisticated. These defects led to the conveyancers devising the second main form of conveyance prior to 1634, the lease and release.

(b) Lease and Release

This form of conveyance avoided some of the disadvantages of a feoffment. It involved a two-stage transaction. First, the grantor granted a lease to the grantee. A leasehold estate was not real property[69] nor did it pass the seisin,[70] so a feoffment with livery of seisin was not necessary at this stage. The grantor then conveyed his fee simple reversion to the grantee which would merge with the lease to give him the fee simple in possession. It is true that the reversion held by the grantor did, technically speaking, involve seisin,[71] but it did not involve actual physical possession of the land and it seems that it was a rule of the common law that feoffment with livery of seisin had to have delivery of possession also.[72] The conveyancers took advantage of this rule to create a form of conveyance which avoided the defects of publicity and formalism that existed with feoffment. It avoided formalism because the reversion could be conveyed by an ordinary deed of release. However, while it avoided the grantor having to enter upon the land and take part in a solemn ceremony, there was one defect from the point of view of the grantee. It was a fundamental rule of the law of leaseholds that a grantee of a lease had to enter into possession of the land before he acquired the estate or term of years granted. Prior to

---

[68] S. 1. S. 3 of the Real Property Act, 1845, provided that a feoffment made after 1845 would be void unless evidenced by deed. See on this section, *Watson* v. *Clooney* (1850) 1 I.C.L.R. 58.

[69] Para. 4.007, *post.*

[70] Para. 4.018, *post.*

[71] *Ibid.*

[72] *Coke Upon Littleton* (19th ed., 1832), 48b.

his entry he had only what was called an *interesse termini*.[73] It was a further rule that a reversion could not be released except to a lessee who had so entered and taken possession. For a lease and release to operate, therefore, the grantee had to enter into possession at some time between the date of execution of the lease and that of the release.[74]

(ii) Post-1634

3.024. The crucial factor which the Statute of Uses (Ireland), 1634, introduced was that it provided that, upon execution of the use *automatically* by the Statute, the *cestui que use* would be "adjudged in lawfull seizin, estate and possession"[75] for the same legal estate as he previously had in the use. The result was that three new forms of conveyance gained prominence.

(a) *Bargain and Sale*

This form had been known prior to the passing of the Statute of Uses, even in England, but it suffered then from the major defect that it created only an equitable estate in the grantee. Very simply, it arose from equity's special regard for a contract to sell land supported by consideration.[76] Equity said that whenever A contracted to sell land to B and B paid the price, A was regarded as having "bargained and sold" the land and, therefore, was deemed to hold it to the use of B.[77] After the Statute of Uses, however, this use raised by equity was automatically executed, thereby passing the legal title to the purchaser without the need for any entry upon the land or formal livery of seisin.

There were also, however, some drawbacks or technicalities about this form of conveyance. First, section 17 of the Irish Statute of Uses[78] specified that no bargain and sale of freeholds would be effective unless indented[79] in writing, sealed and enrolled within six months in one of the King's courts of record at Dublin (and now Belfast for Northern Ireland).[80] Secondly, since it involved the creation of one use there were doubts as to whether further uses could be declared upon this. Indeed, the leading English authority on this point, *Jane Tyrrel's Case*,[81] involved just such a situation. Jane Tyrrel had bargained and sold by deed land to her son to the use of herself for life, remainder to the use of her son in tail. The deed was enrolled as required by the English Statute of Enrolments, 1535, but the court held that, while the use raised in favour of Jane was executed by the Statute of Uses, the uses declared upon it in favour of her son were void. The son, therefore, took the fee simple in law and in equity after the death of Jane. This problem, however, was of little, if any, practical

---

[73] See para. 17.006, *post*.
[74] See further, *Doe* d. *Burne* v. *Saunders* (1822) 1 Fox & Sm. 18.
[75] S. 1.
[76] See further on this in relation to decrees of specific performance, para. 3.144, *post*. Note, however, that for a bargain and sale to raise a use, the consideration must have been paid; the contract is not enough.
[77] *Cf.*, the modern concept of a vendor as constructive trustee for the purchaser, para. 9.061, *post*.
[78] The equivalent in England was the Statute of Enrolments, 1535.
[79] An "indenture" was a deed made in two counterparts, each having an "indented" or irregular edge.
[80] See the discussion by Black L.J. in *Re Sergie* [1954] N.I. 1 (see *A Casebook on Irish Land Law* (1984), p.70). S. 18 exempted land in cities, boroughs, etc., whose mayors, recorders, etc. had authority to enrol deeds.
[81] (1557) Dyer 155a.

significance in Ireland, because by the time the Statute of Uses was passed here it had become fairly settled that equity would, in fact, recognise and enforce uses upon a use,[82] so that a bargain and sale in Ireland after 1634 did not suffer from this drawback.

(b) Covenant to Stand Seised

This form of conveyance had also been recognised in England and Ireland prior to the Irish Statute of Uses. It had been settled that, if the owner of a fee simple entered into a covenant[83] to stand seised of his land in favour of some near relation, equity would raise a use out of this on the ground that "natural love and affection" was good consideration.[84] Once again the use would be executed automatically to pass the legal title and, unlike the bargain and sale, there was the advantage that there was no requirement for enrolment of the covenant. The one serious defect was, however, that this form of conveyance was of limited application only; it could only be used in transactions as between members of the same family, not for transactions with strangers.[85]

(c) Bargain and Sale, Lease and Release Combined

Because of the defects in the above forms of conveyance, conveyancers sought a form of conveyance that would obtain the best of all worlds. The ingenious device they evolved was a combination of the bargain and sale concept recognised by equity and the old lease and release methods so popular prior to the Statute of Uses. This combination became the standard form conveyance in England and Ireland during the seventeenth, eighteenth and early nineteenth centuries, until replaced by the modern deed of conveyance introduced by the Real Property Act, 1845.[86]

The procedure involved two steps. First, the grantor bargained and sold a lease of his land to the grantee, usually for a nominal rent. This raised a use which was automatically executed by the Statute of Uses. The grantee was deemed to be in possession immediately by the Statute, so there was no need for him to enter and take possession. Further, the estate bargained and sold was leasehold, not freehold, so there was no need for enrolment. Secondly, the grantor conveyed his reversion to the grantee by a deed of release, which operated in the usual way at common law, as it had prior to the Statute of Uses. As the use was already vested in the grantee, further uses could be declared in this deed without any doubt as to their validity being raised. As refined by the conveyancers, it became the practice for the bargain and sale and lease and release to be drafted in the one document of conveyance.[87]

---

[82] See para. 3.170, post.

[83] I.e., a promise under seal (in a deed).

[84] On a matter of construction as to the intention of the parties, the presumption might be rebutted and no use raised, Callaghan v. Neville (1856) 1 Ir.Jur. (N.S.) 449.

[85] Doe d. Kerns v. Sherlock (1824) 2 Fox & Sm. 78; Davis v. Davis (1842) 4 Ir.L.R. 353; Re Newton's Estate (1854) 6 Ir.Jur. (O.S.) 153.

[86] Para. 3.026, infra. See also Irish Conveyancing Law (1978), Chs. 15 and 16.

[87] See discussion in Pentland v. Healy (1832) Alc. & Nap. 164. Also Cooper v. Hamilton (1842) 4 Ir.L.R. 225; Malone v. Minoughan (1862) 14 I.C.L.R. 540.

(iii) Statutory Reforms

3.025. The only major statutory reform in the modes of conveyance prior to the nineteenth century was the passing of the Statute of Frauds (Ireland), 1695. Section 1 of this required feoffments to be evidenced in writing, otherwise they were void. It also required leases (unless not exceeding a term of three years) to be in writing signed by the lessor or his agent authorised in writing.[88] In fact, where a lease and release was used by conveyancers a deed was almost invariably used. Then the Conveyance by Release Act, 1841, provided that a release by itself was sufficient as the form of conveyance, illogical though it may have appeared to release the reversion on a lease which had never been created.

3.026. However, the Real Property Act, 1845, soon afterwards simplified matters greatly. Section 2 provided that from 1845 "all corporeal tenements and hereditaments shall, as regards the conveyance of the immediate freehold thereof, be deemed to lie in grant as well as in livery."[89] Since then the ordinary deed of grant has been the standard form of conveyance used in Ireland, as in England. However, unlike England,[90] the old forms of conveyance have never been abolished by statute and may still crop up to cause conveyancers some difficulties. Indeed, a considerable stir was caused by the Northern Ireland case of *Re Sergie*[91] which arose during the early 1950s.

3.027. In that case a block of buildings held under a fee farm grant[92] was mortgaged by demise[93] to a bank for a term of 10,000 years. The demise included a covenant by the mortgagors to stand seised of the fee simple reversion "in trust for any purchaser or purchasers of the premises or to convey and dispose thereof as the covenantees or any such purchaser or purchasers may at any time direct." The object of this covenant was to ensure that the mortgagors still held the legal fee simple under the fee farm grant and were, therefore, still liable for payment of the fee farm rent and responsible to the grantor in respect of the other covenants and conditions in the grant. However, the mortgagees, while thereby absolved from these liabilities, could under the covenant call for the fee simple at any time should they wish so to do, *e.g.*, in order to realise their security. Indeed, this sort of covenant was a standard form in mortgages of land held under fee farm grants.

3.028. Later the bank exercised their mortgagee's power of sale[94] and assigned the buildings to Sergie for the residue of the 10,000-year term.

---

[88] But see now Deasy's Act, 1860, s. 4, para. 17.012, *post*.

[89] In fact, a similar provision had existed in the Transfer of Property Act, 1844, which was replaced by the 1845 Act. For some comments on the 1844 Act, see Lord Upjohn in *Beswick* v. *Beswick* [1968] A.C. 58 at 104.

[90] S. 51 of the Law of Property Act, 1925, provided that "[A]ll lands and all interests therein lie in grant and are incapable of being conveyed by livery or livery of seisin, or by feoffment, or by bargain and sale." A lease and release will still operate in England provided a deed is used, see Megarry and Wade, *The Law of Real Property* (5th ed., 1984), p.1172. Note, however, that s. 3 of the 1845 Act required most feoffments made after 1845 to be *evidenced* by a deed.

[91] [1954] N.I. 1 (see *A Casebook on Irish Land Law* (1984), p.70).

[92] Para. 4.057 *et seq., post*.

[93] Ch. 12, *post*.

[94] Ch. 13, *post*.

However, neither the bank nor Sergie gave the mortgagors any directions with respect to the fee simple reversion. Sergie died and a dispute arose over his will with respect to payment of estate duty. One of the central issues in this dispute was whether Sergie had died holding a *legal* fee simple or a lease for the residue of the 10,000-year term plus an *equitable* fee simple reversion.

3.029. Lord MacDermott L.C.J., at first instance, thought that the covenant to stand seised amounted to a declaration of trust by the mortgagors which was executed by the Statute of Uses (Ireland), 1634, thereby giving the mortgagees the *legal* reversion. By the doctrine of merger,[95] then, his Lordship held, they should have been regarded as holding a legal fee simple, so that Sergie as successor in title died holding a similar title.

3.030. The Northern Ireland Court of Appeal unanimously reversed this decision. Porter L.J. pointed out that, even if the covenant were treated as a declaration of trust, it involved *active* duties on the mortgagors, namely to convey and dispose of the property if called upon, and it was settled law that the Statute of Uses did not execute active uses or trusts.[96] Black L.J. agreed with this point, and made the further point that, of course, the covenant could not operate to create a use like the usual form of covenant to stand seised, because these covenants could only apply in the case of family settlements.[97] The transactions in this case were purely commercial ventures between businessmen for whom "natural love and affection" had no place in their affairs. In Black L.J.'s view, such a covenant should really be construed as a bargain and sale, but this construction meant that the deed should have been enrolled in the Supreme Court at the Royal Courts of Justice in Belfast, under section 17 of the Statute of Uses (Ireland), 1634.[98] His Lordship had diligently searched the Supreme Court's records and could find no trace of any such enrolment, so any use raised by the bargain and sale had not been executed by the Statute and all that Sergie had left was an *equitable* fee simple reversion.[99] This result would certainly seem to conform with the object (mentioned above) of such a covenant in a mortgage of land held under a fee farm grant.[1]

C. JUDICATURE (IRELAND) ACT, 1877

3.031. During the late seventeenth and eighteenth centuries equity was welded into a coherent system of rules and principles. In England this was achieved primarily by a succession of determined Chancellors, beginning with Lord Nottingham in 1673 and culminating with Lord Eldon in the period 1801-27. Gone were the days when the Lord Chancellor was an ecclesiastic, devising new rules and principles more or less at whim. This development took

---

[95] Ch. 24, *post.*
[96] Para. 3.019, *ante.*
[97] Para. 3.024, *ante.*
[98] *Ibid.*
[99] The position would, of course, have been different if a document passing a legal title had been used, *e.g.* a lease and release or a deed of grant, paras. 3.023 and 3.026, *ante.*
[1] The third member of the Court of Appeal, Curran J., simply concurred with the conclusion of the other two members.

place rather later in Ireland,[2] but the practice of appointing English lawyers to the Irish Chancellorship helped to produce parity in developments in Ireland.[3] However, the eighteenth century was a period when ever-increasing complaints were levelled at the Court of Chancery on both sides of the Irish Sea. These arose from the expense of and delays in proceedings in the court.[4] By this time the jurisdiction of the court was covering a wide variety of matters, including remedies like specific performance and injunctions, discovery of documents, fraud, guardianship of minors and lunatics, and trusts. The Chancellor, and his assistant, the Master of the Rolls (later an independent judge),[5] could not cope with the work. It was not until the nineteenth century that substantial reforms took place with respect to the administration of the Court of Chancery in both England and Ireland. Because of the Act of Union of 1800, most of the English reforms were followed in Ireland.

3.032. The Master of the Rolls in Ireland was given judicial functions in 1801.[6] The office of Vice-Chancellor was established in 1867, as was that of Taxing Master.[7] The equity jurisdiction of the Irish Court of Exchequer was transferred to the Court of Chancery in 1850,[8] as was bankruptcy jurisdiction from the Court of Bankruptcy in 1857.[9] A Court of Appeal in Chancery for Ireland was established in 1856.[10] Irish County (or Civil Bill) Courts also enjoyed a limited equitable jurisdiction.[11]

3.033. Some cross-fertilisation of the common law courts and the Court of Chancery also occurred in the nineteenth century. By the Common Law Procedure Amendment (Ireland) Act, 1856, for example, common law courts were given power to compel discovery of documents to the same extent as the Court of Chancery, and a similar provision was made in respect of interrogatories.[12] Discovery of documents is the disclosure on oath before the action is heard by each party of the relevant documents which they have or had in their possession. When a document is "discovered" by one party the other party may inspect it. Thus, when the action is heard, each party knows what documents are in existence and the element of surprise is taken away. On the other hand, the Chancery Amendment Act, 1858, which applied to Ireland, gave the Court

---

[2] During the time of Lord Nottingham, the Irish Chancellor was Michael Boyle, Archbishop of Dublin (and later of Armagh).

[3] See, generally, Keeton and Sheridan, *Equity* (1st ed., 1969), ch. IV. [Note: later editions of this book do not deal with Irish law]

[4] See Howard, *Practice of the Chancery*. Another bone of contention was the fact that appeals from Ireland had to go to Westminster after the passing of the statute of 1719 (6 Geo. 1, c. 5) subordinating the Irish Parliament to Westminster and removing the appellate jurisdiction of the Irish House of Lords. The Irish House of Lords did not recover this appellate jurisdiction until the 1719 Act was repealed in 1782 (22 Geo. 3, c. 53) and a new Act was passed conferring it in 1783 (23 Geo. 3, c. 28).

[5] See on the office of Master of the Rolls, Keeton and Sheridan, *op. cit.*, pp. 132–4.

[6] Master of the Rolls (Ir.) Act, 1801 (41 Geo. 3, c. 25).

[7] Chancery (Ir.) Act, 1867; Richey and Bewley, *Chancery (Ireland) Act, 1867* (1868).

[8] Exchequer Equitable Jurisdiction (Ir.) Act, 1850. *Queen* v. *Jones* (1852) 4 Ir.Jur. (o.s.) 265.

[9] Irish Bankrupt and Insolvent Act, 1857.

[10] Chancery Appeal Court (Ir.) Act, 1856.

[11] See the consolidating County Officers and Courts (Ir.) Act, 1877. Also Connor, *Equity Practice, Rules and Forms of County Courts (Ireland)* (1889); Osborne, *Jurisdiction and Practice of County Courts in Equity and Probate* (1910); Rainey, *Handbook on Jurisdiction and Practice of Irish County Courts* (1906).

[12] Ss. 55–6.

of Chancery a limited power to award damages.[13]

3.034. The culmination of this process of reform and reorganisation in the nineteenth century was the passing of the Judicature (Ireland) Act, 1877.[14] This Act co-ordinated the existing Courts of Queen's Bench, Common Pleas, Exchequer, Admiralty, Probate and Divorce, and the Court of Chancery, into one Supreme Court of Judicature. This Supreme Court was divided into the High Court and the Court of Appeal. The High Court, originally split into five divisions, was reduced to two divisions in 1897, the Queen's Bench and Chancery Divisions,[15] with appeals going to the Court of Appeal. This was, until recently, in practice the position in Northern Ireland,[16] but changes have been made in the Republic.[17] The court structure now consists of district courts, 18 circuit courts,[19] the High Court and the Supreme Court.[20] The High Court is not split into divisions and the Supreme Court is essentially an appeal court.[21] The office of Lord Chancellor of Ireland was abolished in 1922,[22] and his functions are now exercised by the President of the High Court in the Republic and, to some extent, the Lord Chief Justice in Northern Ireland.

3.035. For the purposes of discussion of the development of equity in Ireland, two points in particular must be emphasised with respect to the Judicature (Ireland) Act, 1877. First, the Act purported to co-ordinate only the *administration* of the courts. Thus the traditional view was that it did not purport to bring about "fusion" of the systems of common law and equity as they had developed before the Act. One of the most renowned of Irish nineteenth-century judges, Palles C.B.,[23] himself as expert on the common law, described the effect of the Judicature (Ireland) Act, 1877, thus:

---

[13] In addition to, or in substitution for, an equitable remedy in actions of contract or tort.

[14] The equivalent to the English Judicature Act, 1873.

[15] Judicature (Ireland) (No. 2) Act, 1897.

[16] See McLean, "The Supreme Court of Judicature of Northern Ireland" (1972) 23 N.I.L.Q. 82. The constitution of the Supreme Court of Judicature of Northern Ireland is now governed by the Judicature (Northern Ireland) Act, 1978, which replaced the 1877 Act as regards that part of Ireland. Under Part I of the 1978 Act, the Supreme Court consists of the High Court, the Court of Appeal and the Crown Court. The High Court is split into three divisions, the Chancery Division, the Queen's Bench Division and the Family Division (section 5). Appeals therefrom still lie to the Court of Appeal, which now also exercises the jurisdiction formerly exercised by the Court of Criminal Appeal, which is abolished (section 34). Further appeals still lie to the House of Lords (sections 40–4 and Schedule 1). Some of the functions of the Lord Chancellor of Ireland are no longer to be exercised by the Lord Chief Justice, e.g., that relating to the property and affairs of patients under the Lunacy Regulations (Ireland) Act, 1871 (see para. 25.17, *post*).

[17] See the Courts (Establishment and Constitution) Act, 1961; Courts (Supplemental Provisions) Act, 1961; Courts Act, 1964; Courts (Supplemental Provisions) (Amendment) Act, 1968; Courts Act, 1972. See Grimes and Horgan, *Introduction to Law in the Republic of Ireland* (1981), ch.5.

[18] Northern Ireland has a system of magistrates' courts, see the Magistrates' Courts Act (N.I.), 1964. These and the Republic's district courts have original civil (including equitable) and criminal jurisdiction.

[19] Northern Ireland has a system of county courts, see the County Courts Act (N.I.), 1959; County Court Appeals Act (N.I.), 1964; County Courts (Amendment) Act (N.I.), 1964. These and the Republic's circuit courts also have original civil (including equitable) and criminal jurisdiction.

[20] Irish Free State (Consequential Provisions) Act, 1922.

[21] Its decisions are, of course, final in the Republic. An appeal, however, from the Northern Ireland Court of Appeal still lies to the House of Lords, Government of Ireland Act, 1920, s. 49; Irish Free State (Consequential Provisions) Act, 1922, s. 1; Administration of Justice Act, 1960, ss. 1 (c), 18 (3) and (4); Northern Ireland Act, 1962, s. 1.

[22] See 1920 Act, s. 44; 1922 Act, s. 2. Also, para. 25.17, *post*.

[23] For a biography, see Delany, *Christopher Palles*.

"The same system of jurisprudence now prevails in all Divisions of the High Court; and if, upon the facts pleaded, the Plaintiff could, before the Judicature Act, have had in Equity the relief which he seeks in this action, he is now entitled to it in this court. That Act changed forms of procedure, but did not alter rights or remedies."[24]

In other words, since 1877 every litigant before the superior Courts of Justice in either part of Ireland has been entitled to the full benefit of the common law and equity, no matter in which court the action was brought. Every judge who is a member of these courts has the same all-embracing jurisdiction and the duty to decide all matters at issue in the particular dispute brought before him. In this sense, the Judicature Act involved reforms rather more significant than mere changes in the administration of the courts, and it should be noted that the traditional view of "fusion" has recently been severely questioned by the House of Lords in England, with the apparent subsequent approval of the Republic's Supreme Court.[25] This brings us to the second point to be emphasised with respect to the 1877 Act.

3.036. The duty of judges of the superior courts to operate concurrently the common law and equity could give rise to difficulties in particular cases, *e.g.,* if the rules of the two systems conflicted, as was often the case prior to the Act. As we have already mentioned, the Judicature Act did not purport to fuse the two systems into one cohesive system of law. To meet future cases of conflict, the draftsmen provided in section 28 (11) of the 1877 Act:

In all matters not hereinbefore mentioned,[26] in which there is any con–flict or variance between the rules of equity and the rules of common law, with reference to the same matter, the rules of equity shall prevail."

---

[24] *Barber* v. *Houston* (1884) 14 L.R.Ir. 273 at 276 (aff'd. (1885) 18 L.R.Ir. 475) (see *A Casebook on Equity and Trusts in Ireland* (1985), p.1).

[25] In two cases involving the time-schedule in rent review clauses in leases, *United Scientific Holdings Ltd.* v. *Burnley Borough Council* and *Cheapside Land Development Co, Ltd.* v. *Messels Service Co.,* both reported at [1978] A.C. 904, where the issue was whether time was of the essence of the contracts (on which subject see *Irish Conveyancing Law* (1978), paras. 12.09–24), some members of the House of Lords, in considering the English equivalent, the Judicature Act, 1873, were extremely critical of Ashburner's famous comment that "the two streams of jurisdiction, though they run in the same channel, run side by side and do not mingle their waters" (see *Principles of Equity* (1902), p. 23). Thus Lord Diplock described the metaphor as "both mischievous and deceptive" for in his view "the waters of the confluent streams of law and equity have surely mingled now" (*ibid.,* p. 925; see also Lord Simon of Glaisdale at pp. 944–5 and Lord Fraser of Tullybelton at p. 957). In *Hynes Ltd.* v. *Independent Newspapers Ltd.* [1980] I.R.204 (see *A Casebook on Equity and Trusts in Ireland* (1985), p. 6.), also involving a rent review clause, the Republic's Supreme Court expressly adopted the reasoning of the House of Lords and O'Higgins C.J. stated firmly that the fusion of common-law and equitable rules "was completed by the Courts of Justice Act, 1924, and the Courts (Establishment and Constitution) Act, 1961" (*ibid.,* p. 216). Note also Kenny J.'s criticism of the views expressed by P.V. Baker in "The Future of Equity" (1977) 93 L.Q.R. 529 (*ibid.,* p. 221). See further on "time of the essence" *Macklin* v. *Greacen & Co. Ltd.* [1981] I.L.R.M. 315.

[26] Thus matters dealt with earlier in s. 28 were, *e.g.,* the barring of claims by a beneficiary against an express trustee (subs. (2), see ch. 23, *post*); equitable waste (subs. (3), para. 4.154, *post*); merger by operation of law (subs. (4), ch. 24, *post*); suits for possession of land by mortgagors (subs. (5), ch. 13, *post*); assignment of choses in action (subs. (6)); stipulations as to time of the essence of contracts (subs. (7)). The equivalent of s.28(11) in Northern Ireland is now s.86(1) of the Jidicature (N.I.) Act, 1978, which reads:

"Every court exercising jurisdiction in Northern Ireland in a civil cause or matter shall continue to administer law and equity upon the basis that, wherever there is any conflict or variance between the rules of equity and the rules of common law with reference to the same matter, the rule of equity shall prevail."

As regards the other matters covered by s.28 of the 1877 Act, see now the 1978 Act. ss.87 (assignment of choses in action), 88 (stipulations as to time), 89 (merger), 90 (equitable waste) and 93 (suits for possession by mortgagors).

3.037. This position of pre-eminence given to the rules of equity has ensured that equity has continued to play a vital role in the development of our law, especially our land law.[27] It is true, however, that the great increase in legislation during the twentieth century has reduced to some extent the need for equity that existed in earlier centuries. The legislature can often enact speedier and, significantly, more wide-ranging and comprehensive reforms of the common law than the judges can introduce through decided cases over a period of time.

It is proposed in the next few pages, first, to discuss in general the principal features of modern equity, as it has developed since the Judicature (Ireland) Act, 1877, and then, second, to discuss in some more detail the main principles and doctrines of modern equity, equitable remedies and, since this is primarily a book on land law, equitable interests in land.

D. Modern Equity

There are many aspects of modern equity and it is proposed here to summarise only what may be said to be its main features. More detailed discussion will be found in books specifically devoted to equity as a subject in itself.[28]

3.038. First, there are the cases where the courts since the Judicature (Ireland) Act, 1877, have resolved conflicts between the old common law and equity in favour of equity, as section 28 (11) of the 1877 Act provided, and have thereby produced a common rule of law based upon equitable principles. Perhaps one of the best known illustrations of this type of modern equity is the rule in *Walsh* v. *Lonsdale*,[29] named after a leading English case decided towards the end of the nineteenth century. This rule stems from the different approach of equity to certain contracts, especially those relating to land, in respect of which it is often prepared to grant a decree of specific performance to ensure that the contract is carried out. *Walsh* v. *Lonsdale,* as interpreted by later cases, established the rule that, in cases where a decree of specific performance would be available to enforce an *agreement* for a lease, then the parties would be treated as being in the position of having already a *lease* granted between them, even though the strict statutory formalities for a lease had not been complied with. For most purposes, therefore, an agreement for a lease is as good as a lease itself. This rule will be discussed in more detail in the later chapter on landlord and tenant.[30] Suffice it for the moment to say that the rule in *Walsh* v *Lonsdale* has been adopted by the courts in Ireland.[31] In

---

[27] See Evershed, "Reflections on the Fusion of Law and Equity after 75 Years" (1954) 70 L.Q.R. 326.

[28] See fns. 1 and 2, para. 3.001, *ante.*

[29] (1882) 21 Ch.D. 9. See also *Swain* v. *Ayres* (1888) 21 Q.B.D. 289; *Manchester Brewery Co.* v. *Coombs* [1901] 2 Ch. 608; *Foster* v. *Reeves* [1892] 2 Q.B. 255; *Cornish* v. *Brook Green Laundry Ltd.* [1959] 1 Q.B. 394; *Kingswood Estate Co. Ltd.* v. *Anderson* [1963] 2 Q.B. 169. Note the interesting extension of the rule in *Industrial Properties (Barton Hill) Ltd.* v. *Associated Electrical Industries Ltd.* [1977] Q.B. 614 (see para. 17.017, *post*).

[30] Ch. 17, *post.*

[31] See Sheridan, "*Walsh* v. *Lonsdale* in Ireland" (1952) 9 N.I.L.Q. 190. Also *Archbold* v. *Lord Howth* (1866) 1 I.L.T. 760; *Sweeney* v. *Denis* (1883) 17 I.L.T.R. 76; *Craig* v. *Elliott* (1885) 15 L.R.Ir. 257; *Union* v. *McDermott* (1921) 55 I.L.T.R. 194.

McCausland v. *Murphy*,[32] an agent agreed on behalf of his principal to grant a lease to commence at a future date. This agent had not been authorised in writing, though section 4 of Deasy's Act, 1860,[33] required such written authorisation for an agent to be able to grant a lease. Sullivan M.R. held that there was still in Ireland a distinction to be made between an agreement for a lease and a lease. An agreement to grant a lease to take effect immediately operates as a lease, but an agreement to grant a lease at some future date is an agreement for a lease within the meaning of *Walsh* v. *Lonsdale*.[34]

3.039. The second major aspect of the development of modern equity since the Judicature Act has been the existence of a wide range of equitable remedies available to all the judges of the superior courts. Apart from the traditional equitable remedies of the injunction and specific performance, other important remedies have come to be used by the courts, notably appointment of receivers, rectification of instruments, rescission and cancellation of transactions, accounting and tracing. Each of these remedies stems from equity's traditional function of doing greater justice between the parties by providing a more satisfactory remedy. Apart from the law of trusts and many aspects of the law of mortgages, these remedies form equity's greatest contribution to our modern legal system. They perform a vital function in practically every area of the law. Some are discussed in greater detail later in this chapter.[35]

3.040. The third major aspect of modern equity is the number of important interests in property originally developed by equity and still firmly grounded upon equitable principles. It is the existence of these interests, and the principles governing them, that makes it necessary still in our law to make the distinction between common law and equity. The most obvious and important example of this aspect of modern equity is the trust. Developed from the use which was devised by conveyancers with respect to land (then the primary source of wealth), it has come to be used extensively for both real and personal property. Even in modern times it has retained its original function—tax avoidance. The trust is a vital tool for the lawyer in trying to redistribute the property of his more wealthy clients so as to reduce the effects of modern tax systems. The law of trusts is a subject in itself but, because of its importance in the area of land law, further discussion of it occurs elsewhere in this book.[36] Other important interests derived from equity are those which arise under restrictive covenants on freehold land[37] and under doctrines of the law of mortgages (*e.g.*, the equity of redemption).[38] In recent decades, considerable developments have been taking place with respect to licences.[39] Here again the developments have been particularly significant in respect of land.

---

[32] (1881) 9 L.R.Ir. 9 (see *A Casebook on Irish Land Law* (1984), p. 552).
[33] See para. 17.012, *post*.
[34] Sullivan M.R. described the agreement in *McCausland* thus: "In this case there was authority to make a preliminary agreement for a future tenancy, and a lease was to be executed." *Op. cit.*, p. 15.
[35] Paras. 3.127–69, *post*.
[36] Chs. 9 and 10, *post*.
[37] See ch. 19, *post*.
[38] Ch. 13, *post*.
[39] Ch. 20, *post*.

3.041. The last aspect, and the most controversial, is what might be described as the residual power of equity to do justice in the particular case, by extending the existing remedies to meet a new case or, if necessary, by creating a new interest or right to be protected by the law. This is the most controversial aspect of modern equity because many lawyers, judges and academics have doubted the capacity of equity nowadays in this area. Some would say that equity is now "past the age of childbearing," but others, with Lord Denning, until his recent retirement, in the forefront, vehemently reject this view.[40] Developments in the last few decades would tend to suggest that equity can still create new rights and interests, though many of these instances have occurred in England and have not always been followed in Ireland. This is not necessarily to be taken to mean that Irish judges have taken a different view from their English brethren; the fact is that in some instances cases have not arisen in Ireland putting the matter at issue. Lord Denning had been particularly active in invoking the aid of equity as a residual source of justice to establish, sometimes with the approval of his brother judges, new equitable doctrines, e.g., those of equitable estoppel[41] and licences to occupy land.[42] In other instances, his doctrines have not met with approval, e.g., the deserted wife's equity,[43] third party rights in contract[44] and the "family assets" principle with respect to matrimonial property.[45] Yet, Lord Denning has not been alone in this approach to the role of equity and other new doctrines has been emerging, e.g., the extension of the remedy of tracing discussed so fully in Re Diplock.[46]

III. GENERAL PRINCIPLES

3.042. We come now to some of the main general principles of equity. These

[40] Cf. Denning, "The Need for a New Equity" (1952) 5 C.L.P. 1; Evershed, "Equity Past Childbearing?" (1953) 1 Sydney L. Rev.1; Sugarman, "Equity's Capacity for Childbearing" (1953) 1 Sydney L.Rev. 174; Marshall. "The Reform of Equity" (1967) Law, Justice and Equity 66.

[41] Central London Property Trust Ltd. v. High Trees House Ltd. [1947] K.B. 130; Combe v. Combe [1951] 2 K.B. 215; D. & C. Builders Ltd. v. Rees [1966] 2 Q.B. 617; Crabb v. Arun District Council [1976] Ch. 179; Greasley v. Cooke [1980]1 W.L.R. 1306; Amalgamated Investment and Property Co. Ltd. v. Texas Commerce International Bank Ltd. [1982] Q.B. 84. See discussion in Revenue Commrs. v. Moroney [1972] I.R. 372 and Smith v. Ireland, unreported (see A Casebook on Equity and Trusts in Ireland (1985), p. 80).

[42] Ch. 20, post. See Cullen v. Cullen [1962] I.R. 268 (see A Casebook on Irish Land Law (1984), p. 657).

[43] Bendall v. McWhirter [1952] 2 Q.B. 466; National Provincial Bank Ltd. v. Ainsworth [1965] A.C. 1175. See Wylie, "The End of the Deserted Wife's 'Equity' " (1965) 16 N.I.L.Q. 521. Note, however, that Parliament intervened to vindicate Lord Denning, see the Matrimonial Homes Act, 1967. Cf. the House of Lords decision in Chapman v. Chapman [1954] A.C. 429 (Denning L.J., as he then was, dissented in the Court of Appeal decision), which resulted in the Variation of Trusts Act, 1958, see para. 10.095, post.

[44] Smith and Snipes Hall Farm Ltd. v. River Douglas Catchment Board [1949] 2 K.B. 500; White v. John Warwick & Co. Ltd. [1953] 1 W.L.R. 1285; Drive Yourself Hire Co. (London) Ltd. v. Strutt [1954] 1 Q.B. 250; Beswick v. Beswick [1966] Ch. 538 (C.A.), [1968] A.C. 57 (H.L.). See Wylie, "Contracts and Third Parties" (1966) 17 N.I.L.Q. 351, and "The Third Refusal" (1967) 18 N.I.L.Q. 448. As regards the Beswick case, see the Irish legislation covering the point at issue, the Married Women's Status Act, 1957 (R.I.), s. 8; Law Reform (Husband and Wife) Act (N.I.), 1964, ss. 4–6.

[45] Pettitt v. Pettitt [1970] A.C. 777; Gissing v. Gissing [1971] A.C. 886; Falconer v. Falconer [1970] 3 All E.R. 449. See discussion by the N.I. Court of Appeal in McFarlane v. McFarlane [1972] N.I. 59, espec. at 66–7 (per Lord MacDermott L.C.J.). and, in the Republic, by Kenny J. in Heavey v. Heavey (1977) 111 I.L.T.R. I (see A Casebook on Irish Land Law (1984), p. 714, Finlay P. in W. v. W. [1981] I.L.R.M. 202 and the Supreme Court in M.C. v. M.C., unreported (1982/52). See further, paras. 25.15–6, post.

[46] [1948] Ch. 465. See also Shanahan's Stamp Auctions Ltd. v. Farrelly [1962] I.R. 386 (see A Casebook on Equity and Trusts in Ireland (1985), p. 636) para. 10.109, post. Cf. the courts' struggles over their approach to penalty and forfeiture clauses in contracts, Lombank Ltd. v. Kennedy [1961] N.I. 192 (see ibid., p. 61); Bridge v. Campbell Discount Co. Ltd. [1962] A.C. 600; United Dominions Trust (Commercial) Ltd. v. Ennis [1968] 1 Q.B. 54. See also United Dominions Trust Ltd. v. Patterson [1973] N.I. 142.

are principles which have been established over the centuries as an inherent part of equitable jurisdiction. As such, they clearly pre-date the Judicature Act but, since that Act, have become part of the general law applied in all the superior courts. Yet these principles, and the doctrines which they have established, are still clearly recognisable as having a distinctly equitable flavour. The following discussion is somewhat cursory, for two reasons. First, comprehensive discussion of these principles belongs more properly to a textbook confined to discussion of equity. Secondly, and perhaps because of the early origin of many of these principles, they, or at least the traditional doctrines based upon them, appear to have become less important in practice in recent decades. Certainly the number of cases coming before the courts in England and Ireland seems to have been declining steadily.

A. MAXIMS

3.043. To begin with, a strong word of warning! The so-called maxims of equity[47] must be treated with extreme caution. All too often they appear to be little more than pithy sayings, half-truths which are just as likely to mislead and trap the unwary as they are to inform. Some modern authors on equity, therefore, tend to play down the discussion of the maxims.[48] However, there is no doubt that the maxims have gained a common currency over the centuries. They are frequently cited by judges as convenient short-hand expressions by which to explain the basis of their decision-making. They are sometimes useful in that they often do point towards the underlying principles upon which equitable jurisdiction is founded, and it is probably the case that no discussion of equity is complete without at least a mention of them. The following is an outline of the principal maxims cited in Irish courts.

1. *Equity Acts in Personam*

3.044. This maxim indicates the essential distinction in approach to settlement of a dispute by the common law and equity. Equity concerns itself with the conscience of the parties appearing before the court. Its orders are directed against the parties concerned and so it acts against them personally. Indeed, the original foundation of chancery jurisdiction can be traced to the idea that what the defendant was doing should have been condemned by his "informed" conscience. And it was the obligation of the Chancellor to ensure that the defendant acted in accordance with the dictates of an informed conscience. Failure of a defendant to observe court orders is contempt of court, for which the ultimate sanction is imprisonment at the court's discretion. It is sometimes said, then, that equitable rights are rights *in personam* as opposed to rights *in rem*. Thus a court nowadays has jurisdiction in equity to enforce contracts and trusts relating to property overseas (and, therefore, outside the jurisdiction of the court), provided the party to whom it is sought to address the court's decree

---

[47] See Francis, *Maxims of Equity* (1728); Pound, "The Maxims of Equity" in *Cambridge Legal Essays*, p. 259. For Ireland, Kiely, *The Principles of Equity as Applied in Ireland* (1936), ch. II.
[48] See, *e.g.*, Hanbury and Maudsley, *Modern Equity* (12th ed., 1985 by Martin), p. 26 *et seq.*

is within the jurisdiction, or at least is capable of being served with proceedings if he is outside the jurisdiction.[49] Thus in *Lett* v. *Lett* [50] an injunction was granted to restrain a suit in an Argentine court where the plaintiff in that suit had covenanted not to proceed with his suit. The plaintiff was within the jurisdiction of the Irish court and so equity could act *in personam*. Porter M.R., at first instance, quoted the following passage from *Kerr on Injunctions*[51]—

> "In the exercise of this jurisdiction the Court does not proceed upon any claim of right to interfere with or control the course of proceedings in the tribunals of a foreign country, or to prevent them from adjudicating on the rights of the parties when drawn in controversy and duly presented for their determination. The jurisdiction is founded on the clear authority vested in Courts of Equity over persons within the limits of their jurisdiction, and amenable to process to restrain them from doing acts which work wrong and injury to others, and are therefore contrary to equity and good conscience. As the order of the Court in such cases is pointed solely at the individual, and does not extend to the tribunal where the suit or proceeding is pending, it is wholly immaterial that the party to whom it is addressed is prosecuting his action in the Courts of a foreign country."[52]

3.045. It should be noted, however, that equitable rights have been acquiring in certain circumstances the characteristics of rights *in rem, i.e.,* binding against all-comers as opposed to being enforceable against a limited class of persons only. A traditional example of a right *in personam* is a restrictive covenant which, under the rule in *Tulk* v. *Moxhay*,[53] is not binding on a *bona fide* purchaser of the legal title to the land to be affected by the covenant if the purchaser bought the land without notice of the covenant.[54] This sort of right may be compared with an easement or profit *à prendre*. These are rights *in rem* binding any person who succeeds to the land whether or not he had notice.[55] Recent cases involving the equitable remedy of tracing, *i.e.,* following trust property or other property misappropriated, have shown, however, that the equitable remedies are not only more wide-ranging than the legal remedies in these situations, they may be similar to rights *in rem* in that the *"res"* (the property misappropriated), if traced into the hands of third parties, can be recovered even though it has lost its specific identity (*e.g.,* land sold and converted into money or vice versa). Again one must be careful not to mislead. The remedy of tracing really seems to create "hybrid" rights, because even it may not be invoked in certain circumstances. This remedy is discussed in more detail later in the book.[56]

---

[49] See the leading cases, *Penn* v. *Lord Baltimore* (1750) 1 Ves.Sen. 444; *Rochefoucauld* v. *Boustead* [1897] 1 Ch. 196. See on the latter case, *Gilmurray* v. *Corr* [1978] N.I.99.

[50] [1906] 1 I.R. 618 (see *A Casebook on Equity and Trusts in Ireland* (1985), p.14).

[51] P. 577.

[52] *Op. cit.*, p. 629. His decision was affirmed by the Court of Appeal, *op. cit.*, p. 630.

[53] (1848) 2 Ph. 774.

[54] See ch. 19, *post.* On the doctrine of notice, see para. 3.069, *post.*

[55] See ch. 6, *post.*

[56] Para. 10.108, *post.*

3.046. In Ireland, the right of tracing was regarded as a "mere equity" in *Scott* v. *Scott*,[57] so that a *bona fide* purchaser of an equitable (as opposed to a legal) interest took his interest free of it.[58] Other Irish cases have shown in different contexts a particular regard for the notion that equitable rights are rights *in personam* only. Thus a line of cases has held that beneficiaries' rights under a trust are also mere equities and, therefore, of less value than equitable interests in property created, *e.g.*, by an equitable mortgage.[59] It seems strange nowadays that rights under what has proved to have been equity's greatest creation, the trust, should be accorded such a lowly status and it may be doubted whether these cases would be followed today.[60] They have not, however, been overruled or doubted in Ireland.

2. Equity Follows the Law

3.047. This maxim is a good illustration of the confusion that can be caused by the maxims. It contains an apparent contradiction in terms when compared with section 28 (11) of the Judicature (Ireland) Act, 1877.[61] The maxim's real significance lies in the fact that it indicates the historical approach of equity discussed earlier.[62] In this regard it helps to explain the traditional approach of judges in applying equitable principles, one which survives to the present day.

3.048. Equity never denies the existence of legal rights. What it does do is to work on the conscience of the holders of legal rights, to ensure that these are not exercised unjustly. This approach is well-illustrated by equity's approach to statutes laying down strict requirements for the creation of legal rights, *e.g.*, the Statute of Frauds (Ireland), 1695, or the Wills Act, 1837.[63] Indeed, in these cases the judges frequently cite another maxim or sub-maxim—"Equity will not allow a statute to be used as an instrument of fraud." The result has been the creation of equitable doctrines like those relating to secret trusts[64] and part performance.[65] In each case, equity does not purport to disregard the law laid down by the statute, or strict legal rights acquired under the statute, but it does require the holder of those legal rights not to take unfair advantage of them and certainly not to commit a fraud on the other party by invoking them. An Irish statute in respect of which this approach by equity was frequently adopted was the Registration of Deeds Act (Ireland), 1707.[66] Section 3 of the Act provided for registration of memorials of deeds, conveyances and wills concerning or affecting land. Under section 5, dispositions not registered were to be void as against those which were registered, even though the latter were of later date.

---

[57] [1924] 1 I.R. 141, especially at 150–151.
[58] On the *bona fide* purchaser doctrine, see para. 3.074, *post*.
[59] *Re Ffrench's Estate* (1887) 21 L.R.Ir. 283; *Re Sloane's Estate* [1895] 1 I.R. 146; *Re Bobbett's Estate* [1904] 1 I.R. 461; *Bourke* v. *Lee* [1904] 1 I.R. 280. See para. 3.077, *post*. Also *Allied Irish Banks* v. *Glynn* [1973] I.R. 188 (see *A Casebook on Irish Land Law* (1984), p.85).
[60] See Delany "Equitable Interests and 'Mere Equities' " (1957) 21 Conv. 195.
[61] Or now s.86(1) of the Judicature (N.I.) Act, 1978. See para. 3.036, *ante*.
[62] Para. 3.002, *ante*.
[63] Replaced in the Republic of Ireland by the Succession Act, 1965.
[64] Para. 9.029, *post*.
[65] Para. 3.149, *post*.
[66] See, generally, ch. 22, *post*.

In *Forbes* v. *Deniston*,[67] a lessor granted a lease which was not registered. Later, taking advantage of this, the lessor granted a new lease which was registered, though the lessee knew of the first unregistered lease. The House of Lords held that nevertheless the original lessee had priority over the subsequent lessee, despite the registration of the second lease, for the 1707 Act, itself orginally intended to prevent fraud, should never "be used as a means to cover it."

3.049. The other main illustration of the maxim is that equity in many cases adopted concepts originally derived from common law. Thus it adopted the common law's classification of estates in land, so that an equitable fee simple and fee tail can exist.[68] It even went so far as to adopt rather more technical concepts like the rule in *Shelley's Case*.[69] On the other hand, it did not adopt rules which appeared arbitrary, harsh or out of keeping with present conditions. Equity did not, for example, adopt the highly technical common law contingent remainder rules,[70] nor has it always strictly followed common law requirements like those relating to words of limitation in conveyances.[71]

3. Equitable Remedies are Discretionary

3.050. This maxim illustrates a fundamental principle of equitable jurisdiction, but nowadays the epithet "discretionary" can be misleading. As has already been stated, considerable changes have taken place since the days when equity might vary according to the length of the Chancellor's foot.[72] Today the exercise of the discretion whether or not to grant an equitable remedy is governed by rules that have become settled and clear over the centuries. It is true that some judges, notably Lord Denning, were in the habit of invoking a general discretionary and residual power in equity to do justice, but this claim for equity is rarely made and even more rarely is accepted.[73] As Black L.J. said:

> "The remedy of specific performance still retains the character of an equitable remedy. It is not granted as of right but is a discretionary remedy which may be withheld in cases of a type where the court, having regard to the conduct of the parties and all the circumstances of the case, considers in its discretion that the remedy ought not to be granted. This discretion is not, of course, the arbitrary discretion of the individual judge but is a discretion to be exercised on the principles which have been worked out in a multitude of decided cases."[74]

---

[67] (1722) 4 Bro.P.C. 189.
[68] Ch. 4, *post.*
[69] Para. 4.034, *post.*
[70] Para. 5.012, *post.*
[71] Para. 4.024, *post.*
[72] Para. 3.031, *ante.*
[73] Para. 3.041, *ante.*
[74] *Conlon* v. *Murray* [1958] N.I. 17 at 25 (see *A Casebook on Equity and Trusts in Ireland* (1985), p.22). See also *Smelter Corporation of Ireland Ltd.* v. *O'Driscoll* [1977] I.R. 305 (*ibid.*, p.157).

3.051. There is no doubt, however, that an element of discretion always exists when equitable jurisdiction is invoked. Once a legal right has been established to the satisfaction of the court, it must be enforced and the party granted his legal remedy. Mere proof of infringement of a right recognised in equity, however, does not guarantee the granting of an equitable remedy. As we have said, many rules have been settled governing how the court will exercise its discretion in this regard. For example, it is settled that an equitable remedy, such as an injunction or a decree of specific performance, will not be granted if a common law remedy (*e.g.,* damages) would be an adequate remedy in the opinion of the court.[75] Another settled rule is that, if the party whose rights have been infringed himself acted improperly, the court may refuse him a remedy. Indeed, this rule has come to be cited as another maxim—"He who comes into Equity must come with clean hands."[76]

4. *Where the Equities are Equal, the Law Prevails*

3.052. This maxim states a rule which governed the question of priorities between competing interests in land,[77] where one interest was legal and the other equitable. The rule in effect was that, provided the two owners were equally meritorious in the eyes of equity, the holder of the legal interest would get priority on the ground that the *legal* interest should prevail, because equity came to "fulfil, not to destroy." Once again we see that section 28 (11) of the Judicature (Ireland) Act, 1877 (and section 86 (1) of the Judicature (Northern Ireland) Act, 1978) should not be read too literally.

3.053. Three points have to be emphasised with respect to this maxim. First, the central concept in its application by the courts to decide questions of priority was that of notice. We examine the doctrine of notice, and its application in questions of priority, a little later in this chapter.[78] Secondly, the maxim has been of considerably more limited use in Ireland in relation to land than in England (up to 1925[79]). The reason for this is that priorities in relation to land have been governed primarily in Ireland by the registration of deeds system introduced for the whole country by the Registration of Deeds Act (Ireland), 1707. This system is discussed in much greater detail in a later chapter.[80] For the moment, suffice it to say that this system governs priorities as between registered deeds and unregistered, but registrable, deeds. The doctrine of notice, and the maxim under discussion, will apply only where the issue involves an unregistrable disposition, *e.g.,* an equitable mortgage created by deposit of title deeds, or several unregistered, though registrable, mortgages. A mortgage by deposit only involves no deed or any other written document of which a memorial may be made for the purposes of registration.

---

[75] See further on equitable remedies, para. 3.127, *post.*

[76] Para. 3.058, *post.* Cf., the maxim—"He who seeks Equity, must do Equity," para. 3.055, *post.*

[77] Priorities in equitable interests in personalty were governed by a different principle, known as the rule in *Dearle* v. *Hall* (1823) 3 Russ. 1. See *Survey of the Land Law of Northern Ireland* (1971), paras. 279–80. Also para. 3.092, *post.*

[78] Para. 3.069, *post.*

[79] See now the Land Charges Act, 1972, on the question of priorities and *cf.* Law of Property Act, 1925, s. 198.

[80] Ch. 22, *post* and see para. 3.084, *post.*

Thirdly, the maxim and the doctrine of notice do not normally apply in cases involving registered land, *i.e.*, land the title to which has been registered under the system of registration of title introduced for the whole country by the Local Registration of Title (Ireland) Act, 1891.[81] In this case, transactions with respect to the land must be executed according to Land Registry rules, with appropriate notations on the register, and priorities are governed by the rules relating to this registration of title system.[82]

5. Where the Equities are Equal, the First in Time Prevails

3.054. This maxim is closely connected with the previous one discussed. It governs the case of priorities as between competing equitable interests in land. We shall see later that it is quite common for several successive equitable interests to be created out of land, though there are usually fewer legal interests,[83] in respect of which disputes over priority can arise. Thus it is very common to have one legal mortgage created on a single piece of land, followed by two or three subsequent equitable mortgages.[84] Priorities as between the latter only would be governed by the present maxim, but as between them and the legal mortgage the previous maxim would apply.[85]

6. He Who Seeks Equity, Must Do Equity

3.055. The underlying principle of this maxim is clear. If a party wishes to invoke the aid of equity to pursue his claim, he must be prepared to undertake himself to act in a proper and just manner before equity will grant him any aid. In the case of this maxim, equity is looking towards the party's *future* conduct and this may be compared with the case of the maxim next discussed, where equity looks at his *past* conduct.[86] This maxim has been the foundation of several doctrines of equity over the years.

One of these doctrines is the doctrine of marshalling. This doctrine may be summarised as follows: if A has claims against funds X and Y of B,[87] and C has a claim only against fund X, equity will require A to satisfy himself as far as possible out of fund Y. Equity so requires in an attempt to do justice between A and C, by trying to ensure that each is satisfied in respect of what he is owed as far as possible. If, in our example, A has already satisfied himself out of fund X, equity will not allow its policy to be defeated in this way. Equity will allow C to step into A's shoes and satisfy himself out of fund Y to the extent that A satisfied himself out of fund X. Marshalling, as a principle of equity, has been applied in several situations in Ireland. It has been applied in respect of

---

[81] See now the Registration of Title Act, 1964 (R.I.); Land Registration Act (N.I.), 1970.

[82] See, generally, ch. 21, *post* and para. 3.090, *post*.

[83] See, however, successive legal mortgages by demise, para. 12.38, *post*.

[84] See, generally, ch. 12, *post*.

[85] *Ibid.*

[86] Para. 3.058, *infra*.

[87] Marshalling also applies in the case of a single debtor, *Re Kiely* (1857) 6 Ir.Ch.R. 394. And the two funds should be at this debtor's disposal, *Douglas* v. *Cooksey* (1868) I.R. 2 Eq. 311, 315; *Dolphin* v. *Alyward* (1870) L.R. 4 H.L. 486, 505. See further, ch. 13, *post*.

mortgages and other secured debts,[88] and in respect of judgment mortgages.[89] A right of marshalling may be created when the owner of two estates, both subject to prior mortgages or charges, sells or mortgages again one of them, e.g., to a *bona fide* purchaser for value without notice of the prior charges[90] or with a covenant against incumbrances[91] or further assurances.[92] The equity of marshalling in these cases requires the prior mortgages or charges to be satisfied out of the estate retained by the previous owner of the two estates.

3.056. Marshalling of assets in the administration of estates of deceased persons was once an extremely important subject.[93] Until the Administration of Estates Act, 1833, a distinction exited between specialty creditors, who were entitled to claim against the realty of the deceased persons, and simple contract creditors who were not. This resulted in specialty creditors having two funds to claim against and gave rise to an equity of marshalling in the simple contract creditors, to compel specialty creditors to seek satisfaction as far as possible from the deceased's realty. Since the 1833 Act,[94] however, both realty and personalty are available equally for both types of creditors.[95] Though the doctrine has lost importance in this respect, it is still important in regulating the rights of the beneficiaries *inter se* claiming under the deceased person's estate. The administration of estates legislation lays down the order in which assets are to be applied in payment of debts, subject to variation by a testator.[96] If debts are paid out of assets out of this order this could affect beneficiaries bequeathed specific assets. So the principle of marshalling applies to allow such a beneficiary to have recourse to any property which should have been taken in order before his, and any other beneficiaries affected by this in turn have a right of marshalling.[97] In the Republic of Ireland this principle has been given statutory recognition recently. Section 46 (5) of the Succession Act, 1965,[98] provides:

---

[88] *McCarthy* v. *McCartie (No. 2)* [1904] 1 I.R. 100; *Tighe* v. *Dolphin* [1906] 1 I.R. 305; *Re Archer's Estate* [1914] 1 I.R. 285; *Re Chute's Estate* [1914] 1 I.R. 180; *Smyth* v. *Toms* [1918] 1 I.R. 339; *Re Lysaght's Estate* [1903] 1 I.R. 235.

[89] *Re Lynch's Estate* (1867) I.R. 1 Eq. 396; *Re Scott's Estate* (1863) 14 Ir. Ch.R. 63; *Dolphin* v. *Alyward* (1870) L.R. 4 H.L. 486.

[90] *McCarthy* v. *McCartie (No. 2)*, *op. cit.*

[91] *Avarell* v. *Wade* (1841) 3 Ir.Eq.R. 446; *Ocean Accident and Guarantee Corp.* v. *Collum* [1913] 1 I.R. 337.

[92] *Re Roche's Estate* (1890) 25 L.R.Ir. 271.

[93] Note the controversial question that arose under s. 16 of the Charitable Donations and Bequests (Ir.) Act, 1844 (now repealed by the Charities Act, 1961 (R.I.), and the Charities Act (N.I.), 1964). S. 16 rendered void gifts of land for pious or charitable uses unless the deed was executed and registered or the will executed at least three months before the death of the donor. The question was, if a testator left charitable and non-charitble legacies and charged his realty with payment of legacies and died within three months, could the charitable legatees marshal so as to have the non-charitable legacies satisfied out of the land and thereby save the charitable legacies from s. 16. The question was not settled until the Republic's Supreme Court decided there could be no marshalling in these circumstances, see *Re Solomon* [1949] I.R. 3. See also Newark, "Charities and the Marshalling of Assets" (1944) 6 N.I.L.Q. 36 and 47.

[94] See also the Administration of Estates Act, 1869 (Hinde Palmer's Act).

[95] See now the Succession Act, 1965, s. 45 (R.I.); Administration of Estates Act (N.I.), 1955, s. 29. On the subject of administration of estates, see ch. 16, *post.*

[96] Succession Act, 1965, s. 46 (3); Administration of Estates Act (N.I.), 1955, s. 30 (3).

[97] *Buckley* v. *Buckley* (1887) 19 L.R.Ir. 544 at 559–61.

[98] The equivalent section in the N.I. statute, s. 30 of the Administration of Estates Act (N.I.), 1955, does not contain a similar provision, so marshalling there depends upon case law (as it does in England). See Leitch, *A Handbook on the Administration of Estates Act (N.I.), 1955* (1956), p. 85.

"Where a creditor, a person entitled to a legal right or a personal representative applies an asset out of the order mentioned in Part II of the First Schedule, the persons entitled under the will or on intestacy shall have the right to have the assets marshalled so that a beneficiary whose estate or interest has been applied out of its order shall stand in the place of that creditor or person *pro tanto* as against any property that, in the said order, is liable before his own estate or interest."

3.057. Another illustration of the maxim under discussion, and a very similar doctrine to that of marshalling, is the doctrine of consolidation in the law of mortgages. This doctrine is discussed in a later chapter.[99] Also discussed later are other situations where the maxim has been applied, *e.g.,* the doctrine of election[1] and mutuality (with respect to specific performance),[2] building estate schemes[3] and similar rights as between individual landowners (again based on the concept of mutuality).[4]

7. He Who Comes Into Equity, Must Come with Clean Hands

3.058. This maxim is the corollary of the previous one. Just as equity will have regard to the future conduct of the party claiming its assistance, so it will have regard to his past conduct. If he is to obtain equitable relief he must not have acted in any way improperly in the eyes of equity.[5] This maxim may be illustrated by various rules of the law of trusts, such as the rule that a trustee-beneficiary's beneficial interest will be impounded to make good any breach of trust on his part[6] and that a solicitor-trustee cannot claim contribution from his co-trustees if a full recovery is made against him.[7] Similarly, a beneficiary who has concurred in a breach of trust cannot later sue the trustees in respect of it.[8]

8. Equality is Equity

3.059. It is a principle of equity that, when faced with deciding as between competing claims to property, an equal division amongst the claimants should be made unless there is some good reason for making a division otherwise. This maxim has been applied in several situations by the courts. It has given rise to a sub-maxim—"equity leans against double portions"—which is the corner-stone of the doctrine of satisfaction.[9] It has been used extensively in the law of co-ownership, giving rise to another sub-maxim— "equity leans against joint tenancies."[10] Actually in this context the sub-maxim is accurate, but it is not

---

[99] Para. 13.069 *et seq., post.*
[1] Para. 3.112, *post.*
[2] Para. 3.152, *post.*
[3] Para. 19.34 *et seq., post.*
[4] See the English case of *E. R. Ives Investment Ltd.* v. *High* [1967] 2 Q.B. 379, para. 19.23, *post.*
[5] See the leading English case, *Dering* v. *Earl of Winchilsea* (1787) 1 Cox C.C. 318. See also *Parkes* v. *Parkes,* unreported (see *A Casebook on Equity and Trusts in Ireland* (1985), p. 74).
[6] Para. 10.103, *post.*
[7] Para. 10.101, *post.*
[8] Para. 10.102, *post.*
[9] Para. 3.115, *post.*
[10] See, generally, ch. 7, *post.*

true generally of equity's approach. The concept of a joint tenancy, with its attendant right of survivorship, was used by equity where it was useful, *e.g.*, as between trustees.[11] Equity also invokes the maxim when faced with execution of a power in the nature of a trust which has not been executed by the donee.[12] Finally, it may be noted that the maxim has been cited increasingly in recent years, particularly in England, in disputes over the matrimonial home as between husband and wife.[13]

9. *Equity Looks to the Intent, Not to the Form*

3.060. The essential nature of equity's approach to a document was to look at its substance rather than the form in which it was written or executed. It put primary emphasis on the intention of the parties and strove to put this into effect, if justice required it. One illustration of this approach was equity's attitude towards stipulations as to time in contracts. Failure by one party to perform within the time set was a breach of contract at common law, but equity refused to regard it as a breach which relieved the other party from his contractual obligations, unless the other party had suffered from the delay or time was of the essence of the contract. Section 28 (7) of the Judicature (Ireland) Act, 1877 (now in Northern Ireland section 88 of the Judicature (Northern Ireland) Act 1978), recognised this equitable principle and provided:

> "Stipulations in contracts, as to time or otherwise, which would not before the commencement of this Act have been deemed to be or to have become of the essence of such contracts in a Court of Equity, shall receive in all Courts the same construction and effect as they would have theretofore received in Equity."[13a]

3.061. Perhaps the most important application of the maxim was in respect of mortgages, where the sub-maxim "once a mortgage, always a mortgage" was invoked. Indeed, much of the law of mortgages is founded upon this principle, which led equity to the view that in substance a mortgage transaction was the creation of a secured loan on land only. The modern concept of a statutory charge is essentially an adaptation of this same philosophy and is designed to make the form reflect more accurately the substance of the transaction.[14]

3.062. Some controversy has arisen amongst judges in Ireland and England recently over the scope of the maxim in the context of forfeiture and penalty clauses in contracts, particularly hiring and hire-purchase contracts.[15] In the

---

[11] Para. 10.004, *post.*
[12] Para. 11.11, *post.* Cf. *Re Baden's Deed Trusts* [1971] A.C. 424.
[13] Cf. *Pettitt* v. *Pettitt* [1970] A.C. 777; *Gissing* v. *Gissing* [1971] A.C. 886, paras. 25.15–6, *post.*
[13a] See para. 3.035, fn.25, *ante.*
[14] See, generally, on mortgages, ch. 12, *post.*
[15] On penalty clauses, see *Lombank Ltd.* v. *Kennedy* [1961] N.I. 192; *Bridge* v. *Campbell Discount Co. Ltd.* [1962] A.C. 600; *Financings Ltd.* v. *Baldock* [1963] 2 Q.B. 104; *United Dominions Trust (Commercial) Ltd.* v. *Ennis* [1968] 1 Q.B. 54; *United Dominions Trust Ltd.* v. *Patterson* [1973] N.I. 142. On forfeiture clauses, see *Stockloser* v. *Johnston* [1954] 1 Q.B. 476; *Galbraith* v. *Mitchenall Estates Ltd.* [1965] 2 Q.B. 473. See Wylie, "Judicial Variance on Hire Purchase Agreements: Forfeitures and Penalties" (1965) 16 N.I.L.Q. 94. Note the earlier authority on penalty clauses, *Husband* v. *Grattan* (1833) Alc. & Nap. 389.

Northern Ireland case of *Lombank Ltd.* v. *Kennedy*,[16] Lord MacDermott
L.C.J. found himself in a minority in the Court of Appeal in trying to apply the
principle that "the penalty rule, as a rule of equity, is not to be circumvented by
drafting devices."[17] He went on to state:

> " . . . equitable principles which aim at the promotion of fair dealing
> have a way of outlasting the particular forms of conduct that begot them,
> and the question here, as I see it, is not one of extending the principles of
> the rule but of applying them to a modern form of contract dealing with a
> modern form of transaction. There is certainly no ground for thinking that
> the march of events has outmoded the rule, particularly in these days when
> the desires and needs of the individual so often put him at the mercy of
> documents devised to suit the interests of some powerful corporation."[18]

3.063. These sentiments were echoed by Lord Denning shortly afterwards
in the House of Lords, supported by Lord Devlin, in *Bridge* v. *Campbell
Discount Co.*[19] Yet the majority, in particular Viscount Simonds and Lords
Morton of Henryton and Radcliffe took a different approach to the role of
equity in such cases. Lord Radcliffe stated:

> " 'Unconscionable' must not be taken to be a panacea for adjusting
> any contract between competent persons when it shows a rough edge to
> one side or the other, and equity lawyers are, I notice, sometimes both sur-
> prised and discomforted by the plenitude of jurisdiction, and the im-
> precision of rules, that are attributed to 'equity' by their more enthusiastic
> colleagues. Since the courts of equity never undertook to serve as a general
> adjuster of men's bargains, it was inevitable that they should in the course
> of time evolve definite rules as to the circumstances in which, and the con-
> ditions under which, relief would be given; and I do not think that it
> would be at all an easy task, and I am not certain that it would be a
> desirable achievement, to reconcile all the rules under some simple general
> formula. Even such masters of equity as Lord Eldon and Sir George Jessel,
> it must be remembered, were highly sceptical of the court's duty to apply
> the ephithet 'unconscionable' or its consequences to contracts made
> between persons of full age in circumstances that did not fall within the
> familiar categories of fraud, surprise, accident, etc., even though such
> contracts involved the payment of a larger sum of money on breach of an
> obligation to pay a smaller sum."[20]

10.*Equity Regards as Done What Ought to be Done*

3.064. This maxim underlies several doctrines which are important in the field
of property law. One we have already mentioned, namely, the rule in *Walsh* v.

---

[16] [1961] N.I. 192 (see *A Casebook on Equity and Trusts in Ireland* (1985), p.61).
[17] *Ibid.*, p. 206.
[18] *Ibid.*, p. 208.
[19] [1962] A.C. 600.
[20] *Ibid.*, p. 626. *Cf.* Black and Curran L.JJ. in *Lombank Ltd.* v. *Kennedy, op. cit.*

Lonsdale with respect to agreements for a lease.[21] It has given rise to two important doctrines in the law of trusts, relating to trustees' duty to act impartially as between the beneficiaries with respect to the trust property. These are the rule in *Howe* v. *Lord Dartmouth*[22] and in *Re Earl of Chesterfield's Trusts*.[23] Lastly, the maxim is the basis of the doctrine of conversion, discussed below.[24]

11. *Equity Imputes an Intention to Fulfil an Obligation*

3.065. This maxim forms the basis of the doctrines of satisfaction and performance which are also discussed below.[25]

12. *Delay Defeats Equity*

3.066. An initial point which should be made about this maxim is that it has no application to any action governed by the statutes of limitations.[26] These statutes lay down definite periods of limitation for most actions, and in these cases the statutory provisions will govern the point whether a particular claim is barred. Furthermore, the courts have applied the statutes by analogy in cases not strictly within their terms but nevertheless so closely akin to cases specified in the statutes as to be treated in the same way.[27] Apart from this, however, equity has its own doctrines for dealing with cases clearly not governed by other rules, *e.g.,* breach of fiduciary duties. These are the doctrines of laches and acquiescence. The precise distinction between the two is not always clear.[28] The essence of laches is that a party whose rights have been infringed has failed to pursue his remedy with sufficient speed in the eyes of equity, *i.e.,* the party's inactivity over a lapse of time causes his right of action to be barred in equity.[29] Acquiescence operates more as a kind of estoppel: one party does something to infringe the other's rights but the other, instead of taking action, does nothing and equity infers from this that he has acquiesced in the other's acts and thereby lost his right of action.[30] Obviously, in many cases there will appear to be

---

[21] Para. 3.038, *ante*.
[22] Para. 10.079, *post*.
[23] Para. 10.082, *post*.
[24] Para. 3.094, *post*.
[25] Paras. 3.115, and 3.125, *post*.
[26] Statute of Limitations, 1957 (R.I.); Statute of Limitations (N.I.), 1958. See Brady and Kerr, *The Limitation of Actions in the Republic of Ireland* (1984) and ch. 23, *post*.
[27] See *Hovenden* v. *Annesley* (1806) 2 Sch. & Lef. 607 at 630; *Barber* v. *Houston* (1884) 14 L.R.Ir. 273; (1886) 18 L.R.Ir. 475 (see *A Casebook on Equity and Trusts in Ireland* (1985), p.1); *Salter* v. *Cavanagh* (1837) 1 Dr. & Wal. 668; *Medlicott* v. *O'Donel* (1809) 1 Ba. & B. 156; *Incorporated Society for Protestant Schools* v. *Richards* (1841) 4 Ir.Eq.R. 177; *Rossiter* v. *Rossiter* (1963) 14 Ir.Ch.R. 247.
[28] See the discussion by the Northern Ireland judges in *McCausland* v. *Young* [1948] N.I. 72 at 100–12 (Black J.), [1949] N.I. 49 at 88–9 (Andrews L.C.J.) and 106–8 (Babington L.J.) (see *A Casebook on Equity and Trusts in Ireland* (1985), p.27). Also *Mulhallen* v. *Marum* (1843) 3 Dr. & War. 317; *Dalton* v. *Barry* (1860) 5 Ir.Jur.(N.S.) 271; *Archbold* v. *Scully* (1861) 9 H.L.C. 360; *Horgan* v. *Deasy* (1979) Unrep. (H.C., R.I.) (1976 No.455P); *J.H.* v. *W.J.H.* (1979) Unrep. (H.C., R.I.) (1977 No. 5831P); *Guardian Builders Ltd.* v. *Kelly* [1981] I.L.R.M. 127.
[29] See *Leahy* v. *De Moleyns* [1896] 1 I.R. 206; *Scott* v. *Knox* (1841) 4 Ir.Eq.R. 397; *King* v. *Anderson* (1874) I.R. 8 Eq. 625; *Moore* v. *Blake* (1809) 1 Ba. & B. 62; *Murphy* v. *Harrington* [1927] I.R. 339; *The Goods of Corcoran* [1934] I.R. 571; *Cahill* v. *Irish Motor Traders Association* [1966] I.R. 430.
[30] See *Lydon* v. *Lydon* (1874) 8 I.L.T.R. 85; *Connor* v. *McCarthy* (1878) 12 I.L.T.R. 336; *McCausland* v. *Young*, *op. cit*. See also the discussion of the defence of acquiescence by the English Court of Appeal in *Shaw* v. *Applegate* [1977] 1 W.L.R. 970. *Cf.* invocation of the doctrine of estoppel as a counter to a defence based on lapse of time, e.g., where the words or conduct of one party have induced the other to refrain from instituting

present elements of both laches and acquiescence, the plea of one supporting
the plea of the other.[31]

13. *Equity, like Nature, Does Nothing in Vain*

3.067. This maxim states an important limitation on equitable relief, indeed,
an essentially practical limitation. Equity will not grant relief if it is not going to
be effective or is likely to be of no assistance in the particular case.[32] This
principle is, therefore, the basis of the doctrine of reconversion.[33] It may also
explain why equity will grant a decree of specific performance in certain
circumstances only.[34]

14. *Equity does Not Suffer a Wrong to be Without a Remedy*

3.068. This maxim, perhaps above all the others, must be treated with the
greatest caution. Even in the early stages of development of equitable
jurisdiction it was doubtful if it was strictly accurate. It has been suggested that
the origin of the maxim lies in the early function of the Chancery in issuing new
writs for suits at common law. Whatever its origin, it is a grossly inaccurate
statement of equity's approach in modern times. Much of equity's jurisdiction
nowadays is subject to well-established and well-defined rules and, if a case
cannot be brought within those rules, no remedy will be forthcoming.[35] Of
course, equity will strive to provide a remedy if a substantial grievance is
shown, but there is a tendency nowadays to leave the remedy to the legislature
if something new or wide-ranging is required. This attitude has been
particularly noticeable among English judges in recent decades, hence the
decisions on trustees' investment powers,[36] the deserted wife's equity,[37] the
matrimonial home[38] and penalty clauses.[39] It is true that some judges like Lord
Denning have adopted an attitude closer to a literal interpretation of the
maxim, but many of his brother judges have reacted unfavourably to this
approach and some have scornfully dismissed it as "palm-tree justice."[40]

Despite these remarks, there is little doubt that much of equitable jurisdiction
stems from the desire to carry out the maxim. Much of the law relating to
equitable remedies is derived from the principle enshrined in it.[41]

---

proceedings, see *Doran* v. *Thomas Thompson and Sons Ltd.* [1978] I.R. 223. See also Brady and Kerr, *The
Limitation of Actions in the Republic of Ireland* (1984), p.99 *et seq.*

[31] See also the problem for equity of applying both its doctrine of laches and its principle of relief against
forfeiture (enshrined in the Tenantry Act (Ir.), 1779, para. 4.171, *post*) in cases of leases for lives renewable for
ever. *Ward* v. *Roberts* (1890) 25 L.R.Ir. 224; *Dyott* v. *Massereene* (1874) I.R. 9 Eq. 149.

[32] See *Croskerry* v. *Ritchie* [1901] 1 I.R. 437. See *Lennon* v. *Ganly* [1981] I.L.R.M. 84 (no means of enforcing
interlocutory injunction abroad).

[33] Para. 3.108, *post.*

[34] Para. 3.143, *post.*

[35] *Cf.* Black L.J., para. 3.050, *ante.*

[36] Para. 10.063, *post.*

[37] Para. 3.041, *ante.*

[38] *Ibid.*, and ch. 25, *post.*

[39] Paras. 3.062–3, *ante.*

[40] See *Pettitt* v. *Pettitt* [1970] A.C. 777. Note the review by Lord MacDermott L.C.J. in *McFarlane* v.
McFarlane [1972] N.I. 59.

[41] See paras. 3.127–68, *post.*

B. DOCTRINE OF NOTICE

3.069. It has already been mentioned that the doctrine of notice was evolved by equity to further some of its basic principles.[42] As far as land law is concerned, it has played a vital role in determining the difficult question of priority which can arise when successive interests in land are created. It is, therefore, an important part of the law of mortgages and charges, and we will return to the subject in a later chapter.[43] It was also a doctrine closely linked with a distinction which is a central concept of our land law, the distinction between *legal* estates and interests and *equitable* estates and interests. When the courts were faced with decisions involving questions of priorities, they utilised two concepts: (1) the superior status attributed to a legal interest as against an equitable interest; (2) the doctrine of notice. The past tense is used deliberately here because, as we have also already mentioned,[44] this area of law has been considerably affected by the modern systems of registration introduced by statute.[45] These systems have not, however, entirely displaced the operation of the doctrine of notice in deciding questions of priorities.

It is proposed in the next few pages to discuss the doctrine of notice, its role in deciding questions of priorities in relation to both land and personalty and, briefly, how far it has been affected by modern registration systems.[46] The discussion will be kept brief because several aspects of this subject will be dealt with in greater detail later in the book, particularly in the chapters relating to mortgages and charges[47] and registration.[48]

1. *Elements of Notice*

3.070. The doctrine of notice was particularly relevant in determining the position of purchasers of land already subject to prior interests and charges. In this connection section 3 (1) of the Conveyancing Act, 1882, stated the elements of notice:

"A purchaser shall not be prejudicially affected by notice of any instrument, fact, or thing unless—

(i) It is within his own knowledge, or would have come to his knowledge if such inquiries and inspections had been made as ought reasonably to have been made by him; or

(ii) In the same transaction with respect to which a question of notice to the purchaser arises, it has come to the knowledge of his counsel, as such, or of his solicitor, or other agent, as such, or would have come

---

[42] Para. 3.053, *ante.*
[43] Ch. 13, *post.*
[44] Para. 3.053, *ante.*
[45] See, generally, chs. 21 and 22, *post.*
[46] See Sheridan, "Notice and Registration" (1950) 9 N.I.L.Q. 33, "Registration and Priority of Securities" (1951) 53 J.I.B.I. 259. Also Madden, *Registration of Deeds, Conveyances and Judgment Mortgages in Ireland* (1901); Browning and Glover, *Local Registration of Title in Ireland* (1912); Glover, *Registration of Ownership of Land in Ireland* (1933); Sheridan, *Fraud in Equity* (1957).
[47] Ch. 13, *post.*
[48] Chs. 21 and 22, *post.*

to the knowledge of his solicitor, or other agent, as such, if such
inquiries and inspections had been made as ought reasonably to
have been made by the solicitor or other agent."

There are, therefore, in essence three main types of notice: (i) actual; (ii)
constructive; (iii) imputed.[49]

(i) Actual

3.071. A person has actual notice when he obtains knowledge himself of the
matter in question, *i.e.*, subjectively considered. At first sight this seems to be a
simple and straightforward proposition, but some doubts have been raised.
One doubt is whether the actual knowledge must have been acquired "in the
same transaction." It will be noted that the wording of section 3 (1) of the
Conveyancing Act, 1882, quoted above, contains a significant difference on
this point: the qualification appears in paragraph (ii), but not in paragraph (i).
The apparent conclusion is, then, that the qualification does not apply to the
case of actual notice and that it does not matter in what connection the
knowledge was acquired by the party to the transaction in question, so long as it
was knowledge which was relevant to that transaction.[50] Yet another doubt
which has been raised is whether the knowledge should have been obtained
only from the other party to the transaction or his agent. It seems to be the
settled view that mere "flying reports" or rumours are not knowledge in this
context. The generally accepted principle was stated by Lord Cairns in a
leading English case on the subject, *Lloyd* v. *Banks*[51]—"knowledge which
would operate upon the mind of any rational man, or man of business, and
make him act with reference to the knowledge he had so acquired."[52]

(ii) Constructive

3.072. The concept of constructive notice is really grounded upon the basic
principles of conveyancing.[53] Here the guiding rule of thumb is *caveat emptor*.
The onus is upon the purchaser to take proper steps to ensure that the transaction is carried out and its consequences go according to his plans. The risk is
upon him if anything goes wrong. Upon this principle is based the concept of
investigation of title which is the purchaser's responsibility. It is to this sort of
procedure that section 3 (1) of the 1882 Act is referring when it speaks of
"inquiries and inspections" which "ought reasonably to have been made."

---

[49] See the discussion by Kenny J. in *Bank of Ireland Finance Ltd.* v. *Rockfield Ltd.* [1979] I.R. 21; also *Somers*
v. *W.* [1979] I.R. 94 and *Northern Bank Ltd.* v. *Henry* (para. 3.072, *infra*). See also Garner, "Notice, Registration
and Knowledge" (1959) 23 Conv. 129; Hayton, "Land Law: Getting Priorities Right" (1977) 29 C.L.P. 26; Long,
"Notice in Equity" (1920) 34 H.L.R. 137; Rowley, "Effects of Notice on Contracts for Sale of Land" (1954) 18
Conv. 301; Wade, "Effect of Statutory Notice of Incumbrances" (1954) C.L.J. 89; and fn. 46, *ante.*

[50] See *Irish Conveyancing Law* (1978), para.6.38 *et seq. Cf.* Sugden, *The Law of Vendors and Purchasers* (11th
ed.), p. 1041; Dart, *The Law of Vendors and Purchasers* (6th ed.), vol. 2, p. 267.

[51] (1868) 3 Ch.App. 488. *Cf.* Sugden, *op. cit.*, p. 1040 and Dart, *op. cit.*, p. 267.

[52] *Ibid.*, p. 491. See *O'Connor* v. *McCarthy* [1982] I.R. 161 at 174 (*per* Costello J.). See further on "actual"
notice, *Welch* v. *Bowmaker (Ir.) Ltd.* [1980] I.R. 251. See also *Reeves* v. *Pope* [1914] 2 K.B. 284.

[53] *Abbott* v. *Geraghty* (1854) 4 Ir.Ch.R. 15. See also the discussion by Meredith J. in *Re Riley* [1942] I.R. 416
and generally *Irish Conveyancing Law* (1978), chs. 5–7.

What these are in any particular case depends upon the circumstances, but in essence the general principle is what is regarded as the usual standard conveyancing procedures appropriate for such a case. If the purchaser does not carry these out he will be fixed nevertheless with constructive notice of matters which carrying out such procedures would have brought to his notice. Thus he will not escape being fixed with constructive notice if he knows of certain facts or circumstances which it would be proper conveyancing practice to investigate further.[54] Nor will he escape if he deliberately refrains from any investigation at all and tries to claim that he knew of no circumstances or facts whatsoever to put him to further investigation.[55] Omissions to carry out proper steps due to carelessness or negligence are also caught by this rule. The proper steps in most cases involve two matters of substance, inspection of the property concerned and an investigation of the title to it. These principles were illustrated by the recent *Henry* case decided by the Republic's Supreme Court.

In *Northern Bank Ltd.* v. *Henry*[55a], the wife's father had bought a house for her before her marriage and conveyed it to her only. Sometime after her marriage she and her husband decided to move to a more expensive house. The husband secured a loan from a building society and the new house was transferred to him after the society had investigated the title to it. Later the husband left the wife and went to live elsewhere. He obtained overdraft accommodation from the plaintiff bank and, when he sought to increase this, the bank insisted on getting a mortgage by deed from him of the house. The bank obtained the title deeds and requisitions from the building society, but did not make any requisitions or enquiries themselves, except a search in the Registry of Deeds against the husband. The wife claimed that the house belonged to her in equity and sought a declaration that she was the owner in equity of the house. On the same day as she issued proceedings the husband signed the deed of mortgage to the bank. When the bank brought proceedings against the husband and wife to realise the sum secured by the mortgage, the wife claimed that her interest ranked before that of the bank because, by failing to make requisitions, they had not become aware of her claim and, if they had made them, they would have. The Republic's Supreme Court reviewed the law relating to constructive notice and held that the bank had such notice of the wife's claim and so were postponed to it. If they had made requisitions, they would have discovered that a claim by the wife was pending and was prior in point of time to their mortgage. Commenting on the meaning of section 3 (1)(i) of the Conveyancing Act, 1882, Henchy J. stated:

"In my judgment, the test of what inquiries and inspections ought

---

[54] *Re Flood's Estate* (1862) 13 Ir.Ch.R. 312; *Waldron* v. *Jacob* (1870) I.R. 5 Eq. 131; *Cf. Aldritt* v. *Maconchy* [1908] 1 I.R. 333; *Stephenson* v. *Royce* (1856) 5 Ir.Ch.R. 401.

[55] *Heneghan* v. *Davitt* [1933] I.R. 375; *Justice* v. *Wynne* (1860) 12 Ir.Ch.R. 289 at 310; *Re Olden* (1863) 9 Ir.Jur.(N.S.) 1.

[55a] [1981] I.R. 1 (see *A Casebook on Irish Land Law* (1984), p.87). See also *Somers* v. *W.* [1979] I.R. 94; *O'Connor* v. *McCarthy* [1982] I.R. 161 (see *ibid.*, p.106); *Ulster Bank Ltd.* v. *Shanks and Others* [1982] N.I. 143 (where Murray J. refused to extend the doctrine of constructive notice in a case involving unregistered land which was akin to the situation in *Williams and Glyn's Bank* v. *Boland* [1981] A.C. 487; *Allied Irish Banks Ltd.* v. *McWilliams* [1982] N.I. 156. *Cf. Gahan* v. *Boland* (1984) Unrep. (Sup. Ct., R.I.) (37–1983) (see *A Casebook on Equity and Trusts in Ireland* (1985), p.267).

reasonably to have been made is an objective test, which depends not on what the particular purchaser thought proper to do in the particular circumstances, but on what a purchaser of the particular property ought reasonably to have done in order to acquire title to it . . . Reasonableness in this context must be judged by reference to what should be done to acquire the estate or interest being purchased, rather than by the motive for or the purpose of the particular purchase.

A purchaser cannot be held to be empowered to set his own standard of reasonableness for the purpose of the subsection. He must expect to be judged by what an ordinary purchaser, advised by a competent lawyer, would reasonably inquire about or inspect for the purpose of getting a good title. If his personal preference, or the exigencies of the situation, impel him to lower the level of investigation of title below that, he is entitled to do so, but if he does so, he cannot claim the immunity which s. 3, sub-s. 1, reserves for a reasonable purchaser. And a reasonable purchaser is one who not only consults his own needs or preferences but also has regard to whether the purchase may, prejudicially and unfairly, affect the rights of third parties in the property. In particular, a reasonable purchaser would be expected to make such inquiries and inspections as would normally disclose whether the purchase will trench, fraudulently or unconscionably, on the rights of such third parties in the property."[55b]

Kenny J. pointed out that there was an apparent conflict in section 3 of the 1882 Act, in that subsection (3) purported to preserve the pre-1882 law, under which the standard to be applied was whether the purchaser had been guilty of "gross negligence" (see, e.g., Lord Cranworth in *Ware* v. *Lord Egmont*[55c]), whereas subsection (1) introduced the wider standard of the prudent purchaser who has obtained competent legal advice. Kenny J. refused to take the literal meaning of subsection (3) which would lead to an "absurdity", and pointed out that all the modern textbooks (including the present work) are unanimous that "a purchaser or mortgagee who omits to make such inquiries and inspections as a prudent and reasonable purchaser or mortgagee acting on skilled advice would have made will be fixed with notice of what he would have discovered if he had made the inquiries and inspections which ought reasonably to have been made by him." Henchy J., however, emphasised that there is a distinction between "legal reasonableness" (the proper test) and "business prudence". "The prudence of the worldly wise may justifiably persuade a purchaser that it would be unbusinesslike to stop and look more deeply into certain aspects of the title. But the reasonable man, in the eyes of the law, will be expected to look beyond the impact of his decisions on his own affairs, and consider whether they may unfairly and prejudicially affect his 'neighbour', in the sense in which that word has been given juristic currency by Lord Atkin in *Donoghue* v. *Stevenson*."[55d]

[55b] *Ibid.*, p. 9. See Conlon, "Beneficial Interests, Conveyancers and the Occupation Hazard" (1985), 79 Gaz. I.L.S.I. 59; Pearce, "Joint Occupation and the Doctrine of Notice" (1980) 15 Ir.Jur. (N.S.) 211; Russell, "Williams & Glyn's Bank v. Boland and Brown: The Practical Implications" (1981) 32 N.I.L.Q. 3; Sweeney, "Occupiers' Rights: A New Hazard for Irish Conveyancers?" (1981) 75 Gaz. I.L.S.I. 103.
[55c] (1854) 4 De G. McN. & G. 473.   [55d] [1981] I.R. 1 at 11–12.

(iii) Imputed

3.073. Imputed notice is the actual or constructive notice of an agent employed in the transaction in question. This obviously applies in the case of a solicitor employed to do the conveyancing involved in the transaction.[56] This requirement of the notice being acquired in the same transaction was settled by the Conveyancing Act, 1882, 3 (1) (ii); prior to the Act it would seem that notice gained from previous transactions could be imputed in later ones, but this can no longer be done.[57] In *Re Burmester*[58] it was held that the notice acquired by the agent must be such that it was considered his duty to communicate it to his principal. Thus a principal does not have imputed to him notice acquired by his agent while the latter was engaged in fraudulent dealings.[59]

2. Bona Fide *Purchaser Without Notice*

3.074. The golden rule adopted by equity in dealing with priorities as between successive interests in land was that a *bona fide* purchaser for value of a legal estate or interest in land would take free of an equitable estate or interest of which he had no notice. This was an application of the maxim—"where the equities are equal, the law prevails."[60] There were several elements to this rule as the statement just given indicates. First, the purchaser of the estate had to be *bona fide*, a requirement which reiterates the point that his superiority in terms of priorities was partly based on the fact of his having no notice. Any fraud, or indeed gross negligence,[61] would deprive him of priority.[62] Secondly, he had to be a purchaser for value, *i.e.*, consideration must have been provided, whether in money or money's worth, though not necessarily to full value. "Good" consideration such as natural love and affection between relatives is not enough.[63] Thirdly, to obtain priority over an existing equitable estate or interest the purchaser would have to acquire a legal estate or interest. One of the great English Lord Chancellors, Lord Hardwicke, put the matter thus:

> " . . . as courts of equity break in upon the common law, where necessity and conscience require it, still they allow superior force and strength to a legal title to estates."[64]

---

[56] *Re Rorke's Estate* (1863) 14 Ir.Ch.R. 442; *Re Burmester* (1858) 9 Ir.Ch.R.41. The words "as such" in section 3 (1) (ii) of the Conveyancing Act, 1882, were deleted by section 3 (7) of the Republic's Family Home Protection Act, 1976, thus extending the notion of imputed notice for the purposes of that Act. The effect of section 3 of the 1976 Act was considered by the Supreme Court in *Somers* v. *W.* [1979] I.R. 94. See also *Nestor* v. *Murphy* [1979] I.R. 327; *Guckian* v. *Brennan* [1981] I.R. 478; *Reynolds* v. *Waters* [1982] I.L.R.M. 333; *Weir* v. *Somers* [1983] I.L.R.M. 343. And see generally *Irish Conveyancing Law* (1978), para. 6.31 *et seq.*; Shatter, *Family Law in the Republic of Ireland* (2nd ed., 1981) p.317 *et seq.*

[57] *Nixon* v. *Hamilton* (1838) 1 Ir. Eq.R. 46. *Cf. Marjoribanks* v. *Hovenden* (1843) 6 Ir.Eq.R. 238; *Tucker* v. *Henzill* (1854) 4 Ir.Ch.R. 513; *Re Macnamara's Estate* (1883) 13 L.R.Ir. 158; *Re Stewart's Estate* (1893) 31 L.R.Ir. 405; *Re Hall's Estate* (1893) 31 L.R.Ir. 416; *Re Smallman's Estate* (1867) I.R. 2 Eq. 34.

[58] (1858) 9 Ir.Ch.R. 41. See also *Re Lane's Estate* (1859) 5 Ir.Jur. (N.S.) 32.

[59] *Ibid. Cf. Lenehan* v. *McCabe* (1840) 2 Ir.Eq.R. 342. See also (1862) 10 H.L.C. 90.

[60] Para. 3.052, *ante.*

[61] *E.g.*, in respect of investigation of title. Though in a sense this factor could be regarded as one inducing constructive notice, see para. 3.072, *supra.*

[62] *Re Greer* [1907] 1 I.R. 57.

[63] Megarry and Wade, *The Law of Real Property* (5th ed., 1984), p.143.

[64] *Wortley* v. *Birkhead* (1754) 2 Ves.Sen. 571, 574.

There is one qualification to this third requirement, which is that it is sufficient if the purchaser at least obtains an interest giving him a superior claim on the legal title. For example, instead of taking a conveyance of the legal title to himself directly, the purchaser might have the legal title conveyed to a trustee to be held for him. If neither the trustee nor the purchaser had notice of the prior equitable estate or interest, the doctrine would apply in the normal way and the purchaser will take free of it.[65] Fourthly, the purchaser of the legal title will obtain priority over a prior equitable estate or interest only if he purchased without notice of it. Notice in this context has the meaning discussed above, *i.e.*, actual, constructive or imputed notice.

3.075. This *bona fide* purchaser doctrine, then, governed the question of priorities as between competing legal and equitable estates or interests. Questions of priorities could, however, arise as between successive legal estates or interests and as between successive equitable estates or interests. Here the rule adopted by equity was more straightforward. It was, of course, the other maxim discussed in this connection above—"where the equities are equal, the first in time prevails."[66] As in the case of the *bona fide* purchaser doctrine, an essential condition is that the equities be "equal." Any fraud or gross negligence on the part of the person who would otherwise have priority, in this case the person whose estate or interest was created first, will cause him to lose that priority.[67]

3.076. There is one other much more controversial area of priorities law, namely, that relating to priorities as between equitable estates or interests in land and what are called "mere equities." There has been some considerable discussion in recent years over the precise distinction between an equitable interest and a mere equity, amongst both judges[68] and academic writers.[69] By a "mere equity" is meant an equitable right which does not give an equitable interest in land. The example most frequently cited as a mere equity is a right to special equitable relief, such as the right to have transactions set aside on account of fraud or undue influence,[70] or to have a document rectified for mistake.[71] The courts in England have taken the same view of rights such as those of occupiers of land under a contractual licence[72] and of deserted wives

---

[65] See further on this subject, the doctrine of tacking in relation to mortgages, para. 13.159, *post.*

[66] Para. 3.054, *ante.* See *Tench* v. *Molyneux* (1914) 48 I.L.T.R. 48; *National Bank* v. *Keegan* [1931] I.R. 344.

[67] *Re Lambert's Estate* (1884) 13 L.R.Ir. 234; *Re Roche's Estate* (1890) 25 L.R.Ir. 284.

[68] *Westminster Bank Ltd.* v. *Lee* [1956] Ch. 7; *National Provincial Bank Ltd.* v. *Ainsworth* [1965] A.C. 1175. See also *Allied Irish Banks* v. *Glynn* [1973] I.R. 188 (see *A Casebook on Irish Land Law* (1984), p.85).

[69] Cheshire, "A New Equitable Interest in Land" (1953) 16 M.L.R. 1; Crane "Licensees and Successors in Title of the Licensor" (1952) 16 Conv. 323; "After the Deserted Wife's Licence" (1965) 29 Conv. 254; Delany, "Equitable Interests and 'Mere Equities' " (1957) 21 Conv. 195; Everton, " 'Equitable Interests' and 'Equities'—In Search of a Pattern" (1976) 40 Conv. 209; Marshall and Scamell, "Digesting the Licence" (1953) 31 C.B.R. 847; Maudsley, "Licence to Remain on Land" (1956) 20 Conv. 281; Mitchell, "Learner's Licence" (1954) 17 M.L.R. 211; Sheridan, "Licences to Live in Houses" (1953) 17 Conv. 440; Stoljar, "Licence, Interest and Contract" (1955) 33 C.B.R. 562; Wade, "Licences and Third Parties" (1952) 68 L.Q.R. 337.

[70] See para. 3.157, *post.*

[71] Para. 3.162, *post.*

[72] *Errington* v. *Errington* [1952] 1 K.B. 290; *Westminster Bank Ltd.* v. *Lee* [1956] Ch. 7. *Cf. Woods* v. *Donnelly* [1982] N.I. 257. See ch. 20, *post.*

remaining in possession of the matrimonial home.[73] To be contrasted with such rights are equitable interests in land created by way of charge or mortgage, or interests held under a trust or under a restrictive covenant.[74] In Ireland, however, the category of what are mere equities has been regarded as being rather wider than in England.[75]

3.077. In *Re Ffrench's Estate*[76] trust funds were allowed by trustees to get into the hands of an equitable tenant for life, who mixed them with his own funds and purchased property with the joint fund. Later the tenant for life created an equitable mortgage on the property in favour of a bank. In an action by the beneficiary to trace the trust funds into their converted form, a question of priorities arose between the beneficiary and the bank which had no notice of the fact that trust funds had been converted. It was held that the beneficiary had only a "mere equity" (the right of tracing), whereas the bank had an equitable interest (the mortgage) which, therefore, took priority. This priority was obtained for the bank because the bank took its equitable interest without notice of the prior equity in the beneficiary. This principle has been followed in several Irish cases[77] and seems to be established law in Ireland, though not in England.[78] Yet the soundness of the reasoning in these cases may be questioned on the ground that they seem to involve an unjustifiable demotion of a beneficiary's interest under a trust. Once a trust has been fully established it would seem to be clear that the beneficiary's rights under it amount to an equitable interest.[79] Once that has been established, it is difficult to understand why the beneficiary's rights to protect his interest should be accorded less protection or standing in the eyes of equity or, to put it another way, why misappropriation of the trust funds by the trustee or a third party should automatically reduce the status of the beneficiary's interest. This surely remains an equitable interest which he is entitled to protect by whatever action or remedy (against whatever person) equity affords him. This may be a personal action against the trustees or any person meddling with the trust property, or it may be a remedy to trace the funds into whosoever hands it has come. The nature of the remedy should not affect that which is being protected. In this sense the remedy of tracing is to be distinguished from other remedies like rescission or rectification.[80] These do not exist to protect some equitable interest already in existence. Indeed, until the remedy is invoked, the legal rights created by the transaction in question remain unchallenged by any sort of equitable right—all that exists is the mere possibility of some action being taken to have the

---

[73] *Bendall* v. *McWhirter* [1952] 2 Q.B. 466. But see now *National Provincial Bank Ltd.* v. *Ainsworth* [1965] A.C. 1175 and the Matrimonial Homes Act, 1967. *Cf. Kelaghan* v. *Daly* [1913] 2 I.R. 328. See also *Allied Irish Banks* v. *Glynn* [1973] I.R. 188 at 192 (*per* Kenny J.) (see *A Casebook on Irish Land Law* (1984), p. 85).

[74] *Cave* v. *Cave* (1880) 15 Ch.D. 639; *Rice* v. *Rice* (1853) 2 Drew. 73.

[75] See Delany, "Equitable Interests and 'Mere Equities' " (1957) 21 Conv. 195.

[76] (1887) 21 L.R.Ir. 283. Note the comments on this case by Kenny J. in *Allied Irish Banks* v. *Glynn, op. cit.*, pp. 193–4.

[77] *Re Sloane's Estate* [1895] 1 I.R. 146; *Bank of Ireland* v. *Cogry Flax Spinning Co.* [1900] 1 I.R. 219; *Re Bobbett's Estate* [1904] 1 I.R. 461; *Bourke* v. *Lee* [1904] 1 I.R. 280; *Scott* v. *Scott* [1924] 1 I.R. 141.

[78] *Shropshire Union Railway and Canal Co.* v. *The Queen* (1875) L.R. 7 H.L. 496.

[79] It would seem strange if it were otherwise with respect to equity's greatest creation, see para. 3.046, *ante*.

[80] See paras. 3.157 and 3.162, *post*.

transaction set aside or rectified and, even then, the granting of the remedy in any action lies at the discretion of the court.[81] It is not surprising, then, that rights to bring such actions in equity have been classified as "mere equities" and accorded less status than equitable interests. It is surprising, however, that the Irish courts have treated the right of tracing trusts funds in the same way, especially as the implication seems to be that the beneficiary's interest in those funds should be similarly classified.

3.078. There is something of a paradox here. Part of the reasoning of the Irish courts in these cases seems to have been based on the principle that equitable interests are primarily rights *in personam,* so that the primary remedy for misappropriation is a personal action against the trustee.[82] A right of tracing is not such an action and is, therefore, of less standing. The opposite, however, is really the case. The right of tracing arises where equity is giving greater rather than less protection to the interest involved; this is where equity is providing characteristics more appropriate to a right in *rem.* This is precisely what much of the controversy has been about with regard to the leading English cases on the doctrine of tracing.[83]

3.079. Apart from this doubt about the extension of the notion of mere equities in Ireland, the principle applicable to such rights as regards priorities is clear on both side of the Irish Sea. Mere equities are of less weight than equitable interests so that the *bona fide* purchaser doctrine has been adapted for the case of a dispute between a mere equity and an equitable interest. A *bona fide* purchaser of an equitable interest will take priority over a mere equity of which he has no notice.[84] The purchaser in this case does not have to acquire a *legal* estate or interest to obtain priority. In a dispute between an equitable interest and a mere equity dependent upon the discretion of the court, the "equities" are not equal and so the mere equity cannot claim priority on the basis of being first in time.[85]

It may be useful now to summarise the law relating to priorities as between successive estates or interests in land, apart from questions of registration, which we shall consider in a moment.[86]

(i) Legal v. Legal

3.080. Priorities as between successive legal estates or interests are straight-forward—they have priority in accordance with the dates of their creation. By analogy, the maxim "where the equities are equal, the first in time prevails"

---

[81] Para. 3.050, *ante. Cf.* Kenny J. in *Allied Irish Banks* v. *Glynn* [1973] I.R. 188 at 192: " . . . if the deed was procured by fraud or undue influence, the first-named defendant would acquire an estate in the lands when he succeeded in setting it aside. What he had was a *chose in action* which could become an estate if he brought proceedings and if they were successful."
[82] See *Scott* v. *Scott, op. cit.,* pp. 150–1.
[83] *Re Hallett's Estate* (1880) 13 Ch.D. 696; *Sinclair* v. *Brougham* [1914] A.C. 398; *Re Diplock* [1948] 1 Ch. 465 (C.A.), [1951] A.C. 251 (H.L.) (*sub nom. Ministry of Health* v. *Simpson*). *Cf. Re Reynolds* [1895] 1 I.R. 83; *Re Nolan* [1949] I.R. 197; *Leahy* v. *De Moleyns* [1896] 1 I.R. 206; *Shanahan's Stamp Auctions Ltd.* v. *Farrelly* [1962] I.R. 386 (see *A Casebook on Equity and Trusts in Ireland* (1985), p.636). See paras. 10.108–15, *post.*
[84] *Re Ffrench's Estate, supra.* And see *Rice* v. *Rice* (1853) 2 Drew. 73.
[85] Para. 3.054, *ante.*
[86] Para. 3.084, *infra.*

applies, so that the second in time will gain priority only if the owner of the first in time does something to make the equities unequal, *e.g.*, indulges in fraud or is grossly negligent with the title deeds relating to the property.[87]

(ii) Equitable v. Equitable

The same principles apply as in category (i).

(iii) Legal v. Equitable

3.081. The legal estate or interest gains priority in this case on two grounds. First, on the same principle as applies to categories (i) and (ii), namely, that it is first in time. Secondly, this priority is reinforced by the fact that it is a *legal* estate or interest as opposed to an equitable one and, therefore, should normally be accorded priority. Once again the application of these principles may be upset if the holder of the legal estate or interest does something to render the equities unequal.

(iv) Equitable v. Legal

3.082. This is the classic situation for the application of the *bona fide* purchaser doctrine. If the second in time was a *bona fide* purchaser for value of the legal estate or interest without notice of the equitable estate or interest, he takes priority over that equitable estate or interest. But all these conditions must be met for the equities to remain equal so as to allow the law to prevail.[88]

(v) Mere Equity v. Equitable

3.083. As explained above,[89] in this situation the principle applied in category (iv) is adopted and the *bona fide* purchaser of the equitable estate or interest takes priority over any mere equity of which he has no notice. The "equities" are *unequal* in terms of the status accorded to the respective estates or interests, though, to follow the analogy of the *bona fide* purchaser doctrine, the "equities" in terms of the respective moral positions of the parties (as regards their conduct, etc.) must remain equal.

3. *Registration of Deeds*

3.084. The registration of deeds system introduced for the whole of Ireland by the Registration of Deeds Act (Ireland), 1707, substantially amended the doctrine of notice and the system of priorities based upon it.[90] Under this system, provision was made for registration of "memorials" of all deeds, conveyances and wills[91] affecting lands, tenements and hereditaments.[92] The 1707

---

[87] Para. 3.075, *ante*.
[88] Para. 3.074, *ante*.
[89] To complete classification, a priority in a case of *mere equity* v. *mere equity* would be governed by the same principles as category (ii), *supra*, and *equitable* v. *mere equity* by the principles of category (iii), *supra*.
[90] On this system of registration, see, generally, ch. 22, *post*.
[91] But see now as to wills, para. 22.04, *post*. Note that in *O'Connor* v. *McCarthy* [1982] I.R. 161 (see *A Casebook on Irish Land Law* (1984), p.106), Costello J. accepted the view expressed on p.381 of *Irish*

Act did not make registration of such documents compulsory nor did it specify that registration was a condition of their effectiveness in law, but section 4 provided that registered dispositions would have priority according to their order in time of registration. Section 5 backed this up by providing that a registered disposition would take priority over an unregistered disposition.[93] The precise effect of this system on the doctrine of notice and priorities may now be summarised.

(i) Notice

3.085. The registration of deeds system did have a radical effect on the doctrine of notice in so far as it governed priorities as between successive estates or interests in land. Its effect on priorities we shall discuss in a moment, but first we may consider whether the system affected the doctrine of notice in any other way. The answer seems to be in the negative.[94] The one question that was raised in the early days after introduction of the system was whether registration of a disposition in itself amounted to notice, *i.e.*, once registered, in all subsequent dealings with the land did the parties have notice of the disposition and were they put on inquiries as to its effect? The point was important, *e.g.*, with respect to mortgages to secure further advances.[95] The Irish courts finally decided, however, that registration was not notice in this sense.[96] Lord Redesdale put the matter thus:

> "That the registry is to be considered as notice to all intents and purposes, is, I think, what one would not be inclined to hold when one sees the effect of so considering it: if it is to be considered as notice because it is an intimation of the existence of a deed put upon record, it must be notice of everything contained in that deed, for a party would be bound to inquire after the contents of that deed: if it be notice, it must be notice, whether the deed be duly registered or not; it may be unduly registered, and if it be so the act does not give it a preference, and thus this construction would avoid all the provisions in the act for complying with its requisites."[97]

It should be emphasised that, although sections 4 and 5 of the 1707 Act seemed to displace the doctrine of notice in so far as they applied to the case in question, notice continued to be relevant even in cases within those sections.[98]

Conveyancing law (1978) that a *contract* for the sale of land may be registered in the Registry of Deeds (see further para. 22.03 *post*).

[92] S. 3.

[93] In fact it provided that unregistered deeds would be "void" as against registered deeds, see ch. 22, *post*.

[94] See Sheridan, "Notice and Registration" (1950) 9 N.I.L.Q. 33.

[95] Ch. 13, *post*. See Sheridan, "Registration and the Priority of Securities" (1951) 53 J.I.B.I. 259. Also *Re O'Byrne's Estate* (1885) 15 L.R.Ir. 189.

[96] *Bushell* v. *Bushell* (1803) 1 Sch. & Lef. 90; *Latouche* v. *Dunsany* (1803) 1 Sch. & Lef. 137; *Drew* v. *Norbury* (1846) 9 Ir.Eq.R. 171 and 524. *Cf. Hine* v. *Dodd* (1741) 2 Atk. 275. However, if a purchaser does search the registry of deeds, he is fixed with notice of what it contains, *Bushell* v. *Bushell*, *op. cit.*, p. 103.

[97] *Latouche* . *Dunsany*, *op. cit.*, p. 157. See also *Mill* v. *Hill* (1851) 3 H.L.C. 828.

[98] Para. 3.088, *infra*.

(ii) Priorities

3.086. The registration of deeds system does not entirely displace the rules as to priorities discussed above,[99] for two reasons at least. First, since the Act did not make registration compulsory in the sense of making it a condition of the effectiveness of deeds, it is still possible to have successive dispositions none of which are registered. The Act does not govern priorities as between unregistered dispositions and other unregistered dispositions. Secondly, the Act effected registration by a "memorial"[1] of the *document* in question. If no written document exists with respect to the disposition in question there is nothing from which a memorial can be made and, therefore, nothing to register. The Act cannot govern priorities where an unregistrable disposition is concerned, such as an equitable mortgage created by deposit of title deeds unaccompanied by any written memorandum.[2]

3.087. From these limitations on the effect of the registration of deeds system, we can derive the following rules as to priorities under that registration system.[3]

(a) *Unregistered* v. *Unregistered*

Where successive unregistered dispositions of land are concerned the registration system has no application at all and priorities are governed by the rules discussed above.[4]

(b) *Unregistrable* v. *Registered*

Once again the registration system does not apply and the rules discussed above govern priorities.

(c) *Registered* v. *Registered*

This is the straightforward case governed by sections 4 and 5 of the 1707 Act and, now in Northern Ireland, section 4 of the Registration of Deeds Act (N.I.), 1970. Priorities take effect according to the dates of registration of the instruments relating to the transactions concerning the land,[5] rather than the dates of execution of those instruments. Unlike the rules discussed above, it makes no difference whether the estates or interests created by those instruments were legal or equitable.[6] As Lord Manners put it, once a deed is duly registered, "the question is at an end, for the plea of purchaser for a valuable consideration, without notice, can not avail against a prior duly registered deed; and whether the plaintiff's title be a legal or equitable title, it will have priority from its registration, whether [the defendant] had notice or not."[7]

---

[99] Paras. 3.074–83, *supra.*

[1] A memorandum summarising the principal contents of the document in question, para. 22.05 *et seq. post.*

[2] *Re Burke's Estate* (1881) 9 L.R.Ir. 24; *Re Greer* [1907] 1 I.R. 57; see also *Jennings* v. *Bond* (1845) 8 Ir.Eq.R. 755. *Cf.* if there is a written memorandum, *Fullerton* v. *Provincial Bank of Ireland* [1903] A.C. 309.

[3] See further in relation to mortgages, para. 13.141 *et seq., post.*

[4] Paras. 3.074–83, *supra.*

[5] In Northern Ireland, s. 4 (1) of the 1970 Act provides that the time of priority is now determined by allocation of the serial number to the document in question when lodged for registration, see para.22.09, *post.*

[6] *Eyre* v. *Dolphin* (1813) 2 Ba. & B. 290; *Hamilton* v. *Lyster* (1845) 7 Ir.Eq.R. 560; *Drew* v. *Norbury* (1846) & Ir.Eq.R. 524.

[7] *Eyre* v. *Dolphin, op. cit.,* p. 300.

(d) *Unregistered* v. *Registered*

This case must be distinguished from category (b). Here we have a registrable, but unregistered disposition followed by a registered one. This is clearly governed by section 5 of the 1707 Act and, in Northern Ireland, section 4 of the 1970 Act, and the registered one takes priority despite being later in time. Hargreave J. stated with respect to section 5 of the 1707 Act—

> " . . . [I]n order to bring into operation the nullifying section of the Registry Act, three elements are required, all of which are essential. We must have an unregistered deed, a subsequent registered deed, and we must have a purchaser for value; that is, a person claiming under the deed, and not disabled by the statute relating to voluntary conveyances[8] from asserting his right."[9]

3.088. There is, however, one substantial qualification to be made with respect to this operation of section 5 of the 1707 Act and section 4 of the 1970 Act. It is a qualification which may be compared with the "equities being equal" condition required under the rules discussed above with respect to the unregistered position.[10] The question arose before the Irish courts as to what the position was if the subsequent purchaser who registered first knew of the prior *un*registered deed. Was the statute to be read literally and the purchaser to obtain priority under section 5 despite the existence of the notice? It has been settled by a long line of decisions of the Irish courts, affirmed by decisions of the House of Lords, that such a person cannot in equity so obtain priority.[11] The principle underlying these decisions is the old maxim that "equity will not allow a statute to be used as an instrument of fraud."[12] Lord Hardwicke, in a case relating to the Middlesex Registry of Deeds,[13] put the matter thus:

> " . . . [I]t would be a most mischievous thing, if a person taking the advantage of the legal form appointed by an Act of Parliament, might, under that, protect himself against a person who had a prior equity, *of which he had notice.*"[14]

3.089. It has been settled, however, that for this principle to operate so as to deprive the purchaser registering of the priority he would otherwise have under the Act, he must have *actual* notice of the prior unregistered deed at the time of the second deed's execution or, at least, at the time of its registration,[15] or notice *imputed* to him because of *actual* notice in his agent.[16] It is not enough to

---

[8] Conveyancing Act (Ir.), 1634, ss. 1 and 3, see para. 9.078, *post.*

[9] *Re Flood's Estate* (1862) 13 Ir.Ch.R. 312, 314.

[10] Para. 3.074, *ante.*

[11] *Forbes* v. *Deniston* (1722) 4 Bro.P.C. 189; *Agra Bank Ltd.* v. *Barry* (1874) L.R. 7 H.L. 135; *Workingmen's Benefit Building Society* v. *Higgins* [1945] Ir.Jur. Rep. 38. And see the recent decision of Costello J. in *O'Connor* v. *McCarthy* [1982] I.R. 161 (see *A Casebook on Irish Land Law* (1984), p. 106).

[12] Para. 3.048, *ante.*

[13] Ch. 22, *post.*

[14] *Le Neve* v. *Le Neve* (1748) 3 Atk. 646, 652.

[15] *Eyre* v. *Dolphin* (1813) 2 Ba. & B. 290; *Rochard* v. *Fulton* (1844) 7 Ir.Eq.R. 131; *Nixon* v. *Hamilton* (1838) 1 Ir.Eq.R. 46.

[16] *Forbes* v. *Deniston, op. cit.; Le Neve* v. *Le Neve, op. cit.; Re Morrison* (1856) 1 Ir.Jur. (N.S.) 282; *Smith* v. *Smith* (1834) 2 Law Rec.(N.S.) 157. See further on this distinction the judgment of Kenny J. in *Bank of Ireland Finance Ltd.* v. *Rockfield Ltd.* [1979] I.R.21.

fix him with constructive notice, whether his own or his agent's.[17] These principles were given statutory recognition in Northern Ireland by section 7 of the Registration of Deeds Act (N.I.), 1967,[18] which provision is now contained in section 4 (3) and (4) of the consolidating Registration of Deeds Act (N.I.), 1970.

Section 4 (3) and (4) of the 1970 Act read:

> "(3) Where a person or the agent of that person has actual knowledge of a prior document, which has not been registered [under this Act], affecting any unregistered land, registration of a subsequent document which transfers, or confers an estate in, the land to or on that person shall not operate so as to confer priority on, or make the prior document void in relation to, that subsequent document.
>
> (4) In subsection (3), 'agent' means a person who is generally authorised to act for his principal in respect of dealings in land or who is specially authorised by his principal to deal in the land the subject matter of the prior document and who, in either case, obtains knowledge of the prior document in the course of the same transaction with respect to which the question of knowledge arises."

In enacting provisions which are largely declaratory of the previous case law, this Northern Ireland legislation, it should be noted, has dropped the expression "notice" and has substituted in this context the concept of "knowledge." This avoids the courts having to make distinctions between the various types of notice recognised in equity and in the Conveyancing Act, 1882.[19]

4. Registration of Title

3.090. Priorities between successive estates or interests in land in Ireland may be governed by rules other than those already discussed. This occurs where the land is subject to the system of registration of *title* (as opposed to *deeds*).[20] The difference between the two systems may be summarised by saying that the purpose of the Registry of Deeds system is to disclose the *existence* of a deed while that of the Land Registry system is to show the *effect* of a deed. The two systems are mutually exclusive not in relation to the same *land*, which is the common error made, but in relation to the same *estate* in the land.[21] Until recently in Ireland, the Land Registry system was governed by the Local Registration of Title (Ireland) Act, 1891.[22] Under this system the title to any land may be registered voluntarily, and registration of title to certain land, *e.g.*, agricultural land bought out under the land Purchase Acts,[23] was compulsory.

[17] *Popham* v. *Baldwin* (1837) 2 Jones 320; *Clarke* v. *Armstrong* (1860) 10 Ir.Ch.R. 263; *Stephenson* v. *Royse* (1856) 5 Ir.Ch.R. 401. These first two sentences of para. 3.089 were quoted with approval by Costello J. in *O'Connor* v. *McCarthy* [1982] I.R. 161 at 174.
[18] See Wylie, (1968) 19 N.I.L.Q. 228.
[19] See further, para. 3.070, *ante*.
[20] See, generally, ch. 21, *post*.
[21] See further, para. 21.01, *post*.
[22] See now the Registration of Title Act, 1964 (R.I.); Land Registration Act (N.I.), 1970.
[23] Para. 1.60, *ante*.

Once the title to property is registered all subsequent dealings with respect to that property must generally be done through the Land Registry and appropriate notations made on the registers for the transactions to be effective. The registers, therefore, in general govern priorities. However, it should be noted that certain rights and interests may affect registered land without registration[24]; an equitable mortgage can be created by deposit of the land certificate which is issued to the registered owner of the land to show that he is the registered owner, or even by deposit of the charge certificate issued to the registered owner of a charge on registered land.[25] In these sorts of cases one has to fall back upon the rules of equity as to priorities. In *Tench* v. *Molyneux*,[26] O, the registered owner of land, sold it to A who failed to have himself registered as owner. O later deposited his land certificate with B as security for a loan. In a dispute over priorities between A and B, it was held that the matter had to be determined according to the maxim—"where the equities are equal, the first in time prevails." It was held that equities between A and B were equal and so A as first in time retained priority over B.[27]

5. *Registration of Statutory Charges*

3.091. The Statutory Charges Register Act (N.I.), 1951,[28] introduced a system of registration of public and local authority charges and incumbrances on land, *e.g.*, charges imposed on land under the public health and housing legislation.[29] The 1951 Act was replaced by Part X of the Land Registration Act (N.I.), 1970[30] As regards such charges, priorities are governed according to the dates of registration in the Statutory Charges Register and these charges bind all interests in the land, subsisting or created later.[31] Complicated questions can arise, however, where other interests are created between the date of creation of a statutory charge and the date of its registration, but this subject is better left for discussion in a later chapter.[32]

6. *Personalty*

3.092. This book deals primarily with land rather than personalty, but in passing it may be mentioned that the doctrine of notice plays an important role in Ireland in deciding priorities as between successive equitable interests in personalty. Under the rule in *Dearle* v. *Hall*,[33] where successive interests in

---

[24] Para. 21.36 *et seq. post.*
[25] Para. 12.29, *post.*
[26] (1914) 48 I.L.T.R. 48.
[27] See further on priorities in registered land, *Devoy* v. *Hanlon* [1929] I.R. 246; *Re Strong* [1940] I.R. 382; *Tempany* v. *Hynes* [1976] I.R. 101 (see *A Casebook on Irish Land Law* (1984), p. 485), considered in detail in *Irish Conveyancing Law* (1978), paras. 11.04–6. Glover, *Registration of Ownership of Land in Ireland* (1933), pp. 152–8, and para. 13.127 *et seq., post.*
[28] See Murray, (1951) 9 N.I.L.Q. 90. There is no equivalent legislation in the Republic of Ireland. *Cf.* the English Land Charges Act, 1925.
[29] See, generally, para. 21.57 *et seq.* and *Irish Conveyancing Law* (1978), para. 7.097 *et seq., post.*
[30] Part X was the first part of the 1970 Act to be brought into force (in 1971), see *Irish Conveyancing Law* (1978), para. 21.57.
[31] 1970 Act, ss. 88–9.
[32] Para. 21.63 *et seq., post.*
[33] (1823) 3 Russ. 1. See *Re Henessy* (1842) 5 Ir.Eq.R. 259; *Molloy* v. *French* (1849) 13 Ir.Eq.R. 216.

pure personalty held under a trust are created by way of assignment or charge, priorities are determined by the order in which notice of the respective dealings is received by the debtors or other persons to be charged. The rule applies to pure personalty only in Ireland,[34] though the House of Lords held in *Ward* v. *Duncombe*[35] that this included proceeds of a sale of land held under a trust for sale. It has also been held not to apply to bills of sale.[36]

3.093. The rule was based upon the notion of negligence on the part of an assignee or chargee in not giving notice of his interest, though later cases have tended to apply the doctrine mechanically with little regard to its underlying principle.[37] This negligence may enable the assignor or chargor to represent to other prospective incumbrancers that the property is not already subject to an incumbrance and thereby commit fraud on them. The rule was equity's way of redressing the balance so as to prevent such a fraud. Thus the rule operates to protect a subsequent assignee only if he had no notice at the time his assignment was made. It does not matter that he had notice at the time he served notice of his assignment on the debtor, since it is the former notice which is the very thing likely to spur him into doing that to protect himself.[38] There has, however, been some difficulty where notice has been given to one only of several trustees. The general rule seems to be that notice to one is effective to secure priority as against all subsequent incumbrances created during his trusteeship, and remains so as regards those incumbrances after his death or retirement.[39] But if that trustee dies or retires without communicating the notice to his other trustees, it ceases to be effective as regards incumbrances created after his death or retirement.[40] The obvious procedure to follow to be sure of securing priority in respect of property subject to trusts is to give notice to all the trustees.

C. CONVERSION AND RECONVERSION

1. *Conversion*

3.094. The doctrine of conversion governs the occasions when equity will treat realty as converted into personalty and vice versa, even though the obligation to convert has not in fact been carried out. The underlying principle, then, is the maxim—"equity regards as done what ought to be done."[41] Equity took the

---

[34] *Rochard* v. *Fulton* (1844) 7 Ir.Eq.R. 131; *Dunster* v. *Glengall* (1853) 3 Ir.Ch.R 47; *Justice* v. *Wynne* (1860) 12 Ir.Ch.R. 289. It was extended in England by s. 137 of the Law of Property Act, 1925, to regulate priorities of competing "equitable interests in land, capital money, and securities representing capital money." See the *Survey of the Land Law of Northern Ireland* (1971), para. 279.
[35] [1893] A.C. 369.
[36] *Ex parte Allen* (1870) L.R. 11 Eq. 209. In *Société Générale de Paris* v. *Walker* (1885) 11 App.Cas. 20, it was said not to apply to assignments of shares in a company.
[37] See *Foster* v. *Cockerell* (1835) 3 Cl. & F. 456; *Re Dallas* [1904] 2 Ch. 385; *B. S. Lyle Ltd.* v. *Rosher* [1951] 1 W.L.R. 8.
[38] See *Re Holmes* (1885) 29. Ch.D. 786; *Mutual Life Assurance Soc.* v. *Langley* (1886) 32 Ch.D. 460. On what constitutes notice, see *Re Tichener* (1865) 35 Beav. 317; *Lloyd* v. *Banks* (1868) 3 Ch.App. 488; *Re Worcester* (1868) 3 Ch.App. 555; *Ipswich Permanent Money Club Ltd.* v. *Arthy* [1920] 2 Ch. 257.
[39] *Ward* v. *Duncombe* [1893] A.C. 369.
[40] *Re Hall* (1880) 7 L.R.Ir. 180; *Re Phillip's Trusts*]1903] 1 Ch. 183. See also *Lloyds Bank* v. *Pearson* [1901] 1 Ch. 865.
[41] Para. 3.064, *ante.* See Anderson, "The Proper Narrow Scope of Equitable Conversion in Land Law" (1984) 100 L.Q.R. 86.

view that all parties concerned with the property ought to have their rights and interests determined according to the circumstances as they should exist, and ought not to be put in a different position because the person under the obligation to convert was slow to act.

3.095. The doctrine, until recently, had a vital importance with respect to succession to property on intestacy. Until the passing of the Administration of Estates Act (N.I.), 1955,[42] and the Succession Act, 1965 (R.I.),[43] realty in Ireland devolved when the owner died intestate to the heir-at-law whereas personalty devolved to the next-of-kin.[44] It was, therefore, extremely important to decide which type of property had been owned by the deceased and the doctrine of conversion could be the determining factor. Though this aspect of the doctrine has now lost significance in Ireland, the doctrine still has practical importance. Thus a testator in his will may make residuary dispositions, leaving the residue of his "realty" to one person and the residue of his "personalty" to another. Once again the doctrine of conversion may determine whether particular property is "realty" or "personalty" for the purposes of these gifts of residue.

(i) Contract for Sale or Purchase of Land

3.096. It has been settled that where there is a binding contract for the sale or purchase of land, equity will regard conversion as having taken place from the date of the contract.[45] The key factor in determining whether the doctrine applies is whether a decree of specific performance would be granted in respect of the contract.[46] The effect of the doctrine is to convert the purchaser's interest in the purchase money into realty and the vendor's interest in the land into personalty, and by statute on the death of the purchaser the person taking this realty is generally under an obligation to pay the purchase price.[47] Succession to the vendor's and purchaser's property on their death before completion of the sale by actual conveyance of the land is, therefore, governed by the doctrine.

3.097. This aspect of the doctrine's operation has been extended to options to purchase, so that, even though the option is not exercised until after a testator's death, it is considered to relate back to the date of the original agreement granting the option and may govern succession to property in the meantime, by treating it as converted in equity from the date of the agreement. This was settled by the English case of *Lawes* v. *Bennett,*[48] though the tendency has been since not to extend the doctrine further and to exclude *Lawes* v.

---

[42] Ss. 1 and 6.
[43] Ss. 10 and 66.
[44] See, generally, ch. 15, *post.*
[45] *McDonnell* v. *Stenson* [1921] 1 I.R. 80. This aspect of the doctrine of conversion was discussed at length in *Irish Conveyancing Law* (1978), ch. 11.
[46] See para. 3.142, *post.* See also the discussion in *Tempany* v. *Hynes* [1976] I.R. 101 (see *A Casebook on Irish Land Law* (1984), p. 485).
[47] Real Estate Charges Acts, 1854, 1867 and 1877. See now the Administration of Estates Act (N.I.), 1955, s. 31 and the Succession Act, 1965, s. 47 (R.I.).
[48] (1785) 1 Cox C.C. 167. *Re Isaacs* [1894] 3 Ch. 506 held that it would still operate even though the option

Bennett[49] if there is any evidence indicating such an intention.[50] Palles C.B. quoted with approval the following statement of principle[51]:

> "When you find that in a will, made *after* a contract giving an option to purchase, the testator, knowing of the existence of the contract, devises the specific property which is the subject of the contract without referring in any way to the contract . . . then it is considered that there is sufficient indication of an intention to pass that property, to give to the devisee all the interest, whatever it may be, that the testator had in it."[52]

It has been held that *Lawes* v. *Bennett* does not apply as between a vendor and purchaser,[53] though it has been held that such an option to purchase can be exercised by the personal representatives of a lessee to whom the option to purchase was given.[54] Furthermore, it has been held that such options are governed by the rule against perpetuities.[55]

3.098. A considerable amount of case-law arose in Ireland, relating to the doctrine of conversion in general and the principle of *Lawes* v. *Bennett* in particular, under the Land Purchase Acts.[56] Under the pre-1920 Acts, the land purchase scheme operated on the basis of a voluntary agreement to purchase the freehold between the landlord and tenant, subject to the approval of the Land Commission. Section 32 (4) of the Land Law (Ireland) Act, 1896, provided that such an agreement did not operate in equity to convert the tenant's leasehold interest[57] into realty.[58] Once the agreement received the approval of the Land Commission, however, it was held in several cases that the principle of *Lawes* v. *Bennett* applied and a conversion took place relating back to the date of the original agreement.[59] The post-1920 Acts in both parts of Ireland introduced a compulsory land purchase scheme, based upon an "appointed day" system of vesting the land in the Land Commission subject to the agreement to purchase into which each tenant was deemed to have entered by the Acts.[60] It was held that no conversion in equity took place in respect of property within these Acts prior to the appointed day.[61] However, the Republic's Land Act, 1931, provided expressly for conversion of the landlord's interest into personalty on, whichever was the later, the appointed day or the date of the

could not be exercised until after the testator's death and *Re Carrington* [1932] 1 Ch. 1 applied the doctrine to an option to purchase shares. *Cf. Re Sherman* [1954] Ch. 653.
[49] See also *Re Crofton* (1839) 1 Ir.Eq.R. 204; *Duffield* v. *McMaster* [1896] 1 I.R. 370.
[50] *Miley* v. *Carty* [1927] I.R. 541 at 543–4.
[51] *Per* Page-Wood V.-C. in *Weeding* v. *Weeding* (1861) 1 J. & H. 424 at 431.
[52] *Steele* v. *Steele* [1913] 1 I.R. 292, 305 (see *A Casebook on Equity and Trusts in Ireland* (1985), p. 88). See also *Duffield* v. *McMaster* [1896] 1 I.R. 370; *cf. Re Longworth* (1909) 43 I.L.T.R. 33.
[53] *Re Sherlock's Estate* [1899] 2 I.R. 561 at 608 (*per* Holmes L.J.).
[54] *Belshaw* v. *Rollins* [1904] 1 I.R. 284.
[55] *Re Doyle's Estate* [1907] 1 I.R. 204; *Re Tyrrell's Estate* [1907] 1 I.R. 292. With respect to Northern Ireland, see now the Perpetuities Act (N.I.), 1966, ss. 9 and 10, and para. 5.139, *post.*
[56] Paras. 1.51–6, *ante.*
[57] Which was, of course, personalty, see paras. 2.55, *ante* and 4.008, *post.*
[58] *Re Phelan* [1946] I.R. 451; *Re Foley* (1912) 46 I.L.T.R. 96.
[59] *Re Sherlock's Estate* [1899] 2 I.R. 561; *Re Croker's Estate* [1913] 1 I.R. 522; *Miley* v. *Carty* [1927] I.R. 541; *Mooney* v. *McMahon* [1911] 1 I.R. 125.
[60] See especially the Land Act, 1923 (R.I.), and the Northern Ireland Land Act, 1925, and paras. 1.66 and 1.67, *ante.*
[61] *Re Wright's Estate* (1930) 64 I.L.T.R. 195; *cf. Davies* v. *Alexander* (1929) 63 I.L.T.R. 44.

making of the order or publication of the list of "vested" holdings fixing the appointed day.[62]

3.099. It was an essential part of the pre- and post-1920 land purchase schemes that the title to *all* land bought out by tenants should be registered compulsorily under the Local Registration of Title (Ireland) Act, 1891.[63] By sections 84 and 85 of this Act, registered land devolved on intestacy as personalty rather than realty, thus continuing one previous chattel real characteristic of the tenant's interest. These provisions have caused the Irish courts some difficulty with respect to the doctrine of conversion. In *Re Mary Smith*[64] it was held by the former Irish Court of Appeal that, where a tenant had agreed to purchase and the order vesting the title in him was made before the 1891 Act came into force, the freehold still devolved as realty on death of the tenant before registration of the title under the 1891 Act. This decision has been followed since 1920 in both parts of Ireland in cases involving land bought out *before* the operation of the 1891 Act.[65] However, in the Republic the Court of Appeal held, in *Re Collins' Estate*,[66] that, where a tenant had agreed to purchase and the advance of the purchase-money had been sanctioned, but the tenant died before the freehold was vested in him or registered under the 1891 Act, the land nevertheless devolved on his intestacy as personalty. In this case the land had been bought out under the Irish Land Act, 1903, *i.e., after* the coming into operation of the 1891 Act. These decisions were considered in *Re Desmond*,[67] where the land had been vested in the tenant by a Land Commission order of 1904, *i.e.,* after the 1891 Act, but not registered under the 1891 Act.[68] Overend J. held that the devolution of land remained unaffected by the 1891 Act until actually registered, so that in this case the land devolved as realty and not personalty. The learned judge purported expressly not to follow *McDonnell* v. *Stenson* and *Re Collins' Estate,* and to follow *Re Mary Smith,* despite the fact that a distinction between the two lines of cases can be drawn on the basis of whether the land was bought out before or after the 1891 Act. It is arguable that the statute's conversion provisions should have been interpreted as affecting only the rights of parties in land bought out when the original parties could be said to have its provisions in contemplation when they entered into their *voluntary* agreement to purchase the freehold, *i.e.,* after the coming into force of the 1891 Act.

(ii) Trust for Sale

3.100. The second situation where the doctrine of conversion operates is

---

[62] S. 32. *Re Lyons* (1938) 72 I.L.T.R. 28. It had been held that a binding agreement to sell under the pre-1920 Acts operated to convert the landlord's interest from realty into personalty. *Re Doyle's Estate* [1907] 1 I.R. 204; *Re Sherlock's Estate* [1899] 2 I.R. 561; *Miley* v. *Carty* [1927] I.R. 541. See also *Tuite* v. *Tuite* (1978) Unrep. (H.C., R.I.) (1978 No. 2025P).
[63] Para. 1.60, *ante.*
[64] (1897) 33 I.L.T.R. 69.
[65] *Brady* v. *Brady* [1936] I.R. 431; *Re Stewart* [1956] N.I. 82.
[66] [1924] 1 I.R. 72, following *McDonnell* v. *Stenson* [1921] 1 I.R. 80.
[67] [1943] I.R. 534 (see *A Casebook on Equity and Trusts in Ireland* (1985), p. 97).
[68] As reinforced by s. 51 of the Republic's Land Act, 1927.

where there is a trust for sale,[69] not to be confused with a trust containing a mere *power* of sale. The trustees must be under an obligation to sell, otherwise there is no basis for equity to regard as done what "ought" to be done.[70] Difficulties sometimes arise where clauses exist in the trust instrument restricting the trustees in carrying out their duty to sell. For example, it might be specified that the trustees should obtain a beneficiary's consent before selling. In this sort of case it is a matter of construction whether this gives the beneficiary the power to prevent or upset a sale; if so, there will be no room for the doctrine of conversion.[71] The application of the doctrine depends upon the settlor's or testator's intention, which is also a matter of construction.[72] For example, if a will contains a direction to the trustees to sell *or* retain, it is a matter of construction whether this should be treated as a trust for sale, subject to the doctrine of conversion, or a trust to retain with only a power of sale, and no conversion.[73]

3.101. Once it is decided that there is a trust for sale and there is nothing in the terms of the trust instrument to indicate a contrary intention on the part of the settlor or testator, the doctrine applies and realty is converted into personalty, or vice versa, from the date of execution of the settlement or the death of the testator.

(iii) Order of Court

3.102. Conversion also operates from the date of an order of the court directing the sale (or purchase) of realty or personalty.[74] For the doctrine to operate the order must be final and absolute.[75] Where a court orders a sale of land to discharge incumbrances, for example, and so much is sold as is necessary to discharge these, the surplus of the land unsold remains unconverted.[76] If, however, more land is sold than was strictly necessary to discharge the incumbrances, the surplus of money remains converted as money.[77]

3.103. A court order will not always work a conversion. Section 67 of the Lunacy Regulation (Ireland) Act, 1871, provides that any surplus left over from the sale or mortgage of a lunatic's estate (for such purposes as paying his debts or providing for his maintenance) is to be treated as of the same character

---

[69] See, generally, para. 8.012, *post. Re O'Connor* [1923] 1 I.R. 142; *cf. Re Galway* [1944] N.I. 28. See Boyle, "Trusts for Sale and the Doctrine of Conversion" (1981) Conv. 108. The same principles apply to a trust to purchase land.

[70] *Batteste* v. *Maunsell* (1876) I.R. 10 Eq. 314; *McGwire* v. *McGwire* [1900] 1 I.R. 200; *Owen* v. *Owen* [1897] 1 I.R. 580; *Smithwick* v. *Smithwick* (1861) 12 Ir.Ch.R. 181; *Re Whitty's Trust* (1875) I.R. 9 Eq. 41; *Re Tyndall's Estate* [1941] Ir.Jur.Rep. 51.

[71] *Batteste* v. *Maunsell, op. cit.*

[72] *Kellett* v. *Kellett* (1811) 1 Ba. & B. 533; *McDonagh* v. *Nolan* (1881) 9 L.R.Ir. 262 (see *A Casebook on Equity and Trusts in Ireland* (1985), p. 102); *Norreys* v. *Franks* (1874) I.R. 9 Eq. 18; *Watson* v. *Arundell* (1877) I.R. 11 Eq. 53 (aff'd. *sub nom. Singleton* v. *Tomlinson* (1878) 3 App.Cas. 404).

[73] See further para. 8.047, *post.*

[74] *Re Beamish's Estate* (1891) 27 L.R.Ir. 326; see also *Steed* v. *Preece* (1874) L.R. 18 Eq. 192.

[75] *Re Henry's Estate* (1893) 31 L.R.Ir. 158.

[76] *Sheane* v. *Fetherstonhaugh* [1914] 1 I.R. 268. See also *Re Scanlan's Estate* [1897] 1 I.R. 462; *Re Swanton's Estate* [1898] 1 I.R. 157.

[77] *Re Stinson's Estate* [1910] 1 I.R. 13. *Cf. Scott* v. *Scott* (1882) 9 L.R.Ir. 367.

and nature as the property sold.[78] This provision reflects the courts' general attitude towards lunatics' property. Kennedy C.J. explained the courts' attitude thus:

> "It is the long-settled policy and practice of the court in the administration of lunatics' estates to preserve the character of their property as far as possible, and to avoid disturbing the succession to such property. . . . But that policy and practice is always subject to the paramount obligation and duty upon the court to provide for the maintenance and care of the patient out of his means, and to manage and administer his property in his interest and for his benefit."[79]

Where a sale is ordered not under the 1871 Act, but in the ordinary course of management of a lunatic's estate, it seems that conversion will take place, unless the court orders to the contrary.[80] The rule seems to be the opposite if the sale is out of the ordinary course of management of the estate and the property in this case will retain its original form despite the sale.[81]

(iv) Partnership Land

3.104. Section 22 of the Partnership Act, 1890, provides:

> "Where land or any heritable interest therein has become partnership property, it shall, unless the contrary intention appears, to be treated as between the partners (including the representatives of a deceased partner), and also as between the heirs of a deceased partner and his executors or administrators, as personal or moveable and not real or heritable estate."

This provision recognises the principle of equity followed before the statute and is recognition of the fact that, when a partnership is dissolved, the land will have to be sold anyway and the proceeds divided amongst the partners.

(v) Failure of Objects

3.105. Where property is subject to a duty to convert but the objects of the conversion fail, the question arises as to whether the doctrine of conversion applies.[82] For example, property might be settled on trustees to sell and to pay the income produced by investing the proceeds of sale to A for his life. If A dies before the sale there is a resulting trust[83] of the property in favour of the settlor, but does he take the property in its actual unconverted form or as converted? The answer is that, if there is a *total* failure of the objects, as in the example, there is no conversion, whether the property was settled by deed or will.[84]

---

[78] *Re Stuart* (1939) 73 I.L.T.R. 134. *Cf.* the effect of a sale in the Land Purchase Acts, *Latham* v. *Travers* [1912] 1 I.R. 306.

[79] *O'Connell* v. *Harrison* [1927] I.R. 330 at 337–8; *cf. Kiernan* v. *McGauran* [1922] 1 I.R. 1 at 3 (*per* Powell J.).

[80] *Re Silva* [1929] 2 Ch. 198.

[81] *Batteste* v. *Maunsell* (1876) I.R. 10 Eq. 314; *Att.-Gen.* v. *Marquis of Ailesbury* (1887) 12 App. Cas. 672.

[82] This topic should not be confused with the doctrine of reconversion discussed at para 3.108, *infra.*

[83] See para. 9.055, *post.*

[84] *Donnellan* v. *O'Neill* (1870) I.R. 5 Eq. 523; *Re O'Connor* [1923] 1 I.R. 142.

3.106. The position is more complicated if there is a partial failure of objects only, *e.g.*, a trust for sale for the benefit of A and B and only A dies before the sale. If the property was left by will, a resulting trust of A's share in favour of the testator's estate will occur in respect of the property in its converted form.[85] If, however, the property was settled by deed the general rule applies and the resulting trust is of the property in its unconverted form.[86]

(vi) Settled Land

3.107. It may be noted that a further statutory recognition of the doctrine of conversion is contained in section 22 (5) of the Settled Land Act, 1882, which reads:

> "Capital money arising under this Act while remaining uninvested or unapplied, and securities on which an investment of any such capital money is made, shall, for all purposes of disposition, transmission, and devolution, be considered as land, and the same shall be held for and go to the same persons successively, in the same manner and for and on the same estates, interests, and trusts, as the land wherefrom the money arises would, if not disposed of, have been held and have gone under the settlement."[87]

The operation of this provision will be considered in a later chapter.[88]

2. Reconversion

3.108. Equity sometimes went even further than the doctrine of conversion and held that property regarded as notionally converted should then be regarded as reconverted back into its original form. This principle can, therefore, be distinguished from the principle applied where there is a failure of objects. In the case of the latter there has never been any conversion, even notionally in equity, and the property retains its original form throughout. In the case of the former, notional conversion in equity does take place, followed by a notional reconversion back to the original form. In both cases, of course, the result is the same; the property is regarded as having its original form for the purposes of succession.

Reconversion can take place either by an act of the party concerned with the property or by operation of law.

(i) Act of Party

3.109. Suppose land is left on trust for sale, the proceeds to be held in trust for A until he reaches the age of 21, when he becomes entitled to the capital. The doctrine of conversion applies and the land is regarded in equity as personalty from the death of the testator. But suppose further that the trustees

---

[85] *Re O'Connor, op. cit.*
[86] *Griffith* v. *Ricketts* (1849) 7 Hare 299.
[87] See *Re Tyndall's Estate* [1941] Ir.Jur.Rep. 51.
[88] Para. 8.096, *post.*

fail to sell the land and, when A becomes 21, he asks the trustees to transfer the land to him instead of capital. "Equity, like nature, does nothing in vain"[89] and allows A to elect to take the land, applying the doctrine of reconversion. Even if equity insisted upon the conversion, A could simply reverse this himself by repurchasing land with the capital resulting from an actual conversion.

3.110. A person so electing to reconvert must be *sui juris* and under no disability.[90] However, if it is considered necessary or in the best interests of a person under a disability, such as an infant or a person suffering from mental disorder, the court will elect for him.[91] Where a person is electing, it is not necessary to do so formally; it is sufficient that some act is done clearly indicating the fact that an election has been made, *e.g.*, entering into some transaction with respect to the property and dealing with it in its original form.[92]

(ii) Operation of Law

3.111. Reconversion takes effect automatically, by operation of law, whenever property is "at home," *i.e.*, though originally subject to a trust with an obligation to convert, it has come into the hands of a person now absolutely entitled to it without ever having been converted. In *McDonagh* v. *Nolan*,[93] under a marriage settlement money was vested in trustees to be used to purchase real estate to be held on trust. The only son of the marriage became absolutely entitled to the property held on trust and he died intestate, by which time the money had still not been used to purchase real estate. It was held that the property should be regarded still as money and so it devolved as such to the son's personal representatives on his intestacy.

D. ELECTION

3.112. The basis of the doctrine of election was explained by Lord Hatherley in the following terms,[94] which were quoted with approval by Ronan L.J. in *Re Sullivan*[95]:

"... [T]here is an obligation on him who takes a benefit under a will or other instrument to give full effect to that instrument under which he takes a benefit; and if it be found that the instrument purports to deal with something which it was beyond the power of the donor or settlor to dispose of, but to which effect can be given by the concurrence of him who receives a benefit under the same instrument, the law will impose on him who takes

---

[89] Para. 3.067, *ante*.
[90] *Orr* v. *Alexander* [1925] N.I. 104. A remainderman may elect provided he is entitled to the whole beneficial interest and no contingency still has to be met. No election by him can affect prior interests still outstanding. *Hart* v. *MacDougall* [1912] 1 I.R. 62.
[91] *More-Smyth* v. *Mountcashell* [1895] 1 I.R. 44; *Kiernan* v. *McGauran* [1922] 1 I.R. 1.
[92] *Gaussen and French* v. *Ellis* [1903] I.R. 116; *Hart* v. *MacDougall, op. cit.*
[93] (1881) 9 L.R.Ir. 262 (see *A Casebook on Equity and Trusts in Ireland* (1985), p. 102).
[94] *Cooper* v. *Cooper* (1874) L.R. 7 H.L. 53, 70.
[95] [1917] 1 I.R. 38 (see *A Casebook on Equity and Trusts in Ireland* (1985), p. 106).

the benefit the obligation of carrying the instrument into full and complete force and effect."[96]

The essential ingredients are, therefore, that property is given by deed or will to X and by that same instrument[97] some of X's property is given to a third party. In this case X is put to an election, unless he declines to take the gift altogether; he must take either under the instrument or against the instrument. He cannot claim both the donor's gift and retain his own property for "equity leans against double portions."[98] If he takes under the will, he obtains the donor's property but must transfer his own property to the third party in accordance with the terms of the will. If he elects to take against the will, he retains his own property but must compensate the third party out of the donor's property up to the value of his own property.[99] So in most cases the election will be governed by the respective values of the two properties, the donor's and the donee's, which the donor has purported to give to a third party.[1]

3.113. The doctrine applies to both deeds and wills.[2] The donor must give both some of his own property to the donee[3] and some of the donee's property to a third party.[4] Both of these properties must be freely alienable and disposable, but this does not mean that they may not be subject to contingencies,[5] or to a power of appointment.[6] However, there can be no election if the exercise of the power of appointment violates the rule against perpetuities.[7]

3.114. To a large extent the doctrine is based upon the *presumed* intention of the donor. Thus if it can be shown that there was a contrary intention on his part, there can be no election.[8] If it can be shown that there was no intention by the donor to dispose of property that was not his own (whether or not he was aware of this), there again can be no election.[9] As to what amounts to an

---

[96] *Ibid.*, pp. 42–3.
[97] See *Fearon* v. *Fearon* (1852) 3 Ir.Ch.R. 19 at 24–5 (*per* Blackburne L.C.).
[98] Para. 3.059, *ante.*
[99] *Vane* v. *Lord Dungannon* (1804) 2 Sch. & Lef. 118 at 130; *Hamilton* v. *Jackson* (1845) 8 Ir.Eq.R. 195; *Morrison* v. *Bell* (1843) 5 Ir.Eq.R. 354; *Spread* v. *Morgan* (1859) 9 Ir.Ch.R. 535, (1865) 11 H.L.C. 588.
[1] See *Sadlier* v. *Butler* (1867) I.R. 1 Eq. 415; *Lewis* v. *Lewis* (1876) I.R. 11 Eq. 340; *Coote* v. *Gordon* (1877) I.R. 11 Eq. 279; *Re Woodleys* (1892) 29 L.R.Ir. 304; *Re Saul's Trust* [1951] Ir.Jur.Rep. 34.
[2] *Birmingham* v. *Kirwan* (1805) 2 Sch. & Lef. 444 at 450; *Moore* v. *Butler* (1805) 2 Sch. & Lef. 249.
[3] *Crozier* v. *Crozier* (1843) 3 Dr. & War. 373; *McDonnell* v. *McDonnell* (1843) 2 Con. & L. 481.
[4] *Lewis* v. *Lewis* (1876) I.R. 11 Eq. 340; *Re Woodleys* (1892) 29 L.R.Ir. 304; *Re Irwin's Estate* (1910) 44 I.L.T.R. 50.
[5] *Morgan* v. *Morgan* (1853) 4 Ir.Ch.R. 606.
[6] *Fearon* v. *Fearon* (1852) 3 Ir.Ch.R. 19; *Moriarty* v. *Martin* (1852) 3 Ir.Ch.R. 26; *Ex parte Bernard* (1857) 6 Ir.Ch.R. 133; *Williams* v. *Mayne* (1867) I.R. 1 Eq. 519; *Armstrong* v. *Lynn* (1874) I.R. 9 Eq. 186; *King* v. *King* (1884) 13 L.R.Ir. 531. *Cf. Re Gordon's Will Trusts* [1978] Ch. 145, where the English Court of Appeal held that the doctrine did not apply to a beneficiary whose interest was not available for compensation because it was held on protective trusts (see paras. 9.083–4, *post*). See Pettit, "The Equitable Doctrine of Election and Protective Trusts" (1977) 93 L.Q.R. 65; Watkin, "Election, Compensation and Alienability" (1977) 41 Conv. 188.
[7] *Re Handcock's Trusts* (1888) 23 L.R.Ir. 34: *Re McCormick* (1915) 1 I.R. 315.
[8] *Hall* v. *Hill* (1841) 1 Dr. & War. 94 at 107–8 (*per* Sugden L.C.).
[9] *Michin* v. *Gabbett* [1896] 1 I.R. 1; see also *Henry* v. *Henry* (1872) I.R. 6 Eq. 286; *Galvin* v. *Devereux* [1903] 1 I.R. 185.

election by the donee, this was discussed in some detail by Chatterton V.-C. in *Sweetman* v. *Sweetman*[10]:

> "The requisites for holding a party bound by an election as concluded are, I think, these:—first, he must have a knowledge of his rights, that is to say, he must know that the property, which the testator attempted to give to another person, was not the testator's property, and that it would, upon the testator's decease, become, independently of the testator's will, the property of the party called upon to elect. It must be known by him, as a matter of fact, that the testator had not the power to give the property which he purported to devise, and that it belongs, not by the will, but by an earlier title, to the person who is called upon to elect. Next he must know the relative values of the properties between which he is called upon to elect; and further, he must know, as a matter of fact, and not as a presumption of law, that the rule of equity exists, that he cannot, under such circumstances, take both estates, but must make an election between the two. And, further, the Court must be satisfied that he made a deliberate choice with the intention of making it. . . .
>
> But when I say that these propositions must be established to the satisfaction of the Court, I do not mean to say that there must be in every case actual, direct evidence of the existence of them. From a long course of dealing, from a series of acts, the Court is at liberty, as an inference of fact, to conclude that the party called upon to elect knew his rights, knew the value of both estates, and knew the rule of equity, that he was bound to elect, and had, with that full knowledge, made his choice, with the intention of making it, and of electing between the two estates. To justify the Court, however, in arriving at that conclusion, there must be a series of acts or dealings, consistent only with the knowledge which I have already mentioned, and with the deliberate intention to elect, or, at least, a series of acts or dealings that preponderates so strongly in the mind of the Court, that no person could come reasonably to any other conclusion; and the *onus* of proof must rest always upon the party who alleges that the knowledge existed, and that the deliberate choice was made."[11]

Such an unequivocal decision to elect will be presumed, for example, if the donee deals with the property given to him by the donor,[12] though mere receipt of rents from it is not enough.[13] If the donee is under a disability or suffers from incapacity to elect on his own, the court may act for him in electing as it sees fit.[14]

E. SATISFACTION, ADEMPTION AND PERFORMANCE

Equity has evolved several doctrines founded upon one of its maxims, namely,

---

[10] (1868) I.R. 2 Eq. 141 (see *A Casebook on Equity and Trusts in Ireland* (1985), p. 109). See also *Spread* v. *Morgan* (1865) 11 H.L.C. 588; *Re McCormick* [1915] 1 I.R. 315.

[11] *Ibid.*, pp. 152–3.

[12] *Briscoe* v. *Briscoe* (1844) 1 Jo. & Lat. 334.

[13] *Morgan* v. *Morgan* (1853) 4 Ir.Ch.R. 606.

[14] *Moore* v. *Butler* (1805) 2 Sch. & Lef. 249 at 266–7 (*per* Lord Redesdale); *Morrison* v. *Bell* (1843) 5 Ir.Eq.R. 354.

"equity imputes an intention to fulfil an obligation."[15] These doctrines cover several situations.

1. Satisfaction of Debts by Legacies

3.115. If A owes B a debt of £500 and dies, with the debt still unpaid, but leaving B a legacy of £500, equity presumes that this legacy was given in satisfaction of the debt.[16] Being based upon a presumed intention, the application of this presumption can always be defeated by proof of circumstances indicating a contrary intention. Indeed, the courts have come to show a certain dislike of the principle and the result has been the evolution of a considerable number of restrictions on it.

3.116. First, the legacy left by will must be equal to or greater in value than the debt owed. There is no question of a legacy operating as satisfaction *pro tanto*.[17] This restriction has been carried to the point where the presumption of satisfaction will be rebutted because the legacy is of an uncertain value (*e.g.*, a gift of residue)[18] or of a diffierent character or nature than the debt (*e.g.*, land for personalty[19] or a contingent interest for an immediate debt[20]). Similarly, the presumption will be rebutted if the will was made *before* the debt was incurred, the principle then being that the creditor can take both the legacy and claim satisfaction of his debt out of the estate.[21] It has also been held that the fact that a debt was uncertain at the time of making the will (*e.g.*, liability on a running account) was sufficient to rebut the presumption.[22]

2. Satisfaction of Portions by Legacies

3.117. This aspect of the doctrine of satisfaction arises from the special relationship which exists between a child and his father,[23] or other person *in loco parentis*.[24] A father is deemed in equity to have a moral duty to advance or provide for his child, and a common way of doing this is to undertake to give a "portion" (a substantial sum of money to set the child up in life, as opposed to mere casual payments[25]), usually on some specified occasion, *e.g.*, on marriage or coming of age.

3.118. The general rule is that if a father so enters into an obligation to provide a portion and dies before doing so, but leaving the child a legacy in his

---

[15] See Para. 3.065, *ante*.
[16] *Garner* v. *Holmes* (1858) 8 Ir.Ch.R. 469.
[17] *Coates* v. *Coates* [1898] 1 I.R. 258 (see *A Casebook on Equity and Trusts in Ireland* (1985), p. 114); *Cf. Ellard* v. *Phelan* [1914] 1 I.R. 76. See also *Humphrey* v. *Arabin* (1836) L1. & G. *temp.* Plunk. 318.
[18] *Re Keogh's Estate* (1889) 23 L.R.Ir. 257. *Cf. Re Russell's Estate* (1887) 19 L.R.Ir. 418.
[19] *Coates* v. *Coates* [1898] 1 I.R. 258.
[20] *Peirce* v. *Locke* (1850) 2 Ir.Ch.R. 205; *Haynes* v. *Mico* (1781) 1 Bro. C.C. 129.
[21] *Cranmer's Case* (1701) 2 Salk. 508.
[22] *Buckley* v. *Buckley* (1887) 19 L.R.Ir. 544.
[23] Barton J. said: "My summary of the law is this, that a mother may advance a child, a widowed mother may advance a child, and the difference between a father and a mother is this, that in the one case there is a moral obligation to do so recognised in equity, while in the case of a mother the moral obligation is there, but the Courts of Equity do not recognise it." *Preston* v. *Greene* [1909] 1 I.R. 172 at 177–8. See also *Hayes* v. *Garvey* (1845) 8 Ir.Eq.R. 90.
[24] See *Monck* v. *Monck* (1810) 1 Ba. & B. 298; *Smyth* v. *Gleeson* [1911] 1 I.R. 113; *Longfield* v. *Bantry* (1885) 15 L.R.Ir. 101; *Re Bannon* [1934] I.R. 701.
[25] *Cf.* Blackburne L.J. in *Garner* v. *Holmes* (1858) 8 Ir.Ch.R. 469 at 497.

will, the legacy will be presumed to be in satisfaction of the obligation to give a portion. The child cannot claim both—"equity leans against double portions."[26] Monroe J. explained the basis of the doctrine thus:

> "The question whether a portion given by a settlement is satisfied by a legacy in a subsequent will is entirely one of intention to be gathered in the absence of other evidence, from the terms of the two instruments, subject to this consideration, that the presumption of law is against double portions. If the provision made by the later instrument is equal to or greater than that made by the earlier one and the limitations are substantially the same, double portions will not be allowed; the parties entitled will be put to their election. If the limitations are widely different, the presumption is that the provisions were to be cumulative."[27]

In fact, the application of the doctrine of satisfaction in this situation is even wider than Monroe J. stated. Unlike the case of satisfaction of debts by legacies, here there may be presumed satisfaction *pro tanto* if the legacy is less in value than the portion.[28] However, the learned judge was correct in stating that substantial differences between the two provisions will rebut the presumption. Thus a legacy of a fund to be invested by trustees, inevitably of a fluctuating value, was held not to be in satisfaction of a covenant to stand possessed of a fund secured by a first mortgage on real estate.[29] In the case of satisfaction here, the child has a right to elect[30] between the portion or legacy, his decision in most cases being governed by the respective values of the two provisions.[31] It must not be forgotten, however, that the doctrine of satisfaction is dealing with unfulfilled obligations. It does not apply where an obligation to provide a portion has been carried out by the actual provision of it before the will operates on the father's death.[32]

3. Ademption of Legacies by Portions

3.119. This is the reverse situation of number 2. It also applies only as between a child and his father or person *in loco parentis*. The basis of the doctrine is the same as that applying in satisfaction of portions by legacies. Sullivan M.R. described it thus:

> "[T]here is a presumption raised by the law against double portions; and accordingly, when a parent, or one standing *in loco parentis*, gives

---

[26] Para. 3.059, *ante*. *Re Bannon* [1934] I.R. 701, espec. at 729 (*per* Murnaghan J.). Note the saving in s. 63 (9) of the Republic's Succession Act, 1965.

[27] *Re Battersby's Estate* (1887) 19 L.R.Ir. 359, 363–4 (see *A Casebook on Equity and Trusts in Ireland* (1985), p. 115). See also s. 63 of the Succession Act, 1965 (R.I.), and s. 17 of the Administration of Estates Act (N.I.), 1955.

[28] *Re Moore's Rents* [1917] 1 I.R. 244.

[29] *Smyth* v. *Gleeson* [1911] 1 I.R. 113. See also *Hall* v. *Hill* (1841) 1 Dr. & War. 94; *Peirce* v. *Locke* (1850) 2 Ir.Ch.R. 205; *Keays* v. *Gilmore* (1873) I.R. 8 Eq. 290.

[30] Not to be confused with the doctrine of election discussed paras. 3.112–4, *supra*.

[31] *Chichester* v. *Coventry* (1867) L.R. 2 H.L. 71. *Cf.* s. 63 (8) of the Republic's Succession Act, 1965.

[32] *Noblett* v. *Litchfield* (1858) 7 Ir.Ch.R. 575. For such cases, see Succession Act, 1965, s. 63 (R.I.); Administration of Estates Act (N.I.) 1955, s. 17.

by will a sum of money to a child, and afterwards a like or greater sum is secured by a settlement on the marriage of that child, the law presumes the legacy to be adeemed. But this is only a presumption, and therefore it may be rebutted by evidence of intention to the contrary. The burden of proof of intention to countervail the presumption rests on the person claiming the double portion. Parol evidence is admissible . . . the Court ought to view and examine it with scrupulous care and great discrimination."[33]

There will, however, be ademption *pro tanto* in the case of a portion of less value than the legacy.[34] It must be remembered that the doctrine of satisfaction, or ademption, is in the end based upon equity's presumption of an intention to fulfil an obligation. One important distinction to be made from the case of satisfaction of portions by legacies is, however, that in the case of ademption of legacies by portions there can be no question of election. The Child must take the portion and cannot claim the adeemed legacy.[35] Furthermore, if the portion is actually paid before the will is made, there again can be no question of satisfaction or ademption. No obligation remains to be satisfied by the legacy in the will and at the time of the giving of the portion there is no legacy to be adeemed.[36]

3.120. Finally, it may be noted that the doctrine of ademption is not confined to family relationships. If a person leaves a legacy to some stranger or organisation for a particular purpose and subsequently gives that person or organisation a gift for the same purpose, the subsequent gift adeems the legacy.[37] This application of the doctrine must be distinguished from ademption between parent and child. Porter M.R. explained this matter thus:

"In the case of a parent, or one standing in *loco parentis*, the presumption is that the legacy is adeemed by the advancement. But where the legacy is to a stranger, and not to a child, or a child by adoption, the presumption is that, no matter what the testator does in his lifetime, the legacy is not adeemed. The stranger may take both. But there is another exception in the case of a stranger. Where there is a gift in a will, of money or property, or an expressed object to which it is devoted by the testator, and there is afterwards a donation by the testator in his lifetime for the *same* object, the law presumes that he did not intend that both should take effect, but that the latter should be in substitution for the former gift. The object, however, must be clearly expressed, and it must clearly appear that what he did in his lifetime was done for the same object as that intended in his will—for the same identical object."[38]

---

[33] *Curtin* v. *Evans* (1872) I.R. 9 Eq. 553, 557–8 (see *A Casebook on Equity and Trusts in Ireland* (1985), p. 117). See also *Barry* v. *Harding* (1844) 7 Ir.Eq.R. 313; *Re Wall* [1922] 1 I.R. 59; *Re Nolan* (1923) 58 I.L.T.R. 13.
[34] *Edgeworth* v. *Johnston* (1877) I.R. 11 Eq. 326. *Cf. Re Bannon* [1934] I.R. 701.
[35] *Chichester* v. *Coventry* (1867) L.R. 2 H.L. 71; *Rentoul* v. *Fitzsimmons* (1900) 34 I.L.T.R. 194.
[36] *Re Peacock's Estate* (1872) L.R. 14 Eq. 236.
[37] *Griffith* v. *Bourke* (1887) 21 L,R.Ir. 92 (see *A Casebook on Equity and Trusts in Ireland* (1985), p. 122); *Hodgins* v. *Guinan* [1935] I.R. 464; *Normoyle* v. *Brady* (1947) 81 I.L.T.R. 18. *Cf. Monck* v. *Monck* (1810) 1 Ba. & B. 298 at 304.
[38] *Griffith* v. *Bourke, ibid.*, p. 95.

Considerable confusion is caused by another meaning of the word "ademption." If A leaves a legacy of a specific chattel and that article is subsequently sold or destroyed, the legacy is said to be "adeemed."[38a] This doctrine has no connection whatever with the rules we have been discussing.

4. *Satisfaction of Legacies by Legacies*

3.121. This situation is not really a case where equity applied the doctrine of satisfaction, rather it is a case of equity adopting special rules of construction for wills which seem to involve an element of duplication. In each case where double legacies seem to have been left, the question arises whether, as a matter of construction, these should be regarded as cumulative or substitutional.[39] In dealing with these cases, equity drew one major distinction, between legacies given by the same instrument and those given by different instruments.

(i) Same Instrument

3.122. The rules evolved by equity are as follows. If the legacies are of the *same* value, and given to the same person, the presumption is that they are substitutional and the legatee can take one only.[40] If, however, the legacies given to the same person are of *different* value, then the opposite presumption comes into play.[41] Both presumptions are, of course, rebuttable by evidence showing a contrary intention by the testator, as we discuss further below.

(ii) Different Instruments

3.123. Here the general presumption is that the legacies are cumulative,[42] and a will and codicil are different instruments for this purpose. The legacies will be regarded as substitutional only where the second instrument repeats the first in identical terms or where it makes it clear that it is revising or explaining the first.[43]

(iii) Parol Evidence

3.124. The courts have laid down different rules to govern the admissibility of parol, or other extrinsic, evidence, to show the intention of testators in the various situations outlined above. For the most part these rules operate to the advantage of the legatee.[44] If the rules of construction raise the presumption

---

[38a] See *Tuite* v. *Tuite* (1978) Unrep. (H.C., R.I.) (1978 No. 202 Sp).
[39] See the general discussion in *Quin* v. *Armstong* (1876) I.R. 11 Eq. 161 (see *A Casebook on Equity and Trusts in Ireland* (1985), p. 128).
[40] *Garth* v. *Meyrick* (1779) 1 Bro.C.C. 30.
[41] *Brennan* v. *Moran* (1857) 6 Ir.Ch.R. 126. Cf. *Baylee* v. *Quinn* (1842) 2 Dr. & War. 116.
[42] *Walsh* v. *Walsh* (1869) I.R. 4 Eq. 396; *Pakenham* v. *Duggan* (1951) 85 I.L.T.R. 21.
[43] *Re Armstrong* (1893) 31 L.R.Ir. 154; *Bell* v. *Park* [1914] 1 I.R. 158.
[44] See the discussion by Sugden L.C. in *Hall* v. *Hill* (1841) 1 Dr. & War. 94 at 132–3.

that the legacies are *cumulative*, parol evidence is *not* admissible to rebut this and thereby deprive the legatee of both gifts. If, on the other hand, the presumption is raised that the legacies are *substitutional*, parol evidence *is* admissible to rebut this and to prove that the testator intended the legatee to take both gifts.

5. Performance

3.125. The equitable doctrine of performance, like the doctrine of satisfaction, is based upon the maxim, "equity imputes an intention to fulfil an obligation."[45] The distinction between the two doctrines lies in the theory that satisfaction involves the discharging of a particular obligation by an act different from that contemplated when the obligation was entered into, whereas performance is the actual carrying out of the obligation itself, though there may be some minor differences.[46] The doctrine applies, therefore, where an obligation to do something in the future is entered into and later the obligee does that very thing, or something very similar to it, without reference to the earlier obligation; equity presumes this to be performance of the obligation and thereby discharges the obligee from further liability under it. This future performance of an obligation must be distinguished from present performance as a result of execution of the instrument in which it is expressed.[47] In *Creed* v. *Carey*,[48] a settlor of marriage articles covenanted in the settlement to purchase lands and charge them with a jointure in favour of his wife. A later clause in the settlement actually charged all the settlor's land, of which he was then or later to become seised. It was held that these marriage articles themselves performed the covenant and so created a charge or lien on land subsequently purchased by the settlor, which took priority over a later mortgage created on the purchased land in favour of a purchaser without notice.

3.126. Performance may take place by operation of law. For example, A may covenant to settle property or to leave it to X. If A dies intestate and X receives some of A's property as one of his intestate successors, this is regarded as performance of the covenant *pro tanto*.[49] This presumption can, of course, be rebutted by evidence of a contrary intention.[50]

IV. EQUITABLE REMEDIES

We come now to one of equity's greatest contributions to our law, the creation

---

[45] Para. 3.065, *ante*.
[46] See *Keays* v. *Gilmore* (1873) I.R. 8 Eq. 290. See also the leading English case of *Lechmere* v. *Lechmere* (1735) Cas.*temp*. Talb. 80.
[47] See *Lyster* v. *Burroughs* (1837) 1 Dr. & Wal. 149; *White* v. *Anderson* (1850) 1 Ir.Ch.R. 419; *Re Stack* (1862) 13 Ir.Ch.R. 213; *Galavan* v. *Dunne* (1879) 7 L.R.Ir. 144.
[48] (1857) 7 Ir.Ch.R. 295 (see *A Casebook on Equity and Trusts in Ireland* (1985), p. 133).
[49] *Re Hogan* [1901] 1 I.R. 168; *Re Finegan's Estate* [1925] 1 I.R. 201. *Cf. Re Shine* [1964] I.R. 32, where a charge under a marriage settlement payable on the husband's death was held to be satisfied by the distributive share taken on his intestacy. See also *Richards* v. *Molony* (1850) 2 Ir.Ch.R. 1.
[50] *Re Hood* [1923] 1 I.R. 109.

of a wide variety of remedies to mitigate the rigidity and harshness of the
common law.

A. INJUNCTION

3.127. The injunction is, perhaps, equity's most wide-ranging remedy since it
is one which can be invoked in most areas of the law, private and public. An
injunction is an order of the court requiring a party to do or to refrain from
doing specified acts, when these acts are contrary to law or in breach of another
person's rights.

1. *Classification*

3.128. The following types of injunction may be granted. In some cases the
categorisation is based upon the nature of the direction to the party to be
restrained, in other cases it is based upon the time of operation of the direction.
These categories are not mutually exclusive, indeed invariably it is the case that
a particular order will involve at least two of the categories.

(i) Prohibitory

3.129. This is, perhaps, the most common type of injunction granted by the
courts. It forbids the commission or continuance of a wrongful act, *e.g.,* a
trespass on someone else's land or picketing when there is no trade dispute.

(ii) Mandatory

3.130. This is a much rarer type of injunction. It requires that a party do
something positive to repair a wrong, *e.g.,* pull down buildings erected on land
in violation of a covenant restricting the user of the land. Because this imposes
a heavier obligation it is used sparingly by the courts.[51]

(iii) Quia Timet

3.131. Equity will also grant an injunction in anticipation of wrongful acts. If
it is clearly apprehended that a party is about to commit a wrong, the person
who is likely to suffer substantial injury as a result of such action need not wait
for it to happen and may bring a *quia timet* action to prevent it.[52]

(iv) Perpetual

3.132. This injunction is granted only after the action by the plaintiff has
been fully heard and a judicial decision made upon the arguments. A final
decree may then be made permanently restraining the defendant.[53]

---

[51] See the discussion in *Irish Shell Ltd* v. *Irish Motors Ltd* [1984] I.R. 200 (see *A Casebook on Equity and
Trusts in Ireland* (1985), p. 137). Also *Doupe* v. *Limerick C.C.* [1981] I.L.R.M. 456; *Nova Media Services Ltd.* v.
Minister for Posts and Telegraphs [1984] I.L.R.M. 161; *Woodhouse* v. *Newry Navigation Co.* [1898] 1 I.R. 161;
Att.-Gen. v. *Eastwood* [1949] N.I. 41; *Gaw* v. *C.I.E.* [1953] I.R. 232; *Kelly* v. *Dea* (1966) 100 I.L.T.R. 1.
[52] See *C. & A. Modes* v. *C. &. A. (Waterford) Ltd.* [1976] I.R. 153 (see *ibid.*, p. 153). See also *Att.-Gen.* v.
Rathmines & Pembroke Joint Hospital Board [1904] 1 IR. 161; *Independent Newspapers Ltd.* v. *Irish Press Ltd.*
[1932] I.R. 615; *Radford* v. *Wexford Corporation* (1955) 89 I.L.T.R. 184.
[53] *Taylor* v. *Hughes* (1844) 7 Ir.Eq.R. 529.

(v) Interlocutory

3.133. In certain cases considerable damage to the plaintiff might occur if a full trial of the action had to be awaited, so the courts can in an emergency act more quickly by issuing an interlocutory injunction.[54] This is an interim injunction designed to maintain the *status quo* until the action may be heard more fully and settled one way or the other. Such an injunction may also be granted by a court of first instance pending an appeal to a higher court.[55] Further, in cases where the damage would be irreparable, an injunction may be granted *ex parte, i.e.,* before the defendant has had the opportunity to appear in court and put his side of the case,[56] and the court will limit the time of its operation to a period sufficient to provide that opportunity. Because such an interim injunction might seriously inconvenience the defendant and cause him considerable financial loss, the courts may require a strong *prima facie* case to be made by the applicant[57] and may require him to give an undertaking to pay any damage caused to the defendant by it, if the plaintiff subsequently loses the action.[58] Such considerations often arise when the Court is asked to grant an injunction to prevent the removal or destruction of evidence (a so-called "Anton Piller" order[58a]) or the removal of assets (a so-called "Mareva" injunction[58b]). The English courts have also recently reviewed the principles applicable to the granting of an interlocutory injunction, with the House of Lords decreeing that it is no longer necessary for the applicant to establish a *prima facie* case[58c]; rather the Court should be satisfied that his case is not frivolous or vexatious and that there is a serious question to be tried and, once that is established, the governing principle is whether the "balance of convenience" justifies the grant of the injunction.[58d] The Republic's Supreme Court has since confirmed that essentially the same principles apply in Ireland.[58e]

3.134. It may be noted that the Judicature (Ireland) Act, 1877, abolished another type of injunction, known as a "common" injunction.[59] This was the

[54] See the discussion in *Corporation of Cork* v. *Rooney* (1881) 7 L.R.Ir. 191. Also *Gallaher* v. *Tuohy* (1924) 58 I.L.T.R. 132; *Educational Co. of Ireland Ltd.* v. *Fitzpatrick* [1961] I.R. 323; *Silver Tassie Ltd.* v. *O'Beirne* (1956) 90 I.L.T.R. 90, (1958) 92 I.L.T.R. 29; *Tully* v. *Irish Land Commission* (1963) 97 I.L.T.R. 94; *McMahon* v. *Dunne* (1965) 99 I.L.T.R. 45; *Dublin Post and Docks Board* v. *Britannia Dredging Co. Ltd.* [1968] I.R. 136; *Murtagh Properties Ltd.* v. *Cleary* [1972] I.R. 330.

[55] *O'Malley* v. *O'Malley* (1951) 85 I.L.T.R. 213; *Esso Petroleum Co.* v. *Fogarty* [1965] I.R. 531.

[56] *Browne* v. *Duffy* (1889) 24 L.R.Ir. 13. Cf. *Tyler* v. *Goodwin* (1888) 23 L.R.Ir. 13 (absolute injunction granted *ex parte*, but liberty of defendant to apply to have it dissolved expressly reserved).

[57] *Moore* v. *Att.-Gen.* [1927] I.R. 569; *Sinclair* v. *Gogarty* [1937] I.R. 377; *O'Malley* v. *O'Malley* (1951) 85 I.L.T.R. 213; *McMahon Ltd.* v. *Dunne* (1965) 99 I.L.T.R. 45; *E.I. Co. Ltd.* v. *Kennedy* [1968] I.R. 69; *Darby* v. *Leonard* (1973) 107 I.L.T.R. 82.

[58] *Keenan Bros.* v. *C.I.E.* (1963) 97 I.L.T.R. 54.

[58a] See *Anton Piller K.G.* v. *Manufacturing Processes Ltd.* [1976] Ch. 55.

[58b] See *Mareva Compania Naviera S.A.* v. *International Bulkcarriers S.A.* [1975] 2 Lloyd's Rep. 509. The "Mareva" injunction has recently been recognised in Ireland, see *Fleming and Others* v. *Ranks (Ireland) Ltd* [1983] I.L.R.M. 541 (see *A Casebook on Equity and Trusts in Ireland* (1985), p. 149); *Powerscourt Estates* v. *Gallagher* [1984] I.L.R.M. 123.

[58c] See *American Cyanamid Co.* v. *Ethicon Ltd.* [1975] A.C. 396. See Gray, "Interlocutory Injunctions since *Cyanamid*" (1981) 40 C.L.J. 307.

[58d] This is subject to "special cases" where a "prima facie" case may still be required, *e.g.*, where no trial is likely to take place, see *Cayne* v. *Global Natural Resources plc* [1984] 1 All E.R. 225.

[58e] See *Campus Oil Ltd.* v. *Minister for Industry and Energy* [1983] I.R. 88 (see *A Casebook on Equity and Trusts in Ireland* (1985), p. 143); *Irish Shell Ltd.* v. *Elm Motors Ltd.* [1984] I.R. 200 (see *Ibid.*, p. 137). [59] S.27 (5).

injunction used by the Court of Chancery to restrain persons from enforcing a
judgment obtained in a common law court, when it was contrary to the
principles of equity. The "fusion" of the administration of the two systems of
law and equity by the 1877 Act itself rendered this remedy unnecessary.[60]
However, the court may still issue an injunction to restrain proceedings in a
foreign court or court of inferior jurisdiction.[61]

3.135. Like all equitable remedies, the granting of an injunction lies entirely
within the discretion of the court, which exercises this within the framework of
well-established rules.[62] Disobedience of an injunction is contempt of court,
the ultimate remedy for which is committal to prison.[63] Since the Chancery
Amendment Act, 1858, the court may grant damages in lieu of an injunction, if
it considers this to be the more appropriate remedy in the case.[64] Caution,
however, will be used to ensure that the more wealthy do not thereby buy
themselves out of trouble.

2. Scope

As already mentioned, the scope of the remedy is extremely wide. The
following is a brief list of the areas of law in which the remedy is most often
invoked and granted.[65] Many of these topics are discussed in greater detail
elsewhere in this book.

(i) Real Property

3.136. The injunction is frequently used to protect persons against invasions
of property rights. Thus an injunction may be granted to restrain trespass,[66]
waste[67] and nuisance.[68] It may also be granted to enforce easements and
profits,[69] restrictive covenants[70] and licences.[71]

(ii) Contract

3.137. An injunction can be an extremely useful remedy with respect to

---

[60] See para. 3.035, *ante.* Note the various provisions as to injunctions in the Judicature (N.I.) Act, 1978, e.g.,
ss. 18. (judicial review) and 24 (concerning public offices).

[61] *Lett* v. *Lett* [1906] 1 I.R. 618 (see *A Casebook on Equity and Trusts in Ireland* (1985), p. 14); see also *Re
Belfast Shipowners Co.* [1948] 1 I.R. 321 and *Lennon* v. *Ganly* [1981] I.L.R.M. 84.

[62] Para. 3.050, *ante. Att.-Gen.* v. *Newry No. 1 R.D.C.* [1933] N.I. 50; *Cullen* v. *Cullen* [1962] I.R. 268; *Cahill* v.
Irish Motor Traders Assoc. [1966] I.R. 430.

[63] *Smith-Barry* v. *Dawson* (1891) 27 L.R.Ir. 558; *Gore-Booth* v. *Gore-Booth* (1962) 96 I.L.T.R. 32; *Johnston*
v. *Moore* [1965] N.I. 128.

[64] As regards N.I. see now s. 92 of the Judicature (N.I.) Act, 1978. See *Doherty* v. *Allman* (1878) 3 App. Cas.
709; *Solomon* v. *Red Bank Restaurant Ltd.* [1938] I.R. 793; *Cullen* v. *Cullen* [1962] I.R. 268; *McGrath* v. *Munster
and Leinster Bank Ltd.* [1959] I.R. 313.

[65] See the discussion of the principles for granting injunctions in *Cullen* v. *Cullen* [1962] I.R. 268 at 285–9 (*per*
Kenny J.).

[66] Judicature (Ireland) Act, 1877, s. 28 (8). See *McErlane* v. *O'Neill* (1866) 17 Ir.Ch.R. 86; *Cullen* v. *Cullen*
[1962] I.R. 268; *W.* v. *Somers* [1983] I.R. 122.

[67] See para. 4.149, *post.* Judicature (Ireland) Act, 1877, s. 28 (3) (replaced in N.I. by s. 90 of the Judicature
(N.I.) Act 1978). *Doherty* v. *Allman* (1878) 3 App.Cas. 709; *Re Pigott's Trusts* [1919] 1 I.R. 23. See also
Fishmonger's Co. v. *Beresford* (1818) Beat. 607; *Dunsany* v *Dunne* (1864) 15 Ir.Ch.R. 278.

[68] *Radford* v. *Wexford Corporation* (1955) 89 I.L.T.R. 184; *Halpin* v. *Tara Mines Ltd.* (1976) Unrep.
(H.C.,R.I.) (1973 No. 1516P); *Malone* v. *Clogrennane Lime Co.* (1978) Unrep. (H.C.,R.I.) (1977 No. 1561P).

[69] Ch. 6, *post. Gaw* v. *C.I.E.* [1953] I.R. 232

[70] Ch. 19, *post. Craig* v. *Greer* [1899] 1 I.R. 258.

[71] *King* v. *David Allen & Sons* [1916] 2 A.C. 54. *Cf. Cullen* v. *Cullen* [1962] I.R. 268. See Ch. 20, *post.*

contracts imposing negative or restrictive obligations. We have just mentioned restrictive covenants relating to land. Other areas where similar situations arise are "restraint of trade" agreements in commercial affairs, though here the issue often involves difficult questions of public policy.[72] Furthermore, the courts will generally not issue injunctions in respect of contracts of *personal* service.[73]

(iii) Industrial Property

3.138. The courts have power to grant injunctions to protect industrial and commercial property like patents,[74] copyrights,[75] trade marks[76] and goodwill.[77] There had been much legislation passed to ensure the greater protection of several types of this property during this century.[78]

(iv) Associations

3.139. The injunction has come to play an important semi-public role in the law of associations, especially in restraining breaches of rules and regulations governing companies,[79] unincorporated associations,[80] clubs[81] and trade unions.[82]

(v) Tort

3.140. An injunction is frequently used in many areas of tort law, *e.g.*, libel.[83] In the Republic of Ireland it is also used to restrain picketing when there

---

[72] *Arclex Optical Co. Ltd.* v. *McMurray* [1958] Ir.Jur.Rep. 65; *Esso Petroleum Co.* v. *Fogarty* [1965] I.R. 531; *Irish Shell & B.P. Ltd.* v. *Ryan* [1966] I.R. 75; *Cahill* v. *Irish Motor Traders Association* [1966] I.R. 430; *Continental Oil Co. of Ireland Ltd.* v. *Moynihan* (1977) 111 I.L.T.R. 5; *E.C.I. European Chemicles Industries Ltd.* v. *Bell* [1981] I.L.R.M. 345; *Irish Shell Ltd.* v. *Elm Motors Ltd.* [1984] I.R. 200 (see *A Casebook on Equity and Trusts in Ireland* (1985), p. 136).

[73] See the leading English cases of *Lumley* v. *Wagner* (1852) 1 De G. M. & G. 604; *Wagner Bros. Pictures Inc.* v. *Nelson* [1937] 1 K.B. 209.

[74] *Baxter* v. *Combe* (1851) 3 Ir.Ch.R. 256; *Rawls* v. *Irish Tyre and Rubber Services Ltd.* [1960] I.R. 11. See also *Thomas Hunter Ltd.* v. *James Fox & Co. Ltd.* [1966] I.R. 520.

[75] *Hodges* v. *Welsh* (1840) 2 Ir.Eq.R. 266 (relating to copyright in Crawford and Dix's *Abridged Notes of Cases 1837–8*); *Turner* v. *Robinson* (1860) 10 Ir.Ch.R. 510; *Performing Right Society Ltd.* v. *Bray U.D.C.* (1930) I.R. 509; *McCormick* v. *Emerald Records Ltd.* (1972) 23 N.I.L.Q. 344. See also the Republic's Industrial and Commercial Property (Protection) Act, 1927. *Aston* v. *Independent Newspapers Ltd.* [1931] L.J.Ir. 14.

[76] *Jameson* v. *Dublin Distillers' Co.* [1900] 1 I.R. 43; *Dickson* v. *Dickson* [1909] 1 I.R. 185. See also *Foot* v. *Lea* (1851) 13 Ir.Eq.R. 484; *Kinahan* v. *Bolton* (1864) 15 Ir.Ch.R. 75; *C. & A. Modes* v. *C.&.A. (Waterford) Ltd.* [1976] I.R. 198 (see *A Casebook on Equity and Trusts in Ireland* (1985), p. 153; *Adidas* v. *O'Neill & Co. Ltd.* [1983] I.L.R.M. 112.

[77] *Independent Newspapers Ltd.* v. *Irish Press Ltd.* [1932] I.R. 615.

[78] See the Patents Act, 1964, and Patents (Amendment) Act, 1966 (R.I.); Patents Acts (N.I.), 1949 and 1957; Copyright Act, 1963 (R.I.); Copyright Act (N.I.), 1956 and Design Copyright Act (N.I.), 1968; Trade Marks Act, 1963 (R.I.) and Trade Marks Act, 1938 (U.K.). Also the Industrial and Commercial Property (Protection) Act, 1927 (R.I.). See *Performing Rights Society Ltd.* v. *Marlin Communal Aerials Ltd.* (1975) Unrep. (sup. Ct., R.I.).

[79] *Coubrough* v. *James Panton & Co Ltd.* [1965] I.R. 272.

[80] *Goggin* v. *Fenney* (1949) 83 I.L.T.R. 180.

[81] *Goggin* v. *Fenney, op. cit.*

[82] *Silver Tassie Ltd.* v. *O'Beirne* (1956) 90 I.L.T.R. 90, (1958) 92 I.L.T.R. 29; *Esplanade Pharmacy Ltd.* v. *Larkin* [1957] I.R. 285; *Corry* v. *National Union of Vintners* [1950] I.R. 315; *Roundabout Ltd.* v. *Beirne* [1959] I.R. 423; *Maher* v. *Beirne* (1959) 93 I.L.T.R. 101; *Ardmore Studios (Ireland) Ltd.* v. *Lynch* [1965] I.R. 1; *E.I. Co. Ltd.* v. *Kennedy* [1968] I.R. 69; *Crowley* v. *Cleary* [1968] I.R. 261; *Murtagh Properties* v. *Cleary* [1972] I.R. 330; *Becton, Dickinson & Co. Ltd.* v. *Lee* [1973] I.R. 13; *Crazy Prices (N.I.) Ltd.* v. *Hewitt* [1980] N.I. 151.

[83] *Sinclair* v. *Gogarty* [1937] I.R. 377.

is no "trade dispute" within the meaning of the Trade Disputes Act, 1906.[84] Picketing the premises of another person is a tort. In England recently much controversy has been aroused in respect of its use in the tort of intimidation, as that tort has been applied to trade unions.[85]

(vi) Public Law

3.141. Injunctions can also be invoked in the field of public law, *e.g.*, to ensure that local authorities abide by their bye-laws[86] or any other public body keeps within its statutory powers.[87]

B. SPECIFIC PERFORMANCE

3.142. At common law the remedy for a breach of contract was an action for damages. Yet in many cases this was an inadequate remedy for the aggrieved party and a decree of specific performance was equity's answer to his problem.[88] This is an order of the court requiring a party to a contract to carry it out according to its terms.[89]

3.143. Equity will not grant a decree if it considers that damages would be an adequate remedy in the particular case.[90] Further, under the Chancery Amendment Act, 1858, damages may be awarded by the court in lieu of specific performance.[91] As with all equitable remedies, the question whether to grant a decree lies entirely within the discretion of the court.[92] Thus the court will not grant a decree if the defendant could not possibly carry it out, *e.g.*, being unable to make title to property.[93] Similarly, a court will grant a decree only if it is sure that it will be effective[94] and can be enforced.[95] It follows from these principles that equity will order specific performance of certain types of contracts only. The following is a brief list of the main types.

---

[84] See cases cited in fn. 82, *supra*. Also *Esso Teoranta* v. *McGowan* [1974] I.R. 148; *Ellis* v. *Wright* [1976] I.R. 8; *Goulding Chemicals Ltd.* v. *Bolger* [1977] I.R. 211.

[85] *J. T. Stratford & Son Ltd.* v. *Lindley* [1965] A.C. 269; *Torquay Hotel Co. Ltd.* v. *Cousins* [1969] 2 W.L.R. 289. Cf., *Silver Tassie Ltd.* v. *O'Beirne*, *op. cit.*; *Corry* v. *National Union of Vintners*, *op. cit.*: *Reno Engrais et Produits Chemiques S.A.* v. *Irish Agricultural Wholesale Society Ltd.* (1976) Unrep. (H.C., R.I.) (1976 No. 1494P)

[86] Note also in this field the use of administrative orders like *certiorari, mandamus* or a declaration. *The State* v. *Dublin Corporation* [1953] I.R. 202; *Reg. (McKee)* v. *Belfast Corporation* [1954] N.I. 122.

[87] *Radford* v. *Wexford Corporation* (1955) 89 I.L.T.R. 184; *Transport Salaried Staffs' Assoc.* v. *C.I.E.* [1965] I.R. 180; *Campus Oil Ltd.* v. *Minister for Industry and Energy* [1983] I.R. 88 (see *A Casebook on Equity and Trusts in Ireland* (1985), p. 143) Cf. statutory powers given to private parties, *e.g.*, a mortgagee's power of sale, *Holohan* v. *Friends Provident and Century Life Office* [1966] I.R. 1. Para. 13.036, *post*.

[88] See *Harnett* v. *Yielding* (1805) 2 Sch. & Lef. 549, 553–4 (*per* Lord Redesdale); *Conlon* v. *Murray* [1958] N.I. 17 (see *A Casebook on Equity and Trusts in Ireland* (1985), p. 22).

[89] Except, of course, in respect of the time within which performance was to take place. Specific performance is considered in detail in *Irish Conveyancing Law* (1978), para. 12.36 *et seq*.

[90] *Bagnell* v. *Edwards* (1876) I.R. 10 Eq. 215 at 218 (*per* Chatterton V.-C.) (see *A Casebook on Equity and Trusts in Ireland* (1985), p. 157).

[91] *Murphy* v. *Harrington* [1927] I.R. 339; *Kelly* v. *Duffy* [1922] 1 I.R. 62. As to the time of assessment of damages, see *Vandeleur & Moore* v. *Dargan* [1981] I.L.R.M. 75; *O'Connor* v. *McCarthy* [1982] I.L.R.M.202 (see *A Casebook on Equity and Trusts in Ireland* (1985), p. 205). Cf. *Johnson* v. *Agnew* [1980] A.C. 367. See Ingram and Wakefield, "Equitable Damages under Lord Cairns Act" (1981) Conv. 286.   [92] Para. 3.050, *ante*.

[93] *Kelly* v. *Duffy* [1922] 1 I.R. 62. Cf. *Meara* v. *Meara* (1858) 8 Ir.Ch.R. 37; *Leitch* v. *Simpson* (1871) I.R. 5 Eq. 613.

[94] *Mortal* v. *Lyons* (1858) 8 Ir.Ch.R. 112; *Bagnell* v. *Edwards* (1876) I.R. 10 Eq. 215.

[95] *E.g.*, contracts of personal service will not be specifically enforced, *Gillis* v. *McGhee* (1861) 13 Ir.Ch.R. 48. Para. 3.067, *ante*.

1. *Contracts*

(i) Sale of Land

3.144. A contract for the sale of land is an obvious example of a contract whose breach would rarely be adequately compensated by damages. A particular piece of land usually has certain unique characteristics and it would often be extremely difficult to purchase with any damages awarded another piece of land exactly the same, or even with all the principal characteristics of the piece originally contracted for.[96] Either the vendor or the purchaser may bring this action. If the vendor succeeds, the purchaser is directed to complete the contract and, if he does not do so, the vendor may resell the property and recover any loss from the purchaser. If the purchaser succeeds, the vendor is ordered to complete the contract and, if he does not do so, the court orders the purchaser to lodge the purchase money in court and empowers another person to execute the conveyance in the name and on behalf of the vendor under the Trustee Act.[97]

(ii) Chattels

3.145. Generally contracts relating to chattels are not specifically enforced.[98] unless the chattel in question has some rare or unique value.[99] However, the Sale of Goods Act, 1893, gives the court a discretion to order specific performance of a contract to deliver specific or ascertained goods.[1]

(iii) Building Contracts

3.146. It is now settled that the courts will grant specific performance of building contracts, though there were doubts at one time about the difficulty of supervising the performance of such contracts.[2]

(iv) Separation Deeds

3.147. It was held by the House of Lords that an agreement regulating the position of a husband and wife who have separated will be specifically enforced.[3]

---

[96] *Hughes Dixon & Co. Ltd.* v. *Bernard Hughes Ltd.* [1924] 1 I.R. 113; *Barclays Bank Ltd.* v. *Breen* (1962) 96 I.L.T.R. 179; *Heneghan* v. *Davitt* [1933] I.R. 375; *Sheridan* v. *Higgins* [1971] I.R. 291; *Kennedy* v. *Wrenne* [1981] I.L.R.M. 81; *Tiernan Homes Ltd.* v. *Sheridan* [1981] I.L.R.M. 191. See generally *Irish Conveyancing Law* (1978), para. 12.36 *et seq.*

[97] Trustee Act, 1893, s. 33 (R.I.); Trustee Act (N.I.), 1958, s. 50. See *Moorhead* v. *Kirkwood* [1919] 1 I.R. 225. The court may also make a vesting order in relation to the land, 1893 Act, s. 31; 1958 Act (N.I.), s. 48. See *Re Ruthven* [1906] 1 I.R. 236. See also Harpum, "Specific Performance with Compensation as a Purchaser's Remedy —A Study in Contract and Equity" (1981) 40 C.L.J. 47.

[98] *Buckley* v. *Irwin* [1960] N.I. 98, espec. at 105 (*per* McVeigh J.) (sale of farm together with chattels).

[99] *Falcke* v. *Gray* (1859) 4 Drew. 651. *Cf.* specific restitution in respect of valuable chattels, *Pusey* v. *Pusey* (1684) 1 Vern. 273.

[1] S. 52. In N.I. s. 52 of the 1893 Act has been replaced by s. 52 of the Sale of Goods Act 1979. *Cf.* s. 125 of the English Housing Act, 1974 (relating to a landlord's repairing convenants), fn. 5, para. 3.148, *infra.*

[2] *Rushbrooke* v. *O'Sullivan* [1908] 1 I.R. 232 (see *A Casebook on Equity and Trusts in Ireland* (1985), p. 165); see also *Todd & Co.* v. *M. &. G.W. Rly.* (1881) 9 L.R.Ir. 85; *Armstrong* v. *Courtenay* (1863) 15 Ir.Ch.R. 138; *Bernard* v. *Meara* (1861) 12 Ir.Ch.R. 389. *Cf. Price* v. *Strange* [1978] Ch. 337.

[3] *Wilson* v. *Wilson* (1848) 1 H.L.C. 538.

(v) Partnership Agreements

3.148. The courts will in certain circumstances specifically enforce partnership agreements, provided damages would not be an adequate remedy.[4]

It will be observed, then, that specific performance is a remedy of much narrower scope than an injunction. Indeed, there are a large number of other restrictions still to be mentioned, or "defences" as they are usually described.[5] One obvious restriction is, of course, that equity will not specifically enforce a contract unsupported by consideration—"equity will not assist a volunteer."[6]

2. Defences

The following is a summary of the main defences which can be raised against an application for a decree of specific performance.

(i) Lack of Formalities

3.149. It may be argued that there is no binding contract in existence to be specifically enforced, because some formality necessary for an enforceable contract does not exist. For example, it may be that there has been no offer and acceptance,[7] or that no writing, or other formality required by statute,[8] exists.[9] However, the courts will not allow a statute to be used as an instrument of fraud[10] and so will decree specific performance despite the absence of statutory formalities, provided there has been *part performance* of a contract for the sale of land[11] by the plaintiff.[12] The acts relied upon must be such as to indicate unequivocally the existence of a contract between the parties. In *Lowry* v. *Reid*,[13] Andrews L.J. stated that:

> "[T]he true principle of the operation of the acts of part performance seems only to require that the acts in question be such as must be referred to some contract, and may be referred to the alleged one; that they prove

---

[4] *Cf. Bagnell* v. *Edwards* (1876) I.R. 10 Eq. 215 and *Crowley* v. *O'Sullivan* [1900] 2 I.R. 478.

[5] Note, however, the sweeping statutory provision contained in s. 125 of the English Housing Act, 1974.

[6] Para. 9.040, *post.*

[7] *Swan* v. *Miller* [1919] 1 I.R. 151; *O'Fay* v. *Burke* (1858) 8 Ir.Ch.R. 225 and 511.

[8] *E.g.*, Statute of Frauds (Ir.), 1695, s. 2; Deasy's Act, 1860, s. 4. The need for writing has been abolished in Northern Ireland except in respect of contracts for the sale of land and of guarantee, see Law Reform (Miscellaneous Provisions) Act (N.I.), 1954, ss. 1 and 2. As to s. 2 of the 1695 Statute, see *Boyce* v. *Green* (1826) Batty 608; *Norris* v. *Cooke* (1857) 7 I.C.L.R. 37; *Stinson* v. *Owens* (1973) 24 N.I.L.Q. 218; *Black* v. *Kavanagh* (1974) 108 I.L.T.R. 91. Note also the voluminous case law on both sides of the Irish Sea dealing with "subject to contract" arrangements, admirably surveyed by Keane J, in *Mulhall* v. *Haren* [1981] I.R. 364 (see *A Casebook on Equity and Trusts in Ireland* (1985), p. 167). See also *Irish Conveyancing Law* (1978), para. 9.072 *et seq.*; Clark, "Subject to Contract" [1984] Conv. 173 and 251.

[9] Paras. 9.021–5, *post Cf.* consent required under the Republic's Family Home Protection Act 1976, as to which see *Irish Conveyancing Law* (1978), para. 6.31 *et seq.*; Shatter, *Family Law in the Republic of Ireland* (2nd ed., 1981), p. 317 *et seq.*　　　　　　　　　　[10] Para. 3.048, *ante.*

[11] The limitation of the doctrine to such contracts has been queried, see *Crowley* v. *O'Sullivan* [1900] 2 I.R. 478, especially Palles C.B. at pp. 488–92.

[12] *Devine* v. *Fields* (1920) 54 I.L.T.R. 101; *Clinan* v. *Cooke* (1802) 1 Sch. & Lef. 22. See Thompson, "The Role of Evidence in Part Performance" (1979) Conv. 402.

[13] [1927] N.I. 142 (see *A Casebook on Equity and Trusts in Ireland* (1985), p. 184). See also *Hoon* v. *Nolan* (1967) 101 I.L.T.R. 99; *Glasgow Friendly Soc.* v. *Gilpin Ltd.* (1971) 22 N.I.L.Q. 196.

the existence of some contract and are consistent with the contract alleged."[14]

(ii) Uncertainty

A contract will not be specifically enforced if any essential terms have been left vague or uncertain.[15]

(iii) Incompleteness

3.150. Similarly, there will be no specific performance decree of a contract of which there must be a note or memorandum in writing, if the note or memorandum does not contain all the essential terms of the agreement. Thus the contract should identify clearly the parties,[16] specify the subject-matter[17] and price in the case of a sale,[18] and any other special terms agreed. In *Wyse* v. *Russell*[19] specific performance of an agreement for a lease was refused because the agreement did not specify when the lease was to commence. Failure of the plaintiff to carry out a condition of the contract, *e.g.*, payment of a deposit in cash, will also deprive him of a decree in his favour.[20]

(iv) Want of Fairness

3.151. In this context unfairness must be distinguished from conduct amounting to fraud. Fraud is a ground for invoking a separate equitable remedy, rescission,[21] whereas unfairness is something less than fraud and is a defence to an application for specific performance. In *Conlon* v. *Murray*,[22] Black L.J. put the matter thus:

"And it is well established that there is a class of cases in which a contract may be such and entered into in such conditions that the court will not order it to be rescinded but, at the same time, looking to the substantial justice of the case, will not order it to be specifically performed. It follows naturally . . . that when the aid of a court is sought by way of specific performance of a contract the principles of ethics have a more extensive sway than when a contract is sought to be rescinded. . . .

It was argued on behalf of the plaintiff that cases in which equity refuses the remedy of specific performance fall within one or other of certain

---

[14] *Ibid.*, pp. 159–60. *Cf.* Moore L.C.J. at p. 151. *Mackay* v. *Jones* (1959) 93 I.L.T.R. 177; *Murphy* v. *Harrington* [1927] I.R. 339. Part performance has been reconsidered recently by the House of Lords in *Steadman* v. *Steadman* [1974] 2 All E.R. 977. See Wallace, "Part-Performance Re-Examined" (1974) 25 N.I.L.Q. 453.

[15] *Williams* v. *Kenneally* (1912) 46 I.L.T.R. 292; *Lonergan* v. *McCartney* [1983] N.I. 129.

[16] *McMeekin* v. *Stevenson* [1917] 1 I.R. 348.

[17] *Ibid.*

[18] *Nolan* v. *Graves* [1946] I.R. 376 (see *A Casebook on Equity and Trusts in Ireland* (1985), p. 287).

[19] (1882) 11 L.R.Ir. 173, followed in *O'Flaherty* v. *Arvan Properties Ltd* (1977) Unrep. (Sup. Ct., R.I.) (211–1976). See also *Phelan* v. *Tedcastle* (1885) 15 L.R.Ir. 169; *White* v. *McMahon* (1886) 18 L.R.Ir. 460; *Erskine* v. *Armstrong* (1887) 20 L.R.Ir. 296; *Kerns* v. *Manning* [1935] I.R. 869; *McQuaid* v. *Lynam* [1965] I.R. 564; *Hoon* v. *Nolan* (1967) 101 I.L.T.R. 99.

[20] *Morrow* v. *Carty* [1957] N.I. 174.

[21] See Para. 3.157, *post*.

[22] [1958] N.I. 17 (see *A Casebook on Equity and Trusts in Ireland* (1985), p. 22). See also *Buckley* v. *Irwin* [1960] N.I. 98.

defined categories. I cannot accept this view. Certainly equity acts on certain broad and ascertained principles but it has always refused to be forced into rigid categories."[23]

Connected with the defence of unfairness is what is sometimes classified as a separate defence, namely, hardship. In this context this means some special hardship which would result from specific performance of the contract.[24]

(v) Want of Mutuality

3.152. The theory here is reasonably clear—if specific performance is to be granted it must be mutual and available to both parties. If one party cannot enforce the contract, *e.g.*, for the lack of capacity, he cannot have it specifically enforced against him. However, the scope of this defence has become obscure because the courts have recognised a large number of exceptions to it. For example, where one person only signs the memorandum in writing required by the Statute of Frauds (Ireland), 1695, for a contract for the sale of land, specific performance will be decreed against him, though not against a party not signing, for the party who has not signed makes the remedy mutual by bringing the action.[25]

(vi) Illegality

3.153. Illegality is a defence to any method of enforcing a contract vitiated by such an element, *e.g.*, in restraint of trade[26] or requiring commission of fraud.[27]

(vii) Laches

3.154. As with all equitable remedies, the court may refuse a decree of specific performance because the plaintiff has been guilty of *laches*.[28] It is entirely a matter for the court whether there has been too much delay by the plaintiff in bringing proceedings.[29]

(viii) Misdescription

3.155. Where a substantial misdescription occurs in the contract, the court will usually refuse specific performance and may, indeed, grant instead

---

[23] *Ibid.*, 25–6. *Cf. White* v. *McCooey* (1976) Unrep. (H.C., R.I.) (1973 No. 1412P) (plea of drunkenness); *Smelter Corporation of Ireland Ltd.* v. *O'Driscoll* [1977] I.R. 305 (misrepresentation by defendant).

[24] See the discussion in *Roberts* v. *O'Neill* [1983] I.R. 47 (see *A Casebook on Equity and Trusts in Ireland* (1985), p. 193). See also *Pegler* v. *White* (1864) 33 Beav. 403; *Adams* v. *Weare* (1784) 1 Bro. C.C. 567.

[25] *Lord Ormond* v. *Anderson* (1813) 2 Ba. & B. 363 at 370–1 (*per* Lord Manners L.C.). *Cf. Doherty* v. *Waterford and Limerick Rly. Co.* (1850) 13 Ir.Eq.R. 538 at 543 (*per* Brady L.C.). In *Price* v. *Strange* [1978] Ch. 337, the English Court of Appeal held that the relevant time for considering the issue of mutuality is not the date of the contract but the date of the trial. See also *Sutton* v. *Sutton* [1984] Ch. 184.

[26] *Mulligan* v. *Corr* [1925] 1 I.R. 169.

[27] *Harnett* v. *Yielding* (1805) 2 Sch. & Lef. 549 at 554 (*per* Lord Redesdale). See also *Starting Securities Ltd.* v. *Woods* (1977) Unrep. (H.C., R.I.) (1975 No. 4044P) (fraud on Revenue Commissioners).

[28] See para. 3.066, *ante*. See also *Guardian Builders Ltd* v. *Kelly* [1981] I.L.R.M. 127.

[29] *Crofton* v. *Ormsby* (1806) 2 Sch. & Lef. 583 at 603–4 (*per* Lord Redesdale); *Guerin* v. *Heffernan* [1925] 1 I.R. 57; *Gibson* v. *Butler* (1965) 99 I.L.T.R. 116.

rescission.[30] In fact, often the person suffering from the misdescription can elect either to have the contract rescinded or to carry on with the contract subject to abatement of the purchase price as compensation.[31] The compensation is based upon the difference in value between what was agreed and described in the contract and what is actually received by the purchaser.[32] Compensation will be received only where the misdescription was part of the contract terms.[33] None will be received in respect of defects of which the purchaser should have been aware or have made himself aware.[34]

(ix) Want of Title

3.156. An example in conveyancing of what really amounts to misdescription is another defence known as "want of title," *i.e.,* the vendor cannot obtain a decree of specific performance against the purchaser if he, the vendor, cannot show a good title. Should it occur that the vendor cannot show the title agreed upon to be conveyed, the purchaser may rescind.[35] However, if the purchaser does not repudiate the contract and the vendor can later show the title agreed or one as beneficial, even if only a possessory title, the purchaser may not subsequently be able to resist specific performance.[36]

C. RESCISSION

3.157. In certain circumstances equity will order rescission of a transaction, *i.e.,* that it be set aside.[36a] There are several grounds upon which equity will so avoid a transaction.

1. *Grounds*

(i) Fraud

Equity exercises a general jurisdiction over fraudulent conduct[37] and, like undue influence,[38] this is one of the principal grounds for rescission of a transaction.[39]

---

[30] See para. 3.157, *infra. McMahon* v. *Gaffney* [1930] I.R. 576; *Musgrave* v. *McCullagh* (1864) 14 Ir.Ch.R. 496; *Molphy* v. *Coyne* (1919) 53 I.L.T.R. 177; *Smyth* v. *Lynn* [1951] N.I. 69; *Peilow* v. *O'Carroll* (1972) 106 I.L.T.R. 29 (see *A Casebook on Equity and Trusts in Ireland* (1985), p. 247); *Smelter Corporation of Ireland Ltd.* v. *O'Driscoll* [1977] I.R. 305.

[31] *Leslie* v. *Crommelin* (1867) I.R. 2 Eq. 134.

[32] *Connor* v. *Potts* [1897] 1 I.R. 534; *Perrin* v. *Roe* (1889) 25 L.R.Ir. 37; *Connolly* v. *Keatinge (No. 2)* [1903] 1 I.R. 356.

[33] *Smith* v. *Lynn* [1951] N.I. 69 at 75–8 (*per* Curran J.). See, however, the Misrepresentation Act (N.I.), 1967, with respect to innocent misrepresentation inducing the entering into a contract.

[34] *Re Somerville's Estate* [1895] 1 I.R. 460; *Clements* v. *Conroy* [1911] 2 I.R. 500.

[35] *Maconchy* v. *Clayton* [1898] 1 I.R. 291; *Kelly* v. *Duffy* (1922) 1 I.R. 62. *Cf. McGirr* v. *Devine* [1925] N.I. 94; *McMahon* v. *Gaffney* [1930] I.R. 576; *Mills* v. *Healy* [1937] I.R. 437. See also *United Yeast Co. Ltd.,* v. *Cameo Investments Ltd.* (1977) 111 I.L.T.R. 13 (see *A Casebook on Equity and Trusts in Ireland* (1985), p. 198).

[36] *Ashe* v. *Hogan* [1920] 1 I.R. 159; *Clibborn* v. *Horan* [1921] 1 I.R. 93.

[36a] Rescission is considered in detail in *Irish Conveyancing Law* (1978), para. 12.56 *et. seq.*

[37] See Sheridan, *Fraud in Equity* (1957). Also *National Bank Ltd.* v. *O'Connor* (1969) 103 I.L.T.R. 73; *Northern Bank Finance Corporation Ltd* v. *Charlton* [1979] I.R. 149 (see *A Casebook on Equity and Trusts in Ireland* (1985), p. 210).

[38] See para. 9.075, *post.*

[39] *Carbin* v. *Somerville* [1933] I.R. 276; *Maguire* v. *Conway* [1950] I.R. 44; *Smyth* v. *Lynn* [1951] N.I. 69. *Cf. Hogan* v. *Healy* (1876) I.R. 11 C.L. 119.

(ii) Innocent Misrepresentation

3.158. At common law, an innocent misrepresentation in a term of a contract which amounted to a condition gave the aggrieved party the right to rescind or to sue for damages (but not to do both). If the misrepresentation amounted to a warranty only, there was only an action for damages available. Equity widened relief by granting rescission where the aggrieved party could prove that there was a misrepresentation as to some material fact inducing him to enter into the contract.[40] However, the rule in *Seddon* v. *North Eastern Salt Co. Ltd.*[41] specified that there would be no rescission in equity if the contract had been performed. This rule was doubted in some English cases,[42] but it has been followed in Ireland.[43]

In Northern Ireland, the Misrepresentation Act (N.I.), 1967, provides that the fact that a contract has been accepted or performed is not a bar to rescission. The remedy is now generally available for innocent misrepresentation and the court may award damages in lieu of rescission wherever it thinks this equitable. In the Republic of Ireland this is now the position under section 45 of the Sale of Goods and Supply of Services Act, 1980, but only, under section 43, in respect of contracts for the sale of goods, hire purchase agreements and contracts for the letting of goods and supply of services.[43a]

(iii) Mistake

3.159. At common Law, a contract may be *void*, as opposed to *voidable*, on the ground of a mistake going to the root of the contract and resulting from the fact that the parties were never *ad idem*.[44] In such a case a contract has never come into existence; it is void *ab initio*. In equity, however, a contract not vitiated by any such basic mistake may nevertheless be *voidable* for mistake, *i.e.*, some mistake has occurred which gives at least one of the parties the right to have it avoided.[45] Here the contract remains valid until so avoided; it is not void *ab initio*.

(iv) Non-Disclosure

3.160. Rescission may be granted in equity on the ground of non-disclosure of facts or information in contracts *uberrimae fidei* (of the utmost good faith).

---

[40] *Redgrave* v. *Hurd* (1881) 20 Ch.D. 1. See also *Peilow* v. *O'Connor* [1972] 106 I.L.T.R. 29 (see *A Casebook on Equity and Trusts in Ireland* (1985), p. 247; *Gahan* v. *Boland* (1984) Unrep. (Sup. Ct., R.I.) (37–1983) (*ibid.*, p. 267).   [41] [1905] 1 Ch. 326.
[42] *Solle* v. *Butcher* [1950] 1 K.B. 671, especially at 695 (*per* Denning L.J.); *Leaf* v. *International Galleries* [1950] 2 K.B. 86 at 90 (*per* Denning L.J.). *Cf. Long* v. *Lloyd* [1958] 1 W.L.R. 753 and *Senanayake* v. *Cheng* [1966] A.C. 63. See also *Western Potato Co-operative Ltd.* v. *Durnan* [1985] I.L.R.M. 5.
[43] *Lecky* v. *Walter* [1914] 1 I.R. 378 (see *A Casebook on Equity and Trusts in Ireland* (1985), p. 245).
[43a] See Hannigan and Schuster, "Contractual and Statutory Remedies for Misrepresentation" (1982) 76 Gaz. I.L.S.I. 40.
[44] *J.L. Smallman Ltd.* v. *O'Moore* [1959] I.R. 220. See also *W.* v. *W.* (1978) Unrep. (H.C., R.I.) (1977 No. 2648P); *Dore* v. *Stephenson* (1980) Unrep. (H.C., R.I.) (Cir. App.).
[45] *Cooper* v. *Phibbs* (1867) L.R. 2 H.L. 149; *Gun* v. *McCarthy* (1883) 13 L.R.Ir. 304 (see *A Casebook on Equity and Trusts in Ireland* (1985), p. 268); *Dickie* v. *White* (1901) 1 N.I.J.R. 128; *Monaghan C.C.* v. *Vaughan* [1948] I.R. 306 (see *ibid.*, p. 274); *Nolan* v. *Nolan* (1958) 92 I.L.T.R. 94; *Coleman* v. *Fry* (1873) I.R. 7 C.L. 247; *National Bank Ltd.* v. *O'Connor* (1969) 103 I.L.T.R. 73.

These are contracts regarded in equity as requiring the utmost good faith on the part of one party, largely because he has special knowledge of facts important to that contract. The obvious example is a contract of insurance where the insurer bases his part of the agreement, and calculates the risks he takes, very much upon facts and information supplied by the prospective insured.[46]

2. *Cancellation*

3.161. It used to be common where equity granted rescission for the court, in addition, to order the document in question to be delivered up to the court and cancelled. Thus in *Gun* v. *McCarthy*,[47] where a lessor made a mistake in the rent in a lease he offered to the lessee, the lessor obtained rescission and the court ordered the lease to be delivered up and cancelled. The theory here was that this would safeguard the plaintiff in equity by preventing the document being pleaded in evidence in any subsequent action at law. Since the Judicature (Ireland) Act, 1877, there is no possibility of this happening in view of the fusion of the administration of law and equity in the courts.[48] Since that Act there is really no need for cancellation in this sort of case, though it has been done, as *Gun* v. *McCarthy* itself indicates.

D. RECTIFICATION

3.162. Equity will in certain circumstances order rectification of legal documents to make them conform with what was actually agreed between the parties. It is important to be clear about the basis of equity's jurisdiction here. Equity does not purport to interfere with what the parties agreed, it merely alters the written manifestation of that agreement to make sure that it reflects the agreed terms precisely and accurately. Ball C. put the matter thus:

> "The jurisdiction of a Court of Equity to reform a settlement, in which it is established by evidence that error or mistake has occurred, is undoubted. Parol evidence will suffice, but it is obvious that when the claim for relief rests upon testimony exclusively, and is not supported by any written record of the intention of the parties, especially should time have elapsed since the deed was executed, much vigilance and caution are required on the part of the tribunal which is called upon to exercise the jurisdiction. Still if, after due deliberation, it arrives at the conclusion that the actual contract which was made between the parties differs from that expressed in the instrument, it is, in my judgment, as much bound to act as in any other case depending upon testimony."[49]

Sullivan M.R.[50] listed three classes of case where equity granted rectification:

---

[46] See *Chariot Inns Ltd.* v. *Assicurazioni Generali* [1981] I.R. 199. Also *McMillan* v. *Carey* (1978) Unrep. (H.C., R.I.) (1978 No. 4122P); *Mackender* v. *Feldia A.G.* [1967] 2 Q.B. 590.

[47] (1883) 13 L.R.Ir. 304 (see *A Casebook on Equity and Trusts in Ireland* (1985), p. 268). See also *Field* v. *Boland* (1837) 1 Dr. & Wal. 37.

[48] Para. 3.035, *ante*.

[49] *McCormack* v. *McCormack* (1877) 1 L.R.Ir. 119, 124 (see *A Casebook on Equity and Trusts in Ireland* (1985), p. 271). Bromley, "Rectification in Equity" (1971) 87 L.Q.R. 532.

[50] *Maunsell* v. *Maunsell* (1877) 1 L.R.Ir. 529, 539–40. See also *Rooney & McParland Ltd.* v. *Carlin* [1981] N.I. 138.

(1) mutual mistake in settlements; (2) improper drafting of a settlement in his own favour by a person having a confidential relationship with the settlor; (3) a grantor not knowing the precise effect of a voluntary deed and not authorising the precise detailed drafting.

3.163. It is settled that a voluntary deed will be rectified, even after the death of the donor, provided it is proved the deed did not conform with his intentions.[51] However, rectification will not be granted against a *bona fide* purchaser for value without notice.[52]

3.164. Perhaps the most common case for rectification is where both parties have made a mutual mistake.[53] There will be no relief where one party only claims that the contract has not turned out as he expected.[54] However, Irish courts have granted relief by rectification in cases where one party made a mistake about a particular term in the contract and the other, being aware of his mistake, took advantage of it.[55] It is arguable, however, that this sort of case would be better treated as a case for rescission on the ground of misrepresentation.[56] Often the court grants rectification on the basis of correcting an error on the face of the document in question.[57] Often this is largely a matter of construction of the document, sometimes of the document alone.[58] A document may even be rectified to conform with an earlier agreement, even though there is nothing to connect them positively, provided there is no positive evidence that any other prior agreement was made.[59]

3.165. It is settled that the courts will admit oral evidence to contradict a written document in order to prevent fraud or a mistake and, in the end, to do what is just and equitable.[60] There were some doubts expressed as to whether the memorandum in writing required, by the Statute of Frauds, for a contract for the sale of land could be so rectified. In England, however, it was settled in *Craddock Bros.* v. *Hunt*[61] that a written contract, followed by a conveyance conforming with its terms, could be rectified to conform with an earlier oral agreement, and the conveyance rectified similarly. This was followed in Ireland in *Nolan* v. *Graves.*[62] It was also doubted whether there could be rectification where a contract failed to take effect because it was created by deed and was

---

[51] *McMechan* v. *Warburton* [1896] 1 I.R. 435.

[52] *Alexander* v. *Crosbie* (1835) Ll. & G. *temp.* Sug. 145 at 149; *Alexander* v. *Crosbie* (1844) 7 Ir.Eq.R. 445; *Mortimer* v. *Shortall* (1842) 2 Dr. & War. 363; *Coates* v. *Kenna* (1872) I.R. 7 Eq. 113.

[53] *Collen Bros* v. *Dublin C.C.* [1908] 1 I.R. 503.

[54] *Jackson* v. *Stopford* [1923] 2 I.R.1.

[55] *Monaghan C.C.* v. *Vaughan* [1948] I.R. 306, especially at 312 (*per* Dixon J.) (see *A Casebook on Equity and Trusts in Ireland* (1985), p. 274); *Nolan* v. *Nolan* (1958) 92 I.L.T.R. 94 at 99 (Dixon J.). See also the English cases, *Garrard* v. *Frankel* (1862) 30 Beav. 445; *Harris* v. *Pepperell* (1867) L.R. 5 Eq. 1; *Paget* v. *Marshall* (1884) 28 Ch.D. 255; *Roberts & Co. Ltd.* v. *Leicestershire C.C.* [1961] Ch. 555.

[56] *Gun* v. *McCarthy* (1884) 13 L.R.Ir. 304 (see *A Casebook on Equity and Trusts in Ireland* (1985), p. 268). *Cf. May* v. *Platt* [1900] 1 Ch. 616; *Solle* v. *Butcher* [1950] 1 K.B. 671.

[57] *Annesley* v. *Annesley* (1893) 31 L.R.Ir. 457; see also *Burrowes* v. *Delaney* (1889) 24 L.R.Ir. 503.

[58] *Fitzgerald* v. *Fitzgerald* [1902] 1 I.R. 477 (see *A Casebook on Equity and Trusts in Ireland* (1985), p. 279); *Averall* v. *Wade* (1835) Ll. & G. *temp.* Sug. 252 at 260–1; *Re Davis's Estate* [1912] 1 I.R. 516; *Ex parte Rice* (1896) 30 I.L.T.R. 57. *Cf. Re Adams's Estate* [1965] I.R. 57.

[59] *King* v. *King-Harman* (1873) I.R. 7 Eq. 446 (see *A Casebook on Equity and Trusts in Ireland* (1985), p. 282).

[60] *McCormack* v. *McCormack* (1877) 1 L.R.Ir. 119 (see *ibid.*, p. 271).

[61] [1923] 2 Ch. 136.

[62] [1946] I.R. 376 (see *ibid.*, p. 287).

followed by a contract by deed misstating the terms of the earlier contract, and then by a conveyance conforming with the second deed.[63] However, the view more generally accepted in both Ireland[64] and England[65] now seems to be that equity will rectify in these situations so as to make the rectified deed the deed of the parties from the date of its execution.

E. APPOINTMENT OF A RECEIVER

3.166. A receiver is a person appointed to preserve property which may be disposed of or seized because of insolvency or litigation or any other matter.[66] It is also common to have receivership used as a method of equitable execution, *i.e.,* to take control over assets which could not be seized at common law in satisfaction of a debt.[67] Thus in the Republic of Ireland it has been held that a public service pension may be taken in equitable execution.[68]

3.167. The receiver's general duty is to preserve the property and collect any income coming from it and to pay this to those entitled. It is important to note that he is not necessarily a manager of the property, so he may not have authority to run a business over which he has been appointed receiver. The modern practice, however, is to appoint a person as receiver and manager or to give a receiver power to carry on the business. In this case, if a receiver is appointed, the business ceases as a going concern, its assets are realised, its debts paid and anything left over is paid by the receiver to those entitled to the surplus.[69]

3.168. A receiver may be appointed either by a party entitled to appoint receivers or by the court.[70] Thus a mortgage deed[71] or debenture deed will usually confer such an express power on the mortgagee or the debenture holders.[72] There are various statutes conferring such a power, *e.g.,* on mortgagees.[73] Where a receiver is appointed by the court, he is an officer of the court and any interference with him in carrying out his duties is contempt of court.

V. EQUITABLE INTERESTS IN LAND

3.169. The result of the exercise of equitable jurisdiction over the centuries has

---

[63] See the English cases of *Mackenzie* v. *Coulson* (1869) L.R. 8 Eq. 368, 375 (*per* James V.-C); *Higgins Ltd.* v. *Northampton Corp.* [1927] 1 Ch. 128.

[64] *Collen Bros.* v. *Dublin C.C.* [1908] 1 I.R. 503; *Re Ottley's Estate* [1910] 1 I.R. 1; *Monaghan C.C.* v. *Vaughan* [1948] I.R. 306 (see *A Casebook on Equity and Trusts in Ireland* (1985), p.274).

[65] *Hall-Dare* v. *Hall-Dare* (1885) 31 Ch.D. 251; *Faraday* v. *Tamworth Union* (1916) 86 L.J.Ch. 436; *Carlton Contractors Ltd.* v. *Bexley Corp.* (1962) 60 L.G.R. 331.

[66] See *Commissioners of Church Temporalities* v. *Harrington* (1883) 11 L.R.Ir. 127; *Garrahan* v. *Garrahan* [1959] I.R. 168.

[67] *Glorney Ltd.* v. *O'Byrne* (1951) 85 I.L.T.R. 19.

[68] *Higgins* v. *Higgins* [1951] Ir.Jur.Rep. 29; *Garrahan* v. *Garrahan* [1959] I.R. 168.

[69] *Kernohan Estates Ltd.* v. *Boyd* [1967] N.I. 27.

[70] *Kenealy* v. *O'Keeffe* (1900) 34 I.L.T.R. 75; *McCausland* v. *O'Callaghan* (1903) 3 N.I.J.R. 144; *Langdale Chemical Manure Co.* v. *Ginty* (1907) 41 I.L.T.R. 40.

[71] See ch. 13, *post.*

[72] *Ardmore Studios (Ireland) Ltd.* v. *Lynch* [1965] I.R. 1; *Kernohan Estates Ltd.* v. *Boyd* [1967] N.I. 27; *Industrial Development Authority* v. *Moran* [1978] I.R. 159 (see *A Casebook on Irish Land Law* (1984), p. 419).

[73] Conveyancing Act, 1881, ss. 19 (1) and 24; Conveyancing Act, 1911, s. 3 (1) and (11). Ch. 13, *post.*

been the evolution of several interests in land owing their recognition entirely to equity. Nowadays these interests exist alongside the interests recognised by the common law and, since the Judicature (Ireland) Act, 1877, they must be enforced equally by all the superior courts. It is proposed in the next few pages to list briefly the main creatures of equity in this sense. Each of them will be discussed in much greater detail in the later chapters of this book.

A. TRUSTS

3.170. It was related earlier in this chapter that the Statute of Uses (Ireland), 1634, failed to abolish "uses" for a variety of reasons.[74] In England, much controversy revolved around its Statute of Uses of 1535, and its effect on a "use upon a use."[75] It was clear that the 1535 Statute, like its later Irish counterpart, executed the first use only, but the question remained as to what was the effect of the second use. It was held in *Jane Tyrrel's Case*[76] that the second use was void and no interest was taken by the person in whose favour the second use was created. This position was, however, gradually abandoned by the courts in England. The traditional view is that the new position was firmly established by *Sambach* v. *Dalston*,[77] by coincidence decided about 1634, the same date as the Irish Statute of Uses. It is, however, probably more accurate to say that this case reflected a pattern of decisions that had begun to emerge in England since the end of the sixteenth century.[78] For our purposes, the point to note is that by the time the Irish Statute of Uses was passed it was settled in England that a use upon a use would be recognised and enforced. Since Irish courts followed the English courts at this period in the application of general equitable principles, the development of the modern trust was never really put in doubt by the Statute of Uses in Ireland. The pre-Statute of Uses position of putting property to uses, or trusts as they now came to be called,[79] could be simply preserved by conveying land in the form "to X and his heirs to the use of A and his heirs to the use of [or in trust for] B and his heirs." The Statute executed the first use so as to give A the legal fee simple, X dropping out of the picture, and A had to hold the land in trust for B who took an equitable fee simple. This device led Lord Hardwicke to remark that "by this means a statute made upon great consideration, introduced in a solemn and pompous manner, by this strict construction, has had no other effect than to add, at most, three words to a conveyance."[80]

3.171. From these developments grew the modern law of trusts.[81] Uses were invented for the evasion of feudal dues attaching to land, but modern trusts can

---

[74] Para. 3.021, *ante.*
[75] Para. 3.019. *ante.*
[76] (1557) 2 Dyer 155a. Para. 3.024, *ante.*
[77] (1634) Tothill 168.
[78] See Simpson, *Introduction to the History of Land Law* (1961), pp. 190–1; Barton (1966) 82 L.Q.R. 215; Strathdene (1958) 74 L.Q.R. 550; Yale (1957) C.L.J. 72.
[79] Note that the Statute itself used the word "trust" in the expression "use, confidence or trust," see para. 3,021, *ante.*
[80] *Hopkins* v. *Hopkins* (1738) 1 Atk. 581, 591. Mathematics were evidently not the Lord Chancellor's strong point!
[81] See chs. 9 and 10, *post.*

cover any type of property and, therefore, play a vital role in avoiding the wide-ranging taxation systems of today. So far as land law is concerned, they enabled conveyancers to create a complex system of equitable estates and interests in land to co-exist alongside the system recognised at common law. In this respect, the trust was by far the greatest and most productive factor in creating equitable interests in land.

B. MORTGAGES

3.172. Equity has played a major role in the development of the law of mortgages.[82] First, even where a legal mortgage was created on land as security for a loan by a transfer of the legal ownership in the land to the lender (mortgagee), equity insisted upon the transaction being treated as what it was in substance, a secured loan. Even though the date for redemption (paying back) of the loan had passed, equity refused to allow the mortgagor (borrower) to be deprived of his right to redeem. In fact, as we shall see, equity gave the borrower a right to redeem almost indefinitely and thereby created an equitable interest in land. This "equity of redemption" came to be regarded as something of considerable value which the mortgagor could deal with as a piece of property.[83] Further protection was given to the mortgagor by equity insisting that this equity of redemption could not be unduly restricted by the imposition of "clogs" or the annexation of collateral agreements solely for the benefit of the mortgagee.[84]

3.173. In addition to this encroachment upon legal mortgages, equity greatly facilitated the use of land to secure loans by developing its own equitable forms of mortgage.[85] Perhaps the most common type of mortgage in Ireland is the informal equitable mortgage created by a deposit with the lender of title documents relating to land. This form of mortgage has several advantages. It can be a completely informal transaction (*e.g.,* between the borrower and his bank manager) with no writing or other documentary evidence at all and so there is nothing to be registered in the Registry of Deeds. There is no question of any publicity for what is taking place, unless the borrower is a company, because then particulars of the deposit have to be registered under the companies legislation. Any form of title document will suffice, so this form of mortgage can be used for both registered and unregistered land.[86]

C. RESTRICTIVE COVENANTS

3.174. The third major contribution of equity to land law occurred during the nineteenth century. This was equity's extension of the enforceability of restrictive covenants on freehold land.[87] Most land when it is sold is made

---

[82] See generally chs. 12 and 13, *post.*
[83] Para. 12.05, *post.*
[84] Para. 13. 090 *et seq. post.*
[85] Ch. 12, *post.*
[86] *Ibid.*
[87] See, generally, ch. 19, *post.*

expressly subject to all kinds of restrictions as to its use. These covenants, however, would have had little permanent effect on the future use of the property so long as the common law stuck rigidly to the doctrine of privity of contract and allowed assignment of the benefit of contractual rights only. Equity's contribution was to devise a principle whereby the burden of certain covenants would "run" with the land so as to bind successors in title of the original covenantor. This principle, known as the rule in *Tulk* v. *Moxhay*,[88] ensured that a restrictive covenant on freehold land acquired the attributes of an equitable interest in land, albeit an interest falling short of legal interests like an easement or profit.[89]

3.175. One should add one cautionary note in this context. Restrictive covenants on freehold land are much rarer phenomena in Ireland than in England. The simple reason is that, until recently, most conveyancing in the urban areas (where restrictions as to use are more important and of much greater value) of Ireland was carried out by a *leasehold* rather than a freehold system.[90] The law relating to leasehold covenants had quite a different development and, indeed, the enforceability of such covenants is a much more straightforward matter.[91]

D. LICENCES

3.176. This topic is mentioned because the whole law of licences has been in a state of turmoil in England for the last two or three decades.[92] The reason is that some judges in England seem to have been trying to do for licences what the nineteenth century judges did for restrictive covenants. In other words, licences appear to be acquiring some of the attributes of equitable interests in land. This controversy has also stirred an equally difficult, but no less clear, subject relating to the distinction between "equitable interests" on the one hand and "mere equities" on the other. These thorny questions are better left to discussion in a later chapter.[93]

---

[88] Ch. 19, *post.*
[89] Ch. 6, *post.*
[90] Ch. 19, *post.* Freehold conveyancing has, of course, increased in the Republic as a result of the prohibition of the creation of new ground rents in respect of dwellings by the Landlord and Tenant (Ground Rents) Act, 1978, see para. 1. 75, *ante.*
[91] *Ibid.*
[92] See, generally, ch. 20, *post.*
[93] *Ibid.* and see paras. 3.076–9, *ante.*

PART II

ESTATES AND INTERESTS

CHAPTER 4

ESTATES

I. INTRODUCTION

A. ESTATES IN LAND

4.001. It has already been explained that in this context the word "estate" relates to the duration for which an interest in land may be held by its owner.[1] An initial ambiguity should be pointed out here; the expressions "interest in land" and "estate in land" have tended to assume rather technical meanings in our law. The word *estate* has come to be used in a narrow sense, to refer to the more important (in terms of size and value) interests in land. The word *interest,* whilst having the wider meaning of all interests that can be created in respect of land (thus including estates), can also be used in a narrower sense to refer to minor interests in land of less importance than estates.[2]

4.002. The complexity of land law derives in large part from the diversity in the types of estates and lesser interests in land that can be created. This is one of its distinguishing features when a comparison is made with the law of personal property and chattels, though this distinction is not as clear cut as it used to be. Modern commercial practice has done much in recent decades to break down the concept of absolute ownership of chattels. Indeed, commercial law has adopted many of the concepts originally derived from land law in this respect, so that the leasing and mortgaging of valuable chattels like ships and aircraft is quite common.[3] The point to note here, of course, is that this development has taken place in respect of large, valuable chattels, having a reasonably long life expectancy. This characteristic has a connection with the other main distinguishing feature of land, which facilitates its wide fragmentation of ownership. This is that land is virtually indestructible[4] and so there is little risk in creating a wide range of estates and interests in it, some of which may be postponed in enjoyment and possession for decades ahead.

---

[1] Para. 2.05, *ante.*   [2] *E.g.,* incorporeal hereditaments, see ch. 6, *post.*
[3] Though these concepts may not have the same law and rules applied to them in the case of chattels; *cf. e.g.,* the commercial law concepts of hiring, hire purchase, credit-sale and chartering with leasing. On this subject generally, see Lawson and Rudden, *The Law of Property* (2nd ed., 1982).
[4] Land, since in this context it includes buildings attached to land, is not strictly indestructible since the buildings can be razed to the ground, even though the ground remains. This point has added significance in the case of blocks of flats, where each flat is separately owned and only the ground floor ones, or those below, are attached to the ground. Considerable conceptual problems occur in England where flats held on freehold tenure are quite common: see George and George, *The Sale of Flats* (5th ed., 1984), and the articles cited in fn. 4, para. 1.01, *ante.* In Ireland the conceptual problems are fewer because freehold flats are almost unheard of; as with most urban land, flats, including those for sale (which are becoming quite common in major urban areas), are held on leasehold tenure, ch. 17, *post.* See *Irish Conveyancing Law* (1978), paras. 17.11–22.

B. Classification

4.003. Estates in land fall into two broad categories: *freehold* and *leasehold* estates. It is thus apparent that the epithets "freehold" and "leasehold" are ascribed to two quite distinct concepts, namely, tenure and estates.[5] Generally there is a mutual exclusiveness about these concepts in the sense that one speaks only of land held under freehold tenure for a freehold estate or held under leasehold tenure for a leasehold estate. But in Ireland some confusion occurs because of the practice of creating what appear to be combinations of the concepts. Thus one has concepts like a "lease" for lives renewable for ever. This creates a freehold estate in the land, but by means of a document creating leasehold tenure between the parties.[6] The same occurs in certain types of fee farm grant, where a freehold estate is granted (a fee simple), but the relationship of landlord and tenant (leasehold tenure) exists between the grantor and grantee. These Irish concepts will be examined in detail below.[7]

4.004. As one would expect, freehold estates are those which are connected with the feudal system of tenure and much of the law relating to them is clearly grounded on feudal principles. There are three main types: fee simple, fee tail and life estate.[8] The *fee simple* is the largest estate known to our land law, the estate nearest to absolute ownership. It can rarely be quite absolute because of the notion of tenure which decrees that no matter how large the estate, it must be held of someone else, the State or Crown being the ultimate owner.[9] Furthermore, as we shall see, it is quite common for private parties to impose limitations on the holder for the time being of the fee simple estate, so that it becomes even less absolute.[10] In Ireland, as a result of centuries of conveyancing practice, a fee simple absolute is very rare in urban areas of the country.[11] However, it is a characteristic common to all fees simple that they have the potential to last for ever, with a high probability that they will do so in an age when a last will and testament will avoid the consequences of a death intestate leaving no persons entitled to succeed.[12]

4.005. The *fee tail*[13] is a lesser estate, where the succession is confined to the descendants of the original holder of the estate. This process of succession cannot be disturbed in Ireland by a will (it can in England), so that there is a

---

[5] Distinguished at paras. 2.04–5, *ante.* When the layman talks about a "freehold property" he is probably combining two concepts; he is referring to property held on freehold tenure for a freehold estate.

[6] *Cf.* a lease for lives combined with a term of years, para. 4.177, *post.*

[7] Paras. 4.057 *et seq., post.*

[8] Discussed in detail, paras. 4.021 *et seq.,* 4.112 *et seq.,* and 4.143 *et seq., post.*

[9] In a sense chattels are never owned absolutely either; the State in the Republic of Ireland is ultimate successor to personal property (Succession Act 1965, ss. 14 and 73), and the Crown in Northern Ireland succeeds to personal chattels *inter alia* as *bona vacantia* on the death of the owner intestate with no intestate successor (Administration of Estates Act (N.I.), 1955, ss. 16 and 45), paras. 15.27–8, *post.*

[10] Paras. 4.046 *et seq., post.*

[11] Paras. 4.057 *et seq., post.* In the Republic of Ireland they are becoming more common as a result of the prohibition of the creation of future ground rents in respect of dwellings by the Landlord and Tenant (Ground Rents) Act, 1978, see para. 1.74, *ante.*

[12] Ch. 14, *post.*

[13] Also known as an "estate tail," "entail" or "entailed interest" (though this use of the word "interest," as opposed to "estate," can be confusing, see para. 4.001, *supra*).

much greater probability of an early determination of the estate. The creation of a fee tail estate really belongs to the practices of a bygone age, when land was regarded as the primary and most secure source of wealth. In an age when the paraphernalia of the modern stock market were unknown, most of the wealth of the richer families in the country was tied up with their landed estates and large urban houses, and their lawyer's primary task was to ensure that this land was kept in the family for successive generations. As we shall see, the key tool of the conveyancer in achieving this was the fee tail estate.[14] Nowadays it is rarely created because of two basic reasons. The first is that land is no longer the only main source of wealth, though it remains an investment of considerable value and one of the few which usually increases in value so as to offset, and often outstrip, the fall in the value of money caused by the general inflation which attacks most developed countries' economies. The second is that modern taxation systems impose crippling burdens on many of the older types of family settlement and an estate which decrees a succession to land through various generations incurs heavy capital taxation.[15] Some indication of the problems may be seen from the varied, and often ingenious, attempts in recent decades by owners of large estates and country houses in the British Isles to generate revenue from their estates to pay off tax levies. The only alternative is often the selling up of the estate itself.

4.006. The *life estate* means roughly what the name indicates—an estate to last for someone's life only. The life in question may be that of the grantee, or the grantee may hold for the life of someone else so as to create an estate *pur autre vie*. It should be apparent that without more this estate would be of doubtful commercial value—who is to say how long a life may last? A purchaser is unlikely to risk his money on the basis of an insurance company's actuarial calculations of a person's life expectancy. We shall see that this problem was eventually tackled in a comprehensive manner by legislation.[16] We shall also see that Irish conveyancers provided several variations on this common theme of the life estate, notably the lease for lives renewable for ever[17] and leases for lives combined with terms of years.[18]

There is one important distinction between the first two freehold estates and the third, as their names imply. The fee simple and fee tail are what are known as estates of inheritance, *i.e.*, on the death of the present holder the estate might descend to his heir[19] (now replaced by persons entitled to succeed so far as the fee simple is concerned[20]). The word "fee" also indicates that the

---

[14] Para. 8.005, *post.*
[15] For the Republic, see now the Capital Acquisitions Tax Act, 1976, especially Parts II (gift tax) and III (inheritance tax). This Act imposes a gift tax on gifts taken on or after February 28, 1974 (s.4) and an inheritance tax on an inheritance taken on or after April 1, 1975 (s.10). For Northern Ireland, see the U.K. Finance Act, 1975, which imposes a capital transfer tax on gratuitous *inter vivos* transfers made since March 26, 1974, and on the value of deceased persons' estates since March 12, 1975 (s.19). See *Irish Conveyancing Law* (1978), paras. 1.27–8, 14.42–4 and 17.70.
[16] Ch. 8, *post.*
[17] Para. 4.167, *post.*
[18] Para. 4.177, *post.*
[19] Ch. 15, *post.*
[20] Succession Act, 1965, s. 11(1) (R.I.); Administration of Estates Act (N.I.), 1955, s. 1(3).

duration of the estate could be for ever; the words "simple" and "tail" indicate the classes of heir who could inherit.[21] A life estate, however, is not an estate of inheritance, not even where it is held for a life other than that of the grantee and the grantee predeceases that other person. In that case the grantee's heir does not succeed, instead there are special rules as to succession.[22] A life estate cannot *ex hypothesi* last for ever.

4.007. We turn now to the other main category of estates, namely, *leaseholds*. These are estates which developed much later than freeholds. Indeed, while freeholds were an essential part of the feudal system, leaseholds were never recognized by feudal land law.[23] Prior to the fifteenth century in England they were not even recognized as estates at all nor as creating any interest in land. A lease for a term of years was originally regarded as creating a purely personal contract between the parties and under the doctrine of privity of contract only the original parties to the contract could have any rights or duties under it.[24] It was not until the action of ejectment (a species of the action of trespass[25]) was developed, so as to enable a leaseholder to protect his land and recover it against all comers, that a leasehold could be regarded as an estate in land.[26] Yet it was clear that a lease created a form of tenure and equally clear that it was a new type of tenure, not feudal tenure. Thus statutes like *Quia Emptores* did not apply to leases, so that a leasehold tenant was free to make sub-leases and could be restricted from alienation of his estate, according to the terms of his agreement with his landlord.

4.008. This historical development led to the general principle of our land law that a leasehold estate was always regarded as less than a freehold estate. Indeed, the fundamental distinction was drawn that a leasehold estate was classed as personalty whereas a freehold estate was realty.[27] Freehold estates were classified as realty or real estate because in the early days of the common law an action for their recovery could be brought; the plaintiff got judgment for recovery of the *res,* the thing which was the freehold. But as leaseholds were based on contract there was no known method of getting judgment for their

---

[21] Para. 4.024, *post.*
[22] Para. 4.161, *post.*
[23] Thus a leaseholder had no seisin and was not liable to pay any feudal services nor subject to any feudal incidents, see para. 2.10, *ante* and 4.018, *post.*
[24] Privity of contract is a technical concept dealing with the persons who may sue on a contract. Originally the only persons who could sue were the parties to it; at a later stage their personal representatives could sue and be sued. The next development was that rights under some contracts could be assigned to another person, who could sue on the contract, but this did not become law until the nineteenth century. See, generally, Clark *Contract* (1982), ch. 15; Wylie, "Contracts and Third Parties" (1967) 18 N.I.L.Q. 448.
[25] See, generally, Maitland, *Forms of Action* (eds. Chaytor and Whittaker 1936). The real actions, the original feudal forms of action (such as the writ of right and possessory assizes), were abolished by the Real Property Limitation Act, 1833, s. 36, leaving the action of ejectment as the principal protection for leaseholders *and* freeholders. All forms of action, including ejectment, were abolished by the Common Law Procedure Act, 1852, ss. 168–221, so that in future an action for recovery of land could be instituted by pleading in ordinary language.
[26] See Holdsworth, *History of English Law,* vol. III, p. 4; Megarry and Wade, *The Law of Real Property* (5th ed., 1984), Appendix I.
[27] Note that under the Local Registration of Title (Ir.) Act, 1891, Pt. IV, freehold titles bought by tenants under the Land Purchase Acts and compulsorily registered under the 1891 Act were to descend on intestacy as personalty, not realty. See now the Registration of Title Act, 1964, s. 113 (2) (R.I.); Land Registration Act (N.I.), 1970, s. 97 and Sched. 14. Also para. 3.099, *ante.*

recovery. The action (if any) was for damages and so they were classified as personalty or personal estate. Until recently this was a vitally important distinction because the law of devolution of land on intestacy differed in its application to the deceased's realty and personalty.[28] The distinction remains important because it is quite common for wills to contain general dispositions with respect to the testator's "realty" on the one hand and his "personalty" on the other.[29] But because leaseholds have such a close connection with land and other estates created out of land, they have had a hybrid or composite label ascribed to them. They are frequently called "chattels real"; the word "chattels" indicates the link with personalty and the word "real" the link with realty.

4.009. Another result of this distinction between freehold and leasehold estates was that a freehold estate could not be created out of a leasehold estate in the early stages of development of our land law system. The basic objection to such a grant at common law was that the holder of a freehold estate had seisin and a leaseholder had no seisin to pass to the person to whom he intended to convey a freehold estate.[30] New methods of conveyancing were devised to get round this sort of technical objection.[31]

4.010. There are several types of leasehold estate, which are usually classified into four main categories. It is often said that a major distinguishing feature, in contrast to freehold estates, is the element of certainty of duration attaching to leasehold estates. As we shall see, this is often not a very striking distinction and frequently seems to be a question of degree only.[32] The first category of leasehold estate is one granted for a *certain term*. This sort of estate is common in both Ireland and England, and very long terms of years are particularly common in Ireland.[33] The element of certainty in this case relates to the limit on the estate's duration; there is no certainty at all that such an estate will in fact last for the term agreed, for at least two reasons. One is that something may happen during the course of the lease entitling the lessor to determine it before the term is up.[34] The other is that often a clause is inserted in a lease entitling either party to determine it at any time by serving an appropriate notice to determine on the other party.[35] While there may be a limit on the maximum duration, there is no certainty about the minimum duration.[36]

---

[28] Ch. 15, *post.*

[29] Or expressions having the same meaning, such as "real estate" and "personal estate". One interesting point is that since leaseholds were classified as personalty they could be left by will, whereas freehold land could not be devised by will in Ireland until 1634, para. 3.020, *ante.*

[30] Para. 4019, *post.*

[31] *I.e.*, wills and trusts, see para. 5.019, *post.*

[32] Ch. 17, *post.*

[33] *E.g.*, terms of 999 and 10,000 years. See *Re Sergie* [1954] N.I. 1 (10,000 years) (see *A Casebook on Irish Land Law* (1984), p. 70).

[34] *E.g.*, forfeiture for breach of covenant or ejectment for non-payment of rent, ch. 17, *post.*

[35] Ch. 17, *post.*

[36] Courts in England have from time to time struck down leases which they construed as coming within this category, but which were not certain enough as regards their duration, the most notorious example being a lease "for the duration of the War". *Cf. Lace* v. *Chantler* [1944] K.B. 368 (and see the Validation of War-Time Leases Act, 1944, 62 L.Q.R. 219) and *Re Midland Rly. Co.'s Agreement* [1971] Ch. 725. It is doubtful if this point would have the same force in Ireland, see para. 17.022, *post.*

4.011. The second category of leasehold estate is a *periodic tenancy*. This is sometimes referred to as a fixed term capable of being rendered certain, but this can cause confusion. The only thing that is fixed is the original minimum period (*e.g.*, one week or one month), which will continue for successive periods until such time as either party to the agreement determines the tenancy in the appropriate manner.[37] There is no certainty at all about the maximum duration; if neither party takes any action the successive periods will continue indefinitely, from week to week, month to month or for whatever is the period in question. A maximum limit will be introduced only if and when either party serves a notice to determine the tenancy on a particular date.

4.012. The next category is a *tenancy at will*. As the name implies this is a tenancy which may also continue indefinitely, but which is determinable by either party at any time. The tenant certainly seems to have tenure, but it is questionable whether he can be said to hold for an estate. His tenure is so uncertain and insecure that it is difficult to quantify his estate and he seems to have nothing which he could convey to third parties.[38] Another category rather similar to the tenancy at will is a *tenancy at sufferance*. This arises where a tenant "holds over" after his previous tenancy has terminated. Unlike the tenancy at will, the tenant holds without the landlord's assent or dissent. The reason he is not a trespasser is that his original entry was lawful under the terms of his original tenancy agreement; the landlord must re-enter and re-take possession before he can exclude all others as trespassers. So long as the tenant at sufferance is allowed to remain and the landlord does not accept rent from him, his possession excludes any possession by the landlord.[39] Once again it is questionable whether such an interest should be classified as an estate.[40] In passing, it may be mentioned that there is another type of tenancy which involves the concept of "holding over." This is a *statutory tenancy,* which arises where a tenant is given the right to remain on in possession, subject to the terms and conditions of a previous tenancy agreement,[41] which has since terminated. This sort of tenancy, if it can be called such, is, to some extent, the creation of statute law, such as the rent restriction legislation.[42]

The whole subject of leasehold estates will be dealt with in the later chapter on the law of landlord and tenant.[43]

C. FUTURE INTERESTS

4.013. An estate in land may be enjoyed either at the present time or in the future. In the language of land law, it may be enjoyed in possession, in

---

[37] Para.17.023 *post*.

[38] See further, the discussion in *Binions* v. *Evans* [1972] Ch. 359

[39] Note, however, the landlord's option to treat the tenant overholding as a tenant from year to year under s. 5 of Deasy's Act, 1860, para. 17.024, *post*. On the subject of possession, and its relevance to title to land, see ch. 23, *post*.

[40] See further, ch. 17, *post*.

[41] Which may be replaced in some respects by statute. Thus the Rent Acts control the amount of rent that can be charged to the statutory tenant.

[42] See paras. 18.35 and 18.39 *post*. This sort of statutory tenancy should not be confused with a 15 year *judicial tenancy* granted to an agricultural tenant under the Land Law (Ir.) Act, 1881, see para. 1.49, *ante*.

[43] Ch. 17, *post*.

reversion or in remainder. If an estate is held in possession it means that the holder has an immediate right to possession and enjoyment of the land to which the estate relates. In the case of a reversion or remainder, on the other hand, this right to possession and enjoyment is postponed to some date in the future and someone else is entitled to it in the meantime. A *reversion* arises where a landowner grants away some estate lesser than his own to be enjoyed in possession by some other person. For example, A, owner of the fee simple estate in Blackacre, grants a life estate to B. B holds the life estate in possession and so long as that estate lasts A holds his fee simple in reversion. When B dies, his life estate ends and the land reverts in terms of possession and enjoyment to A; the fee simple in reversion becomes once again a fee simple in possession.

4.014. A *remainder* arises where the grantor creates an estate to be enjoyed in possession in the future by someone other than himself. For example, A, owner of the fee simple in Blackacre, conveys Blackacre to B for life, remainder to C in fee simple. B has a life estate in possession and C has the fee simple in remainder, to be enjoyed in possession when B dies. A has therefore disposed of his entire interest in the property; he has retained no estate or interest in the land, not even a reversion.[44] He would have had a fee simple reversion if instead he had conveyed a fee tail estate only to C.

4.015. The law relating to future interests is, perhaps, one of the most complex aspects of land law. It has become so because of a clash between two competing policies. One is the principle of allowing landowners freedom to deal with their land, coupled with the desire on the part of testators to decree the future enjoyment of their land long after their deaths. The other is the principle of promotion of land as a commercial asset, to be protected from excessive restrictions on its use and alienation and concentration of control of its owner-ship in the hands of a few large landowners. Many rules have been devised by the courts and legislatures over the centuries in an attempt to draw a fair balance between these policies. We shall study these further in a later chapter.[45]

D. Interests Less Than Estates

4.016. Our land law recognises many interests in land which do not come within the classification of estates in land. It is because there are so many types of this sort of interest in land that the fragmentation of ownership of land can be so complex. Whether or not an interest in land has been created or has arisen is often a difficult question. In recent decades, there has been considerable con-troversy in the courts, particularly in England, about this matter.[46] The main criterion by which to judge whether a particular interest is an interest in land

---

[44] The position would be different if a condition precedent were imposed on C's taking possession, so that his remainder was contingent and not vested. This complex subject is discussed in detail in ch. 5, *post*.

[45] Ch. 5,*post*.

[46] See Cheshire, "A New Equitable Interest in Land" (1953) 16 M.L.R. 1; Delany, "Equitable Interests and 'Mere Equities' " (1957) 21 Conv. 195; Stoljar, "Licence, Interest and Contract" (1953) 33 C.B.R. 562; Wade, "Licences and Third Parties" (1952) 68 L.Q.R. 337. Also ch. 20 *post*.

would seem to be whether that interest will bind successors in title of either or both of the original parties to the contract or conveyance creating the interest in the first place. The point is that land law recognises a wide variety of exceptions to the general principle of the law of contract known as the doctrine of privity of contract.[47] If a mere contractual interest has been created, the original parties to the contract only can be affected by it (by gaining rights or becoming subject to duties enforceable by action in court). If, however, an interest in land is created, it will bind successors in title of the original parties, though how far it will bind successors may vary according to the type of interest in land created. A simple illustration may be given in the case of a lease: L leases his house to T for 99 years; some years later T assigns his lease to A. There are two contracts here; one between L and T and one between T and A; L is not a party to the latter contract and A is not a party to the former. Yet under the law of landlord and tenant, A in effect steps into T's shoes and is treated in law almost as if he were T, so that he obtains most rights T had against L under the contract between L and T, and is subject to most of T's duties towards L under that contract. The converse position obtains if L assigns his reversion to X, so that the relationship between X and A is largely governed by the contract between L and T, the original lease, to which neither of them was a party.[48] As we shall see, many cases have arisen recently where a central issue in the dispute was whether the agreement in question created a lease or a mere licence. But the added complication has also arisen that even a licence may in certain circumstances acquire some of the attributes of an interest in land.[49]

4.017. Perhaps the best recognised type of interest in land less than an estate is what is commonly called an *incorporeal hereditament*. These interests are called hereditaments because they were classified as realty, as opposed to personalty, for the purposes of the old law of inheritance, *i.e.*, devolution on intestacy.[50] They are incorporeal because they do not give any rights to physical objects, such as land itself, or buildings (*i.e.*, the *corpus*). They are mere rights over land, usually the land of someone else. Common examples are easements (such as a right of way over a neighbour's land), profits à prendre (such as a right to shoot or fish on someone else's land) and rentcharges (the right to an annuity charged on land). For the most part they are rights attached to specific pieces of land, though for historical reasons this was not always the case.[51]

Other interests in land, apart from incorporeal hereditaments and certain licences, are interests created by conveyancing devices like restrictive covenants[52] or mortgages.[53] In both these cases equity has played an important part in their development.[54]

---

[47] See, generally Clark, *Contract* (1982), ch. 15; Wylie, "Contracts and Third Parties" (1967) 18 N.I.L.Q. 448.
[48] See ch. 17, *post.*
[49] Ch. 20, *post.*
[50] Ch. 15, *post.*
[51] *E.g.*, an advowson, para. 6.018 *post.* Incorporeal hereditaments are discussed in detail in ch. 6, *post.*
[52] Ch. 19, *post.*
[53] Ch. 12, *post.*
[54] On the role of equity in land law generally, see ch. 3 *ante.*

II. FREEHOLD ESTATES

Before discussing the various categories of freehold estates, there are two fundamental concepts relating to such estates which should be mentioned. One is the concept of *seisin* and the other is the concept of *words of limitation*.

A. SEISIN

4.018. Seisin was a concept fundamental to the feudal system as it developed in the early centuries. But it is a concept which defies precise definition.[55] The problem is that the concept involves the notion of possession of land, but it is by no means synonymous with possession. Thus a leaseholder has possession of land but he has no seisin; the seisin is in the freeholder from whom he holds his lease, whether directly or indirectly.[56]

4.019. It eventually became a settled principle under the feudal system that only a freeholder holding under freehold tenure had seisin. So a leaseholder had no seisin, as we have already stated, nor had a copyholder; in a copyholder's case the seisin lay with the lord of the manor. It also became a settled principle that there must always be some person seised at any particular time.[57] Even though a freeholder had parted with possession of the land to someone who could not be seised, the seisin did not lapse and remained in the freeholder. The reasons for these principles were very practical ones. Under the feudal system the services owed could be enforced only against the tenant seised of the land; only those seised were originally recognised by the King's courts. The early actions by which land itself could be recovered, the real actions, could be brought only in respect of disputes over seisin.[58] It was not until several centuries later that the wider concept of possession acquired the same significance and protection in our land law, so that today possession, rather than seisin, is the more important concept.[59]

Seisin had other practical significance. Certain rights on death could be claimed only if the deceased had been seised, *e.g.*, rights of dower for a widow and rights of curtesy for a widower.[60] Only the heir of the tenant seised of the land could succeed to the land on that tenant's death. And, as we have seen,[61] in the early days conveyances of freehold land were very technical and formal exercises. The original method was by feoffment with *livery of seisin*, a symbolic ceremony performed by the parties on the land itself.

---

[55] *Long* v.*Myles* (1822) 1 Fox & Sm. 1. See Williams, *The Seisin of the Freehold* (1878); Bordwell, "Seisin and Disseisin" (1921) 34 H.L.R. 592, 717; Maitland "Mystery of Seisin" (1886) 2 L.Q.R. 481, " Beatitude of Seisin" (1888) 4 L.Q.R. 24, 286; Sweet, "Seisin" (1896) 12 L.Q.R. 239; Thorne, " Livery of Seisin" (1936) 52 L.Q.R. 345.

[56] *E.g.*, in the case of a sub-lessee having possession of the land.

[57] Several rules were derived from the feudal approach to the concept of seisin, sometimes known as the common law seisin rules. They are discussed in ch. 5, *post*.

[58] Maitland, *Forms of Action at Common Law* (eds. Chayton and Whittaker 1936); see also Booth, *Real Actions* (2nd ed., 1811); Lightwood, *Possession of Land* (1894).

[59] Ch. 23, *post*.

[60] Para. 4.157, *post*. See *Long* v. *Myles* (1822) 1 Fox & Sm. 1.

[61] Para. 3.023, *ante*.

B. Words of Limitation

4.020. The concept of words of limitation also derives from the formalistic approach of the feudal system to land transactions. The principle was established that a freehold estate could be created only if the grantor used the words of limitation appropriate for that particular estate. The expression "words of limitation" means, therefore, the words delimiting or defining the estate being conveyed. These words are to be distinguished from "words of purchase," which indicate the person to whom the estate is conveyed. Let us take an example to illustrate the distinction: "to A in fee simple." This would be an appropriate formula to use today, as we shall see.[62] Here the words "to A" are the words of purchase and the words "in fee simple" are the words of limitation. This distinction came to be important, particularly with reference to a principle known as the Rule in *Shelley's Case*.[63]

The appropriate "magic phrases" to be used in connection with the various freehold estates have varied over the centuries, as a result of statutory interventions. The courts took different approaches according to whether the document was a conveyance made *inter vivos* (*i.e.,* between living persons) or a will. These are matters which we shall consider in relation to each particular type of freehold estate, a subject to which we now turn.

III. FEE SIMPLE

A. General

4.021. It has already been explained that the fee simple estate is the largest estate known to our land law, the estate nearest to absolute ownership of land.[64] It has the potential to last for ever and will end only when an owner for the time being dies intestate, leaving no person entitled to succeed.[65] Indeed, in the Republic of Ireland it is arguable that a fee simple cannot end as the State now succeeds as "ultimate intestate successor" when the owner dies leaving no other person entitled to succeed.[66] Nowadays a fee simple is free from most feudal burdens and, in theory, under general land law the owner is free to use and enjoy the land as he pleases. But this statement must be made subject to many qualifications. First, there is nothing to stop parties to a conveyance imposing restrictions on the use and enjoyment of the land to be held in fee simple. It is true that the law may confine this right of private parties within limits, but as we shall see the exercise of the right means that different categories of fee simple can be created. We shall examine these in a moment, and will then go on to examine the special kinds of conveyances creating a fee simple which are so common in Ireland, fee farm grants.[67] A fee farm grant

---

[62] Para. 4.029, *post.*

[63] Para. 4.034, *post.*

[64] Para. 4.004, *ante.* See also Barton, "The Rise of the Fee Simple" (1976) 92 L.Q.R. 108.

[65] See ch. 15, *post.* An interesting point arises in the case of a squatter barring a fee simple owner; if the principle be accepted that there is no statutory transfer of title or Parliamentary conveyance effected by the statute of limitations, presumably the old fee simple disappears and a new one arises in its place. This subject is discussed in ch. 23, *post.*

[66] Succession Act, 1965, s. 73.

[67] Para. 4.057, *post.* It should be noted that the future creation of fee farm grants has been restricted in the

creates a fee simple with many of the usual characteristics of that estate as it developed under English common law, but the real significance of these grants in Ireland is that they create a variety of relationships between the grantors and grantees which could not exist in England. This results in the fee simple estate in these cases acquiring characteristics peculiar to Ireland.

4.022. The second qualification relates to the land held in fee simple. In this context the latin maxim *cuius est solum, eius est usque ad coelum et ad inferos*[68] is often cited. Like many maxims in practice it is only an approximation to the truth. At best it can be regarded as a presumption or a rule of thumb for deciding cases of doubt which cannot be disposed of on any other clearer authority. Several cases have arisen in England involving chattels found under or attached to land belonging to someone else,[69] or becoming affixed to the land so as to become part of it.[70] But the fee simple owner will never enjoy such wide-ranging rights as the maxim suggests. He will be subject to rights others have acquired over his land as a result of other land transactions, *e.g.*, leases and mortgages, or prior sales conferring easements like rights of way. The owner's freedom to do as he pleases on his land is restricted by the general law of tort; he must not cause a public or private nuisance,[71] and may be liable in certain circumstances if dangerous substances escape from his land and injure others,[72] or if others are injured while on his land.[73] The owner's rights are subject nowadays to wide-ranging state control and interference, through legislation like the Public Health Acts, Housing Acts and Planning Acts.[74] Furthermore, the ownership of certain things to be found on land lies elsewhere under our law, either at common law or under statute. Indeed, it seems that some things may not be owned at all, *e.g.*, wild animals,[75] in respect of which the owner of the land on which they are found has only the exclusive right to catch and appropriate.[76] At common law the Crown was entitled to treasure trove, *i.e.*, gold or silver hidden on the land in respect of which the true

Republic by the Landlord and Tenant (Ground Rents) Act, 1978. This Act prohibits the future creation of ground rents in respect of dwellings and for these purposes a "lease" includes a fee farm grant, see para. 4.182, *post*.

[68] Roughly translated: the owner of the soil is to be taken to own also everything up to the sky and down to the centre of the earth. See the interesting discussion of the maxim, and of its limits, in *Baron Bernstein of Leigh* v. *Skyviews and General Ltd.* [1978] Q.B. 479. See also Richardson, "Private Property Rights in Air Space" (1953) 31 C.B.R. 117.

[69] *E.g.*, *Elwes* v. *Brigg Gas Co.* (1886) 33 Ch.D. 562; *South Staffordshire Water Co.* v. *Sharman* [1896] 2 Q.B. 44.

[70] *E.g.*, *Leigh* v. *Taylor* [1902] A.C. 157 (tapestries fastened by tacks to canvas and pieces of wood nailed to the drawing-room wall of a mansion house); *Holland* v. *Hodgson* (1872) L.R. 7 C.P. 328 (mill looms nailed to stone floor of mill). The subject of fixtures in relation to life estate owners and tenants is discussed at paras. 4.155 and 17.060, *post*. See also Bingham, "Some Suggestions Concerning the Law of Fixtures" (1907) 7 Col.L.Rev. 1; Guest and Lever, "Hire-Purchase, Equipment Leases and Fixtures" (1963) 27 Conv. 30; Amos, *Law of Fixtures*.

[71] *McGowan* v. *Masterson* [1953] I.R. 101; see also *McStay* v. *Morrissey* (1949) 83 I.L.T.R. 28; *Cunningham* v. *MacGrath Bros.* [1964] I.R. 209.

[72] *Shell-Mex and B.P. Ltd.* v. *Belfast Corporation* [1952] N.I. 72; *Healy* v. *Bray U.D.C.* [1962–3] Ir.Jur.Rep. 9; see also *Boylan* v. *Dublin Corporation* [1949] I.R. 60.

[73] *Scully* v. *Boland Ltd.* [1962] I.R. 58; *O'Donoghue* v. *Greene* [1967] I.R. 40; see also *Cooney* v. *Dockerell & Sons* [1965] Ir.Jur.Rep. 31. And see as regards Northern Ireland, the Occupiers' Liability Act (N.I.) 1957.

[74] See paras. 1.61–2 and 1.77–9, *ante*.

[75] *Blades* v. *Higgs* (1865) 11 H.L.C. 621.

[76] Subject to statutory limitations and prohibitions, see *e.g.*, Wild Birds Protection Act, 1930 (R.I.); Wild Birds Protection Acts (N.I.) 1931 and 1950; Game Preservation Act, 1930 (R.I.); Game Preservation Act (N.I.), 1928 and Game Law Amendment Act (N.I.) 1951.

owner is unknown. This is still the position in Northern Ireland and in the
Republic treasure trove belongs to the State.[77] The Crown was also entitled to
the foreshore adjoining tidal waters (*i.e.*, the land between high and low water
marks); this is still the position in Northern Ireland,[78] and in the Republic the
foreshore is vested in the State.[79] Other matters have been pre-empted by the
State through legislation. Thus in the Republic the rights to most minerals,
including petroleum,[80] have been vested in the State.[81] A similar development
has recently taken place in Northern Ireland.[82] Restrictions have been put on
the landowner's right to bring actions (for trespass or nuisance) in respect of
infringement of the air-space above his land by, *e.g.*, aircraft.[83]

B. CREATION AND TRANSFER

4.023. Since the Real Property Act, 1845, a fee simple has usually been
granted by a deed, *i.e.*, a document under seal. A deed is not a requirement
because the 1845 Act did not replace the old modes of conveyance, it merely
introduced a more convenient alternative.[84] These other modes of conveyance
were discussed in more detail in the previous chapter,[85] though it should be
noted here that it is extremely unlikely that they would be used today.[86]

C. WORDS OF LIMITATION

4.024. It has already been indicated that under the common law appropriate
words of limitation had to be used to create a fee simple.[87] The rules were
particularly strict in the case of freehold estates of inheritance, *i.e.*, the fee
simple and fee tail, especially where these estates were conveyed *inter vivos*.
The early modes of conveyance *inter vivos* were very solemn and ceremonial

[77] Where treasure is claimed to be found, a coroner is supposed to hold an inquest on the matter, see Coroners Act 1962, s. 49 (R.I.); Coroners Act (N.I.) 1959, s. 33. See Hill, *Treasure Trove in Law and Practice* (1936), especially pp. 263 *et seq.*; Dolly, "The First Treasure Trove Inquest in Ireland?" (1968) 19 N.I.L.Q. 182; (1963) 97 I.L.T.S.J. 39.

[78] Government of Ireland Act, 1920, s. 4 (1); see also the Northern Ireland (Miscellaneous Provisions) Act, 1932, s. 9.

[79] 1937 Constitution, Art. 10; Foreshore Act, 1933. See *Howe* v. *Stawell* (1833) Alc. & Nap. 348; *Hamilton* v. *Att.-Gen.* (1880) 5 L.R.Ir. 555; *Macnamara* v. *Higgins* (1854) 4 I.C.L.R. 326; *Brew* v. *Haren* (1877) 11 I.L.T.R. 66; *Stoney* v. *Keane* (1903) 37 I.L.T.R. 212; *Mahoney* v. *Neenan* [1966] I.R. 559. Lee, "The Right to Take Seaweed from the Seashore" (1967) 18 N.I.L.Q. 33; also (1955) 89 I.L.T.S.J. 131 and 137; Smyth, *The Seashores of Ireland: Public Rights and Restrictions* (1935).

[80] Petroleum and Other Minerals Development Act, 1960.

[81] 1922 Constitution, Art. 11; 1937 Constitution, Art. 10. See also Minerals Development Acts, 1940 and 1979; Minerals Exploration and Development Company Act, 1941; Minerals Company Acts, 1945, 1947 and 1950. See Kelly, *The Irish Constitution* (2nd ed., 1984), pp. 46–50.

[82] Mineral Development Act (N.I.), 1969; Petroleum (Production) Act (N.I.), 1964. The vesting under these Acts was in the then N.I. Ministry of Commerce.

[83] Air Navigation and Transport Act, 1936, s. 55 (R.I.); Northern Ireland is governed by the U.K. Civil Aviation Act, 1949, s. 40. See *Baron Bernstein of Leigh* v. *Skyviews and General Ltd.* [1978] Q.B. 479.

[84] S. 2, replacing ss. 2 and 13 of the Transfer of Property Act, 1844. The old modes of conveyance were abolished in England by the Law of Property Act, 1925, s. 51, under which the deed became the sole method of conveying a fee simple. See paras. 3.025–30, *ante*. See also, generally, *Irish Conveyancing Law* (1978), chs. 16 and 17.

[85] Paras. 3.023–4, *ante*.

[86] Apart from questions of cost and convenience, the old modes do not fit in well with modern conveyancing practice; *e.g.* feoffment with livery of seisin may involve no document capable of registration in the Registry of Deeds, or any title deed or other documentary evidence of title to be supplied to the officials of the Land Registry, see chs. 21 and 22, *post*.

[87] Para. 4.020, *ante*.

affairs[88] and this may explain the courts' strict interpretation of them. For centuries wills were not recognised by the Common Law Courts; eventually they were enforced by the Court of Chancery, and then the Statute of Wills (Ireland), 1634, required the Common Law Courts to enforce them.[89] The Court of Chancery was much more liberal in its interpretation of documents, especially wills, seeking as far as possible to give effect to the intention of the parties.[90] When wills came to be recognised at common law this liberal approach to their interpretation survived and so in the following statement of law a distinction still has to be made between conveyances *inter vivos* and wills. The further complication arises that some amendments in the common law position have been made by statute.

1. *Conveyances Inter Vivos*

(i) At Common Law

At common law a distinction must be made between conveyances to natural persons and conveyances to corporations.

(a) *Natural Persons*

4.025. In this case the proper words of limitation for a fee simple were "and his heirs," to be inserted after the name of the grantee. Thus to convey a fee simple to A one would say: "to A and his heirs." The expression "heirs" was like a magic formula.[91] Failure to use it, or an attempt to use some equivalent expression such as "relatives," "issue," "descendants" or even "in fee simple," gave the grantee a life estate only.[92] The same was the position if expressions like "to A for ever" or "to A absolutely" were used.[93] The use, however, of superfluous words would not invalidate a conveyance of a fee simple so long as appropriate words for a fee simple were included.[94] The word "heir" in the singular was not enough,[95] though adding a description to the word "heirs" did not necessarily prevent the conveyance of a fee simple. Thus it seems that "to A and his heirs male" (not to be confused with the words necessary for a fee tail male, "to A and the heirs male *of his body*"[96]) would still give A a fee simple: the word "male" was ignored by the common law as being a limitation repugnant to the estate purported to be granted and therefore invalid.[97]

---

[88] Para. 3.023, *ante.*

[89] Para. 3.010, *ante.*

[90] See, generally, ch. 14, *post.*

[91] See Challis, *Law of Real Property* (3rd ed.), ch. XV; Megarry and Wade, *Law of Real Property* (5th ed.), pp. 49–53. *Kennedy and Lawler* v. *Ryan* [1938] I.R. 620; see also *Re Fayle and the Irish Feather Co.'s Contract* [1918] 1 I.R. 13.

[92] *Jack* v. *Reilly* (1829) 2 Hud & Br. 301; *Wood* v. *Davis* (1880) 6 L.R.Ir. 50; *Re Coleman's Estate* [1907] 1 I.R. 488; *Re Adams's Estate* [1965] I.R. 57; *Re Houston* [1909] 1 I.R. 319.

[93] *Lysaght* v. *McGrath* (1882) 11 L.R.Ir. 142; *Cf. Twaddle* v. *Murphy* (1881) 8 L.R.Ir. 123 (see *A Casebook on Irish Land Law* (1984), p. 113).

[94] In *Twaddle* v. *Murphy* (1881) 8 L.R.Ir. 123, a conveyance to A and B "their heirs and assigns, for the lives of C, D and E, or for 999 years, or for ever, whichever should last longest" was held to pass a fee simple, in this case subject to a perpetual yearly rent (*i.e.*, a fee farm grant, see para. 4.057, *post*). See the discussion of this case by Murray J. in *Re Courtney* [1981] N.I. 58.

[95] *Mallory's Case* (1601) 5 Co.Rep. 111b at 112a.

[96] Para. 4.128, *post.*

[97] *Idle* v. *Cook* (1705) 1 P.Wm. 70 at 70. On the question of repugnancy generally, see para. 4.052, *post.*

4.026. It was important also be be clear whether the words in question were words of limitation or words of purchase.[98] In the standard formula "to A and his heirs," the words "to A" are the words of purchase only, *i.e.,* A only takes any estate in the land, in this case a fee simple. The words "and his heirs" are words of limitation only, delimiting A's estate; A's "heirs" take no estate at all. Even if at the time of conveyance there is someone who could be regarded as likely to be an "heir" of A, that person has at most a *spes successionis* only, *i.e.,* a hope of succeeding to A's estate should he die intestate as far as that estate is concerned. A's "heirs" or "heir" cannot be determined definitely until A dies. Until recently in Ireland this question of devolution was settled in accordance with the feudal law of primogeniture; A's heir was his eldest surviving son.[99] But the law on this subject has been changed by statute in both parts of Ireland, *for the purposes of devolution on intestacy.* "Heirs" for the purposes of devolution means the persons entitled to succeed on intestacy under Part VI of the Republic's Succession Act, 1965, or Part II of the Administration of Estates Act (N.I.), 1955. These statutes, however, provide that the words "heir" or "heirs" used in any enactment, deed or instrument *as words of limitation,* before or after the enactment of the statutes, have the same effect as if the statutes had not been passed.[1] They also provide that where the words "heir" or "heirs" are used *as words of purchase,* they have the same effect in enactments and deeds, passed or executed *before* the passing of the statutes[2]; in the case of enactments and deeds passed or executed after the passing of the statutes they are to be construed to mean the person or persons entitled to succeed on intestacy (other than a creditor), unless a contrary intention appears.[3] An example of use of the word "heir" as a word of purchase would be "to A's heir and his heirs."[4] If A was dead at the time of the conveyance, the fee simple went to his heir determined in accordance with the rules of primogeniture or, if the conveyance is after the statutes, his successors as determined under Part VI of the Republic's 1965 Act or Part II of Northern Ireland's 1955 Act. If A was alive at the time of the conveyance, the conveyance was void because it purported to convey the estate to someone not yet ascertained, so that an abeyance of seisin would occur which the common law would not allow.[5] Thus the recent statutory provisions on devolution on intestacy avoid upsetting the centuries-old practice of conveyancers in drafting documents of title.

Before leaving the distinction between words of limitation and words of purchase, it should be pointed out that there is one other important aspect of the distinction. This relates to the general principle known as the rule in *Shelley's Case* which we discuss below.[6]

---

[98] See para. 4.020, *ante.*
[99] Ch. 15, *post.*
[1] Succession Act, 1965, s. 15 (1); Administration of Estates Act (N.I.), 1955, s. 5 (1).
[2] 1965 Act, s. 15 (2); 1955 Act (N.I.), s. 5 (2).
[3] 1965 Act, s. 15 (3); 1955 Act (N.I.), s. 5 (3).
[4] It seems that to the same effect would be "to the heirs of A." See Megarry and Wade, *The Law of Real Property* (5th ed.), p. 50.
[5] Para. 5.013, *post.*
[6] Para. 4.034, *post.*

(b) *Corporations*

4.027. Corporations, whether created by charter or by or under statute, have a distinct legal personality of their own, so that they can own property and enter into contracts, and can sue or be sued in contract or tort as entities separate from individuals connected with them, such as directors or share-holders. A corporation may be either a corporation *aggregate* made up of two or more individuals acting as a corporate body (*e.g.*, a limited company or a city corporation), or a corporation *sole* comprising one individual holding an office subject to perpetual succession (*e.g.*, Government Ministers in the Republic[7]). The law relating to words of limitation in conveyances to corporations is different from that relating to conveyances to individuals.

So far as a corporation aggregate is concerned, it has long been settled at common law that a conveyance to the corporation by its corporate name gives it a fee simple without any need for words of limitation.[8] There is nothing surprising about this rule. A corporation is not like a natural person; it cannot die or have "heirs" in the way that a natural person can and it was for this reason that the feudal system, dependent upon revenue generated by deaths, disliked conveyances to corporations, hence the statutes on mortmain.[9]

4.028. In the case of a corporation sole, however, a natural person is involved, who will die even though his office will continue. The rule here is that words of limitation must be used, in this case the words "and his successors." Thus to give the Republic's Minister for Finance a fee simple the expression to be used is: "to the Minister for Finance and his successors."[10] Failure to use these words of limitation would give the Minister a life estate only. A conveyance to the Minister "and his heirs" would also give him a fee simple, but in his private capacity and not as a corporation sole. It is not clear what the position is if a composite expression is used, *e.g.*, "to the Minister for Finance, his heirs and successors." It is a matter of construction whether the conveyance to the Minister is to him in his private or official capacity; use of his official title and of the words "and successors" would seem to suggest a conveyance to him in his official capacity. The question of construction would be more difficult in a case where his individual name was also given or even used without his official title.

(ii) By Statute

4.029. This common law position as regards conveyances *inter vivos* of a fee simple has been modified by statute.[11] By the Conveyancing Act, 1881,[12] the expression "in fee simple" may now be used to convey a fee simple; there is no need to use the older expression "and his heirs," though this expression is still commonly used by conveyancers. The 1881 Act merely provided an alternative

---

[7] Ministers and Secretaries Act, 1924, s. 2.
[8] *Re Woking U.D.C. (Basingstoke Canal) Act, 1911* [1914] 1 Ch. 300 at 312 (*per* Swinfen Eady L.J.).
[9] Para. 2.41, *ante*, and ch. 25, *post*.
[10] *Ex parte Vicar of Castle Bytham* [1895] 1 Ch. 348 at 354 (*per* Stirling J.).
[11] For modifications in the case of fee farm grants in Ireland, see paras. 4.057 *et seq.*, *post*.
[12] S. 51.

form of words of limitation for a fee simple. It has been decided that the 1881 alternative will be construed just as strictly as the courts construed the expression "and his heirs." Thus it has been held that the expression "to A in fee" gives A a life estate only,[13] though it is possible that relief might be given by the court by way of rectification of the conveyance if it could be shown that a mistake had occurred in omitting the word "simple."[14] By its express terms section 51 of the 1881 Act seems to have provided an alternative to the common law formula "and his heirs" only, so that "and his successors" still has to be used to convey a fee simple to a corporation sole in his official capacity.[15]

4.030. There is no equivalent in either part of Ireland of section 60 (1) of the English Law of Property Act, 1925, which abolished the necessity for words of limitation in the case of a fee simple. By that subsection the grantee of a deed of conveyance executed after 1925 takes the fee simple or other whole interest which the grantor had power to convey, unless a contrary intention appears in the conveyance. This reverses the common law position still prevailing in Ireland in respect of conveyances of *unregistered* land that, if appropriate words of limitation are not used, the smallest rather than the largest freehold estate is taken to pass to the grantee.[16] However, in respect of transfers of *registered* land, section 123 of the Republic's Registration of Title Act, 1964, and section 35 of the Land Registration Act (N.I.), 1970, contain a provision similar to section 60(1) of the 1925 Act.

2. *Gifts By Will*

(i) At Common Law

4.031. It has already been stated that the courts took a more liberal approach to the interpretation of wills, so that the requirement of words of limitation was much less strict. Indeed, prior to 1838 all that was necessary was for the will to show an intention to create a fee simple. It was, therefore, a matter of construction whether the words of the will were sufficient to show such an intention, and it was likely that expressions such as "to A for ever" or "to A absolutely" created a fee simple. On the other hand, an expression such as "to A" was before 1838 unlikely to be enough and, without more, would pass a life estate only.

(ii) By Statute

4.032. The position at common law was modified by the Wills Act, 1837.[17] Under this Act, the fee simple or other whole interest of which the testator had

---

[13] *Re Ford and Ferguson's Contract* [1906] 1 I.R. 607 at 610 (see *A Casebook on Irish Land Law* (1984), p. 115). See the comments on this case by Murray J. in *Re Courtney* [1981] N.I. 58 at 63–5. See also the English case of *Re Ethel and Mitchells and Butlers' Contract* [1901] 1 Ch. 945. *Cf. Re Ottley's Estate* [1910] 1 I.R. 1.
[14] *Re Ottley's Estate* [1910] 1 I.R. 1. See also *Banks* v. *Ripley* [1940] Ch. 719.
[15] See Challis, *Law of Real Property* (3rd ed), pp. 224–5.
[16] A provision similar to that in the English 1925 Act has been recommended for Northern Ireland, *Survey of the Land Law of Northern Ireland* (1971), para. 171. See also the Land Law Working Group's Discussion Document No. 4 (*Conveyancing and Miscellaneous Matters*) (1983), paras. 2.10–11.
[17] Ss. 28 and 34.

power to dispose passed to the grantee under any will made or confirmed after 1837, unless a contrary intention was shown.[18] Thus, since 1837 a devise "to A" would raise the presumption that A takes a fee simple. It should be noted, however, that this presumption only arises in respect of an estate or interest already held by the testator, which he is devising in his will. It does not arise where the testator is creating a new interest in his will, *e.g.*, a new rentcharge on land in favour of the devisee. If this is devised simply "to A," A will take a rentcharge for life only.[19]

3. *Equitable Gifts*

4.033. It has been a matter of some controversy over the years whether the rigours of the common law apply to gifts which are equitable only, *e.g.*, an estate conveyed to be held for the grantee under a trust. Here the grantee has an equitable interest only, for the legal estate is vested in the trustees.[20] One would have expected that since equitable estates and interests were originally recognised by the Court of Chancery only,[21] a relaxation of the common law rules would be allowed as in the case of wills. Yet there are Irish authorities suggesting that this is not necessarily the case, so that an equitable fee simple requires the same words of limitation as a legal fee simple.[22] Later cases, however, seem to confine this rule to mean only that, if the settlor uses technical words in delimiting an equitable estate in land, those words will be treated as ordinary words of limitation and given their technical meaning under the common law.[23] Thus a conveyance "to A" would still give A an equitable life estate only. But if no technical words are used or it appears that the settlor is not using conventional conveyancing practice, it seems that the courts will give effect to what appears to be his intention, regardless of the technical requirement of words of limitation at common law.[24] Thus a conveyance "to A

---

[18] Thus the English Law of Property Act, 1925, was merely extending the rule for wills to conveyances *inter vivos, supra*. For a case showing a "contrary intention," see *Re Gannon* [1914] 1 I.R. 86.

[19] *Nichols* v. *Hawkes* (1853) 10 Hare 342. On the subject of rentcharges generally, see paras. 6.131 *et seq., post*.

[20] See, generally, ch. 9, *post*.

[21] See, generally, ch. 3, *ante*.

[22] *E.g., Meyler* v. *Meyler* (1883) 11 L.R.Ir. 522; *Re Bennett's Estate* [1898] 1 I.R. 185; *cf. Re Murphy and Griffin's Contract* [1919] 1 I.R. 187; see Challis, *The Law of Real Property* (3rd ed.), p. 222. It should be noted, however, that equity may rectify a will or settlement on the ground of mistake (*e.g.*, words of limitation omitted); see *Ex parte Rice* (1896) 30 I.L.T.R. 57; *Fitzgerald* v. *Fitzgerald* [1902] 1 I.R. 477 (see *A Casebook on Equity and Trusts in Ireland* (1985), p. 279); *Re Davis's Estate* [1912] 1 I.R. 516.

[23] *Jameson* v. *McGovern* [1934] I.R. 758 (see *A Casebook on Irish Land Law* (1984), p. 116), explaining the English case, *Re Bostock's Settlement* [1921] 2 Ch. 469. This seems to be an example of the maxim "equity follows the law"; see para. 3.047, *ante*. See also the interpretation given in *Savage* v. *Nolan* (1978) Unrep. (H.C., R.I.) (1976 No. 2395P) (see *A Casebook on Irish Land Law* (1984), p. 122), where Costello J. held that "the decision of the Supreme Court in *Jameson* v. *McGovern* can only be interpreted as meaning that an exception to the strict rule in *Bostock's Settlement* does not exist when the settlement being construed contains an agreement to settle the land referred to in the deed on the wife of the intended marriage absolutely." He then held that a remainder over to children of the intended marriage in a trust settlement vested in them the fee simple despite the absence of words of limitation, since the settlor intended that they should take absolutely. He then commented: "I accept that it is well established that the children of an intended marriage are within the consideration of the marriage and that accordingly the settlement constitutes an agreement which is enforceable by them by which they are entitled to absolute interests in the events that have happened." *Cf. Re Hammersly's Estate* (1861) 12 Ir.Ch.R. 319.

[24] *Re Houston* [1909] 1 I.R. 319; *Re Stinson's Estate* [1910] 1 I.R. 47; *Re Cross's Trusts* [1915] 1 I.R. 304; *Re Beer's Estate* [1925] N.I. 191. See also *Re Harte's Settlement* (1955) 89 I.L.T.R. 78, where it was held that an

absolutely" would probably be construed as giving A an equitable fee simple, since the word "absolutely" is clearly not a technical word of limitation at common law. It has been further suggested that the quantum of an equitable estate will not be affected by a failure to convey a legal estate of equal size to the trustees.[25] Thus a conveyance "to A and B on trust for C and his heirs" would still seem to give B an equitable fee simple even though A and B have a legal life estate only.

4. *Rule in Shelley's Case*

4.034. Though this rule takes its name from a case decided in 1581[26] its origin lies in early feudal law.[27] What that origin is precisely, however, has been the subject of some controversy.[28] The rule is usually stated as follows:

> "It is a rule of law that when an estate of freehold is given to a person, and by the same disposition an estate is limited either mediately or immediately to his heirs or to the heirs of his body, the words 'heirs' or 'heirs of his body' are words of limitation and not words of purchase."[29]

The rule may have been connected with an old common law rule forbidding a person's heir to take by purchase from his own ancestor.[30] The common law preferred a person to take land by descent (inheritance) rather than by purchase; there was the doctrine of "worthier title"[31] which stated that, if a person devised land to another person who was in fact his heir, that heir took by descent and not under the devise which became inoperative. No doubt the reasons for these rules lay in the fact that feudal incidents, such as relief, wardship and marriage, arose only in the case of descent.[32] The rule may, therefore, have been another example of the common law trying to prevent evasion of feudal dues. If one approaches the matter from the point of view of general principles of land law, one can see other reasons why the rule was attractive to conveyancers. If the word "heirs" was to be a word of purchase, there was still the question of how an estate could be vested in someone as yet unascertained.[33] Construing the word as a word of limitation avoided this question. That construction also meant that, if there were no intermediate

---

equitable fee simple was created under a trust which was declared by reference to a trust of personal property in the same settlement.
  [25] *White* v. *Baylor* (1846) 10 Ir.Eq.R. 43 at 53 (*per* Smith M.R.).
  [26] (1581) 1 Co.Rep. 88b.
  [27] Challis, *Law of Real Property* (3rd ed.), ch. XIII. See also Brooke-Taylor, "Section 3 of the Inheritance Act 1833 and Shelley's Case, A Forgotten Piece of Learning" [1979] Conv. 164; Hargreaves, "Shelley's Ghost" (1938) 54 L.Q.R. 70; Kales, "Application of Rule in Shelley's Case" (1912) 28 L.Q.R. 148; Megarry, "Shelley's Case and Doctrine of Very Heir" (1943) 59 L.Q.R. 272; "Shelley's Ghost" (1944) 60 L.Q.R. 222.
  [28] *Ibid.*; Megarry and Wade, *Law of Real Property* (5th ed., 1984), Appendix 2. *Van Grutten* v. *Foxwell* [1897] A.C. 658.
  [29] Megarry and Wade, *op. cit.*, p. 1161.
  [30] Challis, *op. cit.*, pp. 166–7.
  [31] This doctrine was abolished by the Inheritance Act, 1833, s. 3. See Brooke-Taylor, "Section 3 of the Inheritance Act 1833 and Shelley's Case, A Forgotten Piece of Learning" [1979] Conv. 164.
  [32] Paras. 2.18–24, *ante*.
  [33] On this subject, see para. 4.026, *ante*.

estate, the fee simple (or fee tail[34]) would merge with the first estate of freehold and take effect in possession immediately. Thus the fee simple would become freely alienable that much earlier.[35] Furthermore, if the remainder to the heirs was treating as containing words of purchase there was a problem as to what estate those "heirs" took. There were no words of limitation delimiting the estate of the heirs, so that in a conveyance *inter vivos* they could take a life estate only, if they were going to take anything.[36] There was also the problem that under the feudal law of inheritance a person could have one heir only (his eldest son), so that the plural form was perplexing as a word of purchase.

(i) General Operation of the Rule

4.035. The rule operates in two basic situations. It operates whenever a conveyance of land is made "to A for life, remainder to A's heirs" or "to B for life, remainder to the heirs of his body." The rule provides that in these examples, both of which appear to involve the granting of a life estate, followed by a remainder to heirs, the remainder does not give the heirs any estate. The rule provides that A has a life estate plus a fee simple in remainder, B a life estate plus a fee tail in remainder, and in both cases the two estates merge.[37] So in the one case A takes an immediate fee simple in possession and not merely a life estate, and in the other case B takes an immediate fee tail in possession and not merely a life estate. The "remainder" clause, in other words, is to be taken as containing words of limitation only and no words of purchase. No estate or interest is to be taken as being conveyed to A's heirs or B's heirs of his body. The result is, therefore, that the conveyances are treated as if they were worded instead: "to A and his heirs" and "to B and the heirs of his body." It cannot be reiterated too often that that is all the rule in *Shelley's Case* does provide; where the wording of the conveyance contains the standard formulae "to A and his heirs" or "to B and the heirs of his body," the rule has no application at all; those formulae create a fee simple or fee tail in the ordinary way and the rule has no application.

It is apparent, then, that the rule applies equally to the fee tail estate, and its application in this case will be considered later in this chapter.[38] For the moment the discussion will be confined to the case of the fee simple.

(ii) Elements of the Rule

(a) *Rule of Law*

4.036. The rule is a rule of law, not a matter of construction of the wording of

---

[34] For the rule's application to the fee tail estate, see para. 4.134, *post*.
[35] See ch. 8, *post*.
[36] See para. 4.025, *ante*.
[37] On the law of merger, see *Keogh* v. *Keogh* (1874) I.R. 8 Eq. 449; *Smith* v. *Smith* (1887) 19 L.R.Ir. 514; *Re Bury's Estate* [1898] 1 I.R. 379; *Re Bayly's Estate (No. 2)* [1898] 1 I.R. 383; *Re Lloyd's Estate* [1903] 1 I.R. 144; *Re Wallace's Estate* [1907] 1 I.R. 91; *Re Butlin's Estate* [1907] 1 I.R. 159; *Re Toppin's Estate* [1915] 1 I.R. 330; *Re Alexander's Estate* [1938] I.R. 23; *Kennedy* v. *Kennedy* [1939] Ir.Jur.Rep. 67. Also ch. 24, *post*.
[38] Para. 4.134, *post*.

the particular conveyance.[39] Thus the rule will apply whatever the declaration of intention on the part of the grantor in the conveyance.[40]

(b) Estate of Freehold

4.037. The rule applies only where an estate of freehold precedes the remainder to the heirs.[41] It applies, therefore, if the first estate is an estate tail, life estate or estate *pur autre vie* (which would include, in Ireland, a lease for lives renewable for ever[42] or a lease for lives and years[43]). It does not apply where the first estate granted is a leasehold estate, *e.g.*, "to A for 99 years, remainder to A's heirs." Here the remainder would have to be treated as containing words of purchase, whose effect would have to be determined under the general law of future interests.[44]

(c) Same Disposition

4.038. The rule applies only where the whole limitation is contained in the same deed, will or other disposition.[45] For these purposes a will and a codicil may be treated as the same disposition,[46] as may be a document creating a power of appointment and the document containing the exercise of that power.[47]

(d) Mediately or Immediately

4.039. It is not necessary that the remainder to the heirs should follow immediately upon the estate of freehold into which it will merge. The rule permits an intervening estate to exist, which may prevent an immediate merger of the freehold estate and the remainder to the heirs.[48] For example, the conveyance might be "to A for life, remainder to B for life, remainder to A's heirs." Here B's vested life estate prevents A's life estate in possession merging with his fee simple in remainder; his fee simple will remain vested in remainder[49] until B dies and a merger can take place.

It may be noted, however, that a merger would occur if B's estate were not vested, but contingent, *e.g.*, subject to some condition being satisfied before it vested in B, such as, that he should marry first or reach the age of 21.[50] In this situation it seems that a merger of A's life estate and fee simple remainder takes effect immediately, but when B's estate ceases to be contingent (*i.e.*, he satisfies the condition for vesting), A's estates separate to let in B's estate and

---

[39] *Cf.* the case of a will, para. 4.041, *infra*.
[40] Except for a special rule in the case of wills, see *Mandeville* v. *Lackey* (1795) 3 Ridgw. P.C. 352; *Van Grutten* v. *Foxwell* [1897] A.C. 659; and para. 4.041, *post*.
[41] *Harris* v. *Barnes* (1768) 4 Burr. 2158.
[42] See para. 4.167, *post*.
[43] See para. 4.177, *post*.
[44] See ch. 5, *post*.
[45] Fearne, *Contingent Remainders* (10th ed.), p. 71; Preston, *Estates* (2nd ed.), vol. 1. p. 309.
[46] *Hayes d. Foorde* v. *Foorde* (1770) 2 Wm.Bl. 698.
[47] *Venables* v. *Morris* (1797) 7 T.R. 342, 347–348; *cf.* Preston, *op. cit.*, p. 310.
[48] Preston, *op. cit.*, pp. 266–267. See further on merger, ch. 24, *post*.
[49] For the meaning of "vested in remainder," see para. 5.008, *post*.
[50] For further discussion of "vested" and "contingent," see ch. 5, *post*.

do not merge again until B's estate ends with his death.[51] A merger would also be prevented if the remainder to A's heirs was contingent.[52]

(e) Heirs

4.040. It has been a matter of some considerable controversy whether the rule requires the use of the word "heirs" (or "heirs of the body") in the plural. In other words, is the rule just as strict as the general common law rules relating to words of limitation?[53] It certainly seems to be the law that one must make a distinction in applying the rule, as one has to in the general law relating to words of limitation, between conveyances *inter vivos,* wills and equitable estates.

So far as conveyances *inter vivos* are concerned, the strict rule applies that the proper words of limitation must be used in the remainder clause—"heirs" or "heirs of the body."[54] The word "heir" in the singular is not a proper word of limitation and, if it is used, the rule will not apply.[55] In such a case, the first grantee would get a life estate only and his heir would take an estate in remainder. That estate in remainder would also be a life estate only unless further words, this time words of limitation, were added to the remainder clause, *e.g.,* "to A for life, remainder to A's heir *and his heirs.*"[56]

4.041. In the case of a will, it seems that the application of the rule was modified to some extent.[57] The courts did not totally abandon the general principle that the rule is a rule of law and not a rule of construction based on the intention of the grantor. But they did decide that a question of construction arose in a will with respect to the words used in the remainder clause. That question was whether the testator intended to give the remainder to the heirs generally (*i.e.,* what lawyers generally understand by the standard words of limitation "and his heirs" or "and the heirs of his body") or to one or more specific persons.[58] If, as a matter of construction, the court decides that the testator intended, by the words he used in the remainder clause, the heirs generally or "the whole class of heirs," then the rule applies, and no other expression of intention on the part of the testator about these words operating as words of purchase will prevent that application. Thus the rule may be held to apply where the expression used in the remainder clause is one like "issue" or "successors" or "children."[59]

If, on the other hand, the court, as a matter of construction of the will,

---

[51] Challis, *Law of Real Property* (3rd ed.), pp. 137–8, 153–4 and 163.

[52] Preston, *op. cit.,* p. 267; Challis, *op. cit.,* p. 163.

[53] Para. 4.025, *ante.*

[54] For a fee tail, see para. 4.128, *post.*

[55] Para. 4.025, *ante.*

[56] Challis, *op. cit.,* pp. 165–6.

[57] *Mandeville* v. *Lackey* (1795) 3 Ridgw.P.C. 352; *Van Grutten* v. *Foxwell* [1897] A.C. 659.

[58] *Ibid.* See also *Herbert* v. *Blunden* (1837) 1 Dr. & Wal. 78; *Crozier* v. *Crozier* (1843) 3 Dr. & War. 373; *Montgomery* v. *Montgomery* (1845) 8 Ir.Eq.R. 740; *Phillips* v. *Phillips* (1847) 10 Ir.Eq.R. 513; *Roddy* v. *Fitzgerald* (1858) 6 H.L.C. 823; *Colclough* v. *Colclough* (1870) I.R. 4 Eq. 263; *Macnamara* v. *Dillon* (1883) 11 L.R.Ir. 28; *Rotheram* v. *Rotheram* (1884) 13 L.R.Ir. 429; *Sandes* v. *Cooke* (1887) 21 L.R.Ir. 445; *Re Keane's Estate* [1903] 1 I.R. 215; *Re Taylor's Trusts* [1912] 1 I.R. 1; *Re Finlay's Estate* [1913] 1 I.R. 143; *Finch* v. *Foley* [1949] Ir.Jur.Rep. 30; *Re Fallon* [1956] I.R. 286.

[59] Challis, *op. cit.,* p. 164 and see cases cited in previous footnote.

decides that the expression used by the testator in the remainder clause was not intended by him to mean the heirs generally, but rather specific persons (*personae designatae*), the rule will not apply. The words will be treated as words of purchase and the *personae designatae* will take their estate accordingly.[60]

4.042. On the question of use of the word "heir" in the singular, it is not clear what the position under a will is. It can be argued that the use of the singular is a clear indication of intention on the part of the testator that a specific person is to take the estate, and not the heirs generally. Yet there are cases, at least in England, where the rule has nevertheless been applied to wills involving use of the word "heir" in the singular.[61] If, however, that word is followed by words of limitation, the rule does not apply whether in a deed or will, and the heir takes the appropriate estate by purchase.[62] Indeed, there is some authority for saying that such "superadded" words of limitation will also prevent the rule's application in a case where "heirs" plural is used in the remainder clause. The principle here seems to be, at least in the case of wills, that such added words of limitation indicate that the first word "heirs" in the clause must be a word of purchase.[63]

So far as equitable estates are concerned, the general maxim applies that equity follows the law. But this, it seems, is so only where both limitations are equitable. If one is legal and the other equitable the rule does not apply, *e.g.,* a grant "to A and B for the life of C on trust for C for his life, then to C's heirs" gives an estate to C's heirs.

D. Classification

4.043. There are several types of fee simple. These are usually divided for the purposes of analysis into two main categories: a fee simple *absolute* and a *modified* fee simple (often referred to by the shorthand description, a "modified fee"). As the term implies, a fee simple absolute forms one category on its own whereas the category of modified fees can be subdivided into several types of fee simple. In other words, by definition any fee simple other than a fee simple absolute is a modified fee.[64]

---

[60] Megarry and Wade, *op. cit.*, p. 1163. *Cf.* the Irish cases of *Finch* v. *Foley* [1949] Ir.Jur.Rep. 30 and *Re Fallon* [1956] I.R. 286 with the English case of *Re Williams* [1952] Ch. 828, see para. 4.134, *post.*

[61] *Whiting* v. *Wilkins* (1612) 1 Bulstr. 219; *Silcocks* v. *Silcocks* [1916] 2 Ch. 161; *Re Hack* [1925] Ch. 633; *cf. Re Davison's Settlement* [1913] 2 Ch. 498; Fearne, *op. cit.*, p. 178.

[62] *Boyley* v. *Morris* (1799) 4 Ves. 788; *Evans* v. *Evans* [1892] 2 Ch. 173. In *Gilbourne* v. *Gilbourne* (1975) Unrep. (H.C.,R.I.) (1974 No. 163 Sp) (see *A Casebook on Irish Land Law* (1984), p. 129), Kenny J. reiterated the principles stated in these paragraphs. That case involved a will under which the remainder after a joint life interest was to go to the "heir-at-law" of the surviving joint tenant. Kenny J. concluded that "the construction of the will indicates that the testator was using the word 'heir-at-law' in the sense that he was referring to a designated person, the individual who would be the heir-at-law of the survivor of Patrick and William [the joint tenants]." Therefore the rule in *Shelley's Case* did not apply in this case, though Kenny J. did expressly recognise that "the word heir-at-law can attract the rule." An appeal against this decision was lodged, but was, with consent, dismissed.

[63] *Hamilton* v. *West* (1846) 10 Ir.Eq.Rep. 75. *Cf.* English cases of *Re Hussey* [1921] 1 Ch. 566; *Re Routledge* [1942] 1 Ch. 457. Challis, *op. cit*, p. 164; Megarry, "Shelley's Case and the Doctrine of Very Heir" (1943) 59 L.Q.R. 272.

[64] See Challis, *Law of Real Property* (3rd ed.), pt. III; Megarry and Wade, *Law of Real Property* (5th ed., 1984), pp. 67–76. It should be noted, however, that the term "modified fee" is sometimes given a wider meaning

1. *Fee Simple Absolute*

4.044. The expression "fee simple absolute" is not a term of art,[65] but in this context is usually taken to mean that the fee simple is held free of all restrictions other than those imposed by the general law, *e.g.*, as a matter of public policy,[66] or by statute, *e.g.*, planning legislation.[67]

4.045. In Northern Ireland the great bulk of agricultural land, which has been bought out under the Land Purchase Acts,[68] will probably be held by its owners in fee simple absolute once the land purchase annuities have been paid off.[69] This is because the statutory restrictions on sub-division and sub-letting on land bought out under the Acts[70] will last only as long as the annuities are being paid. Once these are paid off the land becomes free of such statutory incidents.[71] In the Republic, however, such statutory incidents remain attached to holdings bought out under the Land Purchase Acts after 1923, even when the annuities are paid off (except in the case of what has become or is near to urban land).[72] It is questionable, however, whether continuance of such restrictions after the ending of the land purchase annuity charges would prevent the estates in question from being regarded as held for fees simple absolute, within the above definition. Indeed, it is arguable that those charges themselves do not prevent the estates sold to tenant purchasers being regarded as fees simple absolute.[73]

In respect of urban land in Ireland, however, a fee simple absolute is rare. Here, as we shall see, many fees simple are held in fee farm, *i.e.*, subject to a perpetual rent and various rights and interests retained by the grantor,[74] and most Irish forms of fee farm grant come into the category of modified fees.[75] It should be noted, however, that fee farm grants are much more common in Northern Ireland than in the Republic of Ireland.

2. *Modified Fees*

(i) **Determinable Fee**

4.046. A determinable fee is a fee simple which will determine *automatically*

so as to cover all fees other than a fee simple absolute, so as to include, *e.g.*, a fee tail: see Challis, *op. cit.*, p. 62. And the terms "the fee" or "fee simple" are often taken to mean the fee simple absolute unless the contrary is indicated, Challis, *op. cit.*, p. 438.

[65] *Cf.* the position in England where the term "fee simple absolute in possession" has a statutory definition, Law of Property Act, 1925, ss. 1 (1) (*a*) and 7; Law of Property (Amendment) Act, 1926, Sched. See *Re Claytou's Deed Poll* [1980] Ch. 99. The term has been used recently in an Irish statute, see Land Development Values (Compensation) Act (N.I.), 1965, s. 2. See also *Survey of the Land Law of Northern Ireland* (1971), ch. 2.

[66] Para. 4.052, *post*.

[67] Para. 1.77, *ante*.

[68] Para. 1.67, *ante*.

[69] Para. 1.68, *ante*.

[70] See Irish Land Act, 1903, s. 54 (1). *Poe* v. *Gillen* [1935] N.I. 1; *Moley's Case* [1957] N.I. 130.

[71] Leitch, "Present-Day Agricultural Tenancies in Northern Ireland" (1965) 16 N.I.L.Q. 491.

[72] See Land Acts, 1923, s. 65; 1927, ss. 3 and 4; 1936, s. 44; 1939, s. 23; 1946, ss. 3 and 6; 1965, ss. 12 and 13. *McGillicuddy* v. *Joy* [1959] I.R. 189; *Carew* v. *Jackman* [1966] I.R. 177; *Horgan* v. *Deasy* (1979) Unrep. (H.C., R.I.) (1976 No. 455P). See the discussion in *Irish Conveyancing Law* (1978), ch.8. See further, para. 18.03, *post*.

[73] See Megarry and Wade, *op. cit.*, pp. 142–4.

[74] Para. 4.059, *post*.

[75] *Cf.* the English form, Megarry and Wade, *op. cit.*, p. 127.

on the occurrence of an event which may or may not happen.[76] In other words, should the event in question occur the fee simple will definitely come to an end at that point in time; but it is not certain that the event in question will occur at any particular point in time or, indeed, ever occur at all.[77] In a sense all fees simple are determinable fees, at least in Northern Ireland, because any fee simple may determine if the current holder dies intestate leaving no intestate successor.[78] But that is a rather special case, for here the determination is governed by the general law of intestate succession.[79] The point about a determinable fee, as that expression is usually used, is that the determining event is specified by the original grantor of the estate. Such an estate is similar to another kind of modified fee, a fee simple upon a condition, which is discussed below. Often it is a difficult matter of construction whether the estate is a determinable fee or a fee simple upon a condition. But whatever the questions of construction, the consequences and incidents of the estates are different, as we shall see.[80]

Examples of grants by way of determinable fee would be: "to A and his heirs so long as Northern Ireland remains part of the United Kingdom"; "to B in fee simple until he qualifies as a solicitor."[81]

4.047. There has been some controversy over the years whether a determinable fee could be validly granted, except under statute, since *Quia Emptores*, 1290.[82] The basic argument against validity is that, unlike in the case of a fee simple absolute, the grantor of a determinable fee retains some interest in the property. His interest is called a *possibility of reverter, i.e.,* the possibility of acquiring an estate in the future.[83] It has been suggested that retention of such an interest meant that the grant was a form of subinfeudation, a practice prohibited by *Quia Emptores* in the case of a fee simple. Furthermore, a possibility of reverter has been likened to escheat between lord and tenant.[84] But the generally accepted view now is that *Quia Emptores* did not prohibit the creation of determinable fees.[85] First, it is questionable whether an interest like a possibility of reverter, the most ephemeral of interests in land, should be treated as an estate or interest in land sufficiently substantive as to allow the creation of tenure between the grantor and grantee. It is a mere possibility of an

---

[76] See, generally, Challis, "Determinable Fees" (1887) 3 L.Q.R. 403; Farrer "Reverter to Donor of Determinable Fee" (1935) 49 L.Q.R. 240, (1936) 50 L.Q.R. 33 and (1937) 51 L.Q.R. 361; Gray, "Determinable Fees" (1887) 3 L.Q.R. 399; Hughes, "Reverter to Donor of Determinable Fee" (1937) 51 L.Q.R. 347; Powell, "Determinable Fees" (1923) 23 Col.L.Rev. 207.

[77] Were this not so, the estate would not qualify as a "fee," *i.e.,* an estate which may last for ever, para. 4.004, *ante.*

[78] *Cf.* in the Republic, para. 4.021, *ante.*

[79] Ch. 15, *post.*

[80] Paras. 4.049–55, *post.*

[81] See Challis, *Law of Real Property* (3rd ed.), ch. XVII.

[82] Para. 2.42, *ante.*

[83] This interest may, of course, be destroyed if the event in question becomes impossible, in which case the determinable fee becomes a fee simple absolute, *e.g.,* "a grant by G to A and his heirs until X becomes a solicitor"; if X dies without becoming a solicitor, A is left with a fee simple absolute and G is left with no interest at all in the land.

[84] See Gray, *Perpetuities* (4th ed., 1942), secs. 31 *et seq.* and 774 *et seq.; Hopper* v. *Liverpool Corporation* (1944) 88 Sol.Jo. 213.

[85] Morris and Leach, *The Rule Against Perpetuities* (2nd ed., 1962), pp. 209–10; Megarry and Wade, *The Law of Real Property* (5th ed.), p. 68.

estate in land arising in future, not a present estate or interest.[86] Secondly, it is doubtful if a possibility of reverter has anything to do with the law of escheat: escheat was a general law relating to intestate succession applying to all grants; a possibility of reverter arises only in the special case of a determinable fee and then only by the draftsmanship of the particular grantor or his conveyancer.[87] Thirdly, it has been argued that *Quia Emptores* by implication applied to a fee simple absolute only in prohibiting future subinfeudation.[88] Apart from this, in practice most determinable fees derive from statute, *e.g.*, in respect of land acquired for public purposes, such as railways during the nineteenth century.[89]

(ii) Fee Simple Upon a Condition

4.048. A fee simple upon a condition, often called a conditional fee,[90] is a fee simple to which is attached a condition subsequent, which may cause the estate to be brought to an end.[91] A condition *subsequent* must be distinguished from a condition *precedent*. The latter is a condition which must be satisfied first before the estate or interest becomes vested in the grantee.[92] The former is a condition which may result in forfeiture of an estate already vested in the grantee. Two examples should illustrate the distinction: "to A and his heirs if A reaches the age of 21" (condition precedent; A must become 21 before he gets his fee simple); "to A and his heirs provided A remains a solicitor" (condition subsequent; A has the fee simple from the date of the conveyance but may lose it if he ceases to be a solicitor).

Next the distinction must be drawn between a determinable fee and a fee simple upon a condition. There are two aspects of the distinction to be borne in mind: first, there is the question of how one can recognise which estate is created by the wording of a particular grant and, secondly, there are the different rules applying to the two types of fee simple.

(a) Creation

4.049. Whether a particular conveyance creates a determinable fee or a fee simple upon a condition is largely a matter of the precise wording of the

---

[86] *Att.-Gen.* v. *Cummins* [1906] 1 I.R. 406 (see *A Casebook on Irish Land Law* (1984), p. 131). In this case (heard in 1895) the Irish Court of Exchequer Division, through a judgment delivered by Palles C.B., rejected the suggestion that the rule against perpetuities applied to possibilities of reverter, see para. 4.055, *post*. Pettit, "Determinable Interests and Rule Against Perpetuities" (1957) 21 Conv. 213.

[87] *Cf.* Bennett V.-C. in *Hopper, op. cit.*; Megarry, (1948) 62 L.Q.R. 222

[88] Challis, *Law of Real Property* (3rd ed.), Appendix IV.

[89] See *Pickin* v. *British Railways Board* [1974] A.C. 765. Note also the School Sites (Ir.) Act, 1810, and Leases for Schools (Ir.) Act, 1881, which relate to leasehold land. See the Republic's Charities Act, 1973, s. 6.

[90] Unfortunately, this term is used in several senses; sometimes it covers both determinable fees and fees simple upon a condition (see, *e.g.*, Challis, *op. cit.*, pp. 261–2); sometimes it refers to the special case of a fee tail, *i.e.*, a fee simple conditional upon birth of issue before the statute *De Donis*, 1285 (see para. 4.113, *post*).

[91] See, generally, Benas, "Conditions in Restraint of Religion" (1943) 8 Conv. 6 and 66; Browder, "Conditions and Limitations in Restraint of Marriage" (1949) 47 Mich.L.Rev. 759; Delany, " 'Name and Arms' Clauses" (1951) 17 Ir.Jur. 35; Maitland, "Remainders After Conditional Fees" (1890) 6 L.Q.R. 22; Simes, "Effect of Impossibility Upon Conditions in Wills" (1936) 34 Mich.L.Rev. 909; Squibb, "End of Name and Arms Clause" (1953) 69 L.Q.R. 219; Stone, "Name Worship and Statutory Interpretation in the Law of Wills" (1963) 26 M.L.R. 652; Williams, "Conditions in Restraint of Marriage" (1896) 12 L.Q.R. 36.

[92] *Walker* v. *Lenehan* (1852) 4 Ir.Jur. (o.s.) 310; *Re Doherty* [1950] N.I. 83; *Re Blake* [1955] I.R. 89; *Kiersey* v. *Flahavan* [1905] 1 I.R. 45; *Horrigan* v. *Horrigan* [1904] 1 I.R. 271; *Fitzgerald* v. *Ryan* [1899] 2 I.R. 637; *Re Callaghan* [1937] I.R. 84; *Re Tighe* [1944] I.R. 166; *Re Mansfield* [1962] I.R. 454; *Re Hennessy* (1964) 98 I.L.T.R. 39; *Re Porter's Estate* [1975] N.I. 157; *McKillop* v. *McMullan* [1979] N.I. 85; *Re Gault* [1982] N.I. 170.

conveyance. The theory on this matter is clear. In the case of a determinable fee the words describing the determining event are part of the words of limitation, *i.e.,* they delimit the estate granted.[93] In the case of a fee simple upon a condition, however, the words containing the condition are not part of the words of limitation, they are independent words of condition.[94] These words of condition confer a *right of entry* on the grantor or his successor, which must be exercised to determine the fee simple; a *possibility of reverter* becomes an actual reverter operating automatically when the specified event occurs, because the estate has thereby come to its natural determination according to the words of limitation. The problem in each case is to determine the effect of the particular words used and it is not always an easy problem to solve.[95] The courts have adopted over the years some "rules of thumb" whereby particular words or phrases are taken to indicate one type of estate rather than another. Thus words like "while," "during," "until" and "as long as" tend to be interpreted as words of limitation creating a determinable fee[96]; words like "provided that," "on condition that" and "but if" are usually taken to mean words of condition.[97] The point now seems to have been reached that it is the form that counts, not the substantive intention of the grantor, so that the following two conveyances would be interpreted as passing different estates: "to A and his heirs so long as he remains a solicitor" (determinable fee); "to A and his heirs provided that if he ceases to be a solicitor . . ." (fee simple upon a condition). One Irish judge was moved to describe the distinction between the two types of fee simple as "little short of disgraceful to our jurisprudence."[98] In making this comment, the judge seems to have had in mind wills, which the court usually interpret more liberally than conveyances *inter vivos*. He continued:

> "The distinction is intelligible to a lawyer; but no testator except a lawyer could be expected to understand it, much less to have regard to it in framing his will. We must, however, take the law as we find it."

But however nonsensical the distinction may appear to the layman the fact remains that much depends upon it. Our legal system has devised different rules with respect to the two estates, and some of these rules we now discuss.

(b) *Determination*

4.050. In the case of a determinable fee, when the specified event occurs the fee simple comes to its natural determination according to the words of limitation, and the possibility of reverter takes effect automatically to confer

---

[93] Challis, *The Law of Real Property* (3rd ed.), pp. 252–3, 260–1; *Re King's Trusts* (1892) 29 L.R.Ir. 401 (see *A Casebook on Irish Land Law* (1984), p. 137).

[94] Challis, *op. cit.*, pp. 219–20, 260–1; *Re King's Trusts, op. cit.*

[95] Megarry and Wade, *Law of Real Property* (5th ed.), pp. 69–70.

[96] Challis, *op. cit.*, pp. 255–60; *Att.-Gen.* v. *Cummins* [1906] 1 I.R. 406 (see *A Casebook on Irish Land Law* (1984), p. 131).

[97] *Walsh* v. *Wightman* [1927] N.I. 1.

[98] *Re King's Trusts* (1892) 29 L.R.Ir. 401 at 410 (*per* Porter M.R.) (see *op. cit.*, p. 137).

the fee simple absolute on the grantor (or his successor if he has since died).[99] On the other hand, in the case of a fee simple upon a condition, the occurrence of the specified event, or satisfaction or breach of the condition, merely gives the grantor a right of entry so as to forfeit the grantee's estate.[1] Until that right is exercised, there is no forfeiture and the grantee continues to hold his estate.[2] Rights of entry and forfeiture arise in other areas of land law, and the courts have always been concerned to see that unfair advantage is not obtained through their invocation or exercise. The courts' general approach to conditions subsequent we discuss below.[3]

(c) Alienation

4.051. At common law a possibility of reverter and a right of entry for condition broken were descendible only, i.e., they could be inherited. They were neither alienable *inter vivos* nor devisable by will.[4] The main reason for this rule seems to have been the fact that they did not belong to the category of estates in land, being mere rights or incidents attached to estates.[5] But that common law position has been changed by statute, at least as regards rights of entry for condition broken. Such rights of entry became devisable under the Wills Act, 1837,[6] and alienable *inter vivos* under the Real Property Act, 1845.[7] It was, and is still in Ireland, the case that a right of entry for condition broken could be limited only in a conveyance to the grantor "and his heirs."[8] This rule has been abolished in England by the Law of Property Act, 1925, under which a conveyance may specify that such a right may be exercised by anyone and not merely the grantor and his successors in title.[9]

Possibilities of reverter were also descendible at common law, but it has never been clear whether they were alienable *inter vivos* or devisable by will.[10] The probable rule is that they were not and never have become so because neither the Wills Act, 1837, nor the Real Property Act, 1845, applied to possibilities of reverter. They would seem to suffer from the same flaws as rights of entry in the eyes of the common law and no statute has been passed in Ireland to change that position. The position in England is not much clearer, though the generally accepted view seems to be that the Law of Property Act, 1925, probably assimilated the position in this regard with rights of entry.[11] It is also the case still in Ireland that a possibility of reverter can exist only in the grantor and his heirs; it is a mere possibility of a future interest and, until it becomes an

---

[99] Challis, *op. cit.*, pp. 82–3. See also *Re Drought* (1967) 101 I.L.T.R. 1.

[1] Challis, *op. cit.*, p. 219.

[2] *Ibid.*; *Matthew Manning's Case* (1609) 8 Co. Rep. 94b at 95b.

[3] Para. 4.052, *post*.

[4] Challis, *op. cit.*, pp. 76–7, 176–7 and 228–9.

[5] Challis, *op. cit.*, pp. 76–7.

[6] S. 3.

[7] S. 6.

[8] Challis, *op. cit.*, p. 219.

[9] S. 4 (3). But such rights of entry are now subject to the rule against perpetuities, as are possibilities of reverter, para. 4.055, *post*.

[10] Challis, *op. cit.*, pp. 176–7 and 228–9.

[11] It depends on whether possibilities of reverter come within the expression "future equitable interest" in s. 4 (2) (*a*) of the 1925 Act. See Megarry and Wade, *Law of Real Property* (5th ed., 1984), p. 75.

actuality, there is nothing left in the grantor after his conveyance of the fee simple to be disposed of to someone else.[12]

There is one other matter about alienation to be mentioned. This is the extent to which the courts are prepared to allow grantors to impose restrictions on alienation of property in drafting their provisions about determining events or conditions subsequent. The courts have over the years adopted firm views on this subject as a matter of public policy and we discuss this matter next under the general heading of public policy.

(d) *Public Policy*

4.052. There are several aspects to the courts' approach to determinable fees and fees simple upon condition in matters of public policy. To a large extent a more lenient approach has been taken in the case of determinable fees, no doubt because of the courts' general attitude of strict interpretation of clauses purporting to bring about forfeitures and to make estates and interests void.[13]

(1) GENERAL

4.053. First, the courts will treat as invalid any condition which is illegal, immoral, a violation of constitutional rights under the Republic's Constitution or which otherwise contravenes what they regard as public policy.[14] Perhaps the most frequently litigated example of such conditions are those inserted in conveyances to restrain marriage.[15] Marriage is regarded as an institution essential to our society and so the courts will not allow grantors of property to prevent or discourage it by conditions inserted in their conveyances. It is a matter for the court in each case whether the particular condition will be declared void as contrary to public policy.[16] It seems clear that a *total* restriction will be declared void, *e.g.*, "to A in fee simple but if A marries the grantor has a right to entry," unless the court concludes that the restriction was not intended to prevent A from marrying but was part of a genuine intention by the grantor simply to provide for A for a certain period, *i.e.*, while he remained single.[17] Indeed, in this case the grantor would have been better advised to frame his conveyance in the form of a determinable fee, *e.g.*, "to A in fee simple until he marries." The courts have a quite different approach to such conveyances and rarely hold them void as against public policy.[18] The limitation is regarded as coming to its natural determination and there is no question of a forfeiture.[19] Once again we see that the formula used in the conveyance can make all the

---

[12] *Cf.* Law of Property Act, 1925, s. 4 (3).

[13] See articles cited in fn. 91, para. 4.048, *supra*.

[14] *Massy* v. *Rogers* (1883) 11 L.R.Ir. 409.

[15] *Duddy* v. *Gresham* (1878) 2 L.R.Ir. 442; *Re McLoughlin's Estate* (1878) 1 L.R.Ir. 421; *Gray* v. *Gray* (1889) 23 L.R.Ir. 399. *Cf. Re. Coghlan* [1963] I.R. 246 (see *A Casebook on Irish Land Law* (1984), p. 141).

[16] *Ibid.* See also *Re Armstrong* (1968) 19 N.I.L.Q. 215.

[17] *Duddy* v. *Gresham* (1878) 2 L.R.Ir. 442; *McConnell* v. *Beattie* (1904) 38 I.L.T.R. 133.

[18] *Re King's Trusts* (1892) 29 L.R.Ir. 401 (see *A Casebook on Irish Land Law* (1984), p. 137); *Oliver* v. *Menton* [1945] I.R. 6; *Re Robson* [1940] Ir.Jur.Rep. 72.

[19] *Ibid.*; *Re Elliott* [1918] 1 I.R. 41; *Stewart* v. *Murdoch* [1969] N.I. 78; *Re Dolan* [1970] I.R. 94.

difference to the validity of the grant. Difficult questions arise, however, where there is a *partial* restraint on marriage, *e.g.*, a prohibition against marrying a Protestant or a Catholic, without first obtaining someone else's consent.[20] It is a question of construction whether the particular restriction should be regarded as sufficiently in restraint of marriage (*in terrorem*) as to contravene public policy.[21] And there is always the possibility that a condition may be declared void for uncertainty.[22] Questions of uncertainty have frequently arisen where the condition has related to religious matters, *e.g.*, "practising the Roman Catholic religion,"[23] or bringing up children in the "Roman Catholic faith,"[24] or the taking of a particular name under a "name and arms" clause.[25] If the condition is void for uncertainty, or as being contrary to constitutional rights or public policy, the fee simple becomes a fee simple absolute.[26] In other words, only the condition fails and the fee simple itself remains in effect, provided it is conveyed with the appropriate words of limitation. The contrary is the position in the rare case of a limitation in a grant of a determinable fee being held void as against public policy.[27] Here the words of limitation themselves are defective and so fail to pass the fee simple; the whole grant is ineffective and the grantee

[20] *Lowry* v. *Patterson* (1874) I.R. 8 Eq. 372; *White* v. *McDermott* (1876) I.R. 7 C.L. 1; *Re McLoughlin's Estate* (1878) 1 L.R.Ir. 421; *In b. Knox* (1889) 23 L.R.Ir. 542; *Maguire* v. *Boylan* (1870) I.R. 5 Eq. 90; *Re Greene* [1895] 1 I.R. 130, 142; *Curran* v. *Corbet* [1897] 1 I.R. 343; *Re Burchill's Contract* (1912) 46 I.L.T.R. 35; *Re McKenna* [1947] I.R. 277.

[21] *Greene* v. *Greene* (1845) 8 Ir.Eq.R. 473; *Alleyne* v. *Alleyne* (1845) 8 Ir.Eq.R. 493; *Duggan* v. *Kelly* (1847) 10 Ir.Eq.R. 295; *Hackett* v. *Lord Oxmantown* (1948) 12 Ir.Eq.R. 534; *Adams* v. *Adams* (1858) 8 Ir.Ch.R. 41; *Re Newcomens* (1865) 16 Ir.Ch.R. 315; *Duddy* v. *Gresham* (1878) 2 L.R.Ir. 442; *Gray* v. *Gray* (1889) 23 L.R.Ir. 399.

[22] See, *e.g.*, *Re Coghlan* [1963] I.R. 246; *Re Hennessy* (1964) 98 I.L.T.R. 39. Also *McCausland* v. *Young* [1949] N.I. 49; *Burke and O'Reilly* v. *Burke and Quail* [1951] I.R. 216; *Re Blake* [1955] I.R. 89. Cf. *Duggan* v. *Kelly* (1847) 10 Ir.Eq.R. 295; *Re McKenna* [1947] I.R. 277; *Higgins* v. *Walsh* (1948) 82 I.L.T.R. 10; *Re Parker* [1966] I.R. 309.

[23] *Burke and O'Reilly, op. cit.* Cf. *McCausland* v. *Young* [1949] N.I. 49 (see *A Casebook on Equity and Trusts in Ireland* (1985), p. 27); *Re Vaughan* [1926] I.R. 67.

[24] *Re Blake, op cit.; cf. Higgins* v. *Walsh* (1948) 82 I.L.T.R 10. See the discussion in *Blathwayt* v. *Baron Cawley* [1976] A.C. 397; *Re Tuck's Settlement Trusts* [1978] Ch. 49.

[25] *Re Montgomery* (1955) 89 I.L.T.R. 62; *Bevan* v. *Mahon-Hagan* (1893) 31 L.R.Ir. 342; *Miller* v. *Wheatley* (1885) 28 L.R.Ir. 144; *Vandeleur* v. *Sloane* [1919] 1 I.R. 116; *Re Finlay* [1933] N.I. 89. *Cf. Re Talbot* [1932] I.R. 714; *Re Callaghan* [1937] I.R. 84; *Re De Vere's Will Trusts* [1961] I.R. 224. In *Kearns and McCarron* v. *Manresa Estates Ltd.* (1975) Unrep. (H.C., R.I.) (1974 No. 193 Sp) (see *A Casebook on Irish Land Law* (1984), p. 148), Kenny J. held that a "name and arms" clause was void for uncertainty because it was impossible to state when the disuse or discontinuance of the name in question occurred. In so doing, he followed the *Montgomery* and *De Vere* cases in Ireland and declined to follow the English Court of Appeal decision in *Re Neeld* [1962] Ch. 643 (upholding such a clause, and note that such a clause was also involved in the *Blathwayt* case, *supra*, and was apparently regarded as valid by the House of Lords). He was particularly critical of the English courts' use of the *de minimis* principle to justify disregard of "mistake or forgetfulness" or lapses in use:

> "But it is precisely the question as to what lapses are a disuse or a discontinuance that causes the difficulty for the Court. How many deliberate or unintentional lapses bring the "de minimis" principle into operation? How many lapses are necessary so that it can be said that "de minimis" does not apply? I have the highest respect for any view expressed by Upjohn L.J. (subsequently Lord Upjohn) but invoking the maxim of de minimis seems to me to be a way of avoiding difficulty. None of the judgments in *Re Neeld* deal with the question as to how the Court is to decide that at any given moment of time (and that, as Mr Justice Fry pointed out [in *Re Exmouth* (1883) 23 Ch. D. 158], is the critical question) a person has disused or discontinued to use the surname which he is obliged to assume."

He also pointed out that, since the *Montgomery* and *De Vere* decisions, "titles to property included in the Vernon estate [at issue before him] and in other estates have been accepted on the basis that names and arms are void for uncertainty in Ireland. A decision now that the clauses involved were valid would render these titles bad. Although I am not bound by decisions of other judges of the High Court, the usual practice is to follow them unless I am satisfied that they were wrongly decided. I am not so satisfied: indeed I think that the reasoning of Mr. Justice Dixon [in the *Montgomery* case] is unanswerable."

[26] *Re Coghlan* [1963] I.R. 246; *Re Hennessy* (1964) 98 I.L.T.R. 39. See also *Re Mulcair* [1960] I.R. 321.

[27] *E.g., Re Moore* (1888) 39 Ch.D. 116 (a case of personalty).

is left with nothing.[28] This position should not be confused with the situation where the possibility of reverter becomes impossible because it becomes clear that the determining event will never occur. For example, with a grant "to A and his heirs until B becomes a solicitor," it is possible that B may die without becoming a solicitor. If and when that happens A's estate ceases to be a determinable fee and becomes a fee simple absolute.[29]

(2) RESTRICTIONS ON ALIENATION

4.054. It has been a matter of general policy of our land law from the earliest days that freehold land should be freely alienable.[30] As far as the fee simple is concerned, this general principle was enshrined in *Quia Emptores,* 1290.[31] It is clear that an attempt to impose a condition in total restriction on alienation by the grantee of a fee simple is void.[32] Where the condition is not a total restriction, it is a question for the court as a matter of public policy whether it is so restrictive as to be void. In deciding this the court has to balance the competing interests of free disposition of property by grantors and the general policy of ensuring marketability of freehold land.[33] Thus a covenant by the grantee of a fee simple not to divide it into more than four lots without the consent of the grantor or his successors was held void.[34] A condition in a will devising property to four brothers in fee simple and to two other brothers *pur autre vie,* whereby no brother could sell his interest except to one of his brothers, was held void.[35] Also held void was a provision under which the grantee of a fee simple could not sell it unless all his brothers refused to buy it for £100.[36] However, in Ireland, a fee farm grant may contain a valid restriction on alienation, a subject to which we shall return.[37]

This general rule against inalienability applies in principle to other freehold estates like the fee tail and life estate. In the case of a life estate the courts have been more inclined to regard restrictions on alienation, and similar restrictions, with more leniency and to treat them like limitations rather than conditions. Thus it became common for the courts to recognise and enforce clauses determining life estates on alienation, or on bankruptcy.[38] Restraints upon

[28] Note that this is not the case in N.I. where a possibility of reverter is void under the rule against perpetuities, as amended by the Perpetuities Act (N.I.), 1966, which in such a case renders the fee simple absolute, see para. 5.109, *post.*

[29] Challis, *The Law of Real Property* (3rd ed.), p. 254.

[30] See Gray, *Restraints on the Alienation of Property* (2nd ed.); Manning, "Development of Restraints on Alienation Since Gray" (1935) 48 H.L.R. 373; Smout, "Racial and Religious Restraints on Alienation" (1952) 30 C.B.R. 863; Sweet, "Restraints on Alienation" (1917) 33 L.Q.R. 236 and 342. See discussion in *Re Congested Districts Board* [1919] 1 I.R. 146.

[31] Para. 2.46, *ante.*

[32] *Byrne* v. *Byrne* (1953) 87 I.L.T.R. 183; see also *Waugh* v. *Harshaw* (1902) 36 I.L.T.R. 20; *Re Kelly-Kenny* (1904) 38 I.L.T.R. 163.

[33] *Re McDonnell* [1965] I.R. 354; *Martin* v. *Martin* (1886) 19 L.R.Ir. 72.

[34] *Re Lunham's Estate* (1871) I.R. 5 Eq. 170 (a case of a fee farm grant, see para. 4.110, *post*).

[35] *Crofts* v. *Beamish* [1905] 2 I.R. 349 (see *A Casebook on Irish Land Law* (1984), p. 144). See also *Re Hennessy* (1964) 98 I.L.T.R. 39; *Re McDonnell* [1965] I.R. 354. *Cf.* the famous English case of *Re Macleay* (1875) L.R. 20 Eq. 186, distinguished in *Re Brown* [1954] Ch. 39.

[36] *McGowan* v. *Grimes* (1921) 55 I.L.T.R. 208.

[37] Paras. 4.086 and 4.101, *post.*

[38] *Re Moore's Estate* (1885) 17 L.R.Ir. 549; *Re Walsh's Estate* [1905] 1 I.R. 261. See para. 9.083, *post.*

anticipation so as to prevent married women from disposing of property were also enforced.[39] A restraint upon anticipation was a clause which prohibited a wife to whom a limited estate was given from anticipating the future income of the land. The result was, for example, that she could not mortgage it. The extent to which the courts will go to uphold such restrictions in the case of life estates was indicated by one Irish case in which land was devised to the testator's wife "on condition that she has no power to sign away or will said property to anyone but my brother John." Instead of construing this as a devise of a fee simple subject to a void restraint on alienation, the court construed it as one to the wife for life only, with a remainder to John.[40]

(3) RULE AGAINST PERPETUITIES

4.055. It has been a matter of some controversy whether the rule against perpetuities (which we shall discuss in more detail later[41]) applied at common law to interests like a possibility of reverter or a right of entry for condition broken.[42] The position in England seemed to be that the rule applied at common law both to a possibility of reverter (at least in respect of land)[43] and to a right of entry for condition broken.[44] But whatever was the position in England at common law it has been put beyond doubt by statute that the rule applies now in both cases.[45] In Ireland, however, the courts have taken a contrary view of the common law. In *Att.-Gen.* v. *Cummins*[46] the Irish Exchequer Division, led by Palles C.B., held that the rule did not apply to possibilities of reverter, so that they could operate at any time in the future. In *Walsh* v. *Wightman*,[47] the Northern Ireland Court of Appeal refused to follow the English authorities and held that the rule did not apply to a right of entry for condition broken. This remains the position in the Republic, but Northern Ireland has since passed legislation to conform with English law.[48]

(iii) Base Fee

4.056. A base fee is a special kind of determinable fee which can be created in connection with a fee tail estate. In view of this connection it will be discussed in the section dealing with the fee tail estate.[49]

---

[39] *Re Dillon* (1916) 50 I.L.T.R. 144; *Re Taylor* [1914] 1 I.R. 111; *Re Keller's Estate* (1928) 62 I.L.T.R. 9. Such restraints were abolished in Northern Ireland by the Married Women (Restraint upon Anticipation) Act (N.I.), 1952 and in the Republic by the Married Women's Status Act, 1957. See para. 25.14, *post.*

[40] *Manning* v. *O'Boyle* (1930) 64 I.L.T.R. 43.

[41] Paras. 5.056 *et seq., post.*

[42] See, generally, Gray, *Rule Against Perpetuities* (4th ed., 1942); Morris and Leach, *The Rule Against Perpetuities* (2nd ed., 1962; Supp., 1964); Challis, *The Law of Real Property* (3rd ed.), ch. XIV; Pettit, "Determinable Interests and Rule Against Perpetuities" (1957) 21 Conv. 213.

[43] *Hopper* v. *Corporation of Liverpool* (1944) 88 Sol.Jo. 213 (Megarry, 62 L.Q.R. 222).

[44] *Re Hollis' Hospital* [1899] 2 Ch. 540; *Cf. Third Report of the Real Property Commissioners* (1832), pp. 29 and 36.

[45] Perpetuities and Accumulations Act, 1964, s. 12.

[46] [1906] 1 I.R. 406 (see *A Casebook on Irish Land Law* (1984), p. 131).

[47] [1927] N.I. 1.

[48] Perpetuities Act (N.I.), 1966, s. 13 and see para. 5.108, *post.*

[49] See especially para. 4.136, *post.*

IV. FEE FARM GRANTS

A. GENERAL

4.057. A fee farm grant is a conveyance of a fee simple subject to payment by the grantee and his successors in title to the grantor and his successors in title of a perpetual rent.[50] The fee simple estate so conveyed exhibits the characteristics of the estate just described in the immediately preceding pages, but the significance of fee farm grants lies in the special features attached to that estate in the conveyances that have become so common in Ireland. These are significant because in many respects they are unique in the common law world. It is true that in a few areas of the North and South-West of England, particularly around Manchester and East Lancashire and the Bath, Bristol areas, fee farm grants of a particular type are quite common.[51] These are grants creating perpetual rentcharges which are a rare category in Ireland and which do not exhibit the striking features of other categories more common in Ireland.[52]

In view of the fact that the categories of grants in Ireland have widely divergent origins and characteristics, it is more convenient to discuss matters like their creation, words of limitation and rights of the parties separately in relation to each category.

B. CLASSIFICATION

4.058. Fee farm grants fall into three main categories.[53]: (1) those creating *feudal tenure* between the grantor and grantee; (2) those creating the modern *landlord and tenant* relationship between the grantor and grantee; (3) those creating the relationship of *rentchargor and rentchargee* between the grantor and grantee.[54] These categories are mutually exclusive in relation to the relationship created between the parties to the grants and their successors in title, though they do, of course, share some common features. The most obvious common features are that in every fee farm grant a fee simple estate is conveyed which, in each case, is subject to a perpetual rent.

1. *Feudal Tenure*

4.059. Fee farm grants of this nature create the relationship of lord and tenant as it developed under the feudal system of landholding.[55] This sort of grant,

---

[50] Quoted with approval by Murray J. in *Re Courtney* [1981] N.I. 58 at 62–3. Murray J.'s judgment contains an interesting discussion of several points relating to fee farm grants. See, generally, Mecredy, *The Law of Fee Farm Grants* (1877); Strahan and Baxter, *The Law of Real Property* (3rd ed., 1926); Stubbs and Baxter, *Irish Forms and Precedents*, pp. 87–116; *Survey of the Land Law of Northern Ireland* (1971), ch. 20; Montrose, "Fee Farm Grants" (1938) 2 N.I.L.Q. 194, (1939) 3 N.I.L.Q. 40, 81 and 143, (1940) 4 N.I.L.Q. 40 and 86; Wylie, "Fee Farm Grants—Montrose Continued" (1972) 23 N.I.L.Q. 285.

[51] See Ruoff and Roper, *Registered Conveyancing* (4th ed., 1979), ch. 28; Ruoff, *Rentcharges in Registered Conveyancing* (1961); Rentcharges Act, 1977; Bennett, "Fee Farm Grants Purchased from the Crown" (1903) 19 L.Q.R. 417.

[52] See para. 4.104, *post*.

[53] See Montrose, *op. cit.*

[54] Montrose's series of articles (fn. 50, *supra*) was never completed and does not cover this third category, but see Wylie (*ibid.*).

[55] Ch. 2, *ante*.

therefore, involves the conveyancing process of "subinfeudation" which was prohibited for both England and Ireland by the statute *Quia Emptores,* 1290.[56] Thus for any grant of this nature to exist in England today it would have had to have been created before 1290 and to have survived since then—a highly unlikely event.[57] But in Ireland the story has been somewhat different, at least since the seventeenth century.

It has already been mentioned that during that century much Irish land was confiscated by the Crown and regranted to landowners owing allegiance to the Crown.[58] In making these regrants, usually by letters patent, it became the practice of the Crown to convey the land to the grantee to hold of the Crown subject to a chief rent, known as a "quit rent" in Ireland.[59] The letters patent then usually went on to grant a special dispensation from the statute *Quia Emptores* to the grantee so as to enable him to subinfeudate by way of fee farm grants *"non obstant Quia Emptores* or any other law or custom."[60] The Crown was not mentioned in *Quia Emptores* expressly or by necessary implication, so it was not bound by the statute and could freely make grants of the confiscated Irish land.[61] However, there was some doubt whether the Crown could grant a dispensation to its grantees to enable them to subinfeudate contrary to the statute. Judicial notice was taken of this point in some Irish cases but there seems to be no authoritative decision on the matter.[62] It is extremely doubtful whether it could be argued with much force today for at least two reasons. First, the Irish Parliament passed a series of statutes in the seventeenth century to resolve doubts about, and to quiet the titles to, lands conveyed in such *non obstante* grants.[63] It may be argued that, while it is probable that these were primarily concerned with the original Crown grants, impliedly they confirmed sub-grants made under powers conferred by the original grants.[64] Secondly, whatever the technical doubts, the fact remains that many of the original Crown grantees exercised their powers of subinfeudation and executed a large number of fee farm grants which survive to this day. These grants, and subsequent sub-grants, have been acted upon by all concerned without challenge or question for two centuries. The current holders of land under such grants, and their predecessors before them, have long since acquired good "holding

---

[56] Para. 2.43, *ante.*

[57] Megarry and Wade, *The Law of Real Property* (5th ed., 1984), pp. 818 and 828.

[58] Paras. 1.29–34, *ante.*

[59] See *Corporation of Dublin* v. *Herbert* (1861) 12 I.C.L.R. 502; *Tuthill* v. *Rogers* (1844) 6 Ir.Eq.R. 429; *Massy* v. *O'Dell* (1859) 9 Ir.Ch.R. 441; *Hatton* v. *Waddy* (1834) Hay. and Jon. 601; *Re Maxwell's Estate* (1891) 28 L.R.Ir. 356. Anon., "A Notice on Quit Rents in Northern Ireland" (1952) 10 N.I.L.Q. 30. See para. 6.009, *post.*

[60] See, *e.g.,* the terms of the grant by Charles I to Viscount Montgomery of the Manor of Donaghadee in *Delacherois* v. *Delacherois* (1864) 11 H.L.C. 62.

[61] Para. 2.43, *ante. Re Maxwell's Estate* (1891) 28 L.R.Ir. 356, 358.

[62] *Delacherois* v. *Delacherois, op. cit.; Verschoyle* v. *Perkins* (1847) 13 Ir.Eq.R. 72; *Butler* v. *Archer* (1860) 12 I.C.L.R. 104.

[63] Settlement of Ireland Acts, 1634 (10 Chas. 1, sess. 1, c. 3), 1639 (15 Chas. 1, c. 6), 1662 (14 & 15 Chas. 2, sess. 4, c. 2), 1665 (17 & 18 Chas. 2, c. 3) and 1698 (10 Will. 3, c. 7). These statutes were all repealed in the Republic of Ireland by the Statute Law Revision (Pre-Union Irish Statutes) Act, 1962. As regards N.I., see the Property (N.I.) Order, 1978, art. 16(2) and Sched.2.

[64] For judicial discussion of these Settlement Acts, see *Delacherois* v. *Delacherois, op. cit.; Little* v. *Moylett* [1929] I.R. 439; *Moore* v. *Att.-Gen.* [1934] I.R. 44. See also *Tuthill* v. *Rogers* (1844) 6 Ir.Eq.R. 429; *Tisdall* v. *Parnell* (1863) 14 I.C.L.R. 1.

titles," based on adverse possession,[65] if nothing else.

4.060. Feudal fee farm grants are more common in Northern Ireland than in the Republic of Ireland, for the powers of creating them were standard clauses in the grants made to the participants in the Ulster plantation.[66] It may be questioned whether many could survive after the land purchase operation, which involved the redemption of all superior rents and interests so as to ensure the vesting of a fee simple absolute in the tenant-purchaser (subject to the terminable land purchase annuity).[67] However, it must be remembered that a considerable proportion of the land originally subject to fee farm grants had ceased to be used for agricultural or pastoral purposes by the time of the land purchase scheme and so was outside its scope. This land is now to be found in the urban areas of Ireland that have developed since the seventeenth century and fee farm and sub-fee farm grants remain important links in the chains of title to that land.[68]

(i) Creation

4.061. Feudal grants will have been created either before 1290 or under powers conferred in Crown grants of Irish land of the seventeenth century. The former type are unlikely to be met nowadays by practitioners; any made prior to 1290 would have long since ceased to have effect in view of the turbulent history of Irish land and the frequent changes in its ownership over the centuries since then.[69] As regards the latter any likely exercise of the powers conferred in the Crown grants will have long since been made. Indeed, most, if not all, feudal grants surviving in Ireland today would have been executed originally before 1845, so that the modern deed of conveyance introduced by the Real Property Act, 1845, would not have been used.[70] The modes of conveyance used for such grants would have been those devised by the conveyancers after the Statute of Uses (Ireland), 1634, namely the bargain and sale and lease and release combined,[71] or a covenant to stand seised.[72] These were discussed in more detail in an earlier chapter.[73]

(ii) Words of Limitation

4.062. A fee farm grant involves the conveyance of a fee simple and so the appropriate words of limitation would have to be used in the grant, in accordance with the rules discussed above.[74] However, it should be noted with respect to feudal grants that not all the modes of conveyance likely to be used in

---

[65] Ch. 23, *post.*
[66] Para. 1.30, *ante.*
[67] Paras. 1.51. *et seq., ante.*
[68] For further discussion of this subject, see paras. 4.179 *et seq., post.*
[69] Ch. 1, *ante.* The method of conveyance in such old grants would presumably have been by the old feudal mechanism, namely, feoffment with livery of seisin, para. 3.023, *ante.*
[70] Para. 3.026, *ante.*
[71] See, *e.g., Delacherois* v. *Delacherois* (1864) 11 H.L.C. 62.
[72] See, *e.g., Re Sergie* [1954] N.I. 1 (see *A Casebook on Irish Land Law* (1984), p. 70).
[73] Ch. 3, *ante.*
[74] Para. 4.024, *ante.*

executing these involved a conveyance of the fee simple estate. A feoffment with livery of seisin, the oldest mode of conveyance, did involve such a conveyance and so would require use of appropriate words of limitation.[75] If a lease and release were used, the lease itself did not involve a conveyance of the fee simple and so no words of limitation were required. The release operated to extinguish the reversion on the lease rather than to convey it, so it seems that words of limitation were not required for it either.[76] As regards the bargain and sale and covenant to stand seised, these both raised uses recognised originally only by the Courts of Equity, and it is doubtful if words of limitation were any more necessary than in the case of wills.[77] or equitable interests,[78] though in these cases the uses were executed and created legal estates as a result of the Statute of Uses (Ireland), 1634.[79]

(iii) Fee Farm Rents

4.063. Feudal grants create feudal tenure between the grantor and the grantee and so the rent is what is known as a rent service as opposed to a rent-charge or rent seck.[80] As part of the relationship of lord and tenant the obligation to pay the rent binds the successors in title of the grantee, and the right to receive it accrues to the successors in title of the grantor.

4.064. As a rent service, the fee farm rent is recoverable by, in addition to an ordinary action for debt, the common law remedy of distress, irrespective of any express reservation of this right in the original or any subsequent grant. Distress was, in former times, the main remedy for the recovery of arrears of rent. The landlord entered on the land and seized cattle or other articles belonging to the tenant, which he could later sell and use the proceeds to pay the arrears. As we shall see in a later chapter, there have been many statutory provisions on the subject of distress.[81] In England, because *Quia Emptores*, 1290, prohibited subinfeudation and thereby prevented the subsequent creation of tenure in a grant of a fee simple, a rent service and its attendant right of distress had come to be regarded as existing only where a lease was granted reserving a reversion to the landlord.[82] Irish seventeenth century feudal grants, however, pass a fee simple with no reversion at all left in the grantor, and so there are some doubts as to how many of the statutes relating to distress apply to feudal fee farm grantors. The matter is largely one of construction and the essential issue in each case is whether the particular statute is drafted widely enough to cover such fee farm grants or is confined in its application to the modern landlord and tenant relationship, which can also exist between fee farm grantors and grantees.[83] Thus it may be argued that the early feudal

[75] Para. 3.023, *ante.*
[76] *Coke Upon Littleton* (19th ed., 1832), 193b. *Estoss's Case* (1597) 3 Dy. 263a.
[77] Para. 4.031, *ante.*
[78] Para. 4.033, *ante.*
[79] Para. 3.024, *ante.*
[80] See, generally, para. 6.132, *post.*
[81] Para. 17.064, *post.*
[82] Halsbury, *The Laws of England* (4th ed., 1975), vol. 13, pp. 109–96; Halsbury, *The Statutes of England* (4th ed., 1985), vol. 13, pp. 549–89.
[83] *Cf.* Montrose, (1939) 3 N.I.L.Q. 40 at 44 and at 150–1.

statutes relating to distress cover feudal fee farm grants, *e.g.*, Statute of Marlborough, 1267[84]; Statute of Westminster I, 1275[85]; Statute of Westminster II, 1285[86]; Distress for Rent Acts (Ireland), 1634, 1695, 1712, 1721 and 1751.[87] Whether or not these Acts can be said to have impliedly applied to feudal fee farms grants, the Fee Farm Rents (Ireland) Act, 1851,[88] expressly extended to "all Fee-farm Rents," where the persons to whom such rents were payable had no reversions, all the remedies for recovery of rent provided by sections 20 and 21 of the Renewable Leasehold Conversion Act, 1849,[89] *except* actions of ejectment for non-payment of rent.[90] As regards the later statutes dealing with distress, it is probable that these were meant to be confined to the modern relationship of landlord and tenant and did not extend to feudal fee farm grants.[91] Finally, as regards Northern Ireland, it should be noted that distress as a remedy has recently been abolished and replaced by enforcement of a court judgment through the Enforcement of Judgments Office.[92]

The other main remedy that a grantor might seek in relation to the fee farm rent would be forfeiture of the grant. The subject of forfeiture generally is, perhaps, one of the most difficult aspects of feudal fee farm grants and it is to this subject that we now turn.

(iv) Forfeiture

4.065. It was a general principle of early feudal law that, if the tenant did anything which could be regarded as a denial of his lord's title, his lord had the right to forfeit the tenant's holding, because this amounted to a breach of the basic duty of homage underlying the feudal tenurial relationship.[93] Then the Statute of Gloucester, 1278,[94] expressly provided that a lord who "let his land in fee-farm" and later found that, because of his tenant's mismanagement, there was nothing to distrain for non-payment of the rent, could, after a period of two years, bring an action to demand the land back, "by writ out of the Chancery."[95] The Statute of Westminster II, 1285, provided that such "writs of entry" could be obtained by heirs of the grantor against heirs and alienees of the grantee.[96] Despite these provisions, however, there grew up amongst conveyancers a practice of inserting express provisions with respect to

---

[84] Cc. 1, 2, 4, 9, 15 and 22.
[85] Cc. 16 and 17.
[86] Cc. 2 and 37.
[87] Repealed by Deasy's Act, 1860, only in so far as it related to the modern relationship of landlord and tenant dealt with by the 1860 Act.
[88] The 1851 Act was held to be retrospective in *Major* v. *Barton* (1851) 2 I.C.L.R. 28.
[89] *I.e.*, actions for debt and distress.
[90] S. 1. See ch. 17, *post*. On the 1851 Act, see *Butler* v. *Archer* (1860) 12 I.C.L.R. 104.
[91] *E.g.*, Ejectment and Distress (Ir.) Act, 1846; Landlord and Tenant (Ir.) Act, 1851; Landlord and Tenant Law Amendment Act, Ireland, 1860 (Deasy's Act), s. 51; Law of Distress and Small Debts (Ir.) Act, 1888, and Law of Distress Amendment Act, 1908, s. 10. See para. 17.065, *post*.
[92] Judgments (Enforcement) Act (N.I.), 1969, s. 132, Sched. 6. The 1969 Act has since been consolidated in the Judgments Enforcement (N.I.) Order, 1981.
[93] This right should not be confused with the King's right of forfeiture for treason, see para. 2.23, *ante*.
[94] C. 4.
[95] The statute provided that the tenant could keep the land if he tendered the arrears and any damages due. This action was one of the old real actions (para. 4.008, *ante*), and c. 4 was repealed by the Statute Law Revision (Ir.) Act, 1872.
[96] C. 21.

forfeiture in feudal grants and a general body of law evolved governing these provisions at common law.

4.066. It became a general rule that, before a grantor could rely on the terms of his grant for his right of forfeiture, he had to prove that either the agreement which he claimed had been broken by the grantee had been expressly drafted as a *condition* of the grantee's holding the land, or, if it had been drafted simply as a covenant by the grantee, that there had been included in the grant a separate *forfeiture clause,* reserving to the grantor the express right of forfeiture for breach of any of the grantee's covenants. This rule was later applied to leases so as to govern the modern relationship of landlord and tenant.[97]

4.067. With respect to feudal fee farm grants, it would seem that this general rule about covenants and conditions governs forfeiture both for non-payment of rent and for breach of any other grantee's obligation in the grant. Apart from the very early thirteenth century statutes mentioned above, there would seem to be no later statutes on the matter of non-payment of rent. Certainly the eighteenth and nineteenth Irish statutes governing the action of ejectment for non-payment of rent did not apply.[98] These were confined in scope to the modern relationship of landlord and tenant. Thus the Fee Farm Rents (Ireland) Act, 1851, also mentioned above, in extending sections 20 and 21 of the Renewable Leasehold Conversion Act, 1849, to all fee farm rents, and other rents payable to grantors with no reversion, expressly excluded "the remedy by ejectment for non-payment of rent."[99] This was a special remedy introduced by the Irish Parliament for landlords in Ireland and was governed by statutes designed to get rid of the formalities of the common law of England relating to forfeitures for non-payment of rent. The English position was later consolidated in the Common Law Procedure Act, 1852,[1] but this did not apply to Ireland. The Common Law Procedure Amendment (Ireland) Act, 1853, which corresponded to the English 1852 Act, did not contain provisions relating to forfeiture for non-payment of rent, though it did contain some references to ejectment actions. Thus there seems to be no legislation to cover forfeiture for non-payment of rent by feudal fee farm grantees and common law rules will apply, such as the rule that the grantor must first make a formal demand for the rent before exercising his right of forfeiture and re-entering.[2] The grantee has, however, an equitable right to relief against forfeiture.[3]

4.068. This leaves the question whether later statutes, governing the exercise of a right of forfeiture for breach of obligations other than those relating to rent, apply to feudal fee farm grants. Once again there is a problem of construction caused by the fact that these statutes are English statutes drafted primarily with the English position in mind, namely, that no freehold

---

[97] Megarry and Wade, *The Law of Real Property* (5th ed., 1984), pp. 670–73. See also *Croker* v. *Orpen* (1847) 9 Ir.Eq.R. 563.

[98] See generally, para. 17.098, *post.*

[99] S. 1.

[1] Megarry and Wade, *op. cit.,* pp. 676–8.

[2] Para. 17.098, *post.*

[3] *Ibid.*

subinfeudation could occur after 1290 and the only rights of forfeiture likely to exist were those of landlords in the modern sense. However, while the Conveyancing Acts, 1881 and 1892 (governing forfeiture for breach of covenants other than those relating to rent) speak in terms of "leases," section 14 (3) of the 1881 Act expressly defines "lease" to include a "grant at a fee farm rent." The question of construction remains whether this provision includes feudal fee farm grants creating feudal tenure as opposed to the modern landlord and tenant relationship usually found in leases. There seems to be no authority on the point and one can only state that it would be more convenient and desirable if section 14 were given an interpretation wide enough to cover feudal grants. If it were not given this interpretation, there would seem to be no other statutory provisions to control the grantor's exercise of his right of re-entry or forfeiture. He would not have to comply with any formalities, such as the requirement of serving a notice on the grantee specifying the breach complained of and requesting compensation.[4] Perhaps even more serious, the grantee would appear otherwise to have no claim to equitable relief against forfeiture in such cases, because of the attitude of the courts to relief in cases other than non-payment of rent. In the latter case the courts were always ready to furnish relief in appropriate cases, but in the former case it became the settled rule that relief would not ordinarily be granted.[5] This relief is now grounded entirely on statute law, namely the Conveyancing Acts.[6]

(v) Covenants

4.069. The law relating to covenants in feudal fee farm grants is very obscure in several respects. The reason is that most of the learning relating to freehold covenants is confined to the usual situation in England where the freehold is conveyed without creating any form of tenure between the grantor and the grantee[7]; tenure is created only by leases and the law relating to leasehold covenants is a different subject altogether.[8] It is submitted that Irish feudal fee farm grants which involve the conveyance of a fee simple estate, a freehold, should be governed by the law of freehold covenants rather than that of leasehold covenants. It is difficult, however, to be dogmatic in view of the almost complete absence of authority on the point.[9]

4.070. A first question that may be raised in this context is whether there are restrictions on the type of covenants that could be inserted in a feudal fee farm grant. In particular, when the Crown granted dispensations to its grantees from

---

[4] 1881 Act, s. 14, and 1892, Act, ss. 2 and 4.
[5] Megarry and Wade, *op. cit.*, pp. 675–83. See discussion in *Whipp* v. *Mackey* [1927] I.R. 372.
[6] Paras. 17.088–91, *post.*
[7] See Elphinstone, *Covenants Affecting Land* (1946); Preston and Newsom, *Restrictive Covenants Affecting Freehold Land* (7th ed., 1982). Also ch. 19, *post.*
[8] Megarry and Wade, *op. cit.*, ch 14; also ch. 19, *post.*
[9] Montrose seems to have taken the same view, see (1939) 3 N.I.L.Q. 42–4 and 150–1; (1940) 4 N.I.L.Q. 40. One doubt might be raised on the basis that a right of distress lies in the grantor of a fee farm grant which is a remedy more commonly associated with a lessor. This, however, is an ancient remedy which did originally belong to freehold feudal lords and which later was extended to landlords in the modern sense. In other words part of freehold law became leasehold law also; in the case of covenants, however, no such development took place and the two laws remained divergent on fundamental principles, see ch. 19, *post.*

Quia Emptores, 1290, did this cover all aspects of that statute's provisions? We have already seen that another important principle of our land law, apart from the prohibition of further subinfeudation of freehold land, enshrined in the statute was the right of all free tenants in fee simple to alienate without their lords' consent.[10] This provision established what came to be known as the rule against inalienability, which provides that the grantor of a freehold estate cannot impose restrictions in the grant substantially prohibiting or excessively restricting the grantee's right of alienation.[11] It is submitted that this rule applies to feudal fee farm grants; the fee simple remains a fee simple even though there exists a relationship of lord and tenant between the grantor and grantee. The Crown dispensations of *Quia Emptores* should be regarded as designed only to get round the prohibition against subinfeudation and to facilitate the making of further grants by Crown grantees. They should not be regarded as changing the nature of the estates contained in those grants, which are otherwise governed by the general law relating to freehold estates or by statutes, such as *Quia Emptores* itself. In this sense the dispensations merely conferred powers of granting estates already known to the law. Some support for this view may be gleaned from Irish cases. In *Re Lunham's Estate,*[12] Flanagan J. held that a covenant in a fee farm grant prohibiting assignment and subletting without consent, if this would entail the property being split into more than four divisions or lots, was void and inoperative "as repugnant to the power of alienation necessarily implied in a fee farm grant." It is true that the learned judge decided that the grant in that case created a rentcharge, *i.e.*, that it belonged to the third category of grants found in Ireland,[13] but the implication, and it is no more than that, seems to be that in any grant not creating the modern relationship of landlord and tenant, the second category,[14] such a covenant would be void under the usual law relating to freeholds. A similar implication may be found in some of the second category cases, namely those relating to conversion grants which have special statutory provisions applying to them.[15] The point at issue in these cases seems to stem partly from the view that, but for those special statutory provisions, the covenants in question would be void in fee farm grants as repugnant to the fee simple estates granted.[16]

4.071. Another question with respect to covenants which may be raised relates to what other covenants, apart from those relating to the fee farm rent, may be inserted in feudal grants. By the seventeenth century there were few vestiges of the feudal system remaining in Ireland and the Tenures (Abolition) Act (Ireland), 1662, abolished most services and incidents of feudal tenure, other than monetary ones like fixed rents. Yet it is the case that other covenants

[10] Para. 2.46, *ante.* The Crown could annex a condition against alienation in its grant of a fee simple, *Fowler* v. *Fowler* (1865) 16 Ir.Ch.Rep. 507.
[11] See paras. 5.033 *et seq.*
[12] (1871) I.R. 5 Eq. 170.
[13] Para. 4.104, *post.*
[14] Para. 4.078, *post.*
[15] *Ibid.*
[16] *E.g., Re McNaul's Estate* [1902] 1 I.R. 114 (see *A Casebook on Irish Land Law* (1984), p.41). See paras. 4.085–6, *post.*

were commonly inserted in Irish feudal grants, particularly covenants restricting the user of the land.[17] No doubt these covenants were enforceable as between the original grantor and grantee on the basis of privity of contract, but how far does the benefit and burden of covenants in feudal fee farm grants run with the land and rent so as to bind successors in title of the original grantor and grantee? What significance in this context has the fact that these grants created feudal tenure between the parties?

4.072. This brings us to the medieval law of covenants, which all the authorities categorise as thoroughly unclear.[18] This law was based on the ancient law of warranty,[19] under which an express or implied warranty of title was given by the grantor to the grantee. If his title was impeached, the grantee could "vouch to warranty" the grantor and call for a conveyance of lands of equal value or, later in history, damages for breach of warranty through the old writ of covenant. This law developed into the modern law of covenants for title (relating to a right to convey and for quiet enjoyment), and there grew up alongside it a body of law relating to other covenants contained in conveyances of freehold land. It was eventually resolved that, while the benefit of covenants could be annexed to the land so as to run with the land in favour of successors in title of the grantor,[20] the burden would not run so as to bind successors in title of the grantee.[21] The classic statement of this common law position was given by the English Court of Appeal in *Austerberry* v. *Corporation of Oldham*.[22] Then the modification in the common law position was established in equity to the effect that the burden of a *restrictive* covenant would run with the land so as to bind successors in title of the grantee, provided the covenant "touched and concerned" the land.[23] This rule of equity came to be known as the rule in *Tulk* v. *Moxhay*.[24]

4.073. In conclusion, then, it is submitted that covenants in Irish feudal fee farm grants are governed by the general law relating to freehold covenants. The benefit runs at common law so long as the covenant touches and concerns the land and the benefit is annexed to the legal estate of the covenantee; the burden runs in equity only in respect of restrictive covenants attached to the covenantor's land. Thus a *bona fide* purchaser of the legal estate without notice of such a restrictive covenant theoretically could take the land free of it. It must be mentioned, however, that this is rarely likely to occur in Ireland because of the Registry of Deeds system which was introduced by the Registration of Deeds Act (Ireland), 1707. As we shall see, while registration

---

[17] See the covenants in the *Delacherois* case (1864) 11 H.L.C. 62 (*e.g.,* obligation to grind corn in the manor mills).

[18] See, *e.g.,* Holmes, *The Common Law* (1968; ed. Howe), ch. XI.

[19] Milsom, *Historical Foundations of the Common Law* (1969), pp. 108–9 and 147–8; Bailey, "Warranties of Land in the Thirteenth Century" (1942–4) 8 C.L.J. 274 and (1945–7) 9 C.L.J. 82.

[20] Bailey, "The Benefit of a Restrictive Covenant" (1938) 6 C.L.J. 339; *Report of the Committee on Positive Covenants Relating to Land* (1965; Cmnd. 2719); Preston and Newsom, *Restrictive Covenants Affecting Freehold Land* (7th ed., 1982).

[21] *Ibid.* Also para. 19.21, *post.*

[22] (1885) 29 Ch.D. 750.

[23] See generally, ch. 19, *post.*

[24] (1848) 2 Ph. 774.

itself does not fix subsequent purchasers with *actual* notice, purchasers would normally be fixed with *constructive* or *imputed* notice since a Registry of Deeds search is standard conveyancing practice in Ireland.[25]

(vi) Redemption

Various provisions have been enacted over the years to provide for redemption of fee farm rents and the discharge of covenants and conditions contained in grants, so as to leave the current grantee with a fee simple absolute title. Once again there is the problem of construction as to whether these statutes apply to feudal fee farm grants.

(a) Chief Rents Redemption (Ireland) Act, 1864

4.074. This Act provided for *voluntary* redemption as between the fee farm grantor and grantee through an application to the court. It seems fairly clear from its terminology that the Act was meant to cover all types of fee farm grant including feudal grants.[26] The Act seems to have been invoked rarely and seems to have long since fallen into disuse. Indeed, the advantages of such a statute are doubtful; if the grantor and grantee are agreed voluntarily upon having redemption, why should they incur the trouble and expense of an application to the court? If they cannot agree upon a price for redemption, they might as well arrange their own arbitration rather than submit to the court which has no power under the Act to coerce either party to agree to its award.[27]

(b) Redemption of Rent (Ireland) Act, 1891

4.075. This Act was part of the land purchase scheme and so applied only to fee farm grants of agricultural land being bought out under that scheme.[28] It was used extensively in respect of fee farm grants at the end of the last century,[29] but the question whether it applied to feudal grants caused the courts some difficulty. The reason was that the Act, being linked closely to the land purchase scheme for agricultural tenants, seemed to be more properly confined to the modern relationship of landlord and tenant.[30] It might have been

---

[25] See paras. 3.069–79, *ante* and ch. 22, *post*.

[26] By s. 1, it applied to "*Any* lands or tenements held in Fee Farm, or for Lives renewable for ever . . . " (italics added).

[27] *Survey of the Land Law of Northern Ireland* (1971), para. 472.

[28] See also the Purchase of Land (Ir.) Act, 1885, s. 10; Land Law (Ir.) Act, 1887, ss. 15 and 16; Purchase of Land (Ir.) Act, 1891, s. 20; Land Law (Ir.) Act, 1896, ss. 31, 33 and 37; Irish Land Act, 1903, ss. 61–64. See also the Republic's Land Acts, 1923, s. 38; 1931, s. 44; 1933, s. 42; 1936, s. 43; 1939, ss. 47–9; 1950, ss. 21 and 23. *Re Clements's Estate* [1924] 1 I.R. 165; *Eustace-Duckett* v. *Thompson* (1938) 72 I.L.T.R. 226; *Re Keyser's Estate* [1938] I.R. 326.

[29] *Re Pentland's Estate* (1888) 22 L.R.Ir. 649; *O'Hea* v. *Morrison* (1892) 30 L.R.Ir. 651; *Merry* v. *Irwin* (1894) 28 I.L.T.R. 59; *Gaffney* v. *Trumbull* (1895) 29 I.L.T.R. 129; *Cowell* v. *Buchanan* [1898] 2 I.R. 153; *Mairs* v. *Lecky* [1895] 2 I.R. 475; *Glenny* v. *Bell* [1898] 2 I.R. 233; *Wynne* v. *Wilson* (1901) 35 I.L.T.R. 152; *Cowell* v. *Buchanan* [1903] 1 I.R. 58; *Shiel* v. *Irvine* (1903) 37 I.L.T.R. 92; *Re Barry's Estate* [1917] 1 I.R. 11; *Re Greene's Estate* [1929] I.R. 615.

[30] The Land Law (Ireland) Act, 1896, s. 14 (*b*) seemed to confirm this by providing that with respect to the 1891 Act—"a person shall be a lessee or a grantee under a fee farm grant within the meaning of the said Acts [Land Law Acts], notwithstanding that the instrument under which he holds, *though purporting to create the relation of landlord and tenant*, is dated before the first day of January one thousand eight hundred and sixty-one,

questioned as a matter of policy why a distinction should have been drawn between one type of fee farm grant and another, once the decision had been taken to extend the land purchase scheme to any type of grant at all. Indeed, no less an authority than Palles C.B. stated, albeit obiter, in *Adams* v. *Alexander* that in his view "grants of lands in old manors" were within the 1891 Act.[31] But the majority view amongst Irish judges seems to have been that feudal grants did not come within the 1891 Act, on the ground that it should be read as being *in pari materia* with the Land Law and Land Purchase Acts and thereby confined to grants creating the modern relationship of landlord and tenant. There is not an authoritative decision on the point, but the better view is that a fee farm grant creating the modern relationship of landlord and tenant was a prerequisite to application of the 1891 Act.[32] The point is, of course, largely academic nowadays as most agricultural land has been bought out under the land purchase schemes in both parts of Ireland, and the fee farm rents and other superior interests have been redeemed.[33]

(c) *Landlord and Tenant (Ground Rents) (No.2) Act, 1978 (R.I.)*

4.076. This Act of the Republic replaced, with amendments, the provisions of the Landlord and Tenant (Ground Rents) Act, 1967, which were introduced primarily to give building and proprietary lessees the right of "enfranchisement," *i.e.*, enabling them to buy out superior rents and interests and thereby become holders of the fee simple.[34] The 1967 Act defined "fee simple" as not including the estate of a person holding under a fee farm grant,[35] so that enfranchisement by lessees under that Act and the 1978 Act necessarily entails redemption of superior fee farm rents and other interests held under fee farm grants of any kind. Whether fee farm grantees in occupation of the land can redeem on their own is doubtful since they would not seem to come within the definition of building or proprietary lessees and other lessees on whom the right of enfranchisement was conferred by the 1967 Act, and is now conferred by the 1978 Act.[36]

and by reason of its date does not create *the relation of landlord and tenant* between him and the person to whom money is payable thereunder in respect of the holding, and that person shall be a lessor or grantor in like manner as if the instrument were executed on or after the above-mentioned day" (italics added). The date mentioned relates to the operation of s. 3 of Deasy's Act 1860, as to which see para. 4.091, *post*.

[31] [1895] 2 I.R. 363, 372; *cf.* Barry L.J. at p. 383.

[32] *E.g., Christie* v. *Peacocke* (1892) 30 L.R.Ir. 646; *Kelly* v. *Rattey* (1893) 32 L.R.Ir. 445; *Gormill* v. *Lynne* (1894) 28 I.L.T.R. 44; *Hamilton* v. *Casey* [1894] 2 I.R. 224.

[33] Paras. 1.65–8, *ante*; see also *O'Hea* v. *Morrison* (1892) 30 L.R.Ir. 651. On the post-1920 legislation in the Republic in relation to fee farm rents, see, however, *Re Clements's Estate* [1924] 1 I.R. 165; *Re Greene's Estate* [1929] I.R. 615; *Re Radcliff's Estate* [1939] I.R. 213.

[34] It was based on the recommendations of the Ground Rents Commission's *Report on Ground Rents* (1964; Pr. 7783). The 1978 Act, which was amended by the Landlord and Tenant (Amendment) Act, 1980, added new categories of lessees entitled to buy the fee simple (see ss. 10, 11, 12 and 26).

[35] S. 2 (1).

[36] S. 3 of the 1967 Act and Part II of the 1978 Act, as amended by ss. 70–3 of the Landlord and Tenant (Amendment) Act, 1980. And see the Landlord and Tenant Commission's *Report on Certain Questions arising under the Landlord and Tenant Acts, 1958 and 1967* (1968; Prl. 59), ch. III. The point can also be made that such a grantee has no need to acquire the fee simple to give him security of tenure, as it is already vested in him. He is, however, subject to the fee farm rent and the grantor's right to enforce payment of this (including by way of forfeiture). It is again doubtful whether the new provision in s. 27 of the 1978 Act (abolishing a ground landlord's right to possession of a dwelling house for non-payment of rent) applies to a fee farm grantee, as the section

(d) *Leasehold (Enlargement and Extension) Act (N.I.)*, 1971

4.077. This Act introduces the right of enfranchisement for long lessees in Northern Ireland, and adopts many of the provisions of the Republic's 1967 Act. In particular, in adopting a similar definition of "fee simple,"[37] it indicates that enfranchisement by lessees in Northern Ireland also involves redeeming any superior fee farm rents. Once again this presumably covers feudal grants, as there seems to be no reason why enfranchisement should have a more limited scope. One curious feature of the Northern Ireland Act is, however, that, unlike the Republic's 1967 Act, the 1971 Act's long title states that another purpose of the Act is to enable "grantees of *certain* fee farm grants to redeem their fee farm rents." The implication seems to be that fee farm grantees in occupation of the land can so redeem under the Act, hence the definition of "lease" to include a fee farm grant.[38]

4.078. We come now to a unique feature of Irish land law—a fee farm grant which creates the modern relationship of landlord and tenant between the parties. In other words, this is a grant of a *freehold* estate which creates *leasehold* tenure. To the English conveyancer this seems to be a contradiction in terms, which breaches the fundamental principles of real property law.[39] Yet in Ireland this category is the most common of fee farm grants, largely due to nineteenth-century legislation which applied to Ireland only. The explanation for these grants' prevalence in Ireland lies, therefore, in special statute law rather than in any revolution in the development of the common law.

The first point to be made about these grants is that they fall into two sub-categories. One sub-category consists of "conversion" grants made under statutes like the Renewable Leasehold Conversion Act, 1849, and certain private Acts. This sub-category is dealt with in the next section. The other sub-category relates to grants creating the relationship of landlord and tenant within the meaning of section 3 of the Landlord and Tenant Law Amendment Act, Ireland, 1860, sometimes known as "Deasy's Act grants." This second sub-category will be discussed after the next section of this chapter.

2. *Landlord and Tenant Conversion Grants*

(i) **Creation**

Conversion fee farm grants have all arisen out of leases as a result of statutory provisions.

(a) *Church Temporalities Acts*

4.079. By statutory provisions of the seventeenth century the powers of bishops and other ecclesiastical persons to grant leases of lands belonging to the

---

applies only to persons "entitled to acquire the fee simple" under Part II of the Act.
[37] S. 33.
[38] *Ibid.* See, generally, Wylie, "Leasehold (Enlargement and Extension) Act (N.I.), 1971–A Critique" (1971) 22 N.I.L.Q. 389. The 1971 Act has not been much of a success, see the Land Law Working Group's Interim Report (*Ground Rents and Other Periodic Payments*) (1983), ch. 4. See para. 18.40, *post.*
[39] See paras. 4.007–9, *ante.*

Church of Ireland (then the established Church) were limited.[40] Generally, such persons could not alienate church land except by lease for a period up to 21 years in respect of agricultural land, and up to 40 years for houses in cities and towns.[41] These "bishops' leases," as they were called, became quite common in Ireland and the practice developed of inserting in them covenants for renewal, subject to payment of renewal fines.[42] It was also common to have a *toties quoties* covenant for renewal inserted in sub-leases of lands held under bishops' leases, specifying that, every time the lessee under the head-lease obtained a renewal of the head-lease, he would grant a renewal of the sub-lease.[43] Then the Church Temporalities Act, 1833,[44] gave tenants holding under bishops' leases the right to purchase the fee simple subject to a fee farm rent.[45] The fee farm rent was to be basically the old leasehold rent plus the average annual value of renewal fines due under the old lease, calculated in accordance with the Act.[46] In the case of a sub-lease, if the sub-lessor obtained a fee farm grant he could under the Act compel the sub-lessee to contribute to its purchase price. In that case the sub-lessee became entitled to a sub-fee farm grant.[47] These conversion fee farm grants were, under the 1833 Act, to be subject to the same uses and trusts as the old leases, and the fee farm rents were to be recoverable by the same means as ordinary rents under a lease were recoverable by a landlord.[48] However, the Act disestablishing the Church of Ireland, the Irish Church Act, 1869, prohibited any further conversion grants after January 1, 1874.[49] The main reason for this was that the 1869 Act was, in effect, the first of the Land Purchase Acts, under which eventually most tenants of agricultural land were to buy out the *unincumbered* fee simple of their land, including redemption of any fee farm rents. The Church Temporalities Commissioners established under the 1869 Act, who replaced the Ecclesiastical Commissioners who had operated the earlier 1833 and later Acts, were instructed to sell the unincumbered fee simple of lands still subject to unconverted leases in January, 1874.[50] The position is, therefore, that this category of conversion grant would have had to have been created between 1833 and 1874. Furthermore, as we shall see in a moment, it seems clear that these grants came within the scope of the Land Purchase Acts and the Redemption of Rent (Ireland) Act, 1891, so that most of them would probably have

---

[40]   Ecclesiastical Lands Act (Ir.), 1634, as amended by the Ecclesiastical Lands Act (Ir.), 1795.
[41]   1634 Act, ss. 2 and 3. Leases of up to 60 years might be granted under licence from the Lord Deputy, *ibid.*, s. 3.
[42]   *Brabazon* v. *Lord Lucan* (1849) 12 Ir.Eq.R. 432.
[43]   *Dockrill* v. *Dolan* (1841) 3 Ir.Eq.R. 552; *Bleakely* v. *Collum* (1863) 14 Ir.Ch.R. 375; *Pilson* v. *Spratt* (1889) 25 L.R.Ir. 5.
[44]   See also the Church Temporalities (Ireland) Acts, 1834, 1836 and 1860.
[45]   S. 210. *Clarke* v. *Staples* (1843) 5 Ir.Eq.R. 246; *Hilhouse* v. *Tyndall* (1849) 13 Ir.Eq.R. 209; *Campbell* v. *Ross* (1856) 7 Ir.Ch.R. 222; *Courtenay* v. *Parker* (1864) 16 Ir.Ch.R. 320.
[46]   S. 128. *Betty* v. *Ecclesiastical Commissioners* (1843) 2 Con. & L. 520; *Brabazon* v. *Lord Lucan* (1849) 12 Ir.Eq.R. 432; *Re Jackson* (1861) 11 Ir.Ch.R. 145. In the absence of special circumstances the landlord was not entitled to compensation for mere conversion of his reversion into a fee farm rent, *Re Lawless* (1854) 4 Ir.Ch.R. 230; *Thackwell* v. *Jenkins* (1854) 4 Ir.Ch.R. 243.
[47]   *Poirez* v. *Collum* [1907] 1 I.R. 5; *Carson* v. *Jameson* [1908] 2 I.R. 308.
[48]   S. 146. *Courtenay* v. *Parker* (1864) 16 Ir.Ch.R. 320.
[49]   S. 31. See also the Irish Church Act, 1869, Amendment Act, 1872, s. 12.
[50]   S. 34. *Bernard* v. *Hungerford* [1902] 1 I.R. 89; *McSweeney* v. *Drapes* [1905] 1 I.R. 186.

been subject to redemption under the land purchase scheme.[51] The few that are likely to survive today are probably conversion grants relating to former church property in the urban areas of Ireland.

(b) Trinity College, Dublin, Leasing and Perpetuity Act, 1851

4.080. By the nineteenth century, Trinity College, Dublin owned large estates in many parts of Ireland, but its powers of disposition were limited by statute just as bishops' powers were. The restrictions on the leasing powers of bishops applied also to masters or governors and fellows of colleges,[52] and a similar practice developed of inserting covenants for renewal in college leases.[53] Then the 1851 Act (a local and personal Act) was passed to provide tenants of the College with the right to require the College, at any time within four years of the passing of the Act, to grant them "leases in perpetuity" at a rent.[54] These, in effect, formed another type of conversion fee farm grant.

(c) Renewable Leasehold Conversion Acts

4.081. During the eighteenth and nineteenth centuries there developed in Ireland the practice of large landowners granting leases for lives (usually three) renewable for ever. The lease contained a covenant for renewal by grant of a lease for a new life whenever one of those for whose life the original lease was granted died, subject, of course, to payment of a fine to the landlord. This practice is discussed in more detail later in this chapter.[55] For the moment it may be said that the significance of these leases was that they were also the subject of legislation in the nineteenth century providing for conversion into fee farm grants. The Renewable Leasehold Conversion Act, 1849,[56] gave lessees of such leases (and leases for years with a covenant for perpetual renewal[57]) the right to obtain a fee farm grant from the lessor, subject to a fee farm rent.[58] The fee farm rent was to be the old leasehold rent plus an estimated sum based on the average annual value of renewal fines.[59] Perhaps even more important was the fact that the 1849 Act went on to say that all *future* purported leases for lives renewable for ever (or for perpetually renewable years) were to operate *automatically* as fee farm grants, subject only to the condition that the purported lessor had power to convey a fee simple.[60] It has been stated that not

---

[51] Para. 4.088, *post.*
[52] See statutes cited in fn. 40, para. 4.079, *supra.*
[53] *Orr* v. *Littlewood* (1859) 8 Ir.Ch.R. 348; *Re Conolly's Estate* (1869) I.R. 3 Eq. 339.
[54] S. 3. The College was also given a discretion to grant leases for 99 years (s. 1), and to make perpetuity grants at any time before the expiry of an existing 21 year lease (s. 2).
[55] Paras. 4.167 *et seq., post.*
[56] See also the Renewable Leaseholds Conversion (Ireland) Act, 1868.
[57] See definition of "lease in perpetuity" in s. 38.
[58] S. 1. *Ex parte Waldron* (1850) 1 Ir.Ch.R. 269; *Ex parte Barlow* (1852) 2 Ir.Ch.R. 272; *Re Gore* (1858) 8 Ir.Ch.R. 589; *Palmer* v. *Slaney* (1863) 14 Ir.Ch.R. 540; *Ex parte Murray* (1872) I.R. 6 Eq. 534; *Ex parte Guerin* (1870) I.R. 4 Eq. 467; *Ex parte Walsh* (1874) I.R. 8 Eq. 146; *Ex parte Quinn* [1895] 1 I.R. 187. It seems that some landlords procured private legislation conferring powers to make fee farm grants to tenants on their estates, see *Layard* v. *Donegal* (1861) 8 H.L.C. 460. The Act also applied, at least as regards post–1849 leases, to leases for *years* (as opposed to *lives*) renewable for ever, see s. 37.
[59] S. 2. *Ex parte Keatinge* (1867) I.R. 2 Eq. 26; *Ex parte Hutchinson* (1871) I.R. 6 Eq. 34; *Ex parte Scott* [1906] 1 I.R. 159; *Fitzpatrick* v. *Warren* [1917] 1 I.R. 156.
[60] S. 37. *Forde* v. *Brew* (1865) 17 Ir.Ch.R. 1; *Sheridan* v. *Nesbitt* (1896) 30 I.L.T.R. 39.

as many lessees as might have been expected took advantage of the 1849 Act,[61] and it is impossible to estimate how many grants have come into operation since 1849 under the automatic conversion provisions. However, note that section 74 of the Republic's Landlord and Tenant (Amendment) Act, 1980, now provides that, as from the commencement of the Act, the holder of an interest in land originating under a lease for lives renewable for ever created prior to 1849, and not converted into a fee farm grant under the 1849 Act, holds the land in fee simple, which in this case means one *not* subject to a fee farm rent (see the definition in section 2 (1) of the Landlord and Tenant (Ground Rents) Act, 1967, and section 3 (1) of the Landlord and Tenant (Ground Rents) (No.2) Act, 1978, which was incorporated by section 1 (2) of the 1980 Act). However, subject to that, section 74 provides that the estate so held "shall be deemed to be a graft upon the previous interest and shall be subject to any rights or equities arising from its being such a graft."

(ii) Words of Limitation

4.082. It seems to be settled law that, despite the fact that a conversion grant involves the conveyance of a fee simple estate which would normally require the use of appropriate words of limitation, such words are not necessary in grants purporting to operate under the relevant statutory provisions. It was held in *Re Johnston's Estate*[62] that a conversion grant purporting to have been executed under the Renewable Leasehold Conversion Act, 1849, passed a fee simple despite the absence of any words of limitation. This decision may be taken as indicative of a general judicial attitude to conversion grants to the effect that they are special creatures of statute law and, as such, should not necessarily be subjected to the common law rules relating to conveyances of freehold estates in general, or of a fee simple estate in particular.[62a] We shall see that this attitude has come to light in other contexts in Irish cases.

(iii) Fee Farm Rents

4.083. The various statutes dealing with conversion of leases into fee farm grants usually provided as part of the process of conversion that the fee farm rent was to be recoverable by the same remedies as the old leasehold rents.[63] In other words the fee farm grantor, as he became under the conversion, had the remedies of a landlord, in particular the right of distress and ejectment for non-payment of rent.[64] Thus sections 20 and 21 of the Renewable Leasehold Conversion Act, 1849, provided that the fee farm rents were to be recoverable by a landlord's normal remedies for recovery of a rent service.[65] And in Ireland this included the special statutory remedy of ejectment for non-payment of rent.[66]

---

[61] *Report of the Committee on Registration of Title to Land in Northern Ireland* (1967; Cmd. 512), para. 123.
[62] [1911] 1 I.R. 215.
[62a] Murray J. quoted this sentence as "helpful" in *Re Courtney* [1981] N.I. 58 at 65.
[63] See, *e.g.,* as regards converted bishops' leases, the Church Temporalities Act, 1833, s. 14.
[64] See, generally, ch. 17, *post; Re Hassett's Estate* (1898) 32 I.L.T.R. 115.
[65] *Att.-Gen.* v. *Wilson* (1893) 31 L.R.Ir. 28 at 48–53 (*per* Palles C.B.).   [66] Para. 17.098, *post.*

(iv) Forfeiture

4.084. As regards non-payment of rent, it was unlikely that a conversion fee farm grantor would concern himself with forfeiture since he had the statutory right of ejectment for non-payment of rent. However, there was nothing to prevent reservation of a right of forfeiture in the conversion grant and, indeed, one of the standard precedents included such a right.[67] As has been mentioned earlier,[68] there seems to be no statute law in Ireland governing exercise of a right of forfeiture for non-payment of rent such as that contained in the English Common Law Procedure Act, 1852.

As regards forfeiture for breach of obligations other than those relating to the fee farm rent, it seems clear that conversion fee farm grants come within section 14 of the Conveyancing Act, 1881, as amended by sections 2 and 5 of the Conveyancing Act, 1892. These provisions govern the exercise by the grantor of any powers of re-entry reserved in the grant for breach of the grantee's obligations.[69] A conversion fee farm grant creates the modern relationship of landlord and tenant between the grantor and grantee and so would clearly seem to come within the definition of a lease (as including a fee farm grant) in section 14 (3) of the 1881 Act.[70]

(v) Covenants

4.085. It has been a matter of some controversy whether the ordinary common law with respect to covenants attached to a fee simple estate applies to conversion fee farm grants. The majority view amongst Irish judges has been that these grants are statutory creations to which the common law rules should not necessarily be applied; in particular, they are conversions of leases and this factor should be borne in mind in construing the relevant statutory provisions. Since these provisions usually stated that the covenants contained in the converted lease were to continue in force to the same extent when the conversion to the fee farm grant occurred, the result of the cases has been generally to apply the law of *leasehold* covenants rather than *freehold* covenants to conversion grants.[71] The Church Temporalities Act, 1833, specified that the fee simple conveyed in the conversion grant was to be vested in the grantee "for the like estate, estates or interests, and to and upon the same uses, trusts, intents and purposes respectively (or as near thereto as the nature of each case and the difference of interest will admit)."[72] It is questionable whether the qualification in brackets would prevent the application of the law of leasehold covenants to Church Temporality grants. The judges tended, in construing this provision, to put emphasis on what the position of the lessee was

---

[67] Stubbs and Baxter, *Irish Forms and Precedents* (1910), Precedent No. 1, p. 121.
[68] Paras. 4.065–8, *ante*.
[69] Para. 17.087 *et seq., post*.
[70] Para. 4.068, *ante*. For s. 14's application to a lease for lives renewable for ever, see *Ruttledge* v. *Whelan* (1882) 10 L.R.Ir. 263; to a fee farm grant, *Walsh* v. *Wightman* [1927] N.I. 1.
[71] See ch. 19, *post*.
[72] S. 148. See *Dockrill* v. *Dolan* (1841) 3 Ir.Eq.R. 552; *Clarke* v. *Staples* (1843) 5 Ir.Eq.R. 246; *Hilhouse* v. *Tyndall* (1849) 13 Ir.Eq.R. 209.

under the unconverted lease and, then, to strive to assimilate his position as grantee after the conversion to that as far as possible.[73]

4.086. Section 1 of the Renewable Leasehold Conversion Act, 1849, stated that a conversion grant made under the Act was to be subject to the same "covenants, conditions, exceptions, and reservations" as the lease before conversion (other than, of course, the covenant for renewal).[74] Section 7 stated that the fee simple was to be subject to the same "uses, trusts, provisos, agreements . . . charges, liens, incumbrances, and equities" as the lease before conversion.[75] Section 10 provided that the benefit and burdens of all covenants implied in leases under the general law of landlord and tenant, and all covenants to be contained in grants under the Act, were to run with the land as if the fee farm grantee were the lessee or his assignee and the grantor the lessor or his assignee.[76] Questions arose over these provisions whether they should be interpreted widely to mean that covenants usual and valid when contained in leases could continue as valid and enforceable in the conversion grants of the fee simple, even though under the general common law they could not be attached to a freehold estate. For example, a covenant prohibiting alienation (assignment, subletting or otherwise parting with possession), or restricting it to occasions when the landlord gave consent, was a common clause in a lease, but would usually be invalid in a conveyance of a freehold as infringing the rule against inalienability and, in the case of a fee simple, as being repugnant to the nature of the estate granted.[77] The general judicial view seems to have been that these clauses would continue as valid and enforceable in conversion grants. This was certainly the view of the Court of Appeal in *Re McNaul's Estate*,[78] where the converted lease had contained a covenant by the lessee to pay a higher rent if he alienated without the lessor's consent to someone other than a child or grandchild of the lessor. This covenant was held to be valid in the conversion grant. The court did indicate that it was open to doubt whether such a covenant was properly regarded as a restriction on alienation at all[79] or, if it was, whether it was a sufficient restraint as to be void even in a conveyance of a fee simple at common law.[80] However, an earlier case, *Billing* v. *Welch*,[81]

---

[73] See, *e.g., Campbell* v. *Ross* (1856) 7 Ir.Ch.R. 222; *Re Dane's Estate* (1871) I.R. 5 Eq. 498; *Re Dane's Estate* (1876) I.R. 10 Eq. 207.

[74] *Mahony* v. *Tynte* (1851) 1 Ir.Ch.R. 577; *Kent* v. *Stoney* (1858) 9 Ir.Ch.R. 249; *Gore* v. *O'Grady* (1867) I.R. 1 Eq. 1; *Quinn* v. *Shields* (1877) I.R. 11 C.L. 254; *Fishbourne* v. *Hamilton* (1890) 25 L.R.Ir. 483.

[75] Thus a conversion fee farm grant has been held not to be a good root of title, *Dawson* v. *Baxter* (1886) 19 L.R.Ir. 103; *Re Carew's Estate* (1887) 19 L.R.Ir. 483; *Maconchy* v. *Clayton* [1898] 1 I.R. 291; *Smyth* v. *Shaftesbury* (1901) 1 N.I.J.R. 34; *Re Garde Browne* [1911] 1 I.R. 205; *cf. McClenaghan* v. *Bankhead* (1874) I.R. 8 C.L. 195. *Quaere* whether this is still good law, see *Irish Conveyancing Law* (1978), paras. 13. 11 and 13. 56.

[76] *Re Quin* (1858) 8 Ir.Ch.Rep. 578; *Dooner* v. *Odlum* [1914] 2 I.R. 411. See discussion of parties' position after a grant under the Act by Barry J. in *Morris* v. *Morris* (1872) I.R. 7 C.L. 295, 297–9.

[77] Para. 4.051, *ante*. See *Re Lunham's Estate* (1871) I.R. 5 Eq. 170. The same arguments may arise in respect of the effect of s. 74 of the Republic's Landlord and Tenant (Amendment) Act, 1980, on pre–1849 unconverted renewable leases. As mentioned above (para. 4.081.), this section deems the fee simple to be a "graft" on the previous interest and states that it is subject to the "rights or equities" arising thereby.

[78] [1902] 1 I.R. 114 (see *A Casebook on Irish Land Law* (1984), p. 41).

[79] Thus FitzGibbon L.J. stated that in the court's opinion it was "not a covenant prohibiting alienation—on the contrary, it permitted alienation on the terms of paying the additional rent." *Ibid.*, p. 125. *Cf.* Walker L.J. at p. 133.

[80] Thus Holmes L.J. stated that the "restraint of alienation is of a limited and partial character." *Ibid.*, p. 137.

[81] (1871) I.R. 6 C.L. 88. *Cf. Re Quin* (1858) 8 Ir.Ch.R. 578; *Ex parte Raymond* (1874) I.R. 8 Eq. 231.

which had held that, if a covenant "would be void if contained in an ordinary grant in fee simple, it should be also held void when inserted in a fee simple grant under the Renewable Leasehold Conversion Act,"[82] was expressly overruled by the Court of Appeal in *McNaul's* case in so far as it held void such covenants "upon the ground of repugnancy to a common law estate in fee."[83] As has been stated earlier,[84] the Court of Appeal were agreed that the 1849 Act created a special *statutory* fee simple estate to which were annexed incidents generally recognised as attaching to leasehold estates only.[85]

(vi) Redemption

(a) *Chief Rents Redemption (Ireland) Act, 1864*

4.087. Although by its terms this Act seems to apply to all fee farm grants, it may be doubted whether it was envisaged by its draftsmen that it would extend to special statutory conversion grants. There is no authority at all on the point which must be regarded as unsettled. However, it is no longer of practical importance in view of later legislation.

(b) *Redemption of Rent (Ireland) Act, 1891*

4.088. It has been settled that this Act did apply to fee farm conversion grants so as to facilitate redemption of fee farm rents as part of the land purchase scheme for agricultural holdings. Thus Bewley J. held in *Hamilton* v. *Casey*[86] that a sub-grant under the Church Temporalities Act, 1833, was a fee farm grant within the 1891 Act,[87] and the same was held with respect to a grant under the Trinity College Act, 1851, in *Gormill* v. *Lyne*.[88] It has similarly been held that conversion grants operating under the Renewable Leasehold Conversion Act, 1849, came within the 1891 Act.[89] It is easy to understand these decisions in view of the amount of agricultural land which used to be held under leases for lives renewable for ever and which would probably have become land held under converted fee farm grants.[90] It was important to the

---

[82] *Per* O'Brien J., *ibid.*, p. 103.

[83] *Per* FitzGibbon L.J., *op. cit.*, p. 124, who had earlier stated that the court held, in general, "that the doctrine of repugnancy applicable at common law to an estate in fee is modified, in the case of fee-farm grants founded on renewable leases." *Cf. Bell* v. *Belfast Corporation* [1914] 2 I.R. 1, where the court held that a grantee under a conversion grant was not liable for waste for which a lessee would ordinarily have been liable, para. 17.058, *post*.

[84] Para. 4.082, *ante*.

[85] See *op. cit.*, p. 124 (FitzGibbon L.J.) and p. 133 (Walker L.J.). It may be noted that the Irish Land Act, 1903, s. 70, provided that no restraint on alienation contained in any fee farm grant was to impede a sale under the Land Purchase Acts, whether or not the restraint was valid. For sales under the Land Purchase Acts, with redemption of fee farm rents, see *Re Leader's Estate* [1904] 1 I.R. 368; *Re O'Donoghue's Estate* (1912) 46 I.L.T.R. 83; *Re Dawson's Estate* (1912) 46 I.L.T.R. 288; *Colles* v. *Hornsby* [1913] 2 I.R. 210; *Re Foley* (1912) 46 I.L.T.R. 96; *McCarthy* v. *Anderson* (1912) 46 I.L.T.R. 96; *Re Briscoe's Estate* (1913) 47 I.L.T.R. 64.

[86] [1894] 2 I.R. 224.

[87] See also Palles C.B. in *Adams* v. *Alexander* [1895] 2 I.R. 363 at 372.

[88] (1894) 28 I.L.T.R. 44.

[89] *Gun-Cunningham* v. *Byrne* (1892) 30 L.R.Ir. 384; *Sheridan* v. *Nesbitt* (1896) 30 I.L.T.R. 39; *Langtry* v. *Sheridan* (1896) 30 I.L.T.R. 64. See also Palles C.B. in *Adams* v. *Alexander, op. cit.*

[90] The Devon Commission (para. 1.41, *ante*) reported that about 1/7th of the land in Ireland was held under perpetually renewable leaseholds in the mid-nineteenth century.

land purchase scheme that as much agricultural land as possible should come within its scope.[91]

(c) *Landlord and Tenant (Ground Rents) (No. 2) Act, 1978 (R.I.)*

4.089. It seems clear, for the reasons given earlier,[92] that an urban tenant purchasing the fee simple under this Act would have to redeem any fee farm rents in the chain of title to the fee simple.

(d) *Leasehold (Enlargement and Extension) Act (N.I.), 1971*

4.090. It also seems clear, again for the reasons given earlier,[93] that this Act provides for redemption of fee farm rents as part of the enfranchisement process by urban tenants, and also that it probably provides for redemption by fee farm grantees in occupation of land independent of enfranchisement by "ground" lessees.

3. *Deasy's Act Grants*

4.091. Perhaps the most significant development in the growth of fee farm grants in Ireland was the passing of Deasy's Act—the Landlord and Tenant Law Amendment Act, Ireland, 1860.[94] The reason was the wording of section 3 of that Act—

> "The relation of landlord and tenant shall be deemed to be founded on the express or implied contract of the parties, and not upon tenure or service, *and a reversion shall not be necessary to such relation*, which shall be deemed to subsist in all cases in which there shall be an agreement by one party to hold land from or under another in consideration of any rent."[95]

4.092. The operation of this section on the general law of landlord and tenant will be more fully discussed in a later chapter.[96] For the moment its significance lies in the fact that it facilitated, from January 1, 1861, onwards,[97] the making of fee farm grants creating the full relationship of landlord and tenant between the grantor and grantee. In other words, the grantor and grantee of such a grant were to be treated almost exactly as if the former were a landlord and the latter a tenant as regards their rights and duties and the remedies for enforcement of these.[98] This construction of section 3 obviously

---

[91] See also s. 14 of the Land Law (Ireland) Act, 1896, fn. 30, para. 4.075, *ante.*
[92] Para. 4.076, *ante.*
[93] Para. 4.077, *ante.*
[94] See, generally, ch. 17, *post.*
[95] Italics added. Prior to the Act the common law position had been confirmed in Ireland that a reversion in the landlord was a prerequisite of the relationship, see *Pluck* v. *Digges* (1828) 2 Hud. & Br. 1; *Porter* v. *French* (1844) 9 Ir.L.R. 514. Also *Fawcett* v. *Hall* (1833) Alc. & Nap. 248.
[96] Ch. 17, *post.*
[97] The date of operation of the Act was fixed by s. 105. It was held in *Chute* v. *Busteed* (1865) 16 I.C.L.R. 222 (see *A Casebook on Irish Land Law* (1984), p. 155) that section 3 was not retrospective in operation; see also *McAreavy* v. *Hannan* (1861) 13 I.C.L.R. 70.
[98] See, generally, ch. 17, *post.* Limitations on this statement are considered below, paras. 4.097 *et seq., post.*

had a revolutionary effect on the law of estates in land in Ireland, because the 1860 Act was of general application and not confined to special situations as in the case of conversion grants. For this reason there were some doubts expressed about the application of section 3 to grants of a fee simple, especially since *Quia Emptores* was not included in the repeal schedule of Deasy's Act.[99] This, however, seems to confuse once again the feudal relationship of lord and tenant with the modern relationship of landlord and tenant; *Quia Emptores* did not apply to the latter and section 3 was simply extending its range.[1] The confusion from the common lawyer's point of view is, of course, perfectly understandable because the extension was so revolutionary. It involved an invasion of the territory of the old feudal law (freehold tenure and estates) by modern landlord and tenant law. The wording of section 3, however, seems clearly wide enough to support this broad view of its effect and the fact remains that this view has been generally accepted by Irish conveyancers ever since its enactment. Thus Christian J. in *Chute* v. *Busteed*[2] commented on the effect of section 3:

> "I think it might fairly be argued that an instrument executed after this statute had been passed ought to be construed with reference to the new law founded by the statute; and that if worded as this deed is, like an ordinary lease, it should be held to embody an agreement that the new statutable relation of landlord and tenant should exist—a relationship discharged of the element of tenure and reversion, and resting exclusively on contract."[3]

Numerous grants purporting to operate under Deasy's Act have been made and acted upon without question for decades. The only limitation recognised by the legal profession has been that special care should be taken in drafting the wording of such grants, a matter to which we now turn. Before doing so it may be queried whether the future creation of fee farm grants has been curtailed in the Republic by the Landlord and Tenant (Ground Rents) Act, 1978. Section 2 (1) of this Act renders void a "lease" only if the "lessee" would, apart from the Act, have the right to acquire the fee simple under section 3 of the Landlord and Tenant (Ground Rents) Act, 1967 (since replaced by Part II of the Landlord and Tenant (Ground Rents) (No.2) Act, 1978). But, as mentioned earlier, although a "lease" for these purposes is defined as including a "fee farm grant" (see now section 3 of the Landlord and Tenant (Ground Rents) (No.2) Act, 1978), it is doubtful whether a fee farm grantee who already holds the fee simple can be regarded as having the right to acquire it under the legislation. The most that he could achieve would be redemption of the fee farm rent so as to leave him with an unincumbered fee simple and it is not clear whether the legislation applies to such a limited exercise. It certainly seems to be stretching

---

[99] See *e.g.*, remarks by Christian J. in *Chute* v. *Busteed, op. cit.*, p. 246; also Stubbs and Baxter, *Irish Forms and Precedents* (1910), p. 89.

[1] Para. 4.064, *ante*.

[2] (1865) 16 I.C.L.R. 222.

[3] *Op. cit.*, p. 246. See also *Kelly* v. *Rattey* (1893) 32 L.R.Ir. 445, especially Walker C. at p. 449; *Adams* v. *Alexander* [1895] 2 I.R. 363, especially Barry L.J. at p. 383.

the language to breaking-point to call "redemption of fee farm rents" the "enlargement of [the fee farm grantee's] interest into a fee simple" (section 3 of the Landlord and Tenant (Ground Rents) Act, 1978), or to speak of conveying to or vesting in the grantee an estate which he already holds. If the matter is looked at in terms of the policy of the Landlord and Tenant (Ground Rents) Act, 1978, in prohibiting future creation of ground rents, it can be said, on the one hand, that a fee farm grantee does not suffer from the lack of security of tenure and in particular the danger of losing a home he or his predecessors built at their own expense that a lessee does. And it may be argued that it is these inequities that the legislation is primarily aimed at. On the other hand, a fee farm grantee, like a lessee, is subject to the burden of a form of "ground" rent and, of course, to the grantor's remedy of forfeiture or ejectment for non-payment, and it may be argued that it was also the intention of the legislators to remove such burdens from the Irish scene. Yet it must be remembered that they are as much a part of short-term leasehold arrangements as of long-term ones, or, indeed, as of business or commercial arrangements (the 1978 prohibition is confined to dwelling-houses).

(i) Creation

4.093. From what has already been said, and especially in view of the doubts about the precise effect of section 3, a fee farm grant purporting to operate under Deasy's Act must indicate an intention to create the "relation of landlord and tenant" between the parties.[4] As section 3 says, this may be founded on the "express or implied contract of the parties," and the practice has been adopted by Irish conveyancers of drafting these fee farm grants along the lines of a lease, with appropriate modifications.[5] The precedents for such a grant most commonly used contain a recital which states expressly something like "Whereas the parties hereto have agreed that a contract of tenancy and the relation of landlord and tenant shall be created between them. . . ."[6]

4.094. As regards the instrument of conveyance, a deed is in practice always used for a fee farm grant, as it is for any lease for a substantial term of years. Theoretically there would seem to be no more need for a deed in the case of a grant than in the case of a lease operating under Deasy's Act. Under section 4 of the Act:

> "Every lease *or contract* with respect to lands whereby the relation of landlord and tenant is intended to be created for *any freehold estate or interest*, or for any definite period not being from year to year or any

---

[4] Indeed, it has been suggested that some conveyancers attempted to avoid interpretation problems with such grants by deliberately drafting instead a perpetually renewable lease, which would operate automatically as a fee farm grant under s. 37 of the Renewable Leasehold Conversion Act, 1849 (para. 4.081, *ante*), see Stubbs and Baxter, *Irish Forms and Precedents* (1910), p. 90. In view of the general acceptance now of the validity of Deasy's Act grants this is rarely, if ever, done today.

[5] *E.g.*, the parties are usually referred to as the "grantor" and "grantee," rather than as the "lessor" and "lessee."

[6] See, *e.g.*, Stubbs and Baxter, *op. cit.*, Precedent 2, p. 122. But such a recital is not, apparently, strictly necessary, see *Re Courtney* [1981] N.I. 58 at 63 (*per* Murray J.).

lesser period, shall be by deed executed, *or note in writing* signed by the landlord or his agent thereunto lawfully authorised in writing."[7]

Deasy's Act does expressly amend the Real Property Act, 1845 (section 2 of which introduced the deed as an alternative mode of conveyance for freehold land), so far as section 3 related to the relationship of landlord and tenant in Ireland.[8] So a written instrument in writing not under seal would seem to suffice for a Deasy's Act fee farm grant despite its granting of a fee simple estate, unless a deed is necessary for some special reason, *e.g.,* reservation of an easement.[9]

(ii) Words of Limitation

4.095. It has been suggested that another effect of section 3 of Deasy's Act was that a fee farm grant executed under it could operate without any of the words of limitation requisite at common law in a conveyance of a fee simple.[10] The reasoning is that, since section 3 rests the matter entirely upon the express or implied contract of the parties, all that is necessary is that the particular instrument should indicate an intention to create the relationship of landlord and tenant for an estate in fee simple. Thus, the reasoning continues, a clause such as "to A for ever" would be sufficient in a fee farm grant without any further words of limitation. The only real authority on the point seems to be *Twaddle* v. *Murphy*,[11] which does not support the reasoning. That case involved a deed which granted and demised land to "A and B, *their heirs and assigns*, for the lives of C, D and E, or for 999 years, *or for ever,* whichever should last longest."[12] The court held that this was a fee farm grant, the largest estate (fee simple) absorbing the inferior estates.[13] It is true that the court laid some stress on the words "for ever" as an indication of intention in relation to the question of construction of the wording of the grant,[14] but it did *not* decide that these words were sufficient in themselves to allow the conveyance to operate as a fee farm grant. The fact is that the conveyance in this case did contain appropriate words of limitation for an ordinary conveyance of a fee simple—the words "heirs and assigns." The standard formula in practice used by conveyancers in Ireland for Deasy's Act grants is an *habendum* as follows: "To hold the said premises unto the grantee his heirs and assigns for ever."[15]

---

[7] Italics added. And s. 1 defines "lease" as meaning "any instrument in writing, whether under seal or not, containing a contract of tenancy in respect of any lands, in consideration of a rent or return."

[8] Sched. B.

[9] See *Re Courtney* [1981] N.I. 58 at 67 (*per* Murray J.—deed unnecessary for a conveyance of land held under a fee farm grant). As regards reservation of easements, see para. 6.056 *et seq., post.*

[10] See, *e.g.,* Cherry, *Irish Land Law and Land Purchase Acts* (3rd ed., 1903), p. 5, fn. c, citing *Twaddle* v. *Murphy* (1881) 8 L.R.Ir. 123 and a dictum of Palles C.B. in *Hodges* v. *Clarke* (1883) 17 I.L.T.R. 82 at 84: "When we are obliged to determine for what period a tenant holds, we are bound to look to the agreement of the parties."

[11] (1881) 8 L.R.Ir. 123 (see *A Casebook on Irish Land Law* (1984), p. 113).

[12] Italics added.

[13] Para. 4.025, *ante.*

[14] See May C.J., *op. cit.,* p. 127.

[15] Stubbs and Baxter, *Irish Forms and Precedents* (1910), Precedent 2, p. 123. *Cf.* a conversion grant, Precedent 1, p. 120. The reasoning in this and the next paragraph was adopted expressly by Murray J. in *Re Courtney* [1981] N.I. 58 at 65–6. See also *Irish Conveyancing Law* (1978), para. 17. 42.

4.096. Apart from *Twaddle* v. *Murphy*, it is suggested that, as a matter of principle, Deasy's Act does not dispense with the necessity for words of limitation in a fee farm grant. The crucial point is once again the operation of section 3.[16] The better view is that the section should be regarded only as extending the scope of the relationship of landlord and tenant to cover estates and interests that would not come within that relationship at common law. That does not mean that the section goes further and alters the *nature* of the estate and abolishes *all* its normal incidents. It should be regarded only as doing this where other provisions in Deasy's Act make it clear. Section 3 says only that a reversion is no longer necessary and that the relationship of landlord and tenant can arise when the appropriate intention is shown. Section 4 goes on to talk of an intention to create that relationship "for any freehold estate or interest," but does not say how such an estate is to be created. The implication would seem to be that intention to create a *particular* estate should be indicated in the same way as before the Act; in other words, by the words of limitation appropriate for that estate.[17] As one learned writer on the subject concluded with respect to leases for a term of years, on the one hand, and fee farm grants, on the other hand, executed under Deasy's Act:

> "There is no complete assimilation of the two, no radical change. The creation of the relation of landlord and tenant in fee farm grants means only that certain incidents of leases for years become also incidents of fee farm grants."[18]

It may be convenient then at this point to consider other aspects of Deasy's Act grants in an attempt to clarify the extent of assimilation with leases for years.

(iii) Fee Farm Rents

4.097. Since a Deasy's Act grant creates *ex hypothesi* the relationship of landlord and tenant, a grantor has all the usual remedies of a landlord for recovery of his fee farm rent—action for debt, distress[19] and ejectment for non-payment of rent. These remedies are covered by several other provisions in Deasy's Act itself (it was essentially a consolidating Act for most of the earlier legislation on landlord and tenant).[20] Section 52 of the Act specifically refers to application of the statutory action of ejectment for non-payment of

---

[16] See discussion in Montrose, "Fee Farm Grants" (1939) 3 N.I.L.Q. 143; (1940) 4 N.I.L.Q. 40 and 86.

[17] For some dicta, not always very helpful, on this subject, see *Chute* v. *Busteed* (1862) 14 I.C.L.R. 115 at 130 (FitzGerald B.), (1865) 16 I.C.L.R. 222 at 230 (O'Hagan J.), at 244 (Christian J.) (see *A Casebook on Irish Land Law* (1984), p. 155); *Gordon* v. *Phelan* (1878) 12 I.L.T.R. 70 (FitzGerald B.); *Hodges* v. *Clarke* (1883) 17 I.L.T.R. 82 at 84 (Palles C.B.); *Seymour* v. *Quirke* (1884) 14 L.R.Ir. 455 (C.A.); *Donelly* v. *Galbraith* (1884) 18 I.L.T.R. 54 (Bewley J.); *O'Sullivan* v. *Ambrose* (1893) 32 L.R.Ir. 102 (Madden J.); *Re Maunsell's Estate* [1911] 1 I.R. 271 (Ross J.).

[18] Montrose, (1940) 4 N.I.L.Q. 86, 91. On the basis of this reasoning Murray J. held that words of limitation are necessary in a conveyance of land held under a fee farm grant, even though, in the case of a Deasy's Act grant, s. 9 of Deasy's Act renders a deed unnecessary. See *Re Courtney* [1981] N.I. 58 and para. 17.029, *post*.

[19] Abolished now in Northern Ireland, para. 17. 066, *post*. See *Irish Land Commission* v. *Holmes* (1898) 32 I.L.T.R. 85.

[20] Discussed in more detail in ch. 17, *post*.

rent, dealt with in it and subsequent sections, to "any fee farm, grant."[21] The word "any" would seem to be misleading; this section, like all of Deasy's Act, is confined to grants creating the relationship of landlord and tenant.[22]

(iv) Forfeiture

4.098. Once again, the law relating to landlord and tenant applies. The remedy of ejectment for non-payment of rent may be invoked by the fee farm grantor. The grant may also include an express right of re-entry for non-payment of rent,[23] in which case the grantor may invoke this remedy instead of his statutory action of ejectment. It has already been stated that there appear to be no statutory restrictions on the exercise of such a right of re-entry in Ireland.[24]

As regards forfeiture for breach of covenants other than those relating to rent, Deasy's Act grants would clearly seem to come within section 14 of the Conveyancing Act, 1881, which does certain restrictions on the grantor's exercise of rights under any forfeiture clause relating to such covenants.[25]

(v) Covenants

4.099. Deasy's Act contains various provisions relating to covenants. Section 41 specifies covenants or agreements to be implied in every "lease" on behalf of the "landlord" (for good title and quiet enjoyment) and section 42 covenants or agreements to be implied on behalf of the "tenant" (to pay the rent and taxes, keep in repair and give up peaceable possession on determination of the lease).[26] "Lease" is defined by the Act to mean "any instrument in writing . . . containing a contract of tenancy"; "landlord" is defined as including the person entitled to the landlord's interest "under any lease or other contract of tenancy . . . and *whether he has a reversion or not*"; "tenant" is defined as meaning "the person entitled to any lands under any lease or other contract of tenancy."[27] This wording would seem to be wide enough to cover fee farm grants coming within the Act, so as to assimilate them with leases for the purposes of implied covenants. There seems to be no authority on the point which, in practice, is of academic interest only. Invariably, most fee farm grants, like most leases, have express covenants inserted in them by their draftsmen, who are usually loath to leave such matters to the general law.[28]

---

[21] On s. 52, see *Chute* v. *Busteed* (1862) 14 I.C.L.R. 115; (1865) 16 I.C.L.R. 222; *Mennons* v. *Burke* (1890) 26 L.R.Ir. 193; *Eustace-Duckett* v. *Thompson* (1938) 72 I.L.T.R. 226. The comma is presumably a draftsman's error or idiosyncrasy.

[22] *Cf.* the Fee Farm Rents (Ireland) Act, 1851, which expressly excluded the remedy of ejectment for non-payment of rent, para. 4.064, *ante,* and which was not expressly amended by Deasy's Act.

[23] Thus the precedent in Stubbs and Baxter, *Irish Forms and Precedents* (1910), does contain one, see p. 124.

[24] Para. 4.067, *ante.*

[25] Para. 4.068, *ante,* and see para. 17. 087 *et seq., post.* See also *Walsh* v. *Wightman* [1927] N.I. 1; *Whipp* v. *Mackey* [1927] I.R. 372.

[26] On these covenants generally, see ch. 17, *post.*

[27] S. 1.

[28] See Precedent No. 2 in Stubbs and Baxter, *Irish Forms and Precedents* (1910), pp. 122–3.

4.100. Sections 12 and 13 of Deasy's Act provide for the running of the benefit and burden of landlords' and tenants' covenants or agreements "contained or implied" in "any lease or other contract of tenancy" so as to bind successors in title of both parties.[29] Once again the wording seems to be wide enough to cover fee farm grants operating under the Act. Clearly this was the assumption of the court in *Chute* v. *Busteed*,[30] where the Court of Exchequer held that, since section 3 was not retrospective, the provisions of Deasy's Act relating to covenants did not apply to a fee farm grant executed in 1826.[31]

4.101. Some controversy has arisen, however, in academic circles whether section 10 of Deasy's Act applied to fee farm grants within the Act.[32] This section specified that, if any lease contained an agreement restraining or prohibiting assignment, it was not "lawful" to assign contrary to such agreement without the consent in writing of the landlord or his agent.[33] The question was raised whether this section also applied to fee farm grants, and whether such an agreement in a grant would have been valid generally in the light of *Quia Emptores*. Some have argued that a negative reply should be given to this question, on the ground that the estate granted remained a fee simple and *Quia Emptores* was not expressly repealed by Deasy's Act. It has been argued that the general principle should be maintained that Deasy's Act does not alter the nature of the estate granted and does not decree that a freehold estate should assume the characteristics of a leasehold estate for all purposes. It has been further suggested that section 10 should be read as presupposing that such an "agreement" would have been valid anyway, *i.e.*, judged according to the law before Deasy's Act. This construction, however, is difficult to reconcile with the courts' attitude to other sections in the Act, such as sections 12 and 13.[34] In *Chute* v. *Busteed*, the court discussed *Quia Emptores* in relation to Deasy's Act, and one is left to consider the effect of Christian J.'s *dictum* that "it might fairly be argued that an instrument executed after this statute had been passed ought to be construed with reference to the new law founded by the statute."[35] This could be regarded as an indication that fee farm grants operating under Deasy's Act should be treated in the same way as conversion grants, *i.e.*, creating a special statutory fee simple to which the usual common law characteristics should not necessarily be attached.[36]

(vi) Redemption

(a) *Chief Rents Redemption (Ireland) Act, 1864*

4.102. As a matter of literal construction, the wide wording of this Act

[29] See, generally, ch. 17, *post*.
[30] (1865) 16 I.C.L.R. 222 (see *A Casebook on Irish Land Law* (1984), p. 155).
[31] The successor in title of the original grantor was held not able to enforce (against the successor of the original grantee) a covenant to keep and deliver up in good repair a wall.
[32] See also para. 17.035 *etseq.*, *post*.
[33] S. 10 was repealed in the Republic by s. 35 (1) of the Landlord and Tenant (Ground Rents) Act, 1967.
[34] *Cf.* the question of the necessity for words of limitation, paras. 4.095–6, *supra*.
[35] Para. 4.092, *supra*. *Cf.* Bewley J. in *Donelly* v. *Galbraith* (1894) 28 I.L.T.R. 54; *Re McClatchie and Smyth's Contract* (1904) 38 I.L.T.R. 35.
[36] Para. 4.086, *ante*. *Cf.* Montrose, (1940) 4 N.I.L.Q. 86; Stubbs and Baxter, *Irish Forms and Precedents* (1910), p. 109.

would seem to cover Deasy's Act grants. It might be questioned, though, whether an Act passed only some four years later was intended to allow redemption in the case of grants that could be created only from 1860 onwards. There is no authority on the point.

(b) Redemption of Rent (Ireland) Act, 1891

4.103. This Act, especially in view of the amendment contained in section 14 (*b*) of the Land Law (Ireland) Act, 1896,[37] applied to Deasy's Act grants of agricultural land in order to facilitate redemption as part of the land purchase scheme. Deasy's Act grants create *ex hypothesi* the relationship of landlord and tenant and this, as section 14 (*b*) clearly presupposes and the judges confirmed, was the essential prerequisite for the application of the 1891 Act.[38]

(c) Landlord and Tenant (Ground Rents) (No. 2.) Act, 1978 (R.I.)

It would seem that this Act applies to Deasy's Act grants as much as it does to other fee farm grants.[39]

(d) Leasehold (Enlargement and Extension) Act (N.I.), 1971

This Act would also seem to apply as much to Deasy's Act grants as to other fee farm grants.[40]

4. Rentcharges

4.104. We come now to the third category of fee farm grant to be found in Ireland. This is a grant which creates no form of "tenure," feudal or leasehold, between the grantor and the grantee. These grants are probably more common in England,[41] but it is clear that some are to be found in Ireland.[42] All that is created by the grant is a perpetual *rentcharge* on the land granted.[43] It is doubtful if many grants of this nature have been created since Deasy's Act, 1860, because the rights of a grantor under a Deasy's Act grant are more extensive than those of a perpetual rentchargor. Rentcharge grants in Ireland are usually pre-1860 grants, which were neither executed under a Crown patent

---

[37] See fn. 30, para. 4.075, *ante*.
[38] *Kelly* v. *Rattey* (1893) 32 L.R.Ir. 445; *Adams* v. *Alexander* [1895] 2 I.R. 365; *Wynne* v. *Wilson* (1901) 35 I.L.T.R. 152; *Barton* v. *Fisher* [1901] 1 I.R. 453; *Sheil* v. *Irvine* (1903) 37 I.L.T.R. 92; *Re Maunsell's Estate* [1911] 1 I.R. 271.
[39] See para. 4.076, *ante*.
[40] See para. 4.077, *ante*.
[41] Para. 4.057, *ante*.
[42] For examples, see *Brady* v. *Fitzgerald* (1848) 12 Ir.Eq.R. 273; *Smith* v. *Smith* (1855) 5 Ir.Ch.R. 88; *Delacherois* v. *Delacherois* (1864) 11 H.L.C. 62; *Re Lunham's Estate* (1871) I.R. 5 Eq. 170; *Re Maunsell's Estate* [1911] 1 I.R. 271. Note that in England the creation of many such grants is prohibited by the Rentcharges Act, 1977, which also contains various provisions for redemption or discharge of existing ones. Once again it is doubtful whether the Republic's Landlord and Tenant (Ground Rents) Act, 1978, applies to such grants (see para. 4.092, *ante*). Indeed, it is even more doubtful in this case since there is no landlord and tenant relationship between the rentchargor and rentchargee as there is in the case of a Deasy's Act grant.
[43] The subject of rentcharges is dealt with generally in ch. 6, *post*.

dispensing with *Quia Emptores*[44] nor operating under conversion statutes, or post-1860 grants not purporting to create the relationship of landlord and tenant within section 3 of Deasy's Act.

(i) Creation

4.105. So far as fee farm grants are concerned, a perpetual rentcharge is created by the grant of a fee simple in which a rent is reserved to the grantor and charged on the land. The interest so created is in fact an incorporeal hereditament, a legal interest which will bind all successors to the land.[45] The common law rule was that it had to be created *inter vivos* by deed.[46]

(ii) Words of Limitation

4.106. A rentcharge is governed by the general law, as amended by statute, as to words of limitation in so far as the transfer of an existing rentcharge is concerned.[47] In the case of a fee farm grant annexing the rentcharge to a fee simple, the appropriate words of limitation for a fee simple will have to be used. It has been held that section 28 of the Wills Act, 1837, does not apply to the creation of a new rentcharge, so that the full words of limitation would have to be used in a grant by will.[48]

(iii) Fee Farm Rents

4.107. At common law, a rentcharge could be enforced by an action for the rent as a debt.[49] The action lay against the person known as the "terre tenant," *i.e.*, the *freehold* tenant for the time being of the land, who is the fee farm grantee or his successor in title.[50] The interesting feature of this remedy is that it was a descendant of one of the old real actions and thereby confined to persons seised of the land, so that a lessee in occupation of the land could not be sued for the rent.[51] In this respect such a rentcharge should not be confused with indemnity "rentcharges" which commonly arise as a result of the sub-division of leasehold land and consequent apportionment of head-rents between the sub-divided parts of the land.[52]

However, under the common law a rentcharge, or a rent seck (dry rent) as it

---

[44] An interesting feature of the *Delacherois* case, *op. cit.*, is that the original Crown grant by letters patent did contain the standard dispensation clause conferring a licence to make grants in fee simple "the statute *Quia Emptores* or any other law notwithstanding." But the House of Lords eventually held that the subsequent grants in question were not an exercise of this power; as Lord St. Leonards stated: "There is not that of which the statute *Quia Emptores* complained, that grants were made to hold of the feoffors, and not of the superior Lords." *Op. cit.*, p. 100.

[45] Ch. 6, *post.*

[46] Megarry and Wade, *The Law of Real Property* (5th ed., 1984), p. 822.

[47] *Re Bennett's Estate* [1898] 1 I.R. 185; see also *Plunket* v. *Reilly* (1852) 2 Ir.Ch.R. 585.

[48] *Nicols* v. *Hawkes* (1853) 10 Hare 342.

[49] Megarry and Wade, *op. cit.*, p. 823.

[50] See discussion in *Swift* v. *Kelly* (1889) 24 L.R.Ir. 478, espec. at 481 and 485–6 (Palles C.B.); *Sligo, Leitrim and Northern Rly. Co.* v. *Whyte* (1893) 31 L.R.Ir. 316; *Odlum* v. *Thompson* (1893) 31 L.R.Ir. 394.

[51] But see the Fee Farm Rents (Ireland) Act, 1851, *infra.*

[52] Para. 6.136, *post.* For an example in relation to a conversion grant, see *De Vesci* v. *O'Connell* [1908] A.C. 298.

used to be called, had to be distinguished from a rent service created along with tenure, feudal or otherwise. A rent service had certain incidents automatically annexed to it, including the remedy of distress for rent. The owner of a rentcharge did not have this remedy unless it was expressly reserved in the grant.[53] However, statute law has changed this position. First, the Distress for Rent Act (Ireland), 1712, conferred a statutory right of distress in respect of all rents reserved "upon any grant . . . where no reversion is retained," to be annexed "to the estate in the rent."[54] Then the Fee Farm Rents (Ireland) Act, 1851, extended all the remedies of a landlord for recovery of rent, *except* ejectment for non-payment of rent, to all fee farm rents and other rents with no reversion retained.[55] This Act clearly covered perpetual rentcharges, and it was held to be retrospective in operation.[56]

4.108. Finally, section 44 of the Conveyancing Act, 1881, also contains statutory remedies for recovery of rentcharges, which apply unless they are expressly excluded in the grant.[57] There is an obvious element of duplication here for Ireland so far as fee farm grants are concerned (the 1881 Act also applied to England where it was then the only legislation[58]), as occurs with other provisions of the 1881 Act. Section 44 provides the remedy of distress where the rentcharge is 21 days in arrears,[59] a right of entry into possession if the rentcharge is 40 days in arrears[60] and, also in the latter case, a power to demise the land to a trustee for a term of years on trust to raise the money due, with all costs and expenses.[61]

(iv) Forfeiture

4.109. It is quite common in a rentcharge grant for an express forfeiture clause to be inserted, reserving to the grantor a right of re-entry for non-payment of the rent or breach of any other obligation. Since it is contained in what is otherwise an ordinary conveyance of the fee simple, none of the legislation relating to forfeiture by a landlord applies in this case.[62] In the Republic of Ireland, this right is not confined to the perpetuity period,[63] but in

---

[53] It was in the fee farm grant considered in the *Delacherois* case, (1864) 11 H.L.C. 62. As Lord St. Leonards put it: "The rent is reserved, not as incident to tenure, but with an express power of distress." *Op. cit.*, p. 101. See also *Pennefather* v. *Stephens* (1847) 11 Ir.Eq.R. 61; *Brady* v. *Fitzgerald* (1848) 12 Ir.Eq.R. 273.

[54] S. 7. Replaced as far as the relationship of landlord and tenant was concerned by Deasy's Act, 1860, Sched. B, and repealed altogether in Northern Ireland with the abolition of the remedy of distress by the Judgments (Enforcement) Act (N.I.), 1969. Para. 17.066, *post.*

[55] S. 1.

[56] *Major* v. *Barton* (1851) 2 I.C.L.R. 28.

[57] S. 44 (5). The Act applies only to instruments coming into effect after the Act, s. 44 (6); for before the Act, see *Smith* v. *Smith* (1855) 5 Ir.Ch.R. 88.

[58] Note that s. 45, relating to discharge of rentcharges, did not apply to Ireland, see s. 45 (7).

[59] S. 44 (2), which, of course, no longer applies in Northern Ireland.

[60] S. 44 (3). A *right of entry*, conferring power to take possession and receive the profits of the land until the debt is paid, should not be confused with a *right of re-entry* which effects a forfeiture of the estate granted and determines the grantee's interest in the land as soon as it is exercised, subject to equitable relief against forfeiture, see discussion in *Brady* v. *Fitzgerald* (1847) 11 Ir.Eq.R. 55, (1848) 12 Ir.Eq.R. 273.

[61] S. 44 (4). These remedies were excepted from the rule against perpetuities, Conveyancing Act, 1911, s. 6 (1), and also Perpetuities Act (N.I.), 1966, s. 12.

[62] *Stevelly* v. *Murphy* (1840) 2 Ir.Eq.R. 448. See also ch. 17, *post.*

[63] Para. 5.105, *post.*

Northern Ireland it is not exercisable after the end of that period.[64]

(v) Covenants

4.110. The law applicable to covenants contained in a rentcharge fee farm grant is that applicable generally to freehold covenants.[65] Annexing a rentcharge does not in this regard attach any special characteristics to the conveyance of the fee simple. On the same reasoning, *Quia Emptores* clearly applies, and any attempt to prohibit or unduly restrict alienation by the grantee will be void.[66] Thus a covenant restricting alienation in an 1858 fee farm grant, to which neither the conversion statutes nor Deasy's Act applied, was held void as repugnant to the free power of alienation necessarily implied in the grant. In this case, *Re Lunham's Estate*,[67] Flanagan J. described the grant thus: "In legal effect, it is simply a grant of certain premises from Mr. Stokes to Mr. Lunham in fee simple, and a re-grant of a rent-charge of £400 a year out of these premises."[68]

(vi) Redemption

(a) *Chief Rents Redemption (Ireland) Act, 1864*

4.111. The wide wording of this Act would seem to cover rentcharge fee farm grants.[69]

(b) *Redemption of Rent (Ireland) Act, 1891*

This Act did not apply to rentcharge fee farm grants because they do not purport to create the relationship of landlord and tenant which is the prerequisite for the Act's application.[70]

(c) *Landlord and Tenant (Ground Rents) (No. 2) Act, 1978 (R.I.)*

This Act, however, would seem to apply to rentcharge grants to the same extent as it applies to other fee farm grants.[71]

(d) *Leasehold (Enlargement and Extension) Act (N.I.), 1971*

The same would seem to apply to this Act. There seems to be no good reason for distinguishing between one type of fee farm grant and another for the purposes of this Act.[72]

---

[64] Perpetuities Act (N.I.) 1966, s. 13 (1) (*a*), reversing *Walsh* v. *Wightman* [1927] N.I. 1.
[65] See ch. 19, *post*. Also *Stevelly* v. *Murphy* (1840) 2 Ir.Eq.R. 448.
[66] Para. 4.070, *ante*.
[67] (1871) I.R. 5 Eq. 170.
[68] *Ibid.*, p. 171.
[69] Para. 4.074, *ante*.
[70] Paras. 4.075 and 4.088, *ante*. *Christie* v. *Peacocke* (1892) 30 L.R.Ir. 646; *Kelly* v. *Rattey* (1893) 32 L.R.Ir. 445; *Alexander* v. *Macky* (1893) 32 L.R.Ir. 485.
[71] Para. 4.076, *ante*.
[72] Para. 4.077, *ante*.

V. FEE TAIL

A. GENERAL

4.112. The fee tail estate derives essentially from the early statute *De Donis Conditionalibus*, 1285. This statute was passed at the instigation of landowners who found their settlements being frustrated by the interpretation of the judges. The statute succeeded in the sense that the estate became the cornerstone of the complex system of land settlements which conveyancers in England and Ireland built up over the centuries and which remains in existence in modern times.[73]

1. *Conditional Fee*

4.113. In very early feudal law two freehold estates only were recognised, the fee simple and life estate. But the practice arose of conveying land in fee simple with conditions attached, which attempted to vary the usual mode of descent for a fee simple, *i.e.,* inheritance by general heirs, including collaterals.[74] One form of conveyance subject to a condition was the *maritagium*,[75] usually a conveyance of land by a father to his daughter and her husband "and the heirs of their bodies." In this case, and other similar conveyances, the courts interpretated the words in quotation marks as imposing a condition on the grantees that they must have issue born to them before the fee simple would vest in them.[76] The courts held, however, that, if issue of the marriage was born, the condition was fulfilled and the grantees took a fee simple which they could transfer. Thus the grantor's right to get the land back, when there was a subsequent failure of issue, was defeated and the right of the issue to inherit disappeared. In other words, the conveyance was subject to a condition precedent, which had to be met before the grantee took his estate and could freely alienate it. If no alienation took place the estate was inheritable by the issue, but once the grantee and his issue died the land reverted to the grantor. Such a conditional fee must, therefore, be distinguished from a determinable fee and a fee simple upon a condition, both described earlier.[77] A conditional fee was like a determinable fee in that it *could* determine on a future event, but that event would not necessarily determine it if the fee had been alienated in the meantime, whereby the alienee took a fee simple absolute free of any future interest of the grantor or of the grantee's issue. This fact is what gave rise to much of the criticism by landowners of the courts' interpretation and resulted in the passing of *De Donis*. A conditional fee was like a fee simple upon a condition in that they were both subject to a condition, but in the former case the condition was a condition precedent while in the latter it was a

---

[73] See further on settlements, ch. 8, *post.*
[74] Para. 4.006, *ante.*
[75] See Megarry and Wade, *The Law of Real Property* (5th ed., 1984), pp. 76–7.
[76] See, generally, Challis, *The Law of Real Property* (3rd ed.), ch. XVIII. Until the condition was satisfied the grantees took at most a life estate only.
[77] Paras. 4.046–55, *ante.*

condition subsequent.[78] One governed the vesting of the fee simple in the grantee in the first place, the other governed the grantor's right of forfeiture of the fee simple which had already been vested in the grantee.

2. *De Donis Conditionalibus, 1285*

4.114. *De Donis*[79] was passed to modify the courts' interpretation of conveyances creating a conditional fee. It recorded that lands were many times "given upon condition" and yet, through alienation by the donee after birth of issue, the land did not revert to the grantor or his heirs due to death of the donee without heirs of his body. This, the Act went on, "seemed very hard . . . to the givers and their heirs, that their will being expressed in the gift, was not heretofore, nor yet is observed." Such alienation so as to deprive the grantor of his reversion and the issue of their inheritance was "contrary to the minds of the givers, and contrary to the form expressed in the gift."[80] The statute provided the remedy and enacted that "the will of the giver, according to the form in the deed of gift manifestly expressed, shall be henceforth observed; so that they to whom the land was given under such condition, shall have no power to aliene the land so given, but that it shall remain unto the issue of them to whom it was given after their death, or . . . unto the giver or his heirs, if issue fail."[81]

4.115. Thus the courts' attempt to reinforce the fundamental principle of free alienation of land received a set-back, which was to remain effective for a couple of centuries. As a result of *De Donis*, the conditional fee ceased to be a category of the fee simple estate and really became a separate category of freehold estate. It was an estate of less value than the fee simple, hence the name "fee tail"—"taillé" or "cut down." It was cut down because, while like the fee simple and unlike the life estate it was an estate of inheritance,[82] the heirs capable of inheriting were a limited class, *i.e.*, the legitimate issue of the grantee. Just as significant was the fact that these heirs of the body would always inherit whatever the grantee did with the land. In the case of a fee simple, the grantee's heirs would succeed only if he died without having alienated the land. If the grantee of a fee simple alienated his estate, his heirs had no claim to inheritance; that passed to the alienee's heirs until he in turn alienated and so on. With a fee tail, if the original grantee purported to alienate after *De Donis*, the alienee took an estate *pur autre vie* only, [83] *i.e.*, an estate which would last only for the life-time of the original grantee. On that grantee's death, his issue inherited the land regardless of any claim by the grantee's alienee. This rule applied also to cases where the grantee's interest was determined not by voluntary alienation but by some other means, for the claims of the issue could not be defeated by acts causing an escheat or forfeiture of the grantee's

---

[78] Note the early version of a conditional fee granted in Ireland discussed in (1967) 18 N.I.L.Q. 347–8.

[79] Statute of Westminster II, 13 Edw. 1, c. 1.

[80] *Ibid.*

[81] *Ibid.* Writs of "formedon" were provided to enable the donee's issue, reversioners and remaindermen to claim the land back if necessary: see Brand, "Formedon in the Remainder before 'De Donis' " (1975) 10 Ir.Jur. (n.s.) 318; Milsom, "Formedon Before De Donis" (1956) 72 L.Q.R. 391.

[82] Para. 4.006, *ante*.

[83] Para. 4.160, *post*.

estate.[84] To this extent the statute also modified the feudal incidents normally attaching to freehold estates.[85]

4.116. *De Donis* thus established the basis of the complex system of family settlements of land which was to develop over the centuries and, indeed, despite further reforms facilitated both by the courts and legislatures, has survived down to modern times. It provided the conveyancers with the key instrument by which to ensure that family land and estates were kept within the family.[86] In an age which knew nothing about the modern sources of wealth, government securities and stocks and shares, the desire amongst landowners for such a system was manifold. Yet it had many vices,[87] not the least of which was the fact that it breached completely the fundamental principle of feudal land law that the land should be as freely alienable as possible. As custodians of the common law, it was to be expected that the courts would once again seek ways of curtailing the powers given to landowners and their conveyancers by *De Donis*.

3. *Fines and Recoveries*

4.117 The task facing property lawyers was to find a method of circumventing *De Donis* which the courts could and would enforce. It was clear what their landowner clients wanted. They wanted to be able to sell their entailed land free from restrictions and limitations imposed by the existence of future rights to the land resting in their issue and in reversioners or remaindermen. The courts could not disregard the Act directly, but they might be persuaded to recognise a mechanism which, though it did not directly contravene the Act, did circumvent it indirectly and give the landowners substantially what they wanted. The mechanism devised by the lawyers was the "collusive action," *i.e.*, an action brought against a defendant with his consent—essentially a piece of procedural chicanery but none the less effective at that. Two types of collusive action were devised for tenants in tail, one which was a set of proceedings known as "suffering a recovery" and another known as "levying a fine."[88]

(i) Common Recovery

4.118. The leading authority on this action was an English case decided in the late fifteenth century, usually known as *Taltarum's Case*.[89] The nature of the proceedings was that a stranger to the settlement of the land was persuaded to bring an action claiming the land. The tenant in tail offered no defence to this action, admitted to the court that he had no good title to the land and thereby allowed judgment to be given against him—he suffered a recovery of the

---

[84] Paras. 2.23–4, *ante*.

[85] Entails became subject to forfeiture by the High Treason Act, 1534, 26 Hen. 8, c. 13, s. 5, extended to Ireland by the Treason Act (Ir.), 1537, 28 Hen 8, c. 7 (Ir.), s. 6.

[86] This subject is pursued in greater detail in ch. 8, *post*.

[87] See further ch. 8, *post*.

[88] Challis, *op. cit.*, ch. XXVII.

[89] 12 Edw. 4, pl. 25, f. 19a (Y.B.), translated in Kiralfy, *Source Book of English Law* (1957), p. 86. See *Houlditch* v. *Wallace* (1838) 5 Cl. & F. 629.

land.[90] This judgment would clearly bind the tenant in tail and probably also his issue as claimants through him.[91] It would not on its own bar claimants to the land whose rights did not derive through the tenant in tail, but derived independently from the settlor through the terms of his original settlement. It would not bind, therefore, reversioners (the original settlor and his successors) or remaindermen who would otherwise take the land on failure of the tenant in tail's issue. To achieve this another piece of medieval procedural law was employed, namely, "vouching to warranty."[92] It has already been mentioned that in early feudal law it was the practice for a grantor of land to warrant his title to the land and to undertake to compensate the grantee with lands of equal value should that title subsequently turn out to be bad.[93] Using this principle, the tenant in tail suffering the recovery vouched to warranty some friend or a "man of straw" (any person selected by the parties and accepted without question by the court), who alleged that he had previously conveyed the land to the tenant with the usual warranty of good title. Then, when the tenant in tail disclosed his bad title to the court and suffered the recovery, his "common vouchee"[94] in turn suffered a judgment to be entered against him to make compensation with other land.[95] This judgment was worthless in real terms since it was based entirely on fictitious proceedings, but it had the vital technical function of barring any further claims of reversioners or remaindermen to the land originally conveyed to the tenant in tail and now passing to the person in whose favour the common recovery was suffered. These claims were now supposed to be satisfied out of the judgment given against the common vouchee.[96]

4.119. The result of this collusion, to which the court was an open party, was that the person in whose favour the recovery judgment was given obtained the fee simple absolute in the land. Thus the tenant in tail gained full powers of alienation, subject only to any fee or bribe necessary to secure the co-operation of the other parties to the court action and to the time and trouble involved in the action itself. There was also the limitation that, since the court action was essentially one for the recovery of land, it could be brought only against a person currently seised of the land.[97] A common recovery was effective only if brought against a tenant in tail in possession; if a tenant currently holding only an estate in tail in remainder wished to initiate such proceedings, he would have to enlist the co-operation of the freeholder currently in possession, who would have been seised. It was this limitation which led to the second collusive action for barring entails, the fine.

<hr/>

[90] See *Morrison* v. *Heath* (1818) Rowe 552; *Murphy d. Wray* v. *Humes* (1829) 2 Hud. & Br. 395; *Ellis* v. *Mahony* (1834) 3 Law Rec. (N.S.) 25.
[91] Megarry and Wade, *op. cit.*, p. 79.
[92] *Fitzgerald* v. *Roddy* (1854) 4 I.C.L.R. 74.
[93] Para. 4.072, *ante*.
[94] So-called because the practice developed of some court official acting as the man of straw for any parties requiring him, Challis, *op. cit.*, p. 311. *Fitzgerald* v. *Roddy* (1854) 4 I.C.L.R. 74 (see also 6 H.L.C. 823).
[95] *Hume* v. *Burton* (1784) 1 Ridgw. P.C. 16.
[96] Being a man of straw, he never appeared in court again and so any action to recover against him was doomed from the beginning, Challis, *ibid*.
[97] Para. 4.018, *ante*. *Witham* v. *Notley* [1913] 2 I.R. 281 (see *A Casebook on Irish Land Law* (1984), p. 170).

(ii) Fine

4.120. In this context a fine meant a compromise of an action before any judgment was given by the court, a compromise that was worked out by the parties, approved by the court and then registered in the court's records. The use of such a device to bar entails had been expressly prohibited by *De Donis* itself.[98] However, later legislation reversed this provision, in particular the Fines Act (Ireland), 1634,[99] which provided that all fines levied by tenants in tail in possession, reversion or remainder were "to all intents and purposes" sufficient to bar the entail.

4.121. The significant point about this type of action was that not only a tenant in tail in possession could use it. A tenant in tail in remainder could enter into a compromise agreement with respect to the land, though he could not be sued for recovery of the land itself because he had no seisin.[1] He had no need to get the consent of the tenant in possession who was seised. Yet herein lay the weakness of the device. The tenant in tail's agreement could bind only himself and those claiming through him, his issue; it could not bind reversioners or remaindermen unless they were also made parties to the agreement.[2] If they were not, the stranger who was the other party to the compromise did not obtain a fee simple absolute but instead what was known as a "base fee."[3] This was in substance a determinable fee simple, a fee which would last only until the tenant in tail and his issue died out, at which time the reversion or remainder would take effect.

4.122. To sum up, then, the early law relating to fines and recoveries, they both involved fictitious actions in court to circumvent the clear policy of *De Donis*, which was that the tenant in tail should not be able to bar the entail so as to defeat the future interests in the land of the issue in tail and reversioners or remaindermen to take after them. The common recovery could be used less frequently, since it was confined to tenants in tail in possession. It was also a more complicated and probably more expensive action, though it had a more extensive effect in producing a fee simple absolute. The fine could be used much more frequently by tenants in tail in possession or remainder, and even with contingent interests only. It was a less complicated action, since it did not proceed to judgment, but it had the less extensive effect of producing a base fee only. Both actions exhibited the ingenuity and enterprise of property lawyers and the determination of the courts to abide by the fundamental principles of feudal land law, contrary to the spirit of legislation if necessary. The actions also illustrated some of the striking features of the early common law—the use of legal fictions and the twisting of procedure to provide substantive rights. That substantive rights had been created was made clear by the courts'

---

[98] C. 1.—"And if a fine be levied hereafter upon such lands, it shall be void in the law."

[99] 10 Chas. 1, sess. 2, c. 8 (Ir.). The English equivalent was the Fines Act, 1540 (32 Hen. 8, c. 36) which was considered to confirm the courts' interpretation of an earlier Fines Act of 1489, see Challis, *op. cit.*, pp. 306–7; Megarry and Wade, *op. cit.*, p. 80.

[1] *Jones* v. *Inman* (1794) Ir. Term Rep. 433.

[2] *Carhampton* v. *Carhampton* (1795) Ir. Term Rep. 567.

[3] Discussed more fully, para. 4.136, *post*

insistence that any attempt by settlors expressly to exclude the power to suffer recoveries or levy fines was void as being repugnant to the very nature of a fee tail estate. Such a restriction was regarded by the courts as being as much repugnant to the fee tail estate as a prohibition against alienation was with respect to the fee simple estate. It was essential, however, that the tenant in tail or life tenant in possession should consent to these procedures and he would usually consent only if those entitled on his death settled the land by a resettlement in favour of the family. Thus each generation ensured that the land passed to the next generation as life tenants or tenants in tail and so family estates were preserved.[4]

As the common law developed, it was only a matter of time before legislation would be introduced to get rid of the more absurd aspects of the law of fines and recoveries.

4. Fines and Recoveries (Ireland) Act, 1834

4.123. The Fines and Recoveries (Ireland) Act, 1834,[5] abolished fines and recoveries as methods of barring entails and replaced them with a single and much more simple method, *i.e.,* execution by the tenant in tail of a "disentailing assurance."[6] This means in effect the execution of a conveyance using words which, if executed by the fee simple owner, would convey the fee simple.[7] Failure to execute such a deed meant that the fee tail was not enlarged into a fee simple and what was created was a base fee only,[8] defined by the Act as "that estate in fee simple into which an estate tail is converted where the issue in tail are barred, but persons claiming estates by way of remainder or otherwise are not barred."[9] This was the usual type of base fee, which would arise if the tenant in tail failed to obtain the consent of the protector where necessary.[10] However, it seems that the courts also recognised a more narrowly defined base fee, sometimes referred to as a *voidable* base fee.[11] This has been held to arise where the defect in the disentailing assurance was of a more formal or technical nature. For example, the Act provided that to be effective the disentailing assurance had to be enrolled within six calendar months of its execution in court.[12] Failure to comply with these statutory requirements results, it seems, in the creation of a base fee determinable or voidable by entry of the issue in tail.[13]

---

[4] See further, ch. 8, *post.*

[5] The English equivalent was the Fines and Recoveries Act, 1833, parts of which did also apply to Ireland.

[6] Ss. 2 and 12. *Re Skerrett's Trusts* (1884) 15 L.R.Ir. 1; *Re Gosford's Estate* (1910) 44 I.L.T.R. 234; *Gaussen and French* v. *Ellis* [1930] I.R. 116; *Re Ottley's Estate* [1910] 1 I.R. 1; *Bank of Ireland* v. *Domvile* [1956] I.R. 37 (see *A Casebook on Irish Land Law* (1984), p. 178). (Note that in places the Report of the last case mistakenly refers to the date of the 1834 Act as "1894," see the headnote and p. 43; *cf.* pp. 52 and 58–9.) For the Act's effect on fines and recoveries levied before the Act, see *Davies* v. *D'Arcy* (1853) 3 I.C.L.R. 617.

[7] S. 38. *Nelson* v. *Agnew* (1871) I.R. 6 Eq. 232.

[8] 1834 Act, ss. 12, 38 and 39. See *Re Knox* [1912] 1 I.R. 288.

[9] S. 1.

[10] As in the case of a fine levied before the Act, the tenant in tail would have to get the consent of the freeholder in possession, para. 4.121, *ante.* For "protector," see para. 4.124, *infra.*

[11] See Challis, *The Law of Real Property* (3rd ed.), pp. 322 and 330.

[12] S. 39. Now in the superior Courts of the Republic of Ireland and of Northern Ireland. *Peyton* v. *Lambert* (1858) 8 I.C.L.R. 485 (see *A Casebook on Irish Land Law* (1984), p. 253); *Bank of Ireland* v. *Domvile* [1956] I.R. 37 (see *ibid.,* p. 178).

[13] *Re St. George's Estate* (1879) 3 L.R.Ir. 277; *Witham* v. *Notley* [1913] 2 I.R. 281 (see *A Casebook on Irish*

4.124 The Act recognised, however, one of the features of the previous law, namely, the necessity for consent by the freeholder in possession to a recovery suffered by a tenant in tail in remainder so as to bar the entail effectively. The Act provided that in this case there was to be a person known as the "protector of the settlement," who would have to give his consent to the disentailing assurance. A disentailing assurance executed without his consent created a base fee only.[14] The protector could generally use his discretion about giving consent, but he could not bind himself by agreement to withhold consent in the future.[15] The protector was either the person who would have had to give his consent to a recovery before the Act,[16] or any special protector appointed as such expressly by the settlor, as he was empowered to do by the Act.[17] It was also provided that the protector retained his powers even though he might subsequently part with his own estate.[18]

4.125. The result of this Act was that a tenant in tail in possession acquired the power to dispose of the fee simple estate, provided he followed the procedures laid down. He could either sell it to a third party or enlarge his own previous entailed estate into a fee simple by conveying it to his own use.[19] This disposition had to be by an assurance operating *inter vivos*; it was too late to do it by will. Otherwise, the tenant in tail enjoyed most of the rights and privileges of the fee simple owner. Thus he was not liable for waste, whereas the owner of a mere life estate was.[20] It is true that his ability to grant lesser estates and interests out of his entailed estate, which would be binding on his issue or remaindermen, was curtailed[21] until later settlements legislation radically altered the law in this regard.[22] One further restriction may be noted, which relates to rentcharges held in entail.[23] If a rentcharge already in existence (*in esse*) and held in fee simple were conveyed in fee tail, the tenant in tail could bar the entail by a disentailing assurance under the Act and thereby create a rentcharge in fee simple, for himself or his assignee.[24] Where however the rentcharge had been created for the first time (*de novo*) by the conveyance to the tenant in tail, so that the rentcharge was limited in duration initially to the entailed estate, any assurance under the Act would create a base fee barring the issue in tail only but not remaindermen.[25] Remaindermen would have been

Land Law (1984), p 170); The distinction between the usual base fee and a voidable base fee has been given statutory recognition in New Zealand's Property Law Act, 1952, s. 16, see *Survey of the Land Law of Northern Ireland* (1971), para. 46.

[14] S. 32. As to the type of base fee, see para. 4.121, *ante*.
[15] Ss. 34 and 35.
[16] S. 28. Here the protector was usually the tenant in tail or life tenant in possession of the land, para. 4.121, *ante*.
[17] S. 30, which provided that more than one but not more than three persons could be appointed protectors.
[18] S. 19.
[19] This method of conveyance was explained earlier, para. 3.019, *ante*.
[20] Para. 4.149, *post*.
[21] The Leases Act (Ir.), 1634, 10 Chas. 1, sess. 3, c. 6 (Ir.), enabled the tenant in tail to grant leases for not more than 21 years or a period of 3 lives binding on the issue in tail, though not remaindermen. This Act was replaced by the Settled Estates Act, 1856, s. 35 which was in turn replaced by the Settled Estates Act, 1877 and the Settled Land Acts, 1881–92. See ch. 8, *post*.
[22] Ch. 8, *post*.
[23] See, generally, paras. 6.131 *et seq.*, *post*.
[24] *Re Franks's Estate* [1915] 1 I.R. 387.
[25] *Pinkerton* v. *Pratt* [1915] 1 I.R. 406.

barred, however, if the original conveyance creating the rentcharge had given it in remainder in fee simple to some other party, whom the tenant in tail could bar by enlarging his entailed estate into a fee simple.[26]

B. Creation and Transfer

4.126. Like the fee simple estate, a fee tail has usually been created by deed since the Real Property Act, 1845.[27] A transfer of the estate and its effect is governed by the Fines and Recoveries (Ireland) Act, 1834, which has been discussed.

C. Words of Limitation

4.127. As a freehold estate of inheritance, a fee tail must be created by appropriate words of limitation. Again, as in the case of a fee simple, the law has developed different sets of rules governing the words of limitation according to whether they are contained in a conveyance *inter vivos* or in a will. In the case of a fee tail there is a further complication. A fee simple is an estate which could be inherited by the heirs *general,* whereas a fee tail is an estate inheritable by heirs *special.* The point is however that there can be degrees of speciality and different words have to be used to indicate what degree of speciality in the heirs is required, if any. This problem does not arise in the case of a fee simple where there can be no question of degree in this sense.[28]

1. *Conveyances* Inter Vivos

(i) At Common Law

4.128. The general rule for a fee tail is that the heirs special are always limited to descendants of the holder of the entail. Thus, while the word "heirs" was essential at common law to indicate that the estate granted was a freehold estate of inheritace, that word had to be qualified by additional words indicating that the inheritance was confined to descendants, if it was to create a fee tail. The standard words of limitation for a conveyance *inter vivos* at common law were: to A "and the heirs of his body." Other qualifications of the word "heirs" to the same effect would suffice, *e.g.,* to A "and the heirs of his flesh."[29] Formulae which omitted the vital word "heirs" generally were insufficient in an *inter vivos* conveyance, so that a conveyance to A "and his issue" would not create a fee tail, probably only a joint life estate in A and those of his issue alive at the date of execution of the conveyance.[30]

This was the position for a fee tail *general,* where descendants of every kind could inherit. It was quite possible, however, to restrict the class of descendants further, so as to create a fee tail *special.*[31] Thus a fee tail male could be created

---

[26] *Re Franks's Estate, op. cit.;* Challis, *The Law of Real Property* (3rd ed.), pp. 327–8.
[27] Para. 4.023, *ante.*
[28] *Cf.* the classification of fees simple, para. 4.043, *ante,* with the classification of fees tail, para. 4.135, *post.*
[29] *Cf. Re Smith's Estate* (1891) 27 L.R.Ir. 121.
[30] *Cf.* the case of a will, para. 4.130, *post.*
[31] Sometimes this label is confined to the case of an even further restriction, *i.e.,* to the heirs of the body of a

by the words "and the heirs male of his body," a fee tail female by the words "and the heirs female of his body." In the former case, the entail could last only as long as it could descend through an unbroken line of male descendants; in the latter, it could descend only through an unbroken line of female descendants. Even further restriction could be made by specifying that the heirs of the body could be begotten of one particular spouse only, *e.g,* to A "and the heirs male of his body begotten upon Mary." Here only male descendants of A and Mary could inherit the fee tail.

(ii) By Statute

4.129. The Conveyancing Act, 1881, provided alternative formulae for the creation of fees tail. Section 51 provided that for a fee tail general the words "in tail" were sufficient, for a fee tail special the words "in tail male" and "in tail female." It may be noted that the word "fee" was not mentioned in the section, but there seems to be no reason why "to A in fee tail" should not also create a fee tail.[32]

2. Gifts by Will

(i) At Common Law

4.130. In accordance with the courts' generally more liberal approach to the interpretation of wills,[33] the rule was, and is, that any words sufficient to show an intention on the part of the testator to create a fee tail will suffice. There is, therefore, no need to use technical words and the omission of the word "heirs" will not invalidate the grant. There have been numerous cases holding that expressions like "to A and his issue" or "to A and his descendants" create a fee tail in a will.[34] These expressions indicate that inheritance by a line of descendants is intended.[35] More difficulty was caused by an expression like "to A and his children" which tended to suggest that inheritance was confined to the first generation only. The courts devised a special principle for this sort of case, known as the rule in *Wild's Case*.[36] According to this principle, if A had no children when the will was *made*,[37] the words "and his children" were

---

specified spouse, see Megarry and Wade, *The Law of Real Property* (5th ed., 1984), p. 55 and s. 95 (1) of the Republic of Ireland's Succession Act, 1965, quoted para. 4.131, *post.*

[32] *Cf. Twaddle* v. *Murphy* (1881) 8 L.R.Ir. 123 (a case involving a fee farm grant) (see *A Casebook on Irish Land Law* (1984), p. 113) where the court held that superadded words would not prevent the operation of an otherwise effective conveyance, para. 4.095, *ante. Cf. Roche* v. *O'Brien* (1852) 13 Ir.L.R. 253; *Kempster* v. *Maher* (1903) 37 I.L.T.R. 29.

[33] Para. 4.031, *ante.*

[34] *Mandeville* v. *Earl of Carrick* (1795) 3 Ridgw. P.C. 352; *Bower* v. *Eccles* (1815) Rowe 466; *Manning* v. *Moore* (1832) Alc. & Nap. 96; *Blackwell* v. *Hale* (1850) 11 C.L.R. 612.

[35] Thus it seems that even an expression like "to A and his heirs" (which would normally create a fee simple) might as a matter of construction in a particular case be taken to create a fee tail, see, *e.g., Re Waugh* [1903] 1 Ch. 744.

[36] (1599) 6 Co. Rep. 16b. *Cf. re* personalty, *Heron* v. *Stokes* (1842) 4 Ir.Eq.R. 284.

[37] It is arguable that this was an exception to the general rule that a will speaks from the death of the testator, which is the date at which to judge the validity of limitations operating under it, para. 14.42, *post. Wild's Case* has been expressly reversed in this respect in the Republic of Ireland by the Succession Act, 1965, s. 89, which replaces and extends s. 24 of the Wills Act, 1837 (in force in N.I.), so as to provide that a will always speaks from death, unless a contrary intention appears.

construed as words of limitation and A took a fee tail.[38] The theory was that giving A a fee tail was the only way the testator could have intended to benefit A's children, though A could always prevent this by barring the entail. If, however, A did have children living when the will was made, the words "and his children" were construed as words of purchase and A took jointly with all his children living at the testator's death.[39]

(ii) By Statute

4.131. The above common law position remains the law in Northern Ireland, though recommendations for abolishing the fee tail estate altogether have been made.[40] In the Republic of Ireland the common law position for wills, including the rule in *Wild's Case,* has been reversed by section 95 of the Succession Act, 1965, which reads:

"(1) An estate tail (whether general, in tail male, in tail female or in tail special) in real estate may be created by will only by the use of the same words of limitation as those by which a similar estate tail may be created by deed.

(2) Words of limitation contained in a will in respect of real estate which have not the effect of creating an estate in fee simple or an estate tail shall have the same effect, as near as may be, as similar words used in a deed in respect of personal property."

4.132. These provisions, which may be contrasted with provisions introduced in England in 1925,[41] and which have given rise to considerable controversy there,[42] make the position for entails created by will much stricter than the common law. Subsection (1) means that, if a testator in the Republic wishes nowadays to create a fee tail in his will, he must use the technical expressions required for conveyances *inter vivos* at common law or under the Conveyancing Act, 1881, section 51. These expressions have been discussed above.[43] If a testator fails to use such an expression he fails to create a fee tail; that much at least is clear from subsection (1). What he does create is governed by subsection (2), which is not so clear. The subsection clearly presupposes that the testator has used words of limitation of some sort[44] and these have to be construed so as to have the same effect as in a transfer *inter vivos* of *personal* property, with appropriate allowance made for the different nature of the property transferred. In other words, the subsection applies to what would previously have been regarded as words of limitation, but which now cease to

---

[38] *Clifford* v. *Koe* (1880) 5 App.Cas. 447.
[39] *Re Moyles' Estate* (1878) 1 L.R.Ir. 155. *Cf. Ward* v. *Ward* [1921] 1 I.R. 117.
[40] *Survey of the Land Law of Northern Ireland* (1971), paras. 44–7; Land Law Working Group's Discussion Document No. 2 (*Estates and Interests and Family Dealings in Land*) (1981), p. 16.
[41] Law of Property Act, 1925, s. 130 (1) and (2), though note that other provisions for estates tail were introduced by this Act for England, *e.g.*, making them subsist as equitable estates only after 1925.
[42] See Bailey, (1938) 6 C.L.J. 67; (1947) 9 C.L.J. 185; Megarry, (1947) 9 C.L.J. 46; Morris, (1947) 9 C.L.J. 190.
[43] Paras. 4.025–30, *ante.*
[44] Otherwise the fee simple or other whole estate or interest the testator had power to dispose of by will would pass under the general provision in s. 94 of the 1965 Act.

be effective by virtue of subsection (1) so far as an estate tail is concerned. More difficulty arises with respect to words of limitation not creating an estate in fee simple in a will, because even before the Wills Act, 1837, any words indicating an intention to create a fee simple were sufficient and nothing in the Succession Act, 1965, seems to change this common law position. The subsection would seem to have in mind expressions which were more likely to be regarded as intended to create a fee tail, if any freehold estate, rather than a fee simple, because what was at least clear was that the inheritance was intended to be restricted to a class narrower than heirs general. The subsection seems to apply, therefore, to wills using expressions like "to A and his issue," "to A and his descendants" or "to A and his children." What the effect of such expressions is in a transfer *inter vivos* of personal property is a matter of construction and, in applying this construction to a will, presumably regard should be had to the intention of the testator. Thus "to A and his issue" could be construed as an absolute gift jointly to A and any of his issue living at the testator's death (when the will takes effect). If there are no such issue then living, it could be construed as a gift to A absolutely, *i.e.*, in fee simple where land is concerned, if the testator has power to transmit this.

3. *Equitable Gifts*

4.133. The same rules would seem to apply here as in the case of a fee simple estate. In other words, if a settlor purports to use technical words of limitation in delimiting an equitable fee tail, they will be given their usual meaning under the common law, as amended by statute. It he does not purport to use technical words, the courts will strive to give effect to what appears to have been his intention, by construing them regardless of the usual requirements as to words of limitation, if necessary.[45]

4. *Rule in Shelley's Case*

4.134 The rule in *Shelley's Case*, which was discussed earlier in relation to the fee simple estate,[46] applies equally to the fee tail estate. Thus a conveyance "to A for life, remainder to the heirs of his body" creates a fee tail in A, the remainder being taken, in accordance with the rule, to contain words of limitation only. The same rules apply as in the case of a fee simple estate and there is no need to repeat them here. It may be noted in particular with respect to wills, that, where a testator uses words that are not the normal words of limitation, *e.g.*, "to A for life, remainder to his successors," the general principle is that it is a matter of construction whether the testator meant by that the whole inheritable issue (*i.e.*, the heirs of the body) or *personae designatae*.[47] Thus in *Finch* v. *Foley*,[48] a devise "to A and his first and other sons successively in

[45] See para. 4.033, *ante*, and the authorities therein cited. Also *Crumpe* v. *Crumpe* [1900] A.C. 127; *The Land Purchase Trustee, Northern Ireland* v. *Beers* [1925] N.I. 191.
[46] Paras. 4.034 *et seq.*, *ante*.
[47] Para. 4.041, *ante*. *Re Bishop and Richardson's Contract* [1899] 1 I.R. 71; *Re Keane's Estate* [1903] 1 I.R. 215; *Re Taylor's Trusts* [1912] 1 I.R. 1; *Ward* v. *Ward* [1921] 1 I.R. 117.
[48] [1949] Ir.Jur.Rep. 30 (Kingsmill Moore J.).

remainder one after another according to their respective seniorities in tail male" was held to give A a fee tail. Yet in England a similar devise "to A during his life with . . . remainder to the use of his first and other sons successively according to seniority in tail male" was held not to be a case for the application of *Shelley's Case*.[49] The English judge thought that such a limitation was a common form of settlement designed to convey a life estate, followed by estates tail in succession to *personae designatae*. Yet the fact is that that form covers the persons who would inherit under a fee tail, and the judge interpreted Lord Macnaghten's statement in *Van Grutten* v. *Foxwell*[50] as meaning that this fact was not conclusive of the question of construction as to what the testator intended.[51]

Finally, it may be noted that the rule in *Shelley's Case* was abolished in England in 1925,[52] but this step has not yet been taken in either part of Ireland.[53]

D. CLASSIFICATION

1. *Fees Tail General and Special*

4.135. The distinction between a fee tail general and a fee tail special (which may be one of several kinds) has already been discussed.[54] It should also be noted that in theory there is no reason why a fee tail, general or special, may not be subjected to further restrictions like a fee simple. Thus it may be made determinable or subject to a condition precedent or subsequent.[55]

2. *Base Fee*

4.136. A base fee is essentially a fee simple liable to determine on failure of the heirs of the body of the tenant in tail creating the base fee. This is the usual case which arises where the tenant in tail fails to bar the entail effectively, *i.e.*, so as to bar reversioners or remaindermen due to take the land after failure of the issue of the tenant in tail. The most common occasion for the creation of such a base fee is where a tenant in tail not in possession executes a disentailing assurance without the consent of the protector.[56] There is also the rarer case when the base fee can be determined by entry of the issue in tail, which arises where the failure to bar the entail is caused by a more formal or technical flaw, such as failure to enrol the disentailing assurance within six months of its execution.[57]

---

[49] *Re Williams* [1952] Ch. 828 (Roxburgh J).
[50] [1897] A.C. 659.
[51] *Op. cit.*, pp. 833–4.
[52] Law of Property Act, 1925, s. 131. See Adams, "The Doctrine of Very Heir" (1973) 37 Conv. 113; Farrer, "Law of Property Act, s. 131" (1937) 53 L.Q.R. 371; Hargreaves, "Shelley's Ghost" (1938) 54 L.Q.R. 70; Megarry, "*Shelley's Case* and the Doctrine of Very Heir" (1943) 59 L.Q.R. 272; "Shelley's Ghost" (1944) 60 L.Q.R. 222.
[53] See, however, *Survey of the Land Law of Northern Ireland* (1971), paras. 274–5.
[54] Para. 4.128, *ante*.
[55] Paras. 4.046 *et seq.*, *ante*. *Magee* v. *Martin* [1902] 1 I.R. 367; *Re Elliot* [1916] 1 I.R. 30; *cf. Re Talbot* [1932] I.R. 714.
[56] Para. 4.124, *ante*.
[57] Para. 4.123, *ante*.

4.137 A base fee can be created by the tenant in tail either in some other person in favour of whom the disentailing assurance is executed or in the tenant in tail himself.[58] This sort of estate, however, was obviously an unsatisfactory one, since neither the tenant in tail nor any purchaser from him could be sure when it would end. This made it an extremely unattractive commercial asset. So the law permitted the enlargement of a base fee into a fee simple absolute, thereby producing the same result as a fully effective barring of the entail. Prior to the Fines and Recoveries (Ireland) Act, 1834, this could have been achieved for the owner of the base fee by the tenant in tail suffering a recovery.[59] The 1834 Act, however, abolished recoveries.[60] Since 1834, a base fee can be enlarged by the tenant in tail who created it, if the tenant executes another disentailing assurance either with the consent of the protector this time or after the protectorship has ceased to exist.[61] Thus the tenant in tail could do this on the death of the freeholder in possession, if he had been the protector.[62] If the tenant in tail had died first, the new disentailing assurance could be executed by whoever would have succeeded to the entail (e.g., his eldest son), but it has been held in England that any purchaser to whom the base fee may have been conveyed cannot so enlarge it.[63]

4.138. A base fee may also be enlarged by its current owner, including, therefore, any purchaser from the tenant in tail, buying out the immediate fee simple remainder or reversion. In this case, section 37 of the 1834 Act specifically provides that the base fee will not merge into the fee simple, for otherwise it would have been subject to any charges or incumbrances attaching to the fee simple.[64] Instead, section 37 provides that the base fee "shall be *ipso facto* enlarged into as large an estate as the tenant in tail, with the consent of the protector, if any, might have created by any disposition under this Act, if such remainder or reversion had been vested in any other person." In other words, the base fee is enlarged into a fee simple absolute free of all claims by the issue in tail or any reversioners or remaindermen taking after them.[65]

4.139. Lastly, the current holder of a base fee may enlarge it into a fee simple by acquiring a title to the latter by adverse possession,[66] *i.e.*, by remaining in possession of the land for 12 years after the protectorship has ceased. The original period laid down for this automatic enlargement was twenty years' possession,[67] but this was reduced later to twelve years,[68] which

---

[58] By using an executed use, see paras. 3.019–20, *ante*.
[59] Para. 4.118, *ante*. See Challis, *op. cit.,* pp. 335–8.
[60] S. 2.
[61] S. 16; see also s. 33. *Bank of Ireland* v. *Domvile* [1956] I.R. 37 (see *A Casebook on Irish Land Law* (1984) p. 178).
[62] Para. 4.124, *ante*.
[63] *Bankes* v. *Small* (1887) 36 Ch.D. 716.
[64] As to the law of merger, see ch. 24, *post. Re Wallace's Estate* [1907] 1 I.R. 91.
[65] S. 12.
[66] As to which, generally, see ch. 23, *post*.
[67] Real Property Limitation Act, 1833, s. 23.
[68] Real Property Limitation Act, 1874, s. 6; *Bank of Ireland* v. *Domvile* [1956] I.R. 37 (see *A Casebook on Irish Land Law* (1984), p. 178).

has remained the period in the modern statutes of limitations in both the Republic and Northern Ireland.[69]

3. Entails After Possibility

4.140. Where there is a fee tail special of the kind limiting inheritance to the issue of a specified spouse,[70] the tenant in tail is put in a restricted position if that spouse predeceases him, leaving no such issue. The tenant becomes a tenant in tail "after possibility of issue extinct."[71] Section 15 of the Fines and Recoveries (Ireland) Act, 1834, provided that such a tenant could not bar the entail by executing a disentailing assurance under the Act.[72] Thus the reversion or remainder is bound to take effect on his death, when there will also, *ex hypothesi*, be a failure of the issue in tail. Because his estate is, therefore, really no more than a life estate, a tenant in tail after possibility, like a tenant for life[73] but unlike most tenants in tail,[74] may be liable for waste, at least to some extent. He is probably not liable for voluntary waste,[75] but may be liable for equitable waste, *i.e.*, wanton destruction.[76]

4. Other Unbarrable Entails

4.141. Apart from the special case of an entail after possibility of issue extinct, there are several other kinds of unbarrable entails—despite the general principle that any contract, covenant or other restriction purporting to prevent a tenant in tail from barring the entail is void as repugnant to the nature of an estate in fee tail.[77] In England, for example, certain entails were made expressly unbarrable by statute. Thus entails created by the Crown in lands settled on grantees in recognition of services to the Crown, where the reversion was in the Crown, were unbarrable.[78] But these statutory provisions did not apply to Ireland,[79] so that a reversion in the Crown did not prevent the barring of entails here. Some entails in England were also made unbarrable specifically by special Acts of Parliament, such as those given to the first Duke of Marlborough and Duke of Wellington for public services.[80] There would seem to be no such entails in Ireland.[81]

---

[69] Statute of Limitations, 1957, s. 19 (R.I.); Statute of Limitations (N.I.), 1958, s. 23.

[70] Para. 4.128, *ante*.

[71] See *Re Toppin's Estate* [1915] 1 I.R. 330.

[72] Note, however, that he does have the powers of a tenant for life under the Settled Land Acts, see Settled Land Act 1882, s. 58 (1) (vii), and also para. 8.021, *post*.

[73] Para. 4.149, *post*.

[74] Para. 4.125, *ante*.

[75] Challis, *op. cit.*, p. 292.

[76] Megarry and Wade, *op. cit.*, p. 91.

[77] Para. 4.122, *ante*.

[78] Feigned Recoveries Act, 1542, 34 & 35 Hen. 8, c. 20; Fines and Recoveries Act, 1833, s. 18. See Challis, *op. cit.*, pp. 323–4.

[79] S. 15 of the Fines and Recoveries (Ireland) Act, 1834, which was the equivalent of s. 18 of the English 1833 Act, did not contain the relevant provisions referred to here. Holders of these unbarrable entails were, however, given the powers of a tenant for life under the Settled Land Act, 1882, s. 58 (1) (i), para. 8.021, *post*.

[80] 6 Anne, c. 6, 1706, s. 5; 6 Anne, c. 7, 1706, s. 4; 54 Geo. 3, c. 161, 1814, s. 28.

[81] The holders of such entails purchased by Parliament in England for public services were *not* given the powers of a tenant for life under the Settled Land Act, 1882, s. 58 (1) (i); see *Re Duke of Marlborough's Parliamentary Estates* (1891) 8 T.L.R. 179; *Re Duke of Marlborough's Blenheim Estates* (1892) 8 T.L.R. 582. *Cf.* the English Settled Land Act, 1925, s. 20 (1) (i) and 23 (2).

4.142. Finally, it may be noted that certain persons may be under a disability which prevents them from barring the entails. This is really part of the general law relating to persons under a disability, such as infants, married women and persons suffering from mental disorder. This will be discussed in general in a later chapter,[82] so little need be said here. There is nothing in the Fines and Recoveries (Ireland) Act, 1834, to prevent an infant executing a disentailing assurance, but this would seem to be subject to the general law relating to conveyances and other transactions executed by infants. In other words, the assurance would be valid unless and until revoked by the infant on reaching full age.[83] Restraints on anticipation with respect to a married woman have gone in Ireland and she may now act like a *feme sole* in this regard.[84] Other persons, while they may not act themselves, may have someone else act for them, *e.g.,* a trustee in bankruptcy could bar a bankrupt's entail.

5. *Quasi-Entail*

This subject is discussed below in relation to life estates.[85]

VI. LIFE ESTATE

A. General

4.143. The life estate is the third category of freehold estate, though, unlike the other two categories, the fee simple and fee tail, it is not an estate of inheritance.[86] There are two main types of life estate, one being an estate for the life of the tenant himself and the other being an estate for the life or lives of some person (or persons) other than the life of the tenant holding the estate. The latter is known as an estate *pur autre vie,* and varieties of it were, and still are, extremely common in Ireland, notably the lease for lives renewable for ever and the lease for lives combined with a term of years.[87] These estates in Ireland are somewhat complex in nature because they combine aspects of both freehold estates and leasehold estates. Thus, while they could be discussed in the chapter relating to landlord and tenant,[88] they will be discussed here in view of their close connection with freehold estates. First, however, the discussion will be confined generally to the life estate and estate *pur autre vie,* apart from the Irish variations.

B. Creation and Transfer

4.144. An ordinary life estate or estate *pur autre vie* would, as a freehold estate,

---

[82] Ch. 25, *post.*
[83] Para. 25.06, *post.*
[84] As to the Republic of Ireland, see Married Women's Status Act, 1957; for Northern Ireland, see Law Reform (Miscellaneous Provisions) Act (N.I.), 1937; Married Women (Restraint upon Anticipation) Act (N.I.), 1952, and Law Reform (Husband and Wife) Act (N.I.), 1964.
[85] Para. 4.165, *post.*
[86] Para. 4.006, *ante.*
[87] Paras. 4.167 *et seq., ante.*
[88] Ch. 17, *post.*

be created or transferred by a deed of conveyance under section 2 of the Real Property Act, 1845,[89] or by a will executed in accordance with the statutory provisions.[90]

C. WORDS OF LIMITATION

1. *Conveyances* Inter Vivos

4.145. A life estate, or estate *pur autre vie,* may be created directly by a conveyance using words of limitation such as to A "for life" or "for the life of X." On the other hand, a life estate can be created indirectly by the use of words insufficient to create a fee simple.[91] Thus the courts have held that expressions like "to A" simply, or "to A for ever," in a conveyance *inter vivos* created a life estate only in A.[92] In England this position has been reversed because, under the Law of Property Act, 1925, the whole estate which the grantor had power to convey is presumed to pass unless a contrary intention is shown.[93] No such provision exists in either part of Ireland.[94] An estate *pur autre vie* can be created indirectly by the tenant of a life estate (for his own life) alienating his estate to someone else. All the tenant has to convey is an estate to last for his own life and so his alienee takes an estate *pur autre vie,* the *cestui que vie*[95] being the original tenant.

2. *Gifts by Will*

(i) At Common Law

4.146. The rule at common law for wills was a modification of the rule for conveyances *inter vivos.* The testator might not have to use the technical words of limitation for a fee simple or a fee tail, but he did have to use words showing an intention to create one or other of these freehold estates of inheritance. If he failed to show this intention as a matter of construction, then once again all that would pass to the devisee would be a life estate.[96]

(ii) By Statute

4.147. The Wills Act, 1837, modified the common law in both parts of Ireland by providing that the fee simple or other whole estate of the testator passes unless a contrary intention is shown.[97] So since 1837 a life estate in a will must, in effect, be created expressly or directly rather than indirectly.

---

[89] Para. 3.026, *ante.*
[90] Still principally the Wills Act, 1837, in Northern Ireland, which was replaced in the Republic by the Succession Act, 1965, ch. 14, *post.*
[91] It is unlikely, therefore, that an estate *pur autre vie* could be created indirectly in this way.
[92] *Jameson* v. *McGovern* [1934] I.R. 758 (see *A Casebook on Irish Land Law* (1984), p. 116). See also *Re Courtney* [1981] N.I. 58.
[93] S. 60 (1).
[94] Except in respect of transfers of *registered* land, see para. 4.030, *ante.* But see the recommendations in the *Survey of the Land Law of Northern Ireland* (1971), para. 171; Land Law Working Group's Discussion Document No. 4 (*Conveyancing and Miscellaneous Matters*) (1983), pp. 10–12.
[95] *I.e.,* the person by whose life the duration of the estate is measured. For problems of proof *re* existence of lives, see para. 4.170, *post.*
[96] Para. 4.031, *ante.*
[97] Ss. 28, 30 and 31, replaced in the Republic of Ireland by the Succession Act, 1965, s. 94.

D. Classification

1. *Life Estate*

4.148. The courts developed some special rules to govern the position of a tenant for life to take account of two things. First, there was the fact that his occupation of the property was bound to be for a limited time, so that those taking the property after him should have their interests protected during his tenancy. Secondly, his interest was of uncertain duration, so that he should not be deterred from making the best and fullest use of the property by the fear that he would die before he could enjoy the fruits of his labour. To a large extent, of course, the settlements legislation of the second half of the nineteenth century made the tenant's position much more secure and gave him vastly increased powers in relation to the land. Thus these common law rules are not as significant as they were and some of the statutory modifications have been replaced by the settlements legislation.[98]

(i) Waste

4.149. The law of waste is that which restricts an owner of a limited interest in land from damaging it so as to prejudice those who will take the land after him, whether by way of reversion or remainder. Thus it covers the case of a tenant for life and a tenant holding for a term of years under a lease or tenancy agreement. The law of waste as regards landlords and tenants forms a separate subject now in view of statutory modifications,[99] though the general principles as to what constitutes waste remain those fashioned at common law by the courts.

The general rule is that the reversioner or remainderman may in certain circumstances apply to the court for an injunction to restrain waste being committed by the tenant for life.[1] He may also be able to claim damages if he has suffered loss as a result of the waste[2] or ask the court to order the tenant to account for any profits he has made from the waste.[3] The courts have come to recognise four main types of waste: ameliorating, permissive, voluntary and equitable.[4] In each case the land occupied by the tenant for life has been altered by the waste, but to varying degrees and so his liability varies.

(a) *Ameliorating*

4.150. In a sense this type seems to be a contradiction in terms. The act complained of so far from damaging the property actually benefits or improves it. The element of waste seems to exist in the fact that the nature of the property has been changed, *e.g.*, from residential to business use, however much this

---

[98] This legislation is discussed in detail in ch. 8, *post.*
[99] As to which, see ch. 17, *post.*
[1] *Coppinger* v. *Gubbins* (1846) 9 Ir.Eq.R. 304; see also *Davies* v. *Davies* (1840) 2 Ir.Eq.R. 414.
[2] *Re Dilapidations of the Deanery-house of St. Patrick's, Dublin* (1864) 10 Ir.Jur. (N.S.) 38; *Minister for Local Government and Public Health* v. *Kenny* (1941) 75 I.L.T.R. 26; *Ellis* v. *Dublin Corporation* [1940] I.R. 283.
[3] *Crampton* v. *Bishop of Meath* (1837) S. & Sc. 297.
[4] *Cf.* the concept of "wilful" waste in s. 55 (*b*) of the Republic's Landlord and Tenant Act, 1931, discussed in *Gilligan* v. *Silke* [1963] I.R. 1 and *O'Reilly* v. *East Coast Cinemas Ltd.* [1968] I.R. 56. S. 55 (*b*) of the 1931 Act has

may have increased its value from a purely commercial point of view.[5] Not
surprisingly, perhaps, the courts have shown little enthusiasm for actions
complaining about this sort of waste.[6] It is unlikely that any substantial
damages would be granted because no damage has been suffered. Usually the
reverse is the case, and so the courts are loath to grant an injunction to prevent
such waste. As Lord O'Hagan said in an appeal from Ireland—

> "[T]he waste with which a Court of Equity, or your Lordships acting as a
> Court of Equity, ought to interfere, should not be ameliorating waste, nor
> trivial waste. It must be waste of an injurious character—it must be waste
> of not only an injurious character, but of a substantially injurious
> character, and if either the waste be really ameliorating waste—that is a
> proceeding which results in benefit and not in injury—the Court of Equity,
> and your Lordships acting as a Court of Equity, ought not to interfere to
> prevent it."[7]

That case involved the conversion of store buildings that had become
dilapidated into dwelling-houses and it was held a proper exercise of the court's
discretion to refuse an injunction.[8] In another case, it was held that erecting a
large spirit grocery immediately beside a villa residence, in what had since
become an urbanised area, was not waste, though it clearly altered the
character of that residence.[9]

(b) Permissive

4.151. Permissive waste is the failure to do that which ought to be done, such
as failure to repair property.[10] The general rule is that a tenant for life is *not*
liable for such waste unless an express obligation to this effect has been
imposed upon him, *i.e.*, he has been made impeachable for waste.[11] A tenant

---

been replaced by s. 65 (3) (which retains the concept of "wilful" waste) of the Republic's Landlord and Tenant
(Amendment) Act, 1980. See further on s. 55 of the 1931 Act, *Taylor* v. *Moremiles Tyre Services Ltd.* (1978)
Unrep. (H.C., R.I.) (1975 No. 2646P).

[5] *Cf. Brooke* v. *Kavanagh* (1888) 23 L.R.Ir. 97 (erection of buildings on agricultural land).

[6] See, generally, *Doherty* v. *Allman* (1878) 3 App.Cas. 709 (see *A Casebook on Irish Land Law* (1984), p.
201); *Belton* v. *Nicholl* [1941] I.R. 230. Also *Palmer* v. *McCormick* (1890) 25 L.R.Ir. 110; *Grand Canal Co.* v.
McNamee (1892) 29 L.R.Ir. 131; Bathurst, "Strict Common Law Rules of Waste" (1949) 13 Conv. 278; Yardley,
"Ameliorating Waste in England and the United States" (1956) 19 M.L.R. 150.

[7] *Doherty* v. *Allman, op. cit.*, p. 724. *Cf.* Lord Cairns L.C., who said about ameliorating waste—"Now there
again the course which the Court of Chancery ought undoubtedly to adopt would be to leave those who think they
can obtain damages at common law to try what damages they can so obtain. Certainly, I think here again, the
Court of Chancery would be doing very great injury to the one side for the purpose of securing to the other, that
slightest possible sum which would at common law be considered the full equipment to which he was entitled."
Op. cit., p. 723. For the distinction between common law and equitable remedies, see para. 3.050, *ante*.

[8] In fact the case did not involve a life estate, but a long lease. The same principles apply, however, see ch. 17,
post. See also *Belton* v. *Nicholl* [1941] I.R. 230.

[9] *Craig* v. *Greer* [1899] 1 I.R. 258 (see *A Casebook on Irish Land Law* (1984), p. 616). *Cf. Palmer* v.
McCormick (1890) 25 L.R.Ir. 110 (ploughing pasture land held to be beneficial); *Murphy* v. *Daly* (1860) 13
I.C.L.R. 239 (ploughing ancient meadow land held to be voluntary waste); *Bobbett* v. *Kennedy* (1916) 50
I.L.T.R. 171 (ploughing injurious).

[10] *Cf. White* v. *McCann* (1850) 1 I.C.L.R. 205 (accidental fire not due to negligence by the lessee held not to be
permissive waste). See also *Hughes* v. *Sullivan* (1829) Hay. & Jon. app. xliv; *Shee* v. *Poor Law Commrs.* (1852) 4
Ir.Jur. (o.s.) 346.

[11] *Re Cartwright* (1889) 41 Ch.D. 532; see also *Davies* v. *Davies* (1840) 2 Ir.Eq.R. 414.

for life is rarely made so impeachable but the reverse is the case with a tenant holding under a lease or tenancy agreement.[12]

(c) *Voluntary*

4.152. This is the opposite of permissive waste and is the doing of that which ought not to be done—positive acts as opposed to negative omissions. The general rule is that a tenant for life *is* liable for voluntary waste *unless* expressly made unimpeachable for waste. Thus removing earth or clay from the land would be voluntary waste,[13] as would be cutting down hedges so that they would not grow again or grubbing up the thorns forming the base of the hedge.[14] A common form of waste committed in Ireland was the burning of land and the legislature stepped in to make it an offence for the tenant or occupier of land to burn the surface of land.[15] Under the common law, a tenant for life could not cut down timber on the land except to the extent that he was entitled to reasonable *estovers*. The right to estovers allowed the tenant to cut down suitable timber for such purposes as his own personal fuel, repairing his house or fences and making or repairing farm implements.[16] The tenant was not entitled to cut down more timber than was strictly necessary and suitable for this purpose, nor could he sell such timber for profit, unless he happened to occupy a timber estate on which the cutting and selling of timber was part of the annual income of the occupier.[17] However, the common law position was radically altered by statute.[18] A series of Irish Timber Acts were passed to promote the cultivation of trees in Ireland to replace the numerous forests destroyed over the centuries as a result of the constant changing of ownership of the land and plantation of settlers.[19] These Acts, for example, empowered tenants for life or lives to register by affidavit with the clerk of the peace of the county trees planted by them, whereby they became entitled to cut and sell those trees.[20] Failure to register prevented the tenant from asserting the right to cut down the trees,[21] and, until cut down, the trees remained part of the land and passed with it.[22] So far as tenants holding under leases were concerned, this right was withdrawn by an Act of 1791,[23] which made it an offence to cut down

---

[12] Para. 17.045, *post.*

[13] *Templemore* v. *Moore* (1862) 15 I.C.L.R. 14; *Shaftesbury* v. *Wallace* [1897] 1 I.R. 381.

[14] *Dunn* v. *Bryan* (1872) I.R. 7 Eq. 143.

[15] See Burning of Land Acts (Ireland), 1743, 17 Geo. 2, c. 10 (Ir.); 1763, 3 Geo. 3, c. 29 (Ir.); 1765, 5 Geo. 3. c. 10 (Ir.) 1800, 40 Geo. 3, c. 24 (Ir.). These Acts were replaced as regards tenants holding under leases or tenancy agreements by Deasy's Act, 1860, s. 30.

[16] As regards a tenant for life of land containing a turf bog, see *Jones* v. *Meany* [1941] Ir.Jur.Rep. 50.

[17] *The Fishmongers' Company* v. *Beresford* (1818) Beat. 607; *Gilmore* v. *The O'Connor Don* [1947] I.R. 462 (see *A Casebook on Irish Land Law* (1984), p. 212). See also *Simpson* v. *Simpson* (1879) 3 L.R.Ir. 308; *Marquise de la Bedoyère* v. *Nugent* (1890) 25 L.R.Ir. 143.

[18] See, however, *Kirkpatrick* v. *Naper* (1945) 79 I.L.T.R. 49 (see *op. cit.,* p. 225), where it was held that the common law notion of timber (*i.e.* oak, ash and elm) was also relevant to the Irish Timber Acts.

[19] Timber Acts (Ireland), 1698, 10 Will 3, c. 12 (Ir.); 1705 4 Ann., c. 9 (Ir.); 1710, 9 Ann., c. 5 (Ir.); 1721, 8 Geo. 1, c. 8 (Ir.). Land Improvement Acts (Ireland), 1735, 9 Geo. 2, c. 7 (Ir.); 1765, 5 Geo. 3, c. 17 (Ir.); 1767, 7 Geo. 3, c. 20 (Ir.); 1776, 15 & 16 Geo. 3, c. 26 (Ir.); 1784, 23 & 24 Geo. 3, c. 39 (Ir.). See discussion in *Kirkpatrick* v. *Naper* (1945) 79 I.L.T.R. 49.

[20] *Mountcashel* v. *O'Neill* (1857) 5 H.L.C. 937; see also *Standish* v. *Murphy* (1852) 2 Ir.Ch.R. 264; *Pentland* v. *Somerville* (1851) 2 Ir.Ch.R. 289.

[21] *R.C.B.* v. *Robinson* (1922) 56 I.L.T.R. 123; see also *Re Moore's Estate* (1902) 36 I.L.T.R. 14.

[22] *Alexander* v. *Godley* (1857) 6 I.C.L.R. 445; *Galway* v. *Baker* (1840) 7 Cl. & F. 379.

[23] 31 Geo. 3, c. 40; (Ir.), which excepted leases for lives renewable for ever (see para. 4.167, *post*) and rights of

any tree or wood[24] growing on the land, unless authorised by the terms of the lease or agreement or with the consent in writing of the landlord.[25] Then, nineteenth century settlements legislation provided that, even if a tenant for life is impeachable for waste, he may cut and sell timber ripe and fit for cutting, provided he gets the consent of the trustees of the settlement or an order of the court.[26] Three-quarters of the proceeds are set aside as capital and the tenant for life may keep the remaining one-quarter as income.[27] Finally, it should be noted that nowadays the state may impose restrictions on the felling, uprooting or otherwise damaging of trees, as part of its general protection of the environment and public amenities, such as forests.[28]

4.153. As regards mines and minerals, the rule at common law was that it was voluntary waste for a tenant for life to open and work an unopened mine, whereas it was not waste to continue working a mine already opened on the land.[29] Substantially the same position was enacted by various Irish statutes[30] in respect of mines and quarries for tenants holding under leases and tenancy agreements. As regards tenants for life a series of statutes were passed enabling them to grant mining leases whether or not a mine was already open and whether or not the tenant was impeachable for waste.[31] Now a tenant for life may grant a mining lease for a term of up to 60 years.[32] If the tenant is impeachable for waste, three-quarters of the rent must be set aside as capital, in other cases one quarter only, and the residue he can keep as rents and profits.[33] Most mining and mineral rights are nowadays subject to state ownership and control, so that the law of waste has been largely superseded in this respect.[34]

(d) Equitable

4.154. The courts took the view that, even though a tenant for life was made expressly unimpeachable for waste, he ought not to be allowed to commit acts of wanton destruction.[35] This would be too inequitable as regards the reversioner or remainderman, who could ask the court for an injunction to prevent

tenants with respect to trees already registered under the earlier Acts.

[24] Excepting "willows, osiers, or sallows."

[25] See now Deasy's Act, 1860, s. 31, ch. 17, *post.*

[26] Settled Land Act, 1882, s. 35 (1), para. 8.088, *post.*

[27] *Ibid.,* s. 35 (2).

[28] *E.g.,* Forestry Act, 1946 (R.I.), s. 37, which makes it an offence to uproot any tree over ten years old or to cut down trees other than those specified in the section, without first giving notice to the Gardai. *Cf.* Forestry Act (N.I.), 1953, ss. 4 and 5; Drainage Act (N.I.), 1964, s. 26, Sched. 1.

[29] *Elias* v. *Snowdon Slate Quarries Co.* (1879) 4 App. Cas. 454. *Cf. re* quarries, *Mansfield* v. *Crawford* (1846) 9 Ir.Eq.R. 272.

[30] See Mines Act (Ir.), 1723, 10 Geo. 1, c. 5 (Ir.), ss. 4–7; Mines (Ir.) Act, 1806, ss. 2 and 3, replaced by Deasy's Act 1860, ss. 25–8, ch. 17, *post.*

[31] Mines Acts (Ir.), 1723, 10 Geo. 1, c. 5 (Ir.); 1741, 15 Geo. 2, c. 10 (Ir.); Mining Leases Act (Ir.), 1749, 23 Geo. 2, c. 9 (Ir.); Mines (Ir.) Act, 1806; Mining Leases (Ir.) Act, 1848.

[32] Settled Land Act, 1882, s. 6.

[33] *Ibid.,* s. 11. See, generally, para. 8.075, *post.*

[34] See Minerals Development Acts, 1940 and 1979 (R.I.) and Petroleum and other Minerals Development Act, 1960 (R.I.); Mineral Development Act (N.I.), 1969.

[35] *Cf.* as regards tenants holding under leases or tenancy agreements, "fraudulent or malicious" waste in s. 25 of Deasy's Act, 1860, and "wilful" waste in s. 55 (*b*) of the Republic's Landlord and Tenant Act, 1931. Note again that section 55 (*b*) of the 1931 Act has been replaced by section 65 (3) of the Republic's Landlord and Tenant (Amendment) Act, 1980.

such acts.[36] Equitable waste has been defined as "that which a prudent man would not do in the management of his own property."[37] To escape liability for such acts, the tenant for life would have to prove not only that he was made expressly "unimpeachable for waste" (which would cover voluntary waste only) but for *equitable* waste as well.[38]

(ii) Fixtures

4.155. This is another subject which has relevance in the area of landlord and tenant law, where it has been dealt with by some special legislative provisions.[39] In each case the problem concerns the position of someone who has been in occupation of property for a substantial period of time and who has, during that period, attached fixtures to the land or to buildings on the land. The question is whether those fixtures have been so attached that they become part of the land or buildings and pass with the land or buildings when the tenant for life or years ceases his occupation.[40] Many of the general principles are common to tenants for life and tenants for years and they will be discussed in greater detail later.[41] The general rule as regards tenants for life is that items properly regarded as fixtures, according to the rules governing the degree and purpose of annexation, do pass with the land to the remainderman or reversioner. Certain items have, however, come to be excepted from this general rule, notably trade, ornamental and domestic fixtures.[42] This matter is governed entirely by case law; there is no legislation such as that which governs landlords and tenants.[43]

(iii) Emblements

4.156. Another problem which can arise with respect to an occupier of land for a limited, but uncertain period, whether because his estate is for the period of a life or for a term of years fixed as to maximum duration but determinable within that period,[44] is that the tenant may find that the determination comes unexpectantly. In the case of agricultural land, this could be a serious problem where the tenant has sown crops and his tenancy determines before harvest time. The law dealt with this problem by giving such a tenant a right to *emblements, i.e.,* a right in the tenant, or his personal representatives (in the case of a tenant for life), to enter upon the land after the determination of the tenancy and to reap the crops sown during its currency.[45] This right related to

---

[36] Para. 3.136, *ante.*

[37] *Turner* v. *Wright* (1860) 2 De G.F. & J. 234, 243.

[38] Judicature (Ir.) Act, 1877, s. 28 (3). In Northern Ireland, section 28 (3) of the 1877 Act has been replaced by section 90 of the Judicature (Northern Ireland) Act, 1978 (see para. 3.136, *ante*).

[39] Para. 17.060, *post.*

[40] Amos, *The Law of Fixtures*; Bingham, "Some Suggestions Concerning the Law of Fixtures" (1907) 7 Col.L.Rev. 1; Guest and Lever, "Hire-Purchase, Equipment Leases and Fixtures" (1963) 27 Conv. 30.

[41] Para. 17.060, *post.* See also as regards mortgagors and mortgagees, Para. 13.010, *post.*

[42] As to which, see para. 17.060, *post.* See *Shinner* v. *Harman* (1853) 3 I.C.L.R. 243; *Deeble* v. *McMullen* (1857) 8 I.C.L.R 355.

[43] Para. 17.060, *post.*

[44] Para. 4.010, *ante.*

[45] *Short* v. *Atkinson* (1834) Hay. & Jon. 682; *O'Connell* v. *O'Callaghan* (1841) Long. & Town. 157; *Lalor* v. *Netterville* (1854) 6 Ir.Jur. (o.s.) 261. See Cherry, *Irish Land Law and Land Purchase Acts* (3rd ed., 1903), p.67;

cultivated crops only, like corn, wheat and flax,[46] and arose only in the case of a determination beyond the control of the tenant, such as the tenant's own death or the death of the *cestui que vie* in an estate *pur autre vie*. It would not apply where the tenant brought it upon himself, by serving a notice to determine the tenancy or bringing about an event operating to determine his tenancy (*e.g.*, breaking a condition relating to marriage or bankruptcy).[47]

(iv) Curtesy and Dower

4.157. Rights of curtesy and dower were special kinds of life estate devised by the early common law. The need for them arose from the fact that, under early feudal law, a landowner was not allowed to make a will leaving his land to those members of his family, or in such shares, as he chose. The law of intestate succession or inheritance, as it was then called, was governed by the principle of *primogeniture, i.e.*, the eldest son succeeded to all estates and interests in the land.[48] This was felt to be rather harsh on the surviving spouse of the deceased landowner and rights of curtesy and dower were the common law's solution. These rights have been abolished in relation to those dying after 1955 in Northern Ireland and 1966 in the Republic of Ireland, but the philosophy of ensuring proper provision for certain members of the family lives on.[49]

4.158. Curtesy was the right of a widower to a life estate in the *whole* of the real property of his deceased wife. Dower was the right of a widow to a life estate in *one-third*[50] of the real property of her deceased husband. In each case, the wife or husband must have been entitled during the marriage to a freehold estate of inheritance —there could only be curtesy or dower out of a fee simple or fee tail, not a life estate or leasehold.[51] In each case, the husband or wife must have been seised of the land or entitled in possession to an equitable interest, and no claim could be made if it had been held in a joint tenancy, since the right of survivorship in the other tenant or tenants was inconsistent with curtesy or dower.[52] A husband could not claim curtesy unless issue of the marriage capable of inheriting the land had been born alive, whereas the widow could claim dower if birth of such issue had been *possible,* even if none had in fact been born. A husband could not claim curtesy if his wife had disposed of her land *inter vivos* or by will, to the extent she could do this.[53] As regards dower, the Dower Act, 1833, provided that a widow could not claim it out of any land disposed of by her husband *inter vivos* or by will, or where it had been barred by the husband so declaring by deed or in his will under the Act.[54]

De Moleyns, *Landowners' and Agents' Practical Guide* (8th ed., 1899), ch. 24.
[46] *Flanagan* v. *Seaver* (1858) 9 Ir.Ch.R. 230; see also *Rodwell* v. *Phillips* (1840) 9 M & W. 501.
[47] *Kelly* v. *Webber* (1860) 11 I.C.L.R. 57.
[48] See further on intestate succession, ch. 15, *post*.
[49] Ch. 15, *post*.
[50] *Murland* v. *Despard* [1956] I.R. 170.
[51] *Loyd* v. *Loyd* (1842) 2 Con. & L. 592; *Kernaghan* v. *McNally* (1859) 11 Ir.Ch.R. 52.
[52] Ch. 7, *post*.
[53] Ch. 25, *post*.
[54] Ss. 4, 6 and 7. *Gurly* v. *Gurly* (1840) 2 Dr. & Wal. 463; *Fyan* v. *Henry* (1840) 2 Dr. & Wal. 556; *Killen* v. *Campbell* (1848) 10 Ir.Eq.R. 461; *Cooper* v. *Cooper* (1856) 1 Ir.Jur. (N.S.) 370; *Re Dwyers* (1862) 13 Ir.Ch.R. 431.

4.159. As mentioned above, however, rights to curtesy and dower have been abolished as to the persons dying after 1966 in the Republic of Ireland, by the Succession Act, 1965,[55] and after 1955 in Northern Ireland by the Administration of Estates (N.I.), 1955.[56] These statutes introduced a new law of intestate succession to land whereby the various members of the deceased's family, including a widower or widow, receive specified shares of the estate, real and personal.[57]

2. *Estate* Pur Autre Vie

4.160. The main attributes to this type of life estate have already been mentioned,[58] and it shares many of the features discussed above in relation to the ordinary life estate.[59] At common law, a tenant *pur autre vie* could freely alienate his estate *inter vivos* and it seems that, when he did so, no special words of limitation were necessary to pass the whole of his estate to his assignee.[60] Though there was nothing to prevent the tenant of an estate *pur autre vie* conveying it with an express limitation for life, *i.e.,* the life of the grantee.[61] There are, however, some special features with respect to the estate *pur autre vie,* which arise from the fact that the life determining the duration of the estate is not that of the holder of the estate itself.

(i) Occupancy

4.161. An obvious question that arises is what happens when the holder predeceases the person for whose life the estate was granted. The converse case causes no problems because in that case the estate simply comes to its natural determination while the grantee is still alive. Under early law, a tenant *pur autre vie* could not make a will leaving his estate to someone else in the event of his dying before the expiry of the life in question. Indeed, the early legislation relating to wills of land did not apply to such estates.[62] The common law had to formulate some rules to govern this situation. These rules made up the law of *occupancy.*[63] The general theory of this law was that the estate was succeeded to by the first person to enter and become seised of the land after the death of the tenant. This person did not take as heir, because an estate *pur autre vie* was not an estate of inheritance like a fee simple or fee tail.[64] He took only as the appropriate successor under the peculiar law of occupancy. Originally a distinction had to be made between *general* occupancy and *special* occupancy.

---

[55] S. 11 (2).
[56] S. 1 (4).
[57] See, generally, ch. 15, *post.*
[58] Paras. 4.143–5, *ante. Brenan* v. *Boyne* (1864) 16 Ir.Ch.R. 87; see also *Tisdall* v. *Tisdall* (1839) 2 Ir.L.R. 41.
[59] *E.g.,* the law of waste, para. 4.149, *ante,* fixtures, para. 4.155, *ante,* and emblements, para. 4.156, *ante.*
[60] *McClintock* v. *Irvine* (1860) 10 Ir.Ch.R. 480; *Re Bayley's Estate* (1863) 16 Ir.Ch.R. 215; *Brenan* v. *Boyne* (1864) 16 Ir.Ch.R. 87; *Currin* v. *Doyle* (1878) 3 L.R.Ir. 265; *Horan* v. *Horan* [1935] I.R. 306. *Cf. Dawson* v. *Dawson* (1852) 13 Ir.L.R. 472; *Barron* v. *Barron* (1858) 8 Ir.Ch.R. 366.
[61] *Mitchell* v. *Coulson* (1827) 1 Hud. & Br. 210; *Ryan* v. *Cowley* (1835) Ll. & G. *temp.* Sug. 7; *Crozier* v. *Crozier* (1843) 3 Dr. & War. 373; *Dawson* v. *Dawson* (1852) 13 Ir.L.R. 472; *Rotheram* v. *Rotheram* (1884) 13 L.R.Ir. 429.
[62] *E.g.,* the Statute of Wills (Ir.), 1634.
[63] Challis, *The Law of Real Property* (3rd ed.), pp. 358–62. *Horan* v. *Horan* [1935] I.R. 306.
[64] para. 4.006, *ante.*

(a) *General Occupancy*

4.162. If an estate *pur autre vie* had been granted without any reference to the grantee's heirs or successors in the conveyance, the law of general occupancy applied.[65] Literally the first person to enter upon the land after the grantee's death succeeded to it and remained entitled to it until the estate came to an end with the death of the *cestui que vie.* This rule was connected with the common law's abhorrence of any gap in the seisin and its desire to see that someone, even if a complete stranger to the land, should always be seised at any particular point in time.[66] It may be noted that the general occupant was not liable for any of the grantee's debts.[67]

4.163. It was not a very satisfactory system of devolution to have strangers taking over the ownership of land, and so it is not surprising that legislation abolished general occupancy. The Statute of Frauds (Ireland), 1695, provided that where there was no special occupant, so that normally general occupancy rules would have applied, the estate *pur autre vie* was to descend to the grantee's personal representative for distribution like personalty.[68] The statute provided that in all cases the land so succeeded to was liable for payment of the deceased grantee's debts.[69]

(b) *Special Occupancy*

4.164. Under this law, if the estate *pur autre vie* had been conveyed to the grantee "and his heirs," the heirs (determined under the rules of inheritance) succeeded as *special occupant,* not by way of inheritance.[70] Thus until the passing of the Statute of Frauds (Ireland) the land so taken by the heir was not liable for the deceased's debts.[71]

(c) *Statute of Frauds (Ireland), 1695*

By section 9[72] of this statute a tenant *pur autre vie* became entitled to dispose of his estate by will, thereby displacing the law of occupancy.

(d) *Administration of Estates Act (N.I.), 1955*

Section 1 (3) of this Act abolished the law of special occupancy for the purposes of devolution on intestacy after 1955. Since then, on death of a tenant *pur autre vie* intestate, his land devolves like any other land, other than entailed

---

[65] Challis, *op. cit.*, p. 359.
[66] Challis, *ibid.* And see on the common law seisin rules, para. 5.012, *post.*
[67] Megarry and Wade, *The Law of Real Property* (5th ed., 1984), p. 94.
[68] S. 9, replaced by the Wills Act, 1837, s. 2 (see also ss. 3 and 6); *cf.* the English Statute of Frauds, 1677, s. 12. Plunket v. *Reilly* (1852) 1 Ir.Ch.R. 585; *Mountcashell* v. *More-Smyth* [1896] A.C. 158; *Re King* [1899] 1 I.R. 30; *Re Murray* [1916] 1 I.R. 302. See also Deasy's Act, 1860, s. 9. Para. 17.029, *post.*
[69] *Ibid.*
[70] *Dowell* v. *Dignan* (1826) Batty 698. See also *Kelly* v. *Coote* (1857) 2 Ir.Jur. (N.S.) 195.
[71] The heir still succeeded even if executors and administrators were also referred to in the conveyance. The latter took as special occupants only if the heir or heirs were not referred to. Challis, *op cit.*, pp. 359–61; *Wall* v. *Byrne* (1845) 7 Ir.Eq.R. 578; *Croker* v. *Brady* (1879) 4 L.R.Ir. 653; *Whitehead* v. *Morton* (1887) 19 L.R.Ir. 435; *Horan* v. *Horan* [1935] I.R. 306.
[72] Replaced by ss. 2 and 6 of the Wills Act, 1837.

land.[73] In other words, it devolves on the personal representatives to be administered by them with the rest of the estate in accordance with the Act.[74]

(e) *Succession Act, 1965 (R.I.)*

Section 11 (1) of this Act similarly abolished devolution by special occupancy in the Republic with respect to devolution since 1967. On death of a tenant *pur autre vie* intestate, his land devolves on his personal representatives for distribution with the rest of his estate, real and personal.

(ii) Quasi-Entails

4.165. An estate *pur autre vie* could be conveyed to someone else so as to give him an entailed interest. This estate was not an estate of inheritance and so was outside the scope of *De Donis*, 1285.[75] The courts held that such a conveyance created what was called a quasi-entail in the assignee, *i.e.*, the estate would pass to the heirs of the body of the assignee in the same way as an entail, for so long as the life determining the estate assigned lasted.[76] It was a "quasi" entail only because the successors were not taking by way of inheritance but, in effect, as special occupants. Apart from this, however, the courts strove to apply and develop the rules applying to quasi-entails as closely as possible to those relating to entails.[77] Thus the rights of the heirs as occupants, or of reversioners or remaindermen, could be barred by the quasi-tenant in tail executing a conveyance *inter vivos*.[78] It seems this could be done even before the Fines and Recoveries (Ireland) Act, 1834, so that there was no need to enrol the deed before or after the Act, which applies only to disentailing deeds operating under it.[79] If the quasi-tenant in tail was not in possession he would need the consent of the tenant in possession,[80] and it seems that, as in the case of entails, a quasi-entail could not be barred by will. There was some doubt about this point on the argument that, when estates *pur autre vie* themselves became devisable by will, quasi-entails of them could be similarly barred.[81] This would seem to be a fair argument so far as barring the heirs otherwise succeeding as occupants was concerned, but the Irish courts have consistently questioned the argument and have insisted that at least quasi-remainders over after the quasi-entail could not be so barred.[82]

[73] Para. 15.13, *post*.
[74] Chs. 15 and 16, *post*.
[75] Para. 4.114, *ante*.
[76] Challis, *op. cit.*, pp. 362–3. *Allen* v. *Allen* (1842) 2 Dr. & War. 307; *Batteste* v. *Maunsell* (1876) I.R. 10 Eq. 314; *Re McNeale's Estate* (1858) 3 Ir.Jur. (N.S.) 310; *Lynch* v. *Nelson* (1870) I.R. 5 Eq. 192; *Walsh* v. *Studdert* (1873) I.R. 7 C.L. 482; *MacAndrew* v. *Gallagher* (1874) I.R. 8 Eq. 490; *Betty* v. *Humphreys* (1872) I.R. 9 Eq. 332; *Blackhall* v. *Gibson* (1878) 2 L.R.Ir. 49; *Re Carew's Estate* (1887) 19 L.R.Ir. 483.
[77] For the application of the rule in *Shelley's Case* to estates *pur autre vie*, see *Crozier* v. *Crozier* (1843) 3 Dr. & War. 373, espec. at 381–2 (*per* Sugden L.C.); *Colclough* v. *Colclough* (1870) I.R. 4 Eq. 263; *Macnamara* v. *Dillon* (1883) 11 L.R.Ir. 29.
[78] Para. 4.123, *ante*.
[79] Megarry and Wade, *op. cit.*, p. 95. It was held in *Morris* v. *Morris* (1872) I.R. 7 C.L. 295 that a fee farm grant executed under the Renewable Leasehold Conversion Act, 1849 (para. 4.081, *ante*) barred a quasi-entail. See also *Batteste* v. *Maunsell* (1876) I.R. 10 Eq. 314; *Blackhall* v. *Gibson* (1878) 2 L.R.Ir. 49.
[80] *Allen* v. *Allen* (1842) 2 Dr. & War. 307, espec. at 324–38 (*per* Sugden L.C.). Para. 4.124, *ante*.
[81] Challis, *op. cit.*, p. 363.
[82] *Allen* v. *Allen*, *op. cit.*; *Campbell* v. *Sandys* (1803) 1 Sch. & Lef. 281, espec. at 294–5 (*per* Lord Redesdale);

4.166. As a result of the Administration of Estates Act (N.I.), 1955, and the Republic's Succession Act, 1965, the law relating to quasi-entails has rapidly become obsolete, being applicable now only to estates created before the operation of the Acts. Both Acts abolished all rules, modes and canons of descent and of devolution by special occupancy with a saving only for *descent* of an estate tail.[83] This saving does not cover quasi-entails because the succession in these cases by the heirs of the body is not by descent or inheritance, but by occupancy.[84]

3. *Lease for Lives Renewable for Ever*

4.167. One of the most common methods of holding land in Ireland has been the lease for lives renewable for ever.[85] This sort of grant has rarely occurred on the other side of the Irish Sea, if ever, though a lease for *years* perpetually renewable was quite common until all such leases were converted into leases for 2,000 years by the Law of Property Act, 1922.[86] A "lease" for lives renewable for ever is a curious mixture of land law concepts. It creates leasehold tenure between the parties to the lease, but the estate granted to the lessee is a freehold estate.[87] It is in effect an estate *pur autre vie,* though in this case there are usually three lives named in the lease. The Irish courts have held that in a conveyance *inter vivos* strict words of limitation are not necessary to pass the entire estate of the lessee in a lease for lives renewable for ever. It is sufficient if other words are used indicating such an intention.[88]

4.168. The origin of such leases has been a matter of some controversy over the centuries.[89] One theory is that they gained popularity because those participating in land settlements in the seventeenth century, particularly the Ulster plantation,[90] were given express power to grant leases for lives renewable for ever.[91] Some landowners were given powers by private Acts of Parliament.[92] These leases afforded all the advantages of the relationship of landlord and tenant, especially the extensive landlord's remedies available in Ireland,[93] yet they also gave the tenants a major estate in the land. Indeed, as

---

Dillon v. *Dillon* (1809) 1 Ba. & B. 77, espec. at 95 (*per* Lord Manners); *Hopkins* v. *Ramage* (1826) Batty 365; *Kelly* v. *Kelly* (1901) 35 I.L.T.R. 215. Lyne, *Leases for Lives Renewable for Ever* (1837), pp. 24–6.

[83] 1955 Act, s. 1 (3); 1965 Act, s. 11 (1).

[84] Para. 4.165, *supra.*

[85] See, generally, Lyne, *Leases for Lives Renewable for Ever* (1837); Furlong, *Law of Landlord and Tenant as Administered in Ireland* (2nd ed., 1869), bk. 2, ch. 4; Finlay, *Law of Renewals in Respect of Leases for Lives Renewable for Ever* (1829).

[86] S. 145 and Sched. 15. See *Survey of the Land Law of Northern Ireland* (1971), paras. 61–9; Land Law Working Group's Discussion Document No. 2 (*Estates and Interests and Family Dealings in Land*) (1981), pp. 17-21. Also *Re Hopkins' Lease* [1972] 1 W.L.R. 372.

[87] Paras. 4.003–12, *ante.*

[88] *McClintock* v. *Irvine* (1860) 10 Ir.Ch.R. 480; *Re Bayley's Estate* (1863) 16 Ir.Ch.R. 215; *Brenan* v. *Boyne* (1864) 16 Ir.Ch.R. 87; *Betty* v. *Elliott* (1865) 16 Ir.Ch.R. 110; *Currin* v. *Doyle* (1878) 3 L.R.Ir. 265; *Horan* v. *Horan* [1935] I.R. 306.

[89] See, *e.g.,* Lyne, *op. cit.,* pp. 1–7.

[90] Para. 1.30, *ante.*

[91] See the discussion in *Bateman* v. *Murray* (1785) 1 Ridgw.P.C. 187. The settlers' powers of making fee farm grants have already been discussed, para. 4.060, *ante.*

[92] *E.g.,* the second Duke of Ormonde, see 7 Will. 3, c. i (Ir.). See *Sweet* v. *Anderson* (1788) 2 Bro.P.C. 256; *Boyle* v. *Lysaght* (1787) 1 Ridgw.P.C. 384.

[93] Ch. 17, *post.*

we shall see, the estate came to be regarded almost as equivalent to a fee simple, and ultimately the legislature recognised this in passing the Renewable Leasehold Conversion Act, 1849.[94] Unlike a fee farm grant, which produced a perpetual *fixed* annual income in the shape of the fee farm rent, a lease for lives renewable for ever had the advantage of producing additional *periodic* income in the shape of the fines (sums of money) to be paid to the landlord every time one of the three lives had to be renewed. Such a lease also had the advantage for the landlord over an ordinary lease for a term of years in that the freehold estate carried the parliamentary vote, in the days when this was a qualification, and the landlord could usually expect his tenants to vote for himself or his nominees.[95]

4.169. Whatever the reasons for their creation, there is no doubt that leases for lives renewable for ever became an extremely popular form of tenure in Ireland. So much so that during the nineteenth century it was estimated that up to one-seventh of the entire soil of Ireland was held under such leases.[96] The standard form of lease consisted of a conveyance to the tenant for the lives of three specified persons, with a covenant for perpetual renewal of these lives on payment to the landlord of a specified fine on each renewal.[97] Otherwise, the conveyance took the form of an ordinary lease for years, with various covenants and conditions inserted governing the relationship of the landlord and the tenant. The landlord had all the usual remedies for enforcement of the tenant's obligations, actions for debt, distress and ejectment for non-payment of rent.[98] Yet the fact remained that, although leasehold tenure existed between the parties, the tenant had a freehold estate, an estate *pur autre vie*. Thus succession to his estate, which could be perpetual as new lives were added on each appropriate occasion, was governed by the general law of succession relating to such a freehold estate, *i.e.*, the law of occupancy.[99] It also became very common to make settlements of these estates, which was not surprising in view of the perpetual nature of the estates and of the amount of land in Ireland held subject to them. The effect of limiting a lease for lives to A "and the heirs of his body" was, of course, to create a quasi-entail, a subject we have discussed above.[1] In *Morris* v. *Morris*[2] it was held that a fee farm conversion grant executed under the Renewable Leasehold Conversion Act, 1849,[3] barred a quasi-entail. Not all the law relating to estates *pur autre vie*, however, was strictly applied, for some account had to be taken of the potentially perpetual nature of the tenant's estate. This had more of the attributes of a fee simple,

[94] Paras. 4.081, *ante* and 4.176, *post*.
[95] See also para. 1.35, *ante*.
[96] Lyne, *op. cit.*, p. 1.
[97] See Stubbs and Baxter, *Irish Forms and Precedents* (1910); see also Edge, *Forms of Leases and Other Forms Relating to Land in Ireland* (1884).
[98] For statutory provisions dealing with such remedies against tenants *pur autre vie*, see the Arrears of Rent Act (Ir.), 1634, 10 Chas. 1, sess. 2, c. 5 (Ir.), s. 3; Distress for Rent Act (Ir.), 1710, 9 Ann., c. 8 (Ir.), s. 7; Landlord and Tenant Act (Ir.), 1784, 23 & 24 Geo. 3, c. 46 (Ir.), s. 2.
[99] See paras. 4.161–4, *ante*.
[1] Para. 4.165, *ante*.
[2] (1872) I.R. 7 C.L. 295. See also *Batteste* v. *Maunsell* (1876) I.R. 10 Eq. 314; *Blackhall* v. *Gibson* (1878) 2 L.R.Ir. 49.
[3] Para. 4.176, *post*.

with no reversion or remainder to be protected, than of a life estate. In particular, the law of waste was modified with respect to leases for lives renewable for ever. Thus section 1 of the Land Improvement Act (Ireland), 1765,[4] specified that tenants for lives renewable for ever were *not* impeachable for waste in respect of timber planted by them or their predecessors in title.[5] This was held to apply whether or not the trees had been registered under the Timber Acts (Ireland).[6] Such tenants were excepted from the statutory provisions prohibiting tenants for lives or years from cutting down trees under the guise of *estovers*, unless expressly authorised in the lease or by licence from the landlord.[7] They were also excepted from statutory provisions prohibiting assignment or subletting without licence or consent from the landlord.[8]

4.170. The Irish courts recognised that the estate given to the tenant was potentially perpetual. It is true that the Irish Parliament had in the early days favoured the landlords in passing the Life Estates Act (Ireland), 1695.[9] Section 1 of this Act provided that persons for whose lives estates were granted, who remained "beyond the seas" or absented themselves from Ireland for seven years, were to be presumed dead for the purpose of any action by a lessor or reversioner for recovery of possession of the land.[10] The courts took the view, however, that the estate granted to the tenant was intended to be perpetual, so that not only would the landlord be compelled to perform specifically the covenant to renew the lease at the appropriate times, but relief would be granted in equity against forfeiture by him of the lease for mere lapse of time by the tenant in claiming his renewals on the dropping of the lives in question.[11] The courts developed what was known as the "old equity of the country."[12] This was a general principle that a lessee for lives renewable for ever could always obtain a renewal of his lease even though all the lives had long since died, provided there was no fraud or other misconduct on his part[13] and that he was prepared to compensate the landlord for the arrears in renewal fines which the landlord would have been entitled to had the renewals been obtained when the lives had dropped.[14] Great consternation was caused in Irish legal circles when some members of the House of Lords, notably Lords Mansfield and Thurlow, seemed to call in question the activities of the Irish courts in this

---

[4] 5 Geo. 3, c. 17 (Ir.), one of the Irish Timber Acts (see para. 4.152, *ante*).
[5] See now Deasy's Act, 1860, s. 25. Ch. 17, *post*.
[6] *Pentland* v. *Somerville* (1851) 2 Ir.Ch.R. 289; *Ex parte Armstrong* (1857) 8 Ir.Ch.R. 30; *Re Moore's Estate* (1902) 36 I.L.T.R. 14.
[7] Landlord and Tenant Act (Ir.), 1791, 31 Geo. 3, c. 40 (Ir.); see now Deasy's Act, 1860, s. 31. Ch. 17, *post*.
[8] Assignment and Subletting of Land (Ir.) Act, 1826, 7 Geo. 4, c. 29; see also the Assignment of Leases (Ir.) Act, 1832, 2 & 3 Will. 4, c. 17. See now Deasy's Act, 1860, s. 10, still in force in Northern Ireland, but recently repealed in the Republic by the Landlord and Tenant (Ground Rents) Act, 1967, s. 35 (1). See ch. 17, *post*.
[9] 7 Will. 3, c. 8 (Ir.). See *Aldworth* v. *Allen* (1865) 11 H.L.C. 549; *Secretary of State for War* v. *Booth* [1901] 2 I.R. 692.
[10] S. 3 provided that, if it was later proved that the "lives" were not dead at the time of the action, the lessee could re-enter and recover as damages the full profits received by the lessor in the meantime, plus interest.
[11] *Lennon* v. *Napper* (1802) 2 Sch. & Lef. 682; *Butler* v. *Mulvihill* (1819) 1 Bligh 137.
[12] *Sweet* v. *Anderson* (1722) 2 Bro.P.C. 256; *Worsop* v. *Rosse* (1740) 1 Bro.P.C. 281.
[13] *Lennon* v. *Napper* (1802) 2 Sch. & Lef. 682.
[14] *Sweet* v. *Anderson* (1722) 2 Bro.P.C. 256.

regard towards the end of the eighteenth century.[15] The Irish Parliament reacted swiftly and passed the Tenantry Act (Ireland), 1779.

(i) Tenantry Act (Ireland), 1779

4.171. This Act in effect confirmed the equitable principles enunciated by the Irish courts.[16] It recorded in its preamble that great parts of the lands of Ireland were held under leases for lives with covenants for perpetual renewals, that the tenants and their successors frequently neglected to pay the renewal fines within the time prescribed by the covenants and that "it has been for a long time a received opinion in this kingdom, to which some decisions in courts of equity and declarations of judges have given countenance, that courts of equity would in such cases relieve against the lapse of time upon giving an adequate compensation to the persons, to whom such fines were payable, or their representatives."

Section 1 then enacted:

> "Courts of equity upon an adequate compensation being made shall relieve such tenants and their assigns against such lapse of time, if no circumstance of fraud be proved against such tenants or their assigns; unless it shall be proved to the satisfaction of such courts, that the landlords or lessors, or persons entitled to receive such fines, had demanded such fines from such tenants or their assigns, and that the same had been refused or neglected to be paid within a reasonable time after such demand."

The only change introduced by the statute would seem to be the limited protection it afforded a landlord, in the sense that he could try to limit the tenant's dilatoriness by making a demand for the fine.[17]

Though the 1779 Act was primarily designed for leases for *lives* renewable for ever, it has been held to apply also to the rarer (in Ireland) leases for *years* renewable,[18] and to leases for years determinable on dropping of lives but with covenants for perpetual renewals.[19] It has even been held to apply to a lease for lives renewable for ever without payment of fines.[20]

4.172. No particular form of demand for renewal fines is laid down by Act.[21] So, if it is clear to the tenant, it does not have to be writing. But it must be

---

[15] See *Kane* v. *Hamilton* (1784) 1 Ridgw.P.C. 180 (action begun in Ireland in 1768); *Bateman* v. *Murray* (1785) 1 Ridgw.P.C. 187 (action begun in 1765). In the latter, Lord Thurlow stated that a court of equity would "never assist" a lessee "where he has lost his right by his own gross laches or neglect." Note that these cases were reported long after the passing of the Tenantry Act (Ir.), 1779, which resulted directly from them.

[16] *Alder* v. *Ward* (1845) 8 Ir.Eq.R. 350.

[17] Lyne, *Leases for Lives Renewable for Ever* (1837), p. 170. S. 2 of the Act provided that, if a landlord found it difficult to trace his tenant in order to make such a demand, he could put a notice of the demand for two months in the London and Dublin Gazettes (and now *Iris Oifigiúil* and the Belfast Gazette, S.R. & O. 1921, No. 1804) which "shall be considered to all intents and purposes a demand within this Act."

[18] *McDermott* v. *Caldwell* (1876) I.R. 10 Eq. 504 (lease for 50 years renewable every 31 years for 1,000 years). This decision was queried in *Hussey* v. *Domville* [1900] 1 I.R. 417; see also *Hussey* v. *Domville (No.2)* [1903] 1 I.R. 265.

[19] *Boyle* v. *Lysaght* (1787) 1 Ridgw.P.C. 384; *Freeman* v. *Boyle* (1788) 2 Ridgw.P.C. 69.

[20] *Bond* v. *Slator* (1860) 10 Ir.Ch.R. 472.

[21] *Ex parte Peyton* (1888) 21 L.R.Ir. 371; see also *Butler* v. *Earl of Portarlington* (1841) 4 Ir.Eq.R. 1; *Williamson* v. *Tuckey* (1862) 14 Ir.Ch.R. 407; *Bull* v. *Wigmore* (1860) 5 Ir.Jur. (N.S.) 57.

accurate if it makes statements, *e.g.*, about the dropping of the lives.[22] As regards what amounts to a reasonable time for paying the fine demanded, this is a question for the court to be determined in the light of all the circumstances of the particular case.[23] It should be noted, however, that the tenant cannot claim relief under the Act if time is of the essence under the covenant for renewal, *e.g.*, where it is clear from the covenant that the right of renewal is dependent upon nomination of a new life within the time specified.[24]

4.173. The tenant will get relief only if he is prepared to make *full* compensation to the landlord, *i.e.*, pays any arrears of rent still due, and fines for any renewals required. It was also the practice of the courts to require payment of "septennial" fines where a long period had elapsed from the death of the last life. The theory was that an assumption should be made that it would have been necessary to renew a life every seven years,[25] so that the tenant should be treated as liable to pay a renewal fine for every seven years since the death of the life, plus interest.[26] Thus the court has no discretion to limit the amount of arrears of interest due on renewal fines.[27] Any form of fraud or other improper conduct on the part of the tenant will deprive him of relief under the Act.[28] Thus indulging in tedious and vexatious proceedings against the landlord and ignoring court orders has been held to deprive a tenant of relief.[29]

4.174. The obvious complexities of these combination freehold-leasehold conveyances led to a mounting demand for legislation during the nineteenth century. Landlords found it difficult to keep track of the dropping of lives because these were nominated by the tenant and their deaths were more likely to be within the tenant's knowledge than the landlord's. Yet it was in the tenant's interest to keep quiet about the matter and so escape payment of fines, relying on relief under the Tenantry Act should the landlord later discover that the lives had dropped. The leading writer on the subject catalogued other inconveniences.

> "The obstacles of various kinds, which impede or delay the execution of renewals, hold out perpetual inducements to landlords to rely upon alleged forfeitures of the right of renewal; especially as the tenant, even where he succeeds in establishing his right, has usually to pay the costs of the suit. To such an extent has this litigation prevailed, that Lord

---

[22] *Ex parte Lane* [1907] 1 I.R. 258.

[23] *Dyott* v. *Viscount Massereene* (1874) I.R. 9 Eq. 149; see also *McDonnell* v. *Burnett* (1841) 4 Ir.Eq.R. 216; *Colclough* v. *Smyth* (1861) 14 Ir.Ch.R. 127.

[24] *Hussey* v. *Domville* [1900] 1 I.R. 417; *Hussey* v. *Domville (No. 2)* [1903] 1 I.R. 265; *Cf. McDonnell* v. *Stenson* [1921] 1 I.R. 80.

[25] See also the Life Estates Act (Ir.), 1695, para. 4.170, *ante. Aldworth* v. *Allen* (1865) 11 H.L.C. 549.

[26] *Lord Doneraile* v. *Chartres* (1784) 1 Ridgw.P.C. 122; *Freeman* v. *Boyle* (1788) 2 Ridgw.P.C. 83; *Ware* v. *French* (1863) 14 Ir.Ch.R. 534; *Re Kennedy* (1863) 17 Ir.Ch.R. 162.

[27] *Re McDermott's Estate* [1921] 1 I.R. 114 (see *A Casebook on Irish Land Law* (1984) p. 236), where it was pointed out that, while s. 1 uses the expression "adequate compensation," the preamble uses the phrase "upon making full satisfaction." Campbell C. stated: "This construction is in accordance with what appears to have been the unbroken course of procedure and authority during a lengthy period of years."

[28] Mere non-payment of rent is probably not in itself fraudulent conduct by the tenant, *McDonnell* v. *Burnett* (1841) 4 Ir.Eq.R. 216; *Fitzgerald* v. *O'Connell* (1844) 6 Ir.Eq.R. 455.

[29] *Magrath* v. *Muskerry* (1787) 1 Ridgw.P.C. 469; *cf. Courtenay* v. *Parker* (1864) 16 Ir.Ch.R. 320.

Redesdale states . . . that upon an average throughout Ireland, every lease for lives renewable for ever was the cause of some suit once in every forty or fifty years. In addition to these periodical conflicts with the landlord, other difficulties of an embarrassing nature are constantly arising. The precarious nature of the security afforded by this tenure for the raising or borrowing of money, is a serious inconvenience to persons possessed of an estate, which for many purposes is as beneficial as an inheritance; and when it has been made the subject of incumbrances, the right of renewal is liable to be lost between the delays of parties each of them relying upon the other's taking care of his own interest. Questions, besides, as to the trusts of the renewed lease and the raising and apportioning of renewal fines, where the tenant's interest is in settlement; the frequent disappointment of the settlor's intention, owing to this species of property not being subject to all the laws which regulated the devolution of real estate; the ascertainment of the necessary granting parties, where the lessor's estate has been divided, sold, incumbered, or settled; and many other difficulties . . . create constant perplexity, and involve the parties in serious expense. In a recent case, within the author's knowledge, a treaty for the purchase of a house was protracted for five years, by reason of the difficulty in ascertaining all the necessary parties to a renewal of the lease of it; and when at length it was executed by all of them (fifteen in number, and scattered through various parts of the kingdom) the purchaser, wearied out by the delay, refused to complete the contract."[30]

4.175. The author concluded that "if by some enactment, leases for lives renewable for ever were converted into fee-farm grants, with the remedies incident to the relation of landlord and tenant; it is not easy to see that any injury could be wrought thereby to the landlord, while, on the other hand, the tenant would be relieved from these constant and harassing perplexities."[31] These words were written in 1837 and the legislature obligingly took action some 12 years later.

(ii) Renewable Leasehold Conversion Act, 1849

4.176. This Act[32] gave lessees of leases for lives renewable for ever the right to obtain fee farm grants from their lessors in place of their leases. As regards leases executed after 1849, section 37 of the Act has the effect that they operate automatically as fee farm grants, provided the lessor had power to convey a fee simple, which is usually the case. One point that may be noted here is that section 9 of the 1849 Act provided that no conversion of a lease under the Act was to give any right of dower or curtesy[33] which would not have existed apart from the conversion. This section, however, was held not to deprive claimants'

---

[30] Lyne, *Leases for Lives Renewable for Ever* (1837), pp. 257–9. See also discussion in *Horan* v. *Horan* [1935] I.R. 306.

[31] *Ibid.*, p. 259.

[32] Extended to cover leases granted by governors of colleges, etc. by the Renewable Leaseholds Conversion (Ir.) Act, 1868.

[33] See para. 4.157, *ante*.

rights on the death of a purchaser of a converted lease, *i.e.*, the fee farm grant.[34] These conversion grants have been discussed in detail earlier in this chapter.[35] The result of this legislation has been that renewable leases do not cause as many problems in practice as they used to. Since the land purchase scheme for agricultural land, they are met only in connection with urban land. Here the important point for conveyancers to remember is that a post-1849 lease must usually be treated as a fee farm grant. Pre-1849 unconverted leases, are, however, still quite common, because not as many lessees took advantage of the 1849 Act as might have been expected.[36]

4. Lease for Lives Combined with a Term of Years

4.177. Another common form of conveyance in Ireland is a lease for lives combined with a term of years. Like the lease for lives renewable for ever, this creates an estate *pur autre vie*, a freehold estate,[37] but here there is annexed a leasehold estate as well, a term of years. Also like the lease for lives renewable for ever, a lease for lives with a term of years creates leasehold tenure between the parties, who are subject to the rights and duties of landlords and tenants. Landowners in creating these leases were trying to get the best of both worlds. As Fitzgibbon L.J. explained;

> "Leases for lives, as a matter of history, were commonly adopted because of advantages with respect to the descent of the land, qualification for electoral and other purposes, and other things; and by naming lives these advantages were secured for a great part of the term, without sacrificing the advantage of fixing the time when the tenure would end."[38]

By choosing one's lives carefully, so that they were unlikely to outlast the term of years, and by making the term run concurrently, one ended up with an estate for a certain term but which was freehold for as long as any one of the lives survived.[39] It may be noted, however, that it was not necessarily the case that the term of years was to run concurrently with the estate *pur autre vie*. As Fitzgibbon L.J. again explained:

> "The years are more usually concurrent with the lives, but the term starts from the death of the last surviving life often enough to make it impossible to base a decision upon any presumption that the concurrent construction should prevail in a case otherwise doubtful."[40]

4.178. It is, therefore, a matter of construction in each particular case whether or not the term of years, which usually is for a period of anything between 30 and 99 years, is concurrent or consecutive (or reversionary). In

---

[34] *Robins* v. *McDonnell* (1879) 3 L.R.Ir. 391. See also *Parks* v. *Hegan* [1903] 2 I.R. 643.
[35] Para. 4.079, *ante*.
[36] See the *Report of the Committee on Registration of Title to Land in Northern Ireland* (1967; Cmd. 512), para. 123. The effect of s. 74 of the Republic's Landlord and Tenant (Amendment) Act, 1980, on pre-1849 unconverted leases for lives renewable for ever should be noted, see paras. 4.081 and 4.086, *ante*.
[37] *Batt* v. *Close* (1848) 12 Ir.L.R. 529. *Cf. Trench* v. *Goggins* (1860) 11 I.C.L.R. 477.
[38] *Duckett* v. *Keane* [1903] 1 I.R. 409, 413–4 (see *A Casebook on Irish Land Law* (1984), p. 237).
[39] The freehold being in the eyes of the law always the larger of the two estates, para. 4.008, *ante*.
[40] *Op. cit.*, p. 413.

Duckett v. *Keane*,[41] where the lease was for three lives "and for and during the full end and term of 99 years from thence next ensuing," the Court of Appeal held that the 99-year term was concurrent. In *Adams* v. *McGoldrick*,[42] where a sub-lease was demised for the life of the surviving life named in the head-lease "and for and during the term of 61 years," Wilson J. held the 61-year term was reversionary and not concurrent. He commented on some of the earlier cases:

> "Many cases have been decided on similar words in other cases, and reasons given for coming to directly opposite conclusions. I am not convinced that the reasons given by the learned judges for their decisions are sound and conclusive. Having read these conflicting cases the reasoning seems to me like trying to find some good foundation for a conclusion already held."[43]

VII. PYRAMID TITLES

4.179. It should be apparent from the above discussion that the number and variety of estates in land which can still be created in Ireland may give rise to complications in conveyancing practice. One considerable problem arises in respect of land in urban areas and that is the number of "pyramid" titles which exist. A particular piece of land may have been the subject of a series of successive fee farm grants and sub-grants, long leases and sub-leases. An example may help to illustrate the problem, which is particularly acute in the urban areas of Northern Ireland,[44] probably as a result of the Ulster plantation.[45]

Sample Title

4.180. In—

1860   A was owner in fee simple of 200 acres of largely agricultural land along the banks of the river Lagan.

> [*Note*. This may have been an unincumbered fee simple, or it may have been subject to a burden such as a Crown quit rent, as a result of an earlier confiscation and regrant by the Crown. But the chances are that any such burden would have been since redeemed.[46]]

---

[41] *Op. cit.* See also *Fitzgerald* v. *Vicars* (1839) 2 Dr. & Wal. 298; *Hozier* v. *Powell* (1841) 3 Ir.L.R. 395; *Nesbitt* v. *McManus* (1855) 2 I.C.L.R. 600; *Carpenter* v. *Larkin* (1860) 5 Ir.Jur. (N.S.) 174; *McDonnell* v. *Stenson* [1921] 1 I.R. 80.

[42] [1927] N.I. 127 (see *A Casebook on Irish Land Law* (1984) p. 240). See also *Blackhall* v. *Nugent* (1855) 5 Ir.Ch.R. 323; *Re O'Connor and Small's Contract* (1899) 33 I.L.T.R. 43; *Madden* v. *Maguire* [1910] 2 I.R. 112; *Allman & Co.* v. *McCabe* [1911] 2 I.R. 398. In some cases leases were granted or proposed for *one* life or 21 years, see, *e.g.*, *Wright* v. *St. George* (1861) 12 Ir.Ch.R. 226; *Finucane* v. *Turner* (1862) 13 Ir.Ch.R. 488.

[43] *Ibid.*, p. 130.

[44] See the discussion in the *Report of the Committee on Registration of Title to Land in Northern Ireland* (1967; Cmd. 512), paras. 116–26. Note also the recommendations for dealing with pyramid titles in the *Survey of the Land Law of Northern Ireland* (1971), ch. 20; Land Law Working Group's Discussion Document No. 1 (*Ground Rents and Other Periodic Payments*) (1980) and Interim Report (*Ground Rents and Other Periodic Payments*) (1983). *Cf.* the Republic's *Report on Ground Rents* (1964; Pr. 7783), paras. 7–12.

[45] Para. 1.30,. *ante.*

[46] Para. 6.012, *post.*

1870   A made a fee farm grant to B of 100 of these acres at the yearly fee
       farm rent of £25. In this grant A reserved and excepted to himself and
       his successors in title a wide range of rights and interests, for example,
       all mining and mineral rights, stone and quarrying rights, shooting,
       fishing and sporting rights, rights of way. Further, B entered into
       various covenants on behalf of himself and his successors in title, for
       example, not to assign or sublet the property without first obtaining
       the consent of A or his successors in writing, and restricting the user of
       the property to agricultural or residential purposes.

       [*Note*. The grant was probably made under section 3 of Deasy's
       Act, 1860, so as to create the full relationship of landlord and tenant
       between A and B, that is, A and his successors would have the
       remedies of distress for rent and ejectment for non-payment of rent,
       and the benefit and burden of the covenants on both sides would run
       so as to bind both parties' successors in title like any other leasehold
       covenants.]

1875   B conveyed 20 acres to C subject to all the exceptions and reserva-
       tions, covenants and conditions expressed, implied or contained in
       the 1870 grant. The deed of conveyance expressly charged a £15 rent
       on the 20 acres conveyed to C, which was stated to be an agreed
       apportioned part of the £25 fee farm rent reserved in the 1870 grant. B
       and C, on behalf of themselves and their respective successors in title,
       entered into cross-indemnities in respect of the apportioned parts of
       the head-fee farm rent (£10 and £15) and agreed to indemnify each
       other in respect of all breaches of covenant, condition or agreement
       contained in the 1870 grant, so far as their respective portions of the
       original 100 acres granted were concerned. The deed also created
       mutual rights of way between B and C and their respective successors
       in title, and C undertook to keep all fences, hedges and ditches on the
       boundary betwen the two portions in good repair.

       [*Note*. It must be remembered that this deed of conveyance in
       no way affected A's right to enforce his remedies under the 1870 grant
       against the whole or any part of the 100 acres granted, that is, against
       B or C or both of them. A was not a party to the 1875 deed and was,
       therefore, not bound by it; it created rights only as between B and C
       and their successors in title.]

1880   B made a family settlement whereby he settled 50 acres of his
       remaining 80 acres on his eldest son D for life, with successive
       remainders over to his other sons and grandchildren. The settlement
       contained the usual provisions for jointures and portions charges.

       [*Note*. This settlement was a strict settlement for the
       purposes of the Settled Land Acts, 1882–90, which apply to
       settlements executed before or after 1882.[47]]

---

[47] See generally, ch. 8, *post*.

1884   D, as tenant for life, exercised his powers of leasing under the Settled Land Act, 1882, section 6, and granted with A's consent a building lease of 10 acres to E for 90 years at the annual rent of £35. E covenanted to build 5 dwellinghouses on the property let and that these houses would not be used for purposes other than residential.

[*Note.* Once again these 10 acres will be subject to all the exceptions and reservations, covenants and conditions contained in the 1870 grant.]

1885– E completed the 5 dwellinghouses as specified in the 1884 building
1886   lease and duly sold them by way of sub-leases for the whole of the residue of the 90-year term to F, G, H, I and J. In each sub-lease a ground rent of £25 was reserved and each sub-lessee entered into extensive covenants relating to user of the property (no commercial uses, etc.) and repairs.

[*Note.* Though there was neither privity of contract nor privity of estate between the owners of these houses and owners of superior interests, such as A or B, nevertheless the latter could enforce their rights against the land and anything attached thereto, including buildings, subject, of course, to any equitable relief available to inferior owners. For example, A could seek ejectment for non-payment of rent against B, so as to forfeit B's grant, thereby destroying everything supported by or issuing out of it, but if the owners of inferior interests were in no way to blame for the non-payment of B's rent and had carried out all their responsibilities, they would usually get relief from the forfeiture from the court and be allowed to retain their interests in the land.[48] (See, for example, sections 70 and 71 of Deasy's Act, 1860.) Sub-leasing for the whole term, originating in the activites of the notorious "middlemen," was sanctioned by section 3 of Deasy's Act, which provided that the retention of a reversion was no longer necessary to create the relationship of landlord and tenant. Thus E would remain landlord, with all the usual landlord's remedies, of F, G, H, I and J, who would have had to pay a substantial fine to buy their houses. Indeed, it was and is usually the case in Ireland that the fine represents the full capital value of the property, the ground rents being clear profit for the developer (out of which, of course, he would have to pay his head-rent). It is rarely that the ground rents result in any substantial reduction in the capital price of the property being sold.[49]]

[48] See generally, chs. 17 and 19, *post.*
[49] See ch. 8, *post.*

4.181. This chain of title may be illustrated further by the following diagram:

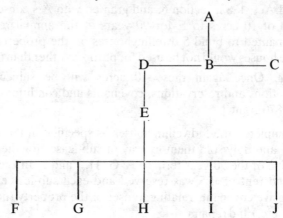

This diagram[50] indicates why such titles are so often said to create a "pyramid of interests" over the land. It should be noted that only part of the probable pyramid of interests has been illustrated, so far as the original 200 acres owned by A in 1860 are concerned. A may have created several parallel tiers in respect of the other 100 acres retained by him after his grant to B, as may have B in respect of the 30 acres retained after his assignment to C and family settlement, and C in respect of the 20 acres assigned to him and so on. In other words, dozens of people may own a wide variety of interests in the pyramid all emanating from A, and the numbers may increase through co-ownership created by intestate succession.[51] In the example given, of course, it would be unlikely that any of the original occupants of the five houses would have survived to 1971. Their houses would now be occupied by their successors in title, either descendants who have succeeded through testate or intestate succession or strangers to their families who have succeeded through assignments (or possibly, though unlikely, sub-leases).

4.182. The pyramid titles make conveyancing in urban areas difficult because an investigation of the title to a particular plot of land may involve tracing the chain of title up through each tier of the pyramid and along the tiers of any parallel pyramid title to neighbouring land emanating from the same original grantor and forming part of the subject-matter of the original grant. This is a particular problem where the land is being bought for development purposes, because the developer may not be prepared to run the risk of some restriction on change of use contained in an earlier grant cropping up later, and so he requires a full investigation of the title.

The example should also help to explain some of the difficulties of extending compulsory registration of title to urban land in Ireland,[52] and the problems faced by lessees wishing to enfranchise, *i.e.,* buy out the freehold, under the

---

[50] *Cf.* the feudal pyramid title, para. 2.07, *ante.* See also the *Survey of the Land Law of Northern Ireland* (1971), para. 464. See ch. 15, *post* and paras. 23.32–4, *post.*
[51] See ch. 15, *post* and paras. 23.40–2, *post.*
[52] See ch. 21, *post.*

recent legislation governing this matter.[53] Finally, a considerable impact on the problem of "pyramid" titles should be made by the recent legislation on ground rents in the Republic. First, there is the prohibition on the future creation of ground rents in respect of dwellinghouses contained in the Landlord and Tenant (Ground Rents) Act, 1978. Secondly, the categories of lessees entitled to enfranchise were extended considerably by the Landlord and Tenant (Ground Rents) (No. 2) Act, 1978, which also introduced a new special enfranchisement procedure to be operated by the Land Registry for a period of 5 years after the Act (since extended). The details of these Acts are considered in a later chapter.[54]

[53] See ch. 18, *post.*
[54] *Ibid.*

CHAPTER 5

FUTURE INTERESTS

I. INTRODUCTION

5.001. Conceptually the law of future interests is, perhaps, the most difficult area of land law to master.[1] It is certainly one of the most technical areas of the law and some of the rules devised by the courts over the centuries may seem now to be subject to little reason. Considerable improvements in this respect have been introduced in recent years in England.[2] and Northern Ireland has largely followed suit.[3] No similar legislation has as yet been introduced in the Republic of Ireland.

5.002. A future interest in land may be described as any interest in land with respect to which the enjoyment of the land is postponed to some time in the future, if that enjoyment is ever going to occur at all. From the earliest days, landowners have attempted to determine the future ownership and enjoyment of their property through succeeding generations and the law has striven to keep this desire within reasonable bounds. Much of the discussion in the ensuing chapters revolves around this constant struggle between the landowners, and their conveyancers, on the one hand, and the judges, and later the legislature, on the other.

II. CLASSIFICATION

5.003. There are two main types of future interest at common law, as has already been briefly explained.[4] These are reversions and remainders. Most of the difficulties in the law of future interests arise in connection with remainders. Indeed, from complexities of the common law rules relating to remainders there developed a new type of future interest, known as an executory interest and recognised in *equity*. Then, as we shall see, the Statute of Uses (Ireland), 1634, had the effect of enabling conveyancers to create *legal* executory interests. Because these interests originally derived from the common law's rules as to remainders they will be discussed under the general heading of remainders.

A. REVERSIONS

5.004. A reversion arises whenever a grantor of land grants away part only of his estate in the land. The reversion is that which is left in him after his grant.

---

[1] See generally, Fearne, *Contingent Remainders* (10th ed., 1844); Challis, *The Law of Real Property* (3rd ed., 1911), chs. XI and XII; Gray, *The Rule Against Perpetuities* (4th ed., 1942); Megarry and Wade, *The law of Real Property* (5th ed., 1984), ch. 7; Maudsley, *The Modern Law of Perpetuities* (1979); Morris and Leach, *The Rule Against Perpetuities* (2nd ed., 1962; supp., 1964).

[2] Law of Property Act, 1925, Part VII; Perpetuities and Accumulations Act, 1964.

[3] Perpetuities Act (N.I.), 1966.

[4] Para. 4.013, *ante.*

For example, A, owner of the fee simple in Blackacre, conveys Blackacre "to B for life." As a result of this conveyance, B holds a life estate and A holds the fee simple in reversion for as long as B's life estate lasts and then, when it ends, his fee simple ceases to be held in reversion and automatically reverts to being held in possession. Thus a reversion lies in the grantor only under a conveyance and operates by operation of law. This is to be contrasted with a remainder, which is a future estate to arise in possession in some person other than the grantor, after the ending of the immediate and prior estate granted. For example, if A instead conveyed Blackacre "to B for life, remainder to C in fee simple," B again takes a life estate immediately in possession and C has the fee simple estate in remainder.[5] The two types of future interest[6] may be illustrated by the following conveyance by A: "to B for life, remainder to C for life." Here B has an immediate life estate in possession, C has a life estate in remainder, which will fall into possession on B's death, and A has a fee simple reversion, which will fall into possession on the death of the survivor of B and C.

5.005. A reversion should be distinguished from two similar future rights which do not amount strictly to either a reversion or a remainder. These are, first a possibility of reverter which exists in the grantor of a determinable fee[7] and, secondly, a right of entry which exists in the grantor of a fee simple subject to a condition subsequent.[8]

5.006. So far the reversions discussed have been freehold reversions and, indeed, according to feudal law these were the only reversions recognised. If A, the owner of the fee simple in Blackacre, granted a lease to B for 99 years, the feudal law took no notice at all of this transaction. Leases were not part of the law of estates and A remained seised of the land and responsible for the feudal dues.[9] As far as feudal law was concerned, no future interest of any kind had been created, reversion or remainder. However, since leases have come to be recognised as part of land law and as belonging to the law of estates in land,[10] it has become proper to refer to a leasehold reversion. In our example, A would hold a leasehold reversion, *i.e.*, the fee simple in reversion which would fall into possession at the end of B's term of years.[11]

B. REMAINDERS

5.007. As we have just explained, a remainder is an estate which comes into possession in the future on determination of a prior estate granted by the same conveyance. Theoretically, there is no limit to the number of remainders that could be limited in any one conveyance. For example, the grantor could convey

---

[5] The further refinements, in this context, of "vested in possession" and "vested in interest" are explained later, paras. 5.008 *et seq., post.*
[6] Note that the word "interest" is more commonly used in this context rather than the technically more accurate word "estate," see para. 4.001, *ante.*
[7] Para. 4.047, *ante.*
[8] Para. 4.049, *ante.*
[9] Para. 4.007, *ante.*
[10] Paras. 4.007–9, *ante.*
[11] Of course, the reversion is in possession during the currency of the lease in the sense that the landlord is entitled to claim the rent annexed to it.

the land for successive life estates *ad infinitum,* but whether all these estates would be valid and enforceable is another matter.[12]

In considering remainders, however, a vital distinction has to be made between those which are "vested" and those which are "contingent." Much of the law and technicalities that surround these interests is based upon this distinction.[13]

1. *Vested and Contingent*

5.008. An immediate problem is that a further distinction must be made with respect to the word "vested." An interest may be vested "in possession" or vested "in interest." If it is the former, the holder of the interest has a present right to *current* enjoyment of the land. In our examples given above, in every case A had such an interest before any of his conveyances; his fee simple was vested in possession. After his conveyances, the only person with such an interest was B who had a life estate vested in possession. On the other hand, if the holder of an interest has a present right to *future* enjoyment of the land, his interest is vested in interest only.[14] It is still vested, because he does have a present right free from any conditions or contingencies upon it vesting. In our examples, in every case A's reversion was vested in interest. Indeed, it is an inherent characteristic of all reversions that they are so vested, because a reversion is what is left in the grantor and this *ex hypothesi* must be a present right. An interest is contingent, therefore, if the holder has no present right and will have none until some condition or contingency is satisfied. For example, A might convey Blackacre "to B for life, remainder to C for life, if C marries B." Here B's life estate is vested in possession, A's fee simple reversion is vested in interest, but C's life estate in remainder is contingent and will not vest in interest unless and until C marries B, and in possession until B dies.

5.009. The rule is, therefore, that an interest is not vested unless not only is the holder ascertained but also his interest can take effect either in possession at once or immediately upon the determination of a prior estate. If either of these two conditions is not satisfied the interest is contingent only.[15] Thus if A conveys Blackacre "B for life, remainder to the first son of B to become a solicitor" and no son of B has yet become a solicitor, the interest remains contingent and will not vest until a son complies with the contingency. It should be noted, however, that the law does not consider personal details of the holders of the interests and does not canvass the probabilities of a particular situation. For example, A might convey Blackacre "to B for life, remainder to

---

[12] See paras. 5.056 *et seq., post.*

[13] Morris and Leach, *The Rule Against Perpetuities,* ch. 2; Foulke, "Vested and Contingent Remainders" (1915) 15 Col.L.Rev. 680; Gluck, "Vested v. Contingent Remainders" (1924) 24 Col.L.Rev. 8; McDougal, "Future Interests Restated: Tradition versus Clarification and Reform" (1942) 55 H.L.R. 1077; Lunes, "Fifty Years of Future Interests" (1937) 50 H.L.R. 749.

[14] *Martin* v. *McCausland* (1842) 4 Ir.L.R. 340; *Roberts* v. *Sampson* (1856) 1 Ir.Jur. (N.S.) 364; *Re Poe* [1942] I.R. 535 (see *A Casebook on Irish Land Law* (1984), p. 268).

[15] See, generally, on contingent remainders, *Jack* v. *Fetherston* (1829) 2 Hud. & Br. 320 (aff'd. *sub nom. Fetherston* v. *Fetherston* (1835) 3 Cl. & F. 67); *Cole* v. *Sewell* (1843) 4 Dr. & War. 1, aff'd. (1848) 2 H.L.C. 186 (see *A Casebook on Irish Land Law* (1984), p. 246); *Re Mansfield* [1962] I.R. 454.

C for life," when B was 10 years of age and C was 80 years of age. The likelihood of C's interest ever vesting in possession is extremely remote, because it is probable that B will outlive C. Yet, so long as C remains alive his interest is vested in interest, because there is no condition or contingency to be satisfied and he is ready to take immediately upon determination of B's prior estate. It is also the case that the question of vesting will not be affected by the fact that the *size* of a person's share is unascertained. This has obvious relevance in the case of a class gift, e.g., a conveyance by A "to B for life, remainder to such of B's children as attain the age of 21 years." Here each of B's children takes a vested interest upon becoming 21 years of age, and that interest remains vested even though it is not certain how many other children may similarly qualify and become entitled to enjoy in possession, on the death of their parent, a share of the land.

5.010. It should be noted that the courts favour the vesting of interests and show this in construing particular conveyances. The result is that what might appear at first sight as a contingent interest may well be construed as a vested interest, but subject to divesting upon the happening of some contingency or the satisfaction of some condition.[16] Thus it is a rule of construction of wills that where property, real or personal, is given to a person "on his attaining" (or "if" or "when" or "as soon as" he attains) a specified age and there is a gift over in the event of his not attaining that age, the primary gift to that person is construed as a vested gift and *not* contingent, but liable to be divested if he fails to attain the age specified.[17] This rule of construction has, however, been criticised recently in Ireland, in the following terms:

> "The reasoning on which the rule was based is plainly fallacious when there is a residuary clause as it is then probable that the testator intended that the income of the property devised on condition should form part of the residuary estate until the attainment of the specified age. The rule did not have its origin in the reasoning which was subsequently developed in its defence but in the common law doctrine that the seisin and legal estate in freehold lands had to have an owner so that the subsequent estate which was contingent would not be destroyed by not having a particular estate to support it. . . .
>
> This history of the rule shows that it was imposed on the Chancery Courts by the Common Law judges. However, despite my objection to it, I feel that the three decisions of the House of Lords compel me to recognise its existence as a rule of construction."[18]

5.011. At common law, contingent remainders by their very nature were interests of little value. At most they conferred only a possibility that an

---

[16] Or sometimes construed as a vested interest but with payment postponed. See *Vize* v. *Stoney* (1841) 4 Ir.Eq.R. 64; *Phipps* v. *Ackers* (1842) 9 Cl. & F. 583; *Kimberley* v. *Tew* (1843) 5 Ir.Eq.R. 389. *Reilly* v. *Fitzgerald* (1843) 6 Ir.Eq.R. 335; *Re Hudsons* (1843) Dr.*temp.* Sug. 6; *Hynes* v. *Redington* (1844) 7 Ir.Eq.R. 405; *Re Brabazon* (1849) 13 Ir.Eq.R. 156; *Re Orme's Settlement Trusts* (1851) 1 Ir.Ch.R. 175; *Dennis* v. *Frend* (1863) 14 Ir.Ch.R. 271; *Love* v. *Love* (1881) 7 L.R.Ir. 306; *Minch* v. *Minch* (1923) 57 I.L.T.R. 135. *Cf. Re Murphy's Estate* [1964] I.R. 308 (see *A Casebook on Irish Land Law* (1984), p. 242).
[17] *McGredy* v. *C.I.R.* [1951] N.I. 155. See also para. 5.059, *post.*
[18] *Re Murphy's Estate* [1964] I.R. 308 at 311 and 313 (*per* Kenny J.).

interest might become vested, and so they were regarded as inalienable *inter vivos* or by will.[19] They do, however, seem to have been inheritable, and equity would grant relief to the extent of requiring an assignor to transfer the property to the assignee if the remainder vested and fell into possession.[20] Contingent remainders were not, however, *bare* possibilities, like possibilities of reverter,[21] and it was decided that the English Statute of Wills 1535 made them devisable by will.[22] This interpretation was adopted for both England and Ireland in the Wills Act, 1837.[23] The Real Property Act, 1845, completed the picture by making contingent remainders alienable *inter vivos* by deed.[24]

2. *Common Law Remainder Rules*

5.012. The early common law's attitude to remainders was determined by the feudal concept of seisin.[25] Since the whole system of services and incidents of tenure, which was the basis of feudal landowning, was dependent upon this concept, the law's primary concern was to see that at any time it was always clear who exactly was seised of the land in question. The result was that a series of rules was devised by the law to govern the validity of dispositions creating remainders which might throw doubt upon this question. Since these rules were largely based upon the doctrine of seisin, they applied to legal remainders of freehold estates only. The following were the four main common law remainder rules. If a remainder did not comply with any of these, it was invalid at common law.

(i) A Remainder must be Supported by a Prior Freehold Estate

5.013. At common law a conveyance could not create a "springing" freehold remainder, *i.e.,* a freehold estate to spring up in the future without any prior freehold estate to support it by carrying the seisin. The feudal system would not countenance an abeyance of the seisin.[26] For example, if A, owner of the fee simple in Blackacre, conveyed the land "to B and his heirs when B marries," and B was unmarried at the date of the conveyance, there would be a gap in the seisin between the date of the conveyance and B's satisfying the contingency that he marry, when a vesting of his interest would take place and he would have the seisin. In this case, at common law B's interest would be void and the entire disposition would fail, leaving the land in A. If the conveyance had been instead "to B for 99 years, remainder to C and his heirs provided C is married," C's contingent remainder would have been similarly void because it was not

---

[19] Challis, *op. cit.,* pp. 76–7.
[20] Megarry and Wade, *op. cit.,* p. 235.
[21] Para. 4.051, *ante.*
[22] *Jones v. Roe d. Perry* (1789) 3 T.R. 88. The Statute of Wills (Ir.), 1634, was the equivalent of the English 1535 Statute.
[23] s. 3. See now, as regards the Republic of Ireland, the Succession Act, 1965, s. 76.
[24] s. 6. The section used the phrase "may be disposed of" which might be said to cover dispositions *inter vivos* or by will. But the Wills Act, 1837, s. 3 was not amended by the 1845 Act, which is usually taken as applying generally to dispositions *inter vivos* only.
[25] Para. 4.018, *ante.*
[26] *Re Murphy's Estate* [1964] I.R. 308 at 311 (*per* Kenny J.) (see *A Casebook on Irish Land Law* (1984), p. 242).

supported by a freehold estate. B's estate, which was valid, was a leasehold estate only which did not carry the seisin and so once again there was an abeyance of seisin. If B had been given a life estate, this would have saved C's contingent remainder—at least initially. As we shall see in a moment, whether C's remainder would continue to be valid would depend on later events.[27] However, the following disposition should be compared with the one just discussed—"to B for 21 years, remainder to C and his heirs." The difference to note here is that C's remainder is not contingent (if C is a living person) and so there is nothing to prevent his fee simple vesting in interest[28] immediately, subject only to B's leasehold estate in possession. There would be, therefore, no abeyance of seisin and, if necessary, B could take livery of seisin[29] on C's behalf in the early days of the feudal system.

(ii) A Remainder Must Not Cut Short a Prior Freehold Estate

5.014. Just as the common law would not allow an abeyance of seisin, it would not permit an arbitrary shifting of the seisin from the holder of one freehold estate to another. Once a freehold estate became vested and the seisin was established in the holder of that estate, the seisin could not be taken from that person, or his successors in title, until the natural determination of the estate originally conveyed. Thus to be a valid remainder at common law, the remainder had to be limited to take effect no earlier than the natural determination of the prior freehold estate. A conveyance "to B for life, but if B marries C, then to D and his heirs" would give B a valid life state, but D's remainder would be void because it was bound to take effect, if at all, by cutting short B's life estate. The result was that B's life estate ceased to be subject to the condition subsequent, became a full life estate and a fee simple reversion remained in the grantor.[30]

5.015. The important point to note here is that this rule applied to protect the natural length of estates. Once again the distinction between an estate subject to a condition and a determinable estate becomes important.[31] If, instead, in the example above the conveyance had been "to B for life or until he marries C, then to D and his heirs," B's life estate would determine naturally according to the words of limitation on his marriage to C and D's fee simple would only take effect at that time. Both interests were, therefore, valid at common law.

(iii) No Remainder after a Fee Simple

5.016. This rule was not so much based upon the concept of seisin as upon the inherent nature of a fee simple estate. That estate comprised the largest

---

[27] Para. 5.017, *post.*
[28] Para. 5.008, *ante.*
[29] Para. 3.023, *ante.*
[30] However, if B married and broke the original condition and the grantor did not exercise his right of entry (see para. 4.049, *ante*), it seems that B's life estate would continue and the remainder would revive and take effect on his death, see Challis, *op. cit.*, pp. 81–2.
[31] Paras. 4.049–51, *ante.*

estate known to the common law and, subject to the concept of tenure,[32] the whole of legal ownership of the land in question. This third rule was speaking the rather obvious truth that, once a grantor has conveyed his fee simple to someone else, he has no estate left over to limit by way of remainder to some further person.[33]

It may be noted that this rule applied not only to a fee simple absolute, but also to a determinable fee simple[34] and a fee simple upon condition.[35] However, where a fee tail, after which there could, of course, be a remainder, was converted into a base fee,[36] this did not destroy the remainders.[37]

(iv) A Remainder Must Vest During or Immediately Upon Determination of the Prior Freehold Estate

5.017. This rule is really a logical conclusion from rules (i) and (ii). For a remainder to be valid there must be no abeyance of seisin (rule (i)) nor any arbitrary shifting of the seisin (rule (ii)), so the remainder must either vest in interest during the continuance of the prior freehold estate or vest in possession immediately upon its determination.[38] An interesting point about this rule (iv), however, was that it was not always clear at the outset whether a particular remainder would violate it. For example, one could compare the following dispositions: "to B for life, remainder to C and his heirs one day after B's death"; "to B for life, remainder to C and his heirs provided C marries D." In the first disposition, the remainder to C is void *ab initio* because an abeyance of seisin for one day after B's death is clear from the beginning. In the second disposition, however, it is *not* clear from the beginning whether an abeyance of seisin will occur on B's death. If C marries D before B's death, there will be no abeyance and, if he does not, there will be an abeyance. So, at common law, in this case one was allowed to "wait and see" and the remainder to C in the second disposition was not regarded as void *ab initio*.[39] This aspect of rule (iv) was significant and especially relevant in connection with a rule devised by the courts much later, known as the rule in *Purefoy* v. *Rogers*.[40]

3. *Equitable Rules*

5.018. The common law remainder rules, as we have discussed, were largely based upon the feudal concept of seisin. Any method of avoiding difficulties over that concept should also have avoided any problems concerning the remainder rules and this is what happened. We have described earlier in this book how landowners avoided feudal rules by conveying property to uses and

---

[32] Ch. 2, *ante.*
[33] *Duke of Norfolk's Case* (1681) 3 Ch.Ca. 1. He can, of course, create a determinable fee and retain a possibility of reverter, but this, like a right of entry, is an interest less than an estate, para. 5.005, *ante.*
[34] Para. 4.046, *ante.*
[35] Para. 4.048, *ante.*
[36] Para. 4.136, *ante.*
[37] Challis, *op. cit.*, p. 325.
[38] *Dawson* v. *Dawson* (1850) 13 Ir.L.R. 472.
[39] *Cf.* the later rule against perpetuities, para. 5.060, *post.*
[40] Discussed para. 5.020, *post.*

creating equitable interests only in the *cestuis que use*.[41] By these conveyances landowners could also create remainders which were equitable only and which did not have to comply with the common law remainder rules.[42] In this case equity did *not* follow the law[43] and for good reason. The seisin was in the feoffees to use and was totally unaffected by any remainders limited to the *cestuis que use*. Springing and shifting uses were, therefore, quite valid, *e.g.*, "to B and his heirs to the use of C and his heirs when C marries" and "to B and his heirs to the use of C for life, but if C marries D, then to the use of D and his heirs." Prior to the Statute of Uses, both dispositions vested the legal fee simple and the seisin in B. The former created a springing use in favour of C and the latter a shifting use in favour of D. Since the common law did not recognise uses, and equitable interests created under them, its courts were not concerned with the application of the remainder rules. A vastly different position was brought about, however, by the passing of the Statute of Uses (Ireland), 1634. As we discussed earlier, this Statute executed uses and converted equitable estates created under uses into legal estates.[44] The effect of the Statute on future interests like springing and shifting uses was, therefore, quite revolutionary; it converted them into legal interests and created a new type of future interest, known as "legal executory interests." These were legal because the use was executed by the Statute and so they had to be distinguished from future equitable interests, often called "future trusts" to conform with the more modern terminology for uses. Yet they had also to be distinguished from legal remainders because they did not comply with the common law remainder rules.

4. *Legal Executory Interests*

5.019. The Statute of Uses (Ireland), 1634, like the English 1535 Statute, took precedence over any judge-made rules, so that any of the common law remainder rules discussed above could be avoided. The Statute specifically stated that the *cestuis que use* were to have "such like estates" as they had in use. Both shifting and springing legal interests could now be created under the Statute.[45] All that was necessary in an *inter vivos* conveyance was that the magic formula "to A and his heirs to the use of . . ." be used. Then, the courts, following their generally more liberal approach to wills,[46] developed the principle that a disposition by will would be read for these purposes as if the magic formula had been used, even if in the particular will it had not been used. Thus legal executory devises (springing and shifting devises) could be created even more easily and with less technicality than legal executory interests in *inter vivos* conveyances.[47]

---

[41] Para. 3.008, *ante.*
[42] *Cf. Sherwin* v. *Kenny* (1864) 16 Ir.Ch.R. 138.
[43] Para. 3.047, *ante.*
[44] Paras. 3.015 *et seq.*, *ante.* See also *Att.-Gen.* v. *Cummins* [1906] 1 I.R. 406 at 410–1 (*per* Palles C.B.) (see *A Casebook on Irish Land Law* (1984), p. 131).
[45] Of course, by the mid-seventeenth century, the feudal revenue aspect of seisin was greatly diminished in importance, as the Tenures Abolition Act (Ir.), 1662, indicated, para. 2.48, *ante.*
[46] Para. 4.031, *ante.* It has been suggested that this may have been due to the courts' interpretation of the wording of the first Statute of Wills (1540 in England, 1634, in Ireland) which gave a testator power to dispose of land "at his free will and pleasure." See Challis, *op. cit.*, p. 169. *Pells* v. *Brown* (1620) Cro.Jac. 590.
[47] *Gwynne* v. *Berry* (1875) I.R. 9 C.L. 494; *Re Conboy's Estate* [1916] 1 I.R. 51; *Re Bellew's Estate* [1924] 1

There was little that the common law could do about this avoidance of the remainder rules by conveyances to uses or wills. In fact, the only major reaction to these developments was a principle developed by the courts known as the rule in *Purefoy* v. *Rogers.*[48]

5. *Rule in Purefoy* v. *Rogers*

5.020. Very briefly this rule required the validity of certain remainders to be governed by one of the common law remainder rules *regardless* of the fact that they were contained in a conveyance to uses or in a will. The remainders to which the rule applied were those which were of uncertain validity under rule (iv) of the common law rules discussed above.[49] Thus the rule did not apply where there was a clear violation of one of the common law rules, *e.g.,* in the case of rules (i)–(iii). Here a conveyance to uses or a will saved the future interest. But in a case where rule (iv) would apply at common law and there would have to be a "wait and see" exercise to determine the remainder's validity (and it complied with the other three rules), the rule in *Purefoy* v. *Rogers* required that the limitation be treated as a common law remainder and that one should wait and see whether or not it was valid under rule (iv). As Sugden L.C. put it in an Irish case, "if there be one rule of law more sacred than another, it is this, that no limitation shall be construed to be an executory or shifting use, which can by possibility take effect by way of remainder."[50]

5.021. Whatever the origin of the rule, and it is usually said to have originated as a rule of construction for carrying out the grantor's intention, it became an inflexible rule of law to be applied regardless of the testator's intentions.[51] In many cases it seems to have been an arbitrary and illogical rule and one cannot help wondering why the courts should have been determined to expose to risk dispositions that might comply with the common law rules, yet allow dispositions, which would otherwise clearly and definitely from the outset violate those rules, to be saved by the conveyance to uses or the will. If one takes the example of a class gift, *e.g.,* "to B for life, remainder to his children who attain 21 years," one can see how the rule operated. In this example, it is not clear from the outset whether any and, if any, how many of B's children will be 21 when B dies, so rule (iv) applies. Only those children who do reach 21 during B's life take to the exclusion of those who do not attain that age until later.[52] Under the rule in *Purefoy* v. *Rogers* this remains the position, even if the disposition is contained in a conveyance to uses or in a will. If, however, the words were added at the end of the limitation "whether before or after B's death," the picture altered completely. Those words made it clear

I.R. 1. Also *Lee* v. *Flinn* (1833) Alc. & Nap. 418; *Tisdall* v. *Tisdall* (1839) 2 Ir.L.R. 41; *Geary* v. *Synan* (1842) 5 Ir.L.R. 509; *Coltsman* v. *Coltsman* (1864) 15 I.C.L.R. 171.

[48] (1671) 2 Wms. Saund. 380. In fact this was a case of a will and the same principle had been held earlier to apply to conveyances *inter vivos* in *Chudleigh's Case* (1595) 1 Co.Rep. 113b at 137b–138a.

[49] Para. 5.017, *ante.*

[50] *Cole* v. *Sewell* (1843) 4 Dr. & War. 1 at 27 (see also (1848) 2 H.L.C. 186) (see *A Casebook on Irish Land Law* (1984), p. 246).

[51] *White* v. *Summers* [1908] 2 Ch. 256.

[52] *Festing* v. *Allen* (1843) 12 M. & W. 279, applied in *Ferguson* v. *Ferguson* (1886) 17 L.R.Ir. 552.

that an abeyance of seisin was to occur, if necessary, to ensure that all the children took and so, the courts held, rule (iv) was clearly violated.[53] There was no element of uncertainty or wait and see and *Purefoy* v. *Rogers* did not apply. Thus a conveyance to uses or a will would save the gift to all the children, who could take whenever they reached 21 regardless of any abeyance of seisin.

5.022. Finally, it must be mentioned that *Purefoy* v. *Rogers* applied only to cases of what would otherwise operate as legal executory interests. It did not apply to purely equitable future interests, *i.e.,* conveyances to uses *not* executed by the Statute of Uses.[54] These continued to be unaffected by the common law remainder rules and this remains the case with respect to equitable interests held under a modern trust. At the risk of repetition, we reiterate the vital point that a conveyance "unto and to the use of the trustees and their heirs" meant that estates which followed that of the trustees were equitable because the Statute of Uses did not apply to convert the later interests into legal estates.[55]

6. *Destruction and Preservation of Contingent Remainders*

5.023. In the sections above we discussed how remainders might be held invalid under various rules of law. This sort of invalidity is usually described as *natural* destruction, *i.e.,* through the normal operation of the rules. However, under early common law, remainders could be subjected to what was called *artificial* destruction. By this was meant acts of the parties in particular cases whereby they caused premature or artificial determination of estates and thereby brought about, *e.g.,* an abeyance of seisin which would not have occurred in the normal course of events, but which destroyed subsequent remainders which were contingent.

(i) Destruction

There were several methods of artificial destruction.

(a) *Disseisin with Loss of Right of Entry*

5.024. This method came from medieval law. It was based upon a distinction made in that law between a right of entry and a right of action. If a tenant for life were disseised of his land he had a right of entry against the disseisor. However, if the latter held the land peaceably for five years[56] and then the land devolved on his heir at his death, it was the rule that the tenant for life thereupon lost his right of entry and from then on could recover the land by one of the old real actions only. It was held that any contingent remainder expectant on the life estate was also destroyed on this conversion of the right of entry into a mere right of action.[57]

---

[53] *Miles* v. *Jarvis* (1883) 24 Ch.D. 633; *Dean* v. *Dean* [1891] 3 Ch. 150.
[54] Para. 3.019, *ante. Lysaght* v. *Scully* (1854) 6 Ir.Jur. (o.s.) 194.
[55] Para. 3.021, *ante.*
[56] See the Disseisin Act (Ir.), 1634, 10 Chas. 1, sess. 2, c. 7 (Ir.) (the equivalent of the English Act of 1540, 32 Hen. 8, c. 33).
[57] *Thompson* v. *Leach* (1697) 1 Ld.Raym. 313, 316.

(b) *Forfeiture*

5.025. The second method of destruction of *contingent* remainders was by a forfeiture of the prior estate so as to give a right of entry to the person with the next *vested* estate (the grantor by way of reversion if no one else had a vested interest). There were several methods of causing a forfeiture under feudal law, *e.g.*, treason or denial of the lord's title.[58] A common method developed by conveyancers was what was known as a *tortious* conveyance.[59] The holder of a lesser freehold estate, *e.g.*, a fee tail or life estate, purported to convey a fee simple by one of the usual methods, *e.g.*, a feoffment[60] or fine and recovery.[61] This was said to operate as a claim by the holder of the lesser estate to a fee simple as a disseisor and a repudiation and destruction of his lesser estate. The next vested remainderman or reversioner had thereupon a right of entry and an exercise of this would destroy any intervening contingent remainders expectant upon that lesser estate.

(c) *Surrender*

5.026. If the holder of a lesser estate surrendered that estate to the holder of the next vested estate, which was of at least as great, if not greater, value, the former estate joined with the latter and any intervening contingent interests expectant on the former were destroyed. This process of destruction by surrender through act of the parties should be distinguished from merger by operation of law,[62] which, in this context, produced the same result.

(d) *Merger*

If a prior freehold estate (other than a fee tail) and a fee simple remainder or reversion became vested in the same person, the two estates merged and destroyed any intervening contingent remainders.[63]

(e) *Disclaimer*

Finally, the grantee of a prior estate could disclaim it, whereupon it reverted to the grantor. Any contingent remainders expectant upon that estate were then destroyed.

(ii) Preservation

5.027. It was not long before the conveyancers devised a method of protecting contingent remainders from this sort of artificial destruction. The device they used was a conveyance to trustees "to preserve contingent remainders" in the event of premature destruction of a prior estate. Thus

---

[58] Para. 2.23, *ante*.
[59] See Challis, *op. cit.*, pp. 135–6.
[60] Para. 3.023, *ante*.
[61] Para. 4.117, *ante*.
[62] See Challis, *op. cit.*, ch. X. Also ch. 24, *post*.
[63] *Cf.* a merger of estates under the rule in *Shelley's Case,* where the merged estates would re-open to let in any remainders subsequently vesting, para. 4.039, *ante*.

protection in a settlement taking the form "to A for life, remainder to his first son to attain 21 in tail male" would be provided by inserting an extra remainder between A's life estate and the contingent remainder to his first son. That extra remainder would be a remainder which provided that, should A's life estate determine for any reason before his death, the land was to vest immediately in trustees to be held in trust by them for A for the remainder of his life and to preserve the contingent remainder, which could then take effect or not take effect according to the ordinary rules governing such remainders.[64] This device should not be confused with an ordinary trust whereby the entire legal estate is vested in the trustees and the entire beneficial estate, and all remainders, are equitable only and unaffected by the common law remainder rules.[65]

(iii) Statutory Reforms

5.028. A series of nineteenth-century statutes have radically altered the law relating to destruction and preservation of contingent remainders.

(a) *Real Property Limitation Act, 1833*

This Act abolished the old distinction between a right of entry and a right of action and prevented the death of a disseisor from destroying a right of entry in the holder of the life estate.[66] Thus one method of destroying contingent remainders was abolished.

(b) *Real Property Act, 1845*

Section 8 of this Act provided that from the end of 1844 a contingent remainder "shall be, and, if created before the passing of this Act, shall be deemed to have been, capable of taking effect, notwithstanding the determination, by forfeiture, surrender, or merger, of any preceding estate of freehold in the same manner in all respects as if such determination had not happened."[67] This Act, therefore, abolished three methods of destruction. It also abolished a special type of forfeiture, namely, the tortious conveyance for section 4 provided that a feoffment made after the first day of 1845 "shall not have any tortious operation."[68] Thenceforth, the capacity of a person to convey an estate greater than that which he held would be governed strictly by the terms of the grant under which he held or the instrument by which he was empowered, or by statute, *e.g.*, the later Settled Land Acts.[69]

---

[64] *Smith d. Dorner* v. *Packhurst* (1740) 3 Atk. 135; *Blackwell* v. *Hale* (1850) 1 I.C.L.R. 612; *Rochford* v. *Fitzmaurice* (1842) 4 Ir.Eq.R. 375.

[65] Para. 5.022, *ante.*

[66] Ss. 4, 5 and 39.

[67] This replaced s. 8 of the Tranfer of Property Act, 1844, which had provided another method of statutory protection, namely, that all contingent remainders should take effect as executory interests. The ill-starred 1844 Act was repealed retrospectively by s. 1 of the 1845 Act.

[68] The Fines and Recoveries (Ir.) Act, 1834, s. had abolished the other main method of execution of a tortious conveyance, the fine and recovery. As regards s. 4 of the 1845 Act, see *O'Reilly* v. *Gleeson* [1975] I.R. 258 at 272 (*per* Henchy J.). See para. 17.067, *post.*

[69] Ch. 8, *post.*

(c) *Contingent Remainders Act, 1877*

5.029. Section 1 of this Act provided:

"Every contingent remainder . . . which would have been valid as a springing or shifting use or executory devise or other limitation had it not had a sufficient estate to support it as a contingent remainder, shall, in the event of the particular estate determining before the contingent remainder vests, be capable of taking effect in all respects as if the contingent remainder had originally been created as a springing or shifting use or executory devise or other executory limitation."

The Act can hardly be described as a model of drafting expertise and to this day its precise application remains unclear. The following are the generally accepted views as to its effect. First, it seems clear that the Act was intended to reverse the rule in *Purefoy* v. *Rogers* and to put an end to destruction of remainders couched as executory uses or devises by the application of rule (iv) (and "wait and see") of the common law remainder rules.[70] Secondly, the Act does not apply to remainders which would be void if treated as executory interests. This is particularly important in view of the modern rule against perpetuities.[71] Under *Purefoy* v. *Rogers* remainders do at least have a chance of survival, because of the wait and see rule. Under the rule against perpetuities there was, and still is in the Republic of Ireland, no general wait and see principle and an executory interest which *might* be too remote in vesting was void *ab initio*.[72] The 1877 Act clearly did not intend that interests which had at least a chance of validity should be construed as executory interests, if this ensured their invalidity. Thirdly, the 1877 Act applied only to the rule (iv) ("wait and see") situation; it did not apply to the common law remainder rules governing springing and shifting interests or remainders after a fee simple. These rules still have to be avoided by conveyances to uses or wills. Fourthly, the Act did not accelerate the vesting of contingent remainders. If the prior estate determined before the vesting of the remainder, the land reverted to the grantor or the testator's estate in the meantime until that vesting occurred. Fifthly, it is not cear whether the Act applied to class gifts, where some members of the class might take a vested interest before determination of the prior estate and some might not.[73] It is arguable that the Act applied only to save remainders where the entire remainder would otherwise fail. It is, however, arguable that the Act applied to save all interests to be taken under a particular remainder, which interests would otherwise fail, whether or not other interests under the same remainder would fail. The point has never been settled,[74] and nowadays has less importance at least so far as wills are concerned.

---

[70] Para. 5.017, *ante.*
[71] Paras. 5.056 *et seq., post.*
[72] This is no longer the position in Northern Ireland as a result of the Perpetuities Act (N.I.), 1966, para. 5.062, *post.*
[73] Para. 5.021, *ante.*
[74] It was raised before Astbury J. in *Re Robson* [1916] 1 Ch. 116, but he decided the case on the basis of the effect of the Land Transfer Act, 1897, on wills, see para. 5.030, *infra.*

(d) *Succession Legislation*

5.030. As a result of a series of statutes dating back to the nineteenth century,[75] all a deceased person's property, real and personal, nowadays vests on his death initially in his personal representatives.[76] These persons are then responsible for its distribution in accordance with the will or the statutory provisions applying in the case of intestacy. The result of these provisions is that the beneficiaries' interests under a will initially are equitable only and remain so as long as the legal estate is vested in the personal representatives— hence the maxim often quoted that "a will operates in equity only." It would seem, therefore, that a will nowadays can create future *equitable* interests only; it cannot create legal remainders or, indeed, legal executory interests and so there is no longer any problem with respect of such interests, so far as remainder rules are concerned. Interests under wills are endangered only by rules which apply also to equitable interests, such as the rule against perpetuities.[77] It might be argued that problems would arise when personal representatives vest the legal estates in the beneficiaries after administration of the estate, but it has been held that this subsequent legal clothing of the equitable interests does not affect their validity.[78] One can argue that the validity of gifts under a will should be determined at the date from which the will operates, namely, the death of the testator. This is the general rule,[79] and at that date, of course, the beneficiaries' interests are equitable only. It would be strange if the personal representatives' carrying out of their trust should alter or destroy this validity retrospectively. The same result could be achieved if the testator had expressly created a trust in his will. While it may be queried whether legislation relating to the administration of estates was originally intended to affect the validity of beneficial interests taken under those estates, there is no doubt that this point was known and argued about long before the passing of the Irish statutes dealing with administration of estates. Yet those statutes contain no provisions reversing the judicial view of the matter.

III. RULES AGAINST REMOTENESS

5.031. It has already been mentioned that our land law has over the centuries constantly striven to restrict the power of landowners to control the ownership and disposition of their land through successive generations.[80] One of the earliest statutes, *Quia Emptores,* 1290, was in some measure devoted to this end.[81] Conversely, the landowners who secured the passing of *De Donis,* 1285,

---

[75] See, *e.g.,* Pt IV of the Local Registration of Title (Ir.) Act, 1891, which applied to freehold agricultural land compulsorily registered under the Act in both parts of Ireland. The Law Reform (Miscellaneous Provisions) Act (N.I.), 1937, s. 1 extended this to all freehold land in Northern Ireland, and the Administration of Estates Act, 1959, s. 6 did so in the Republic of Ireland. These provisions in the Irish 1937 and 1959 Acts corresponded to s. 1 of the English Land Transfer Act, 1897.

[76] Succession Act, 1965, s. 10 (R.I.); Administration of Estates Act (N.I.), 1955, s. 1. See para. 15.06, *post.*

[77] Paras. 5.056 *et seq., post.*

[78] *Re Robson* [1916] 1 Ch. 116.

[79] Para. 14.42, *post.*

[80] Para. 5.002, *ante.*

[81] Para. 2.46, *ante.*

may have thought that they had breached this general attitude of the law,[82] yet
the courts very quickly reasserted the general principle and to such an extent
that the legislature centuries later accepted that principle and facilitated its
enforcement by passing the Fines and Recoveries (Ireland) Act, 1834.[83] The
nineteenth century also saw the culmination of the practice of settling land for
successive generations of the family a practice furthered by the skill and
expertise of conveyancers which had developed over the centuries. This too
was countered by the legislature in the settlements legislation passed later in
the century.[84]

5.032. Apart from these matters, the law has striven to preserve a balance
between the very natural desire of landowners to control the future ownership
and use of their property and the dictates of public policy which require that
owners should be free to deal with their land. If this power of landowners is
restricted, it becomes impossible to raise capital for its development. This
attitude of the law has resulted in the evolution of several rules restricting the
powers of landowners to tie up land in the future. These rules are often, though
somewhat misleadingly, subsumed under the general heading of rules against
remoteness, i.e., they seek to restrict the power of landowners to postpone the
vesting[85] of property beyond a certain time in the future. Four main rules have
come to be recognised, three by the common law and one by statute. The three
established by the common law are the rule against inalienability, the rule in
Whitby v. *Mitchell* and the rule against perpetuities; the rule established by
statute is the rule against accumulations, though this has a very limited
application in Ireland.[86] Each of these rules will now be discussed in turn and it
must be pointed out at the beginning that a distinction has to be made
throughout between the law of the Republic of Ireland and that of Northern
Ireland. The reason is that the Perpetuities Act (N.I.), 1966, which follows
closely the English Perpetuities and Accumulations Act, 1964, has made
considerable changes in the rules against remoteness since 1966 in Northern
Ireland.

A. RULE AGAINST INALIENABILITY

1 *General*

5.033. The so-called rule against inalienability has been a frequent source of
confusion. The reason is that the rule has been invoked in so many quite
distinct situations that it has really become divided into several sub-rules. The
best way to understand the rule is, therefore, to explain the various situations in
which it has been applied.[87]

---

[82]   Para. 4.114, *ante.*
[83]   Para. 4.123, *ante.*
[84]   See ch. 8, *post.*
[85]   For the meaning of "vesting," see para. 5.008, *ante.*
[86]   Para. 5.150, *post.*
[87]   See Morris and Leach, *The Rule Against Perpetuities* (2nd ed., 1962), pp. 307 *et seq.*

2. Land

5.034. We have already discussed this aspect of the rule, which originates in the passing of *Quia Emptores,* 1290.[88] Here the rule states that freehold land must not be conveyed subject to a restriction prohibiting the grantee from alienating the land. To the extent that such a restriction is included in a conveyance of freehold land, it is void as being repugnant to the nature of the estate granted. As we have seen, it is a matter of construction in every case whether the particular restriction offends public policy.[89] Here the rule is usually treated as applying to all freehold estates, though *Quia Emptores* itself was probably confined to the fee simple estate.[90] However, the rule nowadays does not have to be invoked in respect of lesser freehold estates. Wherever such estates are conveyed, a settlement of land within the meaning of the Settled Land Acts is automatically created and under those Acts the tenant for life (again within the meaning of the Acts[91]) is given statutory powers of disposition (including a right to sell, lease and mortgage the land). These statutory powers may not be curtailed by the wording of the conveyance.[92]

3. Trusts

5.035. In the context of trusts, whether of land or personalty, the rule against inalienability is sometimes called the rule against perpetual duration. In a sense this is a more satisfactory label because it does emphasise that this rule is concerned with the *duration* of the gift as opposed to the initial *vesting* of the interest in the beneficiary. The rule must, therefore, be distinguished from the rule against perpetuities.[93] Confusion sometimes arises because the rule against inalienability or perpetual duration has applied the same "perpetuity period" in setting a limit on the duration of certain gifts or on the period when alienation may be restricted. The key to understanding the rule, however, is to remember that its application varies according to the nature of the gift made or the property given.

(i) Charitable Gifts

5.036. It must first be said that the rule against inalienability does not apply to gifts of property to charities, for practical reasons. The very essence of a gift to a charity is that the property can be used only for that charity's purposes and if it were not so restricted the gift would fail to secure for both the donor and donee the very considerable tax advantages which arise from charitable gifts.[94]

It is also important to remember in this context that certain gifts may now be regarded as charitable in both parts of Ireland which are not confined

---

[88] Para. 2.46, *ante.*
[89] Para. 4.054, *ante.*
[90] *Ibid.* and see also para. 2.46, *ante.*
[91] Para. 8.028, *post.*
[92] See generally on settlements ch. 8, *post.*
[93] Discussed at paras. 5.056 *et seq., post.*
[94] On charities, see ch. 9, *post.*

exclusively to charitable purposes.[95] Thus section 49 (1) of the Republic's Charities Act, 1961, provides:

"(1) Where any of the purposes of a gift includes or could be deemed to include both charitable and non-charitable objects, its terms shall be so construed and given effect to as to exclude the non-charitable objects and the purposes shall, accordingly, be treated as charitable."[96]

The effect of so construing a gift in an appropriate case would be, of course, to save the gift if it otherwise infringed the rule against inalienability or perpetual trusts. A provision achieving the same result in similar cases is contained in section 24 of the Charities Act (N.I.), 1964.[97]

(ii) Protective Trusts

5.037. We shall discuss these trusts in a later chapter.[98] The law permits a settlor or testator to dispose of property to a particular person whereby, if that person alienates the property or becomes bankrupt, the property in that event becomes subject to discretionary trusts for the benefit of specified persons (usually the beneficiary and his family). This sort of trust may be created expressly (*i.e.*, by setting out the trusts in detail) or, in Northern Ireland but not in the Republic, by using a shorthand form ("on protective trusts") which incorporates statutory provisions into the trust conveyance.[99] A similar function used to be served with respect to married women by a restraint upon anticipation,[1] preventing a married woman from disposing of her property during her lifetime. Such restraints were abolished in the Republic of Ireland by section 6 of the Married Women's Status Act, 1957, and in Northern Ireland by the Married Women (Restraint upon Anticipation) Act (N.I.), 1952.

(iii) Non-Charitable Purposes

5.038. To the extent that non-charitable purpose trusts are recognised by our law,[2] they are subject to the rule against inalienability or perpetual duration. The general principle is that the property must not be tied to the non-charitable purposes for a period longer than the perpetuity period, which in this case is usually 21 years only. There are usually no "lives in being"[3] because it is a purpose trust; the suggestion in the English case of *Re Dean*,[4] that in the case of a gift for the maintenance of animals the lives of the animals in question may be

---

[95] See further, para. 9.122, *post.*
[96] See also s. 50 of the Republics's 1961 Act, discussed at para. 9.123, *post.*
[97] See *Re McCullough* [1966] N.I. 73. Also Sheridan, "Cy-près in Cyxties: Imperfect Trusts" (1966) 17 N.I.L.Q. 235 and, generally, Keeton and Sheridan, *Modern Law of Charities* (2nd ed., 1971), ch. XVI.
[98] Para. 9.083, *post.*
[99] Trustee Act (N.I.), 1958, s. 34.
[1] *Molony* v. *Harney* [1895] 2 I.R. 169; *Re Lavendar's Policy* [1898] 1 I.R. 175; *Bolster* v. *Bolster* [1916] 1 I.R. 57; *Re Dillon* (1916) 50 I.L.T.R. 144; *Re Dunnill's Trusts* [1926] I.R. 126. See ch. 25, *post.*
[2] See Sheridan, "Trusts for Non-Charitable Purposes" (1953) 17 Conv. 46, "Purpose Trusts and Powers" (1958) 4 A.L.R. 235, "Power to Appoint for a Non-Charitable Purpose: a Duologue or Endacott's Ghost" (1964) 13 De Paul L.Rev. 210. Also para. 9.114, *post.*
[3] Para. 5.067, *post.*
[4] (1889) 41 Ch.D. 552.

counted, is generally discounted by the authorities, including an Irish court.[5] In *Re Kelly*,[6] a gift of £4 a year for the upkeep of the testator's dogs was held by Meredith J. to be a valid annual bequest for each year the dogs lived up to a maximum of 21 years.

5.039. The same principle applies to gifts of property to non-charitable institutions, *e.g.,* unincorporated associations like clubs and societies. Thus, if a capital sum is given to an institution to be devoted to its purposes only, the gift will be void to the extent that the capital sum is tied up for those purposes beyond the perpetuity period. The important point is, however, in every case whether the institution may spend the capital or whether it is tied up. In *Re Fossitt's Estate*[7] a bequest of one-third of the testator's residuary estate was made to the Orange Institution of Ireland "for the upkeep of the Orange Hall, 10 Rutland Square, Dublin." It was held void.[8] On the other hand, in *Re Byrne*,[9] where a gift was made "for the absolute use and benefit of the Jesuit Order of Ireland," it was held valid. The members of the Order could spend the capital at any time and the courts in both parts of Ireland have adopted a similar approach in numerous other cases involving religious bodies.[10] The courts have also upheld similar gifts by construing them not as gifts to the institution as such, but rather as gifts to the individuals making up the institution or society at the time of the gift. If confined to members at the time of the gift and the gift takes effect immediately, there is no problem; if, however, the gift is read as including future members of the institution or society, it would again have to be confined within the perpetuity period.[11]

5.040. Similar problems arise with respect to gifts of income. If property is given to trustees and the income is to be devoted to non-charitable purposes, the gift of income will be void to the extent that it is tied up for those purposes beyond the perpetuity period.[12] However, careful drafting of the disposition may save it. If, instead of providing that the income is to be used indefinitely by an institution for the purposes in question, one provides that the income shall be paid to the institution so long as that purpose is furthered, the gift is valid in law.[13] In this case, the law holds that there is nothing to prevent the institution

---

[5] See *Re Kelly* [1932] I.R. 255 at 260–1 (see *A Casebook on Equity and Trusts in Ireland* (1985), p. 537). The alternative 80 year period introduced for Northern Ireland by the Perpetuities Act (N.I.), 1966, s. 1, does not apply in these cases. S. 16 (4) of the 1966 Act provides: "Nothing in this Act shall affect the operation of the rule of law rendering void for remoteness certain dispositions under which property is limited to be applied for purposes other than the benefit of any person or class of persons in cases where the property may be so applied after the end of the perpetuity period."

[6] *Ibid.*

[7] [1934] I.R. 504.

[8] See also *Stewart* v. *Green* (1870) I.R. 5 Eq. 470; *Morrow* v. *McConville* (1883) 11 L.R.Ir. 236.

[9] [1935] I.R. 782. *Cf. Armstrong* v. *Reeves* (1890) 25 L.R.Ir. 325; *Re Connor* [1960] I.R. 67 (see *A Casebook on Equity and Trusts in Ireland* (1985), p. 536).

[10] *E.g., Re Wilkinson's Trusts* (1887) 19 L.R.Ir. 531; *Re Keogh's Estate* [1945] I.R. 13 (see *A Casebook on Equity and Trusts in Ireland* (1985), p. 534); *Re Rickard* [1954] N.I. 100.

[11] See *Bradshaw* v. *Jackson* (1887) 21 L.R.Ir. 12; *Re Delany's Estate* (1882) 9 L.R.Ir. 226; *Re Lester* [1940] N.I. 92. *Cf. Re Lipinski's Will Trusts* [1976] Ch. 235 and *Re Grant's Will Trusts* [1980] 1 W.L.R. 360.

[12] *Re Hawe* (1959) 93 I.L.T.R. 175. See also *Re Steele* [1976] N.I. 66, espec. at 68 (*per* Murray J.).

[13] See the discussion in the English cases of *Re Chardon* [1928] Ch. 464; *Re Chambers' Will Trusts* [1950] Ch. 267; *Re Wightwick's Will Trusts* [1950] Ch. 260; *Re Dalziel* [1943] Ch. 277. *Cf.* the Irish cases, *Toole* v. *Hamilton* [1901] 1 I.R. 383; *Beresford* v. *Jervis* (1877) 11 I.L.T.R. 128; *cf. Roche* v. *McDermott* [1901] 1 I.R. 394 (capital).

from alienating its determinable interest in the income and the gift remains valid despite the fact that it may be determined later.[14] The only problem that exists is that in Northern Ireland the gift could cease to be determinable under section 13 (3) (*b*) of the Perpetuities Act (N.I.), 1966, which provides that, where a disposition creates a possibility of a resulting trust[15] on the determination of determinable interest in property,[16] the possibility of a resulting trust "shall cease to exist at the end of the perpetuity period, and accordingly the . . . interest in question shall cease to be determinable."

5.041. Finally, it should be noted that a special legislative provision exists in the Republic of Ireland to cover one of the most common cases of dispositions for non-charitable purposes. Section 50 of the Charities Act, 1961, provides:

"(1) Every gift made after the commencement of this Act for the provision, maintenance or improvement of a tomb, vault or grave or of a tombstone or any other memorial to a deceased person or deceased persons which would not otherwise be charitable shall, to the extent provided by this section, be a charitable gift.

(2) Such a gift shall be charitable so far as it does not exceed:
 (*a*) in the case of a gift of income only, sixty pounds a year,
 (*b*) in any other case, one thousand pounds in amount or value."[17]

By treating such a gift as charitable, this section, within the limits it sets, will save the gift from being held void as against the rule against inalienability. No similar provision exists in Northern Ireland[18] nor, indeed, in England.

B. Rule in Whitby *v.* Mitchell

5.042. The rule in *Whitby* v. *Mitchell*,[19] though ascribed to a case decided at the end of the nineteenth century, is a rule of much greater antiquity. Indeed, it is often referred to as the old rule against perpetuities, to be distinguished from the modern rule against perpetuities discussed in the next section of this chapter. It is also, rather more misleadingly, sometimes referred to as the rule

See also Gray, 15 H.L.R. 509; Sweet, 33 L.Q.R. 236 and 357; Hart, 53 L.Q.R. 24; Albery, 54 L.Q.R. 258; Davies, 25 Conv. 56.

[14] The English cases cited in the previous footnote also held that the fact that the capital sum producing the income was tied up in the meantime was immaterial, because the institution to which the income was given could at any time join with those entitled on determination of the trust and put an end to the trust. This principle, known as the rule in *Saunders* v. *Vautier*, is discussed at para. 10.088, *post*.

[15] Defined para. 9.055, *post*.

[16] Other than a possibility of reverter on the determination of a determinable fee simple in land, which is covered by s. 13 (3) (*a*).

[17] See *Re Connor* [1960] I.R. 67 (see *A Casebook on Equity and Trusts in Ireland* (1985), p. 536); see also *Beresford* v. *Jervis* (1877) 11 I.L.T.R. 128; *Toole* v. *Hamilton* [1901] 1 I.R. 383; *Re O'Meara's Will Trusts* (1939) 73 I.L.T.R. 22.

[18] Though in a particular case it may be argued that the purposes in question are wide enough that the property *could* all be used for charitable purposes, etc., so as to come within s. 24 of the Charities Act (N.I.), 1964. S. 24 corresponds more closely to s. 49 of the Republic's 1961 Act (see para. 5.036, *ante*), but its wording is different. However, it is debatable whether its scope is any wider than s. 49. See Lowry J. in *Re McCullough* [1966] N.I. 73 and Sheridan, (1966) 17 N.I.L.Q. 235.

[19] (1890) 44 Ch.D. 85.

against double possibilities, a description perpetuated in the Perpetuities Act (N.I.), 1966.[20]

1. *Origin of the Rule*

5.043. In early common law, it seems that there were several rules included under the general rubric of a so-called rule against double possibilities or against a possibility upon a possibility.[21] One early form of the rule was to the effect that a disposition, which would take effect on some remote or unlikely contingency, was void.[22] This rather vague formulation of the rule, however, was rejected by the House of Lords in the Irish case of *Cole* v. *Sewell*.[23] Another form of the rule against double possibilities was a rule that a disposition would be void if it depended upon more than one possibility or contingency.[24] In this form, too, the general view of the authorities has been to discredit the rule.[25] One leading author has concluded on the controversy surrounding the rule:

> "The maxim against double possibilities, when rightly viewed, is nothing worse than a somewhat clumsy restriction upon the remoteness of legal limitations; and some of the criticisms which have been passed upon it are much more foolish than the maxim itself."[26]

The fact remains that the courts frequently uphold gifts which involve double possibilities in one form or another. A gift "to the first son of A who attains the age of 21" is valid under all rules against remoteness, yet it involves the possibility that, first, A may have no son and, second, even if he has a son, that son may not reach the age of 21.

5.044. This brings us to the third form that the rule against double possibilities was said to take, the rule in *Whitby* v. *Mitchell*. There is no doubt that this rule was recognised by English land law[27] and probably by Irish land law. The slight doubt exists because there is very little authority on the rule in Ireland, though what authority there is seems to support its application here.[28]

The generally accepted view now seems to be that the rule in *Whitby* v.

---

[20] S. 15.

[21] See Challis, *Law of Real Property* (3rd ed.), pp. 116–8 and 215–7; Morris and Leach, *The Rule Against Perpetuities* (2nd ed.), ch. 10; Sweet, "Rule in *Whitby* v. *Mitchell*" (1910) 26 L.Q.R. 3 and (1911) 12 Col.L.Rev. 199, "Limitation of land to Unborn Generations" (1913) 29 L.Q.R. 304 and "Double Possibilities" (1914) 30 L.Q.R. 353; Gray, "*Whitby* v. *Mitchell*" (1913) 29 L.Q.R. 26.

[22] Usually based on *Cholmley's Case* (1597) 2 Co.Rep. 50a (see especially 51a and b). See also *Child* v. *Baylie* (1623) Cro.Jac. 459.

[23] (1848) 2 H.L.C. 186 (see *A Casebook on Irish Land Law* (1984), p. 246); see also (1843) 4 Dr. & War. 1 at 28–9 (*per* Sugden L.C.).

[24] Usually based on the *Rector of Chedington's Case* (1598) 1 Co.Rep. 148b (especially at 156b). See also *Lord Stafford's Case* (1609) 8 Co.Rep. 73a at 75a; *Mayor and Commonalty of London* v. *Alford* (1640) Cro.Car. 576.

[25] See especially Lord Nottingham's attack in the *Duke of Norfolk's Case* (1681) 3 Cha.Ca. 1 at 29. See also the discussion in *Whitby* v. *Mitchell* itself, in *Re Ashford* [1905] 1 Ch. 535 at 543 (*per* Farwell J.) and *Re Nash* [1910] 1 Ch. 1 at 10 (*per* Farwell L.J.).

[26] Challis, *Law of Real Property* (3rd ed.), p. 117.

[27] *Re Ashforth* [1905] 1 Ch. 535; *Re Nash* [1910] 1 Ch. 1.

[28] See *Peyton* v. *Lambert* (1858) 8 I.C.L.R. 485 (see *A Casebook on Irish Land Law* (1984), p. 253); *Cole* v. *Sewell* (1848) 2 H.L.C. 186 (see *ibid*., p. 246). Implied recognition may also be obtained from the fact that the rule was abolished in Northern Ireland by s. 15 of the Perpetuities Act (N.I.), 1966. Though, in the light of the above discussion, note that the marginal note to s. 15 refers to "Abolition of the double possibility rule"! The substantive provisions of the section, however, make it clear that it is dealing with what is generally accepted as being more accurately described as the rule in *Whitby* v. *Mitchell*. S. 15 follows s. 161 of the English Law of Property Act, 1925, in making this reference.

Mitchell should not necessarily be regarded as part of the so-called rule against double possibilities.[29]

2. *General Operation of the Rule*

5.045. The rule is usually stated as follows: where an interest in land is conveyed or given to an unborn person, any remainder over to that unborn person's issue and any subsequent limitations are void. For example, suppose land is conveyed "to A for life, remainder to his son for life, remainder to his son's children in fee simple." If at the date of operation of the conveyance A has no son, the remainder to A's son's children is void because it is a violation of the rule in *Whitby* v. *Mitchell*.

5.046. The most likely explanation for the early common law's establishment of such a rule is that it was part of the courts' policy to prevent settlors and testators creating what would be in effect unbarrable entails.[30] We have already seen how the courts facilitated the use of legal fictions to prevent the standard form of fee tail conveyance from guaranteeing descent to the heirs. The rule in *Whitby* v. *Mitchell* prevented settlors from obtaining largely the same result by a succession of life estates, *e.g.,* to A for life, remainder to his son for life, remainder to his son's son for life, and so on. It is true that nowadays the modern rule against perpetuities will prevent this, but this developed too late to meet the need that arose centuries ago.

3. *Elements of the Rule*

(i) **Property**

5.047. Probably due to its connection with the courts' attitude to successive interests in land, the rule in *Whitby* v. *Mitchell* is confined to dispositions of land. It does not apply to dispositions of personalty[31] and this is a major difference from the modern rule against perpetuities. It has also been argued that the rule, certainly as it originally developed, did not apply to executory future interests, whether legal or equitable.[32] It was the creation of these interests, of course, which really brought about the development of the modern rule against perpetuities, so there may be something to the point that the rule in *Whitby* v. *Mitchell* did not apply to executory interests.

(ii) **Successive Gifts to Unborn Persons**

5.048. The rule is applied strictly according to its terms so that a limitation will fail only if it is to an unborn person *and* it follows upon a prior gift also to an unborn person. This means, of course, that validity to some extent depends upon the form rather than the substance of a conveyance. For example, one

---

[29] See the English authorities cited in fn. 27, *supra.*

[30] See para. 4.141, *ante.*

[31] Though English courts have applied it to trusts for sale of land, under which the land is treated in equity as personalty from the date of execution of the trust, see paras. 3.100, *ante* and 8.043, *post. Re Bullock's Will Trusts* [1915] 1 Ch. 493; *Re Garnham* [1916] 2 Ch. 413.

[32] See Megarry and Wade, *The Law of Real Property* (5th ed., 1984), p. 1188; *cf.* Challis, *The Law of Real Property* (3rd ed.), p. 216.

may compare a disposition "to A for life, remainder to A's son for life, remainder to his son's son for life" with a disposition "to A for life, remainder to A's grandson." If in both cases A had no son at the date of the disposition, the former infringes the rule while the latter does not because it is not preceded by a prior limitation to an unborn person.[33] Whether the latter would infringe the rule against perpetuities is another matter.[34]

5.049. Two further points may be noted in this connection. First, it seems that a slight exception to the rule is allowed where the subsequent gift to an unborn person is to the issue of holders of prior gifts, one of whom may also be unborn. For example, a disposition may be made "to A for life, remainder to his wife for life, remainder to his son in fee simple." If A is unmarried at the date of the disposition, it is possible that he may subsequently marry someone unborn at that date, so that the gift to his unborn son would follow a gift to that son's mother who was also unborn at the date of the disposition. It now seems to be settled in England that the rule would not invalidate the gift to the unborn son in such a case.[35] Secondly, there is no question of a "wait and see" principle operating in application of the rule. If there is a possibility of the rule being infringed, however remote, the offending limitation is void *ab initio*. In this respect, the rule is like the modern rule against perpetuities.[36]

(iii) Vested Remainders Over

5.050. It is a peculiarity of the rule that it also invalidates any remainders over after the invalid remainders to unborn persons, even though those remainders over are vested. Thus in a disposition "to A for life, remainder to his son (unborn) for life, remainder to his son's son for life, remainder to B (born) in fee simple," the remainder to B is void as well as the remainder to A's grandson, despite the fact that the remainder to B is vested because he is alive at the date of the disposition.[37] Even the modern rule against perpetuities was never as harsh as this.[38]

(iv) Estates Tail

5.051. The rule does not apply to the interest taken by a child under a disposition to its parent in fee tail because the words of limitation "in fee tail" do not create a limitation or gift. A disposition "to A (a bachelor who is alive) for life, remainder to his first son in fee tail" will have the result that a child of the first son may ultimately inherit unless the first son has barred the entail. Such a disposition is not invalidated by the rule in *Whitby* v. *Mitchell*.

[33] *Ward* v. *Van der Loeff* [1924] A.C. 653.
[34] The answer would vary according to whether the "common law" rule applicable in the Republic were invoked or the rule amended by the Perpetuities Act (N.I.), 1966, were invoked, see para. 5.060 *et seq.*, *post*.
[35] *Re Bullock's Will Trusts* [1915] 1 Ch. 493. *Re Garnham* [1916] 2 Ch. 413. *Cf. Re Parks' Settlement* [1914] 1 Ch. 595.
[36] Though a "wait and see" principle has now been introduced in Northern Ireland by the Perpetuities Act (N.I.), 1966, see para. 5.062, *post*.
[37] *Brudenell* v. *Elwes* (1801) 1 East 422; *Re Mortimer* [1905] 2 Ch. 502.
[38] Para. 5.091, *post*.

4. *Cy-Près Doctrine*

5.052. The doctrine of *cy-près* was devised by the courts because it was thought that the rule in *Whitby* v. *Mitchell* sometimes operated too harshly. The theory behind the principle of *cy-près* is that, if by construing the terms of a disposition slightly differently the courts can give effect to a testator's intention as nearly as possible (*cy-près*), the courts will adopt that construction. In this respect the doctrine is another illustration of the courts' overriding desire to give effect to the testator's intention in the construction of wills.[39] In relation to the rule in *Whitby* v. *Mitchell,* the operation of the *cy-près* doctrine may be stated as follows: where there is a disposition of land by will to an unborn person for life, with remainder to his children successively in tail or to his issue in a perpetual succession of life estates (which remainder would otherwise be void as infringing the rule in *Whitby* v. *Mitchell*), the court in order to give effect to the testator's intention will construe the disposition as one to the unborn person in fee tail instead of for life.[40] For example, in a conveyance "to A for life, remainder to his eldest son for life, remainder to that son's first and other sons successively in tail male," the remainder to the eldest and other grandsons in tail male infringes the rule in *Whitby* v. *Mitchell,* if A is unmarried. However, there would be no infringement if that remainder were deleted and the remainder to A's eldest son read "in tail male" instead of "for life." This construction would also approximate to the testator's intention in the sense that, if the eldest son did not bar his entail, the land would descend to his eldest son in tail male. Even if he did bar the entail, the eldest son would probably resettle the property so as to benefit his family, and this would always be closer to the testator's intention than the result of a strict application of the rule in *Whitby* v. *Mitchell, i.e.,* giving the eldest son a life estate only and cutting off his successors entirely.

5.053. It is important, however, to note the limitations of the *cy-près* doctrine. First, since it stems from the courts' more liberal approach to the interpretation of wills, it does not apply to deeds. Secondly, like the rule in *Whitby* v. *Mitchell* itself, it is confined to dispositions of land[40a]; apart from that reason, the doctrine required the use of entailed estates and personalty cannot be entailed in Ireland. Thirdly, the doctrine *ex hypothesi* will not be invoked where this would defeat the intention of the testator by, *e.g.,* excluding persons intended to take the property or *vice versa.* Thus, to take the example given above, if the second remainder had been given simply to the eldest son's first son in tail male, *i.e.,* excluding the other sons, construing the first remainder as one to the eldest son in tail male would defeat the testator's intention. If the first son predeceased his father, under the ordinary rules of succession to a tail

---

[39] Para. 4.031, *ante* and 14.36, *post.*
[40] *Peyton* v. *Lambert* (1858) 8 I.C.L.R. 485 (see *A Casebook on Irish Land Law* (1984), p. 253); *East* v. *Twyford* (1853) 4 H.L.C. 517; *Parfitt* v. *Hember* (1867) L.R. 4 Eq. 443.
[40a] In *Bank of Ireland* v. *Goulding* (1975) Unrep. (Sup. Ct., R.I.), the Republic's Supreme Court (Griffin, Budd and Henchy JJ.; O'Higgins C.J. and Walsh J. dissenting) (affirming Kenny J.) upheld the view that the *cy-pres* doctrine is confined to dispositions of land and does not, therefore, apply to personalty.

male the next eldest son would succeed the father, thereby letting in sons other than the first one. It would be different, however, if in the second remainder the word "eldest" were substituted for "first." Similarly, if the second remainder were given to the eldest son's sons in tail general, the first remainder could not be construed as to the eldest son in tail general, because a tail general can be succeeded to by daughters and they were not included by the testator in the second remainder. Again, it would be different in this case if the word "issue" were substituted for "sons" in the second remainder.

5. *Legislative Reform*

5.054. The rule in *Whitby* v. *Mitchell* remains in full force in the Republic of Ireland, at least to the extent that it has ever been applied in Ireland.[41] However, in Northern Ireland it has been abolished, with respect to instruments taking effect after the passing of the Act, by section 15 of the Perpetuities Act (N.I.), 1966, but "without prejudice to the rule against perpetuities."[42] This step had been taken in England in the Law of Property Act, 1925.[43] The reason for this legislative action was that it was considered that the rule had outlived its usefulness. Any need for restriction in the cases covered by the rule would be met by the more modern rule against perpetuities. Indeed, one further reason for abrogating the rule in *Whitby* v. *Mitchell* was that the rule sometimes invalidated gifts which were invalid under the rule against perpetuities. Thus consider a disposition "to A (unmarried) for life, remainder to his first born son for life, remainder to that son's first born son to be born within 21 years of A's death." As was pointed out in *Whitby* v. *Mitchell* itself,[44] the condition attached to the second remainder ensured that there was no infringement of the rule against perpetuities,[45] yet it did involve a gift to the unborn child of an unborn person to whom was given a prior life interest. Thus the disposition, though not infringing the rule against perpetuities, was invalid under the rule in *Whitby* v. *Mitchell*.

5.055. Section 15 does not mention the *cy-près* doctrine, but it is arguable that its operation has ceased in Northern Ireland along with the rule which gave rise to its application by the courts in the first place. However, it has been suggested in England that the repeal of the rule may not have prevented an appeal to the doctrine if, *e.g.*, this would save gifts from the rule against perpetuities.[46]

---

[41] See para. 5.044, *ante*.
[42] The marginal note to s. 15 refers to "Abolition of the double possibility rule," but for the reasons given above (para. 5.044, fn. 28) it is doubtful if the section covers anything more than the rule in *Whitby* v. *Mitchell*. See, however, on the English equivalent, s. 161 of the Law of Property Act, 1925, *Re Leigh's Marriage Settlement* [1952] 2 All E.R. 57. *Cf. Honywood* v. *Honywood* (1905) 92 L.T. 814, especially at 815–6 (*per* Lord Davey).
[43] S. 161.
[44] (1889) 42 Ch.D. 494 at 500–1 (*per* Kay J.).
[45] See para. 5.061, *post*.
[46] See Megarry, (1939) 55 L.Q.R. 422.

C. Rule Against Perpetuities

1. *General*

5.056. The modern rule against perpetuities was devised by the courts to cope with the wholesale evasion of the common law contingent remainder rules which was made possible by conveying land to uses.[47] This matter was made an even greater problem from the common law's point of view by the passing of the Statute of Uses because, as we have seen, the one lasting consequence of that statute was that springing and shifting uses, which could operate to create equitable interests only before the Statute, could after the Statute operate to create legal executory interests.[48]

5.057. The rule lays down limits upon a grantor's power to postpone the "vesting" of the ownership of his property in the future. Any future interest in property, whether real or personal, must nowadays vest within the perpetuity period, as prescribed by the courts or by statute. The period eventually settled by the courts was that of a life or lives in being, plus a further period of 21 years (allowing also for periods of gestation).[49] The rule thus came to be applicable to any kind of property, real or personal, legal or equitable and settled *inter vivos* or by will. Each of the various elements of the rule will be discussed in the next few pages, but first a point already mentioned must be reiterated. Until the twentieth century the rule against perpetuities was developed entirely by the courts and it has been only comparatively recently that legislatures have intervened. Some changes were introduced in England by the Law of Property Act, 1925,[50] but these, of course, did not apply to either part of Ireland. A comprehensive review of the operation of the rule was undertaken some 30 years later by the English Law Reform Committee and its Fourth Report in 1956[51] resulted in the passing of the English Perpetuities and Accumulations Act, 1964.[52] No equivalent of this Act has as yet been passed in the Republic of Ireland, but the Perpetuities Act (N.I.), 1966, was modelled on the English 1964 Act.[53] The position is, therefore, that in the Republic of Ireland

[47] Para. 5.018, *ante*.

[48] Paras. 3.020 and 5.019, *ante*.

[49] See on the history of the rule, Morris and Leach, *The Rule Against Perpetuities* (2nd ed., 1962), ch. 1; see also Gray, *Rule Against Perpetuities* (4th ed., 1942), Maudsley, *The Modern Law of Perpetuities* (1979). Also *Duke of Norfolk's Case* (1681) 3 Ch.Ca. 1; *Thellusson* v. *Woodford* (1805) 11 Ves. 112; *Cadell* v. *Palmer* (1833) 1 Cl. & F. 372; *Lord Dungannon* v. *Smith* (1846) 12 Cl. & F. 546 (on appeal from Ireland, *sub nom. Ker* v. *Lord Dungannon* (1841) 1 Dr. & War. 509).

[50] Ss. 162–3.

[51] Cmnd. 18. Note also the campaigning of the late Professor Barton Leach of Harvard Law School: "Perpetuities in a Nutshell" (1938) 51 H.L.R. 638; "Perpetuities in Perspective: Ending the Rule's Reign of Terror" (1952) 65 H.L.R. 721; "Perpetuities: Staying the Slaughter of Innocents" (1952) 58 L.Q.R. 35; "Perpetuities Legislation: Massachusetts Style" (1954) 67 H.L.R. 1349; "Perpetuities Reform by Legislation" (1954) 70 L.Q.R. 478; (1957) 70 H.L.R. 1411; "Perpetuities: New Absurdity. Judicial and Statutory Corrections" (1960) 73 H.L.R. 1318; "Perpetuities Legislation: Hail, Pennsylvania!" (1960) 108 U.Penn. L.Rev. 1124; (with Logan) "Perpetuities: Standard Saving Clause to Avoid Violations of Rule" (1961) 74 H.L.R. 1141; "Perpetuities: New Hampshire Defertilises the Octogenarians" (1963) 77 M.L.R. 279; "Perpetuities Reform: London Proposes, Perth Disposes" (1963) 6 A.L.R. 11.

[52] See also the earlier Western Australian Law Reform (Property, Perpetuities and Succession) Act, 1962. See Maudsley, *op. cit.*; Morris and Leach, *op. cit.*, 1964 Supp.; Morris and Wade, "Perpetuities Reform at Last" (1964) 80 L.Q.R. 486.

[53] See Gibson, "Perpetuities Act (N.I.), 1966" (1966) 17 N.I.L.Q. 30; also *Survey of the Land Law of Northern Ireland* (1971), ch. 12.

the rule still operates entirely in accordance with the principles developed by the courts, while in Northern Ireland this remains true generally only with respect to instruments taking effect prior to the passing of the 1966 Act.[54] In the ensuing discussion this distinction in the operation of the rule in Ireland since 1966 will be drawn in most sections, since the Northern Ireland 1966 Act, like the English 1964 Act, affects most of the important and fundamental principles evolved by the courts.

2. *Elements of the Rule*

(i) **Vesting**

5.058. The essential requirement of the rule is that a future interest in property must vest in the donee within the perpetuity period. In this context vesting is sufficient if it is vesting *in interest*; the rule does not require that there should be vesting *in possession*.[55] In other words, it is sufficient that the donee is ascertained, his precise share of the property is determined and he is ready to take it, subject only to prior interests. The fact that the donee may not get possession of the property until some date outside the period does not invalidate the gift.

5.059. The most common reason for a gift being held void under the rule is that it is subjected to some contingency which may not be satisfied within the period laid down by the rule. It is important, therefore, to mention once again the approach adopted frequently by the courts in construing conditions attached to gifts. What appears on a first reading to be a contingent gift may instead be construed as a vested gift liable to be divested on failure to comply with what is regarded as a condition subsequent. Thus in *McGredy* v. *C.I.R.*[56] a testator left property to be held in trust "until my said son shall attain the age of 25 years" and then the residue was to be paid to that son "after my said son shall attain that age." The question arose for income tax purposes whether, prior to his attaining 25, the son had a immediate vested interest in the residue. The Northern Ireland Court of Appeal held that, although prima facie he had a contingent remainder only (contingent upon his attaining 25 years), it was a settled rule of construction that, where there is a gift over after a primary gift in the event of the donee not attaining a specified age, the primary gift will be construed so as to confer a vested interest on the donee liable to be divested in the event of death under that age.[57] This rule applies to property of any kind left by will and, being a rule of construction, may be negatived by the terms of the particular will. However, the Northern Ireland court pointed out that, though the justification often given for the rule of construction is that the existence of the gift over shows that the donee of the primary gift was intended to take all except that which was given to the person entitled to the gift over, the

---

[54] 1966 Act, s. 16 (5). The Act was passed on March 24, 1966.
[55] See on this distinction, para. 5.008, *ante*; *Craig* v. *Stacey* (1794) Ir.Term Rep. 249.
[56] [1951] N.I. 155. See also the cases cited in fn. 16, para. 5.010, *ante*.
[57] See the House of Lords speeches in *Phipps* v. *Ackers* (1842) 9 Cl. & F. 583.

rule will not nowadays be negatived merely by the fact that in a particular case there is some disparity between the primary gift and the gift over. Black L.J. commented:

> "The rule, though so firmly settled and repeated in almost identical terms in all the text books, can hardly fail to strike one as a somewhat artificial and technical rule involving, to use Lord Selbourne's words, a rather violent and unnatural construction of words of contingency. . . . But whatever doubts one may have about the soundness of the reasoning on which the rule has been sought to be justified, there can be no doubt that the rule itself, as now enunciated in all the text books, must, for good or for evil, be accepted as a settled rule of construction binding on our courts"[58]

(ii) Wait and See

(a) At Common Law

5.060. One fundamental principle of the rule against perpetuities as evolved by the courts was that there could be no "wait and see" approach[59] to its application to a particular disposition. Each gift had to be regarded at the time of operation of the instrument concerned and, at that point in time, the *possibilities*,[60] not the probabilities and certainly not the actual events which later occurred, had to be taken into account. If there was the slightest possibility that a gift might vest outside the period it was *void ab initio*. In England, this was carried to the extreme of disregarding physical impossibilities, resulting in what Professor Barton Leach castigated as the "fertile octogenarian" and "precocious toddler" cases.[61] For example, a gift "to the first son of A to become a solicitor" would be void under this principle if A were alive and had no son a solicitor at the time of the gift. Any sons A might have might die without becoming a solicitor and A might have a further son (not a life in being at the time of the gift), who might become a solicitor more than 21 years after the death of the lives in being (A and any other sons). The fact that A was a woman well past the age of child-bearing, which was provable as a medical fact, was disregarded by the courts, at least in England.[62] However, in the Republic of Ireland, Gavan Duffy J. (albeit *obiter*) in *Exham v. Beamish*[63] had no doubts as to the absurdity of this aspect of the rule and indicated that he would favour the disregard of English authorities on the point and would be willing to admit evidence, if offered, that a particular woman was past child-

---

[58] *Op. cit.*, pp. 161–2. *Cf.* Kenny J. in *Re Murphy's Estate* [1964] I.R. 308 (see *A Casebook on Irish Land Law* (1984), p. 242), para. 5.010, *ante*.

[59] See para. 5.049, *ante*.

[60] *Re McConnell* [1956] N.I. 151, especially at 155 (*per* Black L.J.); *Re Fallon* [1956] I.R. 286; *Re Adam's Estate* [1965] I.R. 57.

[61] See articles cited in fn. 51, para. 5.057, *supra*.

[62] *Re Dawson* (1888) 39 Ch.D. 155; *Ward v. Van der Loeff* [1924] A.C. 653. *Cf. Re Gaite's Will Trusts* [1949] 1 All E.R. 459, where the court did observe a "legal" impossibility, namely that no legitimate child could be born to a person under the age of 16, since s. 1 of the Age of Marriage Act, 1929, invalidated any marriage by such a person.

[63] [1939] I.R. 336 (see *A Casebook on Irish Land Law* (1984), p. 263).

bearing.[64] There has been no further authority on what the attitude of courts in the Republic is on this point. As far as Northern Ireland is concerned, the English position probably applied prior to 1966, but the matter has become academic since the passing of the Perpetuities Act (N.I.), 1966, as we shall see in a moment.

5.061. Even the English courts recognised two exceptions to the principle against a "wait and see" approach. These exceptions were recognised in the cases of alternative contingencies and powers of appointment.[65] It was also the case that an express saving clause could be inserted in the instrument to ensure that vesting of all gifts took place within the perpetuity period. Thus, in the example given above, the gift to the first son of A would have been saved by insertion of a clause such as "provided that no son may take unless he qualifies as a solicitor within 21 years of A's death." It seems that such a clause must be fairly explicit; a general saving clause, such as one stating that vesting shall be postponed "only so far as the rules of law and equity will permit," will not suffice.[66] It has now become common in settlements to include a clause which gives a longer span to the gifts than would normally occur, but which complies with the rule. Any lives may be selected during which the interests must vest. So a clause providing that the gifts created by the instrument shall continue "during the lives of the issue now living of His Britannic Majesty George V and for 21 years after the death of the survivor of such issue" has the result that the gifts continue during the lives of all the issue (who are many) of George V and for 21 years after the death of the last survivor. Such a clause is now common in settlements and deeds creating discretionary trusts made by persons living in the Republic of Ireland!

(b) *Perpetuities Act (N.I.), 1966*

5.062. This Act radically alters the operation of the rule against perpetuities in Northern Ireland. Indeed, it overturns the basic principle which still operates in the Republic, namely, that there can be no "wait and see" approach to applying the rule to particular dispositions (apart from a few cases like powers of appointment). With respect to instruments taking effect in Northern Ireland after 24th March 1966,[67] section 3 (1) of the 1966 Act provides:

> "Where . . . a disposition would be void on the ground that the interest disposed of might not become vested until too remote a time, the disposition shall be treated, until such time, if any, as it becomes established that the vesting must occur, if at all, after the end of the perpetuity period, as if the disposition were not subject to the rule against perpetuities. . . ."[68]

---

[64] *Ibid.*, pp. 347–51. Note also the decision of Dixon J. in *Re Tennant's Settlement* [1959] Ir.Jur.Rep. 76.

[65] Discussed at paras. 5.092 and 5.118, *post.*

[66] *Portman* v. *Viscount Portman* [1922] 2 A.C. 473. *Cf. Christie* v. *Gosling* (1866) L.R. 1 H.L. 279. Leach and Logan, "Perpetuities: Standard Saving Clause to Avoid Violations of Rule" (1961) 74 H.L.R. 1141.

[67] S. 16 (5).

[68] S. 3 (2) and (3) makes similar provisions for general powers of appointment which would otherwise be held

The important limitation on the application of this provision which must be appreciated is that the "wait and see" principle can be applied only to dispositions which would be void under the common law, *i.e.*, under the rule as it applied in Northern Ireland prior to 1966 and still applies in the Republic. Thus, strictly according to the 1966 Act, one should first apply the pre-1966 rule to the disposition in question and invoke the 1966 Act only if the disposition fails to comply with that rule. In this sense the common law rule against perpetuities has not been displaced in Northern Ireland by the 1966 Act, rather it has been supplemented by the introduction of more "equitable" principles. The practical significance of these principles, however, is enormous.

5.063. From what has been said about the 1966 Act's introduction of the "wait and see" principle, it is clear, as the wording itself implies, that the principle cannot operate where the disposition could not possibly take effect within the perpetuity period. Such a disposition would be void under the common law and the 1966 Act does not change that; it is clear from the beginning that the disposition can take effect only outside the period and there is no point in waiting to see if it will in fact take effect within the period. For example, one may compare the following two dispositions: (1) a devise "to the first son of A to become a solicitor who is born after the testator's death and who survives all lives in being at that date by 25 years"; (2) a devise simply "to the first son of A to become a solicitor." Both these dispositions would be void at common law[69] if A were still alive at the testator's death, but the second only could be saved by the 1966 Act. The first could not be saved for the reason that it is clear from the beginning that there is no possibility of the vesting occurring within the period; the gift can vest only more than 21 years after the death of the lives in being at the testator's death.[70] As regards the second disposition, however, it is not clear at the outset that the vesting could not occur within the period. It is quite possible that a son of A will become a solicitor in A's life-time or at least within 21 years of A's death. The gift would be void at common law because it is not certain that it would so vest within the perpetuity period and one is not allowed to "wait and see," so it would be permissible to invoke the 1966 Act and to "wait and see." If in fact it turns out that vesting does take place within the period, then the disposition is saved under the Act's provisions. Once events take place which indicate that there is no further possibility of such a vesting (*e.g.*, all the lives in being have been dead for over 21 years and the only survivor is a son born after the testator's death who is not a solicitor), the disposition fails.

5.064. Two further points remain to be mentioned with respect to the 1966

---

void because they might not become *exercisable* until too remote a time (see para. 5.117, *post*) and for other powers, options and rights that would be void because they might be *exercised* at too remote a time (see para. 5.133, *post*).

[69] See para. 5.060, *ante*.

[70] Nor would this disposition be saved by another of the 1966 Act's provisions, namely that introducing an "age-reduction" principle, since the condition to be satisfied here is not the attaining of a specified "age" but the survival for a term of years after a specified event. See para. 5.090, *post*.

Act's introduction of the "wait and see" principle in Northern Ireland. Section 3 (1) states that it applies only to dispositions which would be void "apart from the provisions of this section and sections 4 and 5." Sections 4 and 5 we shall discuss later. They introduce further provisions for saving gifts, *e.g.*, by reducing an age to be attained by a beneficiary[71] or excluding members of a class of beneficiaries.[72] The effect of the clause in section 3 (1), just quoted, is to determine the order in which the various saving provisions contained in the 1966 Act should be applied to a particular disposition. The "wait and see" principle should be applied first and the other provisions, such as age-reduction, should be applied only if it turns out that "wait and see" will still not save the gift in question. The theory behind the Act seems to be that there should be the minimum interference with the terms of the settlor's disposition. The "wait and see" principle at least provides the opportunity for the disposition to take effect precisely in accordance with the terms laid down by its draftsman. The other principles, such as age-reduction or class-exclusion, necessarily involve changing the terms of the disposition as originally drafted and to that extent defeat the settlor's intention.

5.065. Section 3 (1) of the 1966 Act also contains an important provision to safeguard persons who might exercise powers while the "wait and see" period is still running. In many cases the disposition concerned will relate to beneficial interests held under a trust and, as we shall see later,[73] trustees often have powers to use trust income for the maintenance of beneficiaries or to use trust capital by way of advancement, even though those beneficiaries still have to comply with contingencies or conditions before their interests under the trust become vested. The question might arise as to what is the position if trustees exercise such powers with respect to a disposition saved only by the "wait and see" principle, and it later turns out after the exercise of the powers that the disposition becomes void because the vesting does not take place within the perpetuity period. Section 3 (1) provides that, where it becomes established after "wait and see" that a disposition is void, this "shall not affect the validity of anything previously done in relation to the interest disposed of by way of advancement, application of intermediate income or otherwise."[74] This serves to emphasise the wide-ranging nature of trustees' powers of maintenance and advancement. Much of the trust property, both capital and income, could be properly applied for the benefit of beneficiaries who later turn out not to be entitled to a penny when the validity of the trust is finally determined; this may have serious financial consequences for those who then become entitled to the trust property.[75]

5.066. Finally, it should be noted that the 1966 Act attempts to get rid of some of the absurd features of the rule which we have already mentioned. In

---

[71] Para. 5.089, *post.*
[72] Para. 5.088, *post.*
[73] Ch. 10, *post.*
[74] See also s. 4 (5).
[75] See generally paras. 10.042–9, *post.*

particular it deals with the "fertile octogenarian" and "precocious toddler" cases.[76] This it does by introducing statutory presumptions as to "future parenthood." Section 2 (1) of the Act provides:

"Where in any proceedings there arises on the rule against perpetuities a question which turns on the ability of a person to have a child at some future time, then—
  (a) subject to paragraph (b), it shall be presumed that a male can have a child at the age of fourteen years or over, but not under that age, and that a female can have a child at the age of twelve years or over, but not under that age or over the age of fifty-five years; but
  (b) in the case of a living person evidence may be given to show that he or she will or will not be able to have a child at the time in question."

Section 2 (3) provides that once a question of this nature is decided in accordance with the statutory presumptions (and it must be emphasised that section 2 (1) clearly indicates that the presumptions are rebuttable, e.g., by medical evidence), that decision will govern the matter in any future proceedings concerning the application of the rule against perpetuities to the disposition in question.[77] However, section 2 (4) provides that the references to "having a child" extend to having a child "by adoption, legitimation or other means." This counters the usual presumption of the law confining references to children to naturally born and legitimate children.[77a] It also opens the way for rather more cases to occur which would negate the statutory presumptions than one would expect to result from "freak" births. Section 2 (2), therefore, assumes all the more signifiance in providing:

"Where any such question is decided by treating a person as unable to have a child at a particular time, and he or she does so, the High Court may on an application made to it make such order as it thinks fit for placing the persons interested in the property comprised in the disposition, so far as may be just, in the position they would have held if the question had not been so decided."

The High Court is clearly given a very wide discretion by this provision and it is by no means certain that a person is going to obtain full restoration of property lost as a result of an earlier decision. In each case due weight must be given to the claims of persons who may have acted in good faith over a considerable period of time on the basis of that decision. It remains to be seen how the courts of Northern Ireland will exercise this discretion.

---

[76] Para. 5.060, ante.

[77] S. 2 (5) provides that these provisions apply to "any question as to the right of beneficiaries to put an end to accumulations of income under any disposition as they apply to any question arising on the rule against perpetuities." Beneficiaries have this right under the rule in Saunders v. Vautier, see Re Deloitte [1926] Ch. 56.

[77a] It may be noted that the usual presumption that references to children are confined to those who are legitimate was abolished in Northern Ireland by Art. 4(8) of the Family Law Reform (N.I.) Order, 1977, which reads: "There is hereby abolished, as respects dispositions made after the commencement of this Article, any rule of law that a disposition in favour of illegitimate children not in being when the disposition takes effect is void as contrary to public policy."

(iii) The Perpetuity Period

(a) *At Common Law*

5.067. At common law it was settled that the period for vesting under the rule against perpetuities was a life or lives in being, plus 21 years thereafter, with allowance for any period of gestation. Each of these elements will now be considered.

(1) LIVES IN BEING[78]

Whilst in theory any person living at the date of the operation of the disposition may be used as a life in being, in practice the rule confines lives to those connected with the disposition in question. This connection may be found in the fact that the persons whose lives are being selected for determining the validity of the gift are expressly mentioned in the disposition, or it may be that the lives of those persons are impliedly mentioned. The key to determining validity in every case is to discover those lives which are relevant to the vesting of the particular gift in question. Since it is the vesting of the gift which is at issue there is usually some contingency involved or some condition to be met and the lives in being will relate to that contingency or condition. If we revert to the example given earlier[79]—a gift "to the first son of A to become a solicitor"— we saw that there, if A were still alive at the time of the gift and had no son a solicitor, A was a life in being, since he was expressly mentioned and his death would obviously affect the vesting of the property, and so also were all his sons alive at the date of the gift, since, although not all mentioned expressly, all of them had a prospect of being the first one to become a solicitor and so each of their lives was relevant to the vesting of the gift. Under the common law rule against perpetuities, the gift would be invalid because of the possibility that A might have another son, born after the date of the gift and therefore *not* a life in being, who might be the first son to become a solicitor and who might do so more than 21 years after the death of A and all the other sons alive at the time of the gift. The fact that there might be other persons in the world alive at the time of the gift still surviving at the date of the vesting would be irrelevant. There is no "wait and see" at common law and, in theory, every other person alive at the date of the gift might die before A's subsequently born son became a solicitor. These other persons were mentioned neither expressly nor by implication and so could not govern the vesting of the property or determine the gift's validity under the rule against perpetuities.

5.068. If, instead, in the example A were dead at the date of the gift, the gift would be valid at common law because any sons capable of qualifying under the terms of the disposition would necessarily be alive at the date of the gift and therefore lives in being. The vesting, therefore, would take place, if ever, clearly within the period, indeed more than 21 years within the period.

---

[78] See generally *Lord Dungannon* v. *Smith* (1846) 12 Cl. & F. 546, espec. at 563 (*per* Cresswell J.).
[79] Para. 5.060, *ante*.

5.069. It should be emphasised that in every case the common law required that the lives in being should be ascertained at the date of the gift. This was the obvious corollary of the principle that the validity of the gift was determined at this date. In the case of an *inter vivos* disposition, the date in question is the date of execution of the instrument and, in the case of a will, the date is the death of the testator. The lives in being have to be alive at those respective dates.

5.070. Finally, a point on which there has been some controversy. It seems to have been settled, at least in England, that any number of lives in being may be chosen for the purposes of the rule against perpetuities. Where a settlor or testator expressly selects lives, it would seem that there is no limit to the number that he selects, hence the "royal lives" clauses which became so popular in the late nineteenth and early twentieth centuries, and still are in the Republic of Ireland.[80] In these cases the lives in being have no connection at all with the gift; they are not beneficiaries nor are they related to the beneficiaries, except that, of course, they have been mentioned expressly in the disposition. Thus in one case in England, capital was not to vest until the expiration of "the period ending at the expiration of 20 years from the day of the death of the last survivor of all the lineal descendants of her late Majesty Queen Victoria who shall be living at the time of my death."[81] In that case the testator died in 1926 and it was calculated that there were about 120 such lives in being. The Court of Appeal upheld the validity of the gift on the ground that the testator had chosen a number of lives reasonably capable of being determined with certainty, so that the date of the death of the last survivor was not beyond the scope of ascertainment by "ordinary legal testimony." The English cases emphasise that "certainty" is the crucial factor where a settlor or testator employs such a clause designed to extend the perpetuity period to its maximum. Thus a clause postponing vesting "until 21 years from the death of the last survivor of all persons who shall be living at my death" was held void for uncertainty.[82] It will also be recalled that the Irish courts have emphasised that the lives in being must be human lives, not, *e.g.*, lives of animals.[83] This problem has become, to a large extent, a matter of academic interest only in Northern Ireland since the passing of the Perpetuities Act (N.I.), 1966, to the provisions of which we shall turn in a moment.[84]

(2) THE 21-YEAR PERIOD

5.071. As we have already stated, the perpetuity period consists of a further 21 years after the death of the last surviving life in being. If no lives in being exist in a particular case, then the period is simply 21 years. This is always the

---

[80] Para. 5.061, *ante.*
[81] *Re Villar* [1929] 1 Ch. 243. See also *Cadell* v. *Palmer* (1833) 1 Cl. & F. 372; *Pownall* v. *Graham* (1863) 33 Beav. 242; *cf. Cole* v. *Sewell* (1848) 2 H.L.C. 186 at 233 (*per* Lord Brougham) (see *A Casebook on Irish Land Law* (1984), p. 246).
[82] *Re Moore* [1901] 1 Ch. 936. *Cf. Re Leverhulme* (*No. 2*) [1943] 2 All E.R. 274.
[83] *Re Kelly* [1932] I.R. 255 at 260–1 (*per* Meredith J.) (see *A Casebook on Equity and Trusts in Ireland* (1985), p. 537); *cf. Re Dean* (1889) 41 Ch.D. 552. See para. 5.038, *ante.*
[84] Para. 5.073, *infra.*

case, for example, where a disposition is made by way of trust for purposes rather than for human objects.[85]

(3) CHILDREN EN VENTRE SA MÈRE

5.072. It was eventually settled at common law that extensions of the perpetuity period would be permitted to take account of children *en ventre sa mère*.[86] Such an extension will be allowed only in respect of a period of gestation which actually exists and where the subsequent birth is relevant to the perpetuity period. For example, taking again the example, "to the first son of A to become a solicitor," if A is dead at the time of the gift but his widow is pregnant with their one and only child, who is born a son, that son is treated as a life in being and the gift is valid at common law. Here the period of gestation operates at the beginning of the perpetuity period. It may also, however, operate so as to extend the period at the end. For example, in the case of a gift "to the first son of A to reach the age of 21," if A is alive at the date of the gift and subsequently dies leaving his wife pregnant with their first child, subsequently born a son who attains 21, the gift is valid despite the fact that the vesting occurs some months outside the normal period. The normal period here would be A's lifetime plus 21 years thereafter, but the courts allowed the extension to cover the period of gestation between A's death and his son's birth.

(b) *Perpetuities Act (N.I.), 1966*

5.073. This Act affects several of the rules relating to the perpetuity period as evolved at common law.

(1) LIVES IN BEING

The Act introduces two major changes in the law relating to lives in being. First, it provides an alternative period of years which a settlor or a testator may adopt instead of the clumsy "royal lives" clauses, and the like, that were used to extend the period as far as possible. Section 1 (1) of the 1966 Act empowers a settlor or testator to select a perpetuity period "of a duration equal to such number of years not exceeding eighty as is specified in that behalf in the instrument." It is clear, then, that the alternative period[87] must be selected expressly in the instrument and must, in view of the last few words of subsection (1), be stated to be the perpetuity period for that disposition. The 80-year period is a maximum limit, so a settlor or testator may select a shorter period. It is also only an alternative period; a "royal lives" clause, or similar device, which must still be used in the Republic of Ireland, can also still be used in Northern Ireland.

---

[85] See the discussion of these cases, paras. 5.038–41, *ante*.

[86] *Thellusson* v. *Woodford* (1805) 11 Ves. 112; *Cadell* v. *Palmer* (1833) 1 Cl. & F. 372.

[87] This alternative period cannot be invoked by the donee of a special power of appointment in his exercise of the power, see s. 1 (2) and para. 5.131, *post*.

5.074. Secondly, the 1966 Act provides a list of statutory "lives in being"[88] to operate where its new "wait and see" provisions come into play.[89] This list, of course, will not operate where lives in being are irrelevant, *e.g.,* where the settlor or testator has selected the 80-year period under section 1 of the Act. Section 3 (4) (*a*) provides that where the Act's "wait and see" principle applies to a disposition after 1966, and the persons listed in the Act are "individuals in being" and "ascertainable at the commencement of the perpetuity period,"[90] then "the duration of the period shall be determined by reference to their lives and no others." However, the paragraph goes on to say that the lives described in the Act "shall be disregarded if the number of persons of that description is such as to render it impracticable to ascertain the date of death of the survivor." If there are no lives in being meeting the Act's description, the period is 21 years.[91]

5.075. Section 3 (5) lists the statutory lives in being as persons coming within the following descriptions:

"(*a*) the person by whom the disposition was made;

(*b*) a person to whom or in whose favour the disposition was made, that is to say—

　(i) in the case of a disposition to a class of persons, any member or potential member of the class;

　(ii) in the case of an individual disposition to a person taking only on certain conditions being satisfied, any person as to whom some of the conditions are satisfied and the remainder may in time be satisfied;

　(iii) in the case of a special power of appointment exercisable in favour of members of a class, any member or potential member of the class;

　(iv) in the case of a special power of appointment, exercisable in favour of one person only, that person or, where the object of the power is ascertainable only on certain conditions being satisfied, any person as to whom some of the conditions are satisfied and the remainder may in time be satisfied;

　(v) in the case of any power, option or other right, the person on whom the right is conferred;

(*c*) a person having a child or grandchild within sub-paragraphs (i) to (iv) of paragraph (*b*), or any of whose children or grandchildren, if subsequently born, would by virtue of his or her descent fall within those sub-paragraphs, or any of whose grandchildren, if subsequently born, would by virtue of his or her birth take a vested interest under the disposition;

(*d*) any person on the failure or determination of whose prior interest the

---

[88] S. 3 (4) and (5).　　　　　　　　　　　　　　　　　　　　　　　[89] Para. 5.062, *ante.*

[90] The 1966 Act excepts from this condition a spouse of a donee of a gift, thereby meeting one of the criticisms made of the English 1964 Act, see s. 3 (4) (*a*) and (5) (*f*). *Cf.* Megarry and Wade, *The Law of Real Property* (5th ed., 1984), p. 256. However, even the 1966 Act was defective and the Q.U.B. Land Law Working Party suggested an amendment to s. 3 (5) (*f*), see *Survey of the Land Law of Northern Ireland* (1971), para. 341.

[91] S. 3 (4) (*b*).

disposition is limited either mediately or immediately to take effect;
(*e*) a person having a child or grandchild within paragraph (*d*);
(*f*) *a spouse of any person within paragraphs* (*b*) (i) to (iv).[92]"

5.076. It would seem from the wording of the Act that successive gifts made in a particular instrument count as separate "dispositions" for the purposes of the above provisions, so that the lives in being have to be calculated separately for each gift. Thus, in a settlement on "the first son of A to become a solicitor but, if no such son becomes a solicitor, then to the first son of B to become a solicitor," there are two dispositions, one to A's son and one to B's son. These gifts would be saved only by the "wait and see" provisions of the 1966 Act and the lives in being under section 3 (5) are different in the two cases. So far as the gifts to A's son is concerned, the most obvious lives in being under section 3 (5) are: (1) the settlor under paragraph (*a*); (2) any sons of A alive at the date of the settlement, under paragraph (*b*) (ii); (3) A himself, if still alive, under paragraph (*c*). With regard to the gift to B's son, the obvious lives in being are: (1) the settlor, under paragraph (*a*); (2) any sons of B alive at the date of the settlement, under paragraph (*b*) (ii); (3) B himself, if still alive, under paragraph (*c*); (4) any sons of A alive at the date of the settlement, under paragraph (*d*); (5) A, if still alive, under paragraph (*e*).[93] It is clear, therefore, that the appropriate lives in being under the Act will vary from one gift to another contained in the same instrument. It is also apparent that the Act differs from the common law rules governing lives in being, quite apart from restricting a settlor's power to select "royal lives" and use similar devices. In the example given above, the settlor would be a life in being in the case of both gifts, yet this would not be true at common law. At common law, the settlor's life has nothing to do with the vesting of the gifts and, because of that irrelevancy, would not count as an appropriate life in being.

(2) THE 21-YEAR PERIOD

5.077. Generally the 1966 Act does not affect the common law on this point. Under both schemes, if there are no lives in being the perpetuity period is 21 years, unless, of course, the alternative fixed statutory period up to 80 years is selected expressly by the settlor or testator.

(3) CHILDREN EN VENTRE SA MÈRE

The 1966 Act does not affect the principles involved here.[94]

(iv) A "Surviving Spouse" Condition
(a) *At Common Law*
5.078. A frequent cause of the failure of many gifts at common law, and this is still the position in the Republic of Ireland, is what has been called, somewhat misleadingly, the "unborn widow" trap. For example, if a testator leaves property "to A for life, then to any widow who should survive A for her

[92] The Q.U.B. Working Party recommended the addition of the words "and (*c*)" here, to allow the spouse of an ancestor of a beneficiary to count as a life in being, see fn. 90, *ante*.
[93] Paragraph (*e*) does not exist in the English 1964 Act, see Megarry and Wade, *op. cit.*, pp. 256–8, and in this respect the 1966 Act is not more restrictive than the common law. [94] Para. 5.072, *ante*.

life, and then to the children of A living at the death of the survivor of A and his widow," the remainder to the children is void at common law. The reason is that the disposition refers to any widow of A and so, at the date of the testator's death, there is the possibility that A may subsequently marry a woman unborn at the testator's death. This woman would, therefore, not be a life in being and there is the further possibility that she may survive A by more than 21 years, so that the remainder to their children may not vest until more than 21 years after the death of the only life in being, namely A. The position would be different, of course, if the clause requiring the children to be living at the death of the survivor of the parents were deleted. If that were done, the children would have no condition to meet other than to be born children of A and his widow. This would occur during A's lifetime, extended, if necessary, by a period of gestation, and so the remainder would vest within the perpetuity period of A's lifetime plus 21 years. The same trap would exist if the roles of the spouses were reversed in the example given above, so that a more accurate label for this problem is one referring to conditions relating to the death of a surviving spouse. This is the description used by the Perpetuities Act (N.I.), 1966, which contains a provision designed specifically to save dispositions in Northern Ireland from the trap.

(b) *Perpetuities Act (N.I.), 1966*

5.079. Section 5 of the 1966 Act provides:

> "Where a disposition is limited by reference to the time of death of the survivor of a person in being at the commencement of the perpetuity period and any spouse of that person, and that time has not arrived at the end of the perpetuity period, the disposition shall be treated for all purposes, where to do so would save it from being void for remoteness, as if it had instead been limited by reference to the time immediately before the end of that period."

The first point to emphasise about this provision is that it can be invoked only if the gift is not saved by applying the Act's new "wait and see" principle. We have already pointed out that section 3 (1) of the Act requires that one should first apply the "wait and see" provisions to a disposition, thereby giving them a chance to conform precisely with the draftsman's wording, before one should alter that wording in an effort to save the gift. However, if the gift still infringes the common law rule despite application of "wait and see," section 5 will save the gift by converting, in the above example, the remainder to the children of A and his widow into one expressed to vest immediately before the end of the perpetuity period. The effect of this will be, of course, that certain children may take a vested interest in the property even though they later predecease the widow and so do not comply with the testator's qualifying condition.[95]

---

[95] It is interesting to note, however, that both the 1966 Act and the English 1964 Act in this regard keep interference with the testator's disposition to the minimum required to save the gift. The English Law Reform Committee (see para. 5.057, *ante*) recommended much greater interference by suggesting that the remainder to the children should be treated as vesting much earlier, namely at the death of the husband (A).

(v) Class Gifts

(a) *At Common Law*

5.080. A class gift to a number of persons, who are linked together in a class or category applying to each of them, so that the share of each member of the class in the property given varies according to the number of members. This last condition is the vital one, which distinguishes a class gift from a series of independent gifts to different people, whose shares are fixed and quantified from the start.[96] Thus one may compare a gift of £1,000 "to those of my sons who reach the age of 21 years" with a gift of £1,000 "to each of my sons." The former is a class gift: the sons will not know what share they will obtain in the £1,000 until the gift operates and until such time passes thereafter as is necessary to determine how many of the surviving sons reach the age of 21 years. The latter is not a class gift: each son gets £1,000 as soon as the gift operates and each son's gift is fixed and quantified from the start. The special principles concerning the application of the rule against perpetuities at common law, which we are going to discuss now, apply only in the case of class gifts.

(1) THE BASIC RULE

5.081. The primary principle applied to class gifts in relation to the rule against perpetuities at common law is that every member of the class must take a vested interest within the perpetuity period, otherwise the whole gift fails.[97] Thus, even if there is only a possibility that one member may take outside the period, all other members of the class lose their interests, even though those members have already complied with any condition or contingency relating to the vesting of the gift.[98] Class gifts are not severable at common law in this regard.

However, the courts sometimes save class gifts which at first sight look like failing entirely. They do this often by invoking one of two principles. These principles are essentially rules of construction, though there has been some controversy about the first principle which some think is more properly regarded as a rule of law.[99]

(2) SEPARATE CLASSES

5.082. The first principle to save gifts at common law is that the courts sometimes regard what appears at first sight to be a single class gift as, instead, two separate gifts, one of which is valid and the other of which is void. This usually arises where one gift is to be substituted for another on the occurrence of some contingency. For example, property might be left "to A for life,

---

[96] See *Re Ewart's Estate* (1967) 18 N.I.L.Q. 463.
[97] *Re Taylor's Trusts* [1912] 1 I.R. 1; *Re Bromhead's Trusts* [1922] 1 I.R. 75; *Re Carney's Will Trusts* [1938] I.R. 292; *Exham* v. *Beamish* [1939] I.R. 336 (see *A Casebook on Irish Land Law* (1984), p. 263); *Re Poe* [1942] I.R. 535 (see *ibid*., p. 268); *Re Burke* [1945] Ir.Jur.Rep. 12.
[98] *Pearks* v. *Moseley* (1880) 5 App.Cas. 714.
[99] See *Re Hooper's Settlement Trust* [1948] Ch. 586, espec. at 591 (*per* Jenkins J.). Morris and Leach, *The Rule Against Perpetuities* (2nd ed.), pp. 104–6; Megarry and Wade, *op. cit.*, p. 263, fn. 19.

remainder to his wife for life, remainder to their children in equal shares, but if any child dies before A or his wife and that child leaves children who do survive A and his wife, those children are to take their parents' share." The important point here is that, although A may be unmarried at the date of the gift, each of A's children takes a vested interest at birth during A's lifetime and, therefore, well within the perpetuity period. It is true that that share may be divested later if the contingency occurs, and that may not occur until outside the period, *e.g.*, the death of a wife who was unborn at the date of the gift, so that the gift to the grandchildren is clearly void at common law. Yet, because the gift to the children is vested, albeit subject to subsequent divesting,[1] their shares will be fixed within the period. Those shares will not alter as a result of some subsequent contingency occurring—the share is vested and on death passes under the child's will or on intestacy. Because of this the courts treat the first gift as a separate and valid gift to the children and the gift to the grandchildren in the proviso as another separate gift which is void as contravening the rule against perpetuities.

5.083. To be compared with the above situation is the type of disposition which was made in the English case of *Pearks* v. *Moseley*.[2] If a testator leaves property "to the issue of A who attain 21, provided that if any issue die under that age, but leaving issue who do attain 21, then that issue shall take the share which the parent would have taken had he attained 21," the whole gift is void, if A is still alive. The crucial point about this disposition is that the children of A do not take a vested interest at birth and the shares which they take will be governed by how many of the grandchildren attain 21, which may not be known until long after the perpetuity period (*i.e.*, A's lifetime, the lifetime of any children born at the date of the gift, plus 21 years). Since the share will not be vested until outside the period, the whole gift is void; there is no possibility of treating them as two separate gifts since the vesting of the children's shares is governed by the too remote contingency relating to the grandchildren. It should be noted, however, that the position would be different if the condition of attaining 21 were deleted from the gift to the children. In that case the children would take a vested interest at birth and their shares would clearly be determined within the perpetuity period. The gift to the children could, therefore, be treated as separate and not invalidated by the proviso for divesting at a time which may be outside the perpetuity period.

(3) CLASS-CLOSING RULES

5.084. The second principle by which the courts save class gifts at common law from total failure is a rule of construction, sometimes known as the rule in *Andrews* v. *Partington*,[3] the leading English case on the subject. The principle

---

[1] *Cf.* the principle of construction discussed at para. 5.059, *ante*.
[2] (1880) 5 App.Cas. 714. See also *Re Lord's Settlement* [1947] 2 All E.R. 685; *Re Hooper's Settlement Trusts* [1948] Ch. 586.
[3] (1791) 3 Bro.C.C. 401. See also *Re Bleckly* [1951] Ch. 740; *Re Clifford's Settlement Trusts* [1981] Ch. 63.

has been recognised and applied in Ireland.[4] It must be emphasised that this rule is a general rule of contruction adopted by courts, which may have the effect of saving a gift from the rule against perpetuities. It is not a rule which was devised specifically with the rule against perpetuities in mind.[5]

5.085. The basic principle is that, where there is a class gift to an unknown number of members, the class closes as soon as the first member of the class becomes entitled to his share, *i.e.*, it becomes vested in possession. Thereupon no member born subsequently can enter the class, but all potential members alive at that time may still qualify to take their shares. In this way the maximum number of shares is fixed and each member will receive his share once he qualifies, the first qualifier who brought about the closing receiving his immediately. Of course, these qualifying members may receive more property as potential members at the date of the closing subsequently fail to qualify, *e.g.*, by not reaching a specified age. The rule seems to apply both to deeds and to wills and, being a rule of construction, is subject to an expression of a contrary intention on the part of the settlor or testator. The question is whether it was intended that every member of the class should take, whatever subsequently happened. The fact that one construction will save a gift from the rule against perpetuities and another will not would seem to be a relevant factor for the court.[6]

5.086. The essential requirement for the class-closing principle to apply is that the first member of the class takes a *vested* interest *in possession*. For example, a devise "to the grandchildren of A who attain 21" will not close until a grandchild reaches 21. If A were alive at the testator's death, the gift would normally be void at common law. However, if also at that date A had a grandchild, *who had attained 21,* the class would close immediately and would be confined to that grandchild and any other grandchildren born at that date. This would save the class gift because it would then be confined to persons who are all lives in being. If, instead, the devise were "to A for life, remainder to the grandchildren of A who attain 21," the same rules apply. The class closes as soon as a grandchild attains 21, *on or after A's death.* The closing cannot take place any earlier than this because the first member must take a vested interest *in possession.* This, however, will not be enough to save the gift at common law because the date for calculating the operation of the rule against perpetuities is the date of the gift, *i.e.,* the testator's death. For the gift to be saved from the rule against perpetuities it must be *certain* that the class will close on A's death, so that the only potential members will be those taking a vested interest within 21 years of his death. The only way this will happen is if A has a grandchild aged 21 at the date of the testator's death, for, even though that grandchild may not survive until A's death, his interest is vested in interest on the testator's death

---

[4] *Re Poe* [1942] I.R. 535 (see *A Casebook on Irish Land Law* (1984), p. 268); *Re Burke* [1945] Ir.Jur.Rep. 12; *Williamson* v. *Williamson* [1974] N.I. 92.
[5] See Morris and Leach, *The Rule Against Perpetuities*, ch. 4.
[6] See *Re Poe* [1942] I.R. 535(see *A Casebook on Irish Land Law* (1984), p. 268).

and will continue vested in interest in his successor, who can claim it on A's death, thereby closing the class.

These principles continue to apply in the Republic of Ireland, but the Perpetuities Act (N.I.), 1966, has introduced some additional rules for Northern Ireland.

(b) Perpetuities Act (N.I.), 1966.

5.087. As with many of its provisions, the position under the 1966 Act is that the gift must first be subjected to the common law rule against perpetuities. Thus the principles just discussed, such as class-closing, will apply. The 1966 Act may be invoked only if the gift would still be void. In that event the 1966 Act will save the gift, at least to some extent. Once again, the Act requires that the "wait and see" principle be applied first, before these further provisions are invoked.[7]

5.088. Section 4 (4) of the Act provides:

"Where . . . it is apparent at the time the disposition is made or becomes apparent at a subsequent time that, apart from this subsection, the inclusion of any persons, being potential members of a class or unborn persons who at birth would become members or potential members of the class, would cause the disposition to be treated as void for remoteness, those persons shall, unless their exclusion would exhaust the class, thenceforth be deemed for all the purposes of the disposition to be excluded from the class."

This provision in effect reverses the common law principle that where any part of the class is affected by remoteness the whole gift fails. It means that any class gift in Northern Ireland from 1966 will at least operate effectively in favour of all those members of the class who do in fact, according to "wait and see", comply with the perpetuities rule.

(vi) Age-Reduction

5.089. This topic is relevant only to Northern Ireland, being based entirely upon statute law. At common law there was no scope for reducing the age required to be attained by a donee in order to save the gift from the rule against perpetuities. The imposition of an "excessive age" condition is a frequent source of failure of gifts at common law, particularly where the age specified exceeds 21 years. Thus a gift "to the first son of A to attain 25" would fail at common law if A were still alive and had no son already 25. Any son he did have might die before 25 and any subsequently born son might attain 25 more than 21 years after the death of the lives in being (A and any other sons alive at the date of the gift).

---

[7] S. 3 (1), and see para. 5.064, *ante*. There is also a special provision in s. 4 (3) relating to class gifts involving an age contingency, which is discussed in the section dealing with "age-reduction" provisions, para. 5.089, *infra*.

5.090. In England, statutory provisions were first introduced by the Law of Property Act, 1925,[8] now replaced and amended by the Perpetuities and Accumulations Act, 1964.[9] Similar statutory provisions have now been introduced for Northern Ireland by section 4 (1)–(3) of the Perpetuities Act (N.I.), 1966. Section 4 (1) provides that, where a gift would not be saved by the Act's "wait and see" principle, and is limited by reference to attainment by a person of an age exceeding 21 years, but would have been valid if the age had been 21 years, that age may be treated as being reduced to whatever age would save the gift from being void for remoteness. Thus the age in question may not necessarily be reduced to 21 years, and the age in question need not be that of the donee of the gift.[10] If a particular disposition requires attainment of different ages by different persons, all the ages may be reduced as necessary.[11] Finally, the 1966 Act permits a combination of age-reduction and class-exclusion.[12] Section 4 (3) provides:

> "Where the inclusion of any persons, being potential members of a class or unborn persons who at birth would become members or potential members of the class, prevents the foregoing provisions of this section [*i.e.,* on age-reduction] from operating to save a disposition from being void for remoteness, those persons shall thenceforth be deemed for all the purposes of the disposition to be excluded from the class, and the said provisions shall thereupon have effect accordingly."

The idea here is that a combination of the two saving provisions may be used where neither one by itself would be sufficient to save the gift, *e.g.,* in a disposition "to all the children of A who attain 25, but if any child should die under 25, then to that child's children who attain the age of 25." Here, merely reducing the age for the grandchildren to 21 years would not make the gift valid, if A were unmarried at the date of the gift and died leaving only children less than 5 years of age. However, if one also operates the class-exclusion provisions, one can close the class after waiting and seeing so as, in the above circumstances, to exclude any grandchildren of A. As regards the children under the age of 5, one can reduce the age, as necessary, to secure vesting within 21 years of A's death.

(vii) Subsequent Gifts

5.091. A question often arises as to what the position is with respect to application of the perpetuities rule to successive gifts. The general rule is that the rule against perpetuities should be applied to each gift separately and each

[8] S. 163.
[9] S. 4. The drafting of this section, in relation to s. 163 of the Law of Property Act, 1925, was not without difficulties, which had to be corrected by the Children Act 1975, 3rd Sched., para. 43, see Megarry and Wade, *The Law of Real Property* (5th ed., 1984), pp 269–70.
[10] *Cf.* s. 163 of the English Law of Property Act, 1925.
[11] S. 4 (2).
[12] It may also be noted in respect of the class-exclusion provisions that there is a saving provision for payments made to potential beneficiaries by way of advancement or application of intermediate income, s. 4 (5), and see para. 5.065, *ante.*

gift's validity should be determined accordingly. However, the difficult question that sometimes arises is what the position is where, by so applying the rule, one discovers that one gift complies and one gift does not. How far does the invalidity of one gift affect the validity of another contained in the same instrument? Once again one has to make a distinction between the common law in force in the Republic of Ireland and the provisions of the Perpetuities Act (N.I.), 1966.

(a) *At Common Law*

5.092. At common law, if a primary gift complies with the rule against perpetuities, it is valid and remains so whatever may be the position with respect to any subsequent gifts. This is fairly straightforward law, though notice should be taken of cases where the primary gift is a class gift with the vesting governed by contingencies which may give rise to substitution of primary members of the class.[13] The problems arise where the primary gift is void but the subsequent gift, on a separate application of the perpetuities rule, is not. How far the subsequent gift is affected by the invalidity of the primary gift depends on the nature of the subsequent gift. If that gift consists of a vested interest, *i.e.*, vested from the date of operation of the instrument, the gift is clearly valid. For example, in a devise " to A for life, remainder for life to A's first son to become a solicitor, remainder to B in fee simple," the second gift to A's first son is void at common law if A is still alive.[14] The remainder to B, however, is vested in interest immediately and so is valid whatever the position with respect to the second gift.

5.093. The complications really only arise where the subsequent gift is contingent, for here the common law drew a distinction between two types of subsequent contingent gifts. One is where the subsequent gift is contingent, but *independent* of the void primary gift.[15] For example, in a devise "to A for life, remainder for life to A's first son to marry, remainder to B if he becomes a solicitor," the gift to B is not vested from the beginning, but contingent upon his becoming a solicitor. This contingency, however, is quite independent of the gift to A's first son and so, according to the common law, the gift can stand or fall on its own. If B is alive, the subsequent remainder to him is valid since he must become a solicitor, if ever, during his own lifetime. To be compared with such a subsequent contingent gift is one which is *dependent* upon the primary gift,[16] *e.g.*, a devise "to A for life, remainder to A's first son to marry in fee simple, but if A has no such son, remainder to B for life." Here B's gift is dependent upon a contingency relating to the gift to A's first son, which is void, so that B's gift is also void. It might be argued that B's gift was vested in that if B were alive he could take immediately, subject only to the prior gift to A's first

---

[13] Discussed at para. 5.082, *ante.*

[14] Para. 5.060, *ante.*

[15] *Re Hay* [1932] N.I. 215 (see *A Casebook on Irish Land Law* (1984), p. 275).

[16] *Armstrong* v. *West* (1863) Ir.Jur. (N.S.) 144; *Re Ramadge's Settlement* [1919] 1 I.R. 205; *Re Manning's Trusts* (1915) 49 I.L.T.R. 143.

son. This, however, ignores the fact that the vesting of B's gift is dependent upon the failure of the prior gift—as it is sometimes put, its operation depends upon the converse contingency to that which invalidated the prior gift. Indeed, it is in the nature of a fee simple estate that any gift which follows it must be contingent.[17] The result is, therefore, that, although B's gift must vest, if at all, within his own lifetime and the perpetuity period, because it is contingent and dependent upon a prior void gift it also is void.

(b) Perpetuities Act (N.I.), 1966

5.094. Section 6 of this Act, which, unlike some of the other provisions of the Act already discussed, is not postponed in operation to the "wait and see" principle, provides:

> "A disposition shall not be treated as void for remoteness by reason only that the interest disposed of is ulterior to and dependent upon an interest under a disposition which is so void, and the vesting of an interest shall not be prevented from being accelerated on the failure of a prior interest by reason only that the failure arises because of remoteness."

Thus, since 1966 in Northern Ireland each subsequent gift, whether dependent or not on a prior gift, stands or falls on its own so far as the rule against perpetuities is concerned. The second part of this provision is designed to resolve doubts that have arisen from a line of English cases about the acceleration of interests.[18] In some of these cases it was argued that the subsequent gift could not take effect where the prior gift was void, if the effect of that was to accelerate the vesting. To the extent that this argument was based upon the presumed intention of the donor (namely that the subsequent gift could take effect only when the prior gift had run its course and become exhausted, not when it was void for remoteness and never operated at all), it was often of questionable merit.[19] Section 6 now makes it clear that acceleration can take place in cases where the prior gift is void for remoteness, but it will not necessarily take place. For example, it will not take place before any condition to be satisfied in respect of the subsequent gift is complied with,[20] or where there is clear evidence of intention to the contrary on the part of the donor.[21]

(viii) Alternative Contingencies

5.095. It sometimes happens that the vesting of property is governed by alternative contingencies, e.g., a gift "to the first son of A to become a solicitor, but if A shall have no son who becomes a solicitor or no son at all, then to B in

---

[17] See para. 5.016, ante, Also Megarry and Wade, op. cit., pp. 270–4.
[18] See Beard v. Westcott (1822) 5 B. & Ald. 801; Monypenny v. Dering (1852) 2 De G.M. & G. 145. Also Morris and Leach, The Rule Against Perpetuities (2nd ed.), pp. 179–81.
[19] Megarry and Wade, op. cit., p. 273.
[20] Re Hubbard's Will Trusts [1963] Ch. 275.
[21] Re Taylor [1957] 1 W.L.R. 1043; Re Young's Settlement Trust [1959] 1 W.L.R. 457.

fee simple." Here the vesting of B's fee simple is expressed to occur on the happening of one of two alternative events, *i.e.*, on A's dying leaving no sons or leaving sons who subsequently all die without becoming solicitors. According to the principles of the rule against perpetuities, at common law the first contingency would not, on its own, prevent the vesting of B's gift within the perpetuity period—the vesting would be determined immediately upon A's death and A is a life in being.[22] The second contingency, however, viewed on its own, would render the gift to B void. In such a case, as we have discussed,[23] if A were alive at the date of the gift, his first son to qualify might be a later-born son who qualified more than 21 years after the death of A and any brothers alive at the date of the gift. The question now is what is the effect of linking together in one disposition, so as to govern the vesting of a particular gift, two contingencies, one of which makes the gift valid on its own, the other of which makes it void on its own.

5.096. The answer to that question is that in such a case the common law allowed the application of a "wait and see" principle. This, of course, was contrary to the general rules governing the application of the rule against perpetuities[24] and it is difficult to see why such cases should have received favoured treatment.[25] Whatever the justification, there is no doubt that "wait and see" applies in such a case.[26] Thus, at common law, in the example given above, B's gift would take effect if A died leaving no sons at all. If, however, A died leaving sons, then the gift would be void.

5.097. One further point should be emphasised. It seems to be settled, at least as far as the English authorities are concerned,[27] that for the "wait and see" principle to operate the alternative contingencies must be stated expressly in the disposition. If the example given above had read—"to the first son of A to become a solicitor but if A shall have no son who becomes a solicitor, then to B in fee simple"—it might be argued that the disposition really involves two contingencies governing the vesting of B's gift. One is the expressed contingency, namely that A leaves no son who becomes a solicitor; the other is an implied one, namely that A dies leaving no son at all. It seems, however, that the courts will not allow such a disposition to be construed in this way, even though in substance there is little difference between the two dispositions.

5.098. Finally, the Perpetuities Act (N.I.), 1966, does not affect the operation of the common law rule against perpetuities in this regard, at least not directly. In the case of alternative contingencies, only one of which would cause an invalidity *ab initio*, one can "wait and see" at common law. If that fails to save the gift, so that at common law the alternative which makes the gift void

---

[22] If he were dead, then, of course, the vesting would be determined even earlier, *i.e.*, the date of the gift.
[23] Para. 5.060, *ante*.
[24] *Ibid.*
[25] For another case receiving similar treatment (powers of appointment), see para. 5.124, *post*.
[26] See the English cases, *Hodgson* v. *Halford* (1879) 11 Ch.D. 959: *Re Curryer's Will Trusts* [1938] Ch. 952.
[27] *Re Harvey* (1888) 39 Ch.D. 289; *Re Bence* [1891] 3 Ch. 242.

governs the matter, the 1966 Act may then save the gift by allowing "wait and see" in respect of that alternative contingency.[28]

(ix) Determinable and Conditional Gifts

5.099. This subject has been one of the most controversial aspects of the rule against perpetuities and it is one which has seen a clear divergence of views amongst the courts of England, on the one hand, and the courts of Ireland, on the other hand. Further complication has recently been added by the fact that the Perpetuities Act (N.I.), 1966, has now reversed the views of the Irish courts (including the Northern Ireland courts), so far as dispositions taking effect in Northern Ireland since 1966 are concerned.[29] We shall discuss first the position at common law.

(a) *At Common Law*

5.100. There are two main categories of future interest to be considered in this context—determinable interests and conditional interests. The distinction between the two has already been discussed.[30]

(1) DETERMINABLE INTERESTS

Perhaps the two most common types of determinable interest are a *possibility of reverter*[31] in respect of land and a *possibility of a resulting trust*[32] in repect of any property (real or personal) held on trust. In these cases, the property reverts to the original grantor automatically on the determination of the immediate gift. The determination may be caused by the happening of an event well outside the perpetuity period. For example, a possibility of reverter may become an actuality many centuries after the original grant of the determinable fee. It was this fact which caused the common law so much difficulty in applying the perpetuities rule.

5.101. It is crucial, however, to draw a distinction between the validity of the determinable interest itself and the validity of a gift or interest or possibility of an interest which arises on the determination of the determinable interest. Let us take an example: "to A in fee simple until the parish church of Dungloe ceases to stand."[33] There are two gifts to be considered here. One is A's determinable fee and the other is the grantor's possibility of reverter. As regards the determinable fee, it seems clear that in both England[34] and Ireland[35] the rule against perpetuities does not apply. The reason usually given

---

[28] See para. 5.062, *ante.*
[29] Section 13 (5) does make an exception to this limitation with respect to interests in property other than land, see para. 5.111, *post.*
[30] Paras. 4.046 *et. seq., ante.*
[31] Para. 4.046, *ante.*
[32] Para. 5.040, *ante* and 9.055, *post.*
[33] One must always bear in mind that problems of certainty may arise over the determining event (or condition in cases of conditional interests), see para. 4.052, *ante.*
[34] *Wainwright* v. *Miller* [1897] 2 Ch. 255; *Att.-Gen.* v. *Pyle* (1738) 1 Atk. 435.
[35] *Att.-Gen.* v. *Cummins* [1906] 1 I.R. 406 (see *A Casebook on Irish Land Law* (1984), p. 131).

is that the rule is concerned with the initial vesting of gifts, not with the duration of gifts already vested. This reasoning applies equally to determinable gifts of personal property.[36]

5.102. The question remains, however, as to what is the position with respect to the possibility of reverter. This sort of interest, it must be remembered, is not vested *ab initio* like a reversion[37]; it is a mere possibility, which *may* become an actuality in the future, and so it is of necessity a contingent interest. As such, one might have expected it to be subject to the rule against perpetuities to the same extent as other contingent gifts, so that, if there was a possibility of the determining event occurring outside the period, the reverter would be void.[38] The Irish courts, however, have not accepted this view and no less an authority than Palles C.B. was adamant that the rule did not apply to possibilities of reverter at common law.[39] In *Att.-Gen.* v. *Cummins*,[40] the Chief Baron dealt at some length with the common law governing the application of the rule against perpetuities to possibilities of reverter and rights of entry for condition broken, and he concluded:

> "Now, there is not a trace in the books of any rule which limited the period during which the determination of an estate by condition should take effect, and it is abundantly clear that the modern rule could not have applied, because the donor took not by way of new limitation, but by the determination of the estate given. . . . Irrespective, therefore, of its non-application to estates, created by Common Law conveyances, the rule against perpetuities could not, from the nature of the estate, apply in a case like the present, without abrogating the elementary principle that, on the happening of the event, the fee in the grantee determined. . . .
>
> Thus the rule as to perpetuities became a Common Law doctrine applicable to springing and shifting uses, and executory and other limitations of property, which could not be created by a Common Law conveyance, and which could only take effect under the Statute of Uses. If I am right in this, the doctrine must be inapplicable to estates created by Common Law conveyances, and especially to estates which reverted to donors on the performance of conditions which determined estates. . . . 'Questions of perpetuity did not arise until the simplicity of the Common Law gave way to the complication of modern conveyancing.'"[41]

This judgment has always been accepted as authoritative in both parts of Ireland, but it has been doubted in England. In *Hopper* v. *Corporation of*

---

[36] *Re Randell* (1888) 38 Ch.D. 213; *Re Blunt's Trusts* [1904] 2 Ch. 767; *Re Chardon* [1928] Ch. 464.
[37] See para. 5.005, *ante*.
[38] See *Fourth Report of the Law Reform Committee* (1956; Cmnd. 18), para. 39; *cf. Third Report of the Real Property Commissioners* (1832), p. 36; Morris and Leach, *The Rule Against Perpetuities* (2nd. ed.), p. 213; Pettit, "Determinable Interests and Rule Against Perpetuities" (1957) 21 Conv. 213.
[39] Palles C.B.'s views were "unhesitantly adopted" and commended "acceptance on both historical and logical grounds" by the Northern Ireland Court of Appeal in *Walsh* v. *Wightman* [1927] N.I. 1, espec. at 15 (*per* Andrews L.J.) and 23 (*per* Best L.J.) (see para. 5.105, *post*).
[40] [1906] 1 I.R. 406 (see *A Casebook on Irish Land Law* (1984), p. 131).
[41] *Ibid.*, p. 409.

Liverpool,[42] Bennett V.-C., following an earlier decision of Byrne J. dealing with rights of entry for condition broken,[43] ruled that a possibility of reverter was subject to the rule against perpetuities, contrary to Palles C.B.'s views. However, this view has not been adopted in England in cases dealing with resulting trusts. Where a beneficial interest has been determined on the occurrence of an event clearly outside the perpetuity period, it has been consistently held for decades in England that a resulting trust in favour of the settlor can take effect, even though a gift over to another donee would fail for perpetuity.[44]

(2) CONDITIONAL INTERESTS

5.103. An equally controversial area of the law has been the application of the rule against perpetuities to conditional gifts. The Irish and English courts here too have held divergent views, especially with respect to gifts of land subject to a condition subsequent, giving rise to a right of entry for condition broken in the grantor.[45]

5.104. Once again it is important to distinguish between the validity of the gift subject to the condition subsequent in the grantee and the right of entry which arises in the grantor if that condition is broken. Provided the conditional interest in the grantee vests within the period, that interest remains valid whatever is the position with respect to the right of entry. For example, in a gift "to A in fee simple provided the parish church of Dungloe remains standing", A's fee simple vests immediately and there is no violation of the rule against perpetuities at common law. Even if the grantor's right of entry were held void, all that this would mean is that A's fee simple would cease to be conditional and would become absolute. The right of entry can divest the fee simple only if it is actually exercised and, if exercise becomes impossible because the right is void, the conditional interest ceases to be subject to the condition. The question remains, however, whether such a right of entry is subject to the rule against perpetuities at common law.

5.105. The Irish courts have held that such a right is not subject to the rule. The leading authority on the point once again was Palles C.B., who dealt with both possibilities of reverter and rights of entry for condition broken in his judgment in *Att.-Gen.* v. *Cummins*.[46] This authority was accepted by the Northern Ireland Court of Appeal in *Walsh* v. *Wightman*.[47] The *Walsh* case concerned a fee farm grant in 1880 to trustees of lands for the building of a

---

[42] (1944) 88 Sol.Jo. 213. See Megarry, 62 L.Q.R. 222.
[43] *Re Hollis' Hospital and Hague's Contract* [1899] 2 Ch. 540 (decided, be it noted, before Palles C.B.'s judgment in *Att.-Gen.* v. *Cummins*). See para. 5.106, *post*.
[44] See *Re Cooper's Conveyance Trusts* [1956] 1 W.L.R. 1096 and the cases on personalty cited in fn. 36, para. 5.101, *ante*.
[45] See further on this subject, para. 4.049, *ante*. It may be noted that little controversy has arisen about the application of the rule against perpetuities to conditions *precedent* (see para. 4.048, *ante*), since gifts subject to such conditions are among the most common to be governed by the rule. A condition precedent prevents the gift vesting from the very beginning and it is precisely the prevention of too great a postponement of initial vesting that the rule was devised at common law.
[46] See para. 5.102, *ante*. (See also *A Casebook on Irish Land Law* (1984), p. 131).
[47] [1927] N.I. 1.

manse for a particular Presbyterian congregation. The grant was made subject
expressly to a proviso that, if that congregation ceased to be connected with the
General Assembly of the Presbyterian Church in Ireland, or became united
with another congregation, or ceased to exist as a separate and independent
congregation, the grant was to become void and a right of entry was reserved
to the grantor. The Court held, *inter alia*, expressly following the earlier judgment
of Palles C.B., that the clause conferring the right of entry was not void as against
the rule against perpetuities and so the right of entry could be exercised over
forty years later.[48] In so holding, the Northern Ireland Court of Appeal laid great
weight on Palles C.B.'s views and expressly rejected the views to the contrary
of English authorities.[49] Andrews L.J. (later Lord Chief Justice of Northern
Ireland) concluded:

> "In the conflict of judicial authority which has arisen and in the clash of
> opinion of the leading textbook writers of the day, I unhesitatingly adopt
> the judgment of the Lord Chief Baron which commends itself to my
> acceptance on both historical and logical grounds. If it be urged that the
> conclusion at which I have arrived is anomalous, having regard to the fact
> that the rule against perpetuities applies to all contingent equitable
> limitations of real estate, I answer that it is our duty only to construe the
> law as we find it, and I add in the words of Mr. Challis[50] that 'when any
> part of the common law is found to require amendment the legislature
> alone is competent to apply the remedy.'"[51]

As we shall see in a moment,[52] the Perpetuities Act (N.I.), 1966, amended the
common law in Northern Ireland, as Andrews L.J. seemed to anticipate some
40 years earlier.

5.106. The authorities in England have generally taken the opposite view on
this subject. In *Re Hollis' Hospital and Hague's Contract*,[53] Byrne J. held that a
proviso in a conveyance of premises, to the effect that the premises would
revert to the grantor if they ceased to be used for specified purposes, was a
common law condition subsequent which was void as against the rule against
perpetuities.[54] This view was accepted as correct by later English authorities[55]
and was given legislative recognition in the Law of Property Act, 1925.[56]

[48] The court held that the procedure laid down in s. 14 of the Conveyancing Act, 1881, had to be followed and
that, in the circumstances, those claiming as fee farm grantors had not given sufficient notice. On this point in
relation to fee farm grants, see paras. 4.068 and 4.084, *ante*.

[49] *E.g.*, *Re Hollis' Hospital and Hague's Contract* [1899] 2 Ch. 540 (see para. 5.106, *infra*). Also *Re Ashforth*
[1905] 1 Ch. 535 (para. 5.114, *post*).

[50] Challis on this subject generally took the view later adopted by the Irish authorities and was supported in
this by Charles Sweet, editor of the third edition of his *Law of Real Property* (1911), see pp. 205–17 of the third
edition.

[51] *Op. cit.*, p. 15.

[52] Para. 5.108, *post*.

[53] [1899] 2 Ch. 540.

[54] Byrne J. expressly rejected the views of Challis, see fn. 50, *supra*, and cited dicta in earlier cases like *Re
Macleay* (1875) L.R. 20 Eq. 186 at 187 (*per* Jessel M.R.); *Dunn* v. *Flood* (1883) 25 Ch.D. 629 at 632–3, (*per* North
J.), on appeal (1885) 28 Ch.D. 586.

[55] *Hopper* v. *Liverpool Corporation* (1944) 88 Sol.Jo. 213 (para. 5.102, *ante*); *Re Da Costa* [1912] 1 Ch. 337;
Imperial Tobacco Co., Ltd. v. *Wilmott* [1964] 1 W.L.R. 902.

[56] S. 4 (3), which provides: "All rights of entry affecting a legal estate which are exercisable on condition
broken or for any other reason may, after the commencement of this Act, be made exercisable by any person and

5.107. So far as the Republic of Ireland is concerned, the position at common law with respect to the application of the rule against perpetuities to determinable and conditional interests remains that determined by the Irish courts. In Northern Ireland, however, the Perpetuities Act (N.I.), 1966, has introduced a major reform.

(b) *Perpetuities Act (N.I.), 1966*

5.108. This Act has, in effect, reversed the views of the Irish courts and has brought the law into line with the views of the English courts and the subsequent English legislation.[57]

(1) DETERMINABLE INTERESTS

5.109. Section 13 (3) of the 1966 Act provides:

"Where a disposition creates—
　(*a*) a possibility of reverter on the determination of a determinable fee simple; or
　(*b*) a possibility of a resulting trust on the determination of any other determinable interest in property;
the possibility of reverter or of a resulting trust, as the case may be, shall cease to exist at the end of the perpetuity period, and accordingly the fee or interest in question shall cease to be determinable."

This subsection must be read together with subsection (4) of the same section. Subsection (4) provides that, where a disposition creates a possibility such as is mentioned in subsection (3), the disposition "shall be treated for the purposes of this Act as including a separate disposition of any rights arising by virtue of the . . . possibility." This is an important provision because it makes it clear that in future in Northern Ireland the words in a conveyance creating a possibility of reverter are treated as a separate disposition for the purposes of the 1966 Act, so that the various saving provisions of that Act can apply to the possibility. Thus the "wait and see" provisions can be applied to see if the possibility becomes an actuality within the period so as to cause a determination of the main gift. If the possibility does not become an actuality within the period, then, after the period has passed, the main gift ceases to be determinable and under subsection (3) becomes absolute. As subsection (3) makes clear, the rule against perpetuities now applies in Northern Ireland to both possibilities of reverter relating to land and to possibilities of resulting trusts in respect of any type of property.

(2) CONDITIONAL INTERESTS

5.110. Section 13 (1) of the 1966 Act provides:

the persons deriving title under him, but, in regard to an estate in fee simple (not being a rentcharge held for a legal estate) only within the period authorised by the rule relating to perpetuities."
[57] *Ibid*. See also Perpetuities and Accumulations Act, 1964, s. 12.

"Subject to the succeeding provisions of this section, the following rights
shall not be exercisable after the end of the perpetuity period:—
> (*a*) a right of entry in respect of a fee simple exercisable on
> condition broken or for any other reason; or
> (*b*) in relation to property other than land, any right equivalent
> to the right mentioned in paragraph (*a*)."

This provision makes the rule against perpetuities apply now in Northern
Ireland to rights arising under conditions subsequent. Subsection (4) of the
same section also applies to these rights, so that the "wait and see" principle
may save them in a particular case.[58] If it does not, then, as in the case of
possibilities, the main gift ceases to be subject to the condition subsequent and
becomes absolute.[58a]

5.111. Section 13 (2) provides that, in relation to conditions subsequent in
the case of land, the rule against perpetuities does not apply to the landlord's
statutory right of ejectment for non-payment of rent conferred by section 52 of
Deasy's Act.[59] This confirms the general principle that the rule against
perpetuities does not apply to interests and rights arising under a lease or
tenancy agreement.[60] The perpetuities rule was devised by the courts to deal
with future interests created in respect of *freehold* land at common law and the
law of leasehold land[61] had a much later and independent development in this
respect.[62] Finally, contrary to the general principle of the 1966 Act,[63] the
provisions of subsection (1), quoted above, in relation to property *other than
land*, apply to instruments coming into operation before or after the passing of
the Act.[64]

(x) Legal Contingent Remainders

(a) *At Common Law*

5.112. This topic is another to be affected by the controversy which
surrounded the courts' attitude to interests like possibilities of reverter and
rights of entry for condition broken. The central argument on one side has been
that the modern rule against perpetuities was devised primarily to deal with
new future interests that were not sufficiently controlled by the common law
contingent remainder rules[65] or the rule in *Whitby* v. *Mitchell*.[66] It was argued
that interests well-established and recognised long before the development of

---

[58] In passing it may be noted that the "wait and see" principle now applies also to conditions *precedent* as it
applies to all contingent gifts in respect of which the initial vesting has been postponed, see fn. 45, para. 5.103,
ante.
[58a] This paragraph was cited with approval by Murray J. in *Re Steele* [1976] N.I. 66 at 68.
[59] Landlord and Tenant Law Amendment Act, Ireland, 1860. See ch. 17, *post*.
[60] Para. 5.144, *post*.
[61] See para. 4.007, *ante* and ch. 17, *post*.
[62] But subs. (2) does not apply to fee farm grants which are, for the most part, governed by leasehold law in
Ireland, ch. 4, *ante*.
[63] S. 16 (5).
[64] S. 13 (5). This was the law applicable to personalty prior to the 1966 Act.
[65] Paras. 5.012 *et seq.*, *ante*.
[66] Paras. 5.042 *et seq.*, *ante*.

the modern rule against perpetuities should continue to be as valid after that development as before. That was essentially the core of Palles C.B.'s attitude to possibilities of reverter and rights of entry for condition broken in *Att.-Gen.* v. *Cummins*,[67] which has been accepted by Irish judges in both parts of Ireland since the beginning of this century and which has been reversed only recently by the legislature in Northern Ireland. The same reasoning can be applied to an ordinary legal contingent remainder, *i.e.*, a remainder unaffected by any uses or trusts or which has not become a legal executory interest under the Statute of Uses.[68] Such a remainder, it may be argued, should continue to be governed only by the common law contingent remainder rules and the rule in *Whitby* v. *Mitchell*. If it is valid under these rules, it should not be struck down by an application of the rule against perpetuities, which was intended to control the new future interests. The earlier rules did not apply where there was a conveyance to uses or a legal executory interest as a result of the operation of the Statute of Uses. If there is no violation of the earlier rules, it is argued that there is no reason to apply the rule against perpetuities in a case where there is no use or trust or legal executory interest.

5.113. The question remains, however, how far this reasoning has been applied in Ireland. Direct authority on the point is scarce. Indeed, at most there can only be regarded as existing in the odd judicial dictum a hint as to the true position, which seems to be that the rule against perpetuities does not apply to legal contingent remainders at common law. This seems to follow from the general discussion of the law applicable to common law future interests by Palles C.B. in *Att.-Gen.* v. *Cummins*,[69] which was accepted by the Northern Ireland Court of Appeal in *Walsh* v. *Wightman*.[70] It also seems to have been the view of some of the judges in *Cole* v. *Sewell*, an Irish case which went to the House of Lords.[71] Support for this reasoning came from writers of some older text books.[72] It would seem that the only relevance of the rule against perpetuities to contingent remainders in Ireland lies in the application of the Contingent Remainders Act, 1877. It will be recalled that this Act reversed the rule in *Purefoy* v. *Rogers* by providing that certain remainders should take effect as executory limitations *if they would be valid as such*.[73] The effect of this provision is, of course, to save gifts which, taken as executory limitations, only are valid under the rule against perpetuities. To this extent the rule applies to contingent remainders even in Ireland.

5.114. In England, however, it is settled, since the beginning of this century, that the rule against perpetuities does apply to legal contingent remainders.

---

[67] [1906] 1 I.R. 406 at 408–12 (see *A Casebook on Irish Land Law* (1984), p. 131.

[68] See para. 5.019, *ante*.

[69] [1906] 1 I.R. 406 at 408–12, para. 5.102, *ante*.

[70] [1927] N.I. 1, para. 5.105, *ante*.

[71] (1843) 4 Dr. & War. 1, espec. at 28 (*per* Sugden L.C.), (1848) 2 H.L.C. 186, espec. at 230–5 (*per* Lord Brougham) (see *A Casebook on Irish Land Law* (1984), p. 246). *Cf.* the explanation of his remarks in *Cole* v. *Sewell* by Lord St. Leonards (formerly Sugden L.C.) in *Monypenny* v. *Dering* (1852) 2 De G.M. & G. 145 at 168.

[72] See, *e.g.*, Challis, *Law of Real Property* (3rd ed.), pp. 200 and 213–7; Williams, *Law of Real Property* (12th ed.), pp. 269 and 318.

[73] See para. 5.029, *ante*.

The leading case on the subject in England is *Re Ashforth*,[74] where Farewell J. applied the rule against perpetuities to a devise of land in the form "to A, B and C for their lives, remainder to their children for their lives, remainder to the surviving child in tail." The result was that the remainder in tail was held void. In Farwell J.'s view, the rule against perpetuities applied to that remainder whether it was legal or equitable. It was plain "that the courts have acted upon the principle that the rule against perpetuities is to be applied where no other sufficient protection against remoteness is attainable."[75] His conclusion was:

> "It would certainly be undesirable to add another to the anomalies that adorn our law, as I should succeed in doing if I held that the rule did not apply to legal contingent remainders."[76]

As we have seen, this approach, which really involves a desire to use the modern rule against perpetuities as a "catch-all," comprehensive method of control of future interests has not found favour with the Irish judges.

(b) *Perpetuities Act (N.I.)*, 1966

5.115. This Act once again brings the law of Northern Ireland into line with that of England (in this case as contained in case law only[77]). Section 14 (1) of the 1966 Act provides:

> "The rule against perpetuities shall not be inapplicable to a disposition by reason only that it creates a contingent remainder."

The reason why this provision is in negative terms seems to be that the draftsman wished to avoid any questions arising about the effect of this provision on the operation of the Contingent Remainders Act, 1877. The effect of that Act was to bring certain contingent remainders within the scope of the rule against perpetuities, in the sense that application of the 1877 Act's provisions so as to save a gift otherwise invalid as a contingent remainder is dependent on the remainder then complying with the perpetuity rule.[78]

(xi) **Powers**

5.116. We shall discuss the subject of powers in much greater detail in a later chapter.[79] For the moment we are concerned with the application of the rule against perpetuities to powers.

It is extremely common for a will or settlement to confer powers of disposition or selection of interests in property. Sometimes the donee (the person on whom the power is conferred) is given power to create interests in other people (the objects of the power) and sometimes power to alter existing

---

[74] [1905] 1 Ch. 535. See also *Re Frost* (1889) 43 Ch.D. 246, espec. at 253–4 (*per* Kay J.).
[75] *Op. cit.*, p. 545.
[76] *Op. cit.*, p. 546.
[77] There can be no legal contingent remainders under the 1925 legislation, see Law of Property Act, 1925, s. 1 and 1st Sched., Pt. I.
[78] See para. 5.029, *ante.*
[79] Ch. 11, *post.*

interests. A power of appointment gives the donee of the power the right to decide who should be the owner. There are, however, other powers which do not give the right to decide who becomes entitled but which are administrative only. An example is a devise "to trustees on trust for the children of A but with power in their discretion to sell the property when they think fit." The application of the rule against perpetuities to a power such as a power of sale at common law is debatable.[80] Nowadays, many powers of this nature are conferred automatically by statute on people occupying a special position, e.g., trustees or mortgagees.[81] It would seem that some types of powers, especially some statutory ones, are outside the scope of the rule against perpetuities simply because it is clear that the legislature intended that the powers in question should be exercisable at any time. Thus the various statutory powers (e.g., of sale and leasing) conferred on a tenant for life of land subject to a settlement within the Settled Land Acts, 1881–90, may be exercised by whoever happens to be the tenant for life at any particular time. As we shall see, the policy of these Acts is that such a limited owner should be as unfettered as possible in dealing with the settled land and application of a restriction such as the rule against perpetuities would offend against the policy.[82] We shall also see later that the Perpetuities Act (N.I.), 1966, has laid down some clear guidelines on this matter for Northern Ireland.[83] First, however, we shall discuss the position at common law, especially as regards one of the most common types of power to be conferred in a will or settlement—a power of appointment.

(a) At Common Law

(1) GENERAL

5.117. The general rule at common law as regards powers is that the power must be exercisable only within the perpetuity period. In some cases it may be clear that this is so, e.g., where the power is conferred only on a person who is a life in being.[84] If, however, the power may be exercised outside the period, it is void. The reason is that, since that exercise creates or alters an interest in property, it affects the vesting of the property and the perpetuity rule is concerned with vesting which is too remote. In passing, however, it may be noted that it is established that a gift over in default of appointment under a power may be valid independently of the power, even though the power is void for remoteness.[85]

(2) POWERS OF APPOINTMENT

5.118. At common law the rule against perpetuities applied to powers of

---

[80] Para. 5.127, post.
[81] See chs. 10 and 13, post.
[82] See, generally, ch. 8, post.
[83] Para. 5.149, post.
[84] Re De Sommery [1912] 2 Ch. 622.
[85] Re Hay [1932] N.I. 215 (see A Casebook on Irish Land Law (1984), p. 275).

appointment in accordance with several principles evolved by the courts. A power of appointment is essentially a power conferring on the donee power to select the objects of the property and/or the size of their shares in the property.

So far as the application of the rule against perpetuities is concerned, two basic distinctions have to be observed. The first is the distinction between a *general* power and a *special* power. The second is the distinction between the validity of the power itself and the validity of appointments made in exercise of a power which in itself is valid.

5.119. I. *General Powers.* It is frequently a difficult question of construction whether a power of appointment can be properly classified as general or special. The English authorities seem to establish that a power of appointment will be special for the purposes of the rule against perpetuities if there is some restriction on its exercise (*e.g.*, the donee must first obtain the consent of the donor or some other person[86]), or the objects are a limited class or even an unlimited class, except that the donee cannot appoint to himself.[87] If, on the other hand, the donee is unfettered in his exercise of the power, so much so that he is to all intents and purposes absolute owner of the property, he has a general power. This is particularly so where the donee has an unrestricted power to appoint himself,[88] for he has only to make such an appointment to become absolute owner. It seems that, where the donee has an unrestricted power to appoint to himself by will only, the power is special so far as the validity of the power is concerned.[89]

5.120. The rule at common law with respect to general powers is that, so far as the power itself is concerned, the rule against perpetuities is irrelevent unless the power may not be acquired until the period has passed. In other words, the standard principle that an interest must vest, if at all, within the period applies.

5.121. With respect to appointments made under such a power, assuming the general power itself is valid, the rule is, as in the case of any absolute owner of property, that the perpetuity period runs from the date of the appointment. The rule against perpetuities is applied to the appointment made at that date and the appointment will be valid unless there is a possibility that the property appointed will not vest in the object selected within the perpetuity period. In this respect there is really no difference from the case of a direct gift of the property by a settlor at the same date as the appointment by the donee of the power of appointment.

5.122. II. *Special Powers.* So far as the validity of a special power itself is concerned, the general rule is that the power is void if it is possible that it may be exercised outside the perpetuity period, which runs from the date of operation of the instrument creating the power. It follows that the donee of the

[86] See, *e.g.*, *Re Watts* [1931] 2 Ch. 302. *Cf. Re Dilke* [1921] 1 Ch. 34; *Re Phillips* [1931] 1 Ch. 347.
[87] *Re Park* [1932] 1 Ch. 580. See also *Re Churston Settled Estates* [1954] Ch. 334; *Re Jones* [1945] Ch. 105.
[88] *Cf. Re Penrose* [1933] Ch. 793 and *Re Harvey* [1950] 1 All E.R. 491.
[89] *Wollaston* v. *King* (1868) L.R. 8 Eq. 165; *Morgan* v. *Gronow* (1873) L.R. 16 Eq. 1. *Cf.* the Irish case, *Re Dunbar-Buller* [1923] 2 I.R. 143, espec. at 144–5 (*per* Moore L.J.) and 148–50 (*per* Andrews L.J.) (relating to estate duty).

power must be ascertained within the period and, even though so ascertained, must not be able subsequently to exercise the power outside the period. However, the mere fact that a particular appointment in exercise of power might be invalid does not mean that the power itself is invalid.[90]

5.123. There is a basic distinction at common law between determination of the validity of appointments under a special power of appointment and determination of the validity of appointments made under a general power of appointment. As stated above, exercise of a general power is in practice treated like a direct disposition of the property by an absolute owner and the perpetuity period runs from the date of the appointment. However, in the case of a special power, it is clear that the property is tied up from the date of creation of the power itself and any appointment under the power is strictly controlled by the terms laid down by the settlor in the instrument creating the power. For this reason, in applying the rule against perpetuities to appointments under special powers, the courts at common law regard the perpetuity period as running from the date of creation of the power, not the date of the appointment.[91] The courts have, however, mitigated the apparent harshness of this principle by adopting other principles, some of which do not conform with the principles usually applied under the rule against perpetuities at common law.

5.124. The courts have held that the mere fact that an invalid appointment could possibly be made does not invalidate the power itself. This, in effect, has meant that the courts have introduced at common law an element of "wait and see" into determination of the validity of appointments under special powers.[92] The method of determination of validity is to wait until an appointment is made. The perpetuity period runs from the date of the instrument creating the power, so that the lives in being must be ascertained according to that date. The really significant point is, however, that the courts allow facts known at the date of the appointment to be taken into account in applying the perpetuity period (calculated as outlined above) to the particular appointment.[93] For example, a conveyance might be made in 1950 "to A for life, remainder to such of his children as he shall appoint." In 1960, A appointed to his son S "provided he reaches the age of 25." If S were unborn at the date of the conveyance, strict application of the rule against perpetuities to the 1960 appointment would render the appointment invalid. A was the only life in being in 1960 and, since S was unborn at that date, he might reach the age of 25 more than 21 years after A's death. However, the courts allow facts known at the date of the appointment to be taken into account and this might save the gift. If S were aged 5 in 1960, he would be bound to take the property, if at all, less than 21 years from his father's death and the existence of this fact saves the appointment at common law.

---

[90] *Slark* v. *Dakyns* (1874) 10 Ch.App. 35.
[91] *Massey* v. *Barton* (1844) 7 Ir.Eq.Rep. 95; *D'Abbadie* v. *Bizoin* (1871) I.R. 5 Eq. 205; *Re Manning's Trusts* (1915) 49 I.L.T.R. 143. See also *Re Thompson* [1906] 2 Ch. 199.
[92] See the discussion in *Re Witty* [1913] 2 Ch. 666.
[93] *Re Hallinan's Trusts* [1904] 1 I.R. 452, espec. at 456 and 460 (*per* Porter M.R.) (see *A Casebook on Irish Land Law* (1984), p. 277); *Davy* v. *Clarke* [1920] 1 I.R. 137, espec. at 148 (*per* Powell J.).

5.125. In short, then, determination of the validity of an appointment under a special power is made by calculating the perpetuity period from the date of the creation of the special power, but by applying that period in the light of facts and circumstances known at the date of the appointment.

5.126. The principles we have been discussing with respect to the application of the rule against perpetuities to powers continue to apply in the Republic of Ireland. In Northern Ireland, however, substantial amendments have been introduced by the Perpetuities Act (N.I.), 1966, and it is to these that we now turn.

(b) *Perpetuities Act (N.I.), 1966*

(1) GENERAL

5.127. The most obvious provision of the 1966 Act to effect a substantial change is, of course, the general "wait and see" provision introduced by section 3. This means that in Northern Ireland a power is no longer subject to the general principle that it is void if it is possible that it may be exercised outside the period. It will be void only if it is in fact exercised outside the period. Furthermore, the donee of a power of appointment is expressly included in the list of persons who are lives in being for the purposes of the 1966 Act.[94] Section 8 of the Act exempts certain powers from the operation of the rule against perpetuities. It provides in subsection (1):

> "The rule against perpetuities shall not operate to invalidate a power conferred on trustees or other persons to sell, lease, exchange or otherwise dispose of any property for full consideration, or to do any other act in the administration (as opposed to the distribution) of any property, and shall not prevent the payment to trustees or other persons of reasonable remuneration for their services."

It should be noted that this concession is confined to trustees' administrative powers,[95] which must be exercised for full consideration. If trustees make gifts of property in the purported exercise of these powers the exercise, if otherwise invalid, will be treated as a disposition to which the perpetuity rule applies. Section 8 (2) provides that the concession made in subsection (1) applies to the exercise, after the Act, of powers conferred by instruments which took effect before the Act. This subsection does not, of course, validate any exercise of a power made before the 1966 Act.

(2) POWERS OF APPOINTMENT

5.128. The first significant provision in the 1966 Act with respect to powers of appointment is that the Act provides a definition of a special power for the purposes of the rule against perpetuities. This should help to resolve the

---

[94] S. 3 (5) (b) (v).
[95] The English Law Reform Committee considered these powers to be inappropriate instances of the perpetuity rule's application, see Cmnd. 18 (1956), para. 34.

difficult questions which frequently arise about particular powers.[96] Section 7
(1) of the Act provides:

> "Subject to subsection (2), for the purposes of the rule against
> perpetuities, a power of appointment shall be treated as a special power
> unless—
>
> (a) in the instrument creating the power it is expressed to be exercisable
> by one person only; and
>
> (b) it could, at all times during its currency when that person is of full age
> and capacity, be exercised by him so as immediately to transfer to
> himself the whole of the interest governed by the power without the
> consent of any other person or compliance with any other condition,
> not being a formal condition relating only to the mode of exercise of
> the power."

This provision seems largely to reflect the result of the considerable case law on the
subject, especially in England.[97] Subsection (2) of the same section also reflects
the case law in providing that, in applying the perpetuity rule to an
appointment under a power exercisable by will only, the power is to be treated
as a general power where it would have been so treated if it had been
exercisable by deed.[98]

5.129. So far as the general application of the 1966 Act to powers of
appointment is concerned, most of the Act's provisions apply to such
transactions as they apply to other transactions. Section 16 (2) of the Act
provides that both the conferring of a power of appointment and the exercise of
a power are "dispositions" within the Act. The same subsection provides that
discretionary powers (more usually referred to as "trusts")[99] are included in the
expression "power of appointment." As far as ascertainment of "lives in being"
under the Act is concerned, both donees and objects (actual or potential) of
powers of appointment are included in the list provided in section 3.[1]

5.130. I. *General Powers.* The main change introduced by the 1966 Act is
that in determination of the validity of a general power itself, the "wait and see"
principle ensures that the power will become invalid only if it later turns out
that in fact it will not be exercisable until outside the perpetuity period. The
same principle applies to the case of the determination of the validity of an
appointment made under a general power.

5.131. II. *Special powers.* The first point to note is that section 1 (2) of the
1966 Act provides that the alternative perpetuity period of not more than 80
years can be used only by the person executing an instrument creating a special
power, in which case the period specified in that instrument will also govern

---

[96] See paras. 5.118–23, *ante.*
[97] See para. 5.119, *ante.* S. 16 (5), however, provides that once a power has been construed to be a special
power under section 7, the Act's provisions apply only where both the instruments creating and exercising the
power are executed after the passing of the Act.
[98] *Rous* v. *Jackson* (1885) 29 Ch.D. 521, espec. at 526 (*per* Chitty J.).
[99] See para. 9.081, *post.*
[1] See s. 3 (5) (*b*) (iii)–(v).

appointments made under the power. If, however, the instrument creating the special power does not specify an alternative period under section 1 (1), the donee of the special power cannot invoke that subsection in his exercise of the power and so the common law period of a life or lives in being plus 21 years will govern the appointment.

5.132. With respect to validity of a special power itself, the "wait and see" principle applies under the Act to such a power as it does in the case of a general power. So far as appointments made under a special power are concerned, apart from the "wait and see" principle other principles introduced by the Act may save particular appointments, *e.g.*, the age-reduction and class-exclusion provisions introduced by section 4.[2] Once again it must be emphasised that these provisions will apply only where the instrument creating the power took effect after the passing of the 1966 Act.

(xii) Contractual and Proprietary Interests

5.133. The general principle is that the rule against perpetuities is concerned with property rights, whether real or personal, legal or equitable. It is not concerned with purely personal or contractual rights. The problem often arises, however, that a particular contract, especially in so far as it can affect third parties, may not only create contractual rights, but also rights which appear to have a proprietary character. The following paragraphs attempt to outline the main situations where the rule against perpetuities has been held to be applicable at common law and then to list the changes introduced for Northern Ireland by the Perpetuities Act (N.I.), 1966.

(a) *At Common Law*

5.134. As already mentioned, the general principle at common law is that personal contractual rights are not subject to the rule against perpetuities. This includes the rights of the original parties to a special contract, such as a contract for the sale of land which is specifically enforceable in equity.[3] These rights are, therefore, enforceable as between the parties regardless as to when they are invoked. To the extent that the benefit (as opposed to the burden) of a contract is assignable, it can be enforced against the original promisor regardless of the rule. However, it seems that the assignment itself, since it purports to transfer rights to another person and to that extent passes property, must take effect within the perpetuity period, which runs from the date of the assignment.[4]

5.135. Some contracts, such as a contract for the sale of land, have proprietary characteristics in that they create interests binding successors in title of the original parties. To the extent that such successors claim interests

---

[2] Paras. 5.088 and 5.089–90, *ante*.

[3] Para. 3.144, *ante*. See the general discussion of the application of the rule against perpetuities in such a case by Jenkins J. in *Hutton* v. *Watling* [1948] Ch. 26 at 36 (on appeal [1948] Ch. 398), where he commented: "specific performance is merely an equitable mode of enforcing a personal obligation with which the rule against perpetuities has nothing to do."

[4] Megarry and Wade, *The Law of Real Property* (5th ed., 1984), p. 289.

arising under the contract, the interests must vest within the perpetuity period. Thus, at common law, a contract by A to sell to B land in 30 years' time, while perfectly enforceable as between A and B in 30 years' time, would not be enforceable by C if B immediately assigned the benefit to C. The contract for sale may raise an equitable interest in the purchaser but here the vesting so far as C is concerned is postponed by more than 21 years.[5]

5.136. Much discussion has taken place about the application of the rule against perpetuities to "options" to purchase property. The general rule at common law seems to be that options must be exercised within the perpetuity period. For example, if L leases land to T and in the lease grants T an option to purchase L's reversion (the freehold or superior leasehold), the option will be void if it is exercisable outside the perpetuity period. In most cases the period will be 21 years from the date of the lease since the life of T has no necessary connection with the exercise of the option. However, the period may be extended by use of a "royal lives" clause.[6]

5.137. The one major exception to this general principle governing options to purchase property at common law is that the perpetuities rule does not apply to options to *renew* leases. It has been long established that such an option belongs to the category of leasehold covenants which run with the land and which are outside the scope of the rule against perpetuities.[7] This is a particularly important exception in Ireland in view of the preponderance here of leases for lives renewable for ever.

(b) *Perpetuities Act (N.I.), 1966*

5.138. This Act contains several provisions dealing with the matter discussed above. First, section 11 provides:

> "Where a disposition inter vivos would fall to be treated as void for remoteness if the rights and duties thereunder were capable of transmission to persons other than the original parties and had been so transmitted, it shall be treated as void as between the person by whom it was made and the person to whom or in whose favour it was made or any successor of his, and no remedy shall lie in contract or otherwise for giving effect to it or making restitution for its lack of effect."

The significance of this provision is that it applies the rule against perpetuities for the first time to purely personal contractual rights. No longer is the rule confined to proprietary rights; it may render void rights claimed by the original

---

[5] C may be alive but his life does not seem to have any necessary connection with the interest that will vest in 30 years and so it seems that he will not be regarded as a life in being. See para. 5.067, *ante*.

[6] Para. 5.070, *ante*.

[7] *L. & S.W. Rly.* v. *Gomm* (1882) 20 Ch.D. 562; *Woodall* v. *Clifton* [1905] 2 Ch. 257. And see the discussion by the Irish Court of Appeal in *Re Tyrrell's Estate* [1907] 1 I.R. 292 and the Republic's Supreme Court in *Jameson* v. *Squire* [1948] I.R. 153 (see *A Casebook on Irish Land Law* (1984), p. 280). See also *Re Garde Browne* [1911] 1 I.R. 205; *Tiernan* v. *Feely* [1949] I.R. 381. See also para. 5.145, *post*. Note, however, that the Law of Property Act, 1922, Sched. 15, para. 7, rendered void in England contracts to renew a lease more than 60 years from the lease's termination. There is no equivalent of this provision in either part of Ireland, see *Survey of the Land Law of Northern Ireland* (1971), para. 65.

parties to a contract. If, applying the 1966 Act's "wait and see" principle, the original parties do not exercise their rights or have rights enforced against them within 21 years, the rights cease to be enforceable by or against them. Thus, in our example above of A contracting to sell land to B in 30 years' time, the contract is void *ab initio* since B cannot exercise his rights within 21 years. If the contract instead gave B an unlimited time in which to purchase, he would have to purchase within 21 years or else the contract would be void for perpetuity. This example involves a contract to sell land, but it should be noted that section 11 is not confined to such contracts. It is, however, confined to contracts where the rights and duties of the original parties are capable of transmission to other parties and have in fact been so transmitted. The word "transmission" in this context includes the passing of the rights on death to personal representatives.

5.139. Section 10 of the 1966 Act deals with options relating to land. Section 10 (1) provides:

> "The rule against perpetuities shall not apply to a disposition consisting of the conferring of an option to acquire for valuable consideration an interest reversionary (whether directly or indirectly) on any lease if—
> (*a*) the option is exercisable only by the lessee or his successors in title; and
> (*b*) it ceases to be exercisable at or before the expiration of one year following the determination of the lease."

This provision, which also applies to an agreement for a lease,[8] alters the common law position as regards options to purchase the freehold reversion or superior leasehold reversion on a lease,[9] within the limits set by the subsection.

Finally section 10 (3) of the Act provides:

> "In the case of a disposition consisting of the conferring of an option to acquire for valuable consideration any interest in land (other than such a disposition as is mentioned in subsection (1)), the perpetuity period under the rule against perpetuities shall be twenty-one years, and section 1 shall not apply."

In other words, in the case of options to purchase land, other than options to purchase the reversion on a lease (and, of course, options to renew leases which remain outside the scope of the rule), the grantor of the option cannot extend the normal 21-year period by specifying a period based on lives in being (*e.g.,* a "royal lives" clause) or the alternative period up to 80 years provided by section 1 of the 1966 Act.[10]

3.   *Exceptions from the Rule*

5.140. There are several future interests which are recognised as being

---

[8] S. 10 (2).
[9] Para. 5.136, *ante.*
[10] The 1966 Act does not contain the exception from this provision, contained in s. 9 (2) of the English Perpetuities and Accumulations Act, 1964, in respect of rights of pre-emption conferred on public or local authorities in respect of land used for religious purposes. See Government of Ireland Act, 1920, s. 5.

excepted from the rule against perpetuities. These exceptions were all recognised at common law and are in addition to any of the exceptions created by statute which have already been mentioned.

(i) Interests after Entails

5.141. Interests limited to take effect after an entailed interest are in a special position since they are liable to be destroyed at any time if the tenant in tail bars the entail.[11] For this reason, it seems that the courts in devising the modern rule against perpetuities were not too concerned about the rule's application to such interests.[12] It became settled law that a contingent remainder would remain valid at common law provided it was bound to vest, if at all, during the period of the entailed interest or, at the latest, at the date of determination of the entail.[13] This remained the case despite the fact that the entailed interest might pass through several generations of a family and last for hundreds of years, during which period the determination of the persons entitled to take the remainder might remain unsettled. If, however, the remainder could possibly vest at a date later than the natural determination of the entail, then the remainder is void at common law.

5.142. This remains the law in the Republic of Ireland. So far as Northern Ireland is concerned, the Perpetuities Act (N.I.), 1966, does not make any specific change but its general provisions may make a difference in a particular case. Thus a remainder void at common law would be saved by the Act's "wait and see" provisions[14] if it vested in fact *within the perpetuity period* (*i.e.*, a life or lives in being plus 21 years). The important point to note is that the Act will save the gift only if the vesting takes place within the normal perpetuity period. The Act does not have any special provision that regard is to be had to the period of the entailed interest as the appropriate perpetuity period in such a case.

(ii) Charitable Gifts

5.143. All too often misleading statements are made about the application of the rule against perpetuities to charitable gifts.[15] The cause of widely existing confusion is that the rule against inalienability[16] does not apply to charitable gifts while the rule against perpetuities does. In fact, the rule applies to such gifts in the same way as it applies to ordinary gifts, with one exception. This is that, where a gift to one charity is followed in the same limitation by a gift to another charity, the courts have long held at common law that the gift over to

---

[11] See paras. 4.117 *et seq.*, *ante*.
[12] Morris and Leach, *The Rule Against Perpetuities* (2nd ed.), p. 195; Challis, *The Law of Real Property* (3rd ed.), p. 180.
[13] *Nicolls* v. *Sheffield* (1787) 2 Bro.C.C. 215.
[14] Para. 5.062, *ante*.
[15] See, generally, Keeton and Sheridan, *The Modern Law of Charities* (2nd ed., 1971), ch. XVII; also Morris and Leach, *The Rule Against Perpetuities* (2nd ed.); Gray, "Remoteness of Charitable Gifts" (1894) 7 H.L.R. 406; Lisle, "Remoteness of Charitable Gifts Once More" (1895) 8 H.L.R. 211.
[16] Para. 5.036, *ante*.

the second charity is not void simply because it may not vest within the perpetuity period.[17] In all other cases the normal principles of the rule against perpetuities apply at common law[18] and no change in this position has been made by legislation in either part of Ireland.

(iii) Rights under Leases

5.144. It has been recognised by the courts of both England and Ireland that rights incident to a lease are exempt at common law from the rule against perpetuities. Any other rule would severely restrict the operation of leasehold interests, which are generally more readily enforceable than freehold interests.[19] Thus under the standard forfeiture clause put in most leases the landlord, and his successors in title, are usually given the right to re-enter the land and forfeit the lease for breach of covenant or condition by the tenant, or his successors in title. This right of re-entry remains a contingent right which may vest in possession, by becoming exercisable at any time during the continuance of the lease, whatever the length of the term of years granted.[20] And it has to be remembered that, in Ireland, this will often be a very substantial period of time, *e.g.*, 999 years, or be annexed to the fee simple under a fee farm grant.[21]

(iv) Rights under Rentcharges

5.145. A right of entry similar to a right of re-entry under a lease is usually inserted in a deed creating a rentcharge, by way of enforcement of the rentcharge against successive owners of the land charged.[22] Such a right is now implied by statute in both parts of Ireland, under section 44 of the Conveyancing Act, 1881, and section 6 (1) of the Conveyancing Act, 1911, provides:

> "For removing doubts, it is hereby declared that the rule of law relating to perpetuities does not apply to any powers or remedies conferred by section forty-four of the Act of 1881, nor to the same or like powers or remedies conferred by any instrument for recovering or compelling the payment of any annual sum within the meaning of that section."

Apart from this provision, it had been held in Ireland that a right to redeem at any time a rentcharge secured by powers of distress and re-entry and exercisable at any time for hundreds of years did not violate the rule against

---

[17] *Christ's Hospital* v. *Grainger* (1849) 1 Mac. & G. 460; *Re Tyler* [1891] 3 Ch. 252; *Re Dalziel* [1943] Ch. 277; *Re Mander* [1950] Ch. 547; *Royal College of Surgeons of England* v. *National Provincial Bank Ltd.* [1952] A.C. 631. *Cf. R.S.P.C.A. of N.S.W.* v. *Benevolent Society of N.S.W.* (1960) 102 C.L.R. 629.

[18] *Commrs. of Charitable Donations and Bequests* v. *Clifford* (1841) 1 Dr. & War. 245; *Re Gordon* (1901) 35 I.L.T.R. 25; *Re Kingham* [1897] 1 I.R. 170; *Re Bowen* [1893] 2 Ch. 491.

[19] *Cf., e.g.*, the law relating to restrictions on alienation (para. 5.034, *ante*, and ch. 19, *post*) and the running of the benefit and burden of convenants (chs. 17 and 19, *post*).

[20] See *Re Tyrrell's Estate* [1907] 1 I.R. 292 at 298 (*per* Walker C.); *Re Garde Browne* [1911] 1 I.R. 205 at 210. See also *Woodall* v. *Clifton* [1905] 2 Ch. 257. *Cf.* the position with respect to common law conditions in defeasance of a freehold estate in England and Ireland, para. 5.103, *ante*.

[21] See ch. 4, *ante*.

[22] On the subject of rentcharges, see ch. 6, *post*.

perpetuities,[23] but this has since been doubted in a number of cases in which provisos for redemption of rentcharges were held void.[24]

5.146. In Northern Ireland, section 6 (1) of the 1911 Act has been replaced by section 12 (1) of the Perpetuities Act (N.I.), 1966, and, in doing so, section 12 (1) extends the exemption from the perpetuity rule to cover *any* powers or remedies for enforcement of a rentcharge or of any term or condition relating to it. This new provision clears up the doubt that still exists in the Republic, which hs no equivalent provision as yet, as to whether the remedies contained in section 44 of the Conveyancing Act, 1881, and which are cross-referred to in section 6 (1) of the 1911 Act, are the only methods of enforcing rentcharges. Thus section 44 does not seem to cover the case of a right of re-entry on non-payment of a rent charged on a fee simple estate, giving power to forfeit that estate altogether. As it happens, the Irish courts quite independently of the statutory provisions decided that such a right of entry for condition broken was exempt from the rule against perpetuities at common law.[25] Those decisions, however, have now been reversed in Northern Ireland by section 13 (1) of the Perpetuities Act (N.I.), 1966, *except* for the case of rentcharges relating to the fee simple. Section 12 (1) of the 1966 Act, in exempting all powers and remedies for enforcement of rentcharges, is stated expressly to operate notwithstanding anything in section 13.

(v) Rights under Mortgages

5.147. It is a well-established principle of the common law that the rule against perpetuities does not apply to mortgages.[26] Thus the mortgagor's right to redeem the property mortgaged may be postponed regardless of the rule against perpetuities,[27] though unreasonable postponement may be controlled in equity by the doctrine relating to clogs on the equity of redemption.[28]

(vi) Rights of Survivorship

5.148. As we shall see,[29] in the case of the form of co-ownership of property known as a "joint tenancy," each joint tenant has a right of survivorship, *i.e.*, the joint tenant who survives the other joint tenants takes the whole property and nothing passes to the deceased joint tenant's or tenants' estates. However, as we shall also see, a joint tenancy can always be "severed" so as to destroy the right of survivorship and for this reason the courts held that there was no more

---

[23] *Switzer & Co.* v. *Rochford* [1906] 1 I.R. 399, but see doubts expressed by the Court of Appeal in *Re Tyrrell's Estate* [1907] 1 I.R. 292. *Cf.* the authorities in Ireland and England relating to rights of entry for condition broken attached to a fee simple estate, para. 5.103, *ante*.

[24] See *Re Donoughmore's Estate* [1911] 1 I.R. 211 and *Re Ramadge's Estate* [1919] 1 I.R. 205, applying *Re Tyrrell's Estate* [1907] 1 I.R. 292.

[25] Para. 5.105, *ante*.

[26] On the subject of mortgages generally, see chs. 12 and 13, *post*.

[27] *Knightsbridge Estates Trust Ltd.* v. *Byrne* [1939] Ch. 441 at 463 (*per* Greene M.R.), aff'd. [1940] A.C. 613.

[28] Ch. 13, *post*.

[29] Ch. 7, *post*.

need to apply the rule against perpetuities to such a destructable right[30] than there was to apply the rule to remainders after an entail.[31]

(vii) Statutory Restrictions

5.149. Section 9 of the Perpetuities Act (N.I.), 1966, lists a series of rights which may operate outside the rule against perpetuities.[32] For the most part these are rights which would be exercised only in respect of other interests in land which are clearly valid at law. Section 9 (1) of the 1966 Act states:

"It is hereby declared that the rule against perpetuities does not apply, and never applied, to—

  (*a*) any power to distrain[33] on or to take possession of land or the income thereof given by way of indemnity against a rent, whether charged upon or payable in respect of any part of that land or not; or

  (*b*) any rentcharge created only as an indemnity against another rentcharge, although the indemnity rentcharge may arise or become payable only on breach of a condition or stipulation; or

  (*c*) any power, whether exercisable on breach of a condition or stipulation or not to retain or withhold payment of any instalment of a rentcharge as an indemnity against another rentcharge; or

  (*d*) any grant, exception, or reservation of any right of entry on, or user of, the surface of land or any easements, rights, or privileges over or under land for the purpose of—

      (i) winning, working, inspecting, measuring, converting, manufacturing, carrying away, and disposing of mines and minerals;

      (ii) inspecting, grubbing up, felling and carrying away timber and other trees, and the tops and lops thereof;

      (iii) executing repairs, alterations, or additions to any adjoining land, or the buildings and erections thereon;

      (iv) constructing, laying down, altering, repairing, renewing, cleansing, and maintaining sewers, water-courses, cesspools, gutters, drains, water-pipes, gas-pipes, electric wires or cables or other like works."

These provisions apply to instruments coming into operation in Northern Ireland before or after the passing of the 1966 Act.[34] No equivalent legislation exists in the Republic of Ireland but, since the Northern statutory provisions seem to be largely declaratory of the common law, the position is probably the same in the Republic.

---

[30] *Re Roberts* (1881) 19 Ch.D. 520.
[31] Para. 5.141, *ante*.
[32] *Cf.* s. 162 of the English Law of Property Act, 1925.
[33] The power of distress was abolished by s. 121 of the Judgments (Enforcement) Act (N.I.), 1969, and enforcement through the Enforcement of Judgments Office was substituted, see para. 17.066, *post*.
[34] S. 9 (2).

D. Rule Against Accumulations

5.150. The rule against accumulations is designed to prevent settlors from directing that the income from property should be tied up, or accumulated, for an unreasonable period of time. In this sense, the rule against accumulations has a purpose similar to that of the rule against inalienability.[35] However, the rule has a very limited application in Ireland.

5.151. At common law the rule against accumulations was simply that a direction that income should be accumulated was invalid only if carrying out the direction involved accumulation beyond the perpetuity period.

A vivid illustration of this rule was afforded by the leading English case of *Thelluson* v. *Woodford*.[36] In this case income had been directed to be accumulated at compound interest during the lives of the testator's sons, grandsons and great-grandchildren living at his death, and on the death of the survivor of these persons the accumulated sum was to be divided among other descendants. Potentially the accumulated fund could have amounted to millions of pounds,[37] yet it was held to be valid at common law. The direction to accumulate was clearly confined to a period of time governed by lives in being and 21 years, and so was within the perpetuity period. This common law position with respect ot accumulations has been followed by the Irish courts.[38]

5.152. In England, however, the *Thelluson* case caused such a storm that Parliament reacted quickly and passed the Accumulations Act, 1800, often referred to as the "Thelluson Act." This Act[39] imposed considerable restrictions on the power to direct accumulation of income, but it did *not* apply to Ireland and so no further discussion of its provisions is warranted here, except for one point. The 1800 Act was amended by the Accumulations Act, 1892, and the 1892 Act for some reason *was* made applicable to Ireland, despite the fact that the principal Act of 1800 did not apply. This seems to be another instance of Westminster legislating for Ireland in the nineteenth century without appreciating the existing legislative position across the Irish Sea.[40]

5.153. The 1892 Act provided that, in the case of a direction to accumulate income for the purchase of land only, the accumulation may not be for any period longer than the duration of the minority or respective minorities of any person or persons who, under the limitations of the instrument directing the accumulation, would for the time being, if of full age, be entitled to the income

---

[35] Discussed at para. 5.033, *ante*.

[36] (1799) 4 Ves. 227; (1805) 11 Ves. 112. See Keeton "The Thelluson Case and Trusts for Accumulation" (1970) 21 N.I.L.Q. 131; Holdsworth, *History of English Law*, vol. VII, pp. 228–30.

[37] In fact, it appears that mismanagement and litigation took its toll, see references in previous footnote. *Cf.* the Irish case of *Londonderry* v. *Londonderry* (1854) 4 Ir.Ch.R. 361.

[38] *Cochrane* v. *Cochrane* (1883) 11 L.R.Ir. 361; *Smith* v. *Cuninghame* (1884) 13 L.R.Ir. 480; *Longfield* v. *Bantry* (1885) 15 L.R.Ir. 101.

[39] Now replaced by the Law of Property Act, 1925, ss. 164–6. For amendments to the 1925 Act, see the Perpetuities Accumulations Act, 1964, s. 13. The fact that the lack of a Thelluson Act sometimes encouraged investment in and transfer of funds to Northern Ireland was brought out in the recent House of Lords decision in *Vestey* v. *I.R.C. (Nos. 1 and 2)* [1979] 3 W.L.R. 915, see especially Lord Wilberforce at p. 920.

[40] For other instances, see para. 17.071, *post*.

so directed to be accumulated.[41] This statutory restriction expressly did not apply to accumulations to be held as capital money under the Settled Land Acts, 1881–90.[42]

[41] See *Shillington* v. *Portadown U.D.C.* [1911] 1 I.R. 247.
[42] See ch. 8, *post*.

CHAPTER 6

INCORPOREAL HEREDITAMENTS

I. INTRODUCTION

6.001. The law of incorporeal hereditaments is concerned with various minor interests in land which have come to be recognised over the centuries. Much of the law is of feudal origin and, indeed, some of it has become of historical interest only. This chapter concentrates on those aspects of the law which remain of practical significance in Ireland today.

II. TERMINOLOGY

6.002. The expression "incorporeal hereditament" itself gives a clue as to its meaning. *Hereditaments* indicates that the rights or interests in question were recognised as part of real property, which, until the recent developments in the law of succession in both parts of Ireland,[1] was governed by the feudal law of inheritance.[2] Thus, on the death intestate of the owner of an incorporeal hereditament, his interest in it descended to his heir-at-law as realty, rather than to his next-of-kin as personalty. Similarly, the feudal system of estates in land,[3] including future interests,[4] applied to incorporeal hereditaments.[5] Incorporeal hereditaments were said to "lie in grant," *i.e.*, they could be created by a deed only.[6]

6.003. The epithet *incorporeal* indicates the distinguishing feature of the hereditaments considered in this chapter when compared with the major estates and interests in land discussed in earlier chapters.[7] A *corporeal* hereditament is one which consists of a physical object, *i.e.*, its ownership confers on the owner the incidents (*e.g.*, the right to possession) of ownership of the physical matter which, being a hereditament, is land, buildings and other things affixed to the land[8] or a part of the land, *e.g.*, minerals. An *incorporeal* hereditament, on the other hand, is not a thing at all, but is a mere right,[9] *i.e.*,

---

[1] See ch. 15, *post*.

[2] Paras. 2.19, *ante* and 7.40, *post*.

[3] Ch. 4, *ante*.

[4] Ch. 5, *ante*.

[5] It seems, however, that not all the incidents of the feudal system applied to incorporeal hereditaments. The view was taken that certain incorporeal hereditaments, *e.g.*, rentcharges and rights of common, were not strictly the subjects of "tenure"—they did not come into the category of "tenements"—and so, *e.g.*, the law of escheat (para. 2.24, *ante*) did not apply. On failure of the heirs, the incorporeal hereditament became extinguished. See Challis, *Law of Real Property* (3rd ed., 1911), p. 38; Pike (1889) 5 L.Q.R. 32. *Cf. Re Franks's Estate* [1915] 1 I.R. 387; *Pinkerton v. Pratt* [1915] 1 I.R. 406.

[6] See further, para. 6.030, *post*.

[7] Especially ch. 4, *ante*. Note the provisions in ss. 8 and 83 of the Republic's Registration of Title Act, 1964, for a Register of Incorporeal Hereditaments to be maintained in the Land Registry; *cf.* Land Registration Act (N.I.), 1970, s. 10(*b*) (Register of Subsidiary Interests). See ch. 21, *post*.

[8] See further on the law of fixtures, para. 4.155, *ante*.

[9] This distinction between rights and things has been much criticised over the centuries but it has been too long established to be ignored now. See, *e.g.*, Austin, *Jurisprudence*, vol. 1, p. 372; Challis, *Law of Real Property* (3rd

its ownership simply confers certain rights over the land in question but not the right to possession of the land itself. In other words, whereas the law of corporeal hereditaments is concerned with the ownership which the holder of the hereditament has in his own land (the "corpus"), the law of incorporeal hereditaments is concerned with the rights which the holder has over someone else's land. In many cases these rights are of a very minor nature, in terms of both the frequency of their exercise in relation to the land in question[10] and the interference with the physical enjoyment of that land by its estate owners.[11] In some cases the rights are of little value in the commercial sense, when compared with the total value of the land to which they relate,[12] though they may be of considerable value to the holder, especially when enjoyed by him as part of his ownership of neighbouring land.[13] Indeed, the law of incorporeal hereditaments is frequently concerned with rights as between neighbouring landowners.[14]

6.004. Finally, incorporeal hereditaments are legal rights which were recognised by the common law and there is generally little problem about their being enforceable by or against successors in title to the parties who originally created them. In this respect they differ considerably from other minor interests or rights which can be created in respect of land but which, though enforceable at common law between the original parties, affect third parties in equity only, e.g., restrictive covenants[15] or licences.[16] One, if not the most, important point to be discussed in relation to such equitable interests in land is the question of their enforceability by and against successors in title.

III. CLASSIFICATION

The following seem to be the main incorporeal hereditaments which have been recognised over the centuries.[17] Several of them are now obsolete and some may have had little recognition in Ireland.

A. EASEMENTS AND PROFITS

6.005. Easements and profits *à prendre* (to give them their full title), are now, perhaps, the most common of incorporeal hereditaments, yet it seems that they have been recognised as coming within this classification only in comparatively

---

ed., 1911) pp. 48–58 (editor Sweet's notes). Also *Lloyd* v. *Jones* (1848) 6 C.B. 81 at 90. *Cf.* the definition of "land" in s. 2 (ii) of the Conveyancing Act, 1881, and of "land" and "estate" in s. 45 (1) (*a*) and (2) of the Interpretation Act (N.I.), 1954. See also ss. 4 and 12 of, and the Sched. to, the Interpretation Act, 1937 (R.I.) Para. 1.01 fn. 3, *ante*.

[10] *E.g.*, a right of way, para. 6.107, *post*. But *cf.* a right of access to an hotel.

[11] *E.g.*, a rentcharge or other periodic rent issuing out of the land, para. 6.007 *et seq.*, *post*. *Cf.* quarrying rights which may exhaust the land.

[12] *E.g.*, periodic rents, *ibid*.

[13] *E.g.*, rights of support or of light, paras. 6.108 and 6.111, *post*.

[14] Para. 6.025, *post*. This is not the only part of land law concerned with rights as between neighbours, see also, *post*, *e.g.*, party walls, para. 7.53, and restrictive covenants, ch. 19, *post*.

[15] See ch. 19, *post*.

[16] See ch. 20, *post*.

[17] *Cf.* Blackstone, *Commentaries on the Laws of England* (15th ed. by Christian, 1809), vol. II, ch. 3.

modern times.[18] Previously, easements and certain profits, *i.e.*, those annexed to a particular piece of land,[19] were regarded as mere rights or privileges appurtenant to corporeal hereditaments, *i.e.*, the lands whose owners held the rights or privileges. Nowadays, however, they are regarded as belonging properly within the category of incorporeal hereditaments with rights which are clearly not appurtenant to land, *e.g.*, profits in gross.[20]

6.006. An easement is a right which a landowner has, by virtue of his ownership of his land, over the land of his neighbour, *e.g.*, rights of way, light, support and water. Many landowners in fact have one or more of these rights. A profit *à prendre* can also exist as between neighbouring landowners, but it is commonly enjoyed "in gross," *i.e.*, independently of any land owned by the holder of the profit. A profit is the right to go on to another person's land and to take from it something regarded as belonging to it naturally, *e.g.*, game, fish, timber, minerals and turf.

The subject of easements and profits is considered in more detail later.[21]

B. Periodic Rents

6.007. One of the striking features of the development of Irish land law has been the number of different periodic rents which have been created to issue out of land.[22] Most of these rents survive to this day and their continued existence is one of the major causes of complexity in the titles to land. The following are the main categories of periodic rents, though it must be emphasised at the outset that these categories are by no means mutually exclusive. Furthermore, the following list does not include perhaps the most common periodic rent,[23] a leasehold rent reserved to a landlord under a lease or tenancy agreement.[24] Such rents did not come within the classification of incorporeal hereditaments and were regarded at common law as being annexed to the landlord's reversion in the same land subject to the rent, *i.e.*, they were not regarded as existing on their own as incorporeal hereditaments held over someone else's land.

1. Crown Rents

6.008. One type of Crown rent was a rent reserved to the Crown on the making of grants of land under the feudal system. Such rents could, of course, be reserved by lords throughout the feudal pyramid of landowners as subinfeuda-

---

[18] Challis, *Law of Real Property* (3rd ed., 1911), pp. 55–6 (Sweet's notes). See also *Hewlins* v. *Shippam* (1826) 5 B. & C. 221; *Hill* v. *Midland Rly.* (1882) 21 Ch.D. 143; *Lord Hastings* v. *North Eastern Rly.* [1900] A.C. 260.

[19] See further, para. 6.036, *post*.

[20] Para. 6.038, *post*.

[21] Paras. 6.022 *et seq.*, *post*.

[22] See further, *Survey of the Land Law of Northern Ireland* (1971), ch. 20; Land Law Working Group's Discussion Document No. 1 (*Ground Rents and Other Periodic Payments*) (1980) and Interim Report (*Ground Rents and Other Periodic Payments*) (1983).

[23] Which may be defined as any rent issuing out of land which is payable on regular recurrent dates, continuing for a set time, an indefinite time (*e.g.*, for life) or for ever (*i.e.*, annexed to a fee simple estate in the land. Note, therefore, that a "periodic" tenancy (para. 4.011, *ante* and ch. 17, *post*) in relation to leasehold land is a much narrower use of the word "periodic".

[24] See ch. 17, *post*.

tion occurred [25] and the common name for such rents, issuing to the Crown or not, was chief rent.[26] However, the prohibition of further subinfeudation of land by *Quia Emptores*, 1290, and the subsequent crumbling of the feudal pyramid of landholding meant that most of these rents disappeared.[27] Those that did survive down to modern times were those reserved directly to the Crown as ultimate feudal owner and it is just possible, though highly unlikely, that some survive in the Republic of Ireland, where, of course, as former Crown rents they belong to the State,[28] or in Northern Ireland, where they remain Crown property. Because of the possibility of the survival of a few such rents[29] even comparatively recent legislation in both parts of Ireland contains references to Crown or, in the Republic, former Crown, rents.[30]

Another type of Crown rent in Ireland is a quit rent, which will be considered next.

2. *Quit Rents*

6.009. Quit rents in Ireland should not be confused with the rents of the same name which used to be common in England. In England, a quit rent was a rent service payable by a copyhold tenant to the lord of his manor, which was so called because it was a rent paid by him in substitution for the agricultural services relating to his tenure which previously had to be performed, *i.e.*, he became "quit" of his services.[31] It is possible that such rents existed also in Ireland in the days when some copyhold tenure was to be found, but any that did exist have long since disappeared along with copyhold, manors and everything that related thereto.[32] What has survived, however, is another form of quit rent peculiar to Ireland, dating from the seventeenth century.[33]

6.010. Irish quit rents are perpetual rents reserved to the Crown under the confiscation and resettlement legislation passed by the Irish Parliament in 1662 and 1665.[34] The Commissioners appointed under this legislation redistributed

[25] Para. 2.35, *ante*.

[26] In fact, it appears that in the very early days of the feudal system chief rents were known as fee farm rents. See *Coke on Littleton* (19th ed., 1832), 143b, n. 5 (by Hargrave). Also Statute of Gloucester, 1278, 6 Edw. 1, para. 1.24, *ante*, and Chief Rents Redemption (Ir.) Act, 1864, para. 4.074, *ante*. *Archbishop of Dublin* v. *Lord Trimleston* (1842) 2 Dr. & War. 535; *Re Scott* (1906) 40 I.L.T.R. 97.

[27] Para. 2.44, *ante*. It is possible that the Chief Rents Redemption (Ir.) Act, 1864, applied to such Crown quit rents, see para. 4.074, *ante*.

[28] State Property Acts, 1954, ss. 13–18 and 24.

[29] Most of these Crown rents will have been redeemed under the Land Purchase Acts, see, *e.g.*, the Republic's State Property Act, 1954, s. 14 and para. 6.012, *infra*.

[30] *E.g.*, in the Republic, Statute of Limitations, 1957, s. 2 (1) (reference in para. (*b*) (i) of definition of "rentcharge"); Registration of Title Act, 1964, s. 72 (1) (*a*). For Northern Ireland, see Statute of Limitations (N.I.), 1958, s. 74 (1) (reference in para. (*b*) (i) of definition of "rentcharge"); Land Registration Act (N.I.), 1970, Sched. 5, Pt. I, para. 1. Of course, strictly speaking Crown rents reserved under the feudal system are not rentcharges, or rents seck, but are rent services. See further on this distinction, paras. 6.015 and 6.131, *post*.

[31] See further, para. 2.30, *ante*.

[32] Para. 2.33, *ante*.

[33] See the useful anonymous note, "A Notice on Quit Rents in Northern Ireland" (1952) 10 N.I.L.Q. 30. Also, *Report of the Departmental Committee on Irish Forestry* (1908, Cmd. 4027), App. VI.

[34] Settlement of Ireland Acts, 1662, 14 & 15 Chas. 2, sess. 4, c. 2 (Ir.) and 1665, 17 & 18 Chas. 2, c. 2 (Ir.). *Cf.* the earlier Settlement Acts of 1634, 10 Chas. 1, c. 3 and 10 Chas. 1. sess. 3, cc. 2 and 3 (Ir.) and 1639, 15 Chas. 1, sess. 2, c. 6 (Ir.). See *Hatton* v. *Waddy* (1837) 2 Jon. 541; *Tuthill* v. *Rogers* (1844) 6 Ir.Eq.R 429; *Massy* v. *O'Dell* (1859) 10 Ir.Ch.R. 22. Paras. 1.31–3, *ante*.

the forfeited land subject to payment of quit rents which were calculated according to the following rates per acre:—Munster 2¾d; Ulster 2d; Connaught 1½d.[35] A rent roll was drawn up showing all the land in Ireland subject to such quit rents, which seems to have been based largely on the maps prepared during Petty's "Down Survey."[36]

6.011. Most of these quit rents came within the land purchase schemes in both the Republic of Ireland and Northern Ireland.[37] The Land Purchase Acts provided that if land being bought out by the tenant was subject to a quit rent, the quit rent could be redeemed.[38] If, as was usual, the quit rent related to a much larger area of land than that of the holding being purchased, the quit rent was apportioned between the holding purchased and the remainder of the denomination subject to the quit rent,[39] and the portion of the quit rent so relating to the holding purchased was then redeemed.

6.012. The operation of the Land Purchase Acts has resulted in a drastic reduction in the number of quit rents due to the State in the Republic or the Crown in Northern Ireland. Yet even in Northern Ireland, where the land purchase scheme was wound up as long ago as 1935,[40] a few have survived. In 1937 some 34 quit rents remained, 15 of these being payable in respect of markets and fairs and 19 in respect of land.[41] However, largely as a result of voluntary redemption since then, it was reported at Westminster on May 15, 1969, that 8 quit rents only were then collected on behalf of the Crown Estate Commissioners in Northern Ireland.[42] The result is, therefore, that practitioners in Ireland will come across such rents very rarely but their continued survival constitutes a nuisance, albeit a minor one, for the purposes of title investigation.[43] It must always be remembered that, even where the title to the land is registered in the Land Registry, in both parts of Ireland a quit rent remains a burden which affects the land *without* registration.[44] As one writer

---

[35] Pre-decimalisation currency. Where land was not entirely re-granted, the undistributed portions were referred to as "plus lands" or "plus acres" and an Act of 1703, 2 Anne, c. 8 (Ir.), vested these portions in the persons then in possession subject to the same quit rent as the remainder of that denomination.

[36] Para. 1.32, *ante*. It seems that Petty prepared his own barony maps as well as official parish maps, but these were captured by the French in 1707 when on their way by ship from Dublin to London and the originals remain in France to this day. Copies were made in 1787 and sent to Ireland, but they were lost in the destruction of the Public Record Office, Dublin in 1922. See (1952) 10 N.I.L.Q. 30 at 31.

[37] Paras. 1.51 *et seq.*, *ante*. See as regards recovery, etc. of quit rents, Crown Lands (Ir.) Act, 1822, ss. 12–13, still in force in both parts of Ireland. Also the Republic's State Property Act, 1954, s. 16.

[38] See, *e.g.*, pre-1920: Purchase of Land (Ir.) Act, 1885, s. 10; Land Law (Ir.) Act, 1887, ss. 15 and 16; Redemption of Rent (Ir.) Act, 1891; Purchase of Land (Ir.) Act, 1891, s. 20; Land Law (Ir.) Act, 1896, ss. 31, 33 and 37; Irish Land Act, 1903, ss. 61–4. Post-1920, Republic of Ireland: Land Acts, 1923, s. 39; 1925, s. 4; 1931, s. 36 (4); 1933, s. 2; 1934, s. 2; 1939 ss. 45, 48 and 52; 1950, ss. 19 and 26; State Property Act, 1954, ss. 14 and 21. See also Northern Ireland Land Act, 1925, s. 20: *Re Clement's Estate* [1924] 1 I.R. 165; *Eustace-Duckett* v. *Thompson* (1938) 72 I.L.T.R. 226; *Re Keyser's Estate* [1938] I.R. 326.

[39] See, as regards apportionment of superior rents, Landlord and Tenant (Ir.) Act, 1870, s. 40; Land Law (Ir.) Act, 1881, s. 38 (2). Also statutes cited in fn. 38, *supra* and the Republic's State Property Act, 1954, s. 13.

[40] Northern Ireland Land Purchase (Winding Up) Act, 1935.

[41] (1952) 10 N.I.L.Q. 30 at 33.

[42] The average annual amount of the rents was reported as being £2. 2s. 4d. and the cost of collection 15s. per annum (pre-decimalisation currency). See *Survey of the Land Law of Northern Ireland* (1971), para. 459.

[43] For comparatively modern references to quit rents, see the Republic's Statute of Limitations, 1957, s. 2 (1) (para. (*b*) (ii) of definition of "rentcharge"). Also Statute of Limitations (N.I.), 1958, s. 74 (1) (para. (*b*) (ii) of definition of "rentcharge").

[44] Registration of Title Act, 1964, s. 72 (1) (*a*); Land Registration Act (N.I.), 1970, Sched. 5, Pt. I, para. 2. See ch. 21, *post*.

has remarked: "The quit rent, like the dead donkey, is not often seen but the young lawyer should know how to deal with any he may stumble across."[45]

3. Fee Farm Rents

6.013. The nature of rents reserved under fee farm grants in Ireland was considered in detail in an earlier chapter.[46] Suffice it to say here that most of these rents in Ireland are leasehold rents, being reserved in grants creating the relationship of landlord and tenant under Deasy's Act, 1860,[47] or renewable leasehold conversion grants.[48] Otherwise they are feudal rents—either ancient ones surviving from the thirteenth century or before, which is highly unlikely,[49] or rents reserved under grants made under Crown letters patent after the seventeenth century plantation schemes, especially the one in Ulster[50]—or they are rentcharges creating no relationship of landlord and tenant.[51] Rentcharges are considered further later in this chapter.[52]

4. Tithe Rentcharges

6.014. The nature of these rentcharges is also discussed in detail later in this chapter.[53] Originally tithes (the right to one-tenth of the produce of all land in a parish) were payable in kind, *i.e.*, in the form of agricultural produce, to the owners, whether clergy, educational institutions or lay persons. Then the Tithe Composition (Ireland) Acts, 1823, 1824, 1827 and 1832,[54] provided for money compositions in lieu of payment in kind. This legislation was followed by the Church Temporalities (Ireland) Acts, 1833, 1834 and 1836, the Tithe Rentcharge (Ireland) Acts, 1838 and 1900, and the Irish Church Acts, 1869, 1872 and 1881,[55] which facilitated redemption of tithes by the landowners and their conversion into fixed rentcharges. A significant number of these tithe rentcharges survived until recently in both parts of Ireland.[56] However, in the Republic, section 7 (3) of the Land Act, 1984, extinguished all tithe rentcharges subsisting on 28th September, 1975, and payable into the Church Temporalities Fund. Section 7 (2) dissolved the Fund and section 7 (3) provided for dispersal of sums in it for the benefit of the Exchequer.

---

[45] Anon., "A Notice on Quit Rents in Northern Ireland" (1952) 10 N.I.L.Q. 30 at 34.

[46] Ch. 4, *ante*.

[47] Paras. 4.091 *et seq.*, *ante*.

[48] Paras. 4.078 *et seq.*, *ante*.

[49] Para. 4.059, *ante*.

[50] Paras. 1.30 and 4.060, *ante*.

[51] Para. 4.104, *ante*.

[52] Paras. 6.015 and 6.131, *post*.

[53] Para. 6.120, *post*.

[54] Note also some local and personal legislation, *e.g.*, Connor Tithes Act, 1824, 5 Geo. 4, c. 80.

[55] See also Purchase of Land (Ir.) Act, 1885, s. 23; Land Law (Ir.) Act, 1887, s. 25; Land Law (Ir.) Act, 1896, s. 26.

[56] Note the references in the Republic's Statute of Limitations, 1957, s. 2 (1) (paras. (*a*) and (*b*) (iii) of the definition of "rentcharge") and Registration of Title Act, 1964, s. 72 (1) (*a*); also Statute of Limitations (N.I.), 1958, s. 74 (1) (paras. (*a*) (ii) and (*b*) (iii) of the definition of "rentcharge") and Land Registration Act (N.I.), 1970, Sched. 5, Pt. I, para. 2.

5. *Rentcharges*

6.015. Rentcharges, to be distinguished from rent services created between landlords and tenants,[57] exist in several forms in Ireland. Tithe rentcharges have just been mentioned. Some fee farm grants create perpetual rentcharges and no relationship of landlord and tenant between the grantor and grantee.[58] It is common for rentcharges, usually known as "pin-money" rentcharges, to be created under settlements of land to provide income for members of the family.[59] Rentcharges may also be created by way of indemnity on the subdivision of land.[60] Finally, certain statutory rentcharges exist in both parts of Ireland, *e.g.*, rentcharges in payment of advances under the Landed Property Improvement (Ireland) Act, 1847.[61] The subject of rentcharges will be considered further later in this chapter.[62]

C. ANNUITIES

6.016. An annuity is a sum of money payable annually. It may be perpetual or for the life of the annuitant. If it is charged on land it usually amounts to a rentcharge,[63] but the common law recognised that an annuity could have an existence independent of any land or charge upon it.[64] Such an annuity was given the rather confusing name of a "personal hereditament." This was meant to indicate that, at common law, the annuity did not issue out of nor was it secured on any land. Furthermore, it was regarded as personalty to the extent that it could not be entailed, was enforceable against the grantor and his estate only and would pass under a general bequest of personalty in a will.[65] On the other hand, such an annuity could be granted or devised to a person and his heirs, in which case it was treated as a hereditament and devolved like land.[66]

6.017. Apart from this, there are certain statutory annuities in Ireland which operate as charges on land. The most common are land purchase annuities charged on land in repayment of sums advanced to tenant farmers under the Land Purchase Acts.[67] Other similar annuities charged on land are those in

---

[57] Para. 6.131, *post*.

[58] Para. 4.104, *ante*.

[59] Para. 8.005, *post*.

[60] Para. 6.136, *post*.

[61] See also the Landed Property Improvement (Ireland) Act, 1849, s. 1.

[62] Paras. 6.131 *et seq.*, *post*.

[63] *Lord de Freyne* v. *I.R.C.* [1916] 2 I.R. 456; *Revenue Commrs.* v. *Malone* [1951] I.R. 269. Note also the definitions of "rentcharge" in the Republic's Statute of Limitations, 1957, s. 2 (1) and Statute of Limitations (N.I.), 1958, s. 74 (1).

[64] Holdsworth, *History of English Law*, vol. III, p. 152; Challis, *Law of Real Property* (3rd ed., 1911) pp. 46–7. Such an annuity may, of course, be a charge on a capital sum, *e.g.*, left by a person's will and held by his personal representatives or trustee, see *Re Lecky* [1949] I.R. 388; *Re Cochrane* [1953] I.R. 160; *Re Vesey* [1958] I.R. 268.

[65] *Aubin* v. *Daly* (1820) 4 B. & Ald. 59. See also *Gibbon* v. *Cloncurry* (1855) 7 Ir.Jur. (o.s.) 171. As to valuation of an annuity, *e.g.*, for tax purposes, see *Re Richardson* [1915] 1 I.R. 39; *Re Esmonde* [1946] I.R. 551; *Re Dunville* [1947] N.I. 50; *Re Cochrane* [1953] I.R. 160. Also *Re Olpherts* (1915) 47 I.L.T.R. 102; *Re Lopdell* [1943] I.R. 50.

[66] *Heron* v. *Stokes* (1842) 12 Cl. & F. 161; *Richardson* v. *Nixon* (1845) 7 Ir.Eq.R. 620. See also *Turner* v. *Turner* (1852) 1 Bro.C.C. 316; *Smith* v. *Pybus* (1804) 9 Ves. 566 at 574. See also ch. 15, *post*.

[67] See, *e.g.*, in the Republic, Land Law Acts, 1923, s. 9; 1931, ss. 4 and 7 and 1953, s. 4 and Sched. For Northern Ireland, see Northern Ireland Land Purchase (Winding Up) Act, 1935, s. 1 (3) and Sched. 2; Finance Act, 1963, s. 73 and Sched. 14. *Provincial Building Society* v. *Brown* [1950] N.I. 163; *Moley's Case* [1957] N.I.

repayment of instalment mortgages payable into the Church Temporalities Fund,[68] purchase annuities payable in respect of cottages subject to a vesting order under the Republic's Labourers Act, 1936,[69] annuities payable in respect of a loan under the Republic's Housing (Gaeltacht) Acts, 1929–67 or, in Northern Ireland, under the Small Dwellings Acquisition Acts (N.I.), 1899–1948.

D. ADVOWSONS

6.018. An advowson[70] was the right of presentation to an ecclesiastical living,[71] *i.e.*, the right of a patron of the church, such as the lord of the manor who, or whose predecessors, had built and endowed it, to nominate the clergyman to succeed a rector or vicar of that church when he died or retired.[72]

6.019. This may appear to have little to do with land law directly, though no doubt it had connections, even if somewhat indirect, with the old feudal system of tenure introduced many centuries ago.[73] Nevertheless, despite its tenuous relationship with land law, an advowson came to be regarded as an incorporeal hereditament.[74] It could be disposed of by will under a general devise of "real property" and, under the old law of intestacy, was subject to rights of dower and curtesy.[75] All this, however, belongs to legal history in Ireland because section 10 of the Irish Church Act, 1869, the Act which disestablished the Church of Ireland, abolished advowsons and they have ever since been left to rest in peace.

E. FRANCHISES

6.020. Another form of incorporeal hereditament recognised at common law was a franchise.[76] Franchises were exclusive rights or privileges granted by the Crown to subjects,[77] the most common being rights to hold fairs and markets,[78]

130; *Re McGowan* [1964] I.R. 16; *Carew* v. *Jackman* [1966] I.R. 177. Note that s. 4 of the Republic's Land Act, 1984, empowers the Minister for Agriculture, with the approval of the Minister for Finance, to waive payment of annuities less than £2 (or such other figure as may be substituted by order from time to time). S. 5 of the 1984 Act dissolved the Purchase Annuities Fund and provided for its dispersal for the benefit of the Exchequer.

[68] See Government of Ireland Act, 1920, s. 31. In the Republic, this Fund has recently been dissolved, see para. 6.014, *ante*. Also paras. 6.128–9, *post*.

[69] Note the termination, etc. of the Labourers' Cottages Fund under the Housing (Amendment) Act, 1958, ss. 5 and 16.

[70] Derived from the Latin *advocatio*—calling to one's aid or to advise.

[71] *Coke upon Littleton* (19th ed., 1832), 17b.

[72] See the *County Palatine of Wexford Case* (1611) Dav. 159; *Thompson* v. *Bishop of Meath* (1794) Ir.Term Rep. 422; *Bishop of Meath* v. *Marquis of Winchester* (1833) Alc. & Nap. 508; *Marquis of Winchester* v. *Bishop of Killaloe* (1846) 9 Ir.L.R. 107; *Reg.* v. *Bishop of Cork* (1848) 11 Ir.L.R. 114; *Re Cuthbert's Estate* (1867) I.R. 4 Eq. 562.

[73] The advowson seems to have been regarded as being held in lieu of the land upon which the church was built, see Challis, *Law of Real Property* (3rd ed., 1911), p. 42.

[74] See the discussion in Challis, *op. cit.*, pp. 46, 50, 52–3, 112 and 236.

[75] *Coke upon Littleton*, 32a.

[76] See Blackstone, *Commentaries on the Laws of England* (15th ed., 1809), vol.I, p. 302; Holdsworth, *History of English Law*, vol. I, p. 87 and vol. III, p. 169. *Case of Proxies* (1604) Dav. 1 at 14; *Case of the Dean and Chapter of Fernes* (1607) Dav. 116; *County Palatine of Wexford Case* (1611) Dav. 159 at 170.

[77] It seems that lords of manors might have special jurisdiction conferred on them by the Crown, *e.g.*, right to chattels of condemned felons, see Pollock and Maitland, *History of English Law* (2nd ed., 1898), vol. I, p. 576 and vol.II, p. 6.

[78] *Cork Corporation* v. *Shinkwin* (1825) Sm. & Bat. 395; *R.* v. *Kelly* (1833) Alc. & Nap. 272; *Russell* v. *Beakey*

the right to run ferries,[79] the right to wrecks[80] and treasure trove[81] and free fishing rights.[82] In both parts of Ireland, franchises remain burdens which affect registered land without having to be registered themselves.[83]

F. TITLES AND OFFICES

6.021. Titles of honour, such as peerages,[84] and offices, such as keeper of the park or master of the hounds,[85] were regarded as incorporeal hereditaments,[86] probably because their conferment was usually accompanied by a grant of land to the office holder.[87] Most grants of offices were for limited periods, *e.g.*, for life, and it is very doubtful if this subject is now of any practical significance in either part of Ireland.[88]

IV. EASEMENTS AND PROFITS

6.022. We now begin more extended treatment of those incorporeal hereditaments which are of practical significance in Ireland today. One of the most common categories is that concerning two very similar interests in land, an easement and a profit *à prendre*. Indeed, much land in both parts of Ireland is subject to interests of this nature, for they include such common matters as rights of way, of light and of support and mining, quarrying, fishing and gaming rights.

(1845) 8 Ir.Eq.R. 559; *Lord Midleton* v. *Power* (1886) 19 L.R.Ir. 1; *Marquis of Downshire* v. *O'Brien* (1887) 19 L.R.Ir. 380. *Cf.* the local authority powers and functions under the Markets and Fairs Clauses Act, 1847. *Mayor of Londonderry* v. *McElhinney* (1874) I.R. 9 C.L. 61; *R.* v. *Wall* [1898] 2 I.R. 762; *Gracey* v. *Banbridge U.D.C.* [1905] 2 I.R. 209; *Newtownards U.D.C.* v. *Tweedie* (1907) 41 I.L.T.R 23; *Lisburn U.D.C.* v. *Shortt* (1912) 46 I.L.T.R. 132. See also the Republic's Local Government Act, 1955, s. 58; Street Trading (Regulation) Act (N.I.), 1929, ss. 10 and 12. And see the recent discussion of a market franchise in *Scottish Co-Operative Wholesale Society Ltd.* v. *Ulster Farmers' Mart Co. Ltd.* [1959] N.I. 46 (H.L.), on appeal from [1958] N.I. 78 (C.A., N.I.); *cf. McCutcheon* v. *Carney* [1938] Ir.Jur.Rep. 73. Also *Duffy* v. *Dublin Corporation* [1974] I.R. 33.

[79] *Hemphill* v. *McKenna* (1845) 8 Ir.L.R. 43; *Leamy* v. *Waterford & Limerick Rly. Co.* (1856) 7 I.C.L.R. 27; *Londonderry Bridge Commrs.* v. *McKeever* (1891) 27 L.R.Ir. 464.

[80] As to Crown or, in the Republic, State rights to property in wrecks, see Merchant Shipping Act, 1894, ss. 523–7. *R.* v. *Forty-Nine Casks of Brandy* (1836) 3 Hagg.Adm. 257. See also *Hamilton* v. *Watt* (1851) 4 Ir.Jur. (o.s.) 253; *The Jeune Adolphe* (1857) 2 Ir.Jur. (N.S.) 285. And (1969) 20 N.I.L.Q. 75. Osborough, "Discoveries from Armada Wrecks" (1970) 5 Ir.Jur. (N.S.) 88.

[81] Which belonged to the Crown at common law, see *Att.-Gen.* v. *Moore* [1893] 1 Ch. 676 at 683; *Att.-Gen.* v. *Trustees of the British Museum* [1903] 2 Ch. 598 at 608–11. See now as to inquests or inquiries by coroners concerning treasure trove, Coroners Act, 1962, s. 49 (R.I.); Coroners Act (N.I.), 1959, s. 33. Dolly, "The First Treasure Trove Inquest in Ireland?" (1968) 19 N.I.L.Q. 182. *Cf.* Mac Niocaill, "Jetsam, Treasure Trove and the Lord's Share in Medieval Ireland" (1971) 6 Ir.Jur. (N.S.) 103.

[82] There has been much litigation in Ireland in recent decades relating to fishing franchises and Crown grants of fishing rights, see *R. (Moore)* v. *O'Hanrahan* [1927] I.R. 406; *Moore* v. *Att.-Gen.* [1934] I.R. 44 (see *A Casebook on Irish Land Law* (1984), p. 5); *Little* v. *Cooper* [1937] I.R. 1; *Foyle and Bann Fisheries Ltd.* v. *Att.-Gen.* (1949) 83 I.L.T.R. 29; *Att.-Gen.* v. *Cooper* [1956] I.R. 1; *Toome Eel Fishery (Northern Ireland) Ltd.* v. *Cardwell* [1966] N.I. 1. See further, para. 6.116, *post.*

[83] Registration of Title Act, 1964, s. 72 (1) (g) (R.I.); Land Registration Act (N.I.), 1970, Sched. 5, Pt. I, para. 8.

[84] *Re Rivett-Carnac's Will* (1885) 30 Ch.D. 136. *Cf.* Lord St. Leonards in the *Berkeley Peerage Case* (1861) 8 H.L.C. 21 at 118 and Lord Macnaghten in *Cowley* v. *Cowley* [1901] A.C. 450 at 456. See also Lord Cairns L.C. in the *Buckhurst Peerage Case* (1876) 2 App.Cas. 1 at 20–1.

[85] See *Coke upon Littleton*, 20c and 233a and b. *Cf. Crosbie* v. *Hurley* (1833) Alc. & Nap. 431.

[86] Note, however, the criticisms by Sweet of this view in his 3rd edition of Challis' *Law of Real Property* (1911), pp. 468–72; *cf.* pp. 42, 45 and 48.

[87] See Lynch, *Legal Institutions, Honorary Hereditary Offices and Feudal Baronies Established in Ireland During the Reign of Henry II* (1850). Also the *Case of the Dean and Chapter of Fernes* (1607) Dav. 116 at 123–4.

[88] Note that dignities or titles of honour were excluded from the legislative powers of the Parliament of Northern Ireland by s. 4 (1) and (5) of the Government of Ireland Act, 1920.

A. Nature

6.023. Though easements and profits have many similar characteristics, there are important points of distinction which should be emphasised. Furthermore there are several other interests in land which are neither easements nor profits. In the next few pages we consider first the nature of easements and profits and then compare them with similar concepts recognised by our land law.

1. *Easements*

6.024. Case law has settled that there are four essential features of an easement.[89]

(i) Dominant and Servient Tenement

6.025. The first essential feature of an easement is that it can exist only if it is *appurtenant* (annexed) to some piece of land, *i.e.*, so as to benefit that land.[90] An easement, unlike a profit *à prendre*,[91] cannot exist *in gross, i.e.*, independently of a piece of land which is benefited by it.[92] The result is, therefore, that the concept of an easement involves the existence of two pieces of land, usually called the *dominant* and *servient* tenements.[93] The dominant tenement is the land benefited by the easement and the servient tenement is the land over which the easement exists, *e.g.*, X, the owner of Blackacre, has a right of way over Whiteacre, which is owned by his neighbour Y.[94]

(ii) Accommodation of Dominant Tenement

6.026. It is not enough that the easement benefits the owner of the dominant land in his personal capacity, it must benefit the land he owns, as the dominant land. The question in each case is whether or not the alleged easement improves the land in some way, whether in terms of amenity, utility or convenience.[95] For example, a right of light may be necessary to make a building serviceable[96] or a diminution in the amount of light previously coming to a building may make it less convenient to use or enjoy.[97] It follows from this that the servient tenement must be in sufficient proximity to the dominant tenement to confer a practical benefit on it. This does not mean that the two

---

[89] See, generally, Morris, *Outline of the Law of Easements* (1869); Gale, *Law of Easements* (14th ed., 1972); Jackson, *The Law of Easements and Profits* (1978).

[90] Hence the argument that an easement was not properly regarded as an incorporeal hereditament but rather a mere right appurtenant or incident to a corporeal hereditament, see Challis, *Law of Real Property* (3rd ed., 1911), pp. 51–2 and 55–6. See also *Associated Properties Ltd.* v. *Representatives of Nolan* (1951) 85 I.L.T.R. 86.

[91] Para. 6.038, *post*.

[92] *Hawkins* v. *Rutter* [1892] 1 Q.B. 668.

[93] See the discussion in *Scott* v. *Goulding Properties Ltd.* [1972] I.R. 200 (see *A Casebook on Irish Land Law* (1984), p. 299).

[94] See *Gaw* v. *C.I.E.* [1953] I.R. 232 (see *ibid.*, p. 622).

[95] *Scott* v. *Goulding Properties Ltd.* [1972] I.R. 200.

[96] *Annally Hotel Ltd.* v. *Bergin* (1970) 104 I.L.T.R. 65.

[97] *McGrath* v. *Munster and Leinster Bank Ltd.* [1959] I.R. 313; *Scott* v. *Goulding Properties Ltd.* [1972] I.R. 200.

tenements must be contiguous, but they must be neighbouring lands.[98] A farmer as owner of land in Cork cannot have a right of way over land in Galway.

6.027. A right which confers a personal advantage only on the owner for the time being of the dominant land is not an easement. Thus a grant of the sole and exclusive right of putting pleasure-boats on a canal to a lessee of land on the canal's bank was held to confer a licence only.[99] In *Ackroyd* v. *Smith*[1] it was held that a grant of a right of way "for all purposes" to the tenant of an estate and his successors in title permitted the right to be used for purposes not necessarily connected with that estate and so it failed to create an easement.[2]

(iii) Ownership or Occupation by Different Persons

6.028. The general rule is that the dominant and servient tenements must be held under separate ownership. An easement, like other incorporeal hereditaments, is essentially an interest held by one person over another person's land.[3] However, this rule is subject to the substantial qualification that an easement may exist in the case of a common "owner" of the two tenements provided the *occupation* of them is not common. The obvious example, which was extremely common in Ireland.[4] though not, perhaps, so common nowadays,[5] is where the dominant and servient tenements are owned by a common landlord but one or other of them or both are occupied by tenants.[6] It is settled that a tenant may have an easement in respect of other land occupied by his own landlord or occupied by another tenant of the same landlord.[7]

6.029. One further point should be noted in this context. While, in general, a landowner cannot have an easement over his own land, his habitual exercise of rights over part of his land does have some significance in our land law. As we shall see later in this chapter,[8] rights so exercised, which would be easements if the other part were owned or occupied by another person, are called "quasi-easements" and may become full easements if the land is subsequently divided into separate parcels in terms of either ownership or occupation.

(iv) Subject-matter of a Grant

6.030. The fourth essential feature of an easement is that the alleged right in

---

[98]   *Bailey* v. *Stephens* (1862) 12 C.B. (N.S.) 91 at 115.

[99]   *Hill* v. *Tupper* (1863) H. & C. 121. See further on licences, para. 6.049, *post*.

[1]   (1850) 10 C.B. 164.

[2]   *Cf. Gaw* v. *C.I.E.* [1953] I.R. 232 at 243 (*per* Dixon J.) (see *A Casebook on Irish Land Law* (1984), p. 622).

[3]   Para. 6.003, *ante*. See also *Re Flanagan and McGarvey and Thompson's Contract* [1945] N.I. 32 (see *ibid.*, p. 317).

[4]   See Chua, "Easements: Termors in Prescription in Ireland" (1964) 15 N.I.L.Q. 489; Delany, "Lessees and the Doctrine of Lost Grant" (1958) 74 L.Q.R. 82. See further, para. 6.078, *post*.

[5]   Due to the disappearance of agricultural tenancies under the Land Purchase Acts, ch. 18, *post*.

[6]   Of course, the tenants are also "owners" of the land in that they hold leasehold estates in the land, as opposed to the freehold estate of the landlord, para. 4.007, *ante*.

[7]   *Hanna* v. *Pollock* [1900] 2 I.R. 664 (see *A Casebook on Irish Land Law* (1984), p. 329); *Flynn* v. *Harte* [1913] 2 I.R. 322; *Tallon* v. *Ennis* [1937] I.R. 549. There has, however, been much controversy in Ireland and England over the question of acquisition of easements *by prescription* in the case of leasehold land, see paras. 6.078–9, *post*.

[8]   Para. 6.061, *post*.

any particular case must be capable of forming the subject-matter of a grant. The general rule is that all easements "lie in grant," *i.e.*, must be created by deed, and so every purported easement must belong to categories of property rights which have over the centuries come to be regarded as capable of being conveyed from one person to another.[9] Thus the following have been recognised as established easements: rights of way,[10] light,[11] support[12] and water.[13] It must be emphasised that these categories or "heads" of easements are very wide ones and numerous kinds of rights may be subsumed within them.[14] Furthermore, it is doubtful whether the categories or list of easements recognised by our law should be regarded as closed, for, as Lord St. Leonards once remarked: "The category of servitudes and easements must alter and expand with the changes that take place in the circumstances of mankind."[15]

6.031. The courts have, however, over the years also taken the view that there must be limits to the rights recognised as easements. They do not look with favour upon novel rights which do not seem to conform with the general nature of easements. Thus it has been held in Ireland that there is no such easement as a right to "shade and shelter" from a hedge,[16] just as in England it was recently held that there was no such easement as a right, in respect of a wall of a house, to protection from weather by an adjoining house.[17] For some time it was thought that a right to use a path or garden for taking walks or wandering around could not be an easement, being a mere *jus spatiandi*.[18] However, it now seems to be recognised that such a right may properly form the subject-matter of an easement in particular cases, *e.g.*, when annexed to a housing estate adjoining parks and gardens.[19] In *Middleton* v. *Clarence*,[20] an Irish court held that the right to throw quarry refuse on another person's land was a proper easement.

6.032. It is part of the principle under discussion that the alleged easement should be capable of precise definition, so that it can, if necessary, be described accurately in a conveyance. It is for this reason that many alleged easements of light fail.[21] Such an easement can be claimed only in respect of a particular window in a building receiving a defined amount of light and there can be no

---

[9] Para. 6.002, *ante*.

[10] *Gaw* v. *C.I.E.* [1953] I.R. 232 (see *A Casebook on Irish Land Law* (1984), p. 622).

[11] *Tisdall* v. *McArthur & Co. (Steel and Metal) Ltd.* [1951] I.R. 228 (see *ibid.*, p. 357); *Annally Hotel Ltd* v. *Bergin* (1970) 104 I.L.T.R. 65; *Scott* v. *Goulding Properties Ltd.* [1972] I.R. 200 (*ibid.*, p. 299).

[12] *Latimer* v. *Official Co-Operative Society* 1885) 16 L.R.Ir. 305 (*ibid.*, p. 293); *Green* v. *Belfast Tramways Co.* (1887) 20 L.R.Ir. 35; *Gateley* v. *Martin* [1900] 2 I.R. 269.

[13] *McCartney* v. *Londonderry and Lough Swilly Rly. Co.* [1904] A.C. 301; *Kelly* v. *Dea* (1966) 100 I.L.T.R. 1.

[14] See further on the various categories of easements, paras. 6.107 *et seq., post*.

[15] *Dyce* v. *Lady James Hay* (1852) 1 Macq. 305 at 312–3. *Cf.* the discussion of ancient lights by the Republic's Supreme Court in *Scott* v. *Goulding Properties Ltd.* [1972] I.R. 200 (*ibid.*, p. 299).

[16] *Cochrane* v. *Verner* (1895) 29 I.L.T. 571.

[17] *Phipps* v. *Pears* [1965] 1 Q.B. 76, followed in *Giltrap* v. *Busby* (1970) 21 N.I.L.Q. 342.

[18] See *Henry Ltd.* v. *McGlade* [1926] N.I. 144 (see *A Casebook on Irish Land Law* (1984), p. 324). See also *International Tea Stores Co.* v. *Hobbs* [1903] 2 Ch. 165, espec. at 172.

[19] *Re Ellenborough Park* [1956] Ch. 131. *Cf. Henry Ltd* v. *McGlade* [1926] N.I. 144 (man carrying pole advertising licensed premises).

[20] (1877) I.R. 11 C.L. 499. *Cf. Wright* v. *Macadam* [1949] 2 K.B. 744 (right to store coal in a shed held to be an easement); *Copeland* v. *Greenhalf* [1952] Ch. 488 (right of a wheelwright to stand an unlimited number of vehicles on a strip of neighbouring land held not to be an easement).

[21] See Bodkin, "Easements and Uncertainty" (1971) 35 Conv. 324.

general right to a view.[22] If such less well-defined rights are sought, the only way to secure them is by a special contract for their protection, which may be drafted in the form of a restrictive covenant.[23]

6.033. Finally, the principle requiring that an easement be capable of forming the subject-matter of a grant implies that there must also be a capable grantor and grantee of the easement. This may give rise to difficulties in a particular case, *e.g.*, where a corporation is involved and it has no power to deal with land.[24]

2. *Profits à Prendre*

6.034. A profit *à prendre*, as the name implies, is a right to take something from another person's land. The general rule is that the something must be a part of the land itself, *e.g.*, minerals[25] or turf,[26] or creatures living naturally on the land which, when taken, are capable of being owned, *e.g.*, wild game[27] or fish.[28]

6.035. The nature of a particular profit *à prendre* depends to some extent on the category of profits to which it belongs. Three categories at least have been recognised over the years.

(i) Appurtenant

6.036. A profit may be created appurtenant to a dominant tenement, like an easement. In such a case the profit must in general comply with the four features necessary for an easement discussed above. It seems that such a profit must be confined to the needs of the dominant tenement, in the absence of a provision to the contrary in the grant.[29]

(ii) Appendant

6.037. A profit appendant is a profit annexed to land by operation of law, as opposed to act of the parties. The most common example was the ancient feudal right of common pasturage, under which a freehold grantee of arable manor land had as appendant to that land a right to pasture certain animals on

---

[22] See the distinction drawn by the Republic's Supreme Court between obstruction of "ancient lights" and reduction of light to "modern" windows in *Scott* v. *Goulding Properties Ltd.* [1972] I.R. 200 (Walsh J. *dissentiente*) (see *A Casebook on Irish Land Law* (1984), p. 299). See also *McGrath* v. *Munster and Leinster Bank Ltd* [1959] I.R. 313; *Annally Hotel Ltd.* v. *Bergin* (1970) 104 I.L.T.R. 65. Hudson, "Parasitic Damages for Loss of Light" (1975) 39 Conv. 116.

[23] Para. 6.046 and ch. 19, *post*.

[24] Ch. 25, *post*.

[25] *Fishbourne* v. *Hamilton* (1890) 25 L.R.Ir. 483; *Earl of Antrim* v. *Dobbs* (1891) 30 L.R.Ir. 424; *Staples* v. *Young* [1908] 1 I.R. 135.

[26] *Convey* v. *Regan* [1952] I.R. 56; *Re Bohan* [1957] I.R. 49. See also *Lowry* v. *Crothers* (1871) I.R. 5 C.L. 98; *Westropp* v. *Congested Districts Board* [1919] 1 I.R. 224.

[27] *Finlay* v. *Curteis* (1832) Hayes 496; *Radcliff* v. *Hayes* [1907] 1 I.R. 101.

[28] *Toome Eel Fishery (Northern Ireland) Ltd.* v. *Cardwell* [1966] N.I. 1. See also *Kerry C.C.* v. *O'Sullivan* [1927] I.R. 26; *Moore* v. *Att.-Gen.* [1934] I.R. 44 (see *A Casebook on Irish Land Law* (1984), p. 5).

[29] *Harris* v. *Earl of Chesterfield* [1911] A.C. 623. See also *Cronin* v. *Connor* [1913] 2 I.R. 119. In *Anderson* v. *Bostock* [1976] Ch. 312, Blackett-Ord V.-C., applying *Harris* v. *Earl of Chesterfield*, held that an exclusive unlimited right to grazing could not exist as a profit appurtenant and, indeed, was a right unknown to the law.

manor waste land.[30] The right was confined to animals necessary for ploughing (horses and oxen) and manuring (cows and sheep) the arable land granted and the number was limited to that which the dominant land could maintain during winter.[31] However, such a grant of freehold land within a manor amounted to subinfeudation and so no new profits appendant of this nature could be created after *Quia Emptores*, 1290.[32] For this reason, it is doubtful if any survive in Ireland today.

(iii) In Gross

6.038. Unlike an easement, a profit can also be enjoyed quite independently of any dominant tenement, *i.e.*, in gross. It is nevertheless regarded as an interest in land and is as much an incorporeal hereditament as a profit appurtenant.[33]

3. *Similar Concepts*

There are several other concepts recognised by our land law which share many of the characteristics of easements and profits, but which must be distinguished from them.

(i) Natural Rights

6.039. Natural rights, which are essentially rights protected by the law of torts,[34] are very like certain easements. There is, however, one major point of distinction. An easement must be acquired whereas a natural right, as the name indicates, exists automatically in respect of the land. This means, of course, that a plaintiff's task in court is considerably easier if he can base his claim on a natural right instead of having to establish an easement. One common natural right is a right of support which can also be acquired as an easement.[35] The natural right of support, which is a right not to have support removed by a neighbour, is confined to support for land in its natural state.[36] No natural right of support exists in respect of buildings on the land; such a right in respect of buildings must be acquired as an easement.[37]

6.040. Another common natural right is the right to water flowing in a defined channel, *e.g.*, the rights enjoyed by the owners of land on the banks of a

---

[30] *Doyle's Case* (1833) Alc.Reg.Cas. 36. See also *Bennett* v. *Reeve* (1740) Willes 227; *Earl of Dunraven* v. *Llewellyn* (1850) 15 Q.B. 791. Note the other form of common of pasturage, *pur cause de vicinage*, see Megarry and Wade, *Law of Real Property* (5th ed., 1984), p. 910.

[31] *Robertson* v. *Hartopp* (1889) 43 Ch.D. 484.

[32] Para. 2.44, *ante*. See also *Baring* v. *Abingdon* [1892] 2 Ch. 374.

[33] Note that there can be a letting of an incorporeal hereditament, *e.g.*, a several fishery, *Bayley* v. *Conyngham* (1863) 15 I.C.L.R. 406 (see *A Casebook on Irish Land Law* (1984), p. 311). Paras. 6.116–7, *post*.

[34] See Salmond, *Law of Torts* (16th ed., 1973).

[35] See the discussion in the leading case of *Dalton* v. *Angus & Co.* (1881) 6 App.Cas. 740, applied in *Latimer* v. *Official Co-Operative Society* (1885) 16 L.R.Ir. 305 (see *A Casebook on Irish Land Law* (1984), p. 293). Garner, "Rights of Support" (1948) 12 Conv. 280, Para. 6.111, *post*.

[36] *Latimer* v. *Official Co-Operative Society* (1885) 16 L.R.Ir. 305.

[37] *Green* v. *Belfast Tramways Co.* (1887) 20 L.R.Ir. 35; *Gateley* v. *Martin* [1900] 2 I.R. 269. See further, para. 6.111, *post*. Also Bodkin, "Rights of Support for Buildings and Flats" (1962) 26 Conv. 210.

river or stream.[38] Such riparian owners, as they are called, may sue to protect their natural rights if the river or stream is dammed or diverted.[39] On the other hand, there is no natural right to water not flowing through a defined channel, *e.g.*, water percolating underground.[40] Rights to water are, however commonly acquire as easements,[41] even in respect of artificial watercourses.[42]

(ii) Public Rights

6.041. Certain public rights are very similar to rights also recognised as easements or profits. For example, there can be a public right of way over land. The essential difference between such a right and an easement is that the public right of way can be invoked by any member of the public regardless of his ownership of any dominant land.[43] At common law, a public right of way was known as a "highway" and could be created by "dedication and acceptance,"[44] *i.e.*, the owner of the land dedicates the way to the public which then accepts that dedication. The dedication is usually made informally and the acceptance inferred from long usage by the public.[45] For the user to raise a presumption of a public right of way, the user must have been open, "as of right" and without interruption.[46] Apart from creation of a public right of way at common law, a public road may, of course, nowadays be adopted by a local authority under statutory powers.[47] The law of nuisance may be invoked to protect public rights of way.[48]

6.042. So far as profits *à prendre* are concerned, perhaps the most obvious analogous public right is the right of the public to fish in the sea and all tidal rivers and waters.[49] In strict theory, this fishing right belonged ultimately to the Crown and now, in the Republic of Ireland, the State.[50] It has now been settled in a series of cases concerning some of the main rivers of Ireland[51] that, while

[38] *Thompson* v. *Horner* [1927] N.I. 191. Brett, "Right to Take Flowing Water" (1950) 14 Conv. 154; Fiennes, "Right to Take Water on the Land of Another" (1938) 2 Conv. 203.

[39] *McClone* v. *Smith* (1888) 22 L.R.Ir. 559; *Massereene* v. *Murphy* [1931] N.I. 192.

[40] *Black* v. *Ballymena Township Commrs.* (1886) 17 L.R.Ir. 459; *cf. Ewart* v. *Belfast Poor Law Commrs.* (1881) 9 L.R.Ir. 172.

[41] *Wilson* v. *Stanley* (1861) 12 I.C.L.R. 345; *Pullan* v. *Roughfort Bleaching and Dying Co. Ltd.* (1888) 21 L.R.Ir. 73; *Craig* v. *McCance* (1910) 44 I.L.T.R. 90.

[42] *Hanna* v. *Pollock* [1900] 2 I.R. 664 (see *A Casebook on Irish Land Law* (1984), p. 329); *Kelly* v. *Dea* (1966) 100 I.L.T.R. 1.

[43] *Att.-Gen. (Cork C.C.)* v. *Perry* [1904] 1 I.R. 247; *Healy* v. *Bray U.D.C.* [1962–63] Ir.Jur.Rep. 9. *Cf. Antrim C.C.* v. *Trustees of Gray* (1930) 64 I.L.T.R. 71.

[44] *Fitzpatrick* v. *Robinson* (1828) 1 Hud. & Br. 585; *Early* v. *Flood* [1953–54] Ir.Jur.Rep. 65; *Browne* v. *Davis* (1959) 93 I.L.T.R. 179. See also *O'Keefe* v. *Dromey* (1898) 32 I.L.T.R. 47; *Smith* v. *Wilson* [1903] 2 I.R. 45; *Giant's Causeway Co.* v. *Att.-Gen.* (1905) 5 N.I.J.R. 301.

[45] *Browne* v. *Davis, op. cit.* See also *Fitzpatrick* v. *Robinson* (1828) 1 Hud. & Br. 585; *Reilly* v. *Thompson* (1877) I.R. 11 C.L. 238; *Neill* v. *Byrne* (1878) 2 L.R.Ir. 287; *O'Connor* v. *Sligo Corp.* (1901) 1 N.I.J.R. 116; *Bruen* v. *Murphy* (1980) Unrep. (H.C., R.I.) (1978 No. 5085P).

[46] *Cf.* the requirements for acquisition of an easement by prescription, para. 6.075, *post.*

[47] See the Republic's Local Government Acts, 1925, s. 25 and 1953, s. 2; Roads Act (N.I.), 1948, s. 16. See also *City Brick and Terra Cotta Co. Ltd.* v. *Belfast Corp.* [1958] N.I. 44.

[48] *Healy* v. *Bray U.D.C* [1962–63] Ir.Jur.Rep. 9; *Cunningham* v. *MacGrath Bros.* [1964] I.R. 209; *Kelly* v. *Mayo C.C.* [1964] I.R. 315; *Wall* v. *Morrissey* [1969] I.R. 10.

[49] *Cf.* non-tidal waters, *Bloomfield* v. *Johnston* (1867) I.R. 8 C.L. 68; *Pery* v. *Thornton* (1889) 23 L.R.Ir. 402. See also *Murphy* v. *Ryan* (1868) I.R. 2 C.L. 143; *Whelan* v. *Hewson* (1871) I.R. 6 C.L. 283.

[50] See especially the detailed discussion of the subject by Kennedy C.J. in *R. (Moore)* v. *O'Hanrahan* [1927] I.R. 406 and Gavan Duffy P. in *Foyle and Bann Fisheries, Ltd.* v. *Att.-Gen.* (1949) 83 I.L.T.R. 29.

[51] *Malcolmson* v. *O'Dea* (1863) 10 H.L.C. 593 (Shannon); *Neill* v. *Duke of Devonshire* (1882) 8 App.Cas. 135

the Crown was free to grant individual or several fishery rights to specified parts of tidal and navigable waters prior to *Magna Carta*, 1215,[52] that charter prohibited the granting of any new fisheries thereafter.[53] It was, however, accepted that those fisheries existing before *Magna Carta*, whose survival in private hands could be established,[54] remain valid to this day.[55]

(iii) Local Customary Rights

6.043. Local customary rights differ from easements in that they are not necessarily annexed to any dominant tenement.[56] They can be invoked by all who come within the custom of the locality regardless of ownership of other land, *e.g.*, the right of parishioners to use a path to their church.[57] Such rights differ from public rights, on the other hand, because they are confined to members of a local community, *e.g.*, the inhabitants of a particular town or village, the fishermen of a port or the tenants of an estate.[58]

6.044. Such local customary rights are recognised at common law provided they satisfy the four basic requirements of being ancient, certain, reasonable and continuous.[59] Being ancient means in theory dating back to or before the beginning of legal memory, *i.e.*, 1189,[60] but in practice courts are prepared to presume such an ancient origin provided long enjoyment of 20 to 40 years is shown and no proof of a later origin is forthcoming.[61]

6.045. It seems that at common law the courts were reluctant to accept customary rights analogous to profits on the ground that, to allow a fluctuating

---

(Blackwater); *R. (Moore)* v. *O'Hanrahan* [1927] I.R. 406 (Erne); *Moore* v. *Att.-Gen.* [1934] I.R. 44 (Erne) (see *A Casebook on Irish Land Law* (1984), p. 5); *Cooper* v. *Att.-Gen.* [1935] I.R. 425 (Ballisodare); *Little* v. *Cooper* [1937] I.R. 1 (Moy); *Foyle and Bann Fisheries, Ltd.* v. *Att.-Gen.* (1949) 83 I.L.T.R. 29 (Foyle).

[52] *I.e.* a franchise, para. 6.020, *ante.*

[53] C. 16. The reported statements of the Irish judges in the *Case of the Royal Fishery of the Banne* (1610) Dav. 149 seem to have been made in ignorance of *Magna Carta* and are, therefore, wrong, see *Moore* v. *Att.-Gen.* [1934] I.R. 44 (see *A Casebook on Irish Land Law* (1984), p. 5); also *Duke of Devonshire* v. *Hodnett* (1827) 1 Hud. & Br. 322. One of the issues also in dispute in these cases was to what extent the Ulster plantation patent grants and seventeenth-century Acts of Settlement (paras. 1.31–3, *ante*) could be regarded as overruling *Magna Carta* on this point and the general view of the judges seems to have been that they should not be so construed. See *Moore* v. *Att.-Gen.* [1934] I.R. 44; *Foyle and Bann Fisheries, Ltd.* v. *Att.-Gen.* (1949) 83 I.L.T.R. 29. *Cf. Little* v. *Moylett* [1929] I.R. 439; *Cooper* v. *Att.-Gen.* [1935] I.R. 425. Note also subsequent private Acts conferring private fisheries, *e.g.*, the "Cooper Act" of 1837, subsequently incorporated in the Fisheries (Ir.) Act, 1842. For litigation on this private legislation, see *Cooper* v. *Att.-Gen.* [1935] I.R. 425; *Att.-Gen. (Mahony)* v. *Cooper* [1956] I.R. 1.

[54] This is a particular problem with respect to those parts of Ireland, *e.g.*, the North West, which did not come under the influence of the English feudal system introduced by the Normans until the late sixteenth or early seventeenth century, paras. 1.27–8, *ante.* Until then the system of law in force in the North West of Ireland was the brehon system, which does not seem to have recognised private property rights in several fisheries, though this is a matter of dispute amongst Irish scholars. Note the evidence given by scholars of ancient Irish law in *R. (Moore)* v. *O'Hanrahan* [1927] I.R. 406; *Moore* v. *Att.-Gen.* [1934] I.R. 44 (see *A Casebook on Irish Land Law* (1984), p. 5); *Foyle and Bann Fisheries, Ltd.* v. *Att.-Gen.* (1949) 83 I.L.T.R. 29.

[55] The court was satisfied as to proof of ownership of a several fishery in the River Moy in Counties Mayo and Sligo prior to *Magna Carta* in *Little* v. *Cooper* [1937] I.R. 1. *Cf.* a fishery in the River Erne in Co. Donegal (the ancient Irish territory of Tirconnaill) in *Moore* v. *Att.-Gen.* [1934] I.R. 44 (see *A Casebook on Irish Land Law* (1984), p.5). See also *Little* v. *Wingfield* (1859) 11 I.C.L.R. 63; *Allen* v. *Donnelly* (1856) 5 Ir.Ch.R. 452; *Ashworth* v. *Browne* (1860) 10 Ir.Ch.R. 421.

[56] *Cf. Re Pews of Derry Cathedral* (1864) 8 Ir.Jur. (N.S.) 115.

[57] *Cf.* a right to use a pew in a church, see *Re Pews of Derry Cathedral, op. cit.*

[58] *Abercromby* v. *Fermoy Town Commissioners* [1900] 1 I.R. 302 (see *A Casebook on Irish Land Law* (1984), p. 294); *Daly* v. *Cullen* (1958) 92 I.L.T.R. 127.

[59] *Daly* v. *Cullen* (1958) 92 I.L.T.R. 127.

[60] Fixed by the Statute of Westminster I, 1275, c. 39. See further para. 6.081, *post.*   [61] Para. 6.081, *post.*

body of persons to take things from the land, might result after a short time in little of the subject-matter of the profit being left.[62] However, the courts have had to recognise that many customary rights regularly invoked and exercised in certain localities for centuries take the form of profits and have enforced them.[63] In fact, in Ireland many such customary rights can be traced to Crown grants resulting from the numerous confiscations and resettlements of Irish land.[64] The Irish courts have often been prepared to explain and elaborate the general words of Crown patents or grants according to the evidence of long user and enjoyment of claimed rights.[65]

(iv) Restrictive Covenants

6.046. As we shall see later,[66] restrictive covenants are very similar to certain easements. The main similarity lies in the feature of both concepts that allows the owner to restrict another person in the use of his land. Thus rights in respect of light, water, air and support may either be acquired as easements[67] on or secured by imposing restrictive covenants[68] on the servient land. The existence of dominant and servient tenements is another common feature of the two concepts.[69]

6.047. There are, however, also distinctions of a fundamental nature. Easements have been recognised by the common law from the earliest stages of development of our land law system. They are usually *legal* interests[70] in land which bind all successors in title to the land. Restrictive covenants became recognised as part of land law only during the early part of the nineteenth century and then as interests enforceable against third parties in equity only.[71] Creating an equitable interest only, a restrictive covenant is often a less secure interest in land because its enforceability may be defeated by the claim of a bona fide purchaser of the legal estate in the land without notice of the covenant.[72] Its enforceability is also based on equitable principles and a court always has a discretion to refuse to grant the equitable remedy usually sought in such cases, namely an injunction.[73]

---

[62] See, *e.g.*, the remarks of Lord Campbell C.J. in *Race* v. *Ward* (1855) 4 E. & B. 702 at 709. *Cf.* Chatterton V.-C. in *Hamilton* v. *Att.-Gen.* (1881) 5 L.R.Ir. 555 at 576.

[63] In England, the courts have been prepared to presume incorporation of a body of persons as recipients of a Crown grant, *Re Free Fishermen of Faversham* (1887) 36 Ch.D. 329, or even to presume a charitable trust or condition binding corporate grantees in favour of the claimants of the customary right, *Goodman* v. *Mayor of Saltash* (1882) 7 App. Cas. 633. See Megarry and Wade, *Law of Real Property* (5th ed., 1984), pp. 854–5. *Cf.* on the *Saltash* principle, *Tighe* v. *Sinnott* [1897] 1 I.R. 140.

[64] There has been much litigation concerning grants made under the Ulster plantation with respect to fishing rights, *Allen* v. *Donnelly* (1856) 5 Ir.Ch.R. 452; *Moore* v. *Att.-Gen.* [1934] I.R. 44 (see *A Casebook on Irish Land Law* (1984), p. 5); *Foyle and Bann Fisheries, Ltd.* v. *Att.-Gen.* (1949) 83 I.L.T.R. 29; *Toome Eel Fishery (Northern Ireland) Ltd.* v. *Cardwell* [1966] N.I.1.

[65] See, *e.g.*, *Hamilton* v. *Att.-Gen.* (1881) 5 L.R.Ir. 555; *Stoney* v. *Keane* (1903) 37 I.L.T.R. 212.

[66] Ch. 19, *post*.

[67] Paras. 6.108–11, *post*.

[68] Ch. 19, *post*.

[69] *I.e.*, if a restrictive covenant is to be enforceable against third parties.

[70] They may, of course, like most legal estates and interests also exist in equity, ch. 4, *ante*.

[71] Ch. 19, *post*.

[72] In practice, however, this claim will rarely succeed in Ireland, paras. 3.069 *et seq.*, *ante* and ch. 22, *post*.

[73] Para. 3.050, *ante* and ch. 19, *post*.

6.048. A restrictive covenant, as the name indicates, confers a purely negative right[74] whereas an easement can have a positive nature, *e.g.*, a right to draw water.[75] Finally, apart from such fundamental points of difference, there are also important differences in detail between the two concepts, *e.g.*, an easement can be acquired through long enjoyment (prescription)[76] whereas a restrictive covenant cannot be so acquired.

(v) Licences

6.049. Licences have really come to be recognised as sometimes creating interests in land only during the past few decades. As we shall see later,[77] there are still several unresolved aspects of their precise status in the sphere of land law, but for the moment it may be said that a degree of similarity with the concept of an easement exists in that a licence can confer rights over another person's land, such as user of a path or driveway. There are, however, as in the case of restrictive covenants, fundamental differences in the nature of the two concepts. To the extent that a licence creates an interest in land, it seems clear from the case law that the interest is equitable only.[78] On the other hand, a licence may be created very informally[79] and may exist in gross, independent of any dominant tenement.[80] A licence may also confer a general right to occupation, indeed exclusive possession of, the servient tenement and in this respect is more like a corporeal hereditament[81] than an incorporeal one,[82] such as an easement.

B. ACQUISITION

There are four ways in which an easement or profit can be acquired: by statute, express grant or reservation, implied grant or reservation and presumed grant (prescription).

1. *Statute*

6.050. Rights in the nature of easements or profits were conferred by statute on private individuals more commonly in past eras. In Ireland, this was particularly the case during the many land disturbances which took place in the seventeenth century and resulted in the confiscation of so much of the land and its regranting by the English Crown. These Crown grants were confirmed by various Acts of Settlement which, *inter alia*, were designed to confirm the grantees' titles and the rights conferred by them.[83] There were also many

---

[74] See further, ch. 19, *post.*
[75] Para. 6.110, *post.*
[76] Para. 6.073, *post.*
[77] Ch. 20, *post.*
[78] *Ibid.*
[79] Para. 20.03, *post.*
[80] In this respect a licence, *vis-à-vis* third parties, differs also from a restrictive covenant, ch. 19, *post.*
[81] *I.e.*, it may appear to confer rights very similar to those granted to a tenant under a tenancy agreement, ch. 17, *post.*
[82] Para. 6.003, *ante.* Cf. *Judge* v. *Lowe* (1873) I.R. 7 C.L. 291; *Atkinson* v. *King* (1877) I.R. 11 C.L. 536; *Stanley* v. *Riky* (1893) 31 L.R.Ir. 196; *Radcliff* v. *Hayes* [1907] 1 I.R. 101; *Whipp* v. *Mackey* [1927] I.R. 372.
[83] Paras. 1.29–33, *ante.* See the discussion of these Acts of Settlement in *Little* v. *Moylett* [1929] I.R. 439; *Moore* v. *Att.-Gen.* [1934] I.R. 44 (see *A Casebook on Irish Land Law* (1984), p. 5).

private and local Acts of Parliament passed as late as the nineteenth century conferring easements and profits, *e.g.*, free fishing rights.[84]

6.051. In more modern times, it has become extremely common for statutory rights equivalent or analogous to easements and profits to be conferred on, or the power of compulsory acquisition to be given to, public and state bodies charged with execution of public undertakings, *e.g.*, in relation to gas, water and electricity supply.[85] In some cases, easements or profits have been expressly conferred on or vested in state bodies by statute.[86]

2. *Express Grant or Reservation*

6.052. Easements and profits may be created expressly by the parties to a land transaction. For example, if X, the owner of Blackacre, sells a part of Blackacre to Y, retaining the other part, he may, as part of the sale, confer on Y various easements (*e.g.*, a right of way) and profits (*e.g.*, fishing rights) to be enjoyed by Y over the part of Blackacre retained by X. In other words, the part sold to Y becomes the dominant tenement and the part retained by X the servient tenement. Quite independently of this transaction, X could grant other profits to be enjoyed in gross, *i.e.*, without any dominant tenement, to other persons (*e.g.*, a right of turbary[87] to Z, who lives in a village some miles away). Both these cases involve an express grant of the easement or profit by X, and it should be noted that a grant of an easement or profit may be made on its own, *i.e.*, independently of any conveyance of either the dominant or servient tenement.

6.053. Alternatively, when selling part of Blackacre to Y, X could reserve easements (*e.g.*, support for farm buildings on the boundary line between the part sold and the part retained) and profits (*e.g.*, quarrying rights) to be enjoyed by him over the part of Blackacre sold to Y. Here the dominant tenement is the part of Blackacre retained by X and the servient tenement is the part sold to Y. The transaction involves an express reservation of easements and profits rather than an express grant.

(i) Grant

6.054. The usual method of expressly granting an easement or profit is by deed.[88] In practice the grant or reservation is usually only part of a larger land

---

[84] See the "Cooper Act" of 1837 relating to a several fishery held by one, Joshua Edward Cooper, in the Ballisodare River and Estuary. The 1837 Act was amended by the Fisheries (Ir.) Act, 1842. See the discussion in *Cooper* v. *Att.-Gen.* [1935] I.R. 425; *Att.-Gen. (Mahony)* v. *Cooper* [1956] I.R. 1. See also *Foyle and Bann Fisheries, Ltd.* v. *Att.-Gen.* (1949) 83 I.L.T.R. 29.

[85] Garner, "Statutory 'Easements' " (1956) 20 Conv. 208.

[86] *E.g.*, fishing rights in rivers vested in the Republic's Electricity Supply Board, see Shannon Fisheries Act, 1938, Pt. II; Electricity (Supply) (Amendment) Act, 1961, ss. 9 and 10; *Daly* v. *Quigley* [1960] Ir.Jur.Rep. 1; *E.S.B.* v. *Gormley* [1985] I.L.R.M. 494. *Cf.* as regards minerals and mining rights, Minerals Development Acts, 1940 and 1979, Minerals Exploration and Development Company Act, 1941, and Minerals Company Acts, 1945, 1947 and 1950 (R.I.); Mineral Development Act (N.I.) 1969. In the Republic, mines and minerals not being worked in 1922 were vested in the State by the 1922 Constitution.

[87] *I.e.*, to cut and take away turf, para. 6.114, *post.*

[88] Since s. 2 of the Real Property Act, 1845, introduced the deed of grant as an alternative to older methods of conveyance, such as feoffment with livery of seisin and the bargain and sale, para. 3.026, *ante.* See the discussion

transaction being executed by that deed. Caution dictates that appropriate words of limitation be used to make it clear for what estate the easement or profit is given. This point is by no means settled in Ireland for there seems to be no authority on it and the controversy which existed in England prior to the 1925 legislation[89] has not yet died down.[90] Such English authority as there was about the pre-1926 position[91] suggests that the appropriate words of limitation for an *inter vivos* conveyance ought to be used, otherwise the grantee may be held to acquire an easement or profit for life only.[92] There is, however, one major point to note about Irish law in this context. The word "lands" is defined in the basic statute dealing with the relation of landlord and tenant in Ireland, Deasy's Act,[93] as including "houses, messuages, and tenements of every tenure, whether corporeal *or incorporeal.*"[94] There can, therefore, be lettings of easements and profits (and they are very common) the formalities of which are governed by Deasy's Act. This means that in most cases writing only is necessary, not a deed (under seal), and, where the letting is at a rent or other return for a period "from year to year or any lesser period", the creation may be oral, with no formalities at all.[95] Thus in *Bayley* v. *Conyngham*[96] a letting by parol of fishing rights in land for a year was upheld as a valid tenancy, creating the relation of landlord and tenant between the grantor and grantee.[97]

6.055. Even if the requisite formalities for creation of a *legal* easement or profit are not met, an easement or profit may come into force *in equity*. Any written document not under seal may be construed as a contract for the grant of an easement or profit and may be enforced in equity through a decree of specific performance.[98] Even an oral agreement for consideration may be enforced in equity, provided there is a sufficient act of part performance to prevent the case coming within the Statute of Frauds (Ireland). 1695.[99]

(ii) Reservation

6.056. A reservation of an easement or profit is also usually contained in a deed. However, there was a problem about this at common law because of the basic rule that a grantor of land could not make a simple reservation to himself.

---

by Monahan C.J. in *Bayley* v. *Conyngham* (1863) 15 I.C.L.R. 406 (see *A Casebook on Irish Land Law* (1984), p. 311).

[89] See, *e.g.*, Sweet, "True Nature of an Easement" (1908) 24 L.Q.R. 259; Underhill, "Words of Limitation and Easements" (1908) 24 L.Q.R. 199; Williams, "Creation of Easements" (1908) 24 L.Q.R. 264.

[90] Megarry and Wade, *Law of Real Property* (5th ed., 1984), p. 856.

[91] *Hewlins* v. *Shippam* (1826) 5 B.& C. 221 at 228–9 (*per* Bayley J.).

[92] Ch. 4, *ante*.

[93] Landlord and Tenant Law Amendment Act, Ireland, 1860. See, generally, ch. 17, *post*.

[94] S. 1 (italics added).

[95] S. 4. See further, para. 17.012, *post*.

[96] (1863) 15 I.C.L.R. 406.

[97] "It occurs to me, and to the majority of the Court, that if we are at liberty to give any effect to the glossary of the Act, the word 'lands' embraces incorporeal hereditaments, and that it was the intention of the Legislature to place lands and incorporeal hereditaments on the same footing, so far as relates to landlord and tenant; and that therefore whatever is sufficient to create the relation of landlord and tenant in corporeal, is sufficient also with respect to incorporeal hereditaments." *Per* Monahan C.J., *ibid.*, p. 412.

[98] Para. 3.144, *ante*.

[99] Para. 3.149, *ante*. See again the discussion in *Bayley* v. *Conyngham* (1863) 15 I.C.L.R. 406 (see *A Casebook on Irish Land Law* (1984), p. 311).

The common law allowed a grantor only to *except* from his grant a part of the land itself or a pre-existing right over it. Things like mines and minerals, stones and quarries are commonly the subject-matter of exceptions.[1] We are considering here the creation of easements or profits for the first time and they *ex hypothesi* could not form the subject-matter of an exception—they come into operation only when the grant of the land is made.[2] The common law did allow some new rights to be reserved, but only if they were to issue out of the land granted, *e.g.*, X in selling Blackacre to Y could reserve to himself a rentcharge of £100 per annum charged on Blackacre.[3] The question, however, is how X could reserve to himself easements and profits over the part of Blackacre sold to Y and to be enjoyed by X as owner of the part of Blackacre retained after that sale to Y.

6.057. In Ireland this object may be achieved in two ways. First, Y could execute the conveyance from X to Y of the part of Blackacre in question. The common law took the view that a conveyance containing a reservation in favour of the grantor and executed by the grantee had a dual operation. The conveyance was regarded as a grant of the land to the grantee followed by a regrant of the reserved right (easement or profit) by the grantee to the grantor.[4] Secondly, since 1881, the grantor may use the Statute of Uses (Ireland), 1634.[5] X could convey the part of Blackacre to Z and his heirs to the use that X should have the easements and profits and, subject to that provision, to the use of Y and his heirs. Prior to 1882, this mechanism did not work[6] because the Statute of Uses (Ireland), 1634, like the English 1535 Statute, applied only where one person (Z in our example) was *seised* of land to the use of another person.[7] Once again we are considering the creation of easements and profits for the first time and Z, the feoffee to uses, could not be seised of them unless they already existed before the feoffment or grant of them to the use of another person.[8] This difficulty was, however, removed by the Conveyancing Act, 1881, s. 62 (1) of which applies the following provision to conveyances made after the Act:

> "A conveyance of freehold land to the use that any person may have, for an estate or interest not exceeding in duration the estate conveyed in the land, any easement, right, liberty, or privilege in, or over, or with respect to that land, or any part thereof, shall operate to vest in possession in that person that easement, right, liberty, or privilege, for the estate or interest

---

[1] *Coke upon Littleton*, 47a. *McDonnell* v. *Kenneth* (1850) 1 I.C.L.R. 113; *Quinn* v. *Shields* (1877) I.R. 11 C.L. 254. See also *McDonnell* v. *McKinty* (1847) 10 Ir.L.R. 514.

[2] Prior to that the rights in question could exist as quasi-easements only, paras. 6.029, *ante* and 6.061, *post*. See the discussion in *O'Donnell* v. *Ryan* (1854) 4 I.C.L.R. 44, espec. at 59–60 (*per* Ball J.).

[3] *Coke upon Littleton*, 143a. See further on rentcharges, para. 6.131, *post*.

[4] *Durham & Sutherland Rly.* v. *Walker* (1842) 2 Q.B. 940, espec. at 967. In the case of a transaction for value, the grantor would have an equitable right to seek specific performance against the grantee, to compel him to execute the conveyance, and in the meantime would have an equitable easement or profit, paras. 3.038, *ante* and 9.061, *post*.

[5] See further, paras. 3.015 *et seq.*, *ante*.

[6] It did, of course, in equity and, if for value (unlikely in the case of a mere conveyancing device), X could enforce the use against Z, para. 9.061, *post*.

[7] S. 1. Para. 3.019, *ante*.

[8] *Ibid*. The 1634 Statute could operate, of course, to transfer an existing easement or profit.

expressed to be limited to him; and he, and the persons deriving title under him, shall have, use and enjoy the same accordingly."[9]

In other words, by virtue of the 1881 Act the use in favour of X relating to the easements and profits would be "executed" so as to vest the legal title to them in X.[10]

(iii) Construction of Grants and Reservations

6.058. The precise effect of a purported grant or reservation of easements or profits is, of course, to a large extent a matter of construction of the particular conveyance. In such questions of construction two principles are most relevant, namely that a grant is in general construed against the grantor and that a man may not derogate from his grant. The first principle means that, in cases of doubt (*e.g.*, over the exact scope of the easement or profit), a grant of an easement or profit will be construed against the grantor in favour of the grantee, whereas a reservation, being treated as a regrant by the grantee,[11] will be construed against him in favour of the grantor.[12] The underlying philosophy is that the person who is in a position to dictate the terms of a transaction, by making the grant, cannot complain if a dispute subsequently occurs and he is not given the benefit of the doubt. Reservations in respect of new easements or profits were treated as a special case[13] because of the common law's view that they should be regarded as regrants by the grantee.

6.059. As regards the rule that a man may not derogate from his grant, the philosophy here is that, when a man transfers his land to another person, knowing that it is going to be used for a particular purpose, he may not do anything which is going to defeat that purpose and thereby frustrate the intention of both parties when the transfer is made.[14] Usually application of this principle creates property rights in favour of the grantee which take the form of restrictions enforceable against the grantor's land. In this respect the rights are similar to restrictive covenants though, it must be emphasised, the principle has nothing to do with the law relating to such covenants. On the

---

[9] In England, the 1881 Act, like the Statute of Uses, 1535, has been replaced by the Law of Property Act, 1925, s. 65 of which now provides that a reservation of a legal estate or interest is effective at law without any execution of the conveyance by the grantee. A similar provision has been recommended for Northern Ireland, see *Survey of the Land Law of Northern Ireland* (1971), paras. 40 and 175; Land Law Working Group's Discussion Document No. 4 (*Conveyancing and Miscellaneous Matters*) (1983), para. 2.15.

[10] Para. 3.016, *ante*.

[11] Para. 6.057, *supra*.

[12] See the discussion in *Neill* v. *Duke of Devonshire* (1882) 8 App.Cas. 135, espec. at 149 (*per* Lord Selborne L.C.). This remains the rule in England despite s. 65 of the Law of Property Act, 1925 (fn. 9, *supra*), see *Bulstrode* v. *Lambert* [1953] 1 W.L.R. 1064; *Johnstone* v. *Holdway* [1963] 1 Q.B. 601; *St. Edmundsbury and Ipswich Diocesan Board of Finance* v. *Clark (No. 2)* [1975] 1 W.L.R. 468; Wade, (1954) C.L.J. 191. The N.I. Land Law Working Group have recommended the reversal of this construction, see Discussion Document No. 4 (*Conveyancing and Miscellaneous Matters*) (1983), p. 15.

[13] Thus, at common law, exceptions and other reservations (*e.g.*, of rent) were construed in the normal way against the grantor making them, *Lofield's Case* (1612) 10 Co.Rep 106a. Bigelow and Madden, "Exception and Reservation of Easements" (1924) 38 H.L.R. 180.

[14] "A grantor having given a thing with one hand is not to take away the means of enjoying it with the other." *Per* Bowen L.J. in *Birmingham, Dudley & District Banking Co.* v. *Ross* (1888) 38 Ch.D. 295 at 313; *cf. Lyttleton Times Co. Ltd.* v. *Warners Ltd.* [1907] A.C. 476 at 481 (*per* Lord Loreburn L.C.). See also *Griffin* v. *Keane* (1927) 61 I.L.T.R. 177; *Kennedy* v. *Elkinson* (1937) 71 I.L.T.R. 153.

other hand, the principle is not confined to the area of easements and profits and may create rights which do not conform strictly with the requirements of easements and profits.[15]

Finally, when considering the effect of the wording of an express grant, the provisions of section 6 of the Conveyancing Act, 1881, must be borne in mind. This is a subject we discuss below.[16]

3. *Implied Grant or Reservation*

Even if a particular conveyance does not mention the creation of easements or profits expressly, they may be created by impication on a true construction of the deed. Once again a distinction has to be drawn between grants in favour of the grantee and reservations in favour of the grantor.[17]

(i) Grant

6.060. The general rule is that a grant is construed in favour of the grantee and this results frequently in the creation of implied easements and, sometimes, implied profits *à prendre*. The following are the main circumstances in which implied grants are construed as taking place.

(a) *Easements of Necessity*

Where X grants part of Blackacre to Y and the only means of access to Y's part is through the part of Blackacre retained by X, then an easement or way of necessity over X's retained land will be implied in favour of Y.[18] This topic is discussed in more detail in relation to implied reservations which is, perhaps, the case more commonly litigated.[19]

(b) *Intended Easements*

Easements which are necessary to carry out the common intention of the parties to the grant will be implied, particularly in favour of the grantee. It is, of course, essential to establish such a common intention, but this can often be inferred from the circumstances of the case,[20] *e.g.*, a sale of one of two attached houses will usually involve an implication of an easement of support for the house sold by the house retained.[21]

---

[15] See the discussion in *Cable* v. *Bryant* [1908] 1 Ch. 259; *Browne* v. *Flower* [1911] 1 Ch. 219. Elliott, "Non-Derogation from Grant" (1964) 80 L.Q.R. 244.

[16] Para. 6.066. *post.*

[17] Stroud, "Implied Grant and Reservation of Easements" (1940) 56 L.Q.R. 93.

[18] *Donnelly* v. *Adams* [1905] 1 I.R. 154. See also *Browne* v. *Maguire* [1922] 1 I.R. 23; *McDonagh* v. *Mulholland* [1931] I.R. 110; *B. and W. Investments Ltd.* v. *Ulster Scottish Friendly Society* (1969) 20 N.I.L.Q. 325.

[19] Para. 6.070, *post.*

[20] *Gogarty* v. *Hoskins* [1906] 1 I.R. 173. *Cf. Annally Hotel Ltd.* v. *Bergin* (1970) 104 I.L.T.R. 65 (doctrine of estoppel also invoked).

[21] *Cf. Latimer* v. *Official Co-Operative Society* (1885) 16 L.R.Ir. 305 (see *A Casebook on Irish Land Law* (1984), p. 293).

(c) Rule in Wheeldon v. Burrows

6.061. The rule in *Wheeldon* v. *Burrows*[22] is an example of the more general principle that a man may not derogate from his grant.[23] It is important to realise the limits to the rule enunciated in that case. First, the rule is confined to cases of implied grant; there can be no application of the rule in cases of implied reservation.[24] Secondly, the rule is confined to cases of creation of easements, and possibly profits,[25] for the first time and does not relate to transfer of easements already existing. In fact, the rule is confined to cases of quasi-easements, *i.e.*, rights exercised by the grantor in respect of the land granted, while it was in his common ownership, which have the potential to become full easements on sale of that part of the land to another person.[26]

6.062. The rule in *Wheeldon* v. *Burrows* lays down that, on the grant of part of land owned by the grantor, there pass to the grantee as easements all rights in the form of quasi-easements over the land retained by the grantor which satisfy three tests, namely, rights which (1) were "continuous and apparent," (2) were necessary to the reasonable enjoyment of the part of the land granted to the grantee and (3) had been, and still were at the time of the grant, used by the grantor for the benefit of the part granted. What is not clear from *Wheeldon* v. *Burrows* itself is the precise relationship between these three tests, in particular whether they are three quite independent tests, each of which must be satisfied for the rule to apply. The first test has given rise to some controversy and it has even been suggested that it was an alien concept imported into the common law from French law.[27] It is also not clear to what extent the first test should be regarded only as an alternative to the second test. The two seem to involve a considerable amount of overlapping when applied to particular cases. Bearing these points in mind, the three tests may be considered in a little more detail.

6.063. With respect to the first, it seems that the grantor need not have exercised the quasi-easement continuously in the strict sense.[28] It has been argued that in this context the word "continuous" is used not in the sense of incessant user but rather in the sense of permanent as opposed to temporary rights.[29] Furthermore, while there is some suggestion in the cases that the rule

---

[22] (1879) 12 Ch.D. 31. For discussion of the rule in Ireland, see *Donnelly* v. *Adams* [1905] 1 I.R. 154; *McDonagh* v. *Mulholland* [1931] I.R. 110; *Re Flanigan and McGarvey and Thompson's Contract* [1945] N.I. 32 (see *ibid.*, p. 317).

[23] Para. 6.059, *supra*. See also *Griffin* v. *Keane* (1927) 61 I.L.T.R. 177.

[24] In fact, this is the actual *ratio decidendi* of *Wheeldon* v. *Burrows* since it concerned a claim that the easements in question were impliedly reserved. See also para. 6.069, *post*. *Wheeldon* v. *Burrows* did not establish the rule either; it merely enumerated principles established by earlier decisions.

[25] It is not clear to what extent, if at all, the rule applies to profits *à prendre* appurtenant, a point on which there is little authority. It is arguable that quasi-profits would not satisfy the test of being "continuous and apparent" in relation to the *servient* tenement, para. 6.062, *infra*. See Megarry and Wade, *The Law of Real Property* (5th ed., 1984), p. 865.

[26] Para. 6.029, *ante*.

[27] Note the remarks of Lord Westbury, in *Suffield* v. *Brown* (1864) 4 De G.J. & S. 185 at 195 and Lord Blackburn in *Dalton* v. *Angus & Co.* (1881) 6 App.Cas. 740 at 821, cited by Barton J. in *Donnelly* v. *Adams* [1905] 1 I.R. 154 at 165–6. See also Gale, *Law of Easements* (1st ed., 1839), p. 53; *Ward* v. *Kirkland* [1967] Ch. 194.

[28] *Suffield* v. *Brown* (1864) 4 De G.J. & S. 185 at 199.

[29] Gale, *Law of Easements* (1st ed., 1839), p. 53.

is confined to passive rights, *i.e.*, rights which do not require the dominant owner to do some acts (*e.g.*, light or support to buildings),[30] there have been cases where this notion has been ignored, *e.g.*, where a right of way, whose exercise necessarily involves positive action, has been held to be created by implied grant under the rule.[31] As regards the requirement of "apparent," this seems to confine the rule to cases where the rights claimed were clearly being exercised over the servient tenement.[32] The courts have taken this to mean that, if the existence of the easement on the servient land cannot be seen or be discovered by a careful inspection of the land, it does not satisfy the test.[33] It is on these grounds primarily that it is argued that the rule in *Wheeldon* v. *Burrows* cannot apply to profits *à prendre*. Profits necessarily involve positive acts on the part of the dominant owner; they are rarely, if ever, exercised continuously[34] and often their exercise is not apparent on the servient land.[35]

6.064. As regards the second test, it is important not to confuse this with the requirements of an easement of necessity. For an easement of necessity to be established it must be one without which the land in question cannot be enjoyed *at all*,[36] whereas the rule in *Wheeldon* v. *Burrows* simply requires that *reasonable* enjoyment of the land cannot be had without the rights in question.

6.065. The third test is a straightforward requirement that the rights should not only have been enjoyed right up to the time of the grant, but also have been enjoyed in respect of the part of the land sold. In other words, the rights in question must have the potential to satisfy the normal requirements of easements (*i.e.*, be quasi-easements in the technical sense), so that, for example, there must be a dominant and servient tenement with the rights, which must accommodate the dominant tenement.[37]

(d) *Conveyancing Act, 1881, s. 6*

6.066. Section 6 of the Conveyancing Act, 1881,[38] is important in the present context because, to some extent, it can perform the same function as the rule in *Wheeldon* v. *Burrows*, in that it may create easements out of quasi-easements. From the outset, however, it must be emphasised that the section does so through giving an extended meaning to general words in an

---

[30] *Worthington* v. *Gimson* (1860) 2 E. & E. 618; *Polden* v. *Bastard* (1865) L.R. 1 Q.B. 156.

[31] *Clancy* v. *Byrne* (1877) I.R. 11 C.L. 355; *Donnelly* v. *Adams* [1905] 1 I.R. 154; *Head* v. *Meara* [1912] 1 I.R. 262; *McDonagh* v. *Mulholland* [1931] I.R. 110. See also *Brown* v. *Alabaster* (1887) 37 Ch.D. 490; *Borman* v. *Griffith* [1930] 1 Ch. 493.

[32] *McDonagh* v. *Mulholland* [1931] I.R. 110. See also *Pyer* v. *Carter* (1857) 1 H. & N. 916 (water from eaves of house running into underground drain); *Watts* v. *Kelson* (1870) 6 Ch.App. 166 (watercourse running through visible pipes).

[33] Thus the rights of way cases have generally been confined to rights over made roads or worn tracks, see cases cited in fn. 31, *supra*.

[34] They can, however, be just as permanent in nature as easements, para. 6.054, *ante*.

[35] *Cf.*, however, mining, quarrying and turbary rights with fishing and sporting rights, paras. 5.113–9, *post*.

[36] Para. 6.070, *post*.

[37] Paras. 6.025–6, *ante*.

[38] *Henry Ltd* v. *McGlade* [1926] N.I. 144 (see *A Casebook on Irish Land Law* (1984), p. 324). For England, see now s. 62 of the Law of Property Act, 1925. See also *Survey of the Land Law of Northern Ireland* (1971), para. 174.

express grant,[39] rather than by way of an implied grant, and the section can bring into operation a much wider range of rights than the rule in *Wheeldon* v. *Burrows*.

Section 6 (1) provides as follows:

"A conveyance of land shall be deemed to include and shall by virtue of this Act operate to convey, with the land, all buildings, erections, fixtures, commons, hedges, ditches, fences, ways, waters, watercourses, liberties, privileges, easements, rights, and advantages whatsoever, appertaining or reputed to appertain to the land, or any part thereof, or at the time of the conveyance demised, occupied, or enjoyed with, or reputed or known as part or parcel of or appurtenant to the land or any part thereof."[40]

This provision applies only to conveyances executed since 1881[41] and in this context a conveyance includes, *inter alia*, an assignment, appointment, lease, settlement and other assurance.[42] It also applies if and so far only as a contrary intention is not expressed in the conveyance and is subject to the terms of the conveyance and its provisions.[43]

6.067. So far as creation of easements and profits is concerned, the following points about section 6 should be noted. First, the section has a much wider scope than the rule in *Wheeldon* v. *Burrows*. It is capable of applying to all kinds of quasi-easements and profits as well as other liberties and privileges.[44] Secondly, the section is not subject to the requirements of *Wheeldon* v. *Burrows*, such as that the quasi-easements must be "continuous and apparent"[45] and must be reasonably necessary to the enjoyment of the land granted. All the section requires is that the rights in question were, or were reputed to be, appertaining to or enjoyed with the land granted. A common example of the operation of the section is where a landlord grants a renewal of a lease and the new lease operates to convert into easements or profits licences or privileges which the landlord previously permitted the tenant to enjoy.[46] Thirdly, it seems clear that section 6 cannot convert into an easement or profit a right which does not comply with the essential requirements of easements and profits. The section is a purely technical conveyancing device intended to shorten conveyances; it is not intended to alter substantive rights or to extend the categories of rights or interests recognised by the law.[47] Fourthly, since the

---

[39] Para. 6.052, *ante*. See also *Geoghegan* v. *Fegan* (1872) I.R. 6 C.L. 139; *Head* v. *Meara* [1912] 1 I.R. 262.

[40] *Jeffers* v. *Odeon (Ireland) Ltd.* (1953) 87 I.L.T.R. 187. Similar provisions for conveyances of land with "houses or other buildings" and "manors" (now obsolete) are contained in s. 6 (2) and (3).

[41] 1881 Act, s. 6 (6).

[42] 1881 Act, s. 2 (v).

[43] 1881 Act, s. 6 (4). *Steele* v. *Morrow* (1923) 57 I.L.T.R. 89.

[44] *Henry Ltd* v. *McGlade* [1926] N.I. 144 (see *A Casebook on Irish Land Law* (1984), p. 324) (right to advertise café by having man stand with pole at entrance to arcade). See also *White* v. *Williams* [1922] 1 K.B. 727 (quasi-profit of a sheepwalk).

[45] *Cf. Titchmarsh* v. *Royston Water Co. Ltd.* (1899) 81 L.T. 673; *Long* v. *Gowlett* [1923] 2 Ch. 177 at 202–4. See also *Ward* v. *Kirkland* [1967] Ch. 194.

[46] *Wright* v. *Macadam* [1949] 2 K.B. 744; *Rye* v. *Rye* [1962] A.C. 496. See also *Jeffers* v. *Odeon (Ireland) Ltd.* (1953) 87 I.L.T.R. 187.

[47] *International Tea Stores Co.* v. *Hobbs* [1903] 2 Ch. 165; *Regis Property Co. Ltd.* v. *Redman* [1956] 2 Q.B. 612; *Phipps* v. *Pears* [1965] 1 Q.B. 76; *Crow* v. *Wood* [1971] 1 Q.B. 77. *Cf.* the controversy over the effect of s. 5 of

section operates by way of express grant, it cannot create rights which the grantor has no power to grant.[48] Fifthly, and this appears to be a considerable restriction on the section's operation, it has been held that the section operates only where there has been a diversity of ownership, or at least of occupation (*e.g.*, as between landlord and tenant), of the dominant and servient tenements *prior* to the conveyance.[49] In other words, it seems that the section cannot be invoked in, perhaps, the most common case for the application of the rule in *Wheeldon* v. *Burrows*, where a *common* owner of quasi-dominant and servient tenements sells the quasi-dominant tenement to another person. The argument in support of this contention is that the section passes rights only in the nature of "liberties," "privileges" and "easements," which are more appropriate expressions for rights over *other* people's property rather than expressions normally used to describe rights which a common owner has over his own property. Yet, the section does also refer to "ways" and "watercourses" and to "rights" and "advantages," which seem equally appropriate in the case of a common owner[50] and it should be noted that the courts have said that the restriction relating to common ownership or occupation does not apply in the case of a right of light.[51] On the other hand, the section appears to be confined to a "conveyance" of *existing* rights, *i.e.*, it does not apply to the "creation" of rights not already in existence.

6.068. One further point should be mentioned with respect to both the rule in *Wheeldon* v. *Burrows* and section 6 of the 1881 Act. Both operate with respect to a *grant* or *conveyance* of land and have nothing to do with the interpretation of any prior *contract* for such grant or conveyance.[52] The rule in *Wheeldon* v. *Burrows* is based on the principle that a man may not derogate from his grant and so can be invoked only after a grant has been made. Section 6 relates only to interpretation of general words in a "conveyance," which, though widely defined in section 2 (v) of the 1881 Act, does not include a contract. Yet it is important to realise that in most cases of a grant or conveyance of land there is initially in force a contract for the sale of the land and questions of its interpretation may arise. What is included in the contract is largely a matter of the intention of the parties as to its scope. It may well be that the contract is intended to include quasi-easements and this may be implied

---

the Real Property Act, 1845 and s. 56 of the Law of Property Act, 1925, see *Beswick* v. *Beswick* [1968] A.C. 58, espec. at 102 (*per* Lord Upjohn). Paras. 3.041, *ante*, and 19.16, *post*.
[48] Note also the saving in s. 6 (5) of the 1881 Act. *Quicke* v. *Chapman* [1903] 1 Ch. 659.
[49] *Long* v. *Gowlett* [1923] 2 Ch. 177. Cf. *Head* v. *Meara* [1912] 1 I.R. 262 at 264–5 (*per* Ross J.); also *Wright* v. *Macadam* [1949] 2 K.B. 744 at 748 (*per* Jenkins L.J.); *Ward* v. *Kirkland* [1967] Ch. 194. Hargreaves, (1952) 15 M.L.R. 265. *Long* v. *Gowlett* was approved by the House of Lords in *Sovmots Investments Ltd.* v. *Secretary of State for the Environment* [1977] 2 W.L.R. 951; see *ibid.*, pp. 958 (*per* Lord Wilberforce), 965 (*per* Lord Edmund-Davies) and 973 (*per* Lord Keith of Kinkel). Note the controversy provoked by this aspect of the decision between Harpum, "Easements and Centre Point: Old Problems Resolved in a Novel Setting" (1977) 41 Conv. 415 and "*Long* v. Gowlett: A Strong Fortress" [1979] Conv. 113, and Smith, "Centre Point: Faulty Towers with Shaky Foundations" [1978] Conv. 449.
[50] See *Head* v. *Meara* [1912] 1 I.R. 262.
[51] *Broomfield* v. *Williams* [1897] 1 Ch. 602. See also *Long* v. *Gowlett* [1923] 2 Ch. 177 at 200–3. Note also, however, that a right of light is a somewhat special case in the law of easements generally, para. 6.097, *post*.
[52] See discussion in *Re Flanagan and McGarvey and Thompson's Contract* [1945] N.I. 32 at 40–1 (*per* Black J.) (see *A Casebook on Irish Land Law* (1984), p. 317); also *Borman* v. *Griffith* [1930] 1 Ch. 493.

from the circumstances of the case.[53] But neither the rule in *Wheeldon* v. *Burrows* nor section 6 of the 1881 Act have any direct relevance to this matter. Furthermore, if the prior contract contained restrictions as to what was to pass with the land, but the subsequent conveyance is drafted in unrestricted form so that, under the rule in *Wheeldon* v. *Burrows* or section 6 of the 1881 Act or both, various rights would be created, it would always be open to the parties to seek rectification of the conveyance in equity on the ground of common mistake.[54] Alternatively, if the purchaser seeks a decree of specific performance against the vendor in relation to the contract, the court will at most oblige the vendor to transfer only those rights which he contracted to sell.[55] The contract may include rights which would pass under the conveyance by virtue of the rule in *Wheeldon* v. *Burrows* or section 6 of the 1881 Act and it may not. In the end of the day, it is entirely a question of the intention of the parties to the contract and the search for this should not be confused by reference to rules or statutory provisions relating to grants or conveyances.

(ii) Reservation

6.069. It is the corollary of the rules just discussed that few easements arise by implied reservation. Since a grant is generally construed against the grantor, he should, if he wishes to reserve easements for himself, do so expressly. However, the courts have been prepared to relax this general rule and to permit easements to arise by implication in at least two cases.

(a) *Easements of Necessity*

6.070. If, on making a grant of part of his land, a grantor cuts himself off from part of his land retained, *e.g.*, it becomes landlocked,[56] there will be implied in his favour a way of necessity.[57] The grantor is given the right to choose a convenient means of access and must thereafter stick to it.[58] Such means of access must be a necessity at the date of the grant[59] and no implied right will arise if there is an alternative route available to the grantor.[60] The grantor will succeed in establishing a way of necessity in the last situation only if he can show that the alternative route is not really open to him, because he has no legal right to it as opposed to permission or a licence which may be revoked at any time, or he has not even permission to use it. The grantor will certainly not succeed if he can show only that the alternative route is inconvenient.

---

[53] *McDonagh* v. *Mulholland* [1931] I.R 110 at 122 (*per* Kennedy C.J.); *Re Flanagan and McGarvey and Thompson's Contract* [1945] N.I. 32 at 40–1 (*per* Black J.). See also *Re Peck and the School Board for London's Contract* [1893] 2 Ch. 315; *Re Walmsley and Shaw's Contract* [1917] 1 Ch. 93; *Borman* v. *Griffith* [1930] 1 Ch. 493.

[54] Para. 3.162, *ante*.

[55] Paras. 3.144 and 3.155, *ante*.

[56] *Maude* v. *Thornton* [1929] I.R. 454. See also *Nickerson* v. *Barraclough* [1981] Ch. 426.

[57] *Nugent* v. *Cooper* (1854) 7 Ir.Jur. (o.s.) 112; *Geraghty* v. *McCann* (1872) I.R. 6 C.L. 411; *Clancy* v. *Byrne* (1877) I.R. 11 C.L. 355; *Browne* v. *Maguire* [1922] 1 I.R. 23. See also the remarks of Black J. in *Re Flanagan and McGarvey and Thompson's Contract* [1945] N.I. 32 at 42 (see *A Casebook on Irish Land Law* (1984), p. 317).

[58] *Cf. Donnelly* v. *Adams* [1905] 1 I.R. 154 (case of implied grant).

[59] *Geraghty* v. *McCann* (1872) I.R. 6 C.L. 411; *Browne* v. *Maguire* [1922] 1 I.R. 23.

[60] *Nugent* v. *Cooper* (1854) 7 Ir.Jur. (o.s.) 112.

6.071. Ways of necessity are by far the most common case of easements arising by implied reservation, but there is no reason why other easements of necessity cannot be established, *e.g.*, an easement of support without which the land or buildings retained could not be enjoyed at all. In each case the grantor has to prove the necessity.[61] Whether the easement ceases to exist subsequently when the necessity ceases, *e.g.*, when an alternative means of access to landlocked property is acquired, is a moot point. There is some authority for saying that the easement does cease[62] but it has been criticised.[63] It is arguable that once the easement comes into existence it cannot be destroyed except in accordance with the usual rules for determination of easements.[64]

(b) Intended Easements

6.072. There is some authority for saying that the courts will imply in favour of the grantor easements required to give effect to the common intention of the parties to the grant. The most commonly cited example is the case of a sale of one of two adjoining houses where the parties can be taken to intend that there should be mutual rights of support.[65] To some extent there seems to be an overlap with cases of necessity, but intended easements may include a wider category.[66] It can be stated with more certainty that the burden of proof on the grantor in such cases is considerable.[67]

4. Presumed Grant or Prescription

6.073. The basis of prescription is the presumption by the courts, on being given evidence of long enjoyment of a right in the nature of an easement or profit, that the right had a lawful origin.[68] In this respect the courts acknowledge the theory that easements lie in grant[69] but in practice they recognise the existence of rights without requiring direct documentary evidence of their creation.[70] The underlying policy is that of "quieting men's titles," a policy that is the foundation of other principles of our land law system.[71]

---

[61] See discussion in *Donnelly* v. *Adams* [1905] 1 I.R. 154 at 161 (*per* Barton J.).

[62] *Holmes* v. *Goring* (1824) 2 Bing. 76. *Cf. Mulville* v. *Fallon* (1872) I.R. 6 Eq. 458 (substituted way and implied release of old one). See also *Clancy* v. *Byrne* (1877) I.R. 11 C.L. 355.

[63] *Barkshire* v. *Grubb* (1881) 18 Ch.D. 616 at 620. See also Garner, "Ways of Necessity" (1960) 24 Conv. 208; Grundes, "Right of Way: Ways of Necessity" (1939) 3 Conv. 425; Simonton, "Ways of Necessity" (1925) 25 Col.L.Rev. 571.

[64] *Cf. Stevenson* v. *Parke* [1932] L.J.Jr. 228. Note also the comments of Meredith J. in *Maude* v. *Thornton* [1929] I.R. 454 at 458 (implied reservation of way of necessity, not simply a licence irrevocable so long as the necessity continues).

[65] *Cf. Gogarty* v. *Hoskins* [1906] 1 I.R. 173. See also *Richards* v. *Rose* (1853) 9 Exch. 218 at 221.

[66] *Jones* v. *Pritchard* [1908] 1 Ch. 630; *Cory* v. *Davies* [1923] 2 Ch. 95. *Cf. Shubrook* v. *Tufnell* (1882) 46 L.T. 886; *Pwllbach Colliery Co. Ltd.* v. *Woodman* [1915] A.C. 634; *Re Webb* [1951] Ch. 808.

[67] *Richards* v. *Rose* (1853) 9 Exch. 218.

[68] This is one point of distinction between prescription and the doctrine of adverse possession, ch. 23, *post.*

[69] Para. 6.030, *ante.*

[70] See the discussion in *Timmons* v. *Hewitt* (1888) 22 L.R.Ir. 627. See also Anderson, "Easement and Prescription—Changing Perspectives in Classification" (1975) 38 M.L.R. 64.

[71] *E.g.*, the doctrine of adverse possession, ch. 23, *post. Cf.* the equitable doctrine of laches, para. 3.066, *ante.*

6.074. Three methods of prescription have come to be recognised over the centuries, namely, prescription at common law, under the doctrine of lost modern grant and by statute.[72] Each of these methods is considered in detail below, but first we must examine certain conditions which must be met for any of those methods to be applicable.

(i) Conditions

The following are the main conditions which must be satisfied for a claim of acquisition of an easement or profit by prescription to succeed.[73]

(a) User as of Right

6.075. The claimant by prescription must show that he has used or enjoyed the easement or profit "as of right," *i.e.*, as if he were entitled to it.[74] This principle follows from the theory that the court makes a presumption on the basis that the right claimed had a lawful origin. If the claimant has acted in a manner to suggest that his right did not have such an origin, then this destroys the theory upon which the court acts and so the claim must fail.[75] On this point the courts have adopted the terminology of Roman law and have reiterated that the user must have been *nec vi, nec clam* and *nec precario, i.e.*, without force, without secrecy and without permission.[76] This shows that the claimant must prove not only that he has used or enjoyed the right in question but also that the servient owner acquiesced in that user or enjoyment, as he would in respect of an established right.[77]

6.076. If the claimant has had user through force or violence on his part only, or the servient owner has permitted user after protest or objection only, it is clear that a claim cannot be established "as of right."[78] Similarly, for the servient owner to acquiesce in the user, he must have knowledge of it and secret user, *e.g.*, in the form of claimed support for a building where the servient owner is unaware that he is providing such support, will not be enough to establish a claim.[79] For this reason also claims in respect of subterranean water often fail.[80]

Finally, the claimant cannot succeed in establishing user "as of right" if, on the contrary, the user has been made under an agreement with or licence from

---

[72] *I.e.*, the Prescription Act, 1832, as applied to Ireland by the Prescription (Ir.) Act, 1858.

[73] Note, however, the special position of rights of light, para. 6.097, *post*.

[74] See the discussion in *Hanna* v. *Pollock* [1900] 2 I.R. 664 (see *A Casebook on Irish Land Law* (1984), p. 329).

[75] *Wilson* v. *Stanley* (1861) 12 I.C.L.R. 345.

[76] *Coke on Littleton* (19th ed., 1832), 114a.

[77] See *Annally Hotel Ltd.* v. *Bergin* (1970) 104 I.L.T.R. 65. Also *Deeble* v. *Linehan* (1860) 12 I.C.L.R. 1. *Cf. Beggan* v. *McDonald* (1877) 2 L.R.Ir. 560. Para. 6.091, *post*.

[78] *Eaton* v. *Swansea Waterworks Co.* (1851) 17 Q.B. 267.

[79] *Gateley* v. *Martin* [1900] 2 I.R. 269.

[80] *Ewart* v. *Belfast Poor Law Commrs.* (1881) 9 L.R.Ir. 172. *Cf. Black* v. *Ballymena Township Commrs.* (1886) 17 L.R.Ir. 459. It seems that the servient owner may not succeed on this ground by simply "turning a blind eye" to the user in question, see *Union Lighterage Co.* v. *London Graving Dock Co.* [1902] 2 Ch. 557, espec. at 571 (*per* Romer L.J.); also *Lloyds Bank Ltd.* v. *Dalton* [1942] Ch. 466.

the servient owner.[81] In such a case the position of the claimant is governed by the terms of the agreement or licence and not by the law of prescription.[82]

(b) *Continuous User*

6.077. It is also a settled principle that the user or enjoyment must be continuous for a claim by prescription to succeed.[83] In the case of certain easements, *e.g.*, a right of way, this has been interpreted as requiring regular user as opposed to intermittent user.[84]

(c) *Leasehold Property*

6.078. In England it has long been a settled principle that the doctrine of prescription is generally confined to freehold property.[85] The theory applied by the English courts seems to have been that prescription involves the notion of a permanent right created at some unspecified date in the past and that this is inconsistent with acquisition in respect of leasehold property.[86] Thus the English Courts have held: (1) there can be no prescription against a landowner who holds a limited freehold estate[87] or a leasehold estate only[88]; (2) where the claimant is himself a limited owner or lessee, he can claim easements by prescription on behalf of the fee simple owner or his landlord only, and so cannot prescribe against other land held by the fee simple owner or the landlord[89]; (3) on the same ground as in (2), one tenant cannot prescribe against another tenant of the same landlord.[90]

6.079. The Irish courts have taken a quite different approach to this subject,[91] which may be partly due to the fact that there was a time when so much of the land in what is still a predominantly agricultural country was subject to tenancies.[92] Furthermore, many of these tenancies were, and still are, in areas which have since become urbanised, for very substantial periods, *e.g.*, 999 and 10,000 years,[93] which for practical purposes seem little different than

---

[81] *Arkwright* v. *Gell* (1839) 5 M. & W. 203.

[82] However, prescription may become relevant if the right continues to be enjoyed after the contract or licence ends, *Gaved* v. *Martyn* (1865) 19 C.B. (N.S.) 732.

[83] *Cf.* the concept of "without interruption" under the Prescription Act, 1832, para. 6.093, *post*.

[84] *Hollins* v. *Verney* (1884) 13 Q.B.D. 304. *Cf.* abandonment through disuse or substitution of an alternative, *Mulville* v. *Fallon* (1872) I.R. 6 Eq. 458; *Stevenson* v. *Parke* [1932] L.J.Ir. 228.

[85] Indeed, confined to the fee simple estate, *Bright* v. *Walker* (1834) 1 Cr. M. & R. 211; *Gayford* v. *Moffat* (1868) 4 Ch.App. 133.

[86] *Wheaton* v. *Maple & Co.* [1893] 3 Ch. 48 at 63 (*per* Lindley L.J.). The English courts have, however, accepted that easements or profits could be acquired in respect of leasehold property by express grant, *Kilgour* v. *Gaddes* [1904] 1 K.B. 457 at 460. See also Kiralfy, "Position of Leaseholder in Law of Easements" (1948) 13 Conv. 104.

[87] *Barker* v. *Richardson* (1821) 4 B. & Ald. 579; *Roberts* v. *James* (1903) 89 L.T. 282. Note, however, that the Settled Land Act, 1882, s. 3 (i) empowered a tenant for life to grant easements in fee simple, ch. 8, *post*.

[88] *Daniel* v. *North* (1809) 11 East 372.

[89] In effect the argument is essentially that the landlord cannot, through his tenant, claim a right against himself, *Gayford* v. *Moffat* (1868) 4 Ch.App. 133.

[90] *Kilgour* v. *Gaddes* [1904] 1 K.B. 457.

[91] See Chua, "Easements: Termors in Prescription in Ireland" (1964) 15 N.I.L.Q. 489; Delany, "Lessees and Doctrine of Lost Grant" (1958) 74 L.Q.R. 82.

[92] Ch. 18, *post*. See also the remarks of Dodd J. in *Flynn* v. *Harte* [1913] 2 I.R. 322 and the discussion by the Court of Appeal in *Hanna* v. *Pollock* [1900] 2 I.R. 664 (see *A Casebook on Irish Land Law* (1984), p. 329).

[93] Note also leases for lives renewable for ever, ch. 4, *ante*.

grants in fee simple so far as the long enjoyment or permanent user of the rights in question is concerned. The result of the Irish courts' reaction to the English decisions[94] is as follows: (1) Prescription against a limited owner or tenant can be claimed under the Prescription Act, 1832,[95] and the doctrine of lost modern grant.[96] There is no authority on whether such a claim can be established at common law.[97] (2) A tenant can probably prescribe against other land held by his own landlord under the Prescription Act, 1832,[98] but not under the doctrine of lost modern grant.[99] Once again there is no authority on the position at common law, but it is likely that a claim would fail as in the case of a claim based on lost modern grant. (3) A tenant can prescribe against another tenant holding under the same landlord under the Prescription Act, 1832,[1] probably also under the doctrine of lost modern grant[2] and possibly even at common law.[3]

6.080. We must now turn to the three methods of prescription recognised by our law. At the outset it must be emphasised that all three methods can still be invoked today and it is usual to plead more than one in a particular case in the hope that the court will find that at least one method is applicable.[4]

(ii) At Common Law

6.081. At common law the courts were prepared to presume that a grant of the easement or profit claimed had been made if user as of right could be shown to have continued from time immemorial,[5] i.e., "from time whereof the memory of men runneth not to the contrary."[6] In fact, the date fixed as the limit of legal memory was 1189,[7] so that a claimant under common law in theory has

---

[94] Especially *Bright* v. *Walker* (1834) 1 Cr. M. & R. 211 and *Gayford* v. *Moffat* (1868) 4 Ch.App. 133.

[95] But in the case of 40 years' enjoyment only, *Wilson* v. *Stanley* (1861) 12 I.C.L.R. 345; *Beggan* v. *McDonald* (1878) 2 L.R.Ir. 560, espec. at 570–1 (*per* May C.J.) (holding this remained the case despite the servient tenant's landlord's absence of knowledge of or non-acquiescence in the enjoyment during the tenancy). In the case of 20 years' enjoyment only, it must be "as of right" under the 1832 Act and this seems to preclude a claim against a tenant so as to bind his landlord, *Wilson* v. *Stanley, op. cit., Cf.* if the claim is for an easement for the period of the servient owner's tenancy only, fn. 96, *infra.*

[96] Provided sufficient evidence of the landlord's knowledge of and acquiescence in the enjoyment is shown, *Deeble* v. *Linehan* (1860) 12 I.C.L.R. 1. It is, of course, possible to argue that in certain cases the easement is to attach to, and to last for the term of, the servient owner's tenancy only, see *O'Kane* v. *O'Kane* (1892) 30 L.R.Ir. 489 at 494 (*per* O'Brien C.J.).

[97] Where the point as been raised, the courts have tended to decide the issue on other grounds, *e.g.*, by holding an easement arose by *implied* grant, see *Timmons* v. *Hewitt* (1887) 22 L.R.Ir. 627. Also *Clancy* v. *Byrne* (1877) I.R. 11 C.L. 355.

[98] Again limited to cases of 40 years' enjoyment. *Fahey* v. *Dwyer* (1879) 4 L.R.Ir. 271. *Cf. Clancy* v. *Byrne* (1877) I.R. 11 C.L. 355.

[99] *Macnaghten* v. *Baird* [1903] 2 I.R. 731.

[1] *Fahey* v. *Dwyer* (1879) 4 L.R.Ir. 271.

[2] *Hanna* v. *Pollock* [1900] 2 I.R. 664 (see *A Casebook on Irish Land Law* (1984), p. 329); *Flynn* v. *Harte* [1913] 2 I.R. 322; *Tallon* v. *Ennis* [1937] I.R. 549; *Tisdall* v. *McArthur & Co. (Steel and Metal) Ltd.* [1951] I.R. 228 at 240–1 (*per* Kingsmill Moore J.) (see *ibid.*, p. 357). Once again the grant may be presumed to relate only to the period of the servient owner's tenancy and not to bind the common landlord, *O'Kane* v. *O'Kane* (1892) 30 L.R.Ir. 489. The courts may also invoke the doctrine of implied grant and hold that the common landlord impliedly granted the easement when demising the dominant tenement, *Timmons* v. *Hewitt* (1887) 22 L.R.Ir. 627 at 637 (*per* Palles C.B.).

[3] *Timmons* v. *Hewitt* (1887) 22 L.R.Ir. 627. See also *Clancy* v. *Byrne* (1877) I.R. 11 C.L. 355.

[4] For reasons which should become clear from the ensuing discussion, it is usual to plead in the order, first, the Prescription Act, second, at common law and, third, the doctrine of lost modern grant. However, practices have varied over the years and there was a time when judges were less reluctant to adopt the doctrine of a lost grant.

[5] *Craig* v. *McCance* (1910) 44 I.L.T.R. 90. See also *Daly* v. *Cullen* (1958) 92 I.L.T.R. 127.

[6] *Coke upon Littleton* (19th ed., 1832), 170.

[7] So fixed by the Statute of Westminster I, 1275, c. 39.

to establish that he and his predecessors in title have enjoyed the easement or profit continuously since 1189.[8] This clearly would be impossible in most, if not all, cases and so the courts for centuries have been prepared to presume such continuous user for a substantial time immediately prior to his action. In practice the courts have been prepared to make this presumption on production of evidence showing 20 years' continuous user,[9] or, sometimes, user since living memory.[10] This reduced considerably the burden of proof on the claimant at common law but there remain two major difficulties in establishing prescription at common law.

6.082. First, the theory of continuous user since 1189 is still the basis of a claim to prescription at common law and the court's presumption in this regard on being shown 20 years' user can easily be rebutted by showing that user was not possible since 1189. Even if the defendant cannot establish exactly the date after 1189 when user began,[11] he can often show that it must have been some time after that date, *e.g.*, where an easement of light is claimed for a building clearly not eight centuries old.[12] Secondly, a claim at common law can also be defeated by showing that at some date since 1189 there has been unity of possession,[13] *i.e.*, that the dominant and servient tenements have been owned and occupied by the same person.[14] It was in an effort to cure these difficulties at common law, especially the first, that the courts devised the second method of prescription, the doctrine of lost modern grant.[15]

(iii) Lost Modern Grant

6.083. Under this doctrine the courts are prepared to indulge in an alleged fiction that the easement or profit claimed was the subject of a grant executed since 1189 but before the action brought by the claimant, and that the deed of grant has been lost and so cannot be produced in evidence.[16] In earlier days juries were instructed to find as a fact that such a grant had been made if they were satisfied that sufficient evidence of long user or enjoyment had been shown,[17] and so the presumption arose that user from living memory or a period of 20 years prior to the action established the existence of a lost grant.[18] Since the doctrine is based on the theory of a grant at some unspecified date in

---

[8] *Abercromby* v. *Fermoy Town Commrs.* [1900] 1 I.R. 302 (see *A Casebook on Irish Land Law* (1984), p. 294). See also *Craig* v. *McCance* (1910) 44 I.L.T.R. 90.

[9] *McCullagh* v. *Wilson* (1838) 1 Jebb & Sym. 120; *O'Brien* v. *Enright* (1867) I.R. 1 C.L. 718; *Powell* v. *Butler* (1871) I.R. 5 C.L. 309; *Timmons* v. *Hewitt* (1887) 22 L.R.Ir. 627.

[10] *Clancy* v. *Whelan* (1958) 92 I.L.T.R. 39. See also *Daly* v. *Cullen* (1958) 92 I.L.T.R. 127.

[11] *Hanna* v. *Pollock* [1900] 2 I.R. 664 (see *A Casebook on Irish Land Law* (1984), p. 329).

[12] *Duke of Norfolk* v. *Arbuthnot* (1880) 5 C.P.D. 390.

[13] *Wilson* v. *Stanley* (1861) 12 I.C.L.R. 345.

[14] Para. 6.106, *post.*

[15] Described by Lush J. as a "revolting fiction" in *Angus & Co.* v. *Dalton* (1877) 3 Q.B.D. 85 at 95, but considered at length and approved in the same case by the House of Lords, *sub nom. Dalton* v. *Angus & Co.* (1881) 6 App.Cas. 740.

[16] See the discussion in *Hanna* v. *Pollock* [1900] 2 I.R. 664. Also *Ingram* v. *Mackey* [1898] 1 I.R. 272; *Whelan* v. *Leonard* [1917] 2 I.R. 323.

[17] *Deeble* v. *Linehan* (1860) 12 I.C.L.R. 1; *O'Kane* v. *O'Kane* (1892) 30 L.R.Ir. 489.

[18] *Deeble* v. *Linehan, op. cit.; O'Kane* v. *O'Kane, op. cit.; Flynn* v. *Harte* [1913] 2 I.R. 322; *Tisdall* v. *McArthur & Co. (Steel and Metal) Ltd.* [1951] I.R. 228 (See *A Casebook on Irish Land Law* (1984), p. 357); *Scott* v. *Goulding Properties Ltd.* [1972] I.R. 200 (*ibid.*, p. 299).

the past, there is no need to prove continued user since 1189. The "fiction" has never been carried to the lengths of requiring findings as to the details of the grant, such as the date of its execution and the names of the parties to it.[19] There are, however, difficulties even with respect to this second method of prescription.

6.084. First, the court will refuse to make the presumption of a lost grant if it can be established that during the period when the grant could have been made, *e.g.*, during the lifetime of the building to which the easement relates, a grant was impossible because of some technicality, such as the servient owner being under a disability, like mental incapacity, or was a corporation prohibited by its articles of association from dealing in land.[20] To this extent, at least, the courts have not treated the matter as being wholly one of fiction. Secondly, even the Irish courts have made it clear in landlord and tenant cases that a grant cannot be presumed in favour of a tenant against his own landlord,[21] though it seems that the courts are prepared to allow the doctrine of lost modern grant to operate as between tenants, even though holding under the same landlord.[22]

6.085. The difficulties over a claim based on prescription at common law and under the doctrine of lost modern grant prompted the enactment of the Prescription Act, 1832. This Act did not apply originally to Ireland but was extended *en bloc* to Ireland by the Prescription (Ireland) Act, 1858, from January 1, 1859.[23]

(iv) Prescription Act, 1832

6.086. Though the 1832 Act did reduce many of the difficulties relating to the concept of prescription as developed by the courts, it has created its own difficulties for, as it was once put in an oft-quoted statement, it is notorious as "one of the worst drafted Acts on the Statute Book."[24] The following is a summary of the Act's main provisions and, at the outset, it should be noted that the Act contains special provisions for rights of lights, which are discussed at the end of this section. As in the case of the other two methods of prescription, the Act applies to profits *à prendre* as well as to easements, though there are

---

[19] *Palmer* v. *Guadagni* [1906] 2 Ch. 494.
[20] *Rochdale Canal Co.* v. *Radcliffe* (1852) 18 Q.B.D. 287. See also *Neaverson* v. *Peterborough R.D.C.* [1902] 1 Ch. 557; *Oakley* v. *Boston* [1976] Q.B. 270.
[21] *Macnaghten* v. *Baird* [1903] 2 I.R. 731, applying the principle laid down by Lord Cairns in *Gayford* v. *Moffat* (1868) L.R. 4 Ch. 133 at 135: ". . . the possession of the tenant of the demised close is in the possession of his landlord, and it seems to be an utter violation of the first principles of the relation of landlord and tenant to suppose that the tenant, whose occupation of a close A was the occupation of his landlord, could by that occupation acquire an easement over close B, also belonging to his landlord. . . ." However, the Irish courts have suggested that a tenant may acquire an easement against his landlord under the doctrine of implied grant, *Timmons* v. *Hewitt* (1887) 22 L.R.Ir. 627 at 637 (*per* Palles C.B.). See fn. 2, para. 6.079, *ante*.
[22] *Hanna* v. *Pollock* [1900] 2 I.R. 664 (see *A Casebook on Irish Land Law* (1984), p. 329). See also *Flynn* v. *Harte* [1913] 2 I.R. 322 at 326 (*per* Dodd J.); *Tisdall* v. *McArthur & Co. (Steel and Metal) Ltd.* [1951] I.R. 228 at 240–1 (*per* Kingsmill Moore J.) (see *ibid.*, p. 357).
[23] 1858 Act, s. 1. Following the English 1832, Act, the 1858 Act's short title stated that it was an Act "for shortening the Time of Prescription in certain Cases in Ireland."
[24] See the English Law Reform Committee's 14th Report, *Acquisition of Easements and Profits by Prescription* (1966; Cmnd. 3100), para. 40.

some differences in detail in its application to the two kinds of incorporeal hereditament. These differences are noted in the following passages of this chapter.

(a) Prescription Periods of User

6.087. Sections 1 and 2 of the 1832 Act lay down two periods of user whereby easements and profits may be acquired by prescription under the Act. In a case of the shorter period only being shown, namely 20 years' user of an easement (other than of light)[25] and 30 years' user of a profit,[26] the Act simply provides that the easement or profit claimed cannot be defeated by showing only that it was first enjoyed at any time prior to the 20 or 30-year period.[27] In other words, where the shorter period of user only can be shown by a claimant, all the Act does is to prevent his claim being defeated by one of the main defences to a claim at common law, *i.e.*, proof that user began after 1189 and so has not continued since time immemorial.[28] In this respect the Act aids a claim to prescription at common law only.[29]

6.088. Where, however, a claimant can show the longer period of user, namely 40 years for an easement (other than of light)[30] and 60 years for a profit,[31] the Act is more positive and provides that the easement or profit is to be "deemed absolute and indefeasible",[32] unless it has been enjoyed by written consent.[33] It is upon the basis of this difference in operation of the Act in the case of user for the longer period that the Irish courts have been prepared to hold not only that prescription under the Act may operate against a tenant so as to bind even his landlord's reversionary estate in certain circumstances,[34] but also that one tenant can prescribe under the Act against another tenant of the same landlord[35] and possibly even directly against his own landlord.[36]

6.089. It must be emphasised again that the 1832 Act provides an *additional* basis for a claim to an easement or profit by prescription and does not exclude the pleading also of the other two alternatives of prescription at common law or acquisition under the doctrine of lost modern grant.[37] Indeed, it is common to

---

[25] S. 2.

[26] S. 1. *Doyle's Case* (1833) Alc.Reg.Cas. 36.

[27] Ss. 1 and 2.

[28] Para. 6.082, *ante*. Thus it is expressly provided in the case of a claim based on one of the shorter periods of user that "such claim may be defeated in any other way by which the same is now liable to be defeated"—see ss. 1 and 2 of the Act.

[29] This seems to have been one of the reasons why the Irish courts have argued that a claim to prescription under the 1832 Act, based on the shorter periods of 20 or 30 years, cannot be made by or against a tenant, see *Wilson* v. *Stanley* (1861) 12 I.C.L.R. 345; *cf. Beggan* v. *McDonald* (1877) 2 L.R.Ir. 560.

[30] S. 2.

[31] S. 1. See *Doyle's Case* (1833) Alc.Reg.Cas. 36; *Lowry* v. *Crothers* (1871) I.R. 5 C.L. 98 (profits *à prendre*).

[32] Ss. 1 and 2.

[33] Discussed further, para. 6.091, *post*.

[34] *I.e.*, if the landlord does not resist the claim within 3 years of determination of the tenant's tenancy under s. 8 of the 1832 Act. See discussion in *Beggan* v. *McDonald* (1877) 2 L.R.Ir. 560, espec. at 570–1 (*per* May C.J.). Also *Wilson* v. *Stanley* (1861) 12 I.C.L.R. 345 at 355 (*per* Pigot C.B.).

[35] *Fahey* v. *Dwyer* (1879) 4 L.R.Ir. 271; *Hanna* v. *Pollock* [1900] 2 I.R. 664 (see *A Casebook on Irish Land Law* (1984), p. 329); *Flynn* v. *Harte* [1913] 2 I.R. 322; *Tallon* v. *Ennis* [1937] 1 I.R. 549.

[36] *Ibid. Cf. Timmons* v. *Hewitt* (1887) 22 L.R.Ir. 627 at 635 (*per* Palles C.B.).

[37] The suggestion in England that lost modern grant can no longer be raised in respect of an easement of light (see, *e.g.*, *Tappling* v. *Jones* (1865) 11 H.L.C. 290) had been doubted in Ireland, see *Tisdall* v. *McArthur & Co.*

plead at least two of the methods of prescription, if not all three, as the Irish cases show.[38] Usually a claim based on the Prescription Act is easier to establish (which is precisely what the Act intends[39]), but it may happen that such a claim fails on a technicality based on other provisions in the Act[40] and so one has to fall back on the other methods of prescription.[41] However, the Act provides expressly that user for *less* than the statutory period is not to give rise to any presumption in favour of the claim in question,[42] though it has been stated that a lost grant may still be presumed from user for less than the statutory period, provided there is some other item of evidence to support that presumption.[43]

(b) *Claim by Litigant*

6.090. It is essential to realise that the Act's provisions are expressly confined to cases where "some suit or action wherein the claim or matter to which such period [of user] may relate shall have been or shall be brought into question."[44] To establish an easement or profit under the Act, the claimant must bring an action for infringement of the alleged right[45] or, if the claimant does not wish to wait for such infringement,[46] he may apply to the court for a declaration that he is entitled to the easement or profit in question.[47] Furthermore, the Act also provides that, when a suit or action is brought, the vital period of user to be considered by the court is the period "next before" that suit or action. In other words, the claimant must not only show the statutory period of user but also show that that user took place immediately prior to his suit or action.[48]

(c) *User as of Right*

6.091. The Act contains the same basic requirement which applies to the other two methods of prescription, namely that the user made by the claimant to the easement or profit was "as of right,"[49] *i.e., nec vi, nec clam* and *nec*

(Steel and Metal) Ltd. [1951] I.R. 228 at 235 and 240–1 (*per* Kingsmill Moore J.) (see *A Casebook on Irish Land Law* (1984), p. 357). See also *Scott* v. *Goulding Properties Ltd.* [1972] I.R. 200 (*ibid.*, p. 299).

[38] *E.g., Wilson* v. *Stanley* (1861) 12 I.C.L.R. 345 (Prescription Act and lost modern grant); *Timmons* v. *Hewitt* (1887) 22 L.R.Ir. 627 (Prescription Act, common law and lost modern grant); *Hanna* v. *Pollock* [1900] 2 I.R. 664 (see *A Casebook on Irish Land Law* (1984), p. 329) (Prescription Act, common law and lost modern grant).

[39] See its short title, fn 23, para. 6.085, *ante.* Thus the Act is usually pleaded first, then prescription at common law, so that a request to the court to adopt a "fiction" is put last. See the remarks of Lord Macnaghten in *Gardner* v. *Hodgson's Kingston Brewery Co. Ltd.* [1903] A.C. 229 at 240.

[40] *E.g.*, consent or interruption, see paras. 6.091 and 6.093, *infra.*

[41] *Hanna* v. *Pollock* [1900] 2 I.R. 664 (see *A Casebook on Irish Land Law* (1984), p, 329).

[42] S. 6.

[43] *Hanmer* v. *Chance* (1865) 4 De G.J. & S. 626 at 631.

[44] S. 4. "The important point is that the fruits of the Act can be reaped only by a litigant." Megarry and Wade, *Law of Real Property* (5th ed., 1984), p. 880.

[45] *Tisdall* v. *McArthur & Co. (Steel and Metal) Ltd.* [1951] I.R. 228 (see *A Casebook on Irish Land Law* (1984). p. 357).

[46] *E.g.*, he may wish to establish the existence of the right prior to selling or otherwise dealing with the dominant land.

[47] *Gaw* v. *C.I.E.* [1953] I.R. 232 (see *A Casebook on Irish Land Law* (1984), p. 622).

[48] *Parker* v. *Mitchell* (1840) 11 Ad. & El. 788.

[49] See ss. 1 and 2 (which refer to any person "claiming right thereto") and 5 (which states that in the pleadings it is sufficient "to allege the enjoyment thereof as of right").

precario.[50] This general principle at least holds good so far as the shorter periods in the Act are concerned, but there is one problem relating to the longer periods whereby easements or profits are deemed absolute and indefeasible. The Act expressly provides that this applies only if the easement or profit was not enjoyed "by some consent or agreement expressly made or given for that purpose *by deed or writing,*"[51] Under the common law rules, however, even *oral* consent or permission will prevent the user from being "as of right" and so the implication seems to be that, under the Act, this does not apply in the case of a claim based on user for one of the longer periods. Yet the Act still requires that (and this applies equally to claims based on the longer periods of user) the claimant should claim "right" to the easement or profit and allege in the pleadings enjoyment "as of right."[52] The House of Lords has suggested[53] that the way to reconcile the apparent conflict between the various provisions of the Act is to hold that, in the case of the longer periods, oral consent or permission will defeat a claim only if it is given during the statutory period of user, or is renewed during that period. Consent given at the beginning of the period only, even if intended to apply throughout, must be in writing.

6.092. It seems to be clear that the consent or permission sufficient to prevent acquisition by prescription may be given by whoever is the current *occupier* of the servient tenement, whether owner of the fee simple, tenant for life or for years or even a squatter.[54] The same applies to acknowledgement of no rights by the occupier of the dominant tenement, so that a tenant may prevent his landlord from acquiring an easement or profit by prescription.[55]

(d) *Without Interruption*

6.093. The Act also provides that the user by the claimant must have been "without interruption."[56] This concept should not be confused with user by consent or permission which also prevents acquisition by prescription under the Act. In the case of user by consent or permission, the user *ex hypothesi* continues, as, indeed, it does where the user is subject to protest.[57] An interruption, on the other hand, involves interference with the enjoyment of the right, if not actual cessation of the enjoyment.[58] The interruption or obstruction may be caused by acts of the servient owner[59] or a stranger,[60] or

[50] Para. 6.075, *ante.*
[51] Ss. 1 and 2 (italics added). See *Lowry* v. *Crothers* (1871) I.R. 5 C.L. 98.
[52] See fn. 49, *supra.*
[53] See the discussion in *Gardner* v. *Hodgson's Kingston Brewery Co. Ltd.* [1903] A.C. 229. Also *Gaved* v. *Martyn* (1865) 19 C.B. (N.S.) 732; *Ward* v. *Kirkland* [1966] 1 W.L.R. 601.
[54] See the discussion in *Lowry* v. *Crothers* (1871) I.R. 5 C.L. 98.
[55] See the discussion in *Hyman* v. *Van den Bergh* [1907] 2 Ch. 500 at 531 (*per* Parker J.), on appeal [1908] 1 Ch. 167 at 179 (*per* Farwell L.J.).
[56] Ss. 1–3. See the discussion in *Tisdall* v. *McArthur & Co. (Steel and Metal) Ltd.* [1951] I.R. 228 (see *A Casebook on Irish Land Law* (1984), p. 357).
[57] See the discussion in *Reilly* v. *Orange* [1955] 1 W.L.R. 616.
[58] *Barry* v. *Lowry* (1877) I.R. 11 C.L. 483.
[59] *Hanks* v. *Cribbin* (1857) 7 I.C.L.R. 489 (see also (1859) 9 I.C.L.R. 312 n.); *Claxton* v. *Claxton* (1873) I.R. 7 C.L. 23; *Geoghegan* v. *Henry* [1922] 2 I.R. 1; *Scott* v. *Goulding Properties Ltd.* [1972] I.R. 200 (see *A Casebook on Irish Land Law* (1984), p. 299). [60] *Davies* v. *Williams* (1851) 16 Q.B. 546.

may be due to natural causes, such as a stream drying up.[61]

6.094. However, the Act goes even further than this and requires that the interruption, to be effective in preventing acquisition of rights by prescription under it, must be "submitted to or acquiesced in for one year after the party interrupted shall have had or shall have notice thereof, and of the person making or authorising the same to be made."[62] Thus the claimant can still establish his right by prescription despite an interruption if he can show that he has not submitted to or acquiesced in that interruption for a period of one year, by, *e.g.*, making protests to the interrupter or, if necessary, commencing an action against him.[63] Furthermore, the one year period does not begin to run until the claimant has notice of both the fact that interruption is taking place and the identity of the person making it.[64] This means that a claimant should succeed in establishing his easement under the Act after 19 years and one day, *provided* he is quick off the mark. It must be remembered that the Act benefits the litigant only, who in this case must show 20 years' uninterrupted user. He must, therefore, issue his summons or writ on the first day of the twenty-first year of his user, for from that day only can he successfully argue that the interruption has not run for one complete year. If he is one day late, the interruption will have run for the full year and he will have lost his claim in respect of the previous twenty years.[65] If he is one day early, he will also fail because he cannot show the full 20 years' user required by the Act.[66] And, of course, this means that the servient owner can still defeat the claim by bringing an action against the dominant owner at any time up to the first day of the twenty-first year of user.[67] Such an action would seem to amount to more than a mere "interruption" of the claimant's user or enjoyment[68] and, apart from that, clearly prevents any subsequent claim by him "as of right."[69]

(e) *Deductions*

6.095. Even though on the face of it a claimant can show user or enjoyment of the right in question for the statutory period, he may still fail because of

---

[61] *Hall* v. *Swift* (1838) 4 Bing.N.C. 381.

[62] S. 4.

[63] *Claxton* v. *Claxton* (1873) I.R. 7 C.L. 23. Presumably protests and, *ex hypothesi*, an action are significant only after the requisite period under the Act has run. Prior to that the claimant has no right to protect and the servient owner is at liberty to interrupt as he pleases and, if necessary, can take action against the claimant. In other words, the references in s. 4 of the Act to submission to or acquiescence in the interruption relate only to the intermediate period between the time *after* the requisite statutory period of user has run and *before* an action is brought to establish the claim. This is simply another illustration of the basic principle that the Act aids a litigant only (para. 6.090, *ante*) and it reiterates the point that, when the action is finally brought, considerably more time may have elapsed than is required by the Act. Yet the crucial period remains that immediately preceding the action and the claimant will fail if interruption has occurred in that period, even though a full uninterrupted period can be established earlier than that, para. 6.090, *ante*. See also *Glover* v. *Coleman* (1874) L.R. 10 C.P. 108.

[64] *Seddon* v. *Bank of Bolton* (1882) 19 Ch.D. 462.

[65] *Flight* v. *Thomas* (1840) 11 Ad. & E. 688 at 771.

[66] *Lord Battersea* v. *Commrs. of Sewers for the City of London* [1895] 2 Ch. 708; *Barff* v. *Mann, Crossman & Paulin Ltd.* (1905) 49 Sol.Jo. 794. Note also s. 6 of the Act, para. 6.089, *ante*.

[67] *Reilly* v. *Orange* [1955] 1 W.L.R. 616.

[68] S. 4 refers to an "act or other matter" in relation to interruption. See Hugessen, "Interruption by Institution of Action" (1954) 32 C.B.R. 582.

[69] Para. 6.091, *ante*.

other special provisions in the Act requiring deductions to be made from the period of user shown. Section 7 provides that, in the case of the *shorter* periods (20 and 30 years) only, there has to be deducted from the period of user any period during which the servient owner was under a disability, such as being an infant, a lunatic or a tenant for life.[70] The same automatic deduction has to be made under section 7 in respect of any period during which an action was pending and actively prosecuted. Section 8 then provides that, where the servient tenement has been held for a "term of life, or any term of years exceeding three years from the granting thereof", that term is to be deducted when computing the *longer* period (40 years) in the case of a "way or other convenient[71] watercourse or use of water",[72] *provided* the claim is resisted by the reversioner within three years of determination of the term.[73] In other words, under section 8 the deduction is not made automatically and depends upon action being taken by the reversioner. This was explained by May C.J. in *Beggan* v. *McDonald*:

> "Assuming that the right has in fact been exercised as of right for forty years, it would become absolute; but if, during the whole or part of this period of forty years, the servient lands were in the occupation of tenants, the period of such tenancies may be excluded, but only subject to the condition that the reversioner shall resist the claim within a certain time. If that condition has not been complied with, the tenancy cannot be excluded from the computation. The right will have been enjoyed for the full period, and becomes *prima facie* absolute, subject to this qualification, that in case the tenancy be not determined, and the reversioner should hereafter upon its determination resist the right, as against him the period of such tenancy cannot be included in computing the term of forty years, and therefore against him the statute will not operate. In the case before the Court, the enjoyment of the right of way took place entirely during the subsistence of a lease demising the servient tenement, and which lease at the time of action brought had not determined. *Non constat* that the landlord ever would or will resist the right; but in the meantime, and before he has done so, what authority can there be for excluding the term from the computation of the period of forty years? And if it be not excluded, then it seems to me that the statute operated to establish a right in favour of the dominant tenement, capable of being challenged and defeated by the reversioner in the case supposed, but otherwise absolute and indefeasible. This result appears to me plainly to follow from a fair construction of the several clauses of the Act."[74]

---

[70] The section also referred to a *feme covert*, but married women are no longer under any disability in law in either part of Ireland, see ch. 25, *post*.

[71] It has been suggested that the word "convenient" here is a misprint for "easement," so that s. 8 should be regarded as applying to all easements; *cf.* the wording of s. 2 of the Act ("way or other *easement*, or of any watercourse . . ."). (Italics added.) See *Laird* v. *Briggs* (1880) 50 L.J.Ch. 260 at 261 (*per* Fry J.); *cf.* the report in 16 Ch.D. 440 at 447 and, on appeal (1881) 19 Ch.D. 22 at 33, 36 and 37.

[72] S. 8 does not apply to profits at all, whereas s. 7 does.

[73] See the discussion of s. 8 in *Wilson* v. *Stanley* (1861) 12 I.C.L.R. 345 and *Beggan* v. *McDonald* (1877) 2 L.R.Ir. 560.

[74] *Op. cit.*, pp. 570–1. Note that s. 8 is expressly confined to a "reversion" and does not seem to cover a

6.096. To summarise, then, the effect of the two sections, section 7 provides for automatic deduction in the appropriate cases whenever a claim is based on the shorter periods of user. Thus if X uses a right of way for 15 years against the fee simple owner of the servient land, followed by 10 years' user against a tenant for life, followed by 5 years' user against the fee simple owner, making 30 years' user in all before an action is brought by him, he succeeds in his claim. The 10 years' user against the tenant for life is deducted, leaving 20 years' user, made up from two periods, as required by the Act.[75] If, instead, the 10 years' user in the example just given had been against a tenant for years, X could have brought his action to establish his right of way after only 5 of those years of user. he would in that case be claiming his right on 20 years' user (15 against the fee simple owner plus 5 against the tenant for years) and section 7 does not allow deductions in the case of terms of years. On the other hand, section 8, which does, does not apply to cases where the claim is based on the shorter period of user. Thus it is preferable from the claimant's point of view to base a case involving leases on the shorter period, if possible, rather than the longer period which may result, as May C.J. indicated, in the claimant establishing a right subject to a condition whereby it may subsequently be defeated.[76] On the other hand, section 8 does not apply to cases of infancy or insanity, so that it is preferable to base a claim in such cases on the longer statutory period of user, if possible, so as to avoid any deduction.

(f) *Easements of Light*

6.097. The 1832 Act contains special provisions relating to easements of light, perhaps for the reason that such easements were the most difficult to establish at common law.[77] Section 3 of the Act provides that, when "the access and use of light to and for any dwelling house, workshop or other building[78] shall have been actually enjoyed" for 20 years "without interruption"[79] the right thereto is to be deemed "absolute and indefeasible, any local usage or custom to the contrary notwithstanding, unless it shall appear that the same was enjoyed by some consent or agreement expressly made or given for that purpose by deed or writing." In other words, contrary to the common law position, acquisition of an easement of light under the Prescription Act is easier than any other kind of easement. This is the case because of the general provision, just quoted, that 20 years' user of an easement of light is equivalent

---

"remainderman" taking after a life owner under a settlement, *Symons* v. *Leaker* (1885) 15 Q.B.D. 629; *cf. Holman* v. *Exton* (1692) Carth. 246.

[75] Ss. 4 and 7.

[76] Note, however, that section 8 also applies to life tenancies, so that deductions in such cases may have to be made whichever period of user is the basis of the claim.

[77] *I.e.*, it can usually be shown that the building to which the light comes has not been standing since 1189, para. 6.082, *ante*.

[78] Held to include a church, *Ecclesiastical Commrs. for England* v. *Kino* (1880) 14 Ch.D. 213, a greenhouse, *Clifford* v. *Holt* [1899] 1 Ch. 698, and a cowshed, *Hyman* v. *Van den Bergh* [1908] 1 Ch. 167. *Cf. Harris* v. *De Pinna* (1886) 33 Ch.D. 238 (structure for storing timber).

[79] See the discussion in *Tisdall* v. *McArthur & Co. (Steel and Metal) Ltd.* [1951] I.R. 228 (see *A Casebook on Irish Land Law* (1984), p. 357).

to 40 years' user of other easements, *i.e.*, the easement is then deemed "absolute and indefeasible."[80] However, there are other important differences in the case of acquisition of easements of light under the Act.

6.098. First, section 3 does not, unlike section 2 of the Act which covers other easements, refer to a person "claiming right" to the easement and so it has been held that it does *not* require user "as of right."[81] For this reason even the English courts have been prepared to permit a tenant to acquire an easement of light against his own landlord[82] or against another tenant of the same landlord.[83] The only aspect of the common law's requirement of enjoyment *nec vi, nec clam* and *nec precario* surviving in the case of an easement of light is that section 3 does state that user by consent *in writing or by deed* defeats a claim.[84]

Secondly, there can be no deduction under sections 7 and 8 in the case of easements of light on the ground of user during periods when some disability affected the servient owner. Section 7 excepts cases where the easement is declared to be "absolute and indefeasible" and section 8 is confined to claims based on 40 years' user.

Thirdly, unlike sections 1 and 2 of the Act, which expressly refer to the Crown, section 3 does not and so it is not possible to acquire easements of light over Crown, or, in the Republic of Ireland, State land.[85]

6.099. Fourthly it seems clear that section 3 of the Act negatives any presumption of a grant in the case of an easement of light, at least to the extent that it does not require user as of right,[86] and so it has been held that such an easement may be acquired against a corporation with no power to grant such a right.[87] Indeed, it has even been suggested by some of the English authorities that the Act has by implication abolished the applicability of the doctrine of lost modern grant to easements of light.[88] This view, however, was doubted in *Tisdall* v. *McArthur & Co.* (*Steel and Metal*) *Ltd.*,[89] where the contrary view was expressed that "since *Hanna* v. *Pollock*[90] it has always been considered to be settled law in Ireland that any easement can be properly claimed on the basis of a lost modern grant."[91]

---

[80] Para. 6.088, *ante.*
[81] *Frewen* v. *Phillips* (1861) 11 C.B. (N.S.) 449, approved by Lawson J. in *Fahey* v. *Dwyer* (1879) 4 L.R.Ir. 271 (which, in fact, involved an easement of way). *Cf. Timmons* v. *Hewitt* (1887) 22 L.R.Ir. 627. Note, however, that s. 5, which governs pleadings in all cases within the Act, does refer to allegations of enjoyment "as of right," a point which the courts hitherto do not seem to have taken.
[82] *Foster* v. *Lyons & Co Ltd.* [1927] 1 Ch. 219 at 227. See also *Frewen* v. *Phillips* (1861) 11 C.B. (N.S.) 449.
[83] *Morgan* v. *Fear* [1907] A.C. 425. See para. 6.078, *ante.*
[84] It seems that a reservation in a lease of the right to rebuild adjoining property may amount to such consent, see *Willoughby* v. *Eckstein* [1937] Ch. 167; *Blake & Lyons Ltd.* v. *Lewis Berger & Sons Ltd.* [1951] 2 T.L.R. 605.
[85] *Wheaton* v. *Maple & Co.* [1893] 3 Ch. 48. Stroud, "Rights of Light over Crown Land" (1942) 58 L.Q.R. 495.
[86] *Tapling* v. *Jones* (1865) 11 H.L.C. 290 at 304 and 318. See also Delany, "Leases and Doctrine of Lost Grant" (1958) 74 L.Q.R. 82 at 86–7.
[87] *Jordeson* v. *Sutton, Southcoates & Drypool Gas Co.* [1898] 2 Ch. 614 at 626, aff'd. [1899] 2 Ch. 217.
[88] *Tapling* v. *Jones* (1865) 11 H.L.C. 290.
[89] [1951] I.R. 228, espec. at 235–8 (see *A Casebook on Irish Land Law* (1984), p. 357).
[90] [1900] 2 I.R. 664 (see *ibid.*, p. 329). See para. 6.079, *ante.*
[91] [1951] I.R. 228 at 241 (*per* Kingsmill Moore J.), aff'd. on appeal by the Supreme Court, which expressly left the point open, *ibid.*, pp. 246 (Maguire C.J.), 247 (Murnaghan J.) and 248 (Black J.).

6.100. Apart from these special provisions in the 1832 Act, which apply to both parts of Ireland, the Rights of Light Act (N.I.) 1961,[92] has to be considered with respect to easements of light in Northern Ireland. This Act, like its English equivalent, was passed to protect owners of land destroyed or badly damaged by bombs or landmines dropped during the Second World War. Several parts of Belfast were severely damaged during the War and this resulted in numerous derelict sites which remained in existence for many years thereafter. As the years went by, rebuilding on many of these sites might have been hampered if neighbouring owners claimed rights of light over the derelict sites and so the 1961 Act introduced first a temporary protection. This took the form of extending the statutory period for prescription under the Prescription Act, 1832, from 20 to 27 years in respect of actions begun before January 1, 1963.[93] This in effect prevented claims based on user since the War air raids being established and gave the site owners time to invoke the permanent provisions of the 1961 Act, which remain in force and have taken on a new significance with the bombing campaigns in the North of recent years. After the Second World War, some derelict site owners attempted to interrupt acquisition of rights of light by erection of screens and hoardings. These were inconvenient, unsightly and scarcely consistent with modern town planning and environmental concepts. The permanent provisions of the 1961 Act enable a site owner to achieve the same result, *i.e.*, interruption of the passage of light, by a much more satisfactory method.

6.101. The 1961 Act enables a servient owner to prevent acquisition of an easement of light by registering in the Statutory Charges Registry[94] of a light obstruction notice which is equivalent to erection of "an opaque structure of unlimited height."[95] This notice must identify the servient land and the dominant building and the servient owner must satisfy the Registrar of Titles[96] that he has given adequate notice of the proposed registration to all concerned and has advertised the same in a newspaper circulating in the district.[97] Registration is effective for one year,[98] unless cancelled before then, and so amounts to an effective interruption under section 4 of the Prescription Act, 1832.[99] However, the dominant owner may bring an action to challenge the registered notice when his right of light has accrued while the notice remains effective[1] and the court is empowered to order cancellation or variation of the registration as may be appropriate.[2] The Act applies to Crown land to the extent of enabling private subjects to resist claims by the Crown, but otherwise

---

[92] Modelled on the English Rights of Light Act, 1959, which was in turn based on the recommendations contained in the *Report of the Committee on Rights of Light* (1958; Cmnd. 473). See Obayan, "The Rights of Light Act (N.I.), 1961" (1964) 15 N.I.L.Q. 248.
[93] S. 3.
[94] Under the Statutory Charges Register Act (N.I.), 1951, Sec. ch. 21, *post.*
[95] S. 1 (3) (f).
[96] Who is responsible for the Statutory Charges Register as well as the Land Registry, ch. 21, *post.*
[97] S. 2 (1).
[98] S. 3.
[99] Para. 6.094, *ante.*
[1] S. 2 (3) and (4).
[2] S. 2 (5).

preserves the immunity of the Crown from prescriptive claims under the Prescription Act.[3]

C. EXTINGUISHMENT

There are three main ways in which an easement or profit can be extinguished or destroyed, *i.e.*, by statute, by release of the right by the owner and by union of ownership and possession of the dominant and servient tenements.[4]

1. *Statute*

6.102. A statute may extinguish an easement or profit expressly or by implication, such as the statutes relating to compulsory acquisition of land in Ireland.[5] In both parts of Ireland, rights which were formally regarded as belonging to the owner of the land because he was owner have been declared to be the property of the State. In the Republic, Article 11 of the 1922 Constitution declared that all the natural resources (including the air and all forms of potential energy) belonged to the State, "subject to any valid private interest therein." Article 10 of the 1937 Constitution makes a similar declaration "subject to all estates and interests therein for the time being lawfully vested in any person or body." Legislation has been passed in both parts of Ireland dealing with mining[6] and petroleum and other minerals.[7] These are not easements or profits in the strict sense, but are rights which formerly were incidents of ownership of the land itself.

6.103. There is no modern legislation in either part of Ireland dealing with extinguishment of common rights of pasturage by approvement and inclosure such as exists in England.[8] At common law, the lord of a manor had a common law right to "approve" the waste land on the manor over which his tenants had rights of pasture, *i.e.*, the lord could take part of that land for his own use. No doubt this law applied equally in the manors in Ireland governed by the feudal system introduced by the Normans in the twelfth century. Indeed, the early English legislation confirming this right of approvement in the lord of a manor was applied to Ireland.[9] Furthermore, even as late as the beginning of the nineteenth century *private* Acts of Parliament were being passed relating to inclosure of land in Ireland.[10] However, later English legislation, especially that

---

[3] S. 4. See para. 6.098, *ante*.
[4] See also Abbott, "Extinguishment of Easements by Impossibility of User" (1913) 13 Col.L.Rev. 409.
[5] *E.g.*, Lands Clauses Consolidation Act, 1845, and the Railways (Ir.) Acts, 1851, 1860 and 1864. See generally Suffern, *Law Relating to Compulsory Purchase and Sale of Lands in Ireland* (1882). Also the Republic's Local Government (Planning and Development) Act, 1963, Pt. 7; Roads Act (N.I.), 1948; Local Government Act (N.I.), 1972 (see also s. 88 of the Land Compensation Act, 1973 (U.K.)). *Comyn* v. *Att.-Gen.* [1950] I.R. 142. See also Housing Act, 1966, s. 83 (R.I.); Housing (Miscellaneous Provisions) and Rent Restriction Law (Amendment) Act (N.I.), 1956), s. 11. See *Irish Conveyancing Law* (1978), para. 9.108 *et seq.*; Trimble, "The Procedure Governing Compulsory Acquisition of Land in Northern Ireland" (1973) 24 N.I.L.Q. 466.
[6] See Minerals Exploration and Development Company Act, 1941 (R.I.); Mineral Development Act (N.I.), 1969. *Cf. Comyn* v. *Att.-Gen.* (*No. 2*) (1951) 85 I.L.T.R. 67.
[7] Minerals Development Acts, 1940 and 1979 and Petroleum and other Minerals Development Act, 1960 (R.I.); Petroleum (Production) Act (N.I.), 1964.
[8] See *Governors of St. Patrick's Hospital* v. *Dowling* (1826) Batty 296.
[9] Statute of Merton, 1235, c. 4; Statute of Westminster II, 1285, c. 46. See para. 1.24, *ante*.
[10] *E.g.*, 55 Geo. 3, c. 35 (1814) and 56 Geo. 3, c 25 (1816). See *Governors of St. Patrick's Hospital* v. *Dowling*

of the second half of the nineteenth century,[11] did not apply to Ireland, presumably because by then the land purchase scheme was sweeping away the remnants of the manorial or copyhold system which had survived the upheavals in land ownership of the previous centuries.[12] Nor did the English Inclosure Acts,[13] which facilitated the discharge of manorial waste land from all rights of common, apply to Ireland and there is no equivalent in either part of Ireland of the English Commons Registration Act, 1965, which requires the registration of rights of common with local authorities.[14] The point is that in Ireland rights of common in agricultural land were or, in the Western parts of the Republic, will be dealt with under the Land Purchase Acts.[15]

2. Release

6.104. The owner of an easement or profit may release it expressly or impliedly. So far as express release is concerned, at common law this has to be executed by deed.[16] However, equity may give effect to an informal release where it can be established that the dominant owner has by his words or conduct led the servient owner into acting on the belief that a release has been made, so that it would be inequitable for the dominant owner to rely on the informality.[17]

6.105. An implied release may arise where it is established that there was an intention on the part of the owner of the easement or profit to abandon it.[18] Such an intention may be presumed from non-user by the dominant owner for a long period, *e.g.*, 20 years.[19] It may also be presumed where an alternative right is granted, *e.g.*, another right of way is substituted for the existing one,[20] or where a substantial alteration is made to either the dominant or servient tenement, so as to make the use or enjoyment of the right impossible or no longer necessary.[21]

(1826) Batty 296; *Jones d. Byrne* v. *Humphreys* (1827) 1 Hud. & Br. 26; *Jones d. Burrowes* v. *Lynam* (1841) 2 Jebb. & Sym. 590.

[11] *E.g.,* Commons Act, 1876 and Law of Commons Amendment Act, 1893. Note, however, that legislation was still being passed in Ireland dealing with commons in the last years of the Irish Parliament before the Act of Union, 1800. See the Commons Act (Ir.), 1789 and the Commons Act (Ir.), 1791, which are still in force in the Republic of Ireland. *Cf.* Criminal Justice (Miscellaneous Provisions) Act (N.I.), 1968, s. 16 and Sched. 4.

[12] Paras. 1.27 *et seq., ante.*

[13] *E.g.,* Inclosure (Consolidation) Act, 1801; Inclosure Act, 1852; Commons Act, 1876. Note, however, the very early legislation in Ireland dealing with inclosure, *e.g.,* 36 Hen. 6, c. 2 (Ir.), 1458 (inclosure of towns and villages).

[14] See the *Report of the Royal Commission on Common Land* (1958; Cmnd. 462).

[15] Para. 6.113, *post.* See also Irish Land Commissioners' *Annual Report, 1971–72*, pp. 6–9.

[16] *Coke upon Littleton* (19th ed., 1832), 264b. *Burke* v. *Blake* (1861) 13 I.C.L.R. 390.

[17] *Cf.,* the converse case of an implied grant in equity, *Annally Hotel Ltd.* v. *Bergin* (1970) 104 I.L.T.R. 65.

[18] *Chambers* v. *Betty* (1815) Beat. 488; *Stevenson* v. *Parke* [1932] L.J.Ir. 228; *Re Bohan* [1957] I.R. 49; *Carroll* v. *Sheridan* [1984] I.L.R.M. 451.

[19] *Moore* v. *Rawson* (1824) 3 B. & C. 32. See also *Swan* v. *Sinclair* [1925] A.C. 227.

[20] *Mulville* v. *Fallon* (1872) I.R. 6 Eq. 458; *Smith* v. *Wilson* [1903] 2 I.R. 45.

[21] *National Guaranteed Manure Co. Ltd.* v. *Donald* (1859) 4 H. & N. 8; *Ecclesiastical Commrs. for England* v. *Kino* (1880) 14 Ch.D. 213. *Cf.* the effect on a right to ancient lights of putting modern windows in an old building, see *Scott* v. *Goulding Properties Ltd.* [1972] I.R. 200 (see *A Casebook on Irish Land Law* (1984), p. 299). Abbott, "Extinguishment of Easements by Impossibility of User" (1913) 13 Col.L. Rev. 409.

3. *Unity of Ownership and Possession*

6.106. If the dominant and servient tenements come into the ownership and the possession of the same person, any easement or profit annexed to those lands is extinguished.[22] Unity of one without the other is not enough. Thus if one person becomes owner of the fee simple in both tenements, but one or other of the tenements is leased, the right may still be exercised by or against the tenant.[23] Similarly, if one person takes a lease of both tenements from their separate fee simple owners any easements or profits are at most suspended until the leases determine.[24]

D. EXAMPLES OF EASEMENTS AND PROFITS

It may be useful at this point to describe in more detail some of the more common types of easement and profit claimed in Ireland. It must be emphasised that the following list should not be taken to be exhaustive.

1. *Easements*

(i) Rights of Way

6.107. Rights of way are, perhaps, the most common type of easement claimed in Ireland today.[25] Such a right may be either *general*, in the sense that it can be used at any time in any way by the dominant owner, or *limited*, in the sense that some restriction binds the dominant owner, *e.g.*, as to the time or mode of user.[26] As a general rule, any works in the nature of construction or repairs to the way have to be executed by the dominant owner, *i.e.*, the grantee, but this is subject to any agreement made by the original parties.[27] It was held in *Gaw* v. *C.I.E.*[28] that the benefit of a covenant by the grantors of a right of way ran with the easement so as to enable a successor in title of the grantee to obtain a mandatory injunction against statutory successors of the grantors, requiring them to execute repairs to the footpath relating to the right of way.

[22] See discussion in *Wilson* v. *Stanley* (1861) 12 I.C.L.R. 345; *Pullan* v. *Roughfort Bleaching and Dyeing Co. Ltd.* (1888) 21 L.R.Ir. 73. Also *Re Flanagan and McGarvey and Thompson's Contract* [1945] N.I. 32 (see *A Casebook on Irish Land Law* (1984), p. 317). See also Brooke-Taylor, "Perdurable Estates" (1977) 41 Conv. 107.
[23] *Richardson* v. *Graham* [1908] 1 K.B. 39.
[24] *Canham* v. *Fisk* (1831) 2 Cr. & J. 126. Suspension operates only as regards pre-existing easements, *B. & W. Investments Ltd.* v. *Ulster Scottish Friendly Society* (1969) 20 N.I.L.Q. 325.
[25] *McCullagh* v. *Wilson* (1838) 1 Jebb. & Sym. 120; *Burke* v. *Blake* (1861) 13 I.C.L.R. 390; *Kavanagh* v. *Coal Mining Co. of Ireland* (1861) 14 I.C.L.R. 82; *Austin* v. *Scottish Widows' Fund Mutual Life Assurance Society* (1881) 8 L.R.Ir. 385; *Head* v. *Meara* [1912] 1 I.R. 262; *Flynn* v. *Harte* [1913] 2 I.R. 322; *Molphy* v. *Coyne* (1919) 53 I.L.T.R. 177; *Cleary* v. *Bowen* [1931] L.J.Ir. 148; *Tallon* v. *Ennis* [1937] 1 I.R. 549; *McCaw* v. *Rynne* [1941] Ir.Jur.Rep. 12; *Dunne* v. *Rattigan* [1981] I.L.R.M. 365; *Flannigan* v. *Mulhall* [1985] I.L.R.M. 134. On ways of necessity, see para. 6.070, *ante*.
[26] *Tubridy* v. *Walsh* (1901) 35 I.L.T. 321 (obligation to close gates). *Cf. Geoghegan* v. *Henry* [1922] 2 I.R. 1; *Griffin* v. *Keane* (1927) 61 I.L.T.R. 177; *Daly* v. *Cullen* (1958) 92 I.L.T.R. 127. See also *St. Edmundsbury and Ipswich Diocesan Board of Finance* v. *Clark (No. 2)* [1975] 1 W.L.R. 468.
[27] *Gaw* v. *C.I.E.* [1953] I.R. 232 (see *A Casebook on Irish Land Law* (1984), p. 622).
[28] *Ibid.*

(ii) Rights of Light

6.108. Rights of light are also common though they can be acquired only in respect of a building, indeed only in respect of a window or other aperture in a building.[29] Long established rights of light are frequently referred to in the courts as "ancient lights."[30] It is now firmly settled that the amount of light to which a dominant owner is entitled in the form of an easement is limited. The quantum of light to which he can successfully lay claim is the amount, according to ordinary user, necessary for the use of the particular building for its particular purpose, *i.e.*, as a dwelling or as business premises or whatever is its purpose.[31] The dominant owner can complain only if the quantum left falls below this amount and a substantial diminution in the amount will not be actionable if that still leaves enough for ordinary user of the premises for their general purpose.[32] It would appear that a case must be decided according to this objective test of the quantum allowable and it is irrelevant that the dominant owner has in fact enjoyed more or less than that quantum.[33] There is no set standard of light which must be applied in all cases, *e.g.*, the so-called 45 degrees rule[34] or according to the "grumble point" limit.[35] To some extent the practice and standard of the particular locality must be taken into account in setting the standard applicable and measuring the quantum allowable.[36]

6.109. If the dominant owner alters the user of his premises or changes his windows, *e.g.*, replacing old ones by more modern ones, he generally cannot object if the nature of the alteration results in less light coming in.[37] Indeed, in

---

[29] *Mackey* v. *Scottish Widows' Fund Life Assurance Society* (1877) I.R. 11 Eq. 541. *Cf. Judge* v. *Lowe* (1873) I.R. 7 C.L. 291.

[30] *Tisdall* v. *McArthur & Co. (Steel and Metal) Ltd.* [1951] I.R. 228 (see *A Casebook on Irish Land Law* (1984), p. 357); *Scott* v. *Goulding Properties Ltd.* [1972] I.R. 200 (*ibid.*, p. 299). See also *O'Connor* v. *Corr* (1826) Batty. 421; Hudson, "Ancient Lights for an Office" (1960) 24 Conv. 424.

[31] *Maguire* v. *Grattan* (1868) I.R. 2 Eq. 246; *Smyth* v. *Dublin Theatre Co.* [1936] I.R. 692. *Cf. Annally Hotel Ltd.* v. *Bergin* (1970) 104 I.L.T.R. 65. In *Allen* v. *Greenwood* [1980] Ch. 119, The English Court of Appeal held that the plaintiff had acquired by prescription rights to the higher degree of light required in the normal use of a greenhouse and the benefits of the rays of sun required to grow plants, and not just the amount of light required for illumination. It was also held that a right to an exceptional or extraordinary amount of light for a particular purpose may be acquired by prescription, but it was expressly left open for decision when a case arises whether, in the case of solar heating, it may be possible and right to separate heat or some other property of the sun from its light (*ibid.*, p. 134, *per* Goff and Orr. L.JJ.).

[32] *Cf. Manning* v. *Gresham Hotel Co.* (1867) I.R. 1 C.L. 115. See also *Gresham Hotel Co.* v. *Manning* (1867) I.R. 1 C.L. 125; *O'Connor* v. *Walsh* (1908) 42 I.L.T.R. 20; *Smyth* v. *Dublin Theatre Co.* [1936] I.R. 692; *Gannon* v. *Hughes* [1937] I.R. 284; *McGrath* v. *Munster and Leinster Bank Ltd.* [1959] I.R. 313. Bodkin, "The Acquisition of Rights of Light for Badly-Lighted Premises" (1974) 38 Conv. 4.

[33] *Cf. Mercer Rice and Co.* v. *Ritchie Hart & Co.* (1903) 3 N.I.J.R. 123 (special quantity). See also *Mackey* v. *Scottish Widows' Fund Life Assurance Society* (1877) I.R. 11 Eq. 541.

[34] *I.e.*, interference by an obstruction rising above an imaginary line drawn at an angle of 45 degrees upwards and outwards from the centre of the window in question. See the discussion in the leading English case on the subject, *Colls* v. *Home and Colonial Stores Ltd.* [1904] A.C. 179, followed by *Smyth* v. *Dublin Theatre Co.* [1936] I.R. 692 and *McGrath* v. *Munster and Leinster Bank Ltd.* [1959] I.R. 313. Note, "Local Standard of Light" (1926) 42 L.Q.R. 443; Merritt, "Rights of Light and Air" (1972) 36 Conv. 15.

[35] *I.e.*, how much of the light, which would reach the outside sill of the window from an unobstructed horizon, reaches parts of the room inside, *e.g.*, taken at a height of three feet above the floor. See *Charles Semon & Co. Ltd.* v. *Bradford Corp.* [1922] 2 Ch. 737 at 747–8; *Fishenden* v. *Higgs & Hill Ltd.* (1935) L.T. 128 at 130. Also Swarbrick *Easements of Light* (1933).

[36] *Mercer Rice & Co.* v. *Ritchie Hart & Co.* (1903) 3 N.I.J.R. 123.

[37] *Scott* v. *Goulding Properties Ltd.* [1972] I.R. 200 (see *A Casebook on Irish Land Law* (1984), p. 299). See the discussion of the *Scott* case in Hudson, "Parasitic Damages for Loss of Light" (1975) 39 Conv. 116.

Scott v. *Goulding Properties Ltd.*,[38] where the dominant owner claimed damages as compensation for the diminution of light and resultant loss of amenity and reduction in value of the property caused by an obstruction of ancient lights, the Republic's Supreme Court held that the amount of compensation should *not* contain an element for the reduction of light to modern windows put in the building. An interesting point about this case, however, was that it seemed to be accepted by all the judges that, if the plaintiff had obtained an injunction, this would have prevented the infringement of the ancient lights and would, of course, have had the incidental effect of protecting the light to the modern windows.[39]

The dominant owner may still claim a right of light even though the light coming to the windows of his building has first to pass through windows or other parts, *e.g.*, a glass roof, of the servient owner's building.[40] However, in assessing whether an actionable diminution of light has occurred, the court will take into account other sources of light to which the dominant owner is entitled, *e.g.*, through a skylight in his own building.[41]

(iii) Rights of Water

6.110. There are many kinds of rights concerning water which have been recognised as easements. In some cases they have been akin to natural riparian rights,[42] *e.g.*, a right to a flow of water from the servient owner's land,[43] or a right to draw water from a well.[44] In other cases, the easement has consisted of a right to the flow of water from or to discharge water through an artificial watercourse,[45] such as a conduit,[46] gullet[47] or drain.[48] In such cases, the dominant owner may be entitled, if necessary, to enter the servient owner's land to remove any obstruction or to clean out a blocked pipe or drain, though he will not usually be entitled to a mandatory injunction[49] to compel the servient owner to clean out a pipe or drain which has become silted up.[50] Other water rights recognised as easements include rights such as a right to water cattle in a stream.[51]

---

[38] *Ibid.* (Walsh J., *dissentiente*).

[39] Walsh J. based his dissent from the Supreme Court's decision in the *Scott* case on the principle that the plaintiff should not have been worse off because she had sought damages instead of an injunction.

[40] *Tisdall* v. *McArthur & Co. (Steel and Metal) Ltd.* [1951] I.R. 228 (see *ibid.*, p. 357).

[41] *Smith* v. *Evangelization Society (Incorporated) Trust* [1933] Ch. 515. See also *Sheffield Masonic Hall Co. Ltd.* v. *Sheffield Corp.* [1932] 2 Ch. 17.

[42] Para. 6.040, *ante*.

[43] *Deeble* v. *Linehan* (1860) 12 I.C.L.R. 1; *Wilson* v. *Stanley* (1861) 12 I.C.L.R. 345. *Cf. McCartney* v. *Londonderry & Lough Swilly Rly.* [1904] A.C. 301; *Thompson* v. *Horner* [1927] N.I. 191. See also *Craig* v. *McCance* (1910) 44 I.L.T.R. 90.

[44] *Macnaghten* v. *Baird* [1903] 2 I.R. 731. See also *Whelan* v. *Leonard* [1917] 2 I.R. 323.

[45] *Hamilton* v. *Fawcett* (1859) 9 Ir.Ch.R. 397; *Powell* v. *Butler* (1871) I.R. 5 C.L. 309; *Pullan* v. *Roughfort Bleaching and Dyeing Co. Ltd.* (1888) 21 L.R.Ir. 73; *McEvoy* v. *G.N.R. Co.* [1900] 2 I.R. 325.

[46] *Hanna* v. *Pollock* [1900] 2 I.R. 664 (see *A Casebook on Irish Land Law* (1984), p. 329).

[47] *Callaghan* v. *Callaghan* (1897) 31 I.L.T. 418.

[48] *Kelly* v. *Dea* (1966) 100 I.L.T.R. 1.

[49] Para. 3.130, *ante*.

[50] *Kelly* v. *Dea* (1966) 100 I.L.T.R. 1. *Cf. Larkin* v. *Smith* (1939) 73 I.L.T.R. 234.

[51] *Re Harding's Estate* (1874) I.R 8 Eq. 620. Water, when taken, is incapable of ownership and so, unlike other things, such as soil, found naturally on land, cannot form the subject-matter of a profit *à prendre*, para. 6.034, *ante*.

(iv) Rights of Support

6.111. Since natural rights of support exist only in respect of the land itself,[52] support for buildings on the land must be acquired as an easement.[53] Mutual rights of support almost invariably exist where buildings keep each other standing and this usually makes demolition work in towns and cities an exercise requiring careful planning.[54] Where an easement of support does exist, it seems that the servient owner is under no duty to keep the supporting building repaired, as opposed actively to removing or damaging it by his own acts, but in such cases it seems that the dominant owner may protect himself by entering and executing the necessary repairs.[55]

(v) Miscellaneous Easements

6.112. From time to time rights which do not seem to come within one of the well-known categories of easements are claimed and often recognised by the courts. Thus in *Middleton* v. *Clarence*[56] a right to throw quarry refuse on another person's land was recognised as an easement. In *Henry Ltd.* v. *McGlade*,[57] the right to have a man stand, at the entrance of an arcade, with a pole advertising licensed premises situated in the arcade was recognised as an easement, or at least a similar right capable of passing on a grant of the dominant land under section 6 of the Conveyancing Act, 1881.[58] The right to use a blacksmith's "shoeing stone" was recognised as an easement in *Calders* v. *Murtagh*.[59] On the other hand, the court in *Cochrane* v. *Verner*[60] refused to recognise a right to "shade and shelter" from a hedge as an easement.

2. *Profits à Prendre*

The following are the most common profits *à prendre*:

(i) Pasturage

6.113. This is the right to graze animals, such as horses, oxen, cows and sheep, on someone else's land. The "taking and carrying away" arises from the cattle's eating of the grass and other vegetation growing naturally on the pasturage land.[61] Frequently these rights in the past have been held in common with other farmers in the neighbourhood[62] and several rights in common

---

[52] Para. 6.039, *ante.*

[53] See discussion in *Carroll* v. *Kildare C.C.* [1950] I.R. 258. Also *Green* v. *Belfast Tramways Co.* (1886) 20 L.R.Ir. 35; *Gately* v. *Martin* [1900] 2 I.R. 169; *Nugent* v. *Keady U.D.C.* (1912) 46 I.L.T.R. 221.

[54] *Latimer* v. *Official Co-Operative Society* (1885) 16 L.R.Ir. 305 (see *A Casebook on Irish Land Law* (1984), p. 293). See also *Hanly* v. *Shannon* (1833) Hay. & Jon. 645; *O'Neill* v. *Grier* (1846) Bl.D. & O. 72; *Toole* v. *Macken* (1855) 7 Ir.Jur. (o.s.) 385.

[55] See the discussion in the English cases of *Jones* v. *Pritchard* [1908] Ch. 630 at 637–8 and *Bond* v. *Nottingham Corp.* [1940] Ch. 429 at 438–9. *Cf.* as regards a right to water flowing through a drain, *Kelly* v. *Dea* (1966) 100 I.L.T.R. 1.

[56] (1877) I.R. 11 C.L. 499.

[57] [1926] N.I. 144 (see *A Casebook on Irish Land Law* (1984), p. 324).

[58] Para. 6.066, *ante.*

[59] [1939] Ir.Jur.Rep. 19.

[60] (1895) 29 I.L.T. 571.

[61] Preston, *Treatise on Estates* (2nd ed., 1827), vol. I, p. 15. See the discussion in *Anderson* v. *Bostock* [1976] ch. 312 (para. 6.036, fn. 29, *ante*).

[62] Para. 6.103, *ante.*

survive in the West of Ireland where the land purchase scheme has not been completed.[63] Also common in Ireland is a system of granting grazing rights known as agistment.[64] An agistment contract in general[65] confers on the grantee rights of grazing only[66] and not possession of the grazing land itself.[67] Though sometimes referred to as a "letting" of the grazing land, it has long been settled in Ireland that an agistment contract does not create the relationship of landlord and tenant nor is the consideration paid by the grantee to be regarded as rent.[68] Thus an agistment arrangement seems to fulfil the essentials for a profit *à prendre*, with one important exception. That is that the arrangement is regarded as a "contract" and so does not have to comply with the general requirement that easements and profits have to be created by deed.[69] In this respect, an agistment contract is more like a licence and it is, perhaps, significant that the Irish courts have often used terminology relating to licences when referring to agistment and to the other very common agricultural system in Ireland—conacre,[70] *i.e.*, the right to till land, sow and harvest crops on it and to enter the land whenever necessary for these purposes.[71] This subject is taken up again in the later chapter dealing with licences.[72]

(ii) Turbary

6.114. Another common profit in Ireland is a right of turbary, *i.e.*, the right to go onto another person's land and to dig and take away turf for use as fuel.[73] In general this right is limited to cutting turf for personal use as fuel,[74] but there is nothing to prevent a grant of the right for commercial purposes, *i.e.*, cutting turf for sale.[75] In the absence of any agreement to the contrary, it seems that a right of turbary includes the right to use bog material for any reasonable

---

[63] See, *e.g.*, *Waterpark* v. *Fennell* (1855) 5 I.C.L.R. 120 (commonage of mountain). Irish Land Commissioners) *Annual Report, 1971–72*, pp. 6–9; *Annual Report, 1982*, p. 7.

[64] Ch. 20, *post*.

[65] To some extent the terms of agistment contracts vary according to the custom and practice of different parts of the country, see *O'Connor* v. *Faul* (1957) 91 I.L.T.R. 7. Also *Fletcher* v. *Hackett* (1906) 40 I.L.T.R. 37.

[66] *Mulligan* v. *Adams* (1846) 8 Ir.L.R. 132; *Hickey* v. *Cosgrave* (1860) 6 Ir.Jur. (N.S.) 251; *Thornton* v. *Connolly* (1898) 32 I.L.T. 216; *Re Moore's Estates* [1944] I.R. 295. See also *O'Flaherty* v. *Kelly* [1909] 1 I.R. 223; *Boothman* v. *Kane* (1923) 57 I.L.T.R. 36.

[67] *Dalton* v. *O'Sullivan* [1947] Ir.Jur.Rep. 25; *Carson* v. *Jeffers* [1961] I.R. 44.

[68] *Allingham* v. *Atkinson* [1898] 1 I.R. 239. *Cf. Crane* v. *Naughten* [1912] 2 I.R. 318. Also *Plunkett* v. *Smith* (1904) 4 N.I.J.R. 136. See also *Collins* v. *O'Brien* [1981] I.L.R.M. 328 (see *A Casebook on Irish Land Law* (1984), p. 679).

[69] Para. 6.054, *ante*.

[70] See especially the discussion in *Dease* v. *O'Reilly* (1845) 8 Ir.L.R. 52 and *Booth* v. *McManus* (1861) 12 I.C.L.R. 418. Also *Westmeath* v. *Hogg* (1841) 3 Ir.L.R. 27; *Carson* v. *Jeffers* [1961] I.R. 44. And see *Maurice E. Taylor (Merchants) Ltd.* v. *Commissioners of Valuation* [1981] N.I. 236 (see *A Casebook on Irish Land Law* (1984), p. 680).

[71] *McKeowne* v. *Bradford* (1861) 7 Ir.Jur. (N.S.) 169; *Evans* v. *Monagher* (1872) I.R. 6 C.L. 526; *Irish Land Commission* v. *Andrews* [1941] I.R. 79.

[72] Ch. 20, *post*.

[73] *Dobbyn* v. *Somers* (1860) 13 I.C.L.R. 293; *Beere* v. *Fleming* (1862) 13 I.C.L.R. 506; *Cochrane* v. *McCleary* (1869) I.R. 4 C.L. 165; *Lowry* v. *Crothers* (1871) I.R. 5 C.L. 98; *Dawson* v. *McGroggan* [1903] 1 I.R. 92; *Convey* v. *Regan* [1952] I.R. 56; *Re Bohan* [1957] I.R. 49.

[74] See, *e.g.*, Landlord and Tenant Law Amendment Act, Ireland, 1860, s. 29. *Lifford* v. *Kearney* (1883) 17 I.L.T.R. 30; *Douglas* v. *McLaughlin* (1883) 17 I.L.T.R. 84. See also Renewable Leasehold Conversion Act, 1849, s. 4; Land Law (Ir.) Act, 1881, s. 17. *R. (Keenan)* v. *Tyrone County Court Judge* [1940] N.I. 108.

[75] *Coppinger* v. *Gubbins* (1846) 9 Ir.Eq.R. 304; *Stevenson* v. *Moore* (1858) 7 Ir.Ch.R. 462. *Cf. Fowler* v. *Blakely* (1862) 13 Ir.Ch.R. 58.

purpose other than fuel, *e.g.*, as manure.[76] However, it seems to be settled that
the soil left over after turf has been cut away is not part of the turbary and must
be left.[77] Similarly it has been held that a right of turbary does not include a
right to take away "scraws," *i.e.*, strips of surface turf.[78] On the other hand,
where a right of turbary over a bog generally has been conferred, the grantee
has the right to exercise it anywhere in the bog and is not confined to a
particular part.[79] In the Republic of Ireland, much land has now been acquired
by a statutory body, Bord na Mòna, for development of the turf industry,[80]
which plays a significant role in the country's economic life.[81]

(iii) Mines and Quarries

6.115. Mining and quarrying rights, whether relating to existing mines or
quarries or for opening new mines or quarries, are another common form of
profit *à prendre*.[82] Such rights are commonly excepted or reserved to the
grantor when he makes a grant of part of his land or even the whole of the land
where the mine or quarry is situated.[83] However, many minerals are extremely
valuable and the pattern of recent decades has been for the State to exercise
increasing control over minerals and their exploitation.[84] We have already mentioned that, in the Republic, all natural resources (including the air and all forms
of potential energy) are vested in the State, so that it is in the position to control
all exploration and development. In Northern Ireland, the Minerals
Development Act (N.I.), 1969,[85] vests, subject to a few exceptions,[86] most
mines and minerals existing in a natural condition in land in the Province, and
all mines for their working, in the Ministry of Commerce[87] which is given wide
powers for securing future prospecting and working or disposal of the mines
and minerals. Following the 1922 Constitution of the Irish Free State, there was
subsequently established in the Republic of Ireland the Minerals Company
(Mianrai Teoranta), which is generally responsible for supervising prospecting

---

[76] *Hutchinson* v. *Drain* (1899) 33 I.L.T.R. 147. See also *Dawson* v. *Baldwin* (1832) Hay. & Jon. 24; *Fitzpatrick*
v. *Verschoyle* [1913] 1 I.R. 8.
[77] *Beere* v. *Fleming* (1862) 13 I.C.L.R. 506; *Oates* v. *Stoney* (1882) 16 I.L.T.R. 30.
[78] *Jameson* v. *Fahey* [1907] 1 I.R. 411.
[79] *Hargrove* v. *Lord Congleton* (1861) 12 I.C.L.R. 362. *Cf. Waterpark* v. *Fennell* (1855) 5 I.C.L.R. 120
(common turbary rights on mountain); also *Knox* v. *Earl of Mayo* (1858) 9 Ir.Ch.R. 192.
[80] Turf Development Acts, 1946, 1950, 1953, 1957, 1958, 1959, 1961, 1965 and 1968. See *O'Brien* v. *Bord na
Móna* [1983] I.L.R.M. 314. Note also turbary regulations made under the Land Purchase Acts in both parts of
Ireland, *Re Drummond's Estate* [1933] I.R. 166; *Re Higginbotham's Estate* [1946] N.I. 208.
[81] *E.g.*, turf-burning power stations for generation of electricity have been established in various parts of the
Republic, see Electricity (Supply) (Amendment) Act, 1941, s. 3.
[82] *Comyn* v. *Att.-Gen.* [1950] I.R. 142. See also *Mansfield* v. *Crawford* (1846) 9 Ir.Eq.R. 271; *Brown* v.
Chadwick (1857) 7 I.C.L.R. 101; *Listowel* v. *Gibbings* (1858) 9 I.C.L.R. 223. *Cf. Atkinson* v. *King* (1877) I.R. 11
C.L. 536; *Stanley* v. *Riky* (1893) 31 L.R.Ir. 196.
[83] *McDonnell* v. *Kenneth* (1850) 1 I.C.L.R. 113; *Fishbourne* v. *Hamilton* (1890) 25 L.R.Ir. 483; *Earl of Antrim*
v. *Dobbs* (1891) 30 L.R.Ir. 424; *Staples* v. *Young* [1908] 1 I.R. 135. See also Landlord and Tenant Law
Amendment Act, Ireland, 1860, ss. 25–8, ch. 17, *post*.
[84] See the Republic's Minerals Development Acts, 1940 and 1979, Minerals Exploration and Development
Company Act, 1941 and Minerals Company Acts, 1945, 1947 and 1950; Petroleum and other Minerals
Development Act, 1960 (R.I.); *Comyn* v. *Att.-Gen.* [1950] I.R. 142. Note also the control of management and
regulation of safety, health and welfare under the Mines and Quarries Act, 1965. *Cf.* Mines Act (N.I.), 1969.
Hamilton v. *Niblock* [1956] N.I. 109; *Gallagher* v. *Mogul of Ireland* [1975] I.R. 204.
[85] See also Petroleum (Production) Act (N.I.), 1964.
[86] 1969 Act, ss. 2–7 and Sched. 1.
[87] S. 1 (now Department of the Environment).

for and development of minerals.[88] The result of this legislation in both parts of Ireland has been to curtail to a considerable extent private rights to mines and minerals.

(iv) Fisheries

.116. Perhaps one of the most litigated subjects in Ireland has been fishing rights. At common law, the right to fish in the sea and all tidal waters belonged to the Crown.[89] The Crown did often grant fishing rights in specified parts of the sea or tidal waters to private individuals, usually in the form of a franchise known as a free or several fishery.[90] However, it has been accepted in Ireland that this practice was prohibited by Magna Carta, 1215, so far as the common law had jurisdiction over the several parts of the island,[91] so that the general public may now in the name of the State or, in Northern Ireland, the Crown, fish freely in the sea and tidal waters,[92] unless some ancient grant survives to restrict that right.[93] The general public has no such rights in respect of non-tidal waters, even if navigable.[94] Much litigation has also arisen in Ireland in the same connection relating to rights to the seashore or foreshore, in particular the right to take seaweed from the shore.[95] At common law, the foreshore was vested in the Crown and this remains the case in Northern Ireland.[96] In the Republic of Ireland it is vested in the State.[97] The foreshore lies between the high-water and low-water marks on land left by ordinary tides occurring between spring and neap tides, which land is covered and left dry alternatively by the flux and reflux of the tide.[98] Thus it is settled that the general public has no right to enter on the foreshore to take away seaweed,[99] but seaweed driven above the high-water mark belongs to the owner of the land upon which it is driven, and seaweed floating in the sea may be recovered by the general public

---

[88] Fn. 84, *ante*.

[89] *Allen* v. *Donnelly* (1856) 5 Ir.Ch.R. 452; *Murphy* v. *Ryan* (1868) I.R. 2 C.L. 143; *Whelan* v. *Hewson* (1872) I.R. 6 C.L. 283.

[90] *Gabbett* v. *Clancy* (1845) 8 Ir.L.R. 299; *Ashworth* v. *Browne* (1860) 10 Ir.Ch.R. 421; *Bristow* v. *Cormican* (1875) 3 App.Cas. 641; *Miller* v. *Little* (1879) 4 L.R.Ir. 302; *Powell* v. *Heffernan* (1881) 8 L.R.Ir. 130.

[91] *Malcolmson* v. *O'Dea* (1863) 10 H.L.C. 593; *R* (*Moore*) v. *O'Hanrahan* [1927] I.R. 406; *Moore* v. *Att.-Gen.* [1934] I.R. 44 (see *A Casebook on Irish Land Law* (1984), p. 5); *Cooper* v. *Att.-Gen.* [1935] I.R. 425; *Little* v. *Cooper* [1937] I.R. 1; *Foyle and Bann Fisheries Ltd.* v. *Att.-Gen.* (1949) 83 I.L.T.R. 29.

[92] *Duke of Devonshire* v. *Hodnett* (1827) 1 Hud. & Br. 322; *Malcolmson* v. *O'Dea* (1863) 10 H.L.C. 593.

[93] *Ashworth* v. *Brown* (1855) 7 Ir.Jur. (o.s.) 315; *Little* v. *Wingfield* (1858) 11 I.C.L.R. 63; *Neil* v. *Duke of Devonshire* (1882) 8 App.Cas. 135; *Att.-Gen* v. *Cooper* [1956] I.R. 1; *Toome Eel Fishery (N.I.) Ltd.* v. *Cardwell* [1966] N.I. 1. Note, however, that the State has in recent decades imposed increasing control and regulation by statute on sea fishing, see the Republic's Whale Fisheries Act, 1937; Sea Fisheries Acts, 1952, 1955, 1956, 1959 and 1963; Maritime Jurisdiction Act, 1959; Fishery Harbour Centres Act, 1968. For Northern Ireland, see the U.K. Sea-Fish Industry Acts, 1933, 1938, 1951, 1959, 1962 and 1967; Herring Industry Acts, 1935, 1938 and 1944; White Fish and Herring Industries Acts, 1948, 1953 and 1957; Fishery Limits Act, 1964.

[94] *Bloomfield* v. *Johnston* (1868) I.R. 8 C.L. 68; *Pery* v. *Thornton* (1889) 23 L.R.Ir. 402; *Re De Burgho's Estate* [1896] 1 I.R. 274; *Johnston* v. *O'Neill* [1911] A.C. 552.

[95] See Lee, "The Right to Take Seaweed from the Foreshore" (1967) 18 N.I.L.Q. 33.

[96] Government of Ireland Act, 1920, s. 4 (1). *Duke of Devonshire* v. *Hodnett* (1827) 1 Hud. & Br. 322; *Hayes* v. *Hayes* (1897) 31 I.L.T. 392; *Att.-Gen.* v. *McCarthy* [1911] 2 I.R. 260.

[97] Foreshore Act, 1933. See also the 1937 Constitution, Art 10. *Linnane* v. *Nestor* [1943] I.R. 200; *cf. Att.-Gen.* v. *McIlwaine* [1939] I.R. 437; *Mahoney* v. *Neenan* [1966] I.R. 559. See Smyth, *The Seashores of Ireland: Public Rights and Restrictions* (1935).

[98] *Casey* v. *McGuanne* (1840) 1 Leg.Rep. 311; *Att.-Gen.* v. *McCarthy* [1911] 2 I.R. 260.

[99] *Howe* v. *Stawell* (1833) Alc. & Nap. 348; *Mulholland* v. *Killen* (1874) I.R. 9 Eq. 471; *Mahoney* v. *Neenan* [1966] I.R. 559.

in exercise of the public right to fish in the sea.[1] Once again, of course, Crown grants of rights to the foreshore, with the right to take seaweed therefrom, have been made from time to time to individuals.[2]

6.117. Apart from such public fishing rights, there exists an abundance of private fishing rights relating to inland rivers and lakes and other non-tidal waters.[3] However, even here there has been a development of public ownership in recent decades.[4] Furthermore, even where private rights have been allowed to remain in existence, their exercise has been strictly controlled and regulated for well over a century[5] by a long series of Fishery Acts.[6] These Acts have been the subject of much litigation.[7]

(v) Other Sporting Rights

6.118. In addition to fishing rights, it is common to have grants or reservations made of other sporting rights, such as hunting and shooting wild animals and fowl.[8] The exercise of such rights is also controlled by statute, *i.e.*, legislation passed for the preservation and protection of game.[9]

(vi) Timber

6.119. Timber may form the subject-matter of a profit in the shape of a right of estovers, *i.e.*, the right to take wood as, in the ancient language of the

---

[1] *Brew* v. *Haren* (1877) I.R. 11 C.L. 198 at 201–2 (*per* Lawson J.).

[2] *Brew* v. *Haren*, *ibid.*; *Hamilton* v. *Att.-Gen.* (1881) 9 L.R.Ir. 271; *Stoney* v. *Keane* (1903) 37 I.L.T.R. 212; *Coppinger* v. *Sheehan* [1906] 1 I.R. 519; *Vandeleur* v. *Glynn* [1907] A.C. 569; *Holien* v. *Tipping* [1915] 1 I.R. 210; *Clancy* v. *Whelan* (1958) 92 I.L.T.R. 39.

[3] *Case of the Royal Fishery of the Banne* (1610) Dav. 149; *Hamilton* v. *Marquis of Donegal* (1795) 3 Ridgw.P.C. 267; *Duke of Devonshire* v. *Hodnett* (1827) 1 Hud. & Br. 322; *Duke of Devonshire* v. *Smith* (1830) 2 Hud. & Br. 512; *Frewen* v. *Orr* (1842) Long. & Town. 601.

[4] See, *e.g.*, the Republic's Foyle Fisheries Act, 1952, Pt II and Sched. 2; Fisheries (Consolidation) Act, 1959. ss. 184–217; *cf.* Foyle Fisheries Act (N.I.), 1952, s. 8 and Sched. 2, and Fisheries Act (N.I.), 1966, ss. 1 and 2.

[5] See Connor, *Fisheries (Ireland) Acts* (1908); Finlay, *Laws of Game and Inland Fisheries in Ireland* (1827); Longfield, *Fishery Laws of Ireland* (1863).

[6] See now the Republic's Freshwater Fisheries (Prohibition of Netting) Act, 1951; Fisheries (Consolidation) Act, 1959; Fisheries (Amendment) Acts, 1962 and 1964. Also Shannon Fisheries Acts, 1935 and 1938, and the Foyle Fisheries Acts, 1952 and 1961. For N.I., see Fisheries Acts (N.I.), 1966 and 1968; Diseases of Fish Act (N.I.), 1967; Development Loans (Agriculture and Fisheries) Act (N.I.), 1968. Also Foyle Fisheries Acts (N.I.), 1952 and 1962. As regards the Fisheries Act (N.I.), 1966, see *D.P.P.* v. *McNeill* [1975] N.I. 177. This decision of the Northen Ireland Court of Appeal raises numerous issues of constitutional and international law which are outside the scope of this book, but see the discussion in Symmons, "Who Owns the Territorial Waters of Northern Ireland?" (1976) 27 N.I.L.Q. 48.

[7] *R. (Hosford)* v. *County Limerick Justices* (1908) 42 I.L.T.R. 105; *King* v. *Russell* [1909] 2 I.R. 25; *McCormack* v. *Carroll* (1911) 45 I.L.T.R. 7; *Irish Society* v. *Fleming* [1912] 1 I.R. 287; *Society of the New Plantation of Ulster* v. *Harold* (1912) 46 I.L.T.R. 273; *Alton* v. *Irvine* [1915] 2 I.R. 72; *Ireland* v. *Quirke* [1928] I.R. 231; *Tangney* v. *Kerry District Justices* [1928] I.R. 358; *Ganley* v. *Minister for Agriculture* [1950] I.R. 191; *Foyle Fisheries Commission* v. *Gallen* [1960] Ir.Jur.Rep. 35. For earlier cases, see books cited in fn. 5, *supra*.

[8] *Finlay* v. *Curteis* (1832) Hayes 496; *Foott* v. *Hudson* (1860) 10 I.C.L.R. 509; *Radcliff* v. *Hayes* [1907] 1 I.R. 101.

[9] See the Republic's Game Preservation Act, 1930, and Wild Birds Protection Act, 1930; *cf.* Game Preservation Act (N.I.), 1928; Wild Birds Protection Acts (N.I.), 1931, 1950 and 1968; Game Law Amendment Act (N.I.), 1951; Protection of Animals Acts (N.I.), 1952 and 1961. Note also earlier legislation applying to the whole of Ireland, *e.g.*, Game Acts (Ir.), 1698 and 1787; Game Act, 1831; Game Trespass Act, 1864; Ground Game Acts, 1880 and 1906. See on this legislation, Connor, *Game Laws of Ireland* (1891); Connor, *Right to Game in Ireland* (1903); Farran, *Game Laws of Ireland* (1907); Finlay, *Laws of Game and Inland Fisheries in Ireland* (1827); Jague, *Irish Game Laws* (1843); Longfield, *Game Laws of Ireland* (1868). *State (Lawlor)* v. *District Justice MacCraith* [1964] I.R. 364.

common law,[10] "house-bote,"[11] "plough-bote"[12] and "hay-bote."[13] We saw earlier that a tenant for life can claim such a right,[14] but it is important to note a vital difference in his case. A tenant for life's right of estovers is exercisable in respect of the same land in which he holds his estate whereas, in the present context, we are concerned with a right of estovers as a profit à prendre, i.e., held by one person in respect of *another* person's land. A right of estovers is usually restricted to some extent, e.g., as to the precise amount of, or, indeed, nature, of the timber which may be cut and taken[15] or limited by reference to the needs of the dominant tenement.[16] Apart from such a right of estovers, a person may acquire much wider timber rights in respect of another's land, in particular the right to cut timber for commercial purposes.[17] Once again there has been the encroachment of statutory regulation, e.g., forestry legislation.[18]

V. TITHE RENTCHARGES

A. TITHES

6.120. As we explained earlier,[19] a tithe was originally an ecclesiastical concept and was the right of a religious institution, usually embodied in the rector of a parish, to one-tenth part of the produce of all the land in the parish.[20] As might have been expected, it was not a popular concept and it has had a turbulent history over the centuries.[21] With the dissolution of monasteries during the reign of Henry VIII, many "rectories" passed into Crown hands, only to be granted to laymen, so that in Ireland, as in Great Britain, "The tithes of religious foundations suppressed at the Reformation passed partly into the possession of secular clergy, partly into that of lay proprietors and partly formed the corpus of collegiate or educational foundations."[22] From the sixteenth century down to the nineteenth century there was much agitation over the payment of tithes, especially to religious and educational institutions. From time to time this rose to such a pitch that the legislature was forced to act. Thus during the eighteenth century there was much opposition to a claim by clergy to tithe agistment for dry and barren cattle, until the Irish Parliament finally barred such claims during its last year of life.[23]

---

[10] *Coke upon Littleton* (19th ed., 1832), 41b and 53b.
[11] *I.e.*, for repairing the house occupied by the holder of the right or for burning in it as fuel.
[12] *I.e.*, for making or repairing agricultural equipment.
[13] *I.e.*, for repairing fences.
[14] Para. 4.152, *ante*.
[15] *Russel and Broker's Case* (1587) 2 Leon. 209; *Brown and Tucker's Case* (1610) 4 Leon. 241.
[16] *Clayton* v. *Corby* (1843) 5 Q.B. 415 at 419–20 (*per* Lord Denman C J.).
[17] *Re Moore's Estate* (1902) 36 I.L.T.R 14; *Rudd* v. *Rea* [1923] 1 I.R. 55.
[18] See the Republic's Forestry Acts, 1946 and 1956; *cf.* Forestry Act (N.I.), 1953, and note the general provisions of the Amenity Lands Act (N.I.), 1965. para.4.152, *ante*.
[19] para. 6.014, *ante*.
[20] *Bradshaw* v. *Cronan* (1818) Rowe 656.
[21] For the Irish background, see O'Brien, "The Story of Tithes" (1910) 27 Ir.Ecc.Rec. (4th Scr.) 458; Woods, "Church Temporalities in Ireland" (1957) 12 N.I.L.Q. 106. Also Dalton, *History of Tithes, Church Lands and Other Ecclesiastical Benefices* (1832); Finlay, *Law of Tithe In Ireland* (1828).
[22] Woods, *op. cit.*, p. 107. Note the Connor Tithes Act, 1824. *Denny* v. *Duke of Devonshire* (1851) 1 Ir.Ch.R. 657; see also *Ellis* v. *O'Neill* (1855) 4 I.C.L.R. 467; *Att.-Gen.* v. *Ashe* (1859) 10 I.Ch.R. 309.
[23] Tithe Agistment (Ir.) Act, 1800.

B. TITHE COMPOSITIONS

6.121. Tithes in kind, *i.e.*, one-tenth of the agricultural produce of the parish, were abolished by the Tithes Composition Acts, 1823–36.[24] There were substituted instead under these Acts money compositions charged on the land previously subject to the tithes in kind.[25]

C. CHURCH TEMPORALITIES

6.122. The passing of the Church Temporalities Act, 1833, was the next stage in the history of tithes.[26] This Act enabled tenants holding land from Bishops or other ecclesiastical persons, or from the Ecclesiastical Commissioners in Ireland, to purchase the fee simple in the land, subject to fee farm or perpetual rents.[27] Estate Commissioners were responsible for fixing the amount of these rents, subject to the terms of the purchase being approved by the Lord Lieutenant.[28] The fee farm or perpetuity rents were variable every seven years according to variations in the average price of wheat or oats during successive periods of seven years.

D. TITHE RENTCHARGES

6.123. The Tithe Rentcharge (Ireland) Act, 1838, abolished tithe compositions[29] and substituted for them annual rentcharges equal to three-quarters of the compositions.[30] For the first time the direct burden of payment of the tithes or their equivalent was removed from the tenants and imposed on the landlords of the lands in question,[31] though no doubt landlords adjusted the rents charged to tenants to take account of this. These tithe rentcharges were given priority by statute over all other charges, liens, mortgages and encumbrances on the land.[32] It has been estimated that by the second half of the nineteenth century much of the income of the Established Church in Ireland was derived from this income from the land.[33] This brings us to the next stage in the history of tithes, the disestablishment of the Church of Ireland.

---

[24] Tithes Composition (Ir.) Acts, 1823, 1824, 1827, 1832 and 1836. See also the Recovery of Tithes (Ir.) Act, 1832. MacKenna, *Rights and Liabilities of Tenants, Landlords and Incumbrancers under Recent Tithe (Ireland) Acts* (1834); O'Leary, *Law of Statutory Composition for Tithes in Ireland* (1835); Ryan, *Directions for Proceedings under the Tithe Acts* (1823).

[25] *R. v. Mackey* (1825) Sm. & Bat. 286; *Carew v. Stuart* (1829) 2 Hud. & Br. 465; *Meade v. Warburton* (1833) Alc. & Nap. 287; *Dickson v. Power* (1833) Hay. & Jon. 267; *Aske v. Locke* (1837) 2 Jones 11; *Armstrong v. Killikelly* (1839) 1 Ir. L.R. 270; *Beresford v. Loughnan* (1839) 1 Ir.L.R. 364; *Fairtlough v. Swiney* (1839) 1 Jebb & Sym. 333; *Lord Shannon v. Stoughton* (1841) 3 Ir.L.R. 521.

[26] See also Church Temporalities (Ir.) Acts, 1834 and 1836.

[27] S. 128. Lyne, *Statute Law of Ecclesiastical Leases in Ireland and Purchases under the Church Temporalities Acts* (1838). *Re Carey Knox's Estate* [1921] 1 I.R. 193.

[28] Ss. 134–5.

[29] S.1.

[30] Ss. 7 and 11. See, generally, Chaytor, *Law and Practice Relating to Variation of Tithe Rent-Charges in Ireland* (1897; Supp. 1900); O'Leary, *Law of Rent-Charges, in lieu of Composition for Tithes in Ireland* (1839). Also Petrie, *Irish Poor Law Rating, as affects Tithe Rent-Charge Property* (6th ed., 1870). Burke v. *Dignam* (1841) 3 Ir.L.R. 368; *Henderson v. Dean of Londonderry* (1842) Ir.Cir.Rep. 631; *Earl of Shannon v. Dowden* (1842) Long. & Town. 529; *Crosthwaite v. Conlan* (1843) 5 Ir.L.R. 534; *Davis v. Fitton* (1847) 10 Ir.L.R. 81.

[31] Ss. 7–9. *Irish Land Commission v. Rowntree* [1896] 2 I.R. 442; *Re Delap's Estate* [1912] 1 I.R. 298.

[32] S. 27. See also Tithe Arrears (Ir.) Act, 1839 and Tithe Rentcharge (Ir.) Act, 1848.

[33] Woods, *op. cit.*, p. 111.

E. Disestablishment of the Church of Ireland

6.124. The Irish Church Act, 1869,[34] disestablished the Church of Ireland from January 1, 1871, and vested its property, real and personal, in a lay corporation called the "Commissioners of Church Temporalities in Ireland". The Commissioners were authorised[35] to purchase the surrender of ecclesiastical leases of rentcharges and thereafter the payers of the tithe rentcharges became entitled to redeem the rentcharges. The Commissioners were empowered to sell any tithe rentcharge either for cash or for credit, *i.e.*, through payment, with interest, over a period not exceeding 52 years.[36] In the case of a sale by credit, the purchase money could be paid by an annuity at £4·9s. per cent.[37] over the period in question.[38] Alternatively, the purchaser could pay at least one-quarter of the purchase price and pay off the balance through an instalment mortgage spread over not more than 64 half-yearly instalments, at a rate of interest of 4 per cent., or through a simple mortgage whereby interest was charged until the balance was repaid.[39] Otherwise, an immediate sale could be made for a sum equal to "22½ years' purchase", *i.e.*, 22½ times the annual rentcharge.[40]

6.125. Various detailed changes in the 1869 scheme were made by subsequent legislation. The Amendment Act of 1872[41] abolished the power to vary tithe rentcharges by reference to the average price of corn[42] and provided that in future an allowance should be made to payers of instalments of annuities on account of income tax, in respect of the part of such instalments representing interest charges.[43] The Commissioners were dissolved by an Act of 1881[44] and all land held by them was vested in the Irish Land Commission, which by then was supervising the general land purchase scheme operating under the Land Purchase Acts.[45] The Commissioners had become one of the largest owners of land in Ireland, with some 11,000 tenants holding under them. They had, however, failed to sell about one-half of the tithe rentcharges originally vesting in them and, though some of them were later redeemed and much of the land on which they were charged was subsequently bought out under the Land Purchase Acts, with the rentcharges being redeemed out of the

---

[34] See also Irish Church Act (1869) Amendment Acts, 1872 and 1881. Atkins, *Irish Church Act, 1869* (1869): Bernard, *Irish Church Acts, 1869 and 1872* (1876); Brooke, *Irish Church Act, 1869* (1870); Todd, *Irish Church Act, 1869* (1869). *Report of the Commissioners of Church Temporalities* (1875; C. 1148).

[35] 1869 Act, ss. 33 and 34.

[36] 1869 Act, s. 32.

[37] Pre-decimalisation currency.

[38] 1869 Act, s. 32 and 1872 Act, s. 7.

[39] 1869 Act, s. 52.

[40] 1869 Act, s. 32.

[41] Irish Church Act (1869) Amendment Act, 1872.

[42] *Reg.* v. *Justices of Mayo* (1857) 7 I.C.L.R. 234; *Reg.* v. *Justices of Cork* (1857) 7 I.C.L.R. 249. See also *Thompson* v. *Shiel* (1840) 3 Ir.Eq.R. 135; *Reg. (Norcott)* v. *Cork Justices* (1890) 28 L.R.Ir. 185; *Reg. (Longfield)* v. *Cork Justices* (1890) 28 L.R.Ir. 369; *R. (Metge)* v. *Justices of Meath* [1898] 2 I.R. 592; *O'Grady* v. *Synan* [1900] 2 I.R. 602.

[43] S. 11 and Sched.

[44] Irish Church Act Amendment Act, 1881.

[45] Para. 1.49, *ante*. See *Conolly* v. *Gorman* [1898] 1 I.R. 20.

purchase price,[46] many of the old tithe rentcharges survive to this day in both parts of Ireland as permanent sources of revenue accruing to the state.

6.126. Other minor changes in the 1869 scheme were introduced by the Purchase of Land (Ireland) Act, 1885,[47] and Land Law (Ireland) Act, 1887,[48] which varied the rate of interest charged on simple and instalment mortgages[49] and the repayment period for instalments in the case of the latter.[50] The Land Law (Ireland) Act, 1896, empowered the Land Commission to convert simple mortgages into mortgages for repayment of capital through an annuity at 4 per cent. per annum, plus interest at 3⅛ per cent.[51] The Tithe Rentcharge (Ireland) Act, 1900, reduced the maximum period for repayment of instalments of purchase money in cases of a credit sale of tithe rentcharges from 52 years to 45 years[52] and provided that, where a hereditament out of which a tithe rentcharge was payable was separately owned by different people, each owner was to be separately liable to a proportion based on the rateable value of the hereditament.[53] Perhaps more importantly, the 1900 Act restored the practice of varying tithe rentcharges which had been abolished by the Irish Church Act of 1872.[54] Sections 2 and 3 of the 1900 Act provided for variation thereafter every 15 years according to the levels of "fair" or "judicial" rents fixed for tenanted land.[55]

6.127. The result was that by 1920 the following were the sources of revenue being collected by the Irish Land Commission: (1) tithe rentcharges; (2) fee farm or perpetuity rents; (3) simple mortgages; (4) instalment mortgages. Tithe rentcharges were those established by the Tithe Rentcharge (Ireland) Act, 1838, and which had neither been sold by the Church Temporalities Commissioners nor been redeemed under the Land Purchase Acts or otherwise.[56] Fee farm or perpetuity rents were those reserved in sales to tenants of ecclesiastical land under the Church Temporalities Acts, 1833–36.[57] Simple mortgages were payable where land had been sold under the Irish Church Act, 1869, the balance of the capital remained unpaid and the mortgages had not been converted into terminable annuities or instalment mortgages under the Land Law (Ireland) Act, 1896.[58] The point to emphasise is that all three of these items of revenue remained permanent until the payers arranged redemption with the Commission. The fourth item, instalment mortgages, was, on the other hand, terminable revenue. These originated also

---

[46] See *Re Mundy's Estate* [1899] 1 I.R. 191; *Re Kemmis's Estate* [1904] 1 I.R. 496; *Re Marquis of Waterford's Estate* (1905) 5 N.I.J.R. 144; *Re Moss's Estate* [1911] 1 I.R. 317; *Re Armstrong's Estate* [1913] 1 I.R. 449; *Re Blackburne's Estate* [1914] 1 I.R. 1; *Re Locke's Estate* [1914] 1 I.R. 302.

[47] S. 23.

[48] S. 25.

[49] Reduced to 3⅛ per cent.

[50] Not to exceed 49 years.

[51] S. 26.

[52] S. 1.

[53] S. 7. Cf. *Irish Land Commission* v. *Kelly* (1900) 34 I.L.T.R. 203.

[54] Para. 6.125, *supra*.

[55] See also s. 8 of the 1900 Act and s. 90 of the Irish Land Act, 1903. As to fair rents, see para. 1.49, *ante*.

[56] Para. 6.123, *ante*.

[57] Para. 6.122, *ante*.

[58] Para. 6.126, *ante*.

under the Irish Church Act, 1869, as amended by subsequent legislation or arose later on conversion of simple mortgages under the Land Law (Ireland) Act, 1896.[59]

F. SINCE 1920

6.128. The Government of Ireland Act, 1920, apportioned the Church Temporalities Fund administered by the old Irish Land Commission between the two parts of Ireland.[60] In the Republic of Ireland, a new Land Commission took over from the old Commission and became responsible for the Fund.[61] So far as tithe rentcharges are concerned, the 15-year variations begun under the 1900 Act[62] were stopped after November 1, 1930, by the Land Act, 1931.[63] Section 49 (1) of that Act provided that sums payable in respect of tithe rentcharges were burdens which affected registered land without registration reduced by 8 per cent. Further provisions as to reduction of tithe rentcharges were contained in the Land Acts, 1933,[64] and 1939.[65] Furthermore, detailed provisions for ascertainment of arrears of and revision of tithe rentcharges, and other rents and sums payable to the Church Temporalities Fund, by the Land Commission were contained in the Land Acts, 1933,[66] and 1939.[67] Such tithe rentcharges could be redeemed as superior interests under section 39 of the Land Act, 1923.[68] Despite these provisions, tithe rentcharges remained in existence and continued to be burdens on land for which conveyancers had to watch out.[69] Tithe rentcharges and payments in lieu of tithes or tithe rentcharges were burdens which affect registered land without registration under the Registration of Title Act, 1964.[70] Finally, it should be noted that section 7 of the Land Act, 1984, extinguished all tithe rentcharges and other rents and payments subsisting on 28th September, 1975, and payable into the Church Temporalities Fund. Section 7 also dissolved the Fund and provided for its dispersal for the benefit of the Exchequer.

6.129. In Northern Ireland, the Church Temporalities Fund was vested in the Ministry of Finance in 1920, as successor to the old Land Commission.[71] Otherwise developments since 1920 have been along the same lines as in the Republic, except that the final act of extinguishment has yet to be taken. The

---

[59] *Ibid.*
[60] S. 31.
[61] Land Act, 1923, espec. S. 24. Irish Land Commissioners' *Annual Report, 1971–72*, pp. 38–9.
[62] Para. 6.126, *ante.*
[63] S. 49 (2).
[64] S. 49.
[65] S. 29.
[66] S. 18.
[67] Ss. 26–8.
[68] See also Land Act, 1931, s. 36 (4); Land Act, 1933, s. 18; Land Act, 1939, s. 45; Land Act, 1950, ss. 19 and 26; Land Act, 1953, s. 4 and Sched.
[69] See the references in the Republic's Statute of Limitations, 1957, s. 2(1) (para. (a) of the definition of "rentcharge"). Note also para. (b) (iii) of the same definition, referring to a "composition rent," see para. 6.121, *ante.*
[70] S. 72 (1) (a). The Registrar may, however, register a notice to the effect that the land is exempt from, or has ceased to be subject to, such burdens, where this is proved to his satisfaction, s. 72 (2).
[71] Government of Ireland Act, 1920, s. 31. See also Church Temporalities Fund Act (N.I.), 1922, and Exchequer and Financial Provisions Act (N.I.), 1923, s. 4 and 1950, s. 28.

Tithe Rentcharge and Variable Rents Act (N.I.), 1930[72] and the Land Law (Miscellaneous Provisions) Act (N.I.),[73] reduced payments of such rents by 8 per cent. in lieu of the 15-year variation due in 1930 under the 1900 Act and repealed the provisions in that Act for further variations. Section 1 of the Finance (Miscellaneous Provisions) Act (N.I.), 1949,[74] permits the Ministry (now Department) to sell any perpetuity rent or tithe rentcharge vested in it "in consideration of a sum which will yield, when invested in securities issued in respect of any loan raised by the Ministry or by the Treasury as the Ministry may determine, such annual amount of interest as is approximately equal to the annual amount of the perpetuity rent or tithe rentcharge as the case may be."[75] In fact, despite several drives by the Ministry to secure redemption of tithe rentcharges over the past few decades, it was reported in 1971 that some 45,000 acres, involving about 1,173 holdings,[76] in Northern Ireland were still subject to such rentcharges.[77] Though some £6,000 annual revenue was produced in this form, the rentcharges attached to particular pieces of property were often of trifling amounts, ranging from 1s. to £21 per annum. Apart from tithe rentcharges collected by the Ministry of Finance, it was also reported that some were still collected on behalf of private owners.[78] It was recommended that these rentcharges should become subject to a compulsory redemption scheme run by the state in order to get rid of burdens on land which had become of nuisance value only.[79]

G. RECOVERY

6.130. Arrears of a tithe rentcharge may be recovered in Northern Ireland by action in the High Court or county court, depending on the amount sought.[80] If the payer is not in occupation of the property or he is not known, a summary petition may be made under section 30 of the Tithe Rentcharge (Ireland) Act, 1838, for appointment of a receiver.[81] If, on the other hand, the payer is in

---

[72] S. 1 (1).

[73] S. 3.

[74] Replacing s. 3 of the Exchequer and Financial Provisions Act (N.I.), 1930, and s. 2 of the Tithe Rentcharge and Variable Rents Act (N.I.), 1930.

[75] If the annual amount of the rent does not exceed 5s. (pre-decimalisation currency), the Ministry may fix the consideration for the sale as it thinks proper.

[76] Varying in size from 406 acres to 1 acre.

[77] See *Survey of the Land Law of Northern Ireland* (1971), para. 459. In 1980, the holdings affected figure had dropped to 343 terminable rents and 31 perpetuity rents, see Land Law Working Group's Discussion Document No. 1 (*Ground Rents and Other Periodic Payments*) (1980), p. 5.

[78] *E.g.*, on behalf of the Shaftesbury and Donegall estates in Belfast and Co. Antrim, *ibid.* In these cases the rentcharges ranged from 1s. 1d. (pre-decimalisation currency) to £3.

[79] *Survey of the Land Law of Northern Ireland* (1971), paras. 459–63, but note that the Land Law Working Group has since favoured a *voluntary* redemption scheme instead, because of the small number of rents and their size, see Interim Report (*Ground Rents and Other Periodic Payments*) (1983), ch. 6. *Cf.* the scheme in England introduced by the Tithe Act, 1936.

[80] Tithe Rentcharge (Ir.) Act, 1838, ss. 27–30. *Blackburne* v. *Gernon* (1899) 33 I.L.T.R. 119; *Irish Land Commission* v. *Ryan* [1900] 2 I.R. 565; *Irish Land Commission* v. *Annesley* [1904] 1 I.R. 272; *Re Moss's Estate* [1911] 1 I.R. 317. Palles C.B. doubted whether the court could order a sale of the land for recovery of a tithe rentcharge, *Re Wade's Estate* (1884) 13 L.R.Ir. 515 at 527; see Chaytor, *Law and Practice Relating to Variation of Tithe Rentcharges in Ireland* (1900 Supp.), pp. 15 *et. seq.*

[81] Provided there are at least 31 days of arrears. See *Kellett* v. *Sturgeon* (1842) 5 Ir.Eq.R. 159; *Macartney* v. *Graydon* (1845) 8 Ir.Eq.R. 99. Also *Mangan* v. *Massy* (1839) 2 Ir.L.R. 106; *Saunderson* v. *Stoney* (1839) 2 Ir.Eq.R. 153.

occupation of the land, the right of distress[82] may no longer be exercised as in Northern Ireland this remedy has been abolished and the plaintiff must proceed through the Enforcement of Judgments Office in such cases.[83]

VI. RENTCHARGES

A. NATURE

6.131. One of the fundamental distinctions in our land law system was that between a rent service and a rentcharge.[84] A rent service is a rent payable by virtue of the feudal relationship of lord and tenant[85] or the modern relationship of landlord and tenant.[86] In Ireland, freehold rent services are still quite common due to the large number of fee farm grants that have been made since *Quia Emptores*, 1290. Some of these grants have created the feudal relationship of lord and tenant *non obstante Quia Emptores*,[87] though most of them create the modern relationship of landlord and tenant by virtue of special statutory provisions, such as section 3 of Deasy's Act, 1860, or the Renewable Leasehold Conversion Act, 1849.[88] Apart from these freehold rent services, the most common rent services are those reserved in grants of leasehold estates.

6.132. To be distinguished from rent services are rents *seck*.[89] These were rents reserved in grants which did not create the relationship of lord and tenant or landlord and tenant. The most significant feature of such rents was that at common law the rent could *not* be enforced automatically by distress.[90] An automatic right of distress could be invoked only by a lord or landlord and at common law a rentchargor had one only if it were granted *expressly* by the instrument creating the rentcharge.[91] This position, however, was later altered by statute,[92] which conferred on owners of rents seck the same rights of distress as landlords, and since then rents seck have usually been referred to as rentcharges.[93] The distinction between the two types of interest still exists. A rent service is generally annexed to the reversion in the land held by the lord or landlord, though this does not always hold good in Ireland where a reversion need not be reserved on the creation of the relationship of landlord and

---

[82] Under s. 29 of the Tithe Rentcharge (Ir.) Act, 1838.
[83] Under the Judgments Enforcement (N.I.) Order, 1981. See para. 17.066, *post*.
[84] Para. 6.015, *ante*.
[85] Ch. 2, *ante*.
[86] Ch. 17, *post*.
[87] Ch. 4, *ante*.
[88] *Ibid*.
[89] From the latin *siccus*, *i.e.*, dry or barren.
[90] Hence the epithet "seck." See further ch. 17, *post*.
[91] *Pennefather* v. *Stephens* (1847) 11 Ir.Eq.R. 61; *Brady* v. *Fitzgerald* (1848) 12 Ir.Eq.R. 273.
[92] See Distress for Rent Act (Ir.), 1712, s. 7 and Landlord and Tenant Act (Ir.), 1741, s. 5. Also Fee Farm Rents (Ir.) Act, 1851, and Conveyancing Act, 1881, s. 44 (2). Para. 6.141, *post*. A right of distress also existed if the rentcharge was created by uses executed by the Statute of Uses (Ir.), 1634, see s. 4 and ch. 3, *ante*.
[93] See Ruoff and Roper, *Registered Conveyancing* (4th ed., 1979), ch. 28; Ruoff, *Rentcharges in Registered Conveyancing* (1961); Law Com. Working Paper No. 24, *Transfer of Land: Rentcharges* (1969). Walford, "Rentcharges and Conveyancing" (1952) 16 Conv. 251; Williams, "Landowner's Liability to Pay Rent-Charges in Fee" (1897) 13 L.Q.R. 288.

tenant.[94] A rentcharge, on the other hand, always stands on its own and comes into the category of an incorporeal hereditament, unless granted for life only.

There are in fact many different situations in which rentcharges are to be found in Ireland nowadays and at this point it may be useful to list the most common ones.

1. *Fee Farm Rents*

6.133. We discussed in an earlier chapter the perpetual rentcharges created in Ireland under fee farm grants.[95] Though fee farm grants of this kind are not very common in Ireland, owing to the existence of the special legislation facilitating creation of the relationship of landlord and tenant in fee farm grants, rentcharge grants have from time to time given rise to litigation.[96]

2. *Settlements*

6.134. One of the common features of a settlement of land is the creation, in addition to the successive estates in the land, of charges on the land to secure income for members of the family not given substantial estates, *e.g.*, a jointure for the settlor's wife and pin-money rentcharges for his younger children.[97] The crucial point to note about such rentcharges is, however, that they are overreachable on a sale of the land by the tenant for life under the Settled Land Acts, 1882–90, and thereafter become charges only on the capital money raised by the sale and paid to the trustees of the settlement.[98] Their days, therefore, as charges on the land and incorporeal hereditaments are usually numbered.

3. *Annuities*

6.135. Quite apart from settlements of land, the provision of an annuity, usually for the grantee's life, is often secured by charging it on a specific piece of land. Where an annuity is charged on land it is subject to the usual rules relating to rentcharges.[99]

4. *Indemnities*

6.136. Indemnity rentcharges are collateral rentcharges which are created independently on the sub-division of land held under a fee farm grant or lease. Usually a sub-division of such land is executed by making sub-grants or subleases and apportioning the head-rent between the sub-divided parts of the

---

[94] Para. 17.005, *post.*

[95] This is the only kind of fee farm grant created in England in modern times, see Law Com. Working Paper No. 24, *op. cit.* Also ch. 4, *ante.*

[96] *Brady* v. *Fitzgerald* (1848) 12 Ir.Eq.R. 273; *Smith* v. *Smith* (1856) 5 Ir.Ch.R. 88; *Delacherois* v. *Delacherois* (1864) 11 H.L.C. 62; *Lunham's Estate* (1871) I.R. 5 Eq. 170; *Re Maunsell's Estate* [1911] 1 I.R. 271.

[97] *Wise* v. *Wise* (1845) 2 Jo. & Lat. 403; *Weir* v. *Chamley* (1851) 1 Ir.Ch.R. 295; *Lord de Freyne* v. *I.R.C.* [1916] 2 I.R. 456; *Revenue Commrs.* v. *Malone* [1951] I.R. 269.

[98] Ch. 8, *post.*

[99] *Re Bermingham's Assignees' Estate* (1870) I.R. 4 Eq. 187; *Re Nicholson's Estate* (1875) I.R. 11 Eq. 177; *Re Matthew's Estate* (1881) 7 L.R.Ir. 269; *Switzer & Co.* v. *Rochford* [1906] 1 I.R. 399; *Hanly* v. *Carroll* [1907] 1 I.R. 166; *Hamilton* v. *Loughhead* [1918] 1 I.R. 227.

land.[1] The sub-divided parts of the head-rent are usually charged on each sub-divided part of the land and cross-indemnity agreements are entered into, indemnifying each sub-divided part of the land from payment of the remainder of the head-rent. It is essential to note that these indemnity rentcharges are collateral to the main fee farm grants or leases and do not bind the head-grantor or lessor, who is at liberty to enforce his head-rent against any part of the original land granted. The rentcharges and cross-indemnity agreements are enforceable only as between the sub-grantor or lessor and the various sub-grantees or lessees and the creation of the rentcharges is to secure the better enforcement of these agreements relating to the sub-division of the head-rent.[2]

5. Statutory

6.137. Over the years many rentcharges have been created by statute in Ireland, usually to secure repayment of money spent on public works relating to the land in question. Such rentcharges have been created in relation to drainage and improvement schemes executed under the Landed Property Improvement (Ireland) Act, 1847.[3] Similar statutory charges on land are land purchase annuities charged on land under the Land Purchase Acts.[4]

B. CREATION

6.138. Apart from statute, legal rentcharges can be created by an *inter vivos* deed or by will. In the case of an *inter vivos* deed, the rentcharge can either be expressly granted to the grantee or reserved to the grantor.[5] Since, unlike an easement,[6] the rentcharge issues out to the land granted, there was no need at common law for the grantee to execute the grant in the case of a reservation to the grantor.[7] An equitable rentcharge may be created more informally, *e.g.* by a specifically enforceable agreement for a legal charge.

6.139. A rentcharge may be created for any of the estates in land recognised by our land law system[8] and, in the case of freehold estates, the appropriate

---

[1] In parts of Northern Ireland, *e.g.*, North Antrim, it is common for such a sub-division to be made by way of assignment rather than sub-grants or sub-leases. The assignment is made subject to an apportioned rent, which is usually charged on the sub-divided part of the land in question, see *Survey of the Land Law of Northern Ireland* (1971), para. 456.

[2] For an illustration of this process in an Irish case, see *De Vesci* v. *O'Connell* [1908] A.C. 298. See also the sample title, para. 4.180, *ante*.

[3] See espec. ss. 22, 38 and 41–52. See also Improvement of Land Act, 1899. Improvement charges may arise under the Settled Land Acts, 1882–90, ch. 8, *post*.

[4] See the Republic's Land Acts, 1923, s. 9; 1931, ss. 4 and 7; 1953, s. 4 and Sched. Also Land Law (Ir.) Act, 1887, ss. 18 and 20; Purchase of Land (Ir.) Act, 1891, ss. 7, 16 and 27. Land Law (Miscellaneous Provisions) Act (N.I.), 1932, s. 2. In both parts of Ireland, land purchase annuities are burdens which affect registered land without registration, see Registration of Title Act, 1964, s. 72 (1) (*c*) (R.I.); Land Registration Act (N.I.), Sched. 5, Pt. 1, para. 3. In the Republic of Ireland, improvement and drainage charges affect registered land without registration, see Registration of Title Act, 1964, s. 72 (1) (*b*). In Northern Ireland, they are registered in the Statutory Charges Register, see Land Registration Act (N.I.), 1970, Sched. 11, para. 1.

[5] See *Hewlins* v. *Shippam* (1826) 5 B. & C. 221, espec. at 229.

[6] Para. 6.056, *ante*

[7] *Coke upon Littleton* (19th ed., 1832), 143a. In fact, legal rentcharges were usually created by uses executed by the Statute of Uses (Ir.), 1634, s. 4 of which, in such cases, conferred the advantages of a right of distress and vesting the seisin in the grantee without the need to await receipt of rent. See *Hanly* v. *Carroll* [1907] 1 I.R. 166.

[8] Ch. 4, *ante*.

words of limitation must be used.[9] Thus, in the case of an *inter vivos* deed,
failure to use the appropriate words of limitation for a fee will mean that a
rentcharge is created or transferred for life only.[10] So far as wills are concerned,
omission of the appropriate words is not disastrous, at least in the case of a
transfer of an existing rentcharge. Under section 28 of the Wills Act, 1837 (in
the Republic a provision now to be found in section 94 of the Succession Act,
1965), the whole interest in the rentcharge held by the testator passes unless a
contrary intention is shown. However, it has been held in England that section
28 is confined to the transfer of an existing interest and does not apply to the
case of creation of the interest *de novo*.[11] This does not appear to have been
challenged in Ireland, so that the rule would still seem to be that a will creating
a rentcharge for the first time must use the words of limitation appropriate for
the estate in question.[12]

C. ENFORCEMENT

There are several ways in which payment of a rentcharge can be enforced by the
rentchargor. To some extent the remedies available depend upon the terms of
the instrument creating the rentcharge and it is usual still to include express
provisions in the instrument itself. Subject to that, remedies may be implied by
the common law or statute.[13]

1. *Action for Money*

6.140. At common law, the rentchargor has an action for the money payable
under the rentcharge as a debt due to him. This remedy in fact is derived from
one of the ancient "real" actions,[14] so that it runs with, and is enforceable
against whoever owns, the land. However, there is one important limitation
and that is that it lies against the *terre tenant* only, *i.e.*, the person currently
seised of the land, namely the *freeholder in possession*.[15] Thus a leasehold
tenant cannot be sued for a rentcharge on the freehold estate, though he can, of
course, be sued where the rentcharge was created for a term of years only.[16]
However, it should be noted that the Fee Farm Rents (Ireland) Act, 1851[17]
extended all the remedies of a landlord under sections 20 and 21 of the
Renewable Leasehold Conversion Act, 1849, except the right of ejectment for

---

[9] *Ibid.*

[10] *Plunket* v. *Reilly* (1852) 2 Ir.Ch.R. 585; *Re Bennett's Estate* [1898] 1 I.R. 185.

[11] *Nichols* v. *Hawkes* (1853) 10 Hare 342. Cf. *Grant* v. *Edmondson* [1941] 1 Ch. 1. Strahan, "Covenants to Pay
Rentcharges" (1931) 47 L.Q.R. 380.

[12] Cf. s. 60 (1) of the Law of Property Act, 1925, about whose scope there are doubts, see Megarry and Wade,
Law of Real Property (5th ed., 1984), p. 823. Note the recommendation to extend the scope of s. 28 of the Wills
Act, 1837, to deal with creation as well as transfer of interests in the *Survey of the Land Law of Northern Ireland*
(1971), para. 357.

[13] Mackey, "Power of Entry to Secure Rentcharges" (1900) 17 L.Q.R. 32; Strahan, "Recovery and
Extinguishment of Rentcharges" (1911) 27 L.Q.R. 341.

[14] Booth, *Real Actions* (2nd ed., 1811); Maitland, *Forms of Action at Common Law* (eds. Chaytor and
Whittaker; 1936), p. 21. *Ahearne* v. *O'Callaghan* (1833) Hay. & Jon. 339

[15] See the discussion in *Swift* v. *Kelly* (1889) 24 L.R.Ir. 478, espec. at 481 and 485–6 (*per* Palles C.B.). Also
Sligo, Leitrim and Northern Rly. Co. v. *Whyte* (1893) 31 L.R.Ir. 316; *Odlum* v. *Thompson* (1893) 31 L.R.Ir. 394.

[16] *Re Herbage Rents* [1896] 2 Ch. 811.

[17] Held to be retrospective in *Major* v. *Barton* (1851) 2 I.C.L.R. 28.

non-payment of rent,[18] to cases of fee farm rents and other rents where the payees have no reversions.[19] This clearly seems to confer the remedy of an action for recovery of a debt in cases of perpetual rentcharges created under a fee farm grant and may extend to all rentcharges.

2. Distress

6.141. No right of distress existed at common law for enforcement of a rentcharge; indeed, this was its distinguishing feature when compared with other rents, such as a rent service.[20] Such a remedy had to be conferred expressly by the instrument creating the rentcharge,[21] until the Distress for Rent Act (Ir.), 1712 conferred a statutory right of distress in respect of all rents seck.[22] Then section 44 (2) of the Conveyancing Act, 1881, conferred on rentcharge owners, subject to a contrary intention in the instrument,[23] a right of distress as soon as the rent or any part of it is 21 days in arrear. In Northern Ireland, of course, this no longer applies since the remedy of distress has been abolished altogether and enforcement through the Enforcement of Judgments Office substituted.[24]

3. Right of Entry

6.142. Section 44 (3) of the Conveyancing Act, 1881, confers a right of entry, whereby the rentcharge owner may take possession[25] of the land charged wherever the rent is 40 days in arrear and take the income from the land until the arrears and all his costs and expenses are recovered. This right of *entry* should not be confused with a right of *re-entry*, which is often conferred expressly by the instrument creating the rentcharge.[26] A right of entry only gives a right to take possession and to receive the rents and profits of the land while in possession, *until* the debt and expenses are paid. A right of re-entry effects a *forfeiture* of the estate granted and, subject to the grantee seeking equitable relief from the court, determines the grantee's interest in the land as soon as it is exercised.[27]

4. Demise to a Trustee

6.143. Section 44 (4) of the Conveyancing Act, 1881, also confers on the

---

[18] *I.e.*, to sue for the debt and the right of distress.

[19] S. 1. See *Butler* v. *Archer* (1860) 12 I.C.L.R. 104.

[20] Para. 6.132, *supra*.

[21] *Pennefather* v. *Stephens* (1847) 11 Ir.Eq.R. 61; *Delacherois* v. *Delacherois* (1864) 11 H.L.C. 62.

[22] S. 7. *Cf.* Fee Farm Rents (Ir.) Act, 1851, Note, however, that a right of distress was conferred on grantees to uses of rentcharges under s. 4 of the Statute of Uses (Ir.), 1634.

[23] S. 44 (5). The remedies conferred by the 1881 Act are expressly excluded from the operation of the rule against perpetuities, Conveyancing Act, 1911, s. 6; Perpetuities Act (N.I.), 1966, s. 12.

[24] Judgments (Enforcement) Act (N.I.), 1969, s. 122. Para. 17.066, *post*.

[25] Without impeachment for waste, para. 4.149, *ante*.

[26] *Stevelly* v. *Murphy* (1840) 2 Ir.Eq.R. 448.

[27] See the discussion in *Brady* v. *Fitzgerald* (1847) 11 Ir.Eq.R. 55, (1848) 12 Ir.Eq.R. 273. A right of re-entry is not restricted by the rule against perpetuities in the Republic of Ireland, *Att.-Gen.* v. *Cummins* [1906] 1 I.R. 406 (see *A Casebook on Irish Land Law* (1984), p. 131); *Walsh* v. *Wightman* [1927] N.I. 1, but it is now so restricted in Northern Ireland, Perpetuities Act (N.I.), 1966, s. 13 (1) (*a*). *Cf.* a proviso for redemption of a rentcharge, *Re Tyrrell's Estate* [1907] 1 I.R. 292; *Re Donoughmore's Estate* [1911] 1 I.R. 211. Para. 5. 145, *ante*.

rentcharge owner, in the case of the rent being 40 days in arrear, the right to demise the land to a trustee for a term of years, with or without impeachment of waste, on trust to raise the money due, plus all costs and expenses, by creating a mortgage, receiving the income or otherwise.[28]

D. Extinguishment

There are two ways in which a rentcharge may be extinguished, apart from the general methods of lapse of time and merger considered in later chapters.[29]

1. *Release*

6.144. A rentcharge owner may release his rentcharge by deed. At common law, a partial release operated to release the entire land from the rentcharge,[30] but section 10 of the Law of Property Amendment Act, 1859, now provides that a release of part of the land charged bars rights to recover any part of the rentcharge out of the land released only and does not prejudice the rights of any person interested in the land remaining unreleased and not concurring in or confirming the release.[31] Thus a partial release may either release the whole land from part of the rent or release part of the land from the whole of the rent. Furthermore, if the rentcharge owner has charges on different lands, he cannot unilaterally increase the liability of one by releasing another from the rentcharge.[32]

2. *Discharge*

6.145. The landowner subject to the rentcharge may be able to obtain a discharge of his land from the rentcharge by invoking statutory provisions. Though section 45 of the Conveyancing Act, 1881, which contained specific provisions for discharge of rentcharges, expressly did not apply to Ireland,[33] there are other provisions which may be used by Irish landowners. First, so far as perpetual rentcharges created under fee farm grants are concerned, these may be redeemed under the Chief Rents Redemption (Ireland) Act, 1864[34] and probably under the Republic's Landlord and Tenant (Ground Rents) (No. 2) Act, 1978 and the Leasehold (Enlargement and Extension) Act (N.I.), 1971.[35] Secondly, the landowner can seek a sale of the land or redemption of

---

[28] *Cf.* appointment of a receiver in cases of mortgages, para. 13.048, *post.* The remedy of appointment of a receiver was conferred in England under s. 122 of the Law of Property Act, 1925, which enabled for the first time the creation of a rentcharge upon a rentcharge. In Ireland a rentcharge can still only be charged on a corporeal hereditament, *Coke upon Littleton* (19th ed., 1832), 47a; *Earl of Stafford* v. *Buckley* (1750) 2 Ves. Sen. 170 at 178; *Re The Alms Corn Charity* [1901] 2 Ch. 750 at 759.

[29] Chs. 23 and 24, *post.*

[30] *Coke upon Littleton* (19th ed., 1832), 147b and 148c.

[31] *Cf.* English Law of Property Act, 1925, s. 70.

[32] *Booth* v. *Smith* (1884) 14 Q.B.D. 318; *Price* v. *John* [1905] 1 Ch. 774.

[33] S. 45 (7). Note the various provisions for the extinguishment of rentcharges in England under the Rentcharges Act, 1977.

[34] This Act seems to have been rarely used, probably because it involves application to the court which seems to have no power to force the parties to accept its terms for redemption, see para. 4.074, *ante.*

[35] Para. 4.111, *ante.* Note that the Redemption of Rent (Ir.) Act, 1891, did *not* apply to rentcharges, *Christie* v. *Peacocke* (1892) 30 L.R.Ir. 646; *Kelly* v. *Rattey* (1893) 32 L.R.Ir. 445; *Alexander* v. *Macky* (1893) 32 L.R.Ir. 485. Para. 4.088, *ante.*

the rentcharge through an application to the Chancery Judge of the High Court of the Republic or Northern Ireland under the Landed Estates Court (Ireland) Act, 1858.[36] Alternatively, he may apply to the court under section 5 of the Conveyancing Act, 1881, to be allowed to pay into court a sum sufficient, when invested, to provide for the rentcharge and thereby obtain an order declaring the land freed from the incumbrance.[37] This section is confined to cases where the land is being sold, whether by the court or out of court.[38]

[36] See espec. ss. 58–9, 68 and 71.

[37] For Irish examples of use of this section, see *Archdale* v. *Anderson* (1888) 21 L.R.Ir. 527; *Re McGuinness's Contract* (1901) 1 N.I.J.R. 49; *Re McSwiney and Hartnett's Contract* [1921] 1 I.R. 178 (see *A Casebook on Irish Land Law* (1984), p. 371); *Re Malone* (1937) 71 I.L.T.R. 26.

[38] S. 5 (1), (2) and (4). See *Survey of the Land Law of Northern Ireland* (1971), paras, 75–6.

PART III

CO-OWNERSHIP

CHAPTER 7

CO-OWNERSHIP

I. GENERAL

7.01. In an earlier chapter we were concerned with the law relating to that part of the fragmentation of ownership of real property which concerns ownership *successively*.[1] We shall return to this subject again in a later chapter.[2] For the moment, however, we must consider another aspect of ownership of real property, namely ownership by two or more persons *concurrently*. The law relating to co-ownership is nothing like as difficult as the law relating to future interests but that is not to say that some very complicated problems do not arise in practice.[3] Indeed, these problems led the draftsmen of the English 1925 legislation to revolutionise the law of co-ownership,[4] but as yet no equivalent provisions have been enacted in either part of Ireland.[5]

II. CLASSIFICATION

7.02. There are four main categories of co-ownership recognised by our law: (1) joint tenancy; (2) tenancy in common; (3) coparcenary; (4) tenancy by the entireties. The use of the word "tenancy" in this context can be misleading. Here the word should be given one of its widest meanings, namely the holding of any estate or interest in land.[6] It is not confined to any particular kind of tenancy, whether freehold or leasehold, legal or equitable, present or future. In all these cases some form of co-ownership may exist, though there may be some problems in particular cases, as we shall see later.[7]

We shall now consider each of the four categories in more detail. The first two, joint tenancy and tenancy in common, bear a close relationship to each other and so will be considered together.

A. JOINT TENANCY AND TENANCY IN COMMON

7.03. In the case of both a joint tenancy and a tenancy in common the land held

---

[1] Ch. 5, *ante.*
[2] Ch. 8, *post.*
[3] See para. 7.12, *post.*
[4] Megarry and Wade, *The Law of Real Property* (5th ed., 1984), ch. 9; Cheshire's *Modern Law of Real Property* (13th ed., 1982), ch. VIII; Potter, "Undivided Shares in Land" (1930) 46 L.Q.R. 71.
[5] See, however, the recommendations in ch. 4 of the *Survey of the Land Law of Northern Ireland* (1971); Land Law Working Group's Discussion Document No. 2 (*Estates and Interests and Family Dealings in Land* (1981), ch. II. The latter raises the controversy arising from the House of Lords decision in *Williams and Glyn's Bank Ltd.* v. *Boland* [1981] A.C. 487.

by the persons concerned is held by them concurrently, so that as far as third parties are concerned the co-owners of the land must be treated as a single unit for the purposes of certain transactions in respect of that land. As between themselves, however, the positions of co-owners holding under a joint tenancy and those holding under a tenancy in common are quite different. This difference may be outlined as follows.

1. *Elements of a Joint Tenancy*

There are two main features which distinguish a joint tenancy from a tenancy in common. These are the so-called *right of survivorship* (*jus accrescendi*) and the *four unities*.

(i) Right of Survivorship

7.04. The central principle of a joint tenancy is that, when one joint tenant dies, his undivided share in the land passes to the surviving joint tenants.[8] As the surviving joint tenants die, their respective shares similarly pass to their survivors until ultimately one only of the original joint tenants survives and becomes thereby sole owner of the land and so free to dispose of it accordingly. It is inherent, therefore, in the nature of this right of survivorship that no joint tenant can defeat it by making a will purporting to leave his share in the land to someone other than his co-tenants.[9] We shall see later, however, that a joint tenant can make an *inter vivos* disposition of his interest in the land, though this will have the effect of ending the joint tenancy as between the purchaser and the other joint tenants.[10]

7.05. The right of survivorship sometimes gives rise to problems. For example, the common law found it difficult to deal with the position of a corporation which, according to the common law's own definition, never dies and so would always be the survivor. In medieval times, "corporation" meant any body corporate and so included what we now call companies. For this reason it became the rule at common law that a corporation could not hold land as a joint tenant and any purported conveyance to that effect operated to create a tenancy in common only. This rule, however, was reversed by the Bodies Corporate (Joint Tenancy) Act, 1899, which still applies in both parts of Ireland. Under this Act, a corporation may acquire and hold property as if it were an individual. This provision was really passed to facilitate banks and similar corporate bodies acting as trustees of property. As we shall see in a later chapter.[11] It is more convenient for trustees to hold as joint tenants because the

---

[6] See para. 2.04, *ante.*

[7] See, *e.g.*, para. 7.18, *post.*

[8] See the discussion in *Cockerill* v. *Gilliland* (1854) 6 Ir.Jur. (o.s.) 357. Also *Reilly* v. *Walsh* (1848) 11 Ir.Eq.R. 22; *Re Barrett* (1858) 8 Ir.Ch.R. 548; *Jury* v. *Jury* (1882) 9 L.R.Ir. 207.

[9] Nor can there be any succession on intestacy—the deceased tenant's estate or interest in the land is deemed to cease on his death where he is survived by another joint tenant, see Administration of Estates Act (N.I.), 1955, s. 44 (*d*) and Succession Act, 1965, s. 4 (*c*) (R.I.).

[10] Para. 7.28, *post.*

[11] Ch. 10, *post.*

right of survivorship ensures the automatic vesting of the trust property in the survivors without the need for any further conveyances.

7.06. Another problem arises in the case of *commorientes*,[12] *i.e.*, where the joint tenants all die together, *e.g.*, in a car crash, and it is impossible to determine whether any one survived the others and, if so, which one. The common law's solution to this problem was to hold that there could be no survivorship and so the heirs of the deceased joint tenants succeeded to the property as joint tenants.[13] In England this rule was reversed by the Law of Property Act, 1925, which introduced for such cases a presumption that the younger survived the elder.[14] In the Republic of Ireland, however, the Succession Act, 1965, preserves the common law rule. Section 5 of that Act provides:

> "Where, after the commencement of this Act, two or more persons have died in circumstances rendering it uncertain which of them survived the other or others, then, for the purposes of the distribution of the estate of any of them, they shall all be deemed to have died simultaneously."

No legislation at all exists on the subject of *commorientes* in Northern Ireland, so the common law position remains in force.[15]

(ii) Four Unities

7.07. The four unities, all of which must be present for a joint tenancy to exist, are the unities of—(a) possession, (b) interest, (c) title and (d) time.

(a) *Possession*

It is inherent in the nature of all forms of co-ownership that each co-owner has as much right to possession of the land held under co-ownership as all the other co-owners.[16] This rule, therefore, applies to a joint tenancy and no joint tenant is entitled to exclude his co-tenants from possession of any part of the land, or to prevent them from taking a share in the rents and profits of the land. However, there was one problem about this matter at common law. Normally if a person entitled to possession of land is excluded or deprived of possession, he has an action in trespass[17] and an action for money had and received or an account for loss of rents and profits.[18] The problem for a co-owner, however,

---

[12] See para. 14.32, *post*.

[13] *Bradshaw* v. *Toulmin* (1784) Dick. 633: "if two persons, being joint tenants, perish by one blow, the estate will remain in joint tenancy, in their respective heirs." *Per* Lord Thurlow L.C.

[14] S. 184. This presumption was, however, made expressly subject to any order of the court, see *Re Lindop* [1942] Ch. 377 and *Hickman* v. *Peacey* [1945] A.C. 304. The presumption was also modified in the case of a husband and wife, where one spouse dies intestate (the intestate is presumed to die later), Intestates' Estates Act, 1952, s. 1 (4). Finally, the old common law rule of simultaneous deaths was restored in England for the purposes of estate duty by the Finance Act, 1958, s. 29 (1), see *Re Scott* [1901] 1 K.B. 228.

[15] See the recommendations in the *Survey of the Land Law of Northern Ireland* (1971), paras. 406–7; *cf.* the Land Law Working Group's Dicussion Document No. 4 (*Conveyancing and Miscellaneous Matters*) (1983), ch. 7.

[16] Challis, *The Law of Real Property* (3rd ed.), pp. 366–7. See also *Reeves* v. *Morris* (1840) 2 Ir.L.R. 309; *Griffith* v. *Leach* (1855) 4 I.C.L.R. 621; *W.* v. *Somers* [1983] I.L.R.M. 122.

[17] See ch. 23, *post*.

[18] *Montgomery* v. *Swan* (1859) 9 Ir.Ch.R. 131.

was that he could not lay claim to possession of any particular part of the land and so could not bring such an action at common law. This problem was resolved by statute. The Administration of Justice Act (Ireland), 1707,[19] conferred on a co-owner the right of action of account against another co-owner who obtains more than his share in a case where the land or its rents and profits yield a net income.[20] If there is no net income, then the only remedy of a joint tenant excluded from possession is to compel a partition of the land, a subject we shall discuss later.[21]

(b) *Interest*

In law all the joint tenants holding a particular piece of land are regarded as a single unit for the purposes of ownership, so that each and every one of them has to join in any transaction relating to that land if it is to be fully effective.[22] This principle led the courts to hold that each joint tenant must hold the same interest in the land, from the point of view of the nature, extent and duration of the interest.[23] Thus one joint tenant may not hold a leasehold interest if another holds a freehold, nor may one hold a fee simple if another holds a fee tail, nor may one have a present interest if another has a future interest only and so on. However, unity of interest is not affected by the fact that one joint tenant has an *additional* interest in the property, *e.g.,* where all the joint tenants have life estates, but one of them has the fee simple remainder.

(c) *Title*

It was also a settled rule at common law that all the joint tenants should have acquired their interests in the land by the same title,[24] whether that source of title lay in a particular document of title or the act of another party or, indeed, the joint tenants' own acts of adverse possession.[25]

(d) *Time*

It was also the rule at common law that the interest of each joint tenant should vest at the same time. The mere fact that there was unity of title was not enough and failure to meet this fourth requirement meant that a tenancy in common was created. However, this fourth unity was not applied to conveyances to uses not to dispositions by will.[26]

---

[19] 6 Ann., c. 10. The English equivalent was the Administration of Justice Act, 1705 (4 & 5 Ann., c. 3), which was repealed by the Law of Property (Amendment) Act, 1924, Sched. 10. Under the Law of Property Act, 1925, joint tenants hold the legal estate in trust for themselves.

[20] S. 23. See *Kearney* v. *Kearney* (1861) 13 I.C.L.R. 314; *Garnett* v. *Cullen* (1863) 8 Ir.Jur. (N.S.) 154; *Montgomery* v. *Swan* (1859) 9 Ir.Ch.R. 131; *Dawson* v. *Baxter* (1886) 19 L.R.Ir. 103.

[21] Para. 7.35, *post.*

[22] Note, however, the position of proving executors, *vis-à-vis* non-proving executors, of a deceased person's estate under the Succession Act, 1965, ss. 20 and 50 (2) and the Administration of Estates Act (N.I.), 1955, s. 32 (2). See para. 16.23, *post.* It appears also that a notice to quit a periodic tenancy does not necessarily have to be served by all the joint landlords or joint tenants, see *Alford* v. *Vickery* (1842) Car. & M. 280; *Morony* v. *Morony* (1874) I.R. 8 C.L. 174; *Hamill* v. *Toomey* (1900) 34 I.L.T.R. 163. *Cf.* service on one of several joint tenants, *Pollok* v. *Kelly* (1856) 6 I.C.L.R. 367; *Biggar* v. *Pyers* (1879) 13 I.L.T.R. 127. Also ch. 17, *post.*

[23] Challis, *The Law of Real Property* (3rd ed.), p. 366.

[24] Challis, *loc. cit.* *Knox* v. *Earl of Mayo* (1858) 9 Ir.Ch.R. 192.

[25] *Cf.* adverse possession as between the joint tenants themselves, para. 23.36, *post.*

[26] Challis, *op. cit.*, p. 367. See the Irish cases of *Hickson* v. *Hill* (1857) 3 Ir.Jur. (N.S.) 165 and espec. the

2. *Elements of a Tenancy in Common*

7.08. The elements of a tenancy in common are best described in contra-distinction to those of a joint tenancy. This remark stems from the basic principle of a tenancy in common which is that each tenant in common holds an *undivided share* in the property.[27] Unlike a joint tenant, a tenant in common from the beginning of his co-ownership has a quite distinct and separate interest or share in the property. He is regarded as a co-owner only because the property has not yet been divided up into the respective shares and, until this is done, it is not possible to say which tenant in common owns which particular part of the property. This principle of undivided shares results in the two basic elements of a tenancy in common.

(i) No Right of Survivorship

7.09. A tenant in common has a distinct share in the property from the date of the commencement of the tenancy in common, so there can be no question of a right of survivorship existing in the other tenants in common.[28] That is not to say, of course, that a grantor of property may not grant in his disposition rights that are equivalent to rights of survivorship. But these rights arise from the express limitations put in the conveyance, not from the creation of a tenancy in common.[29]

(ii) One Unity

7.10. It is also settled that one of the four unities required for a joint tenancy only is required for a tenancy in common.[30] The only unity required is unity of *possession,* though the other three unities may be present in a particular case. However, it is quite permissible for tenants in common to have unequal shares and to hold different estates or interests in the property.

3. *Creation of a Joint Tenancy and Tenancy in Common*

7.11. This is a complicated subject, largely owing to the different attitudes taken by the common law, on the one hand, and equity, on the other, to these two forms of co-ownership. The result is that in considering the effect of a particular disposition one must always distinguish between the legal ownership of the property and the equitable ownership.[31] As we shall see, it will frequently be the case that the co-owners will hold the legal estate or interest in

discussion in *O'Hea* v. *Slattery* [1895] 1 I.R. 7. See also *Kenworthy* v. *Ward* (1853) 11 Hare. 196; *Ruck* v. *Barwise* (1865) 2 Dr. & Sm. 510; *Doe d. Hallen* v. *Ironmonger* (1803) 3 East 533.

[27] *Cockerill* v. *Gilliland* (1854) 6 Ir.Jur. (o.s.) 357; *Knox* v. *Earl of Mayor* (1858) 9 Ir.Ch.R. 192; *Re Robson* [1940] Ir.Jur.Rep. 72.

[28] *McCarthy* v. *Barry* (1859) 9 Ir.Ch.R. 377.

[29] *Re Barrett* (1858) 8 Ir.Ch.R. 548; *Forrester* v. *Smith* (1852) 2 Ir.Ch.R. 70. For the relevance in this context of the intricate conveyancing device of "cross-remainders" in a family settlement, see Challis, *op. cit.,* pp. 370–3. Also *Sutton* v. *Sutton* (1892) 30 L.R.Ir. 251; *Blake* v. *Blake* [1913] 1 I.R. 343. See also *Murray* v. *Murray* (1852) 3 Ir.Ch.R. 120; *Fitzgerald* v. *Fitzgerald* (1861) 12 I.C.L.R. 551; *Taaffe* v. *Conmee* (1862) 10 H.L.C. 64.

[30] Challis, *op. cit.,* p. 370. See the discussion of the rights to occupation of tenants in common *inter se* by the English Court of Appeal in *Jones* v. *Jones* [1977] 1 W.L.R. 438.

[31] See ch. 3, *ante.*

the property as joint tenants, so that the right of survivorship applies, but that that legal estate or interest is held by the joint tenants for themselves in equity as tenants in common. In this case, on the death of one co-owner his legal estate or interest passes to the surviving co-owner, but that survivor must hold the legal estate or interest in trust for the deceased co-owner's estate and it will pass according to the terms of his will or on intestacy. The legal estate or interest in the property, therefore, remains inviolate, whereas the equitable estate or interest becomes the subject of undivided shares held on trust for different people.

We must consider, therefore, the subject of creation of joint tenancies and tenancies in common both at law and in equity. And in this connection it should be noted that there is a special statutory encouragement to create a joint tenancy in the family home contained in section 14 of the Republic's Family Home Protection Act, 1976. This reads:

> "No stamp duty, land registration fee, Registry of Deeds fee or court fee shall be payable on any transaction creating a joint tenancy between spouses in respect of a family home where the home was immediately prior to such transaction owned by either spouse or by both spouses otherwise than as joint tenants."

It is not clear from the section whether it is concerned with legal or equitable "ownership" of the family home, or both, but in terms of policy the protection afforded by the right of survivorship is at its most effective if both legal and equitable ownership are held on a joint tenancy by the spouses (a common conveyancing device).

(i) At Common Law

7.12. The common law preferred a joint tenancy and so there arose a presumption at law in favour of such a tenancy whenever a conveyance to two or more persons was being construed.[32] There were several reasons for the common law's attitude.[33] Some lie in history, *e.g.*, in feudal times it was more convenient to levy feudal services on a small and decreasing number of tenants of land and this a joint tenancy only would ensure. Others are equally relevant today, *e.g.*, joint tenants hold under a single title whereas the title of each tenant in common has to be investigated by conveyancers in a transaction relating to the land held subject to the tenancy in common. With the passage of time, the land held under the tenancy in common may become extremely fragmented as each undivided share is split into more and more parts on the death of each tenant in common and his successors in title. It is quite common today for solicitors to be faced with the daunting task of tracing dozens of shares in what was once a piece of land held by two or three people only as tenants in

---

[32] *McDonnell* v. *Jebb* (1865) 16 Ir.Ch.R. 359; *Re Newsom's Trusts* (1878) 1 L.R.Ir. 373; *Jury* v. *Jury* (1882) 9 L.R.Ir. 207; *Re Wallis' Trusts* (1888) 23 L.R.Ir. 460; *Re Hoban* [1896] 1 I.R. 401; *Welland* v. *Townsend* [1910] 1 I.R. 177; *Kennedy* v. *Ryan* [1938] I.R. 620 (see *A Casebook on Irish Land Law* (1984), p. 372).
[33] See Megarry and Wade, *The Law of Real Property* (5th ed., 1984), p. 424.

common.[34] A particular problem in Ireland involves ownership of distributive shares in land when farmers die intestate.[35]

7.13. This presumption of a joint tenancy at law whenever property is conveyed to two or more people is rebuttable, even at common law. The presumption is rebutted in two main sets of circumstances: (a) lack of one or more of the four unities or (b) use of "words of severance" in the conveyance.

(a) Lack of Unities

7.14. Since all four unities are essential for a joint tenancy,[36] lack of any one of them will prevent the creation of a joint tenancy. If, however, unity of possession exists then a tenancy in common will be created, whatever the position with respect to the other three unities.[37] If there is no unity of possession, then there can be neither a joint tenancy nor a tenancy in common and separate ownership exists between the grantees in the conveyance.

(b) Words of Severance

7.15. It became the settled rule, even at common law, that any words used in the conveyance indicating that the grantees were intended to take distinct shares in the property had the effect of creating a tenancy in common instead of a joint tenancy.[38] The following expressions have been held to be words of severance: "in equal shares"[39]; "equally"[40]; "share and share alike"[41]; "to be divided between"[42]; "between"[43]; "respectively."[44] It must be remembered that this matter is largely one of construction of the particular conveyance, so that absence of such express words of severance does not mean that the court will not find evidence of an intention to create a tenancy in common from other provisions in the conveyance.[45] Thus in one Irish case involving a settlement for infants, which contained a power of advancement conferred on the trustees to benefit any one of the infants, the court held that such a power, which would necessarily have to be exercised by using the "share" of the infant to be advanced,[46] was inconsistent with a joint tenancy and so a tenancy in common was created.[47] FitzGibbon L.J. commented:

---

[34] Hence the radical changes in the law of co-ownership introduced in England by the Law of Property Act, 1925. See also *Survey of the Land Law of Northern Ireland* (1971), ch. 4.

[35] See paras. 23.40–2, *post*.

[36] Para. 7.07, *ante*.

[37] Para. 7.10, *ante*.

[38] *Fleming* v. *Fleming* (1855) 5 Ir.Ch.R. 129, espec. at 134–6 (*per* Brady L.C.).

[39] *Jury* v. *Jury* (1882) 9 L.R.Ir. 207. *Cf. Cockerill* v. *Gilliland* (1854) 6 Ir.Jur. (o.s.) 357.

[40] *Lambert* v. *Browne* (1871) I.R. 5 C.L. 218.

[41] *Clarke* v. *Bodkin* (1851) 13 Ir.Eq.R. 492; *Re Dennehy's Estate* (1865) 17 Ir.Ch.R. 97; *Mill* v. *Mill* (1877) I.R. 11 Eq. 158.

[42] *Crozier* v. *Crozier* (1843) 3 Dr. & War. 373.

[43] *Crozier* v. *Crozier*, *ibid.*; *Murray* v. *Murray* (1852) 3 Ir.Ch.R. 120.

[44] *Fleming* v. *Fleming* (1855) 5 Ir.Ch.R. 129; *Re Wallis' Trusts* (1888) 23 L.R.Ir. 460.

[45] *Bray* v. *Jennings* (1902) 36 I.L.T.R. 6; *Re Gray* (1927) 61 I.L.T.R. 65.

[46] See further on a power of advancement, para. 10.048, *post*.

[47] *L'Estrange* v. *L'Estrange* [1902] 1 I.R. 467 (see *A Casebook on Irish Land Law* (1984), p. 375). See also *Taggart* v. *Taggart* (1803) 1 Sch. & Lef. 84; *Twigg* v. *Twigg* [1933] I.R. 65.

"The incompatibility of a discretionary power of advancement with a joint tenancy is absolute, because the exercise of such a power implies the reduction of several parts of the property into possession."[48]

7.16. On the other hand, it is quite possible that the court may construe the language of a deed or will apparently containing words of severance as nevertheless evincing an intention to create a joint tenancy. And effect to this intention will be given even at law.[49]

7.17. Finally, it has been held in England that in the case of a gift to a "compound" class of beneficiaries (*e.g.,* to the testator's children in equal shares, provided that the children of a deceased child should take his parent's share), compound words of severance should be used, otherwise any substitute children taking a parent's share may take as joint tenants only.[50]

(ii) In Equity

7.18. Equity took a different approach to co-ownership from that of the common law.[51] In fact, equity adopted a contrary view: "equity leans against joint tenancies" was its maxim,[52] based upon what was considered to be a much fairer division of the ownership of property in many cases. This approach resulted in a presumption arising in certain circumstances that the settlor or testator really intended to create a tenancy in common. Equity could not, of course, directly overrule the common law,[53] so frequently today a court will accept that the parties take the property as joint tenants at law, but will insist that they hold it on trust[54] for themselves as tenants in common in equity. In this way, co-ownership nowadays often involves a split in ownership of the property, into the legal ownership on the one hand and the equitable or beneficial ownership on the other hand.

The following are the main circumstances in which the courts will hold that joint tenants in law hold for themselves as tenants in common in equity.

(a) *Purchase Money in Unequal Shares*

7.19. It has been held for many years in both England[55] and Ireland[56] that, if

---

[48] *Ibid.,* p. 469.

[49] Megarry and Wade, *The Law of Real Property* (5th ed., 1984), p. 426. See the Irish case of *Cockerill* v. *Gilliland* (1854) 6 Ir.Jur. (o.s.) 357. Also *Daly* v. *Aldworth* (1863) 15 Ir.Ch.R. 69; *Taaffe* v. *Conmee* (1862) 10 H.L.C. 64.

[50] *Re Brooke* [1953] 1 W.L.R. 439. *Cf. Re Burke* [1945] Ir.Jur.Rep. 12; *Re Froy* [1938] Ch. 566. In a case where a vague expression like "relations" is used in a will, the court may resolve the uncertainty by construing this to mean the deceased's statutory intestate successors, ch. 15, *post.* This does not mean, however, that these successors necessarily take their shares as tenants in common according to the statutory provisions—this remains a question of the intention of the testator and, if no express or implied reference to the statutory provisions can be found, the court is likely to find that the successors take as joint tenants. *Re Gansloser's Will Trusts* [1952] Ch. 30; *Re Kilvert* [1957] Ch. 388. *Cf. Re Burke, op cit.*

[51] Para. 7.11, *ante Fleming* v. *Fleming* (1855) 5 Ir.Ch.R. 129.

[52] See para. 3.059, *ante.*

[53] Para. 3.047, *ante.*

[54] For more on this use of the trust concept see ch. 9, *post.*

[55] *Lake* v. *Gibson* (1729) 1 Eq.Ca.Abr. 290; *Jackson* v. *Jackson* (1804) 9 Ves. 591; *Bull* v. *Bull* [1955] 1 Q.B. 234.

[56] *O'Connell* v. *Harrison* [1927] I.R. 330, espec. at 335–6 (*per* Kennedy C.J.) (see *A Casebook on Irish Land Law* (1984), p. 378.

the purchasers of property provide the purchase-money in *unequal* shares, they will be presumed to take the property in equity as tenants in common. Thus on the death of one co-owner, the survivor takes the whole legal interests in the property himself but he must hold part of the beneficial interest (equivalent to the beneficial share of the deceased co-owner) for the deceased's successors, testate or intestate. On the other hand, if the money was provided in *equal* shares the presumption lies the other way. However, these are presumptions only and it is always open to the court to find the other way as a matter of construction in the particular case.[57] Furthermore, there are special statutory provisions giving the courts jurisdiction to determine matters relating to property as between a husband and wife, which may add an additional dimension in such cases.[58]

(b) *Mortgage Loans*

7.20. In this case equity took the view that lenders of money on mortgage took their legal interest (though equitable mortgages only may also be created) in the property offered as security for the loan[59] as tenants in common, whether the money was lent in *equal or unequal* shares.[60] The usual form of legal mortgage of land not registered under the registration of title legislation is a conveyance of the legal estate to the mortgagee or the creation of a long term of years which is granted to the mortgagee. The reason for the presumption in this case, and again it is a rebuttable presumption only, seems to be that it is in the nature of a mortgage transaction that each lender intends to get back what he has lent. It is essentially a commercial transaction[61] and, as such, the right of survivorship annexed to a joint tenancy seems to be an inappropriate concept to apply to the parties.[62]

(c) *Partnership Property*

7.21. Just as a mortgage transaction was considered in equity to be too much of a commercial transaction for a joint tenancy to be allowed to operate, so equity presumed that land acquired by partners as part of their partnership assets should be presumed to have been acquired on the basis of a tenancy in

---

[57] *Fleming* v. *Fleming* (1855) 5 Ir.Ch.R. 129, espec. at 140–1 (*per* Brady L.C.).

[58] See Married Women's Status Act, 1957, s. 12 (R.I.); Married Women's Property Act, 1882, s. 17 (as explained by s. 3 (7) of the Law Reform (Husband and Wife) Act (N.I.), 1964. As regards s. 12 of the Republic's Married Women's Status Act, 1957, see *C* v. *C* [1976] I.R. 254; *O'D* v. *O'D* (1976) Unrep. (H.C.,R.I.) (1976 No. 77 Sp). It should also be noted that in Northern Ireland s. 17 of the Married Women's Property Act, 1882, and s. 3 of the Law Reform (Husband and Wife) Act, (N.I.), 1964, were extended by art. 55 of the Matrimonial Causes (N.I.) Order, 1978, so as to cover (a) either of the parties to a void marriage, whether or not it has been annulled; (b) either of the parties to a voidable marriage which has been annulled; ;(c) either of the parties to a marriage which has been dissolved. But an application under s. 17 (or as so extended) by a party to a marriage which has been dissolved or annulled cannot be made more than 3 years after the dissolution or annulment, and one by a party to a void marriage, which has not been annulled, cannot be made more than 3 years after the parties have ceased to live with each other in the same household. Para. 25.15, *post.*

[59] On the law of mortgages generally, see ch. 12, *post.*

[60] *Petty* v. *Styward* (1632) 1 Ch.Rep. 57; *Steeds* v. *Steeds* (1889) 22 Q.B.D. 537.

[61] See further ch. 12, *post.*

[62] Note that a "joint account" clause often inserted in a mortgage deed, which purports to make the lenders joint tenants, is intended to govern some matters only relating to the mortgage, *e.g.*, its ultimate discharge, and does not necessarily govern the relations of the mortgagees (lenders) *inter se*, para. 9.050, *post.*

common.[63] Indeed, it seems that equity nowadays would hold this to be the position in most joint undertakings or enterprises of a largely commercial or business nature—whether or not any formal partnership has been entered into by the parties concerned.[64]

(iii) Severance of a Joint Tenancy

7.22. Even at common law it was appreciated that the right of survivorship annexed to a joint tenancy could operate unfairly in some circumstances. So it was recognised that events could occur which would be regarded as "severing" the joint tenancy in the sense that the right of survivorship would be destroyed and the parties thereupon would cease to hold under a joint tenancy and would, instead, hold under a tenancy in common.[65] Severance, therefore, in this context means the conversion of a joint tenancy into a tenancy in common.[66]

7.23. As we discussed above,[67] no joint tenant can be regarded as having any distinct share in the property during the continuance of the joint tenancy, but rather a potential share dependent upon the number of his co-tenants and with prospects of growing larger if he survives them. Thus, on severance of a joint tenancy, the undivided share of each tenant in common, as the surviving joint tenants have become, is an equal share in the property commensurate with the number of co-tenants surviving at the date of severance.

7.24. A joint tenancy may be severed either at law, so as to create a tenancy in common of the legal title to the property, or in equity, so as to leave the legal title held under a joint tenancy but to have this held on trust as to the beneficial ownership under a tenancy in common. There are two main ways of bringing about a severance either at law or in equity, namely (a) by acquisition of some further interest in the property by one of the joint tenants and (b) alienation of his interest in the property by one of the joint tenants. It is apparent, then, that severance of a joint tenancy involves the destruction of one of the four unities[68] essential for such a form of co-ownership. Unity of time cannot, of course, be destroyed because otherwise no joint tenancy would have come into existence in the first place[69] capable of being severed. Further, as we shall see,[70] destruction of unity of possession has even more drastic effects on a joint tenancy than severance and conversion into a tenancy in common; it involves "partition" of the property so as to destroy co-ownership altogether.

(a) Acquisition of Another Interest

7.25. The important point to note here is that a severance will be effected by

---

[63] *Hawkins* v. *Rogers* [1951] I.R. 48; *O'Dwyer* v. *Cafolla & Co.* [1949] I.R. 210; *Meagher* v. *Meagher* [1961] I.R. 96.
[64] See *McCarthy* v. *Barry* (1859) 9 Ir.Ch.R. 377. *Cf. Reilly* v. *Walsh* (1848) 11 Ir.Eq.R. 22.
[65] See *Connolly* v. *Connolly* (1866) 17 Ir.Ch.R. 208; *Butterly* v. *McKechnie* (1902) 36 I.L.T.R. 77; *Re Armstrong* [1920] 1 I.R. 239. See also Garner, "Severance of a Joint Tenancy" (1976) 40 Conv. 77.
[66] It should not be confused with "partition," see para. 7.35, *post.*
[67] Para. 7.03, *ante.*
[68] Para. 7.07, *ante.*
[69] *Ibid.*
[70] Para. 7.37, *post.*

the acquisition of another interest in the property by one of the joint tenants only if that acquisition takes place *after* the joint tenancy has come into existence.[71] The mere fact that, at the date of the creation of the joint tenancy, one of the joint tenants was given some additional interest in the property does not prevent him holding another interest in the same property under a joint tenancy with other co-owners. At that date the four unities may be present as to that other interest. For example, land may be conveyed "to X and Y for life to hold as joint tenants, remainder to X in fee simple." In this case, X and Y would take their joint life estates despite the fact that X also has a fee simple remainder. If, however, in this example the remainder had been conveyed to Z instead of X, and X subsequently bought Z's estate, this subsequent purchase by X would sever the joint tenancy for life X held with Y. The result would be that Y would hold a half-share in the property for life as tenant in common with X, and X's other half-share for life would merge[72] with his fee simple acquired from Z. In other words, X's subsequent purchase of the fee simple destroys the unity of interest that existed between X and Y with respect to the property.

7.26. It will have been noticed that, in the above example, X acquired an estate in the land different from the estate he held as joint tenant with Y. There may occur, however, another situation, *e.g.*, a conveyance "to X, Y and Z as joint tenants in fee simple" and then a release (in effect an alienation, see below) by X of his estate to Y.[73] The effect of this is that a tenancy in common arises as between the one-third share in the property Y has acquired from X, and which he now holds as tenant in common, and the other two-thirds he still holds with Z. But that other two-thirds of the property remains subject to the joint tenancy and is held by Y and Z as joint tenants.[74]

7.27. Furthermore, one must, it seems, distinguish between a conveyance and a surrender of an interest in this context. In the case of a conveyance "to X for life, remainder to Y and Z as joint tenants in fee simple," if X conveys or transfers his estate to Y, the joint tenancy between Y and Z will be severed. If, however, X surrenders his interest to Y, this has the effect of extinguishing[75] that interest, so that the fee simple held jointly by Y and Z thereupon takes effect in possession, *but still subject to the joint tenancy.*[76]

(b) *Alienation*

7.28. The courts have long recognised that a joint tenancy will be severed if any one of the joint tenants alienates his interest in the property, or a part of his interest, by an *inter vivos* transaction.[77] The alienation had to be made *inter*

---

[71] *Connolly* v. *Connolly* (1866) 17 Ir.Ch.R. 208; *Flynn* v. *Flynn* [1930] I.R. 337.

[72] On the doctrine of merger, see ch. 24, *post.*

[73] One joint tenant may subsequently release his interest but one may not disclaim the interest *ab initio* unless the other joint tenants become parties to the disclaimer, *Re Schar* [1951] Ch. 280.

[74] Megarry and Wade, *The Law of Real Property* (5th ed., 1984), p. 433.

[75] See ch. 24, *post.*

[76] See *Coke upon Littleton* (19th ed., 1832), 183a and 192a. This seems to be another example of the form of a transaction governing substantive rights, see para. 3.060, *ante.*

[77] See cases cited in fn. 65, para. 7.22, *ante.* The statement in the text was adopted by McWilliam J. in *Byrne* v. *Byrne* (1980) Unrep. (H.C., R.I.) (1978 No. 402 Sp) (see *A Casebook on Irish Land Law* (1984), p. 376)

vivos for the courts would not allow a will to defeat the right of survivorship.[78]

7.29 No severance occurs if all the joint tenants join together in the alienation,[79] but severance may occur by involuntary alienation, *e.g.*, by the vesting of one joint tenant's property in his trustee in bankruptcy or the Official Assignee.[80] A contract to alienate has the effect of causing a severance in equity[81] until such time as the alienation at law is completed, *e.g.*, by execution of a deed of conveyance relating to land.[82]

7.30. The effect of such an alienation is similar to that of acquisition of another interest. The alienee or purchaser of one joint tenant's interest holds that interest in the property as tenant in common as to that joint tenant's share, the other total share in the property being held in common by the other joint tenants, who still hold it as joint tenants *inter se*.

7.31. A severance is also effected by a partial alienation, *i.e.*, the creation or transfer of a lesser interest in the property. However, it seems that the interest created or transferred must pass such rights in the property as are inconsistent with the right of survivorship. Thus it has been held that the creation of a life estate by a joint tenant will sever the joint tenancy,[83] as will the granting of a mortgage.[84] There has been some dispute amongst the authorities as to the effect of a lease granted by a joint tenant.[85] It seems to be settled now that, if the joint tenant of a lease for a term of years grants a sub-lease for a shorter term, this effects a severance.[86] What is, perhaps, not so clear is the position of a joint tenant in fee simple who grants a lease for a term of years. The majority view seems to be that this too effects a severance.[87] The creation of lesser interests, such as mere incumbrances, will not usually cause a severance, though the registration of a judgment mortgage against the interest of one joint tenant will sever the joint tenancy.[88] Thus it seems to be settled that a rentcharge, which grants no right of occupation of the land itself and which may be satisfied out of one joint tenant's share of the rents and profits issuing out of the land held in joint tenancy,[89] effects no severance.[90]

(c) *In Equity*

7.32. It has already been mentioned that a contract to alienate entered into

---

[78] Para. 7.04, *ante*.

[79] *Re Hayes' Estate* [1920] 1 I.R. 207, espec. at 211 (*per* O'Connor L.J.). See also *Byrne* v. *Byrne*, fn. 77, *supra*.

[80] *Morgan* v. *Marquis* (1853) 9 Exch. 145. The court may sever a joint tenancy in lunacy proceedings, *O'Connell* v. *Harrison* [1927] I.R. 330, espec. at 338 (*per* Kennedy C.J.) (see *A Casebook on Irish Land Law* (1984), p. 378).

[81] *Contra* where the contract is entered into by all the joint tenants, *Re Hayes' Estate* [1920] 1 I.R. 207; *Byrne* v. *Byrne*, fn. 77, *ante*.

[82] In such a case, all the joint tenants hold the whole legal estate in the property on trust as to the share to which one of them becomes entitled as tenant in common in equity, *Brown* v. *Raindle* (1796) 3 Ves. 256.

[83] See the discussion in Challis, *The Law of Real Property* (3rd ed.), p. 367.

[84] *York* v. *Stone* (1709) 1 Salk. 158; *Re Pollard's Estate* (1863) 3 De G.J. & S. 541.

[85] See, *e.g.*, Challis, fn. 83, *supra*.

[86] *Connolly* v. *Connolly* (1866) 17 Ir.Ch.R. 208, espec. at 223 (*per* Walsh M.R.).

[87] *Re Armstrong* [1920] 1 I.R. 239. See also *Clerk* v. *Clerk* (1694) 2 Vern. 323; *Gould* v. *Kemp* (1834) 2 My. & K. 304; *Cowper* v. *Fletcher* (1865) 6 B. & S. 464. *Cf. Harbin* v. *Loby* (1629) Noy 157.

[88] *McIlroy* v. *Edgar* (1881) 7 L.R.Ir. 521. See generally, ch. 13, *post*.

[89] Megarry and Wade, *op. cit.*, p. 431.

[90] Paras. 6.131 *et seq.*, *ante*.

by one of the joint tenants may effect a severance of the joint tenancy in equity.[91] Apart from this, there is no reason why the joint tenants together should not enter into a contract that thenceforward they should hold as tenants in common, and equity will give effect to such a contract. Indeed, the joint tenants may not even formalise their agreement to that extent. There is ample authority in Ireland to the effect that equity will infer such an agreement from the joint tenants' conduct, *e.g.*, where they seem to have treated their interests in the property as severed over a substantial period of time.[92]

(iv) Husband and Wife

7.33. At common law, a husband and wife were treated as one person for many purposes and this gave rise to a number of legal consequences. One was the creation of a separate form of co-ownership, known as a tenancy by the entireties, confined to the husband and wife situation.[93] This we shall discuss in detail later in this chapter.[94] For the moment, however, we are concerned with another consequence of the common law concept of a husband and wife constituting a single unit of ownership. This is that there seems to have arisen a rule of construction (and it is no more than that) that in a conveyance of property to a husband and wife and a third party, the husband and wife between them take one share only and the third party takes the other share.[95] This rule seems to apply whether a conveyance to the three parties was to them as joint tenants or tenants in common.[96] Thus a conveyance "to H and W and X in equal shares" was held to create a tenancy in common as to one half-share held by H and W and the other half held by X.[97] However, the English courts have gone to great lengths to avoid application of this rule to particular cases and much seems to depend upon the precise wording of the conveyance.[98] In view of the nicety of the distinctions drawn sometimes by the English courts, it is questionable how far the Irish courts would follow their decisions and the matter must remain open in the Republic of Ireland until more authoritative guidance is given by the courts.[99] In Northern Ireland the matter has become academic because the rule of construction discussed here has now been

---

[91] *Frewen* v. *Relfe* (1787) 2 Bro.C.C. 220 at 224 (*per* Lord Thurlow L.C.); *Gould* v. *Kemp* (1834) 2 My. & K. 304.

[92] *Wilson* v. *Bell* (1843) 5 Ir.Eq.R. 501; *Roche* v. *Sheridan* (1857) 2 Ir.Jur. (N.S.) 409; *Harris* v. *Harris* (1868) I.R. 3 C.L. 294; *Re Wallis' Trusts* (1888) 23 L.R.Ir. 460. See also *Coughlan* v. *Barry* (1842) 2 Leg.Rep. 195. See also the discussion of how far an intention to sever can be evinced from the conduct of the joint tenants by the English Court of Appeal in *Burgess* v. *Rawnsley* [1975] Ch. 429.

[93] Legislation in the latter half of the nineteenth and this century has gradually whittled away this common law concept, the latest of which is the Married Women's Status Act, 1957 (R.I.), and the Law Reform (Husband and Wife) Act (N.I.), 1964.

[94] Para. 7.47, *post*.

[95] See the discussion of this rule in Megarry and Wade, *The Law of Real Property* (5th ed., 1984) pp. 449–50. All the authorities cited there are English and there seems to be a paucity of Irish authority on this rule of construction. However, the English authorities are many and, at the very least, of persuasive authority on this side of the Irish Sea. See the *Survey of the Land Law of Northern Ireland* (1971), paras. 151–3.

[96] *Re Wylde's Estate* (1852) 2 De G.M. & G. 724; *Re March* (1884) 27 Ch.D. 166; *Warrington* v. *Warrington* (1842) 2 Hare 54.

[97] *Re Wylde's Estate, op. cit.*

[98] Especially the placing of the copulative word "and." See the examples given in Megarry and Wade, *op. cit.*, p. 450.

[99] See *O'Hea* v. *Slattery* [1895] 1 I.R. 7.

abrogated by article 13 of the Property (N.I.) Order, 1978 (as recommended in the *Survey of the Land Law of Northern Ireland* (1971), paragraphs 151–2). Article 13 reads:

> "A husband and wife shall, for all purposes of acquisition of any interest in property under a disposition made or coming into operation after the commencement of this Article, be treated as two persons."[99a]

4. *Determination of Joint Tenancies and Tenancies in Common*

7.34. Apart from determination of a joint tenancy by severance, which has the effect of converting it into a tenancy in common, a joint tenancy *and a tenancy in common* may be determined in other ways. These, unlike severance, involve the determination of the co-ownership of the property altogether. There are two main methods of determination: (i) partition and (ii) union in a sole tenant.

(i) Partition

7.35. First, all the co-owners may voluntarily agree to put an end to their co-ownership and to partition the property in the manner they agree.[1] By statute, such a voluntary partition by joint tenants or tenants in common must be by deed.[2] If, however, the joint tenants or tenants in common could not agree on such a partition, there was no right at common law in any one of them to force a partition on the others.[3] Such a right was first introduced by a statute passed by the Irish Parliament in 1542,[4] which enabled a joint tenant or tenant in common to force a partition of the property on the other co-owners, whether or not it was sensible or convenient to have such a partition.[5] This position was improved considerably by the passing of the Partition Acts, 1868 and 1876, both of which applied to Ireland.

7.36. These Acts gave the court power to order a sale of the property instead of physical partition, and to divide the proceeds amongst the co-owners in accordance with their shares.[6] The obvious situation where this power would be invoked would be where the co-owners had held a single item of property,

---

[99a] As regards the Republic of Ireland, note should again be taken of the statutory encouragement of creation of a joint tenancy as between spouses in the family home contained in section 14 of the Family Home Protection Act, 1976 (see para. 7.11, *ante*).

[1] *Clarke* v. *Bodkin* (1851) 13 Ir.Eq.R. 492.

[2] Real Property Act, 1845, s. 3. The repeal of this section so far as it related to the relation of landlord and tenant in Ireland, by Sched. (B) of Deasy's Act, 1860, expressly excluded from he repeal "partitions."

[3] *Cf.* the position at common law of a co-parcener, para. 7.45, *post*.

[4] 33 Hen. 8, c. 10 (Ir.). The English equivalent legislation were the statutes 31 Hen. 8, c. 1 (1539) and 32 Hen. 8, c. 32 (1540). See also the amending 1697 statutes in Ireland (9 Will. 3, c. 12) and England (8 & 9 Will. 3, c. 31). The Irish statutes have since been repealed as obsolete, see the Statute Law Revision (Ireland) Act, 1878 Statute Law Revision (Pre-Union Irish Statutes) Act, 1962 (R.I.), and Statute Law Revision Act, 1950. In *O'D.* v. *O'D.* (1983) Unrep. (H.C.,R.I.) (1983 No. 20 CA) (see *A Casebook on Irish Land Law* (1984), p. 386). Murphy J. expressed puzzlement at the repeal of the statute establishing the jurisdiction to force partition on the other co-owner. However, he proceeded to decide that case on the assumption that an inherent equitable jurisdiction to partition existed. See also *C.H.* v. *D.G.O'P.* (1978) 109 I.L.T.R. 9.

[5] *Foster* v. *Higgins* (1854) 6 Ir.Jur. (O.S.) 409; *Tottenham* v. *Molony* (1856) 2 Ir.Jur. (N.S.) 88. See also *O'Sullivan* v. *McSweeny* (1843) Dru.temp.Sug. 213; *O'Hara* v. *Strange* (1847) 11 Ir.Eq.R. 262; *Herbert* v. *Hedges* (1844) 10 Ir.Eq.R. 479; *St. Leger* v. *Ferguson* (1860) 10 Ir.Ch.R. 488; *Re Foley's Estate* (1862) 7 Ir.Jur. (N.S.) 402.

[6] *Re Hawkesworth's Estate* (1878) 1 L.R.Ir. 179; *Re Martin's Estate* (1879) 3 L.R.Ir. 255; *Re Balfour's Estate* (1887) 19 L.R.Ir. 487; *Gingles* v. *Magill* [1926] N.I. 234. See also *H.* v. *O.* [1978] I.R. 194.

such as a house or other building, which could not be easily partitioned so as to give each co-owner a viable part.[7]

(ii) Union in a Sole Tenant

7.37. It is axiomatic that co-ownership will determine once the property the subject of the co-ownership becomes vested in one only of the joint tenants or tenants in common. This may occur eventually in the case of a joint tenancy through the operation of the right of survivorship.[8] It will also occur if one of the joint tenants or tenants in common buys out the interests of the other co-owners. The method of transfer required in such a case varies according to whether the co-owners hold under a joint tenancy or tenancy in common.

7.38. A joint tenant's method of transfer is by way of *release* of his interest in the property[9] and any other purported transfer will be construed as a release.[10] This is significant for at least two reasons. First, a release, technically speaking, operates to extinguish an interest rather than to convey it, so words of limitation are not required.[11] Secondly, unlike a surrender,[12] it benefits only the party to whom it is made, so that in the case of three or more joint tenants, a release by one (A) to another (B) of his interest gives that one-third interest only to that other joint tenant (B). He (B) will remain joint tenant with the other joint tenants (C, D, etc.) in respect of the rest of the property (*i.e.*, excluding A's released share).[13] In England, a joint tenant was given the retrospective right to convey his interest to another joint tenant by an ordinary grant in 1925,[14] but there is no equivalent provision in the Republic of Ireland.[15]

7.39. A tenant in common, however, cannot release his interest in the land to his co-tenants, though he may sell or transfer it. As one learned writer put it:

"A tenancy in common, though it is an ownership only of an undivided share, is, for all practical purposes, a sole and several tenancy or ownership; and each tenant in common stands, towards his own undivided share, in the same relation that, if he were sole owner of the whole, he would bear towards the whole. And accordingly, one tenant in common

---

[7] A "good reason to the contrary" against a sale may be shown (1868 Act, s. 4), see, however, *Re Langdale's Estate* (1871) I.R. 5 Eq. 572, espec. at 575–6 (*per* Lynch J.); *Re Whitwell's Estate* (1887) 19 L.R.Ir. 45, espec. at 47–8 (*per* Monroe J.). *Cf., O'Brien & Cronin Ltd.* v. *Dillon* (1977) Unrep. (H.C.,R.I.) (1974 No. 383 Sp). In *O'D* v. *O'D, supra*, fn. 4, *supra*, Murphy J. held that the jurisdiction to order partition or a sale *in lieu* did not overreach the provisions, as to the need for the other spouse's consent to a sale, contained in the Family Home Protection Act 1976. As to the 1976 Act, see *Irish Conveyancing Law* (1978), para. 6.31 *et seq.*; Shatter, *Family Law in the Republic of Ireland* (2nd ed., 1981), ch. 15.
[8] Para. 7.04, *ante*.
[9] See Challis, *The Law of Real Property* (3rd ed.), pp. 368–9.
[10] *Eustace* v. *Scawen* (1624) Cro.Jac. 696; *Chester* v. *Willan* (1670) 2 Wms.Saund. 96. As to a disclaimer, see *Re Schar* [1951] Ch. 280.
[11] *Coke upon Littleton*, 193b.
[12] Para. 7.27, *ante*.
[13] *Coke upon Littleton*, 193a.
[14] Law of Property Act, 1925, s. 72 (4). The power of release was also preserved in the 1925 Act, see s. 36 (2).
[15] One was recommended for Northern Ireland by, the *Survey of the Land Law of Northern Ireland* (1971), Appendix B, Property Bill (N.I.), cl. 93 (3) and this recommendation was given effect to by art. 10 (3) of the Property (N.I.) Order, 1978 (see para. 3.020, fn. 64, *ante*).

must convey his share to another, by some assurance which is proper to convey an undivided hereditament; and he cannot convey by release."[16]

B. COPARCENARY

7.40. The third type of co-ownership known to our law was coparcenary, a subject which has recently been reduced greatly in importance in both parts of Ireland. At common law, coparcenary arose whenever land descended to two or more persons constituting the "heir" of the previous owner.[17] As we shall discuss in greater detail in a later chapter,[18] until recently in Ireland realty on the death of the owner intestate descended to that person's heir-at-law. Under the rules of primogeniture,[19] the heir was the deceased's eldest son (*i.e.,* a single person), but if no sons survived the deceased and the nearest relatives were females (*e.g.,* two or more daughters), then those relatives collectively constituted the heir and took the realty as coparceners. This form of descent on intestacy, however, has been abolished in both parts of Ireland, by the Administration of Estates Act (N.I.), 1955,[20] and the Succession Act, 1965 (R.I.).[21] These provisions prevent coparcenary from arising in Ireland today in the situation where it most frequently arose.[22] That does not mean that such a form of co-ownership is unlikely to arise in future, for there is one situation that can arise quite commonly, which is unaffected by those provisions.[23] Descent to an unbarred entail is still governed by the old rules for ascertainment of a person's heir,[24] and so it is still possible for coparceners to succeed to an entailed estate. For this reason, some further discussion of the nature of coparcenary is required. This is also relevant to investigation of title where the coparcenary arose before the 1955 and 1965 Acts came into force.

1. *Elements of Coparcenary*

7.41. Coparcenary is something of a hybrid form of co-ownership in the sense that it has some of the elements of a joint tenancy and some of the elements of a tenancy in common. For practical purposes, it seems to bear a greater resemblance to a tenancy in common, at least so far as relations between the coparceners themselves are concerned.[25]

(i) No Right of Survivorship

7.42. Like a tenancy in common, there is no right of survivorship attached to

---

[16] Challis, *op. cit.*, pp. 368–9. *Cf. Beauman* v. *Kinsella* (1859) 11 I.C.L.R. 249.

[17] See Challis, *op. cit.*, pp. 373–6.

[18] Ch. 15, *post.*

[19] See para. 2.19, *ante.*

[20]. S. 1 (1) and (3).

[21] Ss. 10 (1) and 11 (1).

[22] Equivalent provisions were introduced earlier in England in the Administration of Estates Act, 1925.

[23] See the 1955 Act, s. 1 (3) and the 1965 Act, s. 11 (1).

[24] Based on primogeniture, as amended by the Inheritance Act, 1833. See Leitch, *A Handbook on the Administration of Estates Act* (*N.I.*), *1955* (1956), pp. 158–62.

[25] See *Cantwell* v. *Hassard* (1857) 7 Ir.Ch.R. 370, espec. at 373–3 (*per* Napier L.C.); see also *McMurray* v. *Spicer* (1868) L.R. 5 Eq. 527 at 538–9 (*per* Malins V.-C.).

coparcenary and the interests of each coparcener passes under her will or on intestacy.[26]

(ii) Four Unities

7.43. More like a joint tenancy, however, the four unities are usually present in a case of coparcenary. Since coparcenary arises in a case of descent, governed by operation of law,[27] all the coparceners usually take the same interest by the same title at the same time. It is sometimes possible, however, for the unities of time, title and interest to be lacking. Thus if one coparcener dies intestate leaving her share to daughters, these daughters also take as coparceners, holding their mother's share in coparcenary with the surviving, original coparceners.[28] This deceased coparcener's share, however, would be split amongst her daughters, who would, therefore, take a different interest than the original coparceners, vesting at a different time and by a different title.

(iii) Undivided Shares

7.44. Each coparcener holds an undivided share in the property and in this respect is like a tenant in common. This share may be equal or unequal to the other coparcener's share, may be alienated *inter vivos* and passed by will or in intestacy.[29] However, unlike a tenant in common, a coparcener is sometimes regarded as jointly seised of the property so that, for example, like a joint tenant, a coparcener can transfer her interest in the property to another coparcener by release.[30]

2. *Determination of Coparcenary*

Coparcenary may be determined in the same ways as a joint tenancy and a tenancy in common.

(i) Partition

7.45. Like joint tenants and tenants in common, coparceners can make a voluntary partition as between themselves, which since 1845 must be by deed.[31] However, unlike joint tenants and tenants in common, one coparcener can compel a partition at common law, regardless of any statutory provisions. The reason for the common law's attitude on this point seems to have been that a coparcenary is created by operation of law, and therefore thrust upon the parties, whereas a joint tenancy or tenancy in common is created by act of parties, albeit frequently by parties other than the co-owners themselves, who

---

[26] *Re Matson* [1897] 2 Ch. 509.
[27] It should be noted that a conveyance "to the heirs of A," who turn out to be several daughters, does not create coparcenary but a joint tenancy, *Owen* v. *Gibbons* [1902] 1 Ch. 636.
[28] Challis, *op. cit.*, pp. 375–6.
[29] Challis, *op. cit.*, p. 374. On alienation by one coparcener, her share is held under a tenancy in common, the other coparceners still holding as such *inter se*, *Coke upon Littleton*, 175a.
[30] *Coke upon Littleton*, 9b and 200b. For the position of coparceners in relation to statutory provisions covering co-owners, see *Re Greenwood's Trusts* (1884) 27 Ch.D. 359.
[31] Para. 7.35, *ante.*

may have had no say in the matter.[32]

(ii) Union in a Sole Tenant

7.46. As in the case of a joint tenancy and tenancy in common, this has the effect of destroying the essential nature of the co-ownership. As mentioned above, a coparcener may achieve such a union by a release[33] of her interest, as a joint tenant can.[34]

C. TENANCY BY ENTIRETIES

7.47. A tenancy by entireties was a form of co-ownership confined to cases of husbands and wives. In essence it was a form of joint tenancy to which the common law ascribed some special characteristics based on its attitude to the relationship of unity between husband and wife.[35] The law on this subject was, however, substantially altered by the Married Women's Property Act, 1882, and so the following discussion will deal with both the pre-1883 position and the post-1883 position.

1. *Elements of Tenancy by Entireties at Common Law*

7.48. The basic rule at common law was that a conveyance of land to a husband and wife, which would create a joint tenancy if they were two single persons, would instead operate to create a tenancy by entireties as between the husband and wife.[36] This remained the position in all cases where a joint tenancy would be created if the husband and wife were unmarried, even where the property was conveyed to them expressly as joint tenants.[37] However, the tenancy by entireties existed only as between the husband and wife. If the conveyance included some additional parties, these third parties took as joint tenants in the normal way and the husband and wife held as joint tenants *vis-à-vis* these other parties.[38] A tenancy by entireties arose only if the husband and wife were married at the date of the conveyance; a conveyance to two single persons as joint tenants was not altered in effect by their subsequent marriage so as to create a tenancy by entireties.[39] On the other hand, a tenancy by entireties was converted into a joint tenancy if the husband and wife were divorced.[40]

The following are the main elements of a tenancy by entireties.

(i) Complete Unity

7.49. It was stated in an Irish case that the husband and wife were seised "per

---

[32] See *Doe d. Crosthwaite* v. *Dixon* (1836) 5 Ad. & E. 834; also *Ballard* v. *Ballard* (1556) 2 Dy. 128a. Challis, *op. cit.*, p. 375.

[33] Para. 7.44, *ante*.

[34] Para. 7.38, *ante*.

[35] *Cf.* the rule of construction discussed at para. 7.33, *ante*. See Challis, *The Law of Real Property* (3rd ed.), pp. 376–9.

[36] *Re Tyrell* [1894] 1 I.R. 267, espec. at 271–2 (*per* Chatterton V.-C.); *Kennedy* v. *Ryan* [1938] I.R. 620 at 625 (*per* Gavan Duffy J.) (see *A Casebook on Irish Land Law* (1984), p. 372.

[37] *Pollok* v. *Kelly* (1856) 6 I.C.L.R. 367, espec. at 373 (*per* Monahan C.J.).

[38] *Back* v. *Andrew* (1690) 2 Vern. 120.

[39] *Symond's Case* (1568) Moo.K.B. 92; *Ward* v. *Walthewe* (1607) Yelv. 101.

[40] *Thornley* v. *Thornley* [1893] 2 Ch. 229.

tout" but not "per my" to the extent that the survivor took the property because
he or she was entitled to it by virtue of the original limitation rather than as the
result of any right of survivorship.[41] The result of this principle was that the
husband and wife were regarded as one single unit of ownership (in those days
the husband being the one[42]), so that no concept of a joint estate, or estate
divided or shared, could arise.

(ii) Unseverable

7.50. As a result of the basic concept of unity, a tenancy by entireties, unlike
a joint tenancy, was unseverable at common law. Neither husband nor wife
could dispose of any interest in the property unless the other joined in the
disposition.[43]

(iii) No Undivided Shares

7.51. Again unlike joint tenants, the husband and wife were not regarded at
common law as having any undivided share in the property. Thus there could
be no division in the rents and profits and in an Irish case it was held that the
husband was entitled to the whole of the interest or income produced by the
property during the spouses' joint lives.[44]

2. Married Women's Property Act, 1882

7.52. The generally accepted view of this Act is that it prevented the creation
of any new tenancy by entireties after 1882.[45] The concept of the wife's separate
estate, freely disposable by her on her own and reinforced by the 1882 Act, is
taken to have resulted in conveyances to husbands and wives creating joint
tenancies rather than tenancies by entireties. This certainly was held to be the
situation in *Kennedy* v. *Ryan,*[46] where no doubts about the point seem to have
been raised.

D. PARTY WALLS

7.53. The subject of party structures often gives rise to disputes concerning
co-ownership. To the extent that it does so, it does not, however, involve any
new form of co-ownership but rather involves the use of the concepts already
discussed. The word "structure" is used here because, of course, the problems
may involve a wide variety of structures on the boundary between two
properties, some of which may not be described very appropriately as a "wall."
As was explained in an Irish case, there is no precise definition of a "party wall" in

---

[41] *Re Tyrell* [1894] 1 I.R. 267 at 271 (*per* Chatterton V.-C.). See Challis, *op. cit.,* p. 377.
[42] See ch. 25, *post.*
[43] *Crofton* v. *Bunbury* (1853) 2 Ir.Ch.R. 465, espec. at 472 (*per* Smith M.R.). It seems that this may not have
been so in the case of a term of years held by entireties, see Challis, *op. cit.,* p. 377.
[44] *Re Tyrell* [1894] 1 I.R. 267.
[45] See ss. 1 and 5. Also *cf.* Challis, *The Law of Real Property* (3rd ed.), pp. 378–9, and *Thornley* v. *Thornley*
[1893] 2 Ch. 229. Palley, "Husbands, Wives and Creditors" (1969) 20 N.I.L.Q. 132, espec. at 139. Also see
further on the 1882 Act, para. 25.12, *post.*
[46] [1938] I.R. 620, espec. at 625 (*per* Gavan Duffy J.) (see *A Casebook on Irish Land Law* (1984), p. 372).

our law.[47] Indeed, it may even be the case that the "party wall" does not stand exactly straight and may lean out of the perpendicular.[48]

7.54. Party walls on the boundary line between two separately owned properties may fall into several categories, only some of which concern us in this chapter. Thus the wall may be owned by one only of the owners of the adjoining properties[49] or the ownership may be divided along its length, so that each neighbour owns his own slice.[50] Even if the wall itself is the subect of single ownership,[51] that owner's neighbour may have an easement in respect of it for its maintenance or repair or for support from it.[52] What we are concerned with for the moment, however, is where such a party wall is held to be subject to some form of co-ownership. On this matter there is a considerable amount of case law in both Ireland[53] and England.[54]

7.55. The general rule at common law is that, in the case of a party wall, there is a presumption that the adjoining property owners are tenants in common of the party wall.[55] It must be emphasised that this is a presumption only, which usually arises where there is evidence that both adjoining owners exercised rights over it. The presumption has been held to be rebutted, however, in the following circumstances, with the consequence that no co-ownership was held to exist: (a) the wall was built entirely on one adjoining owner's land and was held to be his[56]; (b) the wall straddled the boundary line, so that half was on each adjoining owner's land, and a half was held to belong to each of them.[57]

7.56. If the party wall is held to be subject to a tenancy in common, neither tenant in common may pull it down[58] nor prevent the other from enjoying rights over it.[59] However, either tenant in common can insist upon a partition of the wall,[60] though it is doubtful if a sale under the Partition Acts[61] would be an appropriate alternative in these cases.

7.57. It may also be noted that some statutory provisions may be relevant, e.g.,

[47] See the discussion in *Kempston* v. *Butler* (1861) 12 I.C.L.R. 516, espec. at 526 (*per* Christian J.). As to a "party gutter," see *Miley* v. *Hutchinson* [1940] Ir.Jur.Rep. 37.
[48] See the *Survey of the Land Law of Northern Ireland* (1971), para. 154.
[49] *Hanly* v. *Shannon* (1834) Hay. & Jon. 645.
[50] *Matts* v. *Hawkins* (1813) 5 Taunt. 20.
[51] *Hanly* v. *Shannon, op. cit.*
[52] See ch. 6, *ante*. Also *Hanly* v. *Shannon, op. cit.*; *Toole* v. *Macken* (1855) 7 Ir.Jur. (o.s.) 385.
[53] See discussion in *Kempston* v. *Butler* (1861) 12 I.C.L.R. 516 and *Jones* v. *Read* (1876) I.R. 10 C.L. 315 (see *A Casebook on Irish Land Law* (1984), p. 390). Also *Ingram* v. *Mooney*, (1871) I.R. 5 C.L. 357; *Crossin* v. *Hugland* (1897) 31 I.L.T. 418; *Miley* v. *Hutchinson* [1940] Ir.Jur.Rep. 37.
[54] See Megarry and Wade, *The Law of Real Property* (5th ed., 1984), pp. 462–4. The matter is now governed to a large extent in England by legislation, namely the Law of Property Act, 1925, s. 38 and 1st Sched., Pt. v, para. 1.
[55] Frequently because the boundary line was unclear or in dispute, or the site of the wall was clearly held in common.
[56] *Hutchinson* v. *Mains* (1832) Alc. & Nap. 155; *Barry* v. *Dowling* (1968) Unrep.(R.I.) (Kenny J.).
[57] *Kempston* v. *Butler* (1861) 12 I.C.L.R. 516 at 526 (*per* Christian J.). Palles C.B. remarked that in such a case "as a matter of law, the property in the wall followed the property in the land upon which it stood." *Jones* v. *Read* (1876) I.R. 10 C.L. 315, 320 (see *A Casebook on Irish Land Law* (1984), p. 390).
[58] *Jones* v. *Read, op. cit.* There may be an exception to this rule if the pulling down is part of a rebuilding or repairing operation. *Cubitt* v. *Porter* (1828) 8 B. & C. 257; *Jolliffe* v. *Woodhouse* (1894) 38 Sol.Jo. 578.
[59] *Stedman* v. *Smith* (1857) 8 El. & Bl. 1.
[60] *Mayfair Property Co.* v. *Johnston* [1894] 1 Ch. 508.
[61] Para. 7.36, *ante*.

the Boundaries Act (Ireland), 1721,[62] which is still in force in the Republic of
Ireland, though it is rarely invoked nowadays. This was passed to encourage
the building and maintaining of fences, ditches, trenches, banks or walls
between adjoining lands.[63] It enables one owner to build such a fence or wall on
a boundary line, in respect of which there has been no dispute for three years,
and to charge half the cost to his adjoining neighbour, if his neighbour refuses
to join him in sharing the cost from the beginning.[64] The cost is recoverable as a
debt owed and there are various provisions governing the position of landlords
and tenants.[65]

7.58. There may also be local legislation which is relevant. Thus, by the
Dublin Corporation Act, 1890,[66] a local Act, provision is made for the repair of
what the Act calls "party structures." This expression is not defined but
certainly includes party walls and probably boundary walls. It also contains
provisions giving an owner the right to enter on the property of an adjoining
owner to carry out repairs and other works. The operation of the Act was
limited to the municipal boundaries of Dublin but, by an Order made in 1933, it
was extended to all areas added to the City. Under the Act, a person who
wishes to execute any work to a party structure is called "the building owner"
and the owner of the adjoining premises is called "the adjoining owner" and
these terms are used when describing the effect of the Act.

7.59. A building owner is given the right to make good or repair any party
structure which is defective or out of repair and a right to pull down and rebuild
any party structure which is so defective as to make it necessary or desirable to
pull it down. He is also given the right to pull down any party structure which is
of insufficient strength for any building intended to be built, and to rebuild the
same of sufficient strength for this purpose. He is also given the right to cut
away or take down any parts of any wall or building which overhangs his ground
in order to erect an upright wall.

7.60. Before exercising any of these rights, the building owner must give
three months' notice to the adjoining owner of his intention to do the work. If,
within 14 days after service of the notice, the adjoining owner does not give his
consent, he is deemed to have dissented to the work and then a difference is
deemed to have arisen between them. When this happens, the matter is
referred to the arbitration of a mutually agreed arbitrator or to the arbitration
of three arbitrators, one appointed by each party and the third appointed by the
two arbitrators. When they have made their award, the building owner with
workmen may enter on the premises of the adjoining owner for the purposes of
carrying out the work approved by the award of the arbitrators, and any person
who obstructs the workmen is guilty of a criminal offence.

---

[62] 8 Geo. 1, c. 5 (Ir.). It was repealed as obsolete or unnecessary in Northern Ireland by the Property (N.I.)
Order, 1978, article 16 (2) and Schedule 2.
[63] To some extent these provisions were superseded by subsequent legislation relating to public works in
Ireland, see e.g., the Landed Property Improvement (Ireland) Acts, 1847, 1849 and 1866.
[64] Ss. 1 and 8.
[65] E.g., ss. 3–5 and 9–12.
[66] 53 and 54 Vict., c. 246.

7.61. There are elaborate rules for the apportionment between the building owner and the adjoining owner of the expenses of doing the work. The guiding principle of these rules is that the building owner and the adjoining owner are liable "in due proportion regard being had to the use that each owner makes of such structure."

7.62. It is possible that similar provisions are in force in other cities and towns in Ireland but discovery will involve examination of all local Acts passed before 1921 and regrettably there is no index to them after 1907. Few owners have made use of the provisions of the 1890 Act and there is not one reported case on the sections of that Act or on the meaning of the highly ambiguous expression "party structure."

PART IV

SETTLEMENTS, TRUSTS AND POWERS

CHAPTER 8

SETTLEMENTS

I. INTRODUCTION

A. SETTLING FAMILY PROPERTY

8.001 In chapter 7 we considered the law applicable where property owners hold their estates and interests in land concurrently. In this and the following three chapters we return to a topic met in an earlier chapter (chapter 5) which discussed "Future Interests." There we were concerned with the situation where land was held successively and we saw that our law has a series of rules which determine the validity of successive estates and interests in land and, indeed, in other property.[1] Successive ownership is also our concern in this and the next two chapters, though in this context we are more concerned with the devices used by conveyancers to create successive ownership of property and with the rights and duties of the successive owners, on the basis that their estates or interests are valid.

8.002. It is often said that the present topic primarily relates to "family" interests in property as opposed to "commercial" interests, such as those created under leases[2] or mortages.[3] This is a fairly accurate generalisation, though it must always be borne in mind that it is only a generalisation.[4] The point being emphasised by such statements is that conveyancing devices such as a strict settlement of land or a trust of any kind of property are most commonly used to provide for successive family interests in the property concerned. In this sense the word "settlement" may have a wide meaning covering any disposition of any kind of property in favour of successive owners. Thus it may include a marriage settlement *inter vivos,* whereby a husband makes a settlement of his land on the occasion of his marriage, or a will, whereby the testator leaves all his property, real and personal, to trustees to be held for the benefit of various members of his family. This wide meaning of the word "settlement" should be distinguished from a narrowed meaning, which is, perhaps, by tradition the more common usage of the word and the sense in which it is used in the chapter heading. The narrower meaning of the word relates to what has come to be called a strict settlement of land. As we shall see,

---

[1] See para. 5.035, *ante.*
[2] See ch. 17, *post.*
[3] See ch. 12, *post.* See the discussion of the English 1925 legislation from this point of view in the *Survey of the Land Law of Northern Ireland* (1971), ch. 2.
[4] Thus many trusts are created for public rather than private family purposes, see para. 9.004, *post.*

this device usually does not involve the use of any trust, at least not in the original disposition of the land[5] and, unlike the trust concept, it is confined to land. The third device, discussed in chapter 11, a power, is also commonly used in the sphere of family settlements, where one kind of power, a power of appointment, can be particularly useful for achieving the settlor's purposes.[6]

8.003. As we shall see, the areas of law covered by this and the next three chapters have been subject to many changes over the centuries. Sometimes the changes have been caused by the different social and economic demands of the era, at other times brought about by legislation. Frequently, of course, the one source of change has influenced the other, and it is not always clear whether the legislation has merely reflected changed social and economic circumstances or induced further change itself. In law, it is worth noting two particularly significant sources of change. The first is one we have discussed before,[7] namely the general policy of our law, as defined by the judges and recognised by the legislatures, that land should be capable of being freely dealt with. Implementation of this policy means that a limit has to be put on the power of current landowners to determine the succession to their land far into the future. The second influence, which has grown in importance in the twentieth century, is taxation. Nowadays a property owner is not just concerned with settling his property so as to benefit his family. He is also concerned to see that it is settled in such a way that both he and his family reduce the amount of taxation leviable on that property. Indeed, as we have seen,[8] this has been long recognised as a legitimate desire on the part of landowners to which their conveyancers may seek to give the fullest effect. Such, however, is the complexity and severity of our modern taxation system that considerable skill and expertise is needed if a settlement, in its widest sense, is to achieve, and keep on achieving, its taxation avoidance function. The introduction of the concepts of a capital transfer, or acquisition, tax (to replace estate duty) have put a premium on this expertise.[9]

B. HISTORICAL BACKGROUND

1. *Strict Settlements*

8.004. A strict settlement of land was the traditional method at common law of keeping land within the family.[10] It acquired considerable popularity among

---

[5] This qualification is explained later, see para. 8.004 *et seq., post.* The fact, however, that a trust may arise subsequently is one reason for treating these topics together in the introduction to this chapter. Another is that the definition of a settlement in the Settled Land Act, 1882, includes land standing in trust for persons by way of succession, para. 8.020, *post.*

[6] See para. 11.06, *post.*

[7] See ch. 5, *ante.*

[8] *E.g.*, in respect of "uses" of land, see para. 3.008, *ante.*

[9] *Re Dunbar-Buller* [1923] 2 I.R. 143; *Re Magan* [1922] 2 I.R. 208; *Allan* v. *C.I.R.* [1925] N.I. 50; *Re O'Connor's Estate* [1931] I.R. 98; *Re Lord Cloncurry's Estate* [1932] I.R. 687; *Re Stoughton* [1941] I.R. 166; *Re Cullinan* [1941] I.R. 289; *Revenue Commrs.* v. *Matthews* (1958) 92 I.L.T.R. 44; *Revenue Commrs.* v. *Malone* [1951] I.R. 269; *Revenue Commrs.* v. *Jermyn* [1958] I.R. 301; *A.B.K.* v. *MacShamhrain* [1958] I.R. 288; *Re Knox* [1963] I.R. 263. See Harvey, "Tax Avoidance—Illegal, Immoral or Fattening?" (1970) 21 N.I.L.Q. 235. See Bale and Condon, *Capital Acquisitions Tax.*

[10] See generally Professor Harvey's monograph, *Settlements of Land* (1973). See also the excellent essays on the subject in Part A of *Law, Economy and Society* (Eds. Rubin and Sugarman, 1984).

the landed gentry in the British Isles for several centuries and only in recent decades has its popularity declined. In the days before the growth of stocks and shares, and the modern stock market, the primary source of wealth in the community was land. Those families who were fortunate enough to acquire substantial interests in land were, therefore, anxious to see that the land, and thereby their wealth, stayed within the family. Land also carried with it other advantages. Until the mid-nineteenth century, ownership of land was a pre-requisite to having the parliamentary vote.[11] In addition, land ownership was essential if one was to maintain one's standing in the community and secure titles and honours and other benefits of political power.[12]

8.005. The key to a strict settlement was the use by conveyancers of limited freehold estates, *i.e.*, the fee tail and life estate.[13] Thus a simple, but common, form of strict settlement would be a will made by a landowner leaving his property to his eldest son for life, with remainder to that son's eldest son in fee tail.[14] Other members of the family could have special provision made for them. The landowner's widow, if she survived him, could be given an annuity, usually called a jointure. This could be secured by charging it on the land and providing for it to be paid out of the rents and profits of the land.[15] Other children and grandchildren of the landowners could also be provided for. The usual method was to give them what were called portions, *i.e.*, capital sums designed to set them up in life and usually payable on special dates, such as reaching the age of majority or on marriage.[16] These portions were usually raised by mortgaging the land which thereby became subject to mortgage charges.[17] Jointures and portions, however, were largely incidental to the estates in the land held by the favoured successors to the settlor. Yet because of the nature of the estates granted, these successors were in a difficult position at common law. Let us consider the example given above and take first the position of the landowner's eldest son.

8.006. The vitally important point here is that the landowner has left his eldest son with a life estate only in the land. At common law that estate was practically useless as a commercial asset. Few people would be prepared to pay a substantial sum of money to purchase such an estate, because it might end the

---

[11] See para. 4.168, *ante*.

[12] See Harvey, *op. cit.*, ch. 1; Webb, *Modern England* (1973), ch. 1.

[13] See ch. 4, *ante*.

[14] As we shall see, this could tie up succession to the land for many decades, but because the remainder was in fee tail, there was no infringement of the rule against perpetuities, see para. 5.141, *ante*.

[15] See *Fyan* v. *Henry* (1840) 2 Dr. & Wal. 556; *Re Molton* (1852) 2 I.C.L.R. 634. See also *Sullivan* v. *Sullivan* (1844) 7 Ir.Eq.R. 453; *Re Lane's Trusts* (1863) 14 Ir.Ch.R. 523; *Baldwin* v. *Roche* (1842) 5 Ir.Eq.R. 110; *Battersby* v. *Rochfort* (1847) 10 Ir.Eq.R. 439; *Re St. George's Estate* (1863) 14 Ir.Ch.R. 447; *Bannatyne* v. *Ferguson* [1896] 1 I.R. 149; *Re West's Estate* [1898] 1 I.R. 75; *Gilfoyle* v. *Wood-Martin* [1921] 1 I.R. 105; *Gage* v. *Burke* (1946) 80 I.L.T.R. 29. On the subject of rentcharges, see ch. 6, *ante*.

[16] *Leech* v. *Leech* (1842) 2 Dr. & War. 568; *Adams* v. *Adams*(1858) 8 Ir.Ch.R. 41; *Simpson* v. *Frew* (1856) 5 Ir.Ch.R. 517; *Londonderry* v. *Londonderry* (1854) 4 Ir.Ch.R. 361; *L'Estrange* v. *Winniett* [1911] 1 I.R. 62; *Re Beresford's Settlement* [1914] 1 I.R. 222. For the relevance of the doctrine of satisfaction in this context, see para. 3.117, *ante*.

[17] *Re Norcott's Estate* (1863) 14 Ir.Ch.R. 315. *Cf. Re Aylward's Estate* (1862) 13 Ir.Ch.R. 472. See also *Mandeville* v. *Roe* (1844) 7 Ir.Eq.R. 253; *Re Jones's Estate* (1853) 2 Ir.Ch.R. 544; *Wakefield* v. *Richardson* (1883) 13 L.R.Ir. 17, aff'd. *sub nom. Wakefield* v. *Maffett* (1884) 15 L.R.Ir. 218; *Re Leader's Estate* (1885) 17 L.R.Ir. 279; *Cobden* v. *Bagwell* (1886) 19 L.R.Ir. 150; *Re Whitcroft* [1934] I.R. 649.

next day with the sudden death of the vendor. Other commercial dealings were similarly hindered. No lease granted by the life owner was effective after his death and his estate was too precarious to be sufficent security for a mortgage.[18] Thus it was often impossible for the life owner to raise money from the land to pay for improvements and repairs to the property on the land or to the land itself. Some life owners might have private means but many were reluctant to spend their personal fortunes on land which, on their death, would pass to other members of the family according to the terms of the settlement and not as the life owners might decree, if they had been full owners and able to dispose of the land as they wished. Furthermore, the law of waste often restricted exploitation of natural assets which might exist on the land, *e.g.,* minerals or timber.[19] In short, then, so far as the life owner's position was concerned, at common law the land was withheld from the commercial property market, which offended one of the general policies of our law, and proper management and development was severely restricted, which, of course, harmed the family as a whole, socially and economically, and in the end the general economy of the country.

8.007. Let us now turn to the position of the eldest son's eldest son, who was left a remainder in fee tail. So long as his father was alive, the son was rarely better off. First, he had no right to possession of the land, and at most his fee tail was vested in interest only.[20] No doubt this was of value in that a fee tail could be barred so that a fee simple could be transferred, at least since the fifteenth or sixteenth century.[21] But there were several difficulties here. The entail could not be barred at all until the eldest son (the settlor's grandson) reached the age of majority. Even when he reached this age, so long as his father was alive and in possession of the land, the son could not bar the entail entirely on his own. If he tried to do that, he created a base fee only.[22] His father was the protector of the settlement and his consent would be needed to make the barring of the entail effective. This was where family interests played an important role. The father would in most cases be reluctant to give his consent since this might result in the land passing out of the hands of the family altogether, quite apart from any inconvenience it might cause the father himself. So it was always more likely that some compromise would be worked out which would protect the family property and still give the son some more immediate share in the property. What usually happened was that the father and son agreed to bar the entail, but on the basis that they would together resettle the land so as to keep it in the family. As part of the resettlement, the son might be given an immediate annuity on the land or, if he preferred, a lump sum portion raised by mortgage. The resettlement usually took the form of a conveyance to the father for his life, remainder to his eldest son for life,

---

[18] Though the purchaser could try to insure the vendor's life.

[19] To some extent it depended upon whether the tenant for life was made unimpeachable for waste, see generally para. 4.119, *ante.*

[20] See para. 5.008, *ante.*

[21] See para. 4.117, *ante.*

[22] *Bank of Ireland* v. *Domvile* [1956] I.R. 37 (See *A Casebook on Irish Land Law* (1984), p. 178); *Allen* v. *Allen* (1842) 2 Dr. & War. 307. Para. 4.121, *ante.*

remainder to that son's eldest son in tail.[23] The father's position, therefore, remained unchanged but his son's position was even more restricted, because now he had a life estate only, like his father. The fee tail estate had been pushed back for another generation, and no doubt the same sort of compromise was likely to occur in each generation. The result was that this process of settlement and resettlement might tie up the succession to the land from generation to generation. And with each generation's succession the land's condition deteriorated further and much of the potential wealth of the community was confined to a few, often impoverished, landowners. No doubt some enlightened settlors anticipated the problems and made a point of giving their successors express powers of dealing with the land, but these were a small minority.

8.008. In such a situation it was inevitable that Parliament would have to intervene and the nineteenth century saw the passing of much legislation on the subject. Some wealthy landowners in Britain managed to secure private Acts of Parliament, but more general legislation began to appear in Ireland during the eighteenth century and continued into the following century. This took the form of granting limited owners of settled land specific powers of dealing with the land, though in certain respects only.[24] Thus powers to grant mining leases were given by the Mines Act (Ireland), 1723.[25] Powers were given to grant leases of land for places of worship by the Leasing Powers for Religious Worship (Ir.) Acts, 1855 and 1875, and for schools by the Leases for Schools (Ir.) Acts, 1810 and 1881. Similar statutory powers were given in respect of bog reclamation,[26] linen[27] and cotton manufacture[28] and tree planting.[29] The next major step resulted from the economic slump in the first half of the nineteenth century, especially the distressed state of Ireland after the Napoleonic Wars. Many landowners were on the verge of bankruptcy, but because of their limited estates they were incapable of doing much about it. The Parliament at Westminster then passed special legislation for Ireland to try to deal with the situation. The principal Act was the Incumbered Estates (Ireland) Act, 1849, which established an Incumbered Estates Court, consisting of three Commissioners.[30] Their primary function was to supervise the sale of incumbered property so as to pass an absolute title to the purchaser. The proceeds of sale were then used to pay off any incumbrancers or creditors with claims against the previous owner, and any surplus was given to that owner, or was to be held on trust for benefit of those previously interested in the settled

---

[23] See *McCausland* v. *Young* [1949] N.I. 49. Also *Londonderry* v. *Londonderry* (1854) 4 Ir.Ch.R. 361; *Re Domvile and Callwell's Contract* [1908] 1 I.R. 475; *Gaussen and French* v. *Ellis* [1930] I.R. 116.

[24] See para. 1.59, *ante*.

[25] As extended and amended by the Mining Leases Act (Ir.), 1749, and the Mines (Ir.) Act, 1806.

[26] Bog Reclamation Act (Ir.), 1771.

[27] Leasing Powers for Promoting Linen Manufacture Act (Ir.), 1787.

[28] Leases for Cotton Manufacture Act (Ir.), 1800.

[29] Landlord and Tenant (Planting of Trees) Act (Ir.), 1788; *Kirkpatrick* v. *Naper* (1945) 79 I.L.T.R. 49 (see *A Casebook on Irish Land Law* (1984), p. 225).

[30] See para. 1.42, *ante*. See also the Incumbered Estates (Ir.) Acts, 1848, 1852, 1853, 1855 and 1856. *Ex parte Kennedy* (1849) 11 Ir.Eq.R. 171; *Re Wrixon's Estate* (1850) 2 Ir.Jur.(o.s.) 167; *Re Goold's Estate* (1850) 3 Ir.Jur.(o.s.) 181; (1857) 2 Ir.Jur.(n.s.) 387; *O'Donnell* v. *Ryan* (1854) 4 I.C.L.R. 44; *Errington* v. *Rorke* (1859) 7 H.L.C. 617; *Blake* v. *Jenning* (1861) 12 I.C.L.R. 458.

land. In 1858 the Incumbered Estates Court was replaced by the Landed Estates Court with jurisdiction over all estates in Ireland,[31] and the latter became part of the Chancery Division of the High Court under the Judicature (Ireland) Act, 1877.[32] In some respects this legislation brought relief to limited owners, but frequently at a considerable cost to their families. They could apply to the court to have the land sold and a Landed Estates Court conveyance was effective to pass the full title to the purchaser,[33] all previous estates and interests in the land being transferred to the purchase money.[34] But the prevailing economic conditions, and the developing land war,[35] meant that many estates were sold for a mere fraction of what would have been their true value in a reasonably stable property market. Many of the landowners, however, were of British descent and were only too ready to sell up and get out, even if this meant the break up, and sale in portions, of an estate that had been in the family for generations. Yet so chaotic were economic conditions at the time that hundreds of estates were left in the hands of the Court without any prospective purchasers. This problem had to be dealt with later under the Land Purchase legislation.[36]

8.009. Meanwhile, at Westminster, further legislation was being passed to provide for relief of limited owners on that side of the Irish Sea. But like most of the Westminster property legislation of the period it was applied also to Ireland. The first step was the passing of Drainage Acts,[37] which enabled limited owners, with the consent of the Chancery Court, to carry out drainage improvements and charge the cost to the land. These Acts were followed by further measures enabling limited owners to make various improvements to the land, usually by creating rentcharges on the land.[38] Thus the erection and improvement of mansion houses on settled estates was encouraged by the Limited Owners Residences Acts, 1870 and 1871.[39] However, these Acts were

---

[31] Landed Estates Court (Ir.) Act, 1858. See also the Landed Estates Court (Ir.) Acts, 1861 and 1866. See Madden, *Landed Estates Court Act* (1870). *Re Earl of Limerick's Estate* (1861) 7 Ir.Jur.(N.S.) 65; *Re Burmester's Estate* (1862) 14 Ir.Ch.R. 48. Also *Re Pell's Estate* (1860) 6 Ir.Jur.(N.S.) 88; *Re Comyn's Estate* (1861) 11 Ir.Ch.R. 330; *Re Denny's Estate* (1874) I.R. 8 Eq. 427.

[32] S. 7.

[33] *Re Walsh's Estate* (1867) I.R. 1 Eq. 399; *Re Tottenham's Estate* (1869) I.R. 3 Eq. 528; *Sexton* v. *McGrath* (1872) I.R. 6 Eq. 381; *Re Browne's Estate* [1913] 1 I.R. 165; *Re Jackson's Estate* [1922] 1 I.R. 73. The court could, however, sell the land subject to certain incumbrances, including tenancies, see *Lauder* v. *Alley* (1867) I.R. 1 C.L. 82; *Hamilton* v. *Musgrove* (1871) I.R. 6 C.L. 129; *Re Ram's Estate* (1871) I.R. 5 Eq. 503; *Cusack* v. *Hudson* (1880) 6 L.R.Ir. 309; *Oliver* v. *Rooney* [1895] 2 I.R. 660.

[34] *Re Goold's Estate* (1857) 2 Ir.Jur.(N.S.) 387; *Re Knox's Estate* (1858) 3 Ir.Jur.(N.S.) 202; *Re Cuthbert's Estate* (1869) I.R. 4 Eq. 562.

[35] See para. 1.41, *ante*.

[36] *E.g.*, under the Land Law (Ir.) Act, 1896, s. 40, the Land Judge, where three-quarters of tenants on such an estate agreed to purchase the estate, was given power to declare that the remainder were also to be purchasers, so as to dispose of the entire estate. See para. 1.53, *ante*. See also *Re Slack's Estate* [1896] 1 I.R. 191; *Re Owen's Trustees' Estate (No. 1)* [1897] 1 I.R. 200; *Re Wemy's Estate* [1897] 1 I.R. 540; *Re Harkness' Estate (No. 2)* [1898] 2 I.R. 391; *Re Banbury's Estate* [1901] 1 I.R. 248; *Re Stanley's Estates* (1910) 44 I.L.T.R. 18.

[37] *E.g.*, the Acts of 1840 and 1845. See also the Drainage (Ir.) Acts, 1842, 1846 and 1847, and the Landed Property Improvement (Ir.) Acts, 1847, 1849, 1852, 1860 and 1866. *Ex p. Studdert* (1856) 6 Ir.Ch.R. 53; *Re De Salis' Estate* (1869) I.R. 4 Eq. 448; *Re Casey's Estate* (1878) 1 L.R.Ir. 481.

[38] The Settled Land (Ir.) Act, 1847, which does not seem to have had an English equivalent, authorised improvement of settled land by trustees, again with the permission of the Chancery Court. See also the Improvement of Land (Ir.) Act, 1850, and the Improvement of Land Act, 1864.

[39] See also the Limited Owners Reservoirs and Water Supply Further Facilities Act, 1877.

of minor significance when viewed in the light of the more fundamental changes introduced by the Settled Estates Acts,[40] which applied to both England and Ireland. The basic principle of these Acts was that a limited owner could engage in various dealings with the land, including sales, exchanges and leases,[41] *provided* the consent of the court was obtained to the particular transaction. Having to get the consent of the court was an obvious drawback to this scheme in that it involved the limited owner in the time and trouble of an application to the court, which would usually require the agreement of other persons interested in the land before giving its consent to the transaction.[42] The other major drawback to the scheme was that a settlor could contract out of the legislation altogether and thereby defeat its object of giving limited owners special powers of dealing with the settled land.[43]

8.010. These defects in the Settled Estates Acts were later remedied by the Settled Land Acts, 1882–90, which, though they did not, in fact, repeal the Settled Estates Act, 1877,[44] largely replaced it. These Settled Land Acts[45] still today govern the position of a limited owner of land in both parts of Ireland. We shall discuss their provisions in detail later in this chapter, but first we turn to the other major method of settling land, and indeed other property, the trust.

2. *Trusts*

8.011. In an earlier chapter we discussed the development of the trust concept.[46] We saw there how the modern trust grew out of the early concept of uses, which related to land only, so that from the seventeenth century onwards the trust came to be recognised by conveyancers as a useful device for settling any kind of property on successive owners.[47] In the sphere of land it was an obvious alternative to a strict settlement and, as we shall see, quite apart from its wider application to property other than land, it has proved to be an infinitely more flexible device, even taking into account the changes introduced for strict settlements by the Settled Land Acts.

---

[40] Various Acts were passed in the years 1856, 1858, 1864, 1874 and 1876, and then replaced by one major Act, the Settled Estates Act, 1877.

[41] *Re Walsh's Trusts* (1881) 7 L.R.Ir. 554. Strict limits were laid down as to the length of leases which could be granted and there were sometimes special provisions for Ireland. Thus the Settled Estates Act, 1877, s. 4, limited agricultural or occupational leases of 21 years for England, but to 35 years for Ireland. Indeed, under the Act leases up to 21 years (35 years in Ireland) could be granted without the court's consent, though the settlor could prohibit this.

[42] *Ex parte Puxley* (1868) I.R. 2 Eq. 237; *Re Boyd's Settled Estates* (1874) I.R. 8 Eq. 76. The court could dispense with such agreement in certain cases, see the Settled Estates Act, 1877, ss. 26–9.

[43] Settled Estates Act, 1887, s. 38.

[44] Most of the provisions of this Act remain in force in both the Republic of Ireland and Northen Ireland.

[45] They were repealed and replaced in England by the Settled Land Act, 1925. Though the 1925 Act introduced several fundamental changes in the law, it is fair to say that its scheme was largely based on the nineteenth-century system. See Harvey, *Settlements of Land* (1973) and *Survey of the Land Law of Northern Ireland* (1971), ch. 3.

[46] Ch. 3, *ante.* See generally Kiely, *The Principles of Equity as Applied in Ireland* (1936), espec. chs. iii-viii; Keeton and Sheridan, *The Law of Trusts* (9th ed., 1968, with Irish Supp.) (later editions do not have the Irish supplement); Carswell, *The Trustee Acts (Northern Ireland)* (1964). Also chs. 9 and 10, *post.*

[47] Ames, "The Origin of Uses and Trusts" (1908) 21 H.L.R. 261; Hart, "What is a Trust?" (1899) 15 L.Q.R. 294; Maitland, "The Origin of Uses" (1894) 8 H.L.R. 127; Nussbaum, "Sociological and Comparative Aspects of the Trust" (1938) 38 Col.L.Rev. 409; Ryan, "Reception of the Trust" (1961) 10 I.C.L.Q. 265; St. Amond,

8.012. The basic features[48] of a trust are as follows: property, which may be realty or personalty, is transferred by the owner, the settlor or testator, to trustees who are under an obligation to hold the legal title in the property for and on behalf of the beneficiaries designated or for specified purposes. Each of these features is examined in detail later in the next chapter[49] and for the moment we will concentrate on a couple of them. First, it may be noted that, like a strict settlement of land, a trust has as one of its primary functions the determination of the future ownership of property. In particular, in the context of this book, it can provide for the succession to land.[50] Thus, to take the example of a strict settlement given earlier,[51] a landowner could achieve largely the same purpose by leaving his land to X and Y as trustees for his eldest son for life, with remainder on trust for that son's eldest son in fee tail. The essential practical difference is this: whereas in the case of a strict settlement the land is transferred directly to the donees so as to give them the legal ownership in succession, in the case of a trust the entire legal ownership remains intact and is transferred to the trustees, while the donees remain beneficiaries with an equitable title only to the property. At first sight the substantive difference may not appear great, especially when one remembers the duties of trustees[52] and the basic principle that they may not profit from the trust,[53] but from the conveyancing point of view the distinction is fundamental. In the case of a strict settlement the legal title to the property is fragmented in succession, which results in the various hindrances to dealing with the property discussed above.[54] Apart from the question of commercial dealings, the day to day management of the land falls squarely on the current holder of the estate in possession, however limited that estate may be. In the case of a trust, however, the legal title is not fragmented in succession, it is fragmented only in the sense that it may be subject to co-ownership, *i.e.,* the trustees' joint tenancy.[55] But together those co-owners, the trustees, were, prior to the Settled Land legislation, free to deal with the property only because they held the full legal title—in most cases the fee simple absolute in land.[56] The fact that the beneficial or equitable ownership was fragmented was generally irrelevant because, unlike most strict settlements in the early days, settlors of trusts gave the trustees wide powers of dealing with the trust property. Indeed, one common form of trust was what was known as a trust for sale.[57] Here the trustees were put under an obligation to sell the property, invest the proceeds of sale and hold that invested fund on the same trusts as applied to the land or

"Practical Trust Administration" (1954) 56 J.I.B.I. 222; Strathdene, "*Sambach* v. *Dalston*: An Unnoticed Report" (1958) 74 L.Q.R. 550; Vannoman, "Trusts: Restated and Rewritten" (1936) 34 Mich.L.Rev. 1109.

[48] The question of a precise definition has often proved difficult, see the textbooks listed in fn. 46, *supra*. Also ch. 9, *post.*

[49] Ch. 9, *post.*

[50] Thus trusts of land come within a settlement under the Settled Land Acts, 1882–90, para. 8.020, *post.*

[51] See para. 8.005, *ante.*

[52] See Ch. 10, *post.*

[53] Paras. 10.068 *et seq., post.*

[54] Paras. 8.006–7, *ante.*

[55] See chs. 7, *ante,* and 10, *post.*

[56] Nowadays, however, they are subject to the provisions of the Settled Land Acts, 1882–90, which fetter the powers of certain trustees of land, see para. 8.043, *post.*

[57] Note that under the doctrine of conversion the beneficiary's interest is in personalty, para. 3.100, *ante.*

on such further trusts as might have been declared by the settlor. This process whereby the trustees were free to sell the property over the heads of the beneficiaries,[58] so as to give a purchaser a clear legal title to it, with the beneficiaries' interests thereafter attaching to the fund representing the proceeds of sale, was called "overreaching." It was to become a vital feature of our conveyancing system and, as we shall see, was the key factor in the scheme introduced for strict settlements of land by the Settled Land Acts.[59]

8.013. It is clear from this brief description of a trust for sale that such a trust, in so far as it purported to create a settlement of land, had a purpose quite different from a strict settlement. Indeed, it had the opposite purpose. A strict settlement was designed to keep the land within the family whereas a trust for sale of land was designed to ensure that the land was sold out of the family at some date. In a sense, such a trust anticipated the reaction of Parliament to strict settlements. It regarded the land as simply a commercial asset which could, indeed should, be changed into different forms in order to maximise the investment worth of the fund it represented. It was this essential flexibility which explained the growing popularity of trusts in the nineteenth century, when the industrial growth of the country and the development of our modern financial stock market resulted in family fortunes no longer being tied to the land. A device capable of handling all kinds of property was needed and the trust met all the requirements. As the complexity of the family funds grew, so the need for skill in management grew and here the trust also had an advantage. The settlor was free to choose skilled persons as his trustees and leave everything to them. The beneficiaries could enjoy the fruits of the trustees' work without having to assume any of the burdens of management. Here there was a clear contrast with the position of members of the family owning property under a strict settlement.

8.014. So far we have concentrated on the subject of a trust for sale of land, because of the sharp contrast to a strict settlement it presents, but it must be emphasised that this is only one type of trust.[60] There is nothing to stop a settlor creating instead, for example, what might be called a "holding" trust. In other words, no *obligation* to sell the trust property is put on the trustees, so that in this sense the function of the trust bears closer resemblance to that of a strict settlement. The most that the trust may do is to give the trustees a *power* to sell, which they may or may not decide to exercise. But it must be remembered that there is still a trust in existence, so that it differs from a strict settlement in the fundamental respects already mentioned. However, because of such a trust's close affinity to a strict settlement it was brought within the provisions of the Settled Land Acts and so trustees of such a trust nowadays are controlled by that legislation with respect to their powers.

8.015. This example of a holding trust with a power to sell given to the trustees leads us to the third conveyancing device relevant to family

---

[58] Though a settlor might include in his trust provisions for consents or consultation.
[59] Along with the concept of a trust, see para. 8.041, *post.*
[60] The classification of trusts is discussed in general, ch. 9, *post.*

settlements, which is discussed in chapter 11—a power.[61] Such a trust, like most trusts, consists of elements of obligations, which are a prerequisite of a trust, and of powers, which are given to the trustees to enable them to carry out their obligations as effectively as possible. The distinction is this: a trust is obligatory in that, once they have agreed to become trustees, the trustees are obliged to carry it out strictly according to its terms; a power, however, is not obligatory but discretionary only and trustees are usually given a large number of powers under the terms of their trust. How and when, and even if, the trustees exercise their powers is largely a matter for them. The distinguishing feature of a trust for sale, discussed above, is that what is usually only a power, i.e. the power to sell, is turned into an obligation and thereby becomes part of the duties of the trustees.[62]

3. Powers

8.016. To a large extent powers are incidental to the conveyancing devices of strict settlements and trusts.[63] Unlike them, a power in itself confers no interest in property on the donee or objects of the power. Of course the instrument conferring the power may also grant the donee an interest in property, which may or may not be the property to which the power relates. For example, a testator could leave his property to X for life, with remainder to such of his children as X shall appoint. Here X has both a life estate in the property and a power of appointment amongst certain objects, namely his children. As we shall see,[64] this is what is known as a power *in gross, i.e.,* one whose exercise will not affect the interest in property given to the donee. The power may be even more independent than that, in that the donee may be given no interest at all in the property, *e.g.,* a testator simply leaves his property to those of X's children as X appoints.[65] On the other hand, the donee may have a much more direct interest in the exercise of the power, which in this case is known as a power *appendant* or *appurtenant.* For example, if a testator leaves his land to X for life, and expressly confers on him powers to grant leases of the land, exercise of such a power will affect X's enjoyment of his own life interest. The lessee will be entitled to possession of the land according to the terms of the lease, which possession would otherwise be enjoyed by X as life owner. In other words, but for the donee's exercise of his power, his rights to the land would have remained undisturbed.

8.017. This last example indicates that one of the major sources of powers today is a settlement, or a trust, hence our discussion of the subject in the

---

[61] See generally, Farwell, *Treatise on Powers* (3rd ed., 1916); Sugden, *Treatise on Powers* (8th ed., 1861).

[62] Note the operation of the doctrine of conversion in this context, para. 3.100, *ante.* See *Re Whitty's Trust* (1875) I.R. 9 Eq. 41; *Batteste* v. *Maunsell* (1876) I.R. 10 Eq. 314; *McGwire* v. *McGwire* [1900] 1 I.R. 200; *Re O'Connor* [1923] 1 I.R. 142; *Orr* v. *Alexander* [1925] N.I. 104; *Re Tyndall's Estate* [1941] Ir.Jur.Rep. 51.

[63] See discussion in *Bandon* v. *Moreland* [1910] 1 I.R. 220. For further definition of powers, see ch. 11, *post.* Also see Fleming, "Hybrid Powers" (1948) 13 Conv. 20; Hughes, "Classification of Powers of Appointment" (1962) 26 Conv. 25; Marshall, "Trusts and Powers" (1957) 35 C.B.R. 1060; Unwin, "Power or Trust Power" (1962) 26 Conv. 92.

[64] Ch. 11, *post.*

[65] This is known as a power *collateral. Re Dunne's Trusts* (1879) 5 L.R.Ir. 76.

present chapter. Indeed, as we shall see, much of the legislation in Ireland relating to settlements and trusts has as one of its primary functions the conferring of a wide range of statutory powers on certain persons connected with settlements and trusts. Apart from powers connected with such conveyancing instruments, it is also quite common today to have powers created on their own. Thus one common power is a power of attorney whereby one person authorises another to act for him in certain matters, perhaps even to handle his affairs generally, during a period when that person himself is incapable of doing so (due to illness or absence abroad) or does not wish to do so (perhaps for some personal or family reason).[66] From this it is clear that, like trusts, powers can relate to all kinds of property.

Having considered the background to the three property institutions of settlements, trusts and powers, it is time to consider each in more detail. The first is dealt with in the rest of this chapter and the other two are discussed in the following chapters.

II. STRICT SETTLEMENTS

A. GENERAL

8.018. As we have already explained,[67] in both parts of Ireland today strict settlements are governed by the Settled Land Acts, 1882–90. We saw that these Acts were passed primarily in order to give limited owners of land special statutory powers of dealing with the land. As Lord Halsbury put it, when referring to the Settled Land Act, 1882:

> "[W]hat the statute intended to do was to release the land from the fetters of the settlement—to render it a marketable article notwithstanding the settlement."[68]

The Acts did this by giving the limited owner greater powers of dealing with the land than he would otherwise have had as limited owner at common law. The Acts went so far as to give the limited owner the ultimate power to sell the full ownership of the land, the fee simple (or other estate the subject of the settlement), to a purchaser, who would take the title freed entirely of the various interests created by the settlement, whether or not he had notice of them, though not free from interests arising under earlier settlements.[69] It is, therefore, important to determine precisely what land comes within the Acts and what persons can exercise the various powers created by the Acts.

1. *Settled Land*

8.019. Section 2 (3) of the Settled Land Act, 1882, provides the following definition—

---

[66] See ch. 11, *post. O'Connor* v. *Bernard* (1842) 4 Ir.Eq.R. 689: *Langford* v. *Mahoney* (1843) 5 Ir.Eq.R. 569.
[67] Para. 8.010, *supra.*
[68] *Bruce* v. *Ailesbury* [1892] A.C. 356 at 361.
[69] In this respect the Settled Land Acts create a major exception to the general doctrine of notice, see para. 3.069, *ante.*

"Land, and any estate or interest therein, which is the subject of a settlement, is for the purposes of this Act settled land, and is, in relation to the settlement, referred to in this Act as the settled land."

"Land" is defined[70] as including incorporeal hereditaments,[71] and an undivided share in land, *i.e.,* the interest of one of several tenants in common.[72] The key, however, to what is settled land within the above definition is the reference to a "settlement."

2. *Settlement*

8.020. Section 2 (1) of the 1882 Act provides this definition—

"Any deed, will, agreement for a settlement, or other agreement, covenant to surrender, copy of court roll, Act of Parliament, or other instrument, or any number of instruments, whether made or passed before or after, or partly before and partly after, the commencement of this Act, under or by virtue of which instrument or instruments *any land, or any estate or interest in land, stands for the time being limited to or in trust*[73] *for any persons by way of succession,* creates . . . a settlement. . . ." (Italics added.)

Thus any document creating a succession of interests in land is a settlement.[74] The first point to emphasise about this provision is that it applies both to the case of a *strict settlement,* where the land is conveyed directly to persons in succession for legal estates or interests, and *holding trusts,*[75] where the land is conveyed to trustees who hold the legal estate, but on trust for persons in succession who have equitable estates or interests only. Indeed, as we shall discuss in a moment,[76] the 1882 Act had inserted in it a later section[77] bringing within its general provisions *trusts for sale,* despite the obvious distinction in purpose between such trusts, on the one hand, and strict settlements and holding trusts, on the other hand.[78]

8.021. The Settled Land Acts, therefore, apply to the following situations: (1) an *inter vivos* conveyance of land "to X for life, remainder to Y in fee simple"; (2) a devise "unto and to the use of A and B and their heirs on trust for X for life, remainder on trust for Y in fee simple"; (3) a gift by will of a house held under a lease "to my wife Joan for her life and after her death or remarriage to my son John." So long as there is an element of "succession" to the land in each case, there is settled land within the Acts. A succession

---

[70] S. 2 (10) (i).
[71] See ch. 6, *ante.*
[72] See ch. 7, *ante.*
[73] Note the extension of this to cover trusts for sale by s. 63 of the 1882 Act, which was amended by s. 7 of the 1884 Act, see para. 8.043, *post.*
[74] In this sense the word "settlement" in the 1882 Act relates to the document creating the succession of interests rather than the succession itself.
[75] See para. 8.014, *supra.*
[76] Para. 8.043, *post.*
[77] S. 63.
[78] See para. 8.014, *supra.*

obviously arises whenever any limited freehold estate is granted, whether directly or by way of trust,[79] *i.e.,* the various estates in tail and for life discussed in a previous chapter.[80] The element of succession may arise indirectly in the sense that a reversion will always lie in the grantor of a single, limited estate only, *e.g.,* a simple *inter vivos* conveyance by A "to B for life." Such a conveyance leaves the fee simple reversion in A and so the conveyance creates a succession of estates, albeit indirectly.[81] Further guidance on this subject is given by the 1882 Act's definition of a "tenant for life" for the purpose of conferring the powers of dealing with the land on certain persons.[82] From section 58 (1) we see that a settlement exists in the following cases of a strict settlement or conveyance on trust:

(i) a conveyance in tail, including unbarrable entails[83];

(ii) a conveyance in fee simple subject to an executory limitation, gift or disposition over[84];

(iii) a conveyance creating a base fee[85];

(iv) a conveyance of a life estate, an estate *pur autre vie*[85] or for a term of years determinable on life;

(v) a conveyance resulting in a tenancy in tail after possibility of issue extinct,[87] or a tenancy by the curtesy[88];

(vi) a trust providing for income from land to be paid to a person for life or until sale of the land or forfeiture of his interest in the land on that person's bankruptcy or any other event.

8.022. This list, based on the provisions of the 1882 Act relating to persons having the powers of a tenant for life given by the Act, is neither unambiguous nor exhaustive. For example, with reference to category (ii) above, what is the position with respect to a determinable fee[89] and a fee simple subject to a condition subsequent?[90] Such estates are clearly caught if they are subject to a

---

[79] Subject to the special case of trusts for sale, para. 8.043, *post.*

[80] Ch. 4, *ante*

[81] *Re Bective Estate* (1891) 27 L.R.Ir. 364. Further, s. 2 (2) of the 1882 Act provides: "An estate or interest in remainder or reversion not disposed of by a settlement, and reverting to the settlor or descending to the testator's heir, is for the purposes of this Act an estate or interest coming to the settlor or heir under or by virtue of the settlement, and comprised in the subject of the settlement." On this subsection, see *Re Hunter and Hewlett's Contract* [1907] 1 Ch. 46.

[82] We discuss the general position of the person so designated later, see paras. 8.057 *et seq., post.*

[83] S. 58 (1) (i) excluded unbarrable entails in respect of land bought out of money provided by Parliament in consideration of public services by the tenant in tail. See para. 4.141, *ante.* It is doubtful if any such entails existed in respect of Irish land.

[84] This category, perhaps, gives rise to the most difficulty, see para. 8.022, *infra.*

[85] Para. 4.136, *ante.*

[86] This includes the Irish variations, leases for lives renewable for ever and leases for lives and years, see paras. 4.167 *et seq., ante,* both of which create freehold estates and which are not caught by the exception in s. 58 (1) (iv) of tenants for the life of another "not holding merely under a lease at a rent." See *Batt* v. *Close* (1848) 12 Ir.L.R. 529.

[87] See para. 4.140, *ante.*

[88] Note that such a tenancy can no longer come into existence in either part of Ireland, though some may survive to this day, see para. 4.157, *ante.* The 1884 Act resolved a doubt which arose over the fact that a husband's tenancy by the curtesy took effect by operation of law on his wife's death, rather than under a settlement. S. 8 of the latter Act declared that the estate of a tenant by the curtesy "is to be deemed an estate arising under a settlement made by his wife." No such provision was made in respect of a wife's right of dower, though it was later in England, see Settled Land Act, 1925, s. 1 (3).

[89] See para. 4.046, *ante.*

[90] See para. 4.048, *ante.*

limitation over, *e.g.*, a devise "unto and to the use of A in fee simple so long as the parish church of Dungloe stands, then to the use of B in fee simple."[91] In so far as B is entitled to any future interest in the land, there is clearly a succession and the land is settled land within the Acts. However, what if a determinable fee stands on its own, with the only element of "succession" being the automatic operation at law of a possibility of reverter[92] to the grantor? On the one hand, one could argue that this ought to be regarded as creating a settlement just as an automatic fee simple reversion in the grantor of a life estate will be so regarded. On the other hand, a possibility of reverter is not an estate or interest in land like a reversion[93] and it may be questioned whether there is any need to apply the Settled Land Acts to someone who has such a fee simple, albeit a modified one. Looked at from the point of view of the purpose of the legislation, it is doubtful if the owner of a determinable fee needs the special powers given to limited owners by the Settled Land Acts, since in most cases his interest will be secure enough in the eyes of the property market to be freely marketable.[94] This argument, of course, has double force in Northern Ireland now that the Perpetuities Act (N.I.), 1966, causes the determinable fee to become absolute after the perpetuity period passes without a reverter having occurred.[95]

8.023. Then there is the question of what is the position with respect to a fee simple subject to a condition subsequent. Once again, even where the element of succession that exists lies only in the right of entry for condition broken reserved to the grantor of the fee simple, it could be argued that this is sufficient to attract the Settled Land Acts. Some have taken the view that this was the case under the 1882–90 Acts,[96] and the English Settled Land Act, 1925, brought both determinable fees[97] and, apparently, fees subject to a condition[98] within its provisions. However, once again it may be questioned whether the owner of such a fee simple estate should be subject to the provisions of the Settled Land Acts, if he wishes to deal with the property, or whether his estate lacks commercial viability, so that he needs the powers granted by the Acts.[99] And again the question is reinforced in Northern Ireland since the Perpetuities Act (N.I.), 1966, provides that the grantor's right of entry for condition broken

---

[91] Note, however, the operation of the rule against perpetuities on such a devise under the Perpetuities Act (N.I.), 1966, para. 5.109, *ante*.

[92] See para. 4.046, *ante*.

[93] Para. 4.051, *ante*.

[94] This was the view of the Q.U.B. Land Law Working Party, see *Survey of the Land Law of Northern Ireland* (1971), para. 28; *cf.* the Land Law Working Group's Discussion Document No. 2 (*Estates and Interests and Family Dealings in Land*) (1981), ch. 3, which also discusses the not uncommon conveyance of land subject to a power of revocation by the grantor (*ibid.*, para. 3.8). See also Glover, *Registration of Ownership of Land in Ireland* (1933), p. 338.

[95] S. 13 (3) (*a*). See para. 5.109, *ante*.

[96] *E.g.*, Megarry and Wade, *The Law of Real Property* (5th ed., 1984), p. 345.

[97] S. 1 (1) (ii) (*c*).

[98] S. 117 (1) (iv) defies "determinable fee" (used in s. 1 (1) (ii) (*c*) as "a fee determinable whether by limitation or condition." This is rather misleading terminology in view of the basis of the distinction between the two kinds of modified fee, see para. 4.049, *ante*.

[99] The Q.U.B. Working Party took the safe view as they did on the question of determinable fees and recommended the exclusion from the settled land scheme of fees simple subject to a condition, standing on their own; *cf.* the views of the Land Law Working Group. See fn. 94, para. 8.022, *supra*.

ceases to be exercisable after the perpetuity period.[1]

8.024. A similar point arises with respect to another kind of conveyance which is so common in Ireland, namely, a fee farm grant.[2] Although the grantor always has reserved to him in such a grant a whole series of rights connected with the fee farm rent and under several covenants and conditions, including in most cases a right of forfeiture or ejectment,[3] it seems clear that such grants do not come within the Settled Land Acts. Certainly the whole history of Irish land law negates any suggestion that the grantee of land under a fee farm grant lacks any power to deal commercially with his estate. Furthermore, Irish practitioners do not invoke in such dealings the Settled Land Acts' powers, unless, of course, the grantee's fee simple has *subsequently* been settled by him in succession. Even the English 1925 draftsmen realised the dangers of extending the settlements scheme too far and had to ask Parliament to pass a special amending provision[4] to prevent the Settled Land Act, 1925 catching the rentcharge fee farm grants which are common in some parts of the North-West and West of England.[5]

8.025. The question has sometimes arisen as to the position when a settlement appears to come to an end, in that the land no longer is subject to a succession of estates, but is still subject to some family charges, *e.g.,* portions charges.[6] The matter is of obvious importance since, as is always the case whenever the question of whether there is a settlement arises, on it will depend the procedure to be followed by the current holder of the land in selling it and in engaging in other dealings. The point arose in the Irish case of *Re Blake's Settled Estates,*[7] where land came into the hands of a tenant in tail who disentailed. The land up to that point had been subject to a marriage settlement, under which portions charges existed. By disentailing the tenant in tail became holder of the fee simple, subject only to those charges. One of the questions the Republic's Supreme Court had to decide was whether the land in those circumstances was still subject to a settlement. It decided that land held in fee simple and subject only to portions charges was not settled land.[8] Thus on a sale of the

---

[1] S. 13 (1) (a). See para. 5.110, *ante.*

[2] See generally, ch. 4, *ante.*

[3] See para. 4.065, *ante.*

[4] In fact the Schedule to the Law of Property (Amendment) Act, 1926, introduced this amendment by adding a clause to the Law of Property Act, 1925, s. 7 (1), so as to extend the definition of a fee simple *absolute* to cover a fee simple "subject to a legal or equitable right of entry or re-entry." Unfortunately, this amendment is so widely drawn that it seems to apply to all fees simple subject to a condition subsequent, which, it seems, were intended to come within the Settled Land Act, 1925. See Megarry and Wade, *The Law of Real Property* (5th ed., 1984), pp. 127–8 and 345–8.

[5] See para. 4.057, *ante.*

[6] Para. 8.005, *ante.* And see *Re Shine* [1964] I.R. 32.

[7] [1932] I.R. 637 (see *A Casebook on Irish Land Law* (1984), p. 406). See also *Re Domvile and Callwell's Contract* [1908] 1 I.R. 475; *Re Collis's Estate* [1911] 1 I.R. 267.

[8] "It appears to us that the cases which have already been decided do not involve a principle that the mere existence of a portions charge under a settlement which is otherwise spent is enough to create a limitation of lands to or in trust for persons in succession." Per Murnaghan J., *op. cit.,* pp. 647–8. See also the pre-1926 English authorities, *Re Mundy and Roper's Contract* [1899] 1 Ch. 275; *Re Trafford's Settled Estates* [1915] 1 Ch. 9. The Settled Land Act, 1925, s. 1 (1) (v), reversed this position by bringing within its scheme land subject only to family charges. However, this brought much land within the legislative scheme which was previously outside it and caused inconvenience to pre-1926 purchasers of the land, who had secured an indemnity against the charges. The Law of Property (Amendment) Act, 1926, s. 1 was passed to deal with this problem and enabled such purchasers

land such charges would not be overreached, and the owners of the charges had to join in the conveyance.[9]

8.026. The draftsmen of the Settled Land Act, 1882, took the opportunity to deal with one case where, strictly speaking, there is no succession to land, but there was a problem about its commerciability. This is the case where land is granted to an infant.[10] It is still the position in Ireland[11] that an infant can hold an estate in land, but it was long established at common law that any conveyance of the land during his minority was voidable by the infant, though not by his grantee, on the transferor attaining his majority.[12] This rule obviously created a hazardous situation for anyone dealing with an infant and so the draftsmen of the Settled Land Act provided a remedy by including section 59 of the 1882 Act. This states:

"Where a person, who is in his own right seised of or entitled in possession to land, is an infant, then for the purposes of this Act the land is settled land, and the infant shall be deemed tenant for life thereof."

This means that wherever land is held in possession[13] by an infant in Ireland, it now has to be dealt with under the Settled Land Acts, which, as we shall see,[14] contain further provisions governing the procedure for dealing with it.[15] The crucial point for the moment is that anyone dealing with the land can do so in the secure knowledge that, so long as certain of the Acts' procedures are followed, he will obtain a good title unaffected by any rules previously governing an infant's land.

8.027. Considerable controversy has also arisen in both Ireland and England over cases involving some form of right of residence.[16] The common situation is where a testator leaves his property to be enjoyed by various members of his family, but subject to a right in his widow to occupy the family residence for the remainder of her life or, perhaps, so long as she wishes to live there. Sometimes this right of residence is to be enjoyed in common with other beneficiaries' rights of occupation and frequently in a "home-made" farmer's will in Ireland it is expressed in vague terms, *e.g.*, "to Mary for her day." In England, when such rights have been created,[17] they are usually exclusive

---

to sell the land subject to the charges instead of having to go through the Settled Land Act procedures. See *Re Ogle's Settled Estates* [1927] 1 Ch. 229; *Re Ossemsley Estates, Ltd.* [1937] 3 All E.R. 774. See also Megarry and Wade, *op. cit.*, pp. 346–8.

[9] *Re Blake's Settled Estates* was primarily concerned with the problems raised by what are known as *compound settlements*, as to which see para. 8.051, *post.*

[10] See further on this subject, ch. 25, *post.*

[11] In England the Law of Property Act, 1925, s. 1 (6) provided that an infant could not hold a legal estate in land.

[12] *Slator* v. *Trimble* (1861) 14 I.C.L.R. 342. The Infant Settlements Act, 1855, which applied to Ireland, permitted infants of certain ages to make irrevocable marriage settlements. *Re Smith's Trusts* (1890) 25 L.R.Ir. 439. See also the Infant Marriage Act, 1860.

[13] See *Re Scally* (1952) 86 I.L.T.R. 171.

[14] Para. 8.102, *post.*

[15] Thus, while s. 59 states that the infant is the tenant for life under the Act, the statutory powers of dealing with the land normally exercisable by such a person may be exercised by others. See para. 8.028, *post.*

[16] See the detailed analysis in Harvey, "Irish Rights of Residence–The Anatomy of a Hermaphrodite" (1970) 21 N.I.L.Q. 389. Also the same author's *Settlements of Land* (1973), pp. 82–8; ch. 20, *post.*

[17] They do not appear to be as common as in Ireland, see Harvey, *op. cit.*

rights of occupancy conferred on the widow or other devisee and the English courts have generally construed them as conferring a life interest, thereby attracting the provisions of the Settled Land Acts.[18] In Ireland, however, the general conclusion to be drawn from the rather conflicting decisions on the subject seems to be that such a right of residence does *not* confer a life interest and so does not attract the provisions of the Settled Land Acts, 1882–90.[19] At most the right seems to create a form of licence to occupy the land,[20] though one which may bind successors in title.[21] Statutory recognition of this conclusion has now been given in both parts of Ireland, in relation to registered land. The Republic's Registration of Title Act, 1964[22] and the Land Registration Act (N.I.), 1970,[23] provide that a general right of residence, or an exclusive right of residence in or on part of registered land, is to be deemed personal to the person beneficially entitled thereto and not to create an equitable estate in the land or to confer any right of ownership. However, such a right is protected by registration as a burden on the land and thereby may affect successors in title.[24] This complex subject is discussed further in a later chapter.[25]

3. Tenant for Life

8.028. As we have seen the primary object of the Settled Land Acts was to give limited owners of land additional powers of dealing with the land. This the Acts achieve by designating in every case one person as the person who can exercise the statutory powers—referred to in the Act as the "tenant for life." The first point to emphasise, however, is that this is a composite expression covering a large category of landowners, many of whom in fact do not hold a life estate, strictly defined, in the land. To be precise, what section 58 of the Settled Land Act, 1882, does is to enumerate most of the limited owners of land who will have the powers of a tenant for life under the Acts. We have already seen that owners of a fee tail or base fee or even a fee simple with an executory limitation over are such persons.[26] We also saw that section 59 of the 1882 Act

---

[18] See *Re Gibbons* [1920] 1 Ch. 372; *Re Anderson* [1920] 1 Ch. 175; *Re Carne's Settled Estates* [1899] 1 Ch. 324; *Re Baroness Llandover's Will* [1902] 2 Ch. 679; *Re Duce and Boots Cash Chemists Ltd.'s Contract* [1937] Ch. 642; *Re Boyer's Settled Estates* [1916] 2 Ch. 404; *Bannister* v. *Bannister* [1948] 2 All E.R. 133; *Binions* v. *Evans* [1972] Ch. 359. See also some Commonwealth authorities, *e.g., Moore* v. *Royal Trust Co.* [1956] 5 D.L.R. 152 (Canada); *Re Marchetti* (1950) 52 W.A.L.R. 20 (Australia). Also the Scottish case, *Wallace* v. *Simmers*, 1960 S.C. 255. See Hornby, "Tenancy for Life or Licence" (1977) 93 L.Q.R. 561.

[19] See *Kelaghan* v. *Daly* [1913] 2 I.R. 328; *Re Shanahan* [1919] 1 I.R. 131; *National Bank* v. *Keegan* [1931] I.R. 344 (see *A Casebook on Irish Land Law* (1984), p. 673).

[20] For this reason it is discussed more fully in ch. 20, *post.*

[21] The references to its being a "lien" or an "annuity or money charge" in some of the Irish cases are questionable, though the Republic of Ireland's Registration of Title Act, 1964, s. 81 refers to "a right in the nature of a lien for money's worth." (See also s. 69 (1) (*q*) of the 1964 Act.) The Republic's Statute of Limitations, 1957, s. 40 and the Statute of Limitations (N.I.), 1958, s. 42 contain similar references.

[22] S. 81. Note also that in the Republic a surviving spouse has a legal right to one third (or one half, if there are no children) of the deceased spouse's estate, and the surviving spouse may require the family dwelling to be appropriated for this share, Succession Act, 1965, ss. 56 and 111–12, ch. 15, *post.*

[23] S. 47.

[24] 1964 Act, s. 69 (1) (*q*); 1970 Act, Sched. 6, para. 14. Note, however, that s. 81 of the Republic's 1964 Act, unlike s. 47 of the 1970 Act (N.I.), contains no reference to the registration of the burden binding successors in title.

[25] Ch. 20, *post.*

[26] Para. 8.021, *supra.*

designated an infant holding land as a tenant for life under the Act, *whatever* actual estate or interest he held, even a fee simple absolute. However, in the case of an infant, section 60 of the 1882 Act goes on to state that the statutory powers of the tenant for life "may be" exercised on his behalf by the trustees of the settlement or, if there are no such persons, by whoever the court orders. In fact, the courts seem to have interpreted this provision as requiring the trustees of the settlement to act for the infant with respect to dealing with his land, where it is decided to execute some dealing.[27] While the trustees have to act on the infant's behalf, it appears that they may do so without the consent of his parents or guardians.[28] If there are no trustees of the settlement, the court may appoint persons to exercise the power of a tenant for life during an infant's minority, but in such a case the court invariably requires the purchase money to be paid into court.

8.029. Despite the detailed provisions relating to a tenant for life contained in the 1882–90 Acts, these are not exhaustive. It is unfortunately still the position in Ireland that a settlement may exist without there being any person available to exercise the powers of the tenant for life under the Acts. For example, if the land is settled by way of discretionary trusts,[29] so that no beneficiary is *entitled*[30] at any time to any income, there is no one who can exercise the powers of the tenant for life.[31] Similarly, the land held on trust may contain a provision that no income is to be paid to the tenant for life until marriage or there may be a direction to accumulate income until a specified date.[32] The result is that in these cases the land cannot be dealt with at all unless the trustees hold under a *trust* for sale,[33] or the beneficiaries are all *sui juris* and agree to join in the transaction.[34] An express *power* to sell given to the trustees would, of course, be ineffective in that this would be inconsistent with the statutory power to sell conferred on the tenant for life by the Settled Land Acts.[35]

---

[27] Doubtless the wording of the section could not be put in imperative form because it was concerned with *powers* which, by their very nature, are not obligatory, para. 8.016, *ante*. See Re Greenville Estate (1883) 11 L.R.Ir. 138; *Re McClintock* (1891) 27 L.R.Ir. 462; *Re Neill's Estate* (1911) 45 I.L.T.R. 246; *Re Bennett's Estate* (1905) 39 I.L.T.R. 229; *Re Brabazon's Estate* [1909] 1 I.R. 209; *Re Conroy's Trusts* [1938] Ir.Jur.Rep. 26; *Re Scally* (1952) 86 I.L.T.R. 171. See also the following English cases on s. 60 of the 1882 Act: *Re Morgan* (1883) 24 Ch.D. 114; *Re Newcastle's Estates* (1883) 24 Ch.D. 129; *Re Wells* (1883) 48 L.T. 859; *Re Price* (1884) 27 Ch.D. 552; *Re Dudley's Contract* (1887) 35 Ch.D. 338; *Re Simpson* [1897] 1 Ch. 256; *Re Helyar* [1902] 1 Ch. 391; *Re Stamford and Warrington* [1916] 1 Ch. 404. See also the Irish case of *Re Locke's Estate* (1913) 47 I.L.T.R. 147. Harvey, *Settlements of Land* (1973), p. 33. In England the basic change was made that an infant can no longer hold a legal estate in land and this is followed up by providing that both the legal estate and the statutory powers of the tenant for life are vested in the trustees of the settlement, Law of Property Act, 1926, s. 1 (6) and Settled Land Act, 1925, s. 26 (1).

[28] See generally *Re Newcastle's Estates, op. cit.*

[29] See para. 9.081, *post*.

[30] See the 1882 Act, s. 58 (1) (ix).

[31] See *Re Atkinson* (1886) 31 Ch.D. 577; *Re Horne's Settled Estate* (1888) 39 Ch.D. 84. This was remedied in England by s. 23 of the Settled Land Act, 1925, which vested the power of the tenant for life in the trustees as statutory owners in such a case.

[32] *Re Astor* [1922] 1 Ch. 364. This problem was also remedied in England by s. 23 of the Settled Land Act, 1925. See also s. 117 (1) (xxvi).

[33] See para. 8.043, *post*.

[34] See *Registration of Title to Land in Northern Ireland* (Cmd. 512), para. 142 (a); *Survey of Land Law of Northern Ireland* (1971), para. 85.

[35] See para. 8.062, *post*.

8.030. We shall discuss the various powers given to a tenant for life in more detail later in this chapter.[36] Basically these are powers of dealing with the land and of management, including powers to sell, exchange, lease and mortgage it. However, it must be remembered that, while these powers are given solely to the tenant for life for the time being, or to the trustees of the settlement in the case of an infant, the tenant for life or trustees cannot exercise them for his or their own personal benefit. The Act does not go so far as to make the tenant for life trustee of his powers for the benefit of all other persons interested in the land under the settlement, but it does require him, *in the exercise of his powers*, to "have regard to the interests of all parties entitled under the settlement."[37] Thus in relation to the *exercise* of his powers he is "deemed to be in the position and to have the duties and liabilities of a trustee for those parties."[38] The courts have taken this to mean that, while no interference will be made on the grounds of dubious motives or reasons for the exercise of the powers (*e.g.*, out of spite or to clear his own debts), there will be grounds for interference if there is fraud or if the particular transaction is likely to harm the interests of others (*e.g.*, selling the land at a clear undervalue).[39] Furthermore, these statutory powers must remain unfettered so that neither the settlor in his settlement nor the tenant for life, himself, by his subsequent actions can curtail or divest them.[40] From this it is clear that the main control of the settled land was firmly placed in the hands of the tenant for life. This was an obviously risky thing to do since, as one of the people interested in the land, he had his own interest to think about every time he exercised one of the statutory powers. The Act, however, tried to guard against abuse of his powers by the tenant for life in the ways we have just mentioned. Another way was by requiring the appointment of trustees of the settlement, a subject to which we now turn.

4. Trustees of the Settlement

8.031. As we shall discuss later,[41] the trustees of the settlement have largely supervisory functions. The powers of dealing with the land were given by the Acts to the tenant for life and the trustees could exercise these powers only in the case where the tenant for life was an infant. Nevertheless, the trustees have a vital role to play in the legislative scheme, for most dealings with the land executed by the tenant for life cannot be completed effectively without the participation, in some way or other, of the trustees. In some cases they must give a receipt for capital money arising on the disposition of the land,[42] in other cases they must consent to the particular transaction being executed by the tenant for life.[43]

---

[36] Paras. 8.057 *et seq., post.*
[37] 1882 Act, s. 53.
[38] *Ibid.*
[39] See the discussion in *Wheelwright* v. *Walker* (1883) 23 Ch.D. 752; *Hampden* v. *Earl of Buckinghamshire* [1893] 2 Ch. 531; *Re Somers* (1895) 11 T.L.R. 567; *Middlemas* v. *Stevens* [1901] 1 Ch. 574; *Gilbey* v. *Rush* [1906] 1 Ch. 11. See Sweeney, "Abuse of his Statutory Powers by the Tenant for Life" (1976) 70 Gaz. I.L.S.I. 20.
[40] This subject is discussed in detail later, para. 8.060, *post.*
[41] Para. 8.092, *post.*
[42] See para. 8.093, *post.*
[43] See para. 8.101, *post.*

8.032. For the moment, however, we are concerned with identifying the trustees of the settlement in a particular case. Section 2 (8) of the Settled Land Act, 1882, provided the following definition:

"The persons, if any, who are for the time being, under a settlement, trustees with power of sale of settled land, or with power of consent to or approval of the exercise of such a power of sale, or if under a settlement there are no such trustees, then the persons, if any, for the time being, who are by the settlement declared to be trustees thereof for the purposes of this Act, are for the purposes of this Act trustees of the settlement."

An additional provision with respect to trustees was made in section 16 of the Settled Land Act, 1890:

"Where there are for the time being no trustees of the settlement within the meaning and for the purposes of the Act of 1882, then the following persons shall, for the purposes of the Settled Land Acts, 1882 to 1890, be trustees of the settlement; namely,

(i) The persons (if any) who are for the time being under the settlement trustees, with power of or upon trust for sale of *any other land* comprised in the settlement and subject to the same limitations as the land to be sold, or with power of consent to or approval of the exercise of such a power of sale, or, if there be no such persons, then

(ii) The persons (if any) who are for the time being under the settlement trustees with *future power of sale,* or under a *future trust for sale* of the land to be sold, or with power of consent to or approval of the exercise of such a future power of sale, and whether the power or trust takes effect in all events or not."[44]

8.033. It will be noted that the above statutory provisions must be applied in the order in which they have been quoted. Thus to determine who are the trustees of the settlement one must first check to see if there are trustees with a power of sale (or power to consent to a sale) of the settled land in question.[45] If there are, they are the trustees of the settlement for the purposes of the Settled Land Acts, 1882–90, whatever other persons might exist coming into the other categories, *including* persons expressly declared in the settlement to be the trustees of the settlement.[46] Furthermore, it makes no difference that the trustees with the power of sale cannot exercise it because that power is given by the Acts to the tenant for life, so that to the extent that the terms of the settlement conflict with the provisions of the Act the latter prevail.[47] It is sufficient that the settlor attempted to give such a power to the trustees. It

---

[44] Italics added. *Ex p. Patton* (1901) 1 N.I.J.R. 196; *Re Dick's Estate* (1913) 47 I.L.T.R. 149.

[45] It appears that it makes no difference that the trustees' exercise of the power of sale may be subject to some other person's consent, *e.g.*, the tenant for life. *Constable* v. *Constable* (1886) 32 Ch.D. 233. *Cf.*, if the other person's consent cannot be obtained, *Re Johnstone's Settlement* (1886) 17 L.R.Ir. 172.

[46] See *Survey of the Land Law of Northern Ireland* (1971), para. 118.

[47] 1882 Act, s. 56 (2). See para. 8.064, *post*.

appears that the power of sale must be a general power and not one limited to specified purposes, *e.g.*, payment of debts.[48]

8.034. If there are no trustees given such an express power of sale, the next category of persons are persons expressly declared by the settlement to be trustees of the settlement—"for the purposes of the Settled Land Acts, 1882 to 1890."[49] This is probably the most common category in practice and, since 1882, every conveyancer drafting a settlement should have seen to it that such persons were named in the instrument creating the settlement. It is important to appreciate that the appropriate wording must be used. It is not sufficient simply to designate certain persons as "trustees" or even as "trustees of the settlement."[50]

8.035. Failing the existence of persons within the first two categories, the 1890 Act adds two further categories. The first, which is the third altogether in order of priority, relates to persons who are trustees with a power of sale, or trustees for sale, of *other* land which is subject to the same limitations as the settled land in question. Thus the settlement may include two farms, but the trustees named were given power expressly to sell only one of them.[51] The effect of the first part of section 16 of the 1890 Act is to make the trustees the trustees of the settlement as a whole, so that they will act when either farm is sold by the revelant tenant for life. The second part of section 16 of the 1890 Act creates the fourth category of persons and deals with the situation where, for example, the land may be settled on A for life and then is to go to trustees, with a power of sale, who are to hold it for specified beneficiaries.[52] The trustees, in the absence of persons coming within the first three categories, would be the trustees of the settlement for the purposes of any dealings in the land executed by A.

8.036. No further persons are designated as trustees of the settlement in the 1882–90 Acts[53] and, in the ordinary course of events, the lack of such persons would mean that an application would have to be made to the court for the appointment of trustees before any dealing with the land could be carried out. Section 38 (1) of the Settled Land Act, 1882, makes a general provision to this effect:

---

[48] *Re Carne's Settled Estate* [1899] 1 Ch. 324; see also *Re Morgan* (1883) 24 Ch.D. 114.

[49] Note that s. 2 (8) of the 1882 Act, as one would expect, refers only to "for the purposes of this Act" but the later 1890 provision, in s. 16 of the 1890 Act, uses the fuller expression "for the purposes of the Settled Land Acts, 1882 to 1890." The latter is obviously the better expression to use to avoid any question of doubt as to whether powers contained in the Acts after the 1882 Act apply to the particular settlement. Apart from that, s. 2 of the 1890 Act provided that the "Settled Land Acts, 1882 to 1889, and this [1890] Act are to be read and construed together as one Act."

[50] *Re Bentley* (1885) 54 L.J.Ch. 782.

[51] *Re Moore* [1906] 1 Ch. 789.

[52] *Re Pim's Estate* (1905) 39 I.L.T.R. 47; see also *Re Johnson's Settled Estate* [1913] W.N. 222.

[53] The Settled Land Act, 1925, s. 30 (1) (v), added in England a fifth category, namely persons appointed by deed by those able to dispose of the entire equitable interest in the land. Thus in a standard strict settlement of land on A for life, remainder to B in tail, A and B *together* could appoint trustees of the settlement in England, provided, of course, they are both *sui juris* (para. 10.088, *post*). In this example, B could always bar the entail with the protector's (A's) consent and thereby dispose of the entire beneficial interest in the land. *Re Spearman Settled Estates* [1906] 2 Ch. 502; *Re Spencer's Settled Estates* [1903] 1 Ch. 75.

"If at any time there are no trustees of a settlement within the definition in this Act, or where in any other case it is expedient, for the purposes of this Act, that new trustees of a settlement be appointed, the Court may, if it thinks fit, on the application of the tenant for life or any other person having, under the settlement, an estate or interest in the settled land, in possession, remainder, or otherwise, or, in the case of an infant, or his testamentary or other guardian, or next friend, appoint fit persons to be trustees under the settlement for the purposes of this Act."[54]

Section 38 (2) goes on to provide that the survivors of such trustees are to continue to be the trustees of the settlement and, on death of the last surviving or continuing trustee, his personal representatives are to become the trustees of the settlement. In *Burke* v. *Gore*[55] it was pointed out that the court, in exercising its power of appointment under section 38, should require to be satisfied not only as to the fitness of the proposed trustees, but also that the purposes for which their appointment is sought is such as to render their appointment safe and beneficial to all persons interested in the property. The trustees appointed need not be permanently resident in Ireland if the court is convinced that special circumstances justify the appointment of someone outside the jurisdiction, *e.g.*, the tenant for life also has his permanent residence out of the jurisdiction.[56]

8.037. The need for an application to the court in the case of a settlement *by will*, where no trustees have been designated in the will, has now been obviated in both parts of Ireland. Section 50 (3) of the Republic's Succession Act, 1965, provides:

"Where land is settled by will and there are no trustees of the settlement, the personal representatives proving the will shall for all purposes be deemed to be trustees of the settlement until trustees of the settlement are appointed, but a sole personal representative shall not be deemed to be a trustee for the purposes of the Settled Land Acts, 1882 to 1890, until at least one other trustee is appointed."[57]

An identical provision is contained in section 40 (5) of the Administration of Estates Act (N.I.), 1955. It appears from this provision, especially from the phrase "for all purposes," that the personal representatives can make the appointment of trustees of the settlement, including appointment of them-

---

[54] *Re Mulcahy's Estate* (1889) 27 L.R.Ir. 78; *Re Johnstone's Settlement* (1885) 17 L.R.Ir. 172; *Re Kane's Trusts* (1888) 21 L.R.Ir. 112; *Ex p. Patton* (1901) 1 N.I.J.R. 196; *Re Collis's Estate* [1911] 1 I.R. 267; *Ex p. Reid* [1898] 1 I.R. 1; *Re Johnston's Estate* (1906) 40 I.L.T.R. 232; *Re Garde's Estate* (*No. 2*) [1904] 1 I.R. 237; *Re Tweedy's Estate* [1912] 1 I.R. 393; *Re Conroy's Trusts* [1938] Ir.Jur.Rep. 26; *Re Lindsey-Brabazon's Settlement* [1938] I.R. 283; *Re Cox's Settled Estates* (1939) 73 I.L.T.R. 60.

[55] (1884) 13 L.R.Ir. 367, espec. at 371 (*per* Chatterton V.-C.). (see *A Casebook on Irish Land Law* (1984), p. 408).

[56] *Re Lindsey-Brabazon's Settlement* [1938] I.R. 283; *Re Levinge's Trust* [1952] Ir.Jur.Rep. 2; *Re Tyzack* (1964) 98 I.L.T. 396.

[57] The last clause ties in with s. 39 (1) of the Settled Land Act, 1882, requiring capital money to be paid to at least two trustees. However, in Northern Ireland a trust corporation may act instead of two trustees, see Trustee Act (N.I.), 1958, s. 14 (2). No such amendment to s. 39 (1) of the 1882 Act has been made in the Republic of Ireland.

selves.[58] It would seem that the reference to "until trustees of the settlement are appointed" is not to be taken to exclude such an appointment by the personal representatives, unless some other persons have a prior claim to make such an appointment.[59]

8.038. Apart from this general provision relating to settlements by will, section 58 (2) of the Succession Act, 1965, makes a special provision for the case of an infant succeeding to land on intestacy. It provides:

"Where an infant becomes entitled to any estate or interest in land on intestacy and consequently there is no instrument under which the estate or interest of the infant arises or is acquired, that estate or interest shall be deemed to be the subject of a settlement for the purposes of the Settled Land Acts, 1882 to 1890, and the persons who are trustees under section 57[60] shall be deemed to be the trustees of that settlement."

A similar provision is contained in section 38 (3) of the Administration of Estates Act (N.I.), 1955. The wording of these provisions is carefully drafted to make it clear that the infant in such a case takes under a settlement despite the absence of any instrument creating the settlement. This is important because on intestacy an infant, as in other cases of intestacy, succeeds to the property by operation of law, whereas under the Settled Land Acts, 1882–90, settled land is land subject to a settlement which, by section 2 (1) of the 1882 Act, is defined in terms of instruments creating a succession of interests.[61] Following section 60 of the 1882 Act, the trustees appointed under the above provisions may exercise the powers of the tenant for life on behalf of the infant.

8.039. There remains the question as to what is the position after the trustees of the settlement have become trustees or have been appointed in one of the ways mentioned above or by the court. The Settled Land Acts, 1882–90, in fact contain no provisions relating to appointment of new trustees or to the discharge or retirement of existing trustees. However, section 47 of the Trustee Act, 1893, applied all the powers and provisions in that Act relating to the appointment of new trustees, and the discharge and retirement of trustees,[62] to trustees for the purposes of the Settled Land Acts, 1882–90, and this provision

---

[58] See Leitch, *Handbook on the Administration of Estates Act (N.I.), 1955* (1956), p. 123; Carswell, *The Trustee Acts (Northern Ireland)* (1964), p. 137. See further on the appointment of new trustees, etc., ch. 10, *post*.

[59] *E.g.*, persons with an express power of appointment.

[60] S. 57 provides: "(1) Where an infant is entitled to any share in the estate of a deceased person and there are no trustees of such share able and willing to act, the personal representatives of the deceased may appoint a trust corporation or any two or more persons (who may include the personal representatives or any of them or a trust corporation) to be trustees of such share for the infant and may execute such assurance or take such other action as may be necessary for vesting the share in the trustee so appointed. In default of appointment the personal representatives shall be trustees for the purposes of this section. (2) On such appointment the personal representatives, as such, shall be discharged from all further liability in respect of the property vested in the trustees so appointed." A similar provision is to be found in s. 38 (1) of the Administration of Estates Act (N.I.), 1955, under which, however, a trust corporation may not be appointed on its own. These provisions are designed to enable personal representatives to secure a speedy discharge of responsibility for an infant's property and to discourage postponement of administration of the intestate's estate until the infant reaches his majority. See Leitch, *op. cit.* pp. 113–4.

[61] Para. 8.020, *ante*.

[62] *I.e.*, ss. 10, 11, 12, 25 and 37 of the 1893 Act.

remains in force in the Republic of Ireland.[63] In Northern Ireland, section 47 of the 1893 Act has been replaced by section 64 (1) of the Trustee Act (N.I.), 1958.[64] However, section 64 goes on to make the earlier provisions clearer in their application to Settled Land Act trustees in Northern Ireland. Thus section 64 (2) provides:

> "Where, either before or after the commencement of this Act, trustees of a settlement have been appointed by the court for the purposes of the Settled Land Acts, 1882 to 1890, then, after the commencement of this Act:
>
> (a) the person or persons nominated for the purpose of appointing new trustees by the instrument, if any, creating the settlement, though no trustees for the purposes of the said Acts were thereby appointed; or
>
> (b) if there is no such person, or no such person able and willing to act, the surviving or continuing trustees or trustee for the time being for the purposes of the said Acts or the personal representatives of the last surviving or continuing trustee for those purposes;
>
> shall have the powers conferred by this Act to appoint new or additional[65] trustees of the settlement for the purposes of the said Acts."

Having thus made clear who can make the appointments in question, section 64 (3) of the 1958 Act validates retrospectively any appointments made before the Act by persons mentioned in subsection (2), to remove any doubt that might otherwise exist.

8.040. The powers contained in the 1893 and 1958 Acts on this subject are discussed in detail in a later chapter.[66] The only other point on the subject to be mentioned at this stage is to draw attention once again to the statutory power of appointment that now seems to exist in personal representatives in both parts of Ireland in the case of a settlement by will.[67]

5. *Overreaching*

8.041. This is the key concept contained in the Settled Land Acts, 1882–90. The underlying policy of the Acts is to give to the person designated as tenant for life greater powers of dealing with the settled land than he would otherwise have. In particular, as we shall discuss in detail later,[68] the Acts give the tenant for life power to sell the fee simple absolute in the land (or whatever estate was the subject of the settlement), so that the purchaser, provided the proper procedure is observed,[69] obtains the fee simple freed and discharged from all the various estates and interests attaching to the land by or under the settle-

---

[63] See also the Trustee Act, 1931 (R.I.), ss. 3 and 4.

[64] The relevant empowering sections in the 1958 Act are ss. 35–42.

[65] No such power is contained in the 1893 Act and no other statutory power to appoint additional trustees exists in the Republic of Ireland. *Cf.* s. 35 (6) of the Trustee Act (N.I.), 1958.

[66] See ch. 10, *post.*

[67] Para. 8.037, *supra.*

[68] Paras. 8.057 *et seq.*

[69] *E.g.*, payment of purchase money to the trustees of the settlement, para. 8.093, *post.*

ment. After the sale those estates and interests attach to the capital money raised by the sale and protection against squandering of the capital is ensured by the requirement that it be paid to the trustees of the settlement, for them to invest, and not to the tenant for life or any other individual interested in the settlement. This process whereby the land is sold free of all incumbrances created by the settlement, which thereupon are transferred to the capital money, is known as overreaching.[70]

8.042. Apart from the overreaching effect of the tenant for life's power of sale, it may be noted that the tenant for life is given various other powers by the Acts which override the common law position. Thus he is given extensive leasing powers, whereby he may grant leases which will survive his estate or interest in the land, so that his successor to the land under the settlement will take the land subject to those leases.[71] Other statutory powers which he is given, but which the precarious nature of his limited freehold estate would otherwise hinder him in exercising, include the raising of money on mortgage[72] and the making of improvements to the land.[73] We shall examine each of these powers in detail later in the chapter.[74]

6. Trusts for Sale

8.043. We explained earlier that the object of a trust for sale of land is quite different to that of a strict settlement of land or, indeed, a holding trust of land, where the trustees may have, at most, a mere power of sale.[75] In the case of the latter, especially a strict settlement, the object is to keep the land in the family, and the limited powers of successive estate owners at common law under such a settlement further that object. The Settled Land Acts were designed to counter that object and to make land more marketable. On the other hand, that is precisely the policy furthered by a trust for sale of land. The whole object of such a trust is that the land should be sold at the earliest convenient time (though it is usual to give the trustees power to postpone sale at their discretion) and there is no problem about the actual selling since the full legal title is vested in the trustees for sale.[76] One the sale by the trustees the purchaser obtains the full legal title to the property. From the outset, the beneficial interests are regarded as personalty[77] and attach to the capital money raised on the sale and held by the trustees for investment. For this reason, no doubt, the original draft of the Settled Land Act, 1882 did not include trusts for sale within its provisions. Unfortunately, the Westminster Parliament was prompted into adding an amendment to the Bill[78] which was enacted as section

---

[70] In fact the word is not used in the 1882–90 Acts. See especially s. 20 of the 1882 Act, *Connolly* v. *Keating* (No. 1) [1903] 1 I.R. 353. The word is, however, used frequently in the English Law of Property and Settled Land Acts, 1925.

[71] See para. 8.071, *post.*

[72] Para. 8.078, *post.*

[73] Para. 8.081, *post.*

[74] Paras. 8.057 *et seq.*

[75] Para. 8.014, *ante.*

[76] Para. 8.012, *ante.*

[77] See on the doctrine of conversion, para. 3.100, *ante.*

[78] See H.C.Debs., vol. CCLXXII, col. 360 (1882). Also 27 Sol.Jo. 113 and 28 Sol.Jo. 703.

63 of the 1882 Act, subsection (1) of which reads:

"Any land, or any estate or interest in land, which under or by virtue of any deed, will, or agreement, covenant to surrender, copy of court roll, Act of Parliament, or other instrument or any number of instruments, whether made or passed before or after, or partly before or partly after, the commencement of this Act, is subject to a *trust or direction for sale* of that land, estate or interest, and for the application or disposal of the money to arise from the sale, or the income of that money, or the income of the land until sale, or any part of that money or income, for the benefit of any person for his life, or any other limited period, or for the benefit of two or more persons concurrently for any limited period, and whether absolutely, or subject to a trust for accumulation of income for payment of debts or other purposes, or to any other restriction, *shall be deemed to be settled land,* and the instrument or instruments under which the trust arises *shall be deemed to be a settlement;* and the person for the time being beneficially entitled to the income of the land, estate, or interest aforesaid until sale, whether absolutely or subject as aforesaid, *shall be deemed to be tenant for life thereof;* . . . and the persons, if any, who are for the time being under the settlement *trustees for sale* of the settled land, or having power to consent to, or approval of, or control over the sale, or if under the settlement there are no such trustees, then the persons, if any, for the time being, who are by the settlement declared to be trustees thereof for the purposes of this Act, *are for purposes of this Act trustees of the settlement."*[79]

8.044. It is no exaggeration to say that this convoluted provision caused a storm when it was enacted, and with good reason. In effect, it took away from the trustees for sale the vital control over the land which the settlor intended and reduced their functions to the supervisory ones conferred on trustees of the settlement under the 1882 Act. Even worse, it deprived the trustees of the powers of dealing with the land, especially the power to do acts in furtherance of their duty to sell under the trust, and which they were free to do without any statutory provisions. The powers of dealing were given to one of the beneficiaries holding under the trust, no doubt as much to his surprise as to the trustees'. Any exercise of those powers by the tenant for life, including any sale of the land by him, would involve use of the special procedures contained in the Settled Land Act, 1882. It is not surprising, then, that Parliament was quickly persuaded to try to remedy the situation, but, alas, the remedy was hardly satisfactory. Section 6 (1) of the Settled Land Act, 1884, provided:

"In the case of a settlement within the meaning of section sixty-three of the Act of 1882, any consent not required by the terms of the settlement is not by force of anything contained in that Act to be deemed necessary to enable the trustees of the settlement, or any other person, to execute any of the trusts or powers created by the settlement."

[79] Italics added. See *Re Tuthill* [1907] 1 I.R. 305 (see *A Casebook on Irish Land Law* (1984), p. 410); also *Re Iever's Settlements* [1904] 1 I.R. 492.

8.045. The point about this provision was that section 56 (2) of the 1882 Act had provided that the trustees of the settlement could, in cases where the settlor has expressly conferred on them powers granted to the tenant for life by the Act, exercise the powers of the tenant for life, provided he consented to this.[80] Section 6 (1) of the 1884 Act was then followed up by section 7 of the same Act, which provided:

> "With respect to the powers conferred by section sixty-three of the Act of 1882, the following provisions are to have effect:
>
> (i)   Those powers are not to be exercised without the leave of the Court.
>
> (ii)   The Court may by order, in any case in which it thinks fit, give leave to exercise all or any of those powers, and the order is to name the person or persons to whom leave is given.
>
> (iii) The Court may from time to time rescind, or vary, any order made under this section, or may make any new or further order.
>
> (iv)   So long as an order under this section is in force, neither the trustees of the settlement, nor any person other than a person having the leave, shall execute any trust or power created by the settlement, for any purpose for which leave is by the order given, to exercise a power conferred by the Act of 1882.
>
> (v)   An order under this section may be registered and re-registered, as a *lis pendens,* against the trustees of the settlement named in the order, describing them on the register as 'Trustees for the purposes of the Settled Land Act, 1882.'
>
> (vi)   Any person dealing with the trustees from time to time, or with any other person acting under the trusts or powers of the settlement, is not to be affected by an order under this section, unless and until the order is duly registered, and when necessary re-registered as a *lis pendens.*
>
> (vii) An application to the Court under this section may be made by the tenant for life, or by the persons who together constitute the tenant for life, within the meaning of section sixty-three of the Act of 1882.
>
> (viii) An application to rescind or vary an order, or to make any new or further order under this section, may be made also by the trustees of the settlement, or by any person beneficially interested under the settlement.
>
> (ix)   The person or persons to whom leave is given by an order under this section, shall be deemed the proper person or persons to exercise the powers conferred by section sixty-three of the Act of 1882, and shall have, and may exercise those powers accordingly.
>
> (x)   This section is not to affect any dealing which has taken place

---

[80] S. 6 (2) of the 1884 Act amended s. 56 (2) of the 1882 Act to mean that, where two or more persons constitute the tenant for life in the case of a settlement *other than* a trust for sale within s. 63 of the 1882 Act, the consent of one only of those persons is to be deemed necessary to the exercise of the powers by the trustees of the settlement.

before the passing of this Act, under any trust or power to which this section applies."

8.046. The result of these 1884 provisions, which, let it be emphasised, still govern the matter in both parts of Ireland, is as follows. In the case of a trust for sale of land, the trustees may exercise their trusts to the full, including the sale of the land,[81] without the consent of the tenant for life or any other beneficiaries,[82] *provided* the tenant for life has not obtained any order of the court under section 7, which has been duly registered against the trustees. Once such an order has been obtained and registered, however, the tenant for life only may sell the land and exercise the other powers conferred upon him by the Settled Land Acts, 1882–90.[83] The trustees for sale then have only the powers conferred upon the trustees of the settlement by the 1882–90 Acts. It is by no means certain that the tenant for life will obtain such an order of the court, as the Irish case of *Re Tuthill*[84] emphasised, but the general rule seems to be that the tenant for life will obtain an order if he has a direct interest in the administration of the land and no other parties, whether or not connected directly with the trust for sale, will be prejudiced.[85]

8.047. In view of the general policy of the Settled Land Acts of making land more marketable, it is difficult to think of provisions more likely to cause complications for a prospective purchaser of land and his solicitor. The first hurdle that has to be jumped by the purchaser and his solicitor is to determine whether the land in question is subject to a trust for sale or not. If anything at all is clear from the cases on the subject it is that this is by no means an easy question to answer. The problem is that there is nothing to prevent a settlor conferring an express *power* of sale on the persons designated as trustees of the settlement in the case of a strict settlement,[86] or on the trustees of a holding trust creating a succession of interests, and, therefore, settled land.[87] In neither of these cases is there a *trust* for sale, in the sense that an *obligation* to sell is imposed on the trustees.[88] Yet in a particular case it is not always clear which type of settlement has been created and the only way to resolve the matter finally is by litigation. Thus it has been held that there is nothing inconsistent in conferring a power to postpone the sale indefinitely in the case of a trust for sale.[89] Similarly, it has been held that there may still be a trust for sale, where

---

[81] Of course, it was quite possible, though less likely today, that the trustees for sale might have no powers of dealing with the land except by way of sale, *i.e.,* no powers of leasing or mortgaging. This was dependent upon express powers being granted in the trust instrument in the 1880s. For today, see the statutory powers contained in the Trustee Acts, ch. 10, *post.*

[82] Subject, of course, to any express provision in the trust instrument relating to consent.

[83] *Re Longfield's Estate* (1907) 41 I.L.T.R. 124; *Re Iever's Settlements* [1904] 1 I.R. 492; *Finch* v. *Jones* [1912] 1 I.R. 388; *Re Obré* [1920] 1 I.R. 32.

[84] [1907] 1 I.R. 305, espec. at 310 (*per* Meredith M.R.) (see *A Casebook on Irish Land Law* (1984), p. 410). See also *Re Naper* (1952) 86 I.L.T.R. 106.

[85] *Re Naper* (1952) 86 I.L.T.R. 106. See also, *Re Houghton Estate* (1885) 30 Ch.D. 102; *Re Harding's Estate* [1891] 1 Ch. 60; *Re Bagot's Settlement* [1894] 1 Ch. 177; *Re Searle* [1900] 2 Ch. 829.

[86] *Re Babington's Estate* (1905) 39 I.L.T.R. 224; *Re Collis's Estate* [1911] 1 I.R. 267; *Re Dick's Estate* (1913) 47 I.L.T.R. 149.

[87] Para. 8.014, *ante.*

[88] Which may be implied, *Re McCurdy's Estate* (1891) 27 L.R.Ir. 395.

[89] *Re Johnson* [1915] 1 Ch. 435.

the consent of some third party must first be obtained[90] or such a person's request for a sale must be made.[91] On the other hand, if a third party is also given power to instruct the trustees not to sell, which is to be a binding instruction, this will apparently negative the existence of a trust for sale.[92] Further, if some restriction is imposed as to when the trustees can sell, e.g., at some future date only[93] or on the happening of some future event,[94] this will also prevent the trust operating as a trust for sale. Finally, considerable doubts remain as to the proper interpretation to be given to a trust "to retain or sell the land." It seems that the courts will endeavour in such cases to determine whether the general intention of the settlor was that the land should be sold or retained as land.[95] If they construe the general intention as being the former, a trust for sale will operate.

8.048. Assuming that the purchaser and his solicitor get over this hurdle of determining whether or not a trust for sale exists, and find that one does exist, a check must then be made to determine whether or not the tenant for life has obtained an order of court duly registered against the trustees. There is no point in dealing with the trustees if such an order has been obtained and care must be taken to ensure that a *lis pendens* is not registered against the trustees at any time up to the date of completion of the sale. This illustrates the risks and inconveniences for a purchaser dealing with the trustees of a trust for sale of land under the 1884 Act. On the other hand, if it is discovered from the outset that the tenant for life has indeed obtained a court order, which has been registered against the trustees, then the purchaser and his solicitor have to deal with the tenant for life and abide by the procedures of the Settled Land Acts, 1882–90, as if the land were subject to a strict settlement. It is not surprising that the recent government survey of land law in Northern Ireland recommended reforms to deal with this matter.[96]

8.049. One further major problem with respect to trusts for sale of land must be mentioned. When section 7 of the Settled Land Act, 1884, removed the powers of the tenant for life from him until he obtained a court order permitting him to exercise them, it did not say what was to happen in the administration of that property in the meantime. It was true that the trustees for sale could carry out the sale, so long as no court order was obtained, but what about management of the land in the interim period before sale? No powers of management, e.g., relating to leasing, mortgaging and making improvements, were conferred on the trustees for sale by the Settled Land Acts, 1882–90, and they would have no such powers unless they had been conferred upon them, expressly or impliedly, by the trust instrument.[97] Furthermore, if no such powers could

---

[90] *Re Wagstaff's Settled Estates* [1900] 2 Ch. 201; *Re Ffennell's Settlement* [1918] 1 Ch. 91.
[91] *Re Child's Settlement* [1907] 2 Ch. 348.
[92] *Re Goodall's Settlement* [1909] 1 Ch. 440.
[93] *Re Horne's Settled Estate* (1888) 39 Ch.D. 84.
[94] *Re Smith and Lonsdale's Contract* (1934) 78 Sol.Jo. 173.
[95] *Re Johnson* [1915] 1 Ch. 435; *Re White's Settlement* [1930] 1 Ch. 179; *Re Crips* (1907) 95 L.T. 865.
[96] *Survey of the Land Law of Northern Ireland* (1971), ch. 3.
[97] *Stroughill* v. *Anstey* (1852) 1 De G.M. & G. 635; *Re Dimmock* (1885) 52 L.T. 494; *Walker* v. *Southall* (1887) 56 L.T. 882; *Re Bellinger* [1898] 2 Ch. 534. Note that trustees of a trust established by any enactment for the

be found in the trust instrument, the courts were reluctant to confer them, in the absence of exceptional circumstances. Such circumstances might, however, exist in a particular case, so as to persuade the court to exercise its salvage jurisdiction.[98] Thus in *Neill* v. *Neill*,[99] the court authorised expenditure by trustees to render saleable a sheep farm in danger of becoming worthless because it was overrun by rabbits and because of general deterioration. Apart from that sort of exceptional case, the only way to ensure proper management of the land held under a trust for sale was often for the tenant for life to obtain a court order and exercise his powers of management under the Settled Land Acts, 1882–90.[1]

8.050. This remains largely the position in both parts of Ireland, for neither the Trustee Act, 1893, which is still in force in the Republic of Ireland, nor the Trustee Act (N.I.), 1958, conferred powers of management on trustees for sale of land.[2] The only changes are that the Trustee Act (N.I.), 1958, does to some extent extend the trustees' power of sale,[3] and does give the court a new statutory power to grant trustees, including trustees for sale, authority to carry out transactions which the court considers expedient.[4] No equivalent provisions have been enacted in the Republic of Ireland.

7. *Referential and Compound Settlements*

8.051. These are two types of settlement which can give rise to considerable difficulties. Though there is sometimes a confusion between the two,[5] a *referential* settlement arises where one piece of land is settled by reference to the trusts or succession of interests existing under a settlement of *other* land, whereas a *compound* settlement arises where the trusts or succession of interests affecting the *one* piece of land are governed by more than one instrument, *e.g.*, where land already subject to a settlement is resettled by a new instrument.[6] In the one case, there are more than one piece of land involved, though subject to the same or similar trusts or succession of interests; in the other case, there is one piece of land only but it is subject to more than one set of trusts or succession of interests.

8.052. The problems which arise in respect of referential settlements are largely matters of construction. Unless the referential settlement itself is drafted very precisely, questions may arise as to how far reference to the other

provision of dwellings are prevented in the Republic from disposing of those dwellings by way of lease by the Landlord and Tenant (Ground Rents) Act, 1978 (see para. 1.74, *ante*), but instead section 2 (6) of that Act authorises them to dispose of the dwellings to their tenants by the grant of the fee simple.

[98] See para. 10.092, *post*.
[99] [1904] 1 I.R. 513, espec. at 518 (*per* Kenny J.).
[1] See paras. 8.057 *et seq.*, *post*.
[2] In England, s. 28 (1) of the Law of Property Act, 1925, conferred on trustees for sale all the powers of a tenant for life and the trustees of a settlement under the Settled Land Act, 1925.
[3] S. 12. This also gives statutory recognition to decisions holding that a sale may in certain circumstances be carried by granting a sub-fee farm grant or sub-lease, where the land subject to a trust or power of sale is held in fee farm or on lease, see *Re Murphy* [1957] N.I. 156 (see *A Casebook on Equity and Trusts in Ireland* (1985), p. 546), and para. 8.069, *post*.
[4] S. 56.
[5] See, *e.g.*, *Re Byng's Settled Estates* [1892] 2 Ch. 219.
[6] *Gaussen and French* v. *Ellis* [1930] I.R. 116.

settlement may be made. In particular, a doubt may arise when the settlement to which reference is to be made is subsequently varied or modified, *e.g.*, by the court in dealing with some family dispute or on a divorce. It may be questioned whether this variation is to apply to the referential settlement.[7] Then, there may also arise a question as to who are to be the trustees of the referential settlement, if none are appointed expressly by that settlement. Once again a doubt may arise as to whether the reference to the other settlement is sufficient to permit the trustees of that settlement to act as trustees of the referential settlement, and the only way round the difficulty is to make an application to the court for the appointment of trustees.[8] The English Settled Land Act, 1925, gets round this difficulty by providing that, in such a case, the trustees of the referential settlement are to be the trustees of the settlement to which reference is made.[9]

8.053. A compound settlement, perhaps, can give rise to even more difficulties. Such a settlement is commonly created in the following way.[10] First, there is an ordinary settlement, *e.g.*, to A for life, remainder to his son in tail, with other remainders over. When A's son comes of age, he bars the entail with his father's consent and the land becomes subject to a *resettlement*, e.g., to A for life, remainder to his son for life, with remainders over. Thus in subsequent dealings with the land there may be two settlements to consider, the original settlement and the resettlement. However, the Settled Land Act, 1882, also provided that a settlement of land could be created by "any number of instruments"[11] and the courts accepted that in the above situation the instruments concerned could be taken together to create a *compound settlement, i.e.*, there are *three* settlements, not *two*.[12] This could be vitally important subsequently when the tenant for life purported to exercise his powers under the Settled Land Acts, 1882–90. It has been settled that where one person is tenant for life under both the original settlement and the resettlement, or at least tenant for life under the resettlement, he may act as tenant for life under the compound settlement, provided there are trustees of the compound settlement.[13] The result may be, then, that the tenant for life (A in our example given above) may have a choice in the capacity in which he will act in dealing with the land, *i.e.*, as tenant for life of the original settlement, or of the resettlement or of the compound settlement. The following summary of his position may be given—

8.054. (a) He can simply exercise the powers of tenant for life under the

    [7] See *Re Arnell* [1924] 1 Ch. 473; *Re Shelton's Settled Estates* [1928] W.N. 27; *Re Gooch* [1929] 1 Ch. 740.
    [8] See para. 8.036, *ante*.
    [9] S. 32. See *Re Adair* (1927) 71 Sol.Jo. 844.
    [10] See paras. 8.005–6, *ante. Re Meade's Settled Estates* [1897] 1 I.R. 121; see also *Re Lord Annaly's Settled Estates* (1896) 30 I.L.T.R. 45.
    [11] S. 2 (1).
    [12] *Re Earl of Pembroke and Thompson's Contract* [1932] I.R. 493; *Re Blake's Settled Estates* [1932] I.R. 637 (see *A Casebook on Irish Land Law* (1984), p. 406); *Re Domvile and Callwell's Contract* [1908] 1 I.R. 475; *Re Meade's Settled Estates, op. cit.*; *Re Lord Annaly's Settled Estates, op. cit.* Cf. *Re Hayes' Settled Estates* [1907] 1 I.R. 88.
    [13] *Re Mundy and Roper's Contract* [1899] 1 Ch. 275; *Re Phillimore's Estate* [1904] 2 Ch. 460.

original settlement, provided there are trustees of that settlement.[14] The only requirement is that the estate in question, by virtue of which he is tenant for life, should have arisen under the original settlement, whether or not the tenant for life claiming the powers is the original or a subsequent tenant for life.[15] Such an exercise of the powers in question will overreach all interests existing under *both* the original settlement and the resettlement, because the resettlement estates arise under the original settlement.[16] However, there is one major drawback in confining the exercise of the powers to those of tenant for life under the original settlement. This is that, since he is acting under the original settlement only, the tenant for life cannot invoke any *additional* powers conferred on the tenant for life by the resettlement.[17]

8.055. (b) He can exercise the powers of tenant for life under the resettlement, which means that he can, of course, exercise any additional powers conferred by that settlement.[18] However, there may be a problem about interests still subsisting under the original settlement, *e.g.*, jointure or portions charges.[19] These interests are created prior to the resettlement and so cannot be overreached by the exercise of powers subsequently conferred or coming into existence.[20] However, this problem may be avoided by inserting a "restoration and confirmation" clause in the resettlement, *i.e.*, by stating expressly that the life estate granted by the resettlement is in restoration and confirmation of the life estate granted by the original settlement. It is true that there has been some controversy in England over the effect of such a clause. In *Re Constable's Settled Estates*[21] it was suggested that such a clause merely preserved the powers of tenant for life under the original settlement, even though the life estate was not in fact restored and ceased to exist.[22] This view, however, was rejected by the House of Lords in *Parr* v. *Att.-Gen.*,[23] where the majority held that such a clause not only preserved the powers of tenant for life under the original settlement, but also the life estate itself, thereby conferring it on the tenant for life of the resettlement.[24] Whichever view is ultimately upheld in Ireland, the point to remember is that, on *either* construction of such a clause, the tenant for life of the resettlement has the powers of tenant for life of the original settlement and can, therefore, exercise them so as to overreach interests subsisting under the original settlement. Without such a clause he cannot overreach those interests.

---

[14] *Re Cornwallis-West and Munro's Contract* [1903] 2 Ch. 150.
[15] *Re Cope and Wadland's Contract* [1919] 2 Ch. 376; *Re Keck and Hart's Contract* [1898] 1 Ch. 617.
[16] *Re Knowles' Settled Estates* (1884) 27 Ch.D. 707; *Re Lord Wimborne and Browne's Contract* [1904] 1 Ch. 537; *Re Curwen and Frames' Contract* [1924] 1 Ch. 581.
[17] *Re Domvile and Callwell's Contract* [1908] 1 I.R. 475.
[18] *Re Constable's Settled Estates* [1919] 1 Ch. 178.
[19] Para. 8.005, *ante*.
[20] *Re Meade's Settled Estates* [1897] 1 I.R. 121; *Re Mundy and Roper's Contract* [1819] 1 Ch. 275.
[21] *Op. cit.* See also *Re Trafford's Settled Estates* [1915] 1 Ch. 9. *Cf. Re Domvile and Callwell's Contract* [1908] 1 I.R. 475.
[22] Reference was made to s. 50 (1) of the Settled Land Act, 1882, see para. 8.060, *post*. See also *Alexander* v. *Mills* (1870) 6 Ch.App. 124.
[23] [1926] A.C. 239.
[24] This view was given statutory recognition in England, *retrospectively*, by the Settled Land Act, 1925, s. 22 and Sched. 4, para. 8. See *Re Cradock's Settled Estates* [1926] Ch. 944.

8.056. (c) He can exercise the powers of tenant for life under the compound settlement. By doing this he can avoid the main disadvantages of (a) and (b) above, *i.e.*, he can exercise any additional powers conferred by the resettlement and the interests subsisting under *both* the original settlement and the resettlement will be overreached.[25] The trouble is that such powers cannot be exercised effectively unless there exist trustees of the *compound* settlement, which is not often the case.[26] This means that before the tenant for life can secure the advantages of an exercise of such powers, he must incur the trouble and expense of applying to the court for an appointment of trustees of the compound settlement.[27] The alternatives are to forgo exercise of additional powers in the resettlement and to exercise the powers of tenant for life under the original settlement,[28] or, if there is no tenant for life under the original settlement, to exercise the powers of tenant for life under the resettlement and deal with the land either subject to interests subsisting under the original settlement or, possibly, seek leave to pay money into court to discharge any such incumbrances.[29] These problems have been resolved in England,[30] but not yet in either part of Ireland.[31]

B. POWERS OF THE TENANT FOR LIFE

1. *General*

8.057. We are concerned here with an examination of the powers conferred on a tenant for life, as defined in the legislation,[32] by the Settled Land Acts, 1882–90.[33] We are not concerned with the powers of a tenant for life, or other limited owner such as the holder of a fee tail, to deal with his own estate. This subject was discussed in an earlier chapter.[34] So far as his statutory powers are concerned, since the exercise of these can affect materially not only his own interest in the land, but also the interests of others created under the settlement, various provisions are contained in the Acts to protect those other beneficiaries. That protection takes several forms.

[25] *Re Meade's Settled Estates* [1897] 1 I.R. 121; *Re Cowley Settled Estates* [1926] Ch. 725.
[26] *Re Domvile and Callwell's Contract* [1908] 1 I.R. 475. It is doubtful if appointment of the trustees of the original settlement as trustees of the resettlement is sufficient, in itself, to make them also trustees of the compound settlement. See *Re Spencer's Settled Estate* [1903] 1 Ch. 75; Megarry and Wade, *The Law of Real Property* (5th ed., 1984), p. 358.
[27] *Re Lord Annaly's Settled Estates* (1896) 30 I.L.T.R. 45. See also *Re Marquis of Ailesbury and Lord Iveagh* [1893] 2 Ch. 345; *Re Tibbits' Settled Estates* [1897] 2 Ch. 149. Trustees could also, of course, be appointed by *all* the beneficiaries interested in the land joining together, but they must all be *sui juris*, etc. *Re Spearman Settled Estates* [1906] 2 Ch. 502.
[28] Though this is no better course if there are no trustees of the original settlement, *Re Du Cane and Nettlefold's Contract* [1898] 2 Ch. 96; *Re Curwen and Frames' Contract* [1924] 1 Ch. 581.
[29] Under s. 5 of the Conveyancing Act, 1881, as amended by s. 1 of the Conveyancing Act, 1911. See also *Re Cornwallis-West and Munro's Contract* [1903] 2 Ch. 150; *Re Fisher and Grazebrook's Contract* [1898] 2 Ch. 660. These provisions seem to have been rarely invoked in England, but have, perhaps, been invoked more often in Ireland, see *Survey of the Land Law of Northern Ireland* (1971), paras. 75–6, and see para. 6.145, *ante*. See also the Landed Estates Court (Ir.) Act, 1858, para. 8.008, *ante*.
[30] Under the Settled Land Act, 1925, s. 31 (1), as amended by the Law of Property (Amendment) Act, 1926, Sched., the trustees of the original settlement (if still subsisting) or, in default, the trustees of the resettlement, are the trustees of the compound settlement. This applies to settlements coming into existence prior to 1926. *Re Symons* [1927] 1 Ch. 344; *Re Cayley and Evans' Contract* [1930] 2 Ch. 143.
[31] See *Survey of the Land Law of Northern Ireland*, para. 121.
[32] Para. 8.028, *supra*.
[33] See, generally, *Re de Malahide* (1952) 86 I.L.T.R. 191.
[34] Ch. 4, *ante*. See also *Gallagher* v. *Earl of Leitrim* [1948] Ir.Jur.Rep. 23.

(i) Trustee of Powers

8.058. First of all, as we have already mentioned,[35] under section 53 of the Settled Land Act, 1882, the tenant for life must have regard to the interests of all persons entitled under the settlement whenever he exercises any of his statutory powers. Like all trustees,[36] the tenant for life has a certain measure of discretion in the exercise of his powers, and the courts are reluctant to interfere with an exercise which appears on the face of it to have been made bona fide. Thus the courts have refused to interfere just because it appears that the tenant for life may have had dubious motives, *e.g.*, malice or selfishness or spite, provided the transaction was otherwise proper and not liable to harm the other beneficiaries.[37] On the other hand, if it can be shown that the transaction in question is going to harm the other beneficiaries' interests in a material sense, then the courts will intervene.[38] The courts will stop a sale of the land at a clear undervalue,[39] or the imposition of grossly restrictive covenants in a lease, thereby reducing the land's letting value[40] (*e.g.*, no sale of intoxicating liquor in a public-house[41]). On the other hand, the courts will not intervene unless there is clear evidence of harm to other beneficiaries' interests as opposed to a mere possibility of future harm based on largely speculative evidence.[42]

8.059. This position of trusteeship might give rise to difficulty, *e.g.*, if the tenant for life wished to purchase the settled land for his sole purposes. It is a basic rule of our trust law that a trustee must not acquire the trust property directly or indirectly, however fairly and reasonably the trustee acts.[43] While it is true that under the Settled Land Acts, 1882–90, the tenant for life is not trustee of the settled land, but only of his powers to deal with it,[44] it was possible that the courts would extend the trust rule to his situation. So the Settled Land Act, 1890, provides that in dealings between the tenant for life and the settled land, including a sale of the land to him, the trustees of the settlement "shall stand in the place of and represent the tenant for life, and shall, in addition to their powers as trustees, have all the powers of the tenant for life in reference to negotiating and completing the transaction."[45] In certain cases, the tenant for life may be willing to pay a better price for the land than anyone else.

(ii) Powers Not Assignable

8.060. The statutory powers conferred by the Acts are given to the tenant

---

[35] Para. 8.030, *supra*. *Re Fair's Estate* (1907) 41 I.L.T.R. 112 (solicitor-tenant for life selling).
[36] Ch. 10, *post*.
[37] *Cardigan* v. *Curzon-Howe* (1885) 30 Ch.D. 531.
[38] *Re Earl of Radnor's Will Trusts* (1890) 45 Ch.D. 402; *Re Earl of Stamford and Warrington* [1916] 1 Ch. 404; *Re Hunt's Settled Estates* [1906] 2 Ch. 11.
[39] *Wheelwright* v. *Walker* (1883) 23 Ch.D. 752.
[40] *Middlemas* v. *Stevens* [1901] 1 Ch. 574; *Dowager Duchess of Sutherland* v. *Duke of Sutherland* [1893] 3 Ch. 169.
[41] *Re Earl Somes* (1895) 11 T.L.R. 567.
[42] *Thomas* v. *Williams* (1883) 24 Ch.D. 558 (increased value of land due to the passing of a Bill by Parliament for the construction of a railway, possibly to run through the land.)
[43] See para. 10.075, *post*.
[44] He is trustee of both in England under the Settled Land Act, 1952, s. 16 (1). See *Re Boston's Will Trusts* [1956] Ch. 395.
[45] S. 12.

for life and him alone. He cannot assign or release them to anyone else[46] and any contract by him not to exercise them is void.[47] Even if the tenant for life assigns or charges his own estate or interest under the settlement, the powers remain exercisable by the tenant for life (assignor).[48] However, where an assignment has been made for value, the tenant for life cannot exercise his powers so as to prejudice the rights of the assignee, unless the assignee gives his consent.[49] In this context, assignment includes the creation of a mortgage or charge on the land.[50] It has been held that the assignee need give his consent only to the tenant for life's exercise of his powers, he need not become a party to the transaction.[51] Such consent may be implied from the assignee's conduct.[52] However, the tenant for life need not seek the consent of an assignee in the case of granting a lease under the Acts (*i.e.*, at the best rent, without a fine[53]), unless the assignee is actually in possession of the land.[54]

8.061. These provisions are general provisions and in some cases the tenant for life's powers may be exercisable by other persons. We have already mentioned the case of an infant tenant for life, where the powers are exercisable by the trustees of the settlement.[55] Where the tenant for life is a lunatic or person of unsound mind or a mental patient,[56] the powers under the Settled Land Acts may be exercised by a person under order of the President of the High Court in the Republic of Ireland and the Lord Chief Justice of Northern Ireland.[57]

(iii) Powers Cannot Be Curtailed

8.062. Just as the tenant for life cannot do anything to divest himself of his powers, so the settlor in fixing the terms of the settlement cannot attempt to oust, curtail or hamper the powers or their exercise by the tenant for life. In fact there are several provisions in the Settled Land Act, 1882,[58] dealing with this subject and what follows is an attempt to summarise their effect.

8.063. First, the 1882 Act makes it clear that there is nothing to prevent a

---

[46] 1882 Act, s. 50 (1).

[47] 1882 Act, s. 50 (2).

[48] *Re Earl of Pembroke and Thompson's Contract* [1932] I.R. 493. This includes involuntary assignment, *e.g.*, on bankruptcy, 1882 Act, s. 50 (1). In *Re Bruen's Estate* [1911] 1 I.R. 76, however, Wylie J. held that assignment by the first tenant for life of his life estate to the second tenant for life under the settlement, so as to cause a merger, made the statutory powers exercisable by the latter, despite s. 50 of the 1882 Act. *Cf. Re Ker's Estate* [1908] 1 I.R. 293.

[49] 1882 Act, s. 50 (3). It would appear, however, that a purchaser from the tenant for life is not concerned to see whether the consent of the assignee has been obtained, see 1882 Act, s. 54, para. 8.076, *post.*

[50] 1882 Act, s. 50 (4).

[51] *Re Dickin and Kelsall's Contract* [1908] 1 Ch. 213; *Re Davies and Kent's Contract* [1910] 2 Ch. 35.

[52] *Re Kingsley and Holder's Contract* (1903) 115 L.T.Jo. 201.

[53] Para. 8.072, *post.*

[54] 1882 Act, s. 50 (3).

[55] Para. 8.026, *supra.*

[56] See the Lunacy Regulation (Ir.) Act, 1871; Courts (Supplemental Provisions) Act, 1961. s. 9 (R.I.); Mental Health Act (N.I.), 1961.

[57] 1882 Act, s. 62. A petition for such an order may be made by any person interested in the land, *ibid.* See Courts (Supplemental Provisions) Act, 1961, ss. 9 and 55 (1), Sched. 8, para. 14 (R.I.) and S.R. & O. 1921, No. 1802 (Adaptation of Enactments). *Re Bradbury* (1901) 1 N.I.J.R. 187.

[58] Ss. 51, 56 and 57.

settlor conferring *additional* or *larger* powers on the tenant for life.[59] If he does so, these powers are to operate as if they are conferred by the Act itself, unless a contrary intention is expressed in the settlement.[60] It is further emphasised[61] that the Act's powers are cumulative, so that the Act is not to be construed as taking away or prejudicially affecting any power given by the settlement to the tenant for life or to the trustees to be exercised with the consent or on the request of the tenant for life.[62]

8.064. Secondly, if there is any *conflict* between the provisions of a settlement and the provisions of the Acts, the provisions of the Acts relating to the tenant for life's powers must prevail.[63] This has been held to be the case even where the conflicting provision in question was contained in a settlement created by a private Act of Parliament before 1882.[64] This provision is reinforced by another provision in the 1882 Act which renders void any provision in a settlement which "is inserted purporting or attempting, by way of direction, declaration, or otherwise, to forbid a tenant for life to exercise any power under this Act, or attempting, or tending, or intended, by a limitation, gift, or disposition over of settled land, or by a limitation, gift, or disposition of other real or any personal property, or by the imposition of any condition, or by forfeiture, or in any other manner whatever, to prohibit or prevent him from exercising, or to induce him to abstain from exercising, or to put him into a position inconsistent with his exercising any power under this Act."[65] Furthermore, it is also provided that the exercise by the tenant for life of any power under the Act is not to cause a forfeiture, whatever the settlement may say.[66] It is clear that these wide-ranging provisions catch most, if not all, ways in which a settlor might seek to restrict the statutory powers of a tenant for life, be they direct or indirect ways.

8.065. It must, however, be noted that the provisions just quoted are confined to attempts to restrict the tenant for life in the exercise of his *statutory* powers. Thus a forfeiture clause would still operate so as to deprive the tenant for life of his estate in the land where the event causing the forfeiture was *not* his exercising one of his statutory powers, *e.g.*, non-observance of a condition of residence in the mansion-house *before* attempting to exercise the statutory powers.[67] There has been some controversy in England over the case where the

---

[59] S. 57 (1). See *Re Earl of Egmont's Settled Estates* (1900) 16 T.L.R. 360; *Re Duke of Westminster's Settled Estates (No. 2)* [1921] 1 Ch. 585 (*cf.* Settled Land Act, 1925 s. 108 (2)); *Re Cowley Settled Estates* [1926] Ch. 725.
[60] S. 57 (2).
[61] S. 56 (1).
[62] See also s. 56 (2) on powers conferred on trustees by the settlement, para. 8.045, *supra.*
[63] S. 56 (2).
[64] *Re Chaytor's Settled Estate Act* (1884) 25 Ch.D. 651.
[65] S. 51 (1). *Re FitzGerald* [1902] 1 I.R. 162 (see *A Casebook on Irish Land Law* (1984), p. 411); *Re Bellew's Estate* [1924] 1 I.R. 1.
[66] S. 52.
[67] *Cf. Re Thompson's Will* (1888) 21 L.R.Ir. 109; *Re FitzGerald* [1902] 1 I.R. 162. In *Atkins* v. *Atkins* (1976) Unrep. (H.C., R.I.) (1974 No. 74 Sp), Kenny J. held, following *Re Thompson's Will*, that a provision for forfeiture of the tenant for life's estate on ceasing to reside in a property the subject of the settlement was void under section 51 of the Settled Land Act, 1882. See also *Re Haynes* (1887) 37 Ch.D. 306; *Re Trenchard* [1902] 1 Ch. 378. *Cf. Re Paget's Settled Estates* (1880) 30 Ch.D. 161; *Re Gibbons* [1920] 1 Ch. 372; *Re Acklom* [1929] 1 Ch. 195.

settlor provides the tenant for life with separate funds to enable him to pay rates and taxes relative to the property during the tenant for life's occupation. The intention is obviously in such a case to ensure that the tenant for life can occupy the property free of the worry of meeting the expenses of its upkeep. But what if the tenant for life exercises his statutory powers, *e.g.*, to sell or lease the land? The English judges have decided ultimately that the tenant for life can continue to claim the separate funds set aside by the settlor where the land is only *leased*, but not if it is sold by him.[68] However, in the Irish case of *Re FitzGerald*[69] a testatrix gave both her house to the tenant for life and an income of £10,000 for life. Attached to both gifts was a requirement of residence in the house, with a gift over in each case on the tenant for life ceasing to reside there. It was held that, in the event of a sale of the house by the tenant for life under the Settled Land Acts, the gift over relating to the £10,000 income was void under section 51 of the 1882 Act.[70]

2. Sales and Exchanges

8.066. Section 3 of the Settled Land Act, 1882, confers on the tenant for life the power to sell the settled land, or any part of it. "Land" includes any easement, right or privilege of any kind over or in relation to the land.[71] The 1882 Act is clear as to the general duty of the tenant for life when exercising his power of sale. Section 4 (1) provides—

"Every sale shall be made at the best price that can reasonably be obtained."[72]

The tenant for life may choose whether to sell by private treaty or by auction, and may sell the land in one lot or in several lots.[73] If he sells by auction the tenant for life may fix a reserve price and buy the land in at the auction.[74]

8.067. The 1882 Act also confers on the tenant for life a power to make an exchange of the settled land, or any part of it, including an exchange in consideration of money paid for "equality of exchange," *i.e.*, to adjust any difference in value in the terms of property exchanged.[75] Where the settled land is held in undivided shares, the tenant for life may concur in making a partition of the entirety, including a partition in consideration of money paid for equality of partition.[76] Again the Act provides that every exchange and partition shall be made for the best consideration in land or in land and money that can

---

[68] See *Re Ames* [1893] 2 Ch. 479; *Re Eastman's Settled Estates* (1898) 68 L.J.Ch. 122; *Re Trenchard* (1900) 16 T.L.R. 525; *Re Simpson* [1913] 1 Ch. 277; *Re Burden* [1948] Ch. 160; *Re Aberconway's Settlement Trusts* [1953] Ch. 647.

[69] [1902] 1 I.R. 162 (see *A Casebook on Irish Land Law* (1984), p. 411).

[70] *Cf. Sifton* v. *Sifton* [1938] A.C. 656. In the *Atkins* case (fn. 67, *supra*) Kenny J. refused to follow *Sifton* v. *Sifton* and instead followed the decision of the High Court of Australia in *Perpetual Trustees Executors and Agency Company of Tasmania* v. *Walker* (1953) 90 C.L.R. 270 in holding that a condition requiring a beneficiary to make certain premises her principal residence was not void for uncertainty.

[71] S. 3. (i). *Gilmore* v. *The O'Connor Don* [1947] I.R. 462 (see *A Casebook on Irish Land Law* (1984), p. 212).

[72] *Wheelwright* v. *Walker* (*No. 2*) (1883) 31 W.R. 912.

[73] 1882 Act, s. 4 (3). *Re Biggs-Atkinson and Ryan's Contract* [1913] 1 I.R. 125.

[74] *Ibid.*, s. 4 (4).

[75] S. 3 (iii).

[76] S. 3 (iv). On partition in cases of co-ownership, see generally para. 7.35, *ante*.

reasonably be obtained.[77] Section 5 of the Settled Land Act, 1890, added a statutory power to grant or reserve "any easement, right, or privilege of any kind" over the settled land or other land in the case of exchange or partition.

8.068. On such a sale, exchange or partition, restrictions or reservations relating to matters such as user of the land or mines and minerals may be imposed by covenant or condition on either party to the transaction, so far as the general law allows.[78] Furthermore, with respect to existing incumbrances on the land sold, exchanged or partitioned, the tenant for life may, with the consent of the incumbrancer, transfer and charge the incumbrance on any other part of the settled land in exoneration of the land sold, etc.[79]

8.069. One problem in particular sometimes arises in connection with the tenant for life's power to sell the settled land, namely the question whether in exercise of that power he can make a sub-grant of the property in question rather than an out-and-out assignment. Prima facie the answer to this question should be "no." The Acts give a power to sell and say nothing about making sub-grants; if the tenant for life wishes to make such a grant he should instead exercise his statutory powers of leasing, in which case he will be subject to the limitations on leasing imposed by the Acts.[80] However, an out-and-out transfer frequently was neither feasible nor the practice in many parts of Ireland. This occurred in the urban areas of the country, in particular in the larger towns and cities, where so much land is held subject to a fee farm grant or a long lease (e.g., for 999 years). In these situations, where, e.g., the entire row of houses in a street was held under such a grant or lease, the usual method of selling the property was by making sub-grants or sub-leases in lots, reserving in each case a slightly higher rent than the proportionate part of the whole head-rent allocated to each lot.[81] When all the lots had been disposed of in this way, the vendor could then sell off the profit rents which had been created, as and when he chose. The question remains, however, whether a tenant for life of settled land held under such a fee farm grant or long lease can "sell" in this way. Such authority as there is tends to suggest that a tenant for life in Ireland can, indeed, exercise his statutory power of sale in this way, though no longer in respect of dwellings in the Republic where such sub-grants are prohibited by the Landlord and Tenant (Ground Rents) Act, 1978. In *Re Braithwaite's Settled Estate*,[82] Wilson J. held that a tenant for life of land held under a fee farm grant could sell by making a sub-fee farm grant or, indeed, by granting a long lease (10,000 years in this case). Since this amounts to a sale, the profit rents reserved in such a case would have to go to the trustees of the settlement, but this would

---

[77] S. 4 (2).

[78] S. 4 (6).

[79] S. 5. Alternatively, the incumbrance, *e.g.*, a mortgage, can be discharged out of the proceeds of sale, *Re Nepean's Settled Estate* [1900] 1 I.R. 298, or it may be apportioned amongst several lots, *Re Biggs-Atkinson and Ryan's Contract* [1913] 1 I.R. 125.

[80] Para. 8.071, *post*. The power to sell land by way of sub-lease is obviously restricted now in the Republic of Ireland by the Landlord and Tenant (Ground Rents) Act, 1978 (see para. 1.74, *ante*).

[81] Para. 4.180, *ante*.

[82] [1922] 1 I.R. 71. See also *Re Clarke's Will Trusts* [1920] 1 I.R. 47; *McGowan* v. *Harrison* [1941] I.R. 331; *Sims-Clarke* v. *Ilet Ltd.* [1953] I.R. 39.

not seem to create a difficulty. Section 21 (vii) of the Settled Land Act, 1882, authorises the trustees to invest the capital money raised on a sale in the purchase of land.[83] It would appear that in every case the crucial point is whether the tenant for life is simply following the usual conveyancing practice or expedient in the circumstances, so that the transaction is to be regarded as a sale *in substance*. This point was reiterated by Lord MacDermott L.C.J. in his detailed analysis of the authorities on the analogous position of trustees for sale of land, in the case of *Re Murphy*.[84] His Lordship came to the conclusion that trustees for sale could carry out their trust in cases of land held in fee farm or on a long lease by making a sub-fee farm grant or granting a sub-lease, provided in each case that this was simply a conveyancer's expedient for effecting what was in substance a sale. His Lordship considered this to be the case under the Trustee Act, 1893 (still in force in the Republic of Ireland), though no express provisions to this effect are contained therein. However, the point has been settled in Northern Ireland, where the Trustee Act (N.I.), 1958, confers such an express power on trustees for sale or trustees with a power of sale of land[85] held in fee farm or on lease.[86]

8.070. Finally, as in the case of most dealings with the settled land by the tenant for life, he must give at least one month's notice of his intention to make a sale to the trustees of the settlement, under section 45 of the Settled Land Act, 1882. Subsection (3) of this section provides that a person dealing in good faith with the tenant for life is not concerned to inquire whether this notice has in fact been given. We shall return to this provision later when considering the powers and duties of the trustees of the settlement.

3. *Leases*

8.071. Section 6 of the Settled Land Act, 1882, confers various powers on the tenant for life to lease the settled land, or any part of it or any easement, right or privilege over the land.[87] Such a lease will survive for its full term despite the death of the lessor (tenant for life), or other termination of his estate or interest, during the lease's currency, but the Act laid down *maximum* limits on the length of such leases. These limits were: (i) 99 years for building leases; (ii) 60 years for mining leases; (iii) 35 years for other leases.[88] However, where the tenant for life could show, in the case of building or mining purposes, that either it was the custom of the district in which the settled land was situate or it was difficult to make leases or grants except for longer terms or in

---

[83] See also the definition of land in s. 2 (10) of the 1882 Act.

[84] [1957] N.I. 156.

[85] Including cases where, under the Settled Land Act, 1882, s. 56 (2), the trustees can exercise the power only with the consent of the tenant for life, s. 12 (6) and see para. 8.045, *supra*.

[86] S. 12 (2). A similar express power was conferred on personal representatives by s. 40 (1) (c) of the Administration of Estates Act (N.I.), 1955 and, in the Republic of Ireland, by s. 60 (1) (c) of the Succession Act, 1965.

[87] *E.g.*, shooting, fishing or hunting rights.

[88] S. 65 (10) of the 1882 Act made this special provision for Ireland. The maximum limit for England was 21 years for leases other than building and mining leases. The current limits in England and Wales are (i) 999 years for building *or forestry* leases; (ii) 100 years for mining leases: (iii) 50 years for other leases. See Settled Land Act, 1925, s. 41.

perpetuity, he could apply to the court for authority to make longer leases or fee farm grants, as the court thought fit.[89] This is a provision of obvious relevance in the urban areas of Ireland.[90] The 1882 provisions remain in full force in Northern Ireland, but there have been some amendments made in the Republic. First, the limit of 99 years for a building lease was extended by section 62 of the Landlord and Tenant Act, 1931, to 150 years in the case of land situate in an urban area.[91] Under section 60 of the 1931 Act, a person who desired to obtain a building lease of building ground in an urban area could, in certain circumstances, apply to the court for a grant of a building lease for a period not exceeding 150 years[92] and, on such an application, the court could, if it thought fit, dispense with the consent or concurrence of the trustees for the purposes of the Settled Land Acts, 1882–90, of any settlement.[93] Furthermore, under section 43 of the 1931 Act, the leasing powers of tenants for life in respect of leases other than building and mining leases were extended to powers to grant new tenancies up to 99 years where required under the 1931 Act.[94] However, the power to grant building leases was abolished in the Republic of Ireland so far as it relates to "dwellings" by the Landlord and Tenant (Ground Rents) Act, 1978. Subject to that Act, most of the provisions of the Landlord and Tenant Act, 1931, have been replaced by ones in the Landlord and Tenant (Amendment) Act, 1980. The equivalent of section 43 of the 1931 Act is section 79 of the 1980 Act, but it should be noted that there is no equivalent of sections 60 and 62 because of the prohibition in the 1978 Act.

8.072. In making leases under his statutory powers, the tenant for life must

---

[89] 1882 Act, s. 10. See *Re O'Connell's Estate* [1903] 1 I.R. 154 (leave given for grant of building lease for 500 years).

[90] Para. 8.069, *supra*.

[91] Defined in s. 2 of the 1931 Act as "an area which is either a county or other borough, an urban district, a town, or a village." In *Readymix Ltd* v. *Liffey Sandpit Co. Ltd*. (1977) Unrep. (H.C., R.I.), Costello J. held that the applicants' premises on a site "situated in open country approximately 175 yards from the nearest habitation" in the "village" of Palmerston in Co. Dublin were not in an "urban" area within the meaning of the 1931 Act. As to the argument that the entrance to the site was at the end of an avenue in the village, Costello J. stated:

> "It is true that it is a common enough feature of Irish villages to find the entrance of a large estate situated in or close to the village's main street. It is, however, not necessary for me to decide whether the result is that the estate is then 'in' the village. . . In my opinion the mere fact that the entrance to the site is 'in' the village does not result in the site itself being so situated. It seems to me to be clear that the site is situated in open fields outside Palmerston village and that the mode of access to it does not have the effect of bringing it within an 'urban area' as defined in the Act. Indeed, I am satisfied that the Act was not intended to give statutory rights to premises such as the one which I am considering in the present case."

[92] S. 60 (7) (a).

[93] S. 60 (10).

[94] Under s. 29, the court, in the absence of agreement, had power to fix the terms of a new tenancy, which was to be for a minimum of 21 years and a maximum of 99 years. In practice the courts fixed such tenancies for 21 years only and this tended to be the limit adopted in negotiations out of court. In *Byrne* v. *Loftus* [1978] I.R. 211, the Republic's Supreme Court, while recognising that the 1931 Act gave no power to insert a rent review clause in a lease of business premises (common though such a clause was in a business lease), held that it was permissible to fix a rent to take account of inflation, not as had previously been done by Circuit Court Judges by adding 10 per cent to the rent fixed ("an arbitrary and unjust practice"), but by calculating a sum "to provide an aggregate amount of rent over the term of 21 years equal to the total of the rents a willing landlord would obtain by granting a lease for 21 years with a clause providing for periodic rent reviews." As Kenny J. (with whose judgment Parke J. agreed) put it (*ibid.*, pp. 221–2):

> "When there is a finding of fact that a landlord would not willingly make a lease for 21 years of a business premises without inserting a clause for periodic review of the rent, the critical matter, to which the valuers must direct their evidence, is the amount of rent which would be agreed between a lessor

abide by several conditions.[95] First, the lease must be made by deed and take effect in possession not later than twelve months after its date.[96] Secondly, the lease should reserve the best rent that can reasonably be obtained, regard being had to any fine taken[97] and any money laid out for the benefit of the settled land, and generally to the circumstances of the case.[98] However, in the case of a building lease, a peppercorn or nominal or other rent may be payable for up to the first five years of the lease[99] and, in the case of a mining lease, the rent may vary according to the acreage worked or the quantities of minerals taken and disposed of.[1] Thirdly, the lease must contain a covenant by the lessee for payment of the rent, plus a condition of re-entry on the rent not being paid within a specified time not exceeding 30 days.[2] Fourthly, a counterpart of the lease must be executed by the lessee and delivered to the tenant for life, though execution of the lease by the tenant for life is sufficient evidence that this has been done.[3] Fifthly, as in the case of most dealings with the settled land, the tenant for life must give at least one month's notice to the trustees of the settlement of his intention to lease the land.[4] However, section 7 of the Settled Land Act, 1890, makes an exception to this rule in the case of leases for a term not exceeding 21 years[5] at the best rent, without a fine and where the lessee is not made unimpeachable for waste.

8.073. In addition to these general provisions, the Settled Land Act, 1882, contains other special provisions relating to building and mining leases. Section 8 of the 1882 Act provides that every building lease is to be made partly in

anxious to make a letting of the premises for 21 years without a rent review clause and a tenant who is anxious to get them for that period. If the valuer's evidence is that the landlord would not let the premises at a rent less than that which would provide an aggregate amount of rent over the term of 21 years which would be equal to the total of the rents that a landlord would obtain by granting a lease for 21 years with a clause providing for periodic rent reviews, the judge may act on it and fix the rent on that basis. In most cases such evidence could probably be given truthfully but not necessarily in all."

Section 23 (2) of the Landlord and Tenant (Amendment) Act, 1980, now provides that the term of a new tenancy is to be 35 years unless the tenant nominates a shorter term. It should also be noted that section 24 of the 1980 Act provides for application to the Circuit Court for review of the rent every five years where the terms of the new lease were fixed by the Court. See para. 18. 10, *post*.

[95] The court may also grant powers to lease on terms other than those specified in the 1882 Act, under s. 10 of the same Act, see *supra*.

[96] 1882 Act, s. 7 (1). However, by s. 7 (iii) of the Settled Land Act, 1890, a lease at the best rent, etc. without a fine, with the lessee not unimpeachable for waste, may be made in writing only, with an agreement instead of a covenant by the lessee to pay rent, where the term does not exceed 3 years. *Cf.* Deasy's Act, 1860. s. 4, ch. 17, *post*.

[97] A fine received on any lease granted under the Acts is deemed to be capital money arising under the Acts and therefore must be paid to the trustees of the settlement, 1884 Act, s. 4.

[98] S. 7 (2). In *Re Rycroft's Settlement* [1962] Ch. 263, it was held that settled land could not be leased with other land, unless at the least the rent was apportioned between the settled land and the other land.

[99] S. 8 (2).

[1] S. 9 (1) (i). The rent may also vary according to the price of the minerals obtained, whether the saleable price or market value, etc., see s. 8 of 1890 Act.

[2] S. 7 (3).

[3] S. 7 (4).

[4] S. 45. See para. 8.097, *post*. *Hughes* v. *Fanagan* (1891) 30 L.R.Ir. 111 (see *A Casebook on Irish Land Law* (1984), p. 412).

[5] The 1890 Act does not contain any express modification of this period for Ireland, as does the 1882 Act in its general provision as to limits on leases (s. 6) by providing in s. 65 (10) that the maximum limit for leases other than building or mining leases is 35 years in Ireland instead of 21 years. It is arguable that to the extent that s. 7 of the 1890 Act can be regarded as a cross-reference to s. 6 of the 1882 Act, it should be read as subject to the same modification for Ireland as applies to s. 6. This argument may be supported by the general provision in s. 2 of the 1890 Act that it and the Settled Land Acts, 1882–89 "are to be read and construed together as one Act."

consideration of the erection of, improvement of, addition to or repair[6] of buildings, or the agreement to carry out such operations. Until recently, any building erected under such a lease would have reverted automatically along with the settled land itself to the person entitled to the reversion at the expiry of the lease. However, in both parts of Ireland residential lessees can now prevent this by exercising their statutory rights of "enfranchisement" or of getting a reversionary lease, or an extension of the original lease.[7] Where the building land is leased in lots, the rent for the whole land leased may be apportioned among the lots in any manner, subject to certain limitations.[8] Finally, section 2 of the Settled Land Act, 1889, provides that any building lease granted under the 1882 Act may contain an option to purchase the land leased at a price fixed at the time of the lease. The section further provides that the option must have to be exercised within an agreed number of years not exceeding 10 years, and the price fixed must be the best that can reasonably be obtained, having regard to the rent reserved (and be either a fixed sum of money or a sum equal to a stated number of years purchase of the highest rent reserved in the lease). Section 3 of the 1889 Act provides that such price shall for all purposes be capital money arising under the 1882 Act.

8.074. With respect to mining leases, these *may* be made partly in consideration of the lessee having executed, or an agreement to execute, improvements for or in connection with mining purposes.[9] Further, as in the case of a sale, exchange or partition, a mining lease may be made of land with or without an exception or reservation of any of the mines and minerals therein and in such cases with or without a grant or reservation of powers of working, wayleaves or rights of way.[10] In other words, the tenant for life may deal with the surface of the land separately from mines and minerals in such cases.[11]

8.075. As regards the rent reserved in leases of settled land, the general rule is that the tenant for life is entitled to the whole rent as income from the land.[12] The necessary exception to this rule arises in the case of a mining lease, for here the capital value of the land will be diminished by mining and the extraction of

---

[6] *Quaere* whether an ordinary repairing lease comes within these provisions, see Hood and Challis, *Property Acts* (8th ed., 1898), p. 561. It also appears that they do not cover a lease at a low rent in return for repairs or improvements made voluntarily by the tenant, though they do cover a lease requiring a tenant to expend a substantial sum on repairs, usually within a fixed time. *Cf. Re Chawner's Settled Estates* [1892] 2 Ch. 192 and *Re Daniell's Settled Estates* [1894] 3 Ch. 503. See also *Re Earl of Ellesmere* [1898] W.N. 18 and *Re Grosvenor Settled Estates* [1933] Ch. 97.

[7] As to the Republic of Ireland, see the Landlord and Tenant Act, 1931, espec. Part v, Landlord and Tenant (Amendment) Act, 1943, Landlord and Tenant (Reversionary Leases) Act, 1958, and Landlord and Tenant (Ground Rents) Act, 1967, since replaced by the provisions of the Landlord and Tenant (Amendment) Act, 1980. Also, see the *Report on Ground Rents* (Pr. 7783, 1964). As to Northern Ireland, see the Leasehold (Enlargement and Extension) Act (N.I.), 1971. Also, the *Report of the Committee on Long Leases* (Cmd. 509; 1967) and Wylie, "Leasehold (Enlargement and Extension) Act (N.I.), 1971—A Critique" (1971) 22 N.I.L.Q. 389. And, generally, ch. 18, *post.*

[8] 1882 Act s. 8 (3). One limitation is that the rent in any one lease is not to exceed 1/5th part of the full annual value of the land contained in that lease with the buildings thereon, when completed, s. 8 (3) (iii).

[9] S. 9 (2).

[10] S. 17 (1).

[11] See *Re Gladstone* [1900] 2 Ch. 101; *Re Duke of Rutland's Settled Estates* [1900] 2 Ch. 206: *Re Rycroft's Settlement* [1962] Ch. 263.

[12] *Re Wix* [1916] 1 Ch. 279.

minerals. Unless a contrary intention is expressed in the settlement,[13] it is provided by section 11 of the 1882 Act that part of the rent in such a case should from time to time be set aside as capital money, and should not, therefore, be received by the tenant for life. If the tenant for life is impeachable for waste in respect of minerals, three-quarters of the rent should be treated as capital, otherwise one-quarter only. The residue, of course, goes to the tenant for life as income in the usual way. It must be emphasised that these provisions apply only in the case of a mining lease granted under the statutory powers. They do not apply in the case of a mining lease granted under some other power, *e.g.*, an express power in the settlement, where it appears that the tenant for life is entitled to the whole rent, in the absence of a provision to the contrary in the settlement.[14] Nor, of course, do they apply in the situation where the tenant for life does the mining himself. Here his position is governed by the nature of his estate[15] and whether or not he is impeachable for waste.[16]

8.076. The question remains as to what is the effect of a lease granted which does not conform with the requirements of the Settled Land Acts, in particular the requirements of section 7, outlined above. The position in Ireland under the 1882–90 Acts is not as clear as it might be. The doubt exists in the question of how far such a lease remains valid as against successors to the tenant for life under the settlement. The point is that there is nothing in the 1882–90 Acts to indicate whether non-compliance by the tenant for life with the precise requirements of the Acts renders his purported exercise of the statutory powers of leasing void from the outset or merely voidable at the option of other persons, whether the lessee or other beneficiaries under the settlement.[17] The position is complicated by other legislation, in fact passed much earlier in the nineteenth century, namely the Leases Acts, 1849 and 1850. These two Acts remain in force in both parts of Ireland[18] and purport to secure validation of leases otherwise invalid for non-compliance with the terms of the powers under which they were granted. The lessee is given the option to have the lease operate as a contract for the grant of a valid lease, of like effect as the invalid lease but subject to variations necessary to comply with the terms of the power. Such a contract binds the remaindermen entitled to the reversion on the lease on death of the tenant for life. However, these provisions apply only if the lease was made in good faith and the lessee has taken possession under it.[19]

---

[13] *E.g.*, a direction to apply all the rent under a mining lease as income, see *Re Rayer* [1913] 2 Ch. 210. *Cf. Re Daniels* [1912] 2 Ch. 90; *Re Hanbury's Settled Estates* [1913] 2 Ch. 357.

[14] *Re Kemeys-Tynte* [1892] 2 Ch. 211; *Earl of Lonsdale v. Lowther* [1900] 2 Ch. 687; *Re Hall* [1916] 2 Ch. 488; *Re Bruce* [1932] 1 Ch. 316.

[15] *I.e.*, whether he holds a major freehold estate, like a fee simple subject to an executory limitation over, in which case the common law of waste would not apply to him, or a mere life estate, in which case the law of waste would apply, para. 4.149, *ante*.

[16] *Martin* v. *Martin* [1898] 1 I.R. 112. On the law of waste generally, see paras. 4.149 *et seq.*, *ante*.

[17] *Hughes* v. *Fanagan* (1891) 30 L.R.Ir. 111 (see *A Casebook on Irish Land Law* (1984), p. 412) (recovery by remaindermen against lessee). See also *Re Handman and Wilcox's Contract* [1902] 1 Ch. 599. In England, s. 18 (1) of the Settled Land Act, 1925, provides that any unauthorised disposition, etc., is void except to the extent that it binds the beneficial interest of the tenant for life himself.

[18] Their provisions are now contained in England in s. 152 of the Law of Property Act, 1925. The 1849 and 1850 Acts, like s. 152, do not apply to leases of land held on charitable, ecclesiastical or public trusts, see *Survey of the Land Law of Northern Ireland* (1971), para. 298.

[19] *Moffett* v. *Lord Gough* (1878) 1 L.R.Ir. 331.

Furthermore, the courts have tended to apply them only where the invalidity stems from some fairly minor or technical flaw in the exercise of the power to lease, e.g. omission of some restriction or condition.[20] Thus in one case,[21] where a lease made under the Settled Land Acts was defective because it was to commence more than 12 months after its date, it was held not to be validated because the best rent had not been reserved, also a requirement under the Acts.[22] This matter becomes further complicated by a provision in the Settled Land Act, 1882, namely the general provision protecting purchasers and other persons (including lessees) dealing in good faith with the tenant for life.[23] *As against all parties entitled under the settlement*, such a lessee is to be conclusively taken to have given the best rent that could reasonably be obtained by the tenant for life and to have complied with all the requirements of the Acts. It appears, however, that a lessee may have to prove his good faith, *e.g.*, if the lease on its face violates the Acts' provisions.[24]

8.077. Finally, on the subject of leasing powers, it should be noted that the tenant for life is given power to accept surrenders of leases of settled land, to apportion rents on surrender of part only of the land leased and make new leases on surrender.[25] Such new leases must conform with the Settled Land Acts.[26] Furthermore, the statutory leasing powers of a tenant for life extend to leases for special objects, such as giving effect to a contract entered into by his predecessors in title or to a covenant for renewal.[27]

4. *Mortgages*

8.078. The Settled Land Acts, 1882–90, do not confer wide powers of mortgaging the settled land so as to bind the interests of successive owners.[28] Unless the settlement itself confers wider powers,[29] the tenant for life can, in general, mortgage only his own interest under the settlement (*e.g.*, fee tail or life estate). However, the Acts do confer on him limited powers of mortgaging the settled land so as to bind his successors in certain specific cases. Thus section 18 of the Settled Land Act, 1882, confers power to raise money by mortgage, where the money is required for equality of exchange[30] or partition.[31] This power to raise money by mortgage has been extended to cover

---

[20] *Hallett* v. *Martin* (1883) 24 Ch.D. 624; *Brown* v. *Peto* [1900] 1 Q.B. 346; *Re Newell and Neville's Contract* [1900] 1 Ch. 90; *Pawson* v. *Revell* [1958] 2 Q.B. 360.

[21] *Kisch* v. *Hawes Bros*. [1935] Ch. 102. See also *Davies* v. *Hall* [1954] 1 W.L.R. 855. Furthermore, if a power can be exercised with the donor's consent only, it seems that the 1849 and 1850 Acts will validate any exercise of the power without that consent, see *Iron Trades Employers Insurance Association Ltd* v. *Union Land and House Investors Ltd*. [1937] Ch. 313, espec at 323 (*per* Farwell J.).

[22] Para. 8.072, *ante*.

[23] S. 54. *Gilmore* v. *The O'Connor Don* [1947] I.R. 462 (see *A Casebook on Irish Land Law* (1984), p. 212).

[24] *Davies* v. *Hall* [1954] 1 W.L.R. 855. *Cf. Kisch* v. *Hawes Bros*. [1935] Ch. 102, espec. at 109–10 (*per* Farwell J.).

[25] 1882 Act, s. 13.

[26] S. 13 (6).

[27] S. 12.

[28] The English Settled Land Act, 1925, does not alter this position substantially, see ss. 16 and 71.

[29] *E.g.*, to raise money for payment of portions, see para. 8.005, *ante*.

[30] Para. 8.067, *supra*.

[31] *Ibid*. S. 18 also includes "enfranchisement," *i.e.*, purchase of the reversion on a lease, see *Re Corcoran's Settled Estates* [1919] 1 I.R. 283.

satisfaction of claims for compensation under the Republic's Landlord and Tenant (Amendment) Act, 1980,[32] and the Business Tenancies Act (N.I.), 1964.[33] Such a mortgage can be created under the section by conveyance of the fee simple or any other estate or interest the subject of the settlement, or by creation of a term of years.[34] Money so raised by mortgage is to be treated under section 18 as capital money arising under the Act and therefore payable to the trustees of the settlement.[35] This statutory power of mortgaging was extended by the 1890 Act to cover the case of discharging incumbrances on the settled land.[36] However, the incumbrance must be of a permanent nature and not merely an annual sum payable only during a life or lives or for a term of years.[37] This has been held to include charges for making up streets,[38] and to permit the creation of one mortgage to discharge two or more existing mortgages, which were attracting higher rates of interest.[39] The money so raised may be used partly to pay the costs of the mortgage transaction.[40]

8.079. It is important to note that exercise of such statutory powers of mortgaging by the tenant for life overrides the interests of other beneficiaries under the settlement.[41] For this reason, the court will always intervene if it is shown that the tenant for life is exercising the powers in such a way as to prejudice the interests of the other beneficiaries.[42]

5. *Options*

8.080. Section 2 of the Settled Land Act, 1889, provides that any *building lease* granted, or agreement for granting one, under the 1882 Act[43] may contain an option for the lessee to purchase the land leased at a price fixed at the time of making the lease or agreement.[44] Such an option must be exercisable within an agreed number of years not exceeding ten and the purchase price must be the best that can reasonably be obtained, regard being had to the rent under the building lease. When received, the price is to be capital money arising under the 1882 Act.[45]

6. *Improvements*

8.081. In this context, improvements to the settled land means items involving capital expenditure and not merely day-to-day expenses which must be met by

---

[32] S. 79 (3) (replacing s. 43 (3) of the Landlord and Tenant Act, 1931).
[33] S. 49 (2).
[34] Ch. 12, *post*.
[35] Para. 8.093, *post*.
[36] S. 11. *Annesley* v. *Woodhouse* [1898] 1 I.R. 69; *Re Meade's Settled Estates* [1897] 1 I.R. 121.
[37] S. 11 (2).
[38] *Re Smith's Settled Estates* [1901] 1 Ch. 689; *Re Pizzi* [1907] 1 Ch. 67.
[39] *More* v. *More* (1889) 37 W.R. 414. See also *Re Lord Monson's Settled Estates* [1898] 1 Ch. 427.
[40] 1890 Act, s. 11. See also *More* v. *More*, *op. cit.*; *Re Maryon-Wilson's Settled Estates* [1915] 1 Ch. 29.
[41] Para. 8.042, *ante*.
[42] *Hampden* v. *Earl of Buckinghamshire* [1893] 2 Ch. 531; *Re Richardson* [1900] 2 Ch. 778.
[43] Para. 8.071, *Supra*.
[44] *Re Earl of Wilton's Settled Estates* [1907] 1 Ch. 50. S. 51 of the English Settled Land Act, 1925, confers a more general power to grant options to purchase or lease settled land.
[45] 1889 Act, s. 3.

the tenant for life out of his income, *e.g., repairs.*[46] We are concerned with how far the tenant for life can insist upon improvements to the land being paid for out of capital money, whether or not especially raised by mortgage for that purpose.[47] Section 25 of the Settled Land Act, 1882, contains an extensive list of works which may be executed by the use of capital money. This includes the erection of buildings, drainage and irrigation schemes, the building of roads, railways and canals and all the various operations associated with such works. This list has been added to from time to time *e.g.*, by the Settled Land Act, 1890[48] (bridges, additions or alterations to buildings necessary for letting purposes[49] and rebuilding the principal mansion house[50]). If the tenant for life wishes to have capital money devoted to such improvements, he must submit a detailed *scheme* for the approval of the trustees of the settlement or the court, as the case may require.[51] However, under section 15 of the Settled Land Act, 1890, the court is given a discretion, where it appears proper, to make an order directing or authorising expenditure of capital money for any improvement authorised by the 1882–90 Acts, notwithstanding non-submission of a scheme for approval before execution of the improvement, as required by the 1882 Act.[52] Furthermore, the court may authorise improvements by the tenant for life where it considers that these are necessary as a "salvage" operation.[53]

8.082. Where the capital money is in the hands of the trustees, the trustees may apply it to meet the cost of improvements provided there is (a) a certificate of the Commissioners of Public Works in Ireland,[54] or (b) a certificate of a competent engineer or able practical surveyor nominated by the trustees and approved by the Commissioners or the court, that the work has been properly executed and as to the amount properly payable by the trustees,[55] or (c) an order of the court directing or authorising the trustees to apply a specified portion of the capital money.[56] Where the capital money is in court, then, after a scheme is approved by the court, the court may, if it thinks fit, on a report or certificate of the Commissioners, or of a competent engineer, or on such other evidence as it thinks sufficient, order or direct application of the capital money for the improvements.[57] The tenant for life

---

[46] *Standing* v. *Gray* [1903] 1 I.R. 49. And see discussion in *Re O'Farrell* [1959] I.R. 387.

[47] *Re Donoughmore Settlement* (1913) 47 I.L.T.R. 268; *Standing* v. *Gray* [1903] 1 I.R. 49. See also *Re Hotchkin's Settled Estates* (1887) 35 Ch.D. 41; *Re Ormrod's Settled Estate* [1892] 2 Ch. 318.

[48] S. 13. *Standing* v. *Gray* [1903] 1 I.R. 49. And see the Settled Land Act, 1887, ss. 1 and 2 (redemption of rentcharges created by Act of Parliament). See also Landlord and Tenant (War Damage) Act (N.I.), 1941, s. 3 (1) and the Agriculture Act, 1967, s. 36 (5) and (6) (U.K.).

[49] *De Vere* v. *Perceval* [1945] Ir.Jur.Rep. 9 (central heating installed in 150 year old family mansion house).

[50] Provided the sum applied does not exceed ½ of the annual rental of the settled land, s. 13 (iv). *Re Lisnavagh Estate* [1952] I.R. 296; *Re O'Farrell* [1959] I.R. 387.

[51] 1882 Act, s. 26. No such prior scheme is required under the English Settled Land Act, 1925, see s. 84 (1). However, under the 1925 Act the tenant for life may have to repay capital money expended on less permanent improvements, see Pts. II and III of the Third Schedule to the Act.

[52] *Re Donoughmore Settlement* (1913) 47 I.L.T.R. 268; *Re McClure's Trusts* (1900) 34 I.L.T.R. 122; *Boyd-Rochfort* v. *Boyd-Rochfort* [1944] I.R. 415. See also *Re Tucker's Settled Estates* [1895] 2 Ch. 468; *Re Lord Sherborne's Settled Estate* [1929] 1 Ch. 345; *Re Borough Court Estate* [1932] 2 Ch. 39.

[53] *Re Lisnavagh Estate* [1952] I.R. 296.

[54] See 1882 Act, s. 65 (9). In Northern Ireland, the appropriate body is now the Department of the Environment, see Departments (N.I.) Order, 1982, Sched. 1, pt.II.

[55] These certificates are conclusive in favour of the trustees as an authority and discharge for any payment made by them in pursuance thereof, 1882 Act, s. 26 (2) (i) and (ii).

[56] 1882 Act, s. 26 (2). As to a court order, see *Re Keck's Settlement* [1904] 2 Ch. 22.   [57] 1882 Act, s. 26 (3).

may join or concur with any other person interested in executing any improvement authorised by the Acts, or in contributing to its cost.[58]

8.083. Once improvements have been made under the Acts, the tenant for life, and each of his successors in title under the settlement, is obliged, out of his own pocket, to maintain and repair the improvements, and insure them against fire, as the Commissioners of Public Works may prescribe.[59] Any default in this respect by the tenant for life will have the effect of rendering him liable if he is sued by others interested under the settlement and his estate liable to make good any damages on his death.[60] In particular, the 1882 Act provides that the tenant for life and his successors shall not cut down or knowingly permit to be cut down any trees planted as an improvement, except in a proper thinning exercise.[61] Finally, the 1882 Act provides that the tenant for life and his successors, and their employees, can enter on the settled land and execute, inspect, maintain and repair any improvement authorised under the Acts, and do all acts and work necessary in that connection without impeachment of waste by any remainderman or reversioner.[62]

7. Miscellaneous

Various other miscellaneous powers are conferred on the tenant for life by the Acts. The following are the more important ones.

(i) Principal Mansion House

8.084. The Settled Land Acts contain special provisions relating to the "principal mansion house," perhaps reflecting the days when much settled land comprised extensive country estates on which there were large mansion houses. The Settled Land Act, 1890, now covers the case of "the principal mansion house (if any) on any settled land, and the pleasure grounds and park and lands (if any) usually occupied therewith."[63] The 1890 Act provides that the principal mansion house and its grounds may not be sold, exchanged or leased by the tenant for life without the consent of the trustees of the settlement or an order of the court.[64] In this way a check was put on dispositions relating to that part of the settled land which might have special value to other members of the family.[65]

8.085. It must be emphasised that not every settled estate will have a

---

[58] *Ibid.*, s. 27.
[59] *Ibid.*, s. 28 (1). *Re Smyth* [1965] I.R. 595.
[60] S. 28 (5).
[61] S. 28 (2). See further on timber cutting, para. 8.088, *post.*
[62] S. 29.
[63] S. 10 (2), replacing s. 15 of the Settled Land Act, 1882. *Re Bective Estate* (1891) 27 L.R.Ir. 364.
[64] *Ibid.* The 1890 Act does not mention restrictions on other powers of disposition conferred on the tenant for life by the 1882-90 Acts. The English Settled Land Act, 1925, s. 65, however, refers expressly to "powers of disposing" and "disposition" is defined in s. 117 (1) (v) as including a "mortgage" and every "other assurance of property or of an interest therein by any instrument, except a will."
[65] This check is in addition to the check existing in the case of most dispositions by the tenant for life, namely the giving of prior written notice to the trustees of the settlement, para. 8.097, *post.*

principal mansion house. Indeed, the 1890 Act itself exempted a house usually occupied as a "farmhouse" or a house whose site, together with the pleasure grounds, parks and lands, does not exceed 25 acres in extent.[66] On the other hand, where more that one estate is subject to the same settlement, there may be more than one principal mansion house.[67] It is, of course, a question of fact which, if any, of the houses on an estate is the principal mansion house.[68] It may well be that the position will change from time to time as the tenant for life alters his habits of residence,[69] and it certainly cannot be assumed that the largest house on the estate is the principal mansion house.[70]

8.086. The restriction on the tenant for life extends to cover the "pleasure grounds and park and lands" which are "usually occupied" with the principal mansion house. It has been held that the qualification contained in the words "usually occupied therewith" in section 10 (2) of the 1890 Act relates only to the word "lands,"[71] but this seems to be a doubtful construction grammatically[72] and, indeed, in terms of policy.[73] It has also been held that the restriction covers sales and leases of minor interests in or over the settled land, *e.g.*, incorporeal hereditaments such as easements or profits.[74]

8.087. It appears that the trustees must give their consent prior to the transaction in question, though this need not be done formally, *e.g.*, in writing.[75] In considering whether to give their consent the trustees may take into account a variety of factors, as may the court.[76] These may range from family traditions and circumstances[77] to the commercial value of the transaction.[78]

(ii) Timber

8.088. Where a tenant for life is impeachable for waste[79] and there is on settled land timber ripe and fit for cutting, under section 35 (1) of the Settled Land Act, 1882,[80] he may cut and sell that timber, provided he obtains the consent of the trustees of the settlement or an order of the court. If he

---

[66] S. 10 (3).

[67] *Re Wythes' Settled Estates* [1908] 1 Ch. 593.

[68] *Re Thompson's Will* (1888) 21 L.R.Ir. 109. See also *Gilbey* v. *Rush* [1906] 1 Ch. 11; *Re Wythes' Settled Estates, op. cit.*

[69] *Re Feversham's Settled Estate* [1938] 2 All E.R. 210.

[70] *Ibid.*

[71] *Pease* v. *Courtney* [1904] 2 Ch. 503. It is interesting to note, however, that the phraseology in s. 65 (1) of the English 1925 Act has not been altered.

[72] It has been pointed out that, if this was the true intention of the draftsman, one would have expected the word "the" to appear before "lands." See Megarry and Wade, *The Law of Real Property* (5th ed., 1984), p. 368, fn. 62.

[73] *I.e.*, the other members of the family will be primarily interested in a check against disposition of grounds or a park attached to the principal mansion house.

[74] *Dowager Duchess of Sutherland* v. *Duke of Sutherland* [1893] 3 Ch. 169; *Pease* v. *Courtney, op. cit.*

[75] *Gilbey* v. *Rush* [1906] 1 Ch. 11.

[76] *Re Wortham's Settled Estates* (1896) 75 L.T. 293; *Re Marquis of Ailesbury's Settled Estates* [1892] 1 Ch. 506.

[77] *Re Brown's Will* (1884) 27 Ch.D. 179.

[78] See Hood and Challis, *Conveyancing Acts* (7th ed.), p. 582.

[79] *Cf.* where he is unimpeachable, paras. 4.149 *et seq., ante.*

[80] See also the earlier Irish Timber Act, para. 4.152, *ante.*

exercises this power, the tenant for life may keep for himself only one-quarter of the net proceeds of the sale, the remainder being set aside as capital money arising under the Act.[81] There is no definition of "timber" in the Acts and the meaning of the term is uncertain, but trees which have not attained a growth of 21 years are not timber.[82]

(iii) Heirlooms

8.089. The 1882 Act also has a special provision to cover heirlooms.[83] This covers personal chattels settled so as to devolve with the land, such as family pictures, tapestries, antiques and furniture.[84] To this extent the 1882 Act allows an exception to the principle that the settled land legislation is concerned with land only.[85] Part of the reasoning may have been that in many cases such chattels were part and parcel of the family home and, if it could be disposed of, then they should be capable of disposition also. So section 37 (1) confers a power of sale on the tenant for life, which can be exercised only after an order of the court has been obtained.[86] The statutory power is confined to selling and does not extend, *e.g.*, to leasing.[87] Furthermore, the trustees of the settlement cannot sanction any such sale, as is usual in a case of this kind; this must be done by the court. Once again the court will take into account all the circumstances of the case before sanctioning a sale.[88] Thus it is unlikely that the court will sanction the independent sale of heirlooms intimately connected with the family home.[89] On the other hand, chattels not easily removed from the home, or whose removal would seriously detract from the value of the home, would usually be sold with the home.[90]

8.090. The money raised on the sale of such heirlooms is to be treated as capital money arising under the Act and invested accordingly.[91] However, in this case the capital money may be used to purchase other chattels, to be settled and held on the same trusts, and to devolve in the same manner as the chattels sold.[92] Such a purchase of new chattels must also be sanctioned by the court.[93]

---

[81] S. 35 (2).
[82] *Dunn* v. *Bryan* (1872) I.R. 7 Eq. 143. See also *Kirkpatrick* v. *Naper* (1945) 79 I.L.T.R. 49 (see *A Casebook on Irish Land Law* (1984), p. 225).
[83] S. 37.
[84] *Gormanston* v. *Gormanston* [1923] 1 I.R. 137. In this sense the word "heirlooms" is used in a wider sense than in the old law of inheritance, whereby certain chattels descended to the heir. See *Coke on Littleton*, 18b and *Hill* v. *Hill* [1897] 1 Q.B. 483; *Re Johnson* (1884) 26 Ch.D. 538. See also *Beresford* v. *Preston* (1920) 54 I.L.T.R. 48.
[85] Para. 8.002, *supra*.
[86] S. 37 (3). *Gormanston* v. *Gormanston* [1923] 1 I.R. 137. No such power existed before the Act, even if the court considered its exercise would be beneficial, *D'Eyncourt* v. *Gregory* (1876) 3 Ch.D. 635.
[87] *Re Lacon's Settlement* [1911] 1 Ch. 351; [1911] 2 Ch. 17.
[88] *Re Earl of Radnor's Will Trusts* (1890) 45 Ch.D. 402; *Re Hope's Settlement* (1893) 9 T.L.R. 506.
[89] *Re Beaumont's Settled Estates* (1880) 58 L.T. 916. See also the saga of the Hope diamond, *Re Hope* [1899] 2 Ch. 679; *Re Hope's Settled Estates* (1910) 26 T.L.R. 413.
[90] *Browne* v. *Collins* (1890) 62 L.T. 566; *Re Hope's Settled Estates, op. cit.*
[91] S. 37 (2).
[92] *Ibid. Re Lord Stafford's Settlement and Will* [1904] 2 Ch. 72; *Re Earl of Egmont's Settled Estates* [1912] 1 Ch. 251.
[93] S. 37 (3).

(iv) Contracts

8.091. Finally the Settled Land Act, 1882, confers on the tenant for life powers to enter into contracts to make sales, leases and mortgages, and to exercise other powers conferred by the Act.[94] Such contracts are enforceable by or against the tenant for life's successors in title,[95] and the tenant for life may make any conveyance necessary to give effect to such contracts entered into by his predecessor in title.[96] These powers of contracting include powers to vary and rescind the contracts.[97] The court is empowered to give directions as to the enforcement, execution, variation or rescission of such contracts, on the application of the tenant for life or any successor.[98]

C. FUNCTIONS OF THE TRUSTEES OF THE SETTLEMENT

1. *General*

8.092. In the course of the preceding discussion we have mentioned the trustees' functions[99] from time to time. Basically, the trustees fulfil a protective role by ensuring that the exercise by the tenant for life of his statutory powers does not harm the interests of the other beneficiaries interested in the settlement. This is achieved in three main ways, each of which will be considered below. In addition, there are various other miscellaneous functions performed by the trustees and these are also mentioned.

2. *Capital Money*

8.093. We have already explained that an essential part of the overreaching principle[1] enshrined in the Settled Land Acts is the requirement that capital money arising under the Acts be paid to the trustees of the settlement[2] or into court.[3] In this context, "capital money" covers a wide range of sums of money: the proceeds of a sale[4] or mortgage[5] of the settled land; fines[6] paid on the granting of leases; part of the proceeds arising from timber[7] and mining[8] operations; the proceeds of the sale of heirlooms[9]; the price of exercising an option to purchase[10] contained in a building lease. Unless the settlement itself authorises payment of capital money to a sole trustee, it must be paid to at

---

[94] S. 31. *Re Neill's Estate* (1911) 45 I.L.T.R. 246; *Gilmore* v. *The O'Connor Don* [1947] I.R. 462 (see *A Casebook on Irish Land Law* (1984), p. 212).
[95] S. 31 (2).
[96] 1890 Act, s. 6.
[97] 1882 Act, s. 31 (1) (ii), (iii) and (vi) and (2). *Re Locke's Estate* (1913) 47 I.L.T.R. 147.
[98] *Ibid.*, s. 31 (3).
[99] Their appointment, etc. we discussed above, paras. 8.031 *et seq.*
[1] Para. 8.041, *supra.*
[2] 1882 Act, s. 22. *Ex parte Verschoyle* (1885) 15 L.R.Ir. 576; *Gilmore* v. *The O'Connor Don* [1947] I.R. 462 (see *A Casebook on Irish Land Law* (1984), p. 212).
[3] 1882 Act, s. 46 (2). Capital money paid into court may at any time be paid out to the trustees of the settlement, if the court thinks fit, 1890 Act, s. 14. *Re Collis's Estate* [1911] 1 I.R. 267.
[4] Para. 8.066, *supra.*
[5] Para. 8.078, *supra.*
[6] Para. 8.072, *supra.*
[7] Para. 8.088, *supra.*
[8] Para. 8.074, *supra.*
[9] Para. 8.089, *supra.*
[10] Para 8.080, *supra.*

least two trustees.[11] This remains the position in the Republic of Ireland,[12] but in Northern Ireland the modification has been made that payment may be made to a trust corporation acting alone.[13]

8.094. A receipt issued by the trustees (or the court) is essential to discharge, *e.g.,* a purchaser of the settled land from claims by the tenant for life.[14] This receipt forms an essential part of the purchaser's title and the lack of it will be a fatal flaw in his title for the purposes of subsequent transactions relating to the land.[15] It may be noted, however, that the tenant for life has the option to decide whether the capital money is paid to the trustees or into court.[16] It has been suggested that he cannot direct payment into court if there are no trustees.[17] On the other hand, if the purchaser is unaware of the fact that there are no trustees and pays the capital money into court, he still obtains a good discharge and takes the land free of all beneficial interests existing under the settlement.[18] In giving directions as to the investment or application of the capital money, it seems that the tenant for life must act as a trustee.[19]

8.095. Capital money paid to the trustees must be invested or applied by them according to the direction of the tenant for life and, if none is given, at the discretion of the trustees.[20] The 1882 Act lists[21] various ways in which the capital money may be invested or applied: *e.g.,* in government securities and other trustee investments[22]; discharge of incumbrances[23]; payment for improvements authorised under the Acts[24]; purchase of land held in fee simple or for a term of 60 years or more unexpired[25]; any other investment authorised by the settlement itself.[26]

8.096. In accordance with the principle of overreaching, the beneficiaries

---

[11] 1882 Act s. 39 (1) *Re Ardagh's Estate* [1914] 1 I.R. 5.

[12] This is not to say that a corporation cannot act as one of the trustees of the settlement, see *Robinson* v. *Ulster Bank, Ltd.* (1949) 83 I.L.T.R. 105. As to the Public Trustee under s. 52 of the Irish Land Act, 1903 (see para. 10.001, *post*), see *Re Baron Massey's Estate* (1912) 46 I.L.T.R. 87 and *Re Sandes' Trusts* [1920] 1 I.R. 342.

[13] Trustee Act (N.I.), 1958, s. 14 (2). A "trust corporation" is defined in s. 67 of the 1958 Act. Note that this concept has been introduced in the Republic for the purposes of grants of representation, see Bodies Corporate (Executors and Administrators) Act, 1928, and Sucession Act, 1965, s. 30; *cf.* Probates and Letters of Administration Act (N.I.), 1933, and Administration of Estates Act (N.I.), 1955, s. 28 (2). See para. 10.003, *post.*

[14] 1882 Act, s. 40.

[15] *Re Norton and Las Casas' Contract* [1909] 2 Ch. 59.

[16] 1882 Act s. 22 (1).

[17] *Hatten* v. *Russell* (1888) 38 Ch.D. 334 at 345 (*per* Kay J.).

[18] 1882 Act, s. 46 (2). *Re Fisher and Grazebrook's Contract* [1898] 2 Ch. 660 at 662.

[19] *Re Lord Coleridge's Settlement* [1895] 2 Ch. 704; *Re Hotham* [1902] 2 Ch. 575; *Re Sir Robert Peel's Settled Estates*[1910] 1 Ch. 389; *Re Gladwin's Trust* [1919] 1 Ch. 232.

[20] 1882 Act, s. 22 (2). During his life, no investment or application can be altered without the consent of the tenant for life. Money paid into court must be invested or applied under the direction of the court, on the application of the tenant for life or the trustees, 1882 Act, s. 22 (3). In the case of the trustees making investments or applications, it appears that the tenant for life in giving directions cannot insist upon selection of a particular stockbroker, *Re Duke of Cleveland's Settled Estates* [1902] 2 Ch. 350.

[21] S. 21, as amended by s. 1 of the Settled Land Act, 1887.

[22] See para. 10.054, *post.*

[23] Para. 8.078, *supra. Ex parte Dyas* (1888) 21 L.R.Ir. 369. See also *Gage* v. *Burke* (1946) 80 I.L.T.R. 29.

[24] Para. 8.081, *supra.*

[25] S. 21 (vii). See *Re O'Farrell* [1959] I.R. 387. See also s. 21 (viii) as to investment in incorporeal hereditaments, *Re Earl of Portarlington's Settled Estates* [1918] 1 I.R. 362 (sporting rights).

[26] S. 21 (xi). *Re Dick's Estate* (1913) 47 I.L.T.R. 149.

under the settlement of land have the same interests in the capital money, in whatever form it is invested or applied.[27] Thus the income from the investments must be paid or applied as the income from the land would have been under the settlement, had the land not been disposed of.[28] However, despite the conversion[29] of the land into investments (personalty),[30] it is provided that the capital money and any investments representing it are to be treated as land for all purposes of disposition, transmission and devolution.[31] This principle[32] is not, of course, as important as it once was since in both parts of Ireland devolution on intestacy of realty and personalty has been assimilated, as a result of the Succession Act, 1965, and the Administration of Estates Act (N.I.), 1955.[33] The principle can still be vital in determining, *e.g.*, succession under a will making general dispositions of "realty" and "personalty," or of "land" and "money."

3. Notices

8.097. Most of the major powers conferred by the Acts on the tenant for life can be exercised only on his first giving notice to the trustees of the settlement.[34] This check on the tenant for life covers sales, exchanges, leases, mortgages and charges executed by him.[35] The notice need not be a specific one and can be a notice of a general intention to exercise some or all of his powers.[36] The notice must be in writing and posted by registered mail[37] both to the trustees and, if known, to their solicitor.[38] The posting must be done at least one month before the proposed transaction or a contract therefor.[39] Once again the notice must be given to at least two trustees,[40] and in Northern Ireland notice to a trust corporation on its own will not suffice in this situation.[41]

---

[27] Para. 8.041, *supra*.

[28] 1882 Act, s. 22 (6).

[29] See para. 3.094, *ante*.

[30] Note that it may be reconverted by investment in the purchase of land, 1882 Act, s. 21 (v)-(viii), *Re Earl of Portarlington's Settled Estates* [1918] 1 I.R. 362. As to the settlement of such land, see s. 24 and the Conveyancing Act, 1911, s. 9 (4).

[31] 1882 Act, s. 22 (5). See the discussion in *Re Sandes' Trusts* [1920] 1 I.R. 342; *Gilfoyle* v. *Wood-Martin* [1921] 1 I.R. 105; *Bennett* v. *Lucas* [1929] I.R. 606; *Re McDonogh's Trusts* [1932] I.R. 398. See also *Re Cartwright* [1939] Ch. 90. It appears that this principle may not hold good for purposes of taxation, *Earl of Midleton* v. *Baron Cottesloe* [1949] A.C. 418, disapproving of *Re Stoughton* [1941] I.R. 166.

[32] *Cf.* the principle introduced for land compulsorily registered in Ireland under the Local Registration of Title (Ir.) Act, 1891, as a result of the Land Purchase Acts, para. 3.099, *ante*.

[33] Ch. 15, *post*. On the older law, see *Bennett* v. *Lucas* [1929] I.R. 606; *Re McDonogh's Trusts* [1932] I.R. 398.

[34] 1882 Act, s. 45.

[35] S. 45 (1).

[36] 1884 Act s. 5 (1) which excludes the case of mortgages or charges. See *Re Ray's Settled Estates* (1884) 25 Ch.D. 464.

[37] Or by recorded delivery in Northern Ireland, see Recorded Delivery Service Act, 1962, s. 1, Sched. (U.K.).

[38] 1882 Act, s. 45 (1).

[39] *Ibid.* The suggestion in *Duke of Marlborough* v. *Sartoris* (1886) 32 Ch.D. 616 that the notice is valid even if given less than one month before the contract, provided the transaction itself is not completed before one month, does not appear sound on a strict reading of the wording of the Act.

[40] Unless a contrary intention is expressed in the settlement, s. 45 (2).

[41] S. 14 (2) of the Trustee Act (N.I.), 1958, does not expressly amend s. 45 of the 1882, nor does the substance of the section indicate any intention to extend its provisions for a trust corporation to matters other than the matters referred to therein expressly. In England, the proviso to s. 101 (1) of the Settled Land Act, 1925, allows the giving of notice to a trust corporation on its own.

8.098. These requirements as to notice enable the trustees to take action to prevent the tenant for life from executing a transaction which may prejudice the settled land or the interests of other beneficiaries under the settlement, by seeking, if necessary, an injunction to prevent the tenant for life proceeding further.[42] It should be remembered, however, that the trustees are under no obligation to bring any action against the tenant for life, even if they consider that his actions are improper.[43] The obligation to look after the interests of the other beneficiaries in exercising the statutory powers is placed firmly by the Acts on the tenant for life.[44] Furthermore, any person dealing in good faith with the tenant for life is under no obligation to inquire whether or not notice has been given.[45]

8.099. If, however, the purchaser or lessee from a tenant for life has notice that there are no trustees of the settlement, he will not be protected and the transaction will not bind those entitled subsequently. There is a difference between the decisions in Ireland and in England on this important topic. In *Hughes* v. *Fanagan*,[46] the Irish Court of Appeal held that, when a lessee from a tenant for life knew that there were no trustees of the settlement, he was not protected. The English courts have taken a different view.[47]

8.100. The trustees may, in the case of notice of a general intention, request the tenant for life to furnish them with such further particulars and information as they may reasonably require from time to time with reference to transactions effected, in progress or immediately intended.[48] If they wish, the trustees may waive notice in any particular case, or generally, or may accept less than one month's notice, provided they do so in writing.[49]

4. Consents

8.101. In certain cases, the consent of the trustees of the settlement is required for transactions to be executed by the tenant for life.[50] Thus consent must be obtained in the case of a disposition of the principal mansion house and its pleasure grounds.[51] In this case it appears that the consent may be given informally, without the need for any writing.[52] Consent must also be obtained in the case of cutting and selling timber, where the tenant for life is impeachable for waste.[53]

[42] It seems that in certain circumstances the other beneficiaries may obtain an injunction, *Hampden* v. *Earl of Buckinghamshire* [1893] 2 Ch. 531.

[43] This view seems to have been given statutory recognition by the 1882 Act itself, see s. 42. Cf. *Wheelwright* v. *Walker* (1883) 23 Ch.D. 752, espec. at 762 (*per* Pearson J.), where no reference was made to s. 42.

[44] Para. 8.058, *supra*.

[45] 1882 Act, s. 45 (3). "Good faith" involves at least making inquiries as to the vendor's title, *Gilmore* v. *The O'Connor Don* [1947] I.R. 462 (see *A Casebook on Irish Land Law* (1984), p. 212).

[46] (1891) 30 L.R.Ir. 111 (see *ibid.*, p. 412).

[47] In *Chandler* v. *Bradley* [1897] 1 Ch. 315, it was held that a bona fide purchaser will, however, obtain a good title even where there are no trustees if no capital money is raised by the transaction, *e.g.*, the granting of a lease without a fine or premium. See also *Mogridge* v. *Clapp* [1892] 3 Ch. 382.

[48] 1884 Act, s. 5 (2).

[49] *Ibid.*, s. 5 (3).

[50] The alternative in these cases is to obtain an order of the court.

[51] 1890 Act, s. 10 (2). See para. 8.084, *supra*.

[52] *Gilbey* v. *Rush* [1906] 1 Ch. 11.

[53] 1882 Act, s. 35. Again there seems to be requirement of formality in giving consent.

5. *Miscellaneous*

Apart from the above principal functions, the trustees have conferred upon them by the Acts the following functions.

(i) Minors

8.102. We have already explained that where the tenant for life is a minor, his statutory powers, if they are to be exercised at all, must be exercised by the trustees of the settlement or by persons appointed by the court to exercise the powers.[54]

(ii) Dealings between Tenant for Life and the Estate

8.103. In the case of a transaction in respect of the settled land with the tenant for life, such as a sale of it to the tenant, the trustees of the settlement must stand in the place of and represent the tenant for life.[55] In so doing, they have all the powers of the tenant for life for the purposes of negotiating and completing the transaction, in addition to their powers as trustees.[56]

---

[54] 1882 Act, s. 60. See para. 8.026, *supra*.
[55] 1890 Act, s. 12. See para. 8.059, *supra*.
[56] *Ibid*.

CHAPTER 9

TRUSTS

9.001. In this section of the book we are concerned with the general law of trusts in force in Ireland.[1] This is a subject which, because of its complexity and importance in modern law, is frequently given separate treatment by textbook writers on property law.[2] What follows is an attempt to give an outline of the law with particular reference to Irish authorities. Apart from citation for the most part of Irish cases, there will be concentration on the legislation in force in Ireland, which, though largely based on English legislation, contains many differences in detail from the legislation operating across the Irish Sea. In the Republic of Ireland, the basic statute in force remains the Westminster enactment passed at the end of the last century for both Ireland and England, the Trustee Act, 1893.[3] In the field of charitable trusts,[4] however, the Charities Acts, 1961 and 1973, have since been passed in the Republic. In Northern Ireland the 1893 Act has been replaced by the Trustee Act (N.I.), 1958, as amended by the Trustee (Amendment) Act (N.I.), 1962.[5] Again in the field of charities, the Charitable Trusts Validation Act (N.I.), 1954, Recreational Charities Act (N.I.), 1958, and the Charities Act (N.I.), 1964, have been enacted.

I. NATURE OF TRUSTS

A. GENERAL

9.002. We have already discussed briefly the nature of trusts in earlier parts of this book.[6] We saw how the modern concept of a *trust* developed in both Ireland and England from the concept of a *use* which had been devised by conveyancers in feudal times. Precise definition of the modern concept of a

---

[1] See generally, Carswell, *Trustee Acts (Northern Ireland)* (1964); Keeton and Sheridan, *Law of Trusts* (9th ed. with Irish Supp., 1968) (later editions do not have the Irish Supp.); Kiely, *The Principles of Equity as Applied in Ireland* (1936), chs. III-VIII. See also Keeton and Sheridan, *The Comparative Law of Trusts in the Commonwealth and the Irish Republic* (1976).

[2] See the standard English textbooks which have considerable relevance for Irish lawyers in view of the common development of most of the general principles in the law of trusts; Hanbury and Maudsley, *Modern Equity* (12th ed. by Martin, 1985), espec. Pts. 2 and 3; Keeton and Sheridan, *Law of Trusts* (11th ed., 1983); Lewin, *Law of Trusts* (16th ed. by Mowbray, 1964); Parker and Mellows, *Modern Law of Trusts* (5th ed., 1983); Pettit, *Equity and the Law of Trusts* (5th ed., 1984); Underhill, *Law of Trusts and Trustees* (12th ed. by Oerton, 1970). See also Maudsley and Burn, *Trusts and Trustees: Cases and Materials* (3rd ed., 1984). Nathan and Marshall, *Cases and Commentary on the Law of Trusts* (7th ed., 1980). Much learning is further contained in the American treatises, especially Scott, *Law of Trusts* (3rd ed., 1967); see also Bogert and Bogert, *Law of Trusts and Trustees* (2nd ed., 1965); Newman, *Law of Trusts* (2nd ed., 1955).

[3] Replaced in England by the Trustees Act, 1925. See also for England the Variation of Trusts Act, 1958; Trustee Investments Act, 1961. And see the Recreational Charities Act, 1958, and Charities Act, 1960.

[4] See further para. 9.088, *post*.

[5] For a handbook dealing with these Acts, see Carswell, *op. cit.*, fn. 1, *supra*.

[6] Ch. 3, *ante*.

trust has, however, caused many difficulties for writers on the subject,[7] as a result, in some measure, of the wide variety of situations in which it has come to be applied. This breadth of application we shall deal with under the heading of classification of trusts,[8] but first let us say something about the nature or definition of a trust in general.

9.003. Though there may be difficulties in devising a brief verbal formula to cover all the characteristics of all kinds of trusts recognised by our law,[9] it is comparatively easy to state in a few sentences the basic features to be found in all trusts. First, most trusts are established expressly either by a *settlor inter vivos* or by a *testator* in his will. Express trusts form the largest category of trusts coming into existence in our society, but, as we shall see, often trusts come into operation without being expressly created, *e.g.*, implied or constructive trusts.[10] In some of these cases it may be argued that there is still a settlor or testator, at least by implication, though in other cases this appears to be stretching the normal meaning of the words.[11] One important point to emphasise about the settlor of an *inter vivos* trust is that usually he loses all rights to the property put in trust, once the trust has been established. Of course, there is nothing to stop a settlor retaining some measure of control, *e.g.*, by reserving a power of revocation, but this is rarely done because it would usually defeat one of the primary objects in the setting up of the trust in the first place, namely, avoidance of tax.[12] Retention of such an interest in the trust property, however ephemeral it may appear at first sight, will probably be fatal to any scheme whereby the settlor was attempting to avoid income tax leviable against himself[13] or capital taxes leviable against the trust property on his death.[14]

9.004. The second basic feature of the concept of a trust is that the legal title in the trust property is held by persons known as the *trustees*. We shall examine the various powers and duties of the trustees in detail later.[15] For the moment it is sufficient to say that the trustees are obliged not to secure for themselves any personal advantage from their position as legal owners of the trust property.[16] They are obliged to hold that legal ownership in the property for

---

[7] See, *e.g.*, Ames, "The Origin of Uses and Trusts" (1908) 21 H.L.R. 261; Hahlo, "Trust in South African Law" (1961) 78 S.A.L.J. 195; Hart, "What is a Trust?" (1899) 15 L.Q.R. 294; Isaacs, "Trusteeship in Modern Business" (1929) 42 H.L.R. 1048; Maitland, "The Origin of Uses" (1894) 8 H.L.R. 127; Marshall, "Trusts and Powers" (1957) 35 C.B.R. 1060; Nussbaum, "Sociological and Comparative Aspects of the Trusts" (1938) 38 Col.L.Rev. 409; Pascal, "Trust Concept and Substitution" (1959) 19 Louis.L.Rev. 273; Ryan, "Reception of the Trust" (1961) 10 I.C.L.Q. 265; Stone, "Nature of the Rights of the Cestui Que Trust" (1917) 17 Col.L.Rev. 269.

[8] Paras. 9.013 *et seq.*, *post*.   [9] See discussion in textbooks cited in fns. 1 and 2, *supra*.

[10] Paras. 9.045 *et seq.*, *post*.

[11] *E.g.*, where the trust concept is used by a court purely as a remedial device without regard, necessarily, to the precise intention of the parties involved in the case, see paras. 9.059 *et seq.*, *post*. *Cf.* use of the concept in disputes over property as between husband and wife, para. 25.15, *post*.

[12] See Harvey, "Tax Avoidance—Illegal, Immoral or Fattening" (1970) 21 N.I.L.Q. 235. See also *Re Cochrane* [1906] 2 I.R. 200.

[13] See Income Tax Act, 1967, s. 438 (R.I.), and Income and Corporation Taxes Act, 1970, s. 445 (governing N.I. as well as England).

[14] *I.e.* Inheritance tax in the Republic and capital transfer tax in N.I. And see *Re Knox* [1963] I.R. 263 in respect of earlier estate duty.

[15] Ch. 10, *post*. As to the number of trustees, see para. 10.003, *post*.

[16] On the subject of the legal and equitable ownership, see ch. 3, *ante*. See also *R. (Thompson)* v. *Antrim County Court Judge* [1967] N.I. 82.

the benefit of persons who form the third basic feature of a trust, the *beneficiaries* or *cestuis que trust.*[17] The beneficiaries, so long as the trust survives,[18] have equitable interests only. Their interests will, however, always be enforced by the courts against the trustees or third parties, subject only to the limitations such interests involve.[19] In some cases, a trust is established for the furtherance of animals or inanimate objects, or for purposes, rather than for the benefit of specified persons. Charitable trusts are the most common example of this situation and are a well-recognised type of trust.[20] Trusts are sometimes, however, established for non-charitable purposes and there has been considerable controversy recently, especially in England, over the validity of such trusts.[21]

9.005. Finally, there is the feature of the *trust property,* held by the trustees as to the legal title for the benefit of the beneficiaries, who have the equitable title. The important point to note here is that any kind of property capable of private ownership can be held on trust.[22] The trust concept, therefore, applies equally to real and personal property. It is not confined to land as is a strict settlement.[23]

B. DISTINCTION FROM OTHER CONCEPTS

9.006. Perhaps one of the best ways of illustrating the nature of a trust is to compare it with other similar concepts. Each of the following concepts involves more than one person having an interest in a particular item of property, sometimes even involves one person holding property for or on behalf of another, yet does not involve a trust because each lacks some feature or characteristic essential for a trust.

1. *Contract*

9.007. There is a basic distinction between a contract and a trust. A contract is a two-party arrangement, whereby the two sides to the contract create rights and duties as between themselves, whereas a trust is a three-party arrangement as we have explained above, involving the settlor (or testator), trustees and beneficiaries. The significance of the distinction is this. Under a basic principle of Irish and English contract law, known as the doctrine of privity of contract, the parties to the contract only can have any rights or duties under it.[24] Third

---

[17] Of course, if the title transferred to the trustees in the first place is equitable only, then the trustees' title can also be equitable only. This would occur where the settlor or testator himself had an equitable interest only in the property in question: *nemo dat quod non habet.* A trustee may also be a beneficiary of the same trust, *Fausset* v. *Carpenter* (1831) 2 Dow & Cl. 232.

[18] Note in this context the significance of the rule in *Saunders* v. *Vautier,* para. 10.088, *post.*

[19] *E.g.,* the less weight attached by the courts to an equitable claim, as opposed to a legal claim, in a dispute over priorities (see para. 3.069, *ante*) or, indeed, the maxim that equitable remedies are discretionary (para. 3.050, *ante*).

[20] Para. 9.088, *post.*

[21] Para. 9.114, *post.*

[22] Para. 9.017, *post.*

[23] Para. 8.004, *ante.*

[24] *Tweddle* v. *Atkinson* (1861) B. & S. 393; *Dunlop* v. *Selfridge* [1915] A.C. 847; *Beswick* v. *Beswick* [1968] A.C. 58. *Cf. McArdle* v. *Irish Iodine Co.* (1864) 15 I.C.L.R. 146. See Dowrick, "A *Jus Quaesitum Tertio* by Way of Contract in English Law" (1956) 19 M.L.R. 374; Furmston, "Return to *Dunlop* v. *Selfridge*" (1960) 23 M.L.R. 373; Scamell, "Privity of Contract" (1955) C.L.P. 131; Williams, "Contracts for the Benefit of Third Parties" (1944) 7 M.L.R. 723. See also Yates, "Trusts, Contracts and Attornments" (1977) 41 Conv. 49.

persons, *i.e.*, people not "parties" to the contract, in general can have no such rights or duties. It is otherwise, of course, in the case of a trust, because under trust law the beneficiaries have an equitable interest in the trust property although they are not "parties" to the establishment of the trust by the settlor or testator and the trustees. That is not to say, however, that many contracts are not created which expressly purport to confer benefits on third persons. Many such contracts relate to property law[25] and frequently are enforced, as the parties intended, in favour of the "third persons."[26] Furthermore, on occasions the courts have been induced to use a concept of "constructive" trust to provide the third person with a remedy, *i.e.*, the courts have been persuaded to hold that one of the parties to the contract entered into it as "trustee" for the person who was not a party, but whom it was intended to benefit.[27] This use of the trust concept has now been given statutory recognition in both parts of Ireland. Section 7 of the Married Women's Status Act, 1957 (R.I.), and section 4 of the Law Reform (Husband and Wife) Act (N.I.), 1964, provide that life or endowment insurance policies effected by a spouse and expressed to be for the benefit of the other spouse or their children are held on *trust* for the objects so named in the policy.[28] The 1957[29] and 1964[30] Acts further provide that contracts expressed to be for the benefit of, or purporting to confer a benefit upon, the wife, husband or child of one of the contracting parties are enforceable by the third persons in their own names as if they were parties to the contracts. This latter provision, which, it is interesting to note, was a new one having no equivalent in England, drops the use of the trust concept as a means of giving the third person a remedy.

2. Bailment

9.008. Bailment is a concept recognised at common law whereby possession of goods or chattels is held by one person (the bailee) for or on behalf of the owner.[31] A common example of a bailment occurs in the case of carriage of goods, whereby the carrier (the bailee to whom custody of the goods is given) undertakes to deliver the goods in accordance with the owner's instructions. There are several distinguishing features in such an arrangement, which is usually based on contract, when it is compared with a trust. First, the bailor,

---

[25] See, *e.g.*, covenants relating to freehold and leasehold land, ch. 19, *post.*
[26] See generally, Clark, *Contract* (1982), ch. 15. Wylie, "Contracts and Third Parties" (1966) 17 N.I.L.Q. 351; "The Third Refusal" (1967) 18 N.I.L.Q. 448.
[27] See the Irish cases of *Drimmie* v. *Davis* [1899] 1 I.R. 176; *Kenney* v. *Employers' Liability Assurance Corp.* [1901] 1 I.R. 301; *Kelly* v. *Larkin* [1910] 2 I.R. 550; *Cadbury Ireland Ltd.* v. *Kerry Co-operative Creameries Ltd.* [1982] I.L.R.M. 77. See also *Tomlinson* v. *Gill* (1756) Amb. 330; *Les Affréteurs Réunis Société Anonyme* v. *Walford* [1919] A.C. 801. *Cf. Re Schebsman* [1944] Ch. 83; *Green* v. *Russell* [1959] 2 All E.R. 525; *Jackson* v. *Horizon Holidays Ltd.* [1975] 1 W.L.R. 1468; *Swain* v. *The Law Society* [1983] 1 A.C. 598.
[28] Thus replacing and extending s. 11 of the Married Women's Property Act, 1882. See *Re O'Dowd* [1968] N.I. 52.
[29] S. 8. See *Keane* v. *Cotter* (1964) Unrep. (Kenny J.; No. 2228 P.). Insurance policies covered by s. 7 are excluded from this provision.
[30] S. 5. was applied by Murray J. in *Northern Bank Executor and Trustee Co. Ltd.* v. *Manning* (1977) 28 N.I.L.Q. 199, in holding that the widow of a partner could enforce directly rights conferred upon her by the partnership agreement, although she was not a party to it. Insurance policies covered by s. 4 are excluded.
[31] See Beal, *Law of Bailments* (1900); Paton, *Bailment in the Common Law* (1952). Also *British Wagon Co. Ltd.* v. *Shortt* [1961] I.R. 164; *McElwee* v. *McDonald* [1969] I.R. 437.

unlike the settlor of a trust, does not part with ownership of his property; at most he parts with possession only. In this respect the positions of trustee and bailee are quite distinct in nature and purpose. Secondly, enforcement of a bailment is based on rules of common law, whereas enforcement of a trust is based upon equitable principles. Thirdly, a bailment is confined to personal chattels whereas a trust can apply to any kind of property. Fourthly, a bailment usually involves transfer of possession for a limited purpose, *e.g.*, delivery to some other person, whereas a trust involves a transfer of ownership with all the powers of management and disposition associated with ownership.

3. *Agency*

9.009. The relationship of principal and agent shares some of the features of that of trustee and beneficiary, *e.g.*, the agent is accountable to his principal on a fiduciary basis just as a trustee is to his beneficiary.[32] There are, however, several differences. First, an agent has not necessarily any title to any of his principal's property which he may have in his possession. If a principal seeks an account of his agent, he must proceed on the basis of a personal claim. A beneficiary, however, has a proprietary claim to the trust property held by the trustees, since he holds the equitable or beneficial ownership.[33] Secondly, the agent must act on behalf of his principal and is subject to his control and instructions. A trustee is under no such control from either his settlor[34] or beneficiaries.[35] Thirdly, there is always an agreement between the principal and agent which forms the basis of their relationship; there is rarely, if ever, such an agreement between the trustee and his beneficiaries.[36] Fourthly, an agent can commit his principal to liabilities towards third persons, whereas a trustee cannot so commit his beneficiaries. Fifthly, agency can usually be determined at the will of either principal or agent, whereas a trust can rarely be determined by the trustee. Lastly, the law of agency is largely based on common law rules whereas trust law is based on equitable principles.

4. *Personal Representation*

9.010. The position of a personal representative, *i.e.*, the executor or administrator of the estate of a deceased person, is also very like that of a trustee.[37] Indeed, it is common for the same person to act in both capacities

---

[32] See Bowstead, *Law of Agency* (14th ed. by Reynolds and Davenport, 1976); Fridman, *Law of Agency* (4th ed., 1976); Powell, *Law of Agency* (2nd ed., 1961). Also Sweet, "Trusteeship and Agency" (1892) 8 L.Q.R. 220.

[33] See further on recovery of trust property, para. 10.108, *post.*

[34] On this point, see para. 9.003, *supra.*

[35] See further para. 10.030, *post.*

[36] Where a trustee does agree to the terms of the trust, it is usually an agreement between himself and the settlor, see para. 9.029, *post.*

[37] See the discussion in *Re Hayes' Will Trusts* [1971] 1 W.L.R. 758. See also, Ker *Wills, Probate and Administration* (1959); Parry, *Law of Succession* (6th ed., 1972); Williams and Mortimer, *Executors, Administrators and Probate* (ed. Sunnucks, 1970). Also Leitch, *Handbook on the Administration of Estates Act (N.I.), 1955* (1956); Ker, 'Personal Representative or Trustee?" (1955) 10 Conv. 199. Stebbings, "The Transaction from Personal Representative to Trustee" (1984) Conv. 423. And ch. 16, *post.*

with respect to a particular estate, *i.e.*, he first acts as executor during the administration of the estate and then, when the administration is over, takes up his duties as trustee of a trust established for beneficiaries taking under the will. The two offices are quite separate, however, and the person concerned with them rarely acts in both capacities at once. This distinction can be illustrated by reference to the different histories of the development of the two offices: the office of personal representative was governed by the early ecclesiastical courts until their jurisdiction over the grant of probate was transferred to civil courts; trustees were always under the control of the Court of Chancery. This is now recognised in the two distinct schemes of legislation governing the subjects: the Trustee Act, 1893, and the Trustee Act (N.I.), 1958, on the one hand; the Succession Act, 1965, and the Administration of Estates Act (N.I.), 1955. There is, however, some overlap in this legislation. Thus, in both parts of Ireland personal representatives hold the deceased's estate as "trustees" for the persons entitled.[38] Furthermore, the Trustee Act, 1893,[39] and the Trustee Act (N.I.), 1958,[40] define "trust" to include the duties of personal representatives. Yet it is important to keep the distinction between the two offices in mind because sometimes different laws will apply, *e.g.*, different periods of limitation of actions. This might have caused difficulties in view of the provision that a personal representative holds the estate on trust, but the Irish courts eventually took the view that this should not affect a personal representative's position, when acting as personal representative, *vis-à-vis* limitation of actions.[41] This judicial view has now been given statutory recognition in the recent enactments on limitation of actions in both parts of Ireland.[42] It is often difficult to say when persons have ceased to be personal representatives and have become trustees.

5. *Power of Appointment*

9.011. We have already mentioned briefly the subject of powers, including powers of appointment,[43] and the subject is discussed in much greater detail later.[44] While there are obvious similarities to a trust, in that the arrangement involves a three-party transaction (the *donor* giving the *donee* power to appoint property in favour of the *objects* of the power), there are some vital distinctions. First, a trust is imperative since, once he has undertaken the role, the trustee must carry it out according to the settlor's instructions. A

---

[38] Succession Act, 1965, s. 10 (3); Administration of Estates Act (N.I.), 1955, s. 2 (3).

[39] S. 50.

[40] S. 67.

[41] See *Murland* v. *Despard* [1956] I.R. 170; *McNeill* v. *McNeill* [1957] N.I. 10; *Vaughan* v. *Cottingham* [1961] I.R. 184; *Ruddy* v. *Gannon* [1965] I.R. 283.

[42] Statute of Limitations, 1957, s. 2 (2) (R.I.) ("trustee" in the Statute does not include a personal representative in the capacity of personal representative) (see also the Succession Act, 1965, s. 123); Statute of Limitations (N.I.), 1958, s. 47 (1) (personal representative all rights and privileges under the Statute as if not made a trustee under the Trustee Act (N.I.), 1958). It should be noted that the point was given even less force in the Republic because the 1957 Statute, as amended by s. 126 of the Succession Act, 1965, fixed the same general period of limitation (6 years) for actions against both trustees and personal representatives. There remain, however, differences in detail even under these provisions.

[43] Para. 8.016, *ante*.

[44] Ch. 11, *post*.

power, however, is discretionary and the donee may never exercise it.[45] Secondly, and following on from the first point, the objects of a power have no way of forcing the donee to exercise his power, whereas the beneficiaries under a trust can always have recourse to the court to ensure its enforcement.[46] Thirdly, the degree of certainty required with respect to the definition of the objects of a power may not be as great as that required for trusts.[47] This third point has been the subject of some controversy recently in England as a result of the House of Lords decision in *Re Baden's Deed Trusts, McPhail* v. *Doulton*.[48] We shall examine that decision later and consider its applicability to Ireland. For the moment, suffice it to say that the decision does not seem to destroy altogether the distinction between trusts and powers with respect to requirements of certainty.

9.012. Having indicated the basic distinctions between trusts and powers in theory, it is important to add that frequently the two concepts become confused in practice. Thus, on the one hand, there have long been recognised such things as "discretionary trusts" which may be better regarded as a variety of powers.[49] And there have been recognised powers, variously described as "trust-powers", "powers in the nature of a trust" or "powers coupled with a duty," which have at least some of the attributes of trusts, *e.g.*, enforcement by the court in favour of the objects in the absence of execution by the "donees."[50]

II. CLASSIFICATION OF TRUSTS

9.013. Over the years many schemes for classification of trusts have been devised and discussed.[51] In the following pages we discuss in turn most of the main categories of trust now recognised in Ireland. It is hoped that this list is fairly exhaustive but the warning is given that the various categories discussed are not necessarily mutually exclusive. Thus we mention the category of express trusts, primarily to indicate that there are formalities required for the creation of some express trusts, but many of the other categories are usually created expressly.

A. STATUTORY TRUSTS

9.014. Statutory trusts, *i.e.*, trusts coming into operation automatically by virtue of statutory provisions, are a comparatively modern development. In

---

[45] Para. 9.081, *post.*
[46] Para. 10.107, *post.*
[47] Para. 9.018, *post.* See *Brown* v. *Gregg* [1945] I.R. 224.
[48] [1971] A.C. 424.
[49] Para. 9.081, *post.*
[50] *Rorke* v. *Abraham* [1895] 1 I.R. 334; *Matthews* v. *Kieran* [1916] 1 I.R. 289; *Clibborn* v. *Horan* [1921] 1 I.R. 93. See further para. 11.11, *post.* Also Gray, "Powers in Trust and Gifts Implied in Default of Appointment" (1911) H.l.R. 1; Unwin, "Power or Trust Power" (1962) 26 Conv. 92.
[51] See Lord Nottingham's classification in *Cook* v. *Fountain* (1676) 3 Swanst. 585 at 592. Note Megarry V.-C.'s distinction between trusts "in the higher sense" and trusts "in the lower sense" drawn in *Tito* v. *Waddell (No. 2)* [1977] Ch. 106.
[52] *E.g.*, statutory trusts for sale arising in the case of co-ownership of land under ss. 34–8 of the Law of Property Act, 1925 (see ch. 7, *ante*). See Lewis, "Statutory Trusts for Sale" (1940) 56 L.Q.R. 255. See also the proposals for such trusts in the *Survey of the Land Law of Northern Ireland* (1971), espec. chs. 3 and 4. *Cf.* the Land Law Working Group's Discussion Document No. 2 (1981) (*Estates and Interests and Family Dealings in Land*), chs. 10 and 11.

England the most common source of these trusts is the 1925 property legislation,[52] most of which, of course, has no equivalent in Ireland. However, some statutory trusts do exist in Ireland. Under section 10(3) of the Republic's Succession Act, 1965, and section 2(3) of the Administration of Estates Act (N.I.), 1955, the personal representatives of a deceased person hold his real and personal estate *as trustees* for the persons by law entitled thereto.[53]

B. EXPRESS TRUSTS

9.015. The majority of trusts come into this category which covers all trusts expressly created or declared by a settlor or testator. The question remains, however, whether any formalities have to be met by the settlor or testator. The answer in most, if not all, cases is "yes." These formalities take two forms. First, express trusts must comply with what are known as the "three certainties." An Irish judge put the matter thus:

"It has been established that, in order that a trust may be created, the subject-matter must be certain, the objects of the trust must be certain, and the words relied upon as creating the trust must have been used in an imperative sense, so as to show that the testator intended to create an obligation."[54]

Secondly, in some cases further formalities must be complied with because of the nature of the trust property, *e.g.*, land, or the means of execution of the trust, *e.g.*, by a will. We will now consider these matters in turn.

1. *Three Certainties*

The three certainties necessary for the creation of express trusts relate to the *words* indicating the creation of the trust by the settlor or testator, the *subject-matter* of the trust and the *objects* of the trust.[55]

(i) Words

9.016. The first requirement is that the settlor or testator must use words which indicate sufficiently his intention to create a trust rather than simply to transfer the property to the donee or donees for his or their own personal benefit.[56] Much controversy has arisen in this context about the effect of what are called "precatory words," *i.e.*, words, usually contained in a will,[57] which

---

[53] Ch. 16, *post. Cf.* the English equivalent in s. 33 of the Administration of Estates Act, 1925; see *Re Cockburn's Will Trusts* [1957] Ch. 438.

[54] *Chambers* v. *Fahy* [1931] I.R. 17 at 21 (*per* O'Byrne J.) (see *A Casebook on Equity and Trusts in Ireland* (1985), p. 313).

[55] Williams, "The Three Certainties" (1940) 4 M.L.R. 20.

[56] See *Re Humphrey's Estate* [1916] 1 I.R. 21 (see *A Casebook on Equity and Trusts in Ireland* (1985), p. 315); *Re McIntosh* [1933] I.R. 69 (see *ibid.*, p. 317); *Re Coulson* (1953) 87 I.L.T.R. 93.

[57] The issue arises here because, unlike in the case of a deed, the courts strive more to give effect to the testator's intention in construing the terms of a will, see para. 14.36, *post. Greene* v. *Greene* (1869) I.R. 3 Eq. 629; *Reid* v. *Atkinson* (1871) I.R. 5 Eq. 373; *Creagh* v. *Murphy* (1873) I.R. 7 Eq. 182.

do not refer specifically to a trust but which instead refer to the testator's "hope" or "wish" or "desire" or "confidence" as to how the donee or his property will use it.[58] In the past there has been a tendency to construe precatory words in wills as creating trusts[59] but, as Ross J. put it at the beginning of this century, "the tide has now turned and is running against precatory trusts."[60] The rule now is that such words will not create a trust unless the will read as a whole indicates that it was the intention of the testator to create a trust.[61] This must remain a matter of construction in each particular case and mere use of the same precatory words as used in an earlier case will not necessarily determine the matter.[62] Thus a qualification, added to what appears otherwise an out-and-out gift, relating to application of the property, *e.g.*, for maintenance and education of children, may be construed differently in different wills.[63]

If the court decides that there is not sufficient certainty as to words, then there is no trust and the donee of the property takes it beneficially.[64]

(ii) Subject-Matter

9.017. The second requirement to be satisfied is that there must be certainty with respect to the subject-matter of the trust. This means that the settlor or testator must define clearly not only the property to be vested in the trustees but also the precise beneficial interest to be taken in that property by each of the beneficiaries.[65] Failure to comply with this requirement of certainty usually means that the donee of the property takes it beneficially free from any trust. However, if it is clear that the whole of the property transferred by the settlor or left by the testator was to be held on trust, so that the only uncertainty lies in the definition of each beneficiary's interest in the property, then the donee must still hold it on trust – in this case by way of resulting trust[66] for the settlor or the testator's estate.[67]

---

[58] *Lefroy* v. *Flood* (1854) 4 Ir.Ch.R. 1; *McAlinden* v. *McAlinden* (1877) I.R. 11 Eq. 219; *Morrin* v. *Morrin* (1886) 19 L.R.Ir. 37; *Re Byrne's Estate* (1892) 29 L.R.Ir. 250; *Bradshaw* v. *Bradshaw* [1908] 1 I.R. 288; *Berryman* v. *Berryman* [1913] 1 I.R. 21; *Re Blackwood* [1953] N.I. 32; *In b. Fitzgibbon* (1959) 93 I.L.T.R. 56. The use of the word "trust" is not necessarily determinant, see *Tito* v. *Waddell (No. 2)* [1977] Ch. 106.

[59] *Moriarty* v. *Martin* (1852) 3 Ir.Ch.R. 26; *Gray* v. *Gray* (1860) 11 Ir.Ch.R. 218. *Cf. Shaw* v. *Lawless* (1838) 1 Dr. & Wal. 512; *Graves* v. *Graves* (1862) 13 Ir.Ch.R. 182.

[60] *Re Humphrey's Estate* [1916] 1 I.R. 21 at 24 (see *A Casebook on Equity and Trusts in Ireland* (1985), p. 315). See also Dixon J. in *Re Coulson* (1953) 87 I.L.T.R. 93 at 94. The views of Dixon J. were followed by Hamilton J. in *Hillary* v. *Sweeney* (1976) Unrep. (H.C., R.I.) (1974 No. 374 Sp).

[61] *Re Walker and Elgee's Contract* (1919) 53 I.L.T.R. 22; *McCabe* v. *Campbell* [1918] 1 I.R. 429. See also *Berryman* v. *Berryman* [1913] 1 I.R. 390; *Re Sproule* (1915) 49 I.L.T.R. 96; *Murtagh* v. *Murtagh* (1902) 36 I.L.T.R. 129; *Porter* v. *Fay* (1978) Unrep. (H.C., R.I.) (1977 No. 122 Sp); *cf. Re Finnerty's Will Trusts* [1970] I.R. 221.

[62] *Re McIntosh* [1933] I.R. 69, espec. at 71-2 (*per* Kennedy C.J.) (see *A Casebook on Equity and Trusts in Ireland* (1985), p. 317). See also *Re Heron's Estate* (1969) 20 N.I.L.Q. 325.

[63] *Cf. O'Connor* v. *Butler* [1907] 1 I.R. 507 and *Mackett* v. *Mackett* (1872) L.R. 14 Eq. 49. See also *Re Keith's Will Trusts* [1931] I.R. 730.

[64] *McCormick* v. *Grogan* (1869) L.R. 4 H.L. 82; *In b. Fitzgibbon* (1959) 93 I.L.T.R. 56.

[65] *Re King's Estate* (1888) 21 L.R.Ir. 273. The question of definition of the beneficiary's interest in the property can be regarded as part of the third requirement of certainty of objects, *infra*.

[66] See para. 9.055, *post*.

[67] Which means in the case of no residuary legatees or devisees the testator's intestate successors (ch. 15, *post*).

(iii) Objects

9.018. The third requirement is that there must be certainty of objects. In most cases this means that the persons who are to be the beneficiaries under the trust must be clearly identified or, at least, identifiable at the time the trust comes into operation. The general rule is that the trustees or, if necessary, the court, should be able to make an exhaustive list of all the beneficiaries of the trust, otherwise it fails for uncertainty.[68] The rule is different for a mere power of appointment, because here the requirement of certainty is satisfied if a sufficiently precise *criterion* has been provided by the settlor or testator by which to judge whether or not any particular alleged beneficiary can claim under the trust.[69] It is not necessary in the case of a power that one should be able to make an exhaustive list of all the beneficiaries. The House of Lords in *Re Baden's Deed Trusts*[70] has recently held that this "power certainty" rule should be applied to a discretionary trust[71] of income and it appears from the statements of the majority that they felt that the rule should be applied to all discretionary trusts. It does not appear that their Lordships were putting forward the new rule as being any wider than that and they certainly did not suggest or imply that the "trust-certainty" rule should not continue to apply to trusts other than those bearing close similarity to powers, like discretionary trusts.[72] There is little or no authority on this point in Ireland, so the matter remains open. No doubt the recent House of Lords decisions, like *Gulbenkian* and *Baden*, will carry considerable weight in both parts of Ireland, but they are of persuasive authority only.[73]

9.019. So far we have been discussing certainty of objects in the context of a trust for the benefit of persons, but further problems may arise where the trust is instead expressed to be in favour of "purposes." If the purposes are restricted to charitable purposes, then the problems disappear because charities are given favoured treatment in our legal system and one of the features of this treatment is exception from the requirement of certainty of objects.[74] However, if the purposes are not confined to charitable ones, there are considerable problems due to the fact that the courts of Ireland and England do not in general look upon such "trusts" with favour. We return to this subject later.[75]

---

[68] *Re Parker* [1966] I.R. 309. See also *I.R.C.* v. *Broadway Cottages Trust* [1955] Ch. 20; *Re Hain's Settlement* [1961] 1 W.L.R. 440.

[69] *Re Gulbenkian's Settlements* [1970] A.C. 508; see also *Re Gestetner Settlement* [1953] Ch.672.

[70] [1971] A.C.424 (Lords Hodson and Guest *dissentiente*).

[71] See para. 9.081, *post*. To this extent *I.R.C.* v. *Broadway Cottages Trusts, op. cit..*, was overruled. Note the subsequent application of the House of Lords' test in *Re Baden's Deed Trusts (No.2)* [1973] Ch. 9. See also *Re Barlow's Will Trusts* [1979] 1 W.L.R. 278; *Re Hay's Settlement Trusts* [1982] 1 W.L.R. 202.

[72] See Hanbury and Maudsley, *Modern Equity* (12th ed. by Martin, 1985) p.96. Burgess, "The Certainty Problem" (1979) 30 N.I.L.Q. 24; Emery, "The Most Hallowed Principle – Certainty of Beneficiaries of Trusts and Powers of Appointment" (1982) 98 L.Q.R. 551; Grbich, "Baden: Awakening the Conceptually Moribund Trust" (1974) 37 M.L.R. 643; Hopkins, "Certain Uncertainties of Trusts and Powers" (1971) C.L.J. 68; McKay, "Re Baden and the Third Class of Uncertainty" (1974) 38 Conv.269; Martin and Hayton, "Certainty of Objects – What is Heresy?" [1984] Conv. 304; Matthews, "A Certainty and a Half in Certainty of Objects" [1984] Conv. 22. [73] See further on purpose trusts, para. 9.114, *post* and on powers, ch.11, *post*.

[74] See further on charities para. 9.088, *post*.   [75] Para. 9.114, *post*.

9.020. Where a trust fails for want of certainty of objects, the trustee must hold the trust property by way of a resulting trust in favour of the settlor or the testator's residuary estate (or his intestate successors, failing that).[76]

It is now time to turn to the further formalities which may have to be met in creation of a particular trust. These formalities are laid down in Ireland in three basic statutes: the Statute of Frauds (Ireland), 1695, which applies to both parts of Ireland, and the statutes governing wills, the Republic's Succession Act, 1965, and the Wills Act, 1837, in Northern Ireland.

2. Statute of Frauds (Ireland), 1695

(i) Creation of Trusts of Personalty

9.021. Where the trust property consists of pure personalty only, there are no additional formalities to be observed.[77] The trust may be established orally, either by the settlor declaring himself to be trustee of the property or stating that he is transferring it to trustees to be held on trust.[78]

(ii) Creation of Trusts of Land

9.022. In the case of land,[79] however, section 4 of the Statute of Frauds (Ireland), 1695, requires that the trust be *evidenced*[80] in writing signed by some person able to declare the trust, or by his will.[81] There are several points to note about this provision. First, it does not require the declaration of a trust itself to be in writing. All that is required is that some written evidence (be it contained in a letter,[82] memorandum or even in a recital in a deed[83]) exists to evidence the declaration (which may have been oral) before any action is brought connected with the trust.[84] Thus the written evidence may come into existence long after the declaration and operation of the trust.[85] This written evidence must, however, not only prove the existence of the trust but also its essential terms, *i.e.*, the three certainties at least.[86]

9.023. Secondly, lack of written evidence may not be fatal to the establishment of a trust, enforceable in court, because of the principle of equity outlined by Lord Westbury in the Irish case of *McCormick* v. *Grogan*:

"The Court of Equity has, from a very early period, decided that even an

---

[76] *Scott* v. *Brownrigg* (1881) 9 L.R.Ir. 246; *Re Blackwood* [1953] N.I. 32.

[77] Excluding, of course, the case of wills, para. 9.026, *post*.

[78] *Maguire* v. *Dodd* (1859) 9 Ir.Ch.R. 452. See also *Re Rooney* (1931) 65 I.L.T.R. 82.

[79] Including leasehold land, *Donohoe* v. *Conrahy* (1845) 8 Ir.Eq.R. 679.

[80] S.4 uses the words "manifested and proved." In England, the equivalent provision is contained in s.53(1)(*b*) of the Law of Property Act, 1925. See Youdan, "Formalities for Trusts of Land and the Doctrine in Rochefoucauld v. Boustead" (1984) 43 C.L.J. 306.

[81] See para. 9.026, *post*.

[82] *Childers* v. *Childers* (1857) 1 De G. & J. 482.

[83] *Deg* v. *Deg* (1727) 2 P. Wms. 412.

[84] *Donohoe* v. *Conrahy* (1845) 8 Ir.Eq.R. 679 (see *A Casebook on Equity and Trusts in Ireland* (1985), p. 319).

[85] *Per* Sugden L.C., *ibid.*, pp. 682-3.

[86] *Smith* v. *Matthews* (1861) 3 De G.F. & J. 139.

Act of Parliament shall not be used as an instrument of fraud; and if the machinery of perpetrating a fraud an Act of Parliament intervenes, the Court of Equity, it is true does not set aside the Act of Parliament, but it fastens on the individual who gets a title under that Act, and imposes upon him a personal obligation, because he applies the Act as an instrument for accomplishing a fraud. In this way the Court of Equity has dealt with the *Statute of Frauds*, and in this manner, also, it deals with the *Statute of Wills*."[87]

We have discussed this general principle in an earlier chapter.[88] In the present context it has the effect of preventing a successful plea by way of defence to an action to enforce a declaration of trust on the ground that there is no written evidence as required by section 4 of the Statute of Frauds (Ireland), 1695. The point is that the Statute, as its preamble clearly indicated,[89] was passed to prevent fraud and its machinery for doing this was to require objective written evidence of the existence of a trust. Provided there is evidence of a different nature produced in court to prove the existence of a trust, there is every reason for the court to accept that evidence and to further the policy laid down by Parliament.[90] It is on this basis that the doctrine of part performance has been developed.[91] It is also on the application of this principle that the doctrine of secret trusts has evolved in connection with wills, a subject we shall discuss later.[92]

Thirdly, section 4 of the Statute applies to *express* trusts only. There is a specific exclusion of *implied*,[93] *constructive*[94] and *resulting*[95] trusts from the statutory requirements as to written evidence.[96]

(iii) Contracts to Create a Trust in Consideration of Marriage

9.024. In the Republic of Ireland section 2 of the 1695 Statute remains in force. This requires that *contracts* to create a trust in consideration of marriage be evidenced by writing.[97] This provision no longer applies in Northern Ireland where there is now no such formality.[98] However, both parts of Ireland are, of course, still subject to the general provision in section 2 of the Statute, whereby any contract for the *sale of land* must be evidenced by some memorandum or note in writing signed by the party to be charged or his lawfully authorised agent.[99] This has obvious relevance in the case of a contract to transfer land to trustees to be held in trust.

---

[87] (1869) L.R. 4 H.L. 82 at 97.

[88] Para. 3.048, *ante*.

[89] "For prevention of many fraudulent practices which are commonly endeavoured to be upheld by perjury, and subornation of perjury...."

[90] *McGillicuddy* v. *Joy* [1959] I.R. 189. *McGillicuddy* v. *Joy* was followed by Lowry L.C.J. in *Gilmurray* v. *Corr* [1978] N.I. 99, aff'd by the Court of Appeal, *ibid.*, p.106 and (1979) 30 N.I.L.Q. 48.

[91] *Crowley* v. *O'Sullivan* [1900] 2 I.R. 478; *Lowry* v. *Reid* [1927] N.I. 142; *Mackey* v. *Jones* (1959) 93 I.L.T.R. 177, para. 3.149, *ante*.   [94] Para. 9.059, *post*.

[92] Para. 9.029, *post*.   [95] Para. 9.055, *post*.

[93] Para. 9.045, *post*.   [96] 1695 Statute, s.5. See *Peard* v. *Green* (1884) 18 I.L.T.R. 45.

[97] *McAskie* v. *McCay* (1868) I.R. 2 Eq. 447.

[98] Law Reform (Miscellaneous Provisions) Act (N.I.), 1954, s.1. The same position now obtains in England, see Law Reform (Enforcement of Contracts) Act. 1954.   [99] Para. 3.149, *ante*.

(iv) Transfer of an Interest Held Under a Trust

9.025. Once a trust has been created and the beneficial interests have come into existence, the Statute also controls subsequent dispositions of the *beneficial* interests held under the trust. Section 6 provides that such a disposition[1] must be in writing signed by the person making the disposition[2] or be made by will. It is essential to note that this provision requires the disposition itself to be in writing and not merely written evidence of it. Unlike under section 4 of the Statute, an oral disposition backed by written evidence is not enough. Furthermore, section 6 applies to beneficial interests in any kind of property, real or personal, held under a trust. Thus, while a trust of personalty can be *created* orally,[3] any subsequent *disposition* of the beneficial interest must be in writing, otherwise it is void.[4]

2. Wills

9.026. To the extent that a testator purports to create a trust by will, he must comply with the statutory requirements for the making of testamentary dispositions. These are now to be found in section 78 of the Succession Act, 1965, for the Republic of Ireland, replacing section 9 of the Wills Act, 1837, which remains in force in Northern Ireland. As in the case of the Statute of Frauds (Ireland), 1695, the courts have been alerted to see that such statutory provisions are not used as instruments of fraud and the application of this principle has resulted in the establishment of the doctrine of secret trusts, which we discuss below.

(i) Succession Act 1965, s. 78

9.027. This section[5] requires that a will be in writing, signed at the foot or end thereof by the testator (or by some person in his presence and by his direction) and that the testator's signature be made or acknowledged in the presence of two or more witnesses, present at the same time, each of whom shall attest that signature by his own signature. The section in effect lays down the same requirements as section 9 of the Wills Act, 1837, with one exception. The exception is the express provision that the witnesses need not sign in each other's presence, though they usually do so sign. It seems that this was the position also under the Wills Act, 1837.[6]

---

[1] Which may include instructions given by a beneficiary to the trustees to hold the property on some third party's behalf, see *Grey* v. *I.R.C.* [1960] A.C. 1. *Cf. Vandervell* v. *I.R.C.* [1967] 2 A.C. 291; *Re Vandervell's Trusts (No. 2)*[1974] Ch.269. On the Vandervell saga, see Hanbury and Maudsley, *Modern Equity* (12th ed. by Martin, 1985), pp. 81–5.

[2] S.53(1)(c) of the Law of Property Act, 1925, added for England a provision covering that person's agent authorised in writing.

[3] Para. 9.021, *ante.*

[4] See *Oughtred* v. *I.R.C.* [1960] A.C. 206. See Battersby, "Formalities for the Disposition of Equitable Interests under a Trust" [1979] Conv. 17; Green, "Grey, Oughtred and Vandervell – A Contextual Reappraisal" (1984) 47 M.L.R. 385.

[5] Examined in more detail at paras. 14.06 *et seq., post.*

[6] *In b. Webb* (1855) Dea. & Sw. 1.

(ii) Wills Act, 1837, s. 9

9.028. This section lays down for Northern Ireland the same express requirements as section 78 of the Republic's Succession Act, 1965, except for the provision just mentioned.

These, then, are the requirements which a testator normally has to meet if he wishes to create a trust in his will. However, frequently testators wish to conceal the creation of a trust by omitting reference to its existence in the will or, at least, to conceal the identity of the beneficiaries to take under the trust. Many of the older cases involved the creation of such "secret trusts" in favour of the testator's illegitimate children or mistress. Nowadays, testators may be motivated more by a desire to avoid the strict requirements of legislation governing wills, for a secret trust may provide a way of keeping the testator's options open, *i.e.*, the precise definition of the terms of the trust can be left to be determined after the will has been executed, perhaps according to later events. Whatever the motive, the question remains how far such secret trusts are valid in the light of the statutory requirements for wills.

(iii) Secret Trusts

9.029. Perhaps one point should be made clear at the outset. The doctrine of secret trusts has been the subject of some controversy over the years[7] and much of this has raged amongst the judges on both sides of the Irish Sea. It is also fair to say that the Irish judges have not always seen eye to eye with their English brethren on certain aspects of the subject.[8] It does appear, however, that most judges and commentators recognise that there is distinction between two types of secret trust, namely fully secret trusts and half-secret trusts.

(a) Fully Secret

9.030. A fully secret trust arises whenever a testator leaves property in his will to a legatee or devisee and no trust appears on the face of the will. The question, then, arises as to whether the legatee or devisee can keep the property himself or whether he must hold it in accordance with some trust communicated to him *independently* of the will and thereby not complying with the statutory requirements for wills. In fact, a similar secret trust can arise in the case of intestacy, as Lord Westbury explained in *McCormick* v. *Grogan*:[9]

"And if an individual on his deathbed, or at any other time, is persuaded by his heirs-at-law, or his next of kin, to abstain from making a will, or if

---

[7] See Andrews, "Creating Secret Trusts" (1963) 27 Conv. 92; Burgess, "Secret Trust Property" (1972) 36 Conv. 113; Burgess, "The Juridical Nature of Secret Trusts" (1972) 23 N.I.L.Q. 263; Fleming, "Secret Trusts" (1947) 12 Conv. 28; Hodge, "Secret Trusts: The Fraud Theory Revisited" [1980] Conv. 341; Holdsworth, "Secret Trusts" (1937) 53 L.Q.R.501; Matthews, "The True Basis of a Half-Secret Trust" [1979] Conv. 360; Perrins, "Can You Keep Half a Secret?" (1972) 88 L.Q.R. 225 and "Secret Trusts: The Key to the *Dehors*" [1985] Conv. 248; Watkin, "Clothing a Contravention" [1981] Conv. 335.
[8] Sheridan, "English and Irish Secret Trusts" (1951) 67 L.Q.R. 314.
[9] (1869) L.R. 4 H.L. 82 at 97.

the same individual, having made a will, communicates the disposition to the person on the face of the will benefited by that disposition, but, at the same time, says to that individual that he has a purpose to answer which he has not expressed in the will, but which depends on the disponee to carry into effect, and the disponee assents to it, either expressly, or by any mode of action which the disponee knows must give to the testator the impression and belief that he fully assents to the request, then, undoubtedly, the heir-at-law in the one case, and the disponee in the other, will be converted into trustees, simply on the principle that an individual shall not be benefited by his own personal fraud."[10]

9.031. This dictum indicates the basis upon which the Irish, and English, courts enforce fully secret trusts, namely that otherwise the legatee or devisee under the will would be using the statute governing wills as an instrument of fraud.[11] The fraud lies in the legatee or devisee inducing the testator to leave his will as it stands or, in the case of intestacy, the intestate successor inducing the deceased not to make a will. It is essential, therefore, that in each case the elements of *intention, communication* and *acquiescence* should exist.[12] There must have been an intention on the part of the testator or deceased to impose a trust and that intention must have been communicated before the testator's or deceased's death.[13] It appears that there is sufficient communication if the testator gives the legatee or devisee a sealed envelope (containing the instructions to hold the property on trust) during his lifetime, even though this is not to be opened until the testator's death.[14] The communication must specify all the terms of the trust (*i.e.,* comply with the three certainties[15]), otherwise, if an intention to create *a* trust only is evinced, the trust will be a resulting trust for the residuary legatee or devisee or for the intestate successor.

9.032. Difficulties frequently arise where there are several legatees or devisees involved, whether joint tenants or tenants in common,[16] but communication is made to one of them only. Where they are tenants in common, it appears that only those to whom the trust has been communicated are bound by it, the others taking beneficially in their own right.[17] However, the Irish Court of Appeal emphasised[18] that an "innocent" tenant in common takes free

[10] See further on the case of a secret trust arising on intestacy, *Sellack* v. *Harris* (1708) 5 Vin.Ab. 521.

[11] See *Cullen* v. *Att.-Gen. for Ireland* (1866) L.R. 1 H.L. 190; *Turner* v. *Att.-Gen.* (1876) I.R. 10 Eq. 386; *Re King's Estate* (1888) 21 L.R.Ir. 273; *French* v. *French* [1902] 1 I.R. 172; *O'Brien* v. *Condon* [1905] 1 I.R. 51 (see *A Casebook on Equity and Trusts in Ireland* (1985), p. 328); *Re Browne* [1944] I.R. 90 (see *ibid.,* p. 322).

[12] *Per* Viscount Sumner in *Blackwell* v. *Blackwell* [1929] A.C. 318 at 334. See also Chatterton V.-C. in *Riordan* v. *Banon* (1876) I.R. 10 Eq. 469 at 478.

[13] *Re Watters* (1928) 62 I.L.T.R. 61; *Scott* v. *Brownrigg* (1881) 9 L.R.Ir. 246; *Sullivan* v. *Sullivan* [1903] 1 I.R. 193; *Re Ellis* (1919) 53 I.L.T.R. 6. See also *Re Snowden* [1979] Ch. 528, where Megarry V.-C. held that fruad, though a common ingredient of secret trusts, is not an essential one, and in cases not involving fraud the standard of proof is "the ordinary civil standard of proof that is required to establish an ordinary trust"; thus preferring the views of Christian L.J. in the Court of Appeal of Ireland in *McCormick* v. *Grogan* (1867) I.R. 1 Eq. 313 at 328 to those of Brightman J. in *Ottaway* v. *Norman* [1972] Ch. 698 at 712.

[14] *Morrison* v. *McFerran* [1901] 1 I.R. 360; *Re Keen* [1937] Ch. 236; *Re Boyes* (1884) 26 Ch.D. 531.

[15] *Scott* v. *Brownrigg, op. cit.; McCormick* v. *Grogan, op. cit.*

[16] See ch. 7, *ante.*

[17] See *Re Stead* [1900] 1 Ch. 237. *Cf. Tee* v. *Ferris* (1856) 2 K. & J. 357.

[18] *Geddis* v. *Semple* [1903] 1 I.R. 73 (see *A Casebook on Equity and Trusts in Ireland* (1985), p. 324).

of the trust only if his gift can be regarded as an independent one, *i.e.*, that he would have got what he did notwithstanding the undertaking given by his co-tenant in common. If the innocent tenant in common's gift was also induced by the other co-tenant's undertaking, then the Irish judges were of the view that the basic principle that a man should not profit by another's fraud ought to apply here too.[19] Where the legatees or devisees are joint tenants, on the other hand, the Irish judges in the same case took a different view. Holmes L.J. stated:

> "It is, I think, settled that where a gift is given to two persons as joint tenants, a secret trust imparted to one of them will affect the whole gift; but that this arises from the peculiar nature of a joint estate is shown by repeated decisions that this rule does not apply to tenants in common."[20]

It may be questioned, however, whether the nature of a joint tenancy need result in such a rule. If there are difficulties over the fact that the joint tenants hold together, there is nothing to stop the court deciding that the creation of the secret trust to bind one joint tenant severs the joint tenancy and leaves the other tenant as tenant in common in his own right.[21] Thus the basic principle to be applied could be the same as for tenants in common, *i.e.*, an "innocent" joint tenant is bound by the trust unless he can prove that he would still have received his gift without his co-tenant's promise.[22] The principle could also govern the position whether the communication to the one joint tenant took place before the will or after the will.[23] In either case, the test should be whether or not the gift to any particular joint tenant was induced by fraud on the part of any one of the joint tenants. As regards communication after the will was made, all one can say is that it is less likely that the innocent joint tenant's prior gift can be regarded as induced by the subsequent promise of his co-tenant, but no more than that.

9.033. Finally,[24] the legatee or devisee must accept the trust, for otherwise there will be no fraud on his part in not complying with the testator's wishes.[25] The fraud would be perpetrated against the testator and it is arguable that all that is needed to prevent this is to hold that there is a resulting trust[26] for his estate. On this basis, a fully secret trust would appear to be another example of a constructive trust, *i.e.*, one imposed by the courts regardless of the testator's

---

[19] See also *Huguenin* v. *Baseley* (1807) 14 Ves. 273.

[20] [1903] 1 I.R. 73 at 86–7. See also *Stead* [1900] 1 Ch. 237.

[21] See *Turner* v. *Att.-Gen.* (1876) I.R. 10 Eq. 386.

[22] See generally Perrins, (1972) 88 L.Q.R. 225.

[23] Farwell J., with great reluctance, held that the authorities indicated that an innocent joint tenant was bound in the case of his co-tenant's *antecedent* promise but not in the case of his subsequent promise: *Re Stead* [1900] 1 Ch. 237, espec. at 241. See also *Burney* v. *Macdonald* (1845) 15 Sim. 6; *Moss* v. *Cooper* (1861) 1 J. & H. 352. *Cf.* Perrins, *op. cit.* at pp. 235–7.

[24] Of course, the trust must comply with other general requirements relating to trusts, *e.g.*, not be for an illegal purpose. See *Geddis* v. *Semple* [1903] 1 I.R. 73 (see *A Casebook on Equity and Trusts in Ireland* (1985), p. 324); also *O'Brien* v. *Barragry* (1900) 1 N.I.J.R. 117.

[25] *Re Watters* (1928) 62 I.L.T.R. 61; also *Re King's Estate* (1888) 21 L.R.Ir. 273.

[26] See para. 9.055, *post*.

intention in order to prevent fraud, or *by operation of law* as it is sometimes put.[27] Yet the interesting feature of secret trust cases is that, when one is found to exist by the courts, the trust that comes into operation is *not* a resulting trust but is a trust to be carried out in accordance with the testator's secret instructions. On this basis, it is arguable that the secret trust is in fact an express trust.[28] There is some authority for this interpretation in the many judicial statements that secret trusts operate as "declarations *dehors* the will."[29] This interpretation, however, may give rise to difficulties where there are other formalities to be complied with, *e.g.*, an express trust of land must be in writing under the Statute of Frauds (Ireland), 1695, whereas constructive or implied trusts are excepted from this requirement.[30] Another interpretation, then, may be to hold that a secret trust is neither an express nor constructive trust, but instead an implied trust,[31] *i.e.*, one imputed to give effect to the wishes of the testator.[32] On this basis the trust comes into existence to carry out the promise entered into by the legatee or devisee and, in this respect, the doctrine of secret trusts operates like that relating to mutual wills.[33]

(b) *Half-secret*

9.034. A half-secret trust arises when the legatee or devisee of property is designated as trustee of the property given to him by the will, but the objects of the trust are communicated independently. At first sight, this looks like a clear case of an express trust, but even this has been questioned.[34] The point is that only part of the requirements for an express trust are to be found in the will, *i.e.*, the two certainties of words and, usually, subject-matter, but not the objects. The judges in both Ireland[35] and England[36] have insisted that even in this case the secret trust operates "*dehors*" the will.[37] What is enforced is not the trust declared in the will, which would, of course, have to comply with the wills legislation, but an independent trust arising outside the will based upon the undertaking by the legatee or devisee to hold the trust property in accordance with the testator's instructions. Thus the elements of communication and acquiescence[38] must be present also in the case of half-secret trusts.

9.035. The English courts, indeed, seem to have taken an even stricter approach in this case because they have required communication to the trustee

---

[27] Para. 9.059, *post*. See Sheridan, (1951) 67 L.Q.R. 314 at 323–4.
[28] See Hanbury and Maudsley, *Modern Equity* (12th ed. by Martin, 1985), pp. 160–5.
[29] *Blackwell* v. *Blackwell*, *op. cit.*; *Jones* v. *Badley* (1868) 2 Ch.App. 362; *McCormick* v. *Grogan*, *op. cit.*; *Revenue Commrs.* v. *Stapleton* [1937] I.R. 225.
[30] Para. 9.023, *ante*.
[31] Para. 9.045, *post*.
[32] See Burgess, (1972) 23 N.I.L.Q. 263.
[33] Para. 9.051, *post*. See Mitchell, "Some Aspects of Mutual Wills" (1951) 14 M.L.R. 136; Burgess, "Mutual Wills" (1970) 34 Conv. 230.
[34] Burgess, (1972) 23 N.I.L.Q. 263.
[35] *Att.-Gen.* v. *Dillon* (1862) 13 Ir.Ch.R. 127; *Riordan* v. *Banon* (1876) I.R. 10 Eq. 469; *Scott* v. *Brownrigg* (1881) 9 L.R.Ir. 246.
[36] *Blackwell* v. *Blackwell* [1929] A.C. 318.
[37] *Per* Lord Westbury in *Cullen* v. *Att.-Gen. for Ireland* (1866) L.R. 1 H.L. 190 at 198.
[38] Para. 9.031, *supra*.

to take place at or before the execution of the will[39] rather than the testator's death, as is the case with fully secret trusts.[40] It is difficult to follow the reasoning of the English judges in these cases. If the trust enforced by the court operates independently of the will and it is enforced because of the fraud on the part of the legatee or devisee, the date of execution of the will is irrelevant. What is relevant is communication and acquiescence to induce the testator to make or leave unrevoked his will before his death, and so the same rule should apply in the case of both fully and half-secret trusts. To some extent the English judges may have been influenced by another doctrine which is also strictly irrelevant in the present context, namely, the doctrine of incorporation by reference. Under this doctrine, an informal document may be incorporated in a validly executed document, so as to form part of it. It is essential, however, that the informal document should be in existence at the date of execution of the formal document (the will in the present context) and that the formal document refers to the informal document *as an existing document*.[41] By being so incorporated in the will, the informal document is admitted to probate along with the will and so any question of secrecy is excluded. This is really an entirely different situation from a secret trust situation and should not be confused with it.

9.036. It is not surprising, therefore, to find that the Irish courts have not followed their English brethren on this point and have held that in the case of a half-secret trust, as in the case of a fully secret trust, there is need for communication before the testator's death only, whether or not this communication took place before or after the execution of this will.[42] This also seems to be the rule in other jurisdictions.[43]

9.037. One consequence of holding that a half-secret trust operates independently of the will is that the beneficiary may escape rules which would apply if he were regarded as taking under the will. Thus other provisions in the wills legislation may be avoided, such as the restriction on a beneficiary being a witness to the will.[44] In *O'Brien* v. *Condon*,[45] it was held that a witness to the will could still take as beneficiary under a secret trust. In the English case of *Re Gardner*,[46] it was even held that the representatives of the deceased

---

[39] *Johnson* v. *Ball* (1851) 5 De G. & Sm. 85; *Re Keen* [1937] Ch. 236.

[40] Para. 9.031, *supra.*

[41] *In b. Mitchell* (1966) 100 I.L.T.R. 185. See also *In b. Stuart* [1902] P. 238; *Re Jones* [1942] Ch. 328; *Re Tyler* [1967] 1 W.L.R. 1269.

[42] *Riordan* v. *Banon* (1867) I.R. 10 Eq. 469; *Re King's Estate* (1888) 21 L.R.Ir. 273; *Re Browne* [1944] I.R. 90 (see *A Casebook on Equity and Trusts in Ireland* (1985), p. 322). *Cf. Balfe* v. *Halpenny* [1904] 1 I.R. 486. Note, however, that the statements in the Irish cases were largely *obiter*, since they involved *fully* secret trusts, see Land Law Working Group's Discussion Document No. 2 (*Estates and Interests and Family Dealings in Land*) (1981), pp. 53–4.

[43] *E.g.*, U.S.A., Scott, *Law of Trusts*, § 55.8.

[44] Succession Act, 1965, s. 82; Wills Act, 1837, s. 15.

[45] [1905] 1 I.R. 51 (see *A Casebook on Equity and Trusts in Ireland* (1985), p. 328). See also *Re Young* [1951] Ch. 344. *Cf. Re Fleetwood* (1880) 15 Ch.D. 594; *Re Maddock* [1902] 2 Ch. 220.

[46] [1923] 2 Ch. 230.

beneficiary under a secret trust could still claim his share even though the beneficiary had predeceased the testator.[47] This decision involves, in effect, the proposition that a beneficiary's interest under a secret trust vests before the testator's death or, to put it another way, that the secret trust comes into operation as soon as the secret trustee gives his undertaking. The trouble about that proposition is that it seems to ignore the fact that at that point the secret trust, as in the *Gardner* case, may still be incompletely constituted.[48] In most, if not all, cases it will not be completely constituted because the legal title to the trust property has not been vested yet in the trustee and that will not occur until the will comes into operation at the testator's death.[49] Thus in another English case it was held that a secret trust did fail where the trustee predeceased the testator.[50] The better view is that *Re Gardner* was wrongly decided.

C. Executed and Executory Trusts

9.038. The distinction between executed and executory trusts does not appear to be crucial, at first sight, because in both cases there is a valid trust in operation. Sugden L.C. discussed the matter in *Boswell* v. *Dillon*[51] in the following terms:

> "Every trust is in a sense executory; when however there is a mere trust, giving just a legal estate to the trustee, who has a *certain* trust to perform, we are not in the habit of calling that an executory trust. In the proper sense, an executory trust is a trust in which something more is to be done. Executory trusts may thus be of two kinds, one in which something is to be done; yet where the testator has acted as his own conveyancer, as it is called, and the court has nothing to do but to follow out and enforce the limitations. Such trusts do not differ from ordinary estates. They must be construed according to the clear intent of the settlor. The other species of executory trust is, when the testator, intending something beyond what is effected by the words creating the estate, had imperfectly stated what is to be done; and the court is thus invested with a larger discretion, than if the words stood by themselves."[52]

Thus an executory trust usually arises where some further document or instrument must be executed to define more exactly the beneficial interests in that trust. A common example is where marriage articles declare that one of the prospective spouses, usually the husband, will upon the marriage settle certain property on the spouses and their future children. The property

---

[47] Normally a gift by will fails if the donee predeceases the testator: *Underwood* v. *King* (1855) 24 L.J.Ch. 293; *Wing* v. *Angrave* (1860) 8 H.L.C. 183. There are some statutory exceptions to the doctrine of lapse, see Succession Act, 1965, ss. 97 and 98; Wills Act, 1837, ss. 32 and 33. Ch. 14, *post*.

[48] See para. 9.040, *post*.

[49] Para. 14.42, *post*.

[50] *Re Maddock* [1902] 2 Ch. 220, espec. at 231 (*per* Cozens-Hardy L.J.).

[51] (1844) 6 Ir.Eq.R. 389 (see *A Casebook on Equity and Trusts in Ireland* (1985), p. 331). See also *Duncan* v. *Bluett* (1870) I.R. 4 Eq. 469; *Mason* v. *Mason* (1870) I.R. 5 Eq. 288; *Re Dunnill's Trusts* (1872) I.R. 6 Eq. 322; *Dowd* v. *Dowd* [1898] 1 I.R. 244; *Re Jordan's Trusts* [1903] 1 I.R. 119; *Re Dunnill's Trusts* [1926] I.R. 126.

[52] *Ibid*. p. 392.

becomes subject to an immediate trust, but this remains executory until the marriage settlement itself is executed.[53] The other common example occurs in the case of wills, *e.g.*, where a testator gives property in his will to X on trust to settle it on Y when Y reaches the age of majority or marries. The trust again remains executory until X executes the settlement.

9.039. The importance of the distinction lies in the court's attitude to construction of the trust instruments. In the case of an executed trust, the courts construe the trust instrument strictly according to its wording and thus give words their technical meaning.[54] In effect, in this instance equity follows the law[55] even in the case of wills and applies technical rules such as the rule in *Shelley's Case*.[56] If, however, the trust is executory the courts adopt a much more liberal interpretation and give effect to the intention of the settlor or testator, even though this means disregarding the strict, technical meaning of the words used.[57] Thus the terms of marriage articles may be explained by references to other documents,[58] and again from marriage articles it is usually easy to gather an intention to benefit the issue of the marriage and thereby exclude the rule in *Shelley's Case*.[59]

D. COMPLETELY AND INCOMPLETELY CONSTITUTED TRUSTS

9.040. This distinction must not be confused with the one just discussed, where in both cases a valid, completed trust existed. A trust remains incompletely constituted until it is completed by the vesting of the title in the property in the trustees to be held on trust. The importance of the distinction is this: once the trust is completely constituted the beneficiaries can have it enforced even though they are volunteers,[60] *i.e.*, they did not provide any consideration in exchange for the creation of the trust; if the trust is incompletely constituted the beneficiaries cannot have it enforced unless they provided such consideration. If they did, then "equity regards as done what ought to be done."[61] If they did not, then equity will not complete a voluntary incompletely constituted trust[62] or perfect an imperfect gift.[63] There are, however, several ways in which a trust may be completely constituted.

9.041. First, the title to the trust property can be transferred to the trustees *inter vivos* or by will. In each case the appropriate conveyancing formalities

[53] See again Sugden L.C. (later Lord St. Leonards) in *Rochford* v. *Fitzmaurice* (1842) 4 Ir.Eq.R. 375, espec. at 381–2 (see *A Casebook on Equity and Trusts in Ireland* (1985), p. 332). Also *Duncan* v. *Bluett* (1870) I.R. 4 Eq. 469; *Harris* v. *Loftus* (*No. 2*) [1903] 1 I.R. 203.

[54] *Re Bennett's Estate* [1898] 1 I.R. 185; *Boswell* v. *Dillon, op. cit.*; *Delap* v. *Butler* [1919] 1 I.R. 74; *Re Dunnill's Trusts* [1926] I.R. 126.

[55] Para. 3.047, *ante*.

[56] Para. 4.034, *ante*. See *Lowry* v. *Lowry* (1884) 13 L.R.Ir. 317; *Re Keane's Estate* [1903] 1 I.R. 215; *Delap* v. *Butler* [1919] 1 I.R. 74.

[57] *Re Colles's Estate* [1918] 1 I.R. 1 (words of limitation).

[58] *Gaussin and French* v. *Ellis* [1930] I.R. 116. See also *Eustace* v. *Robinson* (1880) 7 L.R.Ir. 83.

[59] *Rochford* v. *Fitzmaurice* (1842) 4 I.Eq.R. 375 (see *A Casebook on Equity and Trusts in Ireland* (1985), p. 332). *Cf.* in the case of wills where a contrary intention usually has to appear on the face of the will, *Delap* v. *Butler* [1919] 1 I.R. 74.

[60] *Blakely* v. *Brady* (1839) 2 Dr. & Wal. 311.   [61] Para. 3.064, *ante*.   [62] *Uniacke* v. *Giles* (1828) 2 Mol. 257.

[63] *Moore* v. *Ulster Banking Co.* (1877) I.R. 11 C.L. 512. Allan, "An Equity to Perfect a Gift" (1963) 79 L.Q.R. 238.

must be complied with according to the nature of the interest to be transferred (e.g., land or personalty, legal or equitable title) and the type of disposition (e.g., inter vivos or by will).[64] However, it appears that this general rule is subject to the qualification that, where the settlor or testator does all that is within his power to effect the transfer of the title to the property, and all that remains to be done is some formality not within his power or control, then the trust is nevertheless regarded as completely constituted despite the fact that, technically speaking, the legal title has not yet been vested in the trustees. This was held to be the case in *Devoy v. Hanlon*[65] where the settlor executed a transfer of registered land which was not registered in the Land Registry and so was technically ineffective. Nevertheless, the Republic's Supreme Court held that the volunteer transferee was entitled to the land as against a devisee of the land in a subsequent will[66] executed by the transferor, provided he proved that the original transfer deed had been delivered. The same principle has been applied in England in cases involving shares, where the legal title is not transferred until there occurs both execution of a written transfer by the existing shareholder *and* registration of the share transfer in its register of shareholders by the company.[67] The same requirement of doing everything in one's power to effect a transfer applies to equitable interests, *e.g.*, interests already held under a trust, though here it is important to note that section 6 of the Statute of Frauds (Ireland), 1695, requires such transfers to be in writing.[68]

9.042. Secondly, the settlor may completely constitute a trust by declaring himself to be trustee, either expressly or by implication. No particular form of words need be used by the settlor provided the declaration is indicated by an instrument leaving "no reasonable doubt as to the purpose with which it was executed."[69] However, no instrument of any kind need be used unless there is some other statutory requirement, such as the need for writing in the case of land.[70] Yet the basic principle holds good that equity will not complete an incompletely constituted trust[71] or perfect an imperfect gift.[72] In this case, of course, the settlor normally retains possession of the property, but it is nevertheless essential that he indicates clearly by his words or actions that he is holding the property on trust for others and that he no longer has power to devote it to his own purposes.[73] The courts will not construe an incompletely constituted trust or an imperfect gift in favour of a volunteer as such a declaration of trust.[74] If consideration has been given by the beneficiaries,

---

[64] *Lee v. Magrath* (1882) 10 L.R.Ir. 45; *Re Carey's Estate* [1901] 1 I.R. 81. See also the discussion in *Milroy v. Lord* (1862) 4 De G.F. & J. 264.

[65] [1929] I.R. 246.   [66] Who did register herself as owner.

[67] *Re Rose* [1949] Ch. 78; *Re Rose* [1952] 1 Ch. 499. See also *Re Fry* [1946] Ch. 312; *Re King* (1879) 14 Ch.D. 179. For the Irish statutory requirements *re* shares, see Companies Act, 1963, ss. 79–90 (R.I.); Companies Act (N.I.), 1960, ss. 75 and 77–8.

[68] *Gason v. Rich* (1887) 19 L.R.Ir. 391.

[69] Per Lord O'Hagan L.C., *Miller v. Harrison* (1871) I.R. 5 Eq. 324 at 346 (see *A Casebook on Equity and Trusts in Ireland* (1985), p. 339). See also *Woodroffe v. Johnston* (1854) 4 Ir.Ch.R. 319.

[70] Para. 9.022, *supra*.   [71] *West v. West* (1882) 9 L.R.Ir. 121.

[72] *Hayes v. Alliance British and Foreign Life and Fire Assurance Co.* (1881) 8 L.R.Ir. 149; *Gason v. Rich* (1887) 19 L.R.Ir. 391; *Vize v. Fitzmaurice* (1905) 39 I.L.T.R. 123.

[73] *Adams v. Lopdell* (1890) 25 L.R.Ir. 311; *Allan v. C.I.R.* [1925] N.I. 50

[74] *Lee v. McGrath* (1882) 10 L.R.Ir. 45; *Towers v. Hogan* (1889) 23 L.R.Ir. 53; *O'Flaherty v. Browne* [1907] 2 I.R. 416. See also cases cited in fns. 72 and 73, *supra*.

then, equity will enforce the incompletely constituted trust in favour of all those within the consideration. In this context, consideration means "valuable" consideration as opposed to what is sometimes called "good" consideration, *i.e.*, based solely on natural love and affection.[75] However, in the case of a marriage settlement, where the consideration is usually the *future*[76] marriage of the parties, it is the general rule that the spouses[77] and their issue[78] come within the marriage consideration and all of them can, therefore, enforce the settlement on that basis. It must be emphasised that this broad interpretation of marriage consideration will not be extended to cover every beneficiary coming within the terms of a marriage settlement. As Christian J. put it, "the question whether it is purchased or whether it is voluntary, must be judged of by the good sense of the case and the intent of the parties."[79]

9.043. There are some other principles to be considered in connection with the rule that equity will not complete an incomplete trust in favour of a volunteer. One is the rule[80] that a gift or trust will be perfected or completed by the donor or settlor appointing the donee or trustee his executor, since the executor will receive the legal title to the property on the donor's or settlor's death.[81] For this rule to apply, the gift or trust must be complete in all respects other than the formality of vesting the legal title in the donee or trustee, which happens on the donor's or settlor's death.[82] Furthermore, for equity to regard the gift or trust as so perfected or completed, there must have been a continuing intention to make the gift or to establish the trust by the donor or settlor up to the date of his death. A second rule is what is known as a *donatio mortis causa*. This is a special kind of gift with its own special rules which seem to be a mixture of those relating to gifts *inter vivos* and gifts by will.[83] The essentials[84] for a *donatio mortis causa* are that, first, there must be a gift made in contemplation of the donor's death,[85] secondly, there must be delivery,[86] actual[87] or

---

[75] See discussion in *Re Browne's Estate* (1862) 13 Ir.Ch.R. 283 and *Mullins* v. *Guilfoyle* (1878) 2 L.R.Ir. 95.

[76] A settlement made in respect of a *past* marriage is not made for valuable consideration, *Re Greer* (1877) I.R. 11 Eq. 502; see also *McAskie* v. *McCay* (1868) I.R. 2 Eq. 447.

[77] *Dennehy* v. *Delany* (1876) I.R. 10 Eq. 377.

[78] *Greenwood* v. *Lutmam* [1915] 1 I.R. 266. It appears that "issue" will normally be construed as confined to "children" (see *Re Dixon's Trusts* (1869) I.R. 4 Eq. 1), but it may sometimes be taken to include a wider class, *e.g.*, grandchildren, see *Re Bromhead's Trusts* [1922] 1 I.R. 75. Fleming, "Position of a Beneficiary within Marriage Consideration under an Incompletely Constituted Trust" (1947) 12 Conv. 132.

[79] *Re Browne's Estate* (1862) 13 Ir.Ch.R. 283 at 295. See also *Re Sheridan's Estate* (1878) 1 L.R.Ir. 54; *Guardian Assurance Co.* v. *Avonmore* (1872) I.R. 6 Eq. 391.

[80] Sometimes known as the rule in *Strong* v. *Bird* (1874) L.R. 18 Eq. 315. See also *Re Freeland* [1952] Ch. 110; *Re Gonin* [1977] 3 W.L.R. 397. Kodilinye, "A Fresh Look at the Rule in Strong v. Bird" [1982] Conv. 14.

[81] *Re Wilson* [1933] I.R. 729 (see *A Casebook on Equity and Trusts in Ireland* (1985), p. 348). Ch. 16, *post*.

[82] *Ibid.*

[83] See Kiely, *Principles of Equity as Applied in Ireland* (1936), ch. xv. See also Fenelou, "Donatio Mortis Causa: A Review and Update" (1984) 78 Gaz. I.L.S.I. 189; Warnock-Smith, " 'Donationes Mortis Causa' and the Payment of Debts" [1978] Conv. 130.

[84] See discussion in *Re Mulroy* [1924] 1 I.R. 98 (see *A Casebook on Equity and Trusts in Ireland* (1985), p. 353).

[85] He must not be in a good state of health (see *Owens* v. *Greene* [1932] I.R. 225, see *Ibid.*, p. 356) nor contemplating suicide (see *Agnew* v. *Belfast Banking Co.* [1896] 2 I.R. 204).

[86] *Re McWey* [1928] I.R. 486; *Re Thompson's Estate* [1928] I.R. 606. *Cf. Re Foran* (1950) 84 I.L.T.R. 187. This includes "symbolic" delivery, such as handing over the key of a locked box containing valuables, see *Re Mulroy* [1924] 1 I.R. 98.

[87] Writing is not necessary, *Fayne* v. *Martin* (1925) 59 I.L.T.R. 14.

constructive,[88] of the gift to the donee before the donor's death[89] and, thirdly, the gift must take effect on the donor's death only, so that it must remain revocable during his lifetime.[90] The doctrine does not apply to land, including leasehold property,[91] but does apply to most kinds of pure personalty.[92] Provided the above essentials are satisfied, the gift will be enforced on the donor's death despite the incompleteness of the gift prior to his death.[93]

9.044. Finally, there appears to be one other case to be considered in Ireland in relation to the rule that equity will not assist a volunteer. This occurs in the case of a joint deposit receipt, *i.e.*, where a person deposits money at a bank and has the receipt for payment made out in favour of himself *and/or other persons*.[94] The Irish courts have held in several cases that such other persons may claim the debt despite being volunteers.[95] The basis for these decisions seems to be that either the relationship between the parties raised a presumption of advancement[96] or else there was sufficient evidence to rebut a resulting trust.[97] The courts seem to have assumed that the action of the depositor in depositing money in his own and another person's name was equivalent to, or, at least, analogous to, purchasing or vesting the legal title to property in that other person's name, so as to raise the presumptions normally raised in such cases.[98] The trouble is that the Irish judges have not made clear why that assumption should be made. Lord Atkin's dictum in *McEvoy* v. *Belfast Banking Co. Ltd.*[99] to the effect that the depositor

---

[88] *E.g.* delivery to an agent or servant, *Re Thompson's Estate* [1928] I.R. 606; *Murphy* v. *Quirke* (1909) 43 I.L.T.R. 225.

[89] The donee permitting retention by the donor after initial delivery may be sufficient, provided it is clear that the donor's possession remains that of custodian only and no longer that of owner, *Re Mulroy* [1924] 1 I.R. 98 (see *A Casebook on Equity and Trusts in Ireland* (1985), p. 353).

[90] *Agnew* v. *Belfast Banking Co.* [1896] 2 I.R. 204; *Keys* v. *Hore* (1879) 13 I.L.T.R. 58.

[91] *Quaere*, a land certificate relating to registered land which under the former law contained in the Local Registration of Title (Ir.) Act, 1891, descended as personalty on death of the registered owner (see para. 3.099, *ante* and ch. 21, *post*), see *Re Longworth* [1910] 1 I.R. 23.

[92] *E.g.*, a chose in action evidence by a deposit receipt (*Cassidy* v. *Belfast Banking Co.* (1887) 22 L.R.Ir. 68) and a Post Office savings book (*Re Thompson's Estate* [1928] I.R. 606 and *Hearty* v. *Coleman* [1953–54] Ir.Jur.Rep. 73); life insurance policy (*Nelson* v. *Prudential Assurance Co. Ltd.* [1929] N.I. 113); "stale" cheques (*Re Mulroy* [1924] 1 I.R. 98). The following have been held not capable of forming the subject-matter of donations: an I.O.U. (*Duckworth* v. *Lee* [1899] 1 I.R. 405; receipts for consideration money relating to stocks and shares (*Re McWey* [1928] I.R. 486); Post Office Savings Certificates of Saorstát Éireann (*Hills* v. *Shields (No. 2)* [1950] I.R. 21, but this has been doubted).

[93] *McGonnell* v. *Murray* (1869) I.R. 3 Eq. 460; *Cross* v. *Cross* (1879) 3 L.R.Ir. 342; *Kelly* v. *O'Connor* [1917] 1 I.R. 312; *Keys* v. *Gilfillan* (1932) 66 I.L.T.R. 127.

[94] See the discussion in Leet, "Deposit Accounts in Joint Names" (1935) 37 J.I.B.I. 31: Montrose, "Deposit Receipts and the Doctrine of Consideration" (1937) 39 J.I.B.I. 232; Corscadden, "Joint Deposit Receipts" (1936–7) 1 N.I.L.Q. 123 and 174; H.A.S., "Relation of Deposit Receipts to Law of Trusts and Contracts" (1938) 72 I.L.T.S.J. 245; Corscadden "Reflections on Irish Deposit Receipts" (1950–2) 9 N.I.L.Q. 148; Montrose, "Joint Deposit Receipts—A Reconsideration" (1950–2) 9 N.I.L.Q. 148; Sheridan, "Reflections on Irish Deposits Receipts" (1950–2) 9 N.I.L.Q. 101; Lyons, "Law Relating to Deposit Receipts" (1956) 56 J.I.B.I. 183 and 258; V.T.H.D., "Joint Deposit Accounts: Some Misconceptions" (1957) 23 Ir.Jur. 31. See also Cullity, "Joint Bank Accounts with Volunteers" (1969) 85 L.Q.R. 530.

[95] *Talbot* v. *Cody* (1875) I.R. 10 Eq. 138: *Re Condrin* [1914] 1 I.R. 89; *Re Hood* [1923] 1 I.R. 109.

[96] See further para. 9.047, *post*. *McEneaney* v. *Shevlin* [1912] 1 I.R. 278; *Owens* v. *Greene* [1932] I.R. 225 (see *A Casebook on Equity and Trusts in Ireland* (1985), p. 356); *McCabe* v. *Ulster Bank Ltd.* [1939] I.R. 1; *Re Walsh* [1942] I.R. 403. See also *Watters* v. *Watters* (1979) 30 N.I.L.Q. 251.

[97] *McDowell* v. *McNeilly* [1917] 1 I.R. 117; *Doyle* v. *Byrne* (1922) 56 I.L.T.R. 125.

[98] The presumption of advancement has even been held to operate in favour of the depositor's wife even though it was not her name endorsed on the receipt made out solely in her husband's name, but that of a third party who was told it was for her, see *Maguire* v. *Maguire* (1927) 61 I.L.T.R. 106. *Cf.* however, *Moore* v. *Ulster Banking Co.* (1877) I.R. 11 C.L. 512.

[99] [1935] A.C. 24.

could be regarded as acting as agent for the other person in entering into the contract with the bank would seem to be disputable in many of the cases.[1] Whatever the basis of these Irish decisions, they mostly involve family arrangements and to that extent the problems have now been solved mostly by statute. Under the Republic's Married Women's Status Act, 1957,[2] and the Law Reform (Husband and Wife) Act (N.I.), 1964,[3] contracts for the benefit of spouses or children are enforceable by the spouses or children in their own names as if they were parties to the contracts. Under these Acts, it is sufficient that the contract is "expressed to be for the benefit of, or by its express terms purports to confer a benefit upon" the third person, and this seems to cover most of the cases where a deposit receipt is made out in the joint names of husband and wife or endorsed in favour of the wife or the children.[4]

E. IMPLIED TRUSTS

9.045. There are several situations recognised in our law where it is held that a trust comes into existence by implication. The underlying basis of the courts' reasoning in such cases is that they are giving effect to the intention of the parties.[5] This distinguishes implied trusts[6] from constructive trusts where the courts hold that a trust exists regardless of any intention on the part of the parties involved to create a trust.[7] It is, of course, often extremely difficult to determine the precise intention of the parties in a particular case (and when the matter comes to court it is usually in their respective interests to put forward conflicting intentions) and so the courts have usually resolved this problem by raising presumptions, normally rebuttable, in different circumstances.[88] The following are the main situations in which the courts find implied trusts.

1. *Purchase in Name of Another*

9.046. Where ownership of property, real or personal,[9] is transferred to one person, but the purchase money is in fact supplied by another person, then the normal presumption is that a resulting trust[10] comes into force by implication. In other words, the person to whom the legal title in the property is transferred is obliged by equity to hold the property in trust for the person who supplied the

---

[1] Note, however, that the fictions of "agency" and "trust" have been used frequently in the past to confer the benefits of a contract on a third person, see Wylie, "Contracts and Third Parties" (1966) 17 N.I.L.Q 351, espec. at 386–402.

[2] S. 8.

[3] S. 5. See Wylie, *op. cit.*, fn. 1, *supra*, pp. 412–14. S. 5 was applied in *Northern Bank Executor and Trustee Co. Ltd* v. *Manning* (1977) 28 N.I.L.Q. 199, see para. 9.007, fn. 30, *ante.*

[4] It would not seem to cover, however, the *Maguire* v. *Maguire* situation, see fn. 98, *supra.*

[5] See the discussion by the Irish House of Lords in *Redington* v. *Redington* (1794) 3 Ridgw. P.C. 106.

[6] And resulting trusts, but see para. 9.055, *post.* Care must be taken in this context to avoid terminological disputes. Many writers nowadays classify what are here described as "implied" trusts as "resulting" trusts, see para. 9.055 *post.* See also Megarry J.'s distinction between "automatic" resulting trusts and "presumed" resulting trusts, *Re Vandervell's Trust (No.2)* [1974] Ch. 269. See also Sweeney, "Presumed Resulting Uses and Trusts: Survivals and a New Arrival?" (1979) Ir.Jur. (N.S.) 282.

[7] Para. 9.059, *post.*

[8] See, *e.g.*, the presumption of advancement, *infra.*

[9] *Per* Pim J., *Re Slattery* [1917] 2 I.R. 278 at 280.

[10] Para. 9.055, *post. McGillicuddy* v. *Joy* [1959] I.R. 189, followed by Lowry L.C.J. in *Gilmurray* v. *Corr* [1978] N.I. 99, aff'd. by Court of Appeal, *ibid.*, p. 106 and (1979) 30 N.I.L.Q. 48.

purchase money.[11] This presumption of a resulting trust is, however, always rebuttable according to the circumstances of each particular case and parol evidence is admissible even in a case involving land.[12]

9.047. Where, on the other hand, the property is bought in the name of the wife,[13] child[14] or other person to whom the purchaser stands *in loco parentis*,[15] there is a contrary presumption known as the presumption of advancement. In other words, a husband will be presumed to be making a gift to his wife and a father to his child.[16] Once again the presumption is rebuttable.[17] The acts and statements of the parties before or at the time of the purchase are admissible for or against the party performing or making them, whereas acts and statements subsequent to the purchase are admissible only against the party concerned.[18]

9.048. There has been much controversy in recent years over the position of husbands and wives with respect to the various "family assets," such as the matrimonial home and its furniture.[19] The point is that a husband and wife rarely keep accurate accounts as to who paid for what and, in the event of a dispute years later when, perhaps, divorce or separation is being considered, it is almost impossible to unravel the history of their financial contributions. In this context, strict adherence to the presumptions we have just discussed may work a very rough justice and some judges have urged application of the "equality is equity" maxim in such cases. Originally the judges sought to solve the difficulties by trying to find the intention of the parties, but domestic relations and property dealings between husband and wife cannot be regarded as forming a matter for contract. The concept of trust has accordingly been adopted and, in the two leading Irish cases on the subject, the approach by contract was rejected and that of a trust adopted.[20] But it has been generally recognised that the traditional concepts, like the presumption of advancement,

---

[11] *Redington* v. *Redington, op. cit.; O'Brien* v. *Sheil* (1873) I.R. 7 Eq. 255 (see *A Casebook on Equity and Trusts in Ireland* (1985), p. 370.

[12] *Nicholson* v. *Mulligan* (1869) I.R. 3 Eq. 308. S. 5 of the Statute of Frauds (Ir.), 1695 excludes trusts arising by implication, para. 9.023, *ante*.

[13] *Re Condrin* [1914] 1 I.R. 89; see also *Talbot* v. *Cody* (1875) I.R. 10 Eq. 138; *C.* v. *C.* (1982) Unrep (H.C., R.I.) (1982 No. 275 Sp).

[14] *O'Brien* v. *Sheil* (1873) I.R. 7 Eq. 255 (see *A Casebook on Equity and Trusts in Ireland* (1985), p. 370); *Re Wall's Estate* [1922] 1 I.R. 59; *Owens* v. *Greene* [1932] I.R. 225 (see *ibid.*, p. 356).

[15] *Re Orme* (1884) 50 L.T. 51. See also *B.* v. *B.* (1978) Unrep. (H.C., R.I.) (1977 No. 500 Sp).

[16] *Alleyne* v. *Alleyne* (1845) 8 Ir.Eq.R. 493; *Irwin* v. *O'Connell* [1936] I.R. 44; *Re Grimes* [1937] I.R. 470. See also the cases on deposit receipts, para. 9.044, *supra*. And *Heavey* v. *Heavey* (1977) 111 I.L.T.R. 1 (see *A Casebook on Irish Land Law* (1984), p. 714).

[17] *Hall* v. *Hill* (1841) 1 Dr. & War. 94; *M* v. *M.* (1978) Unrep. (H.C., R.I.) (1978 No. 155 Sp).

[18] *O'Brien* v. *Sheil* (1873) I.R. 7 Eq. 255; *Morrison* v. *McFerran* [1901] 1 I.R. 360.

[19] See Shatter, *Family Law in the Republic of Ireland* (2nd ed., 1981), ch. 15. See also Law Com. No. 86 (*Third Report on Family Property*); Miller, *Family Property and Family Provision* (2nd ed., 1983); Murphy and Clark, *The Family Home*; Todd and Jones, *Matrimonial Property* (H.M.S.O. 1972). Also Miller, "Expenses of the Matrimonial Home" (1971) 35 Conv, 332, "Trusts for Sale and the Matrimonial Home" (1972) 36 Conv. 99; Nevitt and Levin, "Social Policy and the Matrimonial Home" (1973) 36 M.L.R. 345. See also para. 25.15, *post*.

[20] *McFarlane* v. *McFarlane* [1972] N.I. 59; *Heavey* v. *Heavey* (1977) 111 I.L.T.R. 1 (see *A Casebook on Irish Land Law* (1985), p. 714). *Cf.* the House of Lords decisions in *Pettitt* v. *Pettitt* [1970] A.C. 777 and *Gissing* v. *Gissing* [1971] A.C. 886. See also now in England the Matrimonial Proceedings and Property Act, 1970, s. 37.

look distinctly out-of-date in an era when so many wives go out to work and are financially independent.[21]

2 Joint Purchase and Joint Mortgage

9.049. Here we are dealing with the case where the legal title to the property is taken in the names of all the parties concerned in the purchase or mortgage and they all contribute to the purchase money or money lent on mortgage. Normally, in such a situation a joint tenancy will come into operation and the survivor will succeed to the entire property.[22] Equity, however, leans against joint tenancies[23] and in such situations may require the survivor to hold the legal title to part of the property on trust for the estates of his deceased co-tenants. In the case of a joint purchase, the rule is that, if the co-tenants contributed *unequal* shares of the purchase money, the survivors are trustees for the deceased's estate to the extent of his share; if they contributed *equal* shares, no such presumption of a trust arises and the assumption is that the normal consequences of a legal joint tenancy, with its right of survivorship, follow.[24]

9.050. In the case of money advanced jointly on mortgage, it appears that it makes no difference whether the shares are equal or unequal. In either case a presumption of an implied trust arises on the basis that it was the intention of all the lenders ultimately to get their money back.[25] It seems that insertion of a joint account clause[26] does not necessarily rebut this presumption.[27]

3. Mutual Wills

9.051. Another situation where it is commonly said that an implied trust arises is where two people, usually husband and wife, agree to make mutual wills whereby each agrees to make a will leaving his or her property to the survivor and thereafter to named beneficiaries, probably their children. Once the first of the parties dies, the question arises as to how far the survivor is bound by the original agreement. This could be important if the survivor remarries and decides to make a new will in favour of the second spouse and, perhaps, children of the second marriage who were unlikely to be included in the first, mutual will. Equity steps in and decrees that the survivor holds his or her property under a trust and any new will must take effect subject to that trust.[28] There

---

[21] See Lord Upjohn in *Pettitt* v. *Pettitt, op cit. Cf.* Lord MacDermott in *M'Farlane* and Kenny J. in *Heavey*, paras. 25.15–16, *post*. Note also the subsequent discussion of the *McFarlane* and *Heavey* principles in cases like *McKeown* v. *McKeown* [1975] N.I. 139; *C* v. *C.* [1976] I.R. 254; *McGill* v. *S.* [1979] I.R. 285; *W* v. *W.* [1981] I.L.R.M. 202; *F.G.* v. *F.G.* [1982] I.L.R.M. 155; *N.A.D.* v. *T.D.* [1985] I.R. 153. And see the Republic's Supreme Court's cautionary warning in *McC* v. *McC.* (1984) Unrep. (52/1982).

[22] Ch. 7, *ante*.   [24] *O'Connell* v. *Harrison* [1927] I.R. 330.

[23] Paras. 3.059 and 7.18, *ante*.   [25] *Morley* v. *Bird* (1798) 3 Ves. 631.

[26] Permitting the surviving mortgagee to give the mortgagor a receipt for the entire mortgage debt, now automatically implied in Ireland (subject to a contrary intention expressed in the mortgage), see Convéyancing Act, 1881, s. 61.

[27] *Re Jackson* (1887) 34 Ch.D. 732.

[28] See Burgess, "A Fresh Look at Mutual Wills" (1970) 34 Conv. 230; Graham, "Mutual Wills" (1951) 15 Conv. 28; Goddard, "Mutual Wills" (1919) 17 Mich L.Rev. 677; Mitchell, "Some Aspects of Mutual Wills" (1951) 14 M.L.R. 136; Sheridan, "The Floating Trust; Mutual Wills" (1977) Alberta L. Rev. 211; Youdan, "The Mutual Wills Doctrine" (1979) 29 U. Toronto L.J. 390.

are, however, many uncertainties about this doctrine of mutual wills and, unfortunately, there seems to be no authority in Ireland on the subject.[29]

9.052. First, by tradition the trust in these cases has been classified as an implied one found by the courts in order to give effect to the intention of the parties.[30] However, it has been argued recently that it is more properly regarded as a constructive trust imposed by the courts in order to prevent fraud being committed by the survivor, regardless of any intention to create a trust.[31] It is argued that an analogy can be drawn with the doctrine of secret trusts in that here the deceased has also been induced to leave his or her mutual will as it stood on the basis of the agreement by the survivor to do the same.[32] Certainly both doctrines seem to depend upon this element of agreement between both parties, acted upon by one until death, thereby resulting in equity insisting upon the other keeping to the original agreement. It may be accepted that equity is giving effect to the intention that the agreement for mutual wills should be abided by, but that is not necessarily an intention that a *trust* should come into force. It is arguable that the trust is simply equity's remedy in this situation for enforcement of the contract.

9.053. There are other uncertainties. First, it is not clear when the trust, implied or constructive, should be regarded as coming into force. One possible date is when the original agreement to have mutual wills is made; another is when the first party dies; yet another is when the survivor dies. In practice, the issue arises at the last date. The first date is hardly likely since either party may revoke his or her will before death and, provided the other is given notice, no harm is done. The second date seems more appropriate and it has been held that there is lapse of a beneficiary's interest on his death between that date and the death of the survivor.[33] This may be reinforced on the ground that a special equity arises if and when the survivor receives a benefit from the deceased's will—in effect to prevent unjust enrichment.[34] It is also arguable that in that case the survivor should be put to an election whether to keep to the original agreement for mutual wills and take under the deceased's will or to disclaim the benefits under that will and thereby release himself or herself from the obligations under the agreement.

9.054. Then there is the question as to what property is bound by the trust. Once again there are several possibilities: property the survivor receives under the deceased's will, or all the property the survivor owned at the deceased's death or at the survivor's death or at any time since the deceased's death. It seems clear that it includes the first category, provided, of course, it is in

---

[29] See the English authorities: *Dufour* v. *Pereira* (1769) Dick. 419; *Re Oldham* [1925] Ch. 75; *Re Hagger* [1930] 2 Ch. 190; *Re Green* [1951] Ch. 148.

[30] See, *e.g.* Keeton and Sheridan, *Law of Trusts* (11th ed., 1983), ch. XIII.

[31] See, *e.g.*, Hanbury and Maudsley, *Modern Equity* (12th ed. by Martin, 1985), ch. 12.

[32] But note the same controversy over the true basis of the doctrine of secret trusts, see paras. 9.033–4, *supra*.

[33] *Re Hagger* [1930] 2 Ch. 190. *Cf.* the decision of *Re Gardner* [1923] 2 Ch. 230 on lapse in the case of a secret trust, para. 9.037, *supra*.

[34] See *Hanbury's Modern Equity* (9th ed.), pp. 230–1.

existence after the survivor's death (*e.g.*, a mere life estate left to the survivor would not be). It also seems clear that it includes property the survivor had at the deceased's death[35] and that it is a question of construction of the original agreement whether it extends to after-acquired property.[36]

F. RESULTING TRUSTS

9.055. Since a resulting trust may also be founded by the courts on the intention of the parties, it is to that extent simply another illustration of an implied trust.[37] However, one of the most common examples of such a trust arises where an express trust of property has been set up but this either fails or does not exhaust the entire beneficial interest in the property.[38] For example, a settlor might convey the fee simple in Blackacre to trustees to be held on trust for B for life. In such a case the trustees must hold the fee simple reversion on a resulting trust for the settlor.[39] They cannot benefit from the trust themselves and, arguably, the resulting trust is "automatic" and arises by operation of law, like a constructive trust, independently of the intention of the settlor.[40] Similarly, if B has died before the trust takes effect, so that the objects fail, then the trustees must again hold the property, this time the fee simple in possession, on a resulting trust for the settlor.[41] The resulting trust in each case is in favour of the grantor of the property, *i.e.*, the settlor or the testator's estate. If the settlor is dead, or the testator leaves no residuary estate, then the resulting trust will be in favour of the settlor's (subject to any provision he may have made by will) or the testator's intestate successors.[42] If there are no such persons, nowadays the resulting trust will be in favour of the State in the Republic of Ireland[43] or the Crown in Northern Ireland,[44] in the usual way.[45] The above examples of a resulting trust should not be confused with another common situation where the trust is set up in favour of a beneficiary absolutely (*i.e.*, the entire beneficial interest is disposed of) and that beneficiary dies *after* the trust comes into force. In such a case there is no resulting trust in favour of the settlor and the trustees hold the trust property in favour of the beneficiary's estate, for his testate or intestate successors, as the case requires.[46]

9.056. It is clear that there are certain resulting trusts which are based upon

---

[35] *Re Hagger* [1930] 2 Ch. 190.

[36] *Paul* v. *Paul* (1882) Ch.D. 742; *Re Green* [1951] Ch. 148; *Re Ralli's W.T.* [1964] Ch. 288; *Re Cleaver* [1981] 1 W.L.R. 939.

[37] Costigan, "Classification of Trusts as Express, Resulting and Constructive" (1914) 27 H.L.R. 437; Scott, "Resulting Trusts Arising upon the Purchase of Land" (1927) 40 H.L.R. 669. Thus the examples of implied trusts given earlier can be classified as "presumed" resulting trusts, see fn. 40, *infra*.

[38] See *Scott* v. *Brownrigg* (1881) 9 L.R.Ir. 246

[39] *Chism* v. *Lipsett* [1905] 1 I.R. 60.

[40] See Megarry J.'s analysis of "automatic" resulting trusts and "presumed" resulting trusts in *Re Vandervell's Trust (No. 2)* [1974] Ch. 269. See Sweeney, "Presumed Resulting Uses and Trusts: Survivals and a New Arrival?" (1979) 14 Ir.Jur. (N.S.) 282. See also *In b. Mitchell* (1966) 100 I.L.T.R. 185.

[41] *Scott* v. *Brownrigg* (1881) 9 L.R.Ir. 246.

[42] *Re Lane's Trusts* (1863) 14 Ir.Ch.R. 523; *Re Boyd's Trusts* [1916] 1 I.R. 121. See also *Tuite* v. *Tuite* (1978) Unrep. (H.C., R.I.) (1978 No. 202 Sp.).

[43] Succession Act, 1965, ss. 11 and 73.

[44] Administration of Estates Act (N.I.), 1955, ss. 1 and 16.

[45] See ch. 15, *post*.

[46] *Fenton* v. *Nevin* (1893) 31 L.R.Ir. 478.

the presumed intention of the settlor or testator, and such a resulting trust, always gives way to a contrary intention on the part of the settlor or testator to favour either the trustees or particular beneficiaries. Thus it has been held in Ireland that such a contrary intention may arise in the case of a marriage settlement where, for example, a father settles property in favour of his daughter on her marriage and a resulting trust arises because the trusts have been only partially stated.[47] Normally in such a case the resulting trust is for the benefit of the settlor, the father,[48] but in some Irish cases it has been held to be in favour of the daughter on the ground that there was sufficient evidence of an intention to make an absolute gift to the daughter in the nature of a marriage portion or "fortune," for her to settle in accordance with the trusts in the original settlement[49]

9.057. Another example of a resulting trust arises in the case of a voluntary conveyance, *i.e.*, where a grantor transfers the ownership of property, real or personal, to another person who gives no consideration.[50] In such a case the inference arises that the grantee holds the property by way of resulting trust for the grantor.[51] Once again the inference of a resulting trust may be rebutted,[52] and this would obviously occur in cases where the contrary presumption of advancement arises.[53]

9.058. In the case of a voluntary conveyance of land, prior to the Statute of Uses (Ireland), 1634, the presumption of a resulting *use* in favour of the grantor came into play.[54] The presumption did not arise if either the grantee gave consideration[55] or the conveyance was made expressly to his use, thereby excluding an implied use in favour of the grantor. Indeed, to prevent the question of whether consideration had in fact been given arising in subsequent dealings with the land, it became the practice in most cases when consideration was given by the grantee for the grantor still to convey the land expressly "to the use of the grantee and his heirs." After the passing of the Statute of Uses (Ireland), 1634, which remains in force in both parts of Ireland, the implied resulting use in favour of the grantor of a voluntary conveyance is automatically "executed", with the result that the *legal* estate is vested in the grantor.[56] In other words, since the 1634 Statute a voluntary conveyance of land in Ireland without any uses expressed is ineffective and leaves the legal estate in

---

[47] *Ward* v. *Dyas* (1835) Ll. & G. *temp.*Sug. 177.

[48] *Re Donnelly's Estate* [1913] 1 I.R. 177.

[49] *Ward* v. *Dyas, op. cit; Dennehy* v. *Delaney* (1876) I.R. 10 Eq. 377; *Doyle* v. *Crean* [1905] 1 I.R. 252; *Cummins* v. *Hall* [1933] I.R. 419. *Cf.* the presumption of advancement, para. 9.047, *ante.*

[50] See para. 9.040, *ante.*

[51] *Doyle* v. *Byrne* (1922) 56 I.L.T.R. 125.

[52] *McEneaney* v. *Shevlin* [1912] 1 I.R. 278; *Owens* v. *Greene* [1932] I.R. 225 (see espec. Kennedy C.J. at p. 237) (see *A Casebook on Equity and Trusts in Ireland* (1985), p. 356); *Kiernan* v. *O'Flynn* (1978) Unrep. (H.C., R.I.) (1976 No. 5236 P).

[53] Para. 9.047, *ante.*

[54] See para. 3.018, *ante.*

[55] Including, it seems, "good" as opposed to "valuable" consideration, *e.g.*, a gift to a relative out of "natural love and affection." See *Re Luby's Estate* (1909) 43 I.L.T.R. 141. *Cf. Ellis* v. *Nimmo* (1835) Ll. & G.*temp.*Sug. 333.

[56] Para. 3.016, *ante.*

the land in the grantor. To avoid this happening, it is essential for the convey-ance to use the formula "unto and to the use of" the grantee and his heirs,[57] thereby negativing a resulting use in favour of the grantor and ensuring that the estate passes to the grantee. It is important to note that this formula in such cases simply negatives the presumption of a resulting use; it does not attract the provisions of the Statute of Uses (Ireland), which apply only where a person is seised to the use of *another* person.[58] The legal estate passes to the grantee at common law quite independently of the Statute of Uses (Ireland).[59] Neverthe-less, although the formula "unto and to the use of" is, strictly speaking, necessary in Ireland only in the case of a voluntary conveyance of land, it is the usual practice still to employ it in conveyances involving consideration. This may be partly due to habit and tradition and partly due to a desire to avoid subsequent disputes as to whether or not consideration had been given in previous dealings with the land.

G. CONSTRUCTIVE TRUSTS

9.059. Unlike implied or resulting trusts, a constructive trust is one which arises by operation of law.[60] It is imposed by the courts, not in order to give effect to the intention of the parties, but rather to provide the best remedy or solution for the problem which has occurred, regardless of any intention to create a trust.[61] Over the years constructive trusts have been imposed by the courts in a wide variety of situations and we shall discuss some of them in a moment. The common theme which seems to run through the cases is the con-cern of the Courts of Equity to prevent fraud or unfair advantage or profit being gained in respect of property.[62] Though in many of the cases an express trust has come into existence at some point, and in most at least some kind of fiduciary relationship has arisen, it may be questioned whether these elements are nowadays prerequisites to the finding of a constructive trust. The point is that the concept of a constructive trust has sometimes appeared to assume a purely fictional role in the hands of the courts, where it seems that it has been invoked simply as a remedial device in circumstances where no other con-venient remedy seemed available for the plaintiff. For the most part, however, these developments have occurred in England.[63] In Ireland, at least hitherto,

---

[57] A resulting trust (use) will still arise, of course, if the use does not exhaust the entire beneficial interest in the property, *Lynch* v. *Clarkin* [1900] 1 I.R. 178. The formula is no longer necessary in England, see Law of Property Act, 1925, s. 60 (3) and (4).

[58] Para. 3.019, *ante*.

[59] Of course, the conveyance may go on to impose further trusts on the grantee, see para. 3.021, *ante*. In the event of a failure of those trusts, then the grantee might hold the beneficial or equitable interest in the land on a resulting trust in favour of the grantor, while maintaining his legal estate as trustee.

[60] See generally, Oakley, *Constructive Trusts* (1978); Waters, *The Constructive Trust* (1964).

[61] Costigan, "Classification of Trusts as Express, Resulting and Constructive" (1914) 27 H.L.R. 437; Dewar, "The Development of the Remedial Constructive Trust" (1982) 60 C.B.R. 265; Maudsley, "Constructive Trusts" (1977) 28 N.I.L.Q. 23; Oakley, "Has the Constructive Trust become a General Equitable Remedy?" (1973) C.L.P. 17; Scott, "Constructive Trusts" (1955) 71 L.Q.R. 39.

[62] See generally, Sheridan, *Fraud in Equity* (1957); Goff and Jones, *Law of Restitution* (2nd ed., 1978).

[63] Thus Lord Denning M.R. referred to a "constructive trust of a new model", to be impossed whenever equity, justice and good conscience required it, see *Eves* v. *Eves* [1975] 1 W.L.R. 1338. See also *Hussey* v. *Palmer* [1972] 1 W.L.R. 1286; *Cooke* v. *Head* [1972] 1 W.L.R. 518; *Re Densham* [1975] 1 W.L.R. 1519; *Re Sharpe* [1980] 1 W.L.R. 219. See Cooney, "Wives, Mistresses and Beneficial Ownership" (1979) 14 Ir.Jur. (N.S.) 1; Hodkinson,

except to a limited extent in respect of matrimonial property, a more traditional approach has been adopted by the courts, and in most cases the constructive trust has been founded on the existence of some prior express trust or on a similar fiduciary relationship.

9.060. The following seem to be the main situations in which the courts impose a constructive trust. It must be emphasised that these simply reflect the incidence of litigation up to the present and that they are not to be treated as exhaustive of the categories of constructive trust. Indeed, it is doubtful if one can ever provide an exhaustive list in this sort of area of equitable jurisdiction. To the extent that the constructive trust is simply equity's remedy for dealing with certain kinds of fraud or unfair profit,[64] the concept may be used in any situation where equity finds such fraud or profit. What follow are common examples only.

1. *Vendor*

9.061. It is a principle of long standing that, once a contract for the sale of land has been entered into, the vendor becomes a constructive trustee of the land for the purchaser.[65] To a large extent this notion seems to be based upon the special view taken of such contracts by the Courts of Equity,[66] *i.e.,* that a decree of specific performance will normally be granted to either party to the contract.[67] Following on from this, it is then said that the purchaser may be regarded as the beneficial or equitable owner of the property until such time as completion takes place and the legal ownership is actually transferred to him by the conveyance. Support for the idea that the purchaser is equitable owner during the period between contract and conveyance may be found in the established principle that, upon entering into the contract for sale of the land, the "risk" of damage to the property passes to the purchaser, so that he must thereupon make sure that he is adequately covered by insurance.[68] Yet this very situation illustrates the peculiar nature of the constructive trust which is said to bind the vendor.[69] Thus, for example, it has been held that, while the vendor is constructive trustee of the *land*, he is not, like most trustees, trustee of

"Constructive Trusts: Palm Trees in the Commonwealth" [1983] Conv. 420. But *cf. Burns* v. *Burns* [1984] Ch. 317, a reaction echoed by the Republic's Supreme Court in *McC.* v. *McC.* (1984) Unrep. (52/1982). See para. 25.16, *post.* Note also the trust's use in England in the case of contracts for the benefit of third persons, Wylie, "Contracts and Third Parties" (1966) 17 N.I.L.Q. 351, espec. at 391–402. See also the Republic's Married Women's Status Act, 1957, s. 7; Law Reform (Husband and Wife) Act (N.I.), 1964, s. 4.

[64] Or "unjust enrichment" as it is sometimes called, see generally, Goff and Jones, *Law of Restitution* (2nd ed., 1978). For recognition by the English courts of this "remedial" aspect of the doctrine of constructive trusts, see *Carl Zeiss Stiftung* v. *Herbert Smith & Co.* [1969] 2 Ch. 276; *Chase Manhattan Bank N.A.* v. *Israel-British Bank (London) Ltd.* [1981] Ch. 105. This accords with the American view, see *Restatement of Restitution,* § 160. *Cf. Re Sharpe* [1980] 1 W.L.R. 219.

[65] This subject is discussed in detail in *Irish Conveyancing Law* (1978), ch. 11. See also Waters, "Constructive Trust: Vendor and Purchaser" (1961) 14 C.L.P. 76; Wellings, "Vendor as Trustee" (1959) 23 Conv. 173. See also Jessel M.R. in *Lysaght* v. *Edwards* (1876) 2 Ch.D. 499 at 507.

[66] See para. 3.144, *ante.*

[67] See *Harnett* v. *Yielding* (1805) 2 Sch. & Lef. 549 at 553–4 (*per* Lord Redesdale). Also *Shaw* v. *Foster* (1872) L.R. 5 H.L. 321.

[68] See Foote. "Liability for Fire before 1800" (1969) 20 N.I.L.Q. 141.

[69] See the arguments amongst Cotton, Brett and James L.JJ. in *Rayner* v. *Preston* (1881) 18 Ch.D.1.

anything which is substituted for the land, such as insurance money paid to him under his own insurance policy in respect of damage to the land caused by fire.[70] The purchaser must take out his own insurance policy or else arrange for the vendor's policy to be endorsed in his favour, for, whatever happens to the land, the purchaser will still have to pay, on completion of the sale, the price contracted for.[71] Furthermore, it is also clear that, again unlike most trustees,[72] the vendor may keep the rents and profits of the land until completion takes place and may retain possession of the land until the purchase price is paid by the purchaser. Indeed, even if the land is conveyed before the purchase price is paid, the vendor still has a lien on the land for that purchase price.[73] All this indicates that the trusteeship of a vendor is of a very special kind and, were it not for the long-standing nature of the principle, it might be questioned whether the trust concept should be applied any longer to such cases. It has been argued that nothing of substance seems to be added by reference to a constructive trust in these cases and that it would seem to be perfectly safe to leave it that both parties to a contract for the sale of land, vendor and purchaser, have sufficient remedies by which to protect their respective positions under the contract.[74]

2. *Mortgagee*

9.062. Where a mortgagee of land (*i.e.,* the lender of money on the security of land) exercises his power to sell the land and thereby realise his security, he is obliged to hold the surplus[75] of the proceeds of sale on trust for subsequent mortgagees and, ultimately, the mortgagor.[76] This trust was originally imposed by the Courts of Equity on the basis that a mortgage was only a means of providing security for the debt, so that the mortgagee was entitled to retain only precisely what he was owed and no more. Nowadays, however, this trust is imposed in both parts of Ireland by the Conveyancing Act, 1881.[77]

3. *Fiduciary—Doctrine of Graft*

9.063. It is a basic principle of our law, strictly enforced by the Courts of Equity from their earliest days, that a person in a fiduciary position must not profit from that position.[78] In the case of a fiduciary concerned with property, any

---

[70] *Rayner* v. *Preston* (1881) 18 Ch.D.1.

[71] So that in the *Rayner* case the insurance company was able to reclaim the insurance proceeds from the vendor on the ground that, having received the full purchase price, the vendor had suffered no loss; a contract of insurance is one of indemnity only, see *Gaggin* v. *Upton* (1859) Dru.*temp.*Nap. 427; *Castellain* v. *Preston* (1883) 11 Q.B.D. 380. For England, see now s. 47 of the Law of Property Act, 1925. Also see *Survey of the Land Law of Northern Ireland,* para. 167.

[72] Para. 10.068, *post.*

[73] *Mackreth* v. *Symmons* (1808) 15 Ves. 329; *Davies* v. *Thomas* [1900] 2 Ch. 462. The vendor has a lien on the land for unpaid purchase money and the purchaser has a lien on the land for return of purchase money paid before conveyance, *Rose* v. *Watson* (1864) 10 H.L.C. 672; *Re Strong* [1940] I.R. 382. See also *Bank of Ireland Finance Ltd.* v. *Daly* [1978] I.R. 79.

[74] But *cf. McCarthy & Stone Ltd.* v. *Julian S. Hodge & Co. Ltd.* [1971] 1 W.L.R. 1547.

[75] *I.e.,* after paying the costs of the sale and what he is himself owed by the mortgagor.

[76] See, generally, ch. 13, *post.* Waters, "Constructive Trust: Mortgagor and Mortgagee" (1962) 15 C.L.P. 176.

[77] S. 21 (3).

[78] See further para. 10.068, *post.*

profit or advantage secured by him in relation to that property must be held on a constructive trust by him. Chatterton V.-C. put the matter thus:

> "The funamental principle upon which the doctrine of constructive trusts proceeds is, that no person in a fiduciary capacity shall be allowed to retain any advantage gained by him in his character as trustee. His *cestuis que trust* are entitled to the benefit of any advantage so gained by him, to any addition or accretion to the trust estate which he may have acquired, and to all profit which he may have made with any dealing with it."[79]

In Ireland, such applications of the concept of a constructive trust involve what is known to the Irish courts as the doctrine of *graft*. In equity the profit or accretion is deemed to be "engrafted" upon the original trust property and thereby held upon the same trusts.[80]

9.064. It is clear that the doctrine of graft not only applies to an express trustee[81] but to any person in a fiduciary relationship to another person.[82] It has been applied in Ireland to the following persons acting in a fiduciary capacity: an administrator[83]; executor[84]; guardian of a minor[85]; committee of a lunatic[86]; limited owner[87]; agent[88]; tenant in common[89]; mortgagee[90]; solicitor.[91] A common illustration occurs where a trustee or other fiduciary holds leasehold property on trust and then obtans a renewal of the lease for his own purposes. The doctrine of graft in such a case raises the presumption that the renewed lease is subject to a constructive trust[92] and the onus is on the trustee or other fiduciary to prove to the court that he did not take advantage of his fiduciary position in obtaining the renewal.[93] The doctrine applies whatever the length of the original lease[94] and it matters not that the renewed lease is for a different term[95] or at a different rent.[96] It also applies even though there was no express covenant for renewal in the original lease, nor one implied by custom,[97] and even though the landlord refused to grant a renewal to the

---

[79] *Gabbett* v. *Lawder* (1883) 11 L.R.Ir. 295 at 299 (see *A Casebook on Equity and Trusts in Ireland* (1985), p. 378). *Cf.* Cherry L.J. in *Patten* v. *Hamilton* [1911] 1 I.R. 46 at 60.

[80] See the discussion in *Dempsey* v. *Ward* [1899] 1 I.R. 463 (see *ibid.*, p. 384).

[81] *Moore* v. *McGlynn* [1894] 1 I.R. 74 (see *ibid.*, p. 374); see also *Ker* v. *Lord Dungannon* (1841) 4 Ir.Eq.R. 343; *Coyle* v. *Central Trust Investment Society Ltd* (1978) Unrep. (H.C., R.I.) (1978 No. 531Sp).

[82] *Buggy* v. *Maher* [1926] I.R. 487 at 493 (*per* Fitzgibbon J.). *Cf. Swain* v. *The Law Society* [1983] A.C. 598.

[83] *Gabbett* v. *Lawder* (1883) 11 L.R.Ir. 295. See also *Kelly* v. *Kelly* (1874) I.R. 8 Eq. 403.

[84] *McCracken* v. *McClelland* (1877) I.R. 11 Eq. 172; *Re Egan* [1906] 1 I.R. 320.

[85] *Quinton* v. *Frith* (1868) I.R. 2 Eq. 494; see also *Whyte* v. *Meade* (1840) 2 Ir.Eq.R. 420.

[86] *Smythe* v. *Byrne* [1914] 1 I.R. 53.

[87] *O'Brien* v. *Egan* (1880) 5 L.R.Ir. 633; *Barrett* v. *Hanbury* [1919] 1 I.R. 275; *Re Brady's Estate* [1920] 1 I.R. 170; *Re White and Hague's Contract* [1921] 1 I.R. 138; *Robinson* v. *Crosse and Blackwell Ltd.* [1940] I.R. 56; *O'Donnell* v. *Grogan* [1941] I.R. 557.

[88] *Patten* v. *Hamilton* [1911] 1 I.R. 46; see also *Molony* v. *Kernan* (1842) 2 Dr. & War. 31; *De Montmorency* v. *Devereux* (1840) 2 Dr. & Wal. 410.

[89] *Hunter* v. *Allen* [1907] 1 I.R. 212. See also *Kiernan* v. *McCann* [1920] 1 I.R. 99.

[90] *Nesbitt* v. *Tredennick* (1808) 1 Ba. & B. 29.

[91] *Lawless* v. *Mansfield* (1841) 1 Dr. & War. 557; *Atkins* v. *Delmege* (1847) 12 Ir.Eq.R. 1.

[92] This is also known as the rule in *Keech* v. *Sandford* (1726) Sel.Cas.*temp.* King 61. See also *Re Biss* [1903] 2 Ch. 40.

[93] *Gabbett* v. *Lawder* (1883) 11 L.R.Ir. 295 (see *A Casebook on Equity and Trusts in Ireland* (1985), p. 378).

[94] *Re Egan* [1906] 1 I.R. 320; *Re Tottenham's Estate* (1865) 16 Ir.Ch.R. 115.

[95] Or for lives where the original lease was for a fixed term, *Eyre* v. *Dolphin* (1813) 2 Ba. & B. 290.

[96] *Mulvany* v. *Dillon* (1810) 1 Ba. & B. 409.

[97] *Eyre* v. *Dolphin, supra; Stratton* v. *Murphy* (1867) I.R. 1 Eq. 345 at 354 (*per* Walsh M.R.)

beneficiaries.[98] However, as Fitzgibbon L.J. said: "To have a graft at all, there must still be life in the old stock."[99] He went on to explain what he meant by this remark:

"Where a specific piece of property, such as a tenancy for a fixed term, which is subject to certain rights, comes to its natural end, and ceases to exist, I shall require argument to satisfy me that a person who had an interest in what so came to an end, is under any disability, or is subject to any equity, which will affect him in an honest dealing for a new interest, in any way in which a stranger would not be affected. That does not seem to me to be the case of grafting on an old stock, but of acquiring or planting a new root."[1]

9.065. It appears, therefore, that a trustee may purchase the reversion on a lease, unless the sale to him is made expressly subject to the lease and any right of renewal contained therein.[2] After natural determination of the lease, he may also obtain a renewal for himself provided he acted openly and honestly and did not secure in any way the renewal by reason of his position as trustee of the original lease.[3] Thus he must not surrender the original lease[4] nor suffer an ejectment[5] with a view of obtaining a renewal for himself. Where, however, a trustee who has obtained a renewal or bought the reversion is held to be constructive trustee, he is entitled to be indemnified for his costs and expenses in obtaining the renewal or in purchasing.[6]

9.066. Finally, it is interesting to note that the Irish doctrine of graft was given statutory recognition in the Land Purchase Acts, under which tenant-farmers were given the right to buy out the freehold of their land.[7] Section 14 (3) of the Land Law (Ireland) Act, 1887,[8] provided:

"Any person in occupation of and paying rent for a holding which is held under a contract of tenancy shall have power to enter into an agreement for the purchase thereof. Where a holding shall be conveyed to or vested in any such person, the interest thereby assigned to him *shall be deemed to be a graft upon the previous interest of the tenant* in such holding, and shall be subject to any right or equities *arising from its being such a graft*."[9]

The graft in this instance is not based upon any notice of a constructive trust but is one expressly declared by the statute, so that "the trust is as clearly

[98] *Kelly* v. *Kelly* (1874) I.R. 8 Eq. 403.
[99] *Dempsey* v. *Ward* [1899] 1 I.R. 463 at 474–5 (see *A Casebook on Equity and Trusts in Ireland* (1985), p. 384).
[1] *Ibid.*, p. 474.
[2] *Gabbett* v. *Lawder* (1883) 11 L.R.Ir. 295 (see *ibid.*, p. 378).
[3] *Nesbitt* v. *Tredennick* (1808) 1 Ba. & B. 29; *Re Brady* [1920] 1 I.R. 170; *Re Keogh* [1932] I.R. 406.
[4] *McCracken* v. *McClelland* (1877) I.R. 11 Eq. 172.
[5] *Kelly* v. *Kelly* (1874) I.R. 8 Eq. 403.
[6] *Gabbett* v. *Lawder* (1883) 11 L.R.Ir. 295.
[7] See chs. 1, *ante*, and 18, *post*.
[8] Extending s. 8 of the Purchase of Land (Ir.) Act, 1885.
[9] Italics added.

established as if the purchaser by deed under his hand declared that he held the land purchased under the same trusts and to and for the same purposes as the previous tenancy had been held for.[10]

9.067. When land was purchased under the Land Purchase Acts, no enquiry as to the title of the tenant purchaser was made and the person who entered into or was deemed to have entered into the contract was registered as owner under the Local Registration of Title (Ireland) Act, 1891. The position of those who had a share or interest in the land was protected by the "Note as to Equities" which was entered on the folio.[11] There is no provision in the new registration of title legislation in both parts of Ireland for this note, but it still appears on the folio in all cases of land purchased under the Land Purchase Acts in both parts of Ireland prior to the coming into force of the new legislation. It may also be discharged on proof that the person registered as owner was beneficially entitled to the entire tenant's interest, and the legislation contains provisions for conversion of titles registered.

4. *Stranger*

9.068. A person who is a total stranger to any trust or to any person holding property in a fiduciary capacity may nevertheless become a constructive trustee if he interferes with the trust property or intermeddles in the trust's affairs.[12] Thus, if trust property is transferred in breach of trust to a stranger, he will take the property as constructive trustee, unless he can prove that he received the *legal* title to the property as a *bona fide* purchaser for value without notice of the trust.[13] The stranger will not be protected by lack of notice if he was not a purchaser of the property.[14] Furthermore, any element of fraud on the part of a stranger in obtaining the trust property will have the result that he will be a constructive trustee of the property.[15] Thus, while the agent of a trustee is normally accountable only to his principal, he may be held to be a constructive trustee for the beneficiaries where it is felt that he assumed the character of his principal in dealing with the property or participating in fraud or misappropriation.[16]

H. Void and Voidable Trusts

9.069. A trust may be invalid for a variety of reasons, only some of which can

---

[10] *Per* O'Connor M.R., *Re White and Hague's Contract* [1921] 1 I.R. 138 at 143.

[11] 1891 Act, s. 29. See *Buggy* v. *Maher* [1926] I.R. 487. See further on the "Equities Note," *Report of the Committee on Registration of Title to Land in Northern Ireland* (Cmd. 512; 1967), paras. 29–34; Wallace, "The Untapped Potential of the Land Registration Act (N.I.) 1970" (1974) 25 N.I.L.Q. 1 at 5–8 and 19–20. See also now as to registration subject to equities, the Republic's Registration of Title Act, 1964, s. 35 and Land Registration Act (N.I.), 1970, Sched. 13, Pt. I, para. 2. Ch. 21, *post*.

[12] See discussion by Lord Redesdale in *Adair* v. *Shaw* (1803) 1 Sch. & Lef. 243 at 262. See Harpum, "The Stranger as Constructive Trustee" [1986] Con. 102.

[13] *Thompson* v. *Simpson* (1841) 1 Dr. & War. 459; *Cary* v. *Ryan Ltd.* [1982] I.R. 179 (see *A Casebook on Equity and Trusts in Ireland* (1985), p. 394). See further on the *bona fide* purchaser doctrine, para. 3.074, *ante*. *Cf.* a liability to account, see *Belmont Finance Corporation* v. *Williams Furniture Ltd.* (*No. 2*) [1980] 1 All E.R. 393 at 405 (*per* Buckley L.J.).

[14] *Sheridan* v. *Joyce* (1844) 7 Ir.Eq.R. 115; *McArdle* v. *Gaughran* [1903] 1 I.R. 106.

[15] *Alleyne* v. *Darcy* (1854) 4 Ir.Ch.R. 199 (see *A Casebook on Equity and Trusts in Ireland* (1985), p. 390).

[16] *Alleyne* v. *Darcy, op. cit.* Note the extent to which this principle was carried in *Boardman* v. *Phipps* [1967] 2 A.C. 46; see also *Selangor United Rubber Estates* v. *Cradock* [1968] 1 W.L.R. 1555.

be mentioned here. There is, however, an important distinction to be made in this context. This is the distinction between a ground of invalidity which means that a trust is *void* and one which means that it is voidable only.[17] In the case of the former, the trust is invalid *ob initio* and never in fact comes into operation. In the case of the latter, on the other hand, the trust does come into operation and will remain in force until such time as an action is brought to court to have the trust "avoided." If no such action is ever brought, then the relations of the various persons connected with the trust will continue to be governed by its terms.

1. *Void Trusts*

9.070. The following are the main grounds upon which a trust is void *ab initio*, with the normal consequence that the trust property must then be held by the trustees on a resulting trust for the settlor or testator's estate.[18]

(i) Rules against Perpetuities and Inalienability

Most trusts involve the creation of future interests and so are subject to the general rules governing that subject, such as the rules against perpetuities and inalienability. These rules have been discussed in detail in an earlier chapter and further reference may be made to that discussion.[19]

(ii) Public Policy

In setting up a trust the settlor must beware of offending against public policy or morality as those rather vague concepts are applied by the courts on both sides of the Irish Sea. It is impossible to categorise the various aspects of public policy or morality relevant here, but some common applications may be mentioned.

9.071. A trust in favour of *future* illegitimate children[20] is usually held void as tending to promote immoral conduct. Thus in *Thomson* v. *Thomas*[21] a trust for illegitimate children was held void as to those begotten after the creation of the trust. Similarly, there arises frequently a difficult question of construction as to whether an expression such as "children" or "issue" in a trust by will includes illegitimate children as well as legitimate children.[22] The courts tend to construe such expressions against inclusion of illegitimate children but this view is always subject to a contrary intention being expressed or implied on the

---

[17] See para. 3.159, *ante*.
[18] See Ford, "Illegal Trusts" (1960) 2 U.M.L.R. 165: Schuyler, "Payments under Void Trusts" (1952) 48 H.L.R. 597.
[19] Ch. 5, *ante*.
[20] *Cf.* a trust in a will in favour of the testator's illegitimate children, all of whom must necessarily be born or *en ventre sa mère* when the will and trust comes into operation.
[21] (1891) 27 L.R.Ir. 457 (see *A Casebook on Equity and Trusts in Ireland* (1985), p. 398). See also *Re Connor* (1845) 8 Ir.Eq.R. 401.
[22] As regards adopted children, see the Republic's Adoption Act, 1952, s. 26 (2) (*a*) (and the Succession Act, 1965, s. 110); Adoption of Children Act (N.I.), 1950, s 9 (3) (*a*) (and Administration of Estates Act (N.I.), 1955, s. 46 (*b*) and Sched. 2) and Legitimacy Act (N.I.), 1961, s. 3 (3). See also the Adoption Act (N.I.), 1967, ss. 18–9 and 47.

part of the testator.[23] In Northern Ireland, however, article 4 (8) of the Family Law Reform (N.I.) Order, 1977, abolished, with respect to dispositions made after the commencement of the Order, "any rule of law that a disposition in favour of illegitimate children not in being when the disposition takes effect is void as contrary to public policy." This does not affect the construction of the word "heir" or "heirs" when used to create an entailed interest (article 4 (3)). Furthermore, the presumption that as a matter of construction expressions such as "children" or "issue" are to be taken not to include illegitimate children has been reversed in Northern Ireland by article 4 (1) of the 1977 Order, again with respect to dispositions made after the commencement of the Order.

9.072. In *Re Blake*[24] a trust of capital and income in favour of the testator's grandchildren, but subject to a condition that the children should have been brought up in the Roman Catholic faith, was held void as contrary to the policy of the law. Dixon J. held that it was an attempt to restrict or fetter the right and duty of the parents to provide for the education of their children declared by Article 42 of the Republic's Constitution.[25] This case was, however, not followed by Kenny J. in *Re Doyle*,[26] in which he held that, when a condition precedent attached to a gift is a violation of the donee's constitutional rights in the Republic, the donee takes the benefit of the gift without complying with the condition. Other conditions attached to trusts that might offend against public policy would be ones in restraint of marriage.[27]

(iii) Exchange Control

Under exchange control regulations governing the Republic of Ireland, a trust is invalid to the extent that it purports to confer an interest, involving the transfer of currency, to persons otherwise than as permitted by the regulations.[28]

(iv) Mortmain

Section 16 of the Charitable Donations and Bequests (Ireland) Act, 1844, rendered void in Ireland any gift of land to charity unless the deed was executed and registered or the will made three months before the donor's death. This was designed to prevent deathbed importuning.[29] This mortmain restriction[30]

---

[23] See discussion by Ross J. in *Re B.* [1916] 1 I.R. 364. Also *Andrews* v. *Andrews* (1885) 15 L.R.Ir. 199; *O'Loughlin* v. *Bellew* [1906] 1 I.R. 487. As to the constitutional position of illegitimate children in the Republic, see Kelly, *The Irish Constitution* (2nd ed., 1984), pp. 486–8 and 628–31.
[24] [1955] I.R. 89 (see *A Casebook on Equity and Trusts in Ireland* (1985), p. 399).
[25] See also *Burke* v. *Burke* [1951] I.R. 216. See further on the constitutional position of illegitimate children in the Republic, *The State (Nicolaou)* v. *An Bord Uchtála* [1966] I.R. 567; *The State (G.)* v. *An Bord Uchtála* [1980] I.R. 32; *O'Brien* v. *Stoutt*, (1984) Unrep. (Sup. Ct., R.I.). See also the discussion in Kelly, *The Irish Constitution* (2nd ed., 1984), pp. 458–9, 487 and 628–30.
[26] (1972) Unrep. (H.C., R.I.) (No. 143 Sp).
[27] See para. 4.053, *ante*.
[28] See the Republic's Exchange Control Act, 1954, s. 5 and the Exchange Control (Continuance) Acts, 1966–82; as regards N.I., formerly governed by s. 29 of the Exchange Control Act, 1947 (U.K.), exchange control was suspended in 1979, see Exchange Control (General Exemption) Order 1979 (S.I. 1979 No. 1660).
[29] See *Pollock* v. *Day* (1863) 14 Ir.Ch.R. 371; *Boyle* v. *Boyle* (1877) I.R. 11 Eq. 433; *Murland* v. *Perry* (1879) 3 L.R.Ir. 135; *Re Cresswell* (1899) 33 I.L.T.R. 46; *Re Byrne* [1935] I.R. 782; *Re Scarlett* [1958] N.I. 28.
[30] For avoidance techniques, such as the "O'Hagan Clause," see *Geddis* v. *Semple* [1903] 1 I.R. 73 (see *A Casebook on Equity and Trusts in Ireland* (1985), p. 324); *Hannon* v. *Keane* (1938) 72 I.L.T.R. 113; *Re Meehan's*

has, however, now been removed in both parts of Ireland.[31]

2 *Voidable*

9.073. There are, perhaps, even more ways in which a trust may be voidable at the option of some interested party.

(i) Duress

Any settlor forced into making a trust by duress or force may apply to the court to have it set aside on that ground.[32]

(ii) Mistake

A person interested in a trust may seek to have it set aside or rescinded[33] on the ground of a mistake on his part.[34] Mistake may also be the basis of an action for rectification of the terms of a trust.[35]

(iii) Innocent Misrepresentation

9.074. At common law relief in respect of an *innocent* misrepresentation was confined to the case where the misrepresentation was a term of the contract or trust.[36] Equity, however, developed relief in respect of a misrepresentation of some material fact which induced the plaintiff to enter into a contract or, in the present context, to make the trust in reliance upon the misrepresentation.[37] Such relief can take the form of either rescission or refusal to grant specific performance to other parties, but it appears that no relief was available in equity where property had been conveyed in pursuance of the transaction so induced (usually the case with a trust).[38] The position has since been modified, to a varying extent, in both parts of Ireland. In Northern Ireland changes were introduced by the Misrepresentation Act (N.I.), 1967, to permit both

Estate [1960] I.R. 67. Note also the possible relevance of the doctrine of marshalling (ch. 13, *post*), *Re Solomon* [1949] I.R. 3.

[31] See the Republic's Mortmain (Repeal of Enactments) Act, 1954, and the Charities Act, 1961; Mortmain (Repeals) Act (N.I.), 1960 and Charities Act, 1964.

[32] *Blackwood* v. *Gregg* (1831) Hayes 277; *Smelter Corporation of Ireland* v. *O'Driscoll* [1977] I.R. 305; *cf. Finney* v. *Pardy* (1858) 9 Ir.Ch.R. 347. See also the discussion of duress by the Privy Council in *Barton* v. *Armstrong* [1976] A.C. 104 and *Pao On* v. *Lau Yiu* [1979] 3 W.L.R. 435. In the latter it was emphasised that, while economic duress may render a contract voidable, it must amount to a coercion of will which vitiates consent, i.e., the contract entered into was not a voluntary act. See also Dawson, "Economic Duress; Essay in Perspective" (1947) 45 Mich.L.Rev. 253; "Duress through Civil Litigation" (1947) 45 Mich.L.Rev. 571 and 679. See also on intoxication, *Nagle* v. *Baylor* (1842) 3 Dr. & War. 60; on a threat to take proceedings, *Headfort* v. *Brocket*]1966] I.R. 227.

[33] On rescission for mistake, see para. 3.159, *ante*. Note that where there is a common mistake, so that the parties are not *ad idem*, the trust may be void as opposed to voidable, *ibid*.

[34] *Garvey* v. *McMinn* (1847) 9 Ir.Eq.R. 526. See Kerr, *Law of Fraud and Mistake* (7th ed., 1952); Stoljar, *Mistake and Misrepresentation* (1968).

[35] *Maunsell* v. *Maunsell* (1877) 1 L.R.Ir. 529; *Annesley* v. *Annesley* (1893) 31 L.R.Ir. 457; *Collen Bros* v. *Dublin C.C.* [1908] 1 I.R. 503; *Monaghan C.C.* v. *Vaughan* [1948] I.R. 306; *Nolan* v. *Nolan* (1958) 92 I.L.T.R. 94. See para. 3.162, *ante*. See also *Irish Conveyancing Law* (1978), paras. 12.65–6 and 19.37–8.

[36] If a mere *warranty*, the relief was the award of damages; if a *condition*, then either rescission or damages, but *not* both.

[37] Para. 3.158, *ante*.

[38] *Lecky* v. *Walter* [1914] 1 I.R. 378, following *Seddon* v. *North-East Salt Co.* [1905] 1 Ch. 326. See para. 3.158, *ante*.

rescission and the award of damages in cases of innocent misrepresentation, and performance of the trust or conveyance of property is no longer a bar to rescission. In the Republic of Ireland, section 45 (1) of the Sale of Goods and Supply of Services Act, 1980, created a statutory right to damages for innocent misrepresentation. But, unlike the Northern Ireland 1967 Act, the 1980 Act is confined to contracts for the sale of goods, hire purchase agreements, contracts for the letting of goods and the supply of services.[39]

(iv) Fraud

Equity has always claimed a wide jurisdiction to deal with cases of fraud[40] and trusts induced by fraud are no exception.[41]

(v) Undue Influence

9.075. Equity will also set aside a trust where undue influence has been exercised over the settlor in setting up the trust.[42] Indeed, in certain cases there is a presumption of undue influence and the onus is upon the benefiting party to prove that none was in fact exercised.[43] This presumption arises in the cases of: parent and child,[44] guardian and ward,[45] religious adviser and layman,[46] doctor and patient,[47] solicitor and client,[48] principal and agent[49] and trustee and beneficiary.[50] In *R. (Proctor)* v. *Hutton (No. 2)*,[50a] Lowry L.C.J. (whose decision was affirmed by the Court of Appeal) had this to say about the presumption of undue influence:

> "The relationships which raise the presumption are left unlimited by definition, wide open for identification on the facts and in all the circumstances of each particular case as it arises . . . it is a common *but not necessary* feature of the relationship that the person on whose part undue influence is alleged assumed a responsibility for advising the donor or even managing his property. There are certain relationships

---

[39] Thus the 1980 Act does not apply where land is concerned and even *Lecky* v. *Walter*, fn. 38, *supra*, which involved a sale of shares (choses in action) remains the law. See Clark, *Contract* (1982), p. 109 *et seq*; Hannigan and Schuster, "Contractual and Statutory Remedies for Misrepresentation" (1982) Gaz. I.L.S.I. 76. Also para. 3.158, *ante*.

[40] Para. 3.157, *ante*. See Kerr, *Law of Fraud and Mistake* (7th ed., 1952); Sheridan, *Fraud in Equity* (1957).

[41] *Bowen* v. *Kirwan* (1835) L1. & G. temp. Sug. 47; *Howley* v. *Cook* (1873) I.R. 8 Eq. 570; *Slator* v. *Nolan* (1876) I.R. 11 Eq. 367; *Grealish* v. *Murphy* [1946] I.R. 35; *Buckley* v. *Irwin* [1960] N.I. 98.

[42] Green, "Fraud, Undue Influence and Mental Incompetency" (1943) 43 Col.L.Rev. 176; Winder, "Undue Influence and Fiduciary Relationship" (1940) 4 Conv. 274.

[43] *Gregg* v. *Kidd* [1956] I.R. 183.

[44] *Wallace* v. *Wallace* (1842) 2 Dr. & War. 452; *Croker* v. *Croker* (1870) 4 I.L.T. 181; *McMackin* v. *Hibernian Bank* [1905] 1 I.R. 296.

[45] *Dawson* v. *Massey* (1809) 1 Ba. & B. 219; *Mulhallen* v. *Marum* (1843) 3 Dr. & War. 317; *O'Connor* v. *Foley* [1906] 1 I.R. 20.

[46] *Whyte* v. *Meade* (1840) 2 Ir.Eq.R. 420.

[47] *Ahearne* v. *Hogan* (1844) Dru.*temp*.Sug. 310.

[48] *Taafe* v. *Merrick* (1931) 65 I.L.T.R. 36; see also *Low* v. *Holmes* (1858) 8 Ir.Ch.R. 53; *Fisher* v. *Boston* (1970) 21 N.I.L.Q. 61.

[49] *Molony* v. *Kernan* (1842) 2 Dr. & War. 31.

[50] *Bell* v. *Rogers* (1870) 4 I.L.T. 290; *King* v. *Anderson* (1874) I.R. 8 Eq. 625; *Provincial Bank of Ireland* v. *McKeever* [1941] I.R. 471.

[50a] [1978] N.I. 139.

which are recognised as giving rise to the presumption, but there are also those which, upon a consideration of the particular facts, may raise the same presumption."[50b]

It was held that the relationship of aunt and niece did not give rise to a presumption of undue influence. In *Healy* v. *Lyons,*[50c] Costello J. stated that the authorities established the following principles:

"(1) (a) In equity, persons standing in certain relations to one another are subject to certain presumptions in respect of *inter vivos* transactions. No presumption of undue influence, however, arises in the case of *wills* and the burden of proving undue influence in relation to wills always rests on the person alleging it. . . .

(b) When a person has been instrumental in having a will prepared and takes a benefit under it an onus may be placed on such a person to establish that the testator knew and approved of its contents. . .

(2) The Court may be required to consider whether the testator was a free agent when he made his will. In doing so the Court must be satisfied that the influence alleged amounted to more than mere persuasion. To justify a condemnation of a will the Court must be satisfied that pressure was so exerted as to overpower the volition, without convincing the judgment of the testator. Force need not be used or threatened. But, importunity or threats, such as the testator has not the courage to resist, moral command asserted and yielded to for the sake of peace and quiet, or for escaping from distress of mind or social discomfort, these, if carried to a degree in which the free play of the testator's judgment, discretion or wishes is overborne, will constitute undue influence. . . .

(3) The Court may infer undue influence; it cannot however act on mere surmise or suspicion. If the evidence leaves no other rational hypothesis on which the conduct of the testator can be accounted for then it may find that undue influence was exercised. . . .

(4) It is not sufficient to establish that a person had power unduly to overbear the will of the testator; it must be shown that the power was exercised in fact and that it was by means of it that the will which is being impugned was obtained. . . ."

Like any presumption,[51] it is rebuttable by proper evidence, *e.g.*, that the person seeking to set aside the transaction had independent competent advice.[52] Apart from the question of a presumption arising, there is, of course,

[50b] *Ibid.*, pp. 147–8.
[50c] (1978) Unrep. (H.C., R.I.) (1975 No. 4631P).
[51] *Cf.* the cases of brother and brother (*Armstrong* v. *Armstrong* (1873) I.R. 8 Eq. 1), brother-in-law and sister-in-law (*Evans* v. *Cook* (1874) 8 I.L.T.R. 118) and man and mistress (*Hargreave* v. *Everard* (1856) 6 Ir.Ch.R. 278).
[52] *Cooke* v. *Burtchaell* (1842) 2 Dr. & War. 165; *Provincial Bank of Ireland* v. *McKeever, op. cit.*; *Gregg* v. *Kidd* [1956] I.R. 183. Note, however, that the absence of such advice, even where inequality of bargaining power exists, does not necessarily mean that undue influence exists, see the recent strictures of the House of Lords in *National Westminster Bank plc* v. *Morgan* [1985] A.C. 686. See Barton and Rank, "Undue Influence—A Retreat?" [1985] Conv. 387.

no reason why the existence of undue influence should not be proved as a fact in a particular case.[53]

(vi) Settlements Defrauding Creditors

9.076. There are several provisions in our law designed to prevent debtors from cheating their creditors. One obvious temptation for a debtor is to make a settlement of his property, perhaps in favour of his family, in order to put the property out of the reach of his creditors should he subsequently become insolvent. Section 10 of the Conveyancing Act (Ireland), 1634,[54] provides that any conveyance of property with intent to defraud creditors is "void" as against any person prejudiced. Despite the use of the word "void," it has been taken to mean voidable in the present context.[55] Section 14 of the 1634 Act exempts from the Act cases of property bona fida conveyed on "good" consideration to a person with no notice of the intention to defraud the creditors.[56] It is not surprising that these provisions are not the model of brevity nor entirely free from ambiguity.[57] The following seem to be the main points to note.

9.077. First, it is essential that an intention to defraud creditors be established and, generally, the onus of proof is on the person seeking to have the settlement set aside.[58] However, the surrounding circumstances of the case may raise a presumption of fraud. As Palles C.B. put it:

> "One conveyance, for instance, may be executed with the express intent and object in the mind of the party to defeat and delay his creditors, and from such an intent the law presumes the conveyance to be fraudulent, and does not require or allow such fraud to be deduced as an inference of fact. In other cases, no such intention actually exists in the mind of the grantor, but the necessary or probable result of his denuding himself of the property included in the conveyance, for the consideration, and under the circumstances actually existing, is to defeat or delay creditors, and in such case . . . the intent is, as a matter of law, assumed from the necessary or probable consequences of the act done."[59]

---

[53] *Rossborough* v. *Boyse* (1853) 3 Ir.Ch.R. 629; (1857) 6 H.L.C. 2; *Ahearn* v. *Ahearn* (1911) 45 I.L.T.R. 28. *Smyth* v. *Smyth* (1978) Unrep. (H.C., R.I.) (1975) No. 4369 P); *O'Flanagan* v. *Ray-ger Ltd.* (1983) Unrep. (H.C., R.I.) (1980) No. 2858; *Ryan* v. *Ryan* (1983) Unrep. (H.C., R.I.) (Ct. App.). For improvident settlements, etc, see *O'Rorke* v. *Bolingbroke* (1877) 2 App.Cas. 814; Clark, "The Unconscionability Doctrine Viewed from an Irish Perspective" (1980) 31 N.I.L.Q. 114. See also the Sales of Reversions Act, 1867 (still in force in both parts of Ireland), *Rae* v. *Joyce* (1892) 29 L.R.Ir. 500. And see Clarke, "The Unconscionability Doctrine Viewed from an Irish Perspective" (1980) 31 N.I.L.Q. 114.

[54] 10 Chas. 1, sess. 2, c. 3 See generally on this subject, the Republic's *Bankruptcy Law Committee Report* (1972; Prl. 2714), espec. ch. 23.

[55] See *Re Eichholz* [1959] Ch. 708.

[56] *Bryce* v. *Fleming* [1930] I.R. 376 (see *A Casebook on Equity and Trusts in Ireland* (1985), p. 416).

[57] See discussion of Palles C.B. in *Re Moroney* (1887) 21 L.R.Ir. 27. In *Cadogan* v. *Cadogan* [1977] 3 All E. R. 831, the English Court of Appeal held that the equivalent English statutory provision (section 172 of the Law of Property Act, 1925) may protect persons who could not properly be described as a "creditor" (in that case the wife of the person making a voluntary conveyance of the matrimonial home which defeated her claim to financial relief under the Matrimonial Causes Act, 1973).

[58] *Bryce* v. *Fleming* [1930] I.R. 376 (see *A Casebook on Equity and Trusts in Ireland* (1985), p. 416). See also *Myers* v. *Duke of Leinster* (1844) 7 Ir.Eq.R. 146.

[59] *Re Moroney* (1887) 21 L.R.Ir. 27 at 61–2. *Cf. Smith* v. *Tatton* (1879) 6 L.R.Ir. 32 at 41–2 (*per* Fitzgerlad B.).

Secondly, it is not necessary that the settlor be insolvent when the settlement is made and an intention to defraud future and, even only possible, creditors is enough.[60] However, merely preferring one creditor to another is not, with more, fraudulent.[61] Thirdly, even if the settlor was fraudulent the interest of any person taking under it who provided consideration and who took without notice of the settlor's fraud cannot be set aside.[62] The 1634 Act refers to "good" consideration[63] but it seems that this really means valuable consideration, *i.e.*, it includes marriage consideration[64] but not consideration simply in the form of natural love and affection.[65] Fourthly, the Act applies to any kind of property, real or personal, and is not confined to conveyances of land.[66]

(vii) Voluntary Settlements Defrauding Purchasers

9.078. Section 1 of the Conveyancing Act (Ireland), 1634, provides that any conveyance of land made[67] with intent to defraud subsequent purchasers of the same land is "void"[68] and section 3 excludes bona fide conveyances for "good" consideration.[69] The English equivalent[70] was interpreted to the effect that the mere fact of a conveyance being voluntary made it *ipso facto* void as against any purchaser for value of the same land.[71] So the Westminster Parliament passed the Voluntary Conveyances Act, 1893, which is still in force in both parts of Ireland. This provides that no voluntary conveyance in fact made bona fide and with no fraudulent intent is to be deemed fraudulent and void under section 1 of the 1634 Act. Yet it was held by O'Connor M.R. in *National Bank Ltd.* v. *Behan*[72] that, despite the 1893 Act, the onus of proving that a voluntary conveyance was made bona fide, and without intention to defraud a subsequent purchaser, lay with the person seeking to uphold the voluntary conveyance, rather than the person seeking to set aside the voluntary conveyance having to prove the fraud. The *Behan* decision was questioned in the Court of Appeal in

---

[60] *Murphy* v. *Abraham* (1864) 15 Ir.Ch.R. 371. *Cf. Re Kelleher* [1911] 2 I.R. 1. See also *Re Shilena Hosiery Co. Ltd.* [1979] 3 W.L.R. 332.

[61] *Nolan* v. *Neill* (1899) 33 I.L.T.R. 129; *Rose* v. *Greer* [1945] I.R. 503. Nor would the Act normally catch a disentailing assurance, *Clements* v. *Eccles* (1847) 11 Ir.Eq.R. 229. Note on this point the express exclusion in the English Law of Property Act, 1925, s. 172 (2).

[62] *Bryce* v. *Fleming* [1930] I.R. 376.

[63] S. 14.

[64] Para. 9.042, *ante*. *Stackpole* v. *Stackpole* (1843) 6 Ir.Eq.R. 18.

[65] *Re Rorke's Estate* (1865) 15 Ir.Ch.R. 316; *Bryce* v. *Fleming, op. cit.* This also seems to have been the situation under the earlier English statute, 13 Eliz. 1, c. 5, see *Twyne's Case* (1601) 3 Co.Rep. 80b at 81b; also *Graham* v. *O'Keeffe* (1864) 16 Ir.Ch.R. 1. *Quaere* now under s. 172 (3) of the Law of Property Act, 1925, which refers to both "valuable" and "good" consideration, see *Re Eichholz* [1959] Ch. 708. See Langstaff, "The Cheat's Charter?" (1975), 91 L.Q.R. 86; *Cf.* Elkan, ibid., p. 317. Note that s. 172 has been replaced by s. 212 of the Insolvency Act, 1985, which concerns transactions "at an undervalue."

[66] S. 10.

[67] S. 1 refers to a "conveyance, grant, charge, lease, estate, incumbrance and limitation of use, or uses." See *Blake* v. *Hyland* (1838) 2 Dr. & Wal. 397; *Fitzmaurice* v. *Sadlier* (1846) 9 Ir.Eq.R. 595; *Scott* v. *Scott* (1848) 11 Ir.Eq.R. 487, (1854) 4 H.L.C. 1065.

[68] Again interpreted generally as meaning "voidable." See *Gardiner* v. *Gardiner* (1861) 12 I.C.L.R. 565; *Hamilton* v. *Molloy* (1880) 5 L.R.Ir. 339; *Lee* v. *Matthews* (1880) 6 L.R.Ir. 530.

[69] Again to be interpreted probably as not including natural love and affection, paras. 9.042, *ante* and 9.077, *supra*. *O'Donnell* v. *Murphy* (1824) 2 Fox & Sm. 279; *Gray* v. *Dinnen* (1840) 2 Jebb & Sym. 265. *Cf. Moore* v. *Crofton* (1846) 9 Ir.Eq.R. 344.

[70] 27 Eliz. 1, c. 4.

[71] See also as to the Irish statute, *Gardiner* v. *Gardiner* (1861) 12 I.C.L.R. 565.

[72] [1913] 1 I.R. 512.

Re Moore,[73] but it has not yet been overruled in either part of Ireland.

(viii) Settlements by Bankrupts

9.079. Section 52 of the Bankruptcy (Ireland) Amendment Act, 1872, provides that settlements[74] of property, not being made before or in consideration of marriage, or in favour of a purchaser, or incumbrancer in good faith and for valuable consideration, or settlements made on or for the settlor's wife or children of property accruing after marriage in right of his wife are (1) if the settlor becomes bankrupt within *two* years after the date of the settlement, void as against the assignees or trustee in bankruptcy and (2) if the settlor becomes bankrupt at any subsequent time within *ten* years of the settlement, void as against the assignees or trustee, *unless* the parties claiming under the settlement can prove that at the time of the settlement the settlor could pay all his debts without calling on the property included in the settlement. These provisions remain in force in the Republic but have been replaced, with little substantive amendments, in Northern Ireland by section 12 of the Bankruptcy Amendment Act (N.I.), 1929.[75]

Several points may be noted.

9.080. First, in the case of bankruptcy there is no need to prove a fraudulent intention.[76] What is crucial is the date of the bankruptcy in relation to the date of the settlement. If it occurs within two years, no proof of any fraud at all is necessary; if it occurs within ten years, the only proof required is that the settlor could not pay his debts at the date of the settlement without recourse to the settled property. "Becomes bankrupt" does not mean "is adjudicated bankrupt," but means "commits an act of bankruptcy" and this is the critical date.[77] Secondly, there are the three exceptions made for settlements in consideration of marriage,[78] in favour of a bona fide purchaser for valuable consideration, and in favour of the wife or children in respect of property accruing in right of the wife.[79] Thirdly, once again despite the use of the word "void", it has been taken to mean voidable, *i.e.*, the settlement remains valid until such time as the

---

[73] [1918] 1 I.R. 169 at 177–80 (*per* O'Brien L.C.); *cf.* Ronan L.J. at p. 184 and Molony L.J. at p. 187 (see *A Casebook on Equity and Trusts in Ireland* (1985), p. 421).

[74] S. 52 expressly refers to settlements made by a "trader". S. 17 of the same Act extends the jurisdiction of the court contained in s. 314 of the Irish Bankrupt and Insolvent Act, 1857 to non-traders. See again the Republic's *Bankruptcy Law Committee Report* (1972; Prl. 2714), ch. 23.

[75] See *Re Barnes* (1979) 30 N.I.L.Q. 249. For England, see s. 174 of the Insolvency Act, 1985, replacing s. 42 of the Bankrutpcy Act, 1914.

[76] *Re Moore* (1897) 31 I.L.T.R. 5.

[77] *Re Mackay* [1915] 2 I.R. 347. See also *Re Domvile* (1879) 3 L.R.Ir. 282.

[78] Not necessarily the settlor's marriage, *Re Downes* [1898] 2 I.R. 635. A post-nuptial settlement not in pursuance of an antenuptial agreement is not within this exception, *Re Campbell* (1878) 12 I.L.T.R. 163. See also *Re Densham* [1975] 1 W.L.R. 1519; *Re Windle* [1975] 1 W.L.R. 1628; *Re Bailey* [1977] 2 All E.R. 26; *Re Abbott* [1983] Ch. 45.

[79] This exception obviously had in view a wife's property coming to the husband under the pre-Married Women's Property Act, 1882 law. It has since been held in England to cover property coming to the husband on his wife's intestacy, *Re Bower Williams* [1927] 1 Ch. 441. See now as to insurance policies for the benefit of spouses and children; the Republic's Married Women's Status Act, 1957, s. 7; Law Reform (Husband and Wife) Act (N.I.), 1964, s. 4 (4).

Official Assignee or the trustee in bankruptcy takes steps to have it avoided.[80] Fourthly, a voluntary settlement is void only to the extent necessary to pay the bankrupt's debts and so any surplus remains subject to the terms of the settlement. Fifthly, section 52 of the 1872 At also catches covenants contained in marriage settlements to settle after-acquired property on the wife or children, unless such property was actually paid or transferred under the covenant before the bankruptcy.[81] This prevents a husband covenanting to pay a huge sum in favour of his wife or children so as to enable them to claim priority over subsequent creditors.[82] The position has been amended in Northern Ireland[83] by section 12 (3) of the Bankruptcy Amendment Act (N.I.), 1929, which provides that, even if the property is paid or transferred before the bankruptcy, the trustee in bankruptcy can still avoid the payment or transfer unless the wife or children, as the case may be, can prove (i) that it was made more than two years prior to bankruptcy or (ii) that the settlor could pay all his debts without that property at the date of payment or transfer or (iii) that it was made in pursuance of a covenant to pay or transfer money or property expected to come to the settlor on death of a specified person and it was made within three months of the money or property coming within the settlor's possession or control.[84]

I. DISCRETIONARY AND PROTECTIVE TRUSTS

These are special kinds of trusts which have been growing in popularity in recent years. It is, however, also fair to say that there is not as much law on them in Ireland, especially in the Republic, as in England.

1. *Discretionary*

9.081. A discretionary trust, as the name suggests, is a trust under which the trustees are required to pay the income or capital to the beneficiaries as the trustees in their discretion think fit.[85] Thus no beneficiary has the right to any part of the trust property and receives, if at all, only that which the trustees see fit to give him.[86] At first sight, there seems to be a confusion here between a discretionary trust and a power of appointment and there are certainly similarities.[87] The distinction, however, remains that a trust is obligatory and in the case of a

---

[80] "If the legislature meant to say that the deed was to be void, it would have said it was to be void to all intents and purposes, but where it says the deed is to be void against one particular person on the principle that as to every one else it is valid, it is voidable only and not void." *Per* Palles C.B. in *Re Doyle* (1891) Unreported (C.A.) (quoted in Kiely, *Principles of Equity as applied in Ireland* (1936) pp. 70–1).

[81] *Re McCrohan* (1893) 31 L.R.Ir. 225 (see *A Casebook on Equity and Trusts in Ireland* (1985), p. 429).

[82] The wife and children can, of course, still prove in the bankruptcy along with other creditors, but they will not have priority over creditors for value.

[83] There is no equivalent provision in the Republic.

[84] Where such a payment or transfer is avoided, the persons to whom it was made can claim in the bankruptcy as if the covenant had not been executed at the commencement of the bankruptcy, *i.e.*, they can claim against any surplus left after the other creditors have been paid in full. *Re McCrohan* (1893) 31 L.R.Ir. 225.

[85] Halbach, "Problems of Discretion in Discretionary Trusts" (1961) 61 Col.L.Rev. 1425; Kiralfy, "A Limitations on Discretionary Powers of Trustees" (1953) 17 Conv. 285; Sheridan, "Discretionary Trusts" (1957) 21 Conv. 55.

[86] See *Gray* v. *Gray* (1862) 13 Ir.Ch.R. 404 (see *A Casebook on Equity and Trusts in Ireland* (1985), p. 437).

[87] See Sheridan, *op. cit.*, fn. 85, *supra*.

discretionary trust the trustees are obliged to exercise their discretion, even though this may involve nothing more than a decision not to distribute any of the property to any of the beneficiaries.[88] In the case of a power, at least a bare power, there is no duty to exercise it at all.[89]

9.082. There may be several reasons for creating a discretionary trust. First, the settlor may wish to protect the interest of a particular beneficiary against bankruptcy. We discuss this subject of a protective trust below.[90] Secondly, the settlor may wish to see that control is exercised over young and inexperienced beneficiaries. By giving the trustees a discretion, it is possible to prevent young and, perhaps, foolish beneficiaries from dissipating a large sum through wild and extravagant living. Thirdly, there used to be important tax advantages from such a discretionary trust. With the high levels of taxation on both sides of the Irish Sea, this had become an increasingly important consideration.[91] So far as estate duty was concerned, for example, the fact that no beneficiary was entitled to any interest in the property held under a discretionary trust was vital since estate duty was levied on property passing on death.[92] This method of reducing liability to estate duty was dealt with to some extent in Northern Ireland by the Finance Act (N.I.), 1969, under which duty was chargeable on part of the capital of a fund on death of a member of a discretionary class, which was calculated according to the proportion which the income he had actually received bore to the whole income produced by the fund in the four years immediately prior to his death. In the Republic, a similar provision was contained in section 32 of the Finance Act, 1972, which, as amended by the Finance Act, 1973, had become so obscure as to be impossible of summary. However, the abolition of estate duty in both parts of Ireland and the imposition of new taxes (gift and inheritance tax in the Republic; capital transfer tax in Northern Ireland) has resulted in the advantages of discretionary trusts being largely negated from the tax point of view. Under the new provisions the trust funds are liable to tax at regular intervals even though the trustees have not exercised their discretion and have made no distribution of funds.[93] Finally, it appears that the essential requirements of certainty of objects for trusts may be relaxed in the case of discretionary trusts, as in the case of powers. It is necessary to provide only a sufficiently clear criterion whereby it may be determined whether any particular applicant is within the class of beneficiaries, it is not

---

[88] In practice, therefore, there may appear to be no difference between a decision not to exercise their discretion and a decision to exercise their discretion to the effect that no distribution of property takes place. In theory, however, the distinction is there, *Gartside* v. *I.R.C.* [1968] A.C. 553; *Re Gulbenkian's Settlements* [1970] A.C. 508.

[89] Para. 9.011, *ante* and ch. 11, *post*. Note also a "power in the nature of a trust", para. 11.11, *post*.

[90] Para. 9.083, *post*.

[91] Para. 9.003, *ante*. See *Vestey* v. *I.R.C.* (*Nos. 1 and 2*) [1980] A.C. 1148.

[92] Finance Act, 1894, ss. 1 and 2. For English cases holding that there is no "passing" on death of a member of a discretionary class, see *Gartside* v. *I.R.C.* [1968] A.C. 553; *I.R.C.* v. *Holmden* [1968] A.C. 685; *Re Weir's Settlement Trusts* [1969] 3 W.L.R. 860. See Harvey, (1970) 21 N.I.L.Q. 72. Also Cohen, "Discretionary Trusts and Estate Duty" (1971) 35 Conv. 82; Lovel, "Discretionary Trusts and Estate Duty—The Dutiable Slice" (1970) B.T.R. 220. In the English Finance Act, 1969, the relevant period was 7 years prior to the member's death.

[93] For R.I., see Capital Acquisitions Tax Act, 1976, s. 22; for N.I., see Finance Act, 1975, Sched. 5 (U.K.), as amended by the Finance Act, 1982 (U.K.) (now consolidated in the Capital Transfer Tax Act, 1984, see espec. ss. 64–9 (U.K.)).

necessary to provide an exhaustive list of the members of the class or such a description as to enable the court to make out such a list.[94]

The trustees of a discretionary trust may be given wide powers of management of the trust property and in this respect there is little difference from an ordinary trust.[95]

2. Protective Trusts

9.083. In trying to protect the trust property from bankruptcy a settlor runs against the general policy of the law that a debtor's property should be readily available for his creditors. We have already considered other provisions enforcing this policy.[96] In some jurisdictions, however, it is possible to create "spendthrift" trusts whereby restraints on alienation are imposed on beneficiaries and a life tenant is permitted to retain income despite the claims of his creditors.[97] The nearest our law has come to this was creation of a trust for the separate benefit of a married woman with the imposition of a restraint upon anticipation or alienation by her. This sort of trust was common in the nineteenth century and early part of this century. Restraints upon anticipation, however, can no longer be imposed in either part of Ireland and a married woman is in no special position as regards her husband or creditors in this respect.[98]

9.084. Settlors can, however, achieve a measure of protection by utilising the distinction between an interest subject to a condition subsequent and a determinable interest.[99] A condition subsequent cuts short an otherwise absolute gift and a condition effecting a forfeiture of a beneficiary's interest on alienation or bankruptcy is clearly void.[1] On the other hand, a limitation in a trust to a beneficiary until he becomes bankrupt or alienates the property is valid and this is the key to a protective trust.[2] A protective trust usually consists of, first, a determinable life interest given to a beneficiary, followed by, secondly, the establishment of a discretionary trust in favour of the beneficiary and his family when the prior life interest determines on bankruptcy or attempted alienation or any other determining event specified. A settlor cannot set up such a protective trust to protect himself against bankruptcy,[3] he can create a protective trust only in favour of other beneficiaries. In the Republic of Ireland, it is still necessary to spell out the

---

[94] *Re Baden's Deed Trusts* [1971] A.C. 424. See para. 9.018, *ante.*
[95] Ch. 10, *post.*
[96] Para. 9.076, *supra.*
[97] *E.g.,* U.S.A. See Grisworld, "Reaching the Interest of the Beneficiary of a Spendthrift Trust" (1927) 43 H.L.R. 63; "Spendthrift Trusts for the Benefit of the Settlor" (1930) 44 H.L.R. 203; Scott, "Spendthrift Trusts and the Conflict of Laws" (1964) 77 H.L.R. 845.
[98] See Married Women's Status Act, 1957, s. 6; Law Reform (Miscellaneous Provisions) Act (N.I.), 1937, and Married Women (Restraint Upon Anticipation) Act (N.I.), 1952. Ch. 25, *post.*
[99] Para. 4.046, *ante. Re King's Trusts* (1892) 29 L.R.Ir. 401.
[1] Para. 4.054, *ante.*
[2] *Clarke* v. *Chambers* (1857) 8 Ir.Ch.R. 26; see also *Brandon* v. *Robinscon* (1811) 18 Ves. 429, espec. at 433–4 (per Lord Eldon L.C.); *Rochford* v. *Hackman* (1852) 9 Hare 475. See Sheridan "Protective Trusts" (1957) 2 Conv. 110 and 323.
[3] See para. 9.076, *ante. Re Burroughs-Fowler* [1916] 2 Ch. 251.

details of the protective trust in the trust instrument, but in Northern Ireland this is no longer so, because of section 34 of the Trustee Act (N.I.), 1958. This section contains a piece of legislative "shorthand" whereby the settlor need only direct that the income from the property is to be held "on protective trusts" for the beneficiary's life or any less period.[4] Thereupon, automatically the income must be held for that beneficiary's life or less period or until he does anything which, had he been absolutely entitled, would have deprived himself of the right to receive the income or any part of it.[5] If a beneficiary does do such a thing (*e.g.*, becomes bankrupt), then an automatic discretionary trust arises whereby the trustees have an absolute discretion, for the remainder of the trust period, to apply the income for the maintenance or support or benefit of the beneficiary and his children or remoter issue.[6] As under the general law, a settlor cannot use this statutory form to protect himself against bankruptcy.[7] Furthermore, if the trustees in their discretion decide to make payments to the bankrupt beneficiary they must, as in any discretionary trust, be careful not to pay him more than his basic needs.[8] If they do exceed that limit, the trustee in bankruptcy is entitled to claim the surplus[9] and so part of the object of the protective trust will have failed. While there is nothing to stop the trustees accumulating income in particular years, it seems that they must sometime distribute income to some of the beneficiaries named in the section and certainly cannot retain it indefinitely, regardless of those beneficiaries' needs.[10]

J. Revocable Trusts

9.085. Normally, in the absence of an express clause to the contrary in the trust instrument, a trust is not revocable by the settlor.[11] However, there is one category of trust which has long been recognised to be an exception to that rule, namely trusts for paying the settlor's debts.[12] Sugden L.C. said of such trusts:

[4] The settlor must delimit the beneficiary's interest and not just specify that the property is to be held "on protective trusts." *Re Whittke* [1944] Ch. 166.

[5] S. 34 (1) (*a*). See *Re Gordon's Will Trusts* [1978] Ch. 145 and Pettit, "The Equitable Doctrine of Election and Protective Trusts" (1977) 93 L.Q.R. 65.

[6] S. 34 (1) (*b*). Any unapplied income from a previous year may be used in a subsequent year. If there are no living issue, the persons who would be the beneficiary's next-of-kin, if he or she were dead having been unmarried, may receive income. Under article 4 (4) of the Family Law Reform (N.I.) Order, 1977, the reference in section 34 of the 1958 Act to the children or more remote issue of the principal beneficiary is now to be treated as including any illegitimate child of the principal beneficiary and anyone who would rank as such issue if he, or some person through whom he is descended from the principal beneficiary, had been born legitimate. Furthermore the reference to the issue of the principal beneficiary is to be treated as including anyone who would rank as such issue if he, or some other person through whom he is descended from the principal beneficiary, had been born legitimate.

[7] S. 34 (3).

[8] *Re Coleman* (1888) 39 Ch.D. 443, espec. at 451 (*per* Cotton L.J.).

[9] *Re Ashby* (1892) 1 Q.B. 872. See also *Re Bullock* (1891) 64 L.T. 736.

[10] *Re Gourju's W.T.* [1943] Ch. 24.

[11] Para. 9.003, *ante*.

[12] *Simmonds* v. *Pallas* (1845) 8 Ir.Eq.R. 335 (see *A Casebook on Equity and Trusts in Ireland* (1985), p. 439); see also *Douglass* v. *Allen* (1842) 2 Dr. & War. 213. See Sheridan, "Trusts for Paying Debts" (1957) 21 Conv. 280. The leading English case is *Garrard* v. *Lord Lauderdale* (1830) 3 Sim. 1.

"[I]f a man, without communication with his creditors, behind their backs, makes a provision for them which they are not entitled to require and for which they have not bargained, he may, if he pleases, before the execution of the trusts so created, put an end to them; as he created them so may he destroy them; they remain within his own power."[13]

9.086. There are, however, certain cases where a trust set up to ṛay creditors will be treated as being irrevocable. First, if any creditor is a party to the trust deed, it is irrevocable as against him.[14] Secondly, if the terms of the trust are communicated to the creditors and they act on them, by, *e.g.*, forgoing some rights or remedies they otherwise had and might have enforced, the trust is again irrevocable.[15] Thirdly, the trust will become irrevocable if it is to come into operation on the settlor's death only, since he and he alone can revoke it and, at death, it is too late.[16] Fourthly, if it is shown that the settlor really intended to create a trust and not just to make an arrangement to suit his own purposes, the court will give effect to that intention and enforce the trust.[17]

9.087. Trusts for payment of debts are affected by the deeds of arrangement legislation. Under the Deeds of Arrangement Act, 1887, an assignment of property by a debtor for the benefit of his creditors *generally* must be registered in court within seven days or else it is void.[18] Furthermore, even if such a deed is registered, it may constitute an act of bankruptcy, for section 21 of the Bankruptcy (Ireland) Amendment Act, 1872, includes "a conveyance or assignment of property to a trustee or trustees for the benefit of creditors generally."[19] However, a creditor cannot rely on execution of such a deed as an act of bankruptcy if he stands by and assents impliedly to its execution.[20] However, even an assenting creditor can use it to support a bankruptcy petition if the deed becomes void under the deeds of arrangement legislation.[21] The deed is also void as against the Official Assignee or trustee in bankruptcy if the debtor is adjudged bankrupt on a petition presented within three months of its execution or, in the Republic, commits an act of

[13] *Simmonds* v. *Pallas, op. cit.,* p. 347. See also *Law* v. *Bagwell* (1843) 4 Dr. & War. 398; *Marquis of Donegal* v. *Greg* (1849) 13 Ir.Eq.R. 12; *Gurney* v. *Lord Oranmore* (1855) 4 Ir.Ch.R. 470; *Bentley* v. *Robinson* (1859) 10 Ir.Ch.R. 287.

[14] See *Field* v. *Lord Donoughmore* (1841) 1 Dr. & War. 227; *La Touche* v. *Earl of Lucan* (1840) 2 Dr. & Wal. 432. *Cf. Re Semple* (1846) 3 Jo. & Lat. 488.

[15] *Browne* v. *Cavendish* (1844) 7 Ir.Eq.R. 369 (see *A Casebook on Equity and Trusts in Ireland* (1985), p. 445); *Tommey* v. *White* (1850) 3 H.L.C. 49.

[16] *Bentley* v. *Robinson* (1859) 10 Ir.Ch.R. 287; see also *Hunt* v. *Bateman* (1848) 10 Ir.Eq.R. 360.

[17] *Browne* v. *Cavendish, op. cit.*

[18] Ss. 4 and 5. *Cf. Re Semple* (1848) 12 Ir.Eq.R. 338; *Russell* v. *Murphy* (1865) 16 Ir.Ch.R. 54.

[19] For Northern Ireland, see also s. 1 of the Bankruptcy Amendment Act (N.I.), 1929. Note that, like the 1877 Act, this provision is confined to assignments or trusts for the benefit of creditors *generally*, so that a trust to pay a particular creditor is not covered. See *Re Crossey* [1975] N.I. 1. See also the Republic's *Bankruptcy Law Committee Report* (1972; Prl. 2714), ch. 42.

[20] *Re S.* (1873) I.R. 8 Eq. 51.

[21] Deeds of Arrangements Act, 1887, s. 17 and also, in Northern Ireland, Bankruptcy Amendment Act (N.I.), 1929, s. 2.

bankruptcy within six months of its execution.[22] Thus the trustee cannot safely carry out the trust until three or six months have elapsed, unless all the creditors have assented or are debarred from presenting a petition.

K. CHARITABLE TRUSTS

9.088. The Courts of Equity have long favoured trusts for charitable purposes[23] and our legal system today confers special benefits upon them. These benefits may be summarised in the following manner. First, charities are exempted from income tax in respect of income from investment of the funds held by them for charitable purposes, and on most other income, *e.g.*, sum received under covenants, provided the income is actually applied for charitable purposes.[24] Secondly, an *inter vivos* gift to a charity obtained some relief against estate duty in that the period subsequent to the gift for which the donor had to survive in order to escape duty was less than in the case of other gifts.[25] Furthermore, in the Republic of Ireland relief was given to charities in respect of legacy duty[26] and succession duty.[27] Relief continues under the capital acquisition (R.I.)[28] and transfer (U.K.) taxes.[29] Thirdly, hereditaments occupied by some charities for their charitable purposes are entitled to relief from rates, though this is confined to eleemosynary charities in the Republic.[30] Fourthly, charities have some exemption from corporation tax in

---

[22] Bankrupt and Insolvent (Ir.) Act, 1857, s.328 and Bankruptcy (Ir.) Amendment Act, 1872, s.53, as amended by para.1 of Sched. 11 to the Republic's Companies Act, 1963; also, in Northern Ireland, Bankruptcy Amendment Act (N.I.), 1929, s.13 and Companies Act (N.I.), 1960, Sched. 12. See the Republic's *Report of the Companies Law Reform Committee* (1952), para. 200.

[23] See Brady, *Religion and the Law of Charities in Ireland* (1976); Chesterman, *Charities, Trusts and Social Welfare* (1979); Delany, *Law Relating to Charities in Ireland* (1962); Moore, *Law of Charities in Ireland* (1906); Hamilton, *Law Relating to Charities in Ireland* (1846); O'Leary, *Dispositions of Property for Religious and Charitable Uses* (1847); Picarda, *The Law and Practice Relating to Charities* (1977); Keeton and Sheridan, *The Modern Law of Charities* (3rd ed., 1983); *Tudor on Charities* (7th ed. by Maurice and Parker, 1984). See also Brady, "The Law of Charity and Judicial Responsiveness to Changing Social Need" (1976) 27 N.I.L.Q. 198.

[24] Income Tax Act, 1967, s.334 (R.I.); Income and Corporation Taxes Act, 1970, s.360 (U.K.). *Pharmaceutical Society of Ireland* v. *Special Commrs. of Income Tax* [1938] I.R. 202; *Baptist Union of Ireland* v. *C.I.R.* [1945] N.I. 99; *Pig Marketing Board (N.I.)* v. *C.I.R.* [1945] N.I. 155; *Trustees of Londonderry Presbyterian Church House* v. *C.I.R.* [1946] N.I. 178. Glover, "The Tax Advantages of Charitable Status" (1972) B.T.R. 346; see also the English Goodman Committee *Report on Charity Law and Voluntary Organisations* (1976), ch.5.

[25] Finance (1909-10) Act, 1910, s.59(1) as amended by Finance Act, 1965, s.27(1)(1-5 years)(R.I.); Customs and Inland Revenue Act, 1881, s.38(2)(*a*) as amended by Finance Act (N.I.), 1968, s.1 and Sched. 1, para. 2(1)(1-4 years). There was also, in Northern Ireland, a £50,000 exemption for gifts by will or within one year of death.

[26] Finance Acts, 1932, s.46 and 1934, ss.31 and 32. *Bank of Ireland Trustee Co. Ltd.* v. *Att.-Gen.* [1957] I.R. 257 (see *A Casebook on Equity and Trusts in Ireland* (1985) p.455); see also *Att.-Gen.* v. *Bagot* (1861) 13 I.C.L.R. 48; *Att.-Gen.* v. *Becher* [1910] 2 I.R. 251.

[27] Finance Acts, 1932, s.46 and 1934, s.32. *Revenue Commrs.* v. *Doorley* [1933] I.R. 750. Legacy and succession duty were abolished in Northern Ireland by the Finance Act (N.I.) 1949, s.1.

[28] Capital Acquisitions Tax Act, 1976, s.54.

[29] Capital Transfer Tax Act, 1984, ss.23-6, 58(1)(*a*) and 76 (U.K.).

[30] Poor Relief (Ir.) Act, 1838, s.63; Valuation (Ir.) Amendment Act, 1854, s.2. *O'Neill* v. *Commr. of Valuation* [1914] 2 I.R. 447; *Maynooth College* v. *Commr. of Valuation* [1958] I.R. 189; *Clonmel Mental Hospital Board* v. *Commr. of Valuation* [1958] I.R. 381; see for N.I. *Campbell College* v. *Commr. of Valuation (N.I.)* [1964] N.I. 107; *Poor Clares* v. *Commr. of Valuation*, noted [1971] N.I. 174; *Commr. of Valuation* v. *Redemptorist Order* [1971] N.I. 114; *Dublin Corporation* v. *Dublin Cemeteries Committee* (1975) Unrep. (Sup.Ct., R.I.). See Brady, "Charitable Purposes and Rating Exemption in Ireland" (1968) 3 Ir.Jur. (N.S.) 215; "House of Lords, Charities and Rating Relief in Northern Ireland" (1973) 24 N.I.L.Q. 106; Carswell, "Rating Exemption and Charitable Purposes" (1965) 16 N.I.L.Q. 88; Delany, "Rating Exemption on the ground of Charitable or Public User" (1960) 13 N.I.L.Q. 316; Lowry, "Some Reflections on Rating" (1966) 17 N.I.L.Q. 256. Para. 9.098, *post.*

the Republic of Ireland[31] and corporation tax in Northern Ireland.[32] Fifthly, charitable trust instruments have some exemption from stamp duty.[33] Apart from these fiscal advantages, charitable trusts enjoy several other advantages in our law.

9.089. A charitable trust will not fail for want of certainty. There are two aspects to this principle. First, a charitable trust is not subject to the same extent as other trusts to the requirement of certainty of objects.[34] In particular, there is no difficulty about the objects being purposes as opposed to individuals.[35] Secondly, provided it is clear that the settlor intended the application of the property to charitable purposes only,[36] the court will ensure such an application occurs, by making a scheme of its own, if necessary.[37]

9.090. Charitable trusts may also be of perpetual duration,[38] but they are subject to the rule against perpetuities in that the initial vesting must take place or, in the Republic, must be bound to take place, if at all, within the relevant perpetuity period.[39] However, a gift over from one charity to another is exempted from the rule as to vesting,[40] but not a gift over from a non-charity to a charity.[41]

In view of all these advantages accruing to charitable trusts, it is not surprising that one of the most common grounds of litigation on both sides of the Irish Sea is whether or not a particular trust is for charitable purposes. The reason that this is regularly litigated is that there is no precise definition of a charity in our law,[42] and it is to this subject that we now turn.

1. *Definition*

9.091. Perhaps we may begin by quoting the trenchant remarks of Gavan Duffy J. in *Re Howley's Estate*[43]:

> "'Charity' is in law an artificial conception, which during some 300 years, under the guidance of pedantic technicians, seems to have strayed rather far from the intelligent realm of plain common sense; thus, the

---

[31] Corporation Tax Act, 1976, s.29.

[32] Income and Corporation Taxes Act, 1970, ss.360-1. See also *Association for Industrious Blind* v. *Commr. of Valuation* [1968] N.I. 21. Also capital gains tax in N.I., Capital Gains Tax Act, 1979, ss.145-6 (U.K.).

[33] Finance Act (N.I.) 1963, s.14 (2). *Cf.* Stamp Duties (Ir.) Act, 1842, s.38.

[34] See para. 9.018, *ante.*

[35] This subject is discussed in more detail at para. 9.114, *post.* The Att.-Gen. has jurisdiction over charities and may bring proceedings in relation to them, *Potts* v. *Turnley* (1849) 1 Ir.Jur. (o.s.) 57; *Att.-Gen.* v. *Carlile* (1850) 2 Ir.Jur. (o.s.) 249; *Re Kelly's Will Trusts* (1862) 7 Ir.Jur. (N.S.) 273.

[36] Not even this is strictly necessary in Ireland now, para.9.121, *post.*

[37] See further, para. 9.104, *post.*

[38] Para. 5.036, *ante.*

[39] *Re Gordon* (1901) 35 I.L.T.R. 25; *Re Hawe* (1959) I.L.T.R. 175. For N.I., see the Perpetuities Act (N.I.), 1966. Also para. 5.143, *ante.*

[40] Para 5.143, *ante.*

[41] *Re Macnamara's Estate* [1943] I.R. 372.

[42] None is contained in the recent legislation in the British Isles: Charities Act, 1960; Charities Act, 1961 (R.I.); Charities Act (N.I.) 1964. See the English Nathan *Report on Charitable Trusts* (1952; Cmd. 8710) and the N.I. Newark *Charity Committee Report* (1959, Cmd. 396). See also the English Goodman Committee *Report on Charity Law and Voluntary Organisations* (1976), App.1.

[43] [1940] I.R. 109 at 114 (see *A Casebook on Equity and Trusts in Ireland* (1985), p.450). *Cf.* Andrews L.C.J. in *Londonderry Presbyterian Church House* v. *C.I.R.* [1946] N.I. 178 at 187-8.

textbooks tell us that charity in the eyes of the law includes a bequest for a 'home for Lost Dogs,' as an institution for domestic animals must benefit the human race which they serve, and a legacy to further 'Conservative Principles,' if combined with zeal for mental and moral improvement – so catholic is juristic charity – though it must draw the line at the spiritual exercises of a convent or the plans of an Archbishop conducing to the good of religion in his own diocese; such are the vagaries of Judge-made law."[44]

The starting point of modern charities law,[45] and, in particular, a guide to the definition of charity, is the list of charitable purposes contained in the Statute of Charitable Uses (Ireland) 1634,[46] which provided that dispositions–

". . . for the erection, maintenance or support of any college, school, lecture in divinity, or in any of the liberal arts or sciences, or for the relief or maintenance of any manner of poor, succourless, distressed or impotent persons, or for the building, re-edifying or maintaining in repair of any church, college, school or hospital, or for the maintenance of any minister and preacher of the holy word of God, or for the erection, building, maintenance or repair of any bridges, causeyes, cashes, paces and highways, within this realm, or for any other like lawful and charitable use and uses, warranted by the laws of this realm, now established and in force, are and shall be taken and construed to be good and effectual in law."

Though now repealed,[47] it has long been settled that this statute, along with its English counterpart,[48] is a guide to the Irish courts in determining whether a particular trust comes within the category of charitable trusts.[49] In addition to this guide, judges on both sides of the Irish Sea also turn to the analysis of Lord Macnaghten in *C.I.T.* v. *Pemsel.*[50] Lord Macnaghten classified charitable trusts into four broad categories: advancement of religion, advancement of education, relief of poverty and other purposes beneficial to the community, not falling within the first three categories. The first three categories are reasonably clear, but it is obvious from its general wording that the fourth covers a wide variety of trusts. We shall examine each of these categories in more detail below, but first a few general points must be made.

9.092. First, a particular trust may come within more than one of Lord

---

[44] It should, of course, be noted that the learned judge's remarks were aimed particularly at English decisions!

[45] See Jones, *History of the Law of Charity 1532-1827* (1969); Delany, "Development of Law of Charities in Ireland" (1955) 14 I.C.L.Q. 30.

[46] 10 Chas. 1, sess.3, c.1.

[47] Statute Law Revision (Ir.) Act, 1878.

[48] 43 Eliz. 1, c.4.

[49] *Incorporated Society* v. *Richards* (1841) 1 Dr. & War. 258, espec. at 325-31 (*per* Sugden L.C.)(see *A Casebook on Equity and Trusts in Ireland* (1985), p.487). See also *O'Hanlon* v. *Logue* [1906] 1 I.R. 247 (see *ibid.*, p.473); *O'Neill* v. *Commr. of Valuation* [1914] 2 I.R. 447; *Londonderry Presbyterian Church House* v. *C.I.R.* [1946] N.I. 178.

[50] [1891] A.C. 531 at 583. See also Samuel Romilly's arguments before the courts in *Morice v. Bishop of Durham* (1804) 9 Ves.Jr.399; (1805) 10 Ves.Jr.522.

Macnaghten's categories.[51] Secondly, the public benefit element mentioned in the fourth category should be present in almost all cases[52] of charitable trusts. There has, however, been considerable controversy in Ireland as to whether this element of public benefit is to be found as a question of fact by the court (*i.e.*, an objective test) or whether it may be found simply as a matter of the opinion of the particular donor of the property (*i.e.*, a subjective test). The English courts have favoured the objective test,[53] and this has been accepted as the proper approach in Northern Ireland.[54] Earlier Irish cases, however, held that a gift or trust was charitable if the donor or settlor believed it was for the public benefit and that belief was rational, legal and moral.[55] Dixon J. later held that a subjective test was applicable in the case of religious gifts.[56] There has now been enacted special legislation relating to religious gifts in the Republic of Ireland, but this does not seem to resolve the issue.[57] In *O hUadhaigh* v. *Attorney-General*,[57a] Gannon J. had this to say about the public benefit element of charities:

> "The primary and fundamental inquiry is to ascertain what are the intentions of the testatrix as expressed by her, and whether or not they are to invest the ownership of her property after her death in a charity which is recognised as such in a legal sense. It is this inquiry which explains the use of the expression 'the subjective test' as adopted in Irish courts as against 'the objective test' seemingly applied in England."

9.093. It has been held in Ireland that the relations of the donor do not constitute a section of the community so as to make the gift to them valid as being for the public benefit.[58] For the same reason, gifts to professional bodies and clubs have been upheld as charitable.[59] On the other hand, people

---

[51] See, *e.g., Re Quinn* (1954) 88 I.L.T.R. 161.

[52] See below on poor relations, etc., para. 9.101, *post.* Maurice, "Public Benefit Element in Charitable Trusts" (1951) 15 Conv. 328; Fridman, "Charities and Public Benefit" (1953) 31 C.B.R. 537; Atiyah, "Public Benefit in Charities" (1958) 21 M.L.R. 138; Plowright, "Public Benefit in Charitable Trusts" (1975) 39 Conv.183.

[53] *Re Hummeltenberg* [1923] 1 Ch.237; *National Anti-Vivisection Society* v. *I.R.C.* [1948] A.C. 31. *Cf. Re Watson* [1973] 3 All E.R. 178.

[54] *Re Lester* [1940] N.I. 92; *Commr. of Valuation* v. *Redemptorist Order* [1971] N.I. 114.

[55] *Re Cranston* [1898] 1 I.R. 431 (Holmes L.J. *dissentiente*) (see *A Casebook on Equity and Trusts in Ireland* (1985), p.500); *O'Hanlon* v. *Logue* [1906] 1 I.R. 247 (see *ibid.*, p.487); *Att.-Gen.* v. *Becher* [1910] 2 I.R. 251; *Shillington* v. *Portadown U.D.C.* [1911] 1 I.R. 247. See Brady, (1974) 25 N.I.L.Q. 174.

[56] *Bank of Ireland Trustee Co.* v. *Att.-Gen.* [1957] I.R. 257 (see *A Casebook on Equity and Trusts in Ireland* (1985), p.455).

[57] Charities Act, 1961, s.45 provides: "(1) In determining whether or not a gift for the purpose of the advancement of religion is a valid charitable gift it shall be conclusively presumed that the purpose includes and will occasion public benefit. (2) For the avoidance of the difficulties which arise in giving effect to the intentions of donors of certain gifts for the purpose of the advancement of religion and in order not to frustrate those intentions and notwithstanding that certain gifts for the purpose aforesaid, including gifts for the celebration of Masses, whether in public or in private, are valid charitable gifts, it is hereby enacted that a valid charitable gift for the purpose of the advancement of religion shall have effect and, as respects its having effect, shall be construed in accordance with the laws, canons, ordinances and tenets of the religion concerned." Under subs. (1) the determination still has to be made that the gift advances religion and it does not say which test should be used in making this. Subs. (2) applies only after the determination as to validity is made, *i.e.*, as charitable on the ground of advancement of religion. See also para. 9.096, *infra.*

[57a] (1979) Unrep. (H.C.,R.I.)(1976 No.93 Sp)(see *A Casebook on Equity and Trusts in Ireland* (1985), p.462).

[58] *Re McEnery's Estate* [1941] I.R. 323 (see *A Casebook on Equity and Trusts in Ireland* (1985), p.470). See also *Laverty* v. *Laverty* [1907] 1 I.R. 9. *Cf. Re Lavelle* [1914] 1 I.R. 194. *Cf.* gifts in favour of *poor* relations, or for the relief of poverty of other limited classes, e.g., employees, see para. 9.101, *post.*

[59] *E.g., Miley* v. *Att.-Gen.* [1918] 1 I.R. 455 (Royal College of Surgeons in Ireland).

connected with a particular church in a certain district [60] or children in an area[61] or people affected by a particular disaster[62] may be an appropriate section of the community.

9.094. Until recently in Ireland there was a "mortmain" restriction on gifts of land to charity contained in section 16 of the Charitable Donations and Bequests (Ireland) Act, 1844.[63] This section was confined to land[64] and restricted all pious uses, not only charitable ones.[65] However, the restriction could be avoided by insertion in a will of the "O'Hagan clause" [66] and it was thought at one time,[67] though finally decided to the contrary,[68] that a gift might be saved by applying the doctrine of marshalling of assets.[69] The mortmain restriction has now been removed from both parts of Ireland.[70]

9.095. Finally, the old rule that in order to be valid as a charitable gift the purposes had to be confined to charitable purposes alone[71] has been modified recently again in both parts of Ireland.[72] It is important to emphasise that, in considering a gift today in Ireland, many of the older precedents on charities must be reconsidered in the light of these statutory provisions affecting what were invalid charitable gifts. We consider the subject of imperfect trusts in general later in this chapter.[73]

(i) Advancement of Religion

9.096. Several controversial points have arisen in respect of gifts for

---

[60] *Londonderry Presbyterian Church House* v. *C.I.R.* [1946] N.I. 178. In *Duffy* v. *Doyle* (1979) Unrep. (H.C.,R.I.)(1978 No.696 Sp), McWilliam J. held a gift of the residue of the testator's property to the "Parish of Bray, Co. Wicklow" to be a valid charitable gift.

[61] Cf. *Browne* v. *King* (1885) 17 L.R.Ir. 448 (see *A Casebook on Equity and Trusts in Ireland* (1985), p.497).

[62] *Re Lord Mayor of Belfast's Air Raid Distress Fund* [1962] N.I. 161.

[63] ". . . no donation, devise, or bequest for pious or charitable uses in Ireland shall be valid to create or convey any estate in lands, tenements, or hereditaments for such uses, unless the deed, will or other instrument containing the same shall be duly executed and registered three calendar months at the least before the death of the person executing the same...." The registration referred to was in the Registry of Deeds under the Registration of Deeds Act (Ir.), 1707. See ch.22, *post*.

[64] *Pollock* v. *Day* (1863) 14 Ir.Ch.R. 371; *Murland* v. *Perry* (1879) 3 L.R.Ir. 135; *Re Cresswell* (1899) 33 I.L.T.R. 46; *Re Byrne* [1935] I.R. 782; *Re Scarlett* [1958] N.I. 28. Cf. a foreign bequest to an Irish charity, *McDermott* v. *Anderson* [1915] 1 I.R. 191.

[65] *Boyle* v. *Boyle* (1877) I.R. 11 Eq. 433; *Re Cresswell, op. cit.*

[66] *I.e.*, the trust in favour of the charity was followed by an absolute gift (usually to the same devisee) to take effect free from the trust in the event of the charitable trust being held void – though obviously the hope was that the devisee would use the property for the charitable purpose intended by the donor. See Stubbs and Baxter, *Irish Forms and Precedents* (1910) and Delany, *Law Relating to Charities in Ireland* (1962), pp. 116–17. *Geddis* v. *Semple* [1903] 1 I.R. 73 (see *A Casebook on Equity and Trusts in Ireland* (1985), p.324); *Hannon* v. *Keane* (1938) 72 I.L.T.R. 113; *Re Meehan's Estate* [1960] I.R. 82.

[67] *Biggar* v. *Eastwood* (1886) 19 L.R.Ir. 49; *Re Elwood* [1944] I.R. 344 (wherein Gavan Duffy J. reviewed the English and Irish authorities).

[68] *Re Solomon* [1949] I.R. 3 (Sup. Ct. reversing Gavan Duffy P.) Note also *Re Ryan* [1949] I.R.21.

[69] *I.e.*, where charitable and non-charitable legacies were left by will and realty was charged with payment of legacies, could the charitable legatees marshal so as to have the non-charitable legacies satisfied as far as possible out of the realty? See Newark, "Charities and the Marshalling of Assets" (1944) 6 N.I.L.Q. 36. Also ch.13, *post*.

[70] Mortmain (Repeal of Enactments) Act, 1954, and Charities Act, 1961 (R.I.); Mortmain (Repeals) Act (N.I.), 1960, and Charities Act (N.I.) 1964, Ch.25, *post*.

[71] It seems, however, that a gift which was clearly a general charitable disposition would still be upheld despite the fact that some provision of it, taken out of context, would not be charitable on its own. See *Q.U.B.* v. *Att.-Gen. (N.I.)* [1966] N.I. 115. Cf. *Re McConnell* [1956] N.I. 151.

[72] Charities Act, 1961, ss.49 and 50 (R.I.); Charities Act (N.I.) 1964, s.24. See also the Charitable Trusts (Validation) Act (N.I.) 1954, para. 9.121, *post*.   [73] Para. 9.114 *post*.

religious purposes and the Irish courts have frequently diverged from their English counterparts.[74] The former disabilities in Ireland suffered by certain religious orders, such as the Jesuits,[75] were removed by the Government of Ireland Act, 1920.[76] Such orders are now placed in the same position as other religious communities which were never subject to similar disabilities, such as convents, where the question is whether the gift is for the advancement of religion and contains a sufficient public benefit.[77] It has, however, been settled in Ireland that a gift for Masses is a valid charitable gift, whether the Masses are to be celebrated in public or private.[78] More difficulty has arisen in the case of gifts for contemplative nuns and other enclosed religious orders. In England, such gifts are not charitable for lack of proof of public benefit[79] and it seems that this is also the position in Northern Ireland.[80] In the Republic of Ireland, there is a conflict of authorities.[81] The effect of section 45 (2) of the Republic's Charities Act, 1961,[82] may be to move the issue away from the uncertain concept of public benefit to the question of advancement of religion according to the laws and canons of the particular religion concerned.[83] It remains to be seen whether this will resolve the conflict in the Republic.

9.097. Apart from this, the following gifts have been held in Ireland to come within the category of advancement of religion: a general gift for religious purposes[84]; a gift for the advancement and benefit of the Roman Catholic religion[85]; a gift of two houses to the parish priest of Urney[86]; a gift for decoration and improvement of the Roman Catholic Church of the

[74] See Brady, *Religion and the Law of Charities in Ireland* (1976).

[75] See Roman Catholic Relief Act, 1829, and Charitable Donations and Bequests (Ir.) Act, 1844, s.15. See *Sims* v. *Quinlan* (1864) 17 Ir.Ch.R. 43; *Cullen* v. *Commrs. of Charitable Donations and Bequests* (1870) I.R. 5 Eq. 44; *Roche* v. *McDermott* [1901] 1 I.R. 394; *Cussen* v. *Hynes* [1906] 1 I.R. 539; *Re Greene* [1914] 1 I.R. 305. See also the Republic's Charities Act, 1973, s.5.

[76] S.5. The 1920 Act was repealed for the Republic by the Irish Free State (Consequential Provisions) Act 1922, and freedom of religion is now guaranteed by the 1937 Constitution. See *Gieves* v. *O'Conor* [1924] 2 I.R. 182; *Re Byrne* [1935] I.R. 782.

[77] See *Stewart* v. *Green* (1870) I.R. 5 Eq. 470; *Re Delany's Estate* (1882) 9 L.R.Ir. 226; *Re Wilkinson's Trusts* (1887) 19 L.R.Ir. 531.

[78] *O'Hanlon* v. *Logue* [1906] 1 I.R. 247 (See *A Casebook on Equity and Trusts in Ireland* (1985), p. 473). See also *Read* v. *Hodgens* (1884) 7 Ir.Eq.R. 17; *Att.-Gen* v. *Hall* [1897] 2 I.R. 426; *Re Howley's Estate* [1940] I.R. 109 (see *ibid.*, p. 450). Brady, "Some Problems Touching the Nature of Bequests for Masses in Northern Ireland" (1968) 19 N.I.L.Q. 357; also (1974) 25 N.I.L.Q. 174.

[79] *Cocks* v. *Manners* (1871) L.R. 12 Eq. 574; *Gilmour* v. *Coats* [1949] A.C. 426.

[80] *Commr. of Valuation* v. *Redemptorist Order* [1971] N.I. 114 (Curran L.J. *dissentiente*). See Brady, (1973) 24 N.I.L.Q. 106.

[81] See, holding not charitable, *Commrs. of Charitable Donations and Bequests v. McCartan* [1917] 1 I.R. 388, espec. at 398 (*per* O'Connor M.R.); *Re Keogh's Estate* [1945] I.R. 13 (See *A Casebook on Equity and Trusts in Ireland* (1985), p. 534). Holding charitable, *Re Maguire* [1943] I.R. 238; *Bank of Ireland Trustee Co.* v. *Att.-Gen.* [1957] I.R. 257 (see *ibid.*, p. 455).

[82] Quoted, para. 9.092, fn. 57, *ante*.

[83] It has been suggested that this is the correct criterion by which to decide these cases even in England. Keeton and Sheridan, *Modern Law of Charities* (3rd ed., 1983), p. 86.

[84] *Arnott* v. *Arnott* (*No. 2*) [1906] 1 I.R. 127; *Re Salter* [1911] 1 I.R. 289; *Rickerby* v. *Nicholson* [1912] 1 I.R. 343.

[85] *Copinger* v. *Crehane* (1877) I.R. Eq. 429. *Cf. MacLaughlin* v. *Campbell* [1906] 1 I.R. 588.

[86] *Re Corcoran* [1913] 1 I.R. 1. See also *Re Brown* [1898] 1 I.R. 423 (Christian Brethren); *Cf. MacLaughlin* v. *Campbell* [1906] 1 I.R. 588.

Carmelite Fathers at Clarendon Street, Dublin[87]; a gift to Presbyterian missions and orphans[88]; a gift to the Y.M.C.A.[89] The following gifts or purposes have failed as charitable gifts, though often for rating exemption purposes, as we discuss below: a gift to the Pope to carry out his sacred office (but the case was compromised on appeal and is of doubtful authority)[90]; a gift for Roman Catholic purposes in the parish of Coleraine and elsewhere[91]; a gift of the use of a Presbyterian church hall in Londonderry[92]; various gifts of residences for religious persons [93]; a gift for such missionary purposes in Ireland as the trustees thought fit.[94] It must be emphasised that many of the cases, especially the last category just listed, concern liability for rates and are *not* necessarily authorities on the question whether the objects were otherwise charitable. In the Republic, it remains the case that the tests for exemption from rates on the ground of charity are much narrower than those for determining whether or not an object is otherwise charitable. Thus St. Patrick's College, Maynooth, is unquestionably a charity, but is not exempt from rates.[95]

9.098. The Irish courts put two limitations on exemption of charities from rates. One was to treat the expression "charitable purposes" in rating legislation as co-terminous with the exempt purposes listed in the proviso to section 63 of the Poor Relief (Ireland) Act, 1838, which were essentially eleemosynary purposes.[96] The other limitation was to hold that the character of the occupation of the hereditaments alone was decisive and that it was not permissible to look beyond it. Thus still excluded from exemption were several cases involving residences occupied by persons otherwise solely engaged in activities charitable within the limited meaning of the rating legislation.[97] Both these limitations, however, were removed for Northern Ireland by two House of Lords decisions, the first by *Campbell College* v.

---

[87] *Re Greene* [1914] 1 I.R. 305. In *Re Dunwoodie* [1977] N.I. 141, Murray J. regarded as a valid charitable trust a gift of residue to be held in trust for the Session and Committee of a Presbyterian Church, the wish being expressed that it be used to install bells at the church (see also para. 9.108, *post*).
[88] *Jackson* v. *Att.-Gen.* [1917] 1 I.R. 332. See also *Baptist Union of Ireland* v. *C.I.R.* [1945] N.I. 99; *cf. Re Mulcahy* [1931] I.R. 239.
[89] *Belfast Y.M.C.A.* v. *Commr. of Valuation (N.I.)* [1969] N.I. 3.
[90] *Re Moore* [1919] 1 I.R. 316.
[91] *MacLaughlin* v. *Campbell* [1906] 1 I.R. 588.
[92] *Londonderry Presbyterian Church House* v. *C.I.R.* [1946] N.I. 178. See also *Re Ringsend Methodist Church Hall* [1935] I.R. 607; *Commr. of Valuation* v. *Macausland* [1937] N.I. 132.
[93] *Commr. of Valuation* v. *O'Connell* [1906] 2 I.R. 479; *Dore* v. *Commr. of Valuation* (1916) 50 I.L.T.R. 103; *McKenna* v. *Commr. of Valuation* (1915) 49 I.L.T.R. 103; *Good Shepherd Nuns* v. *Commr. of Valuation* [1930] I.R. 646; *Mulholland* v. *Commr. of Valuation* (1936) 70 I.L.T.R. 253; *Poor Clares* v. *Commr. of Valuation* [1971] N.I. 174. *Cf.* a monastery occupied as a residence for priests and Christian Brothers, *Commr. of Valuation* v. *Redemptorist Order* [1971] N.I. 114; *cf. Sisters of Mercy* v. *Belfast Union* (1860) 4 Ir.Jur.(N.S.) 270; *Hogan* v. *Byrne* (1863) 7 Ir.Jur.(N.S.) 223.
[94] *Scott* v. *Brownrigg* (1881) 9 L.R.Ir. 246. *Cf.* the more modern view, however, in *Dunne* v. *Duignan* [1908] 1 I.R. 228; *Jackson* v. *Att.-Gen.* [1917] 1 I.R. 332.
[95] *College of Maynooth* v. *Commr. of Valuation* [1958] I.R. 189. See *Report on Exemptions from and Remissions of Rates* (1967, Pr. 9373).
[96] *Londonderry Union* v. *Londonderry Commrs.* (1868) I.R. 2 C.L. 577; *Governors of Wesley College* v. *Commr. of Valuation* [1984] I.L.R.M. 117. See discussion in Brady, (1968) 3 Ir.Jur.(N.S.) 215.
[97] *Dore* v. *Commr. of Valuation* (1916) 50 I.L.T.R 105; *Mulholland* v. *Commr. of Valuation (N.I.)* (1935) 75 I.L.T.R. 253; *McLaughlin* v. *Commr. of Valuation (N.I.)* [1937] N.I. 174; *Commr. of Valuation (N.I.)* v. *Fermanagh Hospital Committee* [1974] N.I. 125.

Commission of Valuation (N.I.)[98] and the second by *Glasgow Corp.* v. *Johnstone.*[99] The matter is now dealt with by Article 41 of the Rates Order (N.I.), 1977.[1] Once again, however, it should be remembered that rating cases remain a special category in the Republic of Ireland.

9.099. It is clear that it is often difficult to reconcile the many decisions on what amounts to a charitable trust for the advancement of religion. Perhaps it may be fair to say, however, that the Irish courts tend to favour gifts with a religious content and will strive to uphold them for the reason expressed by Budd J. in *Re Quinn.*[2]

> "It seems to me, in view of the fact that the vast majority of Irish citizens are Christians, that a gift given for the upkeep of a cemetery such as this, which is open to persons of all denominations, is a gift for the advancement of religion."[3]

(ii) Advancement of Education

9.100. Gifts for the advancement of education are another class of gift commonly upheld as charitable in Ireland.[4] This covers gifts to educational institutions, such as schools,[5] though not the provision of residences for teachers,[6] unless, perhaps, they are required to live there for the performance of their duties.[7]

(iii) Relief of Poverty

9.101. Poverty is obviously a central concept in the whole notion of charity, but the courts will not necessarily assume that a gift to someone without

---

[98] [1964] N.I. 107. See Carswell, "Rating Exemption and Charitable Purposes" (1965) 16 N.I.L.Q. 88; Lowry, "Some Reflections on Rating" (1966) 17 N.I.L.Q. 256

[99] [1965] A.C.609, the effect of which was considered in *Poor Clares* v. *Commr. of Valuation*, noted [1971] N.I. 174; *Commr. of Valuation* v. *Redemptionist Order and Commr. of Valuation* v. *Newry Christian Bros.* [1974] N.I. 114. See Brady, (1973) 24 N.I.L.Q. 106

[1] Formerly Article 41 of the Rates (N.I.) Order, 1972, which was amended by article 7 of the Rates (N.I.) Order, 1975 (to include any hereditament used wholly or mainly for purposes declared to be charitable by the Recreational Charities Act (N.I.), 1958) and article 5 of the Rates Amendment (N.I.) Order, 1977 (to include charity shops). The 1972, 1975 and 1977 Orders were consolidated in the Rates (N.I.) Order, 1977, article 41 of which (as amended by articles 3-6 of the Rates Amendment (N.I.) Order, 1979) now deals with exemption from rates of hereditaments used for public, charitable or certain other purposes. See *Royal British Legion Attendants Co. (Belfast) Ltd.* v. *Commr. of Valuation* [1979] N.I. 138. *Cf.* the Republic's Inter-Departmental *Report on Exemptions from and Remissions of Rates* (1967, Pr. 9373). See Brady, (1973) 24 N.I.L.Q. 440.

[2] (1954) 88 I.L.T.R. 161 at 165.

[3] Alternatively Budd J. was prepared to uphold the gift under Lord Macnaghten's 4th category, para. 9.102, *post.*

[4] Note schemes operating under the Educational Endowments (Ir.) Act, 1885, and similar acts. *Re Townsend Street Endowment Trusts* [1956] N.I. 53. See now Charities Act, 1961, s. 30 (R.I.); also N.I. *Charity Committee Report* (1959, Cmd. 396) paras. 83–7. Note also the Leases for Schools (Ir.) Act, 1881, and see now Charities Act, 1973, s. 6 (R.I.).

[5] Including a fee-paying public school, since not a profit-making venture, see *Campbell College* v. *Commr. of Valuation (N.I.)* [1964] N.I. 107. *Cf. Incorporated Society* v. *Richards* (1841) 1 Dr. & War. 258 (see *A Casebook on Equity and Trusts in Ireland* (1985), p.487). See also *Governors of Wesley College* v. *Commr. of Valuation* [1984] I.L.R.M. 117.

[6] *Heron* v. *Monaghen* (1888) 22 L.R.Ir. 532; *Commr. of Valuation (N.I.)* v. *Fermanagh Protestant Board of Education* [1970] N.I. 89; *Poor Clares* v. *Commr. of Valuation* [1971] N.I. 174.

[7] *Commr. of Valuation* v. *Newry Christian Brothers* [1971] N.I. 114.

financial means, *e.g.,* children, qualifies.[8] However, gifts for the relief of poverty are an exception to the general rule that a small group, *e.g.,* the donor's relations or employees, is not a section of the community sufficient for the gift to qualify as being for the public benefit.[9] Thus a gift for the relief of the donor's poor relations is a valid charitable gift.[10]

(iv) Other Charitable Purposes

9.102. Over the years many gifts, covering an enormous variety of situations, have been upheld as coming within this fourth, "catch-all" category. An attempt has been made recently to fit them into some broad sub-categories of their own,[11] such as: animal charities[12]; the old, the bereft and the disabled[13]; health[14] and temperance[15]; benefit of a locality[16]; public works and amenities[17]; armed forces and defence[18]; promotion of economic activity.[19] In *O hUadhaigh* v. *Attorney-General*[19a] Gannon J. held that a gift "for the benefit of the Republic" and "for the benefit of the Republicans of the time according to the objects of the Republicans as they were in the years 1919 to 1921" (as translated from the Irish in which the will was written) was not a charitable one. Gannon J. said of the testatrix:

> "It seems to me she had no clear idea of how the Republicans she considered her trustees would wish to benefit could be recognised, because there appears to be no binding factor or limitation by organisation, by conduct or activity, by location, by regulation or by any unifying factor as a class of the public other than adoption of political

---

[8] *Browne* v. *King* (1885) 17 L.R.Ir. 448 (see *A Casebook on Equity and Trusts in Ireland* (1985), p. 497). *Re Cullimore's Trusts* (1891) 27 L.R.Ir. 18.

[9] Para. 9.093 *ante. Cf.* gifts for the *education* of the donor's relations or employees, *Oppenheim* v. *Tobacco Securities Trust Co. Ltd.* [1951] A.C. 297.

[10] *Mahon* v. *Savage* (1803) 1 Sch. & Lef. 111. See also *Dingle* v. *Turner* [1972] A.C. 601 (poor employees).

[11] Keeton and Sheridan, *Modern Law of Charities* (3rd ed., 1983), chs. VIII–XIII.

[12] *Armstrong* v. *Reeves* (1890) 25 L.R.Ir. 325 (gift to Society of Carlsruhe for Protection of Animals); *Re Cranston* [1898] 1 I.R. 431 (gifts to vegetarian societies) (see *A Casebook on Equity and Trusts in Ireland* (1985), p. 500); *Swifte* v. *Att.-Gen.* [1912] 1 I.R. 133 (gift to Dublin Home for Starving and Forsaken Cats) (see *ibid.*, p. 508).

[13] *Re MacCarthy's Will Trusts* [1958] I.R. 311 (benevolent fund for elderly or infirm nurses). See also *R.* v. *Guardians of Poor of Mitchelstown Union* (1855) 4 I.C.L.R. 590 (houses for poor decayed gentlemen and gentlewomen); *Jackson* v. *Att.-Gen.* [1917] 1 I.R. 332 (Presbyterian missions and orphans); *Baptist Union of Ireland* v. *C.I.R.* [1945] N.I. 99 (annuities for Baptist pastors, evangelists and missionaries and their widows and orphans). *Cf. Att.-Gen. for N.I.* v. *Forde* [1932] N.I. 1 (gift for six widows).

[14] *Barrington's Hospital and City of Limerick Infirmary* v. *Commr. of Valuation* [1957] I.R. 299 (*per* Kingsmill Moore J. at p.324); *Re MacCarthy's Will Trusts* [1958] I.R. 311 (for sick in hospitals); *Down CC.* v. *Commr. of Valuation (N.I.)* [1956] N.I. 173 (N.H.S. hospital); *Armagh County Infirmary Committee* v. *Commr. of Valuation (N.I.)* [1940] N.I. 1 (house for part-time surgeon required to live there for performance of his duties); *Clonmel Mental Hospital Board* v. *Commr. of Valuation* [1958] I.R. 381 (residence for nurses provided as part of hospital premises).

[15] *Clancy* v. *Commr. of Valuation* [1911] 2 I.R. 173 (gift to promote temperance amongst poor and labouring classes).

[16] *Cookstown Roman Catholic Church* v. *C.I.R.* (1953) 34 T.C. 350. *Cf.* Albery, "Trusts for the Benefit of the Inhabitants of a Locality" (1940) 56 L.Q.R. 49.

[17] *Cf. Re Lord Mayor of Belfast's Air Raid Distress Fund*, [1962] N.I. 161 (war memorial in form of building as centre for British Legion and other organisations working for benefit of ex-service community).

[18] *Re Lord Mayor of Belfast's Air Raid Distress Fund, op. cit.*

[19] *C.I.R.* v. *Yorkshire Agricultural Soc.* [1928] 1 K.B. 611 (general promotion of agriculture).

[19a] (1979) Unrep. (H.C.,R.I.)(1976 No.93 Sp)(see *A Casebook on Equity and Trusts in Ireland* (1985), p.462).

thoughts and ideas. Even if she presented her trustees with the Democratic Programme of the Dáil of January 1919 as their directions for the spending of her money she would not thereby demonstrate to her trustees any charitable trust or purpose within the spirit or intendment of the legal standards of charity."

Some difficulty has arisen over gifts for recreational activities. So far as the courts were concerned such gifts in general were not charitable,[20] unless combined with other charitable purposes, such as advancement of education or the general public benefit in a locality.[21] Thus in *Londonderry Presbyterian Church House* v. *C.I.R.*[22] a gift for the purpose of "assisting and helping in the religious moral social and recreative life of those connected with the Presbyterian Church in the City of Londonderry and surrounding district" was held not charitable.

9.103. There is now special legislation affecting recreational charities in force in Northern Ireland, namely the Recreational Charities Act (N.I.), 1958. [23] Section 1 (1) of this Act provides that it shall be and be deemed always to have been charitable to provide, or assist in the provision of, facilities "for recreation or other leisure-time occupation, if the facilities are provided in the interests of social welfare."[24] The proviso is added, however, that such a gift must still be for the public benefit. In *Commr. of Valuation (N.I.)* v. *Lurgan B.C.,*[25] a municipal indoor swimming pool was held to be saved as charitable by section 1 of the 1958 Act. Similarly, the majority of the Northern Ireland Court of Appeal thought that playing fields were within the Act in *City of Belfast Y.M.C.A.* v. *Commr. of Valuation (N.I.).*[26]

2. *Cy-Près Doctrine*

9.104. We have already mentioned that one of the significant aspects of charities law is that a charitable trust will not fail for uncertainty.[27] In other

---

[20] *Clancy* v. *Commr. of Valuation* [1911] 2 I.R. 173 (hall, with various facilities for indoor sport, etc. to promote temperance among poor and labouring classes of Sligo town); *Re Lord Mayor of Belfast's Air Raid Distress Fund,* fn.17 *supra; Northern Ireland Housing Trust* v. *Commrs. of Valuation* (1970) 21 N.I.L.Q. 453 (C.A.)(community centre for residents of housing estate).
[21] *Shillington* v. *Portadown U.D.C.* [1911] 1 I.R. 247 (gift for a quinquennial dinner and fostering healthy recreation, including singing in classes or choruses, for residents of Portadown). *Cf.* cases on sporting activities, *Commr. of Valuation (N.I.)* v. *Fisherwick Presbyterian Church* [1927] N.I. 76; *Belfast Y.M.C.A.* v. *Commr. of Valuation (N.I.)* [1969] N.I. 3.
[22] [1946] N.I. 178. See also *Cookstown Roman Catholic Church* v. *C.I.R.* (1953) 34 T.C. 350; *Commr. of Valuation (N.I.)* v. *Lurgan B.C.* [1968] N.I. 104.
[23] There is no equivalent in the Republic of Ireland. See *re* the English Act of 1958 Hutchinson, "Recreational Charities – A Change of Tactics Required?" [1978] Conv.355; Warburton, "Football and the Recreational Charities Act 1958" [1980] Conv. 173.
[24] This requirement is further emphasised in s.1(2) so as to cover improvement of the conditions of life for those who need such facilities by reason of youth, age, disablement, poverty, etc, or for the public at large. S.1 (3) mentions, in particular, village halls, community centres and women's institutes and the provision and maintenance of recreational or leisure grounds and buildings. In *Northern Ireland Housing Trust* v. *Commr. of Valuation* (1970) 21 N.I.L.Q. 453, the Northern Ireland Court of Appeal held that the residents of a housing estate were not "members of the public at large" within s. 1(2)(*b*)(ii). Note also the discussion of "in the interests of social welfare" in the English Court of Appeal in *I.R.C.* v. *McMullan* [1979] 1 W.L.R. 130 (*cf.* H.L. at [1981] A.C.1).
[25] [1968] N.I. 104 (McVeigh L.J. *dissentiente*).
[26] [1969] N.I. 3 (Curran L.J. disagreeing, *obiter*).   [27] Para. 9.089, *supra*.

words, even though the precise object to be benefited is not clear or the mode of application of the fund is uncertain, the court will still direct a scheme for application of the money, *provided* the original gift was for charitable purposes only. This is known as a *cy-près* application of the funds, *i.e.,* applying them to the next nearest purpose. There is much case law on the *cy-près* doctrine[28] which has recently been extended in both parts of Ireland.[29] The following is a summary of the principles derived from the cases.

(i) General Charitable Intent

9.105. It is clear that, at least in some cases, there must be shown to exist a general charitable intent on the part of the donor of the gift, *i.e.,* an intention to benefit charity in general so that, if the particular method chosen cannot be executed, then another may be selected, under the direction of the court, if need be.[30] In these cases, if no such general charitable intent is established, the gift fails and there is a resulting trust for the settlor or the testator's estate.[31]

9.106. If there is a general charitable intent, the gift will be applied *cy-près*. This is the rule in cases of what is sometimes called "initial impossibility," *i.e.,* where the purpose chosen by the donor is impossible to achieve or illegal,[32] or the purpose has never existed[33] or, if it did exist when the testator made his will, has ceased to exist when he dies and the will becomes operative.[34] In each case it is a question of construction whether or not a sufficient general charitable intent has been shown[35] and the courts may take into consideration a variety of factors, such as the existence of a gift over to another charity or for some non-charitable purpose. In *Re Simpson's Will Trusts*,[36] Gibson J. laid down the following propositions: (1) when deciding whether a general charitable intention has been manifested by a testator, the will is not to be

---

[28] See generally, Sheridan and Delany, *The Cy-Près Doctrine* (1959); Delany, "Some Aspects of the *Cy-Près* Doctrine" (1959) 13 N.I.L.Q. 137; Sheridan, "Cy-Près in the Sixties" (1968) 6 Alberta L.Rev. 16. For early recognition of the doctrine in Ireland, see *Incorporated Society* v. *Price* (1844) 1 Jo. & Lat. 498; *Carbery* v. *Cox* (1852) 3 Ir.Ch.R. 231; *Re Evans' Charities* (1858) 10 Ir.Ch.R. 271; *Daly* v. *Att.-Gen.* (1860) 11 Ir.Ch.R. 41.

[29] Para. 9.108, *post.*

[30] See *Re Templemoyle Agricultural School* (1869) I.R. 4 Eq.295; *Governors of Erasmus Smith Schools* v. *Att.-Gen.* (1932) 66 I.L.T.R. 57; *Re McGwire* [1941] I.R. 33; *Munster and Leinster Bank Ltd.* v. *Att.-Gen.* (1957) 91 I.L.T.R. 34.

[31] Para. 9.055, *ante.*

[32] Cf. *Re Doherty* (1930) 64 I.L.T.R. 50.

[33] *Daly* v. *Att.-Gen.* (1860) 11 Ir.Ch.R. 41; *Re Geary's Trusts* (1890) 25 L.R.Ir. 171; *Re Mulcahy* [1931] I.R. 239.

[34] In *Re Dunwoodie* [1977] N.I. 141 (see para. 9.097, fn. 87, *ante.*), Murray J. held that there was a case of "initial impossibility", because the consent of the church authority in question was necessary for installation of the bells and this was never given. He, therefore, ordered a *cy-près* application on the basis that, on the evidence, there was a general charitable intention to advance religion through the work of a particular church. See also *Re Simpson's Will Trusts, infra.* See also *Makeown* v. *Ardagh* (1876) I.R. 10 Eq. 445. See Hutton "The Lapse of Charitable Bequests" (1969) 32 M.L.R. 283. Problems may be created where an institution is reorganised by statute, such as the change of ownership of hospitals effected in Northern Ireland by the Health Services Act (N.I.), 1948, see *Re Hunter* [1950] N.I. 187; *Re Pearson* [1951] N.I. 152. See also Marshall, "Hospitals and the National Health Service Act" (1952) 5 C.L.P. 81.

[35] *Re Motherwell's Estate* [1910] 1 I.R. 249; *Re Ffrench* [1941] I.R. 49 (see *A Casebook on Equity and Trusts in Ireland* (1985), p.509; *McCormick* v. *Q.U.B.* [1958] N.I. 1.

[36] [1975] 26 N.I.L.Q. 122. See also *Re Deighton* (1952) 86 I.L.T.R. 127.

construed *in vacuo*, and extrinsic circumstances which may explain or clarify the terms of the will may be taken into account, particularly when the document is equivocal; (2) a court nowadays has no religious or other repugnance to declaring void a charitable gift, and so raises no invariable presumption in favour of a general charitable intention if an initial gift fails; (3) if a gift for a designated charitable purpose fails, it cannot be concluded merely from the underlying public benefit which would have been advanced that the court will infer from the frustrated provisions a wider charitable intention; however, a very slight indication of intention to effectuate some general charitable purpose is often sufficient to persuade the court to impute a general charitable intention, although no general rule can be expressed upon how slight that indication may be. In that case it was discovered that the funds available under a residuary gift to be used to found a home for orphan boys were inadequate for the purpose. Gibson J. held that, since the testatrix had no near relations and had made other charitable bequests and since the wording of the gift did not unduly restrict its administration, it could be concluded that she had had a general charitable intention and, therefore, a *cy-près* scheme should be directed. Until recently, major problems could arise in the case of public appeals, *e.g.,* to establish a disaster fund, which ultimately proved impossible of application for some reason or which turned out to have a substantial surplus left over after satisfaction of the appeal purposes. In such a case many contributions (arising, *e.g.,* from jumble-sales and flag-day collections) were anonymous and without any documentary evidence by which to identify the donors. If the particular case was treated as one of initial impossibility,[37] a general charitable intent had to be established, yet, if such an intent was not found, the resulting trust might be unenforceable for want of identity of the objects,[38] and, ultimately, the funds might lie in court until claimed by the State or the Crown as *bona vacantia.*[39] This problem is now covered, however, by section 48 of the Republic's Charities Act, 1961, and section 23 of the Charities Act (N.I.), 1964. Under these provisions, the court[40] may apply property given for specific charitable purposes or (in the Republic of Ireland only) for non-charitable purposes which fail[41] as if it were given for charitable purposes generally, where it belongs:

"(*a*) to a donor who, after such advertisements and inquiries as are reasonable, cannot be identified or cannot be found; or

---

[37] Which presumably should not have been the case where there was simply a surplus left over after application of the funds to the purpose in question, para. 9.107, *post.*

[38] See the discussion in the English cases, *Re North Devon and West Somerset Relief Fund Trusts* [1953] 1 W.L.R. 1260; *Re Hillier's Trusts* [1954] 1 W.L.R. 9 and 700; *Re Ulverston and District New Hospital Building Trusts* [1956] Ch. 622; *Re Gillingham Bus Disaster Fund* [1958] Ch. 300; [1959] Ch. 62. Also see *Munster and Leinster Bank Ltd.* v. *Att.-Gen.* (1957) 91 I.L.T.R. 34.

[39] Ch. 15, *post.*

[40] In the case of less valuable property, the Commissioners of Charitable Donations and Bequests for Ireland (the "Board") may exercise these powers in the Republic (1961 Act, s. 48(7) and the Department of Finance and Personnel may in Northern Ireland (1964 Act, s. 13).

[41] Purposes are deemed to fail where any difficulty in applying property to those purposes makes that property, or the part not applicable *cy-près*, available to be returned to the donors, 1961 Act, s. 48(5); 1964 Act (N.I.), s. 23(5).

(*b*) to a donor who has executed a written disclaimer of his right to have the property returned."[42]

In certain cases[43] it is to be conclusively presumed, without any advertisement or inquiry, that the property belongs to donors who cannot be identified and, in other cases, the court may order it to be treated as such where it would be unreasonable to incur expense, having regard to the amounts likely to be returned to the donors, or for donors to expect the property to be returned, having regard to the nature, circumstances and amounts of the gifts.[44] These provisions are retrospective in both parts of Ireland. [45]

(ii) No General Charitable Intent

9.107. In several situations it has been held that property may be applied *cy-près* despite the lack of a general charitable intent on the part of the donor. This has been held to be the case where there is a "supervening impossibility," *e.g.,* where the purpose ceases to exist after the gift (being an absolute one) has taken effect,[46] whether because an institution has ceased to exist or its objects have come to an end,[47] or where a surplus is left over after providing for a particular purpose.[48]

(iii) Statutory Extension

9.108. The *cy-près* doctrine as it had developed by the mid-twentieth century had become subject to the criticism that its rules were too restrictive in that, first, it was sometimes difficult to establish a case within the strict rules for a *cy-près* application of the fund and, secondly, that the court was hampered in not being able to devise a scheme departing from the original trust.[49] In fact, extensive powers to devise schemes for reorganisation of trusts had been conferred in Ireland under nineteenth-century legislation for certain kinds of trusts,[50] *e.g.,* under the Educational Endowments (Ireland) Act, 1885.[51] A general relaxation of the *cy-près* doctrine has, however, been

---

[42] S. 48(1) of the Republic's 1961 Act adds the proviso that, in applying *cy-près* property given for specific *non-charitable* purposes, regard is to be had to the wishes of the trustees or other persons in charge of the property.

[43] *E.g.,* cash collections through collecting boxes, proceeds of lotteries, competitions, entertainments, etc., see 1961 Act, s. 48(2); 1964 Act (N.I.), s. 23(2).

[44] 1961 Act, s. 48(3); 1964 Act (N.I.), s. 23(3). In cases of a *cy-près* application of property belonging to donors who cannot be identified or found, *other than* property applied under s. 48(2) and (3)(1961 Act) and s. 23(2) and (3)(1964 Act), the donor may make a claim for recovery even after the date of making the scheme, 1961 Act, s. 48(4)(*b*)(within 12 months); 1964 Act (N.I.), s. 23(4)(*b*)(6 months).

[45] 1961 Act, s. 48(8); 1964 Act (N.I.), s. 23(7).

[46] *Munster and Leinster Bank Ltd.* v. *Att.-Gen.* (1957) 91 I.L.T.R. 34. *Cf. Re Hardy* [1933] N.I. 150.

[47] *McCormick* v. *Q.U.B.* [1958] N.I. 1. See Hickling, "Destination of Funds of Defunct Voluntary Associations" (1966) 30 Conv. 117.

[48] *Re Trusts of Rectory of St. John in City of Cork* (1869) I.R. 3 Eq. 335; *Att.-Gen.* v. *Forde* [1932] N.I. 1; *Re Royal Kilmainham Hospital* [1966] I.R. 451 (see *A Casebook on Equity and Trusts in Ireland* (1985), p.514). Winder, "The *Cy-Près* Application of Surplus Charitable Funds" (1941) 5 Conv. 198.

[49] See the Newark *Charity Committee Report* (N.I.) (Cmd. 396, 1958), paras. 22–3.

[50] See General Prisons (Ir.) Act, 1877, s. 58; Charities Act, 1961, s. 29(5)(R.I.). See also Health Services Act (N.I.), 1948, s. 38, as amended by Health Services Act (N.I.), 1953, s. 9.

[51] See also in Northern Ireland, Education Act (N.I.), 1947, 1st Sched., para 4; Education (Amendment) Act (N.I.), 1956, s. 8; Educational Endowments (Confirmation of Schemes) Act (N.I.), 1956. See the Lowry Committee *Report on Schemes made under the Educational Endowments (Ireland) Act, 1885. Re Townsend Street Endowment Trusts* [1956] N.I. 53.

introduced recently in both parts of Ireland. The Republic's Charities Act, 1961,[52] and the Charities Act (N.I.), 1964,[53] now provide a list of the circumstances in which a *cy-pres* application of funds may be made, namely:

"(*a*) where the original purposes, in whole or in part–
(i) have been as far as may be fulfilled; or
(ii) cannot be carried out, or not according to the directions given and to the spirit of the gift, or
(*b*) where the original purposes provide a use for part only of the property available by virtue of the gift; or
(*c*) where the property available by virtue of the gift and other property applicable for similar purposes can be more effectively used in conjunction, and to that end can suitably, regard being had to the spirit of the gift, be made applicable to common purposes; or
(*d*) where the original purposes were laid down by reference to an area which then was but has since ceased to be a unit for some other purpose, or by reference to a class of persons or to an area which has for any reason ceased to be suitable, regard being had to the spirit of the gift, or to be practical in administering the gift; or
(*e*) where the original purposes, in whole or in part, have, since they were laid down–
(i) been adequately provided for by other means; or
(ii) ceased, as being useless or harmful to the community or for other reasons, to be in law charitable; or
(iii) ceased in any other way to provide a suitable and effective method of using the property available by virtue of the gift, regard being had to the spirit of the gift."

9.109. By introducing concepts of "effectiveness," "suitability" and "practicability," the above provisions have relaxed the former requirements of "impossibility" of achieving the original purposes[54] and of application "to the next nearest purpose" only, without substantial deviation from the original purposes.[55] The safeguard for the original donor's wishes is included, however, in the requirement of conformity to the "spirit of the gift."[56] As Lowry J. (as he then was) put it:

"The new statutory approach to *cy-près* is intended not to substitute the trustees' or the court's ideas for those of the donor, but to preserve and

---

[52] S. 47.
[53] S. 22.
[54] Which include purposes modified by a *cy-près* alteration of the original scheme, 1961 Act, s. 47(3); 1964 Act, s. 22(5). In *Re Steele* [1976] N.I. 66, Murray J. applied section 22(1)(*e*)(iii) to a condition attached to land left to the Representative Church Body that the land "be not sold at any time nor ploughed or run out in any way, but let yearly for grazing in conacre." On the other hand, the same judge refused to apply sub-paragraph (iii) in *Re Dunwoodie* [1977] N.I. 141 at 148, though he did still direct a *cy-près* application in that case (see para. 9.106, fn. 34, *supra*).
[55] See *Re Royal Kilmainham Hospital* [1966] I.R. 451, espec. at 482-3 (*per* Budd J.). Also *Q.U.B.* v. *Att.-Gen. for Northern Ireland* [1966] N.I. 115.
[56] S. 22(4) of the Charities Act (N.I.), 1964 provides that this may be ascertained by taking into account the conduct, and any habits or actions, of the donor and any written or oral declarations made by him at any time in relation to the gift. There is no equivalent provision in the Republic's 1961 Act.

promote the spirit of the gift rather than the letter, even where the letter of the gift could be, and according to the former law would have had to be, adhered to."[57]

Indeed, both Acts emphasise that the above provisions do not "affect the conditions which must be satisfied in order that property given for charitable purposes may be applied *cy-près,* except in so far as those conditions require a failure of the original purposes."[58] Thus a general charitable intent is necessary to the same extent as under the former law.[59] The Acts also provide a statutory declaration of a charity trustee's duty, where the case permits and requires the property or some part of it to be applied *cy-près*, to secure its effective use for charity by taking steps to enable it to be so applied.[60]

9.110. Finally, section 4 of the Republic's Charities Act, 1973,[61] introduces new *cy-près* jurisdiction to cover charities established or regulated by statute or charter.[62] Under this section the Commissioners of Charitable Donations and Bequests for Ireland may frame schemes which, after inquiry into the circumstances, they are satisfied would be for the benefit of the charity in question, but which would otherwise be outside their powers by reason of a provision of the statute or charter governing the charity.[63] The Commissioners had before this a very limited power of framing schemes so that charity property was applied *cy-près*. Such a scheme may be made on the application of the trustees and due notice and publicity must be given to bring the proposed scheme to the attention of persons interested.[64]

3. *Administration*

Detailed provisions governing the administration of charities in Ireland are now contained, as to the Republic, in the Charities Acts, 1961, and 1973, and, as to Northern Ireland, in the Charities Act (N.I.), 1964.

(i) Charity Authority

9.111. In the Republic of Ireland, the authority responsible for the general administration of charities is the Board entitled the "Commissioners of Charitable Donations and Bequests for Ireland," first established under a statute of 1844[65] and now controlled by Part II of the Charities Act, 1961, as

---

[57] *Q.U.B.* v. *Att.-Gen. for Northern Ireland,* not included in [1966] N.I. 115 (see p.119), but see (1966) 17 N.I.L.Q. 322 at 331.

[58] 1961 Act, s. 47(2); 1964 Act, s. 22(2).

[59] See para. 9.105, *supra.*

[60] 1961 Act, s. 47(4); 1964 Act, s. 22(6). In fact, English judges had expressed views to this effect, see, *e.g.,* Viscount Simonds in *National Anti-Vivisection Society* v. *I.R.C.* [1948] A.C. 31 at 74; also Upjohn J. in *Vernon* v. *I.R.C.* [1956] 1 W.L.R. 1169 at 1179.

[61] There is no N.I. Equivalent. For England, see Charities Act, 1960, s. 15.

[62] Expressly excluded from this provision are charities covered by the Educational Endowments (Ir.) Act, 1885, as amended by s. 30 of the Charities Act, 1961, see para. 9.108, *supra.*

[63] S. 4(1). *Cf.* Charities Act, 1961, s. 29.

[64] S. 4(5) and (6).

[65] Charitable Donations and Bequests (Ir.) Act, 1844. See also the Acts of 1867 and 1871, and the Republic's Charitable Donations and Bequests (Amendment) Act, 1955.

amended by the Charities Act, 1973. The statutory functions of the Board are many and various: they include the giving of advice to charity trustees,[66] the making of orders for compromise of claims by or against charities,[67] the recovery of misappropriated charitable funds,[68] the institution of legal proceedings in charity matters,[69] the framing of *cy-près* schemes,[70] the investment of charity funds,[71] the authorisation or execution of sales, exchanges, grants and surrenders of leases[72] and the purchase of sites for building,[73] the issuing of receipts,[74] the furnishing of copies of public documents and the examination and searches of records relating to charities,[75] the appointment of new trustees of charities[76] and the making of incorporation schemes for charity trustees.[77] The Board, or High Court, may also establish common investment schemes in which several charities may participate, so as to gain the advantages of investment over a wide range of securities which the pooling of small individual funds into one large fund may achieve.[78] The Board is entitled to notice in writing before legal proceedings are commenced by any person except the Attorney-General,[79] and the Probate Officer is obliged to make an annual return to the Board relating to charitable devises and bequests.[80] The Board itself may apply to the High Court for directions relating to the administration of any charity.[81]

9.112. In Northern Ireland, the Ministry of Finance (now Department of Finance and Personnel) became the Charity Authority in 1921[82] and remains so under the Charities Act (N.I.), 1964.[83] The Department's functions under the Act are very similar to those of the Republic's Board under the Republic's 1961 Act, as outlined above. Perhaps a few points of difference may be mentioned. For example, in addition to having power to make common investment schemes for specific charities, section 25 of the 1964 Act

[66] 1961 Act, s. 21. *Cf.* 1964 Act (N.I.), s. 1.
[67] 1961 Act, s. 22. *Cf.* 1964 Act (N.I.), s. 5.
[68] 1961 Act, ss. 23 and 24. *Cf.* 1964 Act (N.I.), s. 16.
[69] 1961 Act, ss. 25-7. This includes certification of cases to the Attorney-General, s. 26. *Cf.* 1964 Act (N.I.), ss. 2 and 6.
[70] 1961 Act, ss. 29 and 30; 1973 Act, ss. 4 and 8. *Cf.* 1964 Act (N.I.), ss. 13 and 14.
[71] 1961 Act, ss. 32, 33, 38 and 40, as amended by the 1973 Act, ss. 9 and 10. *Cf.* Trustee (Amendment) Act (N.I.), 1962, para. 10.059, *post.*
[72] 1961 Act, ss. 34-7, as amended by the 1973 Act, ss. 11-13. *Cf.* 1964 Act (N.I.), ss. 17-21. See *Re McGarel Buildings Charity* (1966) 17 N.I.L.Q. 514 (duty of trustees to obtain best possible price when selling).
[73] 1961 Act, s. 39.
[74] 1961 Act, s. 41. *Cf.* 1964 Act (N.I.), s. 7.
[75] 1961 Act, s. 42. *Cf.* 1964 Act (N.I.), s. 3.
[76] 1961 Act, s. 43, as amended by 1973 Act, s. 14. See *Re Scott's Trusts* (1962) 96 I.L.T.S.J. 119. *Cf.* 1964 Act (N.I.), s. 12.
[77] 1973 Act, ss. 2 and 3. *Cf.* 1964 Act (N.I.), ss. 10 and 11, replacing the Charitable Trustees (Incorporation) Act (N.I.), 1961.
[78] 1961 Act, s. 46. *Cf.* 1964 Act (N.I.), s. 25.
[79] 1961 Act, s. 53.
[80] 1961 Act, s. 58 *Cf.* 1964 Act (N.I.), s. 30.
[81] 1961 Act, s. 51 *Cf.* 1964 Act (N.I.), s. 29.
[82] The Ministry's succession to the jurisdiction of the Commissioners of Charitable Donations and Bequests for Ireland seems to have been a somewhat obscure process, see the Newark *Charity Committee Report* (1958), para. 41.
[83] Pt. I. In *Re Steele* (see para. 9.109, fn. 54, *ante*), Murray J. held that the "no sale" condition did not take away the jurisdiction of the Department of Finance to authorise a sale under section 18 of the Charities Act (N.I.), 1964.

authorised the Ministry to establish its own "central investment fund" to provide for investment of any charity property of which the Ministry was trustee and to enable any other charity to participate.[84] The Central Investment Fund (N.I.) was in fact set up by the Ministry in 1965 and continues to provide charities in Northern Ireland with a special facility for investment in a fund managed by experts,[85] along the lines of a unit trust.[86] The 1964 Act does not contain any special provisions, other than under common investment schemes, relating to charity trustees' investment powers, because such trustees have the wider powers of investment conferred on trustees generally by the United Kingdom's Trustee Investments Act, 1961, as adapted for Northern Ireland by the Trustee (Amendment) Act (N.I.), 1962.[87]

(ii) Charity Trustees

9.113. Under section 55 of the Republic's 1961 Act, the power to deal[88] with charity property is conferred on a majority of two-thirds of the trustees of a particular charity assembled at a meeting of their body duly constituted. In Northern Ireland, the 1964 Act confines this power of a two-thirds majority to cases where there are four or more trustees for the time being acting in the administration of the charity, and at least two-thirds of the trustees so acting must exercise the powers of the majority conferred by the section.[89] Section 27 of the 1964 Act also imposes on charity trustees in Northern Ireland an express statutory duty to keep proper books of accounts of the affairs of the charity, which books and statements of accounts must be preserved for at least seven years unless the charity ceases to exist and the Department permits destruction or other disposal of them.

Finally, in both parts of Ireland any person,[90] such as a trustee, may apply to the High Court for relief or directions relating to a charity.[91]

L. Purpose Trusts

9.114. The subject of non-charitable purpose trusts, or trusts of imperfect obligation, as they are sometimes called, has, perhaps, been one of the most controversial areas of trust law.[92] There has been much case-law on the

---

[84] S. 25 (8) and (9).

[85] The Department administers and manages the Fund, as trustee (see Charities Central Investment Fund Scheme (N.I.), 1965, para. 4), and invests the Fund after advice from an Advisory Committee comprised of independent experts (para. 12). [86] See para. 13 of the 1965 Scheme. [87] Para. 10.059, *post.*

[88] *I.e.,* to carry into legal effect dispositions of charity property such as sales, exchanges, partitions, mortgages, leases, etc., s. 55 (1). [89] S. 26.

[90] With the consent of the Att.-Gen., 1961 Act, s. 51 (1); 1964 Act (N.I.), s. 29 (3).

[91] This replaces the Charities Procedure Act, 1812 (known as "Romilly's Act") which required the presentation of a petition by "any two or more persons." See *Re Townsend Street Endowment Trusts* [1956] N.I. 53.

[92] See Andrews, "Gifts to Purposes and Institutions" (1965) 29 Conv. 165; Delany, "Bequests for Upkeep of Graves and Tombs" (1951) 17 Ir.Jur. 17; Gravells, "Public Purpose Trusts" (1977) 40 M.L.R. 397; Kirafly, " 'Purpose Trusts', Powers and Conditions" (1950) 14 Conv. 374; Leigh, "Trusts of Imperfect Obligation" (1955) 18 M.L.R. 120; Marshall, "Failure of the Astor Trust" (1953) 6 C.L.P. 151; McKay, "Trusts for Purposes—Another View" (1973) 37 Conv. 420; Sheridan, "Trusts for Non-Charitable Purposes" (1953) 17 Conv. 46; "Purpose Trusts and Powers" (1958) 4 A.L.R. 235; "Power to appoint for a Non-Charitable Purpose: A Duologue or Endacott's Ghost" (1964) 13 De Paul L.Rev. 210; Watkin, "Charity: The Purport of 'Purpose' " [1978] Conv. 277.

subject and, more recently, legislation passed on both sides of the Irish Sea.

1. *Case-law*

9.115. So far as the courts in both Ireland and England were concerned it was a general principle of the law of charities that for a gift to be upheld as charitable it had to be confined to exclusively charitable purposes by its terms. So long as the objects within the scope of the gift were all charitable, it did not matter that a selection had to be made[93] and the courts even went so far as to uphold gifts requiring an apportionment between charitable and non-charitable purposes.[94] In the latter case, the part of the gift to be devoted to the non-charitable purposes usually failed for want of certainty or as infringing the rule against inalienability. This led to the general impression that there cannot be a trust for a non-charitable purpose and it is this proposition that we must now examine in the light of, first, case-law and, secondly, legislation.

(i) General Principle

9.116. Where a gift by its terms seemed to include within its scope both charitable and non-charitable purposes, it was void if the trustees could devote all or some of the fund to the non-charitable purposes.[95] On the other hand, a gift to an institution or organisation whose main work was charitable might still have been upheld even though it engaged in non-charitable activities incidentally.[96] Indeed, in Ireland there were several categories of cases of non-charitable gifts being upheld or, at least, not being held void on the ground of a general principle that such gifts could not be upheld.

(ii) Non-Charitable Religious Purposes

9.117. Perhaps owing to the Irish concern for matters religious, there were many cases where gifts for non-charitable religious purposes were upheld.[97] If such gifts were held void, it was usually on the ground of infringement of the rule against inalienability (*i.e.,* tying up for longer than the perpetuity period).[98]

(iii) Institutions

9.118. There were also many cases of gifts to institutions, whose work or

---

[93] *Commrs. of Charitable Donations and Bequests* v. *Sullivan* (1841) 1 Dr. & War. 501; *Richardson* v. *Murphy* [1903] 1 I.R. 227.
[94] *Re Gavacan* [1913] 1 I.R. 276.
[95] *Boyle* v. *Boyle* (1877) I.R. 11 Eq. 433.
[96] *Clancy* v. *Commr. of Valuation* [1911] 2 I.R. 173, espec. at 183 (*per* Palles C.B.) and 186–7 (*per* Gibson J.).
[97] *Phelan* v. *Slattery* (1887) 19 L.R.Ir. 177; *Bradshaw* v. *Jackman* (1887) 21 L.R.Ir. 12; *Reichenbach* v. *Quin* (1888) 21 L.R.Ir. 138; *Armstrong* v. *Reeves* (1890) 25 L.R.Ir. 325; *Re Gibbons* [1917] 1 I.R. 448; *Re Ryan's Will Trusts* (1926) 60 I.L.T.R. 57; *Re Byrne* [1935] I.R. 782; *Re Keogh's Estate* [1945] I.R. 13 (see *A Casebook on Equity and Trusts in Ireland* (1985), p. 534).
[98] *Dillon* v. *Reilly* (1875) I.R. 10 Eq. 152; *Beresford* v. *Jervis* (1877) 11 I.L.T.R. 128; *McCourt* v. *Burnett* (1877) 11 I.L.T.R. 130; *Kehoe* v. *Wilson* (1880) 7 L.R.Ir. 10; *Morrow* v. *McConville* (1883) 11 L.R.Ir. 236; *Small* v. *Torley* (1890) 25 L.R.Ir. 388; *Laverty* v. *Laverty* [1907] 1 I.R. 9.

functions were not necessarily confined to charitable ones, being still upheld or, if held void, so held on the ground of infringement of other rules, such as the rule against inalienability. Indeed, in these "institution" cases the courts seem to have been concerned only with perpetuity (in the sense of inalienability) problems. Thus gifts have been upheld where it was clear that the institution in question could spend the capital of the fund at any time.[99] In other cases, gifts were upheld by construing them not as gifts to the institutions as such, but rather as gifts beneficially to the individual members who made up the society or institution at the date of the gift, thus avoiding any perpetuity problem.[1] In cases involving gifts of income to non-charitable institutions, once again the courts upheld the gifts provided there was no infringement of the inalienability rule, in the sense that the gift was bound to end or the money could be spent within the perpetuity period.[2]

(iv) Tombs, Graves and Monuments

9.119. There were several cases where the courts upheld gifts for the erection or upkeep of such things as tombs, graves, tablets in churches and other monuments concerned with the dead.[3] Once again the main concern of the courts was whether or not the gift was of indefinite duration, so that there might be an infringement of the rule against inalienability, because it might last longer than the perpetuity period.[4]

(v) Animals

The courts also upheld gifts for the maintenance of the donor's animals provided they complied with the inalienability rule.[5]

9.120. From all this it might have been questioned whether there was much left of the general principle that trusts for non-charitable purposes were invalid *ex hypothesi*. The English courts were adamant, however, that the general principle remained and cases involving animals, graves and monuments, were dismissed as concessions to human weakness or sentiment.[6] The English judges seem to have been particularly concerned about trustees holding large sums of money in trust in situations where no court or other

---

[99] *Re Wilkinson's Trusts* (1887) 19 L.R.Ir. 531 (gift to Superioress of Convent of Mercy); *Armstrong* v. *Reeves* (1890) 25 L.R.Ir. 325 (Society for the Abolition of Vivisection and Society for Protection of Animals); *Re Byrne* [1935] I.R. 782 (Jesuit Order of Ireland); *Re Keogh's Estate* [1945] I.R. 13 (Carmelite nuns and fathers) (see *A Casebook on Equity and Trusts in Ireland* (1985), p. 534); *Re Rickard* [1954] N.I. 100 (convent); *Re Connor* [1960] I.R. 67 (General Cemetery Company of Dublin) (see *ibid.*, p. 536). See paras. 5.039–40, *ante.*

[1] *Re Delany's Estate* (1882) 9 L.R. Ir. 226; *Bradshaw* v. *Jackman* (1887) 21 L.R.Ir. 12. See also *Re Lipinski's Will Trusts* [1976] Ch. 235; *cf. Re Grant's Will Trusts* [1980], W.L.R. 360. See para. 5.039, *ante.*

[2] *Stewart* v. *Green* (1870) I.R. 5 Eq. 470; *Morrow* v. *McConville* (1883) 11 L.R.Ir. 236; *Re Fossitt's Estate* [1934] I.R. 504. Para. 5.040,*ante.*

[3] See now the Republic's Charities Act, 1961, s. 50, para. 9.123, *post.* See also *Re Steele* [1976] N.I. 66.

[4] *Beresford* v. *Jervis* (1877) 11 I.L.T.R. 128; *Toole* v. *Hamilton* [1901] 1 I.R. 383.

[5] *Re Kelly* [1932] I.R. 255, where Meredith J. made it clear that there could be no question of the animals' lives being used as "lives in being" for the purpose of calculating the perpetuity period (see *A Casebook on Equity and Trusts in Ireland* (1985), p. 537). *Cf. Re Dean* (1889) 41 Ch.D. 552.

[6] *Re Astor's Settlement Trusts* [1952] Ch. 534; *Re Endacott* [1960] Ch. 232. *Cf. Re McCauley's Estate* (1967) 18 N.I.L.Q. 462.

body could control them, *i.e.,* there were no beneficiaries to bring an action in court and, since the purposes were *non*-charitable, the Attorney-General had no jurisdiction. It has, however, been pointed out that this fear may have been groundless in that there would always be some person able to bring the matter to court, even if indirectly interested only. If the trustees failed to carry out the purpose trust, it could be argued that the gift itself had failed and so the person entitled on failure could claim the money, were he the settlor or the testator's residuary legatee or devisee or, failing such a person, his intestate successors. But this, and other arguments, such as the argument that purpose gifts should be upheld as being more properly regarded as powers rather than trusts,[7] were never accepted by the English courts. So far as the Irish courts were concerned, the matter was never really considered as one of general principle and so it remained arguable whether it really applied here in the light of the numerous cases upholding non-charitable purpose trusts. The matter has, however, become, to some extent, of historical significance in the light of recent legislation to which we now turn.

2. *Legislation*

9.121. One of the common cases where trusts for non-charitable purposes failed was where the settlor or testator used vague terms to describe the purposes in question, whether by use of several expressions or use of one composite expression, capable of covering both charitable and non-charitable purposes, *e.g.,* "charitable or benevolent purposes" or "charitable and religious purposes." Sometimes such gifts were upheld as charitable, especially when the conjunctive word "and" linked the stated purposes and, in Ireland, when the alternative to charitable purposes was religious purposes. [8] In England, several trusts for apparently worthy causes fell into this trap.[9] The subject is now largely governed by statute law in both parts of Ireland.

(i) Republic of Ireland

9.122. The relevant provisions are contained in sections 49 and 50 of the Charities Act, 1961. Section 49 reads:

"(1) Where any of the purposes of a gift includes or could be deemed to include both charitable and non-charitable objects, its terms shall be so construed and given effect to as to exclude the non-charitable objects and the purpose shall, accordingly, be treated as charitable.
(2) Subsection (1) shall not apply where–
    (*a*) the gift takes effect before the 1st day of January 1960, or

---

[7] See Sheridan, fn. 92, para. 9.114, *supra.*
[8] *Re Sinclair's Trust* (1884) 13 L.R.Ir. 150; *Re Salter* [1911] 1 I.R. 289; *Rickerby* v. *Nicholson* [1912] 1 I.R. 343.
[9] *Oxford Group* v. *I.R.C.* [1949] 2 All E.R. 537; *Chichester Diocesan Fund and Board of Finance* v. *Simpson* [1944] A.C. 341.

(b) (i) the terms of the gift make, or provide for the making of, an apportionment between the charitable and non-charitable objects, and

(ii) the non-charitable objects are identifiable from an express or implied description."

There seems to be no reported Irish authority on the scope of this section, which is modelled on some earlier legislation in Australia.[10] The result of the interpretation of the Australian legislation, by the Australian courts[11] and the Privy Council,[12] seems to be that (1) it covers invalidity contained in both alternative expressions and one compendious expression[13] and invalidity because of both uncertainty and inalienability and (2) probably some "flavour of charity" must be shown in the intention of the donor in making the gift.[14]

9.123. Section 50 of the Republic's 1961 Act, to which there is no equivalent in Northern Ireland[15] or in England, reads:

"(1) Every gift made after the commencement of this Act for the provision, maintenance or improvement of a tomb, vault or grave or for a tombstone or any other memorial to a deceased person or deceased persons which would not otherwise be charitable shall, to the extent provided by this section, be a charitable gift.

(2) Such a gift shall be charitable so far as it does not exceed-

(a) in the case of a gift of income only, sixty pounds a year;

(b) in any other case, one thousand pounds in amount or value."

Under this section gifts within the stated limits are saved by being held charitable. However, if outside the limits, they may still be valid as non-charitable gifts since they are well-recognised exceptions to the general rule (if there be such a thing in Ireland) against such gifts.[16]

---

[10] *I.e.,* Victoria's Property Law Act, 1958, s. 131 (replacing legislation dating back to an Act of 1914) and New South Wales' Conveyancing Act, 1919–1964, s. 37D.

[11] *Re Hollole* [1945] V.L.R. 295; *Union Trustee Co. of Australasia Ltd.* v. *Church of England Property Trust* (1946) 46 S.R. (N.S.W.) 298; *Cf. Roman Catholic Archbishop of Melbourne* v. *Lawlor* (1934) 51 C.L.R. 1; *Re Belcher* [1950] V.L.R. 11.

[12] *Leahy* v. *Att.-Gen. for New South Wales* [1959] A.C. 457.

[13] *I.e.,* one should not apply the so-called "blue pencil" approach whereby the legislation should operate only where the gift mentions at least two distinct objects, one charitable and one non-charitable, in such terms that the court can strike out the words referring to the non-charitable objects, leaving the remaining words referring to charitable objects. See Newark *Charity Committee Report* (1958), App. E; Delany, (1960) 76 L.Q.R. 204.

[14] See generally, Keeton and Sheridan, *Law of Charities* (3rd ed., 1983), ch. xvi; Cullity, "Statutory Salvage of Imperfect Trust Provisions: an Exercise in Comparative Legislation" (1967) 16 I.C.L.Q. 464; Sheridan, "Cy-Près in the Cyxties" (1966) 17 N.I.L.Q. 235.

[15] The Newark *Charity Committee Report* did in fact recommend such a provision for Northern Ireland (para. 21) but this was not adopted in the Charities Act (N.I.), 1964. The English Law Reform Committee's *Report on the Rule Against Perpetuities* (Cmnd. 18, 1956) also recommended a similar provision (paras. 51–3) but this was not adopted in the Perpetuities and Accumulations Act, 1964. Note that under s. 16 (4) of the Perpetuities Act (N.I.), 1966, a prospective donor *cannot* stipulate a special perpetuity period of up to 80 years (under s. 1), instead of the old period of 21 years in the absence of any human lives in being; see para. 5.073, *ante.*

[16] *Re Connor* [1960] I.R. 67 (see *A Casebook on Equity and Trusts in Ireland* (1985), p. 536). Para. 9.119, *supra.*

(ii) Northern Ireland

9.124. The first attempt to deal with imperfect trusts in Northern Ireland was the Charitable Trusts Validation Act (N.I.), 1954, which was modelled on the English Act of the same date. The Act was designed to save imperfect trust provisions, which it defined as "any provision declaring the objects for which the property is to be held or applied, and so describing these objects that, consistently with the terms of the provision, the property could be used exclusively for charitable purposes, but could nevertheless be used for purposes which are not charitable."[17] This Act, however, suffered from two major drawbacks. First, it applied only to trust instruments taking effect *before* December 16, 1952,[18] Secondly, both 1954 Acts were couched in language so vague and obscure that the courts in both England[19] and Northern Ireland[20] had great difficulty in applying the identical provisions of the two 1954 Acts, particularly in finding the existence of an "imperfect trust provision."

9.125. The 1954 Act has been largely replaced by a provision of much wider scope, namely section 24[21] of the Charities Act (N.I.), 1964, which reads:

"(1) Where–
> (*a*) property is given for purposes so described that, consistently with the terms of the gift the property could all be used for charitable purposes but could equally well be used wholly or partly for purposes which are not charitable; and
> (*b*) the gift would, but for this section, be invalid;
the gift shall have effect as a gift for such charitable purposes as may be determined by a scheme made in accordance with subsection (2) by the Court or, if the value of the property comprised in the gift does not exceed five thousand pounds, by the Ministry.

(2) Where the terms of a gift and the surrounding circumstances appear to the Court or, as the case may be, the Ministry to show a predominant intention on the part of the donor to further a particular charitable purpose the Court or, as the case may be, the Ministry shall, in making a scheme under subsection (1), have regard, so far as practicable, to that intention.

(3) Where–
> (*a*) property is disposed of by way of successive gifts so that a gift is dependent upon a prior gift; and
> (*b*) the prior gift has been made the subject of a scheme under this section;

[17] See Maurice, "Validation of Charitable Trusts" (1954) 18 Conv. 532 and (1962) 26 Conv. 200.
[18] The date of publication of the English Nathan *Report on Charitable Trusts* (Cmnd. 8710; 1952).
[19] See *Vernon v. I.R.C.* [1956] 1 W.L.R. 1169; *Re Gillingham Bus Disaster Fund* [1959] Ch. 62; *Re Mead's Trust Deed* [1961] 1 W.L.R. 1244; *Re Wykes* [1961] Ch. 229; *Re Harpur's Will Trusts* [1962] Ch. 78; *Re Saxone Shoe Co. Ltd.'s Trust Deed* [1962] 1 W.L.R. 943.
[20] *Re Lord Mayor of Belfast's Air Raid Distress Fund* [1962] N.I. 161; see (1964) 15 N.I.L.Q. 390.
[21] To some extent based on Western Australia's Trustees Act, 1962, s. 102 and New Zealand's Charitable Trusts Act, 1957, s. 61B (though the wording of these provisions was to some extent based on the English Charitable Trusts Validation Act, 1954).

any gift dependent upon the prior gift shall have the like effect as it would have had if the prior gift had at all times been for the purposes determined by that scheme."

9.126. The effect of this section was considered in *Re McCullough*,[22] which involved a gift of a residuary estate to the West Lancashire Masonic Province so as to form a Memorial Fund, "the interest annually to be used at the sole discretion of the said Provincial Grand Master for such purposes within the province as he shall from time to time direct." In fact the gift was not saved by section 24 because the testator had died before it came into operation, but Lowry J. (as he then was) did make several pertinent remarks about the section:

> ". . . section 24 seems to me to apply without limitation as to the place where the trustee named in the will is to be found or the trust funds are to be applied; the scheme made by the court or the Ministry under section 24 (2) could, in any case, provide for a trustee within the jurisdiction. . . .
>
> Arguing that the purposes required to be specified in order to attract section 24 (1) (*a*), Mr. Higgins [counsel for the next-of-kin] pointed out that the phrase was 'so described that' and no 'such that.' Now, the word 'so' is an adverb, and therefore the question is, 'How are the purposes described?' not, 'What are the purposes described?' Still less the question 'what are the purposes specified?' It seems to me that in ordinary language the purposes have been described in the way Mr. Murray [counsel for the residuary legatee] suggests and that they have, moreover, been 'so described that consistently with the terms of the gift, the property *could* all be used for charitable purposes, but could equally well be used wholly or partly for purposes which are not charitable.'"[23]

Lowry J. took the view that the gift in question would have been saved if the section were retrospective and he doubted the view that, to be saved, "there must be in the will some indication of a charitable intention."[24]

[22] [1966] N.I. 73.

[23] *Ibid.*, pp. 75–6.

[24] *Ibid.*, p. 81. Lowry J. thus doubted the "flavour of charity" view taken by the courts which have considered the Australian legislation, see para. 9.122, *supra*. See further on s. 24, Keeton and Sheridan, *Law of Charities* (3rd ed., 1983), pp. 241–5. See also McClean, "Charitable Trusts, the Rule against Perpetuities, Accumulation and Cy-Près" (1963) 1 U.Brit.Col.L.Rev. 729; Sheridan, "Cy-Près in the Cyxties" (1966) 17 N.I.L.Q. 235.

CHAPTER 10

ADMINISTRATION OF TRUSTS

10.001. We now turn to the important topic of administration of trusts. As no doubt the ensuing pages will show, the position of a trustee is an extremely exacting one and, all too frequently, a thankless one.[1] It is certainly not a task to be undertaken without full consideration of all that it involves and yet often the ordinary layman out of family loyalty commits himself to responsibilities which he is ill-equipped to discharge. Unfortunately, a testator frequently finds himself with the choice of appointing some professional institution, *e.g.*, a bank or a trustee and executor company,[2] which will insist upon being paid its normal fees for acting as trustee, or persuading some member of the family to act even though he has no legal or other relevant professional training, such as in banking or accountancy. His solicitor will usually know better than to commit himself to such responsibilities — unless he too is motivated by loyalty due to a client of long standing, or regards trustee work as one of his firm's specialities.

Much of the law on this subject is contained in statutes in both parts of Ireland. In the Republic the major Act is still the Trustee Act, 1893,[3] while in Northern Ireland the 1893 Act has been replaced by the Trustee Act (N.I.), 1958.[4]

I. GENERAL POSITION OF TRUSTEES

In view of the nature and extent of the responsibilities of trustees great care must be taken over their initial appointment and replacement when necessary, for whatever reason.

---

[1]   See Keeton, "The Changing Conception of Trusteeship" (1950) 3 C.L.P. 14. See also the English Law Reform Committee's 23rd Report, *The Powers and Duties of Trustees* (1982; Cmnd 8733).

[2]   In Ireland, the Public Trustee's functions are confined to matters concerning the Land Purchase Acts (see Irish Land Act, 1903, s. 52) and he cannot undertake other work, see *Re Baron Massey's Estate* (1912) 46 I.L.T.R. 87; *In b. Leeson* [1928] I.R. 168. For the powers and duties of custodian and managing trustees and the office of Public Trustee in England, see Public Trustee Act, 1906. See also the Judicial Trustees Act, 1896, which did not extend to Ireland either.

[3]   As amended, *e.g.*, by the Trustee Act, 1931 and the Trustee (Authorised Investments) Act, 1958.

[4]   As amended by the Trustee (Amendment) Act (N.I.), 1962. See Carswell, *Trustee Acts (Northern Ireland)* (1964). For textbooks, see fns. 1 and 2, para. 9.001, *ante*.

A. APPOINTMENT

10.002. It is obviously wise to appoint as trustee a person who is both prudent and honest. Furthermore, a trustee should also be someone who is independent in the sense that he is not going to find himself with a conflict of interest. For this reason it is unwise to appoint one of the beneficiaries as trustee[5] or, indeed, relatives of the beneficiaries.[6] However, it is not always easy to follow the wisest course and even the court may be forced to make appointments it would not normally make, *e.g.*, persons, including beneficiaries, residing out of the jurisdiction,[7] due to the exceptional circumstances of the particular case.

10.003. Usually at least two trustees are appointed[8] and sometimes two are required, *e.g.*, to give a receipt for money.[9] However, in Northern Ireland a trust corporation may act alone in any case where two trustees would otherwise be required.[10] No such special provision for trust corporations exists in the Republic except that, in the case of personal representatives appointing trustees for the property of an infant, a trust corporation may be appointed as sole trustee.[11] Unlike England,[12] there is no limit in either part of Ireland on the number of trustees who may be appointed, though if there are too many considerable administrative problems may be created.[13]

A distinction has to be drawn between the appointment of the original trustees when the trust is first set up and the appointment of new or additional trustees during the currency of the trust. Let us now consider each subject in turn.

1. *Original Trustees*

10.004. It is usual for the settlor or testator to appoint the original trustees. In the case of a will, the executors and trustees are frequently the same persons. Even if the settlor or testator fails to make such an appointment, as a last resort the court can always make an appointment for equity "will not permit a trust to fail for want of a trustee."[14] This may become necessary in

---

[5] See *Re McCook's Settlement Trusts* (1856) 2 Ir.Jur.(N.S.) 74.

[6] *Re Jackson's Trusts* (1874) 8 I.L.T.R. 174 (husband of beneficiary appointed by court).

[7] *Re Custis's Trusts* (1871) I.R. 5 Eq. 429; *Crofton* v. *Crofton* (1913) 47 I.L.T.R. 24; *Re Tyzack* (1964) 98 I.L.T.R. 396.

[8] Note the confusion caused by the provisions in the will considered in *Re Arnott* [1899] 1 I.R. 201.

[9] See Settled Land Act, 1882, s. 39 (1) (para. 8.093, *ante*) and Trustee Act, 1893, s. 20. See also Trustee Act (N.I.), 1958, ss. 14 and 36 (2).

[10] Trustee Act (N.I.), 1958, s. 14, which amended s. 39 (1) of the Settled Land Act, 1882. See para. 8.093, *ante*.

[11] Succession Act, 1965, s. 57 (1). In Northern Ireland, at least two trustees must still be appointed in such a case even though the personal representatives appoint a trust corporation, Administration of Estates Act (N.I.), 1955, s. 38 (1).

[12] See Trustee Act, 1925, s. 34.

[13] See *Survey of the Land Law of Northern Ireland* (1971), para. 130.

[14] See *Incorporated Society* v. *Richards* (1841) 1 Dr. & War. 258 (see *A Casebook on Equity and Trusts in Ireland* (1985), p. 487); *Pollock* v. *Ennis* [1921] 1 I.R. 181. In the case of infants entitled to possession of land, the court has a statutory power to appoint trustees to manage the land and to receive and apply the income from the land under ss. 42 and 43 of the Conveyancing Act, 1881, as extended in the Republic by s. 58 (4) of the Succession Act, 1965, and in Northern Ireland by s. 38 (4) of the Administration of Estates Act (N.I.), 1955; see also the amendment made by ss. 69 and 70 (2) of the Trustee Act (N.I.), 1958. See *Re Glover* [1899] 1 I.R. 337; *Tuthill* v. *Tuthill* [1902] 1 I.R. 429.

the case of a will where the appointed trustees predecease the testator or refuse to act.[15] In the meantime the testator's personal representatives will hold the property pending the appointment.[16] On appointment of the original trustees, the trust property is invariably vested in them as joint tenants, so that as each one dies the survivors continue as trustees of the entire property without the need for any formal acts of succession.[17] When the sole surviving trustee dies the trust property devolves upon his personal representatives[18] as trustees until new trustees are appointed.[19]

2. New and Additional Trustees

10.005. Once a trust is created, it may be desired or necessary to appoint new or additional trustees. There are three main matters to be considered in this context: who may make such appointments; when may they be made; what method of appointment, or formalities, if any, should be adopted in making the appointment.

10.006. As regards who can make such appointments, the first persons who can do so are persons expressly nominated in the trust instrument.[20] In the case of an *inter vivos* settlement, it appears to be the law that the settlor must expressly reserve such a power, otherwise he will have no power of appointment.[21] Apart from such an express power, a statutory power of appointment is conferred upon certain persons in both parts of Ireland.[22] In the Republic this statutory power is confined to the appointment of replacements for original or substituted trustees,[23] but in Northern Ireland it has been extended to replacement of additional trustees.[24] No statutory power of appointment of additional trustees exists at all in the Republic but one does in Northern Ireland, and the donee of the power may appoint himself.[25] The persons listed in the statutes as having the power of appointment are: (1) the persons nominated in the trust instrument; (2) the existing trustees; (3) the personal representatives of the last surviving or continuing trustee.[26] It has been queried in Ireland whether in this context the

---

[15] See further on appointments by the court, para. 10.007, *post*. See also the statutory power mentioned in fn. 28, para. 10.006, *post*.

[16] Ch. 16, *post*, *Pollock* v. *Ennis* [1921] 1 I.R. 181.

[17] Ch. 7, *ante*.

[18] Succession Act, 1965, s. 10 (5); Administration of Estates Act (N.I.), 1955, s. 44 (*a*) and (*b*). These provisions replace the earlier ones contained in the Conveyancing Act, 1881, s. 30 as to which see *Re Ingleby and Boak's Contract* (1883) 13 L.R.Ir. 326; *In b. Berry* [1907] 2 I.R. 209.

[19] Conveyancing Act, 1911, s. 8 (R.I.); Trustee Act (N.I.), 1958, s. 18 (2). See Smith, "The Chains of Trusteeship" (1977) 41 Conv. 423.

[20] *Kennedy* v. *Turnley* (1844) 6 Ir.Eq.R. 399; *Re Ledwich* (1844) 6 Ir.Eq.R. 561; *Re Byrne* (1844) 6 Ir.Eq.R. 563; *Re Cane's Trusts* [1895] 1 I.R. 172; *Re Kenny's Trusts* [1906] 1 I.R. 531

[21] *Dodkin* v. *Brunt* (1868) L.R. 6 Eq. 580.

[22] Trustee Act, 1893, s. 10; Trustee Act (N.I.), 1958, s. 35. See *Re Kidd's Trusts* (1913) 47 I.L.T.R. 291.

[23] 1893 Act, s. 10 (1).

[24] 1958 Act, s. 35 (1).

[25] 1958 Act, s. 35 (6). *Cf* the English Trustee Act, 1925, s. 36 (6).

[26] 1893 Act, s. 10 (1); 1958 Act, s. 35 (1). It seems that the personal representatives cannot appoint themselves under the 1893 Act, see *Crofton* v. *Crofton* (1913) 47 I.L.T.R. 24, but such a limitation is expressly excluded from s. 35 (1) of the 1958 Act in respect of any of the donees of the statutory power of appointment.

word "person" includes a corporation, but the better view would seem to be that such a body may be appointed to act as trustee under the statutory powers.[27] The statutes provide that the newly appointed trustees have the same powers as if originally appointed under the trust instrument.[28] Apart from conferring a new statutory power to appoint additional, as opposed to new or replacement, trustees,[29] the Trustee Act (N.I.), 1958, contains several new provisions relating to the statutory power of appointment, so as, *e.g.*, to make it applicable where an existing trustee is removed under an express power in the trust instrument[30] or a corporation is dissolved[31] or executors wish to make an appointment but to renounce the offices of executors.[32]

10.007. In addition to persons having an express power of appointment granted by the trust instrument and those having the statutory power, an appointment can be made, if necessary, by the beneficiaries, *provided* they are all *sui juris* and between them absolutely entitled to the entire beneficial interest under the trust.[33] Indeed, such beneficiaries may assume control of the trust and put an end to it altogether, if they wish.[34] Finally, if there is no other method of appointment, an appointment may be made by the court, for it is given a statutory power to make an appointment whenever it is otherwise found "inexpedient, difficult or impracticable"[35] to make one. Furthermore, the court has an inherent jurisdiction to remove trustees and appoint replacements in cases of dishonesty or incompetence.[36]

10.008. To turn now to the question of when such powers of appointment may be exercised, in the case of an express power granted by the trust instrument this is largely a matter of construction of the wording of the particular instrument.[37] So far as the statutory power is concerned, the

[27] See Meredith J. in *Re Longworth* (1900) 34 I.L.T.R. 148. *Cf.* Black L.J. in *Re Robinson* (1949) 83 I.L.T.R. 105, preferring the approach of Swinfen Eady J. in *Re Thompson's Settlement Trusts* [1905] 1 Ch. 229, which does not seem to have been cited before Meredith J. See also *Embankment Properties Ltd.* v. *Calaroga Ltd.* (1975) Unrep. (H.C, R.I.) (where it was apparently accepted by Kenny J. that a corporation had been validly appointed trustee).

[28] 1893 Act, s. 10 (3); 1958 Act, s. 35 (7). Also a new appointment may be made in the case of a nominated trustee who has predeceased the testator, as if that trustee died in office, 1893 Act, s. 10 (4); 1958 Act, s. 35 (8).

[29] S. 35 (6).

[30] S. 35 (2).

[31] S. 35 (3).

[32] S. 25 (5). S. 35 (9) permits replacement of a bare trustee who becomes of unsound mind without the necessity to invoke the powers conferred by the Trustee Acts, 1850 and 1852, and now held by the President of the High Court in the Republic and by the High Court (formerly the Lord Chief Justice) in Northern Ireland (as respective successors to the jurisdiction of the Lord Chancellor), para. 25.17, *post*. See *Re Smith's Trusts* (1870) I.R. 4 Eq. 180; *Re Burton's Trusts* (1872) I.R. 6 Eq. 270; *Re Supple's Trusts* (1903) 37 I.L.T.R. 11.

[33] *Re Miller* [1897] 1 I.R. 290 (see *A Casebook on Equity and Trusts in Ireland* (1985), p. 633.

[34] This is sometimes known as the rule in *Saunders* v. *Vautier* (1841) Cr. & Ph. 240.

[35] 1893 Act, s. 25; 1958 Act, s. 40. *Re Quinlan* (1835) 1 Jones 549; *Re Hossford* (1835) 1 Jones 550; *Re Legg* (1839) 1 Ir.Eq.R. 374; *Re Pennefather* (1842) 2 Dr. & War. 292; *Att.-Gen.* v. *Madden* (1843) 2 Con. & L. 519; *Muley* v. *Smith* (1841) 3 Ir.Eq.R. 497; *Re Kidd's Trusts* (1913) 47 I.L.T.R. 291; *Re C.* [1938] Ir.Jur.Rep.58; *Re Kavanagh's Application* (1984) Unrep. (H.C., R.I.). In the case of a court appointment also, the trustee has the same powers, authorities and discretions as if appointed originally under the trust instrument, 1893 Act, s. 37; 1958 Act, s. 42. The Republic's Trustee Act, 1931, ss. 3 and 4 extend the powers of the High Court to cover the situation where a trustee is such by virtue of holding an office which has ceased to exist or the donee of the power of appointment is the holder for the time being of such an office.

[36] *Moore* v. *McGlynn* [1894] 1 I.R. 74 (see *A Casebook on Equity and Trusts in Ireland* (1985), p. 374); *Arnott* v. *Arnott* (1924) 58 I.L.T.R. 145. See also *Re Wakeford* (1844) 1 Jo. & Lat. 2.

[37] See *Re Walker and Hughes' Contract* (1883) 24 Ch.D. 698; *Re Wheeler and De Rochow* [1896] 1 Ch. 315; *Re Sichel's Settlements* [1916] 1 Ch. 358.

occasions for exercise of the power are listed in the statutes applicable in each part of Ireland.[38] Briefly, these allow replacement of an existing trustee where that trustee: (1) is dead; or (2) remains outside the Republic of Ireland or, in the case of Northern Ireland, the United Kingdom for more than twelve months[39]; or (3) desires to be discharged[40]; or (4) refuses to act[41]; or (5) is unfit to act[42]; or (6) is incapable of acting.[43] With respect to the statutory power, in Northern Ireland only,[44] to appoint additional trustees, this may be exercised where either a sole trustee, other than a trust corporation, is or has been originally appointed or there are not more than three trustees, again other than a trust corporation, whether these are original, substituted or additional trustees and whether appointed by the court or otherwise.[45] Finally, with respect to the court's power of appointment we have already mentioned briefly the occasions for its exercise.[46] In the case of both its statutory powers and its inherent jurisdiction, the general principle operates that the court will act only when there is no other way of appointing trustees.[47]

10.009. We come now to the method of appointment. In the case of an express power of appointment once again the method of appointment, including any formalities, such as a deed or in writing, is governed by the terms of the trust instrument itself. The statutory power of appointment is required only to be exercised in writing.[48] However, in most cases it is desirable to make the appointment by deed because this makes it possible to use the special statutory provisions for vesting the trust property in the new trustees.[49] Under these provisions, as they apply to the Republic of Ireland, a vesting declaration may be inserted in the deed of appointment so as to vest the trust property in the new trustee without the need for any conveyance or

---

[38] 1893 Act, s. 10 (1); 1958 Act, s. 35 (1). In Northern Ireland, subsequent *bona fide* purchasers are protected from having to make inquiries into the validity of appointments and the truth of matters stated in instruments of appointment – a statement reciting one of the grounds listed in s. 35 of the 1958 Act is conclusive evidence of the matter stated, see 1958 Act, s. 37.

[39] Return for a short period, *e.g.*, one week, may prevent the power from becoming exercisable, *Re Walker* [1901] 1 Ch. 259.

[40] See *Re Bailey's Trust* (1854) 3 W.R. 31 (payment into court held to be evidence of desire to be discharged).

[41] This seems to include a trustee disclaiming and never accepting office, *Re Hadley* (1851) 5 De G. & Sm. 67; *Re Birchall* (1889) 40 Ch.D. 436.

[42] *E.g.*, as a result of bankruptcy, *cf. Re Bridgman* (1860) 1 Drew & Sm. 164 and *Re Barker's Trusts* (1875) 1 Ch.D. 43. Also see *Re Roche* (1842) 2 Dr. & War. 287.

[43] *I.e.*, due to some personal incapacity, such as mental illness, *Re Watt's Settlement* (1851) 9 Hare 106; *Re East* (1873) 8 Ch.App. 735.

[44] 1958 Act, s. 35 (6). Prior to the Act, and this would seem to remain the position in the Republic, the number of trustees could be increased only when a vacancy was being filled (see 1893 Act, s. 10 (2) (*a*), though an application could always be made to the court, *Re Gregson's Trusts* (1886) 34 Ch.D. 209. See also the 1958 Act, s. 36 (1) (*a*).

[45] It has been queried whether the first occasion is not covered by the second, see Carswell, *Trustee Acts (Northern Ireland)* (1964), pp. 85–6.

[46] Para. 10.007, *supra*.

[47] See the discussion of the court's exercise of its discretion in making an appointment in *Re Custis's Trusts* (1871) I.R. 5 Eq. 429; *Re Jackson's Trusts* (1874) 8 I.L.T.R. 174; *Pollock v. Ennis* [1921] 1 I.R. 181. See also the discussion in *Re Tempest* (1866) L.R. 1 Ch. 485.

[48] 1893 Act, s. 10 (1); 1958 Act, s. 35 (1).

[49] 1893 Act, s. 12; 1958 Act, s. 39.

assignment of the property.[50] Similar provisions exist in Northern Ireland,[51] but since January 1, 1959, it is no longer necessary to put in such a declaration. The deed of appointment now operates as if it contains such a declaration, unless an express provision is inserted to the contrary.[52] Furthermore, the Northern Ireland provisions cure any defects in deeds of appointment, whenever executed, due to express declarations not listing or referring to the complete number of estates or interests to be vested. Such deeds operate and are to be deemed always to have operated to vest in the new trustees such estates, interests and rights as are capable of being and ought to be vested in the trustees, subject, of course, to any express provision to the contrary.[53] In both parts of Ireland, certain kinds of property are expressly excluded from the statutory provisions for vesting, largely due to special features relating to transfer of ownership of such property or title complications.[54] Thus excepted is land conveyed by way of mortgage to secure money subject to the trust,[55] and stocks and shares transferable only in books kept by a company or other body.[56] In Northern Ireland, the further exception has been added of land held under a lease containing a covenant against assignment without consent.[57]

10.010. In the case of an appointment by the court, the court has wide powers to make vesting orders in both parts of Ireland.[58] Indeed, these statutory powers conferred on the court may be invoked in many different situations, wherever there are difficulties in furnishing a proper title to the trust property.[59] The Trustee Act (N.I.), 1958, resolves several difficulties that existed under the earlier 1893 provisions, which are still in force in the Republic.[60] Thus in Northern Ireland it is no longer necessary in the case of a

---

[50] 1893 Act, s. 12 (1). A similar declaration may be used in a deed discharging a retiring trustee so as to vest the trust property in the continuing trustees, s. 12 (2).

[51] 1958 Act, s. 39 (1) (a) and (2) (b).

[52] 1958 Act, s. 39 (1) (b) and (2) (b).

[53] 1958 Act, s. 39 (3).

[54] 1893 Act, s. 12 (3); 1958 Act, s. 39 (4).

[55] The mortgage term held by the trustees must be conveyed by a separate deed of transfer — trusts should be kept off the mortgagor's title so as to relieve purchasers from making searches when he sells after redeeming the mortgage. Furthermore, persons dealing with the mortgagees (the trustees) in good faith ought not to have to enquire whether they were properly appointed trustees, so long as no notice of the trust appears on the transfers, *Re Blaiberg* [1899] 2 Ch. 340.

[56] These must be transferred in the usual prescribed manner, otherwise people like company registrars would find their duties impossible to perform.

[57] 1958 Act, s. 39 (4) (b). Otherwise, it was felt, in many cases an automatic vesting would amount to a breach of covenant entitling the landlord to invoke a proviso for re-entry. So s. 39 (4) (b) provides that the section will operate only if either the requisite consent or licence is obtained prior to execution of the deed of appointment or the vesting declaration will not operate as a breach of covenant or give rise to a forfeiture in the particular case. As to covenants against assignment in the Republic, see Landlord and Tenant (Amendment) Act, 1980, s. 66; Rent Restrictions Act, 1960, s. 32 (4) (b); Rent Restrictions (Amendment) Act, 1967, s. 10, ch. 17, *post*.

[58] 1893 Act, ss. 26–35; Trustee Act 1893, Amendment Act, 1894; 1958 Act, ss. 43–55. See Carswell, *op. cit.*, pp. 98–111. See also *Re Kavanagh's Application* (1984) Unrep. (H.C., R.I.).

[59] *Re Cane's Trusts* [1895] 1 I.R. 172; *Re Ruthven's Trusts* [1906] 1 I.R. 236; *Re Kenny's Trusts* [1906] 1 I.R. 531; *Re Queenstown Dry Dock Shipbuilding and Engineering Co.* [1918] 1 I.R. 356.

[60] Thus s. 43 (1) (a) of the 1958 Act includes vesting orders in cases where a trustee has been appointed *out of court*, cf. 1893 Act, s. 26 (i); see *Re Ruthven's Trusts* [1906] 1 I.R. 236. Cf. also s. 51 (1) (a) of the 1958 Act and s. 35 (1) (i) of the 1893 Act, see *Re Cane's Trusts* [1895] 1 I.R. 172. S. 43 (1) (b) (iii) includes the case of a corporation which has been dissolved, cf. *Re General Accident Corp.* [1904] 1 Ch. 147 and *Re Taylor's Agreement Trusts* [1904] 2 Ch. 737 and *Re Ruddington Land* [1909] 1 Ch. 701.

trustee becoming of unsound mind to make a petition to the Lord Chief Justice, as successor to the Lord Chancellor of Ireland, for an order to be made under the Trustee Acts, 1850 and 1852.[61] The 1958 Act also confers a new power to make vesting orders in respect of an infant's beneficial interest in property, to facilitate the application of capital or income for the maintenance, education or benefit of the infant.[62]

B. RETIREMENT

10.011. A trustee may retire from a trust in a number of ways. Retirement should not be confused with disclaimer. There is nothing to stop a trustee from the very beginning refusing to take up the office of trustee and it seems that he may still disclaim even though he indicated to the testator of the will establishing the trust that he would act.[63] Once he has accepted the office of trustee, however, he can no longer disclaim (and vice versa),[64] though he may be able to retire. It is wise, therefore, to signify disclaimer by some unequivocal act, such as execution of a deed to that effect.[65] Acceptance of the office of trustee may be implied from the circumstances of the case,[66] Upon disclaimer by one trustee, the trust property is left to be administered by the other trustees and, in the case of disclaimer by a sole trustee, the property reverts on trust to the settlor or, if he is dead, to his personal representatives.[67]

10.012. As we have already stated, once a trustee has accepted the office he cannot disclaim and can only seek retirement.[68] He can always retire if there is an express clause in the trust instrument permitting him to do so. He can also retire if he receives the consent of all the beneficiaries, provided they are *sui juris* and collectively are entitled to the whole beneficial interest held under the trust.[69] Apart from these circumstances, there are statutory provisions for retirement in both parts of Ireland. First, the retirement may be facilitated by exercise of the statutory power of appointment of new

---

[61] 1958 Act, s. 43 (1) (*g*). As to the Republic, see *Re Smith's Trusts* (1870) I.R. 4 Eq. 180; *Re Burton's Trusts* (1872) I.R. 6 Eq. 270; *Re J.J.D.* [1928] I.R. 538; *Re G.H.L.* [1928] I.R. 543.

[62] S. 53, which thus caters for the difficulties which arose in England in respect of an infant's fee tail in remainder (see *Re Hamilton* (1885) 31 Ch.D. 291; *Cadman* v. *Cadman* (1886) 33 Ch.D. 397; *Re Hambrough's Estate* [1909] 2 Ch. 620) and a fee simple reversion after a life estate (see *Re Badger* [1913] 1 Ch. 385); *cf.* a court's power to charge an infant's fee simple in possession with money for past maintenance, *Re Howarth* (1873) L.R. 8 Ch. 415. See now on the English equivalent to s. 53 (Trustee Act, 1925, s. 53), *Re Heyworth's Contingent Reversionary Interest* [1956] Ch. 364; *Re Meux* [1958] Ch. 154. Also Marshall, "Trustee Act, 1925, s. 53" (1957) 21 Conv. 448.

[63] *Doyle* v. *Blake* (1804) 2 Sch. & Lef. 231 at 239 (*per* Lord Redesdale). See also *Plunket* v. *Smith* (1844) 8 Ir.Eq.R. 523; *Re Somerville* (1878) 1 L.R.Ir.293.

[64] *Ibid.* p. 245.

[65] *Bingham* v. *Clanmorris* (1928) 2 Mol. 253; *Burgh* v. *Hickman* (1852) 3 Ir.Jur. (o.s.) 198.

[66] *E.g.*, after lapse of time, *Re Uniacke* (1844) 1 Jo. & Lat. 1; *Re Needham* (1844) 1 Jo. & Lat. 34; *Wise* v. *Wise* (1845) 2 Jo. & Lat. 403, or through acts solely referrable to the office of trustee; *Ward* v. *Butler* (1824) 2 Mol. 533; *Ardill* v. *Savage* (1838) 1 Ir.Eq.R. 79.

[67] *Bayly* v. *Cumming* (1847) 10 Ir.Eq.R. 405.

[68] See discussion of grounds of retirement in *Doyle* v. *Blake* 1804 2 Sch. & Lef. 231.

[69] See para. 10.007, *supra.* It has been queried in England whether the beneficiaries can do so without the consent of the other trustees, see *Re Brockbank* [1948] Ch. 206.

trustees in substitution for existing trustees,[70] which we discussed above.[71] Secondly, a trustee is given a statutory power to retire, without any such substitution of a new trustee, by executing a deed declaring his desire.[72] In this case, however, there must be at least two trustees left to administer the trust or alternatively, in Northern Ireland only, a trust corporation.[73] Furthermore, the other trustees and any other person, if any, empowered to appoint trustees must agree by deed to the retirement, usually by joining in execution of the deed of retirement itself. Again as a last resort, a trustee may seek a court order. Thus the court has a statutory power to appoint new trustees in substitution for existing trustees wherever it is inexpedient, difficult or impracticable to do so without the court's assistance.[74] There is no statutory power to release trustees without a new appointment, though it appears that the court has inherent jurisdiction to release a trustee in an administration action provided there are sufficient continuing trustees.[75] However, a trustee may take advantage of the statutory power to pay *money or securities* belonging to the trust into court and thereby secure a sufficient discharge,[76] which in practice amounts to retirement to that extent.[77] It seems clear from the authorities that this power can be invoked very rarely[78] and, if lodgment of funds in court is made without sufficient reason, the trustees will have to pay the costs of the beneficiaries' application to withdraw the funds.[79]

C. REMOVAL

10.013. A trustee may be removed from his office under an express power in the trust instrument and by the beneficiaries, provided they are all *sui juris*.[80] Apart from these powers, there is power to remove trustees who refuse or are unfit to act by exercise of the statutory power to appoint new trustees,[81] which we discussed above.[82] Finally, the court has an inherent jurisdiction[83] to remove trustees, which it usually exercises in cases of dishonesty or

---

[70]   1893 Act, s. 10; 1958 Act, s. 35.
[71]   Para. 10.006, *supra*.
[72]   1893 Act, s. 11; 1958 Act, s. 38. Like most of these statutory provisions, this power is subject to a contrary intention expressed in the trust instrument, 1893 Act, s. 11 (3); 1958 Act, s. 68 (2).
[73]   *Cf.* 1893 Act, s. 11 (1) and 1958 Act, s. 38 (1). The 1958 Act also permits retirement from a severable part of a trust as well as from the whole trust.
[74]   1893 Act, s. 25; 1958 Act, s. 40. See cases cited in fn. 35, para. 10.007, *ante*.
[75]   See, *e.g., Att.-Gen.* v. *Drummond* (1842) 3 Dr. & War. 162; *Re Chetwynd's Settlement* [1902] 1 Ch. 692. *Cf. Courtenay* v. *Courtenay* (1846) 3 Jo. & Lat. 519.
[76]   1893 Act, s. 42; 1958 Act, s. 63. See *Re Mulqueen's Trusts* (1881) 7 L.R.Ir. 127.
[77]   *Re Murphy's Trusts* [1900] 1 I.R. 145. See also *Re Belfast Empire Theatre Ltd.* [1963] I.R. 41.
[78]   See discussion in Carswell, *Trustee Acts (Northern Ireland)* (1964), pp. 131–5. Also *Re Molony* (1845) 2 Jo. & Lat. 391; *Ex parte Hillis* (1854) 6 Ir. Jur. (o.s.) 26; *Re Godfrey's Trust* (1852) 2 Ir.Ch.R. 105; *Re Belfast Empire Theatre Ltd.* [1963] I.R. 41.
[79]   *Re Wise's Trusts* (1869) I.R. 3 Eq. 599; *Re Fortune's Trusts* (1870) I.R. 4 Eq. 351.
[80]   Para. 10.007, *supra*.
[81]   1893 Act, s. 10; 1958 Act, s. 35.
[82]   Para. 10.008, *supra*.
[83]   *I.e.*, apart from its statutory power to appoint new trustees under the 1893 Act, s. 25 and 1958 Act, s. 40. See para. 10.007, *supra*. See also *Re Dunbar* (1845) 8 Ir.Eq.R. 71.

incompetence.[84] However, the welfare of the beneficiaries is the overriding consideration and in *Arnott* v. *Arnott*[85] a trustee was removed because she would not agree to anything suggested by her co-trustees.

II. POWERS OF TRUSTEES

10.014. It is important that the trustees have sufficient powers to enable them to carry out satisfactorily the day-to-day administration of the trust and management of the trust property.[86] In the early stages of the development of trusts, of course, the onus was on the settlor or testator to see that the requisite powers were granted expressly in the trust instrument. Solicitors drawing up trust instruments may still prefer to include such powers, but the need for them nowadays is much less owing to the provision of statutory powers[87] in both parts of Ireland. For the most part, these statutory powers are additional to any express powers and are subject to any contrary intention expressed in the trust instrument,[88] to which reference should first be made in every case. The following is an outline of the main statutory powers conferred on trustees in Ireland.

A. SALE

10.015. Where a trustee holds property upon trust for sale or with a power of sale,[89] he is given wide statutory powers relating to conduct of the sale, whether by public auction or private contract.[90] While this statutory power would not normally sanction the granting of a lease,[91] it was held by the Irish courts that the Irish conveyancer's practice of selling land held in fee farm or under a lease by way of a sub-fee farm grant or sub-lease was a proper

---

[84]   *Moore* v. *McGlynn* [1894] 1 I.R. 74 (see *A Casebook on Equity and Trusts in Ireland* (1985), p. 347). On the effect of a trustee's bankruptcy, see *Re Barker's Trusts* (1875) 1 Ch.D. 43. Also *Re Roche* (1842) 2 Dr. & War. 287; *Archbold* v. *Commrs. of Charitable Donations and Bequests* (1849) 2 H.L.C. 440.

[85]   (1924) 58 I.L.T.R. 145. In *O'hUadhaigh* v. *O'Loinsigh* (1975) 109 I.L.T.R. 121, Kenny J. ordered the removal of a trustee who was in breach of an undertaking given to the court.

[86]   And, of course, to see to their various duties, which we discuss below, paras. 10.050 *et seq*. See the English Law Reform Committee's 23rd Report, *Powers and Duties of Trustees* (Cmmd. 8733; 1982).

[87]   Including, or course, powers like that of appointment, discussed at para. 10.006, *supra*.

[88]   See generally throughout the Trustee Act, 1893. S. 68 (2) of the Trustee Act (N.I.), 1958, contains a general provision to this effect. Some statutory powers contained in the 1958 Act cannot be negatived by the terms of the trust instrument, *e.g.*, power to raise money (s. 16), protection against liability in respect of rents and covenants (s. 27) and protection by advertisements (s. 28).

[89]   See further on this subject, para. 8.047, *ante*.

[90]   1893 Act, s. 13; 1958 Act, s. 12. In Northern Ireland this includes a sale of part of the trust land, whether the division is horizontal, vertical or made in any other way, 1958 Act, s. 12 (5). In the Republic, only the court can sanction a sale of land separately from its minerals, 1893 Act, s. 44 and see *Re Hallowes' Trusts* [1906] 1 I.R. 526. *Cf.* Settled Land Act, 1882, ss. 33 and 17 (1), para. 8.074, *ante*. See also Samuel, "The Duty of Trustees to Obtain the Best Price" (1975) 39 Conv. 177.

[91]   *Cf.* the position of a trustee, where land is already leased, when it comes into his hands at the inception of the trust, *Drohan* v. *Drohan* (1809) 1 Ba. & B. 185; *Fitzpatrick* v. *Waring* (1882) 11 L.R.Ir. 35 (see *A Casebook in Equity and Trusts in Ireland* (1985), p. 557).

exercise of this statutory power of sale.[92] This view has now been given statutory recognition in Northern Ireland.[93]

10.016. Trustees are further empowered to sell property subject to depreciatory conditions without fear of impeachment by any beneficiary, provided it does not appear that the consideration for the sale is thereby rendered inadequate.[94] Similar protection is afforded the purchaser in such a sale, unless it appears that he was acting in collusion with the trustee when the contract for sale was made.[95] Furthermore, a trustee, whether vendor or, more significantly, a purchaser, may sell or buy land without excluding the rules as to title contained in section 2 of the Vendor and Purchaser Act, 1874.[96]

10.017. Finally, in Northern Ireland, to further the policy of keeping trusts off the title to property, a new statutory provision has been introduced to relieve purchasers of the need to inquire into the trustees' need to raise money by sale of trust property or as to its application.[97] Purchasers from personal representatives are in this position in both parts of Ireland.[98]

B. RECEIPTS

10.018. It is provided by statute in both parts of Ireland that a receipt in writing of a trustee for any money, securities or other personal property or effects payable, transferable or deliverable to him under any trust or power is a sufficient discharge to the person paying, transferring or delivering.[99] Such a receipt effectually exonerates that person from seeing to the application of the money or being answerable for any loss or misapplication.[1] Normally all the trustees should join in issuing a receipt, at least so long as they are performing the role of trustees.[2] In the case of a charitable trust, however, a majority of two-thirds of the trustees[3] may issue a receipt.[4] Though the

---

[92] See on the 1893 Act the discussion of the Irish authorities by Lord MacDermott L.C.J. in *Re Murphy* [1957] N.I. 156 (see *A Casebook on Equity and Trusts in Ireland* (1985), p. 546). *Cf.* the position of a tenant for life in relation to his statutory power of sale under s. 3 of the Settled Land Act, 1882, *Re Braithwaite's Settled Estate* [1922] 1 I.R. 71. See further, para. 8.069, *ante.*

[93] 1958 Act, s. 12 (2) and (3). See also in relation to sales by personal representatives, Administration of Estates Act (N.I.), 1955, s. 40 (1) (*c*).

[94] 1893 Act, s. 14 (1); 1958 Act, s. 13 (1).

[95] 1893 Act, s. 14 (2); 1958 Act, s. 13 (2).

[96] 1893 Act, s. 15; 1958 Act, s. 13 (4).

[97] 1958 Act, s. 17. It is doubtful if this relieves a purchaser with actual knowledge of an improper sale or of misapplication of the purchase money, see Carswell, *op. cit.*, p. 42. See, however, the position of a purchaser who gets a receipt in writing from the trustees, *infra.*

[98] Succession Act, 1965, s. 61 (R.I.); Administration of Estates Act (N.I.), 1955, s. 33.

[99] 1893 Act, s. 20; 1958 Act, s. 14.

[1] In Northern Ireland, s. 14 (1) of the 1958 Act expressly preserves the position under s. 39 (1) of the Settled Land Act, 1882, which requires a receipt for capital money from at least two trustees of the settlement, unless a trust corporation is acting as trustee, see s. 14 (2) of the 1958 Act and para. 8.093, *ante.*

[2] *Lee* v. *Sankey* (1873) L.R. 15 Eq. 204. *Cf.* the power of an executor, *Charlton* v. *Earl of Durham* (1869) 4 Ch.App. 433.

[3] In the Republic, "assembled at a meeting of their body duly constituted" (Charities Act 1961, s. 55); in Northern Ireland, "for the time being acting in the administration of a charity" (Charities Act (N.I.), 1964, s. 26 (1)).

[4] See para. 9.113, *ante.*

statutory provisions do not say so expressly, it seems that a person will not be exonerated where he has prior knowledge that a trustee intends to commit a breach of trust.[5]

C. INSURANCE

10.019. The trustees may insure any trust building or other insurable property against loss or damage by fire, flood, storm and tempest.[6] The premiums may be paid out of trust income without the need to obtain the consent of any person entitled to that income.[7] In the Republic, this power is excluded in the case of any building or property which the trustees are bound forthwith to convey absolutely to any beneficiary upon being requested to do so,[8] but no such exclusion exists now in Northern Ireland.[9] Also in the Republic, the amount of insurance cover is not to exceed three-fourths the full value of the building or property,[10] whereas in Northern Ireland it may now cover up to the full value.[11]

10.020. In Northern Ireland,[12] there is an express provision that insurance money received by trustees or any beneficiary in respect of loss or damage to the trust property[13] is to be treated and applied as capital money for the purposes of the trust.[14] Such money may be used in rebuilding or repairing the damaged property, subject to the consent of any person required by the trust instrument.[15] This provision does not prejudice any other right, statutory or otherwise, which any person may have to require application in rebuilding, reinstating or repairing,[16] such as a lessor or lessee.[17]

D. COMPOUNDING LIABILITIES

10.021. Trustees have a statutory power to compound liabilities as they consider expedient, without being responsible for any loss occasioned by any action or thing done by them in good faith.[18] This covers such things as:

---

[5] *Fernie* v. *Maguire* (1844) 6 Ir.Eq.R. 137.

[6] 1893 Act, s. 18; 1958 Act, s. 19.

[7] *Ibid.* See *Re Kingham* [1897] 1 I.R. 170. In a special case, however, the court may authorise payment out of capital, see *Re Kinahan's Trusts* [1921] 1 I.R. 210 (see *A Casebook on Equity and Trusts in Ireland* (1985), p. 550).

[8] 1893 Act, s. 18 (2).

[9] 1958 Act, s. 19. Of course, such a beneficiary can still stop the trustees insuring at any time by putting an end to the trust under the rule in *Saunders* v. *Vautier*, para. 10.007, *ante*.

[10] 1893 Act, s. 18 (1).

[11] 1958 Act, s. 19.

[12] A similar provision is to be found in s. 20 of the English Trustee Act, 1925.

[13] This provision covers also property subject to a settlement within the Settled Land Acts, 1882–90.

[14] 1958 Act, s. 20. In the case of settled land or chattels, it is deemed to be capital money arising under the Settled Land Acts, 1882–90, see s. 20 (3). Also para. 8.093, *ante*.

[15] S. 20 (4).

[16] S. 20 (4).

[17] Or a mortgagee, see Conveyancing Act, 1881, s. 23 (3).

[18] 1893 Act, s. 21; 1958 Act, s. 15. See remarks of Fitzgibbon L.J. on this power in *Graham* v. *McCashin* [1901] 1 I.R. 404 at 411.

acceptance of any composition or security for any debt claimed; allowing any time for payment of a debt; compromising,[19] compounding, abandoning, referring to arbitration or otherwise settling a debt or claim relating to the trust.[20] In Northern Ireland, there has been added: acceptance of property before the time at which it is made transferable or payable; severance and apportionment of any blended trust funds or property; payment or allowing any debt or claim on any evidence thought sufficient.[21]

10.022. This statutory power also applied expressly to a personal representative,[22] and still does in Northern Ireland, though a separate provision also exists.[23] In the Republic, the earlier provisions in the Trustee Act, 1893, have been replaced by a new statutory provision for personal representatives,[24] which extends the 1893 provisions to the same extent as the Northern Ireland provisions do.[25]

E. RAISING MONEY

10.023. In Northern Ireland only, there is a new statutory power to raise money wherever trustees are authorised to pay or apply capital money subject to the trust for any purpose or in any manner.[26] The money may be raised by sale, conversion, calling in or mortgaging the trust property. Without this statutory power,[27] which cannot be overridden by the trust instrument,[28] it appears, and this would seem to remain the case in the Republic, that a trust for sale will not, on its own, be treated as impliedly conferring a power to raise money by mortgage,[29] nor will a trust to raise money by mortgage be treated ordinarily as conferring a power of sale.[30]

10.024. This power is followed up in Northern Ireland by conferring statutory protection on purchasers and mortgagees dealing with the trustees.[31] Such persons are not to be concerned to see that the money raised

---

[19] See discussion of the power to compromise in *Re Boyle* [1947] I.R. 61 (relating to executors) (see *A Casebook on Equity and Trusts in Ireland* (1985), p. 551) and by the House of Lords in *Chapman* v. *Chapman* [1954] A.C. 429. See also *Graham* v. *McCashin* [1901] 1 I.R. 404. *Cf* the discussion by the English Court of Appeal in *Re Earl of Stafford* [1980] Ch. 28.

[20] 1893 Act, s. 21; 1958 Act, s. 15 (1) (*d*)–(*f*).

[21] 1958 Act, s. 15 (1) (*a*)–(*c*).

[22] 1893 Act, s. 21 (1); 1958 Act, s. 15 (1). See *Re Boyle* [1947] I.R. 61 (see *A Casebook on Equity and Trusts in Ireland* (1985), p. 551).

[23] Administration of Estates Act (N.I.), 1955, s. 40 (9), preserved by the 1958 Act, s. 15 (2).

[24] Succession Act, 1965, s. 60 (8).

[25] Fn. 23, *supra*.

[26] 1958 Act, s. 16. See also s. 16 of the English Trustee Act, 1925.

[27] Which, however, does not apply to charitable trustees (see Charities Act (N.I.), 1964, s. 18) or trustees of a settlement for the purposes of the Settled Land Acts, 1882–90, not being also trustees exercising the powers of tenant for life under s. 60 of the Settled Land Act, 1882, see 1958 Act, s. 16 (2) and para. 8.028, *ante*.

[28] Contrary to the general provision in s. 68 (2) of the 1958 Act.

[29] *Devaynes* v. *Robinson* (1857) 24 Beav. 89, espec. at 91 (*per* Romilly M.R.); *cf.* a power of sale, *Ball* v. *Harris* (1839) 4 My. & Cr. 264 at 267 (*per* Lord Cottenham). However, in *O'Reilly* v. *O'Reilly* (1975) 109 I.L.T.R. 121, Kenny J. held that a trust, under which the trustees were to keep a farming enterprise going "as if they were beneficially entitled thereto", included by implication a power to mortgage the farm land so as to raise money to purchase farm machinery.

[30] *Drake* v. *Whitmore* (1852) 5 De G. & Sm. 619. See Carswell, *Trustee Acts (Northern Ireland)* (1964), pp. 40–1. Also *Lysaght* v. *Warren* (1846) 10 Ir.L.R. 269.

[31] 1958 Act, s. 17. See also s. 17 of the English Trustee Act, 1925.

by the sale or mortgage is wanted, or that no more than is wanted is raised, or otherwise as to the money's application. Though the statute does not say so expressly, it is questionable whether it protects a purchaser or mortgagee who has actual knowledge that the money being raised is excessive or unnecessary.[32]

F. Reversionary Interests

10.025. Again in Northern Ireland only,[33] trustees are given new statutory powers of dealing with reversionary interests [34] settled by the reversioner when they fall into possession in the hands of the trustees.[35] These powers include agreeing or ascertaining the value of the interest as the trustees think fit,[36] accepting authorised investments[37] in satisfaction of such interests[38] and allowing deductions for duties, costs, charges and expenses as they think proper or reasonable.[39] the trustees are not responsible in such cases for any loss occasioned by any act or thing so done by them in good faith.[40]

10.026. Trustees in Northern Ireland are also given a statutory power to carry out valuations of trust property from time to time[41] and to have the trust accounts examined or audited not more than once in three years, unless there is some special reason for doing this more often.[42] Obviously on some of these matters it would be wise of the trustees to exercise their further statutory powers to employ professional agents.[43] In the Republic of Ireland, it is common to have these matters covered by an express clause in the trust instrument, as, indeed, is still often done in Northern Ireland despite the statutory provisions.

G. Deposit of Documents

10.027. A new statutory power to deposit documents relating to the trust or its property for safe custody is conferred in Northern Ireland.[44] The deposit may be made in any bank or any company whose business includes the

---

[32] See para. 10.017, fn. 97, *ante*.

[33] See also s. 22 of the English Trustee Act, 1925.

[34] Para. 5.004, *ante*.

[35] 1958 Act, s. 23.

[36] S. 23 (1) (*a*).

[37] See 1958 Act, s. 67.

[38] S. 23 (1) (*b*).

[39] S. 23 (1) (*c*).

[40] S. 23 (1). See on the subject of "good faith," *Re Greenwood* (1911) 105 L.T. 509. Note also the power of the court to relieve trustees who have acted honestly and reasonably and ought fairly to be excused, para. 10.104, *post*

[41] S. 23 (3).

[42] S. 23 (4).

[43] Para. 10.034, *post*.

[44] 1958 Act, s. 22. Note also the statutory powers of charity trustees in both parts of Ireland, para. 9.111, *ante*. S. 7 of the 1958 Act (N.I.) deals with investment and custody of bearer securities, para. 10.059, *post*.

undertaking of safe custody of documents and the cost is to be paid out of the income of the trust property.[45]

H. RENEWING LEASEHOLDS

10.028.   In both parts of Ireland, trustees of renewable leaseholds, which are so common in many parts of Ireland,[46] have a statutory power to renew such leaseholds and to pay for the renewal out of funds in their hands or, if necessary, by raising funds by mortgage of the land to be comprised in the renewed lease or other land subject to the same trusts.[47] The trustees may, however, be required to use their best endeavours to obtain a renewal by any person having a beneficial interest in the lease.[48]

I. CONCURRING WITH OTHERS

10.029.   In the case of a tenancy in common, from time to time a problem may arise where a trustee or personal representative holds one of the undivided shares in his personal capacity and another as trustee, and it is intended to sell the complete tenancy in the land. Objections may be raised that the trustee or personal representative ought not to act in such a case because of his dual capacity and the danger of a conflict of interest and duty.[49] In Northern Ireland, however, this problem is resolved by giving the trustee or personal representative in such a case of statutory power to concur with other persons in a sale or other exercise of powers, despite his interest in another undivided share of the property.[50] No such statutory power exists in the Republic.

J. DELEGATION

10.030.   The general rule is that a trustee may not delegate his office, *i.e.*, his powers and duties, to anyone else.[51] A trustee has a special fiduciary relationship with his beneficiaries and must look after their interests himself; the maxim *delegatus delegare non potest* applies.[52] Indeed, in *Re O'Flanagan and Ryan's Contract*[53] it was held that the very act of delegation may amount to a breach of trust by the trustee. However, like most general rules, this rule has exceptions and, even before statutory intervention, the courts recognised that it had to give way in certain circumstances.

---

[45]   For the trustees' duties with respect to trust documents of title, etc., see the discussion by Kekewich J. in *Field* v. *Field* [1894] 1 Ch. 425; also *Re Sisson's Settlement* [1903] 1 Ch. 262. Documents may, however, be held by a co-trustee, *Cottam* v. *Eastern Counties Rail Co.* (1860) 1 J. & H. 242.

[46]   Ch. 4, *ante*. Not surprisingly, there is no equivalent of the English Trustee Act, 1925.

[47]   1893 Act, s. 19; 1958 Act, s. 21. As to the trustees' powers of leasing generally, see *Fitzpatrick* v. *Waring* (1882) 11 L.R.Ir. 35 (see *A Casebook on Equity and Trusts in Ireland* (1985), p. 557).

[48]   1893 Act, s. 19 (1); 1958 Act, s. 21 (1).

[49]   See the discussion in *Re Cooper and Allen's Contract* (1876) 4 Ch.D. 802, espec. at 815-7 (*per* Jessel M.R.).

[50]   1958 Act, s. 25.

[51]   See *Carr* v. *Connor* (1929) 63 I.L.T.R. 185.

[52]   Thus the same general rule applies to other fiduciaries, *e.g.*, personal representatives, *Joy* v. *Campbell* (1804) 1 Sch. & Lef. 328.

[53]   [1905] 1 I.R. 280 (see *A Casebook on Equity and Trusts in Ireland* (1985), p. 565).

10.031. First, a trustee may always delegate under an express power granted by the trust instrument, in which case he merely has to ensure that the delegation in question is within the terms of the instrument.[54]

10.032. Secondly, the courts have long recognised that in certain circumstances it is inevitable that some degree of delegation must take place. Indeed, in some situations, it might even amount to a breach of trust *not* to delegate, *e.g.*, where expert help is required to effect a transaction relating to the trust property, such as employment of a solicitor to attend to conveyancing. In matters of this kind, the courts adopted the view that the trustees were entitled to delegate matters which would be delegated in the ordinary course of business, *i.e.*, matters in respect of which it was quite reasonable in all the circumstances to employ agents.[55] Lord Redesdale remarked in one case:

> "He could not transact business without trusting some person, and it would be impossible for him to discharge his duty, if he is made responsible where he remitted money to a person to whom he would himself have given credit, and would in his own business have remitted money in the same way."[56]

This approach to the necessities of administration of a trust has been given some statutory recognition in both parts of Ireland, though statutory intervention in this field has not always been as successful as it might have been.[57]

10.033. Under section 17 of the Trustee Act, 1893, which is still in force in the Republic of Ireland, trustees may entrust solicitors with the receipt of purchase money and allow solicitors or bankers to receive insurance moneys.[58] It appears that a specific authorisation in these matters must be given by the trustees and a general power of attorney to perform administrative acts will not do.[59] In each case the delegation of power to receive money is dependent upon the solicitor having custody of a deed containing, or having endorsed upon it, a receipt for the money or the solicitor or banker having custody of the policy of insurance with a receipt signed by the trustees.[60] In such cases the trustees are not chargeable with

---

[54] *Doyle* v. *Blake* (1804) 2 Sch. & Lef. 231. Note, however, that an express power of delegation in a will concerning charitable funds may be superseded by a scheme approved by the court which provides for delegation. In such a case, delegation may be governed by the terms of the court's scheme and the trustees may be unable to invoke their statutory powers of delegation, it being held that the "instrument creating . . . the trust" is the scheme and not the original will, see *Re Murphy's Trusts* [1967] N.I. 36.

[55] See *Joy* v. *Campbell* (1804) 1 Sch. & Lef. 328; *Rochfort* v. *Seaton* [1896] 1 I.R. 18.

[56] *Joy* v. *Campbell, op. cit.*, p. 341.

[57] See Jones, "Delegation by Trustees: A Reappraisal" (1959) 22 M.L.R. 381; Sheridan, "The Trustee Act, 1966" (1965) 4 *The Solicitor* 186.

[58] In Northern Ireland s. 17 is re-enacted in s. 24 (3) of the Trustee Act (N.I.), 1958, which is made retrospective by s. 24 (4).

[59] See *Re Hetling and Merton's Contract* [1893] 3 Ch. 269.

[60] This may still be the case under s. 24 (3) of the 1958 Act (N.I.), despite the extension generally of the power of delegation in s. 24, see Carswell, *op. cit.*, p. 57. See also *Re Sheppard* [1911] 1 Ch. 50 at 59 (*per* Parker J.).

breach of trust by reason only of making such a delegation, but they remain liable if they permit the money to remain in the hands of solicitors or bankers longer than is reasonably necessary to enable payment to the trustees.[61]

10.034. In Northern Ireland, the trustees' power to delegate administrative matters to professional agents has been considerably extended by section 24 of the Trustee Act (N.I.), 1958.[62] In effect, it enables trustees[63] to make use of experts, such as solicitors, bankers and stockbrokers, in the administration of the trust in much the same way as they would make use of such persons in handling their own private affairs. It is important to realise, however, that the section does not enable the trustees to delegate matters calling for their exercise of a discretion or, indeed, their own judgment. For example, the trustees, and the trustees alone, are fixed with various duties with respect to handling the trust property, including its proper investment.[64] The trustees may seek the *advice* of stockbrokers on the merits of various investments and may employ them actually to make particular investments but the decision whether to make those particular investments rather than other investments must be taken by the trustees and they will remain responsible for any loss suffered.[65] However, they are *not* liable for default of agents employed[66] "in good faith,"[67] though this seems to allow a "foolish, but honest" trustee to be excused, which he might not otherwise be.[68] In equity the rule was that an expert could only be employed to perform functions within his own sphere of expertise,[69] *e.g.*, a solicitor should not be employed as a valuer or an accountant, and this would still seem to apply.

10.035. Under Section 24(2) of the 1958 Act (N.I.), trustees may appoint persons to act as their agents or attorneys in general administration of trust property situated outside the United Kingdom.[70]

10.036. Section 24 of the Trustee Act, 1893, also still in force in the Republic of Ireland,[71] provides a statutory indemnity for trustees in respect of acts and neglects by other trustees, bankers or brokers with whom trust money may be deposited.[72]

---

[61]   1893 Act, s. 17 (3); 1958 Act, s. 24 (5).
[62]   *Cf.* the English Trustee Act, 1925, s. 23. See *Re Murphy's Trusts* [1967] N.I. 36.
[63]   The section also applies to personal representatives, s. 24 (1).
[64]   See para. 10.053, *post.*
[65]   See the discussion by Maugham J. in his controversial decision in *Re Vickery* [1931] 1 Ch. 572 and (1931) 47 L.Q.R. 330 and 463.
[66]   Again the choice of selection of agent must be made by the trustees themselves and not delegated, *Robinson* v. *Harkin* [1896] 2 Ch. 415.
[67]   S. 24 (1). *Cf.* the trustees' non-accountability under s. 31 in respect of money or securities deposited with agents, *infra.*
[68]   In equity, the test was rather one of "reasonableness," *i.e.*, a more objective criterion based on ordinary care and prudence, see *Rochfort* v. *Seaton* [1896] 1 I.R. 18; also *Waring* v. *Waring* (1852) 3 Ir.Ch.R. 331.
[69]   *Re Weall* (1889) 42 Ch.D. 674.
[70]   This may be largely declaratory of the position in equity, *Stuart* v. *Norton* (1860) 14 Moo.P.C. 17. See also *Green* v. *Whitehead* [1930] 1 Ch. 38.
[71]   Re-enacted in s. 31 of the Trustee Act (N.I.), 1958.
[72]   Such an indemnity clause was a common provision inserted in trust instruments executed prior to 1893, *Re Brier* (1884) 26 Ch.D. 238; *Re Munton* [1927] 1 Ch. 262.

10.037. Each trustee is answerable and accountable for his own acts and defaults only, *unless* there is "wilful default"[73] on his part. The section makes it clear that a trustee is not necessarily liable for loss of property simply because he signed,a receipt for sake of conformity,[74] a recognition of the complexity of trust administration in the modern world and the extreme difficulty an individual trustee would have in keeping track of every piece of business. It is also provided that the trustees may reimburse themselves out of the trust property for expenses incurred in execution of the trust or exercise of their powers.[75] This right to expenses, not to be confused with remuneration,[76] incurred in the proper administration of the trust was also recognised at common law.[77]

10.038. Finally, section 26 of the Trustee Act (N.I.), 1958,[78] introduces a new power of delegation for trustees in Northern Ireland. Unlike the powers previously discussed, this power enables trustees to delegate their trust altogether, *i.e.*, so that the agents may exercise all the trustees' powers and discretions and carry out their duties.[79] Section 26 now enables a trustee to delegate all his responsibilities, by a power of attorney, and is no longer restricted to during his absence from the United Kingdom,[80] which delegation is to operate for a period not exceeding 12 months. It is essential to note, however, that in this case the trustee,[81] donor of the power, remains fully liable for all the donee's acts and defaults, as if they were his own.[82]

K. INDEMNITIES

10.039. There are various statutory provisions in force in both parts of Ireland giving trustees indemnities in certain situations. First, there is the general provision that a trustee is chargeable only for money and securities

---

[73] See discussion of this phrase by Maugham J. in *Re Vickery* [1931] 1 Ch. 572. Also Stannard, "Wilful Default" [1979] Conv. 345. It is not easy to reconcile s. 31 with s. 24 of the 1958 Act, see Carswell, *op. cit.*, pp. 55–6.

[74] See also 1958 Act (N.I.), s. 31 (1).

[75] 1893 Act, s. 24; 1958 Act, s. 31 (2). *Hamilton* v. *Tighe* [1898] 1 I.R. 123; *Graham* v. *McCashin* [1901] 1 I.R. 404; *Martin* v. *Wilson* [1913] 1 I.R. 470; *Re White* [1918] 1 I.R. 19; *Fogarty* v. *O'Donoughue* [1926] I.R. 531.

[76] Para. 10.070, *post.*

[77] *Courtney* v. *Rumley* (1871) I.R. 6 Eq. 99, espec. at 106 (*per* Chatterton V.-C. (see *A Casebook on Equity and Trusts in Ireland* (1985), p. 604). See also *De Burgh* v. *McClintock* (1883) 11 L.R.Ir. 220; *Carson* v. *Sloane* (1884) 13 L.R.Ir. 139; *Coppinger* v. *Shekleton* (1885) 15 L.R.Ir. 461.

[78] As substituted by s. 9 of the Powers of Attorney Act (N.I.), 1971. See *Survey of the Land Law of Northern Ireland* (1971), ch. 9. Also *O'Kane* v. *Mullan* [1925] N.I. 1. See generally on the 1971 Act, para. 11.40, *post.*

[79] Thus reversing the general common law position, which remained largely untouched by the Trustee Act, 1893 and which still governs the Republic of Ireland. See para. 10.030, *supra.* See, however, the Conveyancing Acts, 1881, Part XI and 1882, ss. 8 and 9. S 26 (8) removes the necessity for the power of attorney to refer specifically to special powers granted by the instrument, see *Re Donoughmore and Hackett's Contract* [1918] 1 I.R. 359.

[80] *Cf.* the old s. 26 (3). The various requirements for execution of a valid power of attorney are laid down in the Powers of Attorney Act (N.I.), 1971, under which it is no longer necessary to file the instrument creating the power at the Supreme Court; *cf.* the old s. 26 (4) and (5) of the Trustee Act (N.I.), 1958 and Conveyancing Act, 1881, s. 48.

[81] The section also applies to a tenant for life and a trustee exercising the powers of a tenant for life under s. 60 of the Settled Land Act, 1882.

[82] S. 26 (2).

actually received by him, notwithstanding his signing any receipt for the sake of conformity, and is answerable and accountable for his own acts and defaults only[83] and not those of any other trustee or banker with whom trust money may be deposited, nor for any other loss, *unless* this is due to his own wilful default.[84]

10.040. Secondly, section 27 of the Trustee Act (N.I.), 1958, enables a trustee holding land under a fee farm grant or lease[85] and liable in respect of rent, covenants or indemnities to satisfy all liabilities up to date and then to sell or distribute the trust property, thereby freeing himself from further personal liability under the grant or lease.[86] This section in fact extends to trustees in Northern Ireland protection conferred on personal representatives in both parts of Ireland by sections 27 and 28 of the Law of Property Amendment Act, 1859 (Lord St. Leonards' Act). The purpose of the section is to provide statutory protection for trustees and so it operates without prejudice to the right of the fee farm grantor or lessor to follow the trust property into the hands of the beneficiaries.[87] Thirdly, section 28 of the 1958 Act extends to trustees and real property in Northern Ireland the statutory protection introduced in both parts of Ireland for personal representatives in relation to personalty by section 29 of Lord St. Leonards' Act.[88] After making the prescribed advertisements in the *Belfast Gazette* and daily newspapers, giving notice of their intention to convey or distribute trust property, the trustees may proceed with the conveyance or distribution, protected from liability to any creditors or beneficiaries of whose claims they did not receive notice.[89] Once again the right to follow property or trace assets is preserved[90] and the trustees still have the usual duty to make inquiries and searches.[91]

10.041. Fourthly, in both parts of Ireland a trustee acting under a power of attorney is protected against any liability arising from circumstances affecting the validity of the power, *provided* he does not know of those circumstances and acts in good faith.[92] However, this does not prejudice the rights of any person entitled to money paid by the trustee against the payee and, indeed, the plaintiff has the same remedy against the payee as he would have had against the trustee.[93]

---

[83] See para. 10.037, *supra.*

[84] 1893 Act, s. 24; 1958 Act, s. 31. See para. 10.036, *supra.* See also *re* contracts of employment entered into on behalf of the trust, *Wright* v. *Day* [1895] 2 I.R. 337.

[85] Note the wide definitions of these terms in s. 27 (3). *Cf. Millar* v. *Sinclair* [1903] 1 I.R. 150.

[86] Thus dealing with the kind of situation which occurred in *Re Lawley* [1911] 2 Ch. 530.

[87] Which right cannot be removed by an express clause in the trust instrument, s. 27 (2). On the subject of tracing, see *Welwood* v. *Grady* [1904] 1 I.R. 388; *Re Nolan* [1949] I.R. 197; *Shanahan's Stamp Auctions Ltd.* v. *Farrelly* [1962] I.R. 386 (see *A Casebook on Equity and Trusts in Ireland* (1985), p. 636). Para. 10.109, *post.*

[88] See *Stuart* v. *Babington* (1891) 27 L.R.Ir. 551.

[89] S. 28 (2). See *Re Land Credit Co. of Ireland* (1872) 21 W.R. 718.

[90] S. 28 (2) (*a*).

[91] S. 28 (2) (*b*).

[92] 1893 Act, s. 23; 1958 Act, s. 30. See further on powers of attorney, ch. 11, *post.*

[93] 1893 Act, s. 23; 1958 Act, s. 30 (*a*) and (*b*).

L. Maintenance

10.042. Trustees have extensive statutory powers to use trust income for the maintenance of minor beneficiaries in both parts of Ireland.[94] In the Republic of Ireland the matter is governed by section 43 of the Conveyancing Act, 1881,[95] which applies wherever any property is held by trustees in trust for a minor, either for life or for any greater interest and whether absolutely or contingently on his attaining the age of (now) 18 (as a result of section 2 of the Age of Majority Act 1985, though the trustees' powers continue until the minor reaches 21 in respect of instruments made before 1st March 1985, under the Schedule, paragraph 3 (1), to the Act) or on the occurrence of any event before attaining that age, and by section 11 of the Guardianship of Infants Act, 1964, and sections 57 and 58 of the Succession Act, 1965. In cases within section 43 of the 1881 Act, the trustees may, at their sole discretion, pay to the minor's parent or guardian, if any, or otherwise apply for the minor's maintenance, education or benefit, the income of the property, whether or not there is any fund applicable to the same purpose or any person bound by law to provide for the minor's maintenance or education.[96] Surplus income must be accumulated and held on trust as capital, but these accumulations may be drawn on for maintenance in subsequent years.[97]

10.043. This power of maintenance has been extended in Northern Ireland by section 32 of the Trustee Act (N.I.), 1958, to cover all cases where a minor is entitled to any estate or interest whatsoever, whether vested or contingent, including where the vesting is to occur *after* the minor reaches the age of 18.[98] In the last case, once the minor reaches 18 the trustees are *obliged*, unless the trust instrument provides otherwise, to pay the income of the property and any accretions[99] to the minor until he does attain a vested estate or interest therein or dies or until failure of his estate or interest.[1] Section 32 contains a new statutory provision governing the accumulation of income not used for the minor's maintenance, under which the surplus

---

[94] See Bewes, "Maintenance and Education" (1895) 11 L.Q.R. 76; Ker, "Trustees' Powers of Maintenance" (1953) 17 Conv. 273; Nuttal, "Maintenance and Education" (1894) 10 L.Q.R. 330 and (1895) 11 L.Q.R. 172; Vaizey "Maintenance Clauses" (1891) L.Q.R. 370. For similar powers in respect of an intestate's estate, see Succession Act, 1965, s. 58 (4); Administration of Estates Act (N.I.), 1955, s. 38(4). Such powers may be conferred expressly, see *Wilson* v. *Knox* (1884) 13 L.R.Ir. 349; *Re Byrne* (1889) 23 L.R.Ir. 260; *Pierce* v. *Hewson* (1901) 1 N.I.J.R. 65; *Russell* v. *Russell* [1903] 1 I.R. 168; *Duffield* v. *McMaster* [1906] 1 I.R. 333.

[95] See also s. 42, especially subs. (4) and (5), which governs maintenance of minors entitled to settled land. Ss. 42 (4) and (5) and 43 of the 1881 Act have been replaced in Northern Ireland by s. 32 of the Trustee Act (N.I.), 1958. On s. 43 of the 1881 Act, see *Re Lynch's Trusts* [1931] I.R. 517; *Re O'Connell's Estate* [1932] I.R. 298 (see *A Casebook on Equity and Trusts in Ireland* (1985), pp. 567 and 589).

[96] S. 43 (1); *cf.* Trustee Act (N.I.), 1958, s. 32. This power operates only in the absence of a contrary intention and takes effect subject to the terms of the trust instrument 1881 Act, s. 43 (3); 1958 Act, s. 68 (2). Such a power may be conferred expressly by the trust instrument, see *Robinson* v. *Moore* [1962–63] Ir.Jur.Rep. 29; *Re Finnerty's Will Trusts* [1970] I.R. 221.

[97] S. 43 (2); *cf.* 1958 Act, s. 32 (3).

[98] S. 32 (1) (the age being reduced to 18 from 21 by s. 1 (3) of the Age of Majority Act (N.I.), 1969; see also Sched. 1, Pt. I to the 1969 Act). It is also made applicable expressly to the case of a vested annuity, in which case the trustees are to treat the annuity as income from trust property, s. 32 (5).

[99] Due to accumulation of surplus income, see s. 32 (3), *infra*.

[1] S. 32 (1) (*b*).

income must be accumulated in the way of compound interest by investment in authorised securities[2] and the accumulations must then be held on the statutory trusts laid down.[3] Under these trusts, the trustees must hold the accumulations for the minor absolutely[4] if he attains 21 or marries and either by that time he had a vested interest or on occurrence of that event became entitled to the capital absolutely or in tail; otherwise the trustees must hold the accumulations as accretions to capital, subject, however, to their power to use the past accumulations to make up inadequate income in any particular year.

10.044. For both the 1881 and 1958 statutory powers to operate, it is essential that there be income available to the trustees. The general rule laid down by the judges was that no future or contingent gift, *except* residuary personalty, could be regarded as carrying intermediate income which could be applied for maintenance.[5] Like all general rules this one is also subject to exceptions, so that the matter really seems to be one of determining the intention of the settlor or testator in the particular case. In *Johnston* v. *O'Neill*, Chatterton V.-C. put the matter thus:

> "It is, no doubt, the general rule that general legacies payable at a future day, even though vested, do not carry interest before the day of payment, except legacies given to a child by a parent, or a person in *loco parentis*. But to this general rule there are exceptions, one of which is, that where a fund is directed to be presently separated from the general personal estate for the purpose of providing for the future payment of certain legacies, it carries the interest accruing up to the time of payment, to the legatees, with the capital sum. In such cases, the rule that the interest follows the capital prevails, and the legatee gets his legacy with its interim accretions. The effect of a direction to set apart the special fund at once, or at some time prior to the day of payment, is to dedicate that fund, with its increase, from the time appointed for setting it apart, to the particular purpose, and to take it out of the general personal estate, without waiting for the arrival of the time of payment."[6]

An example of the importance, in this question of interpretation of the intention of the donor of the property, of the relationship between the donor and the donee is to be found in *Re Ferguson*,[7] where a contingent specific bequest was held to carry the intermediate income because the testator was *in loco parentis* to the legatee and had made no other provision for the legatee's

---

[2]   Para. 10.059, *post.*

[3]   S. 32 (3).

[4]   This was without prejudice to provisions in any settlement made by the infant under the statutory powers contained in the Infant Settlements Act, 1855, but this Act was repealed by the Republic's Age of Majority Act 1985 and the Age of Majority Act (N.I.), 1969, see para. 25.07, *post.*

[5]   *Gillman* v. *Gillman* (1865) 16 Ir.Ch.R. 461; *Love* v. *Love* (1881) 7 L.R.Ir. 306. See also *Guinness* v. *Guinness* (1862) 14 Ir.Ch.R. 218; *Maher* v. *Maher* (1877) 1 L.R.Ir. 22.

[6]   (1879) 3 L.R.Ir 476 at 480–1 (see *A Casebook on Equity and Trusts in Ireland* (1985), p. 571). See also *Kiersey* v. *Flahavan* [1905] 1 I.R. 45; *Re Ferguson* (1915) 49 I.L.T.R. 110; *Re O'Connell's Estate* [1932] I.R. 298 (see *ibid.*, p. 567)

[7]   (1915) 49 I.L.T.R. 110. See also *Re O'Connell's Estate* [1932] I.R. 298.

maintenance in the period before the bequest vested. Statutory recognition of this principle is contained in section 32 (4) of the Trustee Act (N.I.), 1958.[8]

10.045. The question of interpretation sometimes becomes difficult where the settlor or testator has given an express direction for accumulation of the income. It seems that such a direction in itself will not prevent a finding that the income is nevertheless available for use as maintenance money, though a further direction as to the distribution of such accumulations will prevent such application of the income.[9]

10.046. Under section 11 of the Republic's Guardianship of Infants Act, 1964, the court has power, on the application of a guardian of an infant, to sanction the expenditure of any capital or income to which the infant is entitled for maintenance or education.[10] In the case of persons who died after January 1, 1967, leaving infant children, the personal representatives may appoint a trustee or trustees of the share of the estate to which the infant is entitled and such trustee or trustees may apply the capital or income of such share for the benefit of the infant.[11]

10.047. Finally, on the subject of maintenance of minors, it has long been recognised that the court has an inherent jurisdiction to make an order sanctioning the use by trustees of *capital* for the maintenance of minors.[12] In *Re O'Neill*, Maguire P. had this to say about the court's jurisdiction.

> "I must be satisfied that such a course is not only beneficial but necessary to the welfare of the minors . . . The jurisdiction to make an advance out of the capital is not to be exercised lightly. Where a minor is actually destitute the way is clear, but where the minors, as here, are not destitute, the question of the existence of a sufficient element of necessity becomes a difficult problem."[13]

In Northern Ireland, this jurisdiction has now been given statutory recognition by section 53 of the Trustee Act (N.I.), 1958. This section enables the court to make orders relating to the application of *capital* or *income* of any property for the maintenance, education or benefit of a minor beneficially entitled to that property.[14]

---

[8] It provides: "This section applies in the case of a contingent estate or interest only if the limitation or trust carries the intermediate income of the property, but it applies to a future or contingent legacy by the parent of, or a person standing *in loco parentis* to, the legatee, if and for such period as, under the general law, the legacy carries interest for the maintenance of the legatee, and in any such case as last aforesaid the rate of interest shall (if the income available is sufficient, and subject to any rules of court or county court rules to the contrary) be five pounds per centum per annum."

[9] See *Shaw* v. *McMahon* (1845) 8 Ir.Eq.R. 584; *Kemmis* v. *Kemmis* (1885) 15 L.R.Ir. 90; *King-Harman* v. *Cayley* [1899] 1 I.R. 39; *Re Lynch's Trusts* [1931] I.R. 517; *Re O'Connell's Estate* [1932] I.R. 298 (see *A Casebook on Equity and Trusts in Ireland* (1985), p. 567 and 589).

[10] See *Re Meade* [1971] I.R. 327.

[11] Succession Act, 1965, ss. 57 and 58.

[12] See *Re Moffats* (1850) 2 Ir.Jur.(o.s.) 258; *Re Morgan* [1917] 1 I.R. 181.

[13] [1943] I.R. 562 at 564–5 (the learned judge finally decided to sanction the advance). (See *A Casebook on Equity and Trusts in Ireland* (1985), p. 573).

[14] See cases on the English equivalent (s. 53 of the Trustee Act, 1925), *Re Gower's Settlement* [1934] 1 Ch. 365; *Re Heyworth's Contingent Reversionary Interest* [1956] Ch. 364; *Re Meux* [1958] Ch. 154. *Cf.* the earlier cases, *Re Howarth* (1873) L.R. 8 Ch. 415; *Re Hamilton* (1885) 31 Ch.D. 291; *Cadman* v. *Cadman* (1886) 33 Ch.D. 397; *Re Hambrough's Estate* [1909] 2 Ch. 620.

M. ADVANCEMENT

10.048.   In Northern Ireland there is now a special statutory power to make advancements out of capital to beneficiaries. In the Republic, such a power exists in respect of *minor* beneficiaries.[15] Apart from this, such a power may be expressly conferred by the trust instrument.[16] Under section 33 of the Trustee Act (N.I.), 1958, in the case of *pure personalty*[17] the trustees have an absolute discretion to pay or apply capital money for the advancement *or benefit* of any beneficiary, to be entitled absolutely or contingently, in possession or in remainder or reversion. This power may even be exercised where the beneficiary's interest is liable to be defeated by the exercise of a power of appointment or revocation, or diminished by increase of the class of beneficiaries to which he belongs.[18] However, the amount advanced must not exceed altogether one-half of the beneficiary's share or possible share[19] and, in the event of him later becoming entitled absolutely to a share in the trust property, the amount advanced must be brought into account as part of that share.[20] Exercise of such a power of advancement could obviously prejudice any beneficiary entitled to a prior estate or interest, whether vested or contingent, in the money advanced, so it is provided that no advancement may be made unless such beneficiaries are in existence, of full age and consent in writing to it.[21] It appears that the court has no power to dispense with such consent altogether,[22] though in a particular case it may nevertheless sanction an advance of capital if it considers it appropriate and a prior beneficiary's refusal to give consent unreasonable.[23]

10.049.   At common law, and "advancement" had the rather technical meaning of a capital sum given to a beneficiary with the purpose of giving him a start in life, *e.g.*, by setting him up in business or securing entry into a trade or profession, as opposed to less substantial and more casual payments made at various times during a beneficiary's younger years.[24] No doubt this is still relevant under section 33 of the 1958 Act, but it is significant that the express wording extends the purpose of such payments to cover the alternative of being simply for the "benefit" of the donee. Whatever may be the precise limits of the section, and there is no authority on the Northern Ireland

---

[15]   Guardianship of Infants Act, 1964, s. 11. See also s. 58 (5) and (6) of the Succession Act, 1965, which confer a statutory power of advancement on trustees appointed by personal representatives under s. 57 in the case of a minor sharing in the deceased's estate.

[16]   *Creeth* v. *Wilson* (1882) 9 L.R.Ir. 216; *McMahon* v. *Gaussen* [1896] 1 I.R. 143; *L'Estrange* v. *L'Estrange* [1902] 1 I.R. 467 (see *A Casebook on Irish Land Law* (1984), p. 375).

[17]   S. 33 (2), which excludes personalty regarded as land by the doctrine of conversion (para. 3.094, *ante*) or by statute, *e.g.*, s. 22 (5) of the Settled Land Act, 1925 (para. 8.096, *ante*).

[18]   S. 33 (1).

[19]   S. 33 (1) (*a*).

[20]   S. 33 (1) (*b*).

[21]   S. 33 (1) (*c*).

[22]   *Re Forster's Settlement* [1942] Ch. 199.

[23]   *E.g.*, under s. 56 of the 1958 Act (power of court to authorise transactions relating to trust property) (see para. 10.094, *post*), *Re Beale's Settlement Trusts* [1932] 2 Ch. 15.

[24]   See *Curtis* v. *Curtis* [1901] 1 I.R. 374. Also *Re Aldridge* (1886) 55 L.T. 554; *Taylor* v. *Taylor* (1875) L.R. 20 Eq. 155. *Cf.* Succession Act, 1965, s. 63 (6) (R.I.), para. 15.30, *post*.

section, it is clear from the House of Lords decision in *Pilkington* v. *I.R.C.*[25] on the almost identical English provision[26] that it is considerably wider than the common law notion of advancement and may, indeed, sanction any use of money which will improve the material situation of the beneficiary in question.[27]

III. DUTIES OF TRUSTEES

A. COLLECTION AND DISTRIBUTION OF ASSETS

10.050. One of the first duties of the trustees, after making sure that they understand all the terms of the trust instrument, is to check the state of the trust property and to collect into their hands any assets which should be part of the trust fund.[28] Failure to act with reasonable promptness on matters of this kind may result in the trustees being held liable for a loss suffered thereby.[29] Once the trust assets have been collected in by the trustees, they are under a duty to ensure preservation of the value of the fund. This brings into play their important duties with respect to investment of the trust fund, and the related duties of handling the investments impartially as between the various beneficiaries, all of which we consider below. Finally, the trustees are under a duty to distribute the trust property, capital and income, as instructed by the trust instrument.[30] We have already discussed the powers of the trustees to deal with claims by beneficiaries, in particular their power to discover potential claims through advertisement.[31] Once again failure to discharge this duty may involve the trustees personally in liability for any loss or misapplication of the trust fund. We come back to this subject later.[32]

B. ACCOUNTS AND INFORMATION

10.051. The trustees are under a general duty to keep accounts and thereby to be in a position to produce a record of their management and distribution of the trust property.[33] Should the trustees fail in this duty, a beneficiary, at

---

[25] [1964] A.C., 612, espec. at 632–5 (*per* Viscount Radcliffe). See Waters, (1959) 23 Conv. 423. Also *I.R.C.* v *Bernstein* [1961] Ch. 399.

[26] Trustee Act, 1925, s. 32.

[27] See Waters, " 'New' Power of Advancement" (1958) 22 Conv. 413 and "Creation of Sub-Trusts under Power of Advancement" (1959) 23 Conv. 27.

[28] See *Macnamara* v. *Carey* (1867) I.R. 1 Eq. 9, espec. at 30–2 (*per* Christian L.J.) (see *A Casebook on Equity and Trusts in Ireland* (1985), p. 576).

[29] Para. 10.107, *post*. See also *Waring* v. *Waring* (1852) 3 Ir.Ch.R. 331; *Alexander* v. *Alexander* (1862) 13 Ir.Ch.R. 137; *Macken* v. *Hogan* (1863) 14 Ir.Ch.R. 285.

[30] See Pearce, "Retention of Income by Trustees" (1972) 36 Conv. 38.

[31] Para. 10.040, *supra*.

[32] Para. 10.107, *post*.

[33] *Crawford* v. *Crawford* (1867) I.R. 1 Eq. 436; *Walsh* v. *Murray* (1878) 12 I.L.T.R. 61; *Moore* v. *McGlynn* [1894] 1 I.R. 74 (see *A Casebook on Equity and Trusts in Ireland* (1985), p. 374). See also the statutory duty imposed on charity trustees' para. 9.113, *ante*. Cf. *Nickson* v. *Bank of Ireland* (1975) Unrep. (H.C., R.I.) (1974 No. 15 Sp).

least if he is entitled in possession,[34] can apply for a court order directing that accounts should be prepared. In such a case, Chatterton V.-C. took the view that:

> "It is not necessary for the *cestui que trust* to prove any breach of duty by the trustee for the purpose of having accounts taken of the trust property, as their right to this results from the relation between them."[35]

It should be noted, however, that this duty extends only to *keeping* accounts; there is no duty to have the trust accounts audited. However, the trustees may wish to have this done and it is probably advisable in the case of a particularly large trust. In *Chaine-Nickson* v. *Bank of Ireland*, Kenny J. stated:

> "When a beneficiary has a vested interest in a trust fund so that he has a right to payment of the income, the trustees must at all reasonable times at his request give him full and accurate information as to the amount and state of the trust property and permit him or his solicitor to inspect the accounts and vouchers and other documents relating to the trust . . . When a beneficiary asks for copies of accounts or trust documents, he is bound to pay the copying charges for these."[36]

10.052. The trustees are also under a duty to provide the beneficiaries with information relating to the trust.[37] Furthermore, the beneficiaries can be regarded as having a proprietary interest in documents connected with the trust and, therefore, have a right to inspect them.[38] However, in England it was suggested that in certain cases, *e.g.*, a discretionary trust, some documents may contain confidential information relating to exercise of the trustees' powers and discretions which it might be unreasonable to expect the trustees to disclose to a particular beneficiary.[39] The *Chaine-Nickson* case (para. 10.051, *ante*) involved a discretionary trust and so Kenny J. had to consider the position of potential beneficiaries with no right to be paid capital or income. He went on:

> "All the trust fund is held by the trustees in this case on discretionary trusts and if the plaintiff is not entitled to the trust accounts and particulars of the investments, it follows that none of the potential beneficiaries have a valid claim to any information from the trustees. The result is that the trustees are not under an obligation to account to anyone in connection with their management of the trust fund. This logical conclusion of the defendants' argument leads to remarkable consequences.
> The amount of remuneration to which the trustees are entitled is

---

[34] *Cf.* a potential appointee under the trustees' power of appointment where there is no evidence of misconduct by the trustees, see *Moran* v. *Moran* [1901] 1 I.R. 346; *Nickson, ibid.*

[35] *Moore* v. *McGlynn* [1894] 1 I.R. 74 at 86. See also *Collings* v. *Wade* [1896] 1 I.R. 340; *Clarke* v. *Crowley* (1930) 64 I.L.T.R. 1; *Re Finnerty's Will Trusts* [1970] I.R. 221. See Hanbury, "Forms of Accounts against Executors and Trustees" (1936) 52 L.Q.R. 365.

[36] [1976] I.R. 393 at 396. Note the trustees' statutory power in Northern Ireland, para. 10.026, *supra*.

[37] *Re Ireland* [1905] 1 I.R. 133.

[38] *O'Rourke* v. *Darbishire* [1920] A.C. 581. *Cf. Nickson* v. *Bank of Ireland, op. cit.*

[39] See the discussion by the Court of Appeal in *Re Londonderry's Settlement* [1965] Ch. 918.

specified in the settlement and the potential beneficiaries have an interest in seeing that the amount is not exceeded, for they are the persons who will ultimately benefit by payments of capital and income. The defendants' contention, however, has the result that they do not have to account for or to disclose the amount of their remuneration. This seems to me to be contrary to the basic concept of a trustee being accountable for his management of the trust fund. In a case where the investment powers of trustees under a discretionary trust are limited, the beneficiaries have a clear interest in getting information as to how the trust fund has been invested but again, if the defendants' contention is correct, the potential beneficiaries can never get the details to ascertain whether the trust fund has been invested in accordance with the terms of the settlement. The trustees might indeed make loans out of the trust fund to themselves and the potential beneficiaries would have no means of ascertaining this. These remarkable results of the defendants' argument convince me that the proposition advanced by their counsel is not the law and that a potential beneficiary under a discretionary trust is entitled to copies of the trust accounts and to information as to the investments which represent the trust fund. The obligation of the trustees is not satisfied by giving particulars of the payments made by them."[39a]

However, it appears that trustees are under no obligation to provide information to third parties, *e.g.*, persons negotiating a transaction relating to a beneficiary's interest.[40]

C. INVESTMENT

10.053. Trustees are under a general duty to invest the capital of their trust fund in order to preserve the value of that capital for those beneficiaries who may become entitled to it ultimately, and in order to ensure the flow of a steady income for those beneficiaries currently entitled to such an interest in the trust property.[41] Indeed, in *Re Lynch's Trusts*,[42] Johnston J. held that the

---

[39a] [1976] I.R. 393 at 396–7. Kenny J. regarded this view of the law as being supported by the Irish case of *Moore* v. *McGlynn* [1984] 1 I.R. 73, whereas he distinguished the English case of *Re Londonderry's Settlement* [1965] Ch. 981 on the ground that the daughter in that case, who requested disclosure of information, had a vested interest in the income not distributed under the discretionary trust and was not, therefore, a potential beneficiary only. He went on (*ibid.*, p. 399):

"The case is not a decision that a potential beneficiary is entitled to copies of the trust accounts or as to the information to which he is entitled. It decides only what trustees under a discretionary trust are not obliged to disclose."

[40] *Low* v. *Bouverie* (1891) 3 Ch. 82, reversed in England by s. 137 (8) of the Law of Property Act, 1925, to the extent that trustees may be required to produce notices of dealings with equitable interests to any person "interested." The principle of *Low* v. *Bouverie* should also be considered now in the light of the recent developments in the law of negligent misstatement, see *Hedley Byrne & Co. Ltd.* v. *Heller & Partners* [1964] A.C. 465.

[41] See Keeton, *The Investment and Taxation of Trust Funds*; Carswell, *Trustee Acts (Northern Ireland)* (1964). pp. 13–29 and 166–71. Also Evans, "Enlarging Investment Powers of Trustees" (1963) Conv. 127; Latham, "Trustee Investments and American Practice" (1954) 7 C.L.P. 139; Symposium, "Investment of Trust Funds" (1938) 5 L. & Cont.Prob. 335.

[42] [1931] I.R. 517 (see *A Casebook on Equity and Trusts in Ireland* (1985), p. 589).

court has inherent jurisdiction to disregard an express direction as to the form of investment of trust money and to order instead investment in trustee securities, in order to give effect to the settlor's or testator's objective (in this case, support, maintenance and education of children during their minorities). There are two matters to be considered in this context. First, there is the subject of what powers particular trustees have in making investments with their trust funds. Secondly, in the light of those powers in the particular case, there is the matter of what duties are imposed on the trustees with respect to exercise of their powers. Let us now consider these matters in turn.

1. *Authorised Investments*

10.054.   The extent to which trustees may make any particular investment is governed by two factors, the terms of the trust instrument and statute law. There is nothing to stop the settlor including an investment clause in the trust instrument giving precise details of the trustees' powers of investment. Such a clause may be as restrictive or expansive as is thought necessary and, indeed, there is much to be said[43] for giving the trustees an absolute discretion to make such investments as they think fit.[44] In the absence of such a clause or, if there is one, subject to its terms trustees may invest trust funds, and from time to time vary any such investment, in accordance with the statutory provisions governing these matters in both parts of Ireland.[45] These provisions are respectively, in the Republic of Ireland, Part I of the Trustee Act, 1893, as amended by the Trustee (Authorised Investments) Act, 1958, and, in Northern Ireland, Part I of the Trustee Act (N.I.), 1958, as amended by the Trustee (Amendment) Act (N.I.), 1962.[46]

10.055.   Until the legislation in the last 20 years or so, trustees' authorised securities in both parts of Ireland were in a very limited category, as prescribed by section 1 of the Trustee Act, 1893. Essentially they were limited to British and Commonwealth government stock[47] and stock issued by local authorities and public companies, such as railway or canal companies. Also included was investment on "real or heritable securities in Great Britain or Ireland."[48] The trouble about such securities is that they earn interest at a

---

[43] See further para. 10.062, *post.*

[44] See *Re O'Connor* [1913] 1 I.R. 69 (see a *Casebook on Equity and Trusts in Ireland* (1985), p. 592) and para. 10.065, *infra.* Though the exercise of even so wide a discretion may still be subject to the general law governing the trustees with respect to investments, *ibid.*

[45] Trustee Act, 1893, s. 1, as substituted by s. 1 of the Trustee (Authorised Investments) Act, 1958 (R.I.); Trustee Act (N.I.), 1958, s. 1, as amended by s. 1 of the Trustee (Amendment) Act (N.I.), 1962.

[46] See Carswell, *op. cit.,* pp. 13–29 and 166–71. Also Wylie, (1964) 15 N.I.L.Q. 257.

[47] To which was added later, for the Republic of Ireland, Irish Government stocks and securities, see Adaptation of Enactments Act, 1922, s. 18. *Re Westby* [1932] I.R. 444.

[48] 1893 Act, s. 1 (*b*). A power to lend on "real or heritable" securities was held not to authorise purchase of freehold land, *Robinson* v. *Robinson* (1876) I.R. 10 Eq. 189; *cf. Re O'Connor* [1913] 1 I.R. 69 (see *A Casebook on Equity and Trusts in Ireland* (1985), p. 592). Investment in "real securities" is preserved in the Republic in the new s. 1 of the 1893 Act substituted by the Trustee (Authorised Investments) Act, 1958 and in Northern Ireland by a considerably extended s. 1 (2) of the Trustee Act (N.I.), 1958, as amended by the Trustee (Amendment) Act (N.I.), 1962. See para. 10.059, *post.*

fixed rate only and, if redeemable, are repayable at nominal par value. They do not, therefore, in general safeguard the investor against inflation and for a trust they have the double disadvantage that both current and future beneficiaries suffer. The beneficiaries currently entitled to the income from a fund invested in such securities will find in these days of rampant inflation that the fixed income coming in every year is buying less and less and the beneficiaries ultimately entitled to the capital represented by those securities will find that the capital, while it may be *nominally* the same amount (this depends on the price at which it was originally bought), has been reduced considerably in *real* value, *i.e.*, in terms of what it will purchase in the prevailing market, whether other securities or property such as land or goods and chattels.[49] It has long been recognised that the only way to protect beneficiaries against inflation is to invest in securities that offer the possibility, if not the probability, of a rise in capital value, plus the prospect of a high and, from time to time, rising rate of interest. This necessitates, however, investment in the ordinary stocks and shares of industrial and commercial companies,[50] and in schemes like unit trusts.[51] Prior to the recent legislation in Ireland this was beyond the powers of trustees, unless they were given such power by an express clause in the trust instrument. We must now consider how far the recent statutory provisions have resolved this problem for trustees and have relieved settlors of the need to include an express investment clause in the trust instrument.

10.056. In the Republic of Ireland, a new list of authorised securities was substituted by section 1 of the Trustee (Authorised Investments) Act, 1958, for that in section 1 of the Trustee Act, 1893. The 1958 list, as amended by Ministerial order, authorises investment in securities of, or guaranteed by, the Irish Government,[52] stock of semi-state bodies such as the Bank of Ireland and Allied Irish Banks,[53] E.S.B.[54] and Bord Na Móna,[55] local authorities,[56] loan stock of the Bank of Ireland and bank deposit accounts.[57] So far as industrial and commercial companies are concerned, investment is authorised only in debentures or debenture stock of companies registered in the Republic and quoted on a Stock Exchange, and then only if the debentures or debenture stock of the particular company does not exceed the paid-up share capital and a dividend of not less than five per cent. has been paid on the company's ordinary shares in each of the five years preceding the

---

[49] Note the prophetic words of the English Nathan Committee in its *Report on Charitable Trusts* (1952; Cmd. 8710), para. 286: "If a long view is taken, inflation appears to be a natural tendency of currencies and the trend of the last fifty years may be regarded as merely an acceleration of this natural tendency. The acceleration has, however, become a matter of grave anxiety; the real value of even the soundest currency has been greatly reduced." See Paling, "Trustee Investments in a Time of Economic Depression" (1975) 39 Conv. 318.
[50] Sometimes, rather confusingly for the student of land law, referred to as "equities," *cf.* para. 3.076, *ante.*
[51] See Ford, "Unit Trusts" (1960) 23 M.L.R. 129.
[52] S. 1 (*a*). And the British Government securities inscribed or registered in the Republic, s. 1 (*k*).
[53] S. 1 (*c*).
[54] S. 1 (*d*).
[55] S. 1 (*f*).
[56] S. 1 (*h*).
[57] S. 1 (*j*).

date of the investment.[58] There is no power to invest in the ordinary shares of such a company and so it remains the case that in the Republic of Ireland, with the exception of stock such as that of the Bank of Ireland and Allied Irish Banks, the list of trustees' authorised investments is confined to fixed interest securities,[59] with all that that signifies.[60] This makes it imperative that a settlor or testator weigh carefully whether it would not be wiser to confer wider powers of investment, if not a complete discretion, on the trustees of any trust he is contemplating establishing. In this context it is interesting to note the much wider provisions introduced recently in the Republic with respect to investment of charity funds by section 9 of the Charities Act, 1973.[61] Under this the court may authorise investment of any charity fund in whatever manner the court thinks proper, whether or not the trust instrument authorises such an investment.[62] Furthermore, the Board (i.e., the Commissioners of Charitable Donations and Bequests for Ireland) may invest, or, on application by the trustees, may by order confer power to invest, any charity fund in such manner as they think proper, whether such investment is authorised by the trust instrument or, indeed, by law.[63]

10.057. In addition to the general powers of investment in the Republic just mentioned,[64] there are some further particular powers conferred by statute.[65] Thus section 2 of the Trustee Act, 1893, authorises purchase of securities notwithstanding that they are redeemable and that the price exceeds the redemption value, i.e., purchase at a premium, and retention of such securities until redemption. There were limitations imposed on this power of investment in the 1893 Act,[66] but these have been repealed by the Trustee (Authorised Investments) Act, 1958,[67] which instead authorises trustees to effect redeemable bond insurance policies against redemption and thereby to protect the trust fund from loss by redemption of bonds at par value, where they were purchased at a premium.[68] Section 5 of the 1893 Act provides that an express power of investment in real securities conferred on trustees[69] is to be deemed, subject to any express prohibition in the trust

---

[58] S. 1 (i).

[59] Though s. 2 of the 1958 Act empowers the Minister for Finance to make an order varying the list, by addition or deletion. Thus the list of authorised investments has been extended in recent years so as to permit investments in interest-bearing deposit accounts in various banks, building societies and credit organisations operating in the State, see, e.g. the additions made by the Trustee (Authorised Investments) Order, 1979 (S.I. No. 407) (Norwich Irish Building Society, Irish Intercontinental Bank Ltd., Royal Trust Company (Ireland) Ltd. and Trinity Bank Ltd.).

[60] See remarks at para. 10.055, supra.

[61] Which substitutes a new and amended s. 32 of the Charities Act, 1961.

[62] New s. 32 (1) of the 1961 Act.

[63] New s. 32 (2) and (3) of the 1961 Act. Note also the power of the Board or, if necessary the court, to give leave to trustees to invest a charity fund subject to a prior limited interest, new amended s. 33 of the 1961 Act, as substituted by s. 10 of the 1973 Act.

[64] These investment powers also apply to money under the control or subject to the order of a court, see s. 3 of the Trustee (Authorised Investments) Act, 1958,

[65] See also the discussion of trustees' duties in respect of exercise of investment powers, para. 10.065, post.

[66] S. 2 (2).

[67] S. 6 and Sch.

[68] S. 4.

[69] See Re Tattersall [1906] 2 Ch. 399.

instrument, to include power to invest on mortgage of land held for an unexpired term of not less than 200 years, an express power to invest in companies' mortgages is to include debenture stock and a general power to invest in companies' shares, mortgages and debentures is to include mortgage debentures and those of companies incorporated by or acting under the authority of an Act of Parliament, *e.g.*, the Dublin Gas Co. It is to be noted that the term "real securities" used in section 1 of the 1893 Act does not mean land but money charged on land. Furthermore, a power to invest in the purchase of land or on mortgage of land may be exercised in respect of land notwithstanding that it is subject to drainage charges,[70] unless, again, there is an express prohibition in the trust instrument.[71]

10.058. A limitation of a trustee's power of selecting investments is imposed by section 22 of the Settled Land Act, 1882. Where there is a settlement as defined by that Act, the tenant for life has power to direct the trustees as to how the trust fund is to be invested and they must comply with that direction.[72]

10.059. In Northern Ireland, trustees' powers of investment have been greatly extended recently. Section 1 (1) of the Trustee Act (N.I.), 1958, had authorised trustees in Northern Ireland to invest in such manner as allowed by the existing law in any part of Great Britain. It is arguable, therefore, that the radical changes introduced by the British Trustee Investments Act, 1961,[73] applied automatically to Northern Ireland,[74] but, whether or not that was an accurate view, the 1961 Act was adapted for Northern Ireland by the Trustee (Amendment) Act (N.I.), 1962,[75] section 1 (1) of which substitutes new wording in section 1 (1) of the 1958 Act so as to confer the powers of the 1961 Act, as adapted, on Northern Ireland trustees.[76] This does mean, however, that trustees wishing to take advantage of the statutory powers have to juggle with three different statutes, each of which in itself is a very complicated piece of legislation.

10.060. The 1961 scheme introduces a new list of authorised investments,[77] which are split up into three kinds: (1) *narrower-range investments not requiring advice*, a small class which trustees may use without seeking prior advice, *e.g.*, Defence Bonds and National or Ulster Savings Certificates (2) *narrower-range investments, requiring advice*, a larger class comprising fixed-interest Government securities and similar securities issued by local and

---

[70] Issued under, *e.g.*, the Landed Property Improvement (Ir.) Act, 1847.
[71] 1893 Act, s. 6.
[72] See para. 8.095, *ante*.
[73] See Samuels, (1961) 25 Conv. 372 and (1962) 26 Conv. 351.
[74] See, however, the exclusion in s. 17 (2) of the 1961 Act. Ss. 11 and 16 of the 1961 Act were made expressly applicable to Northern Ireland.
[75] See Wylie, (1964) 15 N.I.L.Q. 257.
[76] Trustees in Northern Ireland were better off under the Trustee Act (N.I.), 1958 than trustees in the Republic in that they could apply under s. 57 of the 1958 Act for a variation of trusts order, conferring wider investment powers, see para. 10.095, *post*.
[77] See Sched. 1.

public authorities in the Commonwealth and the E.E.C.; (3) *wider-range investments, requiring advice*, an entirely new class of securities including those issued by companies incorporated in the U.K., building society shares and units of an authorised unit trust scheme.[78] Category (3) is the most significant because it authorises investment in "equities," though the limitation is imposed that investment may be made only in the shares of a company whose total shares issued and paid up capital exceeds £1m. and which, in each of the 5 years preceding the investment, paid a dividend on all the shares issued.[79] A major drawback for trustees, especially those of comparatively small trusts, is the complexity of the administrative procedures which have to be followed if they are to take advantage of the new powers.

10.061. No wider-range investment may be made unless the trust fund is divided into two equal parts (a narrower-range and wider-range part) and, once made, the division is permanent.[80] Thus a maximum of 50 per cent.[81] only of the fund may be invested in equities. On the other hand, while funds in the narrower-range part must be invested in narrower-range securities, funds in the wider-range part do not have to be invested in wider-range securities.[82] Any transfer of funds from one part of the total fund to another part must be accompanied by a "compensating transfer" in the opposite direction of funds to the same value,[83] and, if any property accrues to the trust, it must be divided between each part so as to increase each by the same amount, unless the accrual falls obviously into one of the parts.[84] On the other hand, where the trustees have power to take property out of the trust fund, they have a complete discretion as to which part they use for the deduction.[85]

10.062. In certain cases, the administration of the trust property under the 1961 Act may become even more complicated. If the trustees have special powers of investment conferred by the trust instrument,[86] or wish to exercise certain other statutory powers of investment,[87] they must exercise these by creating a special-range part of the trust fund.[88] Thus the trustees of a particular trust may find that, in order to take full advantage of the 1961 Act's powers (and this is the position in which they are so often forced by inflation and the pleas of beneficiaries), they have to split the fund into three separate

---

[78] Which are governed by the Prevention of Fraud (Investments) Act (N.I.), 1940, espec. s. 16. See also on advice, para. 10.067, *post*. Note also the special provisions for charity trustees in relation to common investment schemes and the Department of Finance's Common Investment Fund, contained in s. 25 of the Charities Act (N.I.), 1964. See para. 9.112, *ante*.

[79] Sched. 1, Pt. IV, para. 3.

[80] 1961 Act, s. 2 (1).

[81] The British Treasury does have power to alter the proportion of this division, 1961 Act, s. 13 (1).

[82] 1961 Act, s. 2 (2).

[83] S. 2 (1) (*b*).

[84] S. 2 (3).

[85] S. 2 (4).

[86] S. 3

[87] *E.g.*, the power conferred by s. 1 (2) (*a*) and (*c*) of the Trustee Act (N.I.), 1958 to invest in the purchase of an estate or interest in land, see s.1 (2) of the Trustee (Amendment) Act (N.I.), 1962.

[88] 1961 Act, s. 3 (3) and Sched. 2.

parts with all the administrative problems that that will involve. Herein lies one of the most controversial features of the 1961 scheme. In the case of a small trust fund, it may not be worth the trustees' while incurring the trouble and expense of such a complicated exercise[89] and, yet, so often this is precisely the sort of fund hardest hit by inflation. The English Law Society made several suggestions for simplification of the 1961 scheme when it was under consideration as a Bill before Parliament, but these were not adopted. For this reason, it is probably still advisable for a settlor or testator in Northern Ireland to include an investment clause in the trust instrument, drafted in such a way as to give the trustees sufficiently wide powers of investment without the administrative complications of the 1961 scheme.

10.063. Finally, it is interesting to note that section 4 of the Trustee (Amendment) Act (N.I.), 1962, provides that the new scheme in no way lessens the powers of the courts to confer wider investment powers,[90] nor affects the extent of the exercise of such a power. However, the equivalent English provision[91] has been interpreted extremely restrictively, so that it appears that in practice that the courts will rarely grant an extension of the 1961 statutory powers, even in cases where they would have granted wider powers before the 1961 scheme was introduced.[92]

10.064. Apart from the 1961 scheme, as adapted by the Trustee (Amendment) Act (N.I.), 1962, trustees in Northern Ireland have further statutory powers under Part I of the Trustee Act (N.I.), 1958. It is provided that trustees having power, including a statutory power,[93] to invest in mortgages or bonds of a company, may invest in the debenture stock of that company,[94] and, in the case of a power to invest in or on the security of land, may do so notwithstanding that the land is subject to land purchase annuities or drainage charges.[95] Section 7 of the 1958 Act confers a new power to invest in bearer securities provided they are purchased through and, until sold, retained by a bank.[96]

---

[89] Yet failure to make full use of the 1961 powers may involve a breach of the statutory duty imposed by s. 6 of the 1961 Act, see para. 10.067, *post.*

[90] *E.g.*, under s. 57 of the Trustee Act (N.I.), 1958 (the equivalent of the English Variation of Trusts Act, 1958), see para. 10.095, *post.*

[91] S. 15 of the 1961 Act.

[92] See *Re Clarke's Will Trusts* [1961] 1 W.L.R. 1471; *Re Kolb's Will Trusts* [1962] Ch. 531; *Re Cooper's Settlement* [1962] Ch. 826. In *Re Cooper's Settlement* at pp. 829–30, Buckley J. said of the 1961 Act: "In my judgment, the enactment of that Act must have a direct and important bearing on the exercise by this court of its discretion in varying trusts under the Variation of Trusts Act, 1958, in relation to powers of investment. It seems to me that from this time this court will have to be satisfied, whenever applicants under the Variation of Trusts Act ask for relaxation of trustees' powers of investment, that there are special grounds which make it right that trustees should have wider powers of investment than the legislature has indicated in the Trustee Investments Act, 1961, as the normally appropriate powers." See discussion in Wylie, (1964) 15 N.I.L.Q. 257 at 261–3.

[93] See Trustee (Amendment) Act (N.I.), 1962, s. 6. *Cf.* ss. 5 and 6 of the 1893 Act, *Re Tattersall* [1906] 2 Ch. 399.

[94] 1958 Act, s. 4 (1). S. 4 (2) relates to securities of the Isle of Man.

[95] *Ibid.*, s. 6.

[96] *Cf.* s. 7 of the 1893 Act.

2. *Trustees' Duties*

10.065. We now turn to the duties of trustees with respect to exercise of their powers of investment. To a large extent these duties have been established by the courts, but some have been given statutory recognition and others have been established by legislation. One important duty long recognised by the courts is that the trustees must act impartially in making and handling investments to ensure that they do not favour one beneficiary as against another.[97] To some extent, the trustees' duties depend upon the terms of the trust instrument,[98] which may, for example, purport to give them unlimited powers and an absolute discretion as to their exercise. However, even in such a case the trustees find themselves under the control of the courts. In *Re O'Connor*, Meredith M.R. stated:

> "One thing is certain, however unlimited the power of investment may be, the trustee remains subject to the jurisdiction of the court. The trustee has no power to act dishonestly, negligently, or in breach of trust to invest on insufficient security, but, subject to the power of the court to compel a dishonest, grossly negligent, or grossly incompetent trustee to account for money he has so invested, it is in the power of a testator or settlor to place in the hands of his trustee money to be invested in the fullest sense of the word . . ."[99]

10.066. In other words, the trustees must not make unauthorised investments[1] and, in making authorised ones, must still exercise reasonable care. This remains the case despite the statutory provision in both parts of Ireland that the statutory powers of investment are to be exercised according to the discretion of the trustees.[2] On the question of whether or not a particular investment is authorised, it is also provided by statute in both parts of Ireland that trustees may retain investments which have since become unauthorised.[3] Difficulties have often arisen where trustees wished to lend trust money on the security of a mortgage. It has been held that a loan on the security of a judgment mortgage[4] is not a proper investment, unless expressly authorised by the trust instrument.[5] On the other hand, a loan on the security of a second

---

[97] We discuss this duty in more detail later, para. 10.068, *post*.

[98] See, however, the power of the court to override express provisions as to investments discussed in *Re Lynch's Trusts* [1931] I.R. 517 (see *A Casebook on Equity and Trusts in Ireland* (1985), p. 589). *Cf. Cowan* v. *Scargill* [1984] 3 W.L.R. 501, para. 10.053, *ante*.

[99] [1913] 1 I.R. 69 at 75–6 (see *ibid.*, p. 592). See Pearce and Samuels, "Negligent Investment by Trustees" [1983] Conv. 127. In *Gawn* v. *Att.-Gen. for Northern Ireland* (1966) 17 N.I.L.Q. 514, Lowry J. pointed out that trustees in certain circumstances may be relieved of the normal duty to obtain the best price possible – they had to consider the advantage of the trust from all points of view. See discussion of the court's inherent jurisdiction to make orders as to investments in *Re Lynch's Trusts* [1931] I.R. 517 para. 10.053, *ante*.

[1] See further *Waller* v. *Fowler* (1837) S. & Sc. 274; *Fitzgerald* v. *Fitzgerald* (1856) 6 Ir.Ch.R. 145; *Costello* v. *O'Rourke* (1869) I.R. 3 Eq. 172; *Rochfort* v. *Seaton* [1896] 1 I.R. 18; *Webber* v. *Webber* [1922] 1 I.R. 49.

[2] Trustee Act, 1893, s. 3; Trustee Act (N.I.), 1958, s. 2. See *Leoroyd* v. *Whiteley* (1887) 12 App.Cas. 727.

[3] 1893 Act, s. 4; Trustee (Authorised Investments) Act. 1958, s. 5 (R.I.); Trustee Act (N.I.), 1958, s. 3. See discussion in *Re Chapman* [1896] 2 Ch. 763.

[4] See further, ch. 13, *post*. Such a mortgage can no longer be created in Northern Ireland, *ibid*.

[5] *Johnston* v. *Lloyd* (1844) 7 Ir.Eq.R. 252. See also *Lester* v. *Lester* (1857) 6 Ir.Ch.R. 513.

mortgage may be proper in Ireland,[6] since such a mortgage can be protected against *tabula in naufragio* tacking[7] by registration in the Registry of Deeds[8] and against tacking further advances by giving notice to the prior incumbrancer.[9] Normally trustees lending trust money on the security of a mortgage would have to satisfy themselves as to the sufficiency of the value of the security offered and as to the title of the borrower.[10] They have, however, now been relieved of this duty to some extent by statute, whereby it is provided that trustees are not liable by reason only of the proportion borne by the amount of the loan to the value of the security[11] provided that, in making the loan, the trustee was acting on the report of an independent valuer, whom he believed reasonably to be an able practical surveyor or valuer, that the amount of the loan did not exceed two-thirds of the value of the security set out in the report and the loan was made on the advice of the valuer or surveyor expressed in the report.[12] Furthermore, where trustees improperly advance trust money on mortgage security which would, at the time of the investment, have been proper for a smaller sum than that actually advanced, the security is to be deemed an authorised investment for the smaller sum and the trustees are to be liable to make good only the difference with interest.[13] The trustees must show that the loan was proper in all other respects, *i.e.*, except as to value, though they may still invoke the statutory protection where they did not act on the advice of a valuer.[14] In Northern Ireland, only, trustees are given a new statutory power, in the case of lending trust money on mortgage, to contract on certain conditions that the money will not be called in for a period not exceeding 7 years from the date of the loan[15] and, in the case of a sale of land held by trustees in fee simple or for a term with at least 200 years to run, to contract that not more than two-thirds of the purchase money will be secured by a mortgage of the land sold.[16] Under these provisions in Northern Ireland, trustees holding securities in a company are

---

[6] *Smithwick* v. *Smithwick* (1861) 12 Ir.Ch.R. 181 (see *A Casebook on Equity and Trusts in Ireland* (1985), p. 595). Smith M.R. did add, however, at p. 196: "It may be that a trustee lending on a second mortgage should exercise greater caution than if there was no prior incumbrance." See also *Crampton* v. *Walker* (1893) 31 L.R.Ir. 437. In *O'Reilly* v. *O'Reilly* (1975) 109 I.L.T.R. 121 (see also para. 10.023, *ante*), Kenny J. said (p. 122): "It is legally undesirable for trustees to borrow money by equitable deposit of title deeds or Land Certificate." As to such mortgages by deposit, see paras. 12.29 and 12.43–6, *post*.

[7] Ch. 13, *post*.

[8] Ch. 22, *post*.

[9] Ch. 13, *post*. There is no need for protection against foreclosure by the first mortgagee because of the Irish practice of always ordering a sale of the property, para. 13.059, *post*.

[10] *Waring* v. *Waring* (1852) 3 Ir.Ch.R. 331. See also *Mare* v. *Lewis* (1869) I.R. 4 Eq. 219.

[11] *Cf.* the old rules, see *Fitzgerald* v. *Fitzgerald* (1856) 6 Ir.Ch.R. 145; *Crampton* v. *Walker* (1893) 31 L.R.Ir. 437.

[12] 1893 Act, s. 8 (1); 1958 Act, s. 8 (1). Trustees are also permitted in cases of mortgages of leasehold property to dispense with production or investigation of the lessor's title, 1893 Act, s. 8 (2); 1958 Act, s. 8 (2), and in cases of purchase or mortgage of any property to accept a shorter title than that to which they would be entitled to under an open contract, 1893 Act, s. 8 (3); 1958 Act, s. 8 (3), thus permitting conformance with what is standard conveyancing practice.

[13] 1893 Act, s. 9; 1958 Act, s. 9. See the discussion in *Re Somerset* [1894] 1 Ch. 231; *Shaw* v. *Cates* [1909] 1 Ch. 389.

[14] *Jones* v. *Julian* (1890) 25 L.R.Ir. 45, dealing with the earlier provision in s. 5 of the Trustee Act, 1888.

[15] 1958 Act, s. 10 (1). *Cf. Vickery* v. *Evans* (1863) 33 Beav. 376.

[16] 1958 Act, s. 10 (2). This also applies to a sale by a tenant for life.

also given power to concur in schemes or arrangements relating to various matters such as reconstructions, takeover bids and amalgamations.[17]

10.067. Finally, in Northern Ireland, there is now a statutory definition of the trustees' duty in choosing investments. Section 6 (1) of the Trustee Investments Act, 1961 provides:

> "In the exercise of his powers of investment a trustee shall have regard —
> (a) to the need for diversification of investments of the trust, in so far as is appropriate to the circumstances of the trust;
> (b) to the suitability to the trust of investments of the description of investment proposed and of the investment proposed as an investment of that description."

In the light of these duties relating to diversification and suitability it may be questioned whether it would be appropriate for trustees of, say, a relatively small fund to decide that it was not worth the trouble of incurring the administrative difficulties involved to exercise the wider powers of investment under the 1961 Act and to take the easy way out by investing all the funds in narrower-range securities.[18] Apart from this, section 6 goes on to state that the trustees in making the statutory investments requiring advice[19] must obtain and consider proper advice on the questions of diversification and suitability.[20] This advice must be given, or subsequently confirmed, in writing[21] and be obtained from a person who is reasonably believed by the trustees to be qualified in his ability in and practical experience of financial matters.[22] Advice is also required[23] in Northern Ireland where trustees exercise the statutory powers conferred by section 1 (2) (a) of the Trustee Act (N.I.), 1958, to invest trust funds in the purchase of any estate held in fee simple in land in the U.K. (including lands held in fee farm or, in Scotland, in feu).[24]

D. IMPARTIALITY

10.068. In the present context the duty of impartiality has two main aspects. The first covers the general principle which the courts have enforced for centuries, namely that a trustee may not profit from his trust, sometimes referred to as the trustee's duty of loyalty to his trust.[25] This principle has

---

[17]   1958 Act, s. 10 (4) and (5), as amended by s. 3 (1) and (2) of the Trustee (Amendment) Act (N.I.), 1962.
[18]   It is also arguable that it would not be a proper exercise of their discretion as laid down by s. 2 of the Trustee Act (N.I.), 1958, para. 10.066, *supra*.
[19]   Para. 10.060, *supra*.
[20]   S. 6 (2) and (3).
[21]   S. 6 (5).
[22]   S. 6 (4).
[23]   Trustee (Amendment) Act (N.I.), 1962, s. 1 (3), in which the reference to "paragraph (a) of sub-section (1)" should presumably be to "paragraph (a) of sub-section (2)" (*i.e.*, of s..1 of the 1958 Act).
[24]   S. 1 (2) (a) thus considerably extended s. 1 (b) of the 1893 Act, which confined the power to "real or heritable securities" in cases only where an express power to purchase land was conferred by the trust instrument. See *Re Mordan* [1905] 1 Ch. 515; *Re Wragg* [1919] 2 Ch. 58.
[25]   We met this principle earlier in relation to constructive trusts, see para. 9.063, *ante*. See Marshall, "Conflict of Interest and Duty" (1955) 8 C.L.P. 91; Scott, "The Trustee's Duty of Loyalty" (1936) 49 H.L.R. 521.

many applications to administration of trusts, including such matters as trustees' fees and expenses and purchase of trust property. The second aspect of the duty of impartiality is the principle, also derived from case law, that the trustees must not favour one beneficiary as against another and must, if necessary, make apportionments to ensure that this does not happen. This second aspect has obvious relevance to the duties of making and managing investments which we discussed in the previous section.

1. Duty of Loyalty

10.069. The Irish courts have long recognised that a trustee, as Lord Redesdale put it, "shall gain no benefit to himself by an act done by him as Trustee, but that all his acts shall be for the benefit of his *cestui que trust*."[26] There are several examples of the Irish courts' application of this principle.

(i) Fees and Expenses

10.070. Manners L.C. laid down the general rule thus:

"It is a Rule of Equity that in all Matters of Trust, or in the Nature of a Trust, the Trustee is not entitled to Remuneration for any extraordinary Trouble, he may have had in the Business so entrusted to him."[27]

To this general rule that a trustee may not be paid a fee for doing his job, there are several exceptions. First, the trust instrument may authorise such remuneration and, in the case of professional trustees or institutions, such as banks, acting as trustees, it is usual to have such a clause inserted in the instrument.[28] Secondly, such remuneration may be authorised in special cases by the court, a jurisdiction giving statutory recognition in Northern Ireland.[29] Thirdly, the trustees may enter into an arrangement for remuneration with the beneficiaries, provided they are all *sui juris* and together entitled to the whole beneficial interest in the trust.[30] Fourthly, under a peculiar rule relating to solicitor-trustees,[31] it has been established that, while such a solicitor-trustee is normally bound by the general principle, where he acts for himself and his co-trustees in litigation relating to the trust and the costs of his so

---

[26] *O'Herlihy* v. *Hedges* (1803) 1 Sch. & Lef. 123 at 126. Thus a trustee must not bring an action which is contrary to the interests of the trust nor may one of the beneficiaries use his name in bringing an action against other beneficiaries of the trust in a matter contrary to their interests, see *Twigg* v. *Mason* (1916) 50 I.L.T.R. 173. Note the lengths to which the House of Lords applied this notion of loyalty to a solicitor acting for the trustees in *Boardman* v. *Phipps* [1967] 2 A.C. 46. Para. 9.068, *ante*. See also Rider, "The Fiduciary and the Frying Pan" [1978] Conv. 114.

[27] *Re Ormsby* (1809) 1 Ba. & B. 189–90. See Graham, "Remuneration of Trustees" (1952) 16 Conv. 13; Parry, "Remuneration of Trustees" [1984] Conv. 275.

[28] See *Re F.G.D.* (1909) 43 I.L.T.R. 241; *Taafe* v. *Merrick* (1931) 65 I.L.T.R. 36; *Q.U.B.* v. *Att.-Gen. for Northern Ireland* [1966] N.I. 115.

[29] Trustee Act (N.I.), 1958, s. 41. See the review of the court's jurisdiction by the English Court of Appeal in *Re Duke of Norfolk's Settlement Trusts* [1982] Ch. 61.

[30] *Re White* [1918] 1 I.R. 19. As usual, of course, the trustees must beware of exercising undue influence and may be put to proving the absence of such influence in court, see para. 9.075, *ante*.

[31] Sometimes known as the rule in *Cradock* v. *Piper* (1850) 1 Mac. & G. 664.

acting do not exceed the costs which would have been incurred if he had acted for the co-trustees only, he is entitled to be paid his usual costs.[32]

10.071. Though a trustee is not normally entitled to remuneration, he is entitled to expenses incurred in the administration of the trust. In *Courtney* v. *Rumley*, Chatterton V.-C. put the matter thus:

> "The principle upon which this court acts in reference to the allowance of expenses to trustees is, that the trust property shall reimburse them all the charges and expenses incurred in the execution of the trust, and in this the Court will always deal liberally with a trustee acting *bona fide*. But when the costs or expenses claimed have been incurred through the misconduct or negligence of the trustee, he will not be allowed them. The fact of his having been unsuccessful in litigation, either as Plaintiff or Defendant, will not, in the absence of misconduct, disentitle him to be reimbursed his costs."[33]

This right of indemnity in respect of costs and expenses has also been recognised by statute in both parts of Ireland.[34] On the subject of litigation, this may be undertaken to defend the trustees' title[35] or to preserve the trust property and it matters not, as Chatterton V.-C. said, that the litigation turns out to be unsuccessful.[36] But they must not act improperly[37] or unreasonably[38] in the conduct of litigation and it seems that rarely will a trustee be allowed the costs of an appeal; the question of an appeal should be left to the beneficiaries.[39] It also seems that one set of costs only will be allowed between two trustees with no issue at stake between them.[40]

(ii) Director's Fees

10.072. As holders of the legal title of the trust property, which may include shares in a company, the trustees will be the registered shareholders and, as such, may be eligible for appointment as salaried directors of the company. Indeed, if they are majority shareholders, they may be in a position

---

[32] *Re Smith's Estate* [1894] 1 I.R. 60 (see *A Casebook on Equity and Trusts in Ireland* (1985), p. 603). See also *Gomley* v. *Wood* (1846) 9 Ir.Eq.R. 418. It is not clear why a solicitor-trustee should be deprived of costs incurred apart from litigation in similar circumstances, see discussion by the English Court of Appeal in *Re Corsellis* (1887) 34 Ch.D. 675.

[33] (1871) I.R. 6 Eq. 99 at 106 (see *A Casebook on Equity and Trusts in Ireland* (1985), p. 604.). See also *Gomley* v. *Wood* (1846) 9 Ir.Eq.R. 418; *O'Higgins* v. *Walsh* [1918] 1 I.R. 126. See Anon., "Trustee Costs" (1960) 13 N.I.L.Q. 339.

[34] Trustee Act, 1893, s. 24; Trustee Act (N.I.), 1958, s. 31 (2). *Re White* [1918] 1 I.R. 19.

[35] Though not, it seems, to dispute the title of a beneficiary, *Neligan* v. *Roche* (1873) I.R. 7 Eq. 332; see also *Kennedy* v. *Daly* (1804) 1 Sch. & Lef. 355 at 380.

[36] *Hamilton* v. *Tighe* [1898] 1 I.R. 123; *Graham* v. *McCashin* [1901] 1 I.R. 404; *Martin* v. *Wilson* [1913] 1 I.R. 470.

[37] *Fetherstone H.* v. *West* (1871) I.R. 6 Eq. 86; *Twigg* v. *Mason* (1916) 50 I.L.T.R. 173. *Cf. Carson* v. *Sloane* (1884) 13 L.R.Ir. 139.

[38] *Irwin* v. *Rogers* (1848) 12 Ir.Eq.R. 159; *Wren* v. *Swanton* (1857) 6 Ir.Ch.R. 233; *De Burgh* v. *McClintock* (1883) 11 L.R.Ir. 220; *Coppinger* v. *Shekleton* (1885) 15 L.R.Ir. 461; *Re Bayly* (1906) 40 I.L.T.R. 81. *Cf. Norris* v. *Duckworth* (1858) 3 Ir.Jur.(N.S.) 188.

[39] *Fogarty* v. *O'Donoghue* [1926] I.R. 531, espec. at 569 (*per* FitzGibbon J.).

[40] *Nicholson* v. *Falkiner* (1830) 1 Mol. 555; *Hamilton* v. *James* (1877) I.R. 11 Eq. 223. See also *Dudgeon* v. *Corley* (1843) 4 Dr. & War. 158.

to appoint themselves to lucrative posts. This sort of situation was discussed in *Re Egan*,[41] where the general principle was laid down by Davitt P. that a trustee of shares is entitled to keep his director's fees *provided* his appointment as director comes about independently of any use of the trust shares.

(iii) Competition

10.073. The position of a trustee of a business who sets himself up in competition with the trust business was considered in *Moore* v. *McGlynn*,[42] where Chatterton V.-C. enunciated the following principle:

".... I am not prepared to hold that a trustee is guilty of a breach of trust in setting up for himself in a similar line of business in the neighbourhood, provided that he does not resort to deception, or solicitation of custom from persons dealing at the old shop."[43]

While in this case the trustee was allowed to keep his remuneration as postmaster (an appointment which did depend on the trustee's personal merit), despite the fact that previously the post office had been in a shop of which he was now trustee and his predecessor as postmaster had been the testator, the Vice-Chancellor did consider that the setting up of a competing business was a ground for removing the trustee from his trusteeship.[44]

(iv) Other Financial Benefit

10.074. Any other financial benefit obtained by a trustee from the trust property will have to be disgorged. Thus he must not use trust funds to finance his own business operations[45] nor must he indulge in any form of dealing with the trust property from which he may obtain, even indirectly, some financial benefit.[46] We have discussed in the previous chapter the Irish doctrine of graft, which is also relevant in the present context.[47]

(v) Purchase of Trust Property

10.075. Unless authorised by the terms of the trust instrument, the court or the beneficiaries (if they are all *sui juris*, etc.),[48] there is an almost inflexible principle enforced by the courts that a trustee must not purchase

---

[41] [1957] Ir.Jur.Rep. 19. See Lingard, "Directors: Conflict of Interest and Duty" (1960) 24 Conv. 170; Marshall, "Conflict of Interest and Duty" (1955) 8 C.L.P. 91.

[42] [1894] 1 I.R. 74 (see *A Casebook on Equity and Trusts in Ireland* (1985), p. 374).

[43] *Ibid.* p. 89. *Cf.* the English authority of *Re Thomson* [1930] 1 Ch. 203.

[44] Para. 10.013, *ante.*

[45] *Cummins* v. *Cummins* (1845) 8 Ir.Eq.R. 723.

[46] *Armstrong* v. *Armstrong* (1880) 7 L.R.Ir. 207. *Cf. Re Bagnall's Trusts* [1901] 1 I.R. 255 (one of trustees, who paid out of his own pocket the additional premium necessary to convert an insurance policy from one without profits to one with profits, allowed to keep profits or bonus from policy which ultimately accrued). *Quaere*, whether the trustee should have had only a lien for the amount of the extra premiums. See also *Swain* v. *The Law Society* [1983] A.C. 598.

[47] Para. 9.063, *ante.*

[48] *Murray* v. *Palmer* (1805) 2 Sch. & Lef. 474; *Roche* v. *O'Brien* (1810) 1 Ba. & B. 330.

trust property from himself or his co-trustees.[49] Napier C. accepted the following statement of the principle[50]:

> "The principle applies to every case where influence is acquired and abused, where confidence is reposed and betrayed. The relations with which a Court of Equity most ordinarily deals, are those of trustee and *cestui que* trust, and such like. It applies especially to those cases, for this reason and this reason only, that from those relations the court presumes confidence put and influence exerted. Whereas, in all other cases where those relations do not subsist, the confidence and the influence must be proved extrinsically; but where they are proved extrinsically, the rules of reason and of common sense, and the technical rules of a Court of Equity, are just as applicable in the one case as in the other."[51]

Unlike the normal case where there arises a presumption of undue influence,[52] in this case the presumption is irrebuttable. Such a purchase by a trustee will be set aside even without any evidence of unfairness or insufficiency in the price paid or of undue influence exercised or advantage taken by the trustee.[53] Of course, the beneficiaries must take action to have the purchase set aside within a reasonable time,[54] as is always the case with equitable remedies.[55]

10.076. On the other hand, the courts take a less strict view where a trustee purchases the beneficial interest only in the trust property. Here the normal rules apply, *i.e.*, because of the special relationship between trustee and beneficiary, a presumption of undue influence arises[56] and the court will look closely at the transaction to see that full value was given.[57] However, this presumption is rebuttable and the onus is on the trustee to produce appropriate evidence to do this, *e.g.*, that a full disclosure of all material facts was made to the beneficiary or he had the benefit of independent competent advice.[58]

---

[49] See *Nesbitt* v. *Tredennick* (1808) 1 Ba. & B. 29; *Kilbee* v. *Sneyd* (1828) 2 Mol. 186; *Alven* v. *Bond* (1841) Fl. & K. 196; *Ker* v. *Lord Dungannon* (1841) 4 Ir.Eq.R. 343; *Lawless* v. *Mansfield* (1841) 1 Dr. & War. 557; *Murphy* v. *O'Shea* (1845) 2 Jo. & Lat. 422; *O'Shea* v. *O'Shea* (1878) 12 I.L.T.R. 134; *Armstrong* v. *Armstrong* (1880) 7 L.R.Ir. 207. *Cf. Holder* v. *Holder* [1968] Ch. 353.

[50] Given by Lord Kingsdown in *Smith* v. *Kay* (1859) 7 H.L.C. 750 at 779. Also *cf.* a tenant for life under the Settled Land Acts, para. 8.059, *ante*.

[51] *King* v. *Anderson* (1874) I.R. 8 Eq. 625 at 628 (see *A Casebook on Equity and Trusts in Ireland* (1985), p. 611). See Fleming, "Can a Trustee Sell to his Wife?" (1949) 13 Conv. 248; Hinde, "Purchase of Trust Property by Trustee with Approval of Court" (1961) 3 M.U.L.R. 15; Ruoff, "Purchases in Breach of Trust" (1954) 18 Conv. 528.

[52] See para. 9.075, *ante*.

[53] See *Mulvany* v. *Dillon* (1810) 1 Ba. & B. 409.

[54] *Webb* v. *Rorke* (1806) 2 Sch. & Lef. 661 at 672 (*per* Lord Redesdale); *Roche* v. *O'Brien* (1810) 1 Ba. & B. 330.

[55] See further on the doctrine of laches, para. 3.066, *ante*.

[56] See para. 9.075, *ante*.

[57] *Kilbee* v. *Sneyd* (1828) 2 Mol. 186; *King* v. *Anderson* (1874) I.R. 8 Eq. 625 (see *A Casebook on Equity and Trusts in Ireland* (1985), p. 611).

[58] *De Montmorency* v. *Devereux* (1840) 2 Dr. & Wal. 410; *Provincial Bank of Ireland* v. *McKeever* [1941] 471; *Gregg* v. *Kidd* [1856] I.R. 183. In *Smyth* v. *Smyth* (1978) Unrep. (H.C., R.I.) (1975 No. 4369P) (see *A Casebook on Equity and Trusts in Ireland* (1985), p. 410), Costello J. applied the principles set out in this paragraph and held that the defendant-trustee had rebutted the presumption of undue influence by establishing that the beneficiary in that case "freely and with an independent will entered into a bargain with the defendant." He held that this was so despite the absence of "independent professional advice" given to the beneficiary (see also para. 9.075, *ante*).

2. *Apportionments*

10.077. In managing the trust property and, in particular, in handling the investments of the trust property, the trustees must always strive to maintain a balance between the, sometimes conflicting, interests of the various beneficiaries.[59] It must always be remembered that most forms of investment involve some sort of compromise between a desire to preserve, if not to increase, the capital value of the fund invested, which is what a remainderman is primarily interested in, and a desire to ensure that the maximum amount of income is produced by the investment, which is what a current tenant for life is primarily interested in. In general the courts recognise that it is frequently difficult for trustees to draw the appropriate balance between these competing interests and they are reluctant to interfere with the trustees' day-to-day handling of the investments, unless it can be established that there is a clear pattern of evidence showing that the trustees have been in the habit of selecting investments to suit one beneficiary at the expense of another.[60] There are, however, several occasions when the law goes further and says that the trustees are under a duty to convert existing investments into other investments and that failure to do so at the appropriate time, or in some cases the inevitable time gap between when the duty arises and it is carried out, will make it necessary for the trustees to undertake an apportionment to ensure that each beneficiary receives ultimately what he would have received, had the conversion been carried out. Usually such an apportionment had to be made in such cases between the income and capital of the trust fund, *i.e.*, between the tenant for life and the remainderman.[61] We must, therefore, consider both when a duty to convert investments arises and how the apportionments must be made pending conversion.

(i) Duty to Convert

10.078. There are two main situations where the law says that the trustees are under a duty to convert. First, a duty to convert arises where the trustees hold the trust property subject to an express trust for sale.[62] Such a trust for sale ordinarily carries with it a duty to apportion income pending the sale, unless the settlor or testator indicates that the tenant for life is to enjoy the whole income until the sale or conversion takes place. It appears that a power to postpone sale conferred on the trustees is not necessarily to be taken as such an indication.[63]

---

[59] Subject to Settled Land Act, 1882, s. 22, para. 8.095, *ante.*

[60] See the discussion in *Raby* v. *Ridehalgh* (1855) 7 De G.M. & G. 104, espec. at 109.

[61] Hart, "Consequences of Trustee's Failure to Convert as between Tenant for Life and Remainderman" (1906) 22 L.Q.R. 285; Komarofskye, "Apportionment of Annuities between Tenant for Life and Remainderman" (1915) 31 L.Q.R. 421; Stiglitz, "Apportionment and Other Remedies" (1960) 58 Mich.L.Rev. 1049; Walford, "Apportionment of Rent" (1951) 15 Conv. 17.

[62] Not to be confused with a mere power of sale, para. 8.014, *ante.* See further on trusts for sale, para. 8.043, *ante.*

[63] *Blake* v. *O'Reilly* [1895] 1 I.R. 479. See also *Re Chaytor* [1905] 1 Ch. 233; *Re Slater* (1915) 85 L.J.Ch. 432.

10.079.   Secondly, a duty to convert arises under the rule in *Howe* v. *Lord Dartmouth*,[64] which was described by Walker L.C. in *Re Harris's Estate* as follows:

> "The general rule is, that where there is a general residuary bequest of personal estate, including chattels real, to be enjoyed by persons in succession, the Court puts upon the bequest the interpretation that the persons indicated are to enjoy the same thing in succession, and converts the property as the only means of giving effect to that intention . . . the rule in *Howe* v. *Lord Dartmouth* must be applied unless, upon the fair construction of the will, you find a sufficient indication of intention that it is not to be applied, and the burden in every case rests upon the person who says the rule of the Court ought not to be applied in the particular case."[65]

Under the rule the trustees are obliged to convert, on the one hand, wasting, hazardous and unauthorised securities which involve risk to capital in the interests of the remainderman and, on the other hand, future, reversionary or other non-income producing property in the interests of the tenant for life.[66] The rule is confined to wills and is subject to any contrary intention, express or implied, that the property left is to be enjoyed *in specie*. For this reason it is settled that the rule applies only to general as opposed to specific bequests. In *Re Abbott*,[67] there were express directions concerning sale of the property in certain events and it was held, applying the principle *expressio unius est exclusio alterius*, that there was sufficient indication of an intention that the property should be enjoyed *in specie* except in those events. It does not apply to realty though, as was held in *Re Harris's Estate* (referred above),[68] it does apply to leasehold property as well as pure personalty.

10.080.   As mentioned above, wherever the duty to convert arises, the trustees must ensure that a proper apportionment of the property is made pending conversion and, if the trustees fail to apportion or, indeed, fail ultimately to convert, the court will order conversion and the appropriate apportionment. The rules governing apportionment are as follows. In the case of wasting, hazardous or unauthorised assets, the problem is usually that the tenant for life is obtaining a high yield of income at the risk of a loss of capital, so the object of apportionment is to ensure that the tenant for life

---

[64]   (1802) 7 Ves. 137. See Bailey, "Leaseholds and the Rule in *Howe* v. *Lord Dartmouth*" (1934) 4 C.L.J. 357 and "Present State of the Rule in *Howe* v. *Lord Dartmouth*" (1943) 7 Conv. 128 and 191; Fricke, "*Howe* v. *Lord Dartmouth* – An Anachronism?" (1957) 1 M.U.L.R. 193; MacDougall, "*Howe* v. *Lord Dartmouth*: A Reply" (1958) 1 M.U.L.R. 498; Sheridan, "*Howe* v. *Lord Dartmouth* Re-Examined" (1952) 16 Conv. 349.
[65]   [1907] 1 I.R. 32 at 35 (see *A Casebook on Equity and Trusts in Ireland* (1985), p. 618).
[66]   *Arnold* v. *Ennis* (1853) 2 Ir.Ch.R. 601. See further, para. 10.082, *post*.
[67]   [1934] I.R. 189 (see *A Casebook on Equity and Trusts in Ireland* (1985), p. 621).
[68]   [1907] 1 I.R. 32, conversion of the leases of two houses with 30 and 40 years respectively left to run was ordered for benefit of the remainderman. *Cf.* the English position in the light now of s. 73 (1) (xi) of the Settled Land Act, 1925 (leases over 60 years authorised investments), and s. 28 of the Law of Property Act, 1925 (rents and profits of land until sale to be treated as income of investments representing the purchase money payable when sale made), see *Re Brooker* [1926] W.N. 93 and Bailey, (1934) 4 C.L.J. 357.

receives only the current yield from authorised investments[69] and that any surplus actually received is added to the capital.[70] One difficult question is the date at which the capital of the fund should be valued for the purpose of calculating the yield of income to be allowed to the tenant for life. The courts have decided that this should depend upon whether or not there is a power to postpone sale or conversion given to the trustees. If no such power is given, then the trustees are to be taken as governed by the "executor's year," i.e., the one year period during which it is considered that the administration of a deceased's estate should be completed.[71] If the trustees in fact sell during that year, the value is the proceeds of the sale; if they do not, the trust fund should be valued at the end of the one year and the tenant for life allowed the current yield on that value from the date of the death of the testator.[72] On the other hand, if the trustees are given a power to postpone sale there is no question of their being bound by the "executor's year" principle and really no other precise date relevant to actual conversion by them, so the date at which the value of the property should be taken for apportionment purposes is the death of the testator.[73] Before leaving this subject of "wasting or hazardous" securities, it should be stated that the conversion rules in this context have, at times, become divorced from the realities of the 1980s. Where the rules apply, they frequently require, in effect, the sale of equities and re-investment in gilt-edged securities. The traditional theory has always been that this is necessary to protect the remainderman from loss of capital and to reduce the disproportionately high rate of interest received by the tenant for life from such equities. Yet in these days of increasing inflation this may be the very reverse of what the parties would want.

10.081. The pattern of investment performance until recently was that it was gilt-edged securities which involved the greater risk of loss of capital value in real terms, but which did provide a reasonable rate of income or, at least, a rate above what the courts have been in the habit of allowing tenants for life, while only equities offered any safeguard against inflation in terms of capital value, but often produced a very poor rate of return, sometimes well below gilt-edged securities. Thus the tenant for life will often have favoured the sale of equities and investment in gilt-edged securities and the remainderman will have favoured retention of the equities — the reverse of the theories underlying the rules of conversion. Yet the rapid drop in stock market values in the past year or so has made investment in gilt-edged securities much more attractive, and this has illustrated the difficulties for trustees operating between successive periods of "booms" and "slumps." To some extent the investment scheme contained in the Trustee Investments

---

[69] In theory this ought to be governed by current stock market conditions, though the English courts have tended to adopt a fixed figure, e.g., 4 per cent was the figure applied in Re Baker [1924] 2 Ch. 271 and in Re Berry [1962] Ch. 97. Many gilt-edged securities nowadays will yield at least 15 per cent. return.

[70] The tenant for life will, of course, receive an increase in income due to such additions to the capital.

[71] See Re Smith (1914) 48 I.L.T.R. 236.

[72] See Napier v. Staples (1859) 10 Ir.Ch.R. 344.

[73] Brown v. Gellatly (1867) 2 Ch.App. 751; Re Owen [1912] 1 Ch. 519.

Acts, 1961, adapted, as we have seen, for Northern Ireland, recognises these investment facts, yet even under this scheme questions of conversion and apportionment can still arise, because the investments are still unauthorised as being either equities not within the categories of wider-range investments contained in the 1961 Act or, even if within those categories, the requisite expert advice on them has been that they ought not to be retained and should be sold.

10.082. In the case of future or reversionary property, where the tenant for life will receive no income so long as such property remains unconverted, apportionment is governed by the rule in *Re Earl of Chesterfield's Trusts*,[74] which had been applied in Ireland.[75] The only way to provide income is to sell the future or reversionary interest for what it is currently worth and to apportion the proceeds into what remains as capital and what should be taken as representing past income for the tenant for life.[76] This should be done in the following way.[77] The trustees should calculate what sums invested at 4 per cent. interest at the date of the testator's death, accumulating at compound interest with yearly rests,[78] would, after deduction of income tax at the standard or basic rate, produce the actual sum raised by sale of the future or reversionary interest. The sum so calculated should be treated as the capital and the difference between it and the sum received from the sale of the future or reversionary interest should be paid to the tenant for life as income.

It is clear, then, that the trustees could be involved in very complex administrative tasks and for this reason it is common practice for the trust instrument to include a clause exempting trustees from any duties of apportionment such as those discussed above.

(ii) Other Apportionments

10.083. The trustees may find that they have to make various other apportionments during the course of the administration of the trust. Indeed, some apportionments may have to be made at the very beginning of the trust where it arises under a will. A testator's debts must be paid out of his estate and there may be some delay in paying them, in which case the tenant for life would receive income on capital in the estate really needed for purposes other than providing him with income. Subject to a contrary intention, which is in practice usually expressed in wills, an apportionment would have to be made[79] under what is usually known as the rule in *Allhusen v. Whittell*.[80] In

---

[74] (1883) 24 Ch.D. 643.

[75] *Re Ancketills Estate* (1891) 27 L.R.Ir. 331; *Stewart* v. *Kingsale* [1902] 1 I.R. 496 (see *A Casebook on Equity and Trusts in Ireland* (1985), p. 622).

[76] His future income will come from the investments made with part of the proceeds treated as capital.

[77] See Rowland, *Trust Accounts* (3rd ed.), pp. 95 *et seq.*; Chandler, *Trust Accounts* (6th ed.), pp. 117–8.

[78] *I.e.*, adding the interest to the capital each year.

[79] Usually by adding the first year's income to the capital of the estate, then subtracting the sum representing the total of the debts, to give a sum which is taken to represent the true capital value of the estate, after payment of debts, *plus* one year's income.

[80] (1867) L.R. 4 Eq. 295. See Strahan "Rule in *Allhusen* v. *Whittell*" (1914) 30 L.Q.R. 481 and (1916) 32 L.Q.R. 208. And see *Coote* v. *Lord Miltown* (1844) 7 Ir.Eq.R. 391.

other cases, apportionment is decreed by statute, *e.g.*, under the Apportionment Act, 1870,[81] which provides that all rents, annuities, dividends and other periodical payments in the nature of income are to be considered as accruing from day to day and apportionable in respect of time accordingly.[82] Where certain types of investment fail, the trustees may be obliged to apportion the loss between the tenant for life and the remaindermen, *e.g.*, where trust funds are invested on the security of land which later ceases to be adequate security for the loan and interest due on the loan falls into arrears. On a subsequent sale of the land, the trustees may have to apportion the proceeds into the amount to be taken to represent the capital of the trust fund and the amount representing the arrears of income due to the tenant for life.[83]

10.084. The trustees may find themselves faced with problems because of the way in which particular companies, whose shares they hold, make payment to their shareholders. It may not always be clear to the trustees whether a particular payment should be treated *for the purposes of the trust* as a capital payment to be added to the trust fund or as an income payment to be paid to the tenant for life, for him to spend as he pleases. For example, a company may accumulate profits and later distribute them to shareholders as a cash bonus. It has been held in both Ireland[84] and England[85] that trustees must treat such a payment as income for the tenant for life, even though the company may call it a capital distribution, and that there is no need for any apportionment between capital and income. Similarly, any distribution of capital by a company can be made only in the special circumstances where companies are authorised to make such distribution to shareholders, *e.g.*, on liquidation or exercise of power to distribute from the share premium account. However, companies may increase their capital by capitalising profits and using the money to pay up new shares which are then issued to shareholders. It is settled in both Ireland[86] and England[87] that such an issue of bonus shares should be treated by the trustees as a capital distribution only.

10.085. Trustees would also seem to be relieved of any duty to make

---

[81] See also the Apportionment Act, 1834 (apportionment of rents on death). The 1834 Act was excluded in Ireland in the case of rents governed by Deasy's Act (Landlord and Tenant Law Amendment Act, Ireland), 1860, s. 50, see Sched. B.

[82] S. 2. See *Foster* v. *Cunningham* [1956] N.I. 29 (apportionment of conacre and agistment rents).

[83] See *Stewart* v. *Kingsale* [1902] 1 I.R. 496 (see *A Casebook on Equity and Trusts in Ireland* (1985), p. 622). *Cf.* the case of sale of trust property at an "exceptionally high price," *Kirkpatrick* v. *Naper* (1945) 79 I.L.T.R. 49.

[84] *Re Meagher's Will Trusts* [1951] I.R. 100. See also *Ex parte Hodgens* (1847) 11 Ir.Eq.R. 99. *Cf. French* v. *Craig* (1858) 8 Ir.Ch.R. 142.

[85] *Hill* v. *Permanent Trustee Co. of N.S.W.* [1930] A.C. 720; *Re Kleinwort's Settlements* [1951] Ch. 860; *Re Winder's Will Trusts* [1951] Ch. 916; *Re Duff's Settlement* [1951] Ch. 923; *Re Rudd's Will Trust* [1952] 1 All E.R. 254.

[86] *Ex parte Hodgens* (1847) 11 Ir.Eq.R. 99; *Re Carson* [1915] 1 I.R. 321; *Re Gihon's Will Trusts* [1928] N.I. 1; *Bank of Ireland* v. *Geoghegan* [1955–56] Ir.Jur.Rep. 7; *cf. Parkinson* v. *Walker* (1908) 42 I.L.T.R. 114.

[87] *Bouch* v. *Sproule* (1887) 12 App.Cas. 385; *I.R.C.* v. *Blott* [1921] 2 A.C. 171. See Bailey, "Settled Shares in a Company – Income and Capital" (1951) 67 L.Q.R. 195; Goodhart, "Bonus Shares in Lieu of Dividend – Capital or Income?" (1975) 39 Conv. 355; Lingard, "Bonus Shares and the Revenue" (1958) 22 Conv. 458; Strahan, "A Company's Capital or Income" (1930) 46 L.Q.R. 334.

apportionments in the sale of shares ex- or cum-dividend. At first sight this would appear to be a classic case for apportionment, for a sale of shares just before dividend day will result in a price including an allowance for the accrued dividend and a purchase just before dividend will require payment of a price inflated by the immediate prospect of the dividend. In the first case, the trustees would seem in effect to be increasing the capital for the remainderman at the cost of the tenant for life of a dividend he would otherwise have received and, in the second case, they would seem to be using capital to purchase a dividend for the tenant for life. Yet the trustees, especially those with a large fund, will be buying and selling shares regularly and it would impose a considerable burden on them to require them each time to consider such apportionments[88] and this may explain the reluctance on the part of Irish[89] and English judges[90] to impose a duty to make apportionments, in the absence of evidence of manipulation of investments by the trustees to secure advantage for one beneficiary at the expense of another.[91]

10.086. Lastly, the trustees may have to make apportionments of a certain kind where they carry out improvements and repairs to the trust property. In so far as the work involved can be regarded as part of the day-to-day expenses of the upkeep of the property, i.e., ordinary repairs, the cost should be borne by the tenant for life and deducted by the trustees out of income.,[92] On the other hand, in so far as the work can be considered a permanent improvement of the property, its cost should be met out of the capital of the trust and, therefore, borne ultimately by the remaindermen.[93]

IV. VARIATION OF TRUSTS

10.087. We come now to a subject which has assumed increasing importance in recent decades, namely variation of the terms of a trust, particularly those dealing with designation of the beneficial interests, *after* the trust has come into operation.[94] The reason this subject has become so

---

[88] A similar problem arises where a testator dies just before or just after a dividend day, see *O'Brien* v. *Fitzgerald* (1851) 1 Ir.Ch.R. 290 (see *A Casebook on Equity and Trusts in Ireland* (1985), p. 627).

[89] *O'Brien* v. *Fitzgerald, op cit.*

[90] *Scholefield* v. *Redfern* (1863) 2 Dr. & Sm. 173, where Kindersley V.-C. justified the general rule of no apportionment on the ground of the "complicated investigation" that would otherwise arise, so that the "gain to one party or the loss to the other would be far more than compensated by a tenth part of the expense which might be incurred in a complex and difficult case." Later judges in England seem to have recognised that an apportionment may be proper in special circumstances, see *Bulkeley* v. *Stephens* [1896] 2 Ch. 241; *Re Peel's Estate* [1910] 1 Ch. 389; *Re Walker* [1934] W.N. 104; *Re Winterstoke's Will Trusts* [1938] Ch. 158; *Re Firth's Estate* [1938] 1 Ch. 517; *Re Maclaren's Settlement Trusts* [1951] 2 All E.R. 414.

[91] See the discussion in *Raby* v. *Ridehalgh* (1855) 7 De G.M. & G. 104.

[92] *Harris* v. *Bains* (1902) 2 N.I.J.R. 56; *Re Waldron and Bogue's Contract* [1904] 1 I.R. 240. Cf. *Re Kingham* [1897] 1 I.R. 170. See also *McAuliffe* v. *Irish Sailors and Soldiers Land Trust* [1959] I.R. 78.

[93] *Brereton* v. *Day* [1895] 1 I.R. 518 (see *A Casebook on Equity and Trusts in Ireland* (1985), p. 628). Cf. *Martin* v. *Martin* [1898] 1 I.R. 112. Note also the statutory provisions governing payment of repairs and improvements to settled land under Pt. VII of the Settled Land Act 1882, para. 8.081, *ante*. See Willcock, "Repairs to Trust Property" (1956) 20 Conv. 351.

[94] See Harris, *Variation of Trusts* (1975). Also McClean, "Variations of Trusts in England and Canada" (1965) 43 C.B.R. 181; Marshall, "Deviations from Terms of a Trust" (1954) 17 M.L.R. 420; Mowbray, "Varying Trusts" (1958) 2 Conv. 373; Waters, "Variation of Trusts" (1960) 13 C.L.P. 36.

important is, of course, the increasing incidence and rate of taxation which may reduce drastically the value of the trust fund left available for the enjoyment of future beneficiaries. One of the pressing problems nowadays for the trustees, and the beneficiaries, is the protection of the fund from taxation and much ingenuity may be needed to formulate a satisfactory avoidance scheme.[95] Frequently such schemes would involve the variation of the beneficial interests in the trust property designated by the original settlor or testator and so the question remains how far such a variation can be made in Ireland. In considering this subject, a distinction has to be made between a variation without the approval of the court and one which requires such approval.

A. WITHOUT COURT APPROVAL

There are various ways in which a trust may be varied without the need to obtain the approval of the court.

1. *Beneficiaries All* Sui Juris

10.088. As we have mentioned several times before, there is nothing to prevent the beneficiaries, jointly with the trustees altering the trust to suit themselves or, if necessary (*e.g.*, the trustees refuse to agree), putting an end to it by calling upon the trustees to hand over the trust property and then, if they wish, arranging for a completely new trust to be set up. This can be done, however, only if all the beneficiaries are *sui juris, i.e.*, of full age and capacity, and together are entitled to the entire beneficial interest under the trust.[96] In the majority of trusts this, of course, will not be the case since there are usually beneficiaries either under age or not yet born.

2. *Surrender of Life Interest*

10.089. One common way of saving tax, especially estate duty, was for the current life owner of the property immediately to surrender his interest to the remainderman, which he is at liberty to do, provided, of course, that he is *sui juris*. Such a surrender in most cases achieved a saving, even a complete avoidance, of estate duty on the entire capital fund that would otherwise have been levied on the life tenant's death,[97] provided he survived the period applicable under estate duty law for *inter vivos* gifts.[98] Obviously, such a

---

[95] See Harvey, "Tax Avoidance – Illegal, Immoral or Fattening?" (1970) 21 N.I.L.Q. 235. See also Mellows, *Taxation for Executors and Trustees* (6th ed., 1984).

[96] *Saunders* v. *Vautier* (1841) Cr. & Ph. 240. The principle was applied in *Re Miller* [1897] 1 I.R. 290 (see *A Casebook on Equity and Trusts in Ireland* (1985), p. 633).

[97] But *cf.* the position under the new capital acquisition (transfer) tax in both parts of Ireland.

[98] 5 years in the Republic of Ireland, see Finance Act, 1961, s. 24; 4 years in Northern Ireland, see Finance Acts (N.I.), 1960, s. 1 and 1968, s. 1.

scheme was of interest to a life tenant only if he had adequate income for his purpose without recourse to trust income.[99]

3. *Advancement*

10.090. Exercise of an express power of advancement of capital, or of the statutory power,[1] may also be used in a case where the tenant for life does not need all the trust income and is happy to agree to immediate advancement of some of the capital to a remainderman. Once again, for the advancement to secure estate duty relief on the death of the life tenant, he must have survived for the requisite *inter vivos* gift period.

B. WITH COURT APPROVAL

10.091. The necessity for court approval of any scheme for variation of the terms of a trust usually arises where there are unborn or infant beneficiaries who lack the capacity to agree to the scheme devised by the trustees and other *sui juris* beneficiaries, and their advisers. In certain cases an application may be made to the court for its sanction of the scheme on behalf of those beneficiaries who cannot concur in it on their own behalf. This power of the court in Ireland derives partly from the court's inherent jurisdiction and partly from statute law.

1. *Inherent Jurisdiction*

10.092. It seems that the inherent jurisdiction of the court to sanction a variation of the terms of a trust on behalf of beneficiaries who are not *sui juris* is limited to two situations.[2] One situation is where the court's *salvage* or *emergency* jurisdiction may be invoked, *i.e.*, where some emergency situation, unforeseen by the settlor or testator, has arisen and it is necessary to take action not authorised by the terms of the trust to save it from destruction or considerable damage. Generally an application to the court is made simply for the necessary administrative powers to act in the situation and it is doubtful if this salvage jurisdiction could be invoked to alter the beneficial interests.[3] The other situation where the court's sanction can be

---

[99] A surrender cannot be made if the life tenant has only a protected life interest, since an attempt at one will induce a forfeiture of his interest and the operation of the protective trusts, see para. 9.083, *ante*. Such an exercise ceased, of course, to be so effective a tax-saving device when estate duty was replaced by new capital taxes attacking *inter vivos* dispositions as well as ones on death, *i.e.*, capital acquisitions tax (gift and inheritance taxes) in R.I. and capital transfer tax in N.I. Note that, as announced in the British Budget Speech 1986, the latter is to revert to a death only tax.

[1] Para. 10.048, *ante*. Agreement to such an advancement will *not* effect a forfeiture of a protected life interest.

[2] See *Bank of Ireland* v. *Geoghegan* [1955–56] Ir.Jur.Rep. 7. The leading English authority on this subject is *Chapman* v. *Chapman* [1954] A.C. 429.

[3] *Bank of Ireland* v. *Geoghegan*, *op. cit.*; see also *Neill* v. *Neill* [1904] 1 I.R. 513; *Re Johnson's Settlement* [1944] I.R. 529 (see *A Casebook on Equity and Trusts in Ireland* (1985), p. 634). See also *Re De Malahide* (1952) 86 I.L.T.R. 191 (trust property situated in Scotland, where no power to sell it, but testator died domiciled in Ireland, and trustees granted authorisation of Irish Court to apply to Scottish Court for authority to sell). And see *Re Tollemache* [1903] 1 Ch. 457 and 955.

sought is in cases of *compromise* of disputes as between the claims of the various beneficiaries under a trust. The House of Lords held in *Chapman v. Chapman*[4] that for this jurisdiction to operate there must be a genuine dispute between the beneficiaries and not merely a desire to alter the terms of the original trust, however much that may be to the benefit of all concerned, in the light of taxation or in any other way.

2. *By statute*

10.093. In the Republic of Ireland there are no statutory provisions for variation of trusts with the court's approval and so the scope for variation is limited to the situations outlined above. In Northern Ireland, however, there are several statutory provisions granting variation jurisdiction.

10.094. First under Article 26 of the Matrimonial Causes (Northern Ireland) Order, 1978, a court, in granting a decree of divorce or nullity of marriage or judicial separation, is given a wide power to make "property adjustment orders" so as to vary (including alteration of beneficial interests) the trusts in any ante- or post-nuptial settlement made for the benefit of the parties of the marriage or their children.[5] Secondly, section 56 (1) of the Trustee Act (N.I.), 1958, provides:

"Where any transaction affecting or concerning any property vested in trustees, is in the opinion of the court expedient, but the same cannot be effected by reason of the absence of any power for that purpose vested in the trustees by the instrument, if any, creating the trust, or by law, the court may by order confer upon the trustees, either generally or in any particular instance, the necessary power for the purpose, on such terms and subject to such provisions and conditions, if any, as the court may think fit, and may direct in what manner any money authorised to be expended, and the costs of any transaction, are to be paid or borne as between capital and income."

By subsection (3), an application under the section may be made by the trustees, or any of them, or any beneficiaries and subsection (4) applies the section to settlements within the meaning of the Settled Land Acts, 1882–90.[6] Section 56 is clearly confined to authorisation of "transactions" and so relates more to extension of the trustees' powers of management or administration,[7] rather than alteration of the beneficial interests. To some extent it may

---

[4] [1954] A.C. 429. *Cf.* Denning L.J. in the Court of Appeal [1953] Ch. 218.

[5] This replaces the power contained in s. 21 of the Matrimonial Causes Act (N.I.), 1939. In England this power is now contained in ss. 24–6 of the Matrimonial Causes Act, 1973, (as amended by s.3 of the Matrimonial and Family Proceedings Act, 1984) which replaced s. 4 of the Matrimonial Proceedings and Property Act, 1970, which in turn replaced s. 17 of the Matrimonial Causes Act, 1965. See *Thomson* v. *Thomson* [1954] P. 384 (alterations effecting a saving of estate duty). Also *Ulrich* v. *Ulrich* [1968] 1 All E.R. 67; *Muetzel* v. *Muetzel* [1970] 1 W.L.R. 188; *Tinker* v. *Tinker* [1970] P. 136.

[6] S. 56 is thus the equivalent of the English Trustee Act, 1925, s. 57 and Settled Land Act, 1925, s. 57 and Settled Land Act, 1925, s. 64. See generally, Carswell, *Trustee Acts (Northern Ireland)* (1964) pp. 111–15.

[7] See the definition of "transaction" in s. 56 (5).

overlap with the court's inherent salvage or emergency jurisdiction,[8] though it obviously widens that jurisdiction to cover cases of expediency rather than emergency.[9] One of the commonest applications of this jurisdiction, at least in England, was enlargement of trustees' powers of investment but it seems that this may no longer be the case since the passing of the Trustee Investments Act, 1961, despite the apparent provision to the contrary in section 4 of the Trustee (Amendment) Act (N.I.), 1962.[10]

10.095. Thirdly, far and away the widest jurisdiction is conferred by section 57 (1) of the Trustee Act (N.I.), 1958, as amended by section 5 of the Trustee (Amendment) Act (N.I.), 1962,[11] to read:

"Subject to sub-section (2), where property is held on any trusts or settlements arising under any will, settlement or other disposition, the court may if it thinks fit by order approve on behalf of–

(a) any person having, directly or indirectly, an estate or interest, whether vested or contingent, under the trusts or settlements who by reason of infancy or other incapacity is incapable of assenting; or

(b) any person (whether ascertained or not) who may become entitled, directly or indirectly, to an estate or interest under the trusts or settlements as being at a future date or on the happening of a future event a person of any specified description or a member of any specified class of persons so, however, that this paragraph shall not include any person who would be of that description, or a member of that class, as the case may be, if the said date had fallen or the said event had happened at the date of the application to the court; or

(c) any person unborn; or

(d) any person in respect of any discretionary interest of his under protective trusts where the interest of the principal beneficiary has not failed or determined,

any arrangement (by whosoever proposed, and whether or not there is any other person beneficially interested who is capable of assenting thereto) varying or revoking all or any of the trusts or settlements, or enlarging the powers of the trustees of managing or administering any of the property subject to the trusts or settlements.

(2) Except by virtue of paragraph (d) of sub-section (1) the court shall not approve an arrangement on behalf of any person unless the carrying out of the arrangement would be for the benefit of that person."

---

[8] Para. 10.092, *supra*.
[9] See *Re Downshire's Settled Land Estate* (1953) Ch. 218; *Re Cockerell's Settlement Trusts* [1956] Ch. 372.
[10] Para. 10.063, *ante*.
[11] See Carswell, *op cit.*, pp. 116–21. The English equivalent, rushed through Parliament after the House of Lords decision in *Chapman* v. *Chapman*, para. 10.092, *supra*, is the Variation of Trusts Act, 1958.

10.096. It can be seen that section 57 to some extent overlaps with the jurisdiction conferred by section 56 of the 1958 Act,[12] but it is much wider in that it sanctions variation of the beneficial interests under a trust wherever this is considered to be for the benefit of the persons concerned.[13] It is important to note that the court has jurisdiction even under section 57 to sanction a variation only on behalf of those who cannot do so themselves. All beneficiaries who are *sui juris* must agree to any variation on their own behalf.[14] Before giving approval, it seems that the court must be satisfied about the proposed scheme as a whole.[15] It will consider the general welfare of the persons on whose behalf approval is sought and not just their financial interests[16] and consider how far the new scheme is consistent with the general plan of the original settlor or testator.[17] However, it is clear from the English authorities that the new jurisdiction of the court has opened doors to applications whose primary purpose is tax avoidance and, while the English courts will not allow fiscal considerations to override all others, they have shown little diffidence about ignoring the difficulties and doubts expressed by some members of the House of Lords in *Chapman* v. *Chapman*[18] about the propriety of the courts joining battle in this way with Parliament in its efforts to raise revenue by taxation.[19]

V. BREACH OF TRUST

10.097. There are several matters to be considered under this heading.[20] First, there is the question of a trustee's liability to the beneficiaries in respect of a breach of trust by him, both the extent and measure of liability. Secondly, there is the question of liability of the trustees *inter se, i.e.*, to what extent they are jointly and severally liable and the questions of contribution and indemnity. Thirdly, there is the question of how far a trustee is allowed protection in respect of a breach of trust. Lastly, there is the question of the remedies available to the beneficiaries in respect of a breach of trust, in particular remedies available should the trustees turn out to be impecunious.

[12]   S. 57 (6) provides that nothing in the section is to limit the powers conferred by section 56. The overlapping may be explained by the different derivations of the two provisions, namely the English Trustee Act, 1925, s. 57 and the Variation of Trusts Act, 1958,

[13]   But note the exception in subs. (2) for protective trusts, see also subs. (3). *Re Van Gruisen's Will Trusts* [1964] 1 W.L.R. 449.

[14]   The court is also unlikely to override the views of the trustees, see *Re Steed's Will Trusts* [1960] Ch. 407. If beneficiaries are in existence, they should be traced, *Re Suffert's Settlement* [1961] Ch. 1; *Re Clarke's Will Trusts* [1961] 3 All E.R. 1133.

[15]   *Re Burney's Settlement Trusts* [1961] 1 All E.R. 856; *Re Robinson's Will Trusts* [1976] 1 W.L.R. 806; *Re Ball's Settlement* [1968] 1 W.L.R. 899.

[16]   *Re T.'s Settlement Trusts* [1964] Ch. 158; *Re Holt's Settlement* [1969] 1 Ch. 100; *Re Weston's Settlements* [1969] 1 Ch. 223. See Watkin's, "Shifting Interests Overseas" (1976) 40 Conv. 295.

[17]   *Re Steed's Will Trusts* [1960] Ch. 407.

[18]   [1954] A.C. 429 (see especially the opinion of Lord Morton), para. 10.092, *supra*.

[19]   See, *e.g.*, *Re Druce's Settlement Trusts* [1962] 1 W.L.R. 363 (estate duty); *Re Sainsbury's Settlement* [1967] 1 W.L.R. 476 (capital gains tax); *Re Clitheroe's Settlement Trusts* [1959] 1 W.L.R. 1159 (income tax).

[20]   See Delany, "Innocent Participation by Banker in Breach of Trust" (1959) 61 J.I.B.I. 201; Niles, "Trustee Accountability in Absence of Breach of Trust" (1960) 60 Col.L.Rev. 141; Scott, "Deviation from the Terms of a Trust" (1931) 44 H.L.R. 1025; Weston, "Money Stolen from One Trust and Used in Another" (1912) 25 H.L.R. 602. See also the discussion by Megarry V.-C. in *Tito* v. *Waddell (No. 2)* [1977] Ch. 106.

A. TRUSTEE'S PERSONAL LIABILITY

10.098. It is the duty of a trustee to comply with the general law of trusts and the terms of the trust instrument, and, in doing so, to act prudently.[21] Thus it has been held to be a breach of trust in Ireland for a trustee not to register a deed conveying land on trust.[22] The general rule is, however, that a trustee is liable for his own breaches of trust only and not for those of his co-trustees, *i.e.*, personally but not vicariously liable. As we have already seen, this position has been recognised by statute law in both parts of Ireland.[23] This statutory indemnity is expressly subject to a limitation in respect of "wilful default" on the part of a trustee and he will still be liable if he allows property to remain in the complete control of his co-trustees or ignores their breaches of trust.[24] A trustee is not liable for breaches of trust committed before his appointment, unless there is clear evidence of this breach available to him and he ignores it, so that he should examine the books and documents relating to the trust on his appointment.[25] He is liable, however, after retirement for breaches committed by him during his term of office, though not usually for breaches committed after his retirement, unless, *e.g.*, he retired to facilitate a breach.[26]

10.099. At common law a breach of trust was not a crime but some breaches are now in both parts of Ireland. In the Republic of Ireland, a trustee commits a misdemeanour under section 21 of the Larceny Act, 1916, if he appropriates the trust property, with intent to defraud, to his own uses or for any other purpose than a legitimate one.[27] In Northern Ireland, the matter is now governed by the Theft Act (N.I.), 1968,[28] section 1 (1) of which defines "theft" as the dishonest appropriation of "property belonging to another with the intention of permanently depriving the other of it." Section 5 (2) provides that "any person having a right to enforce the trust" is a person to whom the subject-matter of the trust "belongs."[29] Furthermore, under section 5 of the Debtors (Ireland) Act, 1872, in both parts of Ireland a trustee ordered by a court of equity to pay any sum in his possession or under his control may be imprisoned for default of payment for a period not exceeding one year.

---

[21] See *Carr* v. *Connor* (1929) 63 I.L.T.R. 185. See also Hawkins, "The Personal Liability of Charity Trustees" (1979) 95 L.Q.R. 99.

[22] *Macnamara* v. *Carey* (1867) I.R. 1 Eq. 9 (see *A Casebook on Equity and Trusts in Ireland* (1985), p. 576). See also *Townley* v. *Bond* (1843) 4 Dr. & War. 240; *Lester* v. *Lester* (1857) 6 Ir.Ch.R. 513. Ch. 22 *post*.

[23] Trustee Act, 1893, s. 24; Trustee Act (N.I.), 1958, s. 31. See para. 10.036, *supra*. See also *Moore* v. *McGlynn* [1894] 1 I.R. 74, espec. at 88–9 (*per* Chatterton V.-C.) (see *A Casebook on Equity and Trusts in Ireland* (1985), p. 374).

[24] *Featherstone H.* v. *West* (1871) I.R. 6 Eq. 86; *Jones* v. *Fitzgerald* (1931) 65 I.L.T.R. 185. *Cf.* the position of executors, see *Joy* v. *Campbell* (1804) 1 Sch. & Lef. 328; *Lowe* v. *Shields* [1902] 1 I.R. 320 at 323–4 (*per* FitzGibbon L.J.).

[25] Para. 10.050, *supra*.

[26] See Kekewich J. in *Head* v. *Gould* [1898] 2 Ch. 250 at 272.

[27] See *Williams* v. *Bayley* (1866) L.R. 1 H.L. 200; *Jones* v. *Merionethshire Building Society* [1892] 1 Ch. 173.

[28] See Miers, (1969) 20 N.I.L.Q. 455. Also Brazier, "Criminal Trustees?" (1975) 39 Conv. 29.

[29] See also ss. 4 (2) (*a*) (appropriation of "land or anything forming part of it" by a trustee) and 2 (1) (*c*) (theft even though trustee believes the equitable owners cannot be discovered).

10.100. The measure of a trustee's liability in respect of his breach of trust is generally the direct or indirect loss caused to the trust estate. It matters not that the trustee obtained no gain from the breach.[30] If a trustee makes an unauthorised investment he will have to replace the whole fund invested, if necessary.[31] He will also be liable for retaining an unauthorised investment to the extent of the difference between the present value and the price it would have realised if sold at the proper time.[32] Any profit made on unauthorised investments or on any misappropriation of trust funds must be surrendered to the trust.[33] Furthermore, where a trustee is under a liability to replace trust funds, he is chargeable with interest on the sum due. The rate of interest chargeable lies in the discretion of the court[34] and is usually fixed at 4 per cent.[35] However, a trustee guilty of wilful default or gross misconduct may find himself charged with a higher rate[36] and in *Walsh* v. *Murray*[37] 5 per cent. simple interest was ordered for the period a trustee refused to furnish accounts. Where a trustee has used trust funds in a trading or business venture, the beneficiaries may be given the option to claim interest or an account from the trustee of all his dealings including any profits he actually made.[38]

B. TRUSTEES' LIABILITY *Inter Se*

10.101. Where more than one trustee is involved in a breach of trust, liability is joint and several, *i.e.*, the beneficiaries may claim for the entire loss against all or some or any one of the trustees involved and can levy execution against any one.[39] However, if one trustee is thus forced to pay more than his share of liability, he may claim contribution from the other trustees involved in the breach of trust or from their estates.[40] On the other hand, there are occasions where a trustee will not be liable to contribute and will instead be entitled to an indemnity from his co-trustees.[41] Thus where one trustee is fraudulent, he alone will be liable as against his co-trustees. The same is true

---

[30] *Adair* v. *Shaw* (1803) 1 Sch. & Lef. 243. See also *Bradley* v. *Barton* (1847) 10 Ir.L.R. 363; *Bartlett* v. *Barclays Bank Trust Co. Ltd. (No. 2)* [1980] Ch. 515.

[31] *O'Brien* v. *O'Brien* (1828) 1 Mol. 533. See also *Carson* v. *Sloane* (1884) 13 L.R.Ir. 139. And see s. 24 of the Trustee Act, 1893, and s. 31 of the Trustee Act (N.I.), 1958, para. 10.098, *supra*.

[32] *Fry* v. *Fry* (1859) 27 Beav. 144. Note that in Northern Ireland advice must be sought under s. 6 (2) of the Trustee Investments Act, 1961, on the question of retention of certain authorised investments, para. 10.067, *supra*.

[33] Para. 10.068, *supra*.

[34] *Flanagan* v. *Nolan* (1828) 1 Mol. 84.

[35] *McArdle* v. *Gaughran* [1903] 1 I.R. 106; see also *Hamilton* v. *Lane* (1890) 25 L.R.Ir. 188; *Collings* v. *Wade* [1896] 1 I.R. 340. This rate of interest is clearly out of line with modern interest rates and the English courts have recently been inclined to charge a more "commercial" rate, see *Wallsteiner* v. *Moir (No. 2)* [1975] Q.B. 373; *Belmont Finance Corporation* v. *Williams Furniture Ltd (No. 2)* [1980] 1 All ER 393.

[36] *Sheridan* v. *Joyce* (1844) 7 Ir.Eq.R. 115 (6 per cent.).

[37] (1878) 12 I.L.T.R. 61.

[38] *Scott* v. *Scott* [1924] 1 I.R. 141.

[39] *Alleyne* v. *Darcy* (1854) 4 Ir.Ch.R. 199; *cf. Costello* v. *O'Rorke* (1869) I.R. 3 Eq. 172.

[40] *Collings* v. *Wade* [1903] 1 I.R. 89.

[41] See *Adair* v. *Shaw* (1803) 1 Sch. & Lef. 243; *Worthington* v. *Pakenham* (1851) 3 Ir.Jur. (O.S.) 221; *Fetherstone H.* v. *West* (1871) I.R. 6 Eq. 86.

where one trustee is a solicitor and, as such, has exercised a controlling influence over the other trustees, so that they were unable to exercise an independent judgment.[42] If a beneficiary participates in a breach of trust for personal gain, he will have to indemnify the trustees,[43] though some contribution may be claimed if he is also a trustee.[44]

C. PROTECTION OF TRUSTEES

10.102. There are several ways in which a trustee may be protected from the normal consequences of his breach of trust, *i.e.*, being held personally liable.[45] First, a beneficiary has no claim against a trustee if the beneficiary participated, directly or indirectly, in the breach of trust.[46] Such participation may take the form of assisting the trustee in carrying out the activities amounting to the breach or in consenting to it. Secondly, a beneficiary will be deprived of his remedies against the trustee if, subsequent to the breach, he positively confirms it or acquiesces in it.[47] Of course, in this and the previous case, it is essential that the beneficiary was *sui juris*,[48] fully aware of all the facts[49] and exercised a free and independent judgment in the matter,[50] if the trustee is to be protected against a claim by the beneficiary.

10.103. Thirdly, the court has an inherent jurisdiction to impound the interest of a beneficiary who instigated or requested the breach of trust and his interest will be used to indemnify the trustee so far as is possible. There is no necessity to show that the beneficiary benefited from the breach, though there may be in the case of him simply consenting to or acquiescing in it.[51] However, this inherent jurisdiction to impound a beneficiary's interest has been recognised and extended by statute in both parts of Ireland.[52] Under section 45 of the Trustee Act, 1893, and section 62 of the Trustee Act (N.I.), 1958, the court may order the impounding of a beneficiary's interest where a trustee has committed a breach of trust at the instigation or request or with the consent *in writing*[53] of the beneficiary and thereby indemnify the trustee

---

[42] *Head* v. *Gould* [1898] 2 Ch. 250, espec. at 265 (*per* Kekewich J.).

[43] See *French* v. *Graham* (1860) 10 Ir.Ch.R. 522. Note the possibility of impounding the beneficiary's interest, para. 10.103, *infra*.

[44] Under the rule in *Chillingworth* v. *Chambers* [1896] 1 Ch. 685, the beneficiary-trustee's property is taken first to meet claims, so that his co-trustees have an indemnity to that extent. Thereafter the trustees share the liability equally.

[45] See the discussion in *Re Pauling's Settlement Trusts* [1964] Ch. 303.

[46] *Browne* v. *Maunsell* (1856) 5 Ir.Ch.R. 351 (see *A Casebook on Equity and Trusts in Ireland* (1985), p. 635); *Keays* v. *Lane* (1869) I.R. 3 Eq. 1; *O'Shea* v. *O'Shea* (1878) 12 I.L.T.R. 134. See also *McComb* v. *Ulster Bank Ltd.* (1968) 19 N.I.L.Q. 70.

[47] *Re Lynch* (1860) 6 Ir.Jur(N.S.) 143; *Rutherfoord* v. *Maziere* (1862) 13 Ir.Ch.R. 204: *Re McKenna's Estate* (1861) 13 Ir.Ch.R. 239.

[48] *Kilbee* v. *Sneyd* (1828) 2 Mol. 186.

[49] *Roche* v. *O'Brien* (1810) 1 Ba. & B. 330 at 339 (*per* Manners L.C.).

[50] *Bowles* v. *Stewart* (1803) 1 Sch. & Lef. 209.

[51] *Browne* v. *Maunsell* (1856) 5 Ir.Ch.R 351 (see *A Casebook on Equity and Trusts in Ireland* (1985), p. 635); *Keays* v. *Lane* (1869) I.R. 3 Eq. 1; *O'Shea* v. *O'Shea* (1878) 12 I.L.T.R. 154; *Jones* v. *Fitzgerald* (1931) 65 I.L.T.R. 185. See also *Booth* v. *Booth* (1838) 1 Beav. 125; *Chillingworth* v. *Chambers* [1896] 1 Ch. 685.

[52] See *Bolton* v. *Curre* [1895] 1 Ch. 544, espec. at 549 (*per* Romer J.).

[53] The requirement of writing applies only to the case of consent, *Re Somerset* [1894] 1 Ch. 231 at 265 (*per* Lindley L.J.). See also *Fletcher* v. *Collis* [1905] 2 Ch. 24.

or his estate. It must be emphasised that this entire matter lies in the discretion of the court.[54]

10.104. Fourthly, the court is given, though in limited circumstances in the Republic of Ireland, power to excuse trustees from the consequences of a breach of trust. In the Republic this relief is confined to proceedings in relation to any lands sold under the Land Purchase Acts. Under section 51 (4) of the Irish Land Act, 1903, the court may in such cases relieve a trustee from personal liability if he "has acted honestly and reasonably and ought fairly to be excused from the breach of trust."[55] It was held in *Jones* v. *Fitzgerald*[56] that a trustee who placed the trust fund in the hands of the tenant for life was not acting reasonably and so should not be excused. In Northern Ireland the same jurisdiction is conferred on the court by section 61 of the Trustee Act (N.I.), 1958,[57] except that it applies to trustees generally.[58] In exercising its jurisdiction and in deciding whether or not to exercise its discretion to grant relief, the court must consider the three elements mentioned, honesty, reasonableness and fairness.[59] The onus is on the trustee to show that he has acted honestly and reasonably.[60]

10.105. Fifthly, a trustee may be protected from an action for breach of trust under the statutes of limitations. In both parts of Ireland the period of limitation in respect of actions against trustees is 6 years,[61] and time does begin to run against a remainderman until his interest falls into possession.[62] The statutes do not apply to actions against trustees in any case where the claim is founded on any fraud or fraudulent breach of trust to which a trustee was party or privy[63] or the claim is to recover trust property or the proceeds thereof still retained by the trustee, or previously received by him and converted to his own use.[64] Apart from the statutes of limitation, a trustee may be protected by the equitable doctrine of laches,[65] which is particularly relevant in the case of claims not covered by the statutes, *e.g.*, claims for

---

[54] *Jones* v. *Fitzgerald* (1931) 65 I.L.T.R. 185.
[55] See also the court power to relieve a company director in similar circumstances conferred by s. 391 of the Companies Act, 1963 (replacing earlier legislation).
[56] (1931) 65 I.L.T.R. 185.
[57] As to relief of company directors, see s. 394 of the Companies Act (N.I.), 1960.
[58] It was first introduced in England by s. 3 of the Judicial Trustees Act 1896, which did not apply to Ireland. See now the English Trustee Act, 1925, s. 61. See also Maugham, "Excusable Breaches of Trust" (1898) 14 L.Q.R. 159; Sheridan, "Excusable Breaches of Trust" (1955) 19 Conv. 420.
[59] See *Jones* v. *Fitzgerald* (1931) 65 I.L.T.R. 185. Also *Davis* v. *Hutchings* [1907] 1 Ch. 356; *Re Allsop* [1914] 1 Ch. 1; *Mavaden* v. *Regan* [1954] 1 W.L.R. 423.
[60] *Re Stuart* [1897] 2 Ch. 583. On the subject of reasonable conduct, see *Carr* v. *O'Connor* (1929) 63 I.L.T.R. 185. Also *McComb* v. *Ulster Bank Ltd.* (1968) 19 N.I.L.Q. 70. And see *Bartlett* v. *Barclays Bank Trust Co. Ltd. (No. 1)* [1980] Ch. 515.
[61] Statute of Limitations, 1957, ss. 2 (2), 43 and 44 (R.I.); Statute of Limitations (N.I.), 1958, ss. 44–5 and 74 (2). See ch. 23, *post*. See *Carroll* v. *Hargrave* (1870) I.R. 5 Eq. 123; see also *Dunne* v. *Doran* (1844) 13 Ir.Eq.R. 545; *Newport* v. *Bryan* (1856) 5 Ir.Ch.R. 119. Also Delany, (1961) J.I.B.I. 126.
[62] *Collings* v. *Wade* [1896] 1 I.R. 340; *Russell* v. *Crowley* [1907] 1 I.R. 275.
[63] *Ibid.* Brunyate, "Fraud and the Statutes of Limitation" (1931) 4 C.L.J. 174.
[64] *Clarke* v. *Crowley* (1930) 64 I.L.T.R. 1. See 1957 Act, s. 44; 1958 Act (N.I.) s. 45.
[65] See on this para, 3.066, *ante*.

equitable relief by way of specific performance,[66] injunction,[67] rescission[68] or rectification.[69]

10.106. Lastly, it is interesting to note the different effects of bankruptcy of a trustee on his liability for breach of trust in Ireland and England. Under section 58 of the Bankruptcy (Ireland) Amendment Act, 1872, if a trustee becomes bankrupt and obtains a discharge (certificate of conformity), this does *not* relieve him from liability for breach of trust. In England his liability is terminated by his discharge, except in respect of fraudulent breaches of trust.[70] Section 58 of the 1872 Act was repealed in Northern Ireland by the Bankruptcy Amendment (Northern Ireland) Order, 1980, and article 31 of the Order now makes the law in that part of Ireland accord with English law.

D. BENEFICIARIES' REMEDIES

In the event of a breach of trust the beneficiaries have two main types of remedy, sometimes, though not without some confusion, referred to as remedies *in personam* and *in rem*.[71]

1. *In Personam*

10.107. We have already seen that the beneficiaries always have a personal remedy against a trustee for breach of trust, subject, of course, to any protection which the trustee may be able to claim in the particular case.[72] Unfortunately, and especially in cases of fraud, this personal remedy against the trustee usually proves to be of little use because the trustee is impecunious or bankrupt and so not in a position to make good the loss. This means that the second kind of remedy frequently is vital to the beneficiaries, because it does not depend for its efficacy on the financial position of the trustee. Furthermore, such a remedy usually secures priority for the claimant as against unsecured creditors in any bankruptcy or liquidation proceedings.[73]

2. *In Rem*

10.108. By an *in rem* remedy is meant the right of the beneficiaries to follow the misappropriated trust property into whosesoever hands it has come. This is sometimes known as the right of tracing. This remedy of tracing has had a

---

66   Para. 3.142, *ante*.
67   Para. 3.127, *ante*.
68   Para. 3.157, *ante*.
69   Para. 3.162, *ante*.
70   Insolvency Act 1985, s. 128 (3), replacing the Bankruptcy Act, 1914, s. 28.
71   See the discussion in *Re Diplock* [1948] Ch. 465, on appeal *Ministry of Health* v. *Simpson* [1951] A.C. 251. Also by Budd J. in *Shanahan's Stamp Auctions Ltd.* v. *Farrelly* [1962] I.R. 386 (see *A Casebook on Equity and Trusts in Ireland* (1985), p. 636).
72   Paras. 10.098–106, *supra*.
73   See *Re Calvert* [1961] N.I. 58.

long history of development both at common law and equity and what follows is an attempt to summarise the present position in Ireland.[74]

(i) At Common Law

10.109. The common law recognised a proprietary right of tracing to this extent, namely, that the owner of a specified item of property could claim it back from any person who wrongfully received it, on the ground that it was still his property. The owner could continue to lay claim to his item of property so long as it remained identifiable and it mattered not that the property might change form and be substituted for something else.[75] In the case of land, if this is sold to some third party and the proceeds are misappropriated, tracing can proceed against the person who sold the land and, if necessary, a constructive trust will be imposed upon him in relation to the proceeds of the sale.[76] Recently, in *Shanahan's Stamp Auctions Ltd.* v. *Farrelly*,[77] which involved a company organising stamp syndicates, which eventually went into liquidation, Budd J. held that money given by subscribers to the company's scheme to buy stamps was, in effect, held on trust and, while he did not allow a tracing claim against stamps actually purchased,[78] he did find that they were held on trust for sale and subscribers would be entitled *pro rata* to the proceeds of their sale in priority to the claims of ordinary creditors.

10.110. The limitation of the remedy of tracing at common law lies in the fact that once the item of property becomes mixed or intermingled with other property it ceases to be identifiable and so the remedy is lost. It was equity's major contribution to the law of tracing that it overcame the problem of tracing property into a mixed fund, at least to some extent. This limitation of the common law is, of course, in the context of trusts a very significant one, because in most cases such mixing or intermingling does occur, *e.g.*, by the trustee paying trust funds into his own personal bank account.

---

[74] See the discussion in Goff and Jones, *Law of Restitution* (2nd ed., 1978). Also Ames, "Following Misappropriated Property into its Product" (1906) 19 H.L.R. 511; Babafemi, "Tracing Assets: A Case for the Fusion of Common Law and Equity" (1971) 34 M.L.R. 12; Brodhurt, "Following Property in the Hands of an Agent" (1898) 14 L.Q.R. 272; Fleming, "Recovery of Money Mistakenly Paid by Personal Representatives (1947) 11 Conv. 275; Goode, "The Right to Trace and its Impact on Commercial Transactions" (1976) 92 L.Q.R. 360 and 528; Khurshid and Matthews, "Tracing Confusion" (1979) 95 L.Q.R. 76; McLauchlan, "Priorities – Equitable Tracing Rights and Assignments of Book Debts" (1980) 96 L.Q.R. 90; Maudsley, "Restitution in England" (1966) 19 Vand.L.Rev, 1123; McConville, "Tracing and the Rule in Clayton's Case" (1936) 79 L.Q.R. 388; Oakley, "The Pre-requisites of an Equitable Tracing Claim" (1975) C.L.P. 64; Pearce, "A Tracing Paper" (1976) 40 Conv. 277; Scott, "The Right to Follow Money Wrongfully Mingled with Other Money" (1913) 27 H.L.R. 125; Taft, "A Defence of a Limited Use of the Swollen Assets Theory Where Money has Wrongfully been Mingled with Other Money" (1939) 39 Col.L.Rev. 172; Williston, "The Right to Follow Trust Property When Confused with Other Property" (1888) 2 H.L.R. 28.

[75] See *Taylor* v. *Plumer* (1815) 3 M. & S. 562, espec. at 575 (*per* Lord Ellenborough C.J.).

[76] *Carson* v. *Sloane* (1884) 13 L.R.Ir. 139.

[77] [1962] I.R. 386 (see *A Casebook on Equity and Trusts in Ireland* (1985), p. 636). See also *Re Shannon Travel Ltd.* (1972) Unrep. (H.C., R.I.) (1970, No. 3849 P).

[78] On the ground that to hold that there was a trust of these stamps *in specie* was neither intended nor practicable.

(ii) In Equity

10.111. Equity also recognises a right to trace property into an unmixed form or fund, but, as *Shanahan's* case indicates, often provides a more sophisticated remedy by giving the claimant an option. If the misappropriated property is sold and the proceeds of sale are used to purchase other property, the claimant may be given the option either to take the property purchased or to have a charge on it to the amount misappropriated.[79] As Porter M.R. remarked in *Carson* v. *Sloane*:

> ". . . [W]hen trust funds misapplied can be traced into particular invest-
> ments or securities, the latter will be specially charged with their amount.
> In the case of a banker; . . . of a stockbroker; . . . of a solicitor; . . . and
> in numerous other cases of actual or constructive trusts this has been a
> perfectly settled rule."[80]

10.112. In the case of a mixed fund, equity still allows the claimant to prove that his property has become part of that fund (though in this case the remedy is limited to a charge on the mixed fund for the amount claimed[81]) and, if that is done, the only problem is one of sufficient identification of the part of the mixed fund representing the claimant's property. This problem frequently arises in respect of bank accounts, *e.g.*, where the trustee pays trust money into his own bank account and thereafter various deposits and withdrawals occur. The question is how far the beneficiaries can subsequently trace the trust money into the account. It is now settled in both Ireland and England that, in such a claim by the beneficiaries against the trustee or, indeed, as against his unsecured creditors, the ordinary rule of banking appropriation of payments in and out of bank accounts,[82] namely "first in, first out,"[83] does not apply.[84] Rather, when a claim against a trustee is made, the presumption is that he has spent his own money first, so that the surplus belongs to the trust. However, once the balance in the account falls below the amount of trust money originally misappropriated and deposited in the account, the presumption no longer applies and is not extended to presuming

---

[79] *Joy* v. *Campbell* (1804) 1 Sch. & Lef. 328; *Sheridan* v. *Joyce* (1844) 1 Jo. & Lat. 401; *Re Bobbett's Estate* [1904] 1 I.R. 461. See also *Re Hallett's Estate* (1880) 13 Ch.D 696 at 709 (*per* Jessel M.R.).

[80] (1884) 13 L.R.Ir. 139 at 147.

[81] It has been argued that in such a case the beneficiaries ought to have more than a charge for the amount misappropriated, namely a "proportionate share" of the mixed fund, *i.e.*, a share in the proportion to which the original trust funds bore to the mixed fund at the time of mixing. See *Hanbury and Maudsley's Modern Equity* (11th ed. by Martin, 1981), pp. 670–1. Also *Re Tilley's Will Trusts* [1967] Ch. 1179, espec. at 1189 (*per* Ungoed-Thomas J.) and, in Australia, *Scott* v. *Scott* (1963) 37 A.L.J.R. 345. And see Hodkinson, "Tracing and Mixed Funds" [1983] Conv. 135.

[82] Known as the rule in *Clayton's Case* (1817) 1 Mer. 572. See *Re Chute's Estate* [1914] 1 I.R. 180; *Re Hughes* [1970] I.R. 237.

[83] *I.e.*, the first payment in is appropriated to the earliest debt. This rule may apply, however, as between rival claimants under separate trusts or as between two or more beneficiaries or one trust against a single fund unable to meet all claims in full. See *Re Stenning* [1895] 2 Ch. 433; *Re Diplock* [1948] Ch. 465, espec. at 553–4. On the other hand, it can be argued that it is more equitable to order a *pari passu* distribution between the various claimants, see *Sinclair* v. *Brougham* [1914] A.C. 398 and *Shanahan's Stamp Auctions Ltd.* v. *Farrelly* [1962] I.R. 386 (see *A Casebook on Equity and Trusts in Ireland* (1985), p. 636). See para. 10.113, *infra*.

[84] *Re Reynolds* [1895] 1 I.R. 83; *Re Nolan* [1949] I.R. 197. *Cf. Scott* v. *Scott* [1924] 1 I.R. 141; *Re Hughes* [1970] I.R. 237. See also *Re Hallett's Estate* (1880) 13 Ch.D. 696.

that subsequent deposits were intended to replace trust money withdrawn.[85] In such a case the tracing claim is limited to the lowest intermediate balance in the account.[86] It must be remembered, however, that a beneficiary is entitled to a charge on the whole of the mixed fund, so that if the trust money is paid into the trustee's own bank account and is subsequently used to buy land and the balance of the account is then withdrawn the beneficiaries may still trace the trust money into the land. The money used to buy the land was subject to their charge which then attaches to the land and, in such a case, this may be the only remedy available.[87]

10.113. When beneficiaries claim to trace funds which were in the hands of a trustee, there has already been in existence a breach of a fiduciary relationship and it is settled that this secures priority for the beneficiaries' claim as against other, unsecured creditors of the trustee.[88] That is not to say that the existence of a fiduciary relationship is a prerequisite to a tracing action. It is not a prerequisite, but its absence means that the claimant will not be able to claim priority and will simply rank *pari passu* with other claimants.[89] The *pari passu* principle also seems to apply as between the beneficiaries themselves if the fund is not sufficient to meet their claim in full and, as we shall see, as between beneficiaries and other innocent claimants when the mixing is done by an innocent volunteer third party to whom the trustee may have given the money.

10.114. The beneficiaries' right of tracing misappropriated trust property can be invoked not only against the trustees but against any third party into whose hands the trust property comes, *unless* that third party is a bona fide purchaser for value of the legal, or, it appears to be the case in Ireland, of an equitable, interest in the property, without notice of the beneficiaries' right. In England it seems settled that the equitable right of tracing is a proprietary remedy which confers on the claimant an equitable interest in the property, enforceable through a constructive trust or charge,[90] as opposed to a "mere equity" which a person entitled to claim an equitable remedy, like rescission[91] or rectification,[92] has.[93] However, in Ireland there is a line of authority

---

[85]   However, the facts of a particular case may still raise such an inference, see *Re Hughes* [1970] I.R. 237.
[86]   *Re Ulster Land, Building and Investment Co.* (1889) 25 L.R.Ir. 24. See also *Roscoe* v. *Winder* [1915] 1 Ch. 62.
[87]   *Re Oatway* [1903] 2 Ch. 356; *Re Tilley's Will Trusts* [1967] Ch. 1179.
[88]   See the House of Lords discussion in *Sinclair* v. *Brougham* [1914] A.C. 398.
[89]   *Sinclair* v. *Brougham, op cit.; Shanahan's Stamp Auctions Ltd.* v. *Farrelly* [1962] I.R. 386 (see *A Casebook on Equity and Trusts in Ireland* (1985), p. 636). *Cf. Chase Manhattan Bank N.A.* v. *Israel-British Bank (London) Ltd.* [1981] Ch. 105. See Holdsworth, "Unjustifiable Enrichment" (1939) 55 L.Q.R. 37; Stoljar, "Re-examining Sinclair v. Brougham" *(1959)* 22 M.L.R. 21; Wright, "Sinclair v. Brougham" (1938) 6 C.L.J. 305.
[90]   See *Cave* v. *Cave* (1880) 15 Ch.D. 639; *Re Diplock* [1948] 1 Ch. 465. See also *Hanbury and Maudsley's Modern Equity* (11th ed. by Martin), pp. 658–75; Scott, "Constructive Trusts" (1955) 71 L.Q.R. 39.
[91]   Para. 3.157, *ante.*
[92]   Para. 3.162, *ante.*
[93]   See Delany, "Equitable Interests and 'Mere Equities'" (1957) 21 Conv. 195; *Hanbury and Maudsley's Modern Equity* (11th ed.), ch. 24. See also the discussion by Lord Upjohn in *National Provincial Bank Ltd.* v. *Ainsworth* [1965] A.C. 1175.

holding that the right of tracing should be equated to a mere equity on the ground that initially it amounts to a right to apply to the court for a charge on the property only and it does not acquire proprietory characteristics till the court makes an order.[94] Thus it has been held in Ireland that the beneficiaries' right of tracing is ineffective against a bona fide purchaser for value of an *equitable* interest only. *e.g.*, an equitable mortgage subsequently created out of the misappropriated property.[95] It has been argued in an earlier chapter that the principle underlying these cases is questionable and that there is much to be said for the English position.[96] However, it must be emphasised that the existing authorities have yet to be challenged on this point in either part of Ireland.

10.115. Considerable problems arise where the beneficiaries trace the trust property into the hands of a third party who cannot claim the protection we have just mentioned. If the third party has notice[97] of the fact that the property was trust property or was a party to the breach of trust, then he is in no better position than the trustee who committed the original breach. The more difficult questions arise in relation to the innocent volunteer, especially one who has mixed the trust property with his own.[98] It seems to be the position in both Ireland[99] and England[1] that, in such a case, the beneficiaries and the volunteers can both lay claim to the mixed fund on a *pari passu* basis.[2] However, it must be remembered that like all equitable remedies, that of tracing is discretionary and, in certain circumstances, the court may refuse to make an order; *e.g.*, it may refuse a charge on land improved or altered through use of the mixed fund by the innocent volunteer or refuse to allow the beneficiaries to be subrogated to the position of creditors whose debts have been paid off, again out of the mixed fund.[3]

---

[94]   *Re Ffrench's Estate* (1887) 21 L.R.Ir. 283; *Re Sloane's Estate* [1895] 1 I.R. 146; *Bourke* v. *Lee* [1904] 1 I.R. 280; *Re Bobbett's Estate* [1904] 1 I.R. 461; *Scott* v. *Scott* [1924] 1 I.R. 141.

[95]   *Re Ffrench's Estate, op. cit.; Scott* v. *Scott, op cit..*

[96]   Paras. 3.076–9, *ante.*

[97]   *I.e.*, actual, imputed or constructive notice, see paras. 3.070 *et seq., ante.* See also *Sheridan* v. *Joyce* (1844) 1 Jo. & Lat. 401; *Twycross* v. *Moore* (1849) 13 Ir.Eq.r. 250.

[98]   See Denning, "Recovery of Money" (1949) 65 L.Q.R. 37; Higgins, "Re Diplock – A Reappraisal" (1964) 6 U.West.Aust.A.L.Rev. 428; Palmer, "Restitution of Distributions by a Fiduciary to which the Recipient was not Entitled" (1968) 19 Hast.L.J. 993.

[99]   *Leahy* v. *De Moleyns* [1896] 1 I.R. 206 (see *A Casebook on Equity and Trusts in Ireland* (1985), p. 674). *Cf. Welwood* v. *Grady* [1904] 1 I.R. 388.

[1]   *Sinclair* v. *Brougham* [1914] A.C. 398; *Re Diplock* [1948] Ch. 465, on appeal, *sub nom. Ministry of Health* v. *Simpson* [1951] A.C. 251.

[2]   The beneficiaries can, of course, claim return of the entire fund if there has been no mixing with the volunteer's property.

[3]   See discussion in *Re Diplock* [1948] Ch. 465 and criticisms in Maudsley, (1959) 75 L.Q.R. 240, espec. at 248–9. Also Goff and Jones, *Law of Restitution* (2nd ed., 1978), ch. 42.

CHAPTER 11

POWERS

I. GENERAL

11.01. A power may be defined as an authority given to a person whereby that person may determine the legal relations of himself or other persons.[1] The essential difference between a power and a trust is that the latter is obligatory while the former is not.[2] It is apparent from the above definition that the law recognises many kinds of powers and in the following paragraphs an attempt is made at classification. However, extended treatment will be confined to what are, perhaps, the most common powers created (otherwise than by statute) in Ireland today, especially in relation to property, namely, powers of appointment and powers of attorney.

II. CLASSIFICATION

There are several ways in which powers may be classified.

A. Traditional

11.02. The traditional classification of powers[3] is that first there are powers which are *simply collateral*. By this is meant that the donee of the power is given no interest in the property which forms the subject-matter of the power. As we shall see, many powers of appointment and of attorney are of this nature. Secondly, there are powers which are said to be *in gross*. In such a case the donee does have some interest in the property but, and this is also a point of distinction, the exercise of the power cannot affect that interest. For example, a power may be given to the tenant for life of property to make appointments as to the future interests in that property, to take effect on his death. Thirdly, powers may be *appendant* or *appurtenant*, in which case the power relates to and the exercise of the power can affect that interest.[4] For example, property may be given to X with power to appoint by deed or will, in whatever shares or interests X chooses, amongst his children.

---

[1] See Farwell, *Powers* (3rd ed. by Farwell and Archer, 1916); Sugden, *Powers* (8th ed., 1861).

[2] Para. 9.011, *ante*. Even this distinction seems to have become somewhat blurred over the years, see *e.g.*, "discretionary trusts" (para. 9.081, *ante*) and "powers in the nature of a trust" (paras. 9.018, *ante* and 11.11, *post*).

[3] See the discussion in *Re D'Angibau* (1879) 15 Ch.D. 228, espec. at 232–3 (*per* Jessel M.R.) and, on appeal, (1880) 15 Ch.D., espec. at 243–4 (*per* Brett L.J.).

[4] See *Re Greene's Estate* (1863) 14 Ir.Ch.R. 325.

11.03. This traditional classification has little practical significance today. Formerly it was important, *e.g.*, in determining whether a particular power could be released. It was the rule at common law that, while powers in gross and appendant or appurtenant could be released, powers simply collateral could not.[5] However, the Conveyancing Act, 1881, enabled powers simply collateral to be released in both England and Ireland.[6]

B. COMMON LAW AND EQUITY

11.04. The common law's view of powers was fairly limited, in that only certain kinds of powers were recognised.[7] Perhaps the most important common law power for practical purposes was the power of attorney, whereby one person authorises another to do certain acts on his behalf, which might include, for example, power to convey land. The common law, however, did not recognise powers of appointment and, as we discussed in an earlier chapter,[8] resort to the equitable concept of a *use* was a way of getting round the common law's limitations. Prior to the passing of the Statute of Uses (Ireland), 1634, a settlor could, on a conveyance of land, reserve to himself or confer on others a power to revoke the uses he had declared in the conveyance and to declare new uses.[9] Of course, prior to the passing of the Statute such a power, which was, in effect, a power of appointment, could affect the equitable interests in the land only, but after 1634 the uses could be "executed" by the Statute and the equitable interests converted into legal interests.[10] Thus for the first time in Ireland powers of appointment became recognised at common law.

It is still possible to have equitable powers only operating in Ireland by the creation of a modern trust, with the powers conferred on beneficiaries in relation to their equitable interests only.[11]

C. STATUTE

11.05. One of the most common sources of powers in Ireland today is statute law. We have already considered several examples. For example, in chapter 8 we considered the various powers conferred on the tenant for life of settled land under the Settled Land Acts, 1882–90.[12] In chapter 10 we considered the powers conferred on trustees by the legislation in force in the Republic of Ireland and Northern Ireland. Later in this chapter we consider

---

[5] *Digge's Case* (1600) 1 Co.Rep. 173a. See also *Re Dunne's Trusts* (1880) 5 L.R.Ir. 76.
[6] S. 52. See para. 11. 26, *post.*
[7] See, generally, Holdsworth, *History of English Law*, vol. VII, pp. 149–53.
[8] Para. 3.013, *ante.*
[9] Until this power was executed there was a resulting use in favour of the settlor, see para. 3.020, *ante.*
[10] *Ibid.*
[11] Or, in relation to land, by employing a "use upon a use" in the conveyance, see para. 3.021, *ante.*
[12] See especially paras. 8.057 *et seq., ante.* Note also the statutory powers conferred on trustees of the settlement, paras. 8.092 *et seq., ante.*

powers of attorney which are governed largely by statute law in both parts of Ireland.[13]

The above classification relates to powers generally, but, as we shall see in a moment, particular kinds of powers, such as powers of appointment, may themselves be classified into further sub-categories.

III. POWERS OF APPOINTMENT

11.06.   A power of appointment is a power conferred on the donee whereby the donee may appoint the property to which the power relates in accordance with the terms of the power. Powers of appointment are very often conferred by will or trust deed.[14] The person upon whom the power is conferred is known as the *donee* of the power, the persons in whose favour the donee may make an appointment are known as the *objects* of the power and a person in whose favour the donee does in fact make an appointment is an *appointee*.

A. CLASSIFICATION

The following are the generally recognised ways of classifying powers of appointment.[15]

1. *General and Special Powers*

11.07.   A *general* power of appointment is created when the donee may make any appointment, including one in favour of himself.[16] A *special* power of appointment is one where the donee is restricted in the exercise of the power, in that he may appoint among a certain class of persons (objects) only or, indeed, he may be limited to one person only, if any appointment at all is to be made.[17] This distinction between general and special powers is important. For example, the doctrine of fraud on a power, which we discuss below,[18] applies to special powers only. We saw in an earlier chapter that the rule against perpetuities applies in a different way depending upon whether the power is general or special.[19]

11.08.   In recent decades the courts in England have come to recognise a third category of power of appointment which does not seem to fit into the

---

[13]   Para. 11.29, *post*.
[14]   See Casner, "Estate Planning – Powers of Appointment" (1950) 4 H.L.R. 185; Martin, "Observation on Powers of Appointment" (1917) 33 L.Q.R. 256.
[15]   See Gold, "Classification of Some Powers of Appointment" (1942) 40 Mich.L.Rev. 337; H.P., "Classification of Powers" (1932) 48 L.Q.R. 474; Hughes, "Classification of Powers of Appointment" (1962) 26 Conv. 25.
[16]   See *Re Dunbar-Buller* [1923] 2 I.R. 143. And *Lanauze* v. *Malone* (1853) 3 Ir.Ch.R. 354; *Duffy* v. *Duffy* [1941] N.I. 180. Also *Re Churston Settled Estates* [1954] Ch. 334. Campbell, "Enigma of General Powers of Appointment" (1956) 7 Res.Jud. 244; Crane, "Consent Powers and Joint Powers" (1954) 18 Conv. 565.
[17]   See *Re Robertson's and Cardew's Trusts* [1960] I.R. 7 (see *A Casebook on Equity and Trusts in Ireland* (1985), p. 724); *Re Murphy's Marriage Settlement* [1960] I.R. 360; *Re Boland* [1961] I.R. 426. The donee may himself be one of the restricted class. *Re Penrose* [1933] Ch. 793. *Cf*. s. 7 of the Perpetuities Act (N.I.), 1966, para. 5.128, *ante*.
[18]   Para. 11.21, *infra*.
[19]   Paras. 5.116 *et seq.*, *ante*.

dichotomy of general and special powers. This third category consists of what are usually called *hybrid* powers.[20] These are powers where the objects form a very wide class but the class does not include the donee and so he may not make an appointment in favour of himself, or else the class is limited in some other way, *e.g.*, all persons living at the death of the donee.[21] The general view seems to be that such restrictions prevent the power being considered a general power and so it is governed by rules relating to special powers, *e.g.*, the doctrine of fraud on a power and the rule against perpetuities.[22] However, such a *hybrid* power may become general, *e.g.*, because the objects excepted turn out never to have existed and cannot exist when the power may be exercised.[23]

2. Bare and Fiduciary Powers

11.09. Another distinction which may be made with respect to powers of appointment is between *bare* powers and *fiduciary* powers, sometimes referred to as powers *ex officio*.[24] A fiduciary power is conferred where the donee is put under some fiduciary obligation in relation to its exercise, whereas in the case of a bare power the donee has a complete discretion. The common example of a fiduciary power of appointment is one conferred on trustees so that they are required to consider the interests of all the potential appointees. It is vital to note, however, that the mere fact that the power is conferred upon a fiduciary, such as a trustee, does not in itself make the power also a fiduciary one. The trustee must have imposed upon him a fiduciary duty *with respect to the power*. Furthermore, the distinction between bare powers and fiduciary powers should not be confused with the distinction between bare powers and powers in the nature of a trust, which we consider below.

11.10. The significance of the distinction between a bare power and a fiduciary power, apart from the extent of discretion in exercise of such powers, seems to be that a bare power can be exercised only by the individual upon whom it was conferred.[25] A fiduciary power, such as one conferred on trustees, may be executed by the successors[26] of the original donees.[27]

3. Bare Powers and Powers in the Nature of a Trust

11.11. As we have stated several times before, the basic distinction between

---

[20]   See Fleming, "Hybrid Powers" (1948) 13 Conv. 20. See also *Re Manisty's Settlement* [1974] Ch. 17; *Re Hay's Settlement Trusts* [1982] 1 W.L.R. 202.
[21]   *Re Park* [1932] 1 Ch. 580; *Re Jones* [1945] Ch. 105; *Re Harvey* [1950] 1 All E.R. 491.
[22]   In Northern Ireland this is confirmed by s. 7 of the Perpetuities Act (N.I.), 1966, see para. 5.128, *ante*.
[23]   See Vaisey J. in *Re Harvey* [1950] 1 All E.R. 491.
[24]   See *Re Robinson* [1912] 1 I.R. 410.
[25]   See *Re Harding* [1923] 1 Ch. 182; *Re Lysaght* [1966] 1 Ch. 191.
[26]   Or the survivor of more than one donee, see *Bersel Manufacturing Co. Ltd.* v. *Berry* [1968] 2 All.E.R. 552.
[27]   *Re Smith* [1904] 1 Ch. 139; *Re De Sommery* [1912] 2 Ch. 262. See also the statutory provisions relating to the powers of survivors, and personal representatives of the last survivor, of trustees, paras. 10.005 *et seq. ante.*

a power and a trust is that the former is discretionary whereas the latter is imperative or obligatory. However, the courts of Ireland[28] and England[29] have recognised that this distinction may not, in certain cases, be as definite as it appears at first sight. The problem arises where the donor of a special power of appointment makes it clear that he intends the objects of the power to benefit in any event, whether or not the donee makes an appointment. The courts of equity have taken the view that, in such a case, the proper construction is to treat the objects as having a vested interest in the property in equal shares, subject to divestment in the event of an actual appointment by the donee of the power.[30] Hence the description of such a power as being "a power in the nature of a trust,"[31] The difficulty, of course, in each case is to determine whether or not the donor of the power intended it to be in the nature of a trust. It is clear that this cannot be his intention if he has made an express alternative provision to take effect in default of appointment.[32] If no such express provision is made, it is a matter of construction in each case as to what the donor's intention was. The mere absence of such a provision is not *conclusive* evidence that the power is in the nature of a trust, though it may be indicative of such an intention.[33]

B. CREATION

11.12. The general rule is that there are no special formalities for the creation of a power of appointment. In so far as the power is conferred by a deed or will, the power's validity will, of course, be determined by the validity of the deed or will itself. A power of appointment is also subject to general rules of law such as the rule against perpetuities, which applies to determine both the validity of the power itself and appointments made under a valid power.[34] Finally, a power of appointment is subject to the requirements of certainty. Until recently it was thought that there was a basic distinction between the requirements of certainty for trusts and those for powers.[35] In the case of powers, it was thought that the requirements of certainty were met if the donor had provided a sufficiently clear criterion by which to judge

---

[28] *Hutchinson* v. *Hutchinson* (1850) 13 Ir.Eq.R. 332; *Re Hargrove's Trusts* (1873) I.R. 8 Eq. 256; *Ahearne* v. *Ahearne* (1881) 9 L.R.Ir. 144; *Moore* v. *Ffolliot* (1887) 19 L.R.Ir. 499 (see *A Casebook on Equity and Trusts in Ireland* (1985), p. 684).

[29] *Harding* v. *Glyn* (1739) 1 Atk. 469; *Brown* v. *Higgs* (1803) 8 Ves. 561, espec. at 570–1 and 574 (*per* Lord Eldon).

[30] *Re Hargrove's Trusts* (1873) I.R. 8 Eq. 256; *Kelly* v. *Spears* (1952) 86 I.L.T.R. 81. Also *McLaughlin* v. *McPolin* (1903) 3 N.I.J.R. 268; *Re Kieran* [1916] 1 I.R. 289; *Young* v. *Young* (1918) 52 I.L.T.R. 40. *Cf.* where the donor intended the class to take in any event, but *not* equally, so that there can be no vested interests before appointment. Again the court may order a selection or make one itself, but it is not clear that this is a power in the nature of a trust.

[31] See Gray, "Powers in Trusts and Gifts Implied in Default of Appointment" (1911) 25 H.L.R. 1; Harris, "Trust, Power and Duty" (1971) 87 L.Q.R. 31; Marshall, "Trusts and Powers" (1957) 35 C.B.R. 1060; Rood, "Disposition to be made of Property the Subject of a Power if Power is not Exercised" (1915) 15 Mich.L.Rev. 386; Unwin, "Power or Trust Power" (1962) 26 Conv. 92.

[32] *Re Regan's Estate* (1893) 31 L.R.Ir. 246. See also *Tuite* v. *Tuite* (1978) Unrep. (H.C., R.I.) (1978 No. 202 Sp).

[33] *Carberry* v. *McCarthy* (1881) 7 L.R.Ir. 328; *Re Hall's Will Trusts* [1899] 1 I.R. 308; *Re Patterson* [1899] 1 I.R. 324; *Re Burkitt* [1915] 1 I.R. 205. *Clibborn* v. *Horan* [1921] 1 I.R. 93.

[34] See para. 5.118, *ante*.

[35] See para. 9.018, *ante*.

whether or not any particular claimant was properly regarded as an object of the power, and it did not matter that the class of objects was so wide and fluctuating in nature that at any given time it was impossible to make a complete list of all the objects.[36]

11.13. There have been some suggestions in England recently that the requirements of certainty for powers are even less stringent, so that all that is necessary is for one claimant to show that he can satisfy the test or criterion laid down and there is no need to show that a similar decision could be made with equal certainty in the case of every other possible claimant.[37] On the other hand, in the case of a trust, it was considered essential that at any time a complete list of all the beneficiaries could be made and this rule was thought to apply to powers in the nature of a trust.[38] However, once again the House of Lords has recently reconsidered the matter and, in *Re Baden's Deed Trusts*,[39] held that, in the case of a power in the nature of a trust,[40] the requirements of certainty to be satisfied were those relating to powers and not those relating to trusts.[41] It remains to be seen whether the English courts will relax the requirements of certainty for trusts any further than in the kind of case which arose in *Baden*, namely a *discretionary* trust of *income*. Whatever the position in England as a result of these recent developments, the cautionary note must be sounded that this subject has not been considered recently by the Irish courts and it must remain a matter of conjecture how far they would follow the English developments. This is so even in Northern Ireland since the courts there are not bound strictly to follow a House of Lords decision unless given in a case on appeal from Northern Ireland.[42] However, any House of Lords decision is of high persuasive authority, even if given by a three-to-two majority only.

C. Exercise

11.14. The general rule is that the donee in exercising his power of appointment must follow whatever conditions may have been laid down by the donor and the general law, *e.g.*, with respect to formalities for execution

---

[36]   *Brown* v. *Gregg* [1945] I.R. 224; *Re Parker's Will* [1966] I.R. 309 (see *A Casebook on Equity and Trusts in Ireland* (1985), p. 688). See also *Re Gestetner Settlement* [1953] Ch. 672; *Re Sayer* [1957] Ch. 423; *Re Lysaght* [1966] Ch. 191.
[37]   *Re Gibbard's W.T.* [1967] 1 W.L.R. 42 (where Plowman J. applied the test applicable to questions of uncertainty in cases of conditions precedent, see *Re Allen* [1953] Ch. 810; *Re Lysaght* [1966] Ch. 191); *Re Gulbenkian's Settlements* [1968] Ch. 126 (C.A.), [1970] A.C. 508.
[38]   *I.R.C.* v. *Broadway Cottages Trust* [1955] Ch. 20; *Re Hain's Settlement* [1961] 1 W.L.R. 440; *Re Leek* [1968] 2 W.L.R. 1385.
[39]   [1971] A.C. 424 (Lords Hodson and Guest *dissentiente*). See also *Re Baden's Deed Trusts (No. 2)* [1971] 3 W.L.R. 475; *Re Manisty's Settlement* [1973] 2 All E.R. 1203; *Re Hay's Settlement Trusts* [1982] 1 W.L.R. 202.
[40]   Variously described also in the reports of, and comments on, the case as a "trust-power" and "power coupled with a duty."
[41]   See discussion of the case in Hanbury and Maudsley, *Modern Equity* (12th ed. by Martin; 1985), pp. 95–106 and 169–70. See also Burgess, "The Certainty Problem" (1979) 30 N.I.L.Q. 24.
[42]   See generally, Donaldson, *Some Comparative Aspects of Irish Law* (1957), pp. 27–34. On constitutional matters, see Calvert, *Constitutional Law of Northern Ireland* (1968), ch. 7. *Contra* MacDermott, (1977) 28 N.I.L.Q. 108 at 110.

of deeds or wills and compliance with the rule against perpetuities.[43] In both parts of Ireland under section 12 of the Law of Property Amendment Act, 1859, so far as *execution* and *attestation* of a deed executing a non-testamentary power of appointment is concerned, it is sufficient if the deed is executed in the presence of and attested by two or more witnesses, notwithstanding any additional formalities required by the instrument creating the power. With respect to testamentary powers, again so far as execution and attestation is concerned, it is sufficient that the usual formalities for wills are complied with, notwithstanding any additional formalities required by the instrument creating the power.[44] However, the donee may fail to comply with some other requirement and so the question arises as to what the position is in such a case. There are several aspects of this problem to be considered.

1. Defective Execution

Where the donee of a power of appointment fails to comply with the formalities governing exercise of his power, the appointee may be able to have the exercise upheld by reliance on either equity or statute law.

(i) Equity

11.15. Where a donee has by his actions shown that he intended to execute his power, equity will try to give effect to his actions where they have failed because of some formality or technicality.[45] It must be emphasised that equity will not execute a power which the donee fails to execute and will intervene only where the defect is purely formal. Furthermore, equity will intervene only on behalf of certain persons, *e.g.*, creditors or purchasers for value from the donee, not volunteers.[46] No relief will be given if the result would be to further a fraud on the power.[47] It also seems that equitable relief is confined to the case of express powers and cannot be granted in respect of statutory powers.[48]

(ii) Statute

11.16. We mentioned above the relief conferred by statute in the case of

---

[43] *Stuart* v. *Babington* (1891) 27 L.R.Ir. 551; *Re Manning's Trusts* (1915) 49 I.L.T.R. 143.

[44] Succession Act, 1965, s. 79 (R.I.); Wills Act, 1837, s. 10 and Wills Act, 1963, s. 2.

[45] See the discussion in *Pennefather* v. *Pennefather* (1873) I.R. 7 Eq. 300 (see *A Casebook on Equity and Trusts in Ireland* (1985), p. 702). See also *Minchin* v. *Minchin* (1871) I.R. 5 Eq. 258; *L'Estrange* v. *L'Estrange* (1890) 25 L.R.Ir. 399.

[46] *Ibid. Marjoribanks* v. *Hovenden* (1843) 6 Ir.Eq.R. 238. Cf. *Donell* v. *Church* (1842) 4 Ir.Eq.R. 630; *Blake* v. *French* (1855) 5 Ir.Ch.R. 246.

[47] *Brown* v. *Howden* (1900) 34 I.L.T.R. 159. Also *Thompson* v. *Simpson* (1845) 8 Ir.Eq.R. 55; *Marquis of Donegal* v. *Greg* (1849) 13 Ir.Eq.R. 12. See further, para. 11.21, *infra*. See also where the exercise of the power will divest estates, *Re Earl of Kingston's Estate* (1880) 5 L.R.Ir. 169.

[48] See Farwell, *Powers* p. 394. *Att.-Gen.* v. *Ball* (1846) 10 Ir.Eq.R. 146. Also *Steeven's Hospital* v. *Dyas* (1864) 15 Ir.Ch.R. 405. *Cf.*, however, *Dyas* v. *Cruise* (1845) 2 Jo. & Lat. 460 (agreement for lease enforceable against tenant for life acting under a statutory power). See also *Harnett* v. *Yielding* (1805) 2 Sch. & Lef. 549 and Farwell, *op. cit.*, p. 399.

both deeds and wills so far as execution and attestation is concerned. It should be noted that section 12 of the Law of Property Amendment Act, 1859, expressly excludes requirements as to consents to exercise of a non-testamentary power and as to matters not relating to execution and attestation.

11.17. The Leases Acts, 1849 and 1850, validate leases in Ireland otherwise invalid because of non-compliance with the terms of the powers of granting the leases. Provided there was an intention to exercise the power and the lease was executed in good faith and the lessee has entered the property, the invalid lease is to take effect in equity as a contract for the grant of a valid lease under the power.[49] These provisions have been interpreted as applying in cases where the invalidity is due to some minor technicality only, *e.g.*, omission of a condition of re-entry required by the terms of the power to lease.[50] On the other hand, it has been stated that they do not validate a lease executed without the consent of the donor as required by the power.[51] Furthermore, if a lessee wishes to invoke them to save his lease, he must, it seems, prove that the lease is, apart from the defect in question, valid in all other respects and one which the lessor (donee of the power) could properly have granted.[52] Finally, expressly excluded from the saving provisions of the 1849 and 1850 Acts are leases of land held on charitable, ecclesiastical or public trusts.[53]

2. *Excessive Execution*

11.18. As the words indicate, an excessive execution of a power of appointment comes about when the donee in exercising the power exceeds the limits set by the donor or the general law. For example, the donee may appoint to non-objects or give appointees who are objects larger interests than allowed under the power or attach improper conditions to particular appointments.[54] The courts take the general view that they should try to save an appointment if it is at all possible, and so they will try to separate the good aspects of an appointment from the bad. Thus an appointment to persons who include objects and non-objects may be regarded as severable by the court

---

[49] See the discussion in *Moffett* v. *Lord Gough* (1878) 1 L.R.Ir. 331 (see *A Casebook on Equity and Trusts in Ireland* (1985), p. 711).

[50] *Pawson* v. *Revell* [1958] 2 Q.B. 360. (The English provisions are now to be found in s. 152 of the Law of Property Act, 1925.) See Elliott, "Curing a Defective Lease Granted by a Tenant for Life" (1971) 87 L.Q.R. 338.

[51] *Iron Trades Employers' Insurance Association* v. *Union Land and House Investors* [1937] Ch. 313, espec. at 323.

[52] *Kisch* v. *Hawes Bros.* [1935] Ch. 102 (lease, made under Settled Land Acts and defective because it was to commence more than 12 months after its date, held still invalid because the best rent had not been reserved, see para. 8.072, *ante*).

[53] See *Survey of the Land Law of Northern Ireland* (1971), para. 298.

[54] *Hogg* v. *Hogg* (1832) Hay. & Jon. 39; *Lord Trimlestown* v. *Kemmis* (1839) 1 Jebb & Sym. 587; *Caulfield* v. *Maguire* (1845) 8 Ir.Eq.R. 164; *Greene* v. *Greene* (1845) 8 Ir.Eq.R. 473 (see *A Casebook on Equity and Trusts in Ireland* (1985), p. 732); *Bell* v. *Bell* (1862) 13 Ir.Ch.R. 517; *Re Enever's Trusts* [1912] 1 I.R. 511 (see *A Casebook on Equity and Trusts in Ireland* (1985), p. 723); *Holmes* v. *Ulster Bank, Ltd.* (1956) 90 I.L.T.R. 41; *Re Lowry* [1978] N.I. 17.

and valid as to the persons who are objects within the terms of the power.[55] If an unauthorised condition is attached to an appointment, the appointee may be allowed to take the property free from the condition,[56] though it has been held that such a condition may be valid if it is in favour of another object of the power.[57] Where the donee has a special power to appoint by will, it is a matter of construction whether a will executed by him without reference to his special power can be regarded as an exercise of his power.[58]

11.19. The donee of a power of appointment is invested with a discretion and so is caught by the general maxim, *delegatus delegare non potest*.[59] Any attempt by him to make an appointment which involves in effect a delegation of his power is invalid, unless, of course, this is authorised expressly or impliedly by the terms of the power.[60]

3. *Illusory Appointments*

11.20. The law relating to illusory appointments stems from equity's desire to prevent donees of powers making nonsense of their donor's intentions. A distinction was drawn between exclusive powers, under which one or more of the objects might receive no property at all, and non-exclusive powers, under which it was required that each object should receive something.[61] In the case of the latter, the courts of equity took the view that an appointment of a trifling or mere token amount of the property subject to the power should be set aside as an illusory appointment — an object of the power should not be "cut off with a shilling."[62] However, the doctrine proved so difficult for the courts to apply that the Illusory Appointments Act, 1830, was passed, for both Ireland and England,[63] to provide that appointment of a nominal sum is not to invalidate the exercise of the power unless the terms of the power direct otherwise.[64] Then the Powers of Appointment Act, 1874, provided that

---

[55] *Crozier* v. *Crozier* (1843) 5 Ir.Eq.R. 540; *Richardson* v. *Simpson* (1846) 9 Ir.Eq.R. 367; *Re Chambers* (1847) 11 Ir.Eq.R. 518; *Ex parte Bernard* (1857) 6 Ir.Ch.R. 133; *Hutchinson* v. *Tottenham* [1899] 1 I.R. 344; *Re Shekleton's Trusts* [1945] I.R. 115. See also *Re Swinburne* (1884) 27 Ch.D. 696; *Re Latta's Marriage Settlement Trusts* [1949] Ch. 490. *Cf. Re Brown's Trust* (1865) L.R. 1 Eq. 74.
[56] *Butler* v. *Butler* (1880) 7 L.R.Ir. 401; see also *Hay* v. *Watkins* (1843) 5 Ir.Eq.R. 273; *Brereton* v. *Barry* (1860) 10 Ir.Ch.R. 376; *D'Abbadie* v. *Bizoin* (1871) I.R. 5 Eq. 205. *Dowglass* v. *Waddell* (1886) 17 L.R.Ir. 384. See also *Re Hay's Settlement Trusts* [1982] 1 W.L.R. 202.
[57] *Re Leahy* [1920] 1 I.R. 260.
[58] See the discussion in *Re Robertson's and Cardew's Trusts* [1960] I.R. 7 (see *A Casebook on Equity and Trusts in Ireland* (1985), p. 724); *Re Boland* [1961] I.R. 426. See also *Reid* v. *Reid* [1960] I.R. 360.
[59] Para. 10.030, *ante*. See *Hutchinson* v. *Tottenham* [1899] 1 I.R. 344.
[60] *Tredennick* v. *Tredennick* [1900] 1 I.R. 354; *Re Westropp's Estate* (1903) 37 I.L.T.R. 183. See also the discussion in *Re Hay's Settlement Trusts* [1982] 1 W.L.R. 202.
[61] See *Barron* v. *Barron* (1837) 2 Jon. 798; *Woodlock* v. *Mahony* (1857) 6 Ir.Ch.R. 236; *Re Bromhead's Trusts* [1922] 1 I.R. 75.
[62] See the judgment of Lord Nottingham L.C. in *Gibson* v. *Kinven* (1682) 1 Vern. 66. Also *Vanderzee* v. *Aclom* (1799) 4 Ves. 771, espec. at 784–5 (*per* Arden M.R.); Howe, "Exclusive and Nonexclusive Powers and the Illusory Appointment" (1944) 42 Mich.L.Rev. 649.
[63] Now contained for England in s. 158 of the Law of Property Act, 1925. See the discussion of the 1830 Act in *Michin* v. *Michin* (1853) 3 Ir.Ch.R. 167. Also *Barron* v. *Barron* (1837) 2 Jon. 798; *Re Staples* [1933] I.R. 126. *Cf. Re Crofton's Trusts* (1881) 7 L.R.Ir. 279.
[64] See *Gainsford* v. *Dunn* (1874) L.R. 17 Eq. 405, espec. at 407 (*per* Jessel M.R.). Also *Re Stone's Estate* (1869) I.R.3 Eq. 621.

every power of appointment is to be construed as exclusive, so that donees have a complete discretion not to make any appointment at all, *unless* the donor provides expressly to the contrary.[65] As one learned author put it: "The Act of 1830 enabled an appointor to cut off any object of the power with a shilling; the Act of 1874 enables him to cut off the shilling also."[66]

4. *Fraud on a Power*

11.21. The doctrine of fraud on a power is also the creature of equity.[67] Here the court is not concerned with actions such as excessive execution of the power by the donee, but rather with the donee's motives, *i.e.*, an appointment made with an intention on the part of the donee inconsistent with the purposes the donor of the power had in mind. This doctrine applies to special powers of appointment only and the underlying theory is that those persons entitled in default of any appointment have a vested interest in the property, which is subject to divestment on the making of a valid appointment by the donee of the power. Any appointment made for improper motives is to be regarded as fraud on those entitled in default of appointment. Several situations can arise.

(i) **Prior Agreement**

11.22. Unless the donee of the power (*i.e.*, the appointor) is the person entitled in default, an appointment is fraudulent if it is made in pursuance of an agreement or bargain between the donee and the appointee, whereby some person other than an object of the power and not entitled in default is to benefit. This may be illustrated by the Irish case of *Duggan* v. *Duggan*,[68] where the tenant for life of a fund, with power to appoint it among her children, entered into an agreement with those who had attained full age to appoint them on condition that they should purchase her life interest at a valuation and pay the purchase price out of the fund appointed. In fact the mother (tenant for life) used most of the money in question to pay debts for which her children (the appointees) were sureties and which had been incurred for the benefit of the family and to keep up the farm where they all lived. Nevertheless, the Court of Appeal held the appointment to be bad for reasons emphasised by Lord O'Hagan C.:

> "If the primary and simple purpose had been to serve the objects of the power, and if, in serving them, in the peculiar position of affairs, the donee necessarily served herself, there would be no good ground for

---

[65] See on the 1874 Act, *Re Walsh's Trusts* (1878) 1 L.R.Ir. 320; *Moynan* v. *Moynan* (1878) 1 L.R.Ir. 382; *Butler* v. *Butler* (1880) 7 L.R.Ir. 401; *Wybrants* v. *Maude* [1895] 1 I.R. 214; *Brown* v. *Howden* (1900) 34 I.L.T.R. 159; *Re Staples* [1933] I.R. 126; *Re Dolan* [1970] I.R. 94.

[66] Farwell, *Powers* (3rd ed., 1916), p. 427.

[67] See Sheridan, *Fraud in Equity* (1957), ch. 6. Also *Conolly* v. *McDermott* (1819) Beat. 601; *Thompson* v. *Simpson* (1845) 8 Ir.Eq.R. 55.

[68] (1880) 7 L.R.Ir. 152 (see *A Casebook on Equity and Trusts in Ireland* (1985), p. 725). See also *Palmer* v. *Wheeler* (1811) 2 Ba. & B. 18. And *Vatcher* v. *Paull* [1915] A.C. 372.

saying that the execution should be invalidated. But here the primary purpose was to serve the mother; to relieve her embarrassment and discharge her debts; and, although the retention of the farm might possibly benefit her children at some distant day, and under circumstances not to be foreseen, the only immediate and certain advantage was to herself, whilst, as to the debts to the bank, they were merely sureties who could recover against her if they were compelled to pay anything, and find their protection in the mortgage and the insurance."[69]

(ii) Intention Only

11.23. Despite the absence of any agreement or bargain,[70] the courts may still set aside an appointment on the ground that it was made with an improper intention on the part of the donee-appointor.[71] It seems that it must be shown to the satisfaction of the court that the appointor's predominant intention in making the appointment was that a non-object would benefit, *e.g.*, due to strong moral pressure which it was envisaged would affect the appointee.[72] A mere secret hope is not enough, though it does not seem to be necessary that either the appointee should be a party to or know of the appointor's intention or that it should in fact take effect.[73]

(iii) Benefit to Appointor

11.24. It is also fraud on a power for an appointment to be made with the intention of benefiting the appointor (unless, of course, he is an object of the power).[74] Such a benefit may be quite indirect and not out of the property appointed.[75]

(iv) Acquiescence

In *Skelton* v. *Flanagan*,[76] Walsh M.R. stated that, when all the objects of a power concur in or confirm the transaction relating to exercise of a power, they cannot complain that the transaction was a fraud on the power, provided

---

[69] *Ibid.* p. 158.

[70] Note, however, the views of Lynch J. in *Re Dane's Estate* (1871) 5 I.L.T.R. 30: "I have no evidence before me as to any contract made between the [appointee] and her [appointor]; and if the deed does not show this, and if that fact must be inference only or presumption–inasmuch as such a contract would be a fraud–I am not warranted in presuming it without proof."

[71] See the discussion in *Re Crawshay* [1948] Ch. 123, espec. at 134–5.

[72] *Palmer* v. *Wheeler* (1811) 2 Ba. & B. 18; *Hutchins* v. *Hutchins* (1876) I.R. 10 Eq. 453.

[73] *Re Dick* [1953] Ch. 343; *Re Burton's Settlements* [1955] Ch. 82; *Re Brook's Settlement* [1968] 1 W.L.R. 1661. See Cretney, (1969) 32 M.L.R. 317.

[74] *Conolly* v. *McDermott* (1819) Beat. 601; *Hay* v. *Watkins* (1843) 5 Ir.Eq.R. 273; *Hamilton* v. *Kirwan* (1845) 8 Ir.Eq.R. 278; *Weir* v. *Chamley* (1853) 4 Ir.Jur. (O.S.) 1; *Re Sinclaire's Estate* (1867) I.R. 2 Eq. 45.

[75] *Keily* v. *Keily* (1843) 5 Ir.Eq.R. 435; *Jackson* v. *Jackson* (1843) Dru. *temp.* Sug. 91; *Naish Gray* v. *Houghton* (1905) 5 N.I.J.R. 200. Also *Cochrane* v. *Cochrane* [1922] 2 Ch. 230. *Cf.* the case of a power to jointure, *Baldwin* v. *Roche* (1842) 5 Ir.Eq.R. 110.

[76] (1867) I.R. 1 Eq. 362 at 369 (see *A Casebook on Equity and Trusts in Ireland* (1985), p. 728). See also *Hall* v. *Raymond* (1858) 8 Ir.Ch.R. 83; *Clune* v. *Apjohn* (1866) 17 Ir.Ch.R. 25.

there is no imposition or undue influence, though presumably the person entitled in default of appointment can, unless he acquiesces.

(v) Release

The doctrine of fraud on a power does not apply to a release of his power by a donee.[77] Such a release benefits those entitled in default, so they have no cause for complaint, and it seems that the donee generally owes no duty in this regard to deprived appointees.[78]

(vi) Revocation

11.25. The doctrine does not apply either to a revocation of an appointment by a donee of the power.[79] To the extent that a donee has power of revocation it seems that he owes no duties in exercising it to either the deprived appointees or persons entitled in default. That does not mean, of course, that any reappointment, which it was the object of the revocation to facilitate, may not be set aside for fraud.[80]

(vii) Effect of Fraud

Fraud usually affects the whole appointment, which thus fails, leaving the donee of the power free to make a new appointment.[81] However, in certain cases the court may regard the appointment as severable into valid parts and fraudulent parts, in which case the valid part may be allowed to stand.[82]

Where the appointment relates to the legal interest in the property subject to the power, it is *voidable* only, *i.e.*, valid until set aside by the aggrieved party. Thus if the legal interest passes to a bona fide purchaser for value without notice of the fraud, he will take the property free of the aggrieved party's claim.[83] If, however, the appointment relates only to the equitable interest in the property, the appointment is *void ab initio* and a bona fide purchaser from the "appointee" without notice obtains no title.[84]

D. Determination

A power of appointment may be determined either expressly or by implication.

---

[77] *Re Somes* [1896] 1 Ch. 250.
[78] See further on releases of powers of appointment, para. 11.26, *infra*.
[79] See *Rooke* v. *Plunkett* [1902] 1 I.R. 299; *Re Gore-Booth's Estate* [1908] 1 I.R. 387; *Re Reilly and Brady's Contract* [1910] 1 I.R. 258; *Re McClintock* [1943] I.R. 83. Also *Re Greaves* [1954] Ch. 434.
[80] See *Hutchins* v. *Hutchins* (1876) I.R. 10 Eq. 453.
[81] *Greene* v. *Greene* (1845) 8 Ir.Eq.R. 473 (see *A Casebook on Equity and Trusts in Ireland* (1985), p. 732). Also *Topham* v. *Duke of Portland* (1869) 5 Ch.App. 40.
[82] *Harrison* v. *Randall* (1852) 9 Hare 397; *Whelan* v. *Palmer* (1888) 39 Ch.D. 648.
[83] Para. 3.074, *ante*.
[84] *Cloutte* v. *Storey* [1911] 1 Ch. 18. In England, since 1925 all powers of appointment operate in equity only, though some protection is afforded to third parties by s. 157 of the Law of Property Act, 1925.

1. *Expressly*

11.26. The first way in which a power may be determined is by the donee executing a release or entering into a contract not to exercise it.[85] Under section 52 (1) of the Conveyancing Act, 1881, such a release or contract should be by deed. A power in the nature of a trust may not be released since this would amount to a breach of trust,[86] and it is possible that a fiduciary power[87] may not be released either.[88]

11.27. Under section 6 (1) of the Conveyancing Act, 1882, a donee of a power may disclaim it by deed, which does not destroy the power but merely renders that donee incapable of exercising it. The power may still be exercised by other donees or their survivors, unless the contrary is expressed in the instrument creating the power.[89]

2. *Impliedly*

11.28. A power may be regarded by the court as having been determined impliedly due to actions by the donee or dealings with the property clearly inconsistent with further exercise of the power.[90] An implied release may be found where the purposes for which the power was created cease to exist.[91]

IV. POWERS OF ATTORNEY

11.29. A power of attorney comes into operation where one person (the donor) authorises another person to perform certain acts which the donor had power to perform.[92] Such powers are governed by legislation in both parts of Ireland: in the Republic of Ireland by Part XI of the Conveyancing Act, 1881, and sections 8 and 9 of the Conveyancing Act, 1882; in Northern Ireland, the 1881 and 1882 provisions have been replaced by the Powers of Attorney Act (N.I.), 1971.[93] The 1971 Act also replaces the former power of delegation conferred on trustees by a new wider-ranging power to delegate by power of

---

[85] *Re Chambers* (1847) 11 Ir.Eq.R. 518. Hawkins, "The Release of Powers" (1968) 84 L.Q.R. 64. Also *Hanbury's Modern Equity* (9th ed.), pp. 113–6; *Muir* v. *I.R.C.* [1966] 1 W.L.R. 1269.

[86] *Re Will's Trust Deeds* [1964] Ch. 219.

[87] See para. 11.09, *supra*.

[88] *Re Gestetner Settlement* [1953] Ch. 672 at 687 (*per* Harman J.). See also *Re Hay's Settlement Trusts* [1982] 1 W.L.R. 202; *Turner* v. *Turner* [1984] Ch. 100.

[89] 1882 Act. s. 6 (2).

[90] *Stewart* v. *Marquis of Donegal* (1845) 8 Ir.Eq.R. 621; *Stuart* v. *Kennedy* (1852) 3 Ir.Jur. 305. *Cf. Greene* v. *Greene* (1845) 8 Ir.Eq.R. 473 (see *A Casebook on Equity and Trusts in Ireland* (1985), p. 732). See also *Re Hancock* [1896] 2 Ch. 173; *Foakes* v. *Jackson* [1900] 1 Ch. 807; *Re Courtauld's Settlement* [1965] 2 All E.R. 544.

[91] *Wolley* v. *Jenkins* (1856) 23 Beav. 53.

[92] See *Roche* v. *Roche* (1844) 7 Ir.Eq.R. 436; *McLoughin* v. *Strand Housing Ltd.* (1952) 86 I.L.T.R. 167. Also *Booth* v. *McGowan* (1841) 4 Ir.L.R. 188; *Lord Gosford* v. *Robb* (1845) 8 Ir.L.R. 217; *Molesworth* v. *Robbins* (1845) 8 Ir.L.R. 223; *Bank of Ireland* v. *Evans' Trustees* (1855) 5 H.L.C. 389.

[93] This Act, and the English Act of the same year, was based on the recommendations of the Law Commission in its report, *Powers of Attorney*, Law Com. No. 30 (Cmnd. 4473) and the Q.U.B. Land Law Working Party's *Survey of the Land Law of Northern Ireland* (H.M.S.O. 1971), ch. 9. See Oerton, "Powers of Attorney Now" (1971) 112 New L.J. 746, 751, 764, 771 and 795; Ryan, "Powers of Attorney Act 1971" (1971) 115 Sol.Jo. 596; Samuels, "Powers of Attorney Act 1971" (1971) 35 Conv. 310.

attorney, for a period not exceeding 12 months, all or any of the trusts, powers and discretions vested in the trustees.[94]

A. CREATION

Various statutory provisions relating to this subject are in force in both parts of Ireland.

1. *Instruments of Creation*

11.30. In the Republic of Ireland there seem to be no special statutory provisions[95] governing creation of a power of attorney by the donor, though at common law it is necessary for him to execute a deed.[96] In Northern Ireland, section 1 (1) of the Powers of Attorney Act (N.I.), 1971, requires an instrument creating a power of attorney to be signed and sealed[97] by, *or by the direction of and in the presence of,*[98] the donor of the power. Where the instrument is executed by the direction of the donor, two other persons must be present as witnesses and must attest the instrument.[99] The 1971 Act also introduces for the first time a statutory form of a power of attorney, which, if adopted by a donor in Northern Ireland, confers on the donee a general power "to do on behalf of the donor anything which he can lawfully do by an attorney."[1] This form cannot be used to delegate functions which the donor possesses in a fiduciary capacity, *e.g.*, as a trustee.[2] In such a case the specific powers delegated should be spelt out in detail.

2. *Filing*

11.31. In the Republic of Ireland, section 48 (1) of the Conveyancing Act, 1881, provides that an instrument creating a power of attorney, provided its execution is verified by affidavit, statutory declaration or other sufficient evidence, *may* be deposited in the proper office of the Supreme Court, where a file of instruments deposited is kept for searches and inspection.[3] Such filing does not afford any protection against a breach of trust or other abuses, such

---

[94] S. 9, which substitutes a new s. 26 of the Trustee Act (N.I.), 1958 (which, *e.g.*, was confined to delegation during absence abroad). See para. 10.038, *ante.* Also *Re Donoughmore and Hackett's Contract*[1918] 1 I.R. 359.

[95] *I.e.*, apart from the general law with respect to execution of instruments, *e.g.*, creation by a corporation would require the usual actions of affixing the common seal in the presence of officers of the corporation, etc. See *O'Connor* v. *Bernard* (1842) 4 Ir.Eq.R. 689; *Bank of Ireland* v. *Evans' Trustees* (1855) 5 H.L.C. 389. For Northern Ireland, see ss. 1 (3) and 6 of the Powers of Attorney Act (N.I.), 1971.

[96] See *R.* v. *Martin* (1831) Glasc. 33.

[97] The section does not refer to delivery.

[98] This new provision only covers physical, not mental, incapacity.

[99] *Cf.* the statutory provisions for wills in s. 78 of the Succession Act, 1965 (R.I.) and s. 9 of the Wills Act, 1837. Paras. 14.06 *et seq.*, *post.* See also *Burke* v. *Murphy* (1841) Arm.Mac. & Og. 165.

[1] 1971 Act, s. 10 and Sched. 1.

[2] Delegation by trustees is now governed by s. 9 of the 1971 Act, *infra.*

[3] 1881 Act, s. 48 (2), which also entitles the searcher to an office copy of the instrument filed. Memorials of instruments creating powers of attorney can, of course, be registered in the Registry of Deeds, see ch. 22, *post.*

as forgery,[4] and section 2 of the Powers of Attorney Act (N.I.), 1971, abolishes the practice in Northern Ireland.[5]

3. *Proof*

11.32. In the Republic of Ireland the only means of proof of the contents of an instrument creating a power of attorney is production of the original instrument. It would seem that an office copy of the instrument, if it is filed in court under section 48 (1) of the 1881 Act, is not sufficient. Such an office copy did not become, without further proof, sufficient evidence of the contents of the original instrument in England and Northern Ireland until this was provided by section 4 (1) of the Evidence and Powers of Attorney Act, 1940.[6] It must be emphasised that this provision simply provides for proof of the contents of the original instrument, it does not provide for proof of the *truth* of those contents or as to the identity of the person by whom the original was executed.[7] Also in Northern Ireland now, section 3 of the English Powers of Attorney Act, 1971,[8] enables the contents of the original instrument creating the power of attorney to be proved by means of a photographic copy duly certified by a solicitor or stockbroker as a true and complete copy of the original.[9] Furthermore, certified photocopies of a photocopy may be produced as evidence of the contents of the original instrument.[10]

B. EXECUTION

11.33. In the Republic of Ireland, section 46 of the Conveyancing Act, 1881, provides that the donee of a power of attorney may, if he thinks fit, execute or do any assurance, instrument, or thing in and with his own name and signature and his own seal, where sealing is required, by the authority of the donor of the power. Every assurance, instrument and thing so executed and done is effective in law to all intents as if it had been executed or done by the donee in the name and with the signature and seal of the donor.

In *Industrial Development Authority* v. *Moran*,[10a] the Republic's Supreme

---

[4] The N.I. Court of Appeal held that an office copy of an instrument deposited in the Supreme Court could not be taken to be any evidence of the truth of the contents or the genuineness of the execution of the instrument creating the power, see *O'Kane* v. *Mullan* [1925] N.I. 1.
[5] The right to search the file and to obtain an office copy of an instrument already deposited is preserved. The reasons for abolition of filing were that it involved the administrative disadvantages of expense and cumbersome procedure without securing any advantage of protection for interested parties, see *Survey of the Land Law of Northern Ireland* (1971), paras. 256–60.
[6] See also s. 1 (4) of the Execution of Trusts (Emergency Provisions) Act (N.I.), 1939.
[7] See *O'Kane* v. *Mullan* [1925] N.I. 1.
[8] S. 3 of the English 1971 Act was extended expressly to N.I. by s. 11(3) of the Act.
[9] Note the requirement in s. 3 (1) (*b*) (ii) of a certificate at the end of each page of the copy where the original consists of two or more pages. This was not the first time that Westminster recognised the evidentiary value of photographic copies of instruments. Under rules authorised by s. 2 of the Evidence and Powers of Attorney Act, 1943, which extended to N.I., photocopies of instruments creating powers of attorney could be deposited in the proper office of the Supreme Court.
[10] S. 3 (2). Presumably the rule in *O'Kane* v. *Mullan*, fn. 4, *supra* hold good in this regard. See *Survey of the Land Law of Northern Ireland* (1971), para. 259.
[10a] [1978] I.R. 159.

Court held that execution of a deed by a receiver in his own name was effective to vest the fee simple in a company's land in the purchaser under section 46 of the 1881 Act, where the debenture provided that a receiver duly appointed had power to effect a sale of the company's assets and to act as attorney of the company "to execute, seal and deliver" any deed required for such a sale. The debenture had also provided that the receiver could effect a sale "by deed in the name of and on behalf of" the company and the receiver had, in addition, purported to effect execution of the transfer deed (the land was registered land) by the company (as a distinct grantor) by affixing the company's seal opposite the attestation. This was held by the Supreme Court to be ineffective since it was done without the directors' authority, which was required by the company's articles of association. Commenting on such a clause in a debenture, Kenny J. said:

> "When a receiver is selling under such a clause, the more usual and better practice is for him to execute the deed of transfer by writing the name of the company and underneath this to write words that indicate that the name of the company has been written by the receiver as attorney of the company under the power of attorney given by the debenture. In addition, he should execute the deed in his own name. In that way he has the best of both worlds. The writing of the name of the company by the authority of the company given when it executed the debenture brings the case within the words of the debenture itself and execution by the attorney personally gives the advantage of s. 46 of the Conveyancing Act, 1881."[10b]

A similar provision for Northern Ireland is now contained in section 7 of the Powers of Attorney Act (N.I.), 1971.

C. PROTECTION OF DONEE

11.34. The position at common law was that a power of attorney was revoked automatically by the donor's death, insanity, marriage or bankruptcy[11] and was revocable by the donor himself unless "coupled with an interest."[12] There are, however, now in force in both parts of Ireland statutory provisions conferring some measure of protection on donees of powers of attorney. In the Republic of Ireland these provisions are the rather unsatisfactory ones[13] introduced for both Ireland and England by section 47 of the Conveyancing Act, 1881, and section 23 of the Trustee Act, 1893. In Northern Ireland the nineteenth-century provisions have recently been replaced by a new set of provisions.

[10b] *Ibid.*, p. 166.
[11] *Tingley* v. *Muller* [1917] 2 Ch. 144 espec. at 183 (*per Bray* J.).
[12] *Walsh* v. *Whitecomb* (1797) 2 Esp. 565. And see *Abbott* v. *Stratton* (1846) 9 Ir.Eq.R. 233, *Re Parkinson's Estate* (1864) 10 Ir.Jur.(N.S.) 82.
[13] See *Powers of Attorney*, Law.Com. No. 30 (Cmnd. 4473); *Survey of the Land Law of Northern Ireland* (1971), ch. 9.

1. *Republic of Ireland*

11.35. Section 47 (1) of the Conveyancing Act, 1881, provides that "any person"[14] making or doing any payment or act, in good faith, "in pursuance of a power of attorney" is not liable in respect of the payment or act by reason that before the payment or act the donor of the power had died, or become lunatic or of unsound mind, or bankrupt, or had revoked the power, *provided* the fact of death, lunacy or bankruptcy was not at the time of the payment or act known to the person making or doing the payment or act.[15] This protection for the donee acting in good faith against both the donor of the power or third parties claiming there has been a breach of warranty of authority is subject to the qualification that it does not "affect any right against the payee of any person interested in any money so paid; and that person shall have the like remedy against the payee as he would have had against the payer if the payment had not been made by him."[16]

2. *Northern Ireland*

11.36. By section 4 (1) of the Powers of Attorney Act (N.I.), 1971, the donee of a power of attorney, who does not know that the power has been revoked, incurs no liability by reason of the revocation either to the donor or a third party. However, the donee is deemed to know that the power has been revoked if he knows of an event, such as the death of the donor, which has the effect of revoking the power.[17]

D. PROTECTION OF THIRD PARTIES

Again there are statutory provisions in both parts of Ireland conferring some protection on third parties dealing with donees of powers of attorney.

1. *Republic of Ireland*

11.37. In the Republic of Ireland this matter is still governed by the obscure provisions contained in sections 8 and 9 of the Conveyancing Act, 1882, which deal, respectively, with the effect of (a) a power of attorney "given for valuable consideration" and "in the instrument creating the power expressed to be irrevocable" and (b) one "whether given for valuable consideration or not" which is "in the instrument creating the power expressed to be irrevocable for a fixed time therein specified, not exceeding one year from the date of the instrument."[18] Several problems arise from these provisions.

---

[14] Presumably this means only the donee of a power. The side-note to s. 47 refers to "Payment by attorney under power . . ." and this seems to be confirmed by the later phrase in s. 47 (1), "in pursuance of a power of attorney."

[15] This proviso seems to render the earlier reference in s. 47 (1) to "good faith" superfluous, unless it covers turning a "blind eye" to suspicious circumstances.

[16] S. 47 (2). As regards trustees, Trustee Act, 1893, s. 23.

[17] S. 4 (5). *Cf.* where the power is given by way of security, s. 3, see *infra.*

[18] See *Levingston* v. *Somers* [1941] I.R. 183.

11.38. First, it is not clear why a distinction is drawn between powers given for valuable consideration and other powers. As we mentioned above, the significant distinction at common law for the purposes of revocation by the donor was whether or not the power was "coupled with an interest." A power is coupled with an interest where it is given by way of security, *e.g.*, power given to an equitable mortgagee (donee) to convey the legal estate if the mortgagor (donor) defaults on the mortgage.[19] This is a rather different situation from the normal case of a power of attorney, where the donee acts as agent for the donor. In the case of a "security" power, the transaction has proprietary characteristics and the donee in exercising the power acts in his own interests to realise his security rather than as agent of the donor. It is not surprising then that the common law regarded security powers as irrevocable by the donor. Yet this is not the distinction apparently recognised by the Conveyancing Act, 1882. It is true that valuable consideration will be a feature of a security power, but it is not enough on its own to create the proprietary or security element. This brings us to the second major problem about the provisions of the 1882 Act, namely their precise effect with respect to third parties.

11.39. Both sections 8 and 9 provide that "in favour of a purchaser" (a) the power cannot be revoked without the concurrence of the donee; (b) any act done by the donee is effective notwithstanding purported revocation or death, disability or bankruptcy of the donor and (c) neither the donor nor the purchaser is adversely affected by notice of purported revocation[20] or of the donor's death, disability or bankruptcy. The difference between the two sections is that under section 8 the protection lasts for all time, whereas under section 9 it lasts for the fixed time specified in the instrument only. It seems to be clear from the wording of *both* sections that the "donee of the power" and a "purchaser" are different persons[21] and so the person protected in each case is a third party dealing with the donee.[22] Nothing seems to depend upon the existence of consideration as between the two sections and it does not appear that it can be successfully argued that the existence of consideration will extend the protection of irrevocability to the donee of the power. The donee must still rely on the common law and prove the existence of a security interest sufficient to render the power irrevocable as against him. In other words, sections 8 and 9 of the 1882 Act simply give statutory force to a conveyancing device to protect third parties dealing with the donee of the power, including, be it noted, dishonest ones.[23]

---

[19]   See *Abbott* v. *Stratton* (1846) 9 Ir.Eq.R. 233; *McDowell* v. *Reede* (1865) 16 Ir.Ch.R. 430.
[20]   Unless this is done "with the concurrence of the donee," in which case presumably the protection disappears.
[21]   See especially ss. 8 (1) (iii) and 9 (1) (iii). "Purchaser" is defined in s. 1 (4) of the 1882 Act as including "a lessee or mortgagee, or an intending purchaser, lessee or mortgagee, or other person, who, for valuable consideration, takes or deals for property."
[22]   See *Tingley* v. *Muller* [1917] 2 Ch. 144.
[23]   Note that there is no reference to "good faith" in the definition of "purchaser" in s. 1 (4) of the 1882 Act and ss. 8 (1) (iii) and 9 (1) (iii) specifically confer protection on both the donee and "purchaser" even if they have notice of revocation of the power by the donor or by operation of law.

2. *Northern Ireland*

11.40. In Northern Ireland the law on this subject has been overhauled by the Powers of Attorney Act (N.I.), 1971, which does recognise the common law distinction between security powers and other powers.

Under section 3 (1) of the 1971 Act, where a power of attorney is expressed to be irrevocable and is given to secure a proprietary interest of the donee,[24] or the performance of an obligation owed to the donee, then, so long as the donee has the interest or the obligation remains undischarged, the power cannot be revoked either by the donor without the consent of the donee or by the death, incapacity or bankruptcy of the donor or, in the case of a corporation, by its winding up or dissolution.

11.41. This provides protection for the donee of a power of attorney which the Conveyancing Acts, 1881 and 1882, did not provide. Furthermore, to protect third parties, not just purchasers, dealing with the donee, who may have no means of knowing whether the donor has revoked the security power with the donee's consent, section 4 (3) provides that such a third party is entitled to assume that the power is still fully operative, *unless* he knows it has been so revoked. His title will always be good in the absence of such knowledge. However, for this protection to be afforded to the third party, it is essential under section 4 (3) that the power is expressed to be irrevocable and to be given by way of security,[25] *i.e.*, it matters not that it was not *in fact* given by way of security provided that the instrument *says* it was, and, conversely, no protection is afforded even if in fact it was given for security but the instrument does *not* say so.

11.42. So far as other kinds of powers of attorney are concerned, section 4 (2) of the 1971 Act provides that where a third party deals with the donee after such a power has in fact been revoked, but without knowledge of the revocation, the transaction between the donee and third party is to be as valid as if the power were still in existence. However, section 4 (5) provides that knowledge of the occurrence of an event (*e.g.*, death of the donor) causing revocation is equivalent to knowledge of revocation, even though the third party was unaware of the event's effect. To protect a purchaser of such a third party's title, who might find it impossible to discover the state of the third party's knowledge when the third party acquired the property to which the power related, section 4 (4) provides that it is to be conclusively presumed in favour of such a purchaser that the third party did not know of the revocation provided (a) the transaction between the donee and the third party was completed within a year from the date of operation of the power[26] or (b) if the

---

[24] A power of attorney given to secure a proprietary interest may be given, "and shall be deemed to have been capable always of being given," (wording not to be found in s. 4 (2) of the English 1971 Act) to the donee and his successors in title, and the latter are to be deemed donees of the power, so that a transfer of the secured interest does not revoke the power, see s. 3 (2) of the 1971 Act.

[25] *Cf.* s. 3 (1) which requires that the power be expressed to be irrevocable and that it be given to secure, etc.

[26] *I.e.*, the date of the power, unless the instrument creating the power provides otherwise.

transaction is outside that period, the third party makes a statutory declaration, before or within three months of completion of the purchase, that he did not know of the revocation.[27]

11.43. Finally, section 8 of the 1971 Act provides for the delivery of the instrument creating a power of attorney relating to unregistered land (or a copy of it or of material portions of it) to a purchaser of the land, who is entitled to such delivery notwithstanding any stipulation to the contrary.

---

[27] S. 6 provides for a statutory declaration to be made by a properly authorised officer of a company in the case of a company being the third party. See also s. 5 which deals with the case of transferees under stock exchange transactions, who do not sign the form of transfer under the Stock Transfer Act (N.I.), 1963. In such a case the statutory declaration is to be made by the donee of the power.

PART V

MORTGAGES

CHAPTER 12

MORTGAGES

I. NATURE

12.01. The essential feature of a mortgage is the concept of *security*.[1] If a lender of money makes a loan without security he runs the risk of the borrower becoming insolvent and unable to repay anything more than a small fraction of what is owed. The lender's only remedy is to sue for his debt and, if the borrower has become bankrupt, to claim in the bankruptcy proceedings as an unsecured creditor over whom secured creditors will have priority.[2] This is obviously not a very satisfactory position to be in and so many lenders of money make it a practice to insist upon the borrower giving security for the loan. The giving of security usually involves the conferment on the lender of some claim against or interest in an item of property, so that, in the event of the borrower failing to, or becoming unable to, repay the loan, the lender may claim against that property in priority to other creditors. The property may be land which is the traditional subject of a mortgage, or personal property, as it is common to use things like life insurance policies or shares in a company as security. Usually the security is a claim against some specific item of property, but this is not always the case, *e.g.*, it is possible to have a "floating charge" over company assets.[3] Since this book is concerned primarily with land law, the ensuing discussion will concentrate on mortgages of land.

A. HISTORICAL BACKGROUND

1. *Common Law*

12.02. The earliest forms of mortgage recognised at common law seem to

---

[1] See, generally on the law of mortgages, Kiely, *Principles of Equity as Applied in Ireland* (1936), chs. XVI and XVII. Also Coote, *Treatise on the Law of Mortgages* (9th ed. by Ramsbotham, 1927); Fairest, *Mortgages* (1975); Fisher and Lightwood, *Law of Mortgages* (9th ed. by Tyler, 1977); Waldock, *Law of Mortgages* (2nd ed., 1950). See also Jackson, "The Need to Reform the English Law of Mortgages" (1978) 94 L.Q.R. 571.

[2] The subject of priorities is discussed in detail in ch. 13, *post.*

[3] See *Industrial Development Authority* v. *Moran* [1978] I.R. 159; *Kelly* v. *McMahon Ltd.* [1980] I.R. 347; *Crowley* v. *Northern Bank Finance Corporation Ltd.* [1981] I.R. 353; *Re Armagh Shoes Ltd.* [1982] N.I. 59; *Re Keenan Brothers Ltd.* [1985] I.L.R.M. 254. See also *Kreglinger* v. *New Patagonia Meat and Cold Storage Co. Ltd.* [1914] A.C. 25. Farrer, "Floating Charges and Priorities" (1974) 38 Conv. 315 and "The Crystallisation of a Floating Charge" (1976) 40 Conv. 397; Pennington, "The Genesis of the Floating Charge" (1960) 23 M.L.R. 630.

have been of two main kinds.[4] One form was for the borrower of money
(mortgagor) to lease his land to the lender (mortgagee), who went into
possession.[5] This lease was subject to a condition subsequent[6] to the effect
that, if the mortgagor had not repaid the loan by the time the lease expired,
the morgagee's lease was enlarged into a fee simple.[7] If the income from the
land was used to discharge the debt, the mortgage was called a *vivum vadium*,
i.e., a "live" pledge; if not, the mortgage was called a *mortuum vadium*, a
"dead" pledge.[8] The other early form of mortgage was a conveyance of the
fee simple in land by the mortgagor to the mortgagee, subject to a condition
that the mortgagor could re-enter and determine the mortgagee's estate,
provided the loan was repaid on the named date. Again the mortgagee
entered into possession of the land. The crucial factor, however, was that
such a condition was construed strictly at common law. If the mortgagor did
not repay the loan by the set date, the mortgagee's estate in the land became
absolute and the mortgagor found himself in the unfortunate position of being
deprived of his land for ever, yet still liable for the debt. As we shall see, it
was equity's great contribution to the law of mortgages to change this
position.

12.03. These early common law forms of mortgage remain the basis of the
forms used for unregistered land in Ireland today.[9] The major difference that
has developed over the centuries is that nowadays a mortgage by conveyance
of the fee simple or assignment of a lease is subject to a proviso for
redemption in favour of the mortgagor, whereby the mortgagee covenants to
reconvey or reassign the property to the mortgagor on payment of the loan.
Similarly, a mortgage by demise is subject to a proviso for cesser of the lease
or sub-lease on redemption by the mortgagor.

2. *Equity*

12.04. The starting point of equity's approach to a mortgage transaction was
to regard it as being in substance a secured loan only. To the extent that the
mortgagee obtained an interest in property it should be a device to provide
him with security and nothing more. This approach led to the establishment
of several principles which remain to this day cornerstones of the law of
mortgages.

---

[4] See Holdsworth, *History of English Law*, vol. 3, espec. pp. 128–130. Also Barton, "The Common Law
Mortgage" (1967) 83 L.Q.R. 229; Chaplin, "The Story of Mortgage Law" (1890) 4 H.L.R. 1; Hazeltine, "The
Gage of Land in Medieval England" (1904) 17 H.L.R. 549 and (1905) 18 H.L.R. 26. See also the
fourteenth-century example digested at (1967) 18 N.I.L.Q. 348.
[5] This does not conform with the modern form of mortgage and resembles a pledge, see para. 12.18, *post*.
[6] See para. 4.048, *ante*.
[7] There were doubts about the validity of such conditions, see Holdsworth, *op. cit.*, pp. 129–30. See further
on enlargement of leases, chs. 17 and 18, *post*.
[8] The early writers on the common law regarded this as the derivation of the word "mortgage," *i.e.*, mort
(dead) and gage (pledge). See Glanville's *Tractatus de Legibus*, bk. x, 6 and 8; *Coke upon Littleton* (19th ed.,
1832), vol. 2, 205a.
[9] See, further, para. 12.30, *post*.

12.05. Equity regarded it as inconsistent with the concept of security that the mortgagor should lose his property merely because he was late in repaying the loan. Once it was determined that the transaction was a mortgage, and in this equity looked to the intent and not the form,[10] equity would allow the mortgagor to redeem his mortgage, by repayment of the loan and any interest charged thereon, long after the date fixed for redemption. Equity's maxim was "once a mortgage, always a mortgage," and this would be enforced against any attempts to hinder the mortgagor in exercising his right to redeem, *i.e.*, by "clogs" on the equity of redemption.[11] This resulted in the following features of a modern form of mortgage becoming recognised. First, there is what is known as the *legal date for redemption*. This is the date, usually fixed as three or six months from the date of the mortgage, specified in the mortgage instrument for the repayment of the loan. At common law this date was crucial, but because of the attitude of equity it does not mean what it appears to say.[12] No one expects the mortgagor to repay the loan by that date and it is probably in neither party's interest that he should.[13] As we shall see, the main significance of this date today is that it governs the availability of certain of the mortgagee's remedies for realisation of his security in the event of something going wrong with the transaction.[14] Apart from that, both parties usually expect that the loan and any interest charged on it will be repaid over a substantial period of time, frequently running into decades. The second major feature of a mortgage is, therefore, the *equitable right to redeem*, which is exercisable by the mortgagor at any time after the legal date for redemption, though this exercise is always subject to general principles of equity, *e.g.*, "he who comes into equity, must come with clean hands."[15] This second feature of a mortgage is connected with, but must be distinguished from, a third, known as the mortgagor's *equity of redemption*. This is a larger concept than the particular right to redeem and consists of the sum total of the mortgagor's interest in the property which is the security for the loan.[16] It can best be described as ownership[17] of the property subject only to the rights of the mortgagee.[18] While at common law the mortgagee was regarded as owner of the property, in equity the mortgagor is regarded as owner and the mortgagee as an incumbrancer only. This equity of redemption, sometimes

---

[10] See *Goodman* v. *Grierson* (1813) 2 Ba. & B. 274; *Balfe* v. *Lord* (1842) 4 Ir.Eq.R. 648. Also *Hughes* v. *Glenny* (1841) Arm.Mac. & Og. 387. Para. 3.060, *ante*.

[11] See, further, para. 13.088 *et seq.*, *post*.

[12] Maitland thus remarked: "That is the worst of our mortgage deed—owing to the action of equity, it is one long *suppressio veri* and *suggestio falsi*." *Equity* (rev. ed. by Brunyate, 1936), p. 182. See also Lord Macnaghten in *Samuel* v. *Jarrah Timber and Wood Paving Co. Ltd.* [1904] A.C. 323 at 326.

[13] See paras. 12.07–9, *post*.

[14] Ch. 13, *post*.

[15] Para. 3.058, *ante*. See the application of this maxim in the doctrine of consolidation of mortgages, para. 13.069, *post*.

[16] In this context, the distinction between an equitable interest and a mere equity may again be applicable, though rarely, if ever, of practical significance, since the equitable right to redeem is part of the equity of redemption and so at any point in time a mortgagor will not be forced to rely solely on the lesser of the two concepts.

[17] Commensurate, of course, with the interest in the property mortgaged, *i.e.*, freehold, leasehold, etc. See *Wrixon* v. *Vize* (1842) 4 Ir.Eq.R. 463.

[18] See *Blake* v. *Foster* (1813) 2 Ba. & B. 387; *Burrowes* v. *Molloy* (1845) 2 Jo & Lat. 521.

rather loosely referred to as the mortgagor's "equity" in the property,[19] is a valuable interest in property which can be sold, demised or mortgaged, like any other item of property.[20] Furthermore, it is usually quite easy to put a monetary value upon it, especially in these days of high inflation and, until recently, rising property values. For example, if in 1975 X bought a house for IR £20,000 and borrowed IR £18,000 from a building society to help pay for it, he immediately had an equity in the house of about IR £2,000 in value. By 1985 the market value of the house may have risen to IR £40,000, so that by then X had an asset worth IR £40,000 in respect of which the liabilities amounted to rather less than IR £18,000 (assuming he had been repaying capital as well as interest charged on the original loan). Thus his equity in the house had increased in value from IR £2,000 to well over IR £20,000 and, if he sold his house, he could have expected to make a profit of roughly this amount. Instead of selling his house, he might have preferred to make improvements to it and to pay for these by borrowing more money through a second mortgage on the house. Assuming market prices at the very least hold steady, the house will be adequate security for further loans up to the value of the difference between the market value of the house and the amounts of capital outstanding on existing secured loans.

At this point it may be useful to give a few illustrations of the operation of a modern mortgage.

B. MODERN ILLUSTRATIONS

12.06. From the outset it should be emphasised that there are two main aspects to be considered with respect to a mortgage. One may be described as the financial aspect and the other as the conveyancing aspect. By tradition it is the latter which is of primary concern to the lawyer, yet in recent years it has become more common for solicitors to widen their sphere of operation and to be prepared to give their clients what is essentially advice on financial matters. The technical conveyancing aspect of a mortgage transaction is also the aspect with which this book is primarily concerned, but it is useful in considering this to keep in mind the financial aspect which will, after all, be of more concern to the client. This should become clear if we take first what is, perhaps, the most common example of a mortgage, namely the purchase of a house as the private residence of the mortgagor.

1. *House Purchase*

12.07. Let us consider again the example given earlier of X who in 1975 bought a house the purchase price of which then was IR£20,000, but which is now worth IR£40,000 and which X is negotiating to sell to Y. Assuming that Y does not have the cash to pay the full purchase price, which is usually the

---

[19]   See fn. 16, *supra*.
[20]   See *Maxwell* v. *Tipping* [1903] 1 I.R. 498.

case, he will need to borrow money[21] from an institution willing to lend it. In view of the substantial amount of money Y is likely to want to borrow, the repayment of the loan will have to be spread over a substantial period of years.[22] The period for repayment of a house-purchase mortgage can be anything from 15–30 years (and sometimes even longer in special cases), and this generally rules out borrowing from institutions which specialise in short-term lending, e.g., until recently, when they have had a change of policy, banks.[23] Fortunately, there are institutions which specialise in such long-term lending, particularly when it relates to house purchase, e.g., building societies[24] and local authorities.[25] Y will probably find that he is required by X's solicitor or estate agent to pay a deposit on the house, usually 10 per cent. of the purchase price (i.e., IR£4,000). Apart from that, it is comparatively rare for institutions such as building societies to be willing to lend the full 100 per cent. of the purchase price. A common practice is to adopt a rough rule-of-thumb to the effect that normally 80 per cent. of the price only can be borrowed and, if more than that is to be lent to bring, say, the amount borrowed up to 90 or 95 per cent., the society may require the borrower to take out a "mortgage indemnity" insurance policy to cover the excess amount lent.[26] Alternatively, if the building society refuses to advance more than, say, 80 per cent. of the purchase price, Y may be able to obtain a further "topping-up" loan which may be secured on the same house by a

---

[21] In certain cases, however, he may be eligible for a housing grant as opposed to a loan, e.g., in the Republic of Ireland under the Housing Act, 1966, ss. 15–38, or, if the property is in a Gaeltacht area, under the Housing (Gaeltacht) Acts, 1929, ss. 3, 6, 7 and 11; 1949, ss. 5 and 6; 1953, ss. 2 and 3; 1959, ss. 2–4 and 8; 1964, ss. 2–6; 1967, ss. 3 and 4; 1979, ss. 2–6. See also grants in Northern Ireland under the Housing (N.I.) Order, 1981, Pt. IV.

[22] See further on "instalment" mortgages, Re Nepean's Settled Estate [1900] 1 I.R. 298; Re Strabane R.D.C. [1910] 1 I.R. 135; Re Gore Booth's Estate [1910] 1 I.R. 139; Carlow C.C. v. O'Connor [1952] Ir.Jur.Rep. 5.

[23] That does not mean that Y's bank may not have another, but related, part to play in the transaction. If Y is also, as is common, selling his present residence, he may be dependent upon the profit he makes on that sale to meet the deposit required for the purchase of X's house or the difference between the price of X's house and the loan he is seeking for its purchase, which sums incidentally may not be the same. But he may not have that profit or surplus in his hands at the date he is required to pay the deposit on X's house or, indeed, even when he is required to complete the purchase of X's house, in which case he will need a "bridging" loan, i.e., a loan to bridge the gap between the date for payment of the deposit or completion and the date when the sale of his present house is completed and he receives the surplus from that sale (i.e., after redemption of his mortgage, if any, on that house, etc.). Bridging loans, which are usually comparatively short-term loans, are exactly the sort of loans banks are expert in arranging. The subject of finance for land transactions is discussed further in Irish Conveyancing Law (1978), ch. 4.

[24] Whose activities are largely regulated by statute: for the Republic of Ireland, see Building Societies Acts, 1874, 1877, 1884, 1894 and Building Societies Act, 1942, now consolidated in the Building Societies Act, 1976, see Rafferty v. Crowley [1984] I.L.R.M. 350 (see now Building Societies (Amendment) Act, 1983, s. 1); for Northern Ireland, see Building Societies Act (N.I.), 1967. Note also that the Home Purchase Assistance (N.I.) Order, 1978, empowered the N.I. Department of the Environment to make advances to lending institutions to enable them to provide assistance to "first-time" house purchasers. Also Provincial Building Society v. Brown [1950] N.I. 163; Martin v. Irish Industrial Benefit Building Society [1960] Ir.Jur.Rep. 42.

[25] Note the establishment in Northern Ireland of a central housing authority, the Housing Executive, under the Housing Executive Act (N.I.), 1971, see O'Kane, (1971) 22 N.I.L.Q. 530, and in the Republic of the Housing Finance Agency under the Housing Finance Agency Act, 1981.

[26] I.e., this provides the society with an indemnity against loss should it later have to realise its security, perhaps by selling the house, and find that the house's value has by then dropped below the amount borrowed and still outstanding, because this was in excess of the 80 per cent. normally lent. An indemnity policy should not be confused with a "mortgage protection" insurance policy, which is a life insurance policy providing the borrower with cover for the amount borrowed, so that, in the event of the borrower dying before the mortgage is paid off, the insurance company will thereupon pay off the balance outstanding and leave the house discharged from the mortgage.

second mortgage. Such a loan is frequently advanced by employers under a special scheme providing "fringe-benefits" for employees, though some of the larger employers even have full-blown mortgage schemes, under which they are willing not only to advance anything up to 100 per cent. of the purchase price but to do so at very favourable rates of interest. Finally, there is one further consideration to be borne in mind by Y and that is that the lending institution will obviously take into account Y's ability to keep up regular repayments over a substantial period of time in calculating exactly how much money it is prepared to lend him.[27] Here again many institutions adopt a rule-of-thumb whereby they are willing to lend a total amount of only so many times the borrower's gross annual earnings, e.g., two-and-a-half or three times his earnings.[28] Thus, if Y were currently earning a gross income of IR£10,000 per annum, he would find it difficult to persuade many institutions to lend him more than a total of IR£30,000 and, depending upon a variety of circumstances, in particular the general state of the loan market at the time, might well find it impossible to persuade any building society to lend even up to that amount, as has occurred recently.

12.08.   Assuming that Y succeeds in borrowing the amount he needs to buy X's house, let us say, IR£30,000 from a building society, he, then, has to agree with the society how this is to be repaid. Normally, lending institutions like building societies charge interest on the capital sum lent, which interest is charged by a rate calculated on an annual basis. Owing to the present-day difficulties facing most economies and world markets, which has resulted in fluctuating interest rates in the money markets of most developed countries, it is rare nowadays for the rate of interest to be fixed for the duration of the mortgage period, say, 25 years in the case of Y. The result is that over the period of the mortgage Y may find that the rate of interest charged on his loan varies from year to year.[29] The standard repayment mortgage will require Y to make regular payments, usually monthly, to the building society over the 25-year term of the mortgage. Each payment is usually a composite amount representing, partly, repayment of some of the capital originally borrowed and, partly, payment of some of the interest charged on that capital.[30] The

---

[27]   Other matters which may be taken into consideration are such things as Y's sex, marital status and age and the age, state of repair and title (e.g., freehold or leasehold and, if the latter, the term of years remaining on the lease) of the property which is going to be the lender's security. Some institutions are reluctant either to lend to single women, for fear they get married and cease to be wage-earning, or to take into account a working wife's earnings in calculating the sum to be lent to her husband, for fear she has children and ceases to be earning for a substantial part of the period during which the mortgage is to be repaid. As regards the age of the borrowers, the general rule is usually that the older the borrower the more reluctant the institution is to lend and, if it does lend, the shorter the period for repayment.

[28]   Apart from this, a lending institution's offer of a loan will usually be based on its valuation of the property and *not* the purchase price.

[29]   Thus in the early 1970s the rate charged by most building societies fluctuated between 7 per cent. and 11 per cent. per annum; in the late 1970s and 1980s it has usually been over, sometimes well over, 11 per cent.

[30]   In fact, often, due to the way some institutions do their accounting, in the early years of a standard repayment mortgage the payments represent largely payments of interest and this may be significant where the borrower is entitled to income tax relief on the interest charged on the mortgage loan. It will have the effect of reducing the real cost of the mortgage in the early years, which may be a vital factor for a young married couple struggling to make ends meet at the start of the marriage.

result will be, of course, that if Y's mortgage runs for its full term of 25 years, he will have paid to the building society considerably more than IR£30,000, but he will at least have some consolation that, with modern inflation and the steady fall in the value of money, the *real* cost of his mortgage will decrease as the years go by, while the value of the house may increase,[31] though property values are not rising as steeply as they were a few years ago.

12.09. A standard repayment mortgage is not the only kind of mortgage available for someone in Y's position. For example, Y could instead arrange what is usually called an "endowment" mortgage. This is a mortgage linked to a life-endowment insurance policy.[32] The usual procedure is for Y to borrow the capital sum, IR£30,000 in our example, from a building society and, in addition, to take out a life-endowment insurance policy with an insurance company.[33] This insurance policy, as the name implies, combines the elements of life insurance, *i.e.*, payment of a guaranteed sum on the insured's death, and of endowment, *i.e.*, payment of a guaranteed sum on a specified future date. In Y's case the sum in question would be IR£30,000, so that the insurance company would undertake to pay IR£30,000 in 25 years' time (*i.e.*, at the end of the mortgage term) or on Y's death, if this occurs before the 25 years are up (thereby introducing mortgage protection of Y's successors). Because the building society is thereby guaranteed payment of its capital, it will require Y to pay the interest charged on the capital borrowed only during the mortgage term, so that, in this sort of mortgage, Y pays interest (again usually by monthly instalments) to the building society, in respect of which he may obtain tax relief, and premiums to the insurance company, which may also attract tax relief. However, even allowing for any tax relief, it is questionable whether such a mortgage scheme will work out any cheaper than a standard repayment mortgage and, for this reason, such schemes are usually adopted only where the endowment insurance policy is a "with-profits" one. Under such a policy, higher premiums will be charged than in the case of a "without-profits" policy, but, in return for these, the policy-holder is allowed to participate in the profits made by the insurance company on its investments and these profits are accumulated and added to the guaranteed endowment sum payable at the end of the policy. Thus, in Y's case, provided his insurance company has a successful investment record over the 25 years of his mortgage term,[34] not only will he have the IR£30,000 capital owed to the building society paid off at the end of the 25 years, he will also receive an additional lump sum representing his share of the accumulated profits of the company over that 25 years, and sometimes a terminal bonus which represents his share

---

[31] Though in a sense it can be argued that there is no *real* increase in that, if Y decides to realise his "profit," which is due to the rise in property values, by selling his house, he will find that any new house he buys will cost just as much because inflation usually affects the property market generally.

[32] It should not be confused with a mortgage protection insurance policy, see fn. 26, para. 12.07, *ante*.

[33] The building society will probably insist on restricting the insurance companies with which it is willing to arrange such schemes.

[34] There is always an element of risk involved here and this indicates the sort of financial advice that Y may need and which more and more solicitors are becoming skilled in giving.

of the increase in capital value of the company's investments. His share of the accumulated profits could be very large indeed and the principal attraction is that it is a saving built up from payments in respect of which the saver may have received substantial tax relief. However, there is no doubt that such a mortgage involves a higher cost than a standard repayment mortgage and the borrower will need to seek expert advice on which scheme is more suitable for him. It will often require careful calculation in particular cases whether it is more beneficial to choose the cheaper scheme with minimum future benefits or the expensive scheme with maximum future benefits.[35]

2. Consumer Credit

12.10. The history of inflation in the last couple of decades has indicated that land and buildings are one of the very few investments likely to keep pace with the general rise in the cost of living. The result has been that there has been every encouragement for those fortunate enough to have made such an investment, even if it is the family residence only, to maximise its financial potential, especially in terms of security for credit or borrowing transactions. As we pointed out earlier in this chapter, many a house "owner" has been pleasantly surprised in recent years by the growth of his "equity" in his house and has found sometimes that its value has even risen well above the existing debt outstanding on the property under its current first mortgage. The temptation has thus arisen to use this equity for further borrowing, which has not always been confined to what are sometimes referred to as house improvements, *e.g.*, building extensions to the house or installation of major capital items like central heating, to cover the cost of which many building societies are willing to lend additional money, since they increase the value of the security for both the original loan and the additional loan. Sometimes, however, owners of houses subject to a mortgage have been tempted to use the equity as security for borrowing as an alternative to consumer credit arranged through transactions like hire-purchase, and the object has been to raise money for consumer goods like new cars or yachts. This has resulted in an increase in second mortgage borrowing and in England there was much controversy over the activities of several second-mortgage companies,[36] some of whom charged exorbitant rates of interest and, then, ran into considerable

---

[35]   *Cf.* the British "option mortgage" scheme introduced under Pt. II of the Housing Subsidies Act, 1967 (which did not apply to Northern Ireland), under which borrowers from institutions like building societies and insurance companies may have the interest charged to them on their loans reduced by a subsidy paid by the Exchequer as a credit towards their mortgages. This scheme is designed to help those who do not receive much, if any, tax relief in respect of the interest charged on their mortgages and aims at putting them financially in roughly the same position as those who do receive full relief. See Fisher and Lightwood, *Law of Mortgages* (9th ed., 1977), ch. 36. The "option mortgage" scheme was introduced to Northern Ireland by Part II of the Housing (N.I.) Order, 1978. It is operated by the Department of the Environment.

[36]   Sometimes referred to as "secondary" banks (*i.e.*, operating outside the sphere of the central clearing banks), these companies attempted to avoid regulation by the Moneylenders Acts (see the Republic's 1933 Act and the N.I. Acts of 1933 and 1969). See the discussion in the English Crowther Committee *Report on Consumer Credit* (1971, Cmnd. 4596). See also *Premor Ltd.* v. *Shaw Bros.* [1964] 1 W.L.R. 978; *U.D.T. Ltd.* v. *Kirkwood* [1966] 2 Q.B. 431. And now for N.I., the Consumer Credit Act, 1974 (U.K.). See also Adams, "Mortgages and the Consumer Credit Act 1974" (1975) 39 Conv. 94.

liquidity problems. Fortunately, there has been little evidence of similar controversy in Ireland and it is to be hoped that any similar development will be strictly controlled. The dangers of unrestricted and uncontrolled second mortgage schemes have become so apparent now as a result of the English experience that serious consideration, and, above all, expert advice, ought to be taken before a commitment to a second mortgage is entered into.

3. Property Development

12.11. Use of mortgage facilities plays a vital role in property investment and development. Few developers nowadays can afford to pay cash for development sites or properties lest their future development or expansion will be hampered by a lack of capital. Most developers prefer to utilise the mortgage potential of their properties and to get capital loans for development of existing properties, or even for more speculative ventures, by putting down deposits on other properties. The interest charged on such mortgage loans can generally be set against profits and so a policy of "high gearing" is pursued, *i.e.*, as properties increase in value, further loans on their security are taken out to buy more properties, and so on. Sometimes the practice is adopted, *e.g.*, in respect of blocks of office premises, of revaluing the property, raising a new loan on the new value, paying off the old loan and using the difference as fresh capital.[37]

4. Companies

12.12. Companies frequently borrow money for their activities, usually under express powers of borrowing in the memorandum and articles of association.[38] This is usually done by issuing debentures, which may or may not be charged on the company's assets and which are a form of investment like shares.[39] Debentures may be secured by a fixed charge on some specified company property or by a general charge on all or some of the company's lands, present and future.[40] Alternatively, what is known as a "floating" charge on some or all of the company's assets may be created. This form of security, as the name suggests, floats over all the company's assets, but does not attach to any of them until it "crystallises." The advantage of such a charge is that the company is free to use its assets in the ordinary course of business so long as the charge remains floating. The charge will not crystallise

---

[37] *Cf.* "sale and lease-back" operations, whereby the property owner sells the property for a capital sum but on the condition that the purchaser grants a lease-back to the vendor, which provides the vendor with fresh capital, but leaves him with an interest in the property. See the discussion in (1971) 68 L.Soc.Gaz. 346; (1971) 115 Sol.Jo. 87; (1972) 122 New L.J. 429.

[38] See, generally, Keane, *Company Law in Ireland* (1985).

[39] And are maintained on a company register and transferable like shares. See *Alexander Hull & Co. Ltd.* v. *O'Carroll Kent & Co. Ltd.* (1955) 89 I.L.T.R. 70; *Re O'Carroll Kent, Ltd.* (1955) 89 I.L.T.R. 72; *Re White & Shannon Ltd.* [1965] N.I. 15. Also *Norman* v. *Reid* (1846) 10 Ir.L.R. 207.

[40] Frequently such a general charge is created as additional security to a fixed charge on a particular asset.

until some default is made by the company on the charge or steps are taken to enforce the security.[41]

5. *Informal*

12.13. Perhaps one of the most common forms of mortgage in Ireland is the informal mortgage created by deposit of title documents.[42] The Irish banks have long facilitated this method of providing security for an overdraft or other type of bank loan. All the bank customer has to do is to lodge with his bank manager the title documents relating to some item of property, *e.g.*, the title deeds or land certificate[43] relating to land or an insurance policy.[44] There need be no written agreement or any other formality other than the deposit of the documents and it is the attractions of speed, efficiency, informality and secrecy (except in the case of companies) which seem to have led to the popularity of such arrangements with the Irish people.[45]

C. SIMILAR CONCEPTS

12.14. Before considering in detail the technical law of mortgages, it may be useful also to compare briefly with mortgages similar, and, in some cases, related, concepts. Only some of these concepts will be discussed in more detail later in this and the next chapter. Furthermore, it must be emphasised that it is a matter of construction in each particular case as to whether or not the transaction in question amounts to a mortgage. On a question of this kind, equity always looks to the intent and not to the form of any instrument executed and what at first sight may appear to be a sale of property, whether conditional or, even, outright, may nevertheless be construed as a mortgage.[46]

1. *Lien*

12.15. A lien is a concept which has been recognised at common law and in

---

[41]   See *Halpin* v. *Cremin* [1954] I.R. 19; *Re Daniel Murphy Ltd.* [1964] I.R. 1; *Lynch* v. *Ardmore Studios (Ireland) Ltd.* [1966] I.R. 133; *Re Interview Ltd.* [1975] I.R. 382; *Murphy* v. *Revenue Commissioners* [1976] I.R. 101; *Industrial Development Authority* v. *Moran* [1978] I.R. 159; *Kelly* v. *McMahon Ltd.* [1980] I.R. 347; *Crowley* v. *Northern Bank Finance Corporation Ltd.* [1981] I.R. 353; *Re Armagh Shoes Ltd.* [1982] N.I. 59; *Re Keenan Brothers Ltd.* [1985] I.L.R.M. 254. See also *Kreglinger* v. *New Patagonia Meat and Cold Storage Co. Ltd.* [1914] A.C. 25.

[42]   See further, para. 12.43, *post*.

[43]   Depending upon whether or not the title to the land is registered, see ch. 21, *post*. In the case of registered land, where there is a first registered charge on the property, a second, informal mortgage can be created by deposit of the charge certificate, see para. 12.29, *post*.

[44]   Or share certificates, see *Dunster* v. *Lord Glengall* (1853) 3 Ir.Ch.R. 47; *Dunne* v. *Hibernian Bank* (1868) I.R. 2 Eq. 82; *Connolly* v. *Munster Bank* (1887) 19 L.R.Ir. 119.

[45]   See the Lowry Committee's *Report on Registration of Title to Land in Northern Ireland* (Cmd. 512, 1967), paras. 93–6; Corscadden, "Deposit of Title Deeds" (1953) 55 J.I.B.I. 253; Delany, "Company Shares as Security for Bankers' Advances" (1960) 62 J.I.B.I. 263; Greene, "Law Relating to Leaseholds as Security for Bank Advances" (1963) 65 J.I.B.I. 123. Also Holden, *Securities for Bankers' Advances* (5th ed., 1971).

[46]   See the discussion of the principles of construction, including the use of extrinsic evidence to establish the parties' intention, in *Goodman* v. *Grierson* (1813) 2 Ba. & B. 274; *Taylor* v. *Emerson* (1843) 4 Dr. & War 117; *Fee* v. *Cobine* (1847) 11 Ir.Eq.R. 406; *Murphy* v. *Taylor* (1850) 1 Ir.Ch.R. 92; *Re De Freyne's Contract* (1871) 5 I.L.T.R. 193; *O'Reilly* v. *O'Donoghue* (1875) I.R. 10 Eq. 73; *Crone* v. *Hegarty* (1879) 3 L.R.Ir. 50.

equity. A common law lien confers on the holder a mere right of retention of another person's property until such time as a debt is paid, *e.g.*, the right of a garage proprietor to retain a car repaired by him until its owner pays the repair bill.[47] Such a common law lien gives the holder no right (in the absence of a contractual or statutory provision) to sell the property retained or to deal with it in any other way.[48] In this respect, as we shall see, there is a marked difference between a common law lien and a mortgage.[49] Furthermore, if the holder of the lien parts with possession of the property to the debtor or his agent, or to anyone other than his own agent, it is lost.[50] In short, the "security" for the debt is dependent entirely upon the creditor's possession of the property and this too is a point of difference from a modern mortgage.

12.16. In equity a lien arises by operation of law in the sense that, in certain circumstances, general principles of equity require the enforcement of a lien in the form of a charge against property. Because it arises by operation of law such a lien differs from a mortgage which arises by agreement between the mortgagor and the mortgagee.[51] An example of an equitable lien is a vendor's lien for unpaid purchase money, *i.e.*, a vendor who conveys land before he has been paid the full purchase price has a lien on the land for the unpaid balance.[52] Such a lien does not entitle the vendor to claim possession of the land,[53] but it does allow him to apply to the court for a declaration of a charge[54] and enforcement of this by an order for sale[55] of the property, so that he can be recouped out of the proceeds of sale.

12.17. Finally it should be noted that certain bodies and persons have liens on property created by statute, in which case, of course, the liens are governed by the precise terms of the statute in question. Thus a solicitor has a common law lien over his client's documents for his costs,[56] but has a

---

[47] See *Green* v. *All Motors Ltd.* [1917] 1 K.B. 625. And see *re* a horse stable-keeper, *Lee* v. *Irwin* (1852) 4 Ir.Jur.(O.S.) 372 and a shipowner, *Drivar* v. *White* (1820) Rowe 207; *The Princess Royal* (1859) 5 Ir.Jur.(N.S.) 74; *Belfast Harbour Commrs.* v. *Lawther* (1866) 17 Ir.Ch.R. 54. Also Hall, *Possessory Liens in English Law* (1917); Price, *Law of Maritime Liens* (1940). Cf. *re* a claim by auditors to a lien over company books and documents, *Re J. J. Hopkins & Co. Ltd.* (1959) 93 I.L.T.R. 32.

[48] *Mulliner* v. *Florence* (1878) 3 Q.B.D. 484.

[49] Ch. 13, *post.*

[50] *Pennington* v. *Reliance Motor Works Ltd.* [1923] 1 K.B. 127.

[51] Paras. 12.24 *et seq., post.* See further Durfee, "Lien or Equitable Theory of Mortgage: Some Generalisations" (1912) 10 Mich.L.Rev. 587; "Lien Theory of Mortgage: Two Crucial Problems" (1913) 11 Mich.L.Rev. 495.

[52] *Richardson* v. *McCausland* (1817) Beat. 457; *Stuart* v. *Ferguson* (1832) Hayes 452; *Munster and Leinster bank Ltd.* v. *McGlasham* [1937] I.R. 525; *Mackreth* v. *Symmons* (1808) 15 Ves. 329. See also *Eyre* v. *Sadlier* (1863) 14 Ir.Ch.R. 119; (1863) 15 Ir.Ch.R. 1. In effect this reverses the normal position of the vendor being construed in equity as constructive trustee of the land (subject to a contract for sale) for the purchaser; here the purchaser is treated as trustee for the vendor for the amount of unpaid purchase money. See para. 9.061, *ante.* It also seems that, where a purchaser pays the purchase money before the vendor conveys the land to him, the purchaser has a similar lien on the land for the return of his purchase money, see *Rose* v. *Watson* (1864) 10 H.L.C. 672. Also *Woods* v. *Martin* (1860) 11 Ir.Ch.R. 148. See, generally, *Irish Conveyancing Law* (1978), paras. 11.08, 11.10–12 and 11.36.

[53] Cf. a mortgagee's right to possession, ch. 13, *post.* However, it seems that the vendor's lien for unpaid purchase money arises as soon as the contract for sale of the land is entered into, so that his lien does entitle him to *retain* possession in the same way that a creditor can at common law, see *Shaw* v. *Foster* (1872) L.R. 5 H.L. 321; *Re Birmingham* [1959] Ch. 523.

[54] See further on charges, para. 12.47, *post.* Also *Croly* v. *O'Callaghan* (1842) 5 Ir.Eq.R. 25.

[55] Cf. a mortgagee's power of sale, ch. 13 *post..*

[56] *Blunden* v. *Desart* (1842) 5 Ir.Eq.R. 221; *Molesworth* v. *Robbins* (1845) 8 Ir.Eq.R. 223; *Re Bayly's Estate* (1861) 12 Ir.Ch.R. 315.

statutory right to apply to the court for a charging order on property recovered or preserved in litigation.[57]

2. *Pledge*

12.18. A pledge is a transaction whereby chattels are given in possession as security for a loan, *e.g.*, by way of pawn to a pawnbroker. Pawnbrokers' activities are now controlled and regulated in the Republic of Ireland by the Pawnbrokers Act, 1964, and in Northern Ireland by the U.K. Consumer Credit Act, 1974.[58] Apart from the fact that a pledge is confined to chattels,[59] another difference from a mortgage is that the pledgee (lender) obtains no ownership of the chattel pledged.[60] He does obtain possession whereas under a mortgage the borrower usually retains possession until the lender decides to exercise his right to possession. Furthermore, a pledgee, like a mortgagee, does have various powers to realise the security initially conferred upon him by having possession of the chattel, *e.g.*, a power to sell the chattel in the event of the loan not being repaid.[61]

3. *Charge*

12.19. The first point to note is that the word "charge" can have several meanings and in many cases it can be regarded as a form of mortgage.[62] The distinction usually drawn between the two concepts is that a mortgage, by tradition, involves the conveyance of some rights of ownership to the lender whereas a charge involves no transfer of ownership or, indeed, possession, but merely the conferment of rights over the property as security,[63] though,

---

[57]   See   s.   3   of   the   Legal   Practitioners   (Ir.)   Act,   1876,   and   *Re   Legal   Practition-ers (Ir.) Act, 1876* [1951] Ir.Jur.Rep. 1; *Temple Press Ltd.* v. *Blogh* [1955–56] Ir.Jur.Rep. 53. *Cf. Re Kavanagh Ltd.* [1952] Ir.Jur.Rep. 38. See also *Finegan* v. *McGarrell* (1909) 43 I.L.T.R. 184. In N.I., s. 3 of the 1876 Act has been replaced by Article 71 of the Solicitors (N.I.) Order, 1976. *Cf.* a factor's lien against his principal's goods, see Factors Act, 1889, s. 7. Atiyah, *Sale of Goods* (5th ed., 1975); Fridman, *Sale of Goods* (1966); Schmitthoff, *Sale of Goods* (2nd ed., 1966).

[58]   See also the Moneylenders Act, 1933 (R.I.), and former Moneylenders Acts (N.I.), 1933 and 1969; Attenborough, *Law of Pawnbroking* (3rd ed., 1925). See also *Cripps Warbury Ltd.* v. *Cologne Investment Co. Ltd.* [1980] I.R. 321. A pledge may be regarded as a form of bailment, Beal, *Law of Bailments* (1900); Paton, *Bailment in the Common Law* (1952).

[59]   Chattels, as well as land, may be mortgaged by means of a bill of sale. See the Bills of Sale (Ir.) Act, 1879, and the Bills of Sale (Ir.) Act, 1879, Amendment Act, 1883, which still apply to both parts of Ireland. See also *Harries* v. *Handy* (1851) 3 Ir.Jur.(O.S.) 290 (ship); *Dobbyn* v. *Comerford* (1860) 10 Ir.Ch.R. 327 (ship); *Board of Harbour Commrs.* v. *Lawther* (1865) 17 Ir.Ch.R. 54 (ship). Goodeve, *Modern Law of Personal Property* (9th ed., by Kersley, 1949); Crossley Vaines, *Personal Property* (5th ed., 1973); Wilkinson, *Personal Property* (1971); Williams, *Law of Personal Property* (18th ed., 1926); Folsom, "Chattel Mortgages and Substitutes Therefor in Latin America" (1954) 3 A.J.C.L. 477. Furthermore, a deposit of title deeds relating to land (see paras. 12.13, *supra*, and 12.43, *post*) could be regarded as a pledge at common law, but since it has long been regarded as a mortgage in equity the point has little practical significance. See also *Re Morrissey* [1961] I.R. 442 (deposit of share certificates by way of pledge); *cf. Re McClement* [1960] I.R. 141.

[60]   *Re Morritt* (1886) 18 Q.B.D. 222.

[61]   As regards pawnbrokers, see Pawnbrokers Act, 1964, s. 30 (R.I.); Pawnbrokers Act (N.I.), 1954, s. 25, replaced by the Consumer Credit Act, 1974 (U.K.).

[62]   *Cf.* Walker C. in *Shea* v. *Moore* [1894] 1 I.R. 158 at 168: ". . . every charge is not an equitable mortgage, though every equitable mortgage is a charge." See also *Antrim County Land, Building, and Investment Co. Ltd.* v. *Stewart* [1904] 2 I.R. 357 at 369 (*per* Fitz-Gibbon L.J.) (see *A Casebook on Irish Land Law* (1984), p. 426); *Bank of Ireland* v. *Feeny* [1930] I.R. 457 at 469 (*per* Kennedy C.J.).

[63]   See *Northern Banking Co. Ltd.* v. *Devlin* [1924] 1 I.R. 90. Also *National Bank Ltd.* v. *Hegarty* (1901) 1 N.I.J.R. 13.

when these are exercised, there may be little practical difference between the position of a mortgagee and chargee. This point has been underlined in Ireland with respect to registered land which can be mortgaged by the registered owner only by means of a registered charge.[64] Apart from that, an equitable charge on property may be created by an express agreement for such a charge and an attempt to create a legal mortgage which fails for want of some formality may nevertheless be upheld as an equitable charge.[65]

12.20. Not to be confused with these forms of charge are other forms like rentcharges, which are annual sums charged on land by way of security and form a branch of the law of incorporeal hereditaments.[66] Such rentcharges or annuities are commonly created under family settlements of land.[67] Also in Ireland there are land purchase annuities charged on agricultural land, the freehold of which has been bought out by tenant-farmers under the Land Purchase Acts scheme.[68]

4. Judgment-Mortgage

12.21. Under a special statutory scheme introduced in Ireland[69] in the nineteenth century, a judgment creditor became entitled to register[70] his judgment as a mortgage against the land of the judgment debtor. This nineteenth-century legislation remains in force in the Republic of Ireland but has recently been replaced in Northern Ireland as part of the scheme for establishment there of a central Enforcement of Judgments Office.[71] However, under the new scheme the Office has power to make an order charging the land of the debtor which has much the same effect as a judgment-mortgage under the old scheme, except that, as is common practice nowadays when legislatures intervene, a charge only is created and not a mortgage.[72]

In view of the importance of this topic in Ireland, it will be discussed in a separate section in the next chapter.[73]

---

[64] Registration of Title Act, 1964, s. 62 (R.I.); Land Registration Act (N.I.), 1970, s. 41. See further para. 12.24, *post.* Note also orders charging land made under the Judgments (Enforcement) Act (N.I.), 1969 (now consolidated in the Judgments Enforcement (N.I.) Order, 1981), see para. 13.183 *et seq., post.* It is arguable that the concept of charge is a more accurate reflection of the parties' intentions with respect to, and of equity's view of, the effect of a mortgage, see para. 12.04, *supra,* and ch. 13, *post.*

[65] See, further, para. 12.41, *post.* Also Rowley, "Conveyancing and Equitable Charges" (1962) 26 Conv. 445.

[66] See ch. 6, *ante.*

[67] Ch. 8, *ante.* See also as regards quit rents and Crown rents. *Massy v. O'Dell* (1858) 9 Ir.Ch.R. 441, and see ch. 6, *ante.*

[68] Chs. 6, *ante,* and 18, *post.*

[69] See the Judgment-Mortgage (Ir.) Acts, 1850 and 1858. Also the Judgments (Ir.) Acts, 1844 and 1849, and the Judgments Registry (Ir.) Acts, 1850 and 1871. Ch. 13, *post.*

[70] In the Registry of Deeds if the title to the land was unregistered and, later, in the Land Registry if the title became registered, see chs. 21 and 22, *post.*

[71] Under the Judgments (Enforcement) Act (N.I.), 1969; see Trimble (1970) 21 N.I.L.Q. 359. The 1969 Act has now been consolidated in the Judgments Enforcement (N.I.) Order, 1981.

[72] Para. 12.19, *supra.*

[73] Para. 13.163 *et seq., post.*

[74] See Coote, *Law of Mortgages* (9th ed., 1927), ch. III.

5. *Welsh Mortgage*

12.22. A "welsh" mortgage is a special kind of mortgage which has been used quite commonly in Ireland.[74] The following definition has been given:

"[A] welsh mortgage [is] a kind of security which has fallen into disuse, by which, on the one side, the land is assured to the lender as his security–his possession of the land and enjoyment of the profits being in lieu of interest–while, on the other side, the borrower is under no personal obligation to pay the principal money, but yet is entitled to redeem at any time upon its payment."[75]

This differs from an ordinary mortgage in that here the very essence of the transaction is that the lender takes possession of the land. Furthermore, the lender is entitled to receive the rents and profits of the land which are to be applied by him in lieu of interest charged on the capital sum borrowed or, even, sometimes, in lieu of both capital and interest. Because of this, unlike an ordinary mortgage,[76] a welsh mortgagee is not liable to account for the rents and profits received by him.[77] On the other hand, since there is no personal obligation to repay imposed on the borrower[78] and he may redeem at any time, the lender has no right to compel redemption by the borrower or other methods of enforcement of security, such as sale.[79] However, once the debt has been repaid, whether out of the rents and profits or otherwise, the borrower may lose his right of redemption by adverse possession,[80] *i.e.*, it may be barred under the statute of limitations where the lender holds over for the statutory period after such repayment.[81]

12.23. Whether or not a particular arrangement constitutes a welsh mortgage is a matter of construction. The courts usually approach this matter from the standpoint that, if the transaction was intended to create security for a loan, it should be construed as creating an ordinary mortgage, with the usual incidents, unless the terms of the arrangement expressly or impliedly exclude such a presumption.[82] Thus the inclusion of an express power of sale in favour of the mortgagee will negative creation of a welsh mortgage.[83] On the other hand, it seems that inclusion or exclusion of a proviso for redemption will not necessarily determine the issue one way or the other.[84]

---

[75] *Cassidy* v. *Cassidy* (1889) 24 L.R.Ir. 577 at 578–9 (*per* Johnson J.). See also *Montgomery* v. *Rogers* (1903) 37 I.L.T.R. 93.

[76] Ch. 13, *post*.

[77] See *Johnston* v. *Moore* (1904) 4 N.I.J.R. 218. *Cf. Henderson* v. *Burns* (1920) 54 I.L.T.R. 149.

[78] *Cf.* an ordinary mortgagor, ch. 13, *post*.

[79] *Balfe* v. *Lord* (1842) 2 Dr. & War. 480 at 486 (*per* Sugden L.C.). See also *O'Connell* v. *Cummins* (1840) 2 Ir.Eq.R. 251; *Taylor* v. *Gorman* (1844) 7 Ir.Eq.R. 259.

[80] See ch. 23, *post*. Also *Shields* v. *Shields* (1904) 38 I.L.T.R. 188; *Johnston* v. *Moore* (1904) 4 N.I.J.R. 218; *Fenton* v. *Walsh* (1909) 43 I.L.T.R. 54.

[81] *Re Cronin* [1914] 1 I.R. 23.

[82] *Balfe* v. *Lord* (1842) 2 Dr. & War. 480.

[83] *Re Cronin* [1914] 1 I.R. 23.

[84] *Johnston* v. *Moore* (1904) 4 N.I.J.R. 218.

II. CREATION

In considering the creation of mortgages a distinction has to be drawn between registered land and unregistered land.

A. REGISTERED LAND

12.24. Registration of title to land in Ireland[85] is now governed in the Republic of Ireland by the Registration of Title Act, 1964, and in Northern Ireland by the Land Registration Act (N.I.), 1970.[86] These Acts govern the method of creation of mortgages of land the title to which is registered, but they do not prevent the creation of equitable mortgages which do not appear on the registers in the respective Land Registries. Thus, although the distinction between legal and equitable mortgages, which is so vital in the case of unregistered land, is not strictly applicable to registered land, it will be adopted for convenience sake in the following discussion. A legal mortgage of registered land in Ireland is a charge registered in one of the Land Registries.

1. *Legal*

12.25. In both parts of Ireland the only way in which the registered owner of land can create a legal mortgage of the land is to execute a charge which must be registered as such.[87] Such a charge may be created by deed or by will, but, in the case of a deed, it should be in the prescribed form or in such other form as is sufficient[88] to charge the land.[89] Under the earlier statutory provisions contained in the Local Registration of Title (Ir.) Act, 1891,[90] there was some controversy as to the effectiveness of a deed in the form appropriate for a mortgage of *unregistered* land to create a charge on registered land.[91] Section 62 (3) of the Republic's 1964 Act now provides that a mortgage by way of conveyance with a proviso for redemption or by way of demise or sub-demise[92] shall not *of itself* operate to charge registered land or be registrable as a charge on registered land. Taken with the requirement in section 62 (2) of the 1964 Act that the instrument used must be in a form which appears "to the Registrar to be sufficient to charge the land, provided that such instrument

---

[85] Previously governed by the Local Registration of Title (Ir.) Act, 1891, and before that by the Record of Title (Ir.) Act, 1865.

[86] See Ch. 21, *post.*

[87] 1964 Act, s. 62; 1970 Act. s. 41. Both sections refer to charging the land "with payment of money either with or without interest, and either by way of annuity or otherwise."

[88] The Republic's 1964 Act, s. 62 (2), uses the formula–"as may appear to the Registrar to be sufficient"– while the N.I. 1970 Act, Sched. 7, Pt. I, para. 1 does not refer to the Registrar but adds the formula- "and as shall not be calculated to mislead."

[89] The Republic's 1964 Act, s. 62 (2), also adds the proviso, in the case of a form other than the prescribed one, that it must "expressly charge or reserve out of the land the payment of the money secured." *Cf.* Sched. 7, Pt. I, para. 1 of the N.I. 1970 Act.

[90] See especially s. 40 (2).

[91] In *Re Moley* [1957] N.I. 130 at 132, Curran J. expressed doubts on the efficacy of such an instrument and this led to the practice in the N.I. Land Registry of refusing to accept for registration such a deed, unless it also included express words of charge. See Lowry Committee *Report on Registration of Title to Land in Northern Ireland* (1967, Cmd. 512), para. 92.

[92] *I.e.,* the usual forms for unregistered land, paras. 12.30 *et seq., post.*

shall expressly charge or reserve out of the land the payment of the money secured," it would seem that in the Republic a registered owner ought to use express words of charge in his instrument to avoid dispute.[93] In Northern Ireland, paragraph 1 of Part I of Schedule 7 to the 1970 Act expressly excludes from the category of a recognised form, other than the prescribed form of charge, one which is a "purported conveyance or demise (whether or not subject to defeasance)."[94] However, both the 1964 and 1970 Acts contain saving provisions for charges in the form of mortgages which were in fact registered in the respective Land Registries under the 1891 Act. In the Republic, section 63 (1) of the 1964 Act contains a saving for charges registered before the commencement of the 1964 Act to the effect that they are not void or to be deemed ever to have been void either by reason only that they were expressed to have been created by way of mortgage,[95] or by reason only that a requisite consent, from, e.g., the Land Commission or Commissioners of Public Works,[96] was not obtained to any demise or sub-demise expressed to be created by such mortgages, and the registration of such charges as burdens on registered land is, and is deemed always to have been, valid. In Northern Ireland, a similar saving provision is contained in Part III of Schedule 7 to the 1970 Act, except that its operation is confined to charges registered in the Land Registry at July 28, 1957.[97]

12.26. With respect to wills, in the Republic of Ireland these are expressly excluded from the requirement as to execution of an instrument of charge in the prescribed or other suitable form,[98] but it would seem that nevertheless a will must still avoid the trap of using a form appropriate for unregistered land only.[99] In Northern Ireland, it is provided that, where a charge created by will does not expressly charge any registered land with payment to a specified person of a specified amount, with or without interest, or of an annuity, the Registrar is not, unless the court otherwise directs, obliged to register the ownership of that charge in any register.[99a]

12.27. In both parts of Ireland it is provided that any power, howsoever conferred, to borrow or lend money on the security of a mortgage is to be construed as including power to do so on the security of a registered charge.[1]

---

[93] *I.e.*, adopt the warning of Curran J. in *Re Moley*, fn. 91, *supra*.

[94] This furthers the Lowry Committee's view that use of the form of charge, as opposed to a form of mortgage, ought to become standard practice for registered land, see Cmd. 512, para. 92.

[95] Which includes both a mortgage by demise or sub-demise and a mortgage by conveyance or assignment with a proviso for redemption, see s. 63 (2) and paras. 12.30 *et seq.*, *post*.

[96] The Land Purchase Acts imposed such restrictions on sub-division and sub-letting by tenant-purchasers in order to protect the security for the land purchase annuity charged on the land bought under the Acts by way of repayment of the loan advanced for the purchase, see *e.g.*, the Irish Land Act, 1903, s. 54, and the Republic's Land Acts, 1923, s. 65; 1927, ss. 3 and 4; 1936, s. 44; 1939 s. 30; 1946 ss. 3 and 6; 1965, ss. 12 and 13; *Carew* v. *Jackman* [1966] I.R. 177. This was the actual ground for decision in *Re Moley* [1957] N.I. 130, fn. 91, *supra*, and resulted in the N.I. Parliament rushing through the Land Registry Charges Act (N.I.), 1957, to establish the validity of charges already registered.

[97] The date fixed by the Land Registry Charges Act (N.I.), 1957.

[98] 1964 Act, s. 62 (2).

[99] *I.e.*, wills are not excluded from s. 62 (3) of the 1964 Act.

[99a] 1970 Act, s. 41 (3).

[1] 1964 Act, s. 62 (4); 1970 Act, s. 41 (4).

Where a power to charge registered land, or a trust for securing money on registered land, is registered as a burden on the land,[2] it may be exercised or executed by creation of a registered charge and not otherwise.[3] Where a person has a statutory charge on, or a statutory power to charge, registered land, he is to have the same power to create a registered charge on the land as if he were the registered owner of the land.[4]

On registration of the ownership of a charge, the owner is entitled to delivery of a certificate of charge in the prescribed form from the Registrar.[5]

2. *Equitable*

12.28. One of the guiding principles of a registration of title system is that the registers should "mirror" the current title to the land and that all transactions relating to the land should be presented for registration to the Land Registry, for the appropriate consequent amendments to the registers to be made there.[6] However, it has been recognised from the very beginning of the introduction of a registration system in Ireland that, for convenience and administrative reasons, amongst others, the system cannot and, perhaps should not seek to conform with this principle absolutely, and the recent Acts in both parts of Ireland still allow several types of transactions to be effective without registration in the Land Registries and to create interests in the registered land which are not noted on the registers. One of these transactions is the method of informal creation of mortgages which, we pointed out above, is so common in Ireland. It has always been considered that the advantages of such a method of creation of mortgages justify a breach of the "mirror" principle of registration.

12.29. Both the 1964 and 1970 Acts provide that the deposit[7] of a land certificate[8] or certificate of charge[9] has the same effect as a deposit of the title deeds of unregistered land.[10] As Kenny J. recently put the matter: "The right created by the deposit is not limited to keeping the deeds until the money has been paid but gives an equitable estate in the lands."[11] In other words, such a

---

[2] See 1964 Act, s. 69 (1) (*d*) and (*e*); 1970 Act, s. 39 and Sched. 6 Pt. I, paras. 3 and 4.

[3] 1964 Act, s. 76; 1970 Act, s. 42. See also ss. 78 and 79 of the 1964 Act and ss. 45 and 46 of the 1970 Act, which deal with the cases of terms of years vested in trustees or other persons for the purpose of raising money out of registered land and for the purpose of raising money out of or mortgaging land prior to first registration of the title to that land.

[4] 1964 Act, s. 77; 1970 Act, s. 44.

[5] 1964 Act, ss. 62 (5) and 105; 1970 Act, s. 79 (1). *Cf.* custody of the land certificate, ch. 13, *post*.

[6] See further on this subject, ch. 21 *post*.

[7] The Republic's 1964 Act, s. 105 (5) (as did s. 81 (5) of the 1891 Act) refers to— "for the purpose of creating a lien on the land or charge to which the certificate relates." See, on liens and charges, *supra*. The N.I. 1970 Act, s. 50 refers simply to— "for the purposes of giving security for the payment of any sum of money."

[8] Which the Registrar is obliged to deliver on registration of a person as owner of the land, see 1964 Act, s. 28; 1970 Act, s. 79.

[9] Issued to the owner of a registered charge on the land, para. 12.27, *supra*.

[10] 1964 Act, s. 105 (5) (which adds— "or of a charge thereon"); 1970 Act, s. 50. See on the similar s. 81 (5) of the 1891 Act, Glover, *Registration of Ownership of Land in Ireland* (1933), pp. 262–3.

[11] *Allied Irish Banks* v. *Glynn* [1973] I.R. 188 at 192 (see *A Casebook on Irish Land Law* (1984), p. 85). See also *Bank of Ireland Finance Ltd.* v. *Daly* [1978] I.R. 79.

deposit creates an equitable mortgage on the registered land which need not be registered in the Land Registry as a burden on the land[12] in order to secure priority as against subsequent transactions relating to it.[13] The mortgage is protected because subsequent transactions relating to the registered land generally cannot be completed by registration in the Land Registry without production of the land or charge certificate,[14] which the mortgagee holds. However, if the mortgagee wishes, he may lodge a caution with the Registrar against subsequent registered dealings.[15]

B. Unregistered Land

12.30. The two main categories of mortgages of unregistered land are those which are legal and those which are equitable. This distinction is of vital importance when a question of priorities as between successive mortgagees of same land arises.

1. *Legal*

The methods of creation of legal mortgages of unregistered land in Ireland vary according to whether the land is freehold or leasehold.[16]

(i) Freehold

12.31. There are two main ways of mortgaging freehold land, namely (a) by conveyance of the fee simple[17] subject to a proviso for redemption[18] and (b) by demise (*i.e.*, grant of a term of years) subject to a proviso for cessor on redemption. If the parties wish, they may adopt the short-form precedent for a mortgage deed provided by section 26 of, and Part I of the Third Schedule to, the Conveyancing Act, 1881. This provides a statutory form of mortgage for both freehold and leasehold land, through a deed expressed to be made by way of statutory mortgage, in which various covenants are automatically implied by the 1881 Act. In fact, this statutory form is rarely used in Ireland.

(a) *Conveyance of Fee Simple*

12.32. As the name indicates, this form of mortgage involves the borrower (mortgagor) in transferring the legal title to his land to the lender (mortgagee) so as to confer the legal ownership on the lender. Such a

---

[12] *I.e.*, under s. 69 of the 1964 Act and s. 39 of and Pt. I of Sched. 6 to the 1970 Act. See ch. 21, *post.*
[13] It is, however, subject to existing "equities" as discussed in *Tench* v. *Molyneux* (1914) 48 I.L.T.R. 48. The subject of priorities is discussed in detail in ch. 13, *post.*
[14] See 1964 Act, s. 105 (1); 1970 Act, s. 79 (2).
[15] 1964 Act, s. 97; 1970 Act, s. 66. See further, ch. 21, *post.* Note the practice in N.I. under the 1891 Act of entry in the register of a notice of deposit of the land certificate, see *Re Watters* [1934] N.I. 188.
[16] See Sheridan, "Some Aspects of Legal Mortgages" (1949) 52 J.I.B.I. 114.
[17] As regards powers of mortgaging of a tenant of a lesser freehold estate, *i.e.*, a tenant for life under the Settled Land Acts, see ch. 8, *ante.*
[18] This is no longer possible in England where the concept of a "charge by way of legal mortgage" was substituted for a conveyance of the fee simple by s. 85 (1) of the Law of Property Act, 1925. Such a charge has an operation in respect to unregistered land in England similar to that of a registered charge in Ireland.

conveyance is distinguished from a sale by insertion in the conveyance of an express proviso for redemption, usually of a covenant entered into by the mortgagee to reconvey the property to the mortgagor if the money due under the mortgage is paid on a fixed date.[19] We have already discussed the significance of this legal date for redemption and equity's intervention so as to create an equitable right to redeem after this date is passed and despite the wording of the mortgage instrument.[20]

12.33. A mortgage by conveyance is usually executed by deed for the reason that various statutory provisions apply automatically to mortgages by deed.[21]

Since a mortgage by conveyance transfers the legal title to the land to the mortgagee, it follows that any subsequent mortgages created out of the same land by the mortgagor are, of necessity, equitable only, *i.e.*, they are mortgages of the interest in the land retained by the mortgagor after the first legal mortgage, his equity of redemption.[22]

(b) *Demise*

12.34. Instead of conveying the fee simple to the mortgagee, the mortgagor may demise the land for a term of years in favour of the mortgagee. Such a mortgage by demise is made expressly subject to a proviso for cesser of the term of redemption, *i.e.*, on repayment of all monies due under the mortgage. The vital difference from a mortgage by conveyance is, of course, that the mortgagor retains the freehold of the land and to this extent a mortgage by demise accords more with the notion of a mortgage creating security only. As the mortgagee does not get the freehold, it is usual for the mortgagor to appoint the mortgagee his attorney to convey the freehold reversion, so that the mortgagee can sell the freehold[23] and, unless the mortgagee stipulates that he is to have custody of the deeds, he is not entitled to them because he is not entitled to the freehold.[24] It is, however, sometimes convenient in Ireland to create a mortgage by demise where the fee simple is, *e.g.*, held under a fee farm grant.[25] In such a case, it is common practice to mortgage the land by demise for a long term of years, since this avoids imposing on the mortgagee any liability in respect of the fee farm rent and other covenants and conditions attaching to the fee simple estate held by the mortgagor.[26] Furthermore, it is possible to create successive legal

[19] *Gorman* v. *Byrne* (1857) 8 I.C.L.R. 394. *Cf.* the proviso implied in the statutory form under the Conveyancing Act, 1881, s. 26 (2). See further on redemption of mortgages, ch. 13, *post*.
[20] Para. 12.05, *ante*.
[21] *E.g.* under the Conveyancing Acts, 1881–1911, see ch. 13, *post*. Note also the statutory forms provided by Pt. V of the 1881 Act.
[22] See para. 12.39, *post*.
[23] See further on the power of sale, ch. 13, *post*.
[24] Though he will, of course, have his lease. See further, ch. 13, *post*.
[25] See ch. 4, *ante*.
[26] See *Re Sergie* [1954] N.I. 1 (demise for term of 10,000 years) (see *A Casebook on Irish Land Law* (1984), p. 70).

mortgages out of the same land by means of successive demises for terms of years, with the term granted to each successive mortgagee being usually for a slightly longer period than the previous mortgage term.

(ii) Leasehold

12.35. Where the borrower himself holds a leasehold estate only in the land being used as security for the loan, he may again create a mortgage in one of two ways, namely (a) by assignment of his lessee's interest and (b) by sub-demise.

(a) *Assignment*

12.36. A mortgage of leasehold land by assignment[27] involves a transfer of the lessee's interest in the lease to the mortgagee, subject to a proviso for redemption under which the mortgagee covenants to reassign the interest under the lease on repayment on the loan and all other monies due under the mortgage. This form of mortgage is rarely used because it has the effect of making the mortgagee liable to all the obligations in respect of rent and repairs imposed by the lease on the lessee.[28] Further, since the mortgagor has parted with his entire legal estate in the land, he retains his equity of redemption only and any subsequent mortgages created out of the same land will necessarily be equitable only.[29]

(b) *Sub-demise*

12.37. Instead of parting with his entire estate in the land, the mortgagor-lessee may simply sub-demise the land in favour of the mortgagee for a term slightly shorter than the term of the lease. This sub-lease is made expressly subject to a proviso for cesser of the sub-term on redemption of the mortgage. Unlike the case of an assignment, the mortgagee-sub-lessee is under no liabilities in respect of the mortgagor's head-lease, since there is neither privity of contract nor privity of estate between him and the head-lessor.[30]

12.38. Once again, successive legal mortgages may be created by a series of sub-leases, each usually for slightly longer periods than the previous one.[31] For this reason it is wise in the initial sub-lease to leave an adequate gap, say 10 days, between the determination date of the sub-lease and that of the head-lease, *i.e.*, subsequent sub-leases can each be for periods longer by one day than the previous sub-leases until the day before the determination date of the head-lease is reached.[32]

---

[27] See further on assignment of leases, ch., 17, *post.* Mortgages by assignment of leases are also prohibited in England under the Law of Property Act, 1925.

[28] *I.e.* privity of estate arises between the lessor and the mortgagee, see ch. 19, *post.* See *Sligo C.C.* v. *Murrow* [1935] I.R. 771. Also *Re Macartney's Estate* [1933] N.I. 1.

[29] Para. 12.39, *post.*

[30] Ch. 19, *post.*

[31] However, note that in Ireland it is possible to sublet land for the whole term of the head-lease under s. 3 of Deasy's Act, 1860; *Seymour* v. *Quirke* (1884) 14 L.R.Ir. 455. See para. 17.006, *post.*

[32] This probably holds good despite s. 3 of Deasy's Act, in that it makes clear who the immediate reversioner is in respect of a particular mortgage-sub-lease.

2. *Equitable*

There are several methods of creating an equitable mortgage in Ireland.

(i) Equitable Interest

12.39. First, it follows necessarily that, if the mortgagor at the time of creating a mortgage holds an equitable interest only in the land, any mortgage he creates on the security of that land must also be equitable only. We have already mentioned that, if a first legal mortgage on the land has been created by conveyance of the legal estate in the land, any subsequent mortgage can by created out of the mortgagor's equity of redemption only[33] and is equitable. Such a mortgage is often referred to as a puisne mortgage.[34]

Apart from a mortgage of the equity of redemption, an equitable mortgage can be created out of other equitable interests in land, *e.g.*, a beneficiary's interest under a trust.[35]

12.40. A mortgage of an equitable interest in land is usually created formally, by execution of a deed conveying the equitable interest to the mortgagee subject to a proviso for redemption. A deed, however, is not essential. The Statute of Frauds (Ireland), 1695, simply requires that an assignment of an equitable interest *held under a trust* must be in writing signed by the assignor or made by will.[36] Apart from that, there are no requisite formalities and, provided the parties' intentions are clear, equity will give effect to them.[37]

(ii) Agreement for a Legal Mortgage

12.41. As part of its general policy of giving effect to contracts for the creation of legal estates,[38] equity will enforce a contract[39] to create a legal mortgage by its usual remedy of a decree of specific performance.[40] Because of this special approach equity goes further and says that, until the legal mortgage is actually created by conveyance of the legal estate or demise, as the case may be, the intended mortgagee has an equitable mortgage on the land. Thus in *Eyre v. McDowell*.[41] it was held that a covenant by a debtor to

---

[33] Para. 12.33, *ante*.

[34] *Antrim County Land, Building and Investment Co. Ltd.* v. *Stewart* [1904] 2 I.R. 357 (see *A Casebook on Irish Land Law* (1984), p. 426).

[35] Ch. 9, *ante*.

[36] S. 6.

[37] See the discussion in *William Brandt's Sons and Co.* v *Dunlop Rubber Co. Ltd.* [1905] A.C. 454.

[38] See para. 3.144, *ante*.

[39] Note that there must be a "contract"—an *antecedent* debt, *e.g.* is not consideration for an agreement to mortgage, see *Crofts* v. *Feuge* (1854) 4 Ir.Ch.R. 316. If, however, the loan is advanced on the basis of the agreement, then the lender is entitled to specific performance (provided, of course, the borrower is in a position to transfer the legal title) since damages are an inadequate remedy, being an unsecured debt, and an equitable mortgage arises, which is secured and can be realised in priority to other unsecured claims against the debtor, see *Hunter* v. *Lord Langford* (1828) 2 Mol. 272.

[40] Para. 3.142 *et seq.*, *ante*.

[41] (1861) 9 H.L.C. 619 (on appeal from Ireland). See also *Card* v. *Jaffray* (1805) 2 Sch. & Lef. 374; *Abbott* v. *Stratten* (1846) 3 Jo. & Lat. 603; *Re Parkinson's Estate* (1865) 10 Ir.Jur.(N.S.) 82; *Re Hurley's Estate* [1894] 1 I.R. 488.

the effect that, if the debt was not paid by a certain date, the creditor could, by entry, foreclosure, sale or mortgage, levy the amount from the lands of the debtor, was held to create such an equitable mortgage.

12.42. Such an agreement must comply with the Statute of Frauds (Ireland), 1695, section 2 of which requires the agreement to be evidenced in writing and signed by the party to be charged or his authorised agent.[42] Alternatively, there may be sufficient acts of part performance or elements of fraud present to take the case out of the statute.[43]

(iii) Deposit of Title Deeds

12.43 The recognition of a deposit of title deeds as creating an equitable mortgage is often regarded as an extension of the doctrine of part performance.[44] At first sight there appear to be similarities in that it has been settled that a deposit on its own, without any memorandum in writing sufficient to evidence any agreement as required by the Statute of Frauds, will create an equitable mortgage.[45] This, however, involves extending the doctrine beyond its usual limits, one of which is that only the person who performs can take advantage of the performance, as the other party to the transaction is affected by his own fraud.[46] Yet it is the mortgagee who is interested in enforcing the mortgage created by deposit and it is difficult to see what acts of part performance have been done by him.[47] Giving the loan to the mortgagor involves usually payment of money and the general rule is that mere payment of money is not specifically referable to such an agreement for a mortgage.[48] Whatever the difficulties over the underlying theory of deposit of title deeds, the fact remains that it is a well-established method of creating mortgages in both Ireland and England and, as we have seen, has now been given statutory recognition.[49]

12.44. It appears that a mere deposit of the title deeds will be regarded as *prima facie* evidence of an equitable mortgage, unless the deposit is otherwise accounted for, *e.g.*, deposit with a bank for safe keeping.[50] On the other hand, a mere agreement to deposit is not enough if the deeds are not actually

---

[42] See para. 9.024, *ante*. Note that here only evidence of the agreement has to be in writing, whereas under s. 6 of the 1695 Statute the assignment itself must be in writing, *supra*.

[43] Para. 3.149, *ante*.

[44] See Corscadden, "Deposit of Title Deeds" (1953) 55 J.I.B.I. 253. Also para. 3.149, *ante*.

[45] *Bulfin* v. *Dunne* (1861) 12 Ir.Ch.R. 67; *Gilligan* v. *National Bank Ltd.* [1901] 2 I.R. 513; *Northern Banking Co. Ltd.* v. *Carpenter* [1931] I.R. 268; *National Bank Ltd.* v. *McGovern* [1931] I.R. 368. See also the early English authorities, *Russel* v. *Russel* (1783) 1 Bro. C.C. 269; *Edge* v. *Worthington* (1786) 1 Cox C.C. 211; *Hankey* v. *Vernon* (1788) 2 Cox. C.C. 12. *Cf.* The criticisms of the earlier decisions by Lord Eldon in *Ex parte Whitbread* (1812) 19 Ves. 209 at 210; *Ex parte Hooper* (1815) 19 Ves 477 at 478–9.

[46] See para. 3.149, *ante*.

[47] *I.e.*, the acts of part performance must be done by the plaintiff; *cf.* signing of the note or memorandum in writing required by s. 2 of the Statute of Frauds (Ir.), 1695.

[48] Further, even if the mortgagee gives a receipt for the deeds, this is not to his detriment.

[49] Para. 12.28, *ante*.

[50] *McKay* v. *McNally* (1879) 4 L.R.Ir. 438; *Gilligan* v. *National Bank Ltd.* [1901] 2 I.R. 513; *Northern Banking Co. Ltd.* v. *Carpenter* [1931] I.R. 268; *National Bank Ltd.* v *McGovern* [1931] I.R. 368. The deposit of title deeds in one branch of a bank may provide security for loans due in respect of accounts in other branches, see *Bank of Ireland* v. *Macaura* [1934] L.J.Ir. 89.

deposited, though that agreement may create another kind of equitable mortgage.[51] It is not necessary to deposit all the title deeds relating to the land, provided those in fact deposited are material evidence of title and sufficient to indicate the parties' intention.[52] It has also been held in Ireland that a deposit of title deeds with a creditor's solicitor, for the purpose of preparation of a mortgage to secure an antecedent debt and further advances, in itself creates an equitable mortgage without any further agreement.[53] Furthermore, a verbal agreement, supported by parol evidence, to make future advances on a deposit of title deeds as security for a present loan may be sufficient to create an equitable mortgage as security for any subsequent advances.[54]

12.45. The equitable mortgage created by deposit of title deeds gives the mortgagee a lien on the land to which the deeds relate,[55] not on the deeds themselves.[56] Thus an equitable mortgagee may be ordered, without prejudice to his rights, to lodge the deeds in court.[57] Unless the parties agree otherwise, it appears that an equitable mortgage by deposit will carry interest at the rate of 4 per cent. from the date of the deposit,[58] though, if made to a bank, it will secure interest at the current overdraft rate.

12.46 The parties must decide whether to accompany the deposit of the title deeds with any written memorandum. There is no need for any such formality, since the mere deposit is sufficient to create an equitable mortgage and one of the main attractions of such arrangements is their relative informality, which makes them so popular with banks and their customers.[59] On the other hand, if there is no written evidence of the purpose of the deposit there may be disputes later between the parties.[60] Yet if some further document is executed to prevent disputes arising, the parties may find that they are affected by statutory provisions. First, it may be argued that the intention of the parties was not to create a mortgage by deposit but rather to

---

[51] *Simmons* v. *Montague* [1909] 1 I.R. 87. See para. 12.41. *supra. Cf. Ex parte Crossfield* (1840) 3 Ir.Eq.R. 67. *Ex parte Crossfield* and *Simmons* v. *Montague* were followed by Hamilton J. in *Bank of Ireland Finance Ltd.* v. *Daly* [1978] I.R. 79 at 82. An equitable mortgage may still be created even though the depositor has no right to the title deeds, provided the mortgagee advances the money *bona fide*, see *Joyce* v. *De Moleyns* (1845) 8 Ir.Eq.R. 215. *Cf. Purcell* v. *Ruckley* (1849) 12 Ir.Eq.R. 55. The lien is lost if the depositee parts with the deeds, *Re Driscoll's Estate* (1867) I.R. 1 Eq. 285.

[52] *Re Lambert's Estate* (1884) 13 L.R.Ir. 234. See also *C.P.* v. *D.P.* [1983] I.L.R.M. 381.

[53] *Bulfin* v. *Dunne* (1861) 12 Ir.Ch.R. 67. *Cf. Norris* v. *Wilkinson* (1806) 12 Ves. 192. Where an equitable mortgage by deposit of title deeds is followed by execution of a legal mortgage of the same lands, the equitable mortgage does not necessarily merge in the legal one. *Re Smallman's Estate* (1867) I.R. 2 Eq. 34. See further on merger, ch. 24, *post.*

[54] *Bulfin* v. *Dunne, op. cit.* See also *Ex parte Langston* (1810) 17 Ves. 227; *Ex parte Kensington* (1813) 2 V. & B. 79.

[55] *Simmons* v. *Montague* [1909] 1 I.R. 87. Note the references to a "lien on the land" in s. 81 (5) of the Local Registration of Title (Ir.) Act, 1891, and now in s. 105 (5) of the Republic's Registration of Title Act, 1964; *cf.* s. 50 of the Land Registration Act (N.I.), 1970. Para. 12.29, *supra.*

[56] *Gilligan* v. *National Bank Ltd.* [1901] 2 I.R. 513.

[57] *Re Girdwood's Estate* (1881) 5 L.R.Ir. 45.

[58] *Carey* v. *Doyne* (1856) 5 Ir.Ch.R. 104.

[59] See Corscadden, "Deposit of Title Deeds" (1953) 55 J.I.B.I. 253.

[60] And see *Hibernian Bank* v. *Gilbert* (1889) 23 L.R.Ir. 321. Note also *Simmons* v. *Montague* [1909] 1 I.R. 87 (mistake in map lodged with title deeds).

enter into an agreement for a mortgage, in which case the requirements of section 2 of the Statute of Frauds (Ireland), 1695, must be met.[61] Secondly, it has been held that such a written memorandum comes within the Registration of Deeds Act (Ireland), 1707,[62] and so a memorial of it must be registered in a Registry of Deeds to secure priority.[63] This obviously defeats the desire of a bank customer for secrecy and informality in securing a loan or an overdraft. The result is that such a deposit is rarely accompanied by any written memorandum in Ireland.[64]

(iv) Equitable Charge

12.47. An owner of property may appropriate it as security for a debt so as to give the creditor an equitable charge on the property.[65] We have already explained that such a charge is to be distinguished from a mortgage in that it confers only a lien on the land and no legal or equitable estate in the land nor any right to possession.[66] Such a charge may be created by written agreement[67] or by will.[68] Apart from that, no special words are necessary so long as the intention is clear.[69]

---

[61] Para. 12.42, *supra*.

[62] Replaced in Northern Ireland by the Registration of Deeds Act (N.I.), 1970, see ch. 22, *post*.

[63] *Re Lambert's Estate* (1884) 13 L.R.Ir. 234; *Fullerton* v. *Provincial Bank of Ireland* [1903] A.C. 309, on appeal from [1902] 1 I.R. (*sub nom. Re Stevenson's Estate* (see *A Casebook on Irish Land Law* (1984), p. 432). See, further, on priorities, ch. 13, *post*.

[64] Some banks have in the past tried to get round this problem by having the customer read a memorandum containing the terms of the loan at the time of the deposit and then having this signed in the customer's presence by bank officials only as a record of the transaction. This may avoid later disputes in practice and, because the customer-mortgagor has not signed anything, there is no written memorandum coming within the Statute of Frauds, nor, indeed, any deed or conveyance within the Registry of Deeds legislation.

[65] See further, para. 12.19, *ante*.

[66] *Antrim County Land, Building, and Investment Co. Ltd.* v. *Stewart* [1904] 2 I.R. 357, espec. at 369 (*per* Fitzgibbon L.J.) (see *A Casebook on Irish Land Law* (1984), p. 426); *Bank of Ireland Ltd.* v. *Feeney* [1930] I.R. 457, espec. at 469 (*per* Kennedy C.J.).

[67] *Coonan* v. *O'Connor* [1903] 1 I.R. 449. Or, at least, evidenced in writing, see *Matthews* v. *Goodday* (1861) 31 L.J.Ch. 282; *Ex parte Hall* (1878) 10 Ch.D. 615.

[68] *Re Owen* [1894] 3 Ch. 220.

[69] *Coonan* v. *O'Connor* [1903] 1 I.R. 449. See also *Cradock* v. *Scottish Provident Institution* (1894) 70 L.T. 718.

CHAPTER 13

POSITION OF PARTIES UNDER MORTGAGES

13.001. In this chapter we consider the various rights and duties of the mortgagor and mortgagee once a mortgage has been created, including their transfer to other persons. As we shall see, the mortgagor and mortgagee each have their own rights and duties, but some are common to both parties. The nature and extent of these rights and duties depend partly on the contractual terms of the mortgage agreed between the mortgagor and mortgagee and partly on statute law.

I. MORTGAGEE

13.002. In most cases, the mortgagee is a financial institution concerned simply that its loan, plus the interest charged on it, should be repaid according to the terms of the agreement. If the loan and interest are not repaid it can always sue the mortgagor as for any other debt.[1] What makes a mortgage special is the existence of further remedies the mortgagee has for enforcement of his security for the contractual debt. In addition to his various remedies for enforcement of the security, there are several other matters to be considered with respect to the position of a mortgagee *vis-à-vis* the mortgagor and the land which is the security for the debt.

A. TITLE DOCUMENTS

13.003. The general principle is that it is part of a mortgagee's security to have in his possession the title documents relating to the land, because this will protect him against further dealings with the property by the mortgagor without the mortgagee knowing of them, which might affect the priority of his security.[2] There are, however, several situations to be considered.

13.004. First, so far as registered land is concerned, where the security is created by means of a registered charge the chargee is entitled in both parts of Ireland to delivery of a charge certificate.[3] He is not generally entitled to the land certificate relating to the registered ownership of the land which remains in the mortgagor,[4] but he is protected by the fact that his charge is registered and will take priority over any subsequent equitable mortgage created by deposit of the land or charge certificate.[5] It is true that the Registrar, on the application of the registered owner of the land or any person appearing to him

---

[1] Para. 13.011, *infra*.
[2] *Smith* v. *Chichester* (1842) 4 Ir.Eq.R. 580 at 581 (*per* Sugden L.C.). See further on priorities, especially the relevance of negligence as to custody of title documents, para. 13.133, *post*.
[3] Registration of Title Act, 1964, s. 62 (5); Land Registration Act (N.I.), 1970, s. 79 (2) (*a*).
[4] In the Republic of Ireland there is a specific provision to the effect that the registered owner of a charge is not, merely by reason of his being such owner, entitled to possession of the land certificate relating to the registered land which is subject to the charge and any stipulation to the contrary is void, 1964 Act, s. 67 (replacing s. 14 of the Registration of Title Act, 1942). See *Re Associated Banks* [1944] Ir.Jur.Rep. 29. *Cf.* 1970 Act, s. 79 (2) (*a*), which merely provides for rules to be made regarding custody of certificates.
[5] Para. 13.131, *post*.

to be entitled to require it, may order the chargee to produce the certificate to the Registrar for the purpose of a dealing with the land or charge which can be effected without the consent of the person in whose custody it is.[6] This production, however, does not alter the right to custody of the certificate nor any lien created on the land.[7] If an equitable mortgage on the registered land is created by deposit of the land or charge certificate, then, of course, the mortgagee is entitled to custody of the certificate in question since, upon this, his entire position depends.[8]

13.005. Secondly, so far as unregistered land is concerned, if a legal mortgage is created by conveyance of the fee simple, the mortgagee as owner of the fee simple in the land is automatically entitled to the title deeds. If, however, the mortgage is created by demise, the mortgagee will only be entitled to the lease, unless he contracts expressly for surrender of the deeds relating to the freehold.[9] In the case of a mortgage of leasehold property, if created by assignment the mortgagee is entitled to possession of the lease only. If it is created by sub-demise, he is not automatically entitled even to this, though he will usually stipulate expressly for its surrender.[10]

13.006. In the case of an equitable mortgage of unregistered land, the mortgagee obviously has custody of the title deeds where the mortgage is created by their deposit. It is, however, important to remember that the mortgage or lien thereby created relates to the land rather than the deeds,[11] so that the mortgagee may be ordered in certain cases, for example, to lodge the deeds in court.[12] In the case of other equitable mortgages, *e.g.*, a mortgage of an equitable interest only in the property or an agreement for a legal mortgage, the title deeds will be retained by the legal owner of the property. A *fortiori* an equitable chargee who has no estate at all, legal or equitable, in the land has no right to the title deeds.[13]

B. INSURANCE

13.007. In both parts of Ireland a mortgagee has a statutory power to insure the mortgaged property conferred by section 19 of the Conveyancing Act, 1881. This power is implied automatically in mortgages by deed only,[14] but it is provided in both parts of Ireland that a registered charge confers on the owner of the charge all the rights and powers of a mortgagee under a

---

[6]   1964 Act, s. 105 (2); 1970 Act, s. 79 (2) (*b*).

[7]   1964 Act, s. 105 (3); 1970 Act, s. 72 (2) (*b*).

[8]   Para. 12.29, *ante*. His lien is lost if he parts with the certificate, *Re Driscoll's Estate* (1866) I.R. 1 Eq. 285.

[9]   See *Wiseman* v. *Westland* (1826) 1 Y. & J. 117, espec. at 122. *Cf.* the English Law of Property Act, 1925, s. 85 (1) (first long lessee-mortgagee or legal chargee given statutory right to possession of the documents of title).

[10]   *Cf.* Law of Property Act, 1925, s. 86 (1) (first mortgagee of leaseholds same statutory right to possession of documents as if mortgagee by assignment).

[11]   *Gilligan* v. *National Bank Ltd.* [1901] 2 I.R. 513.

[12]   *Re Girdwood's Estate* (1881) 5 L.R.Ir. 45.

[13]   *National Bank Ltd.* v. *Hegarty* (1901) 1 N.I.J.R. 13; *Antrim County Land, Building, and Investment Co. Ltd.* v. *Stewart* [1904] 2 I.R. 357 (see *A Casebook on Irish Land Law* (1984), p. 426); *Bank of Ireland Ltd.* v. *Feeny* [1930] I.R. 457.

[14]   1881 Act, s. 19 (1).

mortgage by deed within the meaning of the Conveyancing Acts.[15] The power to insure may be exercised at any time after the date of the mortgage deed to cover loss or damage by fire to any building, or any effects or property of an insurable nature forming part of the mortgaged property.[16] The premiums are to be a charge on the mortgaged property, in addition to the mortgage debt, with the same priority and with interest at the same rate as that debt.[17] However, the amount of insurance cover is not to exceed the amount specified in the mortgage deed or, if no amount is specified, two-thirds of the amount required to restore the property in the event of total destruction.[18]

13.008. A mortgagee cannot exercise his statutory power to insure in three cases: (i) where there is a declaration in the mortgage deed that no insurance is required; (ii) where an insurance is kept up by or on behalf of the mortgagor in accordance with the mortgage deed; (iii) where the mortgage deed contains no stipulation respecting insurance, and an insurance is kept up by or on behalf of the mortgagor, to the amount in which the mortgagee is by the Act authorised to insure.[19]

13.009. The mortgagee is entitled to require all money received under an insurance effected under the 1881 Act or the mortgage deed to be applied by the mortgagor in making good loss or damage to the mortgaged property,[20] or, subject to any obligation to the contrary imposed by law or a special contract, in discharge of the mortgage debt.[21] It had been held in Ireland that, even though the insurance is effected neither under the 1881 Act nor under the mortgage deed, the mortgagee may still require the insurance money to be applied in discharge of the mortgage debt.[22]

C. FIXTURES

13.010. By virtue of the general definitions in the Conveyancing Act, 1881, of "land" as including houses and other buildings,[23] of a "conveyance" as including an assignment or lease made by deed on a mortgage of property[24] and of a "mortgage" as including any charge on property for securing money or money's worth,[25] there are included in a mortgage of land in Ireland all buildings and fixtures appertaining to that land.[26] It appears that the well-known exceptions which apply as between landlord and tenant[27] do not

---

[15] Registration of Title Act, 1964, s. 62 (6); Land Registration Act (N.I.), 1970, Sched. 7, Pt. I, para. 5.
[16] 1881 Act, s. 19 (1) (ii). [17] *Ibid.* [18] 1881 Act, s. 23 (1). [19] S. 23 (2).
[20] S. 23 (3).
[21] S. 23 (4).
[22] *Re Doherty* [1925] 2 I.R. 246. *Cf. Halifax Building Society* v. *Keighly* [1931] 2 K.B. 248. And in *Myler* v. *Mr. Pussy's Nite Club Ltd.* (1979) Unrep. (H.C., R.I.) (1978 No. 1472 P) (see *A Casebook on Irish Land Law* (1984), p. 445), McWilliam J. applied this principle to a mortgage by deposit of title deeds.
[23] S. 2 (ii).
[24] S. 2 (v).
[25] S. 2 (vi), and note that a registered charge operates as a mortgage by deed within the meaning of the Conveyancing Acts, Registration of Title Act, 1964, s. 62 (6); Land Registration Act, 1970, Sched. 7, Pt. I, para. 5.
[26] 1881 Act s. 6. *Cf. Re Dawson* (1868) I.R. 2 Eq. 218 (growing crops).
[27] *I.e.*, so-called tenant's fixtures which can be removed by him and do not belong to the landlord, *e.g.*, trade or ornamental fixtures, see para. 4.155, *ante* and ch. 17, *post.* Also *Re Dawson* (1868) I.R. 2 Eq. 218 (looms spiked to tiled floor); *Re Calvert* [1898] 2 I.R. 501 (trade fixtures in chemist's shop); *Moore* v. *Merrion Pier and Baths Co.* (1901) 1 N.I.J.R. 184 (gas engine and pump).

apply as between mortgagor and mortgagee.[28] Indeed, the mortgagor may not even be entitled to remove fixtures which he has attached to the property after the date of the mortgage.[29]

D. ACTION FOR DEBT

13.011. It must not be forgotten that a mortgagee, like any other lender of money, is owed a contractual debt and is entitled to sue for it if it is not repaid. One limitation on this right is, of course, that he can sue only after the date for repayment is past and not before then.[30] Furthermore, it appears that the right of action for the debt cannot be considered entirely in isolation from the other remedies the mortgagee has against the land. Central to the concept of a mortgage is the principle that the mortgagor is entitled to have his land back freed from the mortgage once he repays the debt, plus interest, in full. So it has been held that a mortgagee who parts with his interest in the land, and who, therefore, cannot hand it back to the mortgagor on redemption, loses his right to sue on the covenant for the debt.[31]

13.012. The essence of a mortgage, however, is, as we have mentioned several times already, that the mortgagee does not have to rely on such a remedy, which is always subject to the risk that the mortgagor will turn out to be insolvent. If necessary, the mortgagee can seek instead to realise his security and move against the land which forms the subject-matter of the mortgage. It is to the remedies for enforcement of his security that we now turn.

E. ENFORCEMENT OF SECURITY

13.013. The mortgagee's methods of enforcing his security against the land have evolved since mortgages were recognised by the Court of Chancery. The remedies were not created by statute but by the courts and, accordingly, they are the result of constantly changing economic and social factors. Equity, common law, conveyancers, and, subsequently, statute law, have contributed to the present position. We wish to emphasise that in this field there is a significant difference between the practice in Ireland and in England: in England one of the main remedies, when the money due on a mortgage has not been paid, is foreclosure while this is unknown in Ireland. In Ireland the remedies available to a mortgagee when the principal or, in some cases, the interest on the principal, has not been paid are[32]: (1) a court order for possession of the mortgaged property, followed by a sale of that property by the mortgagee out of court; (2) a sale of the mortgaged property without the

---

[28] *Climie* v. *Wood* (1869) L.R. 4 Ex. 328; *Monti* v. *Barnes* [1901] 1 Q.B. 205; *Lyon & Co.* v. *London City & Midland Bank* [1903] 2 K.B. 135. See Firth, "Mortgages and Trade Fixtures" (1899) 15 L.Q.R. 165.

[29] *Longbottom* v. *Berry* (1869) L.R. 5 Q.B. 137; *Reynolds* v. *Ashby & Son* [1904] A.C. 466. *Cf.* fixtures annexed by a third party under an agreement with the mortgagor, *Gough* v. *Wood & Co.* [1894] 1 Q.B. 713.

[30] *Hinds* v. *Blacker* (1878) 1 L.R.Ir. 233; *Sinton* v. *Dooley* [1910] 2 I.R. 162 at 165 (*per* Gibson J.); *Bradshaw* v. *McMullan* [1915] 2 I.R. 187. See also *Bolton* v. *Buckenham* [1891] 1 Q.B. 278.

[31] *Schoole* v. *Sall* (1803) 1 Sch. & Lef. 176. See also *Palmer* v. *Hendrie* (1859) 27 Beav. 349; *cf. Willes* v. *Levett* (1847) 1 De G. & Sm. 392. The same applies where the mortgagee's title is extinguished by adverse possession, see *Beamish* v. *Whitney* [1909] 1 I.R. 360.

[32] See Scanlon, *Practice and Procedure in Administration and Mortgage Suits in Ireland* (1963).

intervention of the court; (3) a court order for the sale of the mortgaged property; (4) the mortgagee going into possession of the mortgaged property and taking the rents and profits of it; (5) the appointment of a receiver, and (6) foreclosure, in theory, though as we stated above, it is never granted in practice.

13.014.   Four of these (a court order for possession followed by a sale out of court, sale of the mortgaged property without the intervention of the court, a court order for the sale of the mortgaged property and foreclosure) are intended to secure repayment of the capital originally borrowed and so have the result that the mortgagee is paid his capital and interest and the mortgage determines. The mortgagee going into possession of the mortgaged property and taking the rents and profits and the appointment of a receiver are designed primarily to secure the regular payment of the outgoings on the property and the interest due on the mortgage and, though they may be preliminary to a sale, they are essentially different from it. A mortgagee may make use of more than one of these remedies at the same time, provided he does not act inconsistently. Thus, in Ireland, a mortgagee may sue the morgager for the debt created by the covenant in the mortgage to repay the principal and interest and may, at the same time, bring proceedings for a court order for the sale of the mortgaged property.[33] This is not the practice in England, but in *Barden* v. *Downes*[34] the Supreme Court in the Republic decided that a mortgagee could bring separate proceedings against the mortgagor to recover judgment for the amount of the mortgage debt and interest when he had already brought proceedings for a court sale.

13.015.   If there are a number of mortgages affecting the land, each of the mortgagees may pursue different remedies so that, while one may sue for his debt, another may apply for a court order for the sale of the mortgaged property.[35] These remedies are not confined to legal mortgages: some of them may be used by equitable mortgagees and special provision has been made by the Registration of Title Act, 1964, in the Republic of Ireland and by the Land Registration Act (N.I.), 1970, in Northern Ireland for a summary remedy by a person who has advanced money on the security of a charge on land which is registered and who seeks to get possession. At one time there existed in Ireland statutory control over the terms on which mortgages could be created through the rent restriction legislation. This control no longer exists in Northern Ireland and has been abandoned in the Republic.[36]

We now proceed to discuss each of these remedies.

1. *Court Order for Possession and Sale out of Court*

13.016.   Until 1950, the most commonly used remedy by a mortgagee when the principal was due, or there had been default in the payment of interest

---

[33]   *Bradshaw* v. *McMullan* [1915] 2 I.R. 187.
[34]   [1940] I.R. 131.
[35]   *Hinds* v. *Blacker* (1877) I.R. 11 Eq. 322; *Sinton* v. *Dooley* [1910] 2 I.R. 162.
[36]   See para. 13.064, *post*.

and he could not get vacant possession of the property, was an application to the court for a declaration that the amount secured by the mortgage was well charged on the mortgagor's interest and for a sale, if the mortgagor did not pay the sum due within three months after service of the court order on him. These proceedings have a number of disadvantages: there is the delay caused by the mortgagor having three months to pay and the inevitable difficulties about a sale by the court. Moreover, the amount realised by a court sale is usually less than the amount that can be realised on a private sale or on a sale which is not advertised as being a court sale. Order 55, rule 7, of the Rules of the Supreme Court (Ireland), 1905, provided that any mortgagee or mortgagor, whether legal or equitable, or any person entitled to or having property subject to a legal or equitable charge or any person having the right to foreclose or redeem any mortgage could take out an originating summons for sale, delivery of possession by the mortgagor, redemption, reconveyance or delivery of possession by the mortgagee.[37]

13.017. The earlier authorities on this rule had decided that an order for possession against a mortgagor would be made in special circumstances only, but in the *Irish Permanent Building Society* v. *Ryan*[38] the Republic's High Court decided that, in a case where the mortgagee had made default in paying instalments on a building society loan, an order that the mortgagor give up possession to the building society should be made as the property, when sold with vacant possession, would realise more.

13.018. In *Re O'Neill*,[39] Lowry J. (as he then was) held that the court had an inherent jurisdiction to put a legal or equitable mortgagee into possession and that such an order could be made not only in the Chancery Division, but also by a judge exercising bankruptcy jurisdiction in the Queen's Bench Division. In that case, the applicant had already obtained a declaration in bankruptcy proceedings that he was mortgagee of the bankrupt's interest and the court had ordered a sale by public auction, the applicant to have carriage of the sale. The applicant later applied for a further order for delivery of possession by the bankrupt, so that the sale could be made with vacant possession. In granting this further order, Lowry J. pointed out for the guidance of the legal profession in Northern Ireland that it will usually be more convenient and less expensive if, in applications for an order for sale of mortgaged premises, the applicant applies for an order for possession at the same time, if such is required.

---

[37] See Wylie, *Judicature Acts (Ireland) and Rules of the Supreme Court (Ireland)* (1906), p. 740. See also discussion in *Re O'Neill* [1967] N.I. 129.

[38] [1950] I.R. 12 (see *A Casebook on Irish Land Law* (1978), p.447).

[39] [1967] N.I. 129. In England there has been considerable judicial controversy recently over the court's power to stay or suspend execution of an order for possession, centering around s. 36 of the Administration of Justice Act, 1970, as amended by s. 8 of the Administration of Justice Act, 1973: see, e.g., *Royal Trust Co. of Canada* v. *Markham* [1975] 1 W.L.R. 1416; *Western Bank Ltd.* v. *Schindler* [1976] 3 W.L.R. 341; *Quennel* v. *Maltby* [1979] 1 W.L.R. 318; *Centrax Trustees Ltd.* v. *Ross* [1979] 2 All E.R. 952. This matter is now dealt with in Northern Ireland in a much more simple manner by s. 86 (3) of the Judicature (Northern Ireland) Act, 1978, which reads:

"Without prejudice to any other powers exercisable by it, a court, acting on equitable grounds, may stay any proceedings or the execution of any of its process subject to such conditions as it thinks fit."

13.019. The 1905 rules have been replaced in the Republic by the 1962 Rules of the Superior Court[40] and this remedy is now dealt with by Order 54, rule 3. The procedure is by special summons. A considerable extension of this useful jurisdiction was made in the Republic by section 13 of the Registration of Title Act, 1942 (now section 62 (7) of the Registration of Title Act, 1964), by which an owner of a registered charge may apply to the court for an order for possession when repayment of the principal money secured by the charge has become due. It had been held by the Court of Appeal in Northern Ireland[41] that an owner of a charge on land registered under the Local Registration of Title (Ireland) Act, 1891, had not got an estate or interest which enabled him to recover possession but, as a result of statutory changes, such an owner may now apply for an order that the mortgagor give up possession of the lands to him. In Northern Ireland this power to award possession to the owner of a registered charge is given by paragraph 5 (2) of Part I of Schedule 7 to the Land Registration Act (N.I.), 1970, and may be exercised when, although payment of the principal has not become due, "there are urgent and special reasons for exercising the power."[42]

13.020. In the Republic, when the rateable valuation of the lands is under £100, the application may be made to the circuit court of the area in which the lands are situate for, although there is nothing in the circuit court's rules corresponding to Order 54, rule 3, of the 1962 Rules of the Superior Court, the mortgagee has a right to possession because either the legal estate has been conveyed to him or he is the owner of a term of years created by sub-demise.[43] Most building society mortgages provide that the sum advanced is to become due within three or six months after the advance, but that the society will not exercise the power of sale or of entering into possession unless there has been a default by the mortgagor in the payment of instalments. The mortgagor usually acknowledges that he is in possession as a tenant of the building society. The result is that proceedings by ejectment may be brought by the building society in the circuit court when there has been default in the payment of the principal moneys or interest secured by the mortgage or, in the case of a mortgage repayable by instalments, when there has been default in the payment of the instalments for the period specified in the mortgage deed.[44] In the case of advances made under the Small Dwellings Acquisition Act, 1899, a special provision is made for recovery of possession in the event of default in the payments secured by the deed of mortgage.[45]

13.021. The order made on an application such as this is that the mortgagor do forthwith upon the service of the court order on him give up

---

[40] S.I. 1962 No., 72. *Cf.* Rules of the Supreme Court (N.I.), 1936, as amended, espec. Ords. 47 and 51.
[41] *Northern Banking Co. Ltd.* v. *Devlin* [1924] 1 I.R. 90.
[42] Para. 5 (3) (*b*).
[43] For N.I., see County Courts Act (N.I.), 1959, s. 16 (*c*) (£75 annual value limit) and see County Court Rules (N.I.), 1965, Ord. 30.
[44] See also County Courts Act (N.I.), 1959, s. 12 (4) and 1965 Rules, Ord. 31.
[45] 1899 Act, ss. 5 (5) and 14 (2). *Cf.* Magistrates' Courts Act (N.I.), 1964, ss. 76–81.

possession of the property to the mortgagee. If he fails to do this, an order of *habere* by which the County Registrar is ordered to put the mortgagee into possession may be obtained in the court offices. When a mortgagee obtains possession, he may sell the property and the principles which we describe in the next part in relation to sale of mortgaged property without the intervention of the court apply. The mortgagee is entitled to pay his costs of the proceedings out of the money realised on the sale and he holds any surplus remaining after payment of the principal and interest and costs as a trustee for any subsequent mortgagees or, if there are none, in trust for the mortgagor.

Finally, in the Republic, under section 7 of the Family Home Protection Act, 1976, the court has power to adjourn proceedings by a mortgagee for possession or sale of a family home on the ground of non-payment of sums due under the mortgage by one spouse. The Court may do so where it appears that the other spouse is desirous and capable of paying the arrears within a reasonable time and future periodical payments falling due under the mortgage, and it would be just and equitable to do so in all the circumstances, having regard to the terms of the mortgage and the interests of the mortgagee and spouses. The adjournment may be for such period and on such terms as appear to the court to be just and equitable, having regard in particular to whether the spouse of the mortgagor has been informed, by or on behalf of the mortgagee or otherwise, of the non-payment of the sums in question or any of them.

2. Sale

13.022.   The second remedy which a mortgagee has is power to sell the mortgaged property without the intervention of the court but, if the mortgagee is unable to obtain vacant possession of the property, he will find considerable difficulty in selling it for no purchaser will buy property in the possession of a mortgagor. If, however, the property mortgaged consists of the right to receive rents, this power of sale without the intervention of the court may be used.

13.023.   In the early days, selling the property was not an effective way of realising the mortgagee's security because neither the common law nor equity recognised any right in the mortgagee to sell the property free from the mortgagor's equity of redemption. The most that the mortgagee was entitled to do was to transfer only the interest he had in the property, *i.e.*, ownership subject to the mortgagor's equity of redemption,[46] and few purchasers could be found who regarded this as a commercial interest in land. The result was that the practice developed of inserting in mortgage deeds an express power of sale enabling the mortgagee to sell the property without the need for any application to the court and free from the mortgagor's equity of redemption. So long as such an express power limited the mortgagee to retaining out of the proceeds of sale only what was due to him in terms of the mortgage debt and

---

[46] See further on transfer of the mortgagee's interest, para. 13.122, *post.*

the costs and expenses of the sale, equity would not intervene. Then in 1860 Lord Cranworth's Act conferred a limited statutory power of sale on mortgagees (*inter alia*)[47] and this was replaced by a wider and more satisfactory power conferred by section 19 of the Conveyancing Act, 1881.[48] The following are the main points to be borne in mind with respect to the statutory power of sale.

(i) Mortgagees Entitled

13.024. Section 19 (1) of the 1881 Act confers the power of sale under the Act on all mortgagees, provided the mortgage was made by *deed* after 1881. This covers most, if not all, in practice, legal mortgages[49] but not some equitable mortgages, *e.g.*, an informal mortgage by deposit of title deeds not accompanied by a memorandum under seal[50] or a contract for a legal mortgage not executed by deed.[51] The most that equitable mortgagees in such cases can do, in the absence of express powers, is to apply to the court for an order declaring the sum due on the mortgage well charged on the land and directing a sale of the land if it is not paid within a specified time (three months).[52] Furthermore, in other cases where a deed is often used, *e.g.*, a mortgage of an equitable interest,[53] there may be difficulties on the ground that the "mortgaged property" within the meaning of section 19 (1) of the 1881 Act,[54] which the mortgagee can sell, is an equitable interest only.[55] To get round this problem the mortgage deed may contain either a power of attorney empowering the mortgagee or his assigns to convey the legal estate[56] or a declaration by the mortgagor that he holds the legal estate on trust for the mortgagee and empowering the mortgagee to convey it.[57]

13.025. So far as an equitable chargee is concerned, if the charge is created by deed, he is in the same position as an equitable mortgagee since the definition of a mortgage in the Conveyancing Act, 1881, includes "any charge on any property for securing money or money's worth."[58] Otherwise, an equitable chargee must apply to the court for an order for sale of the

---

[47] Ss. 11–15.

[48] As extended by s. 4 of the Conveyancing Act, 1911. See also ss. 20–22 of the 1881 Act.

[49] Including registered charges in respect of registered land, see Registration of Title Act, 1965, s. 62 (6); Land Registration Act (N.I.), 1970, Sched. 7 Pt. I, para. 5. *Kidd* v. *O'Neill* [1931] I.R. 664; *Re Neely* [1936] I.R. 381.

[50] Para. 12.46, *ante*.

[51] Para. 12.41, *ante*.

[52] *Shea* v. *Moore* [1894] 1 I.R. 158, espec. at 178–9; (*per* Palles C.B.); *Antrim County Land, Building and Investment Co. Ltd.* v. *Stewart* [1904] 2 I.R. 357 at 369 (see *A Casebook on Irish Land Law* (1984), p. 426). See also *Going* v. *Farrell* (1814) Beat. 472; *Ex parte Domvile* (1862) 14 Ir.Ch.R. 19; *Munster and Leinster Bank* v. *Jervis* (1902) 36 I.L.T.R. 113. Note also the court powers with respect to discharge of incumbrances conferred by s. 5 of the Conveyancing Act, 1881, as amended by s. 1 of the Conveyancing Act, 1911. See para. 6.145, *ante*.

[53] Para. 12.39, *ante*.

[54] *Cf*. the wording of s. 21 (1)–"the property . . . [which] is the subject of the mortgage."

[55] See the discussion in *Re Hodson & Howe's Contract* (1887) 35 Ch.D. 668 and *Re White Rose Cottage* [1965] Ch. 940, espec. at 951 (*per* Lord Denning M.R.). *Cf*. under Lord Cranworth's Act, 1860, *Re Solomon & Meagher's Contract* (1889) 40 Ch.D. 508; *Re Boucherett* [1908] 1 Ch. 180.

[56] See *Re White Rose Cottage* [1965] Ch. 940. Also on powers of attorney, *Industrial Development Authority* v. *Moran* [1978] I.R. 159 (see *A Casebook on Irish Land Law* (1984), p. 419) and generally, ch. 11, *ante*.

[57] *Re Sergie* [1954] N.I. 1.

[58] S. 2 (vi).

property charged.[59] It should also be borne in mind that, once an application is made to the court for a sale and the court orders a sale, the mortgagee's extra-judicial power under the Conveyancing Acts can no longer be exercised since the judicial sale is intended to benefit all incumbrancers and not just the mortgagee who applied for it and then wishes to exercise his statutory power.[60]

(ii) Power Arises

13.026. Section 19 (1) (i) of the 1881 Act provides that the statutory power of sale does not arise until the "mortgage money has become due." In the case of most mortgages this means when the legal date for redemption[61] has passed; in the case of a mortgage "by instalments" it has been held that the power of sale arises as soon as any instalment is in arrear.[62] As we shall discuss in a moment, it is vital for a purchaser from the mortgagee to determine whether or not the power of sale has *arisen*. It is not so important, indeed it is immaterial to him, whether the power is also exercisable, as laid down by the 1881 Act.

(iii) Power Exercisable

13.027. Section 20 of the 1881 Act provides that the power of sale cannot be exercised by the mortgagee unless and until one of three conditions is satisfied, namely:

"(1) Notice requiring payment of the mortgage money has been served on the mortgagor or one of several mortgagors, and default has been made in payment of the mortgage money, or of part thereof, for three months after such service[63]; or

(2) Some interest under the mortgage is in arrear and unpaid for two months after becoming due; or

(3) There has been a breach of some provision contained in the mortgage deed[64] or in this Act,[65] and on the part of the mortgagor, or of some person concurring in and making the mortgage, to be observed or performed, other than and besides a covenant for payment of the mortgage money or interest thereon."

(iv) Protection of Purchaser

13.028. The distinction drawn in the 1881 Act between when the mort-

---

[59] *Antrim Land, Building, and Investment Co. Ltd.* v. *Stewart* [1904] 2 I.R. 357 (see *A Casebook on Irish Land Law* (1984), p. 426); *Bank of Ireland Ltd.* v. *Feeney* [1930] I.R. 457. See also *Bolton* v. *Fairtlough* (1864) 15 Ir.Ch.R. 229.

[60] *Re Beauclerk's Estate* [1907] 1 I.R. 76. See also *Re Prendergast* (1850) 2 Ir.Jur.(O.S.) 145; *Royal Bank of Ireland, Ltd.* v. *Sproule* [1940] Ir.Jur.Rep. 33; *Bagots, Hutton & Kinahan Ltd.* v. *Talbot* (1952) 86 I.L.T.R. 186.

[61] Para. 12.05, *ante.* See, however, *Re Lowe* (1850) 2 Ir.Jur.(O.S.) 131.

[62] *Payne* v. *Cardiff R.D.C.* [1932] 1 K.B. 241. *Cf. Twentieth Century Banking Corporation Ltd.* v. *Wilkinson* [1977] Ch. 99.

[63] It has been held that the mortgagee may instead serve a notice demanding payment in three months' time and, if payment is not made by then, may sell at once, *Baker* v. *Illingworth* [1908] 2 Ch. 20.

[64] *E.g.,* in respect of repairs to or insurance of the mortgaged property.

[65] *E.g.,* in respect of leases granted under the powers conferred by s. 18 of the 1881 Act, *Public Trustee* v. *Lawrence* [1912] 1 Ch. 789. See further para. 13.111, *post.*

gagee's power of sale arises and when it becomes exercisable is crucial from the point of view of a purchaser of the mortgaged land. The significance of the distinction is this. If the power of sale has not arisen, the mortgagee has no statutory power at all and, unless he has an express power of sale under the mortgage instrument, he can only transfer his interest under the mortgage, still subject to the mortgagor's equity of redemption. On the other hand, if the power has arisen and the mortgagee purports to exercise it, even though it is not yet exercisable, the purchaser nevertheless obtains a good title because, as section 21 (2) of the 1881 Act provides:

"Where a conveyance is made in professed[66] exercise of the power of sale conferred by this Act, the title of the purchaser shall not be impeachable on the ground that no case had arisen to authorise the sale, or that due notice was not given, or that the power was otherwise improperly or irregularly exercised; but any person damnified[67] by an unauthorised, or improper, or irregular exercise of the power shall have his remedy in damages against the person exercising the power."

To this section 5 (1) of the Conveyancing Act, 1911, adds:

"Upon any sale made in professed exercise of the power conferred on mortgagees by the Act of 1881, a purchaser is not, and never has been, either before or on conveyance concerned to see or inquire whether a case has arisen to authorise the sale, or due notice has been given, or the power is otherwise properly and regularly exercised."[68]

13.029. These provisions are designed to simplify conveyancing by reducing the enquiries which the purchaser is expected to make. He is only obliged to satisfy himself that the power of sale has arisen, *i.e.*, that the legal date for redemption is passed, and in most cases this can be done very easily by reading the terms of the mortgage deed. He is not obliged to make enquiries, which could become extremely complex, into the detailed relations between the mortgagor and the mortgagee during the currency of the mortgage. In particular, he does not have to look at the accounts, if any, kept by the mortgagor and mortgagee as to payments made and received in respect of the mortgage. However, as is their practice with such a statutory provision,[69] the courts will not allow it to be used as an instrument of fraud and it has been stated that a purchaser with *knowledge* of any impropriety or irregularity about the exercise of the power will not obtain a good title.[70] This does not require of a purchaser from a mortgagee the standard of care in conveyancing matters imposed by the doctrine of notice, but it has been said that he must not shut his eyes to suspicious circumstances.[71]

---

[66] It is no longer necessary in England to state that the sale is made in exercise of the statutory power; this is presumed under s. 104 (2) of the Law of Property Act, 1925.

[67] *E.g.*, the mortgagor.

[68] See discussion in *Re Irish Civil Service Building Society and O'Keeffe* (1880) 7 L.R.Ir. 136.

[69] See para. 3.048, *ante.*

[70] See, *e.g.*, *Lord Waring* v. *London and Manchester Assurance Co. Ltd.* [1935] Ch. 310 at 318 (*per* Crossman J.); *Bailey* v. *Barnes* [1894] 1 Ch. 25 at 30 (*per* Stirling J.). The same principle seems to apply in the case of exercise of an express power of sale, see *Jenkins* v. *Jones* (1860) 2 Giff. 99; *Selwyn* v. *Garfit* (1888) 38 Ch.D. 273.

[71] *Bailey* v. *Barnes, op. cit.*, p. 34.

13.030. Further protection is afforded a purchaser by section 22 (1) of the 1881 Act which provides that a receipt in writing of the mortgagee is a sufficient discharge for any money arising under the statutory power of sale and "a person paying or transferring the same to the mortgagee shall not be concerned to inquire whether any money remains due under the mortgage."

(v) Mode of Sale

13.031. The great advantage the statutory power of sale has over a judicial sale in Ireland[72] is that it can be exercised by the mortgagee without the need to apply to the court for any order. Section 19 (1) (i) of the Conveyancing Act, 1881, confers a wide discretion on the mortgagee as to how he sells the mortgaged property or any part of it, namely–"either subject to prior charges, or not, and either together or in lots, by public auction or by private contract, subject to such conditions respecting title, or evidence of title, or other matter, as he (the mortgagee) thinks fit, with power to vary any contract for sale, and to buy in at an auction, or to rescind any contract for sale, and to re-sell, without being answerable for any loss occasioned thereby." Furthermore, section 4 of the Conveyancing Act, 1911, empowers the mortgagee to impose or reserve covenants and conditions[73] on such a sale and to sell the land or any mines and minerals apart from the surface, with the grant or reservation of rights of way, water and other easements and privileges[74] or the exception or reservation of mines and minerals.[75]

13.032. Section 21 (1) provides that the statutory power may be exercised[76] by deed "to convey the property sold, for such estate and interest therein as is the subject of the mortgage, freed from all estates, interests, and rights to which the mortgage has priority, but subject to all estates, interests, and rights which have priority to the mortgage." Once the power becomes exercisable, the mortgagee can demand and recover from any person, other than a person having priority to the mortgage, all the deeds and documents relating to the mortgaged property and its title which a purchaser is entitled to demand and recover from a mortgagee exercising the power of sale.[77]

13.033. It has been held that the statutory power is exercised once the mortgagee enters into a contract to sell the property. Once the contract comes into existence, the mortgagor loses his right to redeem the mortgage and cannot prevent the sale going through by tendering the money due under the mortgage.[78]

---

[72] S. 21 (5) provides that the statutory power of sale does not affect the right of foreclosure, though it has been held that an order for foreclosure *nisi* renders the statutory power temporarily not exercisable without leave of court, *Stevens* v. *Theatres Ltd.* [1903] 1 Ch. 857. However, foreclosure is never granted in Ireland, para. 13.059, *post.*

[73] *E.g.*, restrictive covenants as to building on or other uses of the land, s. 4 (1) (i).

[74] S. 4 (1) (ii) (*a*).

[75] S. 4 (1) (ii) (*b*). See also s. 4 (1) (ii) (*c*) which permits inclusion of covenants by the purchaser to expend money on the land sold.

[76] By any person for the time being entitled to receive and give a discharge for the mortgage money, see s. 21 (4) of the 1881 Act.

[77] 1881 Act, s. 21 (7).

[78] *Lord Waring* v. *London & Manchester Assurance Co. Ltd.* [1935] Ch. 310; *Property & Bloodstock Ltd.* v. *Emerton* [1968] Ch. 94.

(vi) Duty of Care

13.034. The important point to be considered here is the duty of care imposed on the mortgagee when he exercises his power of sale, a matter upon which there has been considerable controversy over the years. In particular, there has been much discussion over how far the mortgagee, in agreeing to sell the mortgaged land for a certain price, can simply have regard to his own interests, by ensuring that this price at least covers what he is owed, and can disregard the interests of others, *e.g.*, subsequent mortgagees also dependent upon that land for their security. It must always be remembered that the question of a sale usually arises because the mortgagor has defaulted and so is probably not worth suing on his personal covenant for repayment of the debt. The selling mortgagee and any other interested mortgagees are almost certainly dependent entirely on their security in the mortgaged land for repayment of their respective debts. Each of them, therefore, has the most vital of interests in how the mortgagee who does exercise the power of sale in fact carries out the sale. Apart from that, the mortgagor, however precarious his moral position in view of his default which has led to the sale, also has a very clear financial interest in how much money the selling mortgagee raises on the sale, because the mortgagor, as we shall see, is entitled to what is left over from the proceeds of sale after payment off of all the mortgages.

13.035. The only guidance on this matter which the Conveyancing Acts give is contained in section 21 (6) of the 1881 Act, as amended by section 5 (2) of the 1911 Act:

> "The mortgagee, his executors, administrators, or assigns, shall not be answerable for any involuntary loss happening in or about the exercise or execution of the power of sale conferred by this Act or of any trust connected therewith [or of any power or provision contained in the mortgage deed[79]]."

13.036. The result of the courts' interpretation of this rather vague provision may be summarised as follows. First, it seems to be accepted that a mortgagee is not a "trustee" for the mortgagor, or any other interested persons, of his power of sale.[80] The power is conferred on the mortgagee primarily to realise his own security and the question of trusteeship does not arise except in respect of the proceeds of sale which come into his hands after the sale has been completed.[81] Secondly, and following on from this, the mortgagee in general cannot be attacked because of his motives in selling, *e.g.*, out of spite for the mortgagor.[82] Thirdly, the mortgagee must, however, act in good faith and this principle was considered by the Supreme Court of the Republic of Ireland in *Holohan* v. *Friends Provident and Century Life*

---

[79]   Added by s. 5 (2) of the 1911 Act.
[80]   *Kennedy* v. *De Trafford* [1897] A.C. 180; *Haddington Island Quarry Co. Ltd.* v. *Huson* [1911] A.C. 722; *Wright* v. *New Zealand Co-Operative Association of Canterbury Ltd.* [1939] A.C. 439. *Cf.* the position under a judicial sale, *Re Beauclerk's Estate* [1907] 1 I.R. 76.
[81]   Para. 13.038, *infra*.
[82]   *Nash* v. *Eads* (1880) 25 Sol.Jo. 95.

Office.[83] In that case the mortgagor was granted an injunction restraining the mortgagees from exercising an express power of sale. The mortgagees had entered into a contract to sell the mortgaged premises, subject to existing tenancies, as an investment and refused to consider the alternative of selling them with vacant possession, which, it was suggested, would secure a much higher price. Ó'Dálaigh C.J. took the view that the good faith principle really involved a test of what a reasonable man would do in the mortgagee's position.[84] In this respect, good faith is not enough, for there should be no reason to doubt the good faith of the reasonable man. What is required is that the mortgagee should bear in mind the interests of the mortgagor and other subsequent mortgagees interested in the property and should take reasonable precautions or care to see that the fair market price for the property is obtained. Indeed, Ó'Dálaigh C.J. took the view that the reasonable man would strive to get the best price available in the circumstances. While this seems to accord with the views expressed in some of the earlier authorities,[85] it does seem to impose a somewhat stricter duty on mortgagees than seems to have been suggested in some of the other earlier authorities. In particular, it seems to impose a much more positive duty to consider the interests of others and to get a fair price for the property than was implied in judicial statements to the effect that the mortgagee need not delay the sale to obtain a better price[86] or advertise the property or attempt a sale by auction before agreeing to sell by private treaty,[87] or that the court will not interfere with a sale at an apparently low or unusual[88] price unless there is evidence of fraud.[89] In passing it should be noted that in both parts of Ireland this matter has been put beyond doubt by statute so far as building societies acting as mortgagees are concerned. By section 36 of the Building Societies Act (N.I.), 1967,[90] they are under a duty

---

[83]   [1966] I.R. 1 (see *A Casebook on Irish Land Law* (1984), p. 447). Cf. as regards a judicial sale, *Bank of Ireland* v. *Smith* [1966] I.R. 646. In *Van Hool McArdle* v. *Rohan Industrial Estates Ltd.* [1980] I.R. 237, it was held that, when an official liquidator sells "subject to the approval of the High Court" and a higher offer is received before that approval is obtained, the court is not obliged to approve the first sale, even though the liquidator acted with all necessary diligence and in good faith.

[84]   *Ibid.*, p. 21. Lavery and Walsh JJ. concurred with Ó'Dálaigh C.J. Cf. the similar reasoning applied in England by the Court of Appeal in *Cuckmere Brick Co. Ltd.* v. *Mutual Finance Ltd.* [1971] Ch. 949. See also *Standard Chartered Bank Ltd.* v. *Walker* [1982] 1 W.L.R. 1410.

[85]   See, *e.g.*, the House of Lords in *Kennedy* v. *De Trafford* [1897] A.C. 180 and the Court of Appeal in *Tomlin* v. *Luce* (1889) 43 Ch.D. 191. Cf. Lord de Villiers in *Haddington Island Quarry Co. Ltd.* v. *Huson* [1911] A.C. 722 at 727 (there must be "no reckless disregard of the interests of the mortgagors").

[86]   *Davey* v. *Durant* (1857) 1 De G. & J. 535 at 533. Cf. *Farrar* v. *Farrars Ltd.* (1888) 40 Ch.D. 395 at 398 (entitled to proceed to a forced sale); *Jones* v. *Matthie* (1847) 11 Jur. 504 at 506 (court not concerned to see if mortgagee "acted with kindness and charity"). In *Casey* v. *Irish Intercontinental Bank Ltd.* [1979] I.R. 364, the Republic's Supreme Court held that, where mortgagees exercising their power of sale of the mortgaged property accepted an offer to purchase at a price (£111,000) which they considered was the best price available, they could not subsequently rescind the contract upon receiving a higher offer (£190,000). Kenny J. said:

> "The subsequent offer of £190,000 did not in any way invalidate that contract which, in my opinion, Intercontinental were bound to carry out. A mortgagee who enters into a contract for sale at a price which all the circumstances and valuations show is, at the date of the contract, the best price available is not discharged if a higher price is offered after the contract is made."

[87]   *Davey* v. *Durrant, op cit.*, p. 560. Cf. the *Cuckmere* case, fn. 84, *supra.*

[88]   *E.g.*, exactly the right amount needed to cover the debt and costs of mortgagee selling, see *Kennedy* v. *De Trafford* [1897] A.C. 180.

[89]   *Adams* v. *Scott* (1859) 7 W.R. 213; *Warner* v. *Jacob* (1882) 20 Ch.D. 220 at 224; *Wright* v. *New Zealand Farmers Co-Operative Association of Canterbury Ltd.* [1939] A.C. 439.

[90]   The same is the position in England, see now s. 36 of the Building Societies Act, 1962, and *Reliance Permanent Building Society* v. *Harwood-Stamper* [1944] Ch. 362.

"to take reasonable care to ensure that the price at which the estate is sold is the best price which can reasonably be obtained . . . ."[91] By section 82 (1) (*a*) of the Republic's Building Societies Act, 1976, they are obliged to ensure "as far as is reasonably practicable that the estate is sold at the best price reasonably obtainable."

13.037.   Finally, it must be remembered that the mortgagee must carry out a "sale." In particular, he must not try to achieve some other purpose by means of a sale, *e.g.*, acquire the land for himself.[92] Just as the mortgagee cannot sell to himself directly,[93] he cannot acquire the property indirectly through an agent or nominee.[94] Nor may servants of mortgagee institutions purchase mortgaged property in a sale by their employers.[95] However, a second mortgagee of the same land may purchase from the first mortgagee.[96]

(vii) Proceeds of Sale

13.038.   While the mortgagee is not a trustee of his *power* of sale, it is expressly provided by section 21 (3) of the Conveyancing Act, 1881, that he is trustee of the *proceeds* of sale arising from his exercise of the power of sale.[97] Under this trust it is provided that the mortgagee must apply the proceeds in the following order[98]:

(1)   in discharge of prior incumbrances to which the sale is not made subject;

(2)   in payment of all costs, charges, and expenses, properly incurred by him, as incident to the sale or any attempted sale, or otherwise;

(3)   in discharge of the mortgage money, interest, and costs, and other money, if any, due under the mortgage;

(4)   by paying the residue to the person entitled to the mortgaged property,[99] or authorised to give receipts for the proceeds of the sale thereof, *i.e.*, the next mortgagee or, if none, the mortgagor.[1]

Thus the mortgagee is liable to account to subsequent mortgagees[2] and interest may become payable if the money is not paid to those entitled.[3]

---

[91]   See *Survey of the Land Law of Northern Ireland* (1971), para. 228.

[92]   *Farrar* v. *Farrars Ltd.* (1888) 40 Ch.D. 395 at 409.

[93]   *Henderson* v. *Astwood* [1894] A.C. 150.

[94]   *Downers* v. *Grazebrook* (1817) 3 Mer. 200; *Robertson* v. *Norris* (1854) 4 Jur.(N.S.) 443; *Nutt* v. *Easton* [1899] 1 Ch. 873.

[95]   *Martinson* v. *Clowes* (1885) 52 L.T. 706; *Hodson* v. *Deans* [1903] 2 Ch. 647. *Cf.* the case of the mortgage employing his own firm of auctioneers to conduct the sale, *Matthison* v. *Clarke* (1854) 3 Drew. 3 (firm disallowed their commission).

[96]   *Shaw* v. *Bunny* (1865) 2 De G.J. & S. 468; *Kirkwood* v. *Thompson* (1865) 2 De G.J. & S. 613.

[97]   See *Thorne* v. *Heard* [1895] A.C. 495; *Re Counter's Charge* [1960] Ch. 491.

[98]   *Re Thompson's Mortgage Trusts* [1920] 1 Ch. 508.

[99]   At first sight this appears to refer to the purchaser from the selling mortgagee, but it obviously must be taken to mean the person who was entitled to the mortgaged property immediately prior to the sale.

[1]   *West London Commercial Bank* v. *Reliance Permanent Building* (1885) 29 Ch.D. 954.

[2]   *Davey* v. *Durrant* (1857) 1 De G. & J. 535; *Bettyes* v. *Maynard* (1883) 31 W.R. 461; *Belton* v. *Bass, Ratcliffe and Gretton Ltd.* [1922] 2 Ch. 449.

[3]   *Charles* v. *Jones* (1887) 35 Ch.D. 544.

However, if the rights of subsequent mortgagees and the mortgagor have been barred by lapse of time,[4] it appears that the selling mortgagee may keep the entire proceeds of sale for himself.[5]

(viii) Effect of Sale

13.039.   Section 21 (1) of the Conveyancing Act, 1881, provides that a sale of the mortgaged property under the Act passes to the purchaser "such estate and interest therein as is the subject of the mortgage, freed from all estates, interests, and rights to which the mortgage has priority, but subject to all estates, interests, and rights which have priority to the mortgage." Thus, in the case of a legal mortgage created by conveyance of the fee simple, the fee simple passes. In the case of a mortgage by demise or sub-demise, the term of years or sub-term in question only passes.[6] In the case of a registered charge on registered land, the power of sale includes power to sell the estate or interest which is subject to the charge.[7] In the case of an equitable mortgage, the equitable interest mortgaged only will pass unless some conveyancing device such as a power of attorney or declaration of trust has been used to enable the legal estate in the land to be transferred.[8] Apart from that, an application may be made to the court for a sale of the property[9] and the court has a general discretion to make any order for conveyance, or vesting order, to give effect to the sale.[10]

3. Court Order for Sale

13.040.   If the mortgagee cannot or does not wish to bring proceedings for possession and if he cannot sell the property without the intervention of the court, he may bring proceedings to have the property sold by the court and the proceeds applied in discharge of the principal and interest secured by his mortgage. The summons claims a declaration that the sum secured by the mortgage is well charged on the defendant's interest in the lands and a sale. The court order gives the declaration, directs an inquiry as to the amount due on the mortgage for principal and interest, and directs a sale of the property if the amount found due is not paid within 3 months from the date of service of the examiner's certificate finding the amount due on the defendant. The sale is carried out under the control of the court which engages an auctioneer and fixes a reserve price, and the money realised on the sale is paid into court. Although it is a court sale, the vendor is the mortgagee who procures the order for sale and if the mortgagor remains in possession after the prop-

---

[4]   See, further, ch. 23, *post.*

[5]   *Young* v. *Clarey* [1948] Ch. 191. Alternatively, as a "trustee" of the proceeds the mortgagee pays them into court under the statutory power conferred on trustees in Ireland by s. 42 of the Trustee Act, 1893, and s. 63 of the Trustee Act (N.I.), 1958. See as regards mortgagees, *Banner* v. *Berridge* (1881) 18 Ch.D. 254 (surplus proceeds); *Re Walkhampton Estate* (1884) 26 Ch.D. 391 and *Charles* v. *Jones* (1887) 35 Ch.D. 544 (doubt as to proper recipients of proceeds).

[6]   In the case of a sub-demise the mortgagor may make a declaration of trust as to the whole term so as to enable the mortgagee to sell this, see *London & County Banking Co.* v. *Goddard* [1897] 1 Ch. 642.

[7]   Registration of Title Act, 1964, s. 62 (6) (R.I.); Land Registration Act (N.I.), 1970, Sched 7, Pt. 1, para. 5 (1). See *Re Neely* [1936] I.R. 381.

[8]   See para. 13.024, *ante.*

[9]   See s. 5 of the Conveyancing Act, 1881, as amended by s. 1 of the Conveyancing Act, 1911, relating to discharge of incumbrances on land.

[10]   1881 Act, s. 5 (2).

erty has been sold with vacant possession, it is the duty of the mortgagee to apply to the court for an order that the purchaser be put into possession.[11]

13.041.   The order made by the court directing a sale also directs an inquiry as to other mortgages and their priorities and, when the funds in court are being allocated, if there is sufficient to pay the first mortgagee's principal, interests and costs, the balance remaining will be applied in discharge of the amount due to the second mortgagee for principal and interest, and any sum remaining after payment of all the sums due on the mortgages will be paid to the mortgagor. When there is no dispute about the amount due on the mortgage for principal and interest, the court finds the amount due in its original order and does not direct an inquiry as to the amount due. When this is done, the order, and not the examiner's certificate, has to be served on the mortgagor, and the three months run from the date of this service.

4. Taking Possession

13.042.   This is the fourth main remedy available to a mortgagee and the main distinction from the first three is that taking possession does not of itself put an end to the mortgage and secure repayment of the capital debt.[12] It may, of course, be invoked as a preliminary to exercising another remedy, e.g., the power of sale,[13] but for the most part a mortgagee is not interested in taking possession and is happy to allow the mortgagor to keep it.[14] If the mortgagee does take possession it is often to secure regular payment of the interest charged on the capital sum lent, by interception of the rents and profits issuing out of the land.[15]

(i) Mortgagees Entitled

13.043.   Where a legal mortgage is created by conveyance, assignment, demise or sub-demise of a freehold or leasehold estate in the land, it is inherent in the nature of the transaction that the mortgagee is entitled to claim possession of the property as holder of the estate in question as soon as the mortgage is created.[16] He can either claim physical possession or, if this is in the hands of some person with a prior claim to it, e.g., an existing tenant, he can direct that person to pay to him any rents which might otherwise be

---

[11]   *Bank of Ireland* v. *Waldrow* [1944] I.R. 303. Note the power to adjourn proceedings where the sale involves a family home under s. 7 of the Republic's Family Home Protection Act, 1976, see para. 13.021, *ante*.

[12]   See, generally, Rudden, "Mortgagee's Right to Possession" (1961) 25 Conv. 278; Smith, "The Mortgagee's Right to Possession: The Modern View" [1979] Conv. 266.

[13]   *Bank of Ireland Ltd.* v. *Slattery* [1911] 1 I.R. 33; *Royal Bank of Ireland* v. *O'Shea* (1943) 77 I.L.T.R. 4; *Ulster Bank, Ltd.* v. *Conlon* (1957) 91 I.L.T.R. 193. *Cf. Doran* v. *Hannin* (1906) 40 I.L.T.R 186 (to prevent forfeiture of licence of licensed premises).

[14]   Para. 12.15, *ante*.

[15]   *Horlock* v. *Smith* (1842) 6 Jur. 478; *Heales* v. *McMurray* (1856) 23 Beav. 401; *Mexborough U.D.C.* v. *Harrison* [1964] 1 W.L.R. 733. And see Bodkin, "Tenants and Mortgagees" (1952) 16 Conv. 285.

[16]   *Green* v. *Burns* (1879) 6 L.R.Ir. 173. See also *Four-Maids Ltd.* v. *Dudley Marshall (Properties) Ltd.* [1957] Ch. 317; *Birmingham Citizens Permanent Building Society* v. *Caunt* [1962] Ch. 883. If the mortgagee allows the mortgagor to remain in possession, then, subject to the terms of the mortgage, the mortgagor is a tenant at sufferance, but he is entitled to receive and keep all the rents and profits from the land, without accounting for them to the mortgagee. *Ex parte Calwell* (1828) 1 Mol. 259; *Patterson* v. *Reilly* (1882) 10 L.R.Ir. 304; *Campion* v. *Palmer* [1896] 2 I.R. 445.

paid to the mortgagor. So far as a registered chargee on registered land is concerned, since he has no estate in the land it would seem that he has no right initially to take possession of the land.[17] It would seem that the only way to gain possession, if he wants it, is to seek the permission of the chargor or, if that is refused, an order of the court.[18] As we mentioned earlier, in the Republic of Ireland, the registered owner of the charge or his personal representative may apply to the court in a summary manner, under section 62 (7) of the Registration of Title Act, 1964, for possession of the land and, if the court thinks it proper to order possession and the applicant obtains it, he is deemed to be a mortgagee in possession. This power in the Republic is confined to when the principal money secured by the mortgage has become due, but, in Northern Ireland, the power of the court to award possession to the registered owner of a charge under paragraph 5 (2) of Part I of Schedule 7 to the Land Registration Act (N.I.), 1970, though generally similarly confined, may be exercised, under paragraph 5 (3) (b) of the same Part and Schedule, where the court is satisfied that, although payment of the principal sum has not become due, "there are urgent and special reasons for exercising the power."[19]

13.044. So far as an equitable mortgagee is concerned, there has been much controversy as to his right to claim possession.[20] It is clear that he has no right to possession at law since he has no legal estate in the land, unless, of course, the mortgage agreement confers such a right on him.[21] On the other hand, it is arguable that, in equity at least, he ought to be put in the same position as if he had the legal title to the property and there is some authority in Ireland for saying that he is entitled to possession in his own right, especially as against the mortgagor.[22] Whatever an equitable mortgagee's position in theory,[23] it is settled that he can apply to the court for an order for

---

[17]   *Northern Banking Co. Ltd.* v. *Devlin* [1924] 1 I.R. 90. The reference in s. 62 (6) of the Registration of Title Act, 1964 (R.I.) to a registered chargee having "all the rights and powers of a mortgagee under a mortgage by deed" seems to refer back to the earlier reference to "a mortgage by deed within the meaning of the Conveyancing Acts," *i.e.*, it is confined to matters within s. 19 of the 1881 Act–sale, appointment of a receiver, insurance etc. *Cf.* the wording of para. 5 (1) of Pt. I of Sched. 7 to the Land Registration Act (N.I.), 1970, which seems to make this point clearer.

[18]   *Bank of Ireland Ltd.* v. *Feeney* [1930] I.R. 457, espec. at 469 (*per* Kennedy C.J.).

[19]   See *Re Jacks* [1952] I.R. 159.

[20]   See Wade, "Equitable Mortgagee's Right to Possession" (1955) 71 L.Q.R. 205; Willoughby, "Rights of Second Mortgagees Regarding Possession" (1908) 24 L.Q.R. 297. See also Coote, *Law of Mortgages* (9th ed., 1927), p. 823; Waldock, *Mortgages* (2nd ed., 1950), p. 235.

[21]   Or the mortgagor, or first legal mortgagee, subsequently agrees to this. See *Northern Banking Co. Ltd.* v. *Devlin* [1924] 1 I.R. 90 at 92 (*per* Andrews L.J.). *Cf. Ocean Accident & Guarantee Co. Ltd.* v. *Ilford Gas Co.* [1905] 2 K.B. 493.

[22]   See especially the judgment of Palles C.B. in *Antrim County Land, Building and Investment Co. Ltd.* v. *Stewart* [1904] 2 I.R. 357 (see *A Casebook on Irish Land Law* (1984), p. 426). Also *National Bank Ltd.* v. *Hegarty* (1901) 1 N.I.J.R. 13; *Re O'Neill* [1967] N.I. 129. *Cf. Re Gordon* (1889) 61 L.T. 299; *Spencer* v. *Mason* (1931) 75 Sol.Jo. 295; *Barclays Bank Ltd.* v. *Bird* [1954] Ch. 274. See also *Malone* v. *Geraghty* (1852) 1 H.L.C. 89.

[23]   It seems that he cannot intercept the rents and profits from the land, since the right to these belongs to the legal reversioner and there is no legal relationship of landlord and tenant between an equitable mortgagee and a tenant in possession of the mortgaged land, see *Finck* v. *Tranter* [1905] 1 K.B. 427; *Vacuum Oil Co. Ltd.* v. *Ellis* [1914] 1 K.B. 693.

possession[24] and the only restriction is the principle that all equitable remedies are discretionary.[25]

A mere equitable chargee has no right to possession since he has neither a legal nor an equitable estate or interest in the property mortgaged.[26]

(ii) Procedure

13.045.   Should the mortgagor refuse to allow a mortgagee to exercise his right to take possession of the mortgaged land, the mortgagee may initiate an action for ejectment or, if he prefers nowadays, simply make a summary application for an order of possession.[27] This summary procedure, which we mentioned earlier,[28] has removed one of the main reasons for frequent insertion of a particular clause in mortgage deeds, namely, an attornment clause.[29] Through such a clause, the mortgagor usually attorns, *i.e.*, acknowledges, himself to be the tenant of the mortgagee, thereby creating the relationship of landlord and tenant between himself and the mortgagee, so far as this is consistent with the mortgage transaction.[30] The clause may still be relevant today because, *e.g.*, it may provide that the mortgagor's tenancy cannot be determined except by the mortgagee giving a certain period of notice. The necessity for such a notice would obviously restrict the mortgagee in claiming possession of the land.[31] The existence of a relationship of landlord and tenant under an attornment clause may also facilitate the running more widely of the burden of covenants entered into between the mortgagor and mortgagee.[32]

[24]   See Lowry J. in *Re O'Neill* [1967] N.I. 129 at 135: ". . . the Supreme Court has an inherent jurisdiction to make an order putting a legal or equitable mortgagee into possession and . . . such an order may be made not only in the Chancery Division, but also by a judge exercising bankruptcy jurisdiction in the Queen's Bench Division." Para. 13.018, *ante*.

[25]   Para. 3.050, *ante*. The court has no discretion to refuse an order to a legal mortgagee but may grant a short adjournment if there is a reasonable prospect that the mortgagor may redeem the mortgage. See *Birmingham Citizens Permanent Building Society* v. *Caunt* [1962] Ch. 883; *London Permanent Benefit Building Society* v. *De Baer* [1969] 1 Ch. 321. Also Megarry, (1957) 73 L.Q.R. 300.

[26]   *National Bank Ltd.* v. *Hegarty* (1901) 1 N.I.J.R. 13; *Bank of Ireland Ltd.* v. *Feeney* [1930] I.R. 457.

[27]   See *Doran* v. *Hannin* (1906) 40 I.L.T.R. 186; *Bank of Ireland Ltd.* v. *Slattery* [1911] 1 I.R. 33; *Bunyan* v. *Bunyan* [1916] 1 I.R. 70; *National Bank* v. *Shanahan* (1932) 66 I.L.T.R. 120; *Irish Permanent Building Society* v. *Ryan* [1950] I.R. 12; *Ulster Bank Ltd.* v. *Conlon* (1957) 91 I.L.T.R. 193; *Irish Civil Service (Permanent) Building Society* v. *Ingram's Representatives* [1959] I.R. 181. Also *Re Jacks* [1952] I.R. 159 (registered chargee). Note again the power to adjourn proceedings to recover possession of a family home conferred by s. 7 of the Republic's Family Home Protection Act, 1976 (para. 13.021, *ante*). See also s. 86 (3) of the Judicature (N.I.) Act, 1978, and the English cases cited in para. 13.018, fn. 39, *ante*; Smith, "The Mortgagee's Right to Possession: The Modern View" [1979] Conv. 266.

[28]   Paras. 13.019–20, *ante*.

[29]   Gray, "The Attornment Clause" (1948) 13 Conv. 31; Keeton and Sheridan, *Equity* (1969), pp. 232–5. Note also the Form of Attornment (No. 6) by under-tenants or occupiers of land in Sched. A to Deasy's Act, 1860, ch. 17, *post*.

[30]   See the discussion in the English cases, where it has been held that the mortgagor-tenant cannot claim statutory protection under legislation like the Rent Acts or Agricultural Holdings Acts, *Portman Building Society* v. *Young* [1951] 1 All E.R. 191; *Steyning and Littlehampton Building Society* v. *Wilson* [1951] Ch. 1018; *Alliance Building Society* v. *Pinwill* [1958] Ch. 788; *Jessamine Investment Co.* v. *Schwartz* [1977] 2 W.L.R. 145. And see Megarry, (1958) 74 L.Q.R. 348; Baker, (1965) 81 L.Q.R. 341; (1966) 82 L.Q.R. 21. *Cf.* summary recovery of possession of "cottier" tenements under ss. 81–9 of Deasy's Act, 1860, ch. 17, *post*. *Cf.* the English Small Tenements Recovery Act, 1838, see *Dudley and District Benefit Society* v. *Gordon* [1929] 2 K.B. 105.

[31]   *Hinckley and Country Building Society* v. *Henry* [1953] 1 W.L.R. 352. *Cf. Alliance Building Society* v. *Pinwill* [1958] Ch. 788.

[32]   *Regent Oil Co. Ltd.* v. *J.A. Gregory (Hatch End) Ltd.* [1966] Ch. 402. See further on the running of the benefit and burden of covenants, ch. 19, *post*.

(iii) Liability to Account Strictly

13.046. In exercising his right to take possession of the mortgaged land the mortgagee is entitled to safeguard the payments of interest due to him and may, though he is not obliged to do this, devote any surplus rents and profits towards repayment of the capital remaining owing to him.[33] He is also entitled to allowances where he expends money in repairs to the property or in meeting other outgoings, such as head-rents.[34] Section 19 (1) (iv) of the Conveyancing Act, 1881, permits a mortgagee by deed in possession to cut and sell timber and other trees ripe for cutting and not planted or left standing for shelter or ornament. This section also permits the mortgagee in possession to enter into a contract for any such cutting and sale, provided it is to be completed within twelve months from the making of the contract. While the mortgagee is not generally liable for waste, he is not allowed to cut timber other than as allowed under the 1881 Act or to open new mines as opposed to working existing ones.[35] However, in equity he will be allowed to do such things if the land is otherwise insufficient security for the debt, with the qualification that he must not commit "equitable" waste or wanton destruction.[36]

13.047. Apart from this, a mortgagee in possession is liable to account strictly, *i.e.*, on the footing of wilful default, to the mortgagor.[37] He must account not only for the rents and profits which he actually receives but also for those which he would have received, but for his default or mismanagement.[38] If a mortgagee fails to render accounts, he may find himself charged with interest[39] and subsequently deprived of his costs in a redemption suit, even though the entire debt has not been paid.[40] It is part of the same principle of accounting that a mortgagee in possession must try to keep the charges involved as low as possible and so, in general, is not entitled to charge remuneration for any work he does, *e.g.*, in keeping a business going on the mortgaged premises. Indeed, in *Comyns v. Comyns*[41] Sullivan M.R. even held void an express stipulation in the mortgage deed that the mortgagee could have £100 a year for his trouble in managing the mortgaged land.[42]

---

[33] *Nelson v. Booth* (1858) 3 De G. & J. 119; *Wrigley v. Gill* [1905] 1 Ch. 241.

[34] *Burrowes v. Molloy* (1845) 8 Ir.Eq.R. 482. He may also be entitled to make reasonable improvement to the property, chargeable to the mortgagor, so long as these do not hinder the power of redemption, *Shepard v. Jones* (1882) 21 Ch.D. 469 at 479.

[35] See *Millet v. Davey* (1836) 31 Beav. 470; *Elias v. Snowdon Slate Quarries Co.* (1879) 4 App.Cas. 454.

[36] *Sandon v. Hooper* (1844) 14 L.J.Ch. 120; *Millett v. Davey* (1863) 31 Beav. 470 at 476 (*per* Romilly M.R.). See, further, on equitable waste, para. 4.154, *ante*.

[37] *Lord Trimleston v. Hamill* (1810) 1 Ba. & B. 377; *Sloane v. Mahon* (1838) 1 Dr. & Wal. 189. See also *Unthank v. Gabbett* (1830) Beat. 453. And see Markson, "Liability of Lenders in Possession" (1979) 129 New L.J. 334. A first mortgagee in possession may also have to account to subsequent mortgagees, *Ocean Accident and Guarantee Co. Ltd. v. Collum* [1913] 1 I.R. 328.

[38] *Metcalf v. Campion* (1828) 1 Mol. 238; *O'Connell v. O'Callaghan* (1863) 15 Ir.Ch.R. 31. See also *Burke v. O'Connor* (1853) 4 Ir.Ch.R. 418. Cf. *Hughes v. Williams* (1806) 12 Ves. 493; *Marshall v. Cave* (1824) L.J. (O.S.)Ch. 57; *White v. City of London Brewery Co.* (1889) 42 Ch.D. 237.

[39] Where courts have made orders directing accounts against mortgagees in Ireland, the practice seems to have been to make half-yearly rests and not to charge interest on payments received by the mortgagee during intermediate periods, which exceed the interest due, see *Graham v. Walker* (1847) 11 Ir.Eq.R. 415.

[40] *Cassidy v. Sullivan* (1878) 1 L.R.Ir. 313. See also *Burke v. O'Connor* (1853) 4 Ir.Ch.R. 418.

[41] (1871) I.R. 5 Eq. 583.

[42] The learned judge took the view that this amounted to a clog on the equity of redemption, see para. 13.090, *post*.

Sometimes, this principle is put another way, that, having taken possession himself instead of appointing a receiver,[43] the mortgagee cannot turn round and charge a receiver's commission.[44]

Finally, it may be noted that the mortgagee may acquire the full title to the land by adverse possession, *i.e.*, his possession may extinguish the mortgagor's right to redeem under the Statute of Limitations.[45]

5. *Appointment of a Receiver*

13.048.   As we have just discussed, there are many drawbacks about the mortgagee himself taking possession of the mortgaged property and from the earliest stages of development of the law of mortgages it became the practice to achieve the same result, *i.e.*, more efficient management of the property to safeguard the mortgagee's interest payments, by a slightly different means.[46] This was the appointment of a receiver who would be given extensive powers to manage the mortgaged property, a procedure which can most usually be adopted in cases where that property comprises a business, such as an hotel or shop, whose value as security is largely dependent upon the efficient running of the business.[47]

13.049.   In the early days, it seems that receivers were often appointed by the mortgagor at the request of the mortgagee. Then the practice developed of insertion in the mortgage deed of a clause reserving to the mortgagee the right to appoint a receiver.[48] However, this clause would usually state expressly that such a receiver would be deemed to be nevertheless agent of the mortgagor, a theory which, as we shall see, holds good today and avoids many of the difficulties involved in the mortgagee himself taking possession.[49] Then Lord Cranworth's Act, 1860,[50] conferred a limited statutory power to appoint receivers on mortgagees and this was replaced by section 19 (1) of the Conveyancing Act, 1881, which still governs the matter in both parts of Ireland.

(i) Mortgagees Entitled

13.050.   As in the case of the power of sale also conferred by section 19 (1) of the 1881 Act, the power to appoint a receiver[51] is conferred on mortgagees whose mortgages are created by deed and this covers most legal mortgages

---

[43]   See para. 13.048, *infra*.

[44]   *Carew* v. *Johnston* (1805) 2 Sch. & Lef. 280 at 301 (*per* Lord Redesdale). See also *Kavanagh* v. *Workingman's Benefit Building Society* [1896] 1 I.R. 56 (agent appointed to collect rents by mortgagees in possession not allowed commission).

[45]   See ch. 23, *post*.

[46]   One point of distinction from the mortgagee himself taking possession is that the doctrine of adverse possession cannot work in favour of a mortgagee who has appointed a receiver, see ch. 23, *post*.

[47]   See Lyle, *Handbook for Receivers* (1878); also *Alven* v. *Bond* (1841) 3 Ir.Eq.R. 365; *Ardmore Studios (Ireland) Ltd.* v. *Lynch* [1965] I.R. 1; *Kernohan Estates Ltd.* v. *Boyd* [1967] N.I. 27 (see *A Casebook on Equity and Trusts in Ireland* (1985), p. 306).

[48]   See, generally, Kerr, *Law and Practice as to Receivers* (14th ed., by Walton, 1972). Also Molesworth, *Receivers in Chancery in Ireland* (1838). See also *Industrial Development Authority* v. *Moran* [1978] I.R. 159 (para. 11.33, *ante*).

[49]   Para. 13.054, *post*.

[50]   Ss. 17–23.

[51]   See s. 19 (1) (iii).

and registered chargees.[52] It also applies to an equitable mortgagee or chargee if the mortagage or charge is created by deed.[53] If the mortgage or charge is not created by deed, the equitable mortgagee or chargee will have to apply, as can any mortgagee or chargee, to the court for the appointment of a receiver. Prior to the Judicature (Ireland) Act, 1877, the courts of equity claimed jurisdiction to appoint a receiver, who, incidentally, in such a case is not an agent for either party but an officer of the court.[54] Normally relief would be given to equitable mortgagees only, on the ground that a legal mortgagee could help himself by invoking his right to take possession. Now section 28 (8) of the 1877 Act confers jurisdiction on the court to make appointments on such terms as it thinks fit in all cases, including legal mortgages, where it appears to be just or convenient to do so.[55]

(ii) Power Arises

The power to appoint a receiver out of court arises when the mortgage money is due,[56] as in the case of the power of sale out of court.[57]

(iii) Power Exercisable

The power does not become exercisable until one of the three events specified in the 1881 Act[58] for exercise of the power of sale occurs.[59]

(iv) Procedure

13.051. The mortgagee must appoint in writing the person he thinks fit to act as receiver.[60] The mortgagee may also remove the receiver and appoint a new one, again provided he does so in writing.[61] The receiver may be directed in writing by the mortagee to insure and keep insured against loss or damage by fire, out of money received, any building, effects or property comprised in the mortgage, whether affixed to the freehold or not, being of an insurable nature.[62]

(v) Functions

13.052. The main function of a receiver is to manage the mortgaged property and to intercept the rents and profits to ensure that they do not go directly to the mortgagor and that they are first used, *inter alia*, to pay interest

---

[52] Para. 13.024, *ante*. A mortgagee in possession may still appoint a receiver, who will take over possession, see *Refuge Assurance Co. Ltd.* v. *Pearlberg* [1938] Ch. 687.

[53] Para. 13.025, *ante*.

[54] See *Marchioness of Downshire* v. *Tyrrell* (1831) Hayes 354; *Weldon* v. *O'Reilly* (1841) Fl. & K. 320; *Geale* v. *Nugent* (1849) 1 Ir.Jur.(O.S.) 341; *Barber* v. *Roe* (1842) Long. & Town. 655, Reilly, *Practice of High Court of Chancery in Ireland* (1855).

[55] In N.I. s. 28 (8) of the 1877 Act has been replaced by s. 91 of the Judicature (Northern Ireland) Act, 1978 (U.K.). See *Commissioners of Church Temporalities of Ireland* v. *Harrington* (1833) 11 L.R.Ir. 127; *Kennedy* v. *O'Keeffe* (1900) 34 I.L.T.R. 75; *McCausland* v. *O'Callaghan* (1903) 3 N.I.J.R. 144; *Langdale Chemical Manure Co.* v. *Ginty* (1907) 41 I.L.T.R. 40; *Butler* v. *Butler* [1925] 1 I.R. 185; *National Bank Ltd.* v. *Barry* (1966) 100 I.L.T.R. 185.

[56] 1881 Act, s. 19 (1).

[57] Para. 13.026, *ante*.

[58] S. 20, see para. 13.027, *ante*.

[59] 1881 Act, s. 24 (1).

[60] *Ibid.*

[61] 1881 Act, s. 24 (5).

[62] *Ibid.*, s. 24 (7).

due on the loan to the mortgagee.[63] To enable him to carry out these functions, section 24 (3) of the Conveyancing Act, 1881, provides:

"The receiver shall have power to demand and recover all the income of the property of which he is appointed receiver, by action, distress,[64] or otherwise, in the name either of the mortgagor or of the mortgagee, to the full extent of the estate or interest which the mortgagor could dispose of, and to give effectual receipts, accordingly, for the same."[65]

The receiver is entitled to keep out of any money received by him, as remuneration and in satisfaction of all costs, charges and expenses incurred by him as receiver, commission at the rate specified in his appointment, provided this does not exceed 5 per cent. on the gross amount of all money received.[66] If no rate is specified, the rate of commission is to be 5 per cent. or such higher rate as the court thinks fit to allow, on an application made by the receiver for that purpose.[67]

(vi) Application of Receipts

13.053. Section 24 (8) of the Conveyancing Act, 1881, provides that all money received by a receiver must be applied by him in the following order:

(1) In discharge of all rents, taxes, and outgoings whatever affecting the mortgaged property; and

(2) In keeping down all annual sums or other payments, and the interest on all principal sums, having priority to the mortgage in right whereof he is receiver; and

(3) In payment of his commission, and of the premiums on fire, life or other insurances, if any, properly payable under the mortgage deed or under the 1881 Act, and the cost of executing necessary or proper repairs directed in writing by the mortgagee[68]; and

(4) In payment of the interest accruing due[69] in respect of any principal money due under the mortgage; and

(5) In payment of the residue of the money received by him to the person who, but for the possession of the receiver, would have been entitled to receive the income of the mortgaged property, or who is otherwise entitled to that property.[70]

---

[63] *Callaghan* v. *Reardon* (1837) S. & Sc. 682; *Walsh* v. *Walsh* (1839) 1 Ir.Eq.R. 209; *Alven* v. *Bond* (1841) 3 Ir.Eq.R. 365; *Balfe* v. *Blake* (1850) 1 Ir.Ch.R. 365; *Re Annaly* (1891) 27 L.R.Ir. 523 (see *A Casebook on Equity and Trusts in Ireland* (1985), p. 300)

[64] Abolished in Northern Ireland under s. 122 of the Judgments (Enforcement) Act (N.I.), 1969. See ch. 17, *post*.

[65] See *Fairholme and Palliser* v. *Kennedy* (1889) 24 L.R.Ir. 498.

[66] 1881 Act, s. 24 (6).

[67] *Ibid*. Note that a mortgagee in possession may not, in general, charge commission; *Carew* v. *Johnson* (1805) 2 Sch. & Lef. 280 at 301 (*per* Lord Redesdale). See para. 13.047, *ante*.

[68] See *White* v. *Metcalf* [1903] 2 Ch. 567.

[69] Whether before or after the appointment of the receiver, *National Bank Ltd.* v. *Kenney* [1898] 1 I.R. 197. However, the receiver must not pay statute-barred arrears of interest, *Hibernian Bank* v. *Yourell (No. 2)* [1919] 1 I.R. 310. It also seems that the mortgagee is entitled to an account from the receiver in respect of such payments, see *Leicester Permanent Building Society* v. *Butt* [1943] Ch. 308. In England, s. 109 (8) of the Law of Property Act, 1925, added, after no (4), in or towards discharge of the principal money if so directed in writing by the mortgagee.

[70] *I.e.*, normally the mortgagor. A prior mortgagee is normally entitled in priority to a puisne mortgagee, *Lord Lismore* v. *Chamley* (1831) Hayes 329.

(vii) Agent of Mortgagor

13.054. Section 24 (2) of the 1881 Act now provides expressly on this matter:

> "The receiver shall be deemed to be the agent of the mortgagor; and the mortgagor shall be solely responsible for the receiver's acts or defaults, unless the mortgage deed otherwise provides."[71]

The result, therefore, is that by appointing a receiver the mortgagee cannot be regarded as taking possession and so is not liable to account strictly to the mortgagor.[72]

(viii) Protection of Third Parties

13.055. Just as purchasers dealing with a mortgagee exercising his statutory power of sale are given statutory protection,[73] so too are persons paying money to a receiver. Section 24 (4) of the Conveyancing Act, 1881, provides that such persons are not to be concerned to inquire whether any case has happened to authorise the receiver to act. In other words, they are not concerned with whether the mortgagee's power of appointment was exercisable as opposed to whether it had arisen.

6. *Foreclosure*

13.056. Foreclosure is a judicial proceeding by which the mortgagee seeks to have the mortgagor's equitable right to redeem the property declared to be extinguished so that the mortgagee becomes full owner of it. When the principal secured by the mortgage has become due, the mortgagee may bring these proceedings. The initial order is a decree *nisi*, which directs that accounts be taken to establish the amount due and whether other encumbrances affect the land and which provides that unless (*nisi*) the mortgagor redeems the mortgage by a date fixed by the court (usually either 3 or 6 months from the day when the decree *nisi* is made), the order will become absolute and the mortgagor is then foreclosed. Foreclosure means that the mortgagor's equity of redemption is extinguished. It is thus possible that the mortgagee would become owner of a property which was worth considerably more than the amount due to him. It also has the result that mortgagees whose charges are subsequent to that of the first mortgagee are not paid anything unless they redeem the first mortgage, because the first mortgagee, when the order *nisi* becomes absolute, takes the property free of all subsequent mortgages.

13.057. After 1881, the courts in England were given a statutory power to order a sale of the property in a foreclosure action by section 25 of the

---

[71] See also *Chinnery* v. *Evans* (1864) 11 H.L.C. 115.

[72] See *Re Marchesa Della Rocella's Estate* (1899) 29 L.R.Ir. 464 (see *A Casebook on Equity and Trusts in Ireland* (1985), p. 305). Also *Lever Finance Ltd.* v. *Needleman's Estate* [1956] Ch. 375. *Cf.* where the powers of leasing and of accepting surrenders of leases conferred by s. 18 of the Conveyancing Act, 1881, and s. 3 of the Conveyancing Act, 1911, are exercised after a receiver is appointed, see s. 3 (1) of the 1911 Act. Also para. 13.111, *post.*

[73] Para. 13.028, *ante.*

Conveyancing Act, 1881, but this did not apply to Ireland.[74] This provided that any person entitled to redeem mortgaged property could have a judgment for sale instead of for redemption and that in any action, whether for foreclosure or redemption or sale or for the raising and payment of monies due on the mortgage, the court, on the request of the mortgagee or of any person interested either in the mortgage money or in the right of redemption, might, if it thought fit, direct a sale of the mortgaged property.[75]

13.058. The basis of foreclosure was explained by Palles C.B. in this way:

"The essence of a charge by way of mortgage was that a period should be named at which, in the event of non-payment, there should be forfeiture of the estate at law. The contract was to pay at a definite time, but equity, not deeming the time material, gave a further reasonable time for payment; but as it insisted upon the mortgagor losing the estate in case he did not then pay within the further time given, the necessary result was that the estate should be subject to foreclosure as well as redemption."[76]

13.059. Foreclosure as a remedy for a mortgagee has been unknown in Ireland for centuries, though the courts have been careful to state that there is jurisdiction to order foreclosure but that this power will be exercised in exceptional circumstances only. In *Bruce* v. *Brophy*,[77] Walker L.C. remarked: "I do not say that, under special circumstances, and where a special case is made for foreclosure, the court has not power to grant a decree for foreclosure and not a sale."[78] But in the same case he referred to the "settled practice for centuries of decreeing a sale and not foreclosure." Considerable confusion has been caused by the fact that the decree made in Ireland in a mortgage suit was usually called "a decree for foreclosure and sale"[79] although the order made in a mortgage suit has not been given this name during the past 40 years. *Re Power and Carton's Contract*[80] has sometimes been cited as an example of an Irish Court ordering foreclosure, but there the original order for foreclosure was made in England and not in Ireland.

13.060. The reasons why foreclosure was never a remedy in Ireland, and why the relief given to a mortgagee was a sale, arise not from any statutory provision or decision but from the growth of a settled practice which

---

[74] S. 25 (7).

[75] See now for England, Law of Property Act, 1925, s. 91 (2). See also Markson, "Foreclosure for Closure?" (1979) 129 New L.J. 33.

[76] *Shea* v. *Moore* [1894] 1 I.R. 158 at 178. *Cf.* Jessel M.R. in *Carter* v. *Wake* (1877) 4 Ch.D. 605 at 606: "the court simply removes the stop it has itself put on." See also Lord Selbourne L.C. in *Heath* v. *Pugh* (1881) 6 Q.B.D. 345 at 359–61.

[77] [1906] 1 I.R. 611 at 616 (see *A Casebook on Irish Land Laws in Ireland* (1984), p. 456). The learned judge did not elaborate on what he regarded as special circumstances or a special case.

[78] See also McMahon M.R. in *McMahon* v. *Shewbridge* (1814) 2 Ba. & B. 555 at 563 and Holmes L.J. in *Waters* v. *Lloyd* [1911] 1 I.R. 153 at 161–3.

[79] See *Bruce* v. *Brophy, op. cit.* (*per* Barton J.).

[80] (1890) 25 L.R.Ir. 459.

generations of judges have followed. In one case, Fitzgibbon L.J. said that in Ireland foreclosure fell into disuse because there was a special procedure for realising mortgages by court receivers and by sales in the Landed Estates Court.[81] He went on to add, however, that puisne mortgagees had the same right of foreclosure in Ireland as they had in England, but the accuracy of this statement is extremely doubtful. The view that foreclosure fell into disuse because there was a method of getting a sale in the Landed Estates Court does not explain why the relief granted to a mortgagee in Ireland is invariably a sale, because the practice of ordering a sale had become settled long before the Landed Estates Court was established.[82] The more likely explanation is that second and third mortgages were far more common in Ireland than in England and that, as foreclosure as a remedy would have the result that they would get nothing in respect of their principal unless they redeemed the first mortgage, a sale of the property was the only way in which their interests could be safeguarded.

13.061. Although foreclosure as a remedy is unknown in Ireland, the court undoubtedly has jurisdiction to make an order of foreclosure and so we propose to outline the main features of it. Those who want a more detailed account of it should refer to some of the standard English text books on the subject.

(i) Parties Entitled

13.062. An equitable mortgagee may get a foreclosure order and, if he does, it takes the form of a direction to the mortgagor, as holder of the legal title in the land, to convey that title to the mortgagee freed any right of redemption.[83] The right to bring foreclosure proceedings does not arise until repayment of the mortgage becomes due at law, i.e., the legal date for redemption has passed.[84] Foreclosure proceedings are brought against those interested in the equity of redemption relating to the mortgage in question, and so the mortgagor and any subsequent mortgagees must be made defendants.[85] A mortgagee whose encumbrance is prior in point of time to the mortgagee seeking redemption need not be made a party because he will

---

[81]   Antrim County Land, Building, and Investment Co. Ltd. v. Stewart [1904] 2 I.R. 357 at 369: "In Ireland, foreclosure fell into disuse, because there was here a special procedure for realising mortgages by Court Receivers, and by sales in the Landed Estates Court; . . ." (see A Casebook on Irish Land Law (1984), p. 426). See further on sales in the Landed Estates Court, para, 1.42, ante. Cf. Coffin, "Foreclosure and Sale in Nova Scotia" (1954) 32 C.B.R. 217.

[82]   Hulton v. Mayne (1846) 9 Ir.Eq.R. 343. Cf. Loughran v. Loughran (1885) 15 L.R.Ir. 71; Re Lloyd [1911] 1 I.R. 153. See also Greene v. Stoney (1851) 13 Ir.Eq.R. 301; Burrowes v. Molloy (1845) 8 Ir.Eq.R. 482.

[83]   Shea v. Moore [1894] 1 I.R. 158 at 178; Antrim County Land, Building and Investment Co. Ltd. v. Stewart [1904] 2 I.R. 357 at 369 (see A Casebook on Irish Land Law (1984), p. 426). This includes the case of an equitable mortgagee by deposit, see Parker v. Housefield (1834) 2 My. & K. 419 (title deeds); Backhouse v. Charlton (1878) 8 Ch.D. 444 (title deeds); Harrold v. Plenty [1901] 2 Ch. 314.

[84]   Para. 12.05, ante. See the recent discussion on this point in Twentieth Century Banking Corp Ltd. v. Wilkinson [1976] 3 W.L.R. 489, wherein Templeman J. relied heavily on the judgment of Sugden L.C. in the Irish case of Burrowes v. Molloy (1845) 2 Jo. & Lat. 521.

[85]   See Munster Bank Ltd. v. Jervis (1902) 36 I.L.T.R. 113. Also Rolleston v. Morton (1842) 4 Ir.Eq.R. 149; Davis v. Rowan (1843) 3 Dr. & War. 478. Cf. Going v. Farrell (1814) Beat. 472. Also Bishop of Winchester v. Paine (1805) 11 Ves. 194.

not be affected by the foreclosure order,[86] but if the second mortgagee wishes to get a foreclosure order against the mortgagor and to redeem the first mortgagee, he must join him as a party.

(ii) Effect

13.063. The normal effect of the foreclosure becoming absolute is that the mortgagee becomes the owner of the land or, as it was put in one Irish case, "a foreclosure decree is an absolute conveyance,"[87] but the court has jurisdiction to reopen the foreclosure.[88] This will be done in exceptional circumstances only. The reopening of the foreclosure is entirely a matter for the discretion of the court, but the factors which can lead to a decision to reopen the foreclosure and allow the mortgagor to redeem are that the mortgagor was prevented by some misfortune from redeeming between the date of the foreclosure decree *nisi* and when it became absolute, or that there was a considerable difference between the value of the property and the debt owed to the mortgagee.[89] It is, however, settled that, if a mortgagee who has obtained a foreclosure order *nisi*, which has become absolute, sues on the personal covenant of the mortgagor contained in the mortgage deed to pay the debt, this has the effect of reopening the foreclosure and when such an action is brought the mortgagor becomes entitled to redeem.[90]

F. RESTRICTIONS ON MORTGAGEES

13.064. In the Republic of Ireland the powers of mortgagees of enforcing their security were subject to statutory restrictions imposed by the rent restriction legislation or, to give them their full title, the Increase of Rent and Mortgage Interest (Restriction) Acts.[91] The legislation that has been in force for decades in the Republic no longer contains such restrictions on mortgagees.[92]

---

[86]   *Richards* v. *Cooper* (1842) 5 Beav. 304; *cf. Perrott* v. *O'Halloran* (1840) 2 Ir.Eq.R. 428. However, in Ireland, where an order for a sale is invariably given, a puisne mortgagee must obtain the consent of a prior incumbrancer to the carriage of sale being given to the puisne mortgagee, if he is to be allowed the full costs of the sale, see *Wills* v. *Clifford* (1888) 22 I.L.T.R. 51; *Hilliard* v. *Moriarty* [1894] 1 I.R. 316, but the auctioneer's fees will always be given priority over the claim of the prior incumbrancer. *Cf.* the case of a sale of mortgaged property in an administration suit, *Leonard* v. *Kellett* (1891) 27 L.R.Ir. 418; *McAloon* v. *McAloon* [1901] 1 I.R. 470; *Cusack* v. *Cusack* (1903) 37 I.L.T.R. 152; *McSpadden* v. *Patterson* (1905) 5 N.I.J.R. 151. See Bodkin, "Mortgagee's costs" (1954) 18 Conv. 130.

[87]   *Re Power and Carton's Contract* (1890) 25 L.R.Ir. 459. See also *Platt* v. *Mendel* (1884) 27 Ch.D. 246; *Smithett* v. *Hesketh* (1890) 44 Ch.D. 161.

[88]   The leading statement on this subject was given by Jessel M.R. in *Campbell* v. *Holyland* (1887) 7 Ch.D. 166 at 169 and 172–5.

[89]   See the series of eighteenth century English House of Lords decisions in *Wichalse* v. *Short* (1713) 3 Bro.P.C. 558; *Lant* v. *Crispe* (1719) 5 Bro.P.C. 200; *Burgh* v. *Langton* (1724) 5 Bro.P.C. 213; *Jones* v. *Kendrick* (1727) 5 Bro.P.C. 244.

[90]   *Dashwood* v. *Blythway* (1729) 1 Eq.Cas.Abr. 317, pl. 3. *Cf.* if the mortgagee sold the land after foreclosure, *Perry* v. *Barker* (1803) 8 Ves. 527 and (1806) 13 Ves. 198; *Lockhart* v. *Hardy* (1846) 9 Beav. 349. It seems that the foreclosure is not reopened by a suit on the covenant by an incumbrancer, *e.g.* a subsequent mortgagee also foreclosed, other than the foreclosing mortgagee, see *Worthington & Co. Ltd.* v. *Abbott* [1910] 1 Ch. 588. See also *re* an action on the covenant after an application for a sale, *Bradshaw* v. *McMullan* [1915] 2 I.R. 187.

[91]   See the Acts of 1923 and 1926, as extended by the Acts of 1928–31 and subsequent Expiring Law Acts. These earlier Acts were replaced by the Rent Restrictions Act, 1946. See generally Coghlan, *Law of Rent Restrictions in Ireland* (2nd ed., 1950); Hughes, *Increase of Rent and Mortgage Interest (Restrictions) Act, 1923* (1923); Walsh and Cosgrove, *Rent Restrictions Guide* (1943).

[92]   Rent Restrictions Act, 1960; Rent Restrictions (Amendment) Act, 1967. See ch. 18, *post.*

In Northern Ireland the restrictions imposed by the rent restriction legislation[93] remained in force until very recently, though they seemed to have little practical significance.[94]

1. Mortgages Controlled

13.065. The legislation applied to mortgages[95] of dwelling-houses coming within the general control of the Rent Acts, *i.e.*, houses or parts of houses let as separate dwellings, coming within the appropriate rateable valuation limits.[96] The statutory control was designed to give the landlord of property protection against his mortgagee, just as the landlord was himself restricted as regards his tenant. The control took two forms: restriction of the amount of interest that the mortgagor could charge and prevention of the mortgagee enforcing his security against the property.

2. Restrictions on Interest

13.066. In respect of mortgaged property within the Rent Acts, the mortgagee could not charge a rate of interest which exceeded the standard rate permitted.[97] In the case of "old" control houses, the standard rate was the rate fixed on August 3, 1914, or the original rate fixed where the mortgage was created after that date.[98] For "new" control houses, the standard rate was that fixed on September 1, 1939, or the original for mortgages created thereafter.[99]

However, in the case of "old" control houses, the rate could be increased by an amount not exceeding 1 per cent. per annum, up to a "ceiling" of 6½ per cent. per annum.[1] No increase of any kind was permitted for "new" control houses.

3. Enforcement of Security

13.067. The Acts provided that the mortgagee could not call in his mortgage or enforce his security so long as the mortgagor paid his interest (or, at least, was no more than 21 days in arrear), performed and observed the covenants (other than the covenant for repayment of the principal money) and kept the

---

[93] The main Acts still in force were the British Increase of Rent and Mortgage Interest (Restrictions) Act, 1920, and the Rent and Mortgage Interest (Restrictions) Act (N.I.), 1940. See also Rent Restriction Law (Amendment) Act (N.I.), 1951, Housing (Miscellaneous Provisions) and Rent Restriction Law (Amendment) Act (N.I.), 1956, Pt. V and Housing Acts (N.I.), 1961, Pt. III and 1967, Pt. II.

[94] See Frazer and Wylie, "The Rent Restriction Law of Northern Ireland" (1971) 22 N.I.L.Q. 99 at 131–4. Also ch. 18 *post.* The legislation in question was replaced by the Rent (N.I.) Order, 1978, as to which, see para. 18.36 *et seq.*

[95] Including registered charges, 1920 Act, s. 18 (2) (c) and 1940 Act, s. 28 (1), but not a mere equitable mortgage or charge, 1920 Act, s. 12 (4) (a) and (b) and 1940 Act, s. 3 (2). See *London County and Westminster Bank Ltd.* v. *Tompkins* [1918] 1 K.B. 515.

[96] In the case of "old" control governed by the 1920 Act, the Acts did not apply to mortgages created after 1920, see 1920 Act, s. 12 (4) (c). But such mortgages could be subject to "new" control governed by the 1940 Act, s. 3 (1), and there was no limitation re new control for post-1940 mortgages, 1940 Act, s. 3 (2).

[97] 1920 Act, s. 1; 1940 Act, s. 5.

[98] 1920 Act, s. 12 (1) (b).

[99] 1940 Act, s. 28 (1).

[1] 1920 Act, s. 4. It was not clear from the Act whether the mortgagee had to follow any particular procedure, *e.g.*, service of a notice of increase, to claim the increased rate, as the landlord had to do in respect of rent, see Megarry, *The Rent Acts* (10th ed.), p. 492.

property in a proper state of repair, and paid all interest and instalments of principal recoverable under any prior encumbrance.[2] In the case of a mortgage of leasehold property, the county court could authorise the mortgagee to call in the mortgage, if he satisfied the court that his security was seriously diminished in value or otherwise in jeopardy, so that it was reasonable to allow him to enforce it. The court could, however, impose the condition that no enforcement was to take place if the mortgagor, within a set time, paid a portion of the principal sum corresponding to what the court considered to be the diminution in value of the security.[3]

13.068. The major drawback about such controls from the point of view of modern mortgages, apart from the fact that the Rent Acts applied only to properties within certain rateable valuation limits, was that the protection as regards enforcement of security did not apply where the mortgage repayment instalments of principal extended over a term of at least 10 years.[4] In other words, it did not cover the typical building society mortgage or other similar instalment mortgages which are so common nowadays. Furthermore, no protection was afforded as against any power of sale where the mortgagee was in possession on March 25, 1920 ("old" control), or May 1, 1940 ("new" control), or where the mortgagor consented to the exercise of any of the powers conferred by the mortgage.[5] It is not surprising, therefore, that the new legislation obtained in the Rent (N.I.) Order, 1978, follows the Republic's legislation in omitting provisions relating to mortgages.

G. CONSOLIDATION

The doctrine of consolidation is an equitable doctrine intended to protect the mortgagee, but its importance has been greatly reduced by statute. It is also a doctrine which seems to have been recognised with some reluctance on the part of Irish judges.[6]

1. *The Right*

13.069. The doctrine of consolidation comes into operation where a mortgagor mortgages two properties as security for two debts to the same mortgagee. If the value of these two properties then changes, so that one increases in value and the other decreases and the mortgagor seeks to redeem the more valuable one by paying off one debt and thereby to leave the other debt supported by inadequate security, the doctrine gives the mortgagee the right to insist that the mortgagor either redeems both mortgages or neither.[7] In essence, this was an application of the maxim of equity– "He who seeks equity, must do equity."[8] To the extent that the mortgagor seeks to redeem after the legal date for redemption, he is dependent upon equitable relief and

---

[2] 1920 Act, s. 7; 1940 Act, s. 10 (1).
[3] 1920 Act, s. 7 (ii); 1940 Act, s. 10 (1) (iii).
[4] 1920 Act, s. 7 (i); 1940 Act, s. 10 (1) (ii).
[5] 1920 Act, s. 7 (i); 1940 Act, s. 10 (1) (ii).
[6] See the discussion in *Re Thomson's Estate* [1912] 1 I.R. 194 and 460.
[7] *Re Thomson's Estate* [1912] 1 I.R. 460. See also the early English cases, *Lloyd* v. *Cox*, 79 Sel.Soc. 531; *Pope* v. *Onslow* (1690) 2 Vern. 286; *Willie* v. *Lugy* (1761) 2 Eden. 78.
[8] Para. 3.057, *ante*.

equity can impose conditions on the granting of such relief, just as it can extend the right of redemption itself.[9]

13.070. It is settled that the doctrine can be invoked in respect of any kind of mortgage, legal or equitable, of any kind of property. Furthermore, it applies where one mortgage is legal and the other equitable[10] and where one mortgage is of realty and the other of personalty.[11] It also applies where more than two mortgages exist, but it does not necessarily follow that the right to consolidate can be invoked as between each and every one of the mortgages.[12]

2. *Conditions for Exercise*

The following four conditions must be met if a mortgagee is to be able to consolidate.

(i) Right Expressly Reserved

13.071. Unless the mortgages concerned were all made before 1882,[13] at least one of the mortgage deeds must expressly reserve the right to consolidate. The reason for this is the restriction on consolidation, imposed by section 17 (1) of the Conveyancing Act, 1881:

> "A mortgagor seeking to redeem any one mortgage shall, by virtue of this Act, be entitled to do so, without paying any money due under any separate mortgage made by him, or by any person through whom he claims, on property other than that comprised in the mortgage which he seeks to redeem."

This restriction, however, is subject to section 17 (2) which states that it applies "only if and as far as a contrary intention is not expressed in the mortgage deeds or one of them."[14] It is common practice for mortgage deeds to contain such a clause expressing a contrary intention.

(ii) Redemption Dates Passed

13.072. Since the doctrine is an equitable one, it cannot override legal rights,[15] including a legal right to redeem. So the legal dates for redemption must have passed in the case of all the mortgages to which the right to consolidate is being applied.[16]

(iii) Same Mortgagor

It is settled that the right to consolidate can be invoked only where the

---

[9]   Para. 12.05, *ante*.

[10]   *Cracknell* v. *Janson* (1879) 11 Ch.D. 1 at 18. Or both equitable, *Tweedale* v. *Tweedale* (1857) 23 Beav. 341.

[11]   *Tassell* v. *Smith* (1858) 2 De G. & J. 713. Or both of personalty, *Watts* v. *Symes* (1851) 1 De G.M. & G. 240. To the extent that *Re Salmon* [1903] 1 K.B. 147 suggests that there can be consolidation in respect of two mortgages of the *same* property, it must be doubted. See Megarry and Wade, *Law of Real Property* (5th ed., 1984), p. 959, fn. 28. *Cf.* the last phrase of s. 17 (1) of the Conveyancing Act, 1881, *infra*.

[12]   See *Hughes* v. *Britannia Permanent Benefit Building Society* [1906] 2 Ch. 607; *Pledge* v. *White* [1896] A.C. 187.

[13]   Conveyancing Act, 1881, s. 17 (3).

[14]   See *Gore-Hickman* v. *Alliance Assurance Co. Ltd.* [1936] I.R. 721.

[15]   Para. 3.047, *ante*.

[16]   *Cummins* v. *Fletcher* (1880) 14 Ch.D. 699.

mortgages in question were originally created by the same mortgagor.[17] This principle has even been said to apply so as to exclude consolidation where X creates one mortgage and X and Y jointly create the other[18] or Y does so on his own, but as trustee for X.[19] However, it makes no difference whether or not the mortgages are created in favour of the same mortgagee.

(iv) Union of Mortgages and Equities of Redemption

13.073. It also now seems to be settled that there must have been a time during the currency of the mortgages in question when all the mortgages were vested in one person and simultaneously the equities of redemption were vested in another person.[20] It is sufficient that this union occurred at some time and it does not matter that the equities of redemption subsequently become vested in different persons.[21] As regards the mortgagee, all the mortgages must be vested in him when he seeks to exercise his right to consolidate them.[22]

3. Purchaser's Inquiries

13.074. In England the doctrine of consolidation has been criticised[23] because of the dangers involved for a purchaser of property already subject to a mortgage, *i.e.*, a purchaser of the equity of redemption. The point is that in England such a purchaser may find it impossible to discover whether the mortgagor of the property with whom he is dealing has mortgaged *other* property held by a different title and that both mortgages are now held by the same person, who thus may have a right to consolidate them. Even worse from the point of view of such a purchaser, the mortgage on the property he is purchasing may not reserve the right of consolidation and the mortgagee's right may depend upon the terms of the other mortgage of which the purchaser is ignorant. It seems to be settled that the purchaser's lack of notice is no defence, because he is dependent upon an equitable right to redeem which is subject to the prior equitable right to consolidate held by the mortgagee.[24] The result may be, then, that an innocent purchaser suffers as a result of the imprudence of a mortgagee in lending on inadequate security, yet it may be this same mortgagee who is allowed by equity to rescue himself from his own mistake at the expense of an innocent person. In Ireland, however, this criticism does not have the same force because of the Registry of Deeds system which operates throughout both parts of the island.[25] To

---

[17] *Sharp* v. *Richards* [1909] 1 Ch. 109.

[18] *Thorneycroft* v. *Crockett* (1848) 2 H.L.C. 239.

[19] *Re Raggett* (1880) 16 Ch.D. 117 at 119 (*per* James L.J.).

[20] *Pledge* v. *White* [1896] A.C. 187 at 198 (*per* Lord Davey).

[21] *Re Thomson's Estate* [1912] 1 I.R. 460. See also *Hughes* v. *Britannia Permanent Benefit Building Society* [1906] 2 Ch. 607; *cf. Jennings* v. *Jordan* (1881) 6 App.Cas. 698.

[22] *Riley* v. *Hall* (1898) 79 L.T. 244. See further discussion of these rules, with illustrative examples, in Megarry and Wade, *Law of Real Property* (5th ed., 1984), pp. 956–9.

[23] See, *e.g.*, *Pledge* v. *White* [1896] A.C. 187 at 190 (*per* Lord Halsbury) and 192 (*per* Lord Davey).

[24] The purchaser cannot plead that he is bona fide purchaser of a *legal* estate without notice of prior equitable interests (see ch. 3, *ante* and para. 13.145, *post*), even though he purchases the legal title from the mortgagor, where a charge by way of legal mortgage only is created under the Law of Property Act, 1925, because that legal title is subject to the mortgage which can be cleared off the title only by exercising the equitable right to redeem.

[25] See the remarks of Ross J., at first instance, on this matter in *Re Thomson's Estate* [1912] 1 I.R. 194; *cf.* Barry L.C., on appeal [1912] 1 I.R. 460.

protect the priority of his right to consolidate against subsequent dealings with the land,[26] the mortgagee must see that all the mortgages involved are registered in the Registry of Deeds and, since, for the doctrine to apply, the mortgages must all have been made by the same mortgagor, a purchaser of land subject to a mortgage can protect himself by searching the Index of Names of Grantors to see what mortgages have been created by the mortgagor.[27]

H. MARSHALLING

13.075. Marshalling is another doctrine of equity designed to regulate the position of two or more persons interested in the same property. It has particular relevance in the fields of mortgages, but has also played a considerable role in the administration of assets of deceased persons.[28] In essence, the right to marshal arises where one person has an interest in two properties and another has an interest in one of them, and the latter has an equitable right to require the former not to deal with his interests so as to prejudice the latter.[29] In the field of mortgages, the doctrine applies as between successive mortgagees.

1. *The Right*

13.076. Perhaps the most common example of the operation of the doctrine is where the owner of two properties, Whiteacre and Blackacre, mortgages them both to one person, say X, to secure a loan of £10,000. Then he mortgages, for a second time, just one of the properties, Whiteacre, to Y to secure another loan of £5,000. Suppose that some time later X decides to realise his securities to repay his loan of £10,000 and at that time Whiteacre is worth about £10,000 and Blackacre about £8,000. Taken together, the two properties are more than adequate security for X's debt, but Whiteacre is sufficient on its own. The problem is that it is not sufficient to cover also Y's debt of £5,000. If X decides to sell Whiteacre only, this will repay him in full as first mortgagee and leave nothing for Y, whose mortgage is destroyed by the sale. The result would be, then, that but for the doctrine, Y would be reduced to the position of an unsecured creditor of the mortgagor, who, of course, may be insolvent, which is the reason X decided to realise his security. What the courts of equity have said in this situation is that X could have, instead, realised both his securities, *e.g.*, by selling Blackacre as well as Whiteacre, and, had he done this, £18,000 would have been produced, £10,000 of which have gone to X, who would have been obliged to hold the surplus on trust for Y, as second mortgagee, as to £5,000, and for any other mortgagees and, ultimately, the mortgagor, as to the remaining £3,000.[30] Since X is not prejudiced either way, the courts of equity have said that he

---

[26] See further on priorities, paras. 13.127 *et seq., post.*

[27] See ch. 22, *post.*

[28] *Averall* v. *Wade* (1835) Ll. & G.temp.Sug. 252 at 268; *Ellard* v. *Cooper* (1850) 1 Ir.Ch.R. 376; *Buckley* v. *Buckley* (1887) 19 L.R.Ir. 544. See now Succession Act, 1965, s. 46 and 1st Sched., Pt. II (R.I.); Administration of Estates Act (N.I.), 1955, s. 30 and 1st Sched., Pt. II, Ch. 16, *post.* See also Newark, "Charities and the Marshalling of Assets" (1944–6) 6 N.I.L.Q. 36 and *Re Solomon* [1949] I.R. 3.

[29] See the discussion of the doctrine in *McCarthy* v. *McCartie (No. 2)* [1904] 1 I.R. 100. See also *Re Cornwall* (1842) 6 Ir.Eq.R. 63.

[30] Para 13.038, *ante*

ought to act in the way which will leave Y his security and ought to seek satisfaction as far as possible out of the property on which Y has no mortgage, *i.e.*, Blackacre.[31] If X in fact resorts to Whiteacre only, equity will adjust the position of the parties to give effect to Y's equity to the extent of treating Y as if he had a mortgage on Blackacre, thereby protecting his security.[32]

13.077. It is settled in Ireland that the doctrine of marshalling also operates where all the mortgages are not created by the same mortgagor, as in the example given above. In particular, there is a line of decisions to the effect that, under certain circumstances, if the mortgagor, in the above example, sells his equity of redemption in Whiteacre and Blackacre to O who in turn sells his interest in one of the properties to P, P may have a right to invoke the doctrine of marshalling and to insist that the mortgagee satisfy his debt out of the property retained by O. Christian L.J., explained this principle in *Ker* v. *Ker*[33]:

> "When the owner of the incumbered estate sells, or settles for valuable consideration a parcel of it, and there is a covenant against incumbrances,[34] or a declaration that the estate is free from incumbrances[35] or the nature of the dealings shows that the land is sold or settled *as if* free from incumbrances,[36] equity, instead of leaving the purchaser to his action for damages, will specifically perform the covenant, be it express or implied, making the lands, retained by the grantor exonerate those he has sold or settled."[37]

2. Conditions for Exercise

It seems to be settled that the following conditions must be met before a mortgagee or holder of an interest in property can invoke the right to marshal.

(i) Same Mortgagor

13.078. The doctrine normally applies only where the respective mortgages are created by the same person. Thus if A mortgages Whiteacre to X and B mortgages Blackacre also to X, and then A mortgages Whiteacre also to Y, the courts will not compel X to resort primarily to Blackacre in realising his security for his respective loans to A and B.[38] However, we saw above that the Irish courts have relaxed this rule in certain cases.[39]

(ii) Both Properties Available

A subsequent mortgagee can insist on his right of marshalling only if the

---

[31] *Averall* v. *Wade* (1835) Ll. & G.*temp*.Sug. 252 and 268; *Baldwin* v. *Belcher* (1842) 3 Dr. & War. 173; *Re Roddy's Estate* (1861) 11 Ir.Ch.R. 369; *Re Chute's Estate* [1914] 1 I.R. 180. *Cf. Re Jones* (1853) 2 Ir.Ch.R. 544.
[32] *McCarthy* v. *McCartie* (*No. 2*) [1904] 1 I.R. 100.
[33] (1870) I.R. 4 Eq. 15.
[34] See the application of the doctrine in such a case in *Averall* v. *Wade* (1835) Ll. & G.*temp*.Sug. 252.
[35] See *Ocean Accident and Guarantee Co. Ltd.* v. *Collum* [1913] 1 I.R. 337. *Re* a covenant for further assurance, see *Re Roche's Estate* (1890) 25 L.R.Ir. 58.
[36] See *Tighe* v. *Dolphin* [1906] 1 I.R. 305.
[37] (1870) I.R. 4 Eq. 15 at 30–1. See also *McCarthy* v. *McCartie* (*No. 2*) [1904] 1 I.R. 100. at 115 (*per* Walker L.J.).
[38] *Re Keily* (1857) 6 Ir.Ch.R. 394.
[39] Para. 13.077, *supra*.

first mortgagee is in a position to resort to both properties mortgaged to realise his security.[40]

(iii) Notice Irrelevant

It is settled that a subseqent mortagagee can still invoke his right to marshal despite the fact that he had notice of the first mortgage on the same property.[41]

(iv) Third Parties

13.079. There has been much controversy in Ireland over how far marshalling may be allowed in circumstances where it may appear to prejudice third parties. To take again the example of an owner of properties. Whiteacre and Blackacre, who mortgages them both to X and then mortgages Whiteacre only to Y, finally he mortgages Blackacre to Z. If Y is allowed to marshal so as to force X to satisfy himself out of Blackacre, this will have an obvious effect on Z who is also secured on Blackacre. In England, the rule seems to be, as a result of the decision of Knight-Bruce V.-C. in *Barnes* v. *Racster*,[42] that in such circumstances Y and Z *together* can insist on marshalling to the extent of forcing X to satisfy himself out of both Whiteacre and Blackacre rateably, in proportions fixed according to their respective values. The surplus proceeds from the sales of both properties can then be used to satisfy as far as possible the subsequent mortgages on each held respectively by Y and Z. The position in Ireland is not clear, though several authorities have expressly recognised[43] the rule in *Barnes* v. *Racster* and it has even been expressly applied.[44]

13.080. In *Dolphin* v. *Aylward*,[45] the House of Lords, in an appeal from Ireland, laid down the general proposition that there could be no marshalling (by Y in our example) so as to prejudice a third party (Z in our example), whether or not the third party was a volunteer. Irish courts, however, have followed this proposition to the extent only of holding that no prejudice will result if the third party took his mortgage expressly on the terms that it was not to effect or prejudice the rights of prior mortgagees[46] or, indeed, simply if the third party had notice of the prior mortgage.[47] Furthermore, the Irish courts have refused to apply the principle of apportionment laid down in *Barnes* v. *Racster* to cases involving judgment mortgages[48] and have held that

---

[40]   *Douglas* v. *Cooksey* (1868) I.R. 2 Eq. 311 at 315 (*per* Walsh M.R.); *Dolphin* v. *Aylward* (1870) L.R. 4 H.L. 486 at 505.
[41]   *Going* v. *Farrell* (1814) Beat. 472; *Baldwin* v. *Belcher* (1842) 3 Dr. & War. 173; *Re Fox's Estate* (1856) 5 Ir.Ch.R. 541; *Re Roddy's Estate* (1861) 11 Ir.Ch.R. 369.
[42]   (1842) 1 Y. & C.C.C. 401, followed in *Bugden* v. *Bignold* (1843) 2 Y. & C.C.C. 377 and *Wellesley* v. *Mornington* (1869) 17 W.R. 355. See also *Flint* v. *Howard* [1893] 2 Ch. 54; *Re Townley* [1922] 1 Ch. 154.
[43]   E.g. *Re Lawder's Estate* (1861) 11 Ir.Ch.R. 346. *Cf. Tighe* v. *Dolphin* [1906] 1 I.R. 305 and *Re Archer's Estate* [1914] 1 I.R. 285 distinguishing *Barnes* v. *Racster*.
[44]   *Smith* v. *Toms* [1918] 1 I.R. 338.
[45]   (1870) L.R. 4 H.L. 486.
[46]   Including Y's right to marshal against X. See Ross J. in *Re Lysaght's Estate* [1903] 1 I.R. 235 at 244.
[47]   *Re Roche's Estate* (1890) 25 L.R.Ir. 58; *Tighe* v. *Dolphin* [1906] 1 I.R. 305; *Re Archer's Estate* [1914] 1 I.R. 285. *Cf.* however, *Smyth* v. *Toms* [1918] 1 I.R. 388, where Ross J. applied the principle of *Barnes* v. *Racster* in such circumstances.
[48]   See further, paras. 13.163 *et seq., post.*

a judgment mortgagee may marshal so as to affect the rights of a subsequent judgment mortgagee.[49]

II. MORTGAGOR

13.081. We now come to consider the various rights of a mortgagor under a mortgage. Once again these rights depend partly on the general law, including legislation, and partly upon the terms of the mortgage instrument, if any. His most important right, of course, is his right of redemption, *i.e.*, his right to get the property back freed from the mortgage or charge on repayment of the loan and most attention in this section will be paid to the right of redemption. First, however, something must be said of various other rights which a mortgagor usually has.

A. POSSESSION

13.082. Though the mortgagee has in most cases a right to take possession of the mortgaged property,[50] it is common practice for him not to exercise it and to be content to leave the mortgagor in possession so long as he keeps up regular payments due under the mortgage. Though a mortgagor in possession has been described in Ireland as a tenant at sufferance,[51] it has been recognised that he is entitled nevertheless to receive all the rents and profits from the land and to keep them for himself,[52] without the need to account for them to the mortgagee.[53] He is even allowed to commit waste on the land, *e.g.*, cut timber, provided the land will remain adequate security.[54] Otherwise, the mortgagee may be entitled to an injunction to prevent the mortgagor from damaging his security.

B. ACTIONS

13.083. To the extent that a mortgagor was left in possession of the mortgaged property, even at common law he was entitled to maintain actions to protect that possession as against third parties with no better right,[55] *e.g.*, trespassers or neighbours committing a nuisance. He could, indeed, bring an action to recover the land against anyone other than the mortgagee or a person claiming through him. In equity, since the mortgagor was regarded as owner of the land, subject only to the mortgage, he could also apply for

---

[49] *Re Scott's Estate* (1863) 14 Ir.Ch.R. 63; *Re Greene's Estate* (1863) 14 Ir.Ch.R. 325; *Re Lynch's Estate* (1867) I.R. 1 Eq. 396.

[50] See para. 13.042, *ante*.

[51] *Green* v. *Burns* (1879) 6 L.R.Ir. 173. *Cf. Fairclough* v. *Marshall* (1878) 4 Ex.D. 37. See also *Fleming and Moore* v. *Moore* (1891) 28 L.R.Ir. 373. In *Esso Petroleum Co. Ltd.* v. *Alstonbridge Properties Ltd.* [1975] 1 W.L.R. 1474, Walton J. said (at p. 1484):

"I accept that the court will be ready to find an implied term in an instalment mortgage that the mortgagor is to be entitled to remain in possession against the mortgagee until he makes default in payment of one of the instalments. But there must be something on which to hang such a conclusion in the mortgage other than the mere fact that it is an instalment mortgage."

See also *Western Bank Ltd.* v. *Schindler* [1977] Ch. 1; Smith, "The Mortgagee's Right to Possession: The Modern View" [1979] Conv. 266.

[52] *Patterson* v. *Reilly* (1882) 10 L.R.Ir. 304; *Campion* v. *Palmer* [1896] 2 I.R. 445.

[53] *Ex parte Calwell* (1828) 1 Mol. 259.

[54] *King* v. *Smith* (1843) 2 Hare 239; *Harper* v. *Alpin* (1886) 54 L.T. 383.

[55] See, further, on such actions by other mere possessors of land, *e.g.*, a squatter, ch. 23, *post*.

equitable remedies, such as an injunction, and enforce property rights against third parties as allowed in equity only, *e.g.*, freehold restrictive covenants.[56]

13.084. Difficulties used to arise where the property mortgaged was already leased and it was desired to enforce the normal landlord's remedies, *e.g.*, in respect of rent or covenants contained in the lease, against the tenants. If the mortgage was created by assignment of the leasehold reversion[57] the mortgagee became landlord and only he could bring the appropriate actions, even though the mortgagor had been left "in possession", *i.e.*, had the right to receive the rents from the leased premises.[58] This problem was solved by section 28 (5) of the Judicature (Ireland) Act, 1877, which provided that a mortgagor for the time being entitled to the possession of land or to the rents and profits of such land could sign and cause to be served notices to quit, could determine and accept surrenders of leases and sue in his own name for possession or recovery of rents and profits, or to prevent or recover damages in respect of any trespass or other wrong relative to the land.[58a] Such an action is not defeated by proof that the legal estate in the land is vested in the mortgagee. However, such a right of action in the mortgagor is subject to any notice of his intention to take possession or enter into receipt of the rents and profits on the part of the mortgagee and, of course, to any provision to the contrary in the mortgage deed. This provision for mortgagors in possession would appear to be reinforced in part of Ireland by section 10 of the Conveyancing Act, 1881,[59] which deals with the running of the benefit of a lessee's covenants with the reversion and provides that the rent and covenants annexed and incident to the reversion may be recovered, received, enforced and taken advantage of " by the person from time to time entitled . . . to the income of the whole or any part, as the case may require, of the land leased." It has been held in England that section 10 enables a mortgagor in possession to sue the lessee of the mortgaged premises for damages for breach of covenant to repair.[60]

C. Title Documents

13.085. While the mortgagee is, in general, entitled to retain possession of the title deeds relating to the mortgaged property, section 16 (1) of the Conveyancing Act, 1881, provides:

"A mortgagor, as long as his right to redeem subsists, shall, by virtue of this Act, be entitled from time to time, at reasonable times, on his request, and at his own cost, and on payment of the mortgagee's costs and expenses in this behalf, to inspect and make copies or abstracts of or

---

[56] *Fairclough* v. *Marshall* (1878) 4 Ex.D. 37. See also ch. 19, *post.*
[57] Para. 12.36, *ante.*
[58] Para. 13.082, *supra.* See also *Matthews* v. *Usher* [1900] 2 Q.B. 535; *Turner* v. *Walsh* [1909] 2 K.B. 484 at 495.
[58a] In N.I. s. 28 (5) of the 1877 Act was replaced by s. 93 of the Judicature (Northern Ireland) Act, 1978 (U.K.).
[59] See, further, ch. 17, *post.*
[60] *Turner* v. *Walsh* [1909] 2 K.B. 484.

extracts from the documents of title relating to the mortgaged property in the custody or power of the mortgagee."[61]

This right cannot, since 1882, be excluded by any stipulation to the contrary.[62]

13.086. Apart from the right during the currency of the mortgage, the mortgagor is also entitled to have the title deeds restored to his possession on redemption of the mortgage.[63] Should the mortgagee fail to restore the deeds, or lose them, the mortgagor will be able to claim compensation for the mortgagee's default or, alternatively, can seek to set off an amount by way of compensation against the amount due to the mortgagee on the foot of the mortgage at redemption.[64]

D. SALE

13.087. Apart from a sale of the entire interest in the mortgaged property, the mortgagor is free to sell his interest in the property subject to the mortgage, *i.e.*, his equity of redemption.[65] Furthermore, as we shall see, the mortgagor may by statute obtain an order for a sale of the mortgaged property instead of an order for redemption in appropriate cases.[66]

E. REDEMPTION

13.088. The most important right of a mortgagor is his right to redeem the mortgage, *i.e.*, his right to get his property back freed and discharged from the mortgage, by repayment of the capital borrowed plus the interest charged on it. The mortgagor has a *legal* right to redeem on the legal date for redemption specified in the mortgage instrument and thereafter has for an indefinite time an *equitable* right to redeem.[67] It has been stated several times by the Irish judges that, despite the repeal of the usury laws,[68] the courts of equity still have jurisdiction to deal with unconscionable bargains, which may even cover situations previously covered by the usury laws.[69]

1. *Protection of Mortgagor*

As one would expect, the courts have been vigilant over the years to ensure

---

[61] See *Re Lee and the Conveyancing Act* (1902) 36 I.L.T. 79; *Gilligan* v. *National Bank Ltd.* [1901] 2 I.R. 513.

[62] S. 16 (2).

[63] See, further, para. 13.106, *post*.

[64] *Gilligan* v. *National Bank Ltd.* [1901] 2 I.R. 513, where Barton J. also held that there is no implied covenant on the part of a mortgagee to take reasonable care of the title deeds during the currency of the mortgage, so that, until redemption, the mortgagor has no right of action for damages.

[65] Para. 12.05, *ante*.

[66] Para. 13.107, *infra*.

[67] *Burrough* v. *Cranston* (1840) 2 Ir.Eq.R. 203. See further, para. 12.05, *ante*. A mortgage may also be set aside if it involves some form of illegality, see, *e.g.*, *Reilly* v. *Kierans* (1899) 33 I.L.T.R. 59 and *Sheehy* v. *Sheehy* [1901] 1 I.R. 239 (consideration in the supply of liquors contrary to the "Tippling" (Ir.) Acts, 1815 and 1874).

[68] Which originally prohibited the lending of money at a fixed rate of interest and then allowed it within set limits as to the rate of interest, see *e.g.*, Usury Act (Ir.), 1634 (10 Chas. 1, sess. 2, c. 22). The usury laws were finally repealed by the Usury Laws Repeal Act, 1854.

[69] *Chapple* v. *Mahon* (1870) I.R. 5 Eq. 225; *Howley* v. *Cook* (1873) I.R. 8 Eq. 570; *Kevans* v. *Joyce* [1896] 1 I.R. 442. And see now the courts' jurisdiction under the moneylenders' legislation, para. 12.18, *ante*, and, in N.I., the U.K. Consumer Credit Act, 1974, ss. 94, 137–40 and 173. See Adams, "Mortgages and the Consumer Credit Act 1974" (1975) 39 Conv. 94.

that mortgagors are protected in respect of the right which is of such crucial importance to them–indeed, one which is central to the very nature of a mortgage transaction. This has resulted in the following doctrines becoming recognised and enforced by the courts.

(i) Test of Substance

13.089. The equitable maxim "equity looks to the intent, not to the form"[70] has often been applied to mortgage transactions. It means that the courts will ensure what is intended to be as a matter of substance a mortgage will be treated as such, so as to give, in particular, the mortgagor a right to redeem, and it will not matter in what form the transaction has been executed or the legal instruments have been drawn up.[71] Thus what may appear at first sight to be a conditional sale or even an out-and-out conveyance of property may nevertheless, in certain circumstances, be construed, aided, if necessary, by the introduction of parol evidence to show the real intent of the parties to the written instrument, to be a mortgage.[72]

(ii) No Clogs on Equity of Redemption

13.090. It is not only the central principle of equity that the mortgagor should not be prevented from redeeming his property but also that he should get it back free from all the conditions and incidents of the mortgage. As the courts have so often put it, there must be no clog or fetter on the mortgagor's equity of redemption.[73] In the application of this rule, several situations have had to be considered.

(a) *Irredeemability*

13.091. It is clear that a clause in a mortgage instrument purporting to prevent the mortgagor from redeeming altogether will not be enforced by the courts and the mortgagor may redeem without regard to such a restriction.[74] Making the mortgage irredeemable is inconsistent with the very nature of a mortgage. On the same basis, the courts have rejected restrictions or conditions imposed at the time of creation of the mortgage which are designed to enable the mortgagee to become absolute owner of the property. The common example is the conferment on the mortgagee of an option to purchase[75] the mortgaged property, which will be invalid if made a condition

---

[70] See further, para. 3.060, *ante*.

[71] *Goodman* v. *Grierson* (1813) 2 Ba. & B. 274; *Taylor* v. *Emerson* (1843) 4 Dr. & War. 117; *Fee* v. *Cobine* (1847) 11 Ir.Eq.R. 406.

[72] *Neal* v. *Morris* (1818) Beat. 597; *Murphy* v. *Taylor* (1850) 1 Ir.Ch.R. 92; *Re De Freyne's Estate* (1871) 5 I.L.T.R. 193; *O'Reilly* v. *O'Donoghue* (1875) I.R. 10 Eq. 73; *Crone* v. *Hegarty* (1879) 3 L.R.Ir 50. *Cf. Re South City Market Co.* (1884) 13 L.R.Ir. 245 (conveyance with covenant for re-purchase).

[73] See Williams, "The Doctrine of Repugnancy III: 'Clogging the Equity' and Miscellaneous Applications" (1944) 60 L.Q.R. 190; Wyman, "The Clog on the Equity of Redemption" (1908) 21 H.L.R. 459.

[74] *Browne* v. *Ryan* [1901] 2 I.R. 653 at 676 (*per* Walker L.J.) (see *A Casebook on Irish Land Law* (1984), p. 457).

[75] *Re Edward's Estate* (1861) 11 Ir.Ch.R. 367. Such an option should not be confused with a right of pre-emption, which is probably valid, see *Orby* v. *Trigg* (1722) 9 Mod. 2. Such a right, unlike an option to purchase, merely gives the holder a right of first refusal if the mortgagor does decide to sell, but it does not oblige the mortgagor to sell at all to anyone. *Cf.* a conveyance with a covenant for re-purchase, see *Re South City Market Co.* (1884) 13 L.R.Ir. 245.

of the granting of the mortgage.[76] Of course, if the mortgagor, having obtained his mortgage without such a condition attached, subsequently chooses to grant the mortgagee an option to purchase, he is at liberty to do so and the courts will not interfere,[77] unless there are other grounds for doing so.[78]

13.092. Similarly, in *Browne* v. *Ryan*,[79] where, at the time of creation of the mortgage, the mortgagor also agreed to sell within a year the land mortgaged either through the mortgagee, who was an auctioneer, or, if sold otherwise, still paying the mortgagee 5 per cent. commission on the sale, the Court of Appeal held the contract void as a fetter on the equity of redemption.

13.093. While the mortgagor cannot redeem before the legal date for redemption,[80] he can generally redeem in equity at any time thereafter and the courts have been very wary about clauses purporting to postpone the date for redemption for a period much longer than the six month period usually specified in a mortgage deed. It is difficult to be dogmatic on this point, for each case must be considered in the light of the particular circumstances surrounding it. Generally, what the courts in both Ireland[81] and England[82] have said is that they will not enforce such a clause if it is so oppressive and unconscionable that it would be unreasonable for it to be enforced, *e.g.*, because it renders the equitable right to redeem illusory.[83] Thus a long postponement may be unreasonable because the property mortgaged is a wasting asset, *e.g.*, a lease with a limited number of years to run, so that, if redemption is unduly delayed, the mortgagor will get back a "fag end" which is almost worthless.[84] On the other hand, it is often in the interests of the mortgagor, just as much as the mortgagee, to have redemption postponed, which is why so many instalment mortgages are entered into nowadays. The standard building society mortgage nowadays frequently envisages the payment of instalments over a period which can be up to 30 years and, in rare cases, even over 30 years.[85] The important point to note, however, is that, in the case of such mortgages, the mortgagor has a right to redeem long before the end of that mortgage term and, in many cases, the right is exercised.

Finally, it should be noted that a statutory exception to the principle of no

---

[76] *Maxwell* v. *Tipping* [1903] 1 I.R. 498. See also *Samuel* v. *Jarrah Timber and Wood Paving Corp. Ltd.* [1904] A.C. 323; *Lewis* v. *Frank Love Ltd.* [1961] 1 W.L.R. 261.

[77] *Reeve* v. *Lisle* [1902] A.C. 461. *Cf. Alex Lobb (Garages) Ltd.* v. *Total Oil Great Britain Ltd.* [1983] 1 W.L.R. 87.

[78] *E.g.*, fraud, duress, undue influence, etc., see para. 3.157, *ante*.

[79] [1901] 2 I.R. 653 (see *A Casebook on Irish Land Law* (1984), p. 457). See also *Re Edward's Estate* (1861) 11 Ir.Ch.R. 367.

[80] *Burrough* v. *Cranston* (1840) 2 Ir.Eq.R. 203. The mortgagor can so redeem in a case regulated in N.I. by the U.K. Consumer Credit Act, 1974, see ss. 94 and 173.

[81] *Lawless* v. *Mansfield* (1841) 4 Ir.Eq.R. 113; *Re Hone's Estate* (1873) I.R. 8 Eq. 65. See also *Hamill* v. *Matthews* (1910) 44 I.L.T.R. 25.

[82] *Fairclough* v. *Swan Brewery Co. Ltd.* [1912] A.C. 565; *Knightsbridge Estate Trust Ltd.* v. *Byrne* [1939] Ch. 441 (aff'd on other grounds [1940] A.C. 613).

[83] See Bodkin, "Postponement of the Right to Redeem" (1941) 5 Conv. 178.

[84] See, *e.g.*, the *Fairclough* case, fn. 82, *supra*. *Cf. Davis* v. *Symons* [1934] Ch. 442.

[85] See, *e.g.*, *Re Irish Civil Service Building Society and O'Keeffe* (1880) 7 L.R.Ir. 136.

irredeemability exists in both parts of Ireland with respect to company
debentures, which may be made irredeemable or redeemable only on the
happening of some future event or the expiration of a certain period of
time.[86]

(b) *Penalties*

13.094. The courts of equity have always refused to enforce clauses in
contracts which are inserted "in terrorem" of one of the parties.[87] In the law
of mortgages a distinction has been drawn between a clause which provides
for a reduction in the rate of interest otherwise chargeable, if the mortgagor
repays on time, and one which increases the rate of interest otherwise
chargeable if the mortgagor is late with his payments.[88] The former have
generally been upheld[89] and the latter held void.[90] It is difficult to see the
substance of the distinction in terms of the practical position of the mortgagor
but, despite criticism of it,[91] it has not yet been overruled by the courts on
either side of the Irish Sea, though there is a paucity of modern authority on
the subject. In *Burton* v. *Slattery*[92] the House of Lords, in an appeal from
Ireland, held valid a provision that, if interest at the rate of 5 per cent.
became overdue for three months, the rate should rise to 8 per cent. *from the
end of that three months.* In *Chapple* v. *Mahon*[93] a provision that, if the
mortgage was paid off, commission at the rate of 5 per cent. on the sum
advanced should be paid to the mortgagee was held void as a penalty payable
on redemption.

(c) *Collateral advantages*

13.095. The courts have also been concerned to scrutinise any collateral
advantages secured by a mortgagee as part of the mortgage transaction, *i.e.*,
advantages in addition to repayment of the capital advanced plus the interest
charged thereon. FitzGibbon L.J. explained this aspect of the doctrine of
clogs on the equity of redemption as follows:

"The rule originated in that wider principle of equity under which the

---

[86]   Companies Act, 1963, s. 98 (R.I.); Companies Act (N.I.), 1960, s. 88.
[87]   *Kevans* v. *Joyce* [1896] 1 I.R. 442 and 473 (interest at 60 per cent held hard and unconscionable and
reduced to 5 per cent.). See a modern illustration of the penalty principle with respect to hire-purchase
contracts in *Lombank Ltd.* v. *Kennedy* [1961] N.I. 192 (see *A Casebook on Equity and Trusts in Ireland* (1985),
p. 61). See also *United Dominions Trust Ltd.* v. *Patterson* [1973] N.I. 142.
[88]   See Meredith, "A Nicety in the Law of Mortgage" (1916) 32 L.Q.R. 420. In *Multiservice Bookbinding*
Ltd. v. *Marden* [1979] Ch. 84, Browne-Wilkinson J. held that a mortgage under which any sum paid on account
of capital or interest was to be increased or decreased proportionately according to the daily fluctuations in the
rate of exchange between the Swiss franc and pound sterling was valid and not contrary to public policy, even
though during the period of the mortgage the pound greatly depreciated in value against the Swiss franc.
[89]   *I.e.*, if the mortgagor is unpunctual, he must pay the higher rate, see *Re Rocella's Estate* (1898) 32
I.L.T.R. 8; *Re Carroll's Estate* [1901] 1 I.R. 78; *Re Scott's Estate* (1903) 3 N.I.J.R. 119; *Re Jones's Estate* [1914]
1 I.R. 188. See also *Jory* v. *Cox* (1701) Prec.Ch. 160. *Cf. re* an instalment mortgage, *Sterne* v. *Beck* (1863) 32
L.J.Ch. 682.
[90]   *Holles* v. *Wyse* (1693) 2 Vern. 289; *Strode* v. *Parker* (1694) 2 Vern. 316. See also *Chapple* v. *Mahon*
(1870) I.R. 5 Eq. 225. *Cf. Re Armstrong* (1912) 46 I.L.T.R. 46.
[91]   See, *e.g.*, early criticisms, albeit *obiter*, in *Nicholls* v. *Maynard* (1747) 3 Atk. 519 (*per* Lord Hardwicke)
and *Stanhope* v. *Manners* (1763) 2 Eden 197 (*per* Lord Northington L.C.). See also *Brown* v. *Barkham* (1720) 1
P.Wms. 652 (*per* Lord Parker L.C.).
[92]   (1725) 5 Bro.P.C. 233. *Cf. Marquis of Halifax* v. *Higgins* (1690) 2 Vern. 134.
[93]   (1870) I.R. 5 Eq. 225.

Court of Chancery interfered with contracts between parties who were not in a position to deal with each other on equal terms, *e.g.*, 'catching bargains' with expectant heirs, it being deemed inequitable that a lender should, through the necessities of a borrower, obtain any additional or collateral advantage affecting the right of redemption, beyond the payment of principal and interest and costs."[94]

It is important to remember the principle involved here when considering the case law, namely, the supposed inequality in the respective bargaining powers of the mortgagor and mortgagee, leading to the court's interference to prevent an unfair advantage being taken of the former by the latter. This is the explanation for the apparent shift in the attitude of the courts over the last hundred years or so, from one of striking down all collateral advantages[95] to one of considering each case on its own merits and interfering only where a particular provision is unconscionable and a clog on the equity of redemption.[96] Because each case must be considered to that extent on its own, it is not always easy to reconcile past decisions or to draw general principles of universal application. The following, however, is an attempt to give some further guidance on the subject drawn from the existing authorities.

13.096. First, the courts are wary of provisions in mortgages which seem to secure for the mortgagee some financial advantage additional to repayment of the sum advanced and interest charged at a reasonable rate on that sum. Such additional sums–premiums, penalties[97] or however described–will be prohibited by the courts if they are regarded as unconscionable or unreasonable.[98]

13.097. Secondly, the courts have in the past drawn a distinction between collateral advantages which accrue to the benefit of the mortgagee during the currency of the mortgage only, and those which are to accrue after the mortgagor has redeemed the mortgage. The latter constitute clogs on the equity of redemption in the sense that the mortgagor does not get the mortgaged property back as free from incumbrances as it was before it was mortgaged. There were many cases in England during the late nineteenth and the turn of this century where this distinction was drawn in respect of licensed premises mortgaged to brewery companies, which operated "tied houses" schemes, *i.e.*, a provision that the products of a particular brewery company

---

[94] *Browne* v. *Ryan* [1901] 2 I.R. 653 at 685 (see *A Casebook on Irish Land Law* (1984), p. 457). See Firth, "Freedom of Contract in Mortgages" (1895) 11 L.Q.R. 144.

[95] See, *e.g.*, dicta by Hargreave J. to this effect in *Re Edward's Estate* (1861) 11 Ir.Ch.R. 367 at 369. *Cf. Jennings* v. *Ward* (1705) 2 Vern. 520 at 521 (*per* Powle M.R.), overruled expressly by *Kreglinger* v. *New Patagonia Meat and Cold Storage Co. Ltd.* [1914] A.C. 25.

[96] *Browne* v. *Ryan* [1901] 2 I.R. 653 (see *A Casebook on Irish Land Law* (1984), p. 457). See also *Kreglinger* v. *New Patagonia Meat and Cold Storage Co. Ltd.* [1914] A.C. 25; *Multiservice Bookbinding Ltd.* v. *Marden* [1979] Ch. 84, fn. 88, *ante*.

[97] See, further, para. 13.094, *supra*.

[98] *Chapple* v. *Mahon* (1870) I.R 5 Eq. 225; *Browne* v. *Ryan* [1901] 2 I.R. 653 (see *A Casebook on Irish Land Law* (1984), p. 457). See also *Cityland and Property (Holdings) Ltd.* v. *Dabrah* [1968] Ch. 166. *Cf. Santley* v. *Wilde* [1899] 2 Ch. 474, criticised, though not overruled, in *Noakes & Co. Ltd.* v. *Rice* [1902] A.C. 24 and *Bradley* v. *Carritt* [1903] A.C. 253.

and no other's products would be sold on the premises.[99] The courts generally took the view that, if a free house was mortgaged to a brewery company, it was reasonable to allow it to become tied so long as the mortgage lasted, but, once the mortgage ended, the mortgagor should be entitled to redeem a free house.[1] Since then, however, the courts have gone back to first principles and have emphasised that these earlier cases are only examples of the courts' views on what was unconscionable or unreasonable. What has become of increasing importance in recent decades, in the view of many judges, is that proper recognition should be given to commercial practice, so that, in particular, the courts should hesitate before interfering with agreements made between businessmen who, or commercial concerns which, are usually well able to look after their own interests. For this reason, it may be perfectly proper in a particular case to allow a collateral advantage to continue to bind the property after redemption.[2]

13.098. Thirdly, and this follows on from what has just been said, the courts have increasingly viewed such collateral advantages in the light of the common law doctrine of restraint of trade,[3] under which unreasonable restrictions may be struck down, whether because of their effect as between the parties to the transaction in question or their effect on the public interest generally. This has been the approach in both Ireland[4] and England[5] with respect to trading agreements negotiated between oil companies and proprietors of petrol filling-stations or garages.[6]

13.099. Lastly, in deciding whether or not a particular collateral advantage is unreasonable or unconscionable, the courts take into account how far the advantage or provision in question can be regarded as forming part of the mortgage transaction itself.[7] If the advantage is such a part of the granting of the mortgage agreement that it appears to have been almost a condition of the granting of the mortgage,[8] then the court is likely to be less favourable in its treatment of it than it would be if it appears to be an entirely independent matter. In *Maxwell v. Tipping*,[9] a mortgagor, already indebted to the mortgagee for £1,500 at 5 per cent. interest, secured on the mortgaged land,

---

[99]   The modern equivalent, which also applies to Ireland, is the petrol filling-station or garage tied to a particular oil company through a mortgage and a related trading agreement. See para. 13.098, *infra*.
[1]   *Biggs* v. *Hoddinott* [1898] 2 Ch. 307; *Noakes & Co. Ltd.* v. *Rice* [1902] A.C. 24. See also *Bradley* v. *Carritt* [1903] A.C. 253. *Cf. Murphy & Co.* v. *O'Donovan* [1939] I.R. 455, and see *Murphy & Co.* v. *Crean* [1915] 1 I.R. 111 (leases).
[2]   See the discussion in House of Lords in *Kreglinger* v. *New Patagonia Meat and Cold Storage Co. Ltd.* [1914] A.C. 25. Also *De Beers Consolidated Mines Ltd.* v. *British South Africa Co.* [1912] A.C. 52; *Re Cuban Land Development Co. (1911) Ltd.* [1921] 2 Ch. 147.
[3]   See para. 3.137, *ante*.
[4]   *Irish Shell and B.P. Ltd.* v. *Ryan* [1966] I.R. 75. See also *Esso Petroleum Co. (Ireland) Ltd.* v. *Fogarty* [1965] I.R. 531; *Continental Oil Co. of Ireland Ltd.* v. *Moynihan* (1977) 111 I.L.T.R. 5; *Irish Shell Ltd.* v. *Elm Motors Ltd.* [1984] I.R. 200 (see *A Casebook on Equity and Trusts in Ireland* (1985), p. 137.
[5]   *Esso Petroleum Co. Ltd.* v *Harper's Garage (Stourport) Ltd.* [1968] A.C. 269.
[6]   See Swann, "The Solus Site System in Law and Economics" (1967) 18 N.I.L.Q. 1; Whiteman, "Exclusive Distributorship Agreements in the Petrol Industry" (1966) 29 M.L.R. 507.
[7]   See discussion in *Browne* v. *Ryan* [1901] 2 I.R. 653 (see *A Casebook on Irish Land Law* (1984), p. 457). Also by the House of Lords in the *Kreglinger* case, [1914] A.C. 25.
[8]   See, *e.g.*, the agreement in *Browne* v. *Ryan*, para. 13.092, *ante*.
[9]   [1903] 1 I.R. 498.

in consideration of a further advance of £300 entered into a bond[10] with the mortgagee and executed a collateral agreement appointing the mortgagee agent over the mortgaged land and empowering him to charge agent's fees. The mortgagor also agreed to pay 6 per cent. on the entire £1,800 then due. It was held that this subsequent agreement should be regarded as a new contract for fresh consideration and not as a fetter on the equity of redemption. Unfortunately, not all commercial agreements entered into nowadays are as easily "severable," as a study of *solus* agreements drawn up by oil companies will show.[11]

2. Who Can Redeem

13.100. While the right of redemption is usually invoked by the mortgagor, it may be exercised by any person interested in the equity of redemption, *e.g.*, assignees[12] or other successors in title of the mortgagor[13] and subsequent mortgagees.[14] Normally, once a mortgagor has assigned his entire interest he loses his right to redeem,[15] but it has been held that, if he is subsequently sued on his personal covenant for the debt, he acquires a new right of redemption.[16]

3. Mode and Terms of Redemption

In exercising his right to redeem, a mortgagor must comply with certain terms and conditions, some of which have been laid down by the courts and some of which may be specified in the mortgage instrument. For the most part, redemption can be arranged between the parties, but, if necessary, an application may be made to the court.[17]

(i) Notice

13.101. The mortgagor may redeem on the legal date for redemption without the need to give any notice of his intention in this regard. Thereafter the right to redeem is equitable only and must be exercised reasonably and fairly. The general rule laid down by the courts is that the mortgagor must give reasonable notice, usually taken as six months, or, alternatively, must pay six months' interest in lieu of notice.[18] The theory behind this rule of practice is that the mortgagee should be given a reasonable opportunity to find an alternative investment for his capital.[19] However, the rule is not

---

[10]   A judgment was later entered on this and registered as a judgment mortgage against the lands, see para. 13.163, *post*.
[11]   See cases cited in fns. 4 and 5, para. 13.098, *ante*.
[12]   *Howard* v. *Harris* (1683) 1 Vern. 190.
[13]   *Re Harrowby and Paine* [1902] W.N. 137. Even a lessee of a lease granted by the mortgagor but not binding on the mortgagee has been held entitled to redeem, see *Tarn* v. *Turner* (1888) 39 Ch.D. 456.
[14]   *Ocean Accident Corp* v. *Collum* [1913] 1 I.R. 328. See also *Ex parte Hutton* (1849) 11 Ir.Eq.R. 160; *Gregg* v. *Arrett* (1837) S. & Sc. 674.
[15]   *Moore* v. *Morton* [1886] W.N. 196. See also *Cotterell* v. *Price* [1960] 1 W.L.R. 1097.
[16]   *Kinnaird* v. *Trollope* (1888) 39 Ch.D. 636.
[17]   *Hilliard* v. *Moriarty* [1894] 1 I.R. 316; *Giltrap* v. *Byrne* (1902) 2 N.I.J.R. 103.
[18]   *Re Lighton* (1851) 4 Ir.Jur.(O.S.) 35; *Re Kennedy's Estate* (1898) 32 I.L.T.R. 115; *cf. Re Keily's Estate* (1861) 6 Ir.Jur. (N.S.) 184. See also *Cromwell Property Investment Co. Ltd.* v. *Western & Toovey* [1934] Ch. 322, where, at p. 332, Maugham J. described this rule of practice as "harsh." *Cf.* notice to the mortgagor before the mortgagee enforces his security, see *Kelly* v. *Hurley* (1906) 40 I.L.T.R. 117; *Royal Bank of Ireland Ltd.* v. *Daly* [1938] I.R. 192.
[19]   See *Smith* v. *Smith* [1891] 3 Ch. 550. See *Browne* v. *Lockhart* (1840) 10 Sim. 420 at 424.

enforced where the mortgage is of a temporary nature only[20] or the mortgagee has already demanded payment[21] or has taken steps to enforce his security[22], e.g., by taking possession[23] or initiating foreclosure proceedings.[24] If the mortgagor, having given notice, then fails to pay on the proper day, he will usually have to give further reasonable notice or pay interest in lieu thereof.[25]

(ii) Payment of Capital, Interest and Costs

13.102. The general rule is that the mortgagor must on redemption pay the principal sum owing to the mortgagee and the interest charged thereon, plus the proper costs of the mortgagee.[26] If no rate of interest has been fixed by the mortgage instrument, the mortgagee is generally entitled to 4 per cent.[27] Should the mortgagor make overpayments of interest, these may be treated as payments of principal *pro tanto, e.g.*, if they are fairly substantial in relation to the mortgage debt.[28] Otherwise they will be treated as money paid under a mistake of fact which may be set off against the debt owed by the mortgagor, as being a debt *pro tanto* owed by the mortgagee to the mortgagor.[29]

13.103. So far as costs are concerned, the mortgagee is entitled to all reasonable costs incurred by him in maintaining, protecting or realising his security,[30] unless he has been guilty of misconduct.[31] Thus a mortgagee in possession will be deprived of his costs if he fails to account to the mortgagor.[32] Where a redemption suit is brought by a *puisne* mortgagee, the costs of each prior mortgagee are added to his security and the total thus

---

[20]   It was held in *Fitzgerald's Trustee* v. *Mellersh* [1892] 1 Ch. 385 that equitable mortgages by deposit of title deeds are usually so considered.

[21]   *Bovill* v. *Endle* [1896] 1 Ch. 648 at 651; *Edmonson* v. *Copland* [1911] 2 Ch. 301.

[22]   *Re Alcock* (1883) 23 Ch.D. 372 at 376.

[23]   *Bovill* v. *Endle* [1896] 1 Ch. 648.

[24]   *Hill* v. *Rowlands* [1897] 2 Ch. 361 at 363.

[25]   *Re Moss* (1885) 31 Ch.D. 90 at 94. See also *Cromwell Property Investment Co. Ltd.* v. *Western & Toovey* [1934] Ch. 322.

[26]   *Burrowes* v. *Molloy* (1845) 2 Jo. & Lat. 521; *Wynne* v. *Brady* (1843) 5 Ir.Eq.R. 239. See also *Bank of New South Wales* v. *O'Connor* (1889) 14 App.Cas. 273; *Webb* v. *Crosse* [1912] 1 Ch. 323.

[27]   *Carey* v. *Doyne* (1856) 5 Ir.Ch.R. 104. If the mortgagee obtains a judgment debt against the mortgagor, on which interest at 4 per cent is usually allowed, the question may arise as to the appropriate rate to be allowed if the covenant for interest in the mortgage deed stipulates a higher rate of interest. This question seems to depend upon whether the covenant in the deed is to be regarded as being "merged" in the judgment, see *Lowry* v. *Williams* [1895] 1 I.R. 274; *Usbourne* v. *Limerick Market Trustees* [1900] 1 I.R. 103, on appeal, *sub nom. Economic Life Assurance Society* v. *Usbourne* [1902] A.C. 147. Cf. *Kevans* v. *Joyce* [1896] 1 I.R. 442 (6 per cent. interest reduced by court to 5 per cent.). See also the remarks of Kenny J. in *Law* v. *Robert Roberts & Co. (No. 2)* [1964] I.R. 306.

[28]   *Re Carroll's Estate* [1901] 1 I.R. 78.

[29]   *Re Scott's Estate* (1903) 3 N.I.J.R. 119; *Re Jone's Estate* [1914] 1 I.R. 188.

[30]   *Crone* v. *Hegarty* (1879) 3 L.R.Ir. 50; *Re Baldwin's Estate* [1900] 1 I.R. 15. See also *Ennis* v. *Brady* (1839) 1 Dr. & Wal. 720; *Cane* v. *Brownrigg* (1840) 2 Ir.Eq.R. 413; *Bernard* v. *Sadlier* (1841) 4 Ir.Eq.R. 61; *Leonard* v. *Kellett* (1891) 27 L.R.Ir. 418; *Hilliard* v. *Moriarty* [1894] 1 I.R. 316; *McElhinney* v. *Ingram* (1905) 5 N.I.J.R. 167; *Dinsmore* v. *Magowan* (1932) 66 I.L.T.R. 160; *Re Erskine* (1943) 77 I.L.T.R. 66.

[31]   *Loftus* v. *Swift* (1806) 2 Sch. & Lef. 642; *McDonnell* v. *McMahon* (1889) 23 L.R.Ir. 283; *Greene* v. *Murphy* (1901) 1 N.I.J.R. 95.

[32]   *Cassidy* v. *Sullivan* (1878) 1 L.R.Ir. 313. See para. 13.047, *ante.* See also *O'Neill* v. *Innes* (1864) 15 Ir.Ch.R. 527.

arrived at is paid, with interest, according to the respective priority of each mortgage.[33]

13.104. Until the late nineteenth century a solicitor, who was the mortgagee, could not charge his profit costs for professional services against the mortgagor. This position was changed by the Mortgagees Legal Costs Act, 1895, which is still in force in both parts of Ireland. By section 3 of that Act, any solicitor to whom a mortgage is made or in whom it is vested by transfer or transmission, or his firm, is entitled to charge all such usual professional charges and remuneration as he or the firm would otherwise have been entitled to charge against the mortgaged property for all business transacted and acts done by the solicitor or the firm in relation to the mortgage or the property. The mortgage cannot be redeemed without payment of such charges and remuneration, which are, therefore, a charge on the property. Section 2 of the same Act allows a solicitor-mortgagee, or his firm, to charge the costs and expenses of negotiating the loan, deducing and investigating the title to the property and preparing and completing the mortgage to the mortgagor, so as to render them recoverable by action. In this case, however, the costs are not a charge on the mortgaged property.

(iii) Redeem Up, Foreclose Down

13.105. This is a principle insisted upon by the English courts where a subsequent mortgagee brings a redemption suit against a prior mortgagee or foreclosure proceedings against the mortgagor and mortgagees subsequent to him, in which he seeks also to redeem a prior mortgagee. The following example may be used by way of illustration: O mortgages his land in succession to A, B, C, D and E who rank, in terms of priority, in that order. D wishes to improve his position and seeks to redeem B. The accounts in such a case will be extremely complicated and so it is likely that a redemption suit will be brought to court. If that happens, the court will take the view that all those parties who have an interest in what B is entitled to on redemption should be parties to the action and represented in court. The settling of the accounts as between D and B, which is designed to determine exactly what B is owed, is of vital significance to those who are entitled to what is left over after B is paid off, *i.e.*, to those who are subsequent to B in terms of priority, namely C, E and O, who, as mortgagor, comes last of all. A is not concerned because his mortgage has priority to B and, if the property were sold, he would be entitled to be paid first out of the proceeds. If the property is not to be sold as a result of D's redemption suit, A can be left with his first mortgage on it.[34] The principle is, therefore, that a mortgagee who brings a redemption suit against a prior mortgagee must both redeem all mortgagees ranking prior to him and between him and the one being redeemed and foreclose all

---

[33] *Barry* v. *Stawell* (1838) 1 Dr. & Wal. 618; *Snagg* v. *Frith* (1846) 9 Ir.Eq.R. 285; *Handcock* v. *Handcock* (1850) 1 Ir.Ch.R. 444; *Montgomery* v. *Donohoe* (1857) 6 Ir.Ch.R. 168; *Hilliard* v. *Moriarty* [1894] 1 I.R. 316; *Giltrap* v. *Byrne* (1902) 2 N.I.J.R. 103.

[34] *Loughran* v. *Loughran* (1885) 15 L.R.Ir. 71. See also *Rose* v. *Page* (1829) 2 Sim. 471; *Brisco* v. *Kenrick* (1832) 1 L.J.Ch. 116.

subsequent mortgagees and the mortgagor.[35] The applicability of the principle in Ireland is, however, extremely doubtful in view of the fact that redemption suits are extremely rare and foreclosure orders are never made.[36]

4. *Effect of Redemption*

13.106. Normally redemption involves discharge of the mortgage and reconveyance of the property free from the mortgage, *e.g.*, where the mortgagor redeems the only mortgage.[37] Furthermore, by section 15 of the Conveyancing Act, 1881, a mortgagor entitled to redeem may require[38] the mortgagee, instead of reconveying, to assign the mortgage debt and convey the mortgaged property to any third person as the mortgagor directs. This right to compel a transfer of the mortgage instead of redemption was extended to each incumbrancer on the property, and the mortgagor, despite the existence of any intermediate incumbrance, by section 12 of the Conveyancing Act, 1882. In such a case, section 12 provides that a requisition of an incumbrancer prevails over a requisition of the mortgagor and, as between incumbrancers, a requisition of a prior incumbrancer prevails over that of a subsequent incumbrancer.[39] The right to compel a transfer is excluded, however, where a mortgagee is or has been in possession.[40] Such a mortgagee is liable to account strictly to the mortgagor[41] and may be liable for any defaults of the transferee,[42] so it would be unfair to allow the mortgagor to compel him to transfer the mortgage.

5. *Sale*

13.107. Section 25 of the Conveyancing Act, 1881, provided that any person entitled to redeem could apply to the court for an order of sale instead,[43] but this particular section did *not* apply to Ireland[44] and there is no equivalent legislation in force in either part of Ireland. However, the court in any redemption suit has a discretion to order a sale on the request of the mortgagee or any person interested in the proceeds of a sale.[45]

6. *Termination of the Equity of Redemption*

13.108. There are several ways in which the mortgagor may lose his equity of redemption, some of which we have already considered. Apart from the obvious ways, which the mortgagor himself controls, *e.g.*, by redeeming or releasing it,[46] the following should be mentioned.

---

[35] *Farmer* v. *Curtis* (1828) 2 Sim. 466; *Teevan* v. *Smith* (1882) 20 Ch.D. 724. See also *Ocean Accident Corp.* v. *Collum* [1913] 1 I.R. 328. *Cf. McDonough* v. *Shewbridge* (1814) 2 Ba. & B. 555 at 561–2 (*per* McMahon M.R.).
[36] Paras. 13.056–60, *ante*.
[37] See further on discharge of mortgages and charges, para. 13.135, *post*.
[38] This power exists despite any stipulation to the contrary, see s. 15 (3). As to the position before the 1881 Act, see *Colyer* v. *Colyer* (1863) 3 De G.J. & S. 676 at 693.
[39] See *Re Magneta Time Co. Ltd.* (1915) 84 L.J.Ch. 814.
[40] 1881 Act, s. 15 (2). See *Teevan* v. *Smith* (1882) 10 Ch.D. 724.
[41] See para. 13.046, *ante*.
[42] *Hinde* v. *Blake* (1841) 11 L.J.Ch. 26; *Hall* v. *Heward* (1886) 32 Ch.D. 430.
[43] See *Clarke* v. *Pannell* (1884) 29 Sol.Jo. 147.
[44] S. 25 (7).
[45] Para. 13.040, *ante*.
[46] *Reeve* v. *Lisle* [1902] A.C. 461.

(i) Foreclosure

We have already considered this.[47]

(ii) Sale

This too we have considered.[48]

(iii) Lapse of Time

This we consider in a later chapter.[49]

(iv) Merger

The doctrine of merger[50] applies where two estates or interests in the same land come into the same hands and this has obvious relevance where the same person acquires both an interest in the security on the mortgaged property and the equity of redemption.[51] For example, suppose O mortgages his land to A, B and C, who rank in that order for the purposes of priority. If O then redeems A's mortgage, the question arises as to whether a merger takes place or as to whether O can claim to keep A's mortgage alive so as to secure priority over B and C. Similarly, if O sells the equity of redemption to X and X redeems A's mortgage, the question arises as to whether X can keep it alive or, if O releases the equity of redemption to A, can A keep his mortgage alive as against B and C? The following is the position.

13.109. First, where the mortgagor redeems a prior mortgage, it is the general rule of law[52] that this discharges that mortgage and the mortgagor cannot set it up against subsequent mortgagees.[53] Thus, to take the example given above, if O redeems A's mortgage he cannot claim to have kept it alive, so that, if it subsequently turns out that the property is of insufficient value to meet all the parties' claims, O cannot claim priority over B and C to the extent of the amount that was due on A's mortgage. This rule is not so much an application of the doctrine of merger as a special rule governing a mortgagor and his own incumbrancers–he cannot, as it were, derogate from his own grants or bargains[54] in this way.[55]

13.110. Secondly, so far as parties other than the mortgagor are concerned, *i.e.*, subsequent purchasers of the equity of redemption, whether third parties or other mortgagees, they may claim to keep the mortgage in question alive. Here the doctrine of merger does govern the matter. At common law, a merger in cases of the acquisition of two interests in the same land always took place regardless of the intention of the person acquiring

---

[47] Paras. 13.056 *et seq., ante.*
[48] Paras. 13.022 *et seq., ante.*
[49] Ch. 23, *post.* See Statute of Limitations, 1957, ss. 34 (1) (*a*) and 35 (R.I.); Statute of Limitations (N.I.), 1958, ss. 36 and 37.
[50] See further, ch. 24, *post.*
[51] See Randall, "Merger of Charges" (1912) 28 L.Q.R. 348.
[52] It is subject to an agreement to the contrary worked out between the parties concerned, see *Re Cork Harbour Docks and Warehouse Co. Ltd's Estate* (1885) 17 L.R.Ir. 515.
[53] *Re Parnell's Estate* (1901) 1 N.I.J.R. 168. See also *Otter* v. *Lord Vaux* (1856) 6 De G.M. & G. 638.
[54] See further, ch. 24, *post.*
[55] See *Whiteley* v. *Delaney* [1914] A.C. 132 at 145 (*per* Lord Haldane L.C.).

them, the lesser estate or interest merging in the greater.[56] In equity, however, whether or not a merger takes place is entirely a matter of the intention of the person who acquires the two interests[57] and the Judicature (Ireland) Act, 1877, extended this equitable doctrine to common law estates and interests in land.[58] This equitable doctrine now governs the position of holders of an interest in the equity of redemption and an interest in the security relating to mortgaged property, other than the mortgagors who created the mortgages.[59] Generally, the intention is to be found from all the statements and acts of the person in question,[60] though once an intention has been expressed unequivocally it has been doubted if subsequent acts can nullify this.[61] If the court finds it difficult to decipher a precise intention, it will generally presume that it was the intention to adopt the course most advantageous to the person concerned.[62] In most cases where there are mortgages subsequent to the one redeemed, it is to the advantage of the person redeeming to keep that mortgage alive and so no merger will be regarded as having taken place.[63]

(v) Consolidation

We have already discussed the effect of this doctrine on the right to redeem.[64]

III. RIGHTS COMMON TO BOTH PARTIES

We now turn to rights connected with a mortgage which are common to both the mortgagor and the mortgagee. Two such rights, which are connected, exist, the power to grant leases and the power to accept surrenders of leases.

A. LEASES

13.111 A power to grant leases was recognised at common law to a certain extent and there now exists a statutory power of leasing, which is governed by section 18 of the Conveyancing Act, 1881.

1. *At Common Law*

At common law the power of leasing varied according to whether the mortgagor or mortgagee wished to exercise it.

---

[56] See, *e.g.*, *Harnett* v. *Power* (1836) 2 Jones 145; *Williams* v. *Morris* (1849) 13 Ir.Eq.R. 147. *Cf.* where there were two equal estates, *Creagh* v. *Blood* (1845) 8 Ir.Eq.R. 688, or a legal and an equitable estate, *Re Sergie* [1954] N.I. 1; *Re Elliott's Estate* (1873) I.R. 8 Eq. 565.

[57] *Re Butlin's Estate* [1907] 1 I.R. 159; *Re Toppin's Estate* [1915] 1 I.R. 330 (see *A Casebook on Irish Land Law* (1984), p. 703); *Re Alexander's Estate* [1938] I.R. 23. See also *Re Smallman's Estate* (1868) I.R. 2 Eq. 34; *Re Roche's Estate* (1890) 25 L.R.Ir. 284.

[58] S. 28 (4), replaced in N.I. by s. 89 of the Judicature (Northern Ireland) Act, 1978, (U.K.), see para. 24.12, *post.*

[59] *Redington* v. *Redington* (1809) 1 Ba. & B. 131; *Lindsay* v. *Earl of Wicklow* (1873) I.R. 7 Eq. 192; *Church* v. *Church* (1877) 11 I.L.T.R. 163; *Re Howard's Estate* (1892) 29 L.R.Ir. 266.

[60] *Lysaght* v. *Lysaght* (1851) 4 Ir.Jur.(O.S.) 110; *Re Parnell's Estate* (1901) 1 N.I.J.R. 68; *Re Lloyd's Estate* [1903] 1 I.R. 144.

[61] See *Re Godley's Estate* [1896] 1 I.R. 45.

[62] *Re Nunn's Estate* (1888) 23 L.R.Ir. 286 at 300 (*per* Lord Ashbourne C.).

[63] *Keogh* v. *Keogh* (1874) I.R. 8 Eq. 449; *Re Godley's Estate* [1896] 1 I.R. 45. *Cf. Purcell* v. *Purcell* (1854) 5 Ir.Ch.R. 502.

[64] Paras. 13.069 *et seq.*, *ante.*

(i) Mortgagor

13.112. Since the mortgagor is usually allowed to remain in possession of the mortgaged property, he may wish to exercise the usual powers of management of land which would include a power to lease it.[65] Any lease granted by the mortgagor would be binding at common law as between the mortgagor and the tenant, as a lease by estoppel.[66] Thus the mortgagor could exercise as against the tenant the usual rights of a landlord in respect of rent.[67] However, such a lease could be created out of the mortgagor's equity of redemption only and, as such, would not normally bind the mortgagee whose rights under the existing mortgage would be paramount.[68] The mortgagor could not fetter the mortgagee's right to take possession of the land[69] or, if he so chose, of the rents and profits of the land. The mortgagee would be bound by the lease only if he joined in granting it or if he otherwise acknowledged it in such a way as to give rise to an estoppel as against him as well as the mortgagor.[70]

(ii) Mortgagee

13.113. On the other hand, a mortgagee, as holder of the legal right to possession of the land, has power to grant leases.[71] Such leases, however, like the mortgagee's mortgage itself, are subject to the mortgagor's equity of redemption and to that extent a lessee of the mortgagee suffers just as much insecurity of tenure at common law as a lessee of the mortgagor.

2. By Statute

13.114. Section 18 of the Conveyancing Act, 1881, gets over the difficulties of the common law by conferring a statutory power of leasing on both the mortgagor and the mortgagee, while either of them is in possession of the mortgaged land.[72] In the case of a lease made by the mortgagor, it will bind every mortgagee[73] and a mortgagee's lease will bind every prior mortgagee and the mortgagor.[74] In exercising this power, the mortgagor or mortgagee must comply with the detailed provisions laid down by the 1881 Act, otherwise the other party to the mortgage will not be bound by the lease.[75]

---

[65] Cf. a tenant for life of settled land, ch. 8, ante.

[66] See Re O'Rourke's Estate (1889) 23 L.R.Ir. 497; Keenan v. Walsh (1951) 85 I.L.T.R. 86. See also Hassard v. Fowler (1892) 32 L.R.Ir. 49.

[67] See ch. 17, post.

[68] McAreavey v. Hannan (1862) 13 I.C.L.R. 70; Raikton v. Caldwell [1895] 2 I.R. 136. See also Miles v. Murphy (1871) I.R. 5 C.L. 382 (express power). Cf. National Bank v. Lynch (1930) 64 I.L.T.R. 17 (equitable mortgagees bound).

[69] Cf. where the lease is created before the mortgage, or the mortgagee subsequently purchases the equity of redemption, O'Loughlin v. Fitzgerald (1873) I.R. 7 Eq. 483. See also Wyse v. Myers (1854) 4 I.C.L.R. 101.

[70] Roulston v. Caldwell [1895] 2 I.R. 136. See also Smallman Ltd. v. Castle [1932] I.R. 294.

[71] See the discussion in Re O'Rourke's Estate (1889) 23 L.R.Ir. 497. Also Chapman v. Smith [1907] 2 Ch. 97 at 102.

[72] Subject to any express stipulation to the contrary in the mortgage deed or elsewhere in writing.

[73] S. 18 (1). And see Munster and Leinster Bank Ltd. v. Hollinshead [1930] I.R. 187.

[74] S. 18 (2). The powers of leasing are to be exercised by the mortgagee as if he were in possession, where a receiver has been appointed and for so long as the receiver acts, see s. 3 (11) of the Conveyancing Act, 1911. As to appointment of a receiver, see para. 13.048, ante.

[75] Thomas Murphy & Co. Ltd. v. Marren [1933] I.R. 393; Keenan v. Walsh (1951) 85 I.L.T.R. 86. See further, para. 13.116, post.

(i) Limits

Section 18 lays down maximum limits for leases granted by a mortgagor or mortgagee under the statutory power, *i.e.*, 21 years for agricultural or occupational leases, and 99 years for building leases.[76]

(ii) Conditions

13.115. Every lease must comply with certain conditions[77]: it must be made to take effect in possession not later than 12 months after its date[78]; it must reserve the best rent that can reasonably be obtained, regard being had to the circumstances of the case, but without any fine being taken[79]; it must contain a covenant by the lessee for payment of the rent and a condition of re-entry if the rent is not paid within a time therein specified, not exceeding 30 days[80]; a counterpart must be executed by the lessee and delivered to the lessor.[81] Furthermore, in the case of a building lease,[82] it must be made in consideration of the lessee having erected, or agreeing to erect within not more than 5 years from the date of the lease, buildings, new or additional, or having improved or repaired buildings, or agreeing to improve or repair buildings within that time.[83] In the case of a lease by the mortgagor, he must, within one month of making it, deliver to the mortgagee or, if there are more than one, the first mortgagee in priority, a counterpart of the lease duly executed by the lessee, though the lessee is not concerned to see that this provision is complied with.[84]

13.116. Non-compliance with the above conditions does not necessarily mean that a purported exercise of the statutory power fails. First, section 18 (17) of the 1881 Act provides that the provisions in the section referring to a lease "shall be construed to extend and apply, as far as circumstances admit, to any letting, and to an agreement, whether in writing or not, for leasing or letting." It is not clear how far this rather vague provision extends. It seems to say that an oral letting or agreement for a lease may be a valid exercise of the power, but it does not make clear how far precisely the letting or oral agreement must still comply with the conditions laid down in section 18.[85] Secondly, a purported exercise of the power of leasing may be validated under the Leases Act, 1849 and 1850, which are still in force in both parts of Ireland.[86] These provide that, if the exercise of a power was intended, the

---

[76] S. 18 (3). *Cf.* the limits on leases granted by a tenant for life, para. 8.071, *ante*. See also *Brown* v. *Peto* [1900] 2 Q.B. 653; *King* v. *Bird* [1909] 1 K.B. 837.

[77] *Cf.* in the case of a tenant for life, para. 8.072, *ante*.

[78] S. 18 (5).

[79] S. 18 (6). See *Coutts & Co.* v. *Somerville* [1935] Ch. 438.

[80] S. 18 (7). See *Thomas Murphy & Co. Ltd.* v. *Marren* [1933] I.R. 393.

[81] The execution of the lease by the lessor is, in favour of the lessee and his successors in title, sufficient evidence of such execution and delivery, see s. 18 (8).

[82] In which a peppercorn rent, or a nominal or other rent less than the rent ultimately payable, may be made payable for the first 5 years or any less part of the term, s. 18 (10).

[83] Or having executed, or agreeing to execute, within that time, on the land leased, an improvement for or in connection with building purposes, s. 18 (9).

[84] S. 18 (11). See *Public Trustee* v. *Lawrence* [1912] 1 Ch. 789.

[85] Presumably not with the provision as to counterparts in s. 18 (8) in the case of an *oral* letting. See, as regards covenants and conditions of re-entry, *Pawson* v. *Revell* [1958] 2 Q.B. 360.

[86] See para. 11.17, *ante*.

invalid lease can take effect in equity as a contract for a grant of a valid lease, provided the invalid lease was made in good faith and the lessee has entered.[87] These Acts seem designed to save leases otherwise valid but for some minor or technical flaw.[88] Thirdly, by their acts and conduct the parties who would not otherwise be bound by the lease may estop themselves from denying that the lessee in question has a valid tenancy. Bare recognition of the lease in the sense of raising no objection or refraining from eviction is not enough to raise an estoppel.[89] Normally where there is an estoppel the lessee becomes a periodic tenant only, *e.g.*, from week to week or year to year, depending on how the rent is calculated.[90] Only if the confirmatory conduct or acts are such as to make it inequitable to deny the existence of the lease in question will that lease in all its terms and particulars be given recognition.

If a lease is not saved in any of these ways, it is still valid as between the lessor and lessee. The statutory powers of leasing do not prevent the mortgagor and mortgagee from creating leases at common law which do not bind each other.[91]

(iii) Contrary Agreement

13.117. The statutory power of leasing may be either excluded[92] or extended[93] by agreement of the mortgagor and mortgagee expressed in the mortgage deed or otherwise in writing. It is common for mortgage deeds to contain a covenant by the mortgagor not to make any lease or letting without the mortgagee's consent, if the power of leasing is not excluded altogether.

B. Surrenders of Leases

13.118. The question sometimes arises as to how far a lease, already validly created, can be surrendered, usually with a view to granting a new lease. The following is now the position on this matter.

1. *At Common Law*

The position at common law was that the mortgagor could not accept a surrender of a lease granted under the statutory power conferred by the Conveyancing Act, 1881, without the consent of the mortgagee, who was bound by that lease.[94] This position was altered by the Conveyancing Act, 1911, which remains in force in both parts of Ireland.

---

[87] For some reason leases of land "held on charitable, ecclesiastical or public trusts" were expressly excluded from the 1849 and 1850 Acts. See *Survey of the Land Law of Northern Ireland* (1971), para. 298.

[88] See discussion in *Kisch* v. *Hawes Bros.* [1935] Ch. 102; *Iron Trades Employers' Insurance Association* v. *Union Land and House Investors* [1937] Ch. 313, espec. at 323; *Pawson* v. *Revell* [1958] 2 Q.B. 360, dealing with s. 152 of the Law of Property Act, 1925, which replaced the 1849 and 1850 Acts in England.

[89] See the discussion in *Re O'Rourke's Estate* (1889) 23 L.R.Ir. 497. See also *Lever Finance Ltd.* v. *Needleman's Trustee* [1956] Ch. 375; *Taylor* v. *Ellis* [1960] Ch. 368; *Barclay's Bank Ltd.* v. *Kiley* [1961] 1 W.L.R. 1050. Prichard, "Tenancy by Estoppel" (1964) 80 L.Q.R. 370.

[90] See ch. 17, *post.*

[91] Paras. 13.112–3, *ante.*

[92] 1881 Act, s. 18 (13). In Northern Ireland, however, exclusion of the statutory power cannot hamper the power of the court to grant a new lease of business premises under the Business Tenancies Act (N.I.), 1964, see s. 17 (4) of that Act.

[93] S. 18 (14). However, nothing in the Act is to be construed as enabling the mortgagor or mortgagee to make a lease for any longer term or on any other conditions than such as could have been granted or imposed by the mortgagor, with the concurrence of all the incumbrances, before the statutory intervention, s. 18 (15).

[94] *Robbins* v. *Whyte* [1906] 1 K.B. 125.

2. *By Statute*

13.119. Section 3 of the 1911 Act enables a mortgagor or mortgagee in possession[95] to accept a surrender of a lease of the mortgaged land, but for the purpose only of granting a new lease authorised by the 1881 Act or the mortgage deed.[96]

(i) Limits

It is provided that the term of the new lease is not to be less in duration than the unexpired term of the original lease, had it not been surrendered.[97]

(ii) Conditions

Furthermore, a surrender is not valid unless the following conditions[98] are satisfied: an authorised lease of the property is granted to take effect in possession within one month of the surrender[99]; the rent reserved by the new lease is not less than the rent reserved by the surrendered lease.[1] If these conditions are not met the surrender is void.[2]

(iii) Contrary Agreement

Once again the statutory power of accepting surrenders may be excluded or extended[3] by the mortgage deed or otherwise by agreement in writing.

IV. TRANSFER OF RIGHTS

The various rights of a mortgagor and mortgagee may be transferred to third parties both *inter vivos* and on death.

A. MORTGAGOR

1. *Inter Vivos*

13.120. Subject to the terms of the mortgage instrument, there is nothing to prevent a mortgagor making an *inter vivos* transfer of his equity of redemption to some other person.[4] Generally speaking, the assignee takes the property subject to the mortgage. The mortgagor, however, remains liable personally on the covenant to pay the debt,[5] but he will usually require the assignee to enter into a covenant of indemnity in respect of the debt.[6]

---

[95] Including where a receiver has been appointed and is still acting, s. 3 (11).

[96] In certain cases the consent of incumbrancers may be required, see s. 3 (4).

[97] S. 3 (5) (*b*).

[98] There are provisions throughout s. 3 allowing surrender of leases with or without exception of mines and minerals or of part only of the land leased, and for apportionment of rent, etc. See s. 3 (1), (3) and (5).

[99] S. 3 (5) (*a*).

[1] S. 3 (5) (*c*).

[2] *Barclays Bank Ltd.* v. *Stasck* [1957] Ch. 28. Megarry, (1957) 73 L.Q.R. 14.

[3] S. 3 (7) and (8). However, a surrender cannot be accepted which could not have been accepted before the Act by the mortgagor with the concurrence of all the incumbrancers.

[4] *Weatherup* v. *McKelvey* (1933) 67 I.L.T.R. 125. See also the discussion on the propriety of the mortgagee purchasing the equity of redemption in *Kevans* v. *Joyce* [1896] 1 I.R. 442. He also, of course, can mortgage the equity of redemption, see para. 12.05, *ante*. See *Campion* v. *Palmer* [1896] 2 I.R. 445.

[5] *Kinnaird* v. *Trollope* (1888) 39 Ch.D. 636. See also *Re Howard's Estate* (1892) 29 L.R.Ir. 266.

[6] Such a covenant is implied on behalf of an assignee for value, *Adair* v. *Carden* (1891) 29 L.R.Ir. 469. See also *Bridgman* v. *Daw* (1891) 40 W.R. 253; *Mills* v. *United Counties Bank Ltd.* [1912] 1 Ch. 231; *Re Best* [1924] 1 Ch. 42.

If the mortgagor wants to sell the property free from the mortgage he will have to redeem or get the mortgagee to join in the conveyance, which he may be prepared to do if other security is going to replace the property. Otherwise, the mortgagor may seek a discharge of the mortgage by payment of sufficient money into court, under the power conferred by section 5 of the Conveyancing Act, 1881.[7]

2. On Death

13.121. Where a mortgagor dies nowadays in either part of Ireland and his interest in the property passes to a successor, testate or intestate, the general rule is that charges[8] on his property are, as between the different persons claiming through the deceased, to be paid primarily out of the property charged.[9] This, however, is subject to a contrary intention signified by the deceased mortgagor by will, deed or other document.[10]

B. MORTGAGEE

1. Inter Vivos

13.122. A mortgagee is free to transfer his mortgage, i.e., both the debt owed and the security interest in the property, to a third person.[11] A transfer of his interest in the property only will carry the debt with it,[12] whereas a transfer for value of the debt alone will necessitate joining the transferor in any suit to enforce the security.[13] To avoid disputes as to the amount of the debt which is transferred, it may be wise to have the mortgagor join in the transfer, so that he will be bound by the statement as to the amount of the debt.[14] Furthermore, if the mortgagor does not join in the transfer, the transferee ought to give him notice of the transfer to ensure that the debt is not paid to the transferor.[15]

13.123. Instead of making an out-and-out transfer of his mortgage, the mortgagee may instead mortgage it, i.e., create a sub-mortgage.[16] The

---

[7] Para. 6.145, ante.

[8] Including legal and equitable mortgages and charges, and liens for unpaid purchase money. Pim v. Pim (1902) 36 I.L.T.R. 136; Thompson v. Bell [1903] 1 I.R. 489. Also a judgment mortgage, Nesbitt v. Lawder (1886) 17 L.R.Ir. 53.

[9] Succession Act, 1965, s. 47 (R.I.); Administration of Estates Act (N.I.), 1955, s. 31. These provisions replace Locke King's Acts, i.e., the Real Estate Charges Acts, 1854, 1867 and 1877. See ch. 16, post.

[10] Which does not include, e.g., a general direction for payment of debts out of the estate, unless there is further reference to the charge expressly or by necessary implication, 1965 Act, s. 47 (2); 1955 Act, s. 31 (2). See generally, Buckley v. Buckley (1887) 19 L.R.Ir. 544; Thompson v. Bell [1903] 1 I.R. 489.

[11] Re Quinlan's Trusts (1859) 9 Ir.Ch.R. 306. This includes equitable mortgages created by deposit of title deeds, see Re O'Brien (1883) 11 L.R.Ir. 213; Simmons v. Montague [1909] 1 I.R. 87. See the discussion of Re O'Brien by Hamilton J. in Re Sherry-Brennan (1979) Unrep. (H.C., R.I.) (1979 No. 1665). Note the form of statutory transfer of statutory mortgages provided by s. 27 of and in Pt. II of the 3rd Sched. to the Conveyancing Act, 1881. Re Beachey [1904] 1 Ch. 67. As to transfer of a charge on registered land, see Registration of Title Act, 1964, s. 64 (R.I.); Land Registration Act (N.I.), 1970, Sched. 7, Pt. I, para.6.

[12] Jones v. Gibbons (1804) 9 Ves. 407 at 411.

[13] Morley v. Morley (1858) 25 Beav. 253 at 258; Woodford v. Charnley (1860) 28 Beav. 96.

[14] Agnew v. King [1902] 1 I.R. 471; Hicks v. Butler [1932] L.J.Ir. 92; see also Turner v. Smith [1901] 1 Ch. 213.

[15] Dixon v. Winch [1900] 1 Ch. 736 at 742.

[16] Smith v. Chichester (1842) 3 Ir.Eq.R. 580; Connolly v. Munster Bank (1887) 19 L.R.Ir. 119; Feehan v. Mandeville (1890) 28 L.R.Ir. 90. See also, re judgment mortgages, Rossborough v. McNeill (1889) 23 L.R.Ir.

mortgagee may prefer to do this where he wishes to borrow a sum which is small when compared to the debt owed to him by the mortgagor, so that he does not wish to call in that debt. Provided the lender is satisfied that the mortgagee's debt is well-secured, he may be prepared to accept it as security for his loan. The sub-mortgage can then be created by assignment of that debt and transfer of the mortgage subject to a proviso for redemption, or the granting of a sub-lease with a proviso for cesser. The sub-mortgagee for the most part steps into the mortgagee's position and can exercise his rights in respect of the head-mortgage for its enforcement and realisation.[17] He also, of course, exercises his own rights in respect of the sub-mortgage.

2. On Death

13.124. Nowadays, in both parts of Ireland the debt owed to the mortgagee, which is personalty, and the security interest in land devolve alike on the deceased mortgagee's personal representatives, *i.e.*, his executors or administrators, depending upon whether he died testate or intestate.[18]

V. DISCHARGE

13.125. Earlier we considered the subject of redemption of a mortgage by the mortgagor[19] and here we consider the related topic of how the discharge of the land from the mortgage is achieved. Where a legal mortgage has been created by conveyance of the fee simple or assignment of a lease, the discharge must be effected in the Republic by a reconveyance or reassignment of the estate in the land from the mortgagee to the mortgagor, or to his order, and the deed in each case should contain a receipt for the redemption money paid. In the case of a lease, since the passing of the Satisfied Terms Act, 1845,[20] where the purpose for which a term of years was created becomes satisfied (*e.g.*, redemption of the mortgage) the term merges in the reversion[21] expectant thereon (held by the mortgagor) and ceases accordingly. However, this has been held to be inapplicable to sub-terms granted out of leases[22] and so, in the case of a mortgage of leasehold land created by sub-demise, the discharge must be effected by a surrender of the sub-lease. In the case of building society mortgages, discharge is simpler, for it is provided by statute that a special form of receipt indorsed on the

409. See generally, Woodhouse, "Sub-Mortgages: Their Creation, Realization, Transfer and Discharge" (1948) 12 Conv. 171.

[17] By s. 2 (vi) of the Conveyancing Act, "mortgagee" includes "any person from time to time deriving title under the original mortgage." See also *Smith* v. *Chichester* (1842) 4 Ir.Eq.R. 580; *Feehan* v. *Mandeville* (1890) 28 L.R.Ir. 90; *Re Ambrose's Estate* [1914] 1 I.R. 123.

[18] Succession Act, 1965, s. 10 (R.I.); Administration of Estates Act (N.I.), 1955, s. 1. These Acts replace the earlier provision for vesting of an estate or interest in land subject to a mortgage in personal representatives contained in the Conveyancing Act, 1881, s. 30. See ch. 16, *post*. Note also the significance of a "joint account" clause, para. 9.050, *ante*.

[19] Paras. 13.088 *et seq.*, *ante*.

[20] See *Re Sleeman* (1855) 4 Ir.Ch.R. 563.

[21] Note, however, that, under s. 3 of Deasy's Act, 1860, a reversion is no longer necessary to the creation of the relationship of landlord and tenant in Ireland, see para. 17.005, *post*. Also *Survey of the Land Law of Northern Ireland* (1971), para. 79.

[22] *Re Moore & Hulm's Contract* [1912] 2 Ch. 105.

mortgage deed operates both as a discharge of the mortgage and a reconveyance of the property.[23] In Northern Ireland, the Property (Discharge of Mortgage by Receipt) (N.I.) Order, 1983, extends this method to all mortgages.

13.126. Where there is a registered charge on the land, a note put by the Registrar on the register of satisfaction of the charge, or of release of part of the registered land from the charge, has the effect of making the charge cease to operate to that extent.[24] Such a note may be put on the register at the request of[25] the registered chargee or on proof of the satisfaction or release in question. For this it is provided that the receipt of the registered chargee or a release signed by him is sufficient proof of the satisfaction or release.[26]

Finally, it appears that an equitable mortgage is sufficiently discharged by a simple receipt[27] or cancellation of any document executed or by redelivery of the title deeds or other documents deposited.

VI. PRIORITIES

13.127. Since, as we have seen, it is common for more than one mortgage to be created out of the same property, we must consider the subject of priorities as between successive mortgages.[28] We have already considered in an earlier chapter the general principles of the law of priorities[29] and in the following pages we propose to state largely how those principles apply to mortgages of *land*.[30]

In considering the subject of priorities as between successive mortgages of land a distinction must be drawn between registered land, *i.e.*, land the title to which is registered in the Land Registry, and unregistered land.

A. REGISTERED LAND

13.128. The matter of priorities in respect of registered land is governed first and foremost by the Registration of Title Act, 1964, in the Republic, and the Land Registration Act (N.I.), 1970.

1. *Registered* v. *Registered*

13.129. Where there arises a question of priorities as between successive registered charges, the general rule is that priority is governed by the order in

---

[23] Building Societies Act, 1976, s. 84, (R.I.); Building Societies Act (N.I.), 1967, s. 37 and Sched. 6. *Stamers* v. *Preston* (1860) 9 I.C.L.R. 351. See *Irish Conveyancing Law* (1978), paras. 17.55–6. See also *Fourth City Mutual Benefit Building Society* v. *Williams* (1879) 14 Ch.D. 140.

[24] Registration of Title Act, 1964, s. 65 (1) (R.I.); Land Registration Act (N.I.), 1970, s. 49 (1).

[25] 1964 Act, s. 65 (1). Or with his concurrence, 1970 Act (N.I.), s. 49 (1) (a).

[26] 1964 Act, s. 65 (2); 1970 Act (N.I.), s. 49 (2) (which also provides that, where the chargee is a body corporate, a release may be made under the seal of the corporation).

[27] *Firth & Sons Ltd.* v. *C.I.R.* [1904] 2 K.B. 205.

[28] See Sheridan, "Notice and Registration" (1950) 9 N.I.L.Q. 33 and "Registration and the Priority of Securities" (1951) 33 J.I.B.I. 259. Also Ambrose, "Priorities in Registered Estate" (1948) 13 Conv. 100; Crane, "Equitable Interests in Land: Some Problems of Priority" (1956) 20 Conv. 444; Lee, "An Insoluble Problem of Mortgagees' Priorities" (1968) 32 Conv. 325.

[29] Paras. 3.069 *et seq.*, *ante*.

[30] Different rules govern priorities as between successive mortgages of *pure* personalty, see *Rochard* v. *Fulton* (1844) 7 Ir.Eq.R. 131. And see para. 3.092, *ante*.

[31] 1964 Act, s. 74; 1970 Act (N.I.), s. 40. See *Re Mackin* [1938] I.R. 1.

which the charges were registered.[31] In passing, however, it should be noted that a first registered chargee will also take subject to those burdens which affect registered land without registration.[32]

It is common banking practice in Ireland to arrange a mortgage or charge to secure not only past or present advances or loans to a client, but also future advances which may be made. In the case of registered land,[33] it is provided for such a case in both parts of Ireland[34] as follows:

> "Where a registered charge is expressed to be created on any land for the purpose of securing future advances[35] (whether with or without present advances), the registered owner of the charge shall be entitled in priority to any subsequent charge to the payment of any sum due to him in respect of such future advances, except any advances which may have been made after the date of, and with express notice in writing of, the subsequent charge."

2. *Registered* v. *Unregistered*

13.130. As between a registered charge and a subsequent unregistered *but* registrable one, it is clear that the registered one has priority. Even if the subsequent charge is later registered as a charge on the registered land, it can only be registered subject to existing registered rights, so *a fortiori* an existing registered charge has priority before the subsequent one is registered.

3. *Registered* v. *Unregistrable*

13.131. Apart from the burdens to which a registered owner or chargee takes subject without registration,[36] the registration of title systems in both parts of Ireland permit, as we have seen, the creation of informal, equitable mortgages by deposit of the land or charge certificate relating to the registered land.[37] Such informal mortgages are incapable of registration as substantive burdens on the registered land and so a question of priority as between such mortgages and registered charges has to be settled to some extent according to the principles governing unregistered land.[38] However, where the registered charge comes first in time it has the double claim to priority of being first in time and through the principle expressly recognised by the statute governing registration of title, that such equitable mortgages by deposit take effect subject to any registered rights.[39] Apart from that, if what is deposited is a charge certificate, this document in itself indicates the existence of a prior charge on the registered land.

---

[32] *E.g.*, public rights, land purchase annuities and tenancies for terms not exceeding 21 years. See ch. 21, *post*. 1964 Act, s. 72; 1970 Act (N.I.), s. 38 and Sched. 5.

[33] As to unregistered land, see para. 13.161, *post*.

[34] 1964 Act, s. 75 (1); 1970 Act, s. 43 (1).

[35] Which includes sums from time to time due on an account current, and all sums which by agreement or the course of business between the parties are considered to be advances on the security of the charge, 1964 Act, s. 75 (2); 1970 Act (N.I.), s. 43 (2).

[36] Ch. 21, *post*.

[37] 1964 Act, s. 105 (5); 1970 Act (N.I.), s. 50. See para. 12.29, *ante*.

[38] Paras. 13.141 *et seq.*, *post*.

[39] 1964 Act, s. 105 (5); 1970 (N.I.), s. 50 (which refers, *inter alia*, to "any registered burdens and to all other matters appearing from the register to affect the land").

4. *Unregistered* v. *Registered*

13.132. The general principles of registration of title state that the owner of a registered charge on land created for valuable consideration is not affected by any unregistered rights in or over the registered land.[40] Another principle is that a transfer of registered land without valuable consideration is subject to all unregistered rights subject to which the transferor held the land, though not if it is subsequently transferred to some other person for valuable consideration.[41]

5. *Unregistrable* v. *Registered*

13.133. Where an unregistrable mortgage on registered land is created first and subsequently a registered charge is created, the maxim—"where the equities are equal, the first in time prevails"—governs the matter.[42] Normally, of course, the subsequent registered chargee will be put on notice of the prior unregistrable mortgage by the fact that the land certificate is lodged with the mortgagee.[43] Of course, if the equitable depositee joins in a scheme of fraud to induce the subsequent registered chargee to lend on the security of the land, *e.g.*, by surrendering the land certificate to the mortgagor, the "equities" are no longer equal and the equitable depositee will lose the priority he would otherwise have.[44] Furthermore, even if the depositee is innocent of fraud and is induced to surrender the land certificate temporarily by some excuse given by the mortgagor, it seems that the equities are still unequal if the subsequent registered chargee had no notice of the prior equitable mortgage.[45]

6. *Unregistered* v. *Unregistrable*

13.134. Since the only way to create a mortgage on registered land, apart from an equitable mortgage by deposit of the land certificate, is by registered charge and no interest in the land can be created until the charge is registered,[46] a question of priority as between an unregistered charge and an unregistrable mortgage should not arise in practice. However, in *Tench* v. *Molyneux*,[47] where the registered owner of land purported to sell it, but the purchaser failed to get himself registered as the new owner, it was held that the purchaser still could claim priority over a subsequent mortgage on the land created by deposit of the land certificate by the registered owner. The court took the view that the question of priority as between the unregistered

---

[40] Registration of Title Act, 1964, s. 68 (3); *cf.* Land Registration Act (N.I.), 1970, s. 32 (2) (*b*).

[41] 1964 Act, s. 52 (2); 1970 Act (N.I.), s. 34 (5). See *Devoy* v. *Hanlon* [1929] I.R. 246; *Rattigan* v. *Regan* [1929] I.R. 342.

[42] Para. 3.054, *ante*.

[43] The land certificate must be produced, first, to the mortgagee to prove the mortgagor's title and, secondly, to the Land Register to have a registered charge entered on the register. See para. 13.004, *ante*. Also *Re Kellaghan* (1936) 70 I.L.T.R. 193.

[44] See para. 13.137, *post*.

[45] *I.e.*, an application by way of analogy of the "*bona fide* purchaser of the legal estate without notice" doctrine, see para. 3.074, *ante*. See also *Re Mulhern* [1931] I.R. 700. *Cf.* as regards unregistered land, para. 13.145, *post*.

[46] See Registration of Title Act, 1964, s. 68; Land Registration Act (N.I.), s. 32.

[47] (1914) 48 I.L.T.R. 48.

conveyance and the unregistrable mortgage should be settled by application of the maxim–"where the equities are equal, the first in time prevails." The Irish courts seem to have taken the view that an unregistered instrument relating to the registered land could create an equitable estate in the land,[48] a principle which seems to recognise a considerable exception to the central principles which are supposed to govern a registration of title system, namely, that the register should "mirror" the title as far as possible and that all dealings with the land should be presented for registration to the Land Registry, subject to very limited exceptions only.[49]

13.135. To some extent this exception has been recognised by statute in both parts of Ireland. In the Republic of Ireland, section 68 (2) of the Registration of Title Act, 1964, provides that nothing in the Act "shall prevent a person from creating any right in or over any registered land or registered charge, but all such rights shall be subject to the provisions of this Act with respect to registered transfers of land or charges for valuable consideration."[50] Section 68 (3) then provides that an unregistered right in or over registered land, not being a burden to which registered land is subject without registration by virtue of section 72,[51] is *not* to affect the registered owner of a charge created on the land for valuable consideration.[52] In Northern Ireland, there is also a general provision to the effect that nothing in the Land Registration Act (N.I.), 1970, is to prevent a person "creating any estate in any registered land as if that land had been unregistered land,"[53] but section 32 (2) (*b*) provides that, without prejudice to the provisions governing execution of registered charges,[54] "a mortgage or other deed of charge, in whatever form expressed, shall, as far as it relates to registered land, operate only to create a charge and not to vest any freehold or leasehold estate (whether or not subject to defeasance) in the land in the person in whose favour the mortgage or other deed of charge is created."

7. *Unregistered* V. *Unregistered*

13.136. To the extent that unregistered, but registrable, transactions can create interests in land, any question of priorities must be governed by the principles which govern unregistered land. These we discuss below.[55] Furthermore, since we are considering here instruments relating to transactions relating to registered land which are nevertheless registrable in the Land Registry, it would appear that they are caught by the specific exemption of deeds or other documents relating to any estate or interest in registered land

---

[48] See *Devoy* v. *Hanlon* [1929] I.R. 246; *Re Strong* [1940] I.R. 382. See also *Duff* v. *Boushill* [1939] I.R. 160.

[49] Ch. 21, *post.*

[50] *I.e.*, that only the registered owner of land or of a charge can deal with the land or charge by registered disposition, 1964 Act, s. 68 (1). *Cf.* Land Registration Act (N.I.), 1970, s. 32 (1).

[51] Which does not list a mortgage by deposit of the land or charge certificate.

[52] *Cf.* s. 44 of the Local Registration of Title (Ir.) Act, 1891. See *Rattigan* v. *Regan* [1929] I.R. 342. See also the discussion in *Irish Conveyancing Law* (1978), paras. 11.41–4.

[53] S. 32 (2).

[54] Discussed para. 12.25, *ante.*

[55] Paras. 13.141 *et seq., post.*

from registration in the Registry of Deeds.[56] Any question of priority would, therefore, have to be governed by the general maxims of equity.

8. *Unregistrable* v. *Unregistrable*

13.137. Again in practice it should not be common for such a question of priority to arise with respect to registered land, for the reason that one equitable mortgage only at a time should be created. So far as the registered owner is concerned, he can create an unregistrable lien or charge only by deposit of his land certificate[57] and, once he has done this, he should not be able to do so again. However, it is possible that the depositee may be persuaded to hand back the certificate to the registered owner and he may then purport to create another equitable lien or charge by depositing it with another lender. As between the two depositees, the question of priorities would have to be resolved by reference to the principles applying to unregistered land,[58] *i.e.*, as in category 7 above. On the reasoning mentioned above, presumably such transactions are also exempt from the Registry of Deeds system. They would be exempt anyway if no written memorandum or other document accompanied the deposit.[59] If there is such a document, it would seem to relate to the estate registered, to which the land certificate also relates, and so is exempt on that ground.

13.138. So far as creation of an unregistrable charge or lien by deposit of the charge certificate is concerned, this, of course, is a quite different transaction from deposit of the land certificate. The latter creates a charge or lien on the estate held by the registered owner (*e.g.*, the fee simple), whereas the former creates a charge or lien on the charge to which the certificate relates only, in effect the equivalent of a sub-mortgage on unregistered land.[60] Any priority it has is dependent upon the priority which can be claimed for the registered charge itself and, as we saw in category 5 above, as against an unregistrable mortgage on registered land created by deposit of the land certificate, this is also governed by the general rules of equity.

9. *Unregistrable* v. *Unregistered*

13.139. As in category 6 above, to the extent that an unregistered instrument relating to registered land can create an equitable interest or charge on the land, any question of priority as between that instrument and an unregistrable transaction is governed by the maxim—"where the equities are equal, the first in time prevails."

10. *Tacking*

13.140. We discuss below in more detail the doctrine of tacking,[61] which

---

[56] Registration of Title Act, 1964, s. 116 (R.I.); Land Registration Act (N.I.), 1970, s. 72. See ch. 21, *post*.
[57] Para. 12.29, *ante*.
[58] In determining the "equities," the crucial question would be the possible fraud or negligence with respect to the land certificates on the part of the first depositee, see para. 13.145, *post*.
[59] See provisions, cited in fn. 56, *supra*.
[60] Para. 13.123, *ante*.
[61] Para. 13.159, *post*.

allows a mortgagee in certain circumstances to upset the general principles of equity which govern priorities between successive mortgagees. The doctrine of *tabula in naufragio*[62] cannot apply to registered land where the question of priorities is governed by the registration system. It can be invoked only in those cases where the general principles of equity still govern priorities, *e.g.*, where the person seeking to tack has an unregistrable equitable mortgage created by deposit of the land certificate. However, so far as the tacking of further advances is concerned, this is specifically catered for by statute in both parts of Ireland. The provisions of section 75 (1) of the Republic's Registration of Title Act 1964 and section 43 (1) of the Land Registration Act (N.I.) 1970 were quoted earlier.[63] "Future advances" are defined as including "sums from time to time due on an account current and all sums which by agreement or the course of business between the parties are considered to be advances on the security of the charge."[64]

B. Unregistered Land

13.141. As we saw in an earlier chapter, so far as unregistered land in Ireland is concerned, questions of priorities are governed by the registration of deeds system which applies to such land throughout both parts of Ireland.[65] However, because that system applies only where a written document has been used,[66] a memorial of which is registered, some mortgages do not come within the system, *e.g.*, an equitable mortgage by deposit of the title deeds unaccompanied by any written memorandum.[67] In such a case, priorities are governed by the general principles of equity.

The following is a summary of the law of priorities as between mortgages of unregistered land.

1. *Registered* v. *Registered*

13.142. As between registered mortgages, it is specifically laid down by statute that the priorities are governed by the order in which the mortgages are registered in the Registry of Deeds.[68] It does not matter when the mortgages were created and the instruments of creation executed, and the doctrine of notice is irrelevant, except in cases of fraud.[69]

2. *Registered* v. *Unregistered*

13.143. As between a registered mortgage and a subsequent one which is

---

[62] *Ibid.*
[63] Para. 13.129, *ante.* These provisions re-enact s. 77 of the Land Registration of Title (Ir.) Act, 1891.
[64] 1964 Act, s. 75 (2); 1970 Act (N.I.), s. 43 (2).
[65] Ch. 3, *ante* and see also ch. 22, *post.*
[66] S. 3 of the Registration of Deeds Act (Ir.), 1707, and s. 1 of the Registration of Deeds Act (N.I.), 1970, refer to "deeds" and "conveyances" and in *Murphy* v. *Leader* (1841) 4 Ir.L.R. 139 at 142–3 (*per* Pennefather C.J.) this was said to include any instrument in writing. Wills, however, are no longer registrable in either part of Ireland, see ch. 22, *post.*
[67] *Re Burke's Estate* (1881) 9 L.R.Ir. 24; *Re Greer* [1907] 1 I.R. 57.
[68] Registration of Deeds Act (Ir.), 1707, s. 4; Registration of Deeds Act (N.I.), 1970, s. 4 (1). Note that in Northern Ireland, under s. 4 (1) of the 1970 Act, the priority of time of registering a document registered is determined by the serial number allocated to the document (under s. 8) when lodged for registration and not by the actual time of registering the document. See ch. 22, *post.* See also *Moore* v. *Mahon* (1857) 2 Ir.Jur.(N.S.) 277 (registered same day).
[69] *Eyre* v. *Dolphin* (1813) 2 Ba. & B. 290; *Hamilton* v. *Lyster* (1845) 7 Ir.Eq.R. 560; *Drew* v. *Lord Norbury* (1846) 9 Ir.Eq.R. 524. *Cf. Hunter* v. *Kennedy* (1850) 1 Ir.Ch.R. 225.

registerable, but as yet unregistered, the same principle as in category 1 applies *à fortiori*.[70]

3. *Registered* v. *Unregistrable*

13.144. Where, however, the subsequent mortgage is an unregistrable one, *e.g.*, a deposit of the title deeds without any written memorandum or other document, its priority cannot be governed by the registration of deeds system. In such a case one has to fall back on the general principles of equity. Since the subsequent mortgage is equitable only, the registered one, if legal, has a dual claim to priority by being both legal and first in time, if the equities are equal.[71] If the first mortgage is an equitable charge created by deed, which is registered, it still has priority by being first in time when the equities are equal. The equities should always be equal in such a case because, by registering his deed, the prior equitable chargee has done all that could be reasonably expected of him to protect himself. Even if he has left the title deeds in the possession of the mortgagor, who then uses them to create a subsequent equitable mortgage by deposit,[72] normal conveyancing practice in Ireland would require the depositee to protect himself by making a Registry of Deeds search, which would disclose the prior equitable charge.[73] If he does not make such a search, he would nevertheless be fixed with constructive notice[74] and this should remain the case despite the settled rule in Ireland that registration in the Registry of Deeds is not "notice".[75]

4. *Unregistrable* v. *Registered*

13.145. Where the first mortgage is an unregistrable one, its priority as against a subsequent registered mortgage must also be governed by the general principles of equity and the doctrine of notice. If the second mortgage is legal, priorities are in general governed by the maxim "where the equities are equal, the law prevails." However, if the first mortgage is created by deposit of the title deeds, the equities will usually not be equal because the second mortgagee will be fixed either with actual notice of the first mortgage or constructive notice through his neglect in not investigating the reason for non-delivery of the deeds to him.[76] If the subsequent mortgage is also equitable, then the general principle applicable is the maxim, "where the equities are equal, the first in time prevails."[77] Registration of the subsequent mortgage does not *per se* confer any priority as against an unregistrable one nor make the equities unequal.[78] However, the equities may become unequal

---

[70] See *Hamilton* v. *Lyster* (1845) 7 Ir.Eq.R. 560. See also *Ball* v. *Lord Riversdale* (1816) Beat. 550.
[71] See para. 13.131, *ante*. See also *Creed* v. *Carey* (1856) 7 Ir.Ch.R. 295.
[72] *Cf.* where he has not registered his deed, para. 13.146, *post*.
[73] See, *e.g.*, *Re Greer* [1907] 1 I.R. 57, where it was held *not* to be "gross" negligence on the part of a legal mortgagee, who did register his deed, to leave the title deeds with the mortgagor who created a subsequent mortgage by depositing them with the mortgagee. See further, para. 13.146, *infra*.
[74] *Hamilton* v. *Lyster* (1845) 7 Ir.Eq.R. 560.
[75] See para. 13.162, *post*.
[76] See *Re Allen's Estate* (1867) I.R. 1 Eq. 455. See also *Re McKinney's Estate* (1872) I.R. 6 Eq. 445; *Re Stephen's Estate* (1875) I.R.10 Eq. 282.
[77] *Re Burke's Estate* (1881) 9 L.R.Ir. 24.
[78] *Jennings* v. *Bond* (1845) 8 Ir.Eq.R. 755 at 767 (*per* Sugden L.C.).

due to fraud or negligence with respect to the title deeds on the part of the first mortgagee. Since, in this case, his mortgage is dependent upon deposit of the deeds with him, he ought to retain them and if, without good reason, he releases them and thereby enables the mortgagor to induce the second mortgagee into lending money, thinking he is a first mortgagee, he may well lose priority to that second mortgagee. *A fortiori* if he is party to a fraudulent scheme in this regard devised by the mortgagor.[79]

5. *Unregistered* v. *Registered*

13.146. Priority as between an unregistered, but registrable, mortgage and a registered mortgage is clearly governed by the registration of deeds system. It is provided that the unregistered deed is "void" as against the registered one,[80] *i.e.*, it obtains priority by virtue of its first registration, despite being later in time of creation.[81] However, since equity will not allow a statute to be used as an instrument of fraud,[82] the second mortgagee will not gain priority by his registering first where this is fraudulent. It is now settled that it is fraud where he has actual notice of the prior transaction, or the actual notice of his agent is imputed to him.[83] It is not enough if there is constructive notice only on his part or on the part of his agent.[84] It is not entirely clear from the cases whether this notice must be present at the time of execution of the second mortgage or whether it is sufficient for it to be present at the time of the second mortgagee's registration.[85] On principle one might expect the former to be the rule, for then it is clear that the second mortgagee is fraudulent. In the case of the latter, if the second mortgagee has taken his mortgage without actual notice and subsequently discovers the existence of the first one, it may appear to be somewhat hard on him to prevent him from seeking, by

---

[79]   Para. 13.152, *post.*

[80]   Registration of Deeds Act (Ir.), 1707, s. 5; Registration of Deeds Act (N.I.), 1970, s. 4 (2). The Acts expressly exclude from their scope leases for years not exceeding 21 years, where actual possession goes with the lease, see 1707 Act, s. 14; 1970 Act, s. 5 (c); and see *Clarke* v. *Armstrong* (1860) 10 Ir.Ch.R. 263.

[81]   *Re Flood's Estate* (1862) 13 Ir.Ch.R. 312. In this case, Hargreave J. stated that a second registered deed does *not* gain priority over a prior unregistered deed if the second deed was *voluntary* only, see (1862) 13 Ir.Ch.R. 312 at 314–5 and see the quotation at para. 3.087, *ante.* However, if the voluntary donee under the second deed subsequently conveys to a purchaser for value also before the first deed is registered, Hargreave J. held that that subsequent purchaser can rely on the registration of the second deed to gain him priority over the first deed, even if it is later registered. This does not normally apply to mortgage transactions which usually involve consideration. See also *Gardiner* v. *Blesinton* (1850) 1 Ir.Ch.R. 79.

[82]   See para. 3.048, *ante.*

[83]   *Lord Forbes* v. *Deniston* (1722) 4 Bro.P.C. 189; *Nixon* v. *Hamilton* (1838) 1 Ir.Eq.R. 46; *Re Rorke's Estate* (1863) 14 Ir.Ch.R. 442; *Workingmen's Benefit Building Society* v. *Higgins* [1945] Ir.Jur.Rep. 38. And see the statutory recognition of this principle contained in s. 4 (3) and (4) of the Registration of Deeds Act (N.I.), 1970, quoted at para. 3.089, *ante.*

[84]   Para. 3.089, *ante*. See *Marjoribanks* v. *Hovenden* (1844) 6 Ir.Eq.R. 238 at 243 (*per* Sugden L.C.); *Re Burmester* (1859) 9 Ir.Ch.R. 41. *Cf. Tucker* v. *Henzill* (1853) 4 Ir.Ch.R. 513. See also *Lenehan* v. *McCabe* (1840) 2 Ir.Eq.R. 342.

[85]   See cases cited at para. 3.089, *ante*. And see *Riddick* v. *Glennon* (1853) 6 Ir.Jur.(O.S.) 39. It is arguable that even s. 4 (3) and (4) of the Registration of Deeds Act (N.I.), 1970 (para. 3.089, *ante*), are not entirely unambiguous on the point. S. 4 (3) seems to indicate that the knowledge in question is important at the time of "registration of a subsequent document." The reference in s. 4 (4) to obtaining knowledge of the prior document "in the course of the same transaction with respect to which the question of knowledge arises" is also ambiguous since it depends upon what is included in the "course of the same transaction." In Irish conveyancing, most transactions relating to unregistered land would not be regarded as having been completed by the purchaser's solicitor until the purchase deed is registered in the Registry of Deeds. Thus the vendor often does not receive the purchase money until some time after execution, etc. of the deed, to allow for registration of the new deed.

registration, to regain the position he though he held all along, namely first mortgagee with equivalent priority.[86] On the other hand, to the extent that the priority is dependent entirely on the fact of registration, it can be argued that it is an abuse of the system to permit someone who, at the time of registration, is no longer acting in ignorance to take advantage of the prior mortgagee. The point is that the Irish courts have postponed the second mortgagee only in cases of actual notice or knowledge ; he will still succeed in getting priority in some cases where he would fail apart from the registration system, *i.e.*, where he would be fixed with constructive notice or have the constructive notice of his agent (*e.g.*, his solicitor) imputed to him. If, as would often be the case,[87] he or his solicitor would be fixed with constructive notice apart from the registration system, it is arguable that he ought not to be able to take advantage of the system at a time when he has actual notice.

6. *Unregistrable* v. *Registered*

13.147. Where the prior mortgage is not only unregistered but also unregistrable, *e.g.*, an equitable mortgage created by deposit of the title deeds without execution of any written instrument,[88] the Registry of Deeds system cannot govern the matter.[89] As against the prior unregistrable mortgage, the subsequent mortgage gains no additional priority or validity by virtue of its registration.[90] The question of priorities as between such mortgagees must be settled in accordance with the principles of equity we discussed in an earlier chapter.[91] These are the two maxims—"where the equities are equal, the law prevails" and "where the equities are equal, the first in time prevails"—and the doctrine of notice. Thus priorities as between mortgagees governed by these rules depend partly on the nature of the mortgages in question and partly on the notice held by the mortgagees. Since these rules also govern the cases mentioned below, a discussion of their application in all the cases will be postponed to the end of the categorisation of mortgages concerned with unregistered land. Most, if not all, unregistrable mortgages relating to registered lands are equitable mortgages created by deposit of the title deeds and so the rules particularly relevant in this case are those which apply as between an equitable mortgage followed by a legal mortgage[92] and successive equitable mortgages.[93]

---

[86] *Cf.* the rule in relation to the doctrine of tacking, para. 13.169, *post.*

[87] In practice, of course, most cases will fall either into the category where the nature of the prior transaction, *e.g.*, an equitable mortgage created by deposit, with a written memorandum, will result in actual notice, and not just constructive notice, because the subsequent mortgagee's solicitor will make sure that he has all the relevant deeds produced and will discover why they are deposited with some third party, even though the memorandum was never registered; or else the transaction, *e.g.*, an equitable charge in writing only, is unlikely to result in either kind of notice, since the subsequent mortgagee's solicitor, even after a Registry of Deeds search, may quite reasonably be convinced that he has produced all the relevant title documents. The problem will arise only in the rare case where the subsequent mortgagee or his solicitor discovers by accident the existence of the prior charge in the short time between execution of the subsequent mortgage and its registration. Needless to say, the risk of such accidents is reduced by speedy registration!

[88] *Fullerton* v. *Provincial Bank of Ireland* [1903] A.C. 309.

[89] *Re Burke's Estate* (1881) 9 L.R.Ir. 24.

[90] *Jennings* v. *Bond* (1845) 8 Ir.Eq.R. 755 at 767 (*per* Sugden L.C.).

[91] Ch. 3, *ante.*

[92] Para. 13.154, *post.*

[93] Para. 13.156, *post.*

7. *Unregistered* v. *Unregistrable*

13.148.   Priorities as between an unregistered, but registrable mortgage and an unregistrable one are also governed by the rules of equity and the doctrine of notice. In this case the relevant rules are those applying as between a legal mortgage followed by an equitable one[94] and, again, successive equitable mortgages.[95]

8. *Unregistered* v. *Unregistered*

13.149.   In this sort of case, the rules applicable in all four of the categories discussed below are relevant[96] and the ones relevant to the particular case in question are dependent upon whether the mortgages are legal or equitable or both and in which order they were created.

9. *Unregistrable* v. *Unregistrable*

13.150.   Since such mortgages are usually, if not always, equitable[97] the rules applicable in this case are those governing successive equitable mortgages.[98]

10. *Unregistrable* v. *Unregistered*

This is the converse of category 7 above and the rules applicable are those governing an equitable mortgage followed by a legal one[99] and successive equitable mortgages.[1]

11. *Equitable Principles*

It is now time to consider the equitable principles we referred to above. As with conveyances generally, four categories must be considered with respect to successive mortgages.

(i) Legal v. Legal

13.151.   Where both mortgages are legal[2] the usual rule is that they take priority in the order of their creation.[3] However, the first in time only prevails "where the equities are equal" and the prior mortgagee may lose priority if he has been guilty of fraud or "gross negligence" with respect to the title deeds relating to the property, so that it is inequitable for him to have priority over the subsequent mortgagee. We discuss this subject in connection with the next category.

(ii) Legal v. Equitable

13.152.   As we pointed out in an earlier chapter,[4] a prior legal mortgagee

---

[94]   Para. 13.152, *post.*
[95]   Para. 13.156, *post.*
[96]   Paras. 13.151 *et seq.*, *post.*
[97]   See as to informal mortgages, para. 12.29, *ante.*
[98]   Para. 13.156, *post.*
[99]   Para. 13.154, *post.*
[1]   Para. 13.156, *post.*
[2]   *E.g.* grants of successive leases out of freehold land or successive sub-leases out of leasehold land.
[3]   *Hurst* v. *Hurst* (1852) 16 Beav. 372.
[4]   Ch. 3, *ante.*

has the double claim to priority over a subsequent equitable mortgagee of being both first in time and holder of the legal title. However, it is settled that a legal mortgagee may lose priority if he has been guilty of fraud or "gross negligence."[5] The onus of proving fraud or negligence lies on the subsequent equitable mortgagee seeking to displace the presumption of priority in the prior legal mortgagee.[6] "Fraud" is an easily comprehensible concept in this context, e.g., being party to a scheme of deception designed to induce the subsequent mortgagee into thinking he is a first mortgagee.[7] Furthermore, the acts or representations of the first mortgagee may be such as to attract the doctrine of estoppel,[8] so that he is estopped from denying priority to the subsequent mortgagee.[9]

13.153. Gross negligence, usually with reference to the title deeds, is a somewhat vaguer concept. Clearly the principle is that the conduct of the first mortgagee is such that it is considered in certain cases unfair to enforce the normal rules of priority against the second mortgagee.[10] The problem lies in defining precisely what amounts to conduct sufficient to create unfairness. To some extent this must depend upon the facts of each case.[11] If the first legal mortgagee never asks for the title deeds and allows the mortgagor to retain them, he can hardly be said to have acted reasonably or fairly.[12] By his actions he enables the mortgagor to induce the second mortgagee into believing he is a first mortgagee and a proper investigation of the mortgagor's title may not reveal the contrary.[13] On the other hand, he may have acted fairly if he was given a reasonable, albeit false, explanation for non-production of the deeds.[14] He may also act reasonably if he obtains only some of the title deeds, at least if he believes them to be all the relevant deeds.[15] On the other hand, if, having obtained all the deeds, he then fails to retain them and releases them to the mortgagor without good reason, he may again act unfairly towards a subsequent mortgagee dealing with the mortgagor in good faith.[16] Furthermore, quite apart from failing to obtain or retain the title deeds, there is also the possibility in Ireland with respect to unregistered land that failure to register the first mortgage in the Reigistry of Deeds, provided,

---

[5] See discussion in *Re Greer* [1907] 1 I.R. 57.

[6] *Ibid*

[7] See *Peter* v. *Russel* (1716) 1 Eq.Ca.Abr. 321.

[8] See further on estoppel, ch. 20 *post*.

[9] *E.g.*, indorsing a receipt for a mortgage which in fact had not been paid, see *Rimmer* v. *Webster* [1902] 2 Ch. 163. See also *Briggs* v. *Jones* (1870) L.R. 10 Eq. 92; *Brocklesby* v. *Temperance Permanent Building Society* [1895] A.C. 173

[10] *Re. Greer* [1907] 1 I.R. 57.

[11] See *Re Lambert's Estate* (1884) 13 L.R.Ir. 234; *Re Roche's Estate* (1890) 25 L.R.Ir. 284.

[12] *Re Ambrose's Estate* [1914] 1 I.R. 123. See also *Clarke* v. *Palmer* (1882) 21 Ch.D. 124: *Walker* v. *Linom* [1907] 2 Ch. 104. Cf. *Workingmen's Benefit Building Society* v. *Dixon* [1908] 1 I.R. 582 (see *A Casebook on Irish Land Law* (1984), p. 467).

[13] *Cf.*, where the first mortgagee does, however, register his mortage in the Registry of Deeds, *Re Greer* [1907] 1 I.R. 57.

[14] See *Agra Bank Ltd.* v. *Barry* (1874) L.R. 7 H.L. 135.

[15] *Re Lambert's Estate* (1884) 13 L.R.Ir. 234. Cf. *Cottey* v. *National Provincial Bank of England Ltd.* (1904) 20 T.L.R. 607

[16] *Re Glengall Estate* (1860) 5 Ir.Jur. (N.S.) 221. Cf. *Northern Counties of England Fire Insurance Co.* v. *Whipp* (1884) 26 Ch.D. 482.

of course, it is registrable, should in itself be regarded as gross negligence.[17] In view of the crucial part played by a Registry of Deeds search in unregistered conveyancing in Ireland, there is something to be said for this suggestion.

(iii) Equitable v. Legal

13.154. This is the classic case for application of the doctrine of notice and of the maxim— "where the equities are equal, the law prevails." The basic rule is that a subsequent *bona fide* legal mortgagee, being a purchaser for value, takes free of a prior equitable mortgage of which he has no notice.[18] The onus is on the subsequent mortgagee to prove both that he was a purchaser and that he took his mortgage without notice of the prior mortgage,[19] otherwise the equities are not equal. As we discussed in an earlier chapter,[20] notice in such cases may take one of three forms: (1) actual; (2) constructive; (3) imputed.[21] In considering whether or not a mortgagee is affected by actual notice, the courts generally take the view that he is fixed with notice of facts or circumstances brought to his attention which a reasonable mortgagee in his position would take seriously. If these facts or circumstances would lead a reasonable mortgagee to make further enquiries, but the mortgagee in question did not do so, he will be fixed with constructive notice of the information such enquiries would have produced.[22] Furthermore, if the mortgagee fails to follow the usual conveyancing practice in connection with his mortgage, in particular, if he fails to make a proper investigation of title, he will again be fixed with constructive notice of what such investigation would show.[23] Imputed notice[24] is either actual or constructive notice on the part of the mortgagee's agent (usually his solicitor) which is imputed to the mortgagee himself.[25] In general the agent's notice to be so imputed must have been gained in the same transaction,[26] while he was still acting as agent,[27] and be such that he is under a duty to communicate it to his principal.

13.155. On the face of it, then, the usual conveyancing procedures must be carried out if a subsequent legal mortgagee is to be able to invoke the *bona*

---

[17] See on this suggestion *Re Lambert's Estate* (1884) 13 L.R.Ir. 234. *Cf.*, where the first mortgage is registered in the Registry of Deeds, but the title deeds are not obtained, *Re Greer* [1907] 1 L.R. 57 (held not gross negligence). See also *Re Church's Estate* (1878) 1 L.R.Ir. 255.

[18] See discussion in *Re Ffrench's Estate* (1887) 21 L.R.Ir. 283; *Heneghan* v. *Davitt* [1933] I.R. 375.

[19] *Heneghan* v. *Davitt* [1933] I.R. 375.

[20] Ch. 3, *ante*.

[21] Conveyancing Act, 1882, S. 3.

[22] *Re Oldens* (1863) 9 Ir.Jur. (N.S.) 1; *Re Flood's Estate* (1862) 13 Ir.Ch.R. 312. *Cf. Aldritt* v. *Maconachy* [1908] 1 I.R. 333.

[23] *Justice* v. *Wynne* (1860) 12 Ir.Ch.R. 289 at 311 (*per* Ball J.); *Heneghan* v. *Davitt* [1933] I.R. 375. And see *Stewart* v. *Marquis of Conyngham* (1851) 1 Ir.Ch.R. 534. Note also, with respect to an "Equities Note" relating to land bought out under the Land Purchase Acts and registered in the Land Registry, *Re White and Hague's Contract* [1921] 1 I.R. 138. And see ch. 21, *post*.

[24] Note Longfield J.'s remarks on the concept in *Re Rorke's Estate* (1862) 13 Ir.Ch.R. 273 at 281; on appeal (1863) 14 Ir.Ch.R. 442. See also *Marjoribanks* v. *Hovenden* (1834) 6 Ir.Eq.R. 238; *Tucker* v. *Henzill* (1854) 4 Ir.Ch.R. 513.

[25] *Lenehan* v. *McCabe* (1840) 2 Ir.Eq.R. 342; *Richards* v. *Brereton* (1853) 5 Ir.Jur. (O.S.) 366.

[26] Conveyancing Act, 1882, s. 3 (1) (ii); *Re Smallman's Estate* (1868) I.R. 2 Eq. 34; *Re Macnamara* (1884) 13 L.R.Ir. 158; *Re Stewart's Estate* (1893) 31 L.R.Ir. 405; *Re Hall's Estate* (1893) 31 L.R.Ir. 416. *Cf. Nixon* v. *Hamilton* (1838) 1 Ir.Eq.R 46; *Marjoribanks* v. *Hovenden* (1843) 6 Ir.Eq.R.238; *Lenehan* v. *McCabe* (1840) 2 Ir.Eq.R. 342.

[27] *Re Burmester* (1859) 9 Ir.Ch.R. 41. See also *Gerrard* v, *O'Reilly* (1843) 3 Dr. & War. 414; *Re Stewart's Estate* (1893) 31 L.R.Ir. 405.

fide purchaser without notice doctrine and so gain priority. Thus one would expect such a mortgagee to fail to obtain priority if he, or his solicitor, did not see or did not ask to see the title deeds to the property. In particular, failure or inability on the part of the mortgagor to produce the title deeds probably amounts in itself to constructive notice that there is some prior transaction, such as a mortgage, affecting the property. Yet the courts in both Ireland[29] and England[30] have in the past allowed subsequent mortgagees still to gain priority on being given some, apparently flimsy, excuse as to why the title deeds could not be produced. It is questionable how far these cases would be followed today.

(iv) Equitable v. Equitable

13.156. Where there are successive equitable mortgages, the general rule is that they have priority in accordance with their order of creation— "where the equities are equal, the first in time prevails."[31] However, once again the prior mortgagee may lose priority because his fraud or gross negligence[32] renders the equities no longer equal. Thus in Ireland it has been held that a prior equitable mortgagee, whose mortgage was created by deposit of one deed only relating to the property, with an accompanying written memorandum, was negligent in allowing the mortgagor to retain all the other deeds and in not registering the memorandum in the Registry of Deeds.[33]

13.157. It should also be noted that, in Ireland, it has been held in a long line of cases that, where a question of priority arises between an equitable estate or interest in land (such as a mortgage) and a "mere equity" (such as a right to have a transaction set aside through equitable relief for fraud or undue influence[34]), the *bona fide* purchaser for value doctrine may apply.[35] In particular, there is a line of authorities beginning with *Re Ffrench's Estate*[36] holding that a beneficiary's right to trace or follow misappropriated trust property[37] is a "mere equity" which may be postponed in priority to a

---

[28]   *Re Rorke's Estate* (1863) 14 Ir.Ch.R. 273. See also *Atkin's* v. *Delmege* (1847) 12 Ir.Eq.R. 1 (solicitor acting for all parties) and *Moore* v. *Mahon* (1857) 2 Ir.Jur. (N.S.) 277 (same solicitor for successive transactions).

[29]   *Agra Bank Ltd.* v. *Barry* (1874) L.R. 7 H.L. 135; on appeal from (1872) I.R. 6 Eq. 128 (title deeds in Ireland where the property was situated).

[30]   *Hewitt* v. *Loosemore* (1851) 9 Hare 449; *Ratcliffe* v. *Barnard* (1871) 6 Ch.App. 652. *Cf. Oliver* v. *Hinton* [1899] 2 Ch. 264.

[31]   *National Bank* v. *Keegan* [1931] I.R. 344 (see *A Casebook on Irish Land Law* (1984), p. 673).

[32]   In England there is some support in the authorities for the view that an equitable mortgagee may lose priority for a lesser degree of negligence than a legal mortgagee, see *National Provincial Bank of England* v. *Jackson* (1886) 33 Ch.D. 1; *Taylor* v. *Russell* [1891] 1 Ch. 8; on appeal [1892] A.C. 244.

[33]   *Re Lambert's Estate* (1884) 13 L.R.Ir. 234. See also *Re Roche's Estate* (1890) 25 L.R.Ir. 58.

[34]   See, however, Kenny J. in *Allied Irish Banks Ltd* v. *Glynn* [1973] I.R. 188 at 192: "It [the defendant's interest] cannot be classified accurately as having been 'an equity' only for if the deed was procured by fraud or undue influence, the first-named defendant would acquire an estate in the lands when he succeeded in setting it aside. What he had was a *chose in action* which could become an estate if he brought proceedings and if they were successful." This he contrasted with the deserted wife's "equity" discussed in *National Provincial Bank Ltd* v. *Ainsworth* [1965] A.C. 1175.

[35]   *Allied Irish Banks Ltd.* v. *Glynn* [1973] I.R. 188 (see *A Casebook on Irish Land Law* (1984), p. 85.

[36]   (1887) 21 L.R.Ir. 283.

[37]   See further para. 10.108 *ante*.

subsequent equitable estate or interest in land acquired without notice of the prior equity.[38] Though the categorisation of a beneficiary's right to trace as a mere equity may be doubted,[39] the principle that a mere equity is accorded less priority that an equitable estate or interest in land is firmly established.

(v) Salvage Payments

13.158. There is a line of authorities in Ireland holding that the general principles of equity governing priorities discussed above are displaced in a case involving so-called "salvage payments."[40] In such a case, priorities as between successive incumbrancers are subject to the overriding principle that salvage payments are liable to be repaid before all other prior charges on the land in question. In *Re Power's Policies*, Holmes L.J. laid down three conditions which must be satisified for the application of this principle[41]: (1) the payment made in respect of the property must have had the effect of saving it from loss for the benefit of all persons interested in it[42]; (2) the payment must have been made by a person with an interest in or charge on the property[43]; (3) the person making the payment must do so voluntarily and not under any duty or obligation or as agent for someone else. Thus in *Re Power's Policies* itself, a solicitor, who was owed money by a client and took a sub-mortgage from him to secure the debt, paid salaries and rents relating to the property. The solicitor usually acted for that client in the collection of rents, and it was held that he could not claim that the payments he made were salvage payments. He could not show clearly that they were not made as agent for the client.

12. Tacking

Tacking is a method of securing priority for a subsequent mortgage by attaching it to another mortgage with higher priority. Two forms of tacking came to be recognised at common law: (i) *tabula in naufragio*; (ii) tacking of further advances.

(i) Tabula in Naufragio

13.159. *Tabula in naufragio* (literally "the plank in a shipwreck") is a doctrine which seems to owe its development to the deference which our law

---

[38] *Re Sloane's Estate* [1895] 1 I.R. 146; *Re Bobbett's Estate* [1904] 1 I.R. 461; *Bourke* v. *Lee* [1904] 1 L.R. 280; *Scott* v. *Scott* [1924] 1 I.R. 141. See Delany, "Equitable Interests and 'Mere Equities'" (1957) 21 Conv. 195.

[39] In *Allied Irish Banks Ltd.* v. *Glynn* [1973] I.R. 188 at 193–4, Kenny J. in referring to reliance by counsel on "the much discussed decision of the Irish Court of Appeal in *Ffrench's Estate*" commented: "it is not necessary to deal with this difficult and controversial problem on which the Irish Court of Appeal have expressed one view and the House of Lords [*i.e.* in *Shropshire Union Rly. & Canal Co.* v. *The Queen* (1875) L.R. 7 H.L. 496] another."

[40] See the discussion in *Re Power's Policies* [1899] 1 I.R. 6. See also *Munster and Leinster Bank Ltd.* v. *McGlashan* [1937] I.R. 525; *Re Kavanagh, Ltd.* [1952] Ir.Jur.Rep. 38.

[41] *Ibid.* p. 27.

[42] *Hamilton* v. *Denny* (1809) 1 Ba. & B. 199 (mortgagee of leasehold estate paying renewal fines); *Kehoe* v. *Hales* (1843) 5 Ir.Eq.R. 497 (incumbrancer advancing money to save a leasehold estate from forfeiture given priority for his lien *pro tanto* over prior incumbrances). See also *Re Cobden's Estate* [1923] 1 I.R. 1. And *Fetherstone* v. *Mitchell* (1848) 11 Ir.Eq.R. 35; *Locke* v. *Evans* (1823) 11 Ir.Eq.R. 52; *Abercorn* v. *Bristowe* (1855) 1 Ir.Jur. (N.S.) 57; *Hill* v. *Browne* (1844) 6 Ir.Eq.R. 403.

[43] *O'Loughlin* v. *Dwyer* (1884) 13 L.R.Ir. 75 (original lessee sued under covenant in lease unable to claim a salvage payment since he had previously assigned his entire interest in the lease). *Cf. Munster and Leinster Bank Ltd.* v. *McGlashan* [1937] I.R. 525.

gives to the legal estate or interest in land as opposed to an equitable estate or interest. The doctrine applies where successive equitable mortgages are created after a legal mortgage and establishes that, in a question of priority as between the equitable mortgagees, one of them can, in certain circumstances, secure priority by purchasing the legal estate.[44] This might become important where, e.g., the mortgagor manages to conceal the existence of a second mortgage from a third mortgagee, so that the latter is induced into lending rather more than he might otherwise have done—hence the "shipwreck." Thus the owner of Blackacre, worth £10,000, might create a legal mortgage in favour of A, to secure a loan of £6,000, an equitable mortgage in favour of B, for £4,000, and another equitable one in favour of C, also for £4,000. If the owner defaults and the mortgagees decide to realise their respective securities, they may very well find that the property is of insufficient value to cover all their debts. C, as third mortgagee, would normally rank third in priority and so may seek to save himself by purchasing A's mortgage. He will succeed under the doctrine provided two conditions are satisfied: (1) that he had no notice of B's mortgage when he advanced the money in respect of his own[45] and (2) that he acquires a legal estate of some kind in the land.[46] It has even been held that B cannot save himself from being "squeezed out" by giving notice to A.[47] However, it has been held in both Ireland[48] and England[49] that, where A holds the legal estate on trust for B, if C acquires it he is bound by the trust provided he has notice of it and so cannot claim priority over B.

13.160. The doctrine of *tabula in naufragio* had caused considerable controversy in the past. It was actually abolished in Ireland and England by section 7 of the Vendor and Purchaser Act, 1874, but that section was retrospectively repealed as regards Ireland by section 73 of the Conveyancing Act, 1881,[50] and the doctrine survives to this day. However, it rarely has practical effect in respect of land because it cannot operate where priorities are governed by the Registry of Deeds system.[51] It can operate only where priorities are still governed by the general principles of equity, e.g. where the

[44] In effect, by acquiring the legal estate and tacking his equitable mortgage onto it, he is said to be able to claim that the law must then prevail, provided the equities are equal. See *Workingmen's Benefit Building Society* v. *Dixon* [1908] 1 I.R. 582 (see *A Casebook on Irish Land Law* (1984), p. 467). It has been stated that the doctrine can also apply in the reverse situation, *i.e.* a first legal mortgagee can tack onto his first mortgage a subsequent equitable mortgage and gain priority for it over an intermediate equitable mortgage of which he has no notice, see *Morret* v. *Paske* (1740) 2 Atk. 52 at 53.

[45] *Henry* v. *Douglas* (1856) 1 Ir.Jur. (N.S.) 146. It does not matter that he acquires notice later and it is this which induces him to purchase the legal estate to save himself, see *Taylor* v. *Russell* [1892] A.C. 244 at 259. See also *West London Commercial Bank* v. *Reliance Permanent Building Society* (1885) 29 Ch.D. 954 at 963.

[46] *Willoughby* v. *Willoughby* (1756) 1 T.R. 763: *Cooke* v. *Wilton* (1860) 29 Beav. 100. See also *Kirby* v. *O'Shee* (1835) 1 John. 565.

[47] *Peacock* v. *Burt* (1834) 4 L.J.Ch. 33, criticised by Lindley L.J. in *West London Commercial Bank* v. *Reliance Permanent Building Society* (1885) 29 Ch.D. 954 at 963.

[48] *Workingmen's Benefit Building Society* v. *Dixon* [1908] 1 I.R. 582 (see *A Casebook on Irish Land Law* (1984), p. 467).

[49] *Saunders* v. *Dehew* (1692) 2 Vern. 271; *Harpham* v. *Shacklock* (1881) 19 Ch.D. 207.

[50] In England the doctrine was restored by s. 129 of the Land Transfer Act, 1875, see *Robinson* v. *Trevor* (1883) 12 Q.B.D. 423 at 433, but was abolished again as to mortgages by s. 94 (3) of the Law of Property Act, 1925.

[51] See *Survey of Land Law of Northern Ireland* (1971), para. 219. See *Tennison* v. *Sweeny* (1844) 7 Ir.Eq.R. 511. Similarly, if title to the land is registered.

mortgagee seeking to tack holds an unregistrable mortgage[52] or the intervening mortgage is unregistered.[53]

(ii) Tacking Further Advances

13.161. It is common practice in Ireland for a bank to undertake not only to lend money at the present time to a client but also to make further advances in the future on the same security. The question then arises, if the mortgagor in the meantime creates another mortgage in favour of a third party, whether the bank can tack the further advances so as to secure priority for them over the intervening mortgage.[54] The answer to this question has now been settled by the courts. If the intervening mortgagee agreed to tacking, the first mortgagee can tack the further advances whether his mortgage is legal or equitable. In the absence of such an agreement between the parties, tacking can take place either on the ground that the person tacking holds the legal title[55] or is under an obligation to make further advances,[56] but in either case no tacking can take place if the person making the further advance had notice of the intervening mortgage at the time of making that further advance.[57] In the case of an obligation to make further advances, where notice would deprive the person under the obligation of priority, it seems that he is protected by being deemed to be no longer subject to that obligation once the mortgagor creates the intervening mortgage.[58]

13.162. The doctrine survives in Ireland[59] despite the operation of the Registry of Deeds.[60] It was held in *Re O'Byrne's Estate*[61] that, even where the successive mortgages are all registered in the Registry of Deeds, a prior mortgagee can still tack further advances so as to squeeze out of priority an intervening mortgagee, provided he had no notice of the intervening mortgagee when he made his further advance. This ruling results from the earlier decisions of the Irish courts that mere registration in the Registry of Deeds is not "notice" for these purposes.[62] If the intervening registered mortgagee wishes to protect himself, he must give express notice to the prior mortgagee whose mortgage is expressed to secure further advances.

---

[52] *Workingmen's Benefit Building Society* v. *Dixon* [1908] 1 I.R. 582 (mortgage by deposit of deed with Bank).

[53] See *Tennison* v. *Sweeny* (1844) 7 I.R. Eq. R. 511.

[54] See Rowley, "Tacking Further Advances" (1958) 22 Conv. 44.

[55] *Wyllie* v. *Pollen* (1863) 3 De G.J. & S. 596.

[56] Such an obligation might exist in respect of a legal or equitable mortgagee and the intervening mortgagee ordinarily takes subject to it, see *Re O'Byrne's Estate* (1885) 15 L.R.Ir. 373 (see *A Casebook on Irish Land Law* (1984), p. 469). See also *Gannon* v. *Gannon* [1909]1 I.R. 57; *Re Sloane's Estate* [1895] 1 I.R. 146.

[57] *Brown* v. *Lynch* (1838) 2 Jon. 706; *Re Macnamara's Estate* (1884) 13 L.R.Ir. 158; *Re Keogh's Estate* [1895] 1 I.R. 201. See also *Hopkinson* v. *Rolt* (1861) 9 H.L.C. 514; *Bradford Banking Co.* v. *Henry Briggs, Son and Co. Ltd.* (1886) 12 App.Cas. 29; *Union Bank of Scotland* v. *National Bank of Scotland* (1886) 12 App.Cas. 53.

[58] See discussion in *West* v. *Williams* [1899] 1 Ch. 132, espec. at 143 and 146.

[59] Note the modifications in England contained in s. 94 (1) of the Law of Property Act, 1925, para. (c) of which reverses *West* v. *Williams, supra*. See *Survey of the Land Law of Northern Ireland* (1971), para. 220.

[60] As regards unregistered land, see para. 13.140, *ante*.

[61] (1885) 15 L.R.Ir. 373 (see *A Casebook on Irish Land Law* (1984), p. 469).

[62] *Bushell* v. *Bushell* (1803) 1 Sch. & Lef. 90; *Latouche* v. *Dunsany* (1803) 1 Sch. & Lef. 137. Cf. *Ferrall* v. *Boyle* (1839) 1 Ir.Eq.R. 391 at 403 (*per* Plunket L.C.), aff'd. *sub nom. Boyle* v. *Ferrall* (1846) 12 Cl. & F. 740.

VII. JUDGMENT MORTGAGES

13.163. We now come to a subject which is of special significance in Ireland, judgment mortgages.[63] It is a subject which remains to this day of extreme importance with respect to land law practice in the Republic of Ireland. In Northern Ireland the system of judgment mortgages has been replaced by a new one relating to orders charging land made by the Enforcement of Judgments Office established under the Judgments (Enforcement) Act (N.I.), 1969. This new system we consider in a later section of this chapter.[64]

A. JUDGMENTS

13.164. A new method of enforcement of a judgment against the judgment debtor's land was introduced in Ireland in the mid-nineteenth century by the Judgment Mortgage (Ireland) Act, 1850,[65] as amended by the Judgment Mortgage (Ireland) Act, 1858. These two Acts continue to govern the subject for the most part in the Republic of Ireland.

13.165. Essentially what the Acts do is to enable a creditor who obtains a judgment in a court against a landowner to convert that judgment into a mortgage against the land, hence the expression "judgment mortgage." The Acts apply to judgments, including decrees, orders or rules, of the High Court and Supreme Court, provided these require the payment of a sum of money, costs, charges or expenses to the judgment creditor.[66] They also apply in certain cases to judgments of the Circuit Court.[67] The judgment must state in its body the sum payable to the judgment creditor.[68] However, it need not require immediate payment for it appears that a judgment with a stay of execution may still be registered.[69]

The Judgments (Ireland) Act, 1844, also provided a system of registration whereby an action against a landowner may be registered as a *lis pendens*.[70] Prior to this Act, it was settled law in both England[71] and Ireland[72] that, once a suit was instituted, any person subsequently dealing with the land, were he purchaser, lessee or mortgagee, took the land subject to all the rights and liabilities which might be declared in the suit, whether or not he had notice of the suit.[73] This caused considerable hardship to persons dealing with land who often found themselves subject to claims established in actions begun

---

[63] See generally, Madden, *Registration of Deeds, Conveyances and Judgment Mortgages* (2nd ed., 1901); Maguire, *Law and Practice Relating to Registration of Deeds, Wills and Judgment Mortgages* (1912).

[64] The 1969 Act, as amended by the Judgments Enforcement and Debts Recovery (N.I.) Order, 1979, has been consolidated in the Judgments Enforcement (N.I.) Order, 1981. Para. 13.183, *post*.

[65] See also the Debtors (Ir.) Act, 1840, the Judgments (Ir.) Acts, 1844 and 1849 and the Judgments Registry (Ir.) Acts, 1850 and 1871.

[66] Debtors (Ir.) Act, 1840, ss. 27 and 28; Judgment Mortgage (Ir.) Act, 1850, s. 6.

[67] See, generally, Circuit Court (Registration of Judgments) Act, 1937.

[68] *Feeney* v. *Dillon* (1841) 3 Ir.L.R. 503. It seems that the judgment creditor may still register his judgment as a mortgage even though he agrees to take a sum smaller than that marked in the judgment, and payment by instalments, see *Browning* v. *Davis* (1892) 31 I.L.T. 148.

[69] *Barnett* v. *Bardley* (1890) 26 L.R.Ir. 209.

[70] See especially s. 10 of the 1844 Act. See *Dorene Ltd.* v. *Suedes Ltd.* [1981] I.R. 312; *Coffrey* v. *Brunel Construction Co.* [1983] I.R. 36; *Byrne* v. *U.D.T. Bank Ltd.* [1984] I.L.R.M. 418.

[71] *Worsley* v. *Earl of Scarborough* (1746) 3 Atk. 392; *Bishop of Winchester* v. *Paine* (1805) 11 Ves. 194. See also *Bellamy* v. *Sabine* (1857) 1 De G. & J. 566.

[72] *Gaskell* v. *Durdin* (1812) 2 Ba. & B. 167; *Massy* v. *Batwell* (1843) 4 Dr. & War. 58.

[73] See discussion by Kenny J. in *Giles* v. *Brady* [1974] I.R. 462.

many years previously and of which they were totally ignorant. Now section 10 of the 1844 Act provides that no *lis pendens* can bind or affect a purchaser or mortgagee, who has no express notice of it, unless and until a memorandum containing the requisite details[74] concerning the suit is registered in court.[75] Such a registered *lis pendens* may be vacated under an order of the court[76] and the earlier view, that there is no jurisdiction to order a *lis pendens* to be vacated without the consent of the person who registered it until the suit has been determined, has recently been rejected by the Republic's Supreme Court.[77]

B. REGISTRATION

The following are the main rules governing registration of judgment mortgages.

1. *Interests Affected*

13.166. Section 6 of the Judgment Mortgage (Ireland) Act, 1850, provides that a judgment may be registered as a mortgage against a judgment debtor who:

> ". . . is seised or possessed at law or in equity of any lands, tenements or hereditaments, of any nature or tenure, or has any disposing power over any such lands, tenements, or hereditaments which he may without the assent of any other persons exercise for his own benefit. . . ."

This covers a wide range of legal and equitable estates and interests in land and even includes certain powers of appointment.[78] It has been held to apply to, *e.g.*, another judgment mortgage,[79] a jointure annuity,[80] the share of one of a deceased's next-of-kin in leasehold property,[81] a tenancy at will,[82] and

---

[74]   *E.g.*, name and usual or last known abode and title, trade or profession of the person whose estate is intended to be affected by the suit, the court, title of action and day filed. And see *Thornhill* v. *Glover* (1842) 3 Dr. & War. 195; *Att.-Gen.* v. *Corporation of Cashell* (1843) 3 Dr. & War. 294; *Jennings* v. *Bond* (1846) 8 Ir.Eq.R. 755; *Re O'Byrne's Estate* (1885) 15 L.R.Ir. 373 (see *A Casebook on Irish Land Law* (1984), p. 469). *Cf.* the affidavit required for registration of a judgment mortgage, para. 13.168, *post*.

[75]   S. 5 of the Judgment Mortgage (Ir.) Act, 1850, required the memorandum to be registered within 5 years before execution of the conveyance to the purchaser or mortgagee in question.

[76]   Judgments Registry (Ir.) Act, 1871, s. 21. See *Barry* v. *Buckley* [1981] I.R. 306.

[77]   *Flynn* v. *Buckley* [1980] I.R. 423 (see *A Casebook on Irish Land Law* (1984), p. 483), rejecting the view that the Lis Pendens Act, 1867, did not apply to Ireland, as Kenny J. had held in *Giles* v. *Brady* [1974] I.R. 462 (see also *McDonnell* v. *McDonnell* (1908) 42 I.L.T.R. 212; *Jolly* v. *Taylor* (1912) 46 I.L.T.R. 106). Kenny J. had not been followed on this point by McWilliam J. in *Culhane* v. *Hewson* [1979] I.R. 8, nor by Costello J. in *Dunville Investments Ltd.* v. *Kelly* (1979) Unrep. (H.C., R.I.) (1977 No. 640 P). Note, however, that the 1867 Act was *not* listed as applying to N.I. by the H.M.S.O. *Chronological Table of the Statutes Affecting Northern Ireland*.

[78]   See the discussion by Barrington J. in *Murray* v. *Diamond* [1982] I.L.R.M. 113, where it was held that registration against the husband's interest in a family home did not involve a conveyance requiring the consent of his wife under the Family Home Protection Act, 1976. See also *Containercare (Ir.) Ltd.* v. *Wycherley* [1982] I.R. 143. And see *Fletcher* v. *Steele* (1844) 6 Ir.Eq.R. 376.

[79]   *Rossborough* v. *McNeill* (1889) 23 L.R.Ir. 409. But see *Re Blake's Estate* [1895] 1 I.R. 468; *Kennedy* v. *Campbell* [1899] 1 I.R. 59.

[80]   *Re Blake* (1899) 33 I.L.T.R. 182.

[81]   *Tevlin* v. *Gilsenan* [1902] 1 I.R. 514. *Cf. Tench* v. *Glennon* (1900) 34 I.L.T.R. 157. See also *Re Carolan and Scott's Contract* [1899] 1 I.R. 1. In *Kavanagh* v. *Best* [1971] N.I. 89, Gibson J. held that a judgment mortgage registered against the specific devisee under a will, whom the executors let into possession but in whose favour no assent was executed, was well charged on the devisee's interest in the property. In *Munster and Leinster Bank Ltd.* v. *Fanning* [1932] I.R. 671, it was held that a judgment mortgage could be registered against the interest of a sole proving executor of a will, even though the will appointed another executor who had neither renounced nor proved the will.

[82]   *Devlin* v. *Kelly* (1886) 20 I.L.T.R. 76.

lands subject to an order for sale.[83] However, section 6 of the 1850 Act is limited to an estate or interest held by the judgment debtor at the date of registration of the judgment as a mortgage,[84] so that there can be no registration against a future or contingent interest.[85] Furthermore, it has been held that a judgment cannot be registered as a mortgage against a sum of money or a legacy charged on land.[86]

2. Place of Registration

13.167. Section 6 of the 1850 Act also provides that registration of the judgment as a mortgage on the land of the judgment debtor is to be accomplished by filing in the court in which judgment was entered an *affidavit* containing details of the judgment[87] and then a copy of that affidavit should be registered in the Registry of Deeds[88] or, if the title to the land is registered, in the Land Registry.[89]

3. Requirements of Affidavit

13.168. The procedure laid down by statute governing the affidavit must be followed with precision, otherwise the registration is invalid and no mortgage on the land is created.[90] It appears, however, that the insertion of material *in addition* to the statutory requirements, though unnecessary and, perhaps, even inaccurate, will not invalidate the registration, provided the statutory requirements are met.[91]

(i) Who Must Make It

13.169. The general rule is that the affidavit relating to the judgment must be made by the judgment creditor.[92] Where more than one creditor obtains the judgment, any one of them may make the affidavit.[93] If the judgment creditor is a company, it may be made by its secretary or law agent.[94] If a judgment has been obtained against more than one debtor, it may be

---

[83]   *Re Scanlan's Trustees' Estate* [1897] 1 I.R. 462. And see also *Re Swanton's Estate* [1898] 1 I.R. 157.
[84]   *McKinley* v. *Kennedy* [1925] 1 I.R. 34. See also *Lynch* v. *Cooke* (1866) 11 Ir.Jur.(N.S.) 102.
[85]   *Re Rae's Estate* (1877) 1 L.R.Ir. 174. *Cf. Irish Land Commission* v. *Davies* (1891) 27 L.R.Ir. 334. As regards a contract for sale, see *Coffey* v. *Brunel Construction Co.* [1983] I.R. 36.
[86]   *Woodhouse* v. *Annesly* (1899) 33 I.L.T.R. 153; *Re Blake's Estate* [1895] 1 I.R. 168.
[87]   See further, para. 13.168, *infra*. As to lodgment of a certificate of existence of the judgment before registration, see Land Transfer (Ir.) Act, 1848, s. 12; Judgments Registry (Ir.) Act, 1871, s. 22.
[88]   S. 6 provided that the copy of the affidavit is to be treated in the Registry of Deeds as if it were a memorial of a deed, see ch. 22, *post*. See also Judgment Mortgage (Ir.) Act, 1858, ss. 1–4. *Re Flannery* [1971] I.R. 10.
[89]   See Registration of Title Act, 1964, s. 71.
[90]   *Beere* v. *Head* (1846) 9 Ir.Eq.R. 76; *Re Huthwaite* (1851) 2 Ir.Ch.R. 54. Note that a supplemental affidavit may be filed under the Judgment Mortgage (Ir.) Act, 1858, ss. 1–4. See *Re Fitzgerald's Estate* (1861) 11 Ir.Ch.R. 356; *Re Humble's Estate* (1860) 6 Ir.Jur.(N.S.) 140.
[91]   *Nelson* v. *Todd* (1889) 25 L.R.Ir. 17; *Frayne* v. *O'Dowd* (1951) 85 I.L.T.R. 114. Nor can there be more than one valid registration, see *Re Field's Estate* (1877) I.R. 11 Eq. 456.
[92]   Judgment Mortgage (Ir.) Act, 1850, s. 6. See also *Lawless* v. *Doake* (1883) 12 L.R.Ir. 68 (executor). Registration may be made on his behalf in certain circumstances (*e.g.*, judgment creditor abroad) by someone with a power of attorney, see *McLoughlin* v. *Strand Housing Ltd.* (1952) 86 I.L.T.R. 167. See also Judgment Mortgage (Ir.) Act, 1858, s. 3.
[93]   Judgment Mortgage (Ir.) Act, 1858, s. 4. *Re Kane* [1901] 1 I.R. 520. *Cf. Re Ryan* (1853) 3 Ir.Ch.R. 33.
[94]   1858 Act, s. 3. *Munster Bank* v. *Maher* (1885) 16 L.R.Ir. 165. For registration against a company debtor, see *Re Irish Attested Sales Ltd.* [1962] I.R. 70. See as regards personal representatives proceeding as such, *Lawless* v. *Doake* (1883) 12 L.R.Ir. 68 and, as regards a person with power of attorney, *McLoughlin* v. *Strand Housing Ltd.* (1952) 86 I.L.T.R. 167.

registered by one affidavit against the separate property of each of the debtors.[95]

(ii) Contents

13.170. The requisite contents of the affidavit necessary for registration are laid down in section 6 of the Judgment Mortgage (Ireland) Act, 1850. This section is, perhaps, one of the most litigated statutory provisions in force in Ireland. The following are the main particulars which must be in the affidavit. These particulars must all be verified on oath,[96] though, provided the affidavit includes a general swearing clause covering the remaining parts, it is probably not necessary to begin each paragraph with words such as "I swear that" or "I make oath and say that."[97]

(a) Name or Title of Cause or Matter

13.171. The affidavit must contain a statement of the name or title of the cause or matter and of the court in which the judgment relating thereto has been entered up or obtained, plus the date of judgment. The name or title of the cause should consist of the names and description of the parties appearing in the body of the judgment, immediately after the statement of the venue.[98]

(b) Names and Addresses of Parties

13.172. The full names[99] and the "usual or last known place of abode" of the plaintiff and defendant to which the judgment relates must be stated in the affidavit. In *Thorpe* v. *Brown*,[1] Lord Chelmsford summarised the object of requiring the address of each party to be stated:

> "It was not that there should be an exact description of the very place where he was residing, so that any person might resort to him there and ascertain particulars. It was for the purpose of distinguishing him from all other persons, and leaving no doubt whatever as to the identity of the person against whom the judgment which was to be a charge upon the lands had been obtained."[2]

In that case, a description of the defendant as "formerly of Ballina Park, in the County of Wexford, and now of the City of Dublin" was held sufficient in that the reference in the first part of the description so qualified the generality of the last part as to result in sufficiently precise identification to enable a search to be made in the Index of Names kept by the Registry of Deeds.[3]

---

[95]   *Woods* v. *Brown* [1915] 1 I.R. 29 at 36 (*per* Palles C.B.): "Before the [1850] Act there could be no doubt that a judgment against three was a joint judgment against three, and would affect the joint property of the three, and was, in addition, a separate judgement against each which would affect the separate property of each." Cf. *Dunville & Co. Ltd.* v. *McGourty* (1903) 37 I.L.T.R. 177.

[96]   *McDowell* v. *Wheatley* (1858) 7 I.C.L.R. 562. See now Judgment Mortgage (Ir.) Act, 1858, ss. 1–4.

[97]   *Grace* v. *Credit Finance Ltd.* (1972) unrep. (Sup.Ct., R.I.).

[98]   *Wolsey* v. *Worthington* (1863) 14 Ir.Ch.R. 369; *Re Power's Estate* (1860) 11 Ir.Ch.R. 288.

[99]   *Re Humble's Estate* (1861) 11 Ir.Ch.R. 356; *Fowler* v. *Fowler* (1866) 16 Ir.Ch.R. 507. See also *McDowell* v. *Wheatley* (1858) 7 I.C.L.R. 562.

[1]   (1867) L.R. 2 H.L. 220. See also *Re Gray's Estate* (1867) I.R. 1 Eq. 265.

[2]   *Ibid.* p. 232. *Cf. Harris* v. *O'Loghlen* (1888) 23 L.R.Ir. 61. See also *Re Church's Estate* (1878) 1 L.R.Ir. 255.

[3]   See also *Re Fitzgerald's Estate* (1861) 11 Ir.Ch.R. 356; *Re Smith and Ross* (1860) 11 Ir.Ch.R. 397; *Slator* v. *Slator* (1866) 16 Ir.Ch.R. 488; *Re Francis's Estate* (1867) I.R. 1 Eq. 432. See further on Registry of Deeds searches, ch. 22, *post.*

(c) Title, Trade or Profession

13.173. The affidavit must also state the title, trade or profession of the plaintiff and defendant.[4] If a party has a trade or profession, *i.e.*, a calling or business pursued to make a living or to obtain wealth, it is not enough simply to refer to him or her by such description as "Esquire," "gentleman" or "widow."[5] On the other hand, such a description is sufficient if the party in question has no such trade or profession[6] or has retired from it for a long time.[7]

If there is a misdescription, *e.g.*, an agricultural labourer helping without payment in the management of a farm described as a farmer,[8] it invalidates the affidavit and no mortgage is created, whether or not it deceived or misled anyone.[9]

(d) Location of Land

13.174. For unregistered land, the affidavit must specify "the county and barony or the town or county of a city and parish, or the town and parish,"[10] in which the land to which it relates is situated, and if the land lies across two or more counties, baronies, parishes or streets, this must be distinctly stated.[11] Once again any form of misdescription will invalidate the affidavit and so also the registration.[12] The point is that the requirements as to description of the land were probably originally designed to facilitate registration of the judgment against the land to be indicated in the Index of Lands kept by the Registry of Deeds and, if the description was not strictly accurate, incorrect entries would be made in that Index.[13] Thus an affidavit may be invalid if it omits the name of the relevant parish[14] or refers to the wrong parish,[15] or omits the name of the relevant barony[16] or gives the wrong one.[17] The reference in the 1850 Act to a "town" has given rise to some

---

[4]   *Re Ferrall* (1855) 7 Ir.Jur.(O.S.) 307; *Re Assignees of Ferrall* (1860) 5 Ir.Jur.(N.S.) 275; *Re Bagnalstown and Wexford Rly. Co.* (1864) 10 Ir.Jur.(N.S.) 253; *Munster Bank* v. *Maher* (1885) 16 L.R.Ir. 165.
[5]   *Crosbie* v. *Murphy* (1858) 8 I.C.L.R. 301; *Re Doughty's Estate* (1868) I.R. 2 Eq. 235; *Spaddacini* v. *Treacy* (1888) 21 L.R.Ir. 553; *Duffy* v. *Murphy* (1896) 30 I.L.T.R. 108; *Sexton* v. *Valente* (1950) 84 I.L.T.R. 160.
[6]   *Re Swanton's Estate* (1897) 31 I.L.T.R. 166; *Re Edgeworth's Estate* (1860) 11 Ir.Ch.R. 293.
[7]   *Murphy* v. *Lacey* (1897) 31 I.L.T.R. 42.
[8]   *Ibid.* See also *Dardis and Dunns Seeds Ltd.* v. *Hickey* (1974) unrep. (H.C., R.I.) (1972 No. 1165 Sp) (mechanic described as a farmer) (see *A Casebook on Irish Land Law* (1984), p. 479).
[9]   *Crosbie* v. *Murphy* (1858) 8 I.C.L.R. 301; *Dardis and Dunns Seeds Ltd.* v. *Hickey*, *op. cit.*
[10]   This requirement was probably taken from s. 29 of the Registry of Deeds (Ir.) Act, 1832, s. 17 of which provided for the keeping of an Index of Lands in the Registry of Deeds. See ch. 22, *post*. See also *Re Flannery* [1971] I.R. 10.
[11]   *Re Morrow's Estate* (1863) 14 Ir.Ch.R. 44.
[12]   *Cf.*, however, an erroneous description relating to a matter not required to be stated in the affidavit, *e.g.*, the acreage of the land, see *Nelson* v. *Todd* (1889) 25 L.R.Ir. 17.
[13]   See fn. 10, *supra*.
[14]   *Re Earl of Limerick's Estate* (1861) 7 Ir.Jur.(N.S.) 85; *Re Ulster Banking Co.'s Estate* (1896) I.R. 3 Eq. 264. *Cf. Re Edgeworth's Estate* (1860) 6 Ir.Jur.(N.S.) 10.
[15]   *Re Grispi's Estate* (1861) 7 Ir.Jur.(N.S.) 119; *Re Flannery* [1971] I.R. 10 at 14–5 (where Kenny J. pointed out that the reference must be to the list of official names of civil parishes which appears in the 1901 Census, and not to unofficial, religious parishes). *Cf. McIlroy* v. *Edgar* (1881) 7 L.R.Ir. 521.
[16]   *Re Murphy's and McCormack's Contract* [1930] I.R. 322. A list of the baronies of Ireland was contained in the Schedule to the Parliamentary Elections (Ir.) Act, 1850, and judicial notice was taken of this for the purpose of judgment mortgages, see *Gregg & Co.* v. *Boyd* [1915] 1 I.R. 276. See now Electoral Act, 1963.
[17]   *Re Earl of Limerick's Estate* (1861) 7 Ir.Jur.(N.S.) 85; *Harris* v. *O'Loghlen* (1871) I.R. 5 Eq. 514. *Cf. Gregg & Co.* v. *Boyd* [1915] 1 I.R. 276.

difficulty,[18] as the word is nowhere defined in the Act.[19] In *Re Ulster Banking Co.'s Estate*[20] it was held that Omagh, in County Tyrone, was not a town within the 1850 Act, but this seems wrong since it was at the time an assize town.[21] Since the description required is largely for the purposes of identification,[22] it would appear unnecessary to state the parish where the assemblage of buildings in question is all situated in the one parish and that assemblage constitutes a town. If that is the case, it seems to follow that a town for the purposes of the 1850 Act means an assemblage of buildings in two or more parishes.[23]

13.175. Despite these strict requirements as to description of the land laid down in section 6 of the 1850 Act, it seems that an error may not necessarily render the affidavit defective, particularly if it is unlikely to mislead anyone.[24] Apart from that, since the Registry of Deeds in the Republic did for several years cease to put entries in the Index of Lands,[25] it may be questioned whether there is a need for such strict requirements with respect to description of the land,[26] so long as the parties are sufficiently described to facilitate entries in the Index of Names.[27] At the moment they tend to be a trap for conveyancers.

13.176. So far as registered land is concerned, section 71 (2) of the Registration of Title Act, 1964, provides, in relation to affidavits registered after that Act, that the land is sufficiently described by reference to the number of the folio of the register and the county in which the land is situate.[28]

(e) *Amount of Debt and Costs*

13.177. The affidavit must state precisely the amount of the debt, damages, costs or moneys recovered or ordered to be paid by the judgment. Any inaccuracy in this matter will also render the affidavit defective and the

---

[18] In *Archer* v. *Earl of Caledon* [1894] 2 I.R. 473 at 476, Palles C.B. remarked: "'Town' according to my view, like every other word in the English language, will bear a different signification according to the object with which it finds a place in any particular piece of legislation." See also MacDermott, "The Townlands of Ireland" (1972) 3 Cambrian L.Rev. 80; O'Dálaigh, "Linguistically, in the Footsteps of Lord MacDermott" (1972) 3 Cambrian L.Rev. 89. And see *Re Bagnalstown and Wexford Rly. Co.* (1864) 10 Ir.Jur.(N.S.) 253; *Re O'Connor's Estate* [1894] 1 I.R. 408.

[19] Guidance, but no more, may be gained from definitions in other statutes, *e.g.*, Land Law (Ir.) Act, 1881, s. 58, see *Killeen* v. *Lambert* (1882) 10 L.R.Ir. 362 and *McCann* v. *Marquis of Downshire* [1894] 2 I.R. 611; Town Improvements (Ir.) Act, 1854, and see the list of municipal towns within that Act contained in Vanston, *Law Relating to Municipal Towns under the Towns Improvement (Ireland) Act, 1854* (1907), p. 6. The definition in the Interpretation Act, 1937 applies only to the Acts of the Oireachtas. See the discussion in *Irish Conveyancing Law* (1978), para. 8.18 *et seq.*

[20] (1869) I.R. 3 Eq. 264.

[21] See Kenny J. in *Dardis and Dunns Seeds Ltd.* v. *Hickey* (1974) unrep. (H.C., R.I.) (1972 No. 1165 Sp.) (see *A Casebook on Irish Land Law* (1984), p. 479).

[22] See *Thorpe* v. *Brown* (1867) L.R. 2 H.L. 220, para. 13.172, *supra.*

[23] See *Dardis and Dunns Seeds Ltd.* v. *Hickey, op cit.* See also *Re Edgeworth's Estate* (1860) 11 Ir.Ch.R. 293.

[24] *Nelson* v. *Todd* (1889) 25 L.R.Ir. 17; *Grace* v. *Credit Finance Ltd.* (1972) unrep. (Sup. Ct., R.I.). See also *Frayne* v. *O'Dowd* (1951) 85 I.L.T.R. 114.

[25] Ch. 22, *post.*

[26] See the remarks of Kenny J. in *Re Flannery* [1971] I.R. 10 at 15.

[27] Para. 13.172, *supra* and ch. 22, *post.*

[28] Cf. *Re Murphy and McCormack's Contract* [1930] I.R. 322.

registration invalid.[29] If the judgment awards costs, the amount of these must be stated or they must be expressly waived in the affidavit.[30]

(f) Deponent's Statement

13.178. The affidavit must also contain a statement that, "to the best of the knowledge and belief of the deponent," the person against whom the judgment is entered up "is at the time of swearing of such Affidavit so seised or possessed or has such disposing power over" the land in queestion. In *Credit Finance Ltd.* v. *Hennessy*[30a] McWilliam J. held that registration of a judgment mortgage was ineffective to create a charge because the affidavit did not comply with the requirement laid down in the Rules of the Circuit Court (0.22, rr. 5 and 8) (see also Rules of the Superior Courts, 0.40, r.14) that all persons taking affidavits must certify, in the jurat of every affidavit, either that they know the deponent himself or some person named in the jurat who certifies his knowledge of the deponent.

4. Mortgages

13.179. So far as unregistered land is concerned, section 7 of the Judgment Mortgage (Ireland) Act, 1850, provides that registration of the affidavit of judgment in the Registry of Deeds operates "to transfer to and vest in the creditor . . . all the lands, tenements and hereditaments mentioned therein, for all the estate and interest of which the debtor mentioned in such Affidavit shall at the time of such registration be seised or possessed or have disposing power at law or in equity," subject to redemption on payment of the money owing on the judgment. In other words, registration creates a mortgage of the estate or interest in the land held by the judgment debtor in favour of the judgment creditor.[31] Such a mortgage is subject to most of the principles governing mortgages in general. The usual method of enforcement is to bring an action for a declaration that the sum due is well charged,[32] and for a sale if the amount is not paid within a specified period (3 months).[33] Discharge does not require execution of a reconveyance of the land and can be effected simply by entering up a memorandum of satisfaction.[34]

---

[29] Re Pilson's Estate (1861) 7 Ir.Jur.(N.S.) 68; Re Fitzgerald's Estate (1860) 11 Ir.Ch.R. 278; Re Flood's Estate (1865) 17 Ir.Ch.R. 127; Harris v. O'Loghlen (1871) I.R. 5 Eq. 514; McCraith v. Quin (1873) I.R. 7 Eq. 324. Cf. Re Edgeworth's Estate (1860) 11 Ir.Ch.R. 293; Re Ferrall (1855) 7 Ir.Jur.(O.S.) 307; Re Lawler's Estate (1867) I.R. 1 Eq. 268; Re Moorehead's Estate (1870) I.R. 5 Eq. 55; Re Cleland's Estate [1909] 1 I.R. 19.
[30] Madden, Registration of Deeds, Conveyances and Judgments Mortgages (2nd ed. 1901), p. 145.
[30a] (1979) Unrep. (H.C., R.I.) (1979 No. 215Sp).
[31] Ex parte Collins (1857) 6 Ir.Ch.R. 17 at 19 (per Brady L.C.); McAuley v. Clarendon (1858) 8 Ir.Ch.R. 568. See also Hone v. O'Flahertie (1859) 9 Ir.Ch.R. 497; Re Moore's Estate (1885) 17 L.R.Ir. 549 (forfeiture under "alienation" clause): Heeney v. White [1905] 1 I.R. 124; Gowrie Park Utility Society Ltd. v. Fitzgerald [1963] I.R. 436. In McIlroy v. Edgar (1881) 7 L.R.Ir. 521, it was held that registration against the interest of one joint tenant of the land severs the joint tenancy, see ch. 7, ante.
[32] Kavanagh v. Best [1971] N.I. 89; Grace v. Credit Finance Ltd. (1972) unrep. (Sup.Ct., R.I.); Dardis and Dunns Seeds Ltd. v. Hickey (1974) unrep. (H.C., R.I.).
[33] Para. 13.040, ante. The court may also appoint a receiver, see Herbert v. Greene (1854) 3 Ir.Ch.R. 270; Tressillian v. Caniffe (1855) 4 Ir.Ch.R. 399. See also Goldsmidt v. Glengall (1848) 11 Ir.Eq.R. 608; Kenney v. Kenney (1870) I.R. 4 Eq. 181; Holland v. Cork and Kinsale Rly. Co. (1868) I.R. 2 Eq. 417; Re Martin's Estate (1884) 13 L.R.Ir. 43. As regards application of the doctrine of marshalling, see para. 13.080, ante.
[34] Judgment Mortgage (Ir.) Act, 1858, s. 5. See also Land Transfer (Ir.) Act, 1848, ss. 10 and 11; Judgments Registry (Ir.) Acts, 1850, s. 10 and 1871, s. 20.

13.180. With respect to registered land, registration in the Land Registry operates to charge the interest of the judgment debtor and the creditor thereupon has such rights and remedies for enforcement of the charge as may be conferred on him by order of the court.[35]

5. *Priorities*

13.181. So far as unregistered land is concerned, the general rule is that the judgment mortgage registered in the Registry of Deeds takes effect subject to all equities affecting the land at the date of registration, so that a prior unregistered deed still has priority.[36] However, it has been held in Ireland that "a subsequent registered deed carries a judgment mortgage on its back," *i.e.* a subsequent registered deed made for value secures priority for the judgment mortgage over prior unregistered deeds, though only where an issue of priority arises as between the prior unregistered deeds and the subsequent registered one.[37] So far as subsequent mortgages or charges are concerned, the judgment mortgage has, in general, the same priority accorded to it as other registered instuments.[38]

13.182. With respect to registered land, section 71 (4) of the Registration of Title Act, 1964, provides that the charge on the interest of the judgment debtor is subject to existing registered burdens and burdens affecting the interest without registration, and "all unregistered rights subject to which the judgment debtor held that interest at the time of registration of the affidavit." In *Tempany* v. *Hynes*,[39] the Republic's Supreme Court held that a purchaser from the registered owner of the land had such an "unregistered right" under the contract for sale, *i.e.* before execution of the transfer or payment of the purchase money. Therefore, he took free of a post-contract judgment mortgage registered against the vendor.

C. ORDERS CHARGING LAND

13.183. In Northern Ireland, subject to a saving for existing judgment mortgages,[40] the whole system of registration introduced by the Judgment Mortgage (Ireland) Act, 1850, has been swept away as part of the new scheme

---

[35]   Registration of Title Act, 1964 , s. 71 (4). See *Re Moore* (1904) 38 I.L.T.R. 191; *Re Phelan* [1912] 1 I.R. 91; *Roberts* v. *Woods* (1927) 61 I.T.L.R. 132.

[36]   *McAuley* v. *Clarendon* (1858) 8 Ir.Ch.R. 121; *Eyre* v. *McDowell* (1861) 9 H.L.C. 620; *Quinn* v *McCool* [1929] I.R. 620, *Cf. Corbett* v. *De Cantillon* (1856) 5 Ir.Ch.R. 126; *Re Hamilton* (1859) 9 Ir.Ch.R. 512. See also *Johnson* v. *Dublin and Meath Rly. Co.* (1866) 17 Ir.Ch.R. 133; *Re Ryan* (1853) 3 Ir.Ch.R. 33; *Re Jennings' Estate* (1885) 15 L.R.Ir. 277. Note also the application of legislation relating to fraudulent conveyances etc., Judgment-Mortgage (Ir.) Act, 1850, s. 8 and see para. 9.076, *ante.* Also *Dolphin* v. *Aylward* (1870) L.R. 4 H.L. 486 and the Voluntary Conveyances Act, 1893, para. 9.078, *ante.*

[37]   *Latouche* v. *Dunsany* (1803) 1 Sch. & Lef. 137; *Murtagh* v. *Tisdall* (1840) 3 Ir.Eq.R. 85; *Re Scotts' Estate* (1862) 14 Ir.Ch.R. 57.

[38]   *Re Lynch's Estate* (1867) I.R. 1 Eq. 396; *Re Stanley's Estate* (1871) I.R. 5 Eq. 281. See also *Walcott* v. *Lynch* (1850) 13 Ir.Eq.R. 199; *Re Phillips* (1855) 4 Ir.Ch.R. 584. See, however, in relation to registered land, *Re Strong* [1940] I.R. 382. As to priority of judgments *inter se*, see *Borough* v. *Williamson* (1848) 11 Ir.Eq. R. 1; *Hyde* v. *Atkinson* (1852) 2 Ir.Ch.R. 246; *McMinn* v. *McConnell* (1852) 2 Ir.Ch.R. 609.

[39]   [1976] I.R 101 (see *A Casebook on Irish Land Law* (1984), p. 485). See also *Re Murphy and McCormack's Contract* [1930] I.R. 322. Also *Pim* v. *Coyle* [1907] 1 I.R. 334. And see the discussion of this point in *Irish Conveyancing Law* (1978), para. 11. 02 *et seq.*

[40]   Judgments (Enforcement) Act (N.I.), 1969, s. 125.

for enforcement of judgments generally introduced by the Judgments (Enforcement) Act (N.I.), 1969.[41] This Act established a central Enforcement of Judgments Office[42] by or through which most judgments of the High Court or county court must be enforced.[43] To carry out this task, the Office is given a very wide jurisdiction to make what it considers to be the appropriate enforcement order[44] for the judgment in question.[45] The Office must also keep a register of judgments, but pending actions affecting unregistered land must be registered in the Registry of Deeds[46] and those affecting registered land[47] must be registered in the Land Registry.[48]

In the present context, the most relevant provisions in what is now the Judgments Enforcement (Northern Ireland) Order, 1981, are those conferring jurisdiction on the Enforcement of Judgments Office to make orders charging land.[49]

1. *Orders*

13.184. Under Article 45 of the 1981[50] Order a money judgment is enforceable against land only as specified in the Order.[51]

13.185. Article 46(1) gives the Enforcement of Judgments Office power to impose an order charging any of the land or estate in the land of the debtor as it chooses to specify to secure payment of the judgment debt. Such an order may be made whether absolutely or subject to such conditions as may be specified, *e.g.* as to notifying the debtor or as to the time when the charge is to be enforceable.[52] An order charging land and the charge it imposes is to cease to have effect after 12 years[53] from the date of the judgment.[54]

2. *Registration*

13.186. Article 46 (3) provides that an order charging unregistered land has no effect until it is registered by or on behalf of the creditor in the Registry of Deeds. With respect to registered land, the paragraph provides that either the order itself or a notice relating to it must be registered in the Land Registry. The order itself must be registered where the debtor is the registered owner.[55] If, however, the order charges an estate of the debtor in registered land of

---

[41] See Trimble, (1970) 21 N.I.L.Q. 359. The 1969 Act was amended by the Judgments Enforcement and Debts Recovery (N.I.) Order, 1979, both of which have now been consolidated in the Judgments Enforcement (N.I.) Order, 1981. See also *Ulster Bank Ltd.* v. *Chambers* [1979] N.I. 1.

[42] 1969 Act, Pt. II, now 1981 Order, Pt. II.

[43] 1981 Order, Pt. I.

[44] The orders are now dealt with in Pt V of the 1981 Order and included are methods of enforcement such as an attachment of earnings order, see Arts. 73–9.

[45] See Pt. III of the 1981 Order.

[46] Art. 117(*a*). And see Registration of Deeds Act (N.I.) 1970, s. 3.

[47] Art. 117 (*b*). And see Land Registration Act (N.I.) 1970, s. 39 and Sched. 6, Pt. I, para. 8.

[48] Art. 117.

[49] Arts. 46–52.

[50] Replacing s. 45 of the 1969 Act.

[51] *I.e.*, Arts. 46–52.

[52] Art. 46 (2).

[53] The "limitation" period for actions for the recovery of land, see ch. 23, *post.*

[54] Art. 47.

[55] See Land Registration Act (N.I.), 1970, Sched. 6, Pt, I, para. 9.

which the debtor is *not* the registered owner,[56] the order itself cannot be registered, but the creditor may cause a notice of it to be registered.[57] So long as such a notice subsists on the appropriate register, the debtor or any person claiming under him cannot be registered as owner of the land unless the charge has been satisfied or has ceased to have effect or is entered on that register as a burden.[58]

13.187. So far as the actual mechanics of registration are concerned, a person seeking to register an order charging unregistered land must, subject to regulations providing otherwise,[59] lodge in the Registry of Deeds two or, where the debtor is a company, four certified copies of the order. With respect to registered land, a person seeking to register an order charging the land or a notice of it must, subject to Land Registry rules,[60] lodge in the Land Registry, together with such other documents as may be required by law, one certified copy or, where the debtor is a company, three certified copies of the order or notice.

3. Charges

13.188. Article 49 of the 1981 Order provides that an order charging land has the like effect as a charge on the land created by the debtor in favour of the creditor. Article 52 (1) provides that, subject to the terms of the order, the owner of the charge has, for the purpose of enforcing it, the powers of sale of a mortgagee by deed under the Conveyancing Acts, 1881–1911. Furthermore, the owner of the charge has power to convey by deed the estate of the debtor in the land freed from all estates inferior to the charge, though subject to estates having priority to it.[61] To facilitate such a sale, the owner of the charge can apply to the High Court or, in an appropriate case,[62] to the county court for possession of the land.[63] However, no power of sale exists in respect of registered land where the owner of the charge is not the registered owner and has only been able to register a notice relating to the charge,[64] unless he obtains the leave of the court to the sale.[65] Finally, also in the case of registered land, where the owner of a charge has exercised his power of sale the charge and any estate in the land inferior to it are discharged on registration of the purchaser.[66]

---

[56] *E.g.* the debtor holds a lease for a term exceeding 21 years on land of which only the freehold ownership is registered, see ch. 21 *post*.

[57] *I.e.* as a burden on the land under Sched. 6, Pt. I, para. 10 of the Land Registration Act (N.I.), 1970. See ch. 21, *post*.

[58] And the entry relating to such a notice is to state this restrictive effect, see 1981 Order, Art. 48 (2).

[59] See Registration of Deeds Act (N.I.), 1970, S. 19.

[60] Land Registration Act (N.I.), 1970, s. 85.

[61] 1981 Order, Art. 52 (1) (*a*). See *Tubman* v. *Johnston* [1981] N.I. 53; *Allied Irish Banks Ltd.* v. *McWilliams* [1982] N.I. 156.

[62] See County Courts Act (N.I.), 1959, s.12.

[63] 1981 Order, Art. 52 (1) (*b*). The purchaser of the land has the protection afforded by s. 21 (2) of the Conveyancing Act, 1881, and s. 5 (1) of the Conveyancing Act, 1911. See para. 13.028, *ante*.

[64] Para. 13.186, *supra*.

[65] 1981 Order, Art. 52 (3).

[66] 1981 Order, Art. 52 (2). There is a saving from discharge, however, for entries on any register in the Land Registry relating to rights connected with turbary, see Turbary (Ir.) Act, 1891, s.4; Irish Land Act, 1903, s. 21; Northern Ireland Land Act, 1925, s. 26. See 1981 Order, Art. 52 (4).

4. *Priorities*

13.189. Article 51 contains a special provision relating to priority of an order charging land which is founded on a judgment in respect of *rates*. It provides that such a charge has priority over all other charges and incumbrances whatever except Crown rents,[67] quit rents,[68] and tithe rentcharges,[69] and any charge or incumbrance whatsoever securing money due to the Crown. Apart from this provision, orders charging land are subject to the usual rules of priority governing unregistered and registered land. Thus, with respect to unregistered land, section 4 (2) of the Registration of Deeds Act (N.I.). 1970, as amended by the 1981 Order, provides that a deed or conveyance affecting any land which is not registered is void, *inter alia*, "against a registered order charging those lands made under Judgments Enforcement (Northern Ireland) Order 1981." A charge or notice registered as a burden affecting registered land is governed by the rules governing such burdens, *i.e.* burdens "which, if unregistered, would rank in priority according to the date of their creation shall, if created or arising since the first registration of the land, ranking according to the order in which they are entered or deemed to have been entered on the register and not according to the order in which they are created or arise, and shall rank in priority to any other burden (not being a Schedule 5 burden)[70] affecting the land and created or arising since the first registration of the land."[71]

13.190. Finally, a charge on land is void as against the assignees in the bankruptcy of the debtor or the trustee, or, in the case of a company, the liquidator, if, within 28 days of the registration of the charging order or notice, the debtor is adjudged bankrupt[72] or a winding-up order is made in respect of the company.[73]

---

[67] See para. 6.008, *ante*. See the discussion in *Northern Bank Ltd.* v. *Barrington* [1979] N.I. 161.
[68] Para. 6.009, *ante*.
[69] Para. 6.014, *ante*.
[70] *I.e.* burdens which affect registered land without registration, see ch. 21, *post*.
[71] Land Registration Act (N.I.), 1970, s. 40. See ch. 21, *post*.
[72] Or notice of a bankruptcy petition filed by or against the debtor is served on the creditor and an order of adjudication is made at any time on foot thereof, 1981 Order, Art. 93 (*a*).
[73] Or a resolution is passed for its winding up or notice is served on the creditor of presentation of a winding-up petition or of the calling of a meeting at which the voluntary winding up of the company is to be proposed and a winding-up order of resolution results at any time, 1981 Order, Art. 93 (*b*).

PART VI

SUCCESSION

CHAPTER 14

WILLS

14.01. This section of the book deals with the law of succession, *i.e.* that which governs the devolution or transmission of property on death of the owner.[1] Nowadays such transmission of the ownership of property from the deceased owner to the succeeding owner takes place in two stages. The property devolves first by operation of law to persons known as *personal representatives*, namely executors or administrators, and then the beneficial ownership is transferred to the appropriate successors, usually by act of the personal representatives. This process of succession can take one of two forms. There can be either *testamentary* (or *testate*) succession. *i.e.* where the deceased owner has made a valid will disposing of his property on death, or *intestate* succession, *i.e.* where the property has not been disposed of by will, whether because the will is invalid or no will at all has been made or a valid will does not deal with all the testator's property (a partial intestacy). It will be seen, therefore, that there are three main topics to be discussed in the present context, namely wills, intestate succession and the powers, duties and functions of personal representatives.[2] This and the next two chapters deal with each of these topics in turn. First to be considered is the law of wills.[3]

I. INTRODUCTION

14.02. An earlier chapter[4] indicated that the history of the law of wills, especially in relation to land, has been rather chequered. The feudal system of land tenure in effect favoured a system of intestate succession[5] and one of the main objects of the development of uses was the avoidance of this restriction.[6] The fear that the Statute of Uses (Ireland), 1634, might have hindered this development may have been one of the reasons for the passing of the Statute of Wills (Ireland) of the same date, though it is more likely that the Irish Parliament were more concerned at that time with reproducing property legislation passed at Westminster a century earlier.[7] Whatever the reason for its passing, the 1634 statute ensured that the law of wills would

---

[1] See generally, Mellows, *Law of Succession* (4th ed., 1983); Parry and Clark, *Law of Succession* (8th ed., 1983); Williams, Mortimer and Sunnucks, *Executors, Administrators and Probate* (1982).

[2] In the Republic of Ireland the statute law of these matters has not been amassed in one comprehensive statute, namely the Succession Act, 1965. See M'Guire, *The Succession Act, 1965: A Commentary* (2nd ed. by Pearce, 1986). In Northern Ireland, the law of wills is still largely governed by the Wills Act, 1837, though that relating to intestate succession and personal representatives is now to be found largely in the Administration of Estates Acts (N.I.), 1955 and 1971. See Leitch, *A Handbook on the Administration of Estates Act (Northern Ireland), 1955* (1956, with Annot, to 1967).

[3] See further, Bailey, *Law of Wills* (7th ed., 1973); Jarman, *Treatise on Wills* (8th ed. by Jennings, 1951); *Theobald on Wills* (11th ed., by Clark 1971); Williams, *Law Relating to Wills* (3rd ed., 1967).

[4] Ch. 3, *ante.*

[5] Ch. 2, *ante.*

[6] Ch. 3. *ante.*

[7] *I.e.* Statute of Uses, 1535, and Statute of Wills, 1540. See para. 3.015, *ante.*

716

develop in respect of land[8] as it had already developed in respect of personalty,[9] until both realty (except a fee tail) and personalty became freely disposable by will.

14.03. This concept of testamentary freedom of disposition remained an absolute principle until very recent times, when the pendulum has begun to swing back again in favour of restricting a testator's power to dispose of his property as he pleases. In particular, legislatures have been concerned about testators leaving all their property to persons or bodies outside the family, *e.g.* a mistress or housekeeper or a charity, and thereby cutting their families off without a penny and, perhaps, leaving them destitute and a charge upon the state. In England the Inheritance (Family Provision) Act, 1938,[10] gave the court a limited power to make an order modifying the effect of a will, where it was of the opinion that it did not make "reasonable provision" for the maintenance of a "dependant" of the deceased.[11] This legislation did not apply to Northern Ireland, but a similar Act was passed in 1960, the Inheritance (Family Provision) Act (N.I.), 1960, subsequently amended by the Family Provision Act (N.I.), 1969. The English provisions were then overhauled by the Inheritance (Provision for Family and Dependants) Act, 1975, which was followed in Northern Ireland by the Inheritance (Provision for Family and Dependants) (Northern Ireland), Order, 1979. In the Republic of Ireland provisions designed to prevent disinheritance of the deceased's spouse or children, and to confer a "legal right" to part of the estate on the spouse, are contained in Parts IX and X of the Succession Act, 1965, and these provisions, and the Northern Ireland ones, are considered later in this chapter.[12]

II. MAKING OF WILLS

A. CAPACITY

14.04. In the Republic of Ireland, section 77 (1) of the 1965 Act lays down the general rule that, to make a valid will,[13] a person must have attained the age of 18 years, or be or have been married,[14] and be of sound disposing mind. It is a matter for the court to decide whether the instrument in question

---

[8] The Statute of Wills (Ir.), 1634 authorised wills to be made only of land held by certain tenures, *e.g.* socage and knight-service, ch. 3 *ante*. However, the abolition of most forms of tenure on conversion on most land to one tenure, free and common socage, or freehold, by the Tenures (Abolition) Act (Ir.), 1662 completed the process, para. 2.48, *ante*.

[9] See on the early history of wills, Holdsworth, *History of English Law* , vol. III; Pollock and Maitland, *History of English Law* (2nd ed., 1898), vol II pp. 312 *et seq*.

[10] As amended by the Family Provision Act, 1966, Sched. 3 and the Family Law Reform Act, 1969, ss. 5 and 18. See also Pt. II of the Intestates' Estates Act, 1952.

[11] Part II of the Intestates' Estates Act, 1952, gave the court power to modify the usual rules of succession on intestacy.

[12] Paras. 14.55 *et seq., post*

[13] Disposing of all property which he is beneficially entitled to at the time of his death and which devolves then on his personal representatives, s. 76 of the 1965 Act. For Northern Ireland , see s. 3 of the Wills Act, 1837.

[14] However, a person entitled to appoint a guardian of an infant may still make an appointment by will even though he does not comply with any of these provisions, s. 77 (2), replacing s.7 (7) of the Guardianship of Infants Act, 1964. For Northern Ireland, see Wills (Soldiers and Sailors) Act, 1918, s. 4.

was the will of a free and capable testator.[15] A valid will may be made during a "lucid interval" and remains valid despite subsequent mental illness.[16] There are no longer any restrictions on the capacity of married women to make wills.[17]

14.05. In Northern Ireland, the general rule is also that a will to be valid must be made by a person of full age,[18] *i.e.*, 18 years,[19] and of sound mind.[20] There is, however, no provision validating wills of married infants, though one has been recommended.[21] However, there are exceptions which operate in favour of certain testators, so as to render valid wills which may not be properly executed[22] and which have been made by infants.[23] In fact, at common law informal wills of *personalty* could be made by anyone and the Statute of Frauds (Ireland), 1695,[24] preserved this principle in respect of wills made by any soldier "in actual military service,"[25] or any mariner or seaman "being at sea".[26] The same principle for wills of personalty was still preserved by the Wills Act, 1837,[27] which is still in force in Northern Ireland, and has been extended to cover *real* property[28] and airmen[29] by the Wills (Soldiers and Sailors) Act, 1918,[30] also still in force. In each of these cases the will remains valid until revoked, even though the military or other service has ceased.[31] Finally, it should be noted that the testamentary privileges for service personnel contained in these provisions have been repealed in the Republic of Ireland.[32]

---

[15] *Banks* v. *Goodfellow* (1870) L.R. 5 Q.B. 549, espec. at 567 (*per* Cockburn C.J.) See also *In b. Farrell* (1954) 88 I.L.T.R. 57 (insane delusions); *In b. Corboy* [1969] I.R. 148 (arteriosclerosis and speech difficulty); *In b. Mitten* (1934) 68 I.L.T.R. 38 and *Ryan* v. *Ryan* (1904) 4 N.I.J.R. 164 (deaf and dumb). *Cf.* as to undue influence, *Healy* v. *Lyons* (1978) Unrep. (H.C., R.I.) (1975 Nos. 4631 P); *O'Connor* v. *O'Connor* (1978) Unrep. (H.C., R.I.) (1976 No. 4325 P); *In b. Rutledge* [1981] I.L.R.M. 198. As to the presumption of knowledge and approval of the contents of a will duly executed by a testator of sound mind, see *Re Begley* [1939] I.R. 479.
[16] *Re Walker's Estate* (1912) 28 T.L.R. 466. See also *In b. Farrell* (1954) 88 I.L.T.R. 57.
[17] See now Married Women's Status Act, 1957, s. 15 and note the Married Women's Property Acts of the last century, para. 25.10, *post*.
[18] Wills Act, 1837, s. 7.
[19] Age of Majority Act (N.I.), 1969, s. 2 and S.R. & O.(N.I.) 1969 No. 327.
[20] See, generally, the Mental Health Act (N.I.), 1960.
[21] *Survey of the Land Law of Northern Ireland* (1971), para. 352. As regards testamentary freedom for married women, see Married Women's Property Act, 1893, s. 3 and Law Reform (Miscellaneous Provisions) Act (N.I.), 1937, s. 9 (*a*). Also Wills Act, 1837, s. 8.
[22] See further paras. 14.06 *et seq.*, *infra*.
[23] See s. 1 of the Wills (Soldiers and Sailors) Act, 1918. *In b. Anderson* [1945] I.R. 179.
[24] S.19.
[25] See *In b. Schroeder* [1949] I.R. 89 (will made after seeing notice of mobilisation) and also *Re Godley* (1907) 41 I.L.T.R. 160. See further, *Doughty* v. *Mangan* [1943] I.R. 78; *In b. Ryan* [1945] I.R. 174; *In b. Taylor* [1933] I.R.L 709; *In b. Coleman* [1920] 2 I.R. 332.
[26] See *In b. Kearon* [1957] Ir.Jur.Rep. 21 (signed holograph footnote to will written while ship in port); *cf. Barnard* v. *Birch* [1919] 2 I.R. 404 (will signed by captain of Holyhead-Kingstown mail steamer at his home in Holyhead between voyages). In *In b. Hale* [1915] 2 I.R. 362 this statutory provision was held to cover a female typist employed on a liner. It does not seem to matter, in the case of the Navy or Marine Forces, that the seaman has not yet joined his ship, provided he has been called up, see Wills (Soldiers and Sailors) Act, 1918, s. 2 and *In b. Yates* [1919] P. 93. See also *In b. Newland* [1952] P. 71. Note also, as regards Northern Ireland, the powers of the British Board of Trade to distribute property as on an intestacy, instead of in accordance with a will, in certain cases under ss. 176–7 of the Merchant Shipping Act, 1894.
[27] S. 11. See cases cited in fn. 25, *supra*. Also *In b. Anderson* [1945] I.R. 179; *Re Hamilton* [1982] N.I. 197.
[28] 1918 Act, s. 3.
[29] Including members of the R.A.F. etc., 1918 Act, s 5. *Doherty* v. *Mangan* [1943] I.R. 78.
[30] Note also the previous Navy and Marines (Wills) Act, 1914.
[31] *In b. Coleman* [1920] 2 I.R. 352.
[32] See Succession Act, 1965, s. 8 and 2nd Sched., Pt III.

B. Formalities

14.06.   The Statute of Wills (Ireland), 1634,[33] required wills of realty to be in writing, though there was no necessity for a signature nor witnesses. Then the Statute of Frauds (Ireland), 1695,[34] required wills of realty not only to be in writing but also to be signed by the testator and attested in his presence by at least three witnesses and extended the requirements of witnessing to nuncupative, *i.e.* oral, wills of personalty over £30. These early provisions were all replaced by section 9 of the Wills Act, 1837,[35] which laid down a common set of requirements for execution of wills of both realty and personalty. The 1837 provisions remain in force in Northern Ireland but have been replaced in the Republic by provisions, which are, for the most part, to the same effect, contained in section 78 of the Succession Act, 1965.

14.07.   In dealing with questions concerning compliance with these statutory formalities, the courts frequently call in aid the maxim *omnia praesumuntur rite esse acta, i.e.*, everything is presumed to have been properly executed.[36] However, the courts are concerned to see that this presumption is not carried to such lengths that it nullifies the statutory provisions. Thus, in relation to the requirements of attestation by witnesses, Palles C.B. in *Clergy* v. *Barry*[37] emphasised that the maxim should be applied only in such cases as those where, at the time of the dispute, the witnesses are dead, or cannot give evidence through incapacity or their evidence cannot be accepted on account of its unreliability.[38]

The formalities for execution of wills are as follows.

1. *Writing*

14.08.   The first requirement is that a will must be in writing,[39] which may take any form, *e.g.* typewriting or printing.[40] No special form of words need be used provided the document· is intelligible[41] and sufficiently indicates an intention to make a will.[42] In Northern Ireland, section 42 of the Administration of Estates Act (N.I.), 1955, empowers the Lord Chief Justice by order to prescribe and publish forms to which a testator may refer in his

---

[33]   S. 1.

[34]   Ss. 3, 9 and 15–19.

[35]   As amended by the Wills Act Amendment Act, 1852. Note the proposals in the English Law Reform Committee's 22nd Report, *The Making and Revocation of Wills* (Cmnd. 7902; 1980). See also Davey, "The Making and Revocation of Wills" [1980] Conv. 64 and 101. See now for England the Administration of Justice Act, 1982, espec. s. 17.

[36]   As to the limits of application of this maxim see *Clarke* v. *Early* [1980] I.R. 223 (see *A Casebook on Irish Land Law* (1984), p. 496). See further *In b. MacLean* [1950] I.R. 180. Also *Copeland* v. *MacLeod* (1965) 16 N.I.L.Q. 539.

[37] (1889) 21 L.R.Ir. 152.

[38]   See the further discussion in *Rolleston* v. *Sinclair* [1924] 2 I.R. 157.

[39]   1965 Act, s. 78; 1837 Act, s 9.

[40]   *In b. Moore* [1892] P. 378; *In b. Usborne* (1909) 25 T.L.R. 519 *Cf. In b. Adams* (1872) L.R. 2 P. & D. 367 (pencil writing on will in ink excluded from probate).

[41]   *Thorn* v. *Dickens* (1906) W.N. 54.

[42]   *Re Anderson* [1940] Ir.Jur.Rep. 71; *Re Lynch* (1942) Ir.Jur.Rep. 53; *Re Greville* [1942] Ir.Jur.Rep. 1. See also *Re Griffith* [1940] Ir.Jur.Rep.69; *In b. Gilliland* [1937] N.I. 156; *In b. Cullen* [1932] L.J.Ir. 101; *In b. Brennan* [1932] I.R. 633.

will and to give directions as to the manner in which such forms may be
referred to. In fact this power has never been exercised though the similar
power in England has been.[43]

2. *Signature by Testator*

14.09. The will must be signed by the testator or some other person in his
presence and by his direction. [44] Once again the signature may take any form,
so long as there in an intention to execute the will. Thus the following have
been held to constitute a sufficient signature: initials[45]; a mark[46]; a stamped
name[47]; a signature in a former or assumed name[48]; signature by the person
directed by the testator in his own rather than the testator's name.[49] A seal is
not enough, since affixing this does not constitute signing.[50] It seems,
however, that a "holograph" will, *i.e.* written by the testator, may be valid if
the testator's name appears at the end or in the attestation clause, even
though he may not have formally signed it.[51]

14.10. The signature must be "at the foot or end" of the will and in the first
decade or so after the passing of the Wills Act, 1837, this was given a strict
intepretation.[52] This resulted in the passing of the Wills Act Amendment Act,
1852, section 1 of which contained various rules as to the position of the
signature.[53] In the Republic of Ireland, these rules are reproduced in section
78[54] of the Succession Act, 1965. They provide that a will is not to be affected
by the following circumstances:

(a)   that the signature does not follow or is not immediately after the foot
       or end of the will; or

(b)   that a blank space intervenes between the concluding word of the will
       and the signature; or

(c)   that the signature is placed among the words of the testimonium
       clause or of the clause of attestation, or follows or is after or under the
       clause of attestation, either with or without a blank space intervening,

---

[43]   See Law of Property Act, 1925, s. 179 and see S.R. & O. 1925 No. 780.
[44]   1965 Act, s. 78, rule 1; 1837 Act, s. 9. *Clarke* v. *Early* [1980] I.R. 223 (see *A Casebook on Irish Land Law*
(1984), p. 496). See the discussion, especially that relating to the distinction between an assisted signature and
one made by the testator's direction, in *Fulton* v. *Kee* (1961) N.I. 1. See also *In b. Marshall* (1866) 14 L.T. 643.
A directed signature is valid where the testator is blind. *In b. Sullivan* (1944) 78 I.L.T.R. 153; *In b. Dowling*
[1933] I.R. 150; or subject to other physical disability, *In b. Rowan* [1944] Ir.Jur.Rep. 50; or subject to other
physical disability, *In b. Rowan* [1944] Ir.Jur.Rep. 50; or illiterate, *In b. McLoughlin* [1936] I.R. 233.
[45]   *In b. Emerson* (1882) 9 L.R.Ir. 443. *Cf.* a Christian name only, *McConville* v. *McCreesh* (1879) 3 L.R.Ir.
73.
[46]   *In b. Gannon* (1931) 65 I.L.T.R. 113 (no mark, only dot on the "i" of illiterate testator's Christian
name); *In b. Kieran* [1933] I.R. 222 (two undecipherable scrawls held a mark). See also *Re O'Dea* [1932] L.J.Ir.
148; *In b. Smythe* (1915) 49 I.L.T.R. 223; *Ryan* v. *Ryan* (1904) 4 N.I.J.R. 164.
[47]   *Jenkins* v. *Gaisford* (1863) 3 Sw. & Tr. 93. But see *Re Bullock* [1968] N.I. 96, para. 14.12, fn. 66, *post.*
[48]   *In b. Glover* (1847) 11 Jur. 1022; *In b. Redding* (1850 2 Rob.Ecc. 339.
[49]   *In b. Clark* (1839) 2 Curt. 329.
[50]   *Wright* v. *Wakeford* (1811) 17 Ves. 454. *Cf. In b. Lemon* (1896) 30 I.L.T.R. 127; *In b. Emerson* (1882) 9
L.R.Ir. 443.
[51]   *In b. Maguire* (1941) 75 I.L.T.R. 66; *Re Rochford* [1943] Ir.Jur.Rep. 71. See also *Re Faavre* [1937]
Ir.Jur. Rep. 36.
[52]   See, *e.g.*, *Smee* v. *Bryer* (1848) 1 Rob. Ecc. 616.
[53]   The 1852 Act is still in force in Northern Ireland. See *In b. O'Neill* (1916) 50 I.L.T.R. 180. Also *In b.
Graves* (1899) 33 I.L.T.R. 45; *Woodroofe* v. *Creed* [1894] 1 I.R. 508; *In b. Rice* (1871) I.R. 5 Eq. 176; *In b.
Collins* (1879) 3 L.R.Ir. 241.
[54]   Rule 4 (*a*)–(*e*).

or follows or is after, or under, or beside the names or one of the names of the attesting witnesses; or

(d)   that the signature is on a side or page or other portion of the paper or papers containing the will on which no clause or paragraph or disposing part of the will is written above the signature; or

(e)   that there appears to be sufficient space on or at the bottom of the preceding side or page or other portion of the same paper on which the will is written to contain the signature.

Thus while the general rule that the signature must be at the foot or end of the will remains,[55] a fair amount of latitude is allowed in determining whether this requirement is met.[56] Further guidance on this subject is provided by rules 3 and 5 in section 78 of the Republic's 1965 Act.[57] Rule 3 provides with respect to the position of the signature, "it is sufficient if the signature is so placed at or after, or following, or under, or beside, or opposite to the end of the will that it is apparent on the face of the will that the testator intended to give effect by the signature to the writing signed as his will." Rule 5 provides that a signature is not operative to give effect to any disposition or direction inserted after the signature is made.[58]

3. *Witnesses*

14.11.   Section 9 of the Wills Act, 1837, which still governs the matter in Northern Ireland, provided that the testator must either make or acknowledge[59] the signature in the presence of two or more witnesses and either the signing or acknowledgement must be executed when the witnesses are present together at the same time.[60] The same requirement is contained in rule 2 of section 78 of the Republic's 1965 Act.

14.12.   Furthermore, each witness must then attest by his signature[61] the signature of the testator in the presence of the testator, but it is not necessary that they should sign in each other's presence.[62] Nor is a particular form of attestation necessary, *e.g.* an attestation clause (though it is usual to have

[55]   See the final phrase of rule 4 in s. 78 of the 1965 Act; *cf.* s. 1 of the 1852 Act. See now for England the Administration of Justice Act, 1982, s. 17. *Re* N.I., see the Land Law Working Group's Discussion Document No.2 (*Estates and Interests and Family Dealings in Land*) (1981), pp. 46–7.

[56]   *Re Boylan* [1942] Ir.Jur.Rep. 2; *In b. Tiernan* [1942] I.R. 572. See also *In b. Elliott* [1931] I.R. 340; *In b. Reynolds* [1934] L.J.Ir. 151. *Cf.* the *English Practice Direction* [1953] 1 W.L.R. 689.

[57]   *Cf.* s. 1 of the 1852 Act for Northern Ireland. See also the Land Law Working Group's Discussion Document No. 2 (*Estates and Interests and Family Dealings in Land*) (1981), pp. 46–7.

[58]   *Re Lynch* [1942] Ir.Jur.Rep. 53; *In b. Martin* [1928] N.I. 1238. *Cf. In b. Ffrench* (1889) 23 L.R.Ir. 433. See also *In b. White* [1896] 1 I.R. 269; *In b. Madden* [1905] 2 I.R. 612.

[59]   *Cooke* v. *Henry* [1932] I.R. 574; *Kavanagh* v. *Fegan* [1932] I.R. 566. See also *Gillie* v. *Smyth* (1915) 49 I.L.T.R. 36; *In b. Pattison* [1918] 2 I.R. 90; *In b. Ellison* [1907] 2 I.R. 480.

[60]   *In b. MacLean* [1950] I.R. 180; *In b. McDonald* [1942] I.R. 201; *Re Devlin* [1939] Ir.Jur.Rep. 85.

[61]   Mere acknowledgement by a witness is not enough, see *Wyatt* v. *Berry* [1893] P. 5, nor is the appending of his name by a third party, *In b. Mullins* (1944) Ir.Jur.Rep. 21.

[62]   This is now made explicit by rule 2 in s. 78 of the Republic's 1965 Act, but it was probably also the position under s. 9 of the 1837 Act, see *In b. Webb* (1855) Dea. & Sw. 1; *In b. Flynn* [1957] Ir.Jur.Rep. 95. *Cf. In b. MacLean* [1950] I.R. 180; *Re Devlin* [1939] Ir.Jur. Rep. 85; *In b. Smythe* (1915) 49 I.L.T.R. 233. They must, of course, be present together when the testator signs or acknowledges, and the testator must be present when each witness attests, see *Jenner* v. *Finch* (1879) 5 P.D. 106. *Cf. Mulhall* v. *Mulhall* [1936] I.R. 712; *In b. Keane* (1937) 71 I.L.T.R. 90. See also *Wall* v. *Hegarty* (1980) Unrep. (H.C.R.I.) (1979 No. 2552 P) (solicitor held liable in negligence for failure to ensure witness in presence of testator and present when testator signed).

one).[63] The signature of the witnesses may take any form, *e.g.*, initials,[64] a mark[65] or a stamp.[66] It is not necessary that the witnesses should know that they are attesting a will.[67] It is only the testator's signature which must be attested not the will.[68] Furthermore, the witnesses, unlike the testator, need not sign in any particular place, provided it is clear that they are attesting the testator's signature.[69]

14.13. There are generally no special requirements as to the competence of the witnesses, in terms, *e.g.*, of their age or intelligence.[70] Indeed, there is a statutory provision that if a witness is at the time of execution, or at any time afterwards, "incompetent" to be admitted a witness to prove the execution of the will,[71] "the will shall not on that account be invalid."[72] The two important considerations in this regard are that, first, the witnesses may later be called upon to swear affidavits and so should be competent in this respect and, secondly, there are problems about a beneficiary under the will also being a witness, which we consider later.[73] It is also provided by statute that a creditor or his spouse attesting a will dealing with an estate charged with his debt or debts is admissible as a witness,[74] and an executor of a will is not disqualified by reason only of being an executor.[75]

C. ALTERATIONS

14.14. So far as alterations to a will are concerned the following statutory provision exists:

"An obliteration, interlineation, or other alteration made in a will after execution shall not be valid or have any effect,[76] unless such alteration is executed as is required for the execution of the will; but the will, with such alteration as part thereof, shall be deemed to be duly executed if the

---

[63] S. 78, rule 2, 1965 Act; 1837 Act, s. 9. See *In b. Colyer* (1889) 60 L.T. 368; *In b. Denning* [1958] 1 W.L.R. 462; *Clarke* v. *Early* [1980] I.R. 223 (see *A Casebook on Irish Land Law* (1984), p. 486). Note *In b. Tiernan* [1942] I.R. 572 (will on three sheets of paper and third containing the only attestation clause). See also *Scarff* v. *Scarff* [1927] I.R. 13; *cf. Roleston* v. *Sinclair* [1924] 2 I.R. 157. See the discussion in Meredith, "Witnessing and Attestation" (1981) 75 Gaz. I.L.S.I. 219, (1983) 77 Gaz. I.L.S.I. 63.

[64] *In b. Streatley* [1891] P. 172.

[65] *In b. Amiss* (1849) 2 Rob.Ecc. 116

[66] Provided the witness participates by some physical act in affixing his name by means of a stamp, *Re Bullock* [1968] N.I. 96.

[67] *Re Devlin* [1939] Ir.Jur.Rep. 85. See also *Dubourdieu* v. *Patterson* (1920) 54 I.L.T.R. 23. And *Fischer* v. *Popham* (1875) L.R. 3 P. & D. 246; *Daintree* v. *Fasulo* (1888) 13 P.D. 102.

[68] However, a witness cannot attest if he is blind, *In b. Gibson* [1949] P. 434, or otherwise cannot see or know of the testator's signing, *e.g.* being unconscious, *Brown* v. *Skirrow* [1902] P. 3. *Cf.* the case of a testator, see *In b. Sullivan* (1944) 78 I.L.T.R. 153. As regards a witness's illiteracy, see *Clarke* v. *Clarke* (1879) 5 L.R. Ir. 47; *Bells* v. *Hughes* (1880) 5 L.R.Ir. 407.

[69] *In b. Ellison* [1907] 2 I.R. 480. Subsequent erasure of a witness's signature by a third party does not destroy the attestation, *In b. Mullins* (1944) Ir.Jur.Rep. 21.

[70] See, however, fn. 68, *supra*. Also *Smith* v. *Thompson* (1931) 146 L.T. 14 (attestation by infant).

[71] Ch. 16, *post*.

[72] 1965 Act, s. 81; 1837 Act, s. 14.

[73] Para. 14, 34, *post*.

[74] 1965 Act, s. 83; 1837 Act, s. 16.

[75] 1965 Act, s. 84; 1837 Act, s. 17.

[76] S. 21 of the 1837 Act adds—"except so far as the words or effect of the will before such alteration shall not be apparent." See *Townley* v. *Watson* (1844) 3 Curt. 761; *In b. Horsford* (1874) L.R. 3 P. & D. 211; *In b. Itter* [1950] P. 130.

signature of the testator and the signature of each witness[77] is made in the margin or on some other part of the will opposite or near to such alteration, or at the foot or end of or opposite to a memorandum referring to such alteration, and written at the end of some other part of the will."[78]

14.15. If words in a will are completely obliterated, generally the will can take effect as if there are blanks in the space containing those words.[79] The wording of section 21 of the 1837 Act[80] led the courts in Ireland and England to the view that an obliteration is not valid unless it makes that part of the will impossible to read in the normal way, *i.e.*, by the naked eye unassisted by any special scientific device,[81] other than a magnifying glass,[82] or by use of extrinsic evidence to explain the words obliterated.[83] It would appear that this rule may no longer hold good in the Republic of Ireland, since the key phrase in section 21 of the 1837 Act which led to the courts' adoption of the rule does not appear in section 86 of the 1965 Act, quoted above.

14.16. Quite apart from the above statutory provisions, also relevant in this context is the doctrine of incorporation by reference,[84] whereby *un*attested documents may be regarded as part of the will. For this doctrine to operate two conditions must be satisfied: first, the reference to the unattested document in the will must be sufficiently clear, allowing for admission of parol evidence,[85] that the document can be satisfactorily identified[86]; secondly, the document referred to must have been in existence in completed form at the date of execution of the will itself.[87] This second qualification to treating the document as part of the will exists because there must be no infringement of the general principle that a testator cannot reserve to himself power to change his will by a later unattested document.[88]

D. REVOCATION

The general rule is that a will remains revocable until the death of a testator and generally nothing he does or says can change this position.[89] The following are the ways in which a will may be revoked.

[77] Once again initials (put, *e.g.*, in the margin opposite the alteration) are sufficient, see *In b. Blewitt* (1880) 5 P.D. 116.

[78] 1965 Act, s. 86; 1837 Act, s. 21. See *In b. Rudd* [1945] I.R. 180; *In b. Carmody* (1944) 78 I.L.T.R. 112. For a discussion of the subject of interlineations, see *In b. Benn* [1938] I.R. 313. Also *In b. Duffy* (1871) I.R. 5 Eq. 506; *Moore* v. *Moore* (1872) I.R. 6 Eq. 166; *Hutchinson* v. *Hutchinson* (1850) 13 Ir.Eq.R. 332.

[79] *In b. Ibbetson* (1839) 2 Curt. 337. See also *In b. Morell* (1935) 69 I.L.T.R. 79; *Doherty* v. *Dwyer* (1890) 25 L.R.Ir. 297.

[80] Fn. 76, *supra*.

[81] *E.g.*, infra-red photography, *In b. Itter* [1950] P. 130, or chemicals, *Ffinch* v. *Combe* [1894] P. 191. See *In b. Carmody* (1944) 78 I.L.T.R. 112.

[82] *In b. Horsford* (1874) L.R. 3 P. & D. 211; *In b. Brasier* [1899] P. 36.

[83] *Townley* v. *Watson* (1844) 3 Curt. 761; *In b. McCabe* (1873) L.R. 3 P. & D. 94.

[84] See also para. 9.035, *ante*.

[85] See para. 14.40, *post*.

[86] *Re O'Connor* [1937] Ir.Jur.Rep. 67; *In b. Conwell* (1896) 30 I.L.T.R. 23. See also *Re Edward's Will Trusts* [1948] Ch. 440.

[87] *In b. Mitchell* (1966) 100 I.L.T.R. 185. See also *In b. Smart* [1902] P. 238.

[88] See discussion in *Re Keen* [1937] Ch. 236; *Re Bateman's Will Trusts* [1970] 3 All. E.R. 817. See para. 9.051, *ante*.

[89] *Forse and Hembling's Case* (1588) 4 Co.Rep. 61b. See, however, as regards mutual wills, para. 9.051, *ante*.

1. *Another Will or Codicil*

14.17.   It is standard practice to insert in a will a clause expressly revoking all prior wills.[90] Very strong evidence of a contrary intention on the part of the testator would be needed to persuade the court that such a clause does not revoke all previous testamentary dispositions.[91] On the other hand, a mere declaration by the testator that the document is "my last will and testament" is not necessarily enough in itself to revoke prior wills.[92] However, the court may regard revocation as taking place by implication, *e.g.*, if a later will merely repeats a former one or is inconsistent with it.[93] In considering this question of revocation by a subsequent will, it must always be remembered that a testator's "will" may consist of several separate documents, each executed at a different time during a considerable period of years and some partly varied or revoked by subsequent ones.[94] Furthermore, a revocation or cancellation of a particular devise or bequest may be conditional or based on a false assumption, and so may be ineffective if the condition is not met or because of the false premise.[95]

2. *Destruction*

14.18.   Section 85 (2) of the Republic's 1965 Act and section 20 of the Wills Act, 1837, provide that a will is revoked by "burning, tearing, or destruction of it by the testator, or by some person in his presence and by his direction, with the intention of revoking it." There must, therefore, be present the two elements of an act of destruction and an intention to revoke (*animus revocandi*). So far as the former is concerned, there need not be total destruction, provided the part destroyed is so vital or such that it indicates an intention to destroy the whole.[96] Otherwise, the part destroyed only will be regarded as being revoked.[97] Where someone else performs the act, it must be in the presence of and at the direction of the testator; subsequent ratification of an unauthorised destruction is not enough.[98] As regards the

---

[90]   *E.g.*, "I hereby revoke all testamentary dispositions heretobefore made by me and declare this to be my last will." See 1965 Act, s. 85 (2) and 1837 Act, s. 20, which require the revocation to be by will or codicil, executed as required by statute, or by some writing declaring an intention to revoke and executed in the manner required for execution of a will. See *In b. Cullinan* (1951) 85 I.L.T.R. 180; *Pakenham* v. *Duggan* (1951) 85 I.L.T.R. 21.

[91]   *In b. McCullagh* [1949] Ir.Jur.Rep. 49; *In b. Keenan* (1946) 80 I.L.T.R. 1. See also *Stewart* v. *Stewart* (1896) 30 I.L.T.R. 136.

[92]   *In b. Martin* [1968] I.R. 1. See also *In b. Miller* [1940] I.R. 456; *Re Brennan* [1932] I.R. 633. See also *Pepper* v. *Pepper* (1870) I.R. 5 Eq. 85.

[93]   *Caldbeck* v. *Stafford* [1930] I.R. 196; *In b. Martin* [1968] I.R. 1. See also *Pakenham* v. *Duggan* (1951) 85 I.L.T.R. 21. However, it seems that, where there are two wills of the same date containing inconsistent provisions, so that they cannot stand together, neither will be admitted to probate. *In b. Millar* [1913] I.R. 364; *In b. Kernoghan* [1938] N.I. 130. *Cf.* wills of different dates, *In b. Adams* (1911) 45 I.L.T.R. 93; *Hurley* v. *Valentine* (1916) 50 I.L.T.R. 7; *Reeves* v. *Reeves* [1909] 2 I.R. 521. Note the doctrine of "dependent relative revocation", see Newark, (1955) 71 L.Q.R. 374 and para. 14.21, *post.* Also *Re McMullen* [1964] Ir.Jur.Rep. 33; *In b. Cullinan* (1951) 85 I.L.T.R. 180.

[94]   *In b. Wafer* [1960] Ir.Jur.Rep. 19; *In b. M'Carthy* [1965] Ir.Jur.Rep. 56. See also *In b. McLoughlin* (1951) 85 I.L.T.R. 63; *Re Kennedy* [1941] Ir.Jur.Rep. 33; *Pennefather* v. *Lloyd* [1917] 1 I.R. 337.

[95]   *Re Faris (No. 2)* [1911] 1 I.R. 469; *Re Plunkett* [1964] I.R. 259.

[96]   *In b. Gullan* (1858) 1 Sw. & Tr. 23; *In b. Morton* (1887) 12 P.D. 141.

[97]   *Re Wright* (1910) 44 I.L.T.R. 137; *In b. Moore* (1917) 51 I.L.T.R. 136. *Cf. In b. Leeson* [1946] Ir.Jur.Rep. 33 (mutilation). See also *In b. Bentley* [1930] I.R. 455.

[98]   *Gill* v. *Gill* [1909] P. 157; *In b. De Kremer* (1965) 110 Sol.Jo. 18.

requisite intention, it must be an intention to revoke, not merely an intention to destroy; destruction by mistake is not effective revocation.[99]

If a will has been destroyed, but not effectively revoked, it still has force and may be proved by external evidence, *e.g.*, a draft or copy or oral evidence.[1] The same rule applies in the case of a lost will.[2]

3. *Marriage*

14.19. Section 18 of the Wills Act, 1837, provided that every will made by a man or woman is revoked by his or her marriage,[3] with an exception for the case of a will in exercise of a power of appointment, unless, in default of appointment, the property appointed would pass on the intestacy of the testator or testatrix.[4] This remains the position in Northern Ireland, except that the further exception has been added that a will made after June 22, 1954, if *expressed*[5] to be made in contemplation of a marriage, is not revoked by the contemplated marriage.[6]

14.20. In the Republic of Ireland the new statutory provision on the subject of revocation by marriage is contained in section 85 (1) of the Succession Act, 1965, which reads:

"A will shall be revoked by the subsequent marriage of the testator, except a will made in contemplation of that marriage, *whether so expressed in the will or not.*"[7]

Apart from these provisions relating to marriage, the general rule is that no

---

[99] *In b. Walsh* [1947] Ir.Jur.Rep. 44, followed by the Republic's Supreme Court in *In b. Coster* (1979) Unrep. (Sup. Ct., R.I.), wherein Kenny J. stated: "When a testatrix makes a will and retains the original or subsequently comes into possession of it and it cannot be found after her death and there is no evidence to show what has become of it, there is a presumption that she destroyed it with the intention of revoking it." (See *A Casebook on Irish Land Law* (1984), p. 499.) See also *Pinnions* v. *Smith* (1903) 37 I.L.T.R. 116. *Cf. In b. Biggane* [1947] Ir.Jur.Rep. 22 (testator probably unaware of presence of revocation clause in printed form). See also *In b. Paget* (1913) 47 I.L.T.R. 284; *In b. Eyre* [1905] 2 I.R. 540.

[1] *In b. Cullinan* (1951) 85 I.L.T.R. 180; *In b. Regan* [1964] Ir.Jur.Rep. 56. See also *Re Owens* (1907) 41 I.L.T.R. 114. And note the discussion in *Sugden* v. *Lord St. Leonards* (1876) 1 P.D. 154 and *Allan* v. *Morrison* [1900] A.C. 604. S. 90 of the Republic's 1965 Act provides that extrinsic evidence "shall be admissible to show the intention of the testator and to assist in the construction of, or to explain any contradiction in, a will." On the admission of evidence in such cases in Northern Ireland, see Civil Evidence Act (N.I.), 1971; also the Evidence Act (N.I.), 1939 and Statute Law Revision (Northern Ireland) Act, 1973, s. 2 (U.K.). Malcolm, "The Oddity-Section 1 of the Civil Evidence Act (N.I.) 1971" (1973) 24 N.I.L.Q. 94 and "Back to Base?" (1974) 25 N.I.L.Q. 49. See also *Re Gilliland* [1940] N.I. 125.

[2] *In b. Regan* [1964] Ir.Jur.Rep. 56; *In b. Cray* (1967) 101 I.L.T.R. 71. See also *In b. Merrigan* (1899) 33 I.L.T.R. 131; *In b. O'Hare* (1908) 42 I.L.T.R. 75.

[3] *Otway* v. *Sadleir* (1850) 4 Ir.Jur. (N.S.) 97.

[4] *I.e.*, if the "new" family formed on marriage would get the property anyway, if the will were revoked by the marriage and an intestacy thereby occur, allowing the marriage to revoke the will does no harm. See the discussion of this exception in *In b. Gilligan* [1950] P. 32, espec. at 38; followed in *Re Master's Estate* (1968) 19 N.I.L.Q. 216. Also Mitchell, (1951) 67 L.Q.R. 351 and (1952) 68 L.Q.R. 455. *Cf. In b. McVicar* (1869) L.R. 1 P. & D. 671; *Re Paul* [1921] 2 Ch. 1.

[5] This same requirement exists in England under s. 177 of the Law of Property Act, 1925. See *Sallis* v. *Jones* [1936] P. 43; *In b. Langston* [1953] P. 100; *Pilot* v. *Gainfort* [1931] P. 103. See, however, the discussion by Megarry J. in *Re Coleman* [1975] 1 All E.R. 675 and the Law Reform Committee in their 19th and 22nd Reports; *cf.* the N.I. Land Law Working Group's Discussion Document No. 2 (*Estates and Interests and Family Dealing in Land*) (1981), pp. 49–52. And see Edwards and Langstaff, "The Will to Survive Marriage" (1975) 39 Conv. 121. See now as regards England the Administration of Justice Act, 1982, s. 18.

[6] Wills (Amendment) Act (N.I.), 1954.

[7] Italics added. This seems to do away with the need to express the fact of contemplation of marriage altogether.

will is "revoked by any presumption of an intention on the ground of an alteration in circumstances."[8]

4. *Conditional*

14.21. The revocation of a will may be made subject to a condition and remains ineffective until the condition is met.[9] One much litigated illustration of this rule is the so-called "dependent relative revocation."[10] If the revocation is relative to another will and depends upon the validity of that will, the revocation fails if that other will is invalid.[11] This commonly occurs where a new will is to be made with the intention of replacing an old one, which is supposed to be thereby revoked.[12]

E. REPUBLICATION AND REVIVAL

14.22. The general rule is that a duly executed codicil republishes any prior unrevoked will to which it refers.[13] However, any will which has been revoked by destruction and intended to be revoked cannot be revived.[14] Apart from that, a revoked will can be revived provided there is re-execution of it or due execution of a codicil showing an intention to revive it.[15] If a will is revoked by a subsequent will, mere revocation of the latter does not revive the former.[16] Furthermore, if a will is first partly revoked, then wholly revoked, and finally revived, the revival does not extend to the first part which was partially revoked, unless a contrary intention is shown.[17]

14.23. The effect of republication or revival of a will is the same as making a new will on the date of republication or revival.[18] Thus its operation may extend to persons and property who or which have come into existence between the date of the original will and its republication.[19]

---

[8]   So provided expressly by s. 19 of the 1837 Act and still in force in Northern Ireland. No such express provision is included in the Republic's 1965 Act, but may be implied from s. 85.

[9]   *Re Plunkett* [1964] I.R. 259. See also *In b. Groarke* [1949] Ir.Jur.Rep. 8; *Re Faris (No. 2)* [1911] 1 I.R. 469. In *In b. Coster* (1979) Unrep. (Sup. Ct. R.I.) (see *A Casebook on Irish Land Law* (1984), p. 499), Kenny J., following the English Court of Appeal decision in *Re Jones* [1976] 1 All E.R. 593, stated:

"To make a destruction of a will by a testatrix a conditional revocation only, a mere general intention at the time of destruction to make another will is not, in most cases, effective to make the revocation by destruction conditional. The purchase of the printed form of will shows that the deceased had the making of another will in mind but this does not make the revocation conditional."

[10]   See the strictures of Langton J. in *In b. Hope Brown* [1942] P. 136 at 138 and see Newark, (1955) 71 L.Q.R. 374. See also *Re McMullen* [1964] Ir.Jur.Rep. 33; *Re McClintock* [1943] I.R. 83; *In b. Hogan* (1980) Unrep. (H.C., R.I.) (see Brady, "A Case of Dependent Relative Revocation" (1980) 75 Gaz. I.L.S.I. 5).

[11]   Or never made. *Re Cullinan* (1951) 85 I.L.T.R. 180; *In b. McCullagh* [1949] Ir.Jur.Rep. 49. See also *West* v. *West* [1921] 2 I.R. 34; *In b. Irvine* [1919] 2 I.R. 485; *Sterling* v. *Bruce*]1973] N.I. 255.

[12]   *Re McMullen, op. cit.; In b. Walsh* [1947] Ir.Jur.Rep. 44. *Cf. Pinnions* v. *Smith* (1903) 37 I.L.T.R. 116.

[13]   See discussion in *Earl of Mountashell* v. *Smyth* [1895] 1 I.R. 346. See also *Browne* v. *Browne* [1912] 1 I.R. 272; *Grealey* v. *Sampson* [1917] 1 I.R. 286; *In b. Browne* (1902) 2 N.I.J.R. 206; *Re Swiney* (1857) 6 Ir.Ch.R. 455.

[14]   *In b. Reade* [1902] P. 75. See also *Re Hall* [1943] Ir.Jur.Rep. 25.

[15]   1965 Act, s. 87; 1837 Act, s. 22. *In b. Studholme* [1933] L.J.Ir. 178; *In b. Mulock* [1933] I.R. 171. *Cf. In b. Carleton* [1915] 2 I.R. 9.

[16]   *In b. Hodgkinson* [1893] P. 339. *Cf. Davis* v. *Davis* (1868) I.R. 3 C.L. 74.

[17]   1965 Act, s. 87; 1837 Act, s. 22. *Re Mardon's Estate* [1944] P. 109. See also *French* v. *Hoey* [1899] 2 I.R. 472.

[18]   *Rogers* v. *Pittis* (1822) 1 Add. 30 at 38; *Earl of Mountcashel* v. *Smyth* [1895] 1 I.R. 346. See also s. 34 of the Wills Act, 1837; *cf.* s. 99 of the 1965 Act.

[19]   *Grealey* v. *Sampson* [1917] 1 I.R. 286. See also *Re Fraser* [1904] 1 Ch. 726; *Re Hardyman* [1925] Ch. 287.

III. OPERATION

14.24. We now turn to the operation of wills, in particular to a consideration of the operation of the *devises* and *bequests* or *legacies* given by will. A "devise" is the name given to a gift of real property by will and "bequest" or "legacy" is the name given to a gift of personalty.[20]

A. DEVISES AND LEGACIES

14.25. A devise may be either *specific* or *residuary*.[21] A specific devise is one where the testator makes a gift of a specific piece of real property,[22] *e.g.*, "my farm in Kildare."[23] Where a testator disposes of part of his real property by specific devises and then disposes of the rest by a general description, *e.g.*, "the residue of my real estate I leave to my wife," the latter is a residuary devise. The distinction between a specific and residuary devise is important because in both parts of Ireland now property not specifically devised or bequeathed, but included in a residuary gift, constitutes a fund out of which (after undisposed of property) the testator's funeral and testamentary expenses are payable.[24]

14.26. A legacy or bequest may also be *specific* or *residuary*.[25] However, it is also important to distinguish between a specific legacy and a *general* legacy, *i.e.*, a piece of personal estate which the testator has not distinguished from personal property of the same kind, *e.g.*, a bequest of "a horse," of which the testator has several,[26] as opposed to "my horse which won the Irish Sweeps' Derby in 1974."[27] Unlike a specific legacy, a general legacy is not liable to be adeemed by any act of the testator in his lifetime. We have already discussed ademption. It is used in two senses in our law. Here it is the name given to the effect of the thing given ceasing to exist or ceasing to belong to the testator before his death.[28] On the other hand, a specific legacy must be paid or retained by the executor of the will in priority to general legacies and should not be used to satisfy the testator's debts until all undisposed of and residuary property contained in the will have been exhausted.[29] The Irish legislation dealing with administration of assets of

[20] See *McInerney* v. *Liddy* [1945] I.R. 100.
[21] We consider the question of construction of wills later, paras. 14.36 *et seq.*, *post*.
[22] *McCarthy* v. *MacDonald* (1905) 84 I.L.T.R. 33; *Re Bovill* [1957] N.I. 58.
[23] *Cf. Daly* v. *Carroll* (1905) 39 I.L.T.R. 156. See also *Duffield* v. *McMaster* [1896] 1 I.R. 370; *Re Chester* (1915) 49 I.L.T.R. 97.
[24] Succession Act, 1965, 1st Sched., Pt. II, para. 2; Administration of Estates Act (N.I.), 1955, 1st Sched., Pt. II, para. 2. See ch. 16, *post*.
[25] See discussion in *Re Byrne* [1967] I.R. 304; see also *Bothamley* v. *Sherson* (1875) L.R. 20 Eq. 304 at 309 (*per* Jessel M.R.); *Robertson* v. *Broadbent* (1883) 8 App.Cas. 812 at 815 (*per* Lord Selborne). And see *Re Mulcair* [1960] I.R. 321; *Hanton* v. *White* [1958] Ir.Jur.Rep. 68.
[26] *Brennan* v. *Brennan* (1868) I.R. 2 Eq. 321; *Re McAfee* [1909] I.R. 124; *McCoy* v. *Jacob* [1919] 1 I.R. 134.
[27] *Barry* v. *Harding* (1844) 7 Ir.Eq.R. 313; *Re Cranfield* (1895) 1 I.R. 80; *Re Doyle* [1897] 1 I.R. 479; *Kelly* v. *Frawley* (1944) 78 I.L.T.R. 46.
[28] Ch. 3, *ante*. And see *Re Vuille* [1918] 1 I.R. 6; *Guirey* v. *Condon* [1918] 1 I.R. 23. Also *Makeown* v. *Ardagh* (1876) I.R. 10 Eq. 445; *Longfield* v. *Bantry* (1885) 15 L.R.Ir. 101; *Goddard* v. *Overend* [1911] 1 I.R. 165.
[29] Ch. 16, *post*. See *Barry* v. *Harding* (1844) 7 Ir.Eq.R. 313; *Brereton* v. *Day* [1895] 1 I.R. 519; *Kingham* v. *Kingham* [1897] 1 I.R. 170; *Re Smyth* [1965] I.R. 595.

deceased persons also uses the expressions *pecuniary* and *demonstrative* legacies. A pecuniary legacy is defined as including "an annuity, a general legacy, a demonstrative legacy so far as it is not discharged out of the designated property, and any other general direction by a testator for the payment of money, including all death duties free from which any devise, bequest, or payment is made to take effect."[30] A demonstrative legacy is one which is general in nature, but which is directed to be satisfied out of a specified fund or part of the testator's property, e.g., "£1,000 to X to be paid out of my Irish Permanent Building Society Shares."[31] A demonstrative legacy, like a general legacy, is not liable to ademption by act of the testator during his lifetime, but it is not liable to abatement with general legacies.[32]

B. FAILURE OF GIFTS

There are a number of ways in which a gift, whether a devise or a legacy, may fail.

1. *Disclaimer*

14.27. The beneficiary or donee of the gift made by will may disclaim it, *i.e.*, refuse or renounce the gift.[33] Such a disclaimer may be executed formally, *e.g.*, by a deed, or may be implied from conduct.[34] Normally disclaimer of a prior interest accelerates subsequent interests, but this is subject to a contrary intention appearing in the will.[35]

2. *Lapse*

14.28. The general rule is that a devise or legacy lapses if the beneficiary predeceases the testator. In such a case, subject to a contrary intention, the gift falls into the residue and passes as such.[36] If there is no residuary clause in the will, or the lapsed gift is itself residuary, an intestacy occurs with respect to the property in question. The doctrine of lapse derives to some extent from the basic principle that a will is ambulatory, *i.e.*, it has no effect at all until the testator's death and so may be altered and modified from time to time prior to his death.[37] Furthermore, as is now provided by statute,[38] a will, subject to a contrary intention, "speaks from death." In other words it is capable of disposing of all property owned by the testator at the date of his death, *including* property acquired after the date of execution of the will.[39]

There are, however, several exceptions to the general doctrine of lapse of testamentary gifts.

---

[30] 1965 Act, s. 3 (1); 1955 Act (N.I.), s. 45 (1). See also 1st Sched., Pt. II. paras. 1, 2 and 5 to both Acts. And see *Re Connor* [1970] N.I. 159. Also *Re Blake* [1955] I.R. 89.
[31] *McCoy* v. *Jacob* [1919] 1 I.R. 134. *Cf. Barry* v. *Harding* (1844) 7 Ir.Eq.R. 313. See also *Kelly* v. *Frawley* (1944) 78 I.L.T.R. 46; *Boyd* v. *Boyd* [1928] N.I. 14; *Re Cranfield* [1895] 1 I.R. 80; *Conly* v. *Green* (1870) I.R. 5 Eq. 430.
[32] *Re Turner* [1908] 1 I.R. 274.
[33] *Townson* v. *Tickell* (1819) 3 B. & Ald. 31.
[34] *Re Clout and Frewer's Contract* [1924] 2 Ch. 230.
[35] *Re Hodge* [1943] Ch. 300; *Re Harker's Will Trusts* [1969] 1 W.L.R. 1124.
[36] This is now provided by statute, see Succession Act, 1965, s. 91; Wills Act, 1837, s. 25.
[37] *Re Thompson* [1906] 2 Ch. 199.
[38] 1965 Act, s. 89; 1837 Act, s. 24. See *Re Dowse* (1977) Unrep. (H.C., R.I.) (1975 No. 469).
[39] See, further, para. 14.42, *post*.

(i) Moral Obligation

14.29. It is settled that a legacy which is not a mere gift but is designed to fulfil some moral obligation recognised by the testator is not caught by the doctrine of lapse.[40] It is not necessary that the obligation should be a legally enforceable one, *e.g.*, it may be statute-barred or purely moral in nature.[41] In such cases the legatee's personal representatives can claim the legacy.

(ii) Estates Tail

14.30. It is provided by statute[42] that, subject to a contrary intention in the will, there is no lapse if real property is given to a person in tail or quasi entail[43] and that person predeceases the testator, but leaves issue living at the testator's death capable of inheriting under the entail or quasi-entail. It must be noted that this provision does not mean necessarily that the issue will take on death; it merely provides that the gift is to take effect as if the devisee died immediately after the testator, *e.g.*, if the devisee died bankrupt, his trustee in bankruptcy or the Official Assignee can claim the entail.[44]

(iii) Gifts to Issue

14.31. It is also provided by statute,[45] again subject to a contrary intention, that no lapse occurs if any property is given to a child or other issue of the testator who predeceases the testator, but leaves issue living[46] at the testator's death. Once again the gift takes effect as if the donee died immediately after the testator's death, but the provision does not save from lapse gifts which would terminate anyway on the donee's death, *e.g.*, a life interest,[47] or, it appears, certain contingent gifts, *e.g.*, "to A at 21" and A dies aged 20, but would have reached 21 if he survived the testator.[48] It was also held that section 33 of the Wills Act, 1837, and this is still the law in Northern Ireland, did not preserve from lapse appointments made under a *special* power (being confined to property "devised or bequeathed"[49]) nor class gifts (since membership of a class is determined at the testator's death and those

---

[40] *Stevens* v. *King* [1904] 2 Ch. 30; *Re Leach* [1948] Ch. 232.

[41] *Williamson* v. *Naylor* (1838) 3 Y. & C. Ex. 208.

[42] 1965 Act, s. 97; 1837 Act, s. 32.

[43] See para. 4.165, *ante*.

[44] *Re Pearson* [1920] 1 Ch. 247.

[45] 1965 Act, s. 98; 1837 Act, s. 33. See now as regards England, s. 19 of the Administration of Justice Act, 1982.

[46] In *Elliott* v. *Joicey* [1935] A.C. 209 (disapproving of *Re Griffith's Settlement* [1911] 1 Ch. 246), this was held not to include a child *en ventre sa mère*. With respect to section 33 of the Wills Act, Article 5 of the Family Law Reform (N.I.) Order, 1977, now provides that the section is to have effect as if the reference to a child or other issue of the testator included a reference to any illegitimate child of the testator (i.e., the intended beneficiary) and to anyone who would rank as such issue if he, or some other person through whom he is descended from the testator, had been born legitimate. Furthermore, the reference to the issue of the intended beneficiary is to include a reference to anyone who would rank as such issue if he, or some other person through whom he is descended from the intended beneficiary, had been born legitimate. For these purposes, "illegitimate child" includes a child born illegitimate who is a legitimated person within the meaning of the Legitimacy Act (N.I.), 1928, or a person recognised by virtue of that Act or at common law as having been legitimated.

[47] *Re Butler* [1918] 1 I.R. 394.

[48] *Re Wolson* [1939] Ch. 80.

[49] *Holyland* v. *Lewin* (1883) 26 Ch.D. 266. *Cf.* general powers, *Eccles* v. *Cheyne* (1856) 2 K. & J. 676. See also 1965 Act, s. 93 and 1837 Act, s. 27, para. 14.43, *post*.

pre-deceasing him simply fail to qualify *ab initio*).[50] However, in the Republic of Ireland, section 98 of the Succession Act, 1965, refers to property "given" and expressly includes exercise by will of *any* power of appointment and property given whether as a gift to the donee as an individual or as a member of a class. The effect of this is that such gifts do not lapse on the death of the testator, but pass to his issue.

3. *Commorientes*

14.32. Connected with the question of lapse of testamentary gifts is the subject of *commorientes*, *i.e.*, where two or more people die together. If a devisee or legatee, or, indeed, an intestate successor, dies at the same, or nearly the same, time as the testator or intestate deceased, the question arises as to which should be regarded as surviving the other. The answer to this question is crucial to determining whether, in the case of a will, a gift lapses or, in the case of intestacy, the intestate successor's estate has a claim to an intestate share in the other estate. At common law the onus of proof of survivorship, which is the vital factor,[51] lay on the person (or persons claiming through him) asserting it and, in the case of apparently simultaneous, or nearly simultaneous, deaths, it was often impossible to prove this, *e.g.*, where the persons concerned were jointly involved in some disaster such as a road accident or plane crash. In other words, at common law there was in effect a presumption of simultaneous death in cases of uncertainty of survivorship. In the absence of proof of survivorship, none of the persons involved could have a claim under the estates of other persons involved in the same disaster.[52] In England, this difficulty was supposed to be resolved by introduction of a statutory presumption in cases of uncertainty of survivorship to the effect that, subject to any order of the court, the younger person was deemed to survive the elder.[53] This presumption was later modified in the case of a husband and wife, where one of them died intestate,[54] and the common law presumption of simultaneous death was restored for the purposes of estate duty and then capital transfer tax.[55]

14.33. In Northern Ireland the common law presumption of simultaneous deaths in cases of uncertainty of survivorship continues to apply[56] and the same presumption has now been confirmed for the Republic of Ireland by section 5 of the Succession Act, 1965.[57]

---

[50] Nor, it seems, joint gifts, *Joyce* v. *Brew* (1919) 53 I.L.T.R. 119; *cf. Re Beaupre's Trusts* (1888) 21 L.R.Ir. 397. See also *Olney* v. *Bates* (1855) 3 Drew. 319; *Re Harvey's Estate* [1893] 1 Ch. 567. See further on class gifts, paras. 5.080 *et seq., ante.* Also *Re Parker* [1966] I.R. 309; *Re Ramadge* [1969] N.I. 71; *Re Finnerty* [1970] I.R. 221.

[51] The same problem of survivorship arises in respect of a joint tenancy, para. 7.06, *ante.*

[52] *Wing* v. *Angrave* (1860) 8 H.L.C. 183; *Re Phené's Trusts* (1870) 5 Ch.App. 139.

[53] Law of Property Act, 1925, s. 184. See discussion in *Re Lindop* [1942] Ch. 377 and *Hickman* v. *Peacey* [1945] A.C. 304.

[54] Intestates' Estates Act, 1952, s. 1 (4). See also Administration of Estates Act, 1925, s. 46.

[55] Finance Act, 1958, s. 29 (1). *Cf.* Finance Act (N.I.), 1958, s. 2 (1). And see now Finance Act 1975 (U.K.), s. 22 (9).

[56] See *Survey of the Land Law of Northern Ireland* (1971), paras. 406–7. See also the Land Law Working Group's Discussion Document No. 4 (*Conveyancing and Miscellaneous Matters*) (1983), ch. 7.

[57] Which applies "for the purposes of distribution of the estates of any of" the persons dying "in circumstances rendering it uncertain which of them survived the other or others."

4. Gifts to Witnesses

14.34. Section 15 of the Wills Act, 1837,[58] provided that where a person attested the execution of a will, and he or she or his or her spouse was also made a beneficiary of any property under the will, the attestation would be valid but the gift would be void. This provision remains in force in Northern Ireland[59] and a similar one for the Republic of Ireland is now contained in section 82 of the Succession Act, 1965.

The rule against a witness or his or her spouse being a beneficiary does not apply in cases where witnesses are not necessary at all,[60] where the person in question does not sign as a witness,[61] where the gift is made to him or her as trustee and not as beneficiary,[62] where the beneficiary marries the witness after the date of the will[63] nor where the beneficial gift is made or confirmed by any will or codicil *not* attested by the beneficiary.[64] On the other hand, it has been held that the rule still deprives the beneficiary of the gift in cases where there were at least two other witnesses to the will, so that the beneficiary's signature was superfluous.[65] This latter rule has now been reversed in England[66] but as yet no equivalent legislation has been passed in either part of Ireland.[67]

5. Ademption

This subject was discussed in an earlier chapter to which reference may be made.[68]

6. Uncertainty

This subject was also discussed in an earlier chapter.[69]

7. Illegality

Any will made for an illegal purpose or contrary to public policy[70] is void. Illegality may take several forms.

---

[58] Replacing the somewhat odd provisions of s. 3 of the Statute of Frauds (Ir.), 1695, and the Wills Act (Ir.), 1751. See *Hatfield* v. *Thorp* (1822) 5 B. & Ald. 589. See also *Kearney* v. *Kearney* [1911] 1 I.R. 137; *Re McGearey* (1900) 34 I.L.T.R. 43. In *Ross* v. *Caunters* [1980] Ch. 297, Megarry V.-C. held a solicitor liable in negligence for failing to warn a testator that under section 15 of the Wills Act, 1837, attestation by a beneficiary's spouse invalidated a gift made in the will to that beneficiary. The solicitor was held to owe a duty of care to the beneficiary as there was a sufficient degree of proximity between the solicitor and such a third party identified as the person on whom the transaction, which he was employed by his client to carry out, was to confer a benefit. *Cf. Wall* v. *Hegarty* (1980) Unrep. (H.C., R.I.) (1979 No. 2552 P), para. 14.12, fn. 62, *ante*. See also Yale, "Witnessing Wills and Losing Legacies" (1984) (100) L.Q.R. 453.

[59] *Survey of the Land Law of Northern Ireland* (1971), para. 353.

[60] *E.g.* in N.I. wills executed by soldiers or sailors in service, para. 14.05, *ante*.

[61] *In b. Shaw* [1944] Ir.Jur.Rep. 77. See also *In b. Willis* (1927) 61 I.L.T.R. 48; *Re Parker* (1905) 39 I.L.T.R. 6.

[62] *Kelly* v. *Walsh* [1948] I.R. 388.

[63] *Thorpe* v. *Bestwick* (1881) 6 Q.B.D. 311.

[64] *Re Marcus* (1887) 56 L.J.Ch. 830; *Re Trotter* [1899] 1 Ch. 764.

[65] *Randfield* v. *Randfield* (1863) 32 L.J.Ch. 668; *Re Bravda's Estate* [1968] 1 W.L.R. 479.

[66] Wills Act, 1968, s. 1.

[67] But see *Survey of the Land Law of Northern Ireland* (1971), para. 354. *Cf.* the Land Law Working Group's Discussion Document No. 2 (*Estates and Interests and Family Dealings in Land* (1981), pp. 48–9.

[68] Ch. 3, *ante*.

[69] Ch. 4, *ante*.

[70] See further, para. 4.052, *ante*.

(i) Causing Testator's Death

14.35. At common law, the rule[71] developed that a person guilty of murder or manslaughter could take no benefit under the will or intestacy of the victim,[72] unless the killer was insane at the time.[73] The common law continues to govern the matter in Northern Ireland, but in the Republic section 120 (1) of the Succession Act, 1965, provides that a "sane person who has been guilty of murder, attempted murder or manslaughter of another shall be precluded from taking any share in the estate of that other, except a share arising under a will made after the fact constituting the offence."[74] The share which cannot be taken as a result of this provision is to be distributed as if the person precluded died before the deceased.[75]

(ii) Rules against Remoteness

The application of these rules was considered in detail in an earlier chapter.[76]

(iii) Rule against Accumulations

This rule, in its very limited application in Ireland, was also considered earlier.[77]

IV. CONSTRUCTION

The construction of wills is one of the most litigated of subjects and the following is an attempt to state briefly the main rules that have been developed by the courts.[78]

A. GENERAL PRINCIPLES

1. *Intention of Testator*

14.36. In the construction of a will, the primary object of the court is to determine the intention of the testator, as expressed by him in his will.[79] The courts also take the view that the testator's intention must be obtained from

---

[71] Originally the rule was frequently referred to as that relating to "felonious" killing. The distinction between felonies and misdemeanours has been abolished in Northern Ireland, see Criminal Law Act (N.I.), 1967, s. 1.

[72] *In b. Hall* [1914] P. 1; *Re Sigsworth* [1935] Ch. 89; *Re Giles* [1972] Ch. 544.

[73] *Re Pitts* [1931] 1 Ch. 546.

[74] Such a person is also precluded from making an application under s. 117 of the 1965 Act, relating to a testator's failure to make provision for his child, see para. 14.61, *post*. Note the other disqualifications in s. 120 of the 1965 Act relating to the legal right of a spouse to share in the testator's estate, para. 14.63, *post*.

[75] 1965 Act, s. 120 (5). *Cf. Re Callaway* [1956] Ch. 559.

[76] Ch. 5, *ante.*

[77] *Ibid.*

[78] See on jurisdiction of the courts in the Republic of Ireland, s. 6 of the Succession Act, 1965. For Northern Ireland, see Probate and Letters of Administration Act (Ir.), 1857, Court of Probate Act (Ir.) 1859 and Administration of Estates Act (N.I.), 1955, ss. 43, 46–8 and Sched. 3, recently replaced by Parts II and III of the Administration of Estates (N.I.) Order, 1979.

[79] See generally, Hawkins and Ryder, *Construction of Wills* (1965); Law Reform Committee's 19th Report (Cmnd. 5301; 1973); Sherrin, "The Wind of Change in the Law of Wills" (1976) 40 Conv. 66. *Re McCready* [1962] N.I. 43. Also *Re Moore* [1947] I.R. 205; *Oliver* v. *Menton* [1945] I.R. 6; *Johnston* v. *Langheld* [1983] I.L.R.M. 359. As regards emphasis on words and context as opposed to punctuation, see *Re Campbell* [1918] 1 I.R. 429.

reading the will as a whole, so that a general intention overrides a particular one.[80] This overriding principle has in turn led to recognition by the courts of several rules of construction.

2. *Natural Meaning*

14.37. One basic rule is that the words used by the testator ought to be given their natural or ordinary meaning, unless, of course, this would lead to inconsistencies or absurdities.[81] However, merely because a particular provision appears capricious or eccentric is no reason for departing from the ordinary or primary meaning.[82]

3. *Technical Meaning*

14.38. Where, however, a testator uses words which have a generally recognised technical or legal meaning, the assumption to be made is that he intended that technical meaning, unless the will evidences a contrary intention.[83]

4. *Render Operative*

14.39. Apart from statute, the courts tend to give meaning to rather vague phrases, which might otherwise be held void for uncertainty.[84] Thus a phrase like "relations" or "successors" might be construed as a reference to the persons who would have been the testator's intestate successors, had he not made a will.[85] In the Republic of Ireland, section 99 of the Succession Act, 1965 now provides:

> "If the purport of a devise or bequest admits of more than one interpretation, then, in case of doubt, the interpretation according to which the devise or bequest will be operative shall be preferred."[86]

5. *Extrinsic Evidence*

14.40. The common law rule as to extrinsic evidence, *i.e.*, evidence not

---

[80] *Robinson* v. *Moore* [1962–3] Ir.Jur.Rep. 29. See also *Garnett* v. *Garnett* (1854) 5 Ir.Jur. 89. And *I.R.C.* v. *Raphael* [1935] A.C. 96; *Re Mcandrew's Will Trusts* [1964] Ch. 704. In *Fitzpatrick* v. *Collins* (1978) Unrep. (H.C., R.I.) (1978 No. 4122P), McWilliam J., while accepting the general principles stated in this paragraph, refused to disregard the precise terms of a will, although doing so resulted in an intestacy. He stated: "Taking the will as a whole it is reasonably clear that the testator had his mind concentrated solely on the disposition of his property on the basis that his wife would survive him or die very soon after him and that he did not advert at all to the possibility of her predeceasing him. If this is so, he formed no intention with regard to her death before him and died intestate in this respect. It is probable that, had his mind been directed to this possibility, he would have made dispositions similar to those which he made in the event of her dying within two months of his own death but I am not entitled to make a will for a testator to cover circumstances which he has overlooked and such speculation is irrelevant."

[81] *Abbott* v. *Middleton* (1858) 7 H.L.C. 68 at 114. See also *Re Kelly* (1905) 39 I.L.T.R. 158 and the discussion by Lowry L.C.J. in the N.I. Court of Appeal decision in *Heron* v. *Ulster Bank Ltd.* [1974] N.I. 44.

[82] *Bird* v. *Luckie* (1850) 8 Hare 301 at 306.

[83] *Re Harcourt* [1922] 2 A.C. 473; *In b. Gilligan* [1950] P. 32, and see (1951) 67 L.Q.R. 351 and (1952) 68 L.Q.R. 455. *Cf. Oliver* v. *Menton* [1945] I.R. 6; *Re Hogg* [1944] I.R. 244; *Re Gault* [1982] N.I. 170. See also *Mackesy* v. *Mackesy* [1896] 1 I.R. 511; *Davy* v. *Redington* [1917] 1 I.R. 250.

[84] Para. 4.053, *ante*.

[85] *Re Gansloser's Will Trusts* [1952] Ch. 30; *Re Kilvert* [1957] Ch. 388. See para. 7.17, *ante*.

[86] *Cf.* the maxim, *omnia praesumuntur rite et solemniter esse acta*, see *In b. McLean* [1950] I.R. 180. Para. 14.07, *ante*. Note also the comments of O'Higgins C.J. in *Rowe* v. *Law* [1978] I.R. 55 at 66–7 (see *A Casebook on Irish Land Law* (1984), p. 501). *Cf. Re Keoppler's Will Trusts* [1984] All E.R. 111 and *Re Malpass* [1984] 2 All E.R. 313.

gathered from the will itself, was that it was generally inadmissible, *i.e.*, only the words of the will should be considered.[87] However, this rule was subject to several well-recognised exceptions. First, evidence of the "surrounding circumstances" was admissible,[88] *i.e.*, facts and circumstances existing when the will was made, which may be used to explain special terms used or peculiar meanings intended by the testator,[89] or, indeed, mistakes in the words used.[90] This is sometimes called the "armchair principle," for as O'Brien L.C.J. put it: "The court can seat itself in a farmer's chair (if he has one) to construe his will."[91] Secondly, extrinsic evidence could be admitted to explain a latent ambiguity or equivocation in the will, *e.g.*, a description which could apply to more than one person or property referred to in the will.[92] An ambiguity may be latent, *e.g.*, in the sense that it is only when one tries to apply the will that one discovers the ambiguity, or patent, in the sense that the will itself discloses by its words the ambiguity.[93] On the other hand, it seems to be settled that at common law extrinsic evidence was not admissible to explain a contradiction in a will, the rule being that the second expression prevails over the first.[94] However, the courts will make every effort to reconcile apparently conflicting provisions[95] and this is illustrated by the rule in *Lassence* v. *Tierney*.[96] Lord Davey stated this rule as follows:

> "If you find an absolute gift to a legatee in the first instance, and trusts are promulgated or imposed on that absolute interest which fail, either from lapse, or invalidity, or any other reason, then the absolute gift takes effect so far as the trusts have failed to the exclusion of the residuary legatee or next-of-kin, as the case may be."[97]

This rule has been held to apply to both realty and personalty,[98] and to deeds as well as to wills.[99]

---

[87]   *Re Carlisle* [1950] N.I. 105; *Re Bovill* [1957] N.I. 58.
[88]   *Charter* v. *Charter* (1874) L.R. 7 H.L. 364 at 377 (*per* Lord Cairns L.C.); *Boyes* v. *Cook* (1880) 14 Ch.D. 53 at 56 (*per* James L.J.). See also *Re McMullen* [1964] Ir.Jur.Rep. 33.
[89]   *Shore* v. *Wilson* (1839) 9 Cl. & F. 355 at 498.
[90]   *I.e., falsa demonstratio non nocet*, *Sullivan* v. *Sullivan* (1870) I.R. 4 Eq. 457; *Stewart* v. *Barton* (1872) I.R. 6 Eq. 215; *Keogh* v. *Keogh* (1874) I.R. 8 Eq. 449; *Norreys* v. *Franks* (1875) I.R. 9 Eq. 18. *Cf. Re Carlisle* [1950] N.I. 105; *McHugh* v. *McHugh* [1908] 1 I.R. 155. As regards the supplying of omitted words, see *Re Goulding's Will Trusts* (1972) 106 I.L.T.S.J. 355. See also *Re Dowling* (1948) 82 I.L.T.R. 153; *Munro* v. *Henderson* [1908] 1 I.R. 260. Note also where words are omitted from a will by mistake, *Beamish* v. *Beamish* [1894] 1 I.R. 7; *In b. Wrenn* [1908] 2 I.R. 370.
[91]   *Fitzgerald* v. *Ryan* [1899] 2 I.R. 637. *cf. Boyes* v. *Cook* (1880) 14 Ch.D. 53 at 56 (*per* James L.J.). The "armchair principle" has recently been invoked in both parts of Ireland, by Gibson L.J. in *Re Harrison* [1976] N.I. 120 at 122 and Gannon J. in *Northern Bank Ltd.* v. *Allen* (1979) Unrep. (H.C., R.I.) (1978 No. 481 Sp).
[92]   *Re Julian* [1950] I.R. 57; *In b. McLoughlin* (1951) 85 I.L.T.R. 63. See also *Re Buckley* [1942] Ir.Jur.Rep. 43; *Galavan* v. *Walshe* (1937) 71 I.L.T.R. 154. And *Flood* v. *Flood* [1902] 1 I.R. 538.
[93]   *Findlater* v. *Lowe* [1904] 1 I.R. 519; *Henderson* v. *Henderson* [1905] 1 I.R. 353. See also *Wellwood* v. *Wellwood (No. 2)* (1899) 33 I.L.T.R. 18; *Healy* v. *Healy* (1875) I.R. 9 Eq. 418; *Phelan* v. *Slattery* (1887) 19 L.R.Ir. 177.
[94]   *Perkins* v. *Baynton* (1781) 1 Bro.C.C. 118. The rule for deeds is the reverse, *Doe d. Leicester* v. *Beggs* (1809) 2 Taunt. 109 at 113; *Forbes* v. *Git* [1922] 1 A.C. 256 at 259.
[95]   *Wallop* v. *Darby* (1611) Yelv. 209.
[96]   (1849) 1 Mac. & G. 551, applied in *Re Stewart* [1981] N.I. 48.
[97]   *Hancock* v. *Watson* [1902] A.C. 14 at 22. See discussion in *Re Prought* (1967) 101 I.L.T.R. 1. See also *Re Coleman* [1936] Ch. 528; *Re Burton's Settlement Trusts* [1955] Ch. 348.
[98]   *Moryoseph* v. *Moryoseph* [1920] 2 Ch. 33.
[99]   *Att.-Gen.* v. *Lloyds Bank Ltd.* [1935] A.C. 382.

14.41. These rules as to extrinsic evidence continue to apply in Northern Ireland, but in the Republic of Ireland they have been modified by the general statutory provision contained in section 90 of the Succession Act, 1965, which reads:

"Extrinsic evidence shall be admissible to show the intention of the testator and to assist in the construction of, or to explain any contradiction in, a will."

In *Rowe* v. *Law* [99a], the Republic's Supreme Court considered the scope of section 99 of the 1965 Act and the majority (Henchy and Griffin JJ., upholding the view of Kenny J. at first instance and Parke J. in the earlier case of *Bennett* v. *Bennett*[99b] (O'Higgins C.J. dissenting) held that it could *not* be invoked where the express wording of the will being construed was clear and unambiguous. Thus Henchy J. insisted that extrinsic evidence could be received under the section only "if it meets the double requirement of (a) showing the intention of a testator *and* (b) assisting in the construction of or explaining any contradiction in a will."[99c] One or other requirement on its own is not enough. As regards admitting evidence on the first ground alone, he commented:

"Such a sweeping and disruptive change, fraught with possibilities for fraud, mistake, unfairness and uncertainty, should not be read into the section if another and reasonable interpretation is open. . . The plain fact is that the grant of an unlimited and undefined jurisdiction to admit extrinsic evidence to show the testator's intention would be so large in its scope and so untoward in its potential consequences that it would exceed the spirit and purpose of the Act."[99d]

Griffin J. stated:

"If extrinsic evidence of the dispositive intention of a testator is to be admitted without qualification, the effect of this would be that a new will could be written for the testator, this will to be collected from the statements and declarations of the deceased at the time of, before or after the making of the will without compliance with the provisions of section 78. The effect of this would be to nullify those provisions and to render ineffective the safeguards provided therein."[99e]

On the basis of these views, it is doubtful whether the types of case in which extrinsic evidence is admissible have been greatly extended, if they have been extended at all; though once the court agrees that the case is an appropriate one for the admission of extrinsic evidence under section 90, presumably there is no limit to the type of evidence of the testator's intention which the

---

[99a] [1978] I.R. 55 (see *A Casebook on Irish Land Law* (1984), p. 501. See also Brady, "The 'Favor Testamenti' in Irish Law" (1980) 15 Ir.Jur.(N.S.) 1.
[99b] (1977) Unrep. (H.C., R.I.) (1974 No. 1095P)
[99c] *Op. cit.*, p. 72.
[99d] *Ibid.*
[99e] *Ibid.*, p. 77.

court can choose to accept. O'Higgins C.J., who dissented, clearly thought this was inconsistent with what the Oireachtas had in mind, as a reading of the debates would seem to confirm. As he put it:

"The Oireachtas has chosen, and understandably so, to sacrifice the certainty of literal interpretation with its frequently attendant capricious results, in favour of the somewhat more difficult and more understandable task of ascertaining the testator's actual intention."[99f]

B. SPECIFIC RULES

In addition to the general principles of construction outlined above, the following specific rules apply in appropriate cases.

1. *Will Speaks from Death*

14.42. As mentioned earlier in this chapter, it is provided by statute that a will "speaks from death," unless there is a contrary intention shown.[1] This means that the will can dispose of all property owned by the testator at the date of his death, even though some or all of it was acquired after he made his will.[2] However, the rule can apply only to descriptions of a class of objects, *i.e.*, it cannot apply to a gift of a specific object existing at the date of the will.[3] Thus, if the testator leaves by will his piano (and this is described in such a way as to indicate his existing one) to A and subsequently sells that piano, but buys a new one, A cannot claim the new piano.[4] Furthermore, the rule is generally confined to the property disposed of by the will. So far as the persons to whom the gifts are made are concerned, the rule is, at least with respect to individuals, that the relevant date is the date of the will, not the date of the testator's death.[5] However, as we saw in another context,[6] in the case of class gifts, the rule in *Andrews* v. *Partington*,[7] adopted by the courts in order to expedite distribution of shares to members of a class of objects at the earliest rather than the latest date, results in a class of objects generally closing at the date of the testator's death, since this is usually when the first member becomes, or has already become, qualified to take his share.[8]

[99f] *Ibid.*, p. 68. Nevertheless, the majority approach will clearly govern Irish judges until the Oireachtas decides to intervene, see *Gibb* v. *Flynn* (1983) Unrep. (H.C., R.I.) (1981 No. 916 Sp). See also *Fitzpatrick* v. *Collins* (1978) Unrep. (H.C., R.I.) (1978 No. 4122 P).

[1] 1965 Act, s. 89; 1837 Act , s. 24. See *Re Farrelly* [1941] I.R. 261; *Re Atkinson* [1942] I.R. 268. Also *Re White* [1923] 1 I.R. 88; *Murphy* v. *Cheevers* (1885) 17 L.R.Ir. 205. An exception to the principle was the rule in *Wild's Case* (see paras. 4.130, *ante* and 14.47, *post*), but this exception has been destroyed in the Republic of Ireland by s. 89 of the 1965 Act. See also s. 95, para. 14.48, *post*.

[2] *Re Fitzgerald* (1956) 90 I.L.T.R. 2. See also *McHugh* v. *Flood and Smullan* (1950) 84 I.L.T.R. 77. *Cf. Re McAfee* [1909] 1 I.R. 124; *Re Faris* [1911] 1 I.R. 165.

[3] See *Emuss* v. *Smith* (1848) 2 De G. & Sm. 722 at 733 and 736. Also *McHugh* v. *Flood and Smullan* (1950) 84 I.L.T.R. 77; *Ferguson* v. *Ferguson* (1872) I.R. 6 Eq. 199; *Leckey* v. *Watson* (1873) I.R. 7 C.L. 157.

[4] *Re Sikes* [1927] 1 Ch. 364. *Cf.* if the will is confirmed by codicil executed *after* the sale, see *Re Reeves* [1928] Ch. 351. See also *Re Faris* [1911] 1 I.R. 165.

[5] *Amyot* v. *Dwarris* [1904] A.C. 268. However, this rule is also subject to a contrary intention appearing in the will, *Re Daniels* (1918) 87 L.J.Ch. 661.

[6] Para. 5.084, *ante*.

[7] (1791) 3 Bro.P.C. 401.

[8] See the illustration of the class-closing rules given in para. 5.086, *ante*. Also see *Re Goodbody* [1955–56] Ir.Jur.Rep. 73.

2. *Exercise of Powers of Appointment*

14.43. It is provided by statute[9] that a general devise of land or bequest of personalty operates as an exercise of a general power of appointment held by the testator over the property in question, unless a contrary intention appears from the will.[10] Conversely, a special power of appointment cannot be exercised by a general devise or bequest, though this too, like all rules for construction, is subject to a contrary intention.[11]

3. *Doctrine of Satisfaction*

The operation of this doctrine was considered in an earlier chapter to which reference may be made.[12]

4. *"Die without Issue"*

14.44. At common law, a gift by will in the form, "to A, but if he dies without issue, to B" was construed, in the case of land, as giving A a fee tail and, in the case of personalty, A an absolute interest. It was assumed that the intention (though the contrary could be indicated by the testator)[13] was that B was not to take until both A and his issue had died out. In the case of realty, this could be achieved by giving A a fee tail[14] but, since personalty could not be entailed, in that case he took an absolute interest.[15]

14.45. Then section 29 of the Wills Act, 1837, provided that the words should be given their more natural meaning, *i.e.* that A should take a fee simple or, in the case of personalty, an absolute interest, subject in each case to a gift over to B if at A's death there were no living issue.[16] The inconvenience of this for A was obvious, since it would mean that he would never know whether or not B's gift would take effect. Even if he had several children, and even grandchildren, alive, they might all perish in some disaster and so predecease A. Section 10 of the Conveyancing Act, 1882, was passed to deal with this in relation to *land*, by providing that in such a case the executory gift over to B became void as soon as any of A's issue reached the age of 21. Thus A's interest became absolute either when any of his issue reached the qualifying age in his lifetime or, if they had not reached it, there was at least some issue alive at his death. This remains the position in

---

[9] 1965 Act, s. 93; 1837 Act, s. 27. See *Re Thirwell* [1958] Ch. 146 and (1959) 74 L.Q.R. 21.

[10] Or the general power can only be exercised in a certain manner (*e.g.* express reference to the power or property) and this has not been complied with in the will, see *Phillips* v. *Cayley* (1889) 43 Ch.D. 222. *Cf. Hennessey* v. *Murphy* (1953) 87 I.L.T.R. 29. See also *Re Dunbar-Buller* [1923] 2 I.R. 143.

[11] *Re Boland* [1961] I.R. 426; *Re Robertson's and Cardew's Trusts* [1960] I.R. 7. See also *Re Byron's Settlement* [1891] 3 Ch. 474; *Re Ackerley* [1913] 12 Ch. 510.

[12] Ch. 3 *ante*.

[13] *Roe d. Sheers* v. *Jeffrey* (1798) 7 T.R. 589 at 595–6. See also *Shannon* v. *Good* (1886) 15 L.R.Ir. 284.

[14] See ch. 4, *ante*. Also *Croly* v. *Croly* (1825) Batty 1; *Manning* v. *Moore* (1832) Alc. & Nap. 96; *O'Donohoe* v. *King* (1845) 8 Ir.Eq.R. 185; *Jones* v. *Ryan* (1846) 9 Ir.Eq.R. 249; *Hamilton* v. *West* (1846) 10 Ir.Eq.R. 75; *Phillips* v. *Phillips* (1847) 10 Ir.Eq.R. 513.

[15] Being unsupported by an entail, B's gift would infringe the rule against perpetuities, see ch. 5 *ante* and *Candy* v. *Campbell* (1834) 2 Cl. & F. 421. *Cf.* where the limitation to the issue was qualified, *e.g.* "die without *male* issue." See *Upton* v. *Hardman* (1874) I.R. 9 Eq. 157; *Neville* v. *Thacker* (1888) 23 L.R.Ir. 344.

[16] *Re Ball* [1933] N.I. 173; *Re Mooney* (1925) 59 I.L.T.R. 57. See also *Re Sallery* (1860) 11 Ir.Ch.R. 236; *Kirkpatrick* v. *King* (1898) 32 I.L.T.R. 41; *Weldon* v. *Weldon* [1911] 1 I.R. 177; *Re Conboy* [1916] 1 I.R. 51.

Northern Ireland, except that the qualifying age has been reduced to 18 in accordance with the general reduction in the age of majority.[17]

14.46.   In the Republic of Ireland, the 1837 and 1882 provisions have been reproduced in the Succession Act, 1965,[18] but the 1882 restriction on the operation of executory limitations has been extended to cover gifts by will of *any* property[19] and the avoidance of the executory limitation occurs as soon as there is any issue *living*, without the need to reach a qualifying age.[20]

5. *Rule in Wild's Case*

14.47.   We discussed this rule in an earlier chapter.[21] Under it, a limitation in a will in the form "to A and his children" was given a different construction according to when the will was made.[22] If A had no children when the will was made, A took a fee tail, which he could bar and thereby deprive his children of any interest, *i.e.* the words "and his children" were construed as words of limitation.[23] If A did have children when the will was made, the words were treated as words of purchase and A took jointly with those of his children living at the testator's death.[24] Like all rules of construction, it yielded to a contrary intention.[25]

14.48.   The rule in *Wild's Case* continues to govern construction of wills in Northern Ireland, but in the Republic it has been overruled by section 95[26] of the Succession Act, which provides that an estate tail can no longer be created by use of informal words.[27]

6. *Implied Life Estate*

14.49.   There is a rule of construction long recognised whereby a life estate in land or a life interest in property may arise by implication.[28] If property is left by will "to A after B's death" and the income from the property during B's lifetime is not dealt with by a residuary clause, the question arises as to what happens to the income during B's life. If A is the testator's sole intestate successor,[29] the courts take the view that his will evinces an intention that he is not to have any interest in the property so long as B is alive and so a construction must be put on the will to give effect to that intention.[30] Unless

---

[17]   Age of Majority Act (N.I.) 1969, s. 1 (3), Sched. 1 Pt. I; *Survey of the Land Law of Northern Ireland* (1971), paras. 276–7. See also *Re Ball* [1933] N.I. 173.

[18]   Ss. 96 and 100.

[19]   S. 100 (*b*).

[20]   S. 100.

[21]   Para. 4.130, *ante.*

[22]   (1599) 6 Co.Rep. 16b. It did not apply to gifts of personalty, *Heron* v. *Stokes* (1842) 4 Ir.Eq.R. 284.

[23]   *Clifford* v. *Koe* (1880) 6 L.R.Ir. 439.

[24]   *Re Moyles' Estate* (1878) 1 L.R.Ir. 155.

[25]   *Conyingham* v. *Tripp* [1925] 1 I.R. 27.

[26]   See also s. 89, paras. 4.131–2, *ante.*

[27]   The operation of s. 95 considered earlier, para. 4.132, *ante.*

[28]   See also in relation to words of limitation, para. 4.145, *ante.*

[29]   *Aspinall* v. *Petvin* (1824) 1 Sim. & St. 544; *Ralph* v. *Carrick* (1879) 11 Ch.D. 873; *Re Springfield* [1894] 3 Ch. 603.

[30]   *I.e.* an intestacy as to the income should not be allowed to occur, *Gardner* v. *Sheldon* (1671) Vaugh, 259 at 262 (*per* Vaughan C.J.).

the intermediate income is carried,[31] the only other destination for the income would seem to be to hold that it goes to B, *i.e.* B is treated as having a life estate or interest by implication.[32]

7. *Meaning of "Land"*

14.50. Prior to the Wills Act, 1837, a gift by will of "land" included freehold land but not leasehold land, unless the testator owned no freehold land[33] or showed a contrary intention to include leasehold land.[34] Now section 26 of the Wills Act, 1837, for Northern Ireland, and section 92 of the Republic's Succession Act, 1965, provide that a general devise of land is to be construed as including leasehold land as well as freehold land, unless a contrary intention appears from the will. However, problems of construction may still arise if a testator uses phrases such as "real estate" or "realty."[35] It has been held that a gift of "real estate" does not include leasehold land, unless the testator had no freehold land,[36] and that a gift of "real property" does not pass an interest in land held on a trust for sale.[37]

V. CONFLICT OF LAWS

Questions of conflict of laws are now[38] dealt with in the Republic of Ireland by Part VIII of the Succession Act, 1965, and in Northern Ireland by the United Kingdom Wills Act, 1963.

A. GENERAL FORM

14.51. The general rule is that a will[39] is valid as regards the form of its execution if its form complies with the internal law of one of the following[40]: (a) the place the testator made it[41]; (b) the testator's nationality,[42] either when he made the will or when he died; (c) the testator's place of domicile,[43] again either when he made the will or when he died; (d) the place of the

---

[31] See para. 10.044, *ante*, *Cf.* s. 175 of the Law of Property Act, 1925 and see *Survey of the Land Law of Northern Ireland* (1971), para. 356.

[32] *Horton* v. *Horton* (1606) Cro.Jac. 74; *Ralph* v. *Carrick* (1879) 11 Ch.D. 873 at 876.

[33] *Rose* v. *Bartlett* (1631) Cro.Car. 292.

[34] *Hobson* v. *Blackburn* (1833) 1 My. & K. 571.

[35] *Survey of the Land Law of Northern Ireland* (1971), para. 355 and see the recommended statutory presumptions in clause 239 on pp. 344–5. See also *Usher* v. *White* (1830) 2 Hud. & Br. 649; *Crowe* v. *Noble* (1824) Sm. & Bat. 12.

[36] *Butler* v. *Butler* (1884) 28 Ch.D. 66; *Re Holt* [1921] 2 Ch. 17. *Cf. Re Curneen* (1957) 91 I.L.T.R. 55 ("belongings").

[37] *Re Kempthorne* [1930] 1 Ch. 268. *Cf.* "property," *Re Fetherstonhaugh-Whitney's Estate* [1924] 1 I.R. 153; *Casey* v. *Lalor* (1855) 5 I.C.L.R. 507; *Fitzgerald* v. *Westropp* (1858) 3 Ir.Jur. (N.S.) 395.

[38] Replacing the Wills Act, 1861. As regards N.I., note also the provisions relating to the international form of will in Sched. 2 of the UK Administration of Justice Act, 1982 (see also ss. 27 and 28). This adopts the Washington Convention of 26th Oct. 1973 (Uniform Law on the Form of an International Will).

[39] Or "testamentary disposition," which includes any will or testamentary instrument or act, see 1965 Act, s. 101; 1963 Act, s 6 (1).

[40] 1965 Act, s. 102 (1); 1963 Act s. 1 and 2 (1) (*b*). The same applies to a will revoking an earlier one, 1965 Act, s. 102 (2); 1963 Act, s. 2 (1) (*c*), and to joint wills, 1965 Act, s. 105.

[41] See *In b. Keenan* (1946) 80 I.L.T.R. 1. Also *Re Tighe* [1939] Ir.Jur.Rep. 17. *Cf. Murphy* v. *Deickler* [1909] A.C. 446.

[42] See further 1965 Act, s. 102 (3); 1963 Act, s. 6 (2).

[43] Determination of a question of domicile in a particular place is to be governed in the Republic by the law of that place, 1965 Act, s. 102 (4). See also *Re Adams* [1967] I.R. 424; *Re Sillar* [1956] I.R. 344. The place of domicile should not be confused with the place of residence, *Re Welland* [1940] Ir.Jur.Rep. 36.

testator's habitual residence, either when he made the will or when he died; or (e) in the case of immovables, the place they are situated. Construction of a will is not to be altered by reason of any change in the testator's domicile after making the will.[44]

14.52. Any provision of law limiting forms of wills by reference to age, nationality or other personal conditions of the testator, or as to qualification of witnesses are to be treated as pertaining to matters of form in this context.[45] Furthermore, in determining whether a will complies with a particular law, regard is to be had to the requirements of that law at the time of making the will, but this does not prevent account being taken of a subsequent alteration of the law if this enables the will to be treated as valid.[46]

B. Vessels or Aircraft

14.53. A new provision is now made to the effect that a will made on board a vessel or aircraft is valid as regards form if that form complies with the internal law of the place with which, having regard to its registration (if any) and any other relevant circumstances, the vessel or aircraft may be taken to have had the most real connection.[47]

C. Powers of Appointment

14.54. A new provision is also made for powers of appointment, whereby a will is valid so far as it exercises a power if its form complies with the law governing the essential validity of the power.[48] Furthermore, an exercise of a power of appointment by will is not to be treated as invalid as regards form by reason only that its form does not accord with any formal requirements contained in the instrument creating the power.[49]

VI. FREEDOM OF DISPOSITION

14.55. We mentioned earlier in this chapter that there has been statutory interference with a testator's freedom to make whatever testamentary dispositions he pleases in both parts of Ireland. In the Republic of Ireland, provisions on this subject are contained in Parts IX and X of the Succession Act, 1965. All proceedings relating to these parts of the 1965 Act are to be heard in private.[50] In Northern Ireland, the relevant provisions originally to be found in the Inheritance (Family Provision) Act (N.I.), 1960, and the Family Provision Act (N.I.), 1969, are now to be found in the Inheritance (Provision for Family and Dependants) (Northern Ireland) Order, 1979,

---

[44] 1965 Act, s. 107 (1); 1963 Act, s. 4.
[45] 1965 Act, s. 106; 1963 Act, s. 3.
[46] 1965 Act, s. 107 (2); 1963 Act, s. 6 (3)
[47] 1965 Act, s. 103; 1963 Act, s. 2 (1) (a).
[48] 1965 Act, s. 104 (1); 1963 Act, s. 2 (1) (d).
[49] 1965 Act, s. 104 (2); 1963 Act, s. 2 (2)
[50] Ss. 119 and 122.

which was based on the English Inheritance (Provision for Family and Dependents) Act, 1975.[51]

A. REPUBLIC OF IRELAND

The following are the provisions curtailing a testator's testamentary freedom.

1. *Legal Right of Spouse*

14.56. Part IX of the 1965 Act applies to persons dying wholly or partly testate leaving a spouse or children, or both,[52] and generally relates to all the estate to which such testators are beneficially entitled for estates or interests not ceasing on death and remaining after payment of all expenses, debts and liabilities other than estate duty, or now, inheritance tax.[53] Section 111 provides that, if a testator leaves a spouse and no children, that spouse has a *right* to one-half of the estate; if he leaves a spouse and children, the right is to one-third of the estate.[54] Thus the legal right has priority over devises, bequests and shares on intestacy,[55] but it may be renounced in an ante-nuptial contract in writing, made between the parties to an intended marriage, or in writing by the spouse after marriage and during the lifetime of the testator.[56] It seems that, in calculating the value of the estate for these purposes, the value of any immovable property of which the testator was seised or to which he was entitled outside the Republic of Ireland is to be excluded.[57]

14.57. Where a devise or bequest to a spouse is expressed to be *in addition to* the share as a legal right, the testator is to be deemed to have made a gift consisting of both a sum equal to the value of the share as a legal right and the property devised or bequeathed.[58] Otherwise, a devise or bequest is to be deemed to have been intended to be in satisfaction of the share as a legal right.[59] Furthermore, where a testator dies wholly testate and there is a devise or bequest to a spouse, the spouse may elect to take either that devise or bequest or the share to which the spouse is entitled as a legal

---

[51] Replacing the English Inheritance (Family Provision) Act, 1938; Intestates' Estates Act, 1952, Pt. II; Family Provision Act, 1966, Sched. 3. See *Tyler's Family Provision* (2nd ed. by Oughton; 1984); Cadwallader, "A Mistresses' Charter?" [1980] Conv. 46; Farren, "Some Aspects of the Inheritance (Provision for Family and Dependants) Act 1975" [1980] Conv. 60; Sachs, "The Recent Working of the Inheritance (Provision for Family and Dependants) Act 1975" [1985] Conv. 258; Sherrin, "Disinheritance of a Spouse: A Comparative Study of the Law in the United Kingdom and the Republic of Ireland" (1980) 31 N.I.L.Q. 21.
[52] S. 109 (1).
[53] S. 109 (2). The property representing the spouse's share as a legal right bore its due proportion of estate duty payable on the deceased's estate, s. 118. The person taking the inheritance is primarily liable for payment of inheritance tax, see Capital Acquisitions Tax Act, 1976, s. 35. See *Gibb* v. *Flynn* (1983) Unrep. (H.C., R.I.), (1981 No. 916).
[54] See *Bank of Ireland* v. *Gaffin* [1971] 1 I.R. 123. Questions of deducing any relationship for the purposes of this Part of the 1965 Act are to be determined by the Legitimacy Act, 1931, and s. 26 of the Adoption Act, 1952, as those provisions apply in relation to succession on intestacy, see s. 110 of 1965 Act. See O'Connor, "Aspects of our Present law Relating to Illegitimate Children" (1978) 72 Gaz. I. L.S.I. 95.
[55] S 112. See further ch. 15, *post*.
[56] S. 113.
[57] *In b. G.M.* (1972) 106 I.L.T.R 82. (see *A Casebook on Irish Land Law* (1984), p. 535).
[58] S. 114 (1). The court in *In b. G.M.* (1972) 106 I.L.T.R. 82 emphasised that the principle of the 1965 Act is that the testator owes a duty to leave his surviving spouse the legal share in the estate and this duty is *not* based on a duty to provide maintenance.
[59] S. 114 (2). See further on the doctrine of satisfaction, ch. 3 *ante*. Also para. 14. 59, *infra.*.

right.[60] In default of election, the spouse is entitled to take under the will and cannot claim the share as a legal right.[61] Although section 111 provides that, if the testator leaves a spouse and no children, the spouse shall have a right to one-half of the estate and, if he or she leaves a spouse and children, a right to one-third of the estate, the decision of the Supreme Court in *Re Urquhart*[62] establishes that the effect of section 115, dealing with election, is that the spouse does not take the one-half or one-third share ("the legal right") until he or she has elected to do so. If the testator dies partly testate and partly intestate, the spouse may elect to take either the share as a legal right or the share under intestacy, together with any devise or bequest under the will.[63] In default of election, the spouse is entitled only to the latter and not the former.[64]

14.58. In electing to take the share as a legal right, the spouse may further elect to take any devise or bequest less in value than the share in partial satisfaction.[65] It is also the duty of the personal representative to notify the spouse in writing of the right of election.[66] However, the right of election ceases to be exercisable after six months from receipt of such notification or one year from the first taking out of representation of the deceased's estate,[67] whichever is the later.[68]

14.59. Finally, but only in relation to a provision made *before* the commencement of the 1965 Act,[69] where a testator has, during his lifetime, made permanent provision for his spouse, whether under contract or otherwise, all the property which is the subject of that provision (other than periodical payments made for her maintenance during his lifetime) is to be taken as being given in or towards satisfaction of the share as a legal right of the surviving spouse.[70] The value of the property is to be reckoned as at the date of the making of the provision[71] and, if the value is equal to or greater than the share as a legal right, the spouse cannot claim any share as a legal right.[72] If the value of the property is less, the spouse can claim in satisfaction of the share as a legal right only so much of the estate as, when added to the value of the property, is sufficient, as nearly as can be estimated, to make up the full amount of that share.[73]

---

[60]   S. 115. (1) (*a*). See further on the doctrine of election, ch. 3, *ante*. For election in the case of a person of unsound mind, see s. 115 (5).

[61]   S. 115. (1) (*b*).

[62]   [1974] I.R. 197 (see *A Casebook on Irish Land Law* (1984), p. 516).

[63]   S. 115 (2) (*a*).

[64]   S. 115 (2) (*b*). If the surviving spouse fails to elect before his or her death, the right of election does not pass to his or her personal representatives, nor does the property comprising the right form part of the surviving spouse's estate, see *Reilly* v. *McEntree* [1984] I.L.R.M. 572. *Cf.* election but death before distribution, see *Re Hamilton's Estate* [1984] I.L.R.M. 306.

[65]   S. 115 (3).

[66]   S. 115 (4). See also para. 14.60, *infra*.

[67]   Para. 16.03, *post*.

[68]   S. 115 (4).

[69]   S. 116 (5). The Act came into force on January 1, 1967.

[70]   S. 116 (1).

[71]   S. 116 (2).

[72]   S. 116 (3).

[73]   S. 116 (4).

14.60. Section 56 of the Act gives the surviving spouse another valuable right. If the estate of the deceased spouse included a dwelling[74] in which, at the time of the deceased spouse's death, the surviving spouse was ordinarily resident, he or she may require the personal representatives to appropriate the dwelling and any household chattels towards satisfaction of the surviving spouse's share in the estate. This right arises whether the deceased died testate or intestate and includes a case where the surviving spouse elects to take his or her legal right. The personal representatives must notify the surviving spouse of this right,[75] which ceases to be exercisable if the surviving spouse does not elect to exercise the right within six months after the notice or within one year from the date when representation of the estate of the deceased was taken out, whichever is the later.[76] Thus personal representatives have *two* notices to serve, *i.e.* notice of the right of election to take the legal right and notice of the right to require the personal representatives to appropriate the dwelling and household chattels in satisfaction of the share in the estate.

The operation of section 56 of the Succession Act, 1965, was considered by the Republic's Supreme Court in *H* v. *H.*[76a] This case involved construction of subsection (5) (*b*) of the section, which provides that the right to require appropriation is not exercisable in relation to a dwelling in certain cases (e.g., where it is held with agricultural land, used for other than domestic purposes or is an hotel or guesthouse) unless the court, on application by the personal representatives or surviving spouse, is satisfied that its exercise is "unlikely to diminish the value of the assets of the deceased, other than the dwelling, or to make it more difficult to dispose of them in due course of administration" and authorises its exercise. The Supreme Court held that, first (affirming the view of Kenny J. at first instance), the onus of proof under the paragraph lies upon the applicant, secondly (reversing the view of Kenny J.), the reference to assets of the deceased other than the dwelling includes *all* assets, *including* those passing to a spouse who has exercised her legal right to one half of the estate and, thirdly (again reversing the view of Kenny J.), the court must be satisfied that *neither* of the specified eventualities is unlikely to happen. As regards the second point, Kenny J. had taken the view that a residential agricultural holding is invariably more valuable than a non-residential one (and so, unless assets passing to a spouse under her legal right were excluded as well as the dwelling, it would be impossible for any application under the paragraph to succeed in respect of a residential agricultural holding). But Parke J. denied that premise. He stated:

> "The common experience of the Courts affords many examples to the contrary. A large, old and delapidated dwelling will frequently diminish the value of the holding. In cases, common enough nowadays, where

---

[74]   See s. 56 (14). Note the exceptions (*e.g.* a hotel) in s. 56 (6).
[75]   S. 56 (4).
[76]   S. 56 (5).
[76a]   [1978] I.R. 138 (see *A Casebook on Irish Land Law* (1984), p. 526). See also *H* v. *O* [1978] I.R. 194 (*ibid.* p. 529), para. 16.52, *post*; *Re Hamilton's Estate* [1984] I.L.R.M. 306.

there are two dwellings on a holding the exclusion of one of them will probably enhance the value of what is left."[76b]

2. Provision for Children

14.61. Section 117 (1) of the 1965 Act empowers the court, on application by or on behalf of a child of a testator,[77] to make an order for such provision for the child out of the estate as it thinks just, where in the court's opinion "the testator has failed in his moral duty to make proper provision for the child in accordance with his means." The court is to consider such an application from the point of view of a "prudent and just parent, taking into account the position of each of the children of the testator and any other circumstances which the court may consider of assistance in arriving at a decision that will be as fair as possible to the child to whom the application relates and to the other children."[78] However, an order of provision for a child is not to affect the legal right of a surviving spouse or, if the surviving spouse is the mother or father of the child, any devise or bequest to the spouse or any share to which the spouse is entitled on intestacy.[79]

14.62. In the case of *In b. G. M.*,[80] it was held that the question whether a moral duty to make provision for a child exists must be judged according to the facts existing at the date of the testator's death. In particular, it must depend upon the following matters: (1) the amount left to the surviving spouse or the value of the legal right if the spouse elects to take this; (2) the number of the testator's children, their ages and their positions in life at the date of the testator's death; (3) the means of the testator; (4) the age of the child in question and his or her financial position and prospects in life; (5) whether the testator has already in his lifetime made proper provision for the child. It was also emphasised that the 1965 Act was based on the principle that a testator owes a duty to make proper provision for his children in accordance with his means and that that duty was not limited in its application to children who were dependent upon him.

[76b] *Ibid.*, pp. 147–8. The Supreme Court also held that, though s. 56 (11) requires all proceedings under the section to be heard in chambers, this does not mean that the judgment may not be published, so as to promulgate the Court's view as to the correct interpretation of the section (thus following Lord Denning M.R.'s view in *Wallersteiner* v *Moir* [1974] 1 W.L.R. 991). The confidentiality inherent in the requirement as to the hearing can be preserved by omitting all identifying facts and circumstances, including the names of the parties, from the published judgment.

[77] The application must be made within 12 months from the first taking out of representation of the deceased's estate, and the costs in the proceedings are in the discretion of the court, s. 117 (5) and (6). Conduct of the proceedings is in a summary manner, s. 177 (4). See Bacon, "The Rights of Children and the Discretion of the Courts under Section 117 of the Succession Act, 1965" (1983) 77 Gaz. I.L. S.I. 223; Cooney, "Succession and Judicial Discretion in Ireland" (1980) 15 Ir.Jur.(N.S.) 62; Fitzpatrick, "The Succession Act, 1965, Section 117" (1976) 110 I.L.T. S.J. 77, 83, 95 and 101.

[78] S. 117 (2). See the discussion in *In b. G. M.* (1972) 106 I.L.T.R. 82. However, property subject to such an order bore its due proportion of estate duty payable on the deceased's estate, s. 118. *Cf.* inheritance tax, para. 14.56, fn. 53, *ante*.

[79] S. 117 (3).

[80] (1972) 106 I.L.T.R. 82 (see *A Casebook on Irish Land Law* (1984), p. 535). See also *Re Looney* (1969) Unrep. (H.C., R.I.) (No. 126 Sp); *Re McNaughton* (1973) 107 I.L.T.R. 1; *Re McNally* (1974) 108 I.L.T.R. 227; *Woods* v. *Dowd* (1975) Unrep. (H.C., R.I.), (1973 No. 117 Sp); *L.* v. *L.* [1978] I.R. 288; *H.* v. *Allied Irish Banks* (1978) Unrep. (H.C., R.I.) (1978 No. 57 Sp); *J.R.* v. *J.R.* (1979) Unrep. (H.C., R.I.) (1978 No. 661 Sp); *M.P.P.* v. *M.P.* [1981] I.L.R.M. 179; *M.H. and N. McG.* v. *N.M.* [1983] I.L.R.M. 519; *L.* v. *L.* [1984] I.L.R.M. 607.

3. *Unworthiness to Succeed*

14.63. Various categories of person are described in section 120 as being unworthy to succeed and so precluded from a share in the estate, which is then to be distributed as if the person in question had predeceased the deceased.[81] A sane person guilty of murder, attempted murder or manslaughter of another cannot take a share in that other's estate, except a share left by a will made *after* the act constituting the offence, nor can he make any application under section 117 relating to provision for a child.[82] A spouse against whom the deceased obtained a decree of divorce *a mensa et thoro*, or who failed to comply with a decree of restitution of conjugal rights obtained by the deceased or who was guilty of desertion,[83] and any person guilty of an offence against the deceased, his spouse or child,[84] punishable by imprisonment for a maximum of at least two years or a more severe penalty, is precluded from taking any share as a legal right or from making an application in relation to provision for a child.[85]

4. *Disinheritance*

14.64. Under section 121 of the 1965 Act the court is empowered to deal with a disposition,[86] which, it is satisfied, was made for the purpose of defeating or substantially diminishing the share of the disponer's spouse (whether as a legal right or on intestacy), or the intestate share of any of his children, or of leaving any of his children insufficiently provided for. Whether the disponer died testate or intestate, the court can order that the whole, or part, of the disposition[87] be deemed to be a devise or bequest made by will and to form part of his estate, and to have had no other effect.[88] To the extent of such a court order, the disposition is to be deemed never to have had effect and the donee, or any successor in title, is to be a debtor of the estate for such amount as the court may direct.[89] Furthermore, the court is given a general discretion to make such further order in relation to the matter as may appear to the court to be "just and equitable having regard to the provisions and the spirit of this Act and to all the circumstances."[90] If the donee of the property in question disposes of it to a purchaser, the order must be made instead in respect of the consideration given by the purchaser.[91]

---

[81] S. 120 (5).
[82] S. 120 (1).
[83] Or guilty of conduct which justified the deceased in separating and living apart, s. 120 (3).
[84] Including an adopted child or one to whom the deceased was *in loco parentis*, s. 120 (4).
[85] S. 120 (2) and (4).
[86] Including a *donatio mortis causa*, s. 121 (10) and see para. 9.043, *ante*.
[87] This applies only to a non-testamentary and voluntary disposition under which the beneficial ownership of the property vests in possession in the donee within 3 years before the death of the person who made it or on his death or later, s. 121 (1). Accrual by survivorship on the death of a joint tenant constitutes a vesting of the beneficial ownersip of the entire property in the survivor for this purpose, s. 121 (9).
[88] S. 121 (2). See *M.P.D.* v. *M.D.* [1981] I.L.R.M. 179. As to application in favour of a spouse or child, see s. 121 (5)–(7).
[89] S. 121 (3).
[90] S. 121 (4).
[91] S. 121 (8) and fn. 87, *supra*.

B. Northern Ireland

14.65. The Inheritance (Family Provision) Act (N.I.), 1960,[92] as amended by the Family Provision Act (N.I.), 1969, empowered the court[93] to make orders in certain cases where it was of the opinion that a deceased had not, whether by will, intestacy[94] or a combination of both, made reasonable provision for the maintenance of his dependants. The Inheritance (Provision for Family and Dependants) (N.I.) Order, 1979, largely replaces the 1960 and 1969 provisions and confers new powers on the court to make financial provision out of a deceased person's estate. This Order is largely based on the English 1975 Act of the same title.[96]

1. *Reasonable Financial Provision*

14.66. Under Article 3 of the 1979 Order, application for a court order may be made by the wife or husband of the deceased, a former wife or husband of the deceased who has not remarried, a child of the deceased, any person (other than a child) who, in the case of any marriage to which the deceased was at any time a party, was treated by the deceased as a child of the family in relation to that marriage and any other person who immediately before the deceased's death was being maintained wholly or partly by the deceased (i.e., where the deceased, otherwise than for full consideration, was making a substantial contribution in money or money's worth towards that person's reasonable needs).[96] "Child" is defined as including an illegitimate or adopted child (Article 7 of the Family Law Reform (N.I.) Order, 1977, had specified that illegitimate children counted as dependants under the Inheritance (Family Provision) Act (N.I.) 1960). The application is to be made on the ground that the disposition of the deceased's estate effected by his will or the law of intestacy, or a combination of both, is not such as to make "reasonable financial provision" for the applicant. By the definition in Article 2(2) of the words in quotation marks, it is made clear that, in the case of an application by the deceased's wife or husband, such provision is *not* (as in the case of other applications) confined to what would be reasonable for the applicant's "maintenance" (as under the earlier provisions), but extends to such provisions "as it would be reasonable in all the circumstances of the case for a husband or wife to receive, whether or not that provision is required for his or her maintenance." Under Article 6, the application cannot, except with permission of the court, be made after six months from the date when representation to the deceased's estate was taken out.[97]

---

[92] See the Johnson Committee Report, Cmd. 330. Also Hopkins, "Family Provision on Death" (1971) 35 Conv. 72.

[93] The High Court or, in certain cases, the county court, see 1960 Act, s. 8, as amended by s. 5 of the 1969 Act. See *Re Milliken* [1966] N.I. 68; *Allen* v. *Hewitt* (1966) 17 N.I.L.Q. 441.

[94] See ch. 15, *post.*

[95] As to which, see *Tyler's Family Provision* (2nd ed. by Oughton; 1984). See also Cadwallader, "A Mistresses' Charter?" [1980] Conv. 46; Farren, "Some Aspects of the Inheritance (Provisions for Family and Dependants) Act, 1975" [1980] Conv. 60: Sherrin, "Defeating the Dependants" [1980] Conv 13.

[96] See *Re Sehota* [1978] 1 W.L.R. 1506; *Re Fullard* [1982] Fam. 42.

[97] See *Re Salmon* [1981] Ch. 167.

2. *Orders*

14.67. Under Article 4 of the Order, the court may make any one or more of a variety of orders, including, *inter alia*, an order for the making of periodical payments out of the estate, or payment of a lump sum, or a transfer of property or a variation of any anti-nuptial or post-nuptial settlement.[98] The order may contain such consequential and supplementary provisions as the court thinks necessary or expedient to give effect to it or to secure that it operates fairly as between the various beneficiaries of the estate. The court is also given power to make special provision in the case of a person dying within twelve months of the making absolute of a decree of divorce or of nullity of marriage or the making of a decree of judicial separation if no such provision was made at the time of making that decree (i.e., under the Matrimonial Causes (N.I.) Order, 1978), or an application for such provision has been made but the proceedings thereon have not been determined by the time of the applicant's death.[99] The court may also vary or discharge secured periodical payments orders made under the 1978 Order and vary or revoke maintenance agreements relating to the deceased.

14.68. Article 5 of the Order lays down detailed provisions as to the matters to which the court must have regard in making an order, *e.g.*, the financial resources and financial needs of the applicant and any other applicant or of any beneficiary of the estate at the date of application or in the foreseeable future and the size and nature of the deceased's "net estate" available for financial provision.[1]

14.69. As mentioned in the previous paragraph, Article 5 of the Order lays down a number of matters to which the court must have regard and then goes on to specify additional matters to be regarded without prejudice to any matter the court considers relevant, including the conduct of the applicant or any other person, *e.g.*, the age of the applicant and duration of the marriage, the contribution made by him or her to the welfare of the deceased's family and the manner in which he or she was being or might expect to be educated or trained.[2] In considering these matters, the court is to take into account the facts as known to the court at the date of the hearing. Furthermore, under Article 23, statements (written or oral) made by the deceased are admissible as evidence of the facts stated therein as if given by direct oral evidence by the deceased as a witness in court, subject to the provisions of the Article and any rules of court.

14.70. Under Article 21 of the Order, the deceased's will or the law of intestacy has effect from the deceased's death for all purposes subject to the provisions of the court's order. A copy of every court order is to be sent to the Probate and Matrimonial Office of the Supreme Court for entry and filing, and a memorandum of the order is to be endorsed on, or permanently

---

[98] See *Re Campbell* [1983] N.I. 10. See also *Malone* v. *Harrison* [1979] 1 W.L.R. 1353.
[99] Arts. 16–20.
[1] Arts. 10 and 11.
[2] See *Re Campbell* [1983] N.I. 10.

annexed to, the probate or letters of administration to the estate in question. Under Article 8, an order for periodical payments may be varied or discharged and suspended or revived, and, under Article 9, an order for payment of a lump sum may provide for payment of the sum by instalments.

3. *Anti-Avoidance Provisions*

14.71.   The 1979 Order contains important new "anti-avoidance" provisions enabling the court to deal with transactions intended to defeat applications for financial provision. Thus under Article 12 the court may order the donee of property given under a disposition made for less than full valuable consideration and made less than six years before the deceased's death, to provide money or other property for the purposes of making financial provision. Article 13 deals with contracts to leave property by will.

CHAPTER 15

INTESTACIES

15.01. This chapter relates to the other method of succession recognised by our law, intestate succession. This method of succession governs the situation where the deceased person leaves no effective will or, where he dies partly intestate and partly testate, governs succession to the property which is not disposed of by his will. Succession to property on intestacy has had a long and somewhat complex history, but fortunately the subject has been rationalised in recent times in both parts of Ireland — by the Republic's Succession Act, 1965,[1] and the Administration of Estates Acts (N.I.), 1955 and 1971 and the Administration of Estates (N.I.) Order, 1979.[2] These Acts have resulted in the general assimilation of the laws of *devolution* and *distribution* of real (other than entailed property) and personal property on death of the owner intestate.[3] The law of devolution is that which lays down rules as to the persons to whom the ownership of property held by the deceased person passes on his death for the purpose of administration and the law of distribution is that which governs the administration of the assets of the deceased person and the manner in which, and the persons amongst whom, they are to be distributed. These various topics will be dealt with partly in this chapter and partly in the following one.

I. HISTORICAL INTRODUCTION

15.02. In considering the background to the legislation now in operation in Ireland, the important point to remember is that over the centuries the laws of devolution and distribution have varied according to whether the property in question was realty or personalty, as well as whether the deceased died testate or intestate.

A. DEVOLUTION

The law of devolution is best discussed by considering realty and personalty separately.

1. *Personalty*

15.03. The early history of succession to a deceased's personalty is, perhaps, not as clear as it might be.[4] Originally, all the personalty passed to the Bishop Ordinary of the diocese where the deceased lived, to be applied for charitable purposes. Then it was conceded that the family of the dead person had a

---

[1] Especially Parts II–VI.
[2] See generally on this subject, Leitch, *Handbook on the Administration of Estates Act (N.I.), 1955* (1956, Annot. to end of 1967). The 1955 Act followed the recommendations in the *Report of the Committee on Intestate Succession* (Cmd. 308, 1952).
[3] *I.e.* achieving the same purpose as the English Administration of Estates Act, 1925.
[4] See Leitch, *op. cit.*, pp. 2–6.

claim. Then, for some centuries, it appears, a man's wife and children were entitled to two thirds or shares of his personal estate (*pars rationabilis*)[5] and he was free to dispose as he pleased the other third part only. However, by the Statute of Distributions (Ireland), 1695, a man finally became free to dispose of his personal estate as he pleased,[6] though it is interesting to note that this statute recognised the prevailing Irish custom that the wife and children were entitled to two-thirds of the estate.[7] If he left it by will, the personal property did not pass directly to the donees, but vested in his executors.[8] The property was regarded as consisting of assets in their hands for payment of the deceased's debts and then for distribution in accordance with the will.

15.04. If the deceased had made no will, his personal property was liable to be seized by the Crown, but in practice the Crown permitted the Bishop Ordinary of the diocese to seize the intestate's property. The Statute of Westminster II, 1285,[9] made the Ordinary chargeable with the deceased's debts as if he had made a will. The Ordinary did not administer the estate himself, but appointed a deputy or administrator[10] and various enactments were passed relating to the appointment of administrators and their activities.[11] Because the Ordinary was entitled to personal estate on intestacy and because a will deprived him of this right, the grant of a probate of a will was, until 1858, dealt with by the Church Court of the diocese. Probate was the order made by that Court, which showed that the will had been examined by it and had been found to be valid. Then, by the Probates and Letters of Administration Act (Ireland), 1857[12] and the Court of Probate Act (Ireland), 1859,[13] the jurisdiction of the Ordinary in relation to wills and appointment of administrators was transferred to and vested in the Court of Probate and its Probate Judge.[14] The jurisdiction of the Court of Probate was transferred to the High Court by the Judicature (Ireland) Act, 1877, and remains today for the most part with the High Courts of the Republic[15] and Northern Ireland.[16]

2. *Realty*

15.05. Realty at common law was not devisable[17] and, on death, was subject

---

[5]   Confirmed as regards both England and Ireland by Magna Carta, 1225, 9 Hen, 3, c. 18.
[6]   S. 10.
[7]   See the remarks of Walsh J. in *Re Urquhart* [1974] I.R. 197 at 208–9 (see *A Casebook on Irish Land Law* (1984), p. 516).
[8]   Co.Litt. 388a.
[9]   13 Edw. 1, St. 1, c. 19. Extended to Ireland by writ of the same year, confirmed in 1320 by 13 Edw. 2, c. 2 (Ir.) and by Poynings Law 1495, 10 Hen. 7, c. 22 (Ir.).
[10]   See *Harding* v. *Hall* (1842) 10 M & W. 42. See also *In b. Griffen* (1868) I.R. 2 Eq. 320.
[11]   *E.g.* Probate Act (Ir.), 1537, 28 Hen, 8, c. 18 (Ir.), limiting choice of administrator to widow or next-of-kin and allowing administrator to sue as an executor to recover assets.
[12]   S. 6.
[13]   S. 15.
[14]   Note, however, J. R. Lindsay, "The Exempt Jurisdiction of Newry and Mourne" (1954) 11 N.I.L.Q. 3.
[15]   Succession Act, 1965, s. 6, which also confers concurrent jurisdiction on the circuit court in relation to various matters.
[16]   See definition of "Probate Judge" in the Interpretation Act (N.I.), 1954; s. 42 (3), see also Judicature (N.I.) Act, 1978, s. 16. Also Administration of Estates (N.I.), Order, 1979, Art. 12, which also confers some jurisdiction on county courts. See *Briggs* v. *Brennan* (1922) 56 I.LT.R. 92; *In b. Mulligan* [1930] N.I. 185.
[17]   Para. 2.19, *ante*.

to the feudal rules of inheritance, based on the central principle of primogeniture.[18] Realty could be left by will only after the passing of the Statute of Wills (Ireland), 1634.[19] However, in the cases of both intestate and testate succession the basic rule was that the land on death passed *directly* to the heir-at-law or the devisee. It did not devolve upon any personal representative, whether administrator or executor. Furthermore, also unlike personalty, realty did not in general constitute assets available for payment of the deceased's creditors. There were a few exceptions to this rule, *e.g.* Crown debts, judgment and specialty debts,[20] which were extended by the courts of equity until the Administration of Estates Acts, 1833 and 1869 (Hinde Palmer's Act) made realty generally available for all creditors, simple contract as well as specialty, who were to rank equally for payment of debts.

15.06. The first major step in Ireland towards assimilation of the law of devolution of realty and personalty took place under Part IV of the Local Registration of Title (Ireland) Act, 1891.[21] This provided that all land purchased[22] and vested in tenant farmers under the Land Purchase Acts after January 1, 1892, which was thereby converted from chattel real property to realty, should continue on death to devolve to and become vested in personal representatives as if it were still chattel real property. The personal representatives were given the same powers and duties with respect to such realty, which, incidentally, ultimately included most agricultural land in Ireland, as they had in respect of personalty. The ultimate step in the assimilation of the law of devolution (though not distribution) of realty and personalty was first taken in Northern Ireland under the Law Reform (Miscellaneous Provisions) Act (N.I.), 1937,[23] and then in the Republic under the Administration of Estates Act, 1959. The provisions in these Acts have now been replaced by the Republic's Succession Act, 1965,[24] and the Administration of Estates Act (N.I.) 1955.[25] The 1965[26] and 1955[27] Acts now both provide that the real and personal estate of a deceased person on his death, notwithstanding any testamentary disposition, devolves on and becomes vested in his personal representatives. Thus nowadays devolution of a deceased person's estate is generally the same, whether he dies testate or intestate and whether his estate consists of realty or personalty.[28] These Acts also altered the law of distribution.

[18] *Ibid.*
[19] Para. 3.020, *ante.*
[20] *I.e.* debts which the deceased had covenanted on behalf of himself and his heirs to pay.
[21] In fact, prior to the 1891 Act, s. 30 of the Conveyancing Act 1881 provided that trust and mortgage estates should devolve to personal representatives as if chattels real. See also s. 4 of the 1881 Act (personal representatives empowered to convey realty in completion of a contract made by the deceased and enforceable against his heir or devisee).
[22] *Re Smith* (1899) 33 I.L.T.R. 69; *Brady* v. *Brady* [1936] I.R. 431; *Re Desmond* [1943] I.R. 534; *Re Stewart* [1956] N.I. 82. It did not matter that the title was not registered as required by the Act – "equity regards as done what ought to be done." *McDonnell* v. *Stenson* [1921] 1 I.R. 80; *Re Collin's Estate* [1924] I.R. 72. See para. 3.099, *ante.*
[23] See O'Neill, "The Law Reform Act (Northern Ireland) 1937" (1944) 6 N.I.L.Q. 131 and 201; (1946) 7 N.I.L.Q. 215; (1948) 8 N.I.L.Q. 99.
[24] Pt. II.
[25] Pt. I.
[26] S. 10.
[27] S. 1.
[28] See further paras. 15.14 *et seq., post.*

B. Distribution

Once again the history of this subject can be best described by distinguishing between realty and personalty.

1. *Personalty*

15.07. We explained earlier that at common law a man was free to dispose on death of only one-third part of his personal property, the other two parts belonging by right to his wife and children until the Statute of Distributions (Ireland), 1695, gave him complete freedom of disposition.[29] If left by will, it devolved to the executors for payment of the deceased's debts and then distribution amongst the beneficiaries specified in the will.

15.08. If the deceased died intestate, in the early days there was much corruption because, although the administrator was obliged to give effect to the *pars rationabilis* of the wife and children, after payment of debts, he could then appropriate the remainder of the personal estate to his own purposes. This practice was not stamped out in Ireland until the passing of the Statute of Distributions (Ireland), 1695, which required the administrator to distribute the "surplusage," *i.e.*, "what remaineth clear after all debts, funeral charges and just expenses,"[30] in accordance with the Act's provisions.[31] In essence the principles of distribution of personal estate laid down by the 1695 Act were as follows[32]:

(1) if the deceased left a widow and children or other issue, the widow took one-third and the remainder went to the children and those who represented deceased children (*i.e.*, their children);

(2) if no widow survived, the children and their representatives took all;

(3) if there were no issue, the widow took one-half, the other going to those most nearly related by blood, except that a father took to the total exclusion of others.

Then modifications were introduced by the Intestates Estates Act, 1890, under which real and personal property of an intestate, dying after September 1, 1890, and leaving a widow but no issue, passed, if the value did *not* exceed £500, to the widow absolutely. If the value did exceed £500, the widow was entitled to a first charge[33] for £500, at 4 per cent interest, in addition to her share in the residue, as if the residue were the whole estate and the 1890 Act had not been passed. This widow's charge was payable out of realty and personalty on a rateable basis, and the land was to be valued on an artificial basis related to the rateable valuation.

15.09. These rules for distribution of personalty on intestacy remained in force in Northern Ireland until the new scheme was introduced by the

---

[29] Para. 15.03, *ante*.
[30] S. 1.
[31] Ss. 2, 3, 6 and 8.
[32] For details, see Leitch, *op cit*, Appendix 1.
[33] See *McFerran* v. *McFerran* [1897] 1 I.R. 66; *Re McDonagh* [1898] 2 I.R. 79; *In b. Leonard* (1913) 47 I.L.T.R. 113; *Feely* v. *Feely* (1901) 1 N.I.J.R. 115.

Administration of Estates Act (N.I.) 1955.[34] In the Republic of Ireland the 1695 provisions also remained largely in force, but the 1890 modifications were replaced by those introduced by the Intestates' Estates Act, 1954. Under this Act the widow's rights were increased, so that she became entitled to £4,000, or the whole estate if worth less, to be borne rateably by the real and personal estate.[35] Furthermore, if there was no heir according to the rules of descent, but there was a widow, the widow took in preference to escheat to the superior lord or the State.[36] These provisions have now been replaced entirely by the new scheme of distribution introduced by the Succession Act, 1965.[37] We discuss these new schemes below.[38]

2. Realty

15.10.   So far as realty was concerned, one of the central principles of the common law, rooted in the feudal system of tenure introduced into Ireland many centuries ago,[39] was the law of inheritance. This remained a largely judge-made law until it was given statutory recognition, with some modifications, by the Inheritance Act, 1833, and the Law of Property Amendment Act, 1859 (Lord St. Leonard's Act). After the passing of the Statute of Wills (Ireland), 1634, which enabled a person to determine the succession to his realty by will, succession to realty on intestacy was governed by this law of inheritance until comparatively recent times.

15.11.   The main principles of inheritance, or descent to realty (other than entails), which still apply to the estates of persons in the Republic who died before January 1, 1967, and, in Northern Ireland, who died before January 1, 1956, were as follows:

(1) realty descended to the blood relations of the deceased;
(2) since the 1833 Act,[40] descent was traced from the last purchaser, i.e., the person who last acquired the land otherwise than by descent or by escheat,[41] partition[42] or enclosure[43];
(3) inheritance descended lineally, i.e., descendants such as children and grandchildren took preference over other blood relations, such as parents and grandparents;
(4) males were preferred to females;
(5) where there were two or more males of equal degree of relationship, the eldest only inherited, i.e. the principle of primogeniture[44];

---

[34]   Pt. II
[35]   Ss. 3–5.
[36]   S. 6.
[37]   Pt VI.
[38]   Paras. 15.16, et seq., infra.
[39]   Ch. 2, ante
[40]   S. 2.
[41]   Para. 2.24, ante.
[42]   Para. 7.35, ante.
[43]   1833 Act, s . 1. If there was a total failure of heirs of the last purchaser, s. 19 of the 1859 Act allowed descent to be traced from the person last entitled, as if he had been a purchaser, thus minimising cases of hardship arising from cases of escheat.
[44]   Para. 7.40, ante.

(6) females, on the other hand, inherited together as coparceners[45];

(7) lineal descendants of a deceased person who, had he lived, would have inherited, stood in his place, *i.e.*, the doctrine of representation applied[46];

(8) on failure of issue, the inheritance after 1833 descended to the nearest lineal ancestor and his issue, the paternal line being preferred to any of the maternal line[47];

(9) finally, again after 1833, collaterals of the half-blood inherited next after any relative in the same degree of the whole blood and his issue, if the common ancestor was a male, and next after the common ancestor, if the latter was a female.[48]

15.12. In addition, to these principles, the widow of a deceased male was entitled to dower[49] and the widower of a deceased female was entitled to curtesy.[50] On total failure of heirs, the land escheated to the mesne lord and, ultimately, which was what usually happened in the past few centuries in Ireland,[51] to the Crown, or, since 1922 in the Republic of Ireland, the State.

15.13. These complex rules of inheritance of realty on intestacy have now been swept away in both parts of Ireland by the Republic's Succession Act, 1965, and the Administration of Estates Act (N.I.), 1955. Both these Acts abolish "all existing rules, modes and canons of descent and of devolution by special occupancy"[52] and dower and curtesy. Since they came into operation, a deceased person's estate, both real and personal, must be distributed by the personal representatives in the same way, in accordance with the Acts.[53] Furthermore, the law of escheat for want of heirs has been abolished[54] and now a deceased person's estate, on failure of persons entitled to succeed, passes to the State in the Republic of Ireland as "ultimate intestate successor."[55] It passes to the Crown as *bona vacantia* in Northern Ireland,[56] which was the position with respect to personalty in both parts of Ireland prior to the 1965[57] and 1955 Acts.

II. DEVOLUTION

15.14. In both parts of Ireland it is now provided that the real and personal estate of a deceased person on his death, notwithstanding any will he has

---

[45] *Ibid.*

[46] Thus the issue of an elder son took before a younger son or his issue.

[47] 1833 Act, ss. 6 and 7.

[48] 1833 Act, s. 9. However, the whole blood was preferred to the half-blood and this over-rode the usual preference of males over females, *e.g.*, if the deceased left a sister and a half-brother, the former inherited.

[49] Discussed at para. 4.157, *ante.*

[50] *Ibid.*

[51] Para. 2.44, *ante.*

[52] 1965 Act, s. 11 (1); 1955 Act, s. 1 (3). Excepted in both cases is descent of an estate tail, ch. 4 *ante.* As regards special occupancy, see para. 4.164, *ante.*

[53] 1965 Act, Pt VI; 1955 Act. Pt II. See paras. 15.16 *et seq., infra.*

[54] 1965 Act, s. 11 (3); 1955 Act, s. 1 (5).

[55] 1965 Act, s. 73.

[56] 1955 Act, s. 16.

[57] The State succeeding in the Republic since 1922. See para. 2.52, *ante.*

made, devolves on and becomes vested in his personal representatives.[58] The personal representatives hold the estate as trustees for the persons entitled by law,[59] *i.e.* under the will or according to the rules for intestate succession. For these purposes, the deceased's estate includes property over which he exercised by will a general power of appointment[60] and land held on trust[61] or subject to a mortgage.[62]

15.15. The 1965 and 1955 Acts provide for further assimilation of the law respecting real and personal estates of deceased persons by decreeing that all enactments, including the 1965 and 1955 Acts themselves, and rules of law relating to the listed matters, apply, so far as applicable, to real estate as if it were personal estate.[63] The listed matters are: (a) the effect of representation[64] as respects personal estate; (b) the dealing with personal estate before representation; (c) the powers, rights, duties, and liabilities of personal representatives in respect of personal estate; (d) the payment of costs of administration and (e) all other matters with respect to the administration of personal estate. Further discussion of these topics will be found in the next chapter in this part of the book.

III. DISTRIBUTION ON INTESTACY

15.16. Part VI of the Republic's Succession Act, 1965, and Part II of the Administration of Estates Act (N.I.), 1955, provide that all "estate to which a deceased person was [beneficially[65]] entitled for an estate or interest not ceasing on his death and as to which he dies intestate after the commencement of" the Acts are, after payment of all expenses, debts and liabilities properly payable thereout, to be distributed in accordance with those Parts' provisions.[66] Both Acts then make detailed provisions for distribution of the intestate's estate and, in so doing, try to provide for distribution as the deceased might reasonably have been expected to choose, had he made a will, and, in any event, in what the legislatures have adjudged as a fair and just manner.[67]

15.17. In cases of partial intestacy, *i.e.*, where the will of a deceased person effectively disposes of part only of his estate, the remainder is to be

---

[58]   1965 Act, s. 10 (1); 1955 Act, s. 1 (1). S. 10 (2) of the 1965 Act states that they are to be deemed in law the deceased's "heirs and assigns within the meaning of all trusts and powers." *Cf.* s. 1 (2) of the 1955 Act.

[59]   1965 Act, s. 10 (3); 1955 Act, s. 2 (3). See *Re Cockburn's Will Trusts* [1957] Ch. 438.

[60]   1965 Act, s. 10 (4); 1955 Act, s. 1 (6).

[61]   1965 Act, s. 10 (5); 1955 Act, s. 44 (*a*). See *Carroll* v. *Hargreave* (1871) 18 R. 5 Eq. 548

[62]   1965 Act, s. 4 (*a*); 1955 Act, s. 44 (*a*), replacing s. 30 of the Conveyancing Act, 1881, see para. 15.06, *ante*.

[63]   1965 Act, s. 12 (1); 1955 Act, s. 2 (1).

[64]   *I.e.* probate or letters of administration, see 1965 Act, s. 3 (1); 1955 Act, s. 2 (1) (*a*). See ch. 16, *post.*.

[65]   This word is added in the Republic's 1965 Act and is obviously designed to exclude the case where the deceased held property on trust for other persons. Such property devolves, if the deceased was *sole* trustee, in the normal way to his personal representatives (see s. 10 (5) and the definitions of "real estate" in s. 4 (*a*), also s. 14, of the 1965 Act), but it is not to be distributed as other property of the deceased, since it belongs to the beneficiaries of the trust in question. If there are *surviving* trustees, the legal estate held in trust is succeeded to by the survving trustees, under the normal rules as to a joint tenancy (see ch. 7, *ante*, and see s. 4 (*c*) of the 1965 Act). As regards the 1955 Act (N.I.), the same position exists, see s. 44 (*b*) and (*d*).

[66]   1965 Act, s. 566; 1955 Act, s. 6.

[67]   See Leitch, *Handbook on the Administration of Estates Act (N.I.), 1955* (1956), p. 35.

distributed as if he had died intestate and left no other estate.[68] However, in Northern Ireland this rule is subject to the express qualification — "unless it appears by the will that his personal representatives are intended to take beneficially the remainder of his estate." At common law, an executor was entitled to undisposed residuary personalty, whereas in equity there was only a presumption in the executor's favour. The Executors' Act, 1830, reversed this presumption and required the executor to show an intention in the will in his favour[69] and, if he failed, he was obliged to hold the residue for those entitled under the Statute of Distributions.[70] Thus the executors may still succeed in an appropriate case in Northern Ireland, but not in the Republic, in cases of partial intestacy.

The rules for distribution of an intestate's estate in both parts of Ireland may now be summarised as follows.

A. SURVIVING SPOUSE AND ISSUE

15.18. In the Republic of Ireland the surviving spouse of the intestate is entitled to the whole estate, if there are no issue.[71] If the intestate dies leaving both a spouse and issue, the spouse take two-thirds of the estate and the remainder is distributed amongst the issue.[72] If there is no spouse, but there are issue, the estate is again to be distributed among the issue.[73] In both these cases involving issue, distribution is to be made to them in equal shares, provided all the issue are in equal degree of relationship to the deceased.[74] If they are not, distribution is to be made *per stirpes, i.e.*, "any issue more remote than a child of the deceased shall take through all degrees, according to their stocks, in equal shares if more than one, the share which the parent of such issue would have taken if living at the death of the deceased, and no issue of the deceased shall take if the parent of such issue is living at the death of the deceased and so capable of taking."[75]

15.19. In Northern Ireland the surviving spouse takes the personal chattels.[76] If there are issue, the surviving spouse takes, in addition to the personal chattels, the whole of the remaining estate, where the net value[77] of

---

[68]   1965 Act, s. 74; 1955 Act, s. 18.

[69]   *Fuge* v. *Fuge* (1891) 27 L.R.Ir. 59; *Fenton* v. *Neville* (1893) 31 L.R.Ir. 478.

[70]   *Dillon* v. *Reilly* (1881) 9 L.R.Ir. 57. See also para. 15.08, *ante*.

[71]   1965 Act, s. 67 (1). This does not include illegitimate issue, the exclusion of whom has recently been held by the Supreme Court not to be unconstitutional, see *O'B* v. *S* [1984] I.R. 316, [1985] I.L.R.M. 87.

[72]   S. 67 (2). In *Feely* v. *Feely* (1901) 1 N.I.J.R. 115, it was held that no order for administration would be made on the application of the next-of-kin, where the court considered that the value of the estate was less than that to which the surviving spouse was entitled. For adopted children's right, see Adoption Act, 1952, s. 26 (also the Adoption Act 1974) and for illegitimate children, Legitimacy Act, 1931; also 1965 Act, s. 110 (*O'B* v. *S*. fn. 71, *supra*).

[73]   S. 67 (3).

[74]   S. 67 (4).

[75]   S. 3 (3). The same definition will be found for Northern Ireland in s. 15 of the 1955 Act. See further on the distinction between distribution *per stirpes* and *per capita*, *Re Kane* [1940] Ir.Jur.Rep.67; *Re Kinsella* [1944] Ir.Jur.Rep. 15; *Munster and Leinster Bank Ltd.* v. *Fitzgerald* (1947) 81 I.L.T.R. 122. Also *Re Smythe* [1932] I.R. 136.

[76]   1955 Act, s. 7 (1). "Personal chattels" are defined in s. 45 of the 1955 Act. See also Leitch, *op. cit.*, pp. 40–1.

[77]   *I.e.* the estimated market value as at the date of the death of the intestate, after payment of all duties and charges and of debts, funeral expenses and expenses of administration, s. 7 (6). *Cf. Cunningham* v. *Cunningham* [1920] 1 I.R. 119; *Re Dunican* [1920] 1 I.R. 212.

that does not exceed £40,000.[78] If the net value of the remaining estate does exceed £40,000, the surviving spouse takes, in addition to the personal chattels, the sum of £40,000 free of all duties, charges and costs and has a charge on the remaining estate for that amount at 6 per cent. interest from the date of intestate's death to the date of its payment.[79] Furthermore, in addition even to this, the surviving spouse takes one-half of any residue left of the remaining estate, where only one child survives the intestate,[80] or one-third, where more than one child survives.[81] If there are no issue, but the intestate does leave parents or brothers or sisters or issue of deceased brothers or sisters, the spouse takes in addition to the personal chattels, the whole of the remaining estate, where its net value does not exceed £85,000.[82] If it does exceed that value, the spouse is entitled to a sum of £85,000, free of all duties, and charged on the remaining estate at 6 per cent. interest, until payment,[83] plus one-half of any residue left of the remaining estate after provision of that sum and the interest thereon.[84] If the intestate leaves neither issue nor parents nor brothers and so on, the surviving spouse takes the whole estate.[85] Subject to these rights of the surviving spouse, if any, the issue of the intestate are entitled to distribution of the estate *per stirpes* among them.[86]

B. PARENTS

15.20. In the Republic of Ireland, where the intestate dies leaving neither a spouse nor issue, his estate is to be distributed between his parents in equal shares, if both survive.[87] If only one survives, that parent takes the whole estate.[88]

In Northern Ireland, if there are no issue, the parents take equally, or the survivor the whole estate, subject to the rights of the surviving spouse, if any.[89]

---

[78] S. 7 (2) (*a*) and Administration of Estates (Rights of Surviving Spouse) Order (N.I.) 1981 (S.R. No. 124).

[79] S. 7 (2) (*b*) and Art. 41 of Administration of Estates (N.I.) Order, 1979 (see Intestate Succession (Interest) Order (N.I.) 1985, S.R. No. 8). The charge is on the corpus of the estate, not just the income, *Re Saunders* [1929] 1 Ch. 674.

[80] However, if a child predeceased the intestate but leaves issue who do survive the intestate, the surviving spouse takes the same share of the estate as if the child had survived the intestate, s. 7 (3).

[81] S. 7 (2) (*b*) (i) and (ii).

[82] S. 7 (4) (*a*). Note *Feely* v. *Feely* (1901) 1 N.I.J.R. 115, fn. 72, *supra*.

[83] S. 7 (4) (*b*) (i).

[84] S. 7 (4) (*b*) (ii).

[85] S. 7 (5). These provisions do not affect the operation of s. 15 of the Matrimonial Causes Act (N.I.), 1939, under which, in cases of judicial separation, the after-acquired property of a wife who dies intestate devolves as if her husband has been dead, s. 7 (7).

[86] S. 8. As regards adopted children, see Adoption Acts (N.I.), 1950, ss. 9–10 and 1967, ss. 18–19 and 47 and, for illegitimate children, Legitimacy Act (N.I.), 1928, ss. 4, 9 and 11. See *In b. R.* [1946] Ir.Jur.Rep. 7; *In b. Black* [1971] N.I. 68. Also *McDonnell* v. *Alcorn* [1894] 1 I.R. 298. Under Art. 3 (1) of the Family Law Reform (N.I.) Order, 1977, an illegitimate child, or if he is dead, his issue, is entitled to take any interest in the estate of either of his parents on their death intestate which he would have been entitled to if he had been born legitimate. Under Art 3(2) his parents are entitled on the death of an illegitimate child intestate to take any interest they would have been entitled to if he had been born legitimate.

[87] 1965 Act, s. 68.

[88] *Ibid.*

[89] 1955 Act, s. 9.

C. Brothers and Sisters and their Children (or issue)

15.21. In the Republic, if the intestate dies leaving neither a spouse nor issue nor parents, his estate is to be distributed between brothers and sisters in equal shares.[90] The surviving children of any brother or sister who does not survive the intestate, where any other brother or sister survives, are to take in equal shares their parent's share, had that parent survived,[91] *i.e.*, under the principle of "representation." If no brother or sister at all survives the intestate, his estate is to be distributed in equal shares among the children of his brothers and sisters.[92]

15.22. In Northern Ireland, where there is neither spouse nor issue nor parents, the estate is also to be distributed in equal shares between the intestate's brothers and sisters, but if any brother or sister predeceases the intestate, representation is extended to all his or her surviving issue and not confined, as in the Republic, to children.[93] In such a case, the surviving issue of a deceased brother or sister take *per stirpes* the share that brother or sister would have taken, had he or she survived the intestate.[94] In the event of the intestate leaving neither brother nor sister, the estate, subject to the right of any surviving spouse, is to be distributed *per stirpes* among the issue of his brothers and sisters.

D. Next-of-Kin

15.23. In the Republic, where the intestate leaves neither spouse nor issue nor parent nor brother nor sister (nor children of them), the estate is to be distributed in equal shares among his "next-of-kin."[95] In such a case, representation of next-of-kin is not to be admitted amongst collaterals, except in the case of children of brothers and sisters of the intestate, where any other brother or sister survives the intestate.[96] Subject to this, next-of-kin are to be taken as the person or persons who, at the date of the death of the intestate, stand nearest in blood relationship to him.[97] It is then provided:

> "Degrees of blood relationship of a direct lineal ancestor shall be computed by counting upwards from the intestate to that ancestor, and degrees of blood relationship of any other relative shall be ascertained by counting upwards from the intestate to the nearest ancestor common to the intestate and that relative, and then downward from that ancestor to the relative; but, where a direct lineal ancestor and any other relative are so ascertained to be within the same degree of blood relationship to the intestate, the other relative shall be preferred to the exclusion of the direct lineal ancestor."[98]

[90] 1965 Act, s, 69 (1)
[91] *Ibid.*
[92] S. 69 (2).
[93] 1955 Act, s. 10 (1).
[94] *Ibid.*
[95] 1965 Act, s. 70 (1).
[96] S. 70 (2).
[97] S. 71 (1). *Cf. Re Goodbody* [1955–56] Ir.Jur.Rep. 73
[98] S. 71 (2). The same provision for Northern Ireland will be found in s. 12 (2) of the 1955 Act.

In other words, uncles and aunts take before great-grandparents. There is the same degree of blood relationship in their cases, *i.e.*, one degree removed from a grandparent, but it was no doubt considered desirable that the younger generation should take precedence over the older.[99] The same principle applies for even remoter next-of-kin, *e.g.*, grand-uncles and grand-aunts take before great-great-grandparents.

15.24. In Northern Ireland, where the intestate leaves neither spouse nor issue nor parent nor brother nor sister (nor issue of them), the estate is also to be distributed equally among the next-of-kin.[1] Furthermore, it is provided that, where any uncle or aunt of the intestate (being a brother or sister of a parent of the intestate), who would have been, or been included among, the next-of-kin if he or she had survived the intestate, has predeceased him leaving issue, who do survive him, such issue are to represent that uncle or aunt and take *per stirpes* the share the uncle or aunt would have taken, had he or she survived the intestate.[2] However, representation cannot be admitted amongst collaterals except in the case of brothers and sisters of the intestate and issue of uncles and aunts of the intestate.[3] These provisions thus bring within the category of next-of-kin in Northern Ireland first cousins and their descendants.

E. CHILDREN BEGOTTEN BUT NOT BORN

15.25. It is provided in both parts of Ireland now that descendants and relatives of the intestate begotten before his death but born alive thereafter are to inherit as if they had been born in the deceased's lifetime and had survived him.[4]

F. HALF-BLOOD

15.26. It is also provided in both parts of Ireland that relatives of the half-blood are to treated as, and are to succeed or inherit equally with, relatives of the whole blood in the same degree.[5]

G. DEFAULT OF NEXT-OF-KIN

15.27. In the Republic of Ireland, it is provided that, in default of any person taking the estate as intestate successor, the State is to take it as "ultimate intestate successor,"[6] thereby replacing the old law of escheat, as regards realty, and *bona vacantia*, as regards personalty.[7] This change was

[99] See *Evelyn* v. *Evelyn* (1745) 3 Atk. 762.
[1] 1955 Act, s. 11 (1).
[2] S. 11 (2).
[3] S. 11 (3).
[4] 1965 Act, s. 3 (2); 1955 Act, s. 13. *Cf. Elliott* v. *Joicy* [1935] A.C. 209; *Re Castle* [1949] 1 Ch. 46. Also see *Re Allsop* [1968] Ch. 39.
[5] 1965 Act, s. 72; 1955 Act, s. 14. *Cf. In b. McCoy* (1925) 59 I.L.T.R. 130; *In b. McKeon* (1939) 73 I.L.T.R. 51.
[6] 1965 Act, s. 73 (1). It appears that, where there is no next-of-kin, the Att.-Gen. may be named as sole defendant in an administration action brought by a creditor, *Knight* v. *Att-Gen.* [1939] Ir.Jur.Rep. 4 *Cf. Att.-Gen* v. *Sherlock* [1935] Ir.Jur.rep. 36.
[7] See *In b. Doherty* [1961] I.R. 219 (see *A Casebook on Irish Land Law* (1984), p. 52).

made on the ground that a foreign court might treat *bona vacantia* as being a matter of public law and so might not enforce a claim to it. The Minister for Finance may, however, if he thinks proper to do so, waive the right of the State, in whole or in part and in favour of such person and on such terms[8] as he thinks proper, having regard to all the circumstances of the case.[9] Under section 32 of the State Property Act, 1954, land devolving on the State by way of escheat or *bona vacantia* could be disclaimed and this provision is now extended to a grantee's interest under a fee farm grant[10] and a lessee's interest under a lease, where the State has a right to such an interest as ultimate intestate successor.

15.28.   In Northern Ireland, in default of any intestate successor, the estate passes to the Crown as *bona vacantia*,[11] thereby applying the former rule as to personalty to realty. In practice, an estate passing as *bona vacantia* was administered by the Chief Crown Solicitor under section 3 of the Northern Ireland (Miscellaneous Provisions) Act, 1928, as nominee of the British Treasury. It appears that the Treasury frequently made *ex gratia* provisions out of such estates in favour of persons having a claim based on natural kinship or as dependants of the deceased, or who were able to show that the intestate left a document indicative of an intention of benefit them by will.[12] Section 3 of the 1928 Act has been replaced by Article 10 of the Administration of Estates (N.I.) Order, 1979, under which administration of the estate devolving to the Crown is to be granted to the Crown's nominee (either the Treasury Solicitor or some person nominated by him, such as the Crown Solicitor for Northern Ireland). This does not prevent the grant of administration to any other person, where the Treasury Solicitor or other nominee has not made, and has signified his intention not to make, an application for a grant of administration.

H. ADVANCEMENTS TO CHILDREN

15.29.   In both parts of Ireland, any advancements made to a child of the intestate are to be brought into account in reckoning that child's share in the estate.[13] In the Republic, "child" includes a person to whom the deceased was *in loco parentis*[14] and, in Northern Ireland, a grandchild to whom a grandparent dying intestate stood *in loco parentis*.[15] There is no obligation upon issue or brothers and sisters or more remote next-of-kin to bring sums

---

[8]   Whether including payment of money or not.
[9]   S. 73 (2). *Cf.* s. 31 of the State Property Act, 1954.
[10]   See ch. 4, *ante*.
[11]   1955 Act, s. 16 (1). Note the saving in s. 16 (2) as to land subject to a tenancy within s. 3 of the Land Law (Ir.) Act, 1881, which may have escaped the operation of the land purchase scheme in Northern Ireland, see Leitch, *op. cit.*, pp. 51–2. Also *Conroy* v. *Drogheda* [1894] 2 I.R. at 601 *et seq* (*per* Palles C.B.).
[12]   See Leitch, *op. cit.*, pp. 14–15 and 51.
[13]   1965 Act, s. 63 (which also applies to testate succession); 1955 Act, s. 17. S. 63 (9) of the 1965 Act provides expressly that nothing in the section affects any rule of law as to satisfaction of portion debts by legacies, see para. 3.117, *ante*. S. 17 (1) of the 1955 Act refers to advancement "by way of portion" and by s. 17 (4) this includes advancement by settlement from the intestate; *cf.* 1965 Act, s. 63 (6), *infra*.
[14]   1965 Act, s. 63 (10).
[15]   1955 Act, s. 17 (6).

into account,[16] but it appears that a child must do so even in cases of partial intestacy.[17] The advancement is to be reckoned as part of the deceased's estate and its value taken at the date of the advancement.[18] If the advancement is equal to or greater than the share which the child is entitled to receive on intestacy, the child or his issue are excluded from any share in the estate.[19] If the advancement is less than the child's intestate share, the child or issue can receive in satisfaction of that share so much only of the estate as, when added to the advancement is sufficient, as nearly as can be estimated, to make up the full amount of the intestate share.[20] The onus of proving that a child has received an advancement is upon the person asserting it, unless the advancement is expressed in writing by the deceased.[21]

15.30. Section 63 (6) of the Republic's 1965 Act includes a helpful definition of the word "advancement" for these purposes,[22] namely:

". . . a gift intended to make permanent provision for a child and includes advancement by way of portion or settlement, including any life or lesser interest and including property covenanted to be paid or settled. It also includes an advance or portion for the purpose of establishing a child in a profession, vocation, trade or business, a marriage portion and payments made for the education of a child to a standard higher than that provided by the deceased for any other or others of his children."[23]

I. CONSTRUCTION OF DOCUMENTS

15.31. In both parts of Ireland, it is provided[24] that references to any "Statutes of Distribution" in an *inter vivos* instrument made, or will[25] coming into operation, after the 1965 or 1955 Acts, are to be construed respectively, unless the contrary thereby appears, as references to Part VI of the Republic's Succession Act, 1965, or Part II of the Administration of Estates Act (N.I.), 1955, *i.e.*, the provisions discussed above. References in instruments or wills to statutory next-of-kin are to be construed, again unless the contrary appears, as referring to the persons who would succeed on an intestacy under the 1965 or 1955 Acts.

15.32. Furthermore, trusts declared by reference to the Statutes of

---

[16] *Kircudbright* v. *Kircudbright* (1802) 8 Ves. 51; *Re Gist* [1906] 2 Ch. 280. *Cf. Re Hood* [1923] 1 I.R. 109; *Matthews* v. *Donegan and Cooke* [1925] 1 I.R. 201.

[17] 1965 Act, s. 74; 1955 Act, s. 18. See also *Harte* v. *Meredith* (1884) 13 L.R.Ir. 341.

[18] 1965 Act, s. 63 (2); 1955 Act, s. 17 (1) and (2) (which provides, however, that the value has to be reckoned at the date of the advancement only if the intestate has not expressed a value in writing, which expression is to be deemed the value). The personal representative may employ a duly qualified valuer, 1965 Act, s. 63 (7); 1955 Act, s. 17 (5).

[19] 1965 Act, s. 63 (3); 1955 Act, s. 17 (1).

[20] 1965 Act, s. 63 (5); 1955 Act, s. 17 (1) However, s. 63 (8) of the 1965 Act makes it clear that a child is free to retain his advancement and to abandon his intestate share.

[21] 1965 Act, s. 63 (5); 1955 Act, s. 17 (3). See also *McEvoy* v. *Belfast Banking Co. Ltd.* [1934] N.I. 67; *Shephard* v. *Cartwright* [1955] A.C. 431.

[22] See also *Gason* v. *Rich* (1887) 19 L.R.Ir. 391; *Owens* v. *Greene* [1932] I.R. 225; *McCabe* v. *Ulster Bank* [1939] I.R. 1; *Walsh* v. *Walsh* [1942] I.R. 403; para. 10.049, *ante.*

[23] *Cf.* 1955 Act, s. 17 (4).

[24] 1965 Act, s. 75 (1); 1955 Act, s. 19 (1).

[25] See, *e.g.*, *MacLean & Graham* v. *Smith & Mackintosh* [1927] N.I. 109. See also *Re Clarke* (1939) 73 I.L.T.R. 25.

Distribution in an *inter vivos* instrument made, or will coming into operation, before the commencement of the 1965 or 1955 Acts are to be construed, subject to a contrary intention, as referring to the enactments (other than, in the Republic, the Intestates' Estates Act, 1954, or, in Northern Ireland, the Intestates' Estates Act, 1890[26]) relating to distribution of effects of intestates which were in force prior immediately[27] before the commencement respectively of the 1965 and 1955 Acts.[28]

[26]   See *Re Morgan* [1921] 1 Ch. 196.
[27]   Paras. 15.07 *et seq., ante.*
[28]   1965 Act, s. 75 (2); 1955 Act, s. 19 (2).

CHAPTER 16

ADMINISTRATION OF ESTATES

16.01. This chapter deals with the final aspect of the law of succession which requires discussion. The immediately preceding two chapters were concerned with the two types of succession recognised by our law, namely testate and intestate. They showed that in each case the laws of both the Republic of Ireland and Northern Ireland now provide the same system of devolution to personal representatives, whether the deceased's property consists of realty or personalty. Also considered were the schemes of distribution of the deceased's property, by will, if he has made an effective one, or, failing that, according to the rules for intestacy laid down by statute. This chapter fills in the remaining gap in the picture of succession to a deceased person's property, *i.e.*, the administration of his estate from the date of his death until the date of distribution of the estate remaining after that administration amongst the persons entitled under his will or according to the rules for intestacy. In essence this involves a consideration of the functions of personal representatives, *i.e.*, executors or administrators, and, in particular, their powers and duties in administering the deceased's estate.

I. PENDING GRANTS OF ADMINISTRATION

16.02. It is a fundamental principle of our law that there should be no time when property is ownerless.[1] When a person dies, his property devolves to his personal representatives and, in the case of a testator leaving an effective will, there is usually no problem with respect to ownership. This devolves to the executor or executors appointed expressly by his will. The question remains, however, as to what happens if the testator dies either testate, but leaving no executor surviving him, or intestate. In the Republic of Ireland, it is provided that in such a case the deceased's estate, real and personal, vests in the President of the High Court,[2] until administration is granted.[3] In Northern Ireland, the estate vests in the Probate Judge[4] until administration is granted.

16.03. There has been some controversy in Ireland over the precise position of the President of the High Court or the Probate Judge with respect to the property in question,[5] especially where the deceased held a tenancy in

---

[1] See Judicature (Ir.) Act, 1877, s. 36 and Judicature (Ir.) (No. 2) Act, 1897, s. 3. Also *Whitehead* v. *Palmer* [1908] 1 K.B. 151.
[2] Succession Act, 1965, s. 13, which provides that the President is a corporation sole for this purpose. See also *In b. Walsh* (1923) 57 I.L.T.R. 78. It appears that the President should not, however, be joined as a party to proceedings, see *Flack* v. *Flack* (1983) Unrep. (H.C., R.I.) (1983 No. 2955 P). *Cf.* Administration of Estates Act (N.I.) 1955, s. 3.
[3] Paras. 16.04 *et seq., infra.*
[4] Defined by s. 42 (3) of the Interpretation Act (N.I.), 1954, as—"the Judge of the High Court who is for the time being assigned by the Lord Chief Justice" under s. 5 (1) of the Judicature (Ir.) (No. 2) Act, 1897, as amended by Art. 7 of the Supreme Court of Judicature (N.I.) Order, 1921. Also see now Judicature (N.I.) Act, 1978, s. 17.
[5] See, however, *In b. Walsh* (1927) 57 I.L.T.R. 78.

it.[6] It seems to have been settled law in Ireland, since the late nineteenth century, that, if a landlord wishes to serve a notice to quit, he should serve it on the persons remaining in possession, usually relatives of the intestate tenant, rather than on the Probate Judge.[7] This approach seems to have been influenced by the line of Irish decisions to the effect that a landlord, on death of a tenant leaving no legal personal representative, may treat the person left in possession as assignee of the lease.[8] If there is no person left in occupation, it would appear that the general rule must apply and the landlord must serve his notice on the President of the High Court in the Republic, or the Probate Judge in Northern Ireland.[9]

II. GRANTS OF REPRESENTATION

The general rule is that a deceased's personal representatives cannot legally carry out the functions of their office without first obtaining a grant of representation, *i.e.*, either a grant of probate of the testator's will or a grant of letters of administration.[10]

A. PROBATE OF WILLS

1. *Grants of Probate*

(i) Courts

16.04. In both parts of Ireland the jurisdiction to grant probate of wills lies with the High Court,[11] which has a general discretion to deal with matters concerning probate.[12] Generally probate is granted to one or more of the executors named by the testator in his will.[13] However, a person appointed by

---

[6] See discussion in Leitch, *Handbook on the Administration of Estates Act (N.I.), 1955* (1956), pp. 28–30; also Deale, *Law of Landlord and Tenant in Republic of Ireland* (1968), pp. 253–4.

[7] *Sweeny* v. *Sweeny* (1876) I.R. 10 C.L. 375, wherein, incidentally, s. 15 of the Court of Probate Act (Ir.), 1859 (providing for vesting in the Probate Judge pending grant of administration), does not seem to have been cited to the court. See also Harrison, *Ejectments in Ireland* (1903), p. 180. *Sweeny* v. *Sweeny* has been followed in the Republic in *Hill* v. *Carroll* [1953] I.R. 52; *O'Sullivan & Sons Ltd.* v. *O'Mahony* [1953] I.R. 125. Cf. *Apsley* v. *Barr* [1928] N.I. 183. Note also *Kelly* v. *Tallon* (1948) 84 I.L.T.R. 196; *Armstrong* v. *Hall* (1951) 87 I.L.T.R. 68; *O'Connor* v. *Fitzgerald* (1955) 91 I.L.T.R. 32.

[8] *Jones* v. *Murphy* (1840) 2 Jebb. & Sym. 323; *Armstrong* v. *Loughnane* (1851) 2 I.C.L.R. 72; *Shee* v. *Gray* (1864) 15 I.C.L.R. 296; *Rankin* v. *McMurtry* (1889) 24 L.R.Ir. 290; *Dublin Corporation* v. *Personal Representatives of Sheridan* (1976) 111 I.L.T.R. 143. Cherry, *Irish Land Law and Land Purchase Acts* (3rd ed., 1903), p. 233. As regards agricultural land, see Notices to Quit (Ir.) Act, 1876, s. 4; *Rowland* v. *Holland* (1879) 4 L.R.Ir. 421.

[9] In fact the Chief Probate Registrar was authorised to receive it on his behalf, Leitch, *op. cit.*, p. 31. The office of "Chief Probate Registrar" was abolished by s. 40(4)(*b*) of the Judicature (N.I.) Act, 1978, and his functions are now performed by the Master (Probate and Matrimonial) (see s. 70(4)(*a*) of and Sched. 3 to the 1978 Act).

[10] Note, however, that certain small amounts may be distributed before grants are obtained, see Building Societies Act, 1874, s. 29 (since replaced by s. 23 (2) of the Building Societies Act, 1976) and Friendly Societies Act, 1896, s. 58 (R.I.); Administration of Estates (Small Payments) Act (N.I.), 1967.

[11] Succession Act, 1965, ss. 16 and 26; Administration of Estates (N.I.), Order, 1979, Art. 4. Note, however, the role of probate registrars, para. 16.06, *post*. The law relating to grant of probate of wills and grant of administration of estates of deceased persons has been restated in modern form in Northern Ireland by the Administration of Estates (N.I.) Order, 1979 (hereafter referred to in this chapter as the "1979 Order"), especially Parts II and III (thus replacing the provisions on this subject contained in the Probate and Letters of Administration Act (Ir.), 1857, Court of Probate Act (Ir.), 1859, Probate and Letters of Administration Act (N.I.), 1933, and Administration of Estates Act (N.I.), 1955, Part III).

[12] 1965 Act, ss. 6 (2) and 26 (1); 1979 Order, Art. 4(3) and (4). See Mongey, *Probate Practice in a Nutshell* (1980).

[13] *Re Woodroofe* [1953–54] Ir.Jur.Rep. 36; *In b. Martin* [1955–56] Ir.Jur.Rep. 37. See also *Re Kehoe* [1940] Ir.Jur.Rep. 35; *Re Gilpin* [1942] Ir.Jur.Rep. 52; *In b. Drumm* [1931] N.I. 12 (trustees only named).

the testator loses his right to prove the will if, though surviving the testator, he dies before taking out probate or he is cited to take out probate but does not appear to the citation or he renounces probate.[14] The court may revoke, cancel or recall any grant of probate.[15]

(ii) Trust Corporation

If the testator names a trust corporation[16] as executor, whether alone or jointly with another person, the Court may grant probate to the corporation, either solely or jointly.[17]

(iii) Infants

16.05. Where a minor is appointed executor by a will, such appointment will not constitute him a personal representative, as he cannot be granted probate until he reaches the age of majority.[18]

(iv) Separate Grants

A grant of probate may be made either separately in respect of real estate and in respect of personal estate, or in respect of both together, or in respect of real estate although there is no personal estate and *vice versa*.[19] Furthermore, where the estate of the testator is known to be insolvent, the grant cannot be severed except in respect of a trust estate.[20] A grant may also be confined to part only of a will, where the court is not satisfied that the remainder had the approval, or was within the knowledge, of the testator.[21]

2. *Applications*

(i) Office or Registry

16.06. An application for the grant or revocation of probate may be made to the Probate Office in the Republic,[22] or the Probate and Matrimonial

---

[14]   1965 Act, s. 17; 1979 Order, Art. 29. *In b. Bantry White* [1953–54] Ir.Jur.Rep. 47; *In b. Coote* [1932] L.R.Ir. 141; *Searight* v. *Walsh* [1932] L.R.Ir. 136; *In b. Hanlon* [1894] 1 I.R. 551. As regards withdrawal of renunciation, see the new statutory provision in s. 18 of the 1965 Act and Art. 30 of the 1979 Order. *Cf. In b. Lawson* (1933) 67 I.L.T.R. 180 (letters of administration).

[15]   1965 Act, s. 26 (2); 1979 Order, Art. 11. See *In b. Doherty* [1942] N.I. 87; *Vella* v. *Morelli* [1968] I.R. 11. Also *In b. McLean* [1950] I.R. 180; *Mulligan* v. *McKeon* [1955] I.R. 112; *Re Corcoran's Estate* (1945) 79 I.L.T.R. 26.

[16]   Defined in 1965 Act, s. 30 (4) and, for N.I., originally in s. 4 (1) of the Probates and Letters of Administration Act (N.I.), 1933, as extended by s. 28 (2) of the Administration of Estates Act (N.I.), 1955, to meet points discussed by Lord MacDermott L.C.J. in *Re McKee* [1955] N.I. 184. See now 1979 Order, Art. 9 (4). See also *Re Frampton* [1957] N.I. 96.

[17]   1965 Act, s. 30 (1); in N.I. originally the Probates and Letters of Administration Act (N.I.), 1933, s. 4 as amended by 1955 Act, s. 28 (2) (see *Re Frampton* [1957] N.I. 96; *cf. Re McKee* [1955] N.I. 184). See now 1979 Order, Art. 9 (1)–(3). Note also s. 30 (5) of the 1965 Act relating to bodies corporate defined in s. 4 of the Republic's Bodies Corporate (Executors and Administrators) Act, 1928. See *Re Mitchell* [1943] Ir. Jur.Rep. 62 (probate granted to English bank under 1928 Act); *In b. Wallace* [1935] I.R. 68 (leave to apply for letters of administration granted to bank). See also *In b. Andrews* [1931] I.R. 515. *Cf.* S.R. & O. (N.I.) 1956 No. 29, Direction 13. It seems that a testator cannot appoint the English Public Trustee nor the Irish Public Trustee (operating under s. 52 of the Irish Land Act, 1903, para. 10.001, *ante*), *In b. Leeson* [1928] I.R. 168.

[18]   1965 Act, s. 32 (2); 1979 Order, Art. 7. See further, para. 16.09, *infra*.

[19]   1965 Act, s. 28 (1); 1955 Act, s. 1 (2).

[20]   1965 Act, s. 28 (2); 1955 Act, s. 1 (2).

[21]   *Re Shanley* [1941] Ir.Jur.Rep. 73.

[22]   Pt. XII of the Succession Act, 1965, contains various provisions dealing with the Probate Office and district probate registries, *e.g.*, the positions of "Assistant Probate Officer" (s. 128) and acting district probate registrars (s. 131), district registries (s. 129) and fees to be taken there (s. 130).

Office in Northern Ireland,[23] or the district probate registry or branch office in the place where the deceased, at the time of his death, had a fixed place of abode.[24] Any contentious matter arising out of such an application may, in appropriate cases, be referred by the High Court, in the Republic, to the circuit court with jurisdiction in the fixed place of the abode of the deceased,[25] and, in Northern Ireland, to the county court.[26]

(ii) District Registries

16.07.   Grants may be made in the Republic of Ireland by a district probate registrar in common form, in the name of the High Court and under the seal of the registry.[27] No grant may be made in any contentious case until the litigation is disposed of or in any case where the registrar considers there is a need for the direction of the court, in which case a statement is to be sent to the Probate Office for the directions of the High Court, which has wide powers to deal with the matter.[28] A district registrar is also obliged to send to the Probate Office a notice in the prescribed form of every application for a grant and no grant can be made by him until he receives back a certificate that no other application appears to have been made.[29] All notices so transmitted are to be filed and kept in the Probate Office,[30] though directions may be given for disposal, by destruction or otherwise, of such notices as have ceased, owing to lapse of time, to be of any public value.[31] A district registrar is also obliged to transmit regular lists of grants made and copies of wills to which they relate, certified as correct, and he must file and preserve all original wills of which probate has been granted.[32] In Northern Ireland this jurisdiction now resides in the circuit registrar supervising a branch office of the Probate and Matrimonial Office.[32a]

(iii) Caveats

16.08.   Caveats against a grant may be entered in either the Probate Office, or, in Northern Ireland, the Probate and Matrimonial Office, or in district registries or branch offices, which must transmit copies to the central office.[33]

---

[23]   Established by s. 68 (1) of and Sched. 2 to the Judicature (N.I.) Act, 1978. See 1979 Order, Art. 18. This replaced the Principal Probate Registry operating under the Probates and Letters of Administration Act (Ir.), 1857, ss. 50 and 63. See also s. 8 of Court of Probate Act (Ir.), 1859.

[24]   1965 Act, s. 35 (1); 1979 Order, Art. 19.

[25]   1965 Act, s. 35 (3). See also s. 41 (issue of grants in cases of circuit court decrees) and s. 44 (trial by jury of questions of fact).

[26]   County Courts Act (N.I.), 1959, s. 17. And see now 1979 Order, Art. 12. See also 1857 Act, s. 59 (county court decrees) and s. 41 (trial by jury of questions of fact). *In b. Mulligan* [1930] N.I. 185. See also *Briggs* v. *Brennan* (1922) 56 I.L.T.R. 92.

[27]   1965 Act, s. 36 (1).

[28]   1965 Act, s. 36 (2) and (3).

[29]   1965 Act, s. 36 (4), (5) and (7). Furthermore, in the Republic calendars of grants must be kept, see 1965 Act s. 39.

[30]   1965 Act, s. 36 (6).

[31]   1965 Act, s. 36 (10).

[32]   1965 Act, s. 36 (8) and (9).

[32a]   1979 Order, Art. 19. See also Arts. 23 and 24 relating to directions as to keeping and inspection of wills and keeping of records of grants in a branch office.

[33]   1965 Act, s. 38; 1979 Order, Art. 14. *McShane* v. *White* (1935) 69 I.L.T.R. 29; *Re Keegan* [1937] Ir.Jur.Rep. 63.

(iv) Second and Subsequent Grants

Second and subsequent grants are to be made in the registry or office from which the original grant issued.[34]

(v) Original Wills and Copies

Copies of wills, as required,[35] must be sent by the Probate Office, or Probate and Matrimonial Office, or district registries or branch offices to, in the Republic, the Revenue Commissioners and, in Northern Ireland, the Commissioners of Inland Revenue.[36] All original wills of which probate is granted in the Probate Office, or in the Probate and Matrimonial Office, and all copies transmitted from district registries or branch offices, must be deposited and preserved for inspection in the Office,[37] though they may be removed to the Public Record Office for safe-keeping.[38] Official copies of wills may be obtained from the registry or branch office where the will was proved, which copies are sufficient evidence of the grant of representation.[39]

3. Proving

16.09. Generally speaking, proving a will must be done by production of a testamentary instrument duly executed in accordance with the provisions discussed in an earlier chapter.[40] Even if the will was made in a foreign country, it may still be proved in whatever part of Ireland property disposed of by it is situated.[41] The executor must swear on oath as to the precise date and place of the testator's death, or, if that is not possible, when he was last seen alive.[42] He must also deliver to the registry a Revenue affidavit providing particulars of the property to be covered by the grant and of the debts and funeral expenses to be deducted in arriving at the net estate upon which was calculated inheritance tax in the Republic or, in Northern Ireland, capital transfer tax.[43]

The proving can be done in one of two ways, in common form or solemn form.

---

[34]   1965 Act, s. 37; 1979 Order, Art. 14.
[35]   1965 Act, s. 40; Administration of Estates Act (N.I.), 1955, s. 26.
[36]   1965 Act, s. 40; 1979 Order, Art. 26.
[37]   1965 Act, s. 42 (1); 1979 Order, Art. 23.
[38]   1965 Act, s. 42 (2); 1979 Order, Art. 23 (4). *In b. Stuart* [1944] Ir.Jur.Rep. 62.
[39]   1965 Act, s. 43; 1979 Order, Art. 25. Art. 27 governs provisions and management of safe and convenient depositories for the custody of wills of living persons and see also ss. 23–5 of the U.K. Administration of Justice Act, 1982.
[40]   Ch. 14, *ante.*
[41]   See *Robinson* v. *Palmer* [1901] 2 I.R. 489 (testator's domicile in England but assets in Ireland). See further on wills with a foreign element, para. 14.51, *ante.*
[42]   *Re Long-Sutton's Estate* [1912] P. 97. *Cf. Re O'Brien* [1940] Ir.Jur.Rep. 60. As to a presumption of death after disappearance, see *Re Lavelle* [1940] Ir.Jur.Rep. 8; *In b. Griffin* (1931) 65 I.L.T.R. 108. See also *In b. Freytag* (1909) 43 I.L.T.R. 116 (fire at hotel); *In b. Inkerman Brown* (1902) 36 I.L.T.R. 173 (steamer lost at sea).
[43]   As regards returns by personal representatives for the purposes of inheritance tax, see now the Republic's Capital Acquisitions Tax Act, 1976, Part VI. As regards delivery of an account of the deceased's property by personal representatives for the purpose of capital transfer tax in Northern Ireland, see the U.K. Finance Act, 1975, Schedule 4, paras. 2 and 38–40. See also article 20 of the Administration of Estates (N.I.) Order, 1979.

(i) Common Form

16.10. Proof in common form is in practice achieved by producing to the probate registry or office[44] a will which appears to be properly executed and contains a proper attestation clause, so that probate can be granted on the oath of the executor alone. Otherwise, witnesses may be produced to testify by their oaths that the document produced is the true, whole and last will and testament of the deceased. If the original will cannot be produced, *e.g.*, it has been lost or destroyed, probate may be granted of a copy[45] or draft,[46] provided the registry or office is satisfied as to its authenticity, established, if neccesary, by parol evidence.[47] However, such probate is expressed to be limited until the will, or a more authentic copy, is produced. The oath of the proving executor swears or affirms that he believes the will in question is the last will of the testator, that he is the person thereby appointed executor, that he will administer the estate according to law and render just and true accounts when required, and that the gross value of the estate amounts to a particular sum and no more. If the will contains no attestation clause, or the clause is defective,[48] or in other cases of doubt as to due execution, the registrar may require an affidavit from at least one of the attesting witnesses to the effect that the requisite formalities were complied with.[49] Such affidavits may also be required where there appears to be unattested alterations or other forms of interference on the face of the will.[50]

It should be remembered that several wills or documents may together make up the last will of the testator and probate may be granted in respect of them all.[51]

(ii) Solemn Form

16.11. A will is said to be proved in solemn form when it is pronounced to be a valid testament as a result of an action in court.[52] A will so proved is *res judicata* and cannot be impugned by persons party or privy to the action or in a position to intervene,[53] unless, of course, circumstances such as evidence of fraud or discovery of a later will are brought to light.[54]

---

[44] Which may be done through a solicitor, 1965 Act, s. 35 (2); 1979 Order, Art. 18 (2).

[45] *E.g.*, a photocopy of a will already admitted to probate in another jurisdiction, see *Lyons* v. *Chalmers* [1929] I.R. 674; *Lennon* v. *Gray* [1931] I.R. 374. See also *In b. Mulvany* (1902) 36 I.L.T.R. 152; *In b. O'Hare* (1908) 42 I.L.T.R. 75; *In b. Hogan* (1895) 29 I.L.T.R. 64.

[46] *In b. Merrigan* (1899) 33 I.L.T.R. 131.

[47] *In b. Regan* [1964] Ir.Jur.Rep. 56; *In b. Cray* (1967) 101 I.L.T.R. 71. See also *In b. McQuillan* [1953–54] Ir.Jur.Rep. 10; *In b. Collier* [1957] Ir.Jur.Rep. 67; *In b. Cafferty* (1940) 74 I.L.T.R. 161; *In b. O'Callaghan* (1931) 67 I.L.T.R. 43.

[48] Para. 14.12, *ante*. See also *In b. Uniacke* [1964] I.R. 166. *Cf.* if there is a proper attestation clause, *Westby* v. *Westby* (1901) 35 I.L.T.R. 129.

[49] *In b. Miller* [1959] Ir.Jur.Rep. 29. *Cf. In b. Uniacke* [1964] I.R. 166.

[50] *In b. O'Sullivan* [1960] Ir.Jur.Rep. 14; *In b. Corboy* [1969] I.R. 148. See also *In b. Rudd* [1945] I.R. 180; *In b. Leeson* [1946] Ir.Jur.Rep. 33.

[51] *In b. Wafer* [1960] Ir.Jur.Rep. 19; *In b. McCarthy* [1965] Ir.Jur.Rep. 56. See also *In b. McLoughlin* (1949) 85 I.L.T.R. 63; *In b. Strahan* [1907] 2 I.R. 484.

[52] *In b. Corboy* [1969] I.R. 148. See also *Parkinson* v. *Watson* [1956] N.I. 1.

[53] *Young* v. *Holloway* [1895] P. 87; *Re Langton's Estate* [1964] P. 163; *Re Barraclough* [1967] P. 1.

[54] *In b. O'Sullivan* [1960] Ir.Jur.Rep. 14.

B. Letters of Administration

1. *Grants of Administration*

(i) Courts

16.12. In both parts of Ireland, the High Court has power to grant, and to revoke, cancel or recall[55] any grant of, administration to the persons determined in order of priority according to the High Court Rules.[56] It has been held in Ireland that an agreement amongst the deceased's next-of-kin as to who will apply for the grant does not alter the position laid down by the Rules.[57] However, any directions laid down in the Rules may be disregarded if the court considers it necessary or expedient to do so, due to special circumstances.[58]

(ii) Trust Corporation

The provisions mentioned above relating to trust corporations apply to grants of administration as they do to grants of probate of wills.[59]

(iii) Infants

Where an infant is sole executor of a will, administration of the will annexed is to be granted to his guardian, or such other person as the court thinks fit, until the infant attains his majority and applies for and obtains a grant of probate or letters of administration with the will annexed.[60]

(iv) Separate Grants

Letters of administration may also be granted separately in respect of real and personal estate, though generally there can again be no severance of an insolvent estate.[61]

(v) No Estate

16.13. A grant of administration can be made, as can a grant of probate, notwithstanding that the deceased left no estate in the Republic or Northern Ireland.[62] This enables the Irish courts to facilitate foreign grants in respect of the estates of persons still domiciled in Ireland, where the foreign law requires a grant first from the court of domicile. Furthermore, a *de bonis non* or similar grant in respect of an unadministered estate may be made notwithstanding that there is no unadministered estate of the deceased in the Republic or Northern Ireland.[63]

---

[55] *In b. Healy* (1901) 1 N.I.J.R. 77; *In b. Doherty* [1942] N.I. 87. See also *Re O'Brien* [1940] Ir.Jur.Rep. 60; *In b. Hood* [1945] Ir.Jur.Rep. 4.

[56] 1965 Act, s. 27; 1979 Order, Art. 4 replacing Administration of Estates Act (N.I.). 1955, s. 20, and see Leitch, *Administration of Estates Act (N.I.), 1955*, pp. 59–71. The circuit courts in the Republic and the county courts in Northern Ireland also have limited jurisdiction, as in the case of probate of wills, para. 16.06, *ante*.

[57] *Re McMahon* [1941] Ir.Jur.Rep. 70.

[58] 1965 Act, s. 27 (4); 1979 Order, Art. 4 (2).

[59] Para. 16.04, *ante*.

[60] 1965 Act, s. 32 (1); 1979 Order, Art. 7. See *Re Thompson and McWilliam's Contract* [1896] 1 I.R. 362; *In b. Hughes* [1957] Ir.Jur.Rep. 92.

[61] 1965 Act, s. 28; 1955 Act, s. 1 (2).

[62] 1965 Act, s. 29; 1979 Order, Art. 4 (4). See *Re Welsh* [1931] I.R. 161. *Cf. In b. Dyas* [1937] I.R. 479.

[63] *Ibid.* See *Crowley* v. *Flynn* [1982] I.L.R.M. 513 (see *A Casebook on Irish Land Law* (1984), p. 538).

(vi) Grants de Bonis Non

Normally a grant *de bonis non* is made in respect of the unadministered part of a deceased's estate where a personal representative dies before completing administration,[64] but the statutory powers just mentioned even seem to allow an Irish court to grant probate or letters of administration in respect of a deceased's estate which consists entirely of property which passes only outside the jurisdiction.[65]

2. Applications

16.14. The same rules generally govern applications for letters of administration as govern applications in respect of probate of wills.[66] The Irish courts have now been given a very wide discretion as to the persons they may think fit to be appointed administrators, with or without a will annexed,[67] and administrations may also be limited as the courts think fit.[68] Once administration is granted, no person is or may become entitled to administer the estate in question without a grant.[69] Every person to whom letters of administration, with or without will annexed, are granted has, subject to any limitations contained in the grant, the same rights and liabilities and is accountable in the same manner as if he were the executor of the deceased.[70]

(i) Administration Pendente Lite

16.15. In both parts of Ireland the court may appoint an administrator *pendente lite, i.e.,* pending legal proceedings touching the validity of a will or for the obtaining, recalling or revoking of any grant.[71] Such an administrator has all the rights and powers of a general administrator except the right of distributing the estate.[72] He is subject to the immediate control of the court

---

[64] *In b. Robinson* [1949] N.I. 150; *McNeill* v. *McNeill* [1957] N.I. 10. See also *In b. Stuart* [1944] Ir.Jur.Rep. 62; *In b. O'Reilly* [1948] Ir.Jur.Rep. 47; *Re McKay* [1937] Ir.Jur.Rep. 45; *In b. Bradfield* [1922] 2 I.R. 213.

[65] *Re Wayland's Estate* [1951] W.N. 604. *Cf. Re Welsh* [1931] I.R. 161. See also *In b. Dyas* [1937] I.R. 479.

[66] Para. 16.06, *ante.*

[67] 1965 Act, s. 27 (1) and (4); 1955 Act, ss. 20 (2) and 21 (1). See *In b. Reynolds* [1960] Ir.Jur.Rep. 62; *Re McDowell* [1963] N.I. 64. Also *In b. Harte* [1953–54] Ir.Jur.Rep. 68; *In b. Hogan* [1957] Ir.Jur.Rep. 69; *In b. Madden* [1957] Ir.Jur.Rep. 50; *In b. Middleton* [1955] Ir.Jur.Rep. 36; *In b. McKeon* (1939) 73 I.L.T.R. 51; *In b. O'hlladhaigh* (1975) 109 I.L.T.R. 113. *Cf.* s. 78 of the Probate and Letters of Administration Act (Ir.), 1857, which did, however, authorise grants of administration to "strangers" to the deceased if special circumstances justified this, *e.g.*, insolvency or next-of-kin infirm, see *Re Donnelly* [1939] Ir.Jur.Rep. 27; *Re Cole* [1942] Ir.Jur.Rep. 78; *In b. O'Connor* (1945) 79 I.L.T.R. 64; *Re O'Reilly* [1920] 2 I.R. 254; *In b. Bailie* (1919) 53 I.L.T.R. 208.

[68] *Ibid.* See *In b. Knott* [1920] 2 I.R. 397; *In b. Ryan* [1927] I.R. 174; *In b. Eccles* [1929] N.I. 58; *In b. Hogan* [1957] Ir.Jur.Rep. 69. Also *In b. Gilkinson* [1948] N.I. 42; *Munster and Leinster Bank* v. *Murphy* [1942] I.R. 176; *In b. Dyas* [1937] I.R. 479; *In b. Vereker* [1896] 1 I.R. 200. If a temporary administration is revoked while legal proceedings are pending the court may order their continuance by or against the new personal representative as if they had been originally commenced by or against him, subject to such conditions and variations if any, the court directs, 1965 Act, s. 33; 1979 Order, Art. 4 (see also Art. 21).

[69] See *In b. Gilkinson* [1948] N.I. 42; *In b. Hampton Robinson* [1949] N.I. 150. See also 1979 Order, Art. 5(3).

[70] 1965 Act, s. 27 (6); 1979 Order, Art. 33. *Creed* v. *Creed* [1913] 1 I.R. 48. See also para. 16.26, *infra.*

[71] 1965 Act, s. 27 (7); 1979 Order, Art. 6 (1). *Ginty* v. *Costello* (1834) 1 Jones 17. *Re Cullen* (1906) 40 I.L.T. 213; *In b. Gordon* (1867) 7 I.R. 1 Eq. 79; *In b. Colclough* (1887) 19 I.L.R.Ir. 235. Note also power to grant administration notwithstanding any alleged, but unproved, will, *Brennan* v. *Dillon* (1873) I.R. 8 Eq. 94; *Re Leary* (1897) 31 I.L.T.R. 55; *In b. Mullan* (1897) 31 I.L.T.R. 139; *In b. Fitzpatrick* (1902) 2 N.I.J.R. 76.

[72] *Ibid. Re West* [1947] W.N. 2.

and acts under its direction, but he may be paid such reasonable remuneration, as the court thinks fit, out of the deceased's estate.[73] It has been held in Ireland that the costs incurred by a manager appointed by the court in an administration suit take priority over all other costs except those of the executor and of realisation of the assets,[74] and the same may apply to administrators *pendente lite*.

(ii) Special Administration

16.16. The courts may also, on the application of any creditor[75] or other person interested in the estate, grant, in such form as the courts think fit, special administration of the estate if, after twelve months from the death of the deceased, any personal representative to whom a grant was made is residing out of the jurisdiction of the court.[76] Where a special administrator is appointed, the court may order the payment or transfer into court of any money or securities belonging to the estate in question.[77] If the personal representative returns from abroad, however, he must be made a party to any legal proceedings concerning the estate which are pending, and the costs of and incidental to those proceedings and the special administration are to be paid by him and out of such fund as the court in question may direct.[78]

(iii) Administration Bond

16.17. In the Republic of Ireland, every person to whom a grant of administration is made must give an administration bond to the President of the High Court and, if required by the High Court, Probate Office or district probate registrar, with one or more surety or sureties conditioned for duly collecting, getting in and administering the deceased's estate.[79] Such a bond, normally in a penalty of double the amount at which the estate of the deceased is sworn,[80] is not required in the case of the Chief State Solicitor or the Solicitor for the Attorney General,[81] nor are sureties required when a grant is made to a trust corporation.[82] An administration bond issued by a

---

[73] 1965 Act, s. 27 (8); 1979 Order, Art. 6 (2) and (3).
[74] *Ramsey* v. *Simpson* [1899] 1 I.R. 194.
[75] See further as to the claims of creditors *vis-à-vis* next-of-kin, especially where the estate is insolvent, *In b. Hunter* (1902) 2 N.I.J.R. 43; *Re Kelly* (1909) 43 I.L.T.R. 165. See also *In b. Thompson* (1898) 32 I.L.T.R. 76; *In b. Mahon* (1899) 33 I.L.T.R. 24; *In b. Lee* (1899) 33 I.L.T.R. 50; *In b. Moore* (1903) 3 N.I.J.R. 276; *In b. Cooley* (1903) 3 N.I.J.R. 18.
[76] 1965 Act, s. 31 (1); 1979 Order, Art. 8 (1). *In b. Walsh* (1923) 57 I.L.T.R. 78; *In b. Boyd* (1912) 46 I.L.T.R. 294. *Cf. Re Hearst* (1906) 40 I.L.T.R. 198. See also *In b. Kelly* (1897) 31 I.L.T.R. 169; *In b. Lee* [1898] 2 I.R. 81; *In b. Colclough* [1902] 2 I.R. 499. *Cf. Re Walsh* [1931] I.R. 161. Note also a grant to a creditor of one of the next-of-kin where they all fail to appear, *Re Mullins* [1937] Ir.Jur.Rep. 43.
[77] 1965 Act, s. 31 (2); 1979 Order, Art. 8 (2).
[78] 1965 Act, s. 31 (3); 1979 Order, Art. 8 (3).
[79] 1965 Act, s. 34 (1). See *Hibernian Fire Insurance Co.* v. *Dorgan* [1941] I.R. 514; *Gallagher* v. *Connor* [1943] I.R. 194. Also *In b. Leeson* (1937) 71 I.L.T.R. 82; *In b. Corcoran* [1934] I.R. 571; *Lucy* v. *Cronin* (1903) 3 N.I.J.R. 76; *Re Wilson (No. 2)* (1908) 42 I.L.T.R. 39. More than one bond may be required, in order to limit the liability of any surety, 1965 Act, s. 34 (2) (*b*).
[80] 1965 Act, s. 34 (2) (*a*). Also *Att.-Gen* v. *Robinson* [1901] 2 I.R. 73; *In b. Kinsella* (1903) 3 N.I.J.R. 240. It must also include provision for payment of all death duties for which the personal representative is liable and of all income and surtax payable out of the estate, 1965 Act, s. 34 (3). *Cf.* inheritance tax, see Capital Acquisitions Tax Act, 1976, s. 68 (1) (*a*).
[81] 1965 Act, s. 34 (5). *Cf.* an application by the Official Solicitor of England, *In b. Fitzmaurice* (1938) 72 I.L.T.R. 61.
[82] 1965 Act, s. 34 (6), and see para. 16.12, *ante*.

guarantee society or insurance company approved by the President of the High Court is acceptable for these purposes.[83]

16.18. In Northern Ireland, it is now provided that, as a condition of granting administration to any person, the High Court may require one or more sureties to guarantee any loss by breach by the administrator of his duties.[84] This guarantee enures to the benefit of every person interested in the administration, though no action may be brought on the guarantee without the leave of the court.[85] Even prior to this, it had been held in the Republic, in an administration suit, that the court had power to dispense with sureties, on terms, where the excessive premiums asked for made it impossible to obtain sureties.[86]

16.19. The provisions relating to grants of probate concerning district probate registries,[87] notices,[88] caveats,[89] calendars[90] and second and subsequent grants[91] apply equally to grants of administration. An official copy of a grant of representation is sufficient evidence of the grant.[92]

C. General Position of Personal Representatives

16.20. The general position of the personal representatives in relation to the deceased's estate and persons dealing with them may be summarised as follows.[93] In Northern Ireland, it is now laid down by statute that a personal representative is under a duty (a) to collect and get in the estate and administer it according to law; (b) when required by the court, to exhibit on oath in court a full inventory of the estate and, when so required, to render an account of administration to the court; (c) when required by the High Court, to deliver up the grant of probate or administration.[94]

1. *Executor Vis-à-vis Administrator*

16.21. The general rule is that, once an administrator has obtained a grant of administration, he has the same rights and liabilities and is accountable in like manner as if he were the executor of the deceased.[95] However, there is one major distinction which was well-described by Lord Parker of Waddington in these terms:

"It is quite clear that an executor derives his title and authority from the

---

[83] 1965 Act, s. 34 (7). See also *Re Lucas* [1900] 1 I.R. 292.
[84] 1979 Order, Art. 17 (1). See *In b. Walshe* [1897] 1 I.R. 167; *Bannon* v. *Macaire* (1881) 7 L.R.Ir. 221.
[85] 1979 Order, Art. 17 (2) and (3).
[86] *In b. Tynan* [1949] Ir.Jur.Rep. 16. See also *Cochrane* v. *Cochrane* (1859) 5 Ir.Jur.(N.S.) 42; *In b. Gordon* (1867) I.R. 1 Eq. 272; *In b. Elliott* (1879) 3 L.R.Ir. 147.
[87] Para. 16.07, *ante.*
[88] *Ibid.*
[89] Para. 16.08, *ante.*
[90] Para. 16.07, *ante.*
[91] Para. 16.08, *ante.*
[92] 1965 Act, s. 43 (2); 1979 Order, Art. 25 (2).
[93] Note the provisions in s. 65 of the Republic's 1965 Act relating to administration of estates on behalf of the State.
[94] 1979 Order, Art. 35 (1).
[95] 1965 Act, s. 27 (6); 1979 Order, Art. 33.

will of his testator and not from any grant of probate. The personal property of the testator, including all rights of action, vests in him upon the testator's death, and the consequence is that he can institute an action in the character of executor before he proves the will. He cannot, it is true, obtain a decree before probate, but this is not because his title depends on probate but because the production of probate is the only way in which, by the rules of the court, he is allowed to prove his title. An administrator, on the other hand, derives title solely under his grant, and cannot, therefore, institute an action as administrator before he gets his grant."[96]

However, to overcome the inconveniences that this rule might involve, the courts developed the doctrine of "relation back," *i.e.*, that the grant of administration for some purposes[97] would be deemed to relate back to the death of the intestate.[98]

An executor cannot act where administration of the estate has been granted, until the grant has been recalled or revoked or has expired.[99]

2. *Executor of Executor*

16.22. By an early statute,[1] an executor of an executor, *e.g.*, where the sole or last surviving executor of a testator died, could act in addition as executor of the testator without any further grant of probate.[2] Frequently, however, such an executor would be reluctant to become involved in the administration of the first deceased's estate, and section 19 (1) of the Republic's Succession Act, 1965, now prohibits the executor of an executor from acting in such cases. In Northern Ireland the executor of a sole or last surviving executor of a testator is the executor of that testator, but not if he does not prove the will of his testator or where probate is subsequently granted to another surviving executor of the first testator.[3]

3. *Proving Executors*

16.23. In the Republic of Ireland it is now provided that, where probate is granted to one or some of two or more persons named as executors, then, whether or not power is reserved to the other or others to prove, *all* the powers of personal representatives may be exercised by the proving executor

---

[96] *Chetty* v. *Chetty* [1916] 1 A.C. 603 at 608. See also *Creed* v. *Creed* [1913] 1 I.R. 48.
[97] See *Ingall* v. *Moran* [1944] K.B. 160; *Hilton* v. *Sutton Steam Laundry* [1946] 1 K.B. 65; *Fred Long & Son Ltd.* v. *Burgess* [1950] 1 K.B. 115
[98] "It is clear that the title of an administrator, though it does not exist until the grant of administration, relates back to the time of the death of the intestate; and that he may recover against a wrongdoer who has seized or converted the goods of the intestate after his death, in an action of trespass or trover. . . . The reason for this relation . . . is that otherwise there would be no remedy for the wrong done." *Per* Parke B. in *Foster* v. *Bates* (1843) 12 M. & W. 226 at 233.
[99] 1965 Act, s. 21; 1979 Order, Art. 34.
[1] 25 Edw. 3, Stat. 5, c. 5, extended by writ to Ireland in 1351. See Leitch, *op. cit.*, p. 3.
[2] See *In b. Gilkinson* [1948] N.I. 42; *In b. Hampton Robinson* [1949] N.I. 150. See also *Re Owen* (1889) 23 L.R.Ir. 328. *Cf.* as regards administrators, *In b. Griffen* (1868) I.R. 2 Eq. 320. See also *In b. Frengley* [1915] 2 I.R. 1.
[3] 1979 Order, Art. 32.

or executors, or their survivor or survivors, and this is as effectual as if all the persons named as executors had concurred in the exercise of the power in question.[4] A similar provision now exists in Northern Ireland replacing one confined to the personal representatives' powers of sale and to deal with land only.[5] Apart from this, it has been held in Ireland that, where there are two executors and one renounces their office, the acting executor has a good power of sale.[6] Furthermore, it seems that the court has a discretion to authorise a sale by one only of the proving executors.[7]

4. *Administration in Force*

16.24. Once a grant of administration has been made in respect of the deceased's estate, no person may bring any action or otherwise act as executor in respect of that estate until the grant has been recalled or revoked or has expired.[8]

5. *Protection When Acting on Probate or Administration*

16.25. Every person making or permitting any payment or disposition to be made under a representation (and "representation" is defined as meaning probate or administration[9]) is indemnified and protected in so doing, despite any defect or circumstance whatsoever affecting the validity of the representation, *provided* the person acts in good faith.[10] If a representation is revoked, all payments and dispositions made in good faith *to* a personal representative prior to revocation are a valid discharge to the person making them, and the personal representative who acted under the revoked representation may retain and reimburse himself in respect of any payments or dispositions made by him which his successor might have properly made.[11]

6. *Liability of Personal Representatives*

16.26. Personal representatives hold the estate of the deceased person on trust for the persons entitled under the will or the law of intestacy, or as creditors,[12] and are liable generally as express trustees.[13] However, one important exception to this principle in both parts of Ireland is the rule now that a personal representative is not a trustee in his capacity as personal

---

[4] 1965 Act, s. 20. *Cf. Ringland* v. *Ringland* (1901) 1 N.I.J.R. 184.
[5] 1979 Order, Art. 31, replacing Administration of Estates Act (N.I.) 1955, s. 32 (2) (as to which, see *Woods* v. *Magee* (1976) 27 N.I.L.Q. 427).
[6] *Re Fisher and Haslett* (1884) 13 L.R.Ir. 546.
[7] *Re Curry* (1910) 44 I.L.T.R. 66.
[8] 1965 Act, s. 21; in N.I., 1979 Order, Art. 34.
[9] 1965 Act, s. 3 (1); 1979 Order, Art. 2 (2).
[10] 1965 Act, s. 22 (1); 1979 Order, Art. 38 (1).
[11] 1965 Act, s. 22 (2); 1979 Order, Art. 38 (2).
[12] 1965 Act, s. 10 (3); 1955 Act, s. 2 (3). See Clarke, "Some Aspects of the Succession Act, 1965: *Caveat Executors*; New Powers and Burdens for Personal Representatives" (1966) 1 Ir.Jur.(N.S.) 222.
[13] Ch. 10 *ante*. See *Connolly* v. *Connolly* (1866) 17 Ir.Ch.R. 208; *Blount* v. *O'Connor* (1886) 17 L.R.Ir. 620; *Moore* v. *McGlynn* [1894] 1 I.R. 74; *Leahy* v. *De Moleyns* [1896] 1 I.R. 206; *Re Egan* [1957] Ir.Jur.Rep. 19. Also *Minford* v. *Carse* [1912] 2 I.R. 245; *Re Gunning* [1918] 1 I.R. 221. As regards remuneration, see *Taafe* v. *Merrick* (1931) 65 I.L.T.R. 36. As regards joint and several liability, see *Lowe* v. *Shields* [1902] 1 I.R. 320; *Scully* v. *Delany* (1839) 2 Ir.Eq.R. 165; *Bowen* v. *Lindsay* (1854) 5 Ir.Jur. 129; *Clarke* v. *Pope* (1862) 13 Ir.Ch.R. 91.

representative for the purposes of the Statute of Limitations.[14] Prior to the intervention of legislation on this subject, there was much controversy in Ireland as to whether for the purposes of limitation of actions a personal representative was to be treated as an express trustee[15] or an implied one only.[16] It is also provided now that "trustee" in the Statute of Limitations does not include a person whose fiduciary relationship arises merely because he is in possession of property comprised in the estate of a deceased person in the capacity of bailiff for another person.[17]

7. Liability of Personal Representative's Estate

16.27. Where a personal representative of a deceased person, including an executor de son tort (in his own wrong),[18] wastes or converts to his own use any part of the deceased's estate and then dies, his personal representative is liable and chargeable to the extent of the available assets of the defaulting representative as the defaulter would have been if he had survived.[19]

8. Executor de Son Tort

16.28. If any person, in defraud of creditors or without full valuable consideration,[20] obtains, receives or holds any part of the estate of a deceased person, or effects the release of any debt or liability due to the estate, he is chargeable as executor in his own wrong (de son tort) to the extent of the estate received or coming into his hands, or the debt or liability released.[21] However, a deduction should be made for any debt for valuable consideration and without fraud due to the person concerned from the deceased at his death, and for any payment made which might properly be made by a personal representative.[22]

III. ADMINISTRATION OF ASSETS

We now turn to the second main topic to be considered in this chapter, namely the powers and duties of the personal representatives in the administration of the deceased person's assets.[23]

---

[14] 1965 Act, s. 123 (1) in substitution for s. 2 (2) (d) of the Statute of Limitations, 1957; Statute of Limitations (N.I.), 1958, s. 74 (2) (b), (see also s. 47 (1)). See further, ch. 23, post. Also Ruddy v. Gannon [1965] I.R. 283, espec. at 290 (per O'Dálaigh C.J.).

[15] See Re Loughlin [1942] I.R. 15; Owens v. McGarry [1948] I.R. 226; McNeill v. McNeill [1957] N.I. 10. See also Graham v. Chambers (1898) 36 I.L.T.R. 108.

[16] See Bermingham v. Bermingham [1918] I.R. 437; Mallon v. McAlea [1923] I.R. 30; Murland v. Despard [1956] I.R. 170; Vaughan v. Cottingham [1961] I.R. 184. See also Re McCausland [1908] I.R. 327; McEneaney v. McEneaney (1920) 54 I.L.T.R. 199.

[17] 1965 Act, s. 124, reversing Rice v. Begley [1920] 1 I.R. 243. Cf. Statute of Limitations (N.I.), 1958, s. 74 (2) (a).

[18] See heading 8, infra.

[19] 1965 Act. s. 24; 1979 Order, Art. 40. Ennis v. Rochford (1844) 14 L.R.Ir. 285.

[20] Defined in 1965 Act, s. 23 (2) as "such valuable consideration as amounts or approximates to the value of that for which it is given." Cf. 1979 Order, Art. 39 (1).

[21] 1965 Act, s. 23 (1); in N.I., Administration of Estates Act (Ir.), 1634. See McAllister v. McAllister (1883) 11 L.R.Ir. 533; Blackstaff Flax Co. v. Camera [1899] 1 I.R. 252; In b. Leeson (1937) 71 I.L.T.R. 82.

[22] Ibid. Re Ryan [1897] 1 I.R. 513; Earl of Westmeath v. Coyne [1896] 2 I.R. 436. See also Beatty v. Porter (1861) 7 Ir.Jur.(N.S.) 31; McCarthy v. Donovan (1863) 13 I.C.L.R. 195.

[23] See generally the Republic's Succession Act, 1965, Pt. V and the Administration of Estates Act (N.I.), 1955, Pt. IV. Also Keeton and Sheridan, Equity (1969), ch. VII; Kiely, Principles of Equity as Applied in Ireland (1936), ch. XIV; Leitch, Administration of Estates Act (N.I.), 1955 (1956), pp. 81–127. Note also 1979 Order Act, Art. 35 (1), para. 16.20, ante.

A. Assets

16.29. Without prejudice to the right of incumbrancers,[24] in both parts of Ireland the estate, real and personal, whether legal or equitable,[25] of a deceased person, and the estate of which he disposes by will in pursuance of a general power, are assets for payment of the funeral, testamentary and administrative expenses, debts (whether by specialty or simple contract) and liabilities relating to the estate, to the extent of the deceased's beneficial interest.[26] Any disposition by will which is inconsistent with this rule is void as against the creditors[27] and, in the Republic of Ireland, a spouse in respect of the legal right to a share in the estate.[28] If necessary, the court is under an obligation to administer the estate for the purpose of payment of the expenses, debts and liabilities.[29]

B. Administration of Assets

The order in which the personal representatives are to administer the assets is laid down by statute and a distinction is drawn between the estate of a deceased person which is insolvent and one which is solvent.[30]

1. *Insolvent Estate*

16.30. Though the statutes refer only to insolvent estates,[31] it appears that the order in question should be followed until it becomes clear that there are sufficient assets to pay the expenses and debts in full.[32] The rules in both parts of Ireland as to the order of application of assets in payment of debts where the estate is insolvent[33] are now as follows:[34]

(1) The funeral, testamentary and administration expenses have priority;
(2) Subject to that, the same rules are to prevail and to be observed as to the respective rights of secured and unsecured creditors and as to debts and liabilities provable and as to the valuation of annuities and future and contingent liabilities, respectively, and as to the priorities of debts and liabilities as may be in force for the time being under the

---

[24] 1965 Act, s. 45 (2); 1955 Act, s. 29 (2). See para. 16.40, *infra.*
[25] As to the importance of this distinction formerly, see *Hanley* v. *McDermott* (1874) I.R. 9 Eq. 35; *Re Drew* [1923] 1 I.R. 35.
[26] 1965 Act, s. 45 (1); 1955 Act, s. 29 (1). These provisions replace the Statute of Westminster II. 1285, 13 Edw. 1, c. 19 (Administration of Estates); Administration of Estates Act, 1357, 31 Edw. 3, Stat. 1, c. 11; Statute of Frauds (Ir.), 1695, ss. 7 and 8; Administration of Estates Act, 1833; Administration of Estates Act, 1869 (Hinde Palmer's Act). See para. 15.05, *ante* and *Hanley* v. *McDermott* (1874) I.R. 9 Eq. 35; *Re Drew* [1923] 1 I.R. 35. In the Republic of Ireland, the liabilities include the legal right of the spouse to share in the estate under s. 111 of the 1965 Act, para. 14.56, *ante.*
[27] *Ibid.*
[28] *Ibid.*
[29] *Ibid.* See *Re Colclough* [1965] I.R. 668.
[30] 1965 Act, s. 46; 1955 Act, s. 30.
[31] 1965 Act, s. 46 (1); 1955 Act, s. 30 (1), replacing s. 28 (1) of the Judicature (Ir.) Act, 1877. See *O'Brien* v. *Gillman* (1883) 13 L.R.Ir. 6; *Scott* v. *Murphy* (1884) 13 L.R.Ir. 10.
[32] *Re Milan Tramways Co.* (1883) 22 Ch.D. 122; *Re McMurdo* [1902] 2 Ch. 684. See also *Re O'Toole* (1930) 64 I.L.T.R. 124.
[33] *I.e.*, if the assets are not sufficient to pay all funeral, testamentary and administration expenses, plus the debts, *Re Leng* [1895] 1 Ch. 652.
[34] 1965 Act, 1st Sched., Pt. I; 1955 Act, 1st Sched., Pt. I.

law of bankruptcy with respect to the assets of persons adjudged bankrupt.[35]

(3) In the application of the rules as to bankruptcy the date of the death of the deceased is to be substituted for the date of adjudication in bankruptcy.[36]

(i) Funeral, Testamentary and Administration Expenses

16.31. Funeral[37] and testamentary[38] expenses have long been entitled to priority, where the estate of the deceased was being administered by the court.[39] Administration expenses include such things as the personal representatives' costs and the costs of realisation of assets.[40] However, a claim against the estate of a deceased person will, in the absence of corroboration, be viewed with suspicion.[41]

(ii) Preferential Debts

16.32. After payment of funeral, testamentary and administration expenses, the personal representatives must apply the assets in payment of "preferential" debts as laid down by the bankruptcy legislation.[42] Such debts are rates and taxes due at the deceased's death,[43] wages or a salary of a clerk or servant for services rendered during the four months prior to death,[44] wages of any labourer or workman for services rendered during the four months preceding death[45] and amounts due in respect of contributions payable by the deceased during the twelve months prior to bankruptcy under social welfare[46] or national insurance legislation.[47] These debts rank equally as between themselves and must be paid in full unless the property is

---

[35] See *Bankruptcy Law Committee Report* (1972; Prl. 2714), ch. 40 (R.I.).

[36] See previously as to N.I., s. 1 (8) of the Preferential Payments in Bankruptcy Act (N.I.), 1933.

[37] See *Re McIntyre* (1930) 64 I.L.T.R. 179 (erection of tombstone). Also *Magennis* v. *Dempsey* (1868) I.R. 3 C.L. 327; *Turner* v. *McGeagh* (1894) 28 I.L.T.R. 38.

[38] *Gillooly* v. *Plunkett* (1882) 9 L.R.Ir. 324; *Re Hanratty* (1905) 39 I.L.T.R. 132; *Re Blake* [1955] I.R. 89.

[39] See Judicature (Ir.) Act, 1877, s. 28 (1). See on this, *Moore* v. *Smith* [1895] 1 I.R. 512; *McCausland* v. *O'Callaghan* [1904] 1 I.R. 376. As regards administration by the court, see *Sweeney* v. *Gallagher* (1888) 22 I.L.T.R. 82; *McFerran* v. *McFerran* [1897] 1 I.R. 66; *Johnston* v. *Lowry* [1900] 1 I.R. 316; *Thompson* v. *Hurley* [1905] 1 I.R. 588; *McSweeney* v. *Murphy* [1919] 1 I.R. 16.

[40] *McFeeley* v. *Boyle* (1886) 17 L.R.Ir. 633; *Kelly* v. *Kelly* (1888) 21 L.R.Ir. 243; *Ramsey* v. *Simpson* [1899] 1 I.R. 194; *Hibernian Bank* v. *Lauder* [1898] 1 I.R. 262; *McSpadden* v. *Patterson* (1905) 39 I.L.T.R. 122; *Re Hanratty* (1905) 39 I.L.T.R. 132; *Re O'Kean* [1907] 1 I.R. 223.

[41] *Re Boak* (1881) 7 L.R.Ir. 322; *Re Harnett* (1886) 17 L.R.Ir. 543, as explained in *Somers* v. *Erskine (No. 2)* [1944] I.R. 368.

[42] *I.e.*, in the Republic, the Irish Bankrupt and Insolvent Act, 1857, s. 249, Bankruptcy (Ir.) Amendment Act, 1872, s. 49 and Preferential Payments in Bankruptcy (Ir.) Act, 1889; *cf.* Bankruptcy (Amendment) (N.I.) Order, 1980, Arts. 18–26, replacing the Preferential Payments (Bankruptcies and Arrangements) Act (N.I.), 1964 and Preferential Payments in Insolvency (N.I.) Order, 1977. See *Re Lindsay* [1926] N.I. 128. Also *Bankruptcy Law Committee Report* (1972; Prl. 2714), ch. 55 (R.I.).

[43] *Re D.* [1927] I.R. 220.

[44] *Re M.* [1956] N.I. 182, where it was held that a skilled craftsman is a "labourer or workman" rather than a "clerk or servant" in this context.

[45] *Ibid.*

[46] *E.g.*, in the Republic Insurance (Intermittent Unemployment) Act, 1942, s. 27 (3); Social Welfare Act, 1952, s. 58 (3); Finance (No. 2) Act, 1959, s. 12 (1); Redundancy Payments Act, 1967, s. 42 (3); Health Contributions Act, 1971, s. 11 (3); Social Welfare Act, 1976, s. 7. See *Re Hennessy* [1932] I.R. 11; *Re W.* [1933] I.R. 202; *Graham* v. *Tinode Brick and Tile Co.* [1942] I.R. 258; *Re Farmer Bros.* [1964] I.R. 513.

[47] *E.g.*, National Insurance (Industrial Injuries) Act (N.I.), 1946; National Insurance Act (N.I.), 1946. Bankruptcy (Amendment) (N.I.) Order, 1980, Arts. 19–21. See *Re P.F. and M.L.F.* [1952] N.I. 172.

insufficient, in which case they abate equally.[48] After they have been paid, all other debts proved are generally paid *pari passu*.[49]

(iii) Secured Creditors

16.33. In the administration of an insolvent estate, the general bankruptcy rules as regards secured creditors apply.[50] A secured creditor has several options, *e.g.*, he may rely entirely on his security and not prove for the debt or surrender the security and prove for the whole debt[51]; he may also realise his security, usually by exercising a power of sale or applying to the court for a sale, and prove for any deficiency remaining after realisation,[52] or set out particulars of his security, value it and then prove for any deficiency thereby disclosed.[53]

(iv) Priorities

16.34. A testator's creditors have priority over creditors in respect of trading carried on after the testator's death,[54] though they may lose priority if they assent to the trading.[55] Furthermore, where an executor carries on authorised trading, and is entitled to an indemnity out of the general assets for any debt properly incurred by him, his creditor may be entitled to a direct claim against the estate under the principle of subrogation.[56]

(v) Debts Provable

16.35. The general bankruptcy rules as to debts which are provable also apply in the administration of an insolvent estate, *i.e.*, all debts and liabilities, present or future, certain or contingent, incurred by the deceased may be proved, subject to certain exceptions, *e.g.*, in respect of claims for unliquidated damages.[57]

(vi) Retainer and Preference

16.36. The rights of retainer and preference were two special rights recognised apart from general bankruptcy law, which could be invoked by executors. Where an executor was also a creditor of the estate, he could not sue himself and get priority by obtaining judgment, so he was given the right

---

[48] Preferential Payments in Bankruptcy (Ir.) Act, 1889, s. 1; 1980 (N.I.) Order, Art. 18.

[49] *E.g.* Crown debts (see *Re Galvin* [1897] 1 I.R. 530; *Re K.* [1927] I.R. 260) and specialty and simple contract debts (see *Re Leinster Contract Corporation* [1903] 1 I.R. 517; *McCausland* v. *O'Callaghan* [1904] 1 I.R. 376). See also as regards deferred debts, Partnership Act, 1890, s. 3; Moneylenders Act, 1933, s. 16 (R.I.); *cf.* Consumer Credit Act, 1974 (U.K.).

[50] See Bankruptcy (Ir.) Amendment Act, 1872; Bankruptcy Amendment Acts (N.I.), 1929, 1963 and 1980.

[51] *Ex parte Robinson* (1886) 15 L.R.Ir. 496; *Re MacEntee* [1960] Ir.Jur.Rep. 55. See also *Beattie* v. *Cordner* [1904] A.C. 1; *Cooper* v. *Teahan* (1890) 23 L.R.Ir. 203.

[52] *Re Love* (1883) 9 L.R.Ir. 6; *Re MacEntee* [1960] Ir.Jur.Rep. 55. See also *Re Johnston* (1890) 23 L.R.Ir. 50; *Ross* v. *Ross* (1892) 29 L.R.Ir. 318; *Hilliard* v. *Moriarty* [1894] 1 I.R. 316.

[53] *Re Greer* (1877) I.R. 11 Eq. 502; *Findlater* v. *Butler* (1880) 5 L.R.Ir. 95; *Re Robinson* [1958] N.I. 166; *Re Clenaghan* (1959) 95 I.L.T.R. 89; *Re Sythes* [1962] N.I. 38.

[54] *Re Morris* (1889) 23 L.R.Ir. 333; *McAloon* v. *McAloon* [1900] 1 I.R. 367; *Re O'Kelly* [1920] 1 I.R. 200.

[55] *Re Hodges* [1899] 1 I.R. 480; *Kirkwood* v. *Hamilton* (1902) 36 I.L.T.R. 155; *Scott* v. *Scott* [1924] 1 I.R. 141; *McGinley* v. *Gallagher* [1929] I.R. 307.

[56] *Moore* v. *McGlynn* [1904] 1 I.R. 334; *O'Neill* v. *McGrorty* [1915] 1 I.R. 1; *Re Byrne* (1913) 47 I.L.T.R. 301; *Re Geary* [1939] N.I. 152. See also *I.R.C.* v. *Walsh* [1951] N.I. 88.

[57] *Re Calvert* [1961] N.I. 58; *Davoren* v. *Wootten* [1900] 1 I.R. 273. See, however, Civil Liability Act, 1961, s. 10 (R.I.); Law Reform (Miscellaneous Provisions) Act (N.I.), 1937, s. 14.

to pay the debt due to himself in priority to any debt of an equal priority to his own debt.[58] The right of retainer could also be invoked by an administrator, though this was subject to the terms of his bond upon taking out letters of administration.[59] In the Republic, a personal representative's right of retainer may now be exercised in respect of all the deceased's asssets, but only for debts owing to the personal representative "in his own right," whether solely or jointly with another person.[60] However, it is expressly provided that the right of retainer is not exercisable where the estate is insolvent.[61] In Northern Ireland, the right of retainer has recently been abolished altogether.[62]

16.37. The right of preference was the right of a personal representative to prefer one creditor as against another to the same extent as the representative could retain, *i.e.*, in respect of debts of equal, but not superior, priority. This right of preference is preserved in the Republic of Ireland and also applies to all the assets of the deceased.[63] In Northern Ireland, however, it too has recently been abolished.[64] But, a personal representative either who, in good faith and at any time had no reason to believe the deceased's estate was insolvent, pays a debt of one of the deceased's creditors (including himself), or to whom administration is granted solely as a creditor and who in good faith pays the debt of another creditor, is not liable to account to a creditor of the same degree or the paid creditor, if it subsequently appears that the estate was insolvent.[65]

2. *Solvent Estate*

16.38. Where the deceased's estate is solvent, then, subject to rules of court and provisions as to charges on the deceased's property, or contained in his will, the assets, real and personal, are to be applied in discharge of the funeral, testamentary and administration expenses, debts and liabilities and, in the Republic of Ireland, any legal right of a spouse in the following order[66]:

(1)   property of the deceased undisposed of by will, subject to the retention thereout of a fund sufficient to meet any pecuniary legacies[67];

(2)   property of the deceased person not specifically devised or bequeathed but included (either by a specific or general description)

---

[58]   See discussion in *Hanley* v. *McDermott* (1874) I.R 9 Eq. 35; *Re Owen* (1890) 23 L.R.Ir. 328; *Taaffe* v. *Taaffe* [1902] 1 I.R. 148; *Re Lynch* (1915) 49 I.L.T.R. 78; *Re Carey* (1915) 49 I.L.T.R. 226; *Olpherts* v. *Coryton* [1913] 1 I.R. 211; *Olpherts* v. *Coryton (No. 2)* [1913] 1 I.R. 381.
[59]   Para. 16.17, *ante*. See also *Re Simpson* [1895] 1 I.R. 530; *Re Carey* (1915) 49 I.L.T.R. 226; *Re Harty* [1955–56] Ir.Jur.Rep. 76. As regards the right of retainer in the case of administration by the court, see *Hanley* v. *McDermott* (1874) I.R. 9 Eq. 35 and, in the case of an executor *de son tort*, *Whalley* v. *Galbraith* (1841) 2 Cr. & Dix 146.
[60]   1965 Act, s. 46 (2). See *Att.-Gen.* v. *Jackson* [1932] A.C. 365. Also *Featherstone H.* v. *West* (1871) I.R. 6 Eq. 86. *Cf.* a debt owed by a legatee to the executor, *Jackson* v. *Yeats* [1912] 1 I.R. 267.
[61]   1965 Act, s. 46 (2) (*a*).
[62]   Administration of Estates Act (N.I.), 1971, s. 3 (1) (repealing s. 30 (2) of 1955 Act).
[63]   1965 Act, s. 46 (2). *Fitzpatrick* v. *Purcell* (1837) Cr. & Dix, Abr. Cas. 297.
[64]   1971 Act, s. 3 (1). See now Administration of Estates (N.I.) Order, 1979, Art. 37 (1).
[65]   1971 Act, s. 3 (2). See now 1979 Order, Art. 37 (2).
[66]   1965 Act, s. 46 (3) and 1st Sched., Pt. II; 1955 Act, s. 30 (3) and 1st Sched., Pt. II. As to the former law, see Kiely, *Principles of Equity as Applied in Ireland* (1936), pp. 234–47.
[67]   As to the meaning of pecuniary legacies, see para. 14.26, *ante*.

in a residuary gift,[68] subject to the retention out of such property of a
fund sufficient to meet any pecuniary legacies, so far as not provided
for as aforesaid;

(3)   property of the deceased person specifically[69] appropriated or devised
or bequeathed (either by specific or general description) for the
payment of debts;

(4)   property of the deceased person charged with, or devised or
bequeathed (either by a specific or general description) subject to a
charge for the payment of debts[70];

(5)   the fund, if any, retained to meet pecuniary legacies[71];

(6)   property specifically devised or bequeathed, rateably according to
value[72];

(7)   property appointed by will under a general power, rateably according
to value.

This order of application may be varied by the deceased's will[73] and it is not to
affect the liability of land to answer the death duty imposed thereon in
exoneration of other assets.[74]

(i) Spouse's Legal Right

16.39.   In the Republic of Ireland, the spouse's claim to a share as a legal
right or on intestacy in the deceased's estate,[75] which is a claim against the
assets to a sum equal to the value of the share,[76] is not affected by the order of
application given above.[77]

(ii) Creditors

Similarly, in both parts of Ireland, the order does not affect the rights of
creditors of the deceased who may resort to any part of the estate.[78]

(iii) Marshalling

If any injustice occurs as a result of a creditor's, or in the Republic of
Ireland, a spouse's application of assets, or, of course, if the personal
representatives apply the assets out of order, the doctrine of marshalling[79]

---

[68]   Para. 14.26, *ante*. Also *Re Wolfe* [1919] 2 I.R. 491; *Bagge* v. *Bagge* [1921] 1 I.R. 213; *Re Kelly* [1932] I.R.
255.

[69]   Para. 14.26, *ante*. *Re McAfee* [1909] 1 I.R. 124; *McCoy* v. *Jacob* [1919] 1 I.R. 134.

[70]   See *Harding* v. *Grady* (1841) 1 Dr. & War. 430; *Elliott* v. *Montgomery* (1872) I.R. 5 Eq. 214; *Henry* v.
Henry (1872) I.R. 6 Eq. 286.

[71]   See *Boyd* v. *Boyd* [1928] N.I. 14. As regards annuities, see *Re Esmonde* [1946] I.R. 551; *Re Cochrane*
[1953] I.R. 160.

[72]   Specific legacies and devises abate rateably *inter se*, *Re Turner* [1908] 1 I.R. 274.

[73]   1965 Act, 1st Sched., Pt. II, para. 8 (*a*); Administration of Estates Act (N.I.) 1955, 1st Sched., Pt. II,
para. 8 (*a*). *Re Worthington* [1933] Ch. 771; *Re Berrey's Will Trusts* [1959] 1 W.L.R. 30.

[74]   1965 Act, 1st Sched., Pt. II, para. 8 (*b*); 1955 Act, 1st Sched., Pt. II, para. 8 (*b*).

[75]   Para. 14.56, *ante*.

[76]   1965 Act, s. 46 (6).

[77]   1965 Act, s. 46 (4).

[78]   1965 Act, s. 46 (4). See also Leitch, *Administration of Estates Act (N.I.), 1955* (1956), p. 85.

[79]   *Cf.* paras. 13.075 *et seq.*, *ante*. *Douglas* v. *Cooksey* (1868) I.R. 2 Eq. 311; *Hanley* v. *McDermott* (1874)
I.R. 9 Eq. 35. Note the discussion of the applicability of the doctrine to save a legacy from the mortmain
restriction in s. 16 of the Charitable Donations and Bequests (Ir.) Act, 1844 (now repealed in both parts of
Ireland, para. 9.072, *ante*) in *Re Clancy* [1943] I.R. 23; *Re Elwood* [1944] I.R. 344; *Re Morrissey* [1944] I.R.
361; *Aitken* v. *Att.-Gen* [1945] I.R. 419; *Ryan* v. *Murphy* [1948] 82 I.L.T.R. 2; *Re Solomon* [1949] I.R. 3.

may be applied to correct it.[80] Indeed section 46 (5) of the Republic's Succession Act, 1965 now contains an express provision to this effect:

"Where a creditor, a person entitled to a legal right or a personal representative applies an asset out of the order mentioned in Part II of the First Schedule, the persons entitled under the will or on intestacy shall have the right to have the assets marshalled so that a beneficiary whose estate or interest has been applied out of its order shall stand in the place of that creditor or person *pro tanto* as against any property that, in the said order, is liable before his own estate or interest."

(iv) Charges on Property

16.40. At common law the rule was that, where land was mortgaged or contracted to be sold when the mortgagor or vendor died, the mortgage debt or purchase money was payable primarily out of the deceased's personal estate. This rule was reversed by Locke King's Acts[81] so that, thereafter, the burden generally descended with the property in question. These Acts have now been replaced in both parts of Ireland and extended to cover charges on personalty as well as realty.[82] Where a person dies possessed of, or entitled to, or, under a general power of appointment, by his will disposes of, an interest in property, which at his death is charged[83] with payment of money, then, subject to a contrary or other intention,[84] the interest so charged is, as between the different persons claiming through the deceased, to be primarily liable for payment of the charge.[85] A contrary or other intention is not to be deemed to be signified (a) by a general direction for the payment of debts or of all the debts of the testator out of his estate, or any part of it[86]; or (b) by a charge of debts upon any such estate,[87] unless such intention is further signified by words expressly or by necessary implication referring to all or some part of the charge.[88]

C. DISTRIBUTION OF ASSETS

1. *Procedure*

16.41. It is the duty of the personal representatives to distribute the

---

[80] See *Averall* v. *Wade* (1835) Ll. & G. *temp.* Sug. *252; Ellard* v. *Cooper* (1860) 11 Ir.Ch.R. 376; *Buckley* v. *Buckley* (1887) 19 L.R.Ir. 561.

[81] *I.e.*, Real Estate Charges, Acts, 1854, 1867 and 1877. See *Dowdall* v. *McCartan* (1881) 5 L.R.Ir. 642; *Nesbitt* v. *Lawder* (1886) 17 L.R.Ir. 53; *Given* v. *Massey* (1892) 31 L.R.Ir. 126; *Pim* v. *Pim* (1902) 36 I.L.T.R. 136; *Caldwell* v. *Ball* (1902) 36 I.L.T.R. 206; *Thompson* v. *Bell* [1903] 1 I.R. 489; *Re McCluskin* (1899) 33 I.L.T.R. 70.

[82] 1965 Act, s. 47; 1955 Act, s. 31.

[83] Whether by way of legal or equitable mortgage or charge or otherwise (including a lien for unpaid purchase money), *ibid.*

[84] Signified by will, deed or other document, *ibid.* See *Givan* v. *Massey* (1892) 31 L.R.Ir. 126; *Reynolds* v. *McGloughlin* (1883) 9 L.R.Ir. 405.

[85] This does not affect the right of the chargee to obtain payment or satisfaction out of other assets of the deceased or otherwise, 1965 Act, s. 47 (3); 1955 Act, s. 31 (3). See *Re Neeld* [1962] Ch. 643, overruling *Re Biss* [1956] 2 W.L.R. 94. Note also the operation of the doctrine of marshalling in the event of a chargee resorting to the wrong assets, para. 16.39 *supra* and see *Re Bobbett's Estate* [1904] 1 I.R. 461; *Buckley* v. *Buckley* (1887) 19 L.R.Ir. 544.

[86] 1965 Act, s. 47 (2) (*a*); 1955 Act, s. 31 (2) (*a*). Cf. *Buckley* v. *Buckley* (1887) 19 L.R.Ir. 544; *Thompson* v. *Bell* [1903] 1 I.R. 489.

[87] 1965 Act, s. 47 (2) (*b*); 1955 Act, s. 31 (2) (*b*).

[88] Cf. *Rawson* v. *McCausland* (1874) I.R. 8 Eq. 617; *Corballis* v. *Corballis* (1883) L.R.Ir. 309.

deceased's assets amongst those entitled under his will, or on his intestacy, after payment and discharge of all debts and liabilities of the deceased. The following points may be noted about the execution of this duty.

(i) Notice to Creditors

16.42. The personal representatives should not distribute the assets until notices have been given to creditors and others to send in their claims against the estate and the time allowed to them for the sending in of the claims has expired.[89]

The representatives are not liable to any person for the assets or any part of them so distributed, unless at the time of distribution they had notice of that person's claim.[90] In such a situation, the creditor or other claimant may, however, be able to invoke his right to follow the assets into the hands of any person who may have received them.[91]

(ii) Executor's Year

16.43. For centuries the general rule had been that the personal representatives had a period of one year from the testator's death in which to complete the administration of the estate, so that they could not be sued by a beneficiary for non-distribution before expiration of the "executor's year."[92] This remains the general position,[93] except that proceedings may be brought now for failure to distribute provided leave of the court is granted.[94] This is also the position now in Northern Ireland in respect of actions in the county court for recovery of legacies and distributive shares,[95] a jurisdiction first conferred by the Civil Bill Courts (Ir.) Act, 1851.[96] It should, however, be noted that creditors of the deceased are still free to bring proceedings against his personal representatives before the expiration of one year from his death.[97]

Though the personal representatives have the protection of the executor's

---

[89] 1965 Act, s. 49 (1); in N.I., Law of Property Amendment Act, 1859, s. 29. *Filgate* v. *Lindsay* (1874) I.R. 8 Eq. 61. For a discussion of the required notices (usually one month's notice by advertisements in two local newspapers and *Iris Oifigiúil* or Belfast *Gazette*), see *Stuart* v. *Babington* (1891) 27 L.R.Ir 551; *Re Beatty* (1892) 29 L.R.Ir. 290.

[90] 1965 Act, s. 49 (2); in N.I., 1859 Act, s. 29.

[91] 1965 Act, s. 49 (3); in N.I., 1859 Act, s. 29. See para. 16.63, *post.*

[92] Statute of Distributions (Ir.), 1695, s. 4. *Dowzer* v. *Dowzer* (1914) 48 I.L.T.R. 236; *Re Lopdell* [1943] I.R. 50. *Cf.* bringing an administration suit, *Wallis* v. *Wallis* (1883) 9 L.R.Ir. 511; *Re McGuinness* (1918) 52 I.L.T.R. 64; but see *Ryan* v. *Tobin* (1895) 29 I.L.T. 252; *Re Smith* (1914) 48 I.L.T.R. 236. See also *O'Higgins* v. *Walsh* [1918] 1 I.R. 126.

[93] But the 1965 and 1955 Acts now put a more positive duty on the personal representatives to act with dispatch—they "shall distribute [the deceased's] estate as soon after his death as is reasonably practicable having regard to the nature of the estate, the manner in which it is required to be distributed and all other relevant circumstances." 1965 Act, s. 62 (1); 1955 Act, s. 41 (1). *Cf.* 1971 Act (N.I.), s. 2 (1), para. 16.20, *ante.*

[94] 1965 Act, s. 62 (1); 1955 Act, s. 41 (1). General legacies carry interest at 4 per cent. from the date one year from the testator's death. *Re Hall* [1951] W.N. 231. *Cf.* specific legacies (*McCoy* v. *Jacob* [1919] 1 I.R. 134), legacies charged on land (*Pearson* v. *Pearson* (1802) 1 Sch. & Lef. 10; *Purcell* v. *Purcell* (1842) 2 Dr. & War. 217) and where the testator was parent, or stood in *loco parentis*, of the legatee (*Re Ferguson* (1915) 49 I.L.T.R. 110; *Re O'Connell* [1932] I.R. 298).

[95] County Courts Act (N.I.), 1959, s. 11.

[96] S. 49, repealed in the Republic by the Succession Act, 1965 (see s. 8 and 2nd Sched.), under which, subject to limits, the circuit courts have concurrent jurisdiction with the High Court, see s. 6. On s. 49 of the 1851 Act, see *Molyneux* v. *Scott* (1852) 3 Ir.Ch.R. 297; *Sweeney* v. *Gallagher* (1888) 22 I.L.T.R. 82.

[97] 1965 Act, s. 62 (2); 1955 Act, s. 41 (3).

year, they are, of course, free to distribute the assets *before* the year is up, if they so choose.

(iii) Assents

16.44. The actual transfer of the assets by the personal representatives to the persons entitled under the will or on intestacy[98] is usually carried out by means of an "assent."[99] In the case of personalty, the assent to the property vesting in the persons entitled may be oral and the transfer effected by delivery or handing over the property in question.[1] In the case of land, however, the assent must be in writing to be effectual to pass any estate or interest in the land.[2] Such an assent vesting land in the beneficiaries may be made subject to a charge for payment of any money which the personal representatives are liable to pay[3] and, in such a case, the representatives cease to be liable in respect of the land, except as to acts done or contracts entered into before the assent.[4] Generally speaking,[5] some or one only of several joint personal representatives cannot execute an effective assent, without the leave of the court.[6]

There are also special provisions in both parts of Ireland relating to assents of registered and unregistered land.

(a) *Registered Land*

16.45. On death of the registered owner of land in either part of Ireland, his personal representatives alone are to be recognised by the Registrar as having any right to deal with the registered land.[7] Production of an assent or transfer in the prescribed form from them authorises the Registrar to register the person named in the assent or transfer as owner.[8]

(b) *Unregistered Land*

16.46. An assent to the vesting of any estate or interest in unregistered land of a testator or intestate must, in both parts of Ireland—(1) be in writing; (2) be signed by the personal representatives; (3) be deemed, for the purposes of the Registry of Deeds legislation,[9] to be a conveyance of that estate or

---

[98] Including the trustees or personal representatives of such persons, 1965 Act, s. 52 (1) (*b*); 1955 Act, s. 34 (1) (*b*).

[99] 1965 Act, ss. 52–4; 1955 Act, ss. 34–6. See *Vahy* v. *Vahy* (1903) 3 N.I.J.R. 15.

[1] *Quinton* v. *Frith* (1868) I.R. 2 Eq. 494; *Hunter* v. *Hunter* (1870) I.R. 3 C.L. 40; *McKinley* v. *Kennedy* [1925] 1 I.R. 34.

[2] 1965 Act, s. 52 (5); 1955 Act, s. 34 (4). The statutory covenants implied where a person is expressed in a deed to convey as personal representative are also implied in any assent signed by a personal representative, unless the assent otherwise provides, 1965 Act, s. 52 (6); 1955 Act, s. 34 (5). As to these covenants, see Conveyancing Act, 1881, s. 7, and *Survey of the Land Law of Northern Ireland* (1971), paras. 180–1. See also *Irish Conveyancing Law* (1978), para. 19.05 *et seq.* These provisions as to assents of land do not attract stamp duty, 1965 Act, s. 52 (8); 1955 Act, s. 34 (8).

[3] 1965 Act, s. 52 (2); 1955 Act, s. 34 (2). See *Re Thompson* (1904) 4 N.I.J.R. 100.

[4] 1965 Act, s. 52 (3); 1955 Act, s. 34 (2).

[5] *Cf.* the case of proving executors, 1965 Act, s. 20; 1955 Act, s. 34 (6) (*a*) and (*b*).

[6] 1965 Act, s. 52 (7); 1955 Act, s. 34 (6).

[7] Registration of Title Act, 1964, s. 61 (2) (R.I.); Land Registration Act (N.I.), 1970, Sched. 4 para. 1. See *Shiels* v. *Flynn* [1975] I.R. 296 (see *A Casebook on Irish Land Law* (1984), p. 540).

[8] 1964 Act, s. 61 (3) (as substituted by s. 54 (2) of the Succession Act, 1965); 1970 Act, Sched. 4, para. 4.

[9] *I.e.*, Registration of Deeds Act (Ir.), 1707; Registration of Deeds Act (N.I.), 1970. See ch. 22, *post.*

interest from the personal representatives to the person entitled; (4) operate, subject to the provisions of the Registry of Deeds legislation with respect to priorities,[10] to vest that estate or interest in the person entitled subject to such charges and incumbrances, if any, as may be specified in the assent and as may otherwise affect that interest; (5) subject to the said provisions, be deemed (unless a contrary intention appears therein), for all purposes necessary to establish the title of the person entitled to intervening rents and profits, to relate back to the date of the death of the deceased, but this is not to enable any person to establish a title inconsistent with the will of the deceased.[11] Any beneficiary in whose favour an assent or conveyance has been made may call upon the personal representatives to register, at the beneficiary's own expense, the assent or conveyance in the Registry of Deeds.[12] It is also provided in the Republic that an assent is, in favour of a purchaser, *conclusive*[13] evidence that the beneficiary is the person entitled to have the estate or interest vested in him, but it is not to prejudice otherwise the claim of any person originally entitled to it or to any mortgage or incumbrance thereon.[14]

(c) *Court Order*

16.47. If, after one year from the deceased's death, the personal representatives have, on request, failed to execute an assent or transfer of land to the person entitled, the latter may apply to the court for an appropriate order.[15] The court may, if it thinks fit and after notice to the personal representatives, order the transfer to be made and, in default of compliance with such an order within the time specified, may make an order vesting the land in the person entitled as fully and effectively as a transfer by the personal representatives.[16] Apart from this, the court has an inherent jurisdiction to compel the personal representatives to make an assent or transfer where they unreasonably withhold an assent or refuse to execute a transfer.[17] Finally, the court has power to require the personal representatives to exhibit on oath in court a "true and perfect" inventory and account of the deceased's estate.[18]

---

[10] Chs. 3 and 13, *ante.*

[11] 1965 Act, s. 53 (1); 1955 Act, s. 35 (1).

[12] 1965 Act, s. 53 (2); 1955 Act, s. 35 (2). See *Stinson* v. *Crozier* [1936] N.I. 203.

[13] In Northern Ireland it is only "sufficient" evidence (see 1955 Act, s. 35 (3)) and, in *Re Duce and Boots Cash Chemists (Southern), Ltd.'s Contract* [1937] Ch. 642, Bennett J. held that the similar provision in s. 36 (7) of the English Administration of Estates Act, 1925, did *not* mean "conclusive" evidence, *i.e.*, it is sufficient only until, on a proper investigation of title by the purchaser, facts indicating the contrary come to light. The English provision has obvious relevance in the context of the "curtain" principle of the 1925 legislation, and the policy of keeping trusts off the title, hence the difficulty in transporting it to a jurisdiction lacking similar legislation. See Leitch, *Handbook on Administration of Estates Act (N.I.), 1955* (1956), pp. 103–4.

[14] 1965 Act, 53 (3). This seems to remove the difficulties raised by *Re Duce and Boots Cash Chemists (Southern), Ltd.'s Contract*, fn. 13, *supra*, and relieves a purchaser from the beneficiary from investigating the administration of the deceased's estate by the personal representative (payments of debts, etc.), and, apparently, even the will and its probate, *i.e.*, he need inspect the grant of representation and the vesting assent or transfer only.

[15] 1965 Act, s. 52 (4); 1955 Act, s. 34 (3).

[16] *Ibid.* See *Re Patrick Lavin* [1931] L.R.Ir. 130.

[17] *Martin* v. *Wilson* [1913] 1 I.R. 470. See also *Coppinger* v. *Sheckleton* (1885) 15 L.R.Ir. 461.

[18] 1965 Act, s. 64; in N.I., 1971 Act, s. 2 (1) (*b*), replacing Administration of Estates Acts, 1357 (31 Edw. 3, Stat. 1, c. 11); Probate Act (Ir.), 1537 (28 Hen. 8, c. 18 (Ir.)); Statute of Distributions (Ir.), 1695, s. 1 (7 Will. 3, c. 6 (Ir.)); Probate and Legacy Duties (Ir.) Act, 1814, s. 4.

2. *Powers*

The following are the main statutory powers conferred upon personal representatives with respect to distribution of the deceased's assets.

(i) Sale

16.48. The personal representatives may sell the whole or any part of the deceased's estate not only in order to pay the debts, but also, whether or not there are debts, to facilitate distribution amongst the persons beneficially entitled.[19] Before selling for the purposes of distribution they must, so far as practicable, give effect to the wishes of the beneficiaries of the property to be sold, provided they are of full age, or, if there is a dispute, the majority according to the value of their combined interests.[20] However, a purchaser is not to be concerned to see if the personal representatives have so complied with the beneficiaries' wishes[21] nor is it necessary for the beneficiaries to concur in any sale.[22] It would seem that, while an executor can enter into a contract of sale before probate, he cannot make title until probate is granted.[23]

16.49. Generally speaking all the personal representatives must join together in disposing of land or otherwise dealing with the deceased's estate,[24] unless the leave of court is granted to some or one of them to act.[25] However, in the case of a grant of probate to one or more of executors named in the will, the proving executors may dispose of land without leave of the court.[26] If there are two executors and one renounces his office, the acting executor may sell on his own.[27] Furthermore, the court has a discretion to authorise a sale by one only of the proving executors.[28]

16.50. It is provided that a *bona fide* purchaser for value[29] from the personal representatives is entitled to hold the property freed and discharged from any debts or liabilities of the deceased (except those charged otherwise than by his will), and from all claims of those entitled to a share in the estate, and such a purchaser is not concerned to see to the application of the

---

[19] 1965 Act, s. 50 (1); 1955 Act, s. 32 (1). See *Re Thompson and McWilliam's Contract* [1896] 1 I.R. 362. See also *Crawford* v. *Carlin* (1904) 4 N.I.J.R. 150. *Cf.* where the personal representative have already executed an assent, *Re Byrne and Great Northern Rly. Co.'s Contract* (1901) 35 I.L.T.R. 214. A testator may, of course, confer an express or implied power of sale or even impose a duty to convert the property, see *Re Waldron* [1956] I.R. 315. Also *Re Robinson* [1912] 1 I.R. 410; *Carlisle* v. *Cooke* [1905] 1 I.R. 269; *Keeffe* v. *Kirby* (1857) 6 I.C.L.R. 591.

[20] *Ibid.*

[21] 1965 Act, s. 50 (1) (*a*); 1955 Act, s. 32 (1) (*a*).

[22] 1965 Act, s. 50 (1) (*b*); 1955 Act, s. 32 (1) (*b*).

[23] *Lynch* v. *Harper* (1911) 43 I.L.T.R. 95. *A fortiori* an administrator prior to a grant of letters of administration, see para. 16.21, *ante*.

[24] See further, para. 16.56, *post*.

[25] 1965 Act, s. 50 (2); 1955 Act, s. 32 (2). See *Woods* v. *Magee* (1976) 27 N.I.L.Q. 427.

[26] 1965 Act, s. 20; 1955 Act, s. 32 (2). *Cf. Ringland* v. *Ringland* (1901) 1 N.I.J.R. 184.

[27] *McKenna* v. *Eager* (1875) I.R. 9 C.L. 79; *Re Fisher and Haslett* (1882) 13 L.R.Ir. 546.

[28] *Re Curry* (1912) 44 I.L.T.R. 66.

[29] A sale will, of course, be set aside in cases of fraud, *e.g.*, where the purchaser connives with the personal representatives to obtain the estate at a nominal price or a gross undervalue, *Boothman* v. *Brown* (1901) 1 N.I.J.R. 41.

purchase money.[30] The debts and liabilities, and the beneficiaries' claims, are, in effect, overreached and attach to the purchase money.[31] A conveyance by the personal representatives also remains valid despite a subsequent revocation or variation of the grant of probate or letters of administration.[32] There are several authorities in Ireland concerning the situation where personal representatives purport to sell in the course of administration of the estate many years after the death of the deceased and the suspicion arises that, in fact, the debts have long since been paid and that this is not the reason for the sale.[33] Indeed, there is some suggestion in the Irish cases that a presumption arises after 20 years from the death of the deceased that the debts have been paid and that any sale is not made as part of the administration of the estate.[34]

16.51. Section 51 of the Succession Act, 1965, has altered this for the Republic of Ireland and a purchaser from an executor or adminstrator of a deceased person who died more than 20 years before the sale is now protected. A *bona fide* purchaser for value of the deceased's estate from a beneficiary in whom it has been vested by the personal representatives is entitled, as he is also in Northern Ireland, to hold it freed and discharged from other beneficiaries' claims and those of the deceased's creditors, unless the purchaser has actual or constructive notice of the claims.[35]

(ii) Appropriation

16.52. Personal representatives now have very wide statutory powers to appropriate any part of the deceased's estate, in its actual condition or as invested, in or towards satisfaction of any legacy or any other interest or share in the deceased's property, whether settled or not, according to the respective rights of the persons interested in the estate.[36] In making such an appropriation,[37] the personal representatives must not affect prejudicially any specific devise or bequest[38] and must serve notices on parties entitled to a

---

[30] 1965 Act, s. 51 (1); 1955 Act, s. 33 (1). *Re Thompson and McWilliam's Contract* [1896] 1 I.R. 362. This rule does *not* apply to registered land, 1965 Act, s. 51 (2) (*a*); *cf.* 1955 Act, s. 33 (3). A purchaser from the personal representatives is also entitled to assume that the personal representatives are acting correctly and within their powers, 1965 Act, s. 61 (this section applies whether the deceased died before or after 1st Jan. 1967); in N.I., Law of Property Amendment Act, 1859, s. 17; see also 1955 Act, s. 40 (3).

[31] *Cf.* a sale of settled land, ch. 8, *ante*.

[32] 1965 Act, s. 25. See also *McParland* v. *Conlon* [1930] N.I. 138; *cf. Dooley* v. *Dooley* [1927] I.R. 190. *Cf.* a sale after a judgement for administration but before it is registered as a *lis pendens, Re Hoban* [1896] 1 I.R. 401.

[33] *Re Molyneux and White* (1885) 15 L.R.Ir. 383; *Re Anderson* (1897) 31 I.L.T.R. 175; *Re Higgins and Stevenson's Contract* [1906] 1 I.R. 656; *Re Fitzwilliam* (1907) 41 I.L.T.R. 143; *McDonnell* v. *Branigan* (1922) 56 I.L.T.R. 143.

[34] See, *e.g.*, discussion by Chatterton V.-C. in *Re Ryan and Cavanagh's Contract* (1886) 17 L.R.Ir. 42. See also *Re Anderson* (1897) 31 I.L.T.R. 175. And *Shiels* v. *Flynn* [1975] I.R. 296 (see *A Casebook on Irish Land Law* (1984), p. 540); *Crowley* v. *Flynn* [1983] I.L.R.M. 538 (see *ibid.*, p. 530).

[35] *Cf.* 1965 Act, s. 51 (2) (*b*); 1955 Act, s. 33 (2). See *Shiels* v. *Flynn, op. cit.* and *Crowley* v. *Flynn, op. cit.*

[36] 1965 Act, s. 55; 1955 Act, s. 37. See *Re Mill* [1923] 1 I.R. 78. As regards fixing values, and employment of valuers, see 1965 Act, s. 55 (10); 1955 Act, s. 37 (3). Also *Re Esmonde* [1946] I.R. 551; *Re Richardson* [1915] 1 I.R. 39.

[37] S. 37 (1) of the 1955 Act expressly limits appropriations to those which may seem "just and reasonable" to the personal representatives. No such words appear in s. 55 (1) of the 1965 Act.

[38] 1965 Act, s. 55 (2) (which excepts an appropriation of the deceased's dwelling and household chattels for the surviving spouse, see *infra*); 1955 Act, s. 37 (1) (*a*) (i).

share in the estate[39] and obtain consents from persons absolutely entitled in possession to the property in question[40] or, in the case of settlements, trustees or the persons entitled for the time being to the income.[41] Property duly appropriated in this way is to be treated as an authorised investment and may be retained or dealt with accordingly,[42] thus excluding the need for apportionments as between tenant for life and remainderman.[43] Subject to any court order, such an appropriation binds all persons interested in the property whose consent is not required,[44] but who are entitled to notice.[45] If, after property has been appropriated to a person,[46] that person disposes of it, the appropriation is to be deemed to have been properly made in favour of a purchaser.[47] The extent of the court's power to interfere with the exercise of the personal representatives' power of appropriation under section 55 of the Republic's Succession Act, 1965, was considered by the Supreme Court in *H. v. O.*[47a] Henchy J. stated:

"The section is silent as to how the court is to exercise its jurisdiction, which is essentially supervisory and prohibitive. So it must be assumed, having regard to the tenor, the scope and purpose of the section, that the court should prohibit an intended appropriation only (a) when the conditions in the section have not been complied with; or (b) when, notwithstanding such compliance, it would not be just or equitable to allow the appropriation to take place, having regard to the rights of all persons who are or will become entitled to an interest in the estate; or (c) when apart from the section, the appropriation would not be legally permissible. Since the personal representatives hold the estate under s. 10 sub-s. 3, as trustees for the persons by law entitled thereto, the exercise of the statutory discretion to appropriate must be viewed as an incident of the trusteeship, so that it is the court's duty to prohibit the appropriation if it is calculated to operate unjustly or inequitably by unduly benefiting one beneficiary at the expense of another. But otherwise, where the conditions of the sections have been observed and the personal representatives have made a bona fide decision to appropriate, the exercise of their discretion to appropriate should not be intereferd with unless for some reason unrelated to the terms of the

---

[39] 1965 Act, s. 55 (3) (again excepting an appropriation for the surviving spouse); 1955 Act, s. 37 (1) (a) (ii). Any one of these parties then has six weeks in which to apply to the court to prohibit the appropriation.
[40] 1965 Act, s. 55 (4) (a); 1955 Act, s. 37 (1) (b) (i).
[41] 1965 Act, s. 55 (4) (b); 1955 Act, s. 37 (1) (b) (ii). See also as regards consents, 1965 Act, s. 55 (5)–(8) and 1955 Act, s. 37 (1) (b)–(e), dealing with the cases of infants, persons of unsound mind, or coming into existence after appropriation or who cannot be found or ascertained, and where, independently of the personal representatives, there is no trustee of a settled share. The personal representatives do have to have regard to the rights of such persons, even if their consent is not required, 1965 Act, s. 55 (12); 1955 Act, s. 37 (5).
[42] 1965 Act, s. 55 (9); 1955 Act, s. 37 (2).
[43] Ch. 10, *ante*.
[44] 1965 Act, s. 55 (11); 1955 Act, s. 37 (4).
[45] Para. 16.42, *ante* and fn. 41, *supra*.
[46] Note as regards stamp duty, 1965 Act, s. 55 (17); 1955 Act, s. 37 (10). *Cf. Dawson v. I.R.C.* [1905] 1 I.R. 69.
[47] 1965 Act, s. 55 (14); 1955 Act, s. 37 (7).
[47a] [1978] I.R. 194 (see *A Casebook on Irish Land Law* (1984), p. 529).

section the appropriation would be legally unacceptable, e.g., if it would amount to a sub-division prohibited by law."[47b]

In the Republic of Ireland, where the deceased's estate includes a dwelling[48] in which, at the deceased's death, the surviving spouse was ordinarily resident, the surviving spouse may require the personal representatives in writing to appropriate the dwelling, under the above provision, in or towards satisfaction of any share of the surviving spouse.[49] We mentioned this matter in an earlier chapter.[50]

(iii) Infant's Property

16.53.   To facilitate distribution of an infant's share in the deceased's estate,[51] it is now provided in both parts of Ireland that the personal representatives may, where there are no trustees of the infant's share able and willing to act, appoint a trust corporation[52] or any two or more persons (including any of the personal representatives or a trust corporation) to be trustees of the infant's share and may vest that share in them.[53] Such appointment of trustees and vesting of the infant's property in them operates to discharge the personal representatives from all further liability in respect of that property.[54] The trustees may retain the property in its existing state or re-invest it in trustee securities.[55]

16.54.   Where an infant becomes entitled to any estate or interest in land on intestacy and so there is no instrument under which it arises or is acquired, the estate or interest is deemed to be the subject of a settlement for the purposes of the Settled Land Acts, 1882–90, and the persons appointed trustees under the above provisions are the trustees of the settlement.[56]

16.55.   Trustees so appointed are to be deemed trustees for the purposes of sections 42 and 43 of the Conveyancing Act, 1881, as amended in Northern Ireland by the Trustee Act (N.I.), 1958,[57] which confer wide powers of management on trustees during the infant's minority, including powers to advance capital and to apply income for maintenance, education or benefit.[58] Without prejudice to those powers, the trustees may pay or apply the capital

---

[47b]   *Ibid.*, pp. 206–7.

[48]   Note the exclusion of certain dwellings in s. 56 (6) of the 1965 Act, *e.g.*, a hotel or guest house or dwelling held with agricultural land also part of the estate, unless the court is satisfied that there is unlikely to be a diminution in the value of the assets other than the dwelling, etc. "Dwelling" is defined in s. 56 (14). *Cf.* the definition in the Rent Restrictions Act, 1960, s. 2 (1).

[49]   1965 Act, s. 56 (1). See further on the surviving spouse's legal right, para. 14.56, *ante.*

[50]   Para. 14.60, *ante.*

[51]   As to the previous position, see *McCreight* v. *McCreight* (1849) 13 Ir.Eq.R. 314 (receipt of testamentary guardian for infant's legacy good discharge under Tenures Abolition Act (Ir.), 1662); *Crawford* v. *Carlin* (1904) 4 N.I.J.R. 150 (payment into court good discharge).

[52]   Under s. 38 (1) of the 1955 Act (N.I.), a trust corporation may be only one of the trustees appointed. *Cf.* Trustee Act (N.I.), 1958, s. 14.

[53]   1965 Act, s. 57 (1); 1955 Act, s. 38 (1).

[54]   1965 Act, s. 57 (2); 1955 Act, s. 38 (2).

[55]   1965 Act, s. 58 (1); 1955 Act, s. 38 (2). As to trustee securities, see ch. 10, *ante.*

[56]   See further, ch. 8, *ante.*

[57]   Ss. 69 and 70 (2). See also s. 32 of the 1958 Act. *Re Lynch's Trusts* [1931] I.R. 517; *Re O'Connell* [1932] I.R. 298.

[58]   See ch. 10, *ante.* As to express powers, see *K'Eogh* v. *K'Eogh* [1911] 1 I.R. 396.

of any infant's share for his advancement or benefit in such manner as the trustees, in their absolute discretion, think fit.[59] In particular, the trustees may carry on any business in which the infant is entitled to a share.[60]

(iv) Dealing with Estate

16.56. Personal representatives in both parts of Ireland are given several statutory powers to deal with the deceased's estate.[61] All these powers are subject to the terms of the will of the testator, if there is one, and he is free to enlarge or restrict the statutory powers.[62]

(a) Leases

16.57. At common law, the view was taken that the primary function of the personal representatives was to administer the estate and making leases or sub-leases was not normally part of that exercise, unless, of course, the deceased has contracted to make the lease before his death.[63] Thus, while the Irish courts recognised that the representatives could make leases, they insisted that any lessee or sub-lessee had to prove that his lease was made in the usual administration of the estate.[64] It is now provided that the personal representatives may make such leases of the deceased's land[65] as may be reasonably necessary for the administration of the estate.[66] Such leases are often made in respect of a business, where it is necessary to keep it going for a period to enable stock to be disposed of or, in the case of manufacturing, orders to be completed.[67] Generally, however, the courts still do not approve of personal representatives carrying on a business for any lengthy period, unless the deceased clearly authorised this.[68]

16.58. The personal representatives may also make leases for such term and on such conditions as they think proper, with the consent of the beneficiaries or the approval of the court.[69] Where the land is already subject

---

[59] 1965 Act, s. 58 (5) (replacing Guardianship of Infants Act, 1964, s. 11); Trustee Act (N.I.), 1958, s. 33 (extending s. 38 (5) of the 1955 Act). See *Re Meade* [1971] I.R. 327.

[60] 1965 Act, s. 58 (5). *Cf.* personal representatives, *Re Hodges* [1899] 1 I.R. 480. These powers of the trustee may also be exercised in the Republic by the surviving spouse as trustee of any property of an infant appropriated under s. 56 of the 1965 Act, see s. 58 (6).

[61] *Cf.* trustees, ch. 10, *ante* and the tenant for life of settled land, ch. 8, *ante*.

[62] 1965 Act, s. 60 (9); 1955 Act, s. 40 (10).

[63] The personal representatives are generally under a duty to complete contracts enforceable against the testator or intestate at his death as part of the administration of the estate, see 1965 Act, s. 60 (4); 1955 Act, s. 40 (6). *Re O'Leary* [1961] Ir.Jur.Rep. 45.

[64] *Keating* v. *Keating* (1835) Ll. & G. *temp.* Sug. 113; *Hackett* v. *Macnamara* (1836) Ll. & G. *temp.* Plunk. 203. See also *Drohan* v. *Drohan* (1809) 1 Ba. & B. 185.

[65] If the deceased held leasehold property, the personal representatives may take possession, see *Minford* v. *Carse* [1912] 2 I.R. 245.

[66] 1965 Act, s. 60 (1) (*a*); 1955 Act, s. 40 (1) (*a*). Such leases are not caught by the restrictions on recovery of possession contained in rent restriction legislation (ch. 18, *post*) or, in N.I., business tenancies legislation (*ibid*), 1965 Act, s. 60 (2); 1955 Act, s. 40 (2).

[67] *Perry* v. *Perry* (1869) I.R. 3 Eq. 452; *Re Hodges* [1899] 1 I.R. 480; *I.R.C.* v. *Walsh* [1951] N.I. 88. The testator may, of course, direct his executors to keep the business going, in which case the executors are entitled to an indemnity as against creditors of the business, see *Hall* v. *Fennell* (1875) I.R. 9 Eq. 615; *Gallagher* v. *Ferris* (1882) 7 L.R.Ir. 489; *De Malahide* v. *Moran* (1883) 8 L.R.Ir. 307; *Morris* v. *Latchford* (1889) 23 L.R.Ir. 333; *McAloon* v. *McAloon* [1900] 1 I.R. 367; *Moore* v. *McGlynn* [1904] 1 I.R. 344 (see *A Casebook on Equity and Trusts in Ireland* (1985), p. 374).

[68] *National Bank Ltd.* v. *Hamrock* (1928) 62 I.L.T.R. 165. See also *Re Hickey* (1891) 27 L.R.Ir. 65; *Devitt* v. *Kearney* (1885) 13 L.R.Ir. 45. *Gallagher* v. *Ferris* (1882) 7 L.R.Ir. 489; *Boylan* v. *Fay* (1882) 8 L.R.Ir. 374.

[69] 1965 Act, s. 60 (1) (*b*); 1955 Act, s. 40 (1) (*b*).

to a fee farm grant or lease, which would frequently be the case in the major towns and cities of both parts of Ireland,[70] the personal representatives may make a sub-grant or sub-lease where this would amount in substance to a sale of the property and they have satisfied themselves that it is the most appropriate method of disposing of the land in the course of administration of the estate.[71] Sale by way of sub-grant or sub-lease, followed by sale of the profit rents reserved in each case, is the standard method of disposal of much city land in Ireland, where whole streets or rows of houses may be held ultimately under one single head-grant.[72]

(b) Mortgages and Charges

16.59. The personal representatives may from time to time raise money by way of mortgage or charge for payment of expenses, debts, liabilities and, in the Republic of Ireland, any legal right of the surviving spouse.[73] They may also raise money for the erection, repair, improvement or completion of buildings, or the improvement of lands forming part of the deceased's estate, *provided* they obtain the approval of all the beneficiaries being *sui juris* or the court.[74]

(c) Settled Land

16.60. Where land is settled by will and there are no trustees of the settlement,[75] the personal representatives proving the will are for all purposes to be deemed to be the trustees of the settlement until others are appointed.[76] If there is only one personal representative, he is not deemed a trustee until at least one other is appointed.[77]

(d) Distress

16.61. In the Republic of Ireland, personal representatives may distrain for arrears of rent due to the deceased.[78] They may also distrain for arrears of a rentcharge.[79] In Northern Ireland, the right of distress was abolished by the Judgments (Enforcement) Act, 1969,[80] and the personal representatives must proceed through the Enforcement of Judgments Office.[81]

---

[70] Ch. 4, *ante*.

[71] 1965 Act, s. 60 (1) (c). Cf. *Alexander v. Clarke* [1920] 1 I.R. 47; *Re Braithwaite's Settled Estate* [1922] 1 I.R. 71; *Sims-Clarke v. Ilet Ltd.* [1953] I.R. 39; *Re Murphy* [1957] N.I. 156 (see *A Casebook on Equity and Trusts in Ireland* (1985), p. 546). The purchaser or lessee from the personal representatives is entitled to assume that their powers in this regard have been validly exercised, so that such a person is not obliged to see to the application of any money or rent paid by him, 1965 Act, s. 61; 1955 Act, s. 40 (3).

[72] Paras. 4.179–81, *ante*.

[73] 1965 Act, s. 60 (3); 1955 Act, s. 40 (4). See *Clarke v. Connor* (1887) 31 I.L.T. 429; *Re O'Donnell* [1905] 1 I.R. 406. Also *Douglas v. Douglas* (1883) 9 L.R.Ir. 548; *Re Queste's Estate* (1886) 17 L.R.Ir. 461; *Connolly v. Munster Bank* (1888) 19 L.R.Ir. 119; *Re Roulston's Trusts* (1889) 21 L.R.Ir. 503; *Telvin v. Gilsenan* [1902] 1 I.R. 514.

[74] *Ibid*. Cf. settled land, ch. 8, *ante*. *Re Smyth* [1965] I.R. 595.

[75] Ch. 8, *ante*.

[76] 1965 Act, s. 50 (3); 1955 Act, s. 40 (5). Note also the provision where an infant becomes entitled to land on an intestacy, para. 16.54, *supra*.

[77] *Ibid*.

[78] 1965 Act, s. 60 (5) and (6). See further on distress for rent, ch. 17, *post*.

[79] 1965 Act, s. 60 (7). See further on rentcharges, ch. 6, *ante*.

[80] S. 122. The 1969 Act thus repealed s. 40 (7) and (8) of the Administration of Estates Act (N.I.), 1955.

[81] See now the consolidating Judgments Enforcement (N.I.) Order, 1981, for the various enforcement orders which can be made by the Office.

(e) *Settlement of Claims*

16.62. Personal representatives are given a variety of powers to enable them to settle claims and disputes and perform similar functions without being personally responsible for any loss, provided they acted in good faith.[82] These powers include such things as: payment or allowance of any debt or claim on any evidence they may reasonably deem sufficient[83]; acceptance of any composition or security for debts or property claimed[84]; compromise, compounding or settlement of any debts, amounts, disputes and claims relating to the estate[85]; and settlement on reasonable terms of remuneration for any trust corporation appointed to act as trustee for an infant[86] in case of intestacy.[87]

3. *Following Property*

16.63. Even though the personal representatives have distributed the deceased's property to the persons entitled, creditors have a right, recognised by statute, to follow the property into the beneficiaries' hands.[88] It is provided that, where the personal representatives have conveyed property to any person other than a purchaser for value taking it in good faith, the property, so long as it remains vested in that person, or any person, other than a *bona fide* purchaser, claiming under him, remains liable to answer the debts of the deceased and any share in the estate to which it was liable when vested in the personal representatives.[89] It is also provided that, where the transferee from the personal representatives, or volunteer claiming under them, sells or mortgages the property, the seller or mortgagor remains personally liable for such debts or share in the estate to the extent to which the property was liable when vested in the personal representatives.[90]

---

[82] 1965 Act, s. 60 (8); 1955 Act, s. 40 (9).

[83] 1965 Act, s. 60 (8) (*b*); 1955 Act, s. 40 (9) (*b*).

[84] 1965 Act, s. 60 (8) (*c*); 1955 Act, s. 40 (9) (*c*).

[85] 1965 Act, s. 60 (8) (*e*); 1955 Act, s. 40 (9) (*e*). It appears that rights under a claim adverse to the estate cannot be determined on an originating summons, *Re McQuillan* [1939] N.I. 164. See also *Macredy* v. *Brown* [1906] 2 I.R. 437; *Re Atkinson* (1908) 42 I.L.T.R. 226; *Ormsby* v. *Good* [1895] 1 I.R. 103; *McKenna* v. *McKenna* [1901] 1 I.R. 484; *Graham* v. *McCashin* [1901] 1 I.R. 404; *Smithwick* v. *Hayden* (1889) 23 L.R.Ir. 475.

[86] See para. 16.53, *supra*.

[87] 1965 Act, s. 60 (8) (*f*); 1955 Act, s. 40 (9) (*f*). *Cf.* inherent jurisdiction of court to award remuneration to a solicitor acting as administrator, *Re Bowden* [1957] Ir.Jur.Rep. 61. See also *Re Naish* (1905) 39 I.L.T.R. 249.

[88] *Cf.* tracing trust property, ch. 10, *ante*.

[89] 1965 act, s. 59 (1); 1955 Act, s. 39. See *National Assurance Co.* v. *Scott* [1909] 1 I.R. 325. See further on tracing orders with respect to assets, *Duane* v. *Lee* (1884) 14 L.R.Ir. 56; *Leahy* v. *De Moleyns* [1896] 1 I.R. 206; *Welwood* v. *Grady* [1904] 1 I.R. 388. Note the protection personal representatives have in distribution after advertisements, etc., para. 16.42, *ante*.

[90] 1965 Act, s. 59 (2); 1955 Act, s. 39. See also *Hamill* v. *Murphy* (1884) 12 L.R.Ir. 400; *Duane* v. *Lee* (1884) 14 L.R.Ir. 56.

PART VII

LANDLORD AND TENANT

CHAPTER 17

LANDLORD AND TENANT

I. INTRODUCTION

17.001. The law of landlord and tenant is one of the most important areas of land law[1] and, in Ireland, it has played a central role in our history.[2] It must be emphasised from the outset that in this chapter we are concerned with the modern relationship of landlord and tenant, which must be distinguished from the feudal relationship of lord and tenant, though it has many similarities to that ancient form of tenure. We discussed the distinction between these two forms of tenure earlier in the book.[3]

17.002. Perhaps the most striking feature of landlord and tenant law in Ireland, as in other countries, has been the extent to which the legislation has sought to control the agreements made between landlords and tenants. The result has been that in the case of many, if not most, agreements entered into in Ireland today, the relationship of the landlord and tenant is largely governed by statute rather than by the terms of the contract entered into by the parties. Thus the law relating to tenancies of *agricultural* property has been revolutionised by the Land Law and Land Purchase Acts of the last hundred years or so.[4] Certain urban *residential* tenancies are subject to rent restriction legislation which was introduced during the First World War and now exists as a complex form of statutory regulation in both parts of Ireland.[5] In the Republic of Ireland, certain tenants of land in urban areas have statutory rights to new leases of ground originally let for building purposes, to new tenancies of tenements and reversionary leases and, in both parts of Ireland, certain urban lessees have the right to acquire the fee simple of land occupied by them.[6] Urban tenants of *business* properties also have statutory

---

[1] For a modern treatment of the subject, see Deale, *Law of Landlord and Tenant in the Republic of Ireland* (1968). See also the same author's *Landlord and Tenant Acts, 1931 and 1943* (1953), which, however, deals with legislation applicable in the Republic only. Earlier treatises, which are still helpful, are Cherry, *Irish Land Law and Land Purchase Acts, 1860–1901* (3rd ed., 1903; Supp. 1910); De Moleyns, *Landowner's and Agent's Practical Guide* (8th ed., 1899); Edge, *Forms of Leases and Other Forms Relating to Land in Ireland* (2nd ed., 1884); Ferguson and Vance, *Tenure and Improvement of Land in Ireland* (1851); Furlong, *Law of Landlord and Tenant as Administered in Ireland* (2nd ed., 1869). Note also the review of the law in the *Survey of the Land Law of Northern Ireland* (1971), ch. 11.

[2] See, generally, ch. 1, *ante*.

[3] Ch. 2, *ante*.

[4] Chs. 1, *ante*, and 18, *post*.

[5] Ch. 18, *post*.

[6] *Ibid*.

rights, though there is special legislation on this subject in Northern Ireland.[7]

17.003. One final point may be noted about Irish landlord and tenant law. There are several areas, as we shall see, where duplicate statutory provisions, which are not, however, identical, exist. What usually has happened is that provisions passed at Westminster primarily intended for England have been made applicable also to Ireland, probably without realisation that separate provisions applicable to Ireland only were already in force. The classic example of this phenomenon is the fact that the parts of the Conveyancing Acts, 1881-1911, relating to landlord and tenant law in some places cover ground already dealt with by the Landlord and Tenant Law Amendment Act, Ireland, 1860.

II. NATURE OF THE RELATIONSHIP

17.004. In an earlier chapter, we saw that the feudal system for tenure introduced into Ireland by the Normans did not recognise as part of land law the modern relationship of landlord and tenant.[8] Grants of land for a period of years were regarded as creating personal contracts only, even though some of the characteristics of feudal tenure were present, *e.g.*, service, in the form of rent, was due to the grantor. The grantee had no estate in the land and the grantor had no right to escheat; later, even when an estate was recognised, on death of the grantee intestate his leasehold interest in the land was regarded as personalty only.[9] The result was that in the early days of the common law, a tenant who had been wrongfully ejected could not bring an action for recovery of the land.

17.005. Gradually, however, a term of years came to be regarded as an estate in land, known as a chattel real estate to distinguish it from real estates such as the fee simple or life estate.[10] At common law the concept of tenure was applied to grants of terms of years by analogy with feudal tenure, so that the tenant held under the landlord through a grant made in return for service, usually payment of rent.[11] Thus it was a condition at common law that the landlord should retain a reversion in the land granted to his tenant and this was reiterated by the House of Lords in an appeal from Ireland.[12] This had obvious inconvenience for "middlemen" in Ireland, *i.e.*, agents of absentee landlords who often granted their entire interests to tenants and who might then find themselves unable to invoke landlord remedies, such as the right of distress.[13] The common law remains the basis of the relationship of landlord

[7] *Ibid.*
[8] Ch. 2, *ante.*
[9] Ch. 4, *ante.*
[10] See the discussion in Megarry and Wade, *Law of Real Property* (5th ed., 1984), App. 1.
[11] Thus the rent is a rent service and not a rentcharge, para. 6.131, *ante.*
[12] *Pluck* v. *Digges* (1832) 5 Bligh (N.S.) 31, reversing the Irish Court of Exchequer Chamber (1828) 2 Hud. & Br.1.
[13] See *Porter* v. *French* (1844) 9 Ir.L.R. 514. See also *Ireland* v. *Landy* (1888) 22 L.R.Ir. 403 at 416 (*per* Palles C.B.).

and tenant in England, but in Ireland the nature of the relationship must be considered in the light of section 3 of the Landlord and Tenant Law Amendment Act, Ireland, 1860,[14] which provides:

> "The relation of landlord and tenant shall be deemed to be founded on the express or implied contract of the parties, and not upon tenure or service, and a reversion shall not be necessary to such relation, which shall be deemed to subsist in all cases in which there shall be an agreement by one party to hold land from or under another in consideration of any rent."[15]

Much controversy has existed over the precise effect of this section ever since it became law. However, we can see now after over a hundred years that, while it no doubt had great importance, especially in establishing or confirming concepts and practices which became common in Ireland during the eighteenth and nineteenth centuries, it did not have the striking or revolutionary effect on the development of the law that might appear from a first reading of it. Indeed, to some extent there is still uncertainty as to all its consequences and this tends to give credence to the view that much of the controversy has been of academic significance only.

17.006. Some of its consequences seem to be clear. By abolishing the need for a reversion in the landlord, it opened the way for creation of the relationship of landlord and tenant in situations where this was impossible at common law, as it still is in England and other common law countries.[16] In an earlier chapter we discussed the creation of fee farm grants under the section.[17] The section also facilitated middleman grants, *i.e.*, subletting for the whole term held by the landlord himself,[18] so that unlike in the case of an assignment, which is how such a grant would be treated at common law,[19] the grantor has the usual landlord's remedies for enforcement of the tenant's obligations.[20] On the other hand, while the section extended the situations where the relationship may arise, it is doubtful if it changed the nature of the estate granted in a particular case. We have already queried the suggestion that it abolished, for example, the need for appropriate words of limitation in a fee farm grant[21] – a fee simple is still the estate granted and nothing in the Act seems to change that. Indeed, it was even held that the rent reserved in a

---

[14] Known throughout Ireland as "Deasy's Act," a reference to the Att.-Gen. for Ireland of the day, who sponsored the Act in the Westminster House of Commons. In fact Deasy himself made it clear that the Bill which he introduced was substantially the same as one drafted and introduced in the Commons in 1852 by Napier and Whiteside, then respectively Att.-Gen. and Sol.-Gen. for Ireland, see Hansard, vol. 158, col. 1346, and vol. 159, col. 260. The 1852 Bill lapsed with the fall of Lord Derby's Government, was re-adopted by the new Liberal Government, passed by the Commons, but rejected by the House of Lords in 1853.

[15] S. 3 was held not to be retrospective in *Chute* v. *Busteed* (1865) 16 I.C.L.R. 222.

[16] See the discussion in *McAreavy* v. *Hannan* (1862) 13 I.C.L.R. 71; *Gordon* v. *Phelan* (1881) 15 I.L.T.R. 70; *Twaddle* v. *Murphy* (1881) 8 L.R.Ir. 123 (see *A Casebook on Irish Land Law* (1984), p. 113); *Irish Land Commission* v. *Holmes* (1898) 32 I.L.T.R. 85 (see ibid., p. 551).

[17] Ch. 4, *ante.*

[18] See *Seymour* v. *Quirke* (1884) 14 L.R.Ir. 455.

[19] *Beardman* v. *Wilson* (1868) L.R. 4 C.P. 57.

[20] Paras. 17.061 *et seq., post.*

[21] Para. 4.095, *ante.* See also *Twaddle* v. *Murphy* (1881) 8 L.R.Ir. 123 (see *A Casebook on Irish Land Law* (1984), p.113); *Hodges* v. *Clarke* (1883) 17 I.L.T.R. 83.

lease made under the Act remains a rent service with the usual common law incidents, such as a right of distress,[22] though the express wording of section 3 seems to the contrary.[23] In other respects the normal incidents of the common law have been altered by Deasy's Act, *e.g.*, the extent to which covenants or agreements bind successors in title to the original parties.[24] It is also arguable that section 3 abolished the common law doctrine of *interesse termini*, *i.e.*, that the tenant had no *estate* in the land until he entered the property and, until he did, had a *right* to enter only. It would appear from section 3 that the relationship of landlord and tenant arises immediately upon the making of the agreement and so the tenant thereupon has his estate, which he can assign to another person, without the need for entry.

The Act applies to incorporeal hereditaments,[25] so that the relationship of landlord and tenant can be created by a grant of a minor interest in land only, *e.g.*, shooting or fishing rights.[26]

17.007. Finally, before proceeding further, it may be useful to add a note concerning the terminology employed in this chapter, since this is a frequent source of confusion. It must be emphasised that the following note must be treated as a guide for this chapter only and as to what is common usage amongst lawyers.[27] As the chapter heading indicates, the expressions "landlord" and "tenant" are wide terms referring to parties as between whom the relationship of landlord and tenant exists.[28] They include, therefore, cases where the relationship is created by a written document, a "lease," and orally. If there is a lease,[29] whether written only or also under seal (*i.e.*, a deed), the landlord and tenant may instead be referred to as the "lessor" and "lessee." Either party may transfer outright his entire interest in the property and this is called an "assignment." The transferor is usually called the "assignor" and the transferee the "assignee." The lessee or tenant may instead make a sub-grant out of his interest, in which case he may be called the sub-lessor or sub-landlord[30] and his grantee the sub-lessee or sub-tenant. The original agreement under which the sub-lessor or tenant holds can then be called the head-lease or head-tenancy and the corresponding expressions, "head-lessor or landlord" and "head-lessee or tenant" are also often used. Another word commonly used in this content is "demise," which is a technical conveyancing term which can be used as either a verb or a noun. As

---

[22] *Gordon* v. *Phelan* (1881) 15 I.L.T.R. 70.

[23] Note, however, the *statutory* right of distress conferred by s. 51 of the Act, para. 17.064, *post*.

[24] Para. 17.072, *post*.

[25] S. 1 defines "lands" as including "houses, messuages and tenements of every tenure, whether corporeal *or incorporeal*" (italics added).

[26] *Bayley* v. *Conyingham* (1863) 15 I.C.L.R. 406. See ch. 6, *ante*.

[27] Note that some of these terms may have been defined in statutes for the purposes of their provisions, see, *e.g.*, s. 1 of Deasy's Act, 1860, and s. 2 of the conveyancing Act, 1881.

[28] "Landlord" and "tenant" can, of course, be used in the narrower sense in contradistinction to "lessor" and "lessee," *i.e.*, where the relationship is created without a lease. For the most part in this chapter "landlord" and "tenant" are used in the wider sense indicated.

[29] The word "lease" is also often used to describe the estate in the land conferred on the lessee as well as the document conferring it, so that sometimes the expression "oral lease" is used. *Cf.* s. 1 of Deasy's Act, 1860.

[30] *I.e.*, he has the dual position of tenant under the original lease and landlord under the subsequent sub-lease.

a verb it means "letting" or "leasing"[31] land and, as a noun, a "tenancy" or "lease." Frequently, the land in question is referred to as the "demised premises." "Term of years" describes a particular estate that can be granted to a lessee or tenant, though other kinds of "leasehold" estate or interest may be granted.[32]

III. CREATION OF THE RELATIONSHIP

17.008. To create the relationship of landlord and tenant the parties must intend that it should come into existence between them and comply with any formalities laid down by the law. Furthermore, it is settled that in general the relationship does not exist unless the tenant is given exclusive possession of the land in question.

A. EXCLUSIVE POSSESSION

17.009. Until recently it was thought that the concept of exclusive possession was the main distinguishing feature of a tenancy as compared with, for example, a licence. It has come to be realised, however, at least in England,[33] that a licence may confer a right to occupation similar to that conferred by a tenancy and so some other test must be used to determine which type of interest has in fact been granted.[34] There are, indeed, two extremely common types of grant in Ireland which, it is settled, do not create a tenancy. These are "lettings" in conacre and agistment which, despite the usual ascription of the word "letting" to the grants, create at most licences. A conacre letting is like a form of profit à prendre[35] and confers the right to till the land, sow a crop and reap the harvest in due course, coupled with a right to enter the land in exercise of those rights.[36] Agistment is the right to graze livestock.[37] The general rule is that grants of conacre or agistment do not create the relationship of landlord and tenant[38]; indeed, the grantor is usually regarded

---

[31] Corresponding to "landlord" and "tenant" and "lessor" and "lessee," see fn. 28, *supra*.

[32] Ch. 4, *ante*.

[33] Mainly as a result of cases concerning the application of rent restriction and similar legislation, see, *e.g.*, *Marcroft Wagons Ltd.* v. *Smith* [1951] 2 K.B. 496; *Facchini* v. *Bryson* [1952] 1 T.L.R. 1386; *Murray Bull & Co.* v. *Murray* [1953] 1 Q.B. 211; *Isaac* v. *Hotel de Paris Ltd.* [1960] 1 W.L.R. 239. *Cf. Great Southern Rlys.* v. *Bergin* (1937) 71 I.L.T.R. 276; Hargreaves, "Licensed Possessors" (1953) 69 L.Q.R. 466; Sheridan, "Licences to Live in Houses" (1953) 17 Conv. 440.

[34] The courts in England usually fell back on the notion of the intention of the parties viewed as a matter of substance, *Addiscombe Garden Estates Ltd.* v. *Crabbe* [1958] 1 Q.B. 513. *Cf. Whipp* v. *Mackey* [1927] I.R. 372 at 382. See also *Trappe* v. *Halpin* (1928) 62 I.L.T.R. 15. However, recently the House of Lords has preferred the test of whether exclusive possession for a fixed or periodic term at a rent has been granted. If so, a tenancy is to be presumed and expressions of intention are irrelevant. See *Street* v. *Mountford* [1985] 2 All E.R. 289. It remains to be seen whether the Irish courts will adopt this approach.

[35] Chs. 6, *ante*, and 20, *post*.

[36] See, generally, *Dease* v. *O'Reilly* (1845) 8 Ir.L.R. 52; *Booth* v. *McManus* (1861) 12 I.C.L.R. 418; *Evans* v. *Monagher* (1872) I.R. 6 C.L. 526; *Irish Land Commission* v. *Lawlor* [1944] Ir.Jur.Rep. 55; *Scully* v. *Corboy* [1950] I.R. 140. For criticism of the system, which is still prevalent in both parts of Ireland, from the point of view of the agriculture industry, see *Survey of the Land Law of Northern Ireland* (1971), para. 287. Also ch. 20, *post*.

[37] See, generally, *Mulligan* v. *Adams* (1846) 8 Ir.L.R. 132; *Thornton* v. *Connolly* (1898) 32 I.L.T.S.J. 216; *Allington* v. *Atkinson* [1898] 1 I.R. 239; *Fletcher* v. *Hackett* (1906) 40 I.L.T.R. 37; *Re Moore's Estate* [1944] I.R. 295.

[38] *Cf. Irish Land Commission* v. *Andrews* [1941] I.R. 79. See also *Crane* v. *Naughten* [1912] 2 I.R. 318.

as retaining possession of the land, so that, where he is a lessee, such a grant would not be in breach of a covenant against subletting or otherwise parting with possession.[39]

The rule now may be stated that, if the "grantee" of the land in question does not have possession of it, he is clearly not a tenant. If he does have possession, he may be a tenant but this is not necessarily the case.[40]

B. INTENTION

17.010. The parties to the agreement in question must intend to create the relationship of landlord and tenant and not some other relationship, such as that of licensor and licensee.[41] The fact that their agreement uses the terminology appropriate for the landlord and tenant relationship ("landlord" and "tenant" and "rent"), or *vice versa*, does not necessarily determine the issue. What the parties intended must be viewed as a matter of substance rather than of form.[42]

17.011. If the intention to create the relationship of landlord and tenant is clearly established, but the lease or agreement does not accurately reflect what the parties intended, the parties may be able to obtain rectification of the lease or agreement, *e.g.*, if there has been a mutual mistake.[43]

C. FORMALITIES

17.012. Certain formalities may have to be followed by the parties if they are to create the relationship of landlord and tenant between them. In considering this question one important distinction should be borne in mind, that between a contract for the future grant of an estate or interest in land and the actual grant itself.[44] Prior to Deasy's Act this distinction was clearly established because the Statute of Frauds (Ireland), 1695, governed contracts[45] and the Real Property Act, 1845, governed grants.[46] Some controversy has existed over the effect of section 4 of Deasy's Act on these

---

[39] See, especially, *Dease* v. *O'Reilly* (1845) 8 Ir.L.R. 52 at 59 (see *A Casebook on Irish Land Law* (1984), p. 678). *Cf. Evans* v. *Monagher* (1872) I.R. 6 C.L. 526. See also *McKenna* v. *Herlihy* (1920) 7 T.C. 762.

[40] This view of the law was accepted by the Republic's Supreme Court in *Gatien Motor Co. Ltd.* v. *Continental Oil Co. of Ireland Ltd.* [1979] I.R. 406 (see *A Casebook on Irish Land Law* (1984), p. 543) (relating to a "caretaker's agreement" and holding it did not create a tenancy despite exclusive possession). See also *N.I. Housing Executive* v. *McCann* [1979] N.I. 39; *Bellew* v. *Bellew* [1982] I.R. 447; *Irish Shell and B.P. Ltd.* v. *Costello Ltd.* [1985] I.L.R.M. 554. For earlier authorities see *Kelly* v. *Woolworth & Co. Ltd.* [1922] 2 I.R. 5; *MacGinley* v. *National Aid Committee* [1952] Ir.Jur.Rep. 43. See also *Boylan* v. *Dublin Corporation* [1949] I.R. 60 at 68. *Cf. Street* v. *Mountford* [1985] 2 All E.R. 289, fn. 34, *supra*.

[41] *King* v. *David Allen & Sons (Billposting) Ltd.* [1915] 2 I.R. 448 (C.A.); [1916] 2 A.C. 54 (H.L.). See also *Isitt* v. *Monaghan C.C.* (1905) 5 N.I.J.R. 118; *Hickey* v. *Tipperary (South Riding) C.C.* [1931] I.R. 621; *Belton* v. *Kirwan* [1943] I.R. 525. *Cf.* a lodger, *Wauchob* v. *Reynolds* (1850) 1 I.C.L.R. 142.

[42] Fn. 34, para. 17.010, *ante*. See also *Whyte* v. *Sheehan* [1943] Ir.Jur.Rep. 38.

[43] *Gun* v. *McCarthy* (1883) 13 L.R.Ir. 304 (see *A Casebook on Equity and Trusts in Ireland* (1985), p. 268); *Jackson* v. *Stopford* [1923] 2 I.R. 1; *Irish Dunlop Co. Ltd.* v. *Ralph* (1961) 95 I.L.T.R. 70; *Rosborough* v. *Stevenson* (1968) 19 N.I.L.Q. 458. Para. 3.162, *ante*. It is not clear how far *Street* v. *Mountford*, fn. 34, para. 17.010, *ante* affects this principle.

[44] Para. 6.068, *ante. Leitrim* v. *Geelan* (1873) I.R. 8 C.L. 122; *Erskine* v. *Armstrong* (1887) 20 L.R.Ir. 296. *Cf. Jones* v. *Inman* (1794) Ir. Term. Rep. 433; *Jones* v. *Duggan* (1841) 4 Ir.L.R. 86.

[45] S. 2. See para. 3.149, *ante*.

[46] S. 3 (requiring a deed).

provisions. Section 4 provides:

> "Every lease[47] or contract with respect to lands whereby the relation of landlord and tenant is intended to be created for any freehold estate or interest, or for any definite period of time not being from year to year or any lesser period, shall be by deed executed, or note in writing signed by the landlord or his agent thereunto lawfully authorised in writing."

It has been suggested that this section is so widely drafted that it impliedly repeals section 2 of the Statute of Frauds relating to contracts.[48] This, however, seems to confuse the distinction between contracts and grants and it is significant that Deasy's Act expressly repealed the provisions of the Real Property Act, 1845, only. Furthermore, this repeal was confined to the relationship of landlord and tenant within the meaning of Deasy's Act.[49] It did not repeal expressly section 2 of the Statute of Frauds and the better view would seem to be that section 2 is still in force and governs contracts for the future creation of the relationship.[50] The confusion is, of course, understandable because section 3 of Deasy's Act makes it clear that an agreement or contract may create the relationship of landlord and tenant without more, *i.e.*, operate as a grant, and so it may not always be easy to determine in practice whether the parties intended a contract only[51] or a grant. As we shall see in a moment, the point can, however, have practical importance where the formalities laid down in section 4 have *not* been complied with.

1. *Freeholds and Terms of Years*

17.013. In the case of freehold estates[52] and terms of years, section 4 requires writing only, though in most cases it is the practice still to execute a deed, which is also mentioned as an alternative by the section. The written agreement must be signed by the landlord[53] or by his agent, who must be lawfully authorised in writing.[54] It seems that the agent's authority must exist at the time of signature or execution of the lease and there can be no subsequent ratification by his principal of unauthorised acts.[55]

It is important to note that section 3 of Deasy's Act confines the Act's operation to cases where the relationship of landlord and tenant is created "in

---

[47] Defined in s. 1 as "any instrument in writing, whether under seal or not, containing a *contract of tenancy* in respect of any lands, in consideration of a rent or return" (italics added).

[48] See the discussion in *Bayley* v. *Conyngham* (1863) 15 I.C.L.R. 406 (see *A Casebook on Irish Land Law* (1984), p. 311).

[49] S. 104 (which adds "but not otherwise" twice) and Sched. (B). Note also that s. 1 of the Statute of Frauds (Ir.), 1695, *is* repealed.

[50] *McCausland* v. *Murphy* (1881) 9 L.R.Ir. 9 (see *A Casebook on Irish Land Law* (1984), p. 552). See also Sheridan, "Walsh v. Lonsdale in Ireland" (1952) 9 N.I.L.Q. 190.

[51] In effect a "contract for a contract" in certain cases, see Sheridan, *op. cit.*, pp. 192–3.

[52] *I.e.*, fee farm grants and leases for lives renewable for ever, ch. 4, *ante*.

[53] *Archbold* v. *Howth* (1866) I.R. 1 C.L. 608; *Babington* v. *O'Connor* (1887) 21 I.L.T.R. 41.

[54] *Cf.* s. 2 of the Statute of Frauds (Ir.), 1695, which does *not* require the authorisation to be in writing. *McCausland* v. *Murphy* (1881) 9 L.R.Ir. 9 (see *A Casebook on Irish Land Law* (1984), p. 552).

[55] *Byrne* v. *Rorke* (1869) I.R. 3 Eq. 642.

consideration of any rent."[56] If a gratuitous lease or a lease in return for a lump sum (a fine) only,[57] without reservation of a rent, is granted, presumably the matter is still governed by the Real Property Act, 1845,[58] whereby a deed may be used instead of one of the other forms of conveyance.[59]

2. Periodic Tenancies

17.014. Section 4 of Deasy's Act makes it clear that periodic tenancies, *i.e.*, tenancies from year to year, month to month or week to week,[60] may be created without any formal document, *i.e.*, orally.[61] Even if a document is executed by the tenant only, the tenancy is still valid in such cases without the landlord's or his agent's signature,[62] provided the terms have been agreed orally.

17.015. The same rules apply where there is a grant for a term certain, or as section 4 puts it, for a "definite period of time," which is less than "from year to year." This clearly covers periods of less than one year, *e.g.*, 6 months,[63] but there has been some controversy over the case of a grant for one year certain.

3. One Year Certain

17.016. On the face of it, a grant for one year certain is less than a grant from year to year,[64] or at least is no greater than it, and so there is no need for a deed or writing. A grant from year to year will last at least one year and may, of course, last considerably longer. A grant for one year certain cannot last any longer. Nevertheless, the Irish Court of Exchequer Chamber, in *Wright* v. *Tracey*,[65] by a majority of 4:3[66] held that a tenancy for a year certain was not less than a tenancy from year to year. The majority took the view that a tenancy from year to year was technically a tenancy "at will" and could be treated as equivalent to a tenancy for a year by construction of law only,[67] whereas a tenancy for a year certain was such by express contract of the parties.[68]

---

[56] See also the definition of "lease" in s. 1 ("in consideration of a rent or return").

[57] *Quaere* whether the reference to a "return" in s. 1 of Deasy's Act brings such a case within the Act; *cf*. s. 3 which does not refer to a return, but only to rent.

[58] Hence the limited repeal by Deasy's Act, fn. 49, *supra*. [59] S. 3. See para. 3.026, *ante*. [60] Para. 4.011, *ante*.

[61] *Bayley* v. *Conyngham* (1863) 15 I.C.L.R. 406 (see *A Casebook on Irish Land Law* (1984), p. 311); *Union* v. *McDermott* (1921) 55 I.L.T.R. 194; *Landy* v. *Power* [1962–63] Ir.Jur.Rep. 45.

[62] *Jagoe* v. *Harrington* (1882) 10 L.R.Ir. 335. The absence of the landlord's or his agent's signature may, however, impair the enforceability of covenants or conditions against him, paras. 17.061 *et seq.*, *post*.

[63] *Crane* v. *Naughten* [1912] 2 I.R. 318.

[64] This was the view of the English Court of Appeal in *Bernays* v. *Prosser* [1963] 2 Q.B. 592 in relation to the similar wording of s. 2 (1) of the Agricultural Holdings Act, 1948.

[65] (1874) I.R. 8 C.L. 478, which concerned the similar wording of s. 69 (2) of the Landlord and Tenant (Ir.) Act, 1870. The English Court of Appeal refused to follow the decision in *Bernays* v. *Prosser*, *op. cit*.

[66] Palles C.B., Whiteside C.J., Fitzgerald J. and Fitzgerald B.; Deasy and Dowse BB. and O'Brien J. *dissentiente*. [67] Paras. 4.011–2, *ante*.

[68] Lord Denning M.R. remarked in *Bernays* v. *Prosser*: "It seems to me absurd to say that a tenancy for 'one year certain' is *equal* to a tenancy 'from year to year.' It is not equal to it: and, as it is not equal to it, it must be *less* than it. A tenancy from year to year is not only a tenancy for one year certain. It is something more, because the tenant, unless a notice to quit has been given, has a right to stay on after the end of the year and so on from year to year" [1963] 2 Q.B. 592 at 598. *Cf*. Dowse B. in *Wright* v. *Tracey* (1874) I.R. 8 C.L. 478 at 481–2. *Cf. McGrath* v. *Travers* [1948] I.R. 122. See also *Esso Teoranta* v. *Wong* [1975] I.R. 416.

4. *Rule in Walsh v. Lonsdale*

17.017. The question remains as to what the position is if the formalities required by section 4 of Deasy's Act are not complied with in cases within the section. At common law the rule was that an "informal" lease was void. However, if the tenant took possession with the landlord's consent, a tenancy at will arose[69] and, if rent was paid and accepted, a periodic tenancy arose whose length depended upon the way in which the rent was calculated rather than how it was paid.[70] If the rent was expressed to be a yearly rent, but payable monthly, a tenancy from year to year arose. However, apart from this, even at common law an informal lease might be saved by construing it as a contract to grant a lease. To be enforceable at common law it would have to comply with the formalities for contracts laid down by the Statute of Frauds (Ireland), 1695, *i.e.*, there would at least have to be a note or memorandum in writing signed by the party to be charged or his authorised agent.[71] If these formalities[72] are not met, the contract may still be enforceable in equity through a decree of specific performance, provided there is a sufficient act of part performance to take the case out of the Statute of Frauds.[73] The result is, therefore, that an informal lease for valuable consideration may be validated by construing it as a specifically enforceable contract and, applying the maxim "equity regards as done what ought to be done," the doctrine was developed by the courts that the parties would be treated in equity as being in the same position from the beginning as if a proper formal lease had been executed. In other words, until a formal lease is executed, if necessary as a result of a decree of specific performance, the parties' position is still governed by the terms of the informal lease but with one major qualification. Until execution of the formal lease, their rights are equitable only. This doctrine, sometimes, though rather misleadingly, summarised as "a contract for a lease is as good as a lease," is known as the rule in *Walsh* v. *Lonsdale.*[74]

17.018. As stated above, it would seem that the doctrine may still be invoked in Ireland in cases where the formalities of section 4 of Deasy's Act have not been complied with, *e.g.*, a two-year lease made orally only, or signed by the tenant only, or by the landlord's agent not authorised in writing.[75] The last situation arose in *McCausland* v. *Murphy*,[76] where Sullivan

---

[69] *Ward* v. *Ryan* (1876) I.R. 10 C.L. 17.

[70] Para. 4.011, *ante.*

[71] S. 2. See para. 3.149, *ante.* Also *Scott* v. *McComb* (1965) 16 N.I.L.Q. 122; (1966) 17 N.I.L.Q. 418; *Conaty* v. *Ulster Development Ltd.* (1966) 17 N.I.L.Q. 162.

[72] Here writing is required in *all* cases, though the landlord's agent need not be authorised in writing; *cf.* s. 4 of Deasy's Act.

[73] See the discussion at para. 3.149, *ante.* In *Industrial Properties (Barton Hill) Ltd.* v. *Associated Electrical Industries Ltd.* [1977] Q.B. 614, the English Court of Appeal stated that the doctrine of *Walsh* v. *Lonsdale* need not be limited to a case where there is one agreement only nor to a case where there is a direct contractual relationship between the lessee and the holders of the legal estate.

[74] (1882) 21 Ch.D. 9. Para. 3.038, *ante.*

[75] Sheridan, "Walsh *v.* Lonsdale in Ireland" (1952) 9 N.I.L.Q. 190.

[76] (1881) 9 L.R.Ir. 9. See also *Leitrim* v. *Geelan* (1873) I.R. 8 C.L. 122; *Babington* v. *O'Connor* (1887) 21 I.L.T.R. 41.

M.R. granted specific performance of the preliminary agreement between the landlord's agent and the tenant, on the terms contained in a draft lease prepared by the agent and read to the tenant.

17.019. It is important to appreciate the limits of this doctrine. First, it is dependent upon the availability of the remedy of specific performance in the particular case, a matter which lies within the discretion of the court.[77] If this would not be available the doctrine cannot apply and the parties' arrangements may still have no effect.[78] Secondly, even if specific performance would be granted, it must be remembered that it is an equitable remedy only and so the parties' rights are also equitable only. This may have an important bearing on any question of priorities which may arise, though in Ireland such a question may be resolved if the document executed, if any, is registered in the Registry of Deeds.[79] Thirdly, to the extent that the parties' rights are based on contract only, they are subject to the general privity of contract doctrine and cannot affect third parties,[80] whereas, as we shall see, if a proper lease is granted successors in title to both the lessor and lessee may have rights and duties under it.[81] Fourthly, various statutory provisions apply to leases only and do not apply to contracts for leases.[82]

5. *Attornment*

17.020. An occupier of land may "attorn" or acknowledge himself to be the tenant of the owner of the land. Thus section 94 of Deasy's Act enables a writ or decree for possession to be executed without removing from possession sub-tenants or occupiers of the land who sign an attornment or acknowledgment form.[83] Mortgages often contain attornment clauses whereby the mortgagor attorns himself tenant of the mortgagee, so that possession of the land can be recovered on that basis.[84]

A conveyance of the reversion on a lease is now valid without any attornment by the lessee, though the lessee is not liable in respect of payment of rent to the assignor before notice of the assignment is given to him.[85] However, an attornment by a lessee to a person claiming to be the landlord is void, unless made with the consent of his lessor.[86]

D. CLASSIFICATION OF TENANCIES

The various categories of tenancies known to our law were discussed in an

---

[77] Para. 3.050, *ante.* [78] *Cf. Kingwood Estate Co., Ltd.* v. *Anderson* [1963] 2 Q.B. 169.
[79] Ch. 3, *ante.*
[80] Wylie, "Contracts and Third Parites" (1966) 17 N.I.L.Q. 351.
[81] Para. 17.069, *post.*
[82] *E.g.*, a contract is not a "conveyance" for the purpose of rights and interests pasing under s. 6 of the Conveyancing Act, 1881, para. 6.066, *ante.*
[83] See the forms (Nos. 6 and 7) in Sch. (A). *Corr* v. *Harris* (1889) 23 I.L.T.R. 82; *Ulster Bank* v. *Woolsey* (1890) 24 I.L.T.R. 65.
[84] Para. 13.020, *ante.*
[85] Administration of Justice Act (Ir.), 1707, ss. 9 and 10.
[86] Or pursuant to a judgment to a mortgagee where the mortgagor's right of redemption is barred or to any other rightful successor in title to the lessor, Landlord and Tenant [Distress for Rent] Act (Ir.), 1741, ss. 7 and 8.

earlier chapter and little need be added here.[87] The following is brief summary of the main categories.

1. *Freehold*

17.021. Various kinds of freehold grants are common in Ireland under which the relationship of landlord and tenant may be created. The most common are fee farm grants,[88] leases for lives renewable for ever[89] and leases for lives combined with a concurrent or reversionary term of years.[90]

2. *Terms Certain*

17.022. Tenancies for a fixed period, or term certain, are also very common. The terms granted can range from periods of a week's duration to very long periods, such as 999 or even 10,000 years.[91] In England there has been some controversy, which has recently broken out again, as to how far certainty of duration is a prerequisite for a lease. During the Second World War, the Court of Appeal held that a lease "for the duration of the war" was void for uncertainty,[92] but the modern view seems to be that the principle of certainty discussed in that case should be applied to grants purporting to create a fixed term only. It should not be extended, *e.g.*, to periodic tenancies which involve inherently an element of uncertainty as to their maximum duration.[93] This issue does not seem to have arisen in Ireland and it has been suggested that there may be no requirement of certainty even for fixed term tenancies because section 3 of Deasy's Act bases the relationship of landlord and tenant entirely on contract. If the grant purports to create a tenancy for a single period of uncertain duration, it has been argued that this would be valid so long as it was clear what the parties agreed. The continued prevalence of leases for freehold estates,[94] a major characteristic of which is their uncertainty of duration, seems to support the notion that the Irish courts would not concern themselves with such questions of certainty with respect to the relationship of landlord and tenant.[95] On the other hand, it can be argued once again that section 3 of Deasy's Act should not be read as changing the

---

[87] Paras. 4.010–2, *ante.*

[88] Para. 4.057, *ante.*

[89] Para. 4.167, *ante.*

[90] Para. 4.177, *ante.*

[91] There is no limit in theory, but terms exceeding 10,000 years are very rare.

[92] *Lace* v. *Chatler* [1944] K.B. 368, reversed as regards its particular facts by the Validation of War-Time Leases Act, 1944. See also *M.W. Investments Ltd.* v. *Kilburn Envoy Ltd.* [1947] Ch. 370. For a *contract* for a lease to be enforceable, the lease's date of commencement and duration must be certain, see *Kerns* v. *Manning* [1935] I.R. 869; *McQuaid* v. *Lynam* [1965] I.R. 564. See also *O'Flaherty* v. *Arvan Propeties Ltd.* (1977) Unrep. (Sup.Ct., R.I.) (211/1976); *Law* v. *Murphy* (1978) Unrep. (H.C.,R.I.) (1976 No. 4328P).

[93] *Re Midland Rly. Co's Agreement* [1971] Ch. 725; *Centaploy Ltd.* v. *Matlodge Ltd.* [1973] 2 All. E.R. 720. *Cf. Cavendish Furniture Co. Ltd.* v. *Chalfont* [1967] N.I. 1.

[94] Note, however, the recommendations in the *Survey of the Land Law of Northern Ireland* (1971), ch. 2. Perpetually renewable leases and leases for lives cannot be created in England since the Law of Property Acts, 1922 and 1925, a factor which may have influenced the reasoning of the Court of Appeal in *Lace* v. *Chantler.*

[95] Frequently the Irish courts have construed apparently uncertain grants as leases for lives or for as long as the lessor's interest lasts, see *Re Connolly's Estate* (1869) I.R. 3 Eq. 339; *Re Coleman's Estate* [1907] 1 I.R. 488; *Stafford* v. *Rosenberg* [1932] L.J.Ir. 26. See also *Holmes* v. *Day* (1874) I.R. 8 C.L. 235; *Wood* v. *Davis* (1880) 6. L.R.Ir. 50.

nature of the estate granted so that, to the extent that the grant purports to create a leasehold estate for a term certain, the common law requirements for such an estate should still be met, including any necessary element of certainty of duration.

3. Periodic Tenancies

17.023. Periodic tenancies determinable by either party by notice, *e.g.*, weekly, monthly and yearly tenancies, may also be created either expressly or by implication, *e.g.*, by the tenant taking possession and the landlord accepting rent.[96] The type of periodic tenancy so created by implication depends on how the rent accepted by the landlord is calculated rather than how it is paid, *i.e.*, the yearly rent of a tenancy from year to year may be paid by weekly or monthly instalments.[97] Section 6 of Deasy's Act provides that, where the tenancy is from year to year, it is presumed to have commenced on the last "gale" day[98] of the calendar year on which the rent has become due, unless the contrary appears.

17.024. If a tenant "holds over," *i.e.*, continues in possession, after expiration or determination of his lease[99] for more than one month after a demand for possession from his land,[1] the latter is given the option by section 5 of Deasy's Act of deeming the tenant's continued possession to be a new tenancy from year to year, subject to the same rent and such agreements in the old tenancy as may be applicable to the new periodic one.[2] The court may, however, take the view that the parties' actions since expiration or determination of the old tenancy indicate the creation of a tenancy other than a yearly one[3] or one containing different terms.[4] All this, however, is subject to the considerable statutory changes introduced this century, *e.g.*, under the rent restriction legislation relating to tenants of unfurnished accommodation in both parts of Ireland, which permits tenants to continue on in possession as statutory tenants on expiration or determination of contractual tenancies.[5] In these cases the position of the tenant is governed by the rent restriction legislation itself.[6]

[96] *Hurly* v. *Hourahan* (1867) I.R. 1 C.L. 700; *Fahy* v. *O'Donnell* (1871) I.R. 4 C.L. 322; *Leader* v. *Manning* (1886) 20 I.L.T.R. 55; *Commrs. of Public Works* v. *Mackey* [1941] I.R. 207.

[97] Para. 17.017, *ante. Cinnamon* v. *O'Hara* (1844) 3 Cr. & Dix 199; *Wren* v. *Buckley* (1904) 4 N.I.J.R. 171. See also *Beauchamp* v. *Kenny* (1930) 64 I.L.T.R. 30.

[98] *I.e.*, a day on which a periodic payment of rent is due. This expression is commonly used in Ireland and appears in several parts of Deasy's Act, see also, *e.g.*, ss. 15, 20–1, 34 and 47.

[99] This provision does not apply where the original tenancy was created orally.

[1] Under s. 76 of Deasy's Act a tenant "wilfully" overholding is liable to pay *double* rent for the period he overholds, see *Beck* v. *Creggan* (1879) 13 I.L.T.R. 79. *Survey of the Land Law of Northern Ireland* (1971), para. 327. See also para. 17.097, *post*. Under Art. 66 of the Rent (N.I.) Order, 1978, a tenant is not to be deemed for the purposes of s. 76 of the 1860 Act wilfully to hold over by reason of his remaining in possession under or by virtue of the Order.

[2] *Morragh* v. *Alleyne* (1873) I.R. 7 Eq. 487; *Meath* v. *Megan* [1897] 2 I.R. 477. *Cf. Cusack* v. *Farrell* (1886) 18 L.R.Ir. 494, aff'd. (1887) 20 L.R.Ir. 56.

[3] *Phoenix Picture Palace Ltd.* v. *Capitol and Allied Theatres Ltd.* [1951] Ir.Jur.Rep. 55.

[4] *Nixon* v. *Darby* (1868) I.R. 2 C.L. 467; *O'Keeffe* v. *Walsh* (1880) 8 L.R.Ir. 184.

[5] Ch. 18, *post*. Note also s. 28 of the Republic's Landlord and Tenant (Amendment) Act, 1980 (tenant of a "tenement" entitled to retain possession until final determination by the court of his application for a new tenancy – see *Cook* v. *Dillon* (1959) 93 I.L.T.R. 48) and s. 40 of the 1980 Act (lessee entitled to retain possession until reversionary lease granted or he is declared not entitled to one). See further on this Act, ch. 18, *post*.

[6] *McCombe* v. *Sheehan* [1954] I.R. 183. See also *Healy* v. *Armstrong* [1949] Ir.Jur.Rep. 18.

4. *Tenancies at Will and at Sufferance*

17.025. These categories were dealt with in an earlier chapter[7] and what has just been said about tenants "holding over" relates to tenancies at sufferance.

5. *Statutory Tenancies*

These are dealt with in the next chapter.[8]

6. *Tenancy by Estoppel*

17.026. Once the tenant goes into possession of the property, the doctrine of estoppel prevents the tenant from denying his landlord's title and the landlord from denying his tenant's.[9] Furthermore, even though in fact the landlord had no title to pass to the tenant under a tenancy agreement, a periodic tenancy by estoppel may still arise on the basis of the tenant's possession and the landlord's acceptance of the rent.[10] If the landlord later obtains title to the property, this "feeds" the estoppel and the tenant becomes tenant under the original tenancy agreement.[11]

IV. ASSIGNMENT AND SUBLETTING

17.027. At common law, an assignment of a tenancy involves an out-and-out transfer of the entire tenant's interest, so that he retains nothing[12] and the assignee succeeds to his rights and duties. A subletting, on the other hand, involves a sub-grant for a period less than the tenant's (sub-lessor's) term, so that the tenant retains a reversion on the sub-lease and remains liable on the covenants and conditions of the head-lease. In Ireland, this theoretical distinction remains but in practice the two concepts have become blurred as a result of section 3 of Deasy's Act, which permits subletting for the whole of the tenant's term, even though he retains no reversion.[13] It may, therefore, be a difficult question of construction whether an assignment or subletting has occurred.[14] If a fine (lump sum) only is paid by the transferee, it is probably an assignment; if rent is to be paid, it is probably a subletting, whether or not a fine is paid.[15]

17.028. The importance of the distinction is this: an assignment creates

---

[7] Para. 4.012, *ante.* See the recent discussion in *Binions* v. *Evans* [1972] Ch. 359.

[8] Ch. 18, *post.*

[9] *Gowrie Park Utility Society Ltd.* v. *Fitzgerald* [1963] I.R. 436. *Cf. Levingston* v. *Somers* [1914] I.R. 183. See also *Lennon* v. *Meegan* [1905] 2 I.R. 189; *Byrne* v. *O'Neill* (1979) Unrep. (Sup. Ct., R.I.) (16/1976). Martin, "Tenancies by Estoppel, Equitable Leases and Priorities" [1978] Conv. 137.

[10] *Ward* v. *Ryan* (1875) I.R. 10 C.L. 17; *Commrs. of Public Works* v. *Mackey* [1941] I.R. 207; *Keenan* v. *Walsh* (1951) 85 I.L.T.R. 86; *Cook* v. *Dillon* (1959) 93 I.L.T.R. 48.

[11] *Sturgeon* v. *Wingfield* (1846) 15 M. & W. 224.

[12] Excluding things like rentcharges, ch. 6, *ante.*

[13] Para. 17.007, *ante. Survey of the Land Law of Northern Ireland* (1971), paras. 307–10.

[14] *Seymour* v. *Quirke* (1884) 14 L.R.Ir. 455. See also *Re Doyle and O'Hara's Contract* [1899] 1 I.R. 113.

[15] See also *O'Reilly* v. *O'Donoughue* (1875) I.R. 10 Eq. 73; *Foley* v. *Gallagher* (1879) 2 L.R.Ir. 389; *Cork C.C.* v. *O'Shea* [1947] I.R. 369; *McGinley* v. *National Aid Committee* [1952] Ir.Jur.Rep. 43.

privity of estate[16] between the landlord and the tenant's assignee and this means that covenants, conditions and agreements contained in the original tenancy agreement are generally enforceable as between the landlord[17] and the assignee. No privity of estate is created between the head-landlord and a sub-tenant, who is liable only to his sub-landlord, *i.e.*, the tenant of the head-lease or tenancy agreement who remains liable to the head-landlord.[18]

A. METHODS

1. *Assignment*

17.029. Section 9 of Deasy's Act lays down the various ways in which a tenancy, including an oral one,[19] may be assigned,[20] namely, by deed, or instrument in writing[21] signed by the assignor, or his agent lawfully authorised in writing, or by devise or bequest,[22] or act and operation of law.[23] This list seems to be exhaustive, though section 9 adds the words "and not otherwise," which seem to contemplate some other methods, not indicated, which are unlawful. There seems to be no authority on what these other methods might be.[24]

17.030. Sections 11–16 of Deasy's Act then state the legal position of the landlord (or his successors in title), the tenant-assignor and his assignee after an assignment has been made. Section 11 states that the assignee is subject to all agreements in respect of assignment or subletting to the same extent as his assignor.[25] This provision may not have been strictly necessary in view of the more general provisions in sections 12 and 13, which make the burden and benefit of agreements contained or implied in leases or tenancy agreements enforceable by or against successors in title of both the landlord and tenant.[26] So far as the tenant-assignor is concerned, section 16 provides that an assignment of his interest under a lease[27] with the landlord's consent releases

---

[16] See ch. 19, *post.*

[17] Or the assignee of his reversion, para. 17.071, *post.*

[18] However, the sub-tenant may become liable indirectly, in that enforcement of the landlord's remedies against the head-tenant may involve destruction of the head-lease and, therefore, of everything created out of it, including the sub-lease. Note, however, the provisions in ss. 19–21 of Deasy's Act, para. 17.034, *post.*

[19] It is doubtful if it covers tenancies at will, which may not be assignable anyway, see *Murphy* v. *Ford* (1855) 5 I.C.L.R. 19; *Ward* v. *Ryan* (1875) I.R. 10 C.L. 17.

[20] This assumes that assignment is permissible in the particular case and is subject to any covenant or condition in the tenancy agreement prohibiting or restricting assignment, see para. 17.035, *post.*

[21] No special words need be used provided the intention is clear, *Doran* v. *Kenny* (1869) I.R. 3 Eq. 148; *Manning* v. *Saul* (1890) 26 L.R.Ir. 640. Cf. *Magowan* v. *Telford* (1909) 43 I.L.T.R. 237. Also in *Re Courtney* [1981] N.I.58, Murray J. held that words of limitation are necessary for a conveyance of land held under a fee farm grant, even though under Deasy's Act no deed is necessary.

[22] See *Parnell* v. *Boyd* [1896] 2 I.R. 571.

[23] *E.g.* on the tenant's bankruptcy, Bankruptcy (Ir.) Acts, 1857, s. 271 (see *Re McCafferty* [1974] I.R. 471; *Re Keaney* [1977] N.I. 67) and 1872, s. 97 (see *Hanway* v. *Taylor* (1874) I.R. 8 C.L. 254; *Re Connor* (1874) 8 I.L.T.R 71; *Re Deane's Trusts* [1909] 1 I.R. 334) or death, Succession Act, 1965, s. 10 and Administration of Estates Act (N.I.), 1955, s. 1 (see *Nixon* v. *Quinn* [1868] I.R. 2 C.L. 248; *Wallis* v. *Wallis* (1884) 12 L.R.Ir. 63). Cf. *Foley* v. *Galvin* [1932] I.R. 339.

[24] *Survey of the Land Law of Northern Ireland* (1971), para. 307.

[25] See *Norbury* v. *McDonald* (1853) 4 I.C.L.R. 137. The original tenant's position, however, has been considerably altered recently in the Republic of Ireland, para. 17.038, *post.*

[26] These provisions are discussed later, para. 17.072, *post.*

[27] Note that the section is so restricted.

and discharges him from all future liability under the lease. This alters the common law position, under which the original tenant remained liable even after assignment of his interest, because the assignment did not destroy the privity of contract existing between him and the original landlord.[28]

17.031. So far as the assignee is concerned, section 14 largely confirms the common law position that the assignee is liable only in respect of the obligations under the lease for the period he is tenant, *i.e.*, so long as privity of estate exists between him and the landlord. He is not generally liable in respect of breaches occurring before the assignment to him,[29] nor is he liable, section 14 provides, after he further assigns the tenancy to someone else, *provided* he gives written notice of the particulars of this assignment[30] to the landlord.[31] The one exception to this general rule is provided by section 15 which states that the assignee is liable for payment of the rent up to and including the next gale day following service of the notice of assignment required by section 14.

2. Subletting

17.032. No specific provision as to the modes of effecting a subletting are contained in Deasy's Act, presumably by the ground that, since it involves the creation of a new relationship of landlord and tenant between the parties to the subletting, the matter is governed by the general formalities contained in section 4.[32]

17.033. Where a sub-tenancy is created with the consent of the head-landlord,[33] the receipt of the sub-landlord (head-tenant) for the rent paid by the sub-tenant under the sub-tenancy is a full discharge to the latter and the land sublet as against the head-landlord,[34] unless the head-landlord has previously served a notice on the sub-tenant requiring him to pay the sub-rent or part of it directly to him rather than the sub-landlord.[35] It would seem from the wording of the section[36] that it contemplates the issue of some documentary receipt by the sub-landlord, yet there appears to be no reason why the sub-tenant cannot prove payment in another way if the sub-landlord refuses to issue a receipt, *e.g.*, production of a cleared cheque (which operates as a receipt) used to pay the rent.[37] No discharge, however, is

---

[28] The usual method of protection was to insert an indemnity clause in the assignment, whereby the assignee undertook to indemnify the assignor against all future liability and, indeed, this is frequently still inserted in Ireland despite s. 16.

[29] Where the tenant-assignor defaults in paying rent, the assignee is liable only for the part of the rent apportioned in respect of the period running from the date of the assignment, *Glass* v. *Patterson* [1902] 2 I.R. 660. For apportionment of rent, see Apportionment Act, 1870, s. 3.

[30] *I.e.*, its mode, date and the parties thereto, *Powell* v. *Adamson* [1895] 2 I.R. 41.

[31] *Cottingham* v. *Manning* (1897) 3 Ir.W.L.R. 43.

[32] Para. 17.012, *ante*.

[33] To some extent this provision seems to relate to s. 18 of Deasy's Act, though that section has been repealed in the Republic without any amendment of the provision under discussion, para. 17.038, *infra*.

[34] Deasy's Act, s. 19, which adds the proviso that the discharge does not prevent the landlord pursuing his remedies for the balance of rent owed, against the sub-landlord or other land out of which it is due.

[35] *Ibid.*, s. 20.

[36] *I.e.*, receipt "of" rather than "by" the head-tenant (sub-landlord).

[37] Cheques Act, 1959, s. 3 (R.I.); Cheques Act, 1957, s. 3 (U.K.).

obtainable in the case of a "building lease,"[38] though it is arguable that this is the very case where sub-tenants are most likely to need a safeguard against forfeiture of the sub-landlord's interest for default on his part and action by the head-landlord. Frequently the tenant of a building lease is a building developer and builders have a notorious propensity for getting into financial difficulties.[39]

17.034. If a tenant, who has sublet, fails to pay rent for at least one month after one gale of the rent has accrued due under the head-tenancy, the head-landlord can give written notice[40] to the sub-tenant requiring him to pay to the head-landlord so much of the sub-rent as is sufficient to discharge the amount of the head-rent still owing.[41] Such payment directly to the head-landlord with issue of receipt discharges the sub-tenant in respect of his obligations *pro tanto* to his sub-landlord and the head-landlord has the same remedies for enforcing payment of the rent as the sub-landlord had. Even if the landlord does not serve a notice requiring payment directly to him, the sub-tenant can voluntarily pay his sub-rent directly to the head-landlord after at least one gale of the head-rent is overdue and the receipt of the head-landlord or his agent is again a full discharge.[42] It seems that the sub-tenant can deduct such voluntary payments from rent due to the sub-landlord, though he cannot sue for them.[43]

B. RESTRICTIONS

17.035. Sections 10 and 18 of Deasy's Act contain restrictions on a tenant's right to assign or sublet which remain in force in Northern Ireland[44] but have recently been repealed in the Republic of Ireland.[45] Section 10 provides that, where a lease contains an agreement restraining or prohibiting assignment,[46] it is "not lawful" to assign the lands or any part thereof without the consent in writing of the landlord or of his agent lawfully authorised in writing.[47] Section 18 contains a similar provision for consent where the lease contains an agreement against subletting *or letting in conacre*.[48] These provisions have given rise to some difficulties of interpretation.

[38] Not defined in the Act, but presumably it means a lease granted for the purpose of erection or completion of buildings on the demised land.
[39] *Survey of the Land Law of Northern Ireland* (1971), para. 310.
[40] Delivered or left at the sub-tenant's usual place of abode with some member of his family over 16 years of age.
[41] S. 20. See *Buck* v. *Sullivan* (1902) 2 N.I.J.R. 164.
[42] S. 21. See *Grogan* v. *Regan* [1902] 2 I.R. 196.
[43] Unless they have been adopted by the sub-landlord and he has obtained a credit from the head-landlord in respect of them. See the discussion in *Ahearne* v. *McSwiney* (1874) I.R. 8 C.L. 570. Salvage payments are still recoverable, *O'Geran* v. *McSwiney* (1874) I.R. 8 Eq. 624.
[44] See, however, the recommendations in the *Survey of the Land Law of Northern Ireland* (1971), para. 309.
[45] Landlord and Tenant (Ground Rents) Act, 1967, s. 35. Note, however, s. 10 of the Rent Restrictions (Amendment) Act, 1967, which restricts assignment of a "controlled dwelling," ch. 18, *post*.
[46] And this has not been waived, para. 17.037, *infra*.
[47] Testified by his being an executing party to the instrument of assignment, or by an indorsement on or subscription of the instrument.
[48] On conacre, see ch. 20 *post*. Note also that under s. 18 the agent need not be authorised *in writing*. It is not clear why this distinction was made. In *Northern Ireland Carriers Ltd.* v. *Larne Habour Ltd.* [1981] N.I. 171, Murray J. drew the further distinction between ss. 10 and 18 that s. 18 applies only to agreements prohibiting subletting, not to one simply regulating or restraining it by, *e.g.*, requiring consent to it.

17.036. First, there is the meaning of the expression "not lawful." At common law, an assignment or subletting in breach of contract still passed an estate to the assignee, though this might be subject to a right of forfeiture in the landlord where the agreement was a condition of the lease or subject to a proviso for re-entry for breach of covenant.[49] In other words, the assignment or subletting was at most voidable and not void *ab initio.*[50] It is not clear whether sections 10 and 18 alter the common law and render the transactions void. Monahan C.J. took the view that the common law was so altered,[51] yet, in another case in which he also was a member of the court, it was held that such a "void" assignment still enabled the landlord to invoke a forfeiture clause.[52] In other words, it could not be successfully argued that, since the purported assignment was void and, therefore, a nullity, there had been no breach of covenant.

17.037. Secondly, sections 10 and 18 operate so long only as the agreements against assignment or subletting have not been waived. At common law, waiver can take one of two forms. It can either be a *general* waiver of the entire clause or term of the lease, so that it ceases to operate thereafter, or it can be a waiver of one particular breach of the clause or term only, so that the clause or term remains as part of the lease and may be invoked in the case of subsequent breaches. The question arises whether another section in Deasy's Act, section 43, recognises this distinction in providing that no act of a landlord is to be deemed to be a dispensation with the tenant's conditions, covenants or agreements or a waiver of the benefit of them in respect of any breach, unless the dispensation or waiver is signified by the landlord or his authorised[53] agent in writing. Palles C.B. seemed to think that section 43 applied to general waivers only, so that an oral waiver of a particular breach would still bar the landlord taking action in respect of that breach,[54] but this view has been queried.[55] Apart from this, section 18 specifically provides that, in the case of a subletting, no receipt of rent by the landlord or his agent is to be deemed a waiver of the agreement against subletting.[56] Furthermore, section 22 of Deasy's Act provides that a subletting with the landlord's consent is not to be deemed a general waiver of the benefit of any agreement against subletting. To some extent this duplicates sections 1 and 2 of the Law of Property Amendment Act, 1859, which reversed the common law rule that

[49] Para. 17.067, *post.*

[50] Para. 3.159, *ante. Cf.* the prohibition on sub-division or sub-letting under the land Purchase Acts, *Moley's Case* [1957] N.I. 130; *Carew* v. *Jackman* [1966] I.R. 177.

[51] *Butler* v. *Smith* (1864) 16 I.C.L.R. 213. See also *Ferris* v. *Mairs* (1903) 37 I.L.T.R. 614; *Knight* v. *Smith* [1947] Ir.Jur.Rep. 17. Thus the landlord cannot recover rent from the purported assignee but can sue the assignor who also cannot recover from the assignee. Note that s. 10 (3) of the Republic's Rent Restrictions (Amendment) Act, 1967, states that an assignment in contravention of the section is "void."

[52] *Clifford* v. *Reilly* (1870) I.R. 4 C.L. 218.

[53] Again note no requirement of authorisation in writing.

[54] *Foott* v. *Benn* (1884) 18 I.L.T.R. 90. *Cf.* as regards the pre-1860 position, *Midleton* v. *Wallis* [1914] 1 I.R. 35 at 42 (*per* Cherry L.J.). See also *Clifford* v. *Reilly* (1870) I.R. 4 c.L. 218.

[55] *E.g. McIlvenny* v. *McKeever* [1931] N.I. 161 at 167–8 (*in arguendo*) and at 174 (*per* Andrews L.J.); *cf.* Best L.J. at 185. See also *Donoughmore* v. *Forrest* (1871) I.R. 5 C.L. 470 at 474–5 (*per* Cherry L.J.); *Noonan* v. *Reddy* (1925) 59 I.L.T.R. 131; *Creed* v. *Forde* (1932) 66 I.L.T.R. 76; *Reynolds* v. *McKane* (1958) 92 I.L.T.R. 86.

[56] See *O'Toole* v. *Lyons* [1948] I.R. 115.

a licence to assign or sublet operated as a total or general waiver of a condition against assignment or subletting,[57] and section 6 of the Law of Property Amendment Act, 1860, which provides that a waiver of a particular breach of a covenant or condition is to be confined to that breach only and is not to operate as a general waiver, unless a contrary intention appears. The 1859 and 1860 provisions remain in force in both parts of Ireland.[58]

17.038. Though sections 10 and 18 of Deasy's Act have been repealed in the Republic of Ireland, it is still possible to insert express provisions prohibiting or restricting assignment or subletting in leases or tenancy agreements and, indeed, this is still commonly done even in Northern Ireland where the sections remain in force. Such an express clause may take the form of an absolute prohibition[59] or restriction of assignment or subletting to cases where the consent, oral or written, of the landlord is obtained. In Northern Ireland, the only legislation affecting such express clauses, apart from Deasy's Act, is section 3 of the Conveyancing Act, 1892, which provides that no "fine" (lump sum) or similar sum is to be payable for the landlord's licence or consent, unless the lease expressly provides for it.[60] In the Republic of Ireland, however, certain express covenants in leases are in addition modified by what is now section 66 of the Landlord and Tenant (Amendment) Act, 1980.[61] Under this, leases of "tenements"[62] containing absolute prohibitions or general or particular restrictions on "alienation"[63] are to have effect as if the prohibition or restriction reads that such alienation is prohibited or restricted without the licence or consent of the lessor.[64] If the lease contains or has implied in it[65] a covenant permitting alienation but with the licence or consent of the lessor only, the covenant, condition or agreement in question is deemed to be subject to the proviso that such licence or consent shall not be "unreasonably withheld."[66] In the case of a building lease for more than 40 years, the proviso is that no licence or consent is needed for an alienation effected more than seven years before the expiry of the lease, *provided* written notice of the transaction is given to the lessor within one month of its being affected.[67] If an alienation causes a transfer or increase of any rates, taxes or other burdens to or of the lessor, the proviso is that the lessee must reimburse all expenditure incurred by the lessor.[68]

---

[57] *Dumpor's Case* (1603) 4 Co.Rep. 119b.

[58] *Survey of the Land Law of Northern Ireland* (1971), paras. 299–300.

[59] Note the problems, however, concerning certain fee farm grants, ch. 4, *ante*.

[60] See also the Republic's Landlord and Tenant, 1931, s. 57.

[61] Reenacting s. 56 of the Landlord and Tenant Act, 1931. *Cf.* the English Landlord and Tenant Act, 1927, and see *Survey of the Land Law of Northern Ireland* (1971), para. 309. See also the Land Law Working Group's Discussion Document No.3. (*Landlord and Tenant*) (1982), ch. 4.

[62] See the definition in s. 2. *McEvoy* v. *Gilbeys of Ireland Ltd.* [1964] I.R. 30.

[63] It is not clear whether this includes subletting. *Cf.* s. 17 (2)(*d*)(iii) of the Labourer's Act, 1936, and see *Westmeath C.C.* v. *Claffey* [1952] I.R. 1.

[64] S. 66 (1). *Curragh Bloodstock Agency* v. *Warner* [1959] Ir.Jur.Rep. 73.

[65] See, *e.g.*, Landlord and Tenant (Ir.) Act, 1826, repealed with saving by Deasy's Act, s. 104 and Sched. (B).

[66] S. 66 (2)(*a*). But the lessor can charge reasonable expenses incurred in connection with the licence or consent.

[67] S. 66 (2)(*b*).

[68] S. 66 (2)(*c*).

17.039. There has been much litigation on the proviso relating to unreasonable withholding of consent.[69] The onus of proving that consent has been unreasonably withheld lies on the lessee.[70] It is usually not unreasonable where the landlord can show that his financial circumstances are going to be worsened[71] and in one case it was held reasonable where the proposed assignee was a Jew and the landlord a Christian.[72] On the other hand, it has been held unreasonable where the landlord was a local authority, which had leased the house under the Housing (Ireland) Act, 1919, and had not required its maintenance as accommodation for members of the working classes, and the proposed assignee was not such a member.[73] In *White* v. *Carlisle Trust Ltd.*[73a] McWilliam J. summarised the principles arising from the authorities on the question of unreasonable withholding of consent as follows:

"From these cases it appears to be established that the onus is on the plaintiff to establish that the consent has been unreasonably withheld, that 'reasonably' may be contrasted with 'arbitrarily' or 'capriciously', that a landlord may reasonably base a refusal of consent upon grounds of policy in relation to the management of his estate, and that the question whether the grounds alleged for the refusal of consent are reasonable or not in any particular case is a matter for the Court."

Finally, as regards tenancies coming within the rent restriction legislation,[74] it remains the position in Northern Ireland that a statutory tenancy is personal to the tenant and is not assignable *inter vivos* or by will.[75] In the Republic of Ireland, it is a condition of a statutory tenancy that the tenant will not assign it without the consent in writing of the landlord, but that consent may be withheld only if greater hardship[76] would, owin to the special circumstances of the case, be caused by granting consent than by withholding it.[77] However, in the case of tenancies of controlled dwellings *other than* those used in part for business, trade or professional purposes, or tenancies held under a lease for a term of more than 21 years, it is now provided that the tenant cannot assign without the consent in writing of the landlord unless the tenancy

---

[69] Note that this proviso also applies where an absolute prohibition is modified to one needing licence or consent by s. 66(1). *Cf.* s. 19 of the English Landlord and Tenant Act, 1927, *F.W. Woolworth & Co. Ltd.* v. *Lambert* [1937] Ch. 37 at 58–9.

[70] *Cahill & Co.* v. *Mayor of Drogheda* (1924) 58 I.L.T.R. 26; *Rice & Kennedy* v. *Dublin Corporation* [1947] I.R. 425 (see *A Casebook on Irish Land Law* (1984), p. 562).

[71] *Burns* v. *Morelli* [1953–54] Ir.Jur.Rep. 50; *Curragh Bloodstock Agency* v. *Warner* [1959] Ir.Jur.Rep. 73; *W. & L. Crowe Ltd.* v. *Dublin Port & Docks Ltd.* [1962] I.R. 194. See also *Egan Film Service* v. *McNamara* (1952) 86 I.L.T.R. 189.

[72] *Schlegel* v. *Corcoran* [1942] I.R. 19, provoking the following comment by a distinguished author: "This is the dark side of a remarkable judge." See kelly, *The Irish Constitution* (2nd ed., 1984), p. 665., fn. 2. *Cf.* English Race Relations Act, 1976, ss. 21–4. See Brooke-Taylor, "Racial and Religious Restrictive Covenants" [1078] Conv. 24.

[73] *Boland* v. *Dublin Corporation* [1946] I.R. 88. See also *Hervey-McLeay* v. *Patton* [1946] N.I. 118.

[73a] (1977) Unrep. (H.C..R.I.)(Cir.App.).

[74] Ch. 18, *post.*

[75] See *Drury* v. *Johnston* [1927] N.I. 25 at 30 (*per* Moore L.C.J.). See also the discussion in *McCullough* v. *Ministry of Commerce for N.I.* [1960] N.I. 75.

[76] On this concept, see *O'Farrell* v. *Woods* [1957] Ir.Jur.Rep. 26. Also *Cooley* v. *Walsh* [1926] I.R. 239; *G.N.R.* v. *O'Toole* [1934] L.J.Ir. 83.

[77] Rent Restrictions Act, 1960, s. 32 (4)(*b*).

contract is in writing and authorises assignment without consent.[78] Consent may be withheld only if the assignment is to anyone except to a member of the tenant's family[79] who is *bona fide* residing with him at the time of assignment.[80] An assignment in contravention of these provisions is void.[81]

There is no prohibition in the rent restriction legislation of either part of Ireland in respect of subletting a statutory tenancy and this remains a matter of contract.[82]

V. COVENANTS AND AGREEMENTS

17.040. The rights and duties of the landlord and tenant depend upon the covenants, conditions and agreements which are contained in the lease or other tenancy agreement. These fall into two main categories, those which are inserted in the lease or agreement *expressly* and those which are *implied* by the general law (by common law and statute) in the absence of express agreement.

A. EXPRESS

17.041. To a large extent the parties[83] are free to determine the express terms to insert in their agreement, though, as we shall see, some of these terms may be modified automatically by statute or even declared void. Furthermore, some covenants or agreements may be appropriate to certain types of tenancy only, *e.g.*, a covenant restricting user of the premises to private residential purposes is appropriate only where the original lease itself relates to residential premises. The following are the covenants or agreements most commonly found in a lease or tenancy agreement.

1. *Landlord*

17.042. It is quite usual for the lease or tenancy agreement to contain no covenants or agreements on behalf of the landlord, other than a covenant for "quiet enjoyment," *i.e.*, that the tenant will not be disturbed by any acts of the landlord or any other person for whom he is responsible.[84] However, in certain cases, *e.g.*, a short-term residential tenancy, the landlord may undertake to pay some of the outgoings of the demised premises, *e.g.*, the rates and, possibly, gas and electricity charges.[85] The landlord may also undertake

---

[78] Rent Restrictions Act, 1967, s. 10 (2)(*a*), as amended by Landlord and Tenant (Amendment) Act, 1971, s. 11. S. 32 (4)(*b*) of the 1960 Act is expressly excluded from application to statutory tenancies of controlled dwellings within this section, see s. 10 (6) of the 1967 Act.

[79] See s. 31 (5) (*a*)-(*d*) of the 1960 Act.   [80] S. 10 (2)(*b*).   [81] S. 10 (3).

[82] *Enniskillen U.D.C.* v. *Bartley* [1947] N.I. 177; *Waldron* v. *Burbage* (1957) 91 I.L.T.R. 30.

[83] Though in practice the lease is often drawn up by the landlord or his agent or solicitor and presented to the lessee as a *fait accompli*, at least in the case of short term residential leases. Negotiations over a draft lease is common only in the cases of a long term residential lease or a business lease. See *Irish Conveyancing Law* (1978), para. 15.04.

[84] *FitzGerald & Co. Ltd.* v. *O'Mahony* (1955) 89 I.L.T.R. 153; *Lapedus* v. *Glavey* (1965) 99 I.L.T.R. 1. See Russell, "Landlord's Covenant for Quiet Enjoyment" (1976) 40 Conv. 427.

[85] *O'Donnell* v. *Prices Tailors (Ir.) Ltd.* [1949] Ir.Jur.Rep. 32; *Keating* v. *Turner* [1953] I.R. 1.

to be responsible for certain repairs to the demised premises; the shorter the term of the tenancy or the less valuable the tenant's estate, the more likely it is that the landlord will be responsible for repairs.[86] Even in the case of long-term residential tenancies, it is common for the landlord to be responsible for repairs to the structure and exterior of the premises and, indeed, for their regular maintenance and redecoration.[87] Such a covenant is often accompanied by one giving the landlord, or his agent or workmen, the right to enter, view and inspect the premises at reasonable times, usually on giving notice to the tenant[88] and the tenant usually undertakes to afford the landlord or his workmen reasonable facilities for execution of any necessary repairs.[89] Apart from his contractual liability in respect of repairs, the landlord may be liable in tort for negligence if he has retained control or possession of part of the premises.[90]

17.043. The lease or tenancy agreement may include a covenant by the landlord to renew the lease or agreement. Perpetually renewable leases were once extremely common in Ireland,[91] but any created since 1849 by a fee simple owner operate automatically as fee farm grants.[92] Instead of a covenant for renewal by the landlord, the lease or agreement may give the tenant an option to have the lease renewed[93] or, even, to purchase the landlord's freehold reversion.[94]

2. *Tenant*

Most of the express covenants or agreements contained in a lease or tenancy agreement are entered into by the tenant and impose obligations upon him. The following are the most common express covenants or agreements.

(i) Rent, Taxes, Rates and Other Outgoings

17.044. The tenant will usually undertake to pay a specified rent,[95] at the

---

[86] *Scales* v. *Vandeleur* (1914) 48 I.L.T.R. 36; *Lapedus* v. *Glavey* (1965) 99 I.L.T.R. 1. *Cf. Carroll* v. *Routledge* [1925] N.I. 1; *McBride* v. *Boyle* (1928) 62 I.L.T.R. 104. See Smith, "Remedies of Tenant for Breach of Landlord's Covenant to Repair" (1980) 130 New L.J. 330.

[87] *Cf. Murphy* v. *Hurley* [1921] 2 I.R. 335; *Cowan* v. *Factor* [1948] I.R. 128. See also *Gray* v. *Siev* (1949) 83 I.L.T.R. 67; *Lapedus* v. *Glavey* (1965) 99 I.L.T.R. 1.

[88] This is the only limitation on the tenant's right to exclusive possession (para. 17.009, *supra*) and the landlord is not otherwise entitled to enter the premises and come and go as he pleases.

[89] *Cf.* Deasy's Act, s. 38 and the Republic's Rent Restrictions (Amendment) Act, 1967, s. 11, para. 17.057, *infra*.

[90] *O'Reilly* v. *Doherty* [1928] N.I. 32; *Conway* v. *Davin* (1935) 69 I.L.T.R. 33; *Geraghty* v. *Montgomery* [1953] I.R. 89; *Victor Weston (Eire) Ltd.* v. *Kenny* [1954] I.R. 191. *Cf. Beaver* v. *McFarlane* [1932] L.J.Ir. 128; *Poole* v. *Siev* (1942) 76 I.L.T.R. 191. See also *Chambers* v. *Cork Corp.* (1959) 93 I.L.T.R. 45; *Scully* v. *Boland Ltd.* [1962] I.R. 58; *Bowes* v. *Dublin Corp.* [1965] I.R. 476; *McCauliffe* v. *Moloney* [1971] I.R. 200. See also Russell, "Nuisance by Landlords" (1977) 40 M.L.R. 651. And note as regards N.I. the Defective Premises (N.I.) Order, 1975, as to which see *Irish Conveyancing Law* (1978), para. 5.24.

[91] See discussion, ch. 4, *ante*.

[92] Renewable Leasehold Conversion Act, 1849, s. 37.

[93] *Allen* v. *Murphy* [1917] 1 I.R. 484.

[94] *Jameson* v. *Squire* [1948] I.R. 153 (see *A Casebook on Irish Land Law* (1984), p. 280). See also *Tiernan* v. *Feely* [1949] I.R. 381; *Cassidy* v. *Baker* (1969) 103 I.L.T.R. 40.

[95] See the definition in s. 1 of Deasy's Act, 1860. See also *Donegal* v. *Verner* (1872) I.R. 6 C.L. 504; *Carson* v. *Jameson* [1908] 2 I.R. 308; *Lloyd* v. *Keys* [1901] 2 I.R. 416; *Freeman* v. *Att.-Gen.* [1949] Ir.Jur.Rep. 61.

regular intervals stated,[96] and may also be responsible for paying the rates[97] and other outgoings[98] *e.g.*, gas and electricity charges, relating to the demised premises.

(ii) Repairs

17.045. The tenant will usually be responsible to some extent for repairs to the demised premises. He frequently undertakes to keep the premises "in good and substantial" repair or to use them in a "tenantable" or "tenantlike" manner.[99] However, he is often expressly excepted from liability in respect of "fair wear and tear,"[1] as he probably is even in the absence of an express exception.[2] In the case of "tenements" within the Republic's Landlord and Tenant (Amendment) Act, 1980, a tenant's liability for breach of an express or implied repairing covenant is limited to the diminution in the value of the reversion and, unless the lessee has caused wilful damage, is excluded where repair is impossible, due to the age and condition of the tenement, or its cost would be excessive or, even if carried out, the tenement could not be profitably used, unless re-built or re-constructed.[3]

(iii) User of Premises

17.046. It is usual for the tenant to be restricted in the user he makes of the demised premises. Such restrictions protect the landlord who may own neighbouring property and who anyway will eventually get the property back and will not want its value reduced by the use made of it by the tenant in the meantime. In the case of residential premises, there is usually a covenant or agreement by the tenant to use the premises as a private dwelling-house only,[4] or not to use them for the purposes of carrying on any business, trade or profession.[5] Sometimes the covenant prohibits use for the purposes of

[96] Often in advance, *Malone* v. *Manton* (1879) 13 I.L.T.R. 144; *National Telephone Co.* v. *Clothworthy* (1902) 2 N.I.J.R. 25. See also *Smallman Ltd.* v. *Castle* [1932] I.R. 294; *Hennessy* v. *Cahill* [1945] I.R. 55.

[97] Generally charged on the occupier of land, *Leathley* v. *Dublin Corporation* [1942] Ir.Jur.Rep. 20; *R.C.B.* v. *Dublin Board of Assistance* [1948] I.R. 287; *Keating* v. *Turner* [1953] I.R. 1; *Harris* v. *Minister for Finance* [1966] I.R. 27.

[98] And Sched. A income tax which is still payable generally by occupiers of land in the Republic of Ireland, see Income Tax Act, 1918, and also Income Tax Act, 1967, ss. 14–17 and 20–28. *Bloomfield Land & Building Co.* v. *Lytle* (1903) 3 N.I.J.R. 88; *Wycherley* v. *Flynn* [1922] 2 I.R. 28.

[99] *Rushbrooke* v. *O'Sullivan* [1908] 1 I.R. 232; *Fleming* v. *Brennan* [1941] I.R. 499; *Groome* v. *Fodhla Printing Co.* [1943] I.R. 380; *Watters* v. *Creagh* (1958) 92 I.L.T.R. 196.

[1] *Cowan* v. *Factor* [1948] I.R. 128; *cf. Kiernan* v. *O'Connell* (1938) 72 I.L.T.R. 196.

[2] *McEvoy* v. *O'Donnell* [1946] Ir.Jur.Rep. 38. See Smith, "Repair, Renewal and Improvement" [1979] Con. 429.

[3] S. 65, replacing s. 55 of the Landlord and Tenant Act, 1931. *Groome* v. *Fodhla Printing Co.* [1943] I.R. 380; *Watkins, Jameson, Pim & Co. Ltd.* v. *Stacy & Harding Ltd.* (1961) 95 I.L.T.R. 122; *Gilligan* v. *Silke* [1963] I.R. 1; *O'Reilly* v. *East Coast Cinemas Ltd.* [1968] I.R. 56 (see *A Casebook on Irish Land Law* (1984), p. 557); see also *Fethersonhaugh* v. *Smith* (1979) Unrep. (H.C.,R.I.) (1976 4574 P); *cf. Taylor* v. *Moremiles Tyre Service Ltd.* (1978) Unrep. (H.C.,R.I.) (1975 No. 2636 P) (covenant for *insurance*, and *not* for *repair*). It should be noted that by s. 64 of the 1980 Act, s. 65 now applies to yearly tenancies arising by operation of law or by inference on expiration of a lease and to a statutory tenancy implied by holding over premises on the expiration of a lease. In *Whelan* v. *Madigan* (1978) Unrep. (H.C.,R.I.) (1978 No. 191 P), Kenny J. held that section 55 of the 1931 Act was confined to covenants in a lease and did not apply where a tenant held over after his contractual tenancy had expired.

[4] *Belton* v. *Nicholl* [1941] I.R. 230. See also *Bray* v. *Fogarty* (1869) I.R. 4 Eq. 544; *Domville* v. *Colville* (1873) I.R. 7 C.L. 68.

[5] *Kinsella* v. *Caroll* (1953) 87 I.L.T.R. 27. See also *Corry* v *Hatch* (1934) 68 I.L.T.R. 241; *Bryne* v. *Fox* [1938] I.R. 682; *O'Farrell* v. *Woods* [1957] Ir.Jur.Rep. 26.

"offensive" trades or businesses, *e.g.*, fish-frying or sale of intoxicating liquor.[6] On the other hand, where the covenant restricts user to or permits a specific trade or business, user for another kind of trade or business is not necessarily a breach of covenant.[7] If the premises are licensed premises, it is usual to have a covenant by the tenant not to do anything to endanger the licence or to cause a licensing conviction.[8] Where the landlord in such a case is the brewery or distilling company, there may be a covenant restricting the licensee-tenant to sale of the company's products,[9] *i.e.*, creating a "tied" house.[10]

17.047. Covenants restricting user can, of course, hinder future development of the property, especially in later years when the character of the neighbourhood may have so changed that the covenants have become obsolete. This problem is to some extent met in the Republic of Ireland in the case of leases of tenements within the Landlord and Tenant (Amendment) Act, 1980.[11] Section 67 (1) of that Act automatically modifies covenants, conditions or agreements absolutely prohibiting alteration of user of the tenement and makes alterations subject to the licence or consent of the lessor only. Section 67 (2) (*a*) then provides that the licence or consent, whether required expressly or impliedly under subsection (1), is subject to the proviso that it cannot be unreasonably withheld,[12] though the lessor may charge for his legal or other expenses in relation to the licence or consent. There is the further proviso that there can be no fine or other sum charged or an increase of rent payable for the licence or consent, unless the alteration involves the erection, provision or reconstruction[13] of any building or structure.[14] The court may authorise the user prohibited by the lease if the lessor of a tenement is not known to and cannot be found by the lessee in order to obtain the licence or consent.[15]

(iv) Alterations and Improvements

17.048. It is also common to have a covenant by the tenant not to alter the structure of the demised premises or to make improvements thereto.[16] This may again be an absolute prohibition or simply subject to obtaining the

---

[6] *Pembroke* v. *Warren* [1896] 1 I.R. 76; *Vernon* v. *Small* [1936] I.R. 677; *Byrne* v. *Fox* [1938] I.R. 683; *Dublin (South) City Markets Co.* v. *McCabes Ltd.* [1953] I.R. 283.

[7] *Re Cullen's and Rial's Contract* [1904] 1 I.R. 206; *cf. O'Farrell* v. *Stephenson* (1879) 13 I.L.T.R. 161. See also *Lynam* v. *O'Reilly* [1898] 2 I.R. 48.

[8] *Brown* v. *Watson* [1904] 2 I.R. 218; *Maguire* v. *Day* [1926] N.I. 80; *Heathcote* v. *Maguire* [1929] I.R. 170; *McIlvenny* v. *McKeever* [1931] N.I. 161; *Watkins, Jameson, Pim & Co. Ltd.* v. *Coyne* [1904] Ir.Jur.Rep. 28.

[9] *O'Leary* v. *Deasy* [1911] 2 I.R. 450; *Murphy & Co.* v. *O'Donovan* [1939] I.R. 455.

[10] This may also be achieved where the premises are mortgages, see para. 13.097, *ante*.

[11] S. 67, replacing s. 57 of the Landlord and Tenant Act, 1931 (as amended by s. 27 of the Landlord and Tenant (Ground Rents) Acts, 1967). There is no equivalent in N.I., but see *Survey of the Land Law of Northern Ireland*, para. 309. See also Land Law Working Group's Discussion Document No. 3 (*Landlord and Tenant*) ch. 4. And note Pt. II of the Property (N.I.) Order, 1978, see para. 19.46, *post*.

[12] See *O'Neill* v. *Murphy* [1948] I.R. 72; *O'Gorman* v. *Dublin Corporation* [1949] I.R. 40; *Lloyd* v. *Pembroke* (1955) 89 I.L.T.R. 40; *W. & L. Crowe Ltd.* v. *Dublin Port and Docks Board* [1962] I.R. 294.

[13] Not being an "improvement" as defined by subs. (3).

[14] S. 67 (2) (*b*), *W. & L. Crowe Ltd.* v. *Dublin Port and Docks Board* [1962] I.R. 294.

[15] S. 69, replacing s. 59 of the Landlord and Tenant Act, 1931, *Freeman* v. *Att.-Gen.* [1949] Ir.Jur.Rep. 61.

[16] *White* v. *Ryan* [1932] I.R. 169. See also *O'Neill* v. *Murphy* [1948] I.R. 72; *Killeen* v. *Talbot de Malahide* [1951] Ir.Jur.Rep. 19.

landlord's licence or consent. Once again the Republic's Landlord and Tenant (Amendment) Act, 1980, modifies such covenants in leases of tenements, so that at most the lessor's licence or consent is required and this may not be unreasonably withheld nor may it be a ground for charging a fine or higher rent.[17] Quite apart from the landlord's consent, alterations and improvements are likely to be subject to public control under planning legislation.[18] Furthermore, in the Republic of Ireland, certain improvements by a building or proprietary lessee[19] in breach of covenant remain valid if they are permitted or exempted development under the Local Government (Planning and Development) Act, 1963.[20] Also, in both parts of Ireland, improvements made by the tenant may entitle him to compensation in certain cases when he has to quit the premises.[21]

(v) Assignment and Subletting

17.049. It is important for the landlord to choose his tenant carefully for the latter will be in possession of a valuable capital asset during the tenancy. Apart from the danger of damage to the premises, the landlord will also want to be sure that the tenant will pay his rent promptly and carry out his other obligations.[22] These objects may be frustrated if the tenant is free to assign, sublet or otherwise part with possession to third parties unknown to the landlord, and so it is usual to insert in the lease or agreement an express covenant or agreement by the tenant that he will not assign or sublet the whole or any part of the property let to him without the consent in writing of the landlord.[23] We discussed earlier in this chapter the extent to which such covenants are modified by statute in the Republic of Ireland.[24] It is settled that conacre and agistment "lettings" ususally[25] neither create the relationship of landlord and tenant nor involve parting with possession and so do not infringe such covenants, unless they are expressed in even wider terms to cover such lettings.[26]

(vi) Insurance

17.050. The tenant may undertake to insure the demised premises,

---

[17] S. 68, replacing s. 58 of the Landlord and Tenant Act, 1931 (as amended by s. 28 of the Landlord and Tenant (Ground Rents) Act, 1967). Note also the definition of "improvement" in s. 67 (3) of the 1980 Act, which also applies to s. 29 of the 1967 Act, see fn. 20, *infra*, which is relevant in this context, see 1980 Act, s. 68 (4): *O'Gorman* v. *Dublin Corporation* [1949] I.R. 40.

[18] See generally the Local Government (Planning and Development) Act, 1963 (R.I.); Planning (N.I.) Order, 1972.

[19] Ch. 18, *post*.

[20] Landlord and Tenant (Ground Rents) Act, 1967, s. 29.

[21] Ch. 18, *post*.

[22] The landlord may insist on the tenant producing references as to his reputation and conduct in previous tenancies and on some third party becoming a surety to guarantee payment of the rent, see *Roper* v. *Cox* (1882) 10 L.R.Ir. 200; *O'Connor* v. *Sorahan* [1933] I.R. 591; *Jackson* v. *Hayes* [1939] Ir.Jur.Rep. 59; *Jordan* v. *McArdle* (1940) 74 I.L.T.R. 31.

[23] *Goldstone* v. *Annfield Holdings Ltd:* [1966] N.I. 148. As regards covenants against alienation in fee farm grants, see ch. 4, *ante*.

[24] Para. 17.038, *ante*.

[25] *Cf. Crane* v. *Naughten* [1912] 2 I.R. 318; *Irish Land Commission* v. *Andrews* [1941] I.R. 79.

[26] Note the terms of the implied covenant in s. 18 of Deasy's Act, 1860. See generally, para. 17.035, *ante*.

probably in the joint names of himself and the landlord, through a named insurance company and for a specified sum.[27] In the Republic of Ireland, such a covenant in a building or proprietary lease within the Landlord and Tenant (Reversionary Leases) Act, 1958,[28] is to be construed and have effect as though the lessee were to insure either directly, or through an agent as the case may be, with an insurer licensed under the Insurance Act, 1936.[29]

(vii) Costs

17.051. It has been the custom in Ireland that a lessee was responsible for paying the lessor's costs in relation to the lease, and often a contractual liability existed.[30] In the Republic of Ireland, however, a party to a lease is not responsible now for the other party's solicitor's costs and any contractual provision to the contrary is void.[31] In Northern Ireland, a similar restriction existed in the Costs of Leases Act, 1958,[32] but this was subject to any contrary agreement in writing. The Costs of Leases Act, 1958, was repealed, as regards Northern Ireland, by Article 70(5) of the Solicitors (N.I.) Order, 1976, Article 70(2) of which now provides:

> "A grantor or lessor who grants or leases any property for ever or for any term of years may as a condition of the grant or lease lawfully require that it be prepared by his solicitor but may not require the grantee or lessee to pay any costs of such solicitor in connection therewith."

B. IMPLIED

Even if the lease or tenancy agreement contains no express covenants, conditions or agreements, which is very unusual, several will be implied by the general law, mostly by statute.

1. *Landlord*

17.052. Under section 41 of Deasy's Act, unless the lease expressly provides otherwise, two covenants are implied in it on behalf of the landlord.[33] These are, first, that the landlord has a good title to make the lease[34] and, secondly, that the tenant will have quiet and peaceable enjoyment without interrruption

---

[27] *Re Lecky and Aiken's Contract* (1906) 40 I.L.T.R. 65. See also *Taylor* v. *Moremiles Tyres Service Ltd.* (1978) Unrep. (H.C.,R.I.) (1975 No. 2646 P). *cf. Sheppard* v. *Rennick* (1977) 111 I.L.T.R. 136 (covenant in lease by tenant not to do anything to render landlord's insurance policy void).

[28] Ch. 18, *post.*

[29] Landlord and Tenant (Ground Rents) Act, 1967, s. 30.

[30] A similar custom existed in the sale and purchase of land with respect to estate agents' and solicitors' fees. See the discussion in the *Survey of the Land Law of Northern Ireland* (1971), ch. 6 and now the Commission on Sales of Land Act (N.I.), 1972. Kerr, "Estate Agents' Commission in Northern Ireland" (1973) 24 N.I.L.Q. 1. *Cf.* as regards documents or certificates required by the purchaser to be produced by the vendor, Conveyancing Act, 1881, s. 3 (6). *Re Murray and Hegarty's Contract* (1885) 15 L.R.Ir. 510; *Re Furlong* (1889) 23 L.R.Ir. 407. See *Irish Conveyancing Law* (1978), paras. 13.49–50.

[31] Landlord and Tenant (Ground Rents) Act, 1967, s. 32.

[32] S. 1 (U.K.).

[33] *Leonard* v. *Taylor* (1874) I.R. 8 C.L. 300; *Murphy* v. *Brandon Co-Operative Society* (1911) 2 I.R. 631. See also *Colhoun* v. *Foyle College Trustees* [1898] 1 I.R. 233.

[34] *Knight* v. *Smith* [1947] Ir.Jur.Rep. 17; *Downes* v. *Hannon* (1949) 83 I.L.T.R. 78.

of the landlord "or any person whomsoever"[35] during the term of the lease, so long as the tenant performs his obligations under the lease.[36] Apart from these, the common law implies a covenant, in the case of a letting of *furnished* accommodation, that the premises are fit for human habitation at the beginning of the tenancy,[37] though this covenant does *not* extend to the currency of the tenancy thereafter.[38] However, section 114 of the Republic's Housing Act, 1966,[39] implies such an extended condition to keep houses or parts of houses, let at a rent not exceeding £130 per annum for a term of not less than three years,[40] in all respects reasonably fit for human habitation.[41] No such provision exists in Northern Ireland, though statutory provisions exist enabling the Housing Executive to serve a repairs notice[42] on the owner of a building unfit for human habitation.[43] There is also in both parts of Ireland, quite apart from liability under express or implied covenants, the sanction against landlords, who allow property to become unfit for human habitation or overcrowded, that the housing authority may serve a repairs notice or even, in extreme cases, a closing or demolition order relating to the premises.[44]

17.053. With respect to weekly or monthly lettings of controlled dwellings within the Republic's Rent Restrictions (Amendment) Act, 1967, there is now an implied covenant by the landlord to keep in repair the structure[45] and exterior of the dwelling, and to keep in repair and working order water, gas and sanitation installations,[46] having regard to the age, condition, character, situation and prospective life of the dwelling.[47] There is a corresponding implied covenant by the tenant that the landlord or his agents may, on giving 24 hours' written notice, enter and view the state and condition of the

[35] An express covenant is usually confined to interruption by the lessor or those lawfully claiming through him, para. 17.042, *supra*. See discussion in *Bowes* v. *Dublin Corp.* [1965] I.R. 476. *Cf.* derogation from grant, *Kennedy* v. *Elkinson* (1937) 71 I.L.T.R. 153. See also Russell, "Landlord's Covenant for Quiet Enjoyment" (1976) 40 Conv. 427.

[36] *Doyle* v. *Hort* (1880) 4 L.R.Ir. 455; *Kennedy* v. *Elkinson* (1937) 71 I.L.T.R. 153; *Solomon* v. *Red Bank Restaurant* [1938] I.R. 793; *Bowes* v. *Dublin Corporation* [1965] I.R. 476; *Lapedus* v. *Glavey* (1965) I.L.T.R. 1. See also the discussion by Kenny J. in *Whelan* v. *Madigan* (1978) Unrep. (H.C.,R.I.) (1978 No. 1918).

[37] *Wilson* v. *Finch Hatton* (1877) 2 Ex.D. 336. *Cf.* an unfurnished house, *Murray* v. *Lace* (1872) I.R. 8 C.L. 396; *Beaver* v. *McFarlane* [1932] L.J.Ir. 128. See also the discussion in *Siney* v. *Dublin Corporation* [1980] I.R. 400.

[38] *Sarson* v. *Roberts* [1895] 2 Q.B. 395.

[39] Replacing the earlier provisions of s. 31 of the Housing (Miscellaneous Provisions) Act, 1931, which still govern lettings made up to July 12, 1966, see 1966 Act, s. 121 (1) (*b*).

[40] Not determinable at the option of either party before the expiration of the 3 years.

[41] *McGowan* v. *Harrison* [1941] I.R. 331; *O'Neill* v. *Cork Corp.* [1947] I.R. 103; *Cooke* v. *McCabe* [1948] Ir.Jur.Rep. 6; *Conway* v. *Smith* [1950] Ir.Jur.Rep. 3. See also *Drayson* v. *Galbraith* [1955] N.I. 168. In *Siney* v. *Dublin Corporation* [1980] I.R. 400, the Supreme Court held that s. 114 of the 1966 Act did not apply to a housing authority (which was under a statutory duty to provide and let only dwellings complying with the terms of the section) *without regard* to the limits as to rent contained therein. The Court also held that the Corporation were liable in negligence, following the recent developments in this area in English case law (as to which, see *Irish Conveyancing Law* (1978), paras. 5.17–8.). As regards N.I., see the Defective Premises (N.I.) Order, 1975 (*Irish Conveyancing Law*, paras. 5.24–8.).

[42] Housing (N.I.) Order, 1981, Arts. 41–2.

[43] As regards the standard of such fitness, see *ibid*. Art. 46.

[44] Housing Act, 1966, ss. 65–72 (R.I.); Housing (N.I.) Order, 1981, Arts. 35–40.

[45] And the ceiling where the dwelling is a room or flat, 1967 Act, s. 11 (2) (*d*).

[46] 1967 Act, s. 11 (2) (*a*)–(*c*).

[47] S. 11 (5).

premises at reasonable times of the day and be afforded all reasonable facilities for execution of repairs.[48] The landlord, however, is not liable in respect of repairs for which the tenant is responsible by covenant,[49] or in respect of the tenant's fixtures.[50]

In Northern Ireland, the landlord under a regulated tenancy coming under the Rent (N.I.) Order, 1978, is now under a duty to keep in repair the structure and exterior of the dwelling-house comprised in the tenancy and the interior thereof (subject to the tenant's responsibilities) and in proper working order the installations for supply of water, gas and electricity and for sanitation, space heating or water heating (Article 41 of the Order). Under Article 43, the landlord is under a duty to keep in good order any part of a building or curtilage used by the tenant for access or other purposes and to ensure that any such part used for access is adequately lit and safe to use. These duties apply only in so far as they are not inconsistent with any express provision in the tenancy agreement (Article 40) and they do not require the landlord to carry out works or repairs for which the tenant is responsible or to keep in repair or maintain anything not constructed or provided by the landlord or any person from whom he derives title or which the tenant is entitled to remove from the dwelling-house (Article 44). Nor do they require him to rebuild or re-instate the dwelling-house in the case of destruction or damage by fire, flood or other inevitable accident, or to carry out works unless he has actual knowledge (whether because of notice given by the tenant or otherwise) of the need for those works. In determining the standard of repair under Article 45(1) regard is to be had to the age, character and prospective life of the premises. On application, under Article 46 the district council is to cause the premises to be inspected for breaches of such covenants and, if confirmed, is to issue a certificate of disrepair requiring them to be made good. Such a certificate is enforceable by order of a court of summary jurisdiction under Article 48. Failure to comply with such an order is a criminal offence and the council may carry out the works specified in the certificate of disrepair and recover the cost as a civil debt.

17.054. Finally, a landlord of a "cottier tenancy"[51] is under an implied obligation to keep and maintain the dwelling house[52] in tenantable condition and repair,[53] and, if the house is unfit for occupation through the landlord's default, no rent is recoverable for as long as it so remains.[54] This reverses the general common law rule that a tenant may not withhold his rent for breach of the landlord's obligations.[55]

---

[48] S. 11 (6).

[49] S. 11 (3), (4) (a) and (8). Nor as regards destruction by fire, flood or other inevitable accident, s. 11 (4) (b).

[50] S. 11 (4) (c).

[51] See Deasy's Act, 1860, s. 81. R. (Connor) v Londonderry Justices (1894) 29 I.L.T.R. 92. See also Cottier Tenant (Ir.) Act, 1856, and Labourers (Ir.) Act, 1883, s. 13 (both Acts now repealed in N.I.). Survey of the Land Law of Northern Ireland (1971), para. 338.

[52] S. 81 of the 1860 Act requires such a house or cottage to be let without land, or a portion not exceeding a ½ acre, at a rent not exceeding £5 p.a., for a term of 1 month, or from month to month or any lesser period of time.

[53] This is also part of the definition in s. 81.

[54] Deasy's Act, 1860, s. 83, Counihan v. Scariff R.D.C. [1914] 2 I.R. 81; Bartley v. Fagan [1938] I.R. 733.

[55] Corkerry v. Stack (1948) 82 I.L.T.R. 60.

2. *Tenant*

Various covenants or agreements are implied by statute on the part of the tenant and his successors in title.

(i) Rent, Taxes, Rates and Other Outgoings

17.055. Section 42 implies an agreement in leases that the tenant and his successors will pay the rent reserved, when due, and all taxes and other impositions payable by the tenant, *e.g.*, rates and taxes.[56]

(ii) Give Up Peaceable Possession and Repairs

17.056. Section 42 of Deasy's Act also implies in leases a covenant that the tenant or his successors will give up peaceable possession of the premises in good and substantial repair and condition, on determination of the lease.[57] This is subject to the tenant's right, if any, to remove fixtures,[58] to compensation for improvements,[59] to surrender in cases of destruction[60] and, in the Republic of Ireland, the obligation does not apply in cases of controlled dwellings under the Rent Restrictions (Amendment) Act, 1967.[61]

(iii) Waste

17.057. Connected with the question of repairs is the extent to which a tenant is liable for waste,[62] a subject on which there are several provisions in Deasy's Act. At common law, unless there is an agreement to the contrary, a tenant for years is liable generally for permissive and voluntary waste and, *a fortiori*, equitable waste.[63] In England, however, it has been queried whether a tenant with a short term or certain periodic tenants, *e.g.*, a weekly tenant, should be liable for permissive as opposed to voluntary waste,[64] and the view has been expressed that such a tenant's obligation is, in view of his very limited estate, a duty to use the premises in a "tenantlike manner" only, *e.g.*, generally a duty not to commit voluntary waste, "fair wear and tear excepted."[65] In Ireland the law of waste is now largely governed by Deasy's

---

[56] *Reardon* v. *O'Donnell* (1897) 31 I.L.T.S.J. 165; *Vandeleur* v. *McAuliffe* (1904) 38 I.L.T.R. 95; *Tyson* v. *Holmes* [1941] Ir.Jur.Rep. 41. See also para. 17.044, *ante*.

[57] Expected are cases of accidents by fire without the tenant's default. *Kiernan* v. *O'Connell* (1938) 72 I.L.T.R. 205; *cf. Cowan* v. *Factor* [1948] I.R. 128.

[58] Para. 17.060, *infra*.

[59] Para. 17.048, *ante*.

[60] Para. 17.059, *infra*.

[61] 1967 Act, s. 11 (8)

[62] See also on Waste, para. 4.149, *ante*.

[63] See Statute of Marlborough (sometimes spelt "Marlbridge" or "Marlebridge"), 1267, c. 23. Also Statute of Gloucester, 1278, c. 5. *Survey of the Land Law of Northern Ireland* (1971), paras. 311–16.

[64] *Yellowly* v. *Gower* (1885) 11 Exch. 274; *Doherty* v. *Allman* (1878) App. Cas. 709; *Woodhouse* v. *Walker* (1880) 5 Q.B.D. 404; *Warren* v. *Keen* [1954] 1 Q.B. 15; *Regis Property Co.* v. *Dudley* [1959] A.C. 370.

[65] See especially the discussion by Denning L.J. (as he then was) in *Warren* v. *Keen, op cit.* In N.I. Article 42 of the Rent (N.I.) Order, 1978, imposes on a tenant of a regulated tenancy various duties, namely to take proper care of the premises as a good tenant (and in particular to keep in repair such items as open fireplaces, glass (both external and internal), tap washers and boundary walls constructed by him or a predecessor in title), to make good any damage wilfully or negligently done or caused by him, any tenant of his or any other person lawfully living in or visiting the premises, to keep the interior of the dwelling-house in reasonable decorative order, not to carry out any alterations without the consent of the landlord (which consent is not to be unreasonably withheld) and to clear any blockage in pipes and drains.

Act, which in some respects confirms the common law and in others modifies it. These provisions are generally subject to any express provision to the contrary in the lease.

17.058. Section 25 of Deasy's Act renders fee farm grantees[66] and lessees of perpetually renewable leases[67] unimpeachable for waste other than "fraudulent or malicious" waste.[68] Tenants for lives renewable for ever are also expressly unimpeachable for waste under the Irish Timber Acts in respect of timber or woods planted by them or their predecessors.[69] Tenants under leases for lesser interests[70] may not, unless given previous written consent by the landlord or his authorised agent, open new mines or quarries on the demised land or otherwise commit waste thereon,[71] unless the land was leased for this purpose or with such consent or licence.[72] The landlord may work or lease mines and minerals excepted from a grant or lease of lands, but compensation[73] must be paid for any damage caused thereby to the tenant.[74] However, the tenant may work already opened or worked mines[75] and quarries, though, in the case of the latter, for the purposes of agriculture and good husbandry only and not trade or profit.[76] A tenant may also cut turf, but again not for trade or profit, where the land demised includes a turf bog or the lease confers a right of turbary.[77] Tenants with less than a perpetual interest in the land[78] are prohibited from burning the soil or surface of the land, unless they have the written consent of the landlord, and the landlord may recover a penalty not exceeding £20 per statute acre or part of an acre burned.[79] Nor may such tenants cut or lop trees or woods, without the landlord's written agreement or consent, for which there is a penalty not exceeding £5 per tree.[80] This restriction, however, does not apply to trees registered under the Irish Timber Acts[81] nor to "willows, osiers, or sallows." These provisions largely replace the common law right of estovers[82] and section 34 of Deasy's Act

---

[66] Of grants executed after Jan. 1, 1861. Excluded from this provision are grants under the Renewable Leasehold Conversion Act, 1849 (ch. 4, *ante,* but see *Bell* v. *Belfast Corporation* [1914] 2 I.R. 1) and grants executed after 1860 under an agreement for renewal in a lease made after 1860 under an agreement for renewal in a lease made before 1860 (see *Hamilton* v. *Casey* [1894] 2 I.R. 224).

[67] See the definition of "perpetual interest" in s. 1 of the Act.

[68] The Act does not define these terms, whch may mean "voluntary and equitable" waste. Note also "wilful" waste under s. 65 (3) of the Landlord and Tenant (Amendment) Act, 1980, replacing s. 55 (*b*) of the Republic's Landlord and Tenant Act, 1931. See *Gilligan* v. *Silke* [1963] I.R. 1.

[69] 5 Geo. 3, c. 17, s. 1 (1765). *Pentland* v. *Somerville* (1851) 2 Ir.Ch.R. 287; *Ex parte Armstrong* (1857) 8 Ir.Ch.R. 30; *Re Moore's Estate* (1902) 2 N.I.J.R. 127.

[70] Which presumably includes fee farm conversion grants excluded from s. 25, fn. 66, *supra.*

[71] Subject to ss. 27–31, *infra.*

[72] S. 26. Note that mining and mineral rights are now largely controlled by the state in both parts of Ireland, para. 6.115, *ante.*

[73] Assessed, if necessary, by a circuit court or, in Northern Ireland, county court judge, s. 33.

[74] S. 32.

[75] S. 27.

[76] S. 28. Also unlike s. 27 which is confined to "leases," s. 28 includes "demises" which covers oral tenancies, *Re Brown's Estate* (1874) I.R. 8 Eq. 297; *Wakefield* v. *Hendron* (1883) 11 L.R.Ir. 505; *Lifford* v. *Kearney* (1883) 17 I.L.T.R. 30. *Cf.* s. 29, *infra.*

[77] S. 29. See further on the right of turbary, para. 6.114, *ante.* Note also s. 4 of the Renewable Leasehold Conversion Act, 1849, *Gore* v. *O'Grady* (1886) I.R. 1 Eq. 1.

[78] See s. 1 of the Act.

[79] S. 30, replacing the Burning of Lands Acts (Ir.), 1743, 1763, 1765, and 1800.

[80] S. 31. *Townsend* v. *Lucey* (1897) 31 I.L.T.R. 124, *Cf. Dunn* v. *Bryan* (1872) I.R.Eq. 143.

[81] Para. 4.152, *ante.*

[82] *Ibid. Hayes* v. *Bridges* (1974) Ir. Term Rep. 390; *Dobbyn* v. *Somers* (1860) 13 I.C.L.R. 293.

permits a tenant to hold over until the last gale day of the "current" year[83] in lieu of a right to emblements.[84]

(iv) Assignment and Subletting

The implied position of a tenant in this regard was discussed earlier.[85]

(v) Insurance

17.059. Where there is no express covenant or agreement by the tenant to repair the demised premises, section 40 of Deasy's Act permits him to surrender[86] his tenancy on the destruction or rendering uninhabitable of the premises by fire or other inevitable accident due to no default of his, and thereby discharge himself from all future obligations. It would appear, therefore, that the tenant may pocket the proceeds of any insurance he took out to cover the premises, unless there is some term to the contrary in his lease or agreement.[87] The same would seem to apply to the landlord in respect of insurance he takes out, so that his tenant under an express obligation to repair may have to rebuild the property at his own expense.[88] In England, in such a case the tenant may be able to request the insurance company to apply the money in rebuilding the premises under the Fires Prevention (Metropolis) Act, 1774,[89] which never[90] applied to Ireland.[91] This makes it all the more imperative that the question of insurance be covered by an express agreement, as it usually is.[92] However, it is common for insurance companies to insert an exclusion clause for damage resulting from "riot or civil commotion." Moreover, in such cases the landlord or tenant may have a right to compensation from public funds, a subject of vital importance in view of recent events in Northern Ireland.[93]

(vi) Fixtures

17.060. At common law the general rule was that fixtures attached to the demised premises by the tenant belonged to the landlord and had to be surrendered along with the premises on determination of the tenancy.

---

[83] Held in *Earl of Derby* v. *Sadlier* (1866) 11 Ir.Jur. (N.S.) 171 to mean the current year of the tenancy rather than the calendar year. See *Survey of the Land Law of Northern Ireland* (1971), para. 314.

[84] *Hibernian Bank* v. *Harrington* (1912) 46 I.L.T.R. 27. As to emblements, see *Short* v. *Atkinson* (1834) Hay. & Jon. 682; *O'Connell* v. *Tyndall* (1834) 2 Jon. 20. Also para. 4.156, *ante.*

[85] Paras. 17.029 *et seq., ante.*

[86] See further, para. 17.084, *post.*

[87] See *Survey of the Land Law of Northern Ireland* (1971), paras. 319–21.

[88] See *Re King* [1963] Ch. 459; *Mumford Hotels* v. *Wheler* [1964] Ch. 117. *Cf. Lapedus* v. *Glavey* (1965) 99 I.L.T.R. 1.

[89] See s. 83. Also Foote, "Liability for Fire before 1800" (1969) 20 N.I.L.Q. 141.

[90] It was amended by s. 7 of the Law of Property Amendment Act, 1859, which section was repealed by the Conveyancing Act, 1881, both of which applied to Ireland. However, the 1774 Act was originally thought to be confined in application to London and was only later interpreted as applying throughout England. *Ex parte Goreley* (1864) 4 De G.J. & J. & S. 477.

[91] *Andrews* v. *Patriotic Assurance Co.* (1886) 18 L.R.Ir. 355 at 366–9 (*per* Palles C.B.).

[92] Para. 17.050, *ante.* And see *Lapedus* v. *Glavey* (1965) 99 I.L.T.R. 1 (landlord's covenant to repair). See also *Taylor* v. *Moremiles Tyre Services Ltd.* (1978) Unrep. (H.C., R.I.) (1975 No. 2646P).

[93] See Criminal Damage (Compensation) (N.I.) Order, 1977. Greer and Mitchell, *Compensation for Criminal Damage to Property.*

Gradually the courts relaxed this rule and permitted the tenant to retain trade, ornamental and domestic fixtures, provided they could be removed without doing substantial damage to the premises.[94] Then section 3 of the Landlord and Tenant Act, 1851, permitted tenants to remove agricultural or trade and agricultural fixtures and buildings erected on farms, provided the land was left in as good a condition as before and prior notice in writing was given to the landlord, who could elect to purchase them instead.[95] To a large extent the common law and the 1851 provisions seem to have been superseded by the general provisions in section 17 of Deasy's Act[96] which covers "personal chattels, engines, and machinery, and buildings accessorial thereto, erected and affixed to the freehold by the tenant at his sole expense, for any purpose of trade, manufacture, or agriculture, or for ornament, or for the domestic convenience of the tenant in his occupation of the demised premises." The tenant, or his successor, is entitled to remove such fixtures where they are so attached that they can be removed "without substantial damage"[97] to the freehold or the fixture itself, unless the lease or agreement provides otherwise, and in any event the landlord is entitled to compensation for any damage that does occur. However, the section also provides that the tenant must remove the fixtures either "during the tenancy"[98] or while he is still in possession or, where the tenancy determines by some uncertain event and without the act or default of the tenant, within two calendar months of the determination.

C. ENFORCEMENT OF OBLIGATIONS

17.061. The remedies available to the landlord and tenant for enforcement of their respective obligations under the tenancy depend partly on the terms of the tenancy agreement and partly on the general law. Since the agreement is usually drawn up by the landlord, it tends to favour him by concentrating largely on his remedies against the tenant and, until recent times, the general law also tended to favour the landlord. The advent of public control during the latter half of the nineteenth century and this century has evened up the scales in favour of the tenant.[99] It is important to remember that under the law of landlord and tenant obligations may be enforceable by and against not only the original parties to the tenancy agreement but also their successors in title.

---

[94] *Poole's Case* (1703) 1 Salk. 368; *Spyer* v. *Phillipson* [1931] 2 Ch. 183. See also *Hodges* v. *Dick* (1828) 1 L.Rec. (o.s.) 392; *Barnett* v. *Lucas* (1873) I.R. 6 C.L. 247. The tenant may remove landlord's fixtures for safe-keeping during the tenancy, *White* v. *Ryan* [1932] I.R. 169, and the terms of the lease may make the tenant's fixtures become part of the landlord's property, see *Lombard and Ulster Banking Ltd.* v. *Kennedy* [1974] N.I. 20 (machine hired to tenant becoming landlord's property).

[95] *Shinner* v. *Harman* (1853) 3 I.C.L.R. 243.

[96] See also s. 4 of the Landlord and Tenant (Ir.) Act, 1870, giving tenants of agricultural buildings a right to compensation for improvements on quitting possession. *Cosby* v. *Shaw* (1890) 23 Ir.L.R. 181.

[97] It is not clear whether this criterion differs from the common law approach to the quantum of damage or degree of annexation, which approach is now largely based on the intention of the party affixing the articles, see *Leigh* v. *Taylor* [1902] A.C. 157.

[98] See the discussion in Cherry, *Irish Land Law and Land Purchase Acts, 1860–1901* (3rd ed., 1903), p. 46. It is not clear why the tenant should not be allowed to remove fixtures within a reasonable time of a fixed term's expiry. *Deeble* v. *McMullen* (1857) 8 I.C.L.R. 355.

[99] See, further, ch. 18, *post*.

This is one of the distinguishing features of such an agreement when compared with contracts in general.[1]

1. *Original Parties*

So far as the original parties to the tenancy agreement are concerned there are several remedies which may be invoked, depending upon the nature of the obligation broken and to which party it relates.

(i) Action

17.062. To the extent that the obligations arise from agreements entered into by the landlord and tenant, either party can sue the other for breach of contract and recover damages suffered. For example, the tenant invariably agrees to pay the rent and the landlord can sue him for breach of contract if he fails to pay. Quite apart from contract, section 45 of Deasy's Act confers a statutory right to sue for rent in arrear.[2] Even if there is no relationship of landlord and tenant, *e.g.*, in a conacre or agistment letting,[3] and no "rent" is specified, the grantor has an action to recover "reasonable satisfaction" for use and occupation.[4] At common law, the tenant can set off amounts due to him by the landlord arising out of the same transaction, *e.g.*, breach of covenants in the same tenancy agreement. However, section 48 allows him to make a deduction or set-off in respect of "all just debts" due to him by the landlord, which may not be confined to debts arising from the tenancy agreement.[5] The landlord may also be prevented or estopped from recovering the full rent if he has agreed to an abatement or reduction and this has been acted upon by the tenant.[6]

17.063. So far as other obligations are concerned, *e.g.*, the tenant's obigation not to commit waste or in respect of restricted user of the premises, the landlord will often prefer to seek an injunction.[7] Indeed, in respect of waste, sections 35-7 of Deasy's Act provide a special summary remedy of a district justice's or, in Northern Ireland, Resident Magistrate's, precept[8] to restrain it.[9]

---

[1] Wylie, "Contracts and Third Parties" (1966) 17 N.I.L.Q. 351 at 358–61.

[2] *Pringle* v. *McDonnell* (1903) 3 N.I.J.R. 212; *Smallman Ltd.* v. *Castle* [1932] I.R. 294. See also s. 50 for apportionment on determination before the day rent is payable, *Re Leeks* [1902] 2 I.R. 339. *Cf.* if the rent is penal, *Wright* v. *Tracey* (1873) I.R. 7 C.L. 134; *Dickson* v. *Lough* (1887) 18 L.R.Ir. 518; *Bradshaw* v. *Lemon* [1929] N.I. 159.

[3] Ch. 20, *post.*

[4] S. 46. *Shine* v. *Dillon* (1867) I.R. 1 C.L. 277; *Donegal* v. *Verner* (1872) I.R. 6 C.L. 504; *Markey* v. *Coote* (1876) I.R. 10 C.L. 146; *Downing* v. *Low* (1884) 13 L.R.Ir. 556; *Power* v. *Condon* (1926) 60 I.L.T.R. 6; *Lynham* v. *Butler* (1933) 67 I.L.T.R. 121.

[5] *Mullarkey* v. *Donohoe* (1886) 16 L.R.Ir. 355; *Butcher* v. *Ruth* (1879) 22 L.R.Ir. 380. See also ss. 20 and 21. *Cf.* the Republic's Landlord and Tenant (Amendment) Act, 1980, s. 87 and Rent Restrictions Act, 1960, s. 44 *Higgins* v. *Monaghan* (1933) 67 I.L.T.R. 253.

[6] *Lefroy* v. *Walsh* (1851) 1 I.C.L.R. 311; *McKay* v. *McNally* (1879) 4 Ir.L.R. 438; *Bishop of Cork* v. *Lawton* (1940) 74 I.L.T.R. 163. See also *Re Ashe & Hogan's Contract* [1920] 1 I.R. 159.

[7] *Belton* v. *Nicholl* [1941] I.R. 230; *Dublin (South) City Markets Co.* v. *McCabes Ltd.* [1953] I.R. 283.

[8] See the form (No. 1) in Sched. (A) to the Act.

[9] *Ex p. Donaghty* (1869) I.R. 2 C.L. 22; *Brady* v. *Slator* (1863) 9 Ir.Jur. (N.S.) 152; *Kelly* v. *Drought* (1887) 21 I.L.T.R. 31. *Survey of the Land Law of Northern Ireland* (1971), para. 316.

(ii) Distress

17.064. In the Republic of Ireland the landlord can still probably exercise the ancient right of distress for rent, a "self-help" remedy recognised since the introduction of the feudal system.[10] As distress is rarely, if ever, used as a remedy, the question whether it is inconsistent with the 1937 Constitution has not been litigated. Distress involves the seizure of the goods of one person by another without any court order and so may be inconsistent with certain of the provisions of the Constitution.[11] At common law, distress is the taking or seizure of goods and chattels[12] on the demised premises, or which have been fraudulently or clandestinely removed by the tenant from there.[13] The goods should be impounded or secured on the premises as security for payment of the rent,[14] but, if they are not redeemed within 8 days, they are sold to the highest bidder at a public auction.[15] Any surplus from the proceeds of sale, after payment of the rent due, goes to the person from whom the goods were distrained. Frequently the right is provided for expressly in the tenancy agreement,[16] but section 51 of Deasy's Act provides that no distress can be taken for rent due more than a year before the distress.[17] Apart from this, exercise of the remedy is hindered by all kinds of restrictions which make most landlords hesitate before invoking it.

17.065. First, there are various statutory requirements as to procedure: a proper demand for the rent must be made[18]; distress can be made by the landlord or his known or authorised agent only[19]; entry on the premises cannot be made by breaking open an outer door[20]; distress cannot be made on a Sunday[21] nor between sunset and sunrise.[22] Secondly, various goods and chattels are protected or exempt from distress, both at common law, *e.g.*, perishable goods,[23] tenant's fixtures[24] and animals on the way to market,[25] and by statute, *e.g.*, certain clothing and bedding,[26] gas and electricity fittings[27] and

---

[10] Ch. 2, *ante*. See *Gordon* v. *Phelan* (1881) 15 I.L.T.R. 70. Longfield, *Distress and Replevin in Ireland* (1841); Stewart, *Law and Practice of Distress in Ireland* (1844).

[11] *E.g.*, Art. 43, see para. 1.83, *ante*.

[12] Including the tenant's cattle, Distress for Rent Act, 1741, s. 5. Even an innocent stranger's goods could be seized at common law (*Juson* v. *Dixon* (1813) 1 M. & S. 601), but it has been queried whether this is now constitutional, see 1937 Constitution, Arts. 40 and 43. Deale, *Law of Landlord and Tenant in the Republic of Ireland* (1968), p. 142.

[13] Provided they have not been sold to a *bona fide* purchaser for value without notice, *ibid.*, ss. 1 and 2.

[14] See Distress for Rent Act (Ir.), 1741. s. 6; Pounds (Provision and Maintenance) Act, 1935. Also Law of Distress and Small Debts (Ir.) Acts, 1888, s. 10 and 1893, s. 3 (Dublin City).

[15] Distress for Rent Acts (Ir.) 1741, s. 5 and 1751, s. 5.

[16] *Wright* v. *Tracey* (1874) I.R. 8 C.L. 478; *Nestor* v. *O'Neill* [1939] Ir.Jur.Rep. 80.

[17] *Tracey* v. *Brennan* (1874) I.R. 8 C.L. 527.

[18] *Ejectment and Distress* (Ir.) Act, 1846, ss. 10 and 14. *McLeary* v. *Davis* (1869) I.R. 2 C.L. 236; *Croghan* v. *Maffett* (1891) 26 L.R.Ir. 664.

[19] *Ibid.*, s. 12. See also Law of Distress and Small Debts (Ir.) Act, 1888, s. 7 (Dublin).

[20] *Gordon* v. *Phelan* (1881) 15 I.L.T.R. 70; *Re Cassidy* [1904] 2 I.R. 427.

[21] Sunday Observance Act (Ir.), 1695, s. 7. *Werth* v. *London & Westminster Loan Co.* (1889) 5 T.L.R. 521.

[22] *Tutton* v. *Darke* (1860) 5 H. & N. 647.

[23] *Darby* v. *Harris* (1841) 1 Q.B. 895. *Cf.* corn or hay in a barn or granary, Distress for Rent Act (Ir.) 1695, ss. 4 and 5.

[24] *Crossley Bros.* v. *Lee* [1908] 1 K.B. 86.

[25] *Nugent* v. *Kirwan* (1838) 1 Jebb & Sym. 97.

[26] Law of Distress and Small Debts (Ir.) Act, 1888, ss. 3 and 5.

[27] Gas Works Clauses Act, 1847, s. 14; Electricity (Supply) Act, 1927, s. 49 (7).

sub-tenants, lodgers and hire-purchase companies may succeed in having their goods exempted,[28] where a superior landlord makes a distress. Thirdly, no distress can be taken, or it may be restricted, in certain special cases, such as bankruptcy or insolvency,[29] winding up of a company[30] and controlled tenancies under the Rent Restrictions Act, 1960.[31]

17.066. If a wrongful distress is made, the tenant or other person whose goods are seized may seek an injunction,[32] sue for recovery of the goods[33] and damages.[34]

In Northern Ireland, the right of distress was abolished by section 122 of the Judgments (Enforcement) Act (N.I.), 1969, and a landlord must now, first, obtain a judgment for the rent due and, then, if necessary, have this enforced by or through the Enforcement of Judgments Office. The Office has power to make several different kinds of enforcement orders, *e.g.*, for payment by instalments, seizure and sale or delivery of goods and attachment of debts or wages.[35]

(iii) Re-entry or Forfeiture

17.067. At common law, the landlord can re-enter the property, or, as the Courts of Equity referred to it, forfeit the lease or tenancy agreement, for breach of a *condition* of the agreement by the tenant.[36] A denial of his landlord's title by the tenant in legal proceedings also effects a forfeiture,[37] though the landlord can waive the disclaimer.[38] It does not seem to have been argued in any of the Irish cases that forfeiture of the tenant's interest by his denial of the landlord's title in legal proceedings was the result of a breach of the obligation of loyalty arising from the feudal concept of tenure.[39] Yet, since the relationship of landlord and tenant has been based on contract and not on tenure since 1860,[40] it is arguable that the whole basis of the doctrine has disappeared. If the tenant's covenants or agreements are not made conditions of the agreement, it is usual to include a proviso for re-entry or forfeiture clause to cover breach of covenant or agreement.[41] Such a proviso or clause

---

[28] Law of Distress Amendment Act, 1908, ss. 1–5. See also Lodgers' Goods Protection Act, 1871 (largely replaced by the 1908 Act, s. 8).
[29] Irish Bankrupt and Insolvent Act, 1857, s. 321. *Re McQuillan* (1895) 29 I.L.T.R. 4; *Ex p. Shaw* (1895) 29 I.L.T.R. 6.
[30] Companies Act, 1963, ss. 219 and 285 (9).
[31] S. 43.
[32] *Re Cassidy* [1904] 2 I.R. 427.
[33] Dublin Police Act, 1842, s. 67; Lodgers' Goods Protection Act, 1871, s. 1; Law of Distress and Small Debts (Ir.) Act, 1888, s. 13; Law of Distress Amendment Act, 1908, ss. 1 and 2.
[34] Ejectment and Distress (Ir.) Act, 1846, ss. 16, 18 and 20; Civil Bill Courts (Ir.) Act, 1851, ss. 38–9; Law of Distress Amendment Act, 1908, s. 2.
[35] See generally Pts. III and V of the consolidating Judgments Enforcement (N.I.) Order, 1981.
[36] *Doe d. Henniker v. Watt* (1828) 8 B. & C. 308.
[37] *Congested Districts Board v. Connor* [1916] 2 I.R. 611; *Wallace v. Daly & Co. Ltd.* [1949] I.R. 352; *Gowrie Park Utility Society Ltd. v. Fitzgerald* [1963] I.R. 436. Cf. *Levingston v. Somers* [1941] I.R. 183. See also *O'Reilly v. Gleeson* [1975] I.R. 258 (see *A Casebook on Irish Land Law* (1984), p. 600), *infra*.
[38] *Bailey v. Mason* (1851) 2 I.C.L.R. 582.
[39] Ch. 2, *ante*.
[40] Para. 17.005, *ante*.
[41] *Bennett v. Kidd* [1926] N.I. 50; *Re Drew* [1929] I.R. 504; *Kelly v. Murnaghan* [1948] I.R. 38; *Breaden v. Fuller & Sons* [1949] I.R. 290.

may cover both non-payment of rent and breach of any other covenant or agreement by the tenant and, in case of the former, should not be confused with the Irish statutory right of ejectment discussed in the next section of this chapter.[42] The procedure for exercise or a right of re-entry or forfeiture, and how far a tenant is entitled to relief are discussed later.[43]

In *O'Reilly* v. *Gleeson*[43a] the Republic's Supreme Court held that, in the absence of an appropriate forfeiture or re-entry clause in the lease, a disclaimer of title by the lessee by an act *in pais* [i.e., without any legal proceedings] is *not* sufficient to ground a forfeiture of the lessee's interest under a lease for a fixed term. Henchy J. stated:

> "It is fundamental to the relationship of landlord and tenant that the tenant is estopped from denying (i.e., disclaiming) his landlord's title. That is to say, he cannot assert the rights of a tenant and at the same time say, in effect, that there is no tenancy because the landlord had not title to grant the tenancy, or because the title is in himself or in someone else. He cannot have it both ways. If what he does is a repudiation of the relationship of landlord and tenant, then in the case of a periodic tenancy determinable by notice to quit, he is debarred from insisting on the necessity for a notice to quit if the landlord chooses to eject him without serving one. The reason is that a notice to quit is necessary only when there is an admitted tenancy, so when the tenant repudiates the existence of a tenancy he thereby admits that there is nothing to terminate and that a notice to quit is unnecessary. However, as I have pointed out, in the case of a lease for a fixed term not determinable by notice to quit, the estate of the lessee in the land is not defeasible by mere disclaimer of title on his part.
>
> But even if a lease for a fixed term could be forfeited by disclaimer – or if a notice to quit, in the case of a periodic tenancy, is rendered unnecessary because of a disclaimer – the disclaimer must be not of some particular aspect of the landlord's title but of the landlord's whole title as landlord. If it were otherwise,the tenant could question, only at the peril of forfeiture or ejectment, any error, large or small, in the extent of the land leased or let, or in the terms of the lease or tenancy, or in the extent of the rights or duties (such as the use of furniture, or trading restrictions) incorporated in the lease or tenancy. The landlord could question such mistakes with impunity and have them rectified, whereas the lessee or tenant would imperil his leasehold or tenancy if he raised them. If that were the law, it would be unequal and oppressive."[43b]

It should also be noted that statutory restrictions on the landlord's right of re-entry have been imposed recently in both parts of Ireland. In the Republic, section 27 of the Landlord and Tenant (Ground Rents) (No.2) Act, 1978,

---

[42] *Russell* v. *Moore* (1882) 8 L.R.Ir. 318; *Gaffrey* v. *Bailey* (1883) 17 I.L.T.R. 89; *Sweeney Ltd.* v. *Powerscourt Shopping Centre Ltd.* [1985] I.L.R.M. 442.

[43] Para. 17.087, *post.*

[43a] [1975] I.R. 258 (see *A Casebook on Irish Land Law* (1984), p. 600).

[43b] *Ibid.*, pp. 272–3.

provides that a landlord can no longer invoke a covenant for re-entry and taking possession for non-payment of rent in respect of a dwelling-house whose tenant has a right under Part II of the Act to acquire the fee simple. In Northern Ireland, Article 55 of the Rent (N.I.) Order prohibits enforcement of a right of re-entry or forfeiture otherwise than in pursuance of proceedings in court in respect of any premises let as a dwelling-house on a lease subject to such right, so long as any person is lawfully residing in the premises or any part of them. Article 54 of the same Order creates the criminal offence of unlawful eviction and harrassment of an occupier of a dwelling-house and Article 56 prohibits eviction without due process of law of any occupier continuing to reside in a dwelling-house after determination of a tenancy.

(iv) Ejectment

17.068. Landlords in Ireland have long had, in addition to their contractual remedies for enforcement of their tenants' obligations, a special statutory right of ejectment for non-payment of rent.[44] A similar right exists in respect of deserted premises and overholding tenants. This whole subject is dealt with later in this chapter.[45]

2. *Successors in Title*

17.069. Having considered the position of the original landlord and tenant, we must now consider to what extent their respective successors in title become subject to the terms of the original lease or tenancy agreement. In Ireland, this subject is complicated by the fact that the common law rules have been subjected to statutory intervention at least twice, and the statutory provisions are not easily reconcilable.[46]

(i) At Common Law

17.070. The common law position was that generally the benefit and burden of the landlord's and tenant's covenants ran with the land and the reversion respectively,[47] *i.e.*, a successor in title to the landlord could sue a successor in title to the tenant on the tenant's covenants and *vice versa*. The two conditions that had to be met were: (1) the successor had to succeed to the estate of the original party, *i.e.*, privity of estate had to exist[48]; (2) the covenant had to "touch and concern" the land, *i.e.*, not depend upon personal characteristics of the particular parties or be collateral to the tenancy agreement.[49]

---

[44] Harrison, *Law and Practice Relating to Ejectment in Ireland* (1903). See also Longfield, *Action of Ejectment in Superior Courts of Ireland* (1846).

[45] Paras. 17.092, *post*.

[46] See the discussion in Bready, "Covenants Affecting Land" (1944) 6 N.I.L.Q. 48. Also Wylie, "Contracts and Third Parties" (1966) 16 N.I.L.Q. 351 at 358–61. As regards liability of a deceased landlord's or tenant's estate, see *Re Smyth* [1965] I.R. 595.

[47] Statute of Reversions (Ir.), 1634; *Spencer's Case* (1583) 5 Co.Rep. 16; *Butler* v. *Archer* (1861) 12 I.C.L.R. 104.

[48] Para. 17.028, *ante*.

[49] *Athol* v. *Midland G.W. Rly.* (1868) I.R. 3 C.L. 333. See further, ch. 20, *post*.

17.071. These rules were later given statutory recognition by sections 10 and 11 of the Conveyancing Act, 1881,[50] the only difference being that these sections used the expression having "reference to the subject-matter of the lease" instead of "touch and concern" the land. This, however, was held to mean the same as the common law expression[51] and most of the usual covenants or agreements one expects to find in leases nowadays have long since been held to satisfy the test.[52] The 1881 provisions applied, like most of the Act, to Ireland, despite the fact that provisions had already been enacted for Ireland in sections 12 and 13 of Deasy's Act, 1860. The two sets of statutory provisions overlap to a large extent, though in some cases one set only can apply, *e.g.* the 1881 Act applies to leases only, whereas Deasy's Act applies to all tenancies; on the other hand, Deasy's Act applies where the relationship of landlord and tenant is created in consideration of a rent or other return only, whereas the 1881 Act may cover gratuitous leases.[53]

(ii) Deasy's Act

17.072. Sections 12 and 13 of Deasy's Act provide that the benefit of agreements in leases or tenancy agreements can be enforced against successors in title of the tenant and landlord respectively by the successors in title of the landlord and tenant respectively. The essential difference from the common law rules or sections 10 and 11 of the 1881 Act is that there is no reference to "touch and concern" the land nor having "reference to the subject-matter" of the lease or tenancy agreement. All that is required is that the agreements be "contained or implied" in the lease or agreement,[54] though curiously section 13 adds the words "concerning the land," which suggests a condition similar to the common law's "touch and concern" the land.[55] It is arguable, then, that, at least under section 12, covenants or agreements may bind successors in title of the tenant which would not do so at common law or under the 1881 Act and such authority as there is on the point seems to support this view. Thus, in *Liddy* v. *Kennedy*[56] Lord Hatherley remarked on the effect of Deasy's Act on this subject:

> "It appears to me that this Statute has been framed for the express
> purpose of removing some of the technical difficulties which stood in the
> way of justice, and which, though devised originally with logical regard
> to consequences, have been found in practice to involve far more
> frequently the failure of justice than to secure any beneficial result to the

---

[50] See also Conveyancing Act, 1911, s. 2.

[51] *Davis* v. *Town Properties Investment Co. Ltd.* [1903] 1 Ch. 797; *Breams Property Investment Co. Ltd.* v. *Stroulger* [1948] 2 K.B. 1.

[52] *Brereton* v. *Tuohey* (1857) 8 I.C.L.R. 190 (renew lease); *Athol* v. *Midland G.W. Rly.* (1868) I.R. 3 C.L. 333 (use of conduit and water); *Morris* v. *Kennedy* [1896] 2 I.R. 247 (make street). *Cf. Costello* v. *Brice* (1932) 66 I.L.T.R. 146 (concerning adjoining land).

[53] See Sheridan, *The United Kingdom* (eds. Keeton and Lloyd), ch. 20.

[54] Or be "incident to the tenancy," *Burrowes* v. *Delany* (1889) 24 L.R.Ir. 503 at 517 (*per* Andrews J.), *Cf. Lyle* v. *Smith* [1909] 2 I.R. 58 at 89 (*per* Kenny J.) (see *A Casebook on Irish Land Law* (1984), p. 575).

[55] *Cf.*, however, *Burrowes* v. *Delaney, op. cit.*

[56] (1871) L.R. 5 H.L. 134.

parties; it carries into effect the true meaning of the contracts into which they had entered."[57]

17.073. The only full judicial discussion in Ireland occurred in *Lyle* v. *Smith*,[58] where at least some members of the Court of Appeal[59] held that a covenant to repair a sea wall did not run with the land, but did bind the lessee's assignee under section 12 of Deasy's Act. Gibson J. remarked:

> "The express language of sections 12 and 13 cannot be restricted or altered by forcing on it *Spencer's Case* applicable to the law of covenants at common law, which was so precious in the eyes of legal schoolmen that they could hardly conceive a statute disregarding it. We construe the enactment as it stands. It introduced a wholly new and revolutionary principle, substituting contract for ancient property law."[60]

The approach of some Irish judges seems to have been that Deasy's Act usually makes it unnecessary to decide questions such as whether the covenant "touches and concerns" the land,[61] yet a curious point is the number of cases where counsel have argued and judges have decided cases according to the common law rules without any apparent reference at all to Deasy's Act.[62]

17.074. Two further points should be mentioned with respect to the position of successors in title. First, it is the general rule that an assignee can recover damages only for a breach of covenant which occurs during the time when he was assignee.[63] Secondly, the common law rule that an assignee is no longer liable on the covenants once he ceases to be assignee[64] is modified by sections 14 and 15 of Deasy's Act. The assignee secures no discharge until he gives notice in writing to the landlord of the assignment by him[65] and, if it occurs between two gale days, he remains liable up to and including the next gale day following service of the notice.

VI. DETERMINATION OF RELATIONSHIP

There are many ways in which the relationship of landlord and tenant may determine. In considering the ways mentioned in the following paragraphs, the overriding point should be borne in mind that this is one of the main areas of statutory control, which is discussed later.[66]

---

[57] *Ibid.*, p. 143, *Cf.* Madden J. in *Lyle* v. *Smith, op. cit.* at p. 78; "privity of contract is substituted for privity of estate," and see Lord O'Brien C.J. at p. 70.

[58] [1909] 2 I.R. 58 (see *A Casebook on Irish Land Law* (1984), p. 575).

[59] Lord O'Brien C.J. and Gibson J.; *cf.* Madden and Kenny JJ.

[60] [1909] 2 I.R. 58 at 76. *Cf.* Madden J. at p. 78.

[61] *E.g.*, Madden J. in *Burrowes* v. *Delaney* (1889) 24 L.R.Ir. 503 and Kenny J. in *Lyle* v. *Smith, op. cit.*

[62] *E.g.* *Athol* v. *Midland G.W. Rly* (1868) I.R. 3 C.L. 333; *O'Leary* v. *Deasy* [1911] 2 I.R. 450; *Fitzgerald* v. *Sylver* (1928) 62 I.L.T.R. 51; *Costello* v. *Brice* (1932) 66 I.L.T.R. 146.

[63] *Doyle* v. *Hort* (1880) 4 L.R.Ir. 455 at 467.

[64] *Cf.* the position of the original tenant after he has assigned, para. 17.030, *ante.*

[65] *Powell* v. *Adamson* [1895] 2 I.R. 41; *Cottingham* v. *Manning* (1897) 3 Ir.W.L.R. 43.

[66] See ch. 18, *post.*

A. EXPIRY

17.075. The first obvious way in which a tenancy may determine is its expiry, *e.g.*, at the end of the term where this was fixed.[67] No notice to quit is needed in such circumstances.[68] In Ireland it is still common to find leases for lives, where the tenancy ends on an uncertain date, *i.e.*, the dropping of the last life.[69] It must also be remembered that, even in the case of a fixed term tenancy, there may be a special clause enabling the landlord, and, perhaps, the tenant also, to serve notice determining the tenancy before the fixed term is up.[70] Apart from that, it is usual to have a proviso for re-entry or forfeiture clause enabling the landlord to determine the tenancy prematurely for breach of covenant or agreement by the tenant.[71] This right of re-entry is now invariably enforced by an action for recovery of possession.

B. NOTICE TO QUIT

17.076. A notice to quit is the usual method of determining a periodic tenancy, *e.g.*, a weekly or monthly tenancy.[72] It can also be used in respect of a tenancy at will or at sufferance, but it is not necessary in this case.[73] There are various formalities required for a valid notice to quit.

1. *Form*

17.077. So far as agricultural and pastoral holdings are concerned, and note that these are rare in Ireland today,[74] a landlord's notice to quit must be printed or in writing, signed by the landlord or his lawfully authorised agent, and duly stamped.[75] As regards other holdings or tenancies, there is no need for any writing unless the agreement so provides.[76] If a particular form of writing is required, this must be followed strictly.[77]

17.078. Apart from the landlord, a notice to quit may be signed by the landlord's authorised agent,[78] but not by a rent collector.[79] One of two joint

---

[67] See *O'Farrell* v. *Woods* [1975] Ir.Jur.Rep. 26.

[68] *Wright* v. *Tracey* (1874) I.R. 8 C.L. 478; *McGrath* v. *Travers* [1948] I.R. 122. See also *Essor Teoranta* v. *Wong* [1975] I.R. 416.

[69] Ch. 4, *ante*. See also *Secretary of State for War* v. *Booth* [1901] 2 I.R. 692; *Allman* v. *McCabe* [1911] 2 I.R. 398.

[70] *Watters* v. *Creagh* (1958) 92 I.L.T.R. 196; *Cavendish Furniture Co. Ltd.* v. *Chalfont* [1967] N.I. 1.

[71] Para. 17.087, *post*.

[72] Para. 17.023, *ante*.

[73] *Ward* v. *Ryan* (1875) I.R. 9 C.L. 51 at 54 (*per* Morris J.) (reversed on another point, (1875) I.R. 10 C.L. 17); *Wilkinson* v. *Morris* (1883) 17 I.L.T.R. 153.

[74] Ch. 18, *post*.

[75] Landlord and Tenant (Ir.) Act, 1870, ss. 58 and 71: Notice to Quit (Ir.) Act, 1876, s. 6. *McDonnell* v. *Blake* (1890) 28 L.R.Ir. 395; *Avonmore* v. *Hobbs* (1897) 31 I.L.T.R. 53.

[76] *Doolan* v. *Cooney* [1949] Ir.Jur.Rep. 35.

[77] *Hamill* v. *Toomey* (1900) 34 I.L.T.R. 163; *Lamb* v. *Spacek* [1947] Ir.Jur.Rep. 39.

[78] *Erne* v. *Armstrong* (1873) I.R. 6 C.L. 279; *Sligo* v. *Davitt* (1840) 3 Ir.L.R. 146; *Listowel R.D.C.* v. *O'Connor* (1907) 41 I.L.T.R. 50; *Doody* v. *Byrne* [1950] Ir.Jur.Rep. 43.

[79] *Frewen* v. *Ahern* (1842) 4 Ir.L.R. 181; *Meath Board of Health* v. *Reilly* (1942) 76 I.L.T.R. 124; *Naas U.D.C.* v. *Herbert* [1960] Ir.Jur.Rep. 20.

tenants may give notice,[80] as may a mortgagor in possession[81] and a receiver appointed by the court.[82]

2. *Contents*

17.079. The general rule is that the notice must indicate clearly an intention to determine the tenancy. This may, however, be implied from a demand for a higher rent, which may be treated as an offer of a new tenancy.[83]

The parties may specify in the original tenancy agreement the length of notice required, though it has been quite common for them to contract that no notice will be given so long as the rent is paid.[84] If they do not, the common law lays down different periods according to the type of periodic tenancy.[85]

17.080. For a *weekly* tenancy one week's notice only is required,[86] and it seems that it may expire on any day of the week.[87] A monthly tenancy requires a month's notice,[88] which should expire on a gale day[89] or at the end of the monthly period.[90] In the case of a *yearly* tenancy, however, six month's notice is required and should expire at the end of a year of the tenancy.[91] If the date of commencement of the yearly tenancy is not known, it is presumed to have begun on the last gale day of the calendar year on which rent has become due.[92]

17.081. So long as it is clear when the tenant must leave, the notice to quit need not specify the day. If it is not clear, *e.g.*, because it is uncertain what is the nature of the tenancy or when it began, the notice should specify alternative dates, *i.e.*, "on 1st June next ensuing the date hereof, provided your tenancy originally commenced on 1st June, or if otherwise at the expiration of the year of your tenancy which will expire next after the end of

---

[80] *Hamill* v. *Toomey* (1900) 34 I.L.T.R. 163. *Cf.* tenants in common, *Morony* v. *Morony* (1874) I.R. 8 C.L. 174.

[81] Judicature (Ir.) Act, 1877, s. 28 (5); for N.I., see now Judicature (N.I.) Act, 1978, s. 93 (U.K.).

[82] *Keating* v. *Cleary* (1844) 6 Ir.L.R. 221.

[83] *Inchiquin* v. *Lyons* (1888) 20 L.R.Ir. 474.

[84] *Holmes* v. *Day* (1874) I.R. 8 C.L. 235; *Wood* v. *Davis* (1880) 6 L.R.Ir. 50, *Ryan* v. *Stapleton* (1906) 40 I.L.T.R. 614; *Stafford* v. *Rosenberg* [1932] L.J.Ir. 26.

[85] In Northern Ireland, Art. 62 of the Rent (N.I.) Order, 1978, now provides that a notice by a landlord or tenant to quit a dwelling-house let (before or after the commencement of the Order) under a tenancy is not valid unless given not less than four weeks before the date on which it is to take effect. In England there is also a minimum requirement of four weeks' notice for dwellings, Rent Act, 1957, s. 16, as amended by Housing Act, 1974, s. 123. See also Notices to Quit (Ir.) Act, 1876, ss. 1 and 6. *Survey of the Land Law of Northern Ireland* (1971), paras. 331–2.

[86] Six days is not enough, *Graham* v. *Donoghue* [1939] Ir.Jur.Rep. 45. See also *McErlane* v. *McGowan* (1944) 78 I.L.T.R. 106.

[87] *Harvey* v. *Copeland* (1893) 30 L.R.Ir. 412; *Fleury* v. *O'Reilly* (1906) 40 I.L.T.R. 12; *Skelly* v. *Thompson* (1911) 45 I.L.T.R. 138; *Sullivan* v. *Sheehan* (1916) 50 I.L.T.R. 41; *Doolan* v. *Cooney* [1949] Ir.Jur.Rep. 35.

[88] *Beamish* v. *Cox* (1886) 16 L.R.Ir. 458; *Hardwicke Ltd.* v. *Dolan* [1957] I.R. 35.

[89] *Coyle* v. *Duddy* (1899) 33 I.L.T. 322.

[90] *Kane* v. *McCabe* [1952] Ir.Jur.Rep. 41.

[91] *Ashtown* v. *Larke* (1872) I.R. 6 C.L. 270; *Wright* v. *Tracey* (1874) I.R. 8 C.L. 478. *Cf. Smith* v. *Foley* (1909) 43 I.L.T.R. 258.

[92] Deasy's Act, 1860, s. 6. It is not clear whether a contrary intention can be implied in a lease or has to be expressed, *Fitzwilliam* v. *Dillon* (1875) I.R. 9 C.L. 251; *Murphy* v. *McCormick* (1876) I.R. 10 C.L. 326; *R.C.B.* v. *McQuinn* (1877) I.R. 11 C.L. 218. See *1971 Survey (N.I.)*, para. 333.

one half-year from the service of this notice."[93] It seems that an error in the description of the demised premises may not be fatal to the notice, provided this does not mislead the tenant.[94]

3. Service

17.082. Normally the notice to quit must be served on the tenant, though, subject to statutory requirements,[95] it may be sufficient to serve it at his house and hand it to his wife or other member of his family.[96] Putting through the letterbox[97] or, indeed, service through the post is sufficient.[98] If the tenant is dead, service may be made on his personal representatives; if no representation is taken out, it may be made on the President of the High Court or, in Northern Ireland, the Probate Judge,[99] or on the persons in possession of the premises.[1] Service on one of several joint tenants is *prima facie* service on all of them.[2] In Northern Ireland, Article 73 of the Rent (N.I.) Order, 1978, provides that any document required or authorised by the Order to be served on a landlord of a dwelling-house is to be deemed to be duly served on him if it is served on any agent of the landlord named as such in the rent book or on the person who receives the rent.

4. Waiver

17.083. A notice to quit may be waived either expressly or by implication arising from the parties' conduct, *e.g.*, acceptance of rent after the notice has expired.[3] Section 35 of the Republic's Rent Restrictions Act, 1960, permits a landlord to accept rent in respect of controlled premises for three months after the expiration of a notice to quit, without waiving the notice. Waiver by implication depends upon the parties' intention[4] and it is not necessarily found where a demand, or even acceptance, is made of rent accruing due *after* expiration of the notice.[5]

C. Surrender

17.084. Section 7 of Deasy's Act, 1860, provides that a lease or tenancy may

---

[93] *Ashtown* v. *Larke* (1872) I.R. 6 C.L. 270; *Colfix (Dublin) Ltd.* v. *Hendron Bros. (Dublin) Ltd.* [1948] I.R. 119; *White* v. *Mitchell* [1962] I.R. 348. See also *Dempsey* v. *Tracey* [1924] 2 I.R. 171; *1971 Survey (N.I.)*, para 333. Key and Elphinstone, *Precedents in Conveyancing* (10th ed.), vol. II, p. 370.
[94] *McFarlane* v. *Lawless* [1944] Ir.Jur.Rep. 23; *Bank of Ireland* v. *Lyons* [1951] Ir.Jur.Rep.3. *Cf. Pryce* v. *McLoughlin* (1982) Unrep. (H.C.,R.I.) (1976 No. 2760P).
[95] *E.g.*, the Republic's Rent Restrictions Act, 1960, ss. 47 (1) and (2) and 54 (2) (v).
[96] *Warden* v. *Shea* (1905) 5 N.I.J.R. 7. *Cf. Lamb* v. *Spacek* [1947] Ir.Jur.Rep. 39.
[97] *Judd* v. *Cochrane* (1926) 60 I.L.T.R. 152.
[98] *Wilkins* v. *McGinty* [1907] 2 I.R. 660.
[99] Para. 16.03, *ante. Cf.* Notice to Quit (Ir.) Act, 1876, s. 4.
[1] *Kelly* v. *Tallon* (1950) 84 I.L.T.R. 196; *Hill* v. *Carroll* [1953] I.R. 52; *O'Sullivan & Sons* v. *O'Mahony* [1953] I.R. 125.
[2] *Pollok* v. *Kelly* (1856) 6 I.C.L.R. 367; *Biggar* v. *Pyers* (1879) 13 I.L.T.R. 127.
[3] *Hall* v. *Flanigan* (1877) I.R. 11 C.L. 470; *Earl of Listowel* v. *Kelly* (1883) 17 I.L.T. 285.
[4] *Pile* v. *Kent* (1930) 64 I.L.T.R. 17; *Lyons* v. *Johnston* (1944) 78 I.L.T.R. 19. *Cf.* Rent Restrictions Act, 1960, s. 35 (R.I.). *Sheppard* v. *Collins* (1927) 61 I.L.T.R. 124.
[5] *McGeough* v. *Gray* (1872) 6 I.L.T.R. 64; *McGilliard* v. *Crooks* (1903) 37 I.L.T.R. 187; *Murphy* v. *Kinsella* (1928) 62 I.L.T.R. 62.

be surrendered in one of the ways listed in that section only, namely, by deed, or writing signed by the tenant or his agent lawfully authorised in writing, or by act or operation of law.[6] The tenant does not have a right to surrender unless this is conferred expressly by the lease or statute; otherwise he can surrender with the landlord's consent only. It seems that an express right conferred by the lease will be construed strictly and its terms must be completely complied with.[7] Under section 40 of Deasy's Act, the tenant can surrender on destruction of the demised premises by accidental fire or other inevitable accident,[8] and a disclaimer of a bankrupt's lease by his assignee in bankruptcy operates as a surrender from the date of adjudication.[9]

17.085. Surrender by act or operation of law may be inferred from the acts or conduct of the parties.[10] A purported express surrender which fails to comply with the requirements of section 7 of Deasy's Act may nevertheless operate as a surrender by operation of law, because the landlord or tenant has become estopped from relying on the absence of the formalities.[11] A surrender may also be indicated by delivery to and acceptance by the landlord of possession of the premises,[12] admission of a new tenant with the former tenant's consent[13] or, indeed, acceptance of a new tenancy agreement by the tenant.[14] If the tenant assumes any other status which is inconsistent with that of tenant, *e.g.*, caretaker or licensee, this will effect a surrender.[15]

17.086. A surrender must operate immediately and cannot take effect *in futuro*,[16] though, of course, a contract for a future surrender may be entered into and must comply with the Statute of Frauds (Ireland), 1695.[17]

A surrender of part of demised premises only does not prejudice the rights of the landlord in respect of the remainder of the premises.[18] Where a surrender of a lease is made to obtain a renewal, any sub-tenancies do not have to be surrendered and the grantees of the renewed lease have the same rights against the sub-tenants as they would have had if no surrender had been

---

[6] See also Land Law (Ir.) Act, 1887, s. 8. *Trench* v. *Daly* [1899] 2 I.R. 41. And Rent Restrictions Act, 1960, s. 32(1) (R.I.).

[7] *McGrath* v. *Shannon* (1866) 17 I.C.L.R. 128; *Hodges* v. *Clarke* (1883) 17 I.L.T.R. 83; *Perrot* v. *Dennis* (1887) 18 L.R.Ir. 29; *Wilkins* v. *McGinty* [1907] 2 I.R. 660.

[8] Para. 17.059, *ante.*

[9] Bankruptcy (Ir.) Amendment Act, 1872, s. 97. See also Bankruptcy (Amendment) Act (N.I.); 1963, s. 2 (1). *O'Farrell* v. *Stephenson* (1879) 12 I.L.T.R. 161; *Re Brownrigg* (1886) 17 L.R.Ir. 589; *Re Keane* [1922] 2 I.R. 198.

[10] See *Lynch* v. *Lynch* (1843) 6 Ir.L.R. 131 at 138 (*per* Brady C.B.) (see *A Casebook on Irish Land Law* (1984), p. 592).

[11] *Bronsan* v. *Dobson* (1897) 2 Ir.W.L.R. 181; *Glynn* v. *Coghlan* [1918] 1 I.R. 482.

[12] *E.g.*, the tenant giving the key and moving out, see *McMurtry* v. *McGivern* (1898) 32 I.L.T.R. 154, *Cf. Sexton* v. *Kelly* (1903) 3 N.I.J.R. 60.

[13] *Doran* V. *Kenny* (1896) I.R. 3 Eq. 148. There must, however, be a change of possession, *Bourke* v. *Bourke* (1874) I.R. 8 C.L. 221; *McCracken* v. *Ross* (1886) 20 I.L.T.R. 65; *Anderson* v. *Anderson* (1887) 21 I.L.T.R. 35. See also *McSweeney* v. *McKeown* (1970) Unrep. (H.C., R.I.).

[14] Here a change of possession is not necessary, *Conroy* v. *Drogheda* [1894] 2 I.R. 590; *Butler* v. *O'Mahoney* (1898) 32 I.L.T.R. 93. *Cf. Booth* v. *Daly* (1855) 6 I.C.L.R. 460.

[15] *Lambert* v. *McDonnell* (1865) 15 I.C.L.R. 136. See also *Gray* v. *Gray* [1894] 1 I.R. 65.

[16] *Neville* v. *Harman* (1883) 17 I.L.T.R. 86.

[17] S. 2. *Ronayne* v. *Sherrard* (1877) I.R. 11 C.L. 146; *D'Arcy* v. *Castlemaine* [1909] 2 I.R. 474.

[18] Deasy's Act, s. 44. *Irish Society* v. *Tyrrell* (1866) 16 I.C.L.R. 249; *Mercer* v. *O'Reilly* (1862) 13 I.C.L.R. 153.

made.[19]

D. FORFEITURE

17.087. We pointed out earlier that the landlord may forfeit the tenant's interest and re-enter the premises for breach of condition or under a proviso for re-entry for breach of covenant.[20] The Irish action of ejectment for non-payment of rent we discuss below.[21] Forfeiture or re-entry for breach of condition or covenant relating to matters other than non-payment of rent is now governed by the Conveyancing Acts, 1881[22] and 1892,[23] though these Acts do not apply to certain covenants or conditions[24] and here the landlord can forfeit or re-enter without restriction.

17.088. Section 14 (1) of the 1881 Act requires the lessor to serve a notice on the lessee before he enforces any right of forfeiture, whether by re-entry or action for possession. This notice must: (1) specify the breach complained of[25]; (2) require it to be remedied, if it is capable of remedy[26]; (3) require the lessee to make compensation for the breach, if the lessor wants this.[27] In addition to the complications of this procedure,[28] landlords intending to re-enter without judicial proceedings must beware of infringing the forcible entry legislation,[29] especially if the tenant refuses to give up possession peaceably.

Where the lessor is proposing to exercise his right of forfeiture or re-entry or to bring proceedings for possession, the lessee can apply[30] to the court for relief against the forfeiture and the court has a general discretion to grant whatever relief it thinks fit in the light of the parties' conduct and all the other circumstances of the case.[31] There are no fixed rules for the exercise of this

[19] Deasy's Act, s. 8. See the discussion in *Hayes* v. *Fitzgibbon* (1870) I.R. 4 C.L. 500 (see *A Casebook on Irish Land Law* (1984) p. 597. Also *1971 Survey (N.I.)*, para. 329.

[20] Para. 17.067, *ante*.   [21] Para. 17.098, *infra*.

[22] S. 14, extended in the Republic to cover covenants or conditions against assignment, subletting, parting with possession or disposing of land by s. 35 (1) of the Landlord and Tenant (Ground Rents) Act, 1967. *Ashby* v. *Rave* [1932] L.J.Ir. 73; *McEvoy* v. *Arnott* [1943] I.R. 214.

[23] Ss. 2, 4 and 5. *Mercer's Co.* v. *McKeefrey* (1896) 30 I.L.T.R. 41; *Ferguson* v. *Ferguson* [1924] 1 I.R. 22; *M.C.B. (Galway) Ltd.* v. *Industrial Development Authority* [1981] I.L.R.M. 58 (see *A Casebook on Irish Land Law* (1984), p. 604); *O'Connor* v. *Mooney & Co. Ltd.* [1982] I.L.R.M. 373 (*ibid.*, p. 606); *Enock* v. *Jones Estates Ltd.* [1983] I.L.R.M. 532.

[24] *E.g.* covenants in mining leases or conditions against bankruptcy of the lessee or the taking of the lessee's interest in execution, see 1881 Act, s. 14 (6) and 1892 Act, s. 2. *Re Drew* [1929] I.R. 504; *Monument Creameries Ltd.* v. *Carysfort Estates Ltd.* [1967] I.R. 462. Covenants against assignment, etc. are also still excluded in N.I., fn. 22, *supra*. Also para. 17.091, *post*.

[25] *Mercer's Co.* v. *McKeefrey* (1896) 30 I.L.T.R. 41; *McIlvenny* v. *McKeever* [1931] N.I. 161; *Minister for Local Government* v. *Kenny* (1941) 75 I.L.T.R. 26.

[26] *Walsh* v. *Wightman* [1927] N.I. 7. See also *Rugby School* v. *Tannahill* [1935] 1 K.B. 87; *Glass* v. *Kencakes* [1964] 3 All E.R. 807.

[27] *Lock* v. *Pearce* [1893] 2 Ch. 271. See also *McIlvenny* v. *McKeever*, *op. cit.*

[28] See the criticisms in Law Com. W.P. No. 16, *Termination of Tenancies* (1968). See also *Sweeney Ltd.* v. *Powerscourt Shopping Centre Ltd.* [1985] I.L.R.M. 442.

[29] Forcible Entry Acts, 1381, 1391 and 1429; Forcible Entry Acts (Ir.) 1634 and 1786. See also the Republic's Forcible Entry and Occupation Act, 1971.

[30] Or counterclaim in, or raise it in defence to, any action for possession by the lessor. *Minister for Local Government* v. *Kenny* (1941) 75 I.L.T.R. 26. See also *Powerscourt* v. *Doran* [1941] Ir.Jur.Rep. 83 (application on appeal).

[31] *Watkins, Jameson, Pim & Co. Ltd.* v. *Coyne* [1940] Ir.Jur.Rep. 28; *Treanor* v. *Watchman & Keenan* [1942] Ir.Jur.Rep. 40. *Cf. Ferguson* v. *Ferguson* [1924] 1 I.R. 22; *Maguire* v. *Day* [1926] N.I. 80; *Breaden* v. *Fuller & Son Ltd.* [1949] I.R. 290. See also *Walsh* v. *Legge* (1976) Unrep. (H.C., R.I.) (1972 No. 3328 P).

discretion which is administered by the courts on general equitable principles.[32] It is important to note that relief in these cases must be sought *before* the forfeiture or re-entry is completed and the lessee should apply as soon as he receives the statutory notice under section 14 of the 1881 Act.[33]

17.089. Normally, forfeiture of a lease terminates all interests derived from the lease, including sub-leases or mortgages. However, a sub-lessee[34] now has a statutory right to apply for relief from the court, which may take the form of an order vesting the whole term (but no longer) of the lease in the sub-lessee, on such terms and conditions as the court thinks fit.[35]

17.090. The 1881 and 1892 Acts do not cover forfeiture or re-entry for non-payment of rent[36] and there seem to be no statutory provisions governing the subject in Ireland, corresponding to the English provisions in sections 210–212 of the Common Law Procedure Act, 1852.[37] The only requirement would seem to be the common law one that the landlord must make a formal demand for the rent, unless the tenancy agreement exempts him from this.[38] The tenant is entitled to equitable relief against the forfeiture for non-payment of rent.[39] However, in cases of non-payment of rent, the landlord can, and usually does, invoke the statutory remedy of ejectment which is largely governed by Deasy's Act. In Northern Ireland, section 94 of the Judicature (N.I.) Act, 1978, now confers jurisdiction on the court to grant relief after a judgment or decree for possession in any action of ejectment for non-payment of rent, including an action for forfeiture for non-payment of rent.

17.091. Section 14 of the 1881 Act did not apply to a covenant or condition against assignment or subletting the land leased, but this limitation on the right to relief was repealed in the Republic by section 35 of the Landlord and Tenant (Ground Rents) Act, 1967. Section 14, as originally enacted, did not apply to a condition for forfeiture on the bankruptcy of the lessee and, by the definition section, section 2, bankruptcy included the liquidation of a company, whether voluntary or by the court. The Conveyancing Act, 1892, section 2, amended this by providing that the exemption of the case of the tenant's bankruptcy or liquidation from section 14 was to apply only after the expiration of one year from the bankruptcy, and was not to apply at all if the

---

[32] *Breaden* v. *Fuller & Son Ltd., op. cit.*; *M.C.B. (Galway) Ltd* v. *Industrial Development Authority* [1981] I.L.R.M. 58 (see *A Casebook on Irish Land Law* (1984), p. 604); *O'Connor* v. *Mooney & Co. Ltd.* [1982] I.L.R.M. 373 (*ibid.*, p. 606); *Enock* v. *Jones Estates Ltd.* [1983] I.L.R.M. 532. See also *Hyman* v. *Rose* [1912] A.C. 623; *Belgravia Insurance Co. Ltd.* v. *Meah* [1964] 1 Q.B. 436.

[33] *Cf.* cases of non-payment of rent, para. 17.104, *infra*.

[34] But not a squatter, *Tickner* v. *Buzzacott* [1965] Ch. 426, para. 23.11, *post*.

[35] 1892 Act, ss. 4 and 5. See *O'Connor* v. *Mooney & Co. Ltd.* [1982] I.L.R.M. 373 (see *A Casebook on Irish Land Law* (1984), p. 606; *Enock* v. *Jones Estates Ltd.* [1983] I.L.R.M. 532.

[36] 1881 Act, s. 14 (8).

[37] *Cf.* Common Law Procedure Amendment (Ir.) Act, 1853.

[38] *Barry* v. *Clover* (1859) 10 I.C.L.R. 113, *Cf. Kelly* v. *Murnaghan* [1948] I.R. 38. See also *Rosborough* v. *Steenson* [1968] 19 N.I.L.Q. 458.

[39] *Whipp* v. *Mackey* [1927] I.R. 372; *Blake* v. *Hogan* (1933) 67 I.L.T.R. 237; *Ennis* v. *Rafferty* (1938) 72 I.L.T.R. 56.

lessee's interest was sold within one year of the bankruptcy or liquidation.[39a]

E. EJECTMENT

17.092. An action of ejectment is the legal remedy by which a landlord seeks to recover possession of property which has been let to a tenant.[40] It is a form of the general action for recovery of possession. If an owner brings proceedings for recovery of possession against a person who has no title to the property, the action is usually called an action for possession or an ejectment on the title. This type of action may be brought against a tenant whose tenancy has determined by passage of time or has been determined by a notice to quit or which has been forfeited so that the landlord is entitled to re-enter. However, when a landlord seeks to recover possession of lands from a tenant whose tenancy has expired or has been determined by notice to quit, it is more usual to bring an ejectment for overholding and, in the Republic, when the rateable value of the property does not exceed £100, such an action may be brought in the Circuit Court. In Northern Ireland, such an action may be brought in the County Court where the annual value of the land does not exceed £75.[41] Ejectment for overholding as a form of action has the advantage that the plaintiff may apply for final judgment for possession when the defendant enters an appearance and is thus more expeditious than other forms of action for recovery of possession. The ejectment for overholding was not, as is commonly believed, created as a form of action by Deasy's Act. Section 72 of that Act was intended to give jurisdiction to the Civil Bill Court to hear ejectments for overholding when the rent did not exceed £100. Deasy's Act also covers another type of ejectment action, the ejectment for non-payment of rent, which can be brought during the currency of the term created by the lease.

17.093. Every form of ejectment proceeding is an action for possession but, in order to give an outline of an extremely complicated subject in which there is a bewildering variety of terminology, we propose to use the term "action for possession" as meaning: (a) an action in which a person claims possession of property on the ground that he is the owner of it and that the person in possession has no title or has a defective title; *and* (b) an action in which the landlord claims possession on the ground that the tenant's interest under a lease has been forfeited and that the landlord is entitled to re-enter.

17.094. On this basis, the types of action in Ireland for ejectment may be broadly (if somewhat inaccurately) classified as: (1) an action for possession, or as it is sometimes called, an ejectment on the title; (2) an ejectment for

---

[39a] See *M.C.B. (Galway) Ltd.* v. *Industrial Development Authority* [1981] I.L.R.M. 58 (see *A Casebook on Irish Land Law* (1984), p. 604).

[40] Harrison, *Law and Practice Relating to Ejectments in Ireland* (1903); Deale, *Law of Landlord and Tenant in the Republic of Ireland* (1968), ch. 8.

[41] See further, para. 17.096, *post.*

overholding; (3) an ejectment for non-payment of rent; (4) an ejectment in respect of deserted premises; (5) an ejectment in respect of cottier tenancies; (6) an ejectment against persons who hold premises as servants, herdsmen or caretakers; (7) an ejectment against a cottier tenant or a tenant holding for a shorter period than one month on the ground that the tenant has maliciously or wilfully injured or destroyed the premises let to him.

We now propose to deal with each of these in a summary form.

1. Action for Possession

17.095. An action for possession is sometimes called an ejectment on the title. In so far as the relationship of landlord and tenant is concerned, this is the type of action which a landlord brings when he claims possession on the ground that the tenant's interest under a lease has been forfeited and that the landlord is entitled to re-enter. It is also the type of action which is brought by a landlord when there has been a tenancy but some person is in possession who has not succeeded to the tenant's interest and so cannot claim through that interest.

2. Overholding

17.096. If a tenant does not give up possession when his tenancy determines either by the expiration of the term for which it was granted or by a notice to quit, the landlord may bring an ejectment for overholding.[42]

17.097. The Rules of Court in the Republic and in Northern Ireland provide that, when the defendant enters an appearance to a summons or writ for ejectment for overholding, the landlord may apply to the court for final judgment and, unless the defendant can show that he has a defence, the landlord will be awarded an order for possession. Section 75 of Deasy's Act authorises the court to order the tenant in an ejectment for overholding to enter into a recognisance with two sureties in respect of the costs, damages and mesne profits to be recovered by the landlord but this has been made obsolete by the summary procedure for final judgment.[43] Every person in possession of any part of the lands must be served with a copy of the summons. Any tenant or other person in possession under him or with his collusion, who "wilfully" overholds, is liable to pay *double* the rent for the period of the overholding, but claims for this double rent are rarely made.[44] In Northern Ireland this provision for double rent has been excluded in cases of ejectment proceedings in a magistrate's court, where the tenant is liable only for an amount equal to the rent which would have been payable had the tenancy not been

---

[42] Deasy's Act, s. 72, replaced in N.I. by County Courts Act (N.I.), 1959, s. 12 (5) (*b*). See also Magistrates' Courts Act (N.I.), 1964, s. 76 (3) (*a*). Wylie v. Boyce (1929) 63 I.L.T.R. 85; Flynn v. Sweeney (1933) 67 I.L.T.R. 228; Bray U.D.C. v. Skelton [1947] Ir.Jur.Rep. 33; McArdle Moore & Co. Ltd. v. Kelly (1960) I.L.T.R. 48.

[43] Cherry, *Irish Land Law and Land Purchase Acts 1860–1901* (3rd ed. 1903), p. 133; Deale, *Law of Landlord and Tenant in the Republic of Ireland* (1968), p. 67. Domville v. Brack (1864) 16 I.C.L.R. 167; King v. Williams (1864) 16 I.C.L.R. App. vi; Armstrong v. Massey (1871) 5 I.L.T.R. 136.

[44] Deasy's Act, s. 76. Beck v. Creggan (1879) 13 I.L.T.R. 79.

determined.[45] The amount payable by a former tenant in respect of his occupation from the date of the determination of his tenancy to the date when possession is recovered is called mesne rent or mesne profits.

3. *Non-Payment of Rent*

17.098. Under section 52 of Deasy's Act, ejectment proceedings may be brought against a tenant for recovery of possession when a year's rent is in arrear,[46] but the tenancy must be one from year to year or for a longer term.[47] Most leases contain a re-entry clause under which the landlord may re-enter if the rent is in arrear for 21 days and, if the landlord wishes to avail of this remedy, he proceeds not by ejectment for overholding or by ejectment for non-payment of rent, but by an action for possession. At common law, a formal demand for rent had to be made before there could be a forfeiture and so in well-drawn leases there is invariably a provision that the landlord may bring proceedings for re-entry if the rent is 21 days in arrear, whether any formal or legal demand thereof shall have been made or not. In the Republic, section 7 of the Family Home Protection Act, 1976, confers jurisdiction on the court to adjourn proceedings by a lessor for possession of a house on the ground of non-payment of rent by one spouse, where it appears that the other spouse is capable of paying the arrears and it is just and equitable in all the circumstances so to adjourn the proceedings. Furthermore, section 27(2) of the Landlord and Tenant (Ground Rents) (No.2) Act, 1978, provides that section 52 of Deasy's Act is not to apply to a dwelling-house in respect of which the tenant is entitled to acquire the fee simple under Part II of the Act. When it is proposed to bring an ejectment for non-payment of rent, the effect of section 53 of Deasy's Act is that it is not necessary to make any demand for the rent and the absence of a clause of re-entry in the lease is not an answer to a claim for ejectment for non-payment of rent. The section also provides that it is not necessary that there should be a legal reversion in the landlord and the only requirement is that there should be a tenancy between the parties, whether by original contract or by lawful assignment, devise, bequest or act and operation of law and that there should be one year's rent in arrear. The proceedings must be brought by the landlord[48] or other person "substantially and beneficially" entitled to the rent.[49] Proceedings may be brought in the High Court or, in the Republic or Ireland, in the circuit or district court[50] or, in Northern Ireland, in the country or magistrates' court.[51]

---

[45] Magistrates' Courts Act (N.I.), 1964, s. 78. *1971 Survey (N.I.)*, para. 327.

[46] *Chester* v. *Beary* (1852) I.C.L.R. 120; *Lloyd* v. *Keys* [1902] 2 I.R. 416; *Smallman Ltd.* v. *Castle* [1932] I.R. 294; *Eustace-Duckett* v. *Thompson* (1938) 72 I.L.T.R. 226; *Hardman* v. *White* [1946] Ir.Jur.Rep. 68.

[47] *O'Sullivan* v. *Ambrose* (1893) 32 L.R.Ir. 102; *Batt* v. *Carr* (1895) 1 Ir.W.L.R. 22. Included are fee farm grants (*Chute* v. *Busteed* (1865) 16 I.C.L.R. 222 (see *A Casebook on Irish Land Law* (1984), p. 155); *Mennons* v. *Burke* (1890) 26 L.R.Ir. 193), but probably not tenancies of incorporeal hereditaments (*Irish Societies* v. *Crommelin* (1869) I.R. 2 C.L. 324; *Associated Properties Ltd.* v. *Nolan* (1951) 85 I.L.T.R 86).

[48] *Staples* v. *Bell* (1887) 21 I.L.T.R. 28. See also *Farrell* v. *Kennedy* [1936] L.R. 14.

[49] *E.g.*, a personal representative (*Doyle* v. *Maguire* (1885) 14 L.R.Ir. 24), mortgagee (*Smallman Ltd.* v. *Castle* [1932] I.R. 294) or receiver (*Lyons-Montgomery* v. *Dolan* (1899) 33 I.L.T.R. 144).

[50] Courts of Justice Act, 1924, s. 77; Courts (Supplemental Provisions) Act, 1961, 3rd Sched.; Courts Act, 1971, ss. 2 (1) (*d*) and 7 (*a*) (ii).

[51] County Courts Act (N.I.), 1959, s. 12 (2); Magistrates' Courts Act (N.I.), 1964, ss. 76–81.

4. Deserted Premises

17.099. Ejectment proceedings may be brought in respect of deserted or abandoned premises or uncultivated or unemployed lands, where half a year's rent is in arrear and there is no sufficient distress.[52] The district justice, or, in Northern Ireland, two or more justices of the peace may view and inspect the premises and issue a certificate of desertion or abandonment, which is evidence of the facts stated "unless the same shall be disproved" to the satisfaction of the circuit court judge in the Republic of Ireland and the county court judge in Northern Ireland.[53] These proceedings must be brought in the circuit court in the Republic or in the county court in Northern Ireland.[54] This form of ejectment has become completely obsolete and though the section creating it has not been repealed, we are not aware of any case where this remedy has been used during the last 50 years.

5. Cottier Tenancies

17.100. Summary proceedings maybe brought in the district court or, in Northern Ireland, the magistrates' court for possession of property held under a cottier tenancy.[55] This is defined by Deasy's Act as a letting by agreement or memorandum in writing of a dwelling-house or cottage without land or with any portion of land not exceeding half an acre, at a rent not exceeding £5 per year for one month or from month to month or for any lesser period and under which the landlord is bound to keep and maintain the dwelling-house or cottage in tenantable condition and repair.[56] Cottier tenancies were very common about 100 years ago but have become obsolete.

6. Servants, Herdsmen or Caretakers

17.101. Section 86 of Deasy's Act deals with a case of "any person [who] shall have been put or shall be put into possession of any lands or premises by permission of the owner, as servant, herdsman or caretaker."[57] Summary proceedings for ejectment may be brought in the district court or, in Northern

---

[52] Deasy's Act, s. 78, replaced in N.I. by County Courts Act (N.I.), 1959, s. 12 (3). See *Orpen-Palmer* v. *Gilman* [1936] Ir.Jur.Rep. 70; *Nestor* v. *O'Neill* [1939] Ir.Jur.Rep. 80.

[53] S. 79. See *1971 Survey (N.I.)*, para. 327.

[54] See fn. 51, *supra*.

[55] Deasy's Act, ss. 84 (wilful injury by tenant) and 85 (non-payment of rent); replaced in N.I. by Magistrates' Courts Act (N.I.), ss. 76–81. *Bartley* v. *Grey* (1938) 72 I.L.T.R. 105; *Bartley* v. *Fagan* [1938] I.R. 733.

[56] Deasy's Act, s. 81 Note the landlord's duty to keep in repair and the tenant's right to withhold rent if he fails (s. 83, *Counihan* v. *Scariff R.D.C.* [1914] 2 I.R. 81) and to compensate for loss of crops where he serves a notice to quit (s. 82). See also Cottier Tenant (Ir.) Act, 1856 (repealed in N.I., Summary Jurisdiction and Criminal Justice Act (N.I.), 1935, ss. 15 (9) and 62; *1971 Survey (N.I.)*, para. 338.)

[57] But not, apparently, other licensees, *Cody* v. *Houlihan* [1955–56] Ir.Jur.Rep. 61; *cf. R (Mahony)* v. *Cork JJ.* [1910] 2 I.R. 38 at 42 (*per* Holmes J.). See also *R. (Corcoran)* v. *Wicklow JJ.* [1912] 2 I.R. 349; *R. (Walshe)* v. *Swifte* [1913] 2 I.R. 113; *Gowrie Park Utility Society Ltd.* v. *Fitzgerald* [1963] I.R. 436; *Davies* v. *Hilliard* (1967) 101 I.L.T.R. 50; *Gatien Motor Co. Ltd.* v. *Continental Oil Co. of Ireland Ltd.* [1979] I.R. 406 (see *A Casebook on Irish Land Law* (1984), p. 543).

Ireland, in the county or magistrates' court against such persons when a demand for possession to them has been made and they have refused or omitted to leave.[58] Similar proceedings may be brought against any other person in actual occupation of the demised premises, *e.g.*, a trespasser, who fails to give up possession on demand.[59]

7. *Cottier Tenants*

17.102. Section 84 of Deasy's Act provides for summary proceedings for possession against any cottier tenant or any tenant for a shorter period than a month or at will or by sufferance who has maliciously or wilfully injured or destroyed any part of the premises let to him and which the landlord is bound to keep in repair.

17.103. Various provisions relating to procedure in all these cases of ejectment are contained in Deasy's Act and remain in force in the Republic of Ireland.[60] In Northern Ireland, these have mostly been replaced by later legislation.[61]

In any ejectment under Deasy's Act, it is not necessary to allege or prove the making of any preliminary demand for possession,[62] except in certain cases.[63] The contents of a lease may be proved by its counterpart or, if there is no counterpart, or it has been lost or destroyed, by a copy of the original lease or counterpart.[64] If the landlord's title is derivative, *i.e.*, he cannot claim under the original lease or tenancy agreement, *prima facie* proof of his title is receipt by him of at least one year's rent, or receipt of such rent by his immediate predecessor in title within three years before transmission of the title.[65] A landlord recovering possession by ejectment proceedings is still entitled to recover all arrears of rent on the basis that the tenancy remains in force until the order for possession is executed.[66]

---

[58] Deasy's Act, s. 86; County Courts At (N.I.), 1959, s. 12 (5) and Magistrates' Courts Act (N.I.), 1964, s. 76 (1) (*b*) and (3) (*b*) (see also s. 80 (*a*)). A demand must be made for possession, *Killarney R.D.C.* v. *Grady* [1912] 2 I.R. 545. *Hughes* v. *O'Gorman* (1944) 78 I.L.T.R. 16.

[59] Deasy's Act, s. 86; Magistrates' Courts Act (N.I.), 1964, s. 76 (3) (*a*). *Tullamore R.D.C.* v. *Burke* (1902) 2 N.I.J.R. 55; *Bartley* v. *Grey* (1938) 72 I.L.T.R. 105. See also *Limerick Corp.* v. *Holmes* [1947] Ir.Jur.Rep. 53. *Cf. Waterford C.C.* v. *Dunne* (1962) 96 I.L.T.R. 52.

[60] *E.g.*, ss. 54–60 (civil bills) and ss. 61–4 (lodgment of rent in court and tender before execution). *Chartres* v. *Muldoon* (1923) 57 I.L.T.R. 102; *Murphy* v. *Kenny* (1930) 64 I.L.T.R. 179.

[61] *E.g.*, County Courts Act (N.I.), 1959, Pt. VIII.

[62] S. 53, which is unqualified and misleading to a certain extent, fn. 63, *infra. Malton* v. *Maguire* (1877) I.R. 11 C.L. 4; *Kelly* v. *Murnaghan* [1948] I.R. 38.

[63] Ss. 75 (security from overholding tenants), 76 (double rent for overholding) and 86 (permissive occupants).

[64] This applies in all suits and proceedings by or on behalf of the landlord, s. 23. *Jagoe* v. *Harrington* (1882) 10 L.R.Ir. 335.

[65] S. 24 *Beatty* v. *Leacy* (1886) 16 L.R.Ir. 132; *Dempsey* v. *Ward* [1899] 1 I.R. 463; *Annaly* v. *Harrington* (1928) 62 I.L.T.R. 13. To the extent that this section encourages devolution without taking out a grant of representation, it has a questionable policy, *1971 Survey (N.I.)*, para. 295. *Cf.* fee farm conversion grants, Renewable Leasehold Conversion Act, 1849, s. 20 (3 year's receipt).

[66] S. 66. *Kennedy* v. *Gannon* (1901) 35 I.L.T.R. 188; *Hardman* v. *White* [1946] Ir.Jur.Rep. 68. *Cf. Hall* v. *Flanagan* (1877) I.R. 11 C.L. 470; *Wilson* v. *Burne* (1890) 24 L.R.Ir. 14.

17.104. Where a decree of possession or writ of *habere facias*[67] has been granted to the landlord in a case of ejectment for non-payment of rent, the tenant may still apply to the court within six months after its execution for an order restoring him to possession.[68] The court may determine such a claim in a summary manner,[69] after payment or lodgment of money to cover any arrears of rent and costs, and award, on the general principles of equitable relief,[70] restitution of possession to the tenant.[71] This restores the original tenancy and all interests derived from it, *e.g.*, sub-tenancies.[72] It also, of course, puts the landlord in a difficult position, since he may feel unable to deal with the property effectively for at least six months after recovering possession.[73]

In Northern Ireland, sections 70 and 71 of the Deasy's Act have been replaced by section 94 of the Judicature (N.I.) Act, 1978, which (following a recommendation in the *Survey of the Land Law of Northern Ireland* (1971)) drops the six month period for application and instead specifies that the tenant must make his application "at the earliest opportunity at which he can reasonably do so." Unless and until such an application is made, section 95(2) provides that the landlord holds the premises freed and discharged from the lease, but subject to any appeal from the original decree or judgment in his favour. For these purposes a "lease" includes a fee farm grant (section 94(3) and (4)).

F. MERGER

17.105. Merger is the converse of surrender of an estate or interest in land, though the result is the same. In the case of leasehold property, surrender occurs where the landlord acquires the tenant's interest,[74] whereas merger occurs where the tenant retains his interest and acquires the immediate reversion, or a third party acquires both the tenant's and landlord's interest.[75] In each case the lesser interest is absorbed in the greater.

17.106. At common law, no merger can take place unless the reversion and tenancy vests in the same person in the same right and there is no vested intervening estate. Thus there is no merger where the landlord takes possession as mortgagee of the tenancy,[76] nor will a legal lease merge in an

---

[67] Or, in Northern Ireland, an order for delivery of possession of the land, Judgments (Enforcement) (N.I.), 1969, s. 53 and Sched. 4.

[68] Deasy's Act, s. 70. *O'Farrell* v. *Cloran* (1871) I.R. 5 C.L. 442; *Rochfort* v. *Bermingham* (1873) I.R. 7 C.L. 508; *Hackett* v. *Fluche* [1927] I.R. 257.

[69] It is not clear what this means – perhaps by originating summons, or in the judge's private room or chambers? *1971 Survey (N.I.)*, para. 326.

[70] *Chester* v. *Farrell* (1883) 17 I.L.T.R. 73; *Wilson* v. *Burne* (1890) 24 L.R.Ir. 14; *Ennis* v. *Rafferty* (1938) 72 I.L.T.R. 56; *Delany* v. *Jones (No. 2)* [1939] I.R. 623.

[71] S. 71. *Newenham* v. *Mahon* (1841) 3 Ir.Eq.R. 304; *Fitzgerald* v. *Hussey* (1841) 3 Ir.Eq.R. 319. S. 71 refers to a "writ" of restitution, but such "writs" have been abolished in N.I., see Judgments (Enforcement) Act (N.I.), 1969, s. 121 and Sched. 3, Pt. I.

[72] *Lombard* v. *Kennedy* (1889) 21 L.R.Ir. 201; *Wilson* v. *Burne* (1890) 24 L.R.Ir. 14.

[73] *1971 Survey (N.I.)*, para. 326.

[74] Para. 17.084, *ante*.

[75] *Lennon* v. *Mark* [1899] 1 I.R. 416.

[76] *Farrelly* v. *Doughty* (1881) 15 I.L.T.R. 100. *Cf. Hurley* v. *Hurley* [1910] 1 I.R. 86. Also *Chambers* v. *Kingham* (1878) 10 Ch.D. 743.

equitable fee simple.[77] No merger can occur between a sub-tenancy and the head-reversion because of the intervening tenancy, which is an important point to remember in Ireland where so much urban land is held on "pyramid" titles made up of fee farm and sub-fee farm grants and long leases and sub-leases.[78] Indeed, since in such cases the intermediate tenancy usually relates to a much larger plot of land than the sub-tenancy, it is questionable whether there can be merger between the head-reversion and the intervening tenancy where the sub-tenant exercises his right to buy out the fee simple.[79] Thus even the common rule that merger or surrender of the intermediate lease destroyed the incidents and obligations attaching to it with respect to the sub-lease was reversed by the Real Property Act, 1845,[80] which provides, in effect, that the merger or surrender is to operate as an assignment of the intermediate lease for the purpose of preserving those incidents and obligations as would have existed but for the merger or surrender.

17.107. In equity no merger occurs unless this was intended by the party who acquires the two estates or interests[81] and there is a presumption against merger where this is contrary to his interest.[82] This is now the universal rule since the Judicature (Ireland) Act, 1877, provided that there is no merger by operation of law only of any estate which would not be deemed to be merged in equity.[83]

G. ENLARGEMENT

17.108. There are various statutory provisions enabling certain lessees to enlarge their interests into a fee simple, *e.g.*, under the Renewable Leasehold Conversion Act, 1849,[84] and the recent enfranchisement legislation in both parts of Ireland.[85] Section 65 of the Conveyancing Act, 1881, also enables lessees[86] of certan long leases granted rent free, or at a peppercorn or valueless rent, to execute a deed declaring the term to be enlarged into a fee simple.[87] The fee simple is to be subject to all the same trusts, powers and rights and all the same covenants and conditions as the leasehold term, but it is not clear if this includes restrictive covenants against alienation that would not normally attach and run with the fee simple.[88]

---

[77] *Re Sergie* [1954] N.I. 1.
[78] Ch. 4, *ante*.
[79] Ch. 18, *post*.
[80] S. 9. *1971 Survey (N.I.)*, para. 297.
[81] *Re Lloyd's Estate* [1903] 1 I.R. 144; *Re Alexander's Estate* [1938] I.R. 23.
[82] *Graig* v. *Greer* [1899] 1 I.R. 258; *McIlvenny* v. *McKeever* [1931] N.I. 161. *Cf. Re Toppin's Estate* [1915] 1 I.R. 330.
[83] S. 28 (4), replaced in N.I. by s. 89 of Judicature (N.I.) Act, 1978. See further on merger, ch. 24, *post*.
[84] Ch. 4, *ante*.
[85] Landlord and Tenant (Ground Rents) Act, 1967, as amended substantially by the Landlord and Tenant (Ground Rents) (No. 2) Act, 1978, Landlord and Tenant (Ground Rents) (Amendment) Acts, 1983 and 1984 and Landlord and Tenant (Amendment) Act, 1984 (R.I.); Leasehold (Enlargement and Extension) Act (N.I.), 1971, ch. 18, *post*.
[86] With an original term of not less than 300 years and an unexpired residue of not less than 200 years.
[87] S. 65 (1)–(3). See also Conveyancing Act, 1882, s. 11. *Re Waugh's Estate* [1943] Ir.Jur.Rep. 50.
[88] Para. 4.051, *ante*. See Taylor, "Enlargement of Leasehold to Freehold" (1958) 22 Conv. 101; *1971 Survey (N.I.)*, para. 330.

H. FRUSTRATION

17.109. Apart from the special statutory right to surrender in the case of destruction of the premises by fire or other inevitable accident,[89] it is not clear to what extent the doctrine of frustration of contract applies to leases or tenancy agreements in Ireland.[90] The traditional view was that it did not and the tenant remained liable whatever disaster befell the subject-matter of the lease or agreement,[91] but a relaxation of this rule has been recommended for Northern Ireland, allowing the court to order termination where the purposes of the lease or agreement can no longer be fulfilled substantially in accordance with the intention of the parties.[92] The House of Lords has recently expressed the view that the doctrine may apply in exceptional cases in England.[93]

---

[89] Para. 17.059, *ante*. Note also the special provisions in the Landlord and Tenant (War Damage) Act (N.I.), 1941.

[90] See the discussion in *Cricklewood Property and Investment Trust* v. *Leighton's Investment Trust* [1945] A.C. 221 and *National Carriers Ltd.* v. *Panalpina (Northern) Ltd.* [1981] A.C. 675.

[91] *Denman* v. *Brise* [1949] 1 K.B. 22; *Cusak-Smith* v. *London Corp.* [1956] 1 W.L.R. 1368.

[92] *1971 Survey (N.I.)*, para. 334. *Cf*, the views of the Land Law Working Group in Discussion Document No. 3 (*Landlord and Tenant*) (1982), pp. 9–13.

[93] *National Carriers Ltd.* v. *Panalpina (Northern) Ltd.* [1981] A.C. 675.

CHAPTER 18

STATUTORY CONTROL OF TENANCIES

18.01. There is now an enormous amount of legislation dealing with statutory control over most kinds of lease and tenancy agreement and this chapter is an attempt to summarise the main schemes in operation in both parts of Ireland. There has been considerable divergence between the two parts of the island on this subject, despite the fact that much of the original legislation applied to the entire island.

I. AGRICULTURAL AND PASTORAL HOLDINGS

18.02. The first obvious scheme of control to mention is that relating to lettings for agricultural or pastoral purposes which was introduced during the nineteenth century.[1] This included the Landlord and Tenant (Ireland) Act, 1870, which "legalised" the Ulster tenant-right custom and extended it throughout Ireland, and the Land Law (Ireland) Acts, 1881 and 1896, which introduced the "three F's" (free sale, fixity of tenure and fair rents) and provided for compensation for improvements and disturbance. However, this legislation was largely superseded by the Land Purchase Acts,[2] which enabled tenants to buy out the freehold of their land under a State-financed scheme. This scheme continued in operation after 1920, under legislation passed in both parts of Ireland. In Northern Ireland, the scheme was wound up under the Northern Ireland Land Purchase (Winding Up) Act, 1935, and thereafter only the collection of the annuities charged on the land bought out remains to be done. In the Republic, the purchase scheme has almost been completed and the main emphasis now lies on land settlement, relief of congestion and enlargement of uneconomic holdings.[3]

18.03. The result of the land purchase scheme has been, of course, that agricultural tenancies are now extremely rare in both parts of Ireland and most agricultural land is held for a fee simple estate, with the title compulsorily registered in the Land Registry. The rarity of agricultural tenancies will continue to be the case for some time to come, especially in Northern Ireland, because, so long as the land purchase annuity is being paid off, the land cannot be let, sublet or sub-divided without the written consent of the Republic's Land Commission[4] or the Northern Ireland Department of Agriculture.[5] However, in the Republic there was launched in 1983 by Allied Irish Banks and the Irish Farmers' Association, with the co-operation of the

---

[1] Ch. 1, *ante.*
[2] Beginning with the Irish Church Act, 1869. Ch. 1, *ante.*
[3] *Annual Report of the Irish Land Commissioners, 1982*, p.5.
[4] Land Act, 1965, s. 12.
[5] Irish Land Act, 1909, s. 32 (4) but note the relaxation in cases of tenancies not exceeding 31 years, Administrative and Financial Provisions Act (N.I.), 1956, s. 1. See the Departments (N.I.) Order, 1982, Art. 3.

Incorporated Law Society and the Royal Institution of Chartered Surveyors, a "Master Lease" aimed at promoting long-term leasing of agricultural land. The conveyancers, however, had to bear in mind that, as more and more land became freed from restrictions,[6] it might become subject to the old Land Law Acts of the nineteenth century, which had not at that point been repealed in either part of Ireland.[7] Not surprisingly there was then enacted in the Republic the Land Act 1984, section 2 of which excludes the "troublesome" provisions[8] in the old Acts from applying to agricultural leases. Arguably this is a stop-gap measure only and it may be that a new scheme of control for the agricultural tenancies of the future will be needed,[9] and this could also deal with the existing problems created by the conacre and agistment "lettings" which are still common in both parts of Ireland.[10]

II. BUSINESS TENANCIES

18.04. The Town Tenants (Ireland) Act, 1906,[11] conferred two main rights on tenants of premises held on tenancies for not less than one year. First, it gave tenants of premises situated in towns or villages, and used wholly or partly for business purposes, a right to compensation for improvements on quitting the premises, based on the capitalised value of the addition to the letting value resulting from the improvement.[12] Secondly, it gave tenants of premises, wherever situated but used wholly or substantially for business purposes, a right to compensation for loss of goodwill and removal expenses on disturbance without good and sufficient cause.[13] Unfortunately, this Act was not a success and it soon became a dead letter.[14] One reason was that the tenant had no right to compensation for improvements if the landlord made a reasonable offer of an extension of the existing tenancy or a new tenancy.[15] Compensation for disturbance could be claimed only after the tenant had quit

---

[6] In the Republic, before an agricultural holding can be let, sublet or sub-divided without the Commission's consent, not only must the annuity be paid off but also the holding must now be in an urban area or certified by the Land Commission as required for urban development, by reason of its proximity to such an area, Land Act, 1965, s. 12(4). See *Irish Conveyancing Law* (1978), ch. 8; *Horgan* v. *Deasy* (1979) Unrep. (H.C.,R.I.) (1976 No. 455P).

[7] See Leitch, "Present-Day Agricultural Tenancies in Northern Ireland" (1965) 16 N.I.L.Q., 491; *Survey of the Land Law of Northern Ireland (1971)*, paras. 286-8. See also the Land Law Working Group's Discussion Document No. 3 *(Landlord and Tenant)* (1982), ch.6.

[8] *E.g.*, Landlord and Tenant (Ir.) Act, 1870, ss. 3, 4 and 7 (compensation for disturbance and improvements) and Land Law (Ir.) Act, 1881, ss. 1, 4, 13 and 22 (sale of lease without consent, compensation for disturbance or depreciation and sale after execution of a writ for possession).

[9] *Cf.* the English Agricultural Holdings Act, 1948, as amended by the Agriculture Acts, 1954–70.

[10] See *1971 Survey (N.I.)*, para. 287. See also the Land Law Working Group's Discussion Document No. 3 *(Landlord and Tenant)* (1982), ch. 6. And see ch. 20, *post*.

[11] *Cf.* the English Landlord and Tenant Act, 1927. Brown, *Town Tenants and Landlords* (1906); Clery, Kennedy and Dawson, *Town Tenants (Ir.) Act, 1906* (1913); Lehane and Coles, *Town Tenants (Ir.) Act, 1906* (1906); Muldoon and McSweeny, *Town Tenants Act* (1907).

[12] Ss. 1-4 and 13. *MacIntosh* v. *Brosnan* (1907) 41 I.L.T.R. 246; *Wallace* v. *McCracken* (1910) 44 I.L.T. 178; *Bates* v. *Lawler* (1924) 58 I.L.T.R. 142.

[13] Ss. 5 and 7. *Cronin* v. *Kiely* (1910) 44 I.L.T.R. 205; *Allman & Co.* v. *McCable* [1911] 2 I.R. 398; *Cassidy* v. *McMahon* (1911) 45 I.L.T.R. 272.

[14] See the Republic's *Report of the Town Tenants Commission* (1928); *Report on Reversionary Leases under the Landlord and Tenant Acts* (1954, Pr. 2532), para. 21; *Report on Occupational Tenancies under the Landlord and Tenant Act, 1931* (1967, Pr. 9685), para. 21.

[15] *Bloomer* v. *O'Hara* (1917) 51 I.L.T.R. 71,. See also *Pim* v. *Day* (1911) 45 I.L.T.R. 265; *Hogan* v. *O'Grady* (1912) 46 I.L.T.R. 50, *Crowley* v. *Enright* (1913) 47 I.L.T.R. 222; *Porter* v. *Corscadden* [1931] N.I. 141.

the premises and, even then, was hedged in with conditions, *e.g.*, where the landlord had refused an extension or new lease without "good and sufficient" cause.[16] It was also fairly easy for landlords to grant tenancies outside the control of the Act.[17]

The 1906 Act was repealed and replaced in the Republic of Ireland by the Landlord and Tenant Act, 1931,[18] and superseded, though not repealed, in Northern Ireland by the Business Tenancies Act (N.I.), 1964.[19]

A. Landlord and Tenant (Amendment) Act, 1980

18.05. Here we are concerned primarily with Parts I, II, IV and VI of the 1980 Act,[20] which govern the rights of tenants of "tenements" to compensation for improvements and to new tenancies or compensation for disturbance.[21] Section 5 of the 1980 Act amended the definition of "tenement" contained in section 2 of the 1931 Act, as recommended by the Landlord and Tenant Commission in its 1967 Report.[22] First, it removes the distinction between an "urban" and "non-urban" area[23] and now a tenement is required to consist only of land covered wholly or partly by buildings or a defined portion of a building.[24] Secondly, it removes various disabilities which existed under section 2 of the 1931 Act because of the requirement of actual occupation[25] of the tenant, *viz.* (1) where the tenancy is held by one State authority (e.g., the Commissioners of Public Works), but occupied by another (see subsection (2)); (2) where the tenant is an individual carrying on a business in the premises [26] through a private company or is a holding company whose subsidiary company is in occupation (see subsections (3) and (4)). Section 3 (1) of the 1980 Act extends the meaning of "business" to cover usage of premises for any activity providing "cultural, educational, social or sporting

---

[16] *Haughton* v. *Ross* (1915) 49 I.L.T.R. 72. See also *O'Leary* v. *Deasy* [1911] 2 I.R. 450; *Samuels* v. *O'Brien* (1914) 48 I.L.T.R. 249; *O'Reilly* v. *Leahy* [1931] I.R. 474; *Corway* v. *Smith* [1931] I.R. 505.

[17] See the definitions in s. 18. *Heron* v. *O'Donnell* (1908) 42 I.L.T.R. 227; *Forte* v. *Wright* (1908) 42 I.L.T.R. 264; *Byrnes* v. *Rohan* (1909) 43 I.L.T.R. 229; *Porter* v. *Pigeon* (1912) 46 I.L.T.R. 16; *Storey* v. *Day* (1913) 47 I.L.T. 139; *McFarlane* v. *Montgomery* [1926] N.I. 119.

[18] S. 9. See also Landlord and Tenant (Amendment) Act, 1943; *Agreed Report of the Town Tenants (Occupational Tenancies) Tribunal* (1941). The 1931 Act, which was not confined in operation to business or commercial premises, but applied also to residential premises (see para. 18. 19, *post*), was replaced by the Landlord and Tenant (Amendment) Act, 1980, with amendments suggested by the Landlord and Tenant Commission's *Report on Occupational Tenancies under the Landlord and Tenant Act, 1931* (1967; Pr. No. 9685). See also the Landlord and Tenant (Amendment) Act, 1984.

[19] See also the Business Tenancies (Amendment) Act (N.I.), 1968.

[20] For detailed coverage of the provisions replaced, Pts. I - IV of the Landlord and Tenant Act, 1931, see Deale, *Landlord and Tenants Acts, 1931 and 1943* (1953) and *Law of Landlord and Tenant in the Republic of Ireland* (1968), ch. 7.

[21] Pt. III deals with reversionary leases.

[22] Pr. No. 9685, para. 84.

[23] As to which see *Readymix Ltd.* v. *Liffey Sandpit Co. Ltd.* (1977) Unrep. (H.C., R.I.), see para. 8.071, *ante.*

[24] S.5(1)(*a*)(i). Land not covered by buildings must be subsidiary and ancillary to the buildings, s. 5(1)(*a*)(ii). *Lynch* v. *Simmons* (1954) 88 I.L.T.R. 3.

[25] See *McManus* v. *E.S.B.* [1914] I.R. 371; *Corr* v. *Ivers* [1949] I.R., 245; *McEvoy* v. *Gilbeys of Ireland Ltd.* (1964) I.R. 30. In *Calaroga Ltd.* v. *O'Keefe* [1974] I.R. 450, Kenny J. held an apparent weekly tenant was not "entitled" to occupation under section 2 of the 1931 Act because the person who created the tenancy had only a two-thirds interest in the premises. In *Fetherstonhaugh* v. *Smith* (1979) Unrep. (H.C.R.I) (1976) No. 4574P), Costello J. held that the plaintiff was in "occupation" of the premises even though she resided only in an upper storey of the front portion of the premises with her husband and he used the rest, with her permission, for his solicitor's practice.

[26] *O'Reilly* v. *Kevans* (1935) 69 I.L.T.R. 1.

services" and for the activities of local authorities, health boards and harbour authorities. [27] However, section 4 of the 1980 Act, as amended by section 14 of the Landlord and Tenant (Amendment) Act, 1984, now contains a new provision that the Act does not bind a State authority in its capacity as *lessor* or immediate *lessor* of any premises.

1. *Improvements*

18.06. Under Part IV of the 1980 Act a tenant of a tenement is entitled to compensation from his landlord, on quitting the tenement on expiration of his tenancy,[28] for every improvement made by him or his predecessors in title which adds to the letting value and is suitable to the character of the tenancy. The amount of compensation may be agreed between the landlord and tenant, otherwise it will be fixed by the circuit court[29] as the capitalised value of the addition to the letting value of the tenement at the termination of the tenancy, having regard to the probable duration of the addition and probable life of the improvement.[30] Deductions must be made for benefits received by the tenant or his predecessors, *e.g.*, by way of deduction of rent,[31] and there is a maximum limit for the amount of compensation of fifteen times the annual amount of the addition to letting value.[32] Part IV of the 1980 Act also contains new provisions, some of which were recommended by the Landlord and Tenant Commission. Thus section 60 enables a landlord, in certain circumstances, to obtain an order terminating an occupational tenancy in obsolete buildings or buildings in an obsolete area before the tenancy expires, subject to compensation being made to the tenant.[33] The provisions of this section depart in some respects from the Commission's recommendations, *e.g.*, they are restricted to cases where the tenancy has not only more than three years to run but also not more than twenty-five years to run.[34] Section 53 now makes it clear that where, *e.g.*, a landlord of a controlled dwelling executes an improvement at his own expense,[35] he is not entitled to increase the rent to a level above the "lawful rent" as defined by section 11 of the Rent Restrictions Act, 1960.

18.07. To be able to take advantage of the Act, the tenant must serve a notice of intention to execute the improvement in question, giving details of

[27] *Cf.* the definition in the Rent Restrictions Act, 1960, s. 54. See para. 90 of the 1967 Report. *Cf.* 1931 Act, s. 3. *Rice* v. *Dublin Corp.* [1947] I.R. 425 (see *A Casebook on Irish Land Law* (1984), p. 562); *Byrne* v. *Dun Laoghaire Corp.* [1949] Ir.Jur.Rep. 44. S.3 of the 1931 Act has been replaced by s. 6 of the 1980 Act, which extends the provision to confer on business tenants of housing authorities the same rights as business tenants of private landlords, see 1967 Report (Pr. No. 9685), para. 307.

[28] Otherwise than by surrender or ejectment for non-payment of rent, s. 46(1)(*b*). S.10 of the 1931 Act has been replaced by s. 46 of the 1980 Act, subsection (1)(*b*)(ii) of which amends the provision contained in s. 10(1) as recommended by the Landlord and Tenant Commission, see 1967 Report (Pr. No. 9685), para. 123, the disentitlement to compensation now clearly applies in any case where termination is based on non-payment of rent, whether the proceedings are framed as an ejectment for non-payment of rent, an ejectment for overholding or an ejectment on the title based on forfeiture.

[29] S.8.

[30] S. 47 (1) and (4).

[31] S.47(2). See also s. 47(3), dealing with compensation by an intermediate landlord to a superior landlord.

[32] S.47(4).

[33] Pr. No. 9685, para. 222.

[34] See proviso to subs.(2).

[35] See s. 51.

the work and estimates of its cost.[36] The landlord then has one month in which to do one of three things: (a) consent and serve an improvement consent[37]; (b) object and serve an objection notice; or (c) serve an improvement undertaking agreeing to do the work himself and asking for an increased rent in the future.[38] In the case of an improvement consent, the tenant has one year within which to execute the improvement.[39] In the case of an objection notice, the tenant can (but only if he holds for a term of over 5 years, or on a lease for life or lives or shows occupancy for more than 5 years by himself or his predecessors in title) refer the objection to the circuit court, which has power to authorise the improvement with or without modification.[40] The court is to reject the tenant's application only if it is satisfied that he holds the tenement otherwise than under a lease for a term of which at least five years were unexpired at the time the improvement notice was served and that he would not be entitled to a new tenancy under Part II of the 1980 Act.[41] In the case of an improvement undertaking and demand for increased rent, the tenant can object to the increase and, if necessary, refer it to the circuit court to be fixed or have the matter dealt with on the basis that there has been an improvement objection.[42] To assist a claim which may be made many years after execution of the improvements, the landlord must give the tenant an improvement certificate of completion, which is conclusive evidence in any future proceedings.[43]

2. New Tenancies

18.08. Part II of the 1980 Act gives tenants[44] of certain tenements the right to a new tenancy on satisfaction of certain conditions. In this respect the 1980 Act made several modifications[45] to the provisions of the 1931 Act, which

---

[36] Ss. 48 and 54. See also s. 49, dealing with procedure where a sanitary authority requires works to be executed under the Public Health or Housing Acts.

[37] He is deemed to consent after one month if he does nothing, s. 50.

[38] A superior landlord can only adopt course (a) or (b), s.48(4). S. 48 of the 1980 Act replaced s. 12 of the 1931 Act with some modifications. Subs. (1) simplifies the requirements as to the documentation to be supplied by the tenant, e.g., instead of plans and specifications, a copy of the planning permission will do (where this is required). Subs. (2) reduces the time-limit for the landlord serving an improvement consent, etc. from two months to one month. Subs. (3) now limits the grounds of objection by a landlord to two grounds, viz., that the tenant holds the tenement otherwise than under a lease for a term of which at least five years are unexpired when the improvement notice is served, or the tenant would not be entitled to a new tenancy under Part II of the 1980 Act (on any of the grounds specified in s. 17(2)(a)). S. 17 of the 1931 act has been replaced by s. 54 of the 1980 Act, again with modifications. First, s. 17(1) and (6) were not re-enacted, so that if there are still landlords and tenants who were excluded from compensation in respect of improvements made between 1907 and 1931 for failure to serve a notice under the Town Tenants (Ir.) Act, 1906 (see para. 18.04, ante), they are no longer excluded. Secondly, the provision in s. 17(3) of the 1931 Act disentitling the tenant if he failed to serve an improvement notice has been modified by s. 54(2) to provide that he is disentitled where no notice is served only if the landlord can satisfy the court that he has been prejudiced by the non-service or that the improvement is in contravention of a covenant in the tenancy agreement or that it injures the amenity or convenience of the neighbourhood.

[39] Or where consent is deemed, s. 50.

[40] S. 52. The tenant can instead withdraw his improvement notice, s. 52(1)(a) and (2).

[41] S. 52(4).

[42] S. 51.

[43] S. 55.

[44] Pt.III of the 1980 Act replaces Pt.III of the 1931 Act. In *Gatien Motor Co. Ltd.* v. *Continental Oil Co. of Ireland Ltd.* [1979] I.R. 406 (see *A Casebook on Irish Land Law* (1984), p. 543), the Republic's Supreme Court reiterated that these provisions can be invoked only by a "tenant" and not someone in exclusive possession of the premises in some other capacity, e.g., as a "caretaker" (see para. 17.009, ante).

were much criticised.[46] So far as business tenants are concerned, under section 13 (1) (*a*) of the 1980 Act the right to a new tenancy is now given to all such tenants of three year's standing regardless of the nature of their existing tenancy and, under section 13(2), regardless of a temporary break in the use of the tenement if the court considers it reasonable to disregard it.[47] Apart from that, the tenant may base his claim on a "long occupation" equity (20 years' continuous occupation),[48] or an "extensive improvement" equity (more than half the letting value of tenement).[49] Finally, business tenancies[50] decontrolled by the Rent Restrictions Act, 1960,[51] and lettings of houses or self-contained flats decontrolled by the Rent Restrictions (Amendment) Act, 1967,[52] now come to some extent within the provisions for new tenancies in the 1980 Act.

18.09. The tenant has no right to a new tenancy if the existing one is terminated by ejectment for non-payment of rent or for breach of condition, or by his surrender of the tenancy, or his tenancy terminated otherwise than by a notice to quit and the landlord either refused a new tenancy for a good and sufficient reason, or, if he had been asked to renew the tenancy, would have had a good and sufficient reason to do so.[53] Furthermore, he is not entitled if it appears to the court that the landlord *bona fide* intends or has agreed to execute a demolition and rebuilding or reconstruction scheme or requires vacant possession for a development scheme, a new tenancy would be inconsistent with good estate management[54] or, where the landlord is a planning authority, the tenement is within an area for which the development

[45] One is the removal of the "artificial" termination provisions in s. 19 of the 1931 Act. Under the 1980 Act the right to a new tenancy may be established as soon as the necessary conditions are satisfied, which may be before the termination of the existing tenancy.

[46] See *Report on Occupational Tenancies under the Landlord and Tenant Act, 1931* (1967, Pr. 9683), paras. 144-6. See also *Farrell* v. *Barron* [1938] Ir.Jur.Rep. 19, overruled by *Bauman* v. *Elgin Contractors Ltd.* [1972] I.R. 169.

[47] Replacing 1931 Act, s. 19(1)(*a*) *Ennis Cinemas Ltd.* v. *Ennis U.D.C.* [1953–54] Ir.Jur.Rep. 1; *Butler* v. *Fitzgerald* [1955] I.R. 308. In *Esso Teoranta* v. *Wong* [1975] I.R.416, Finlay P. held that a business tenant was not entitled to a new tenancy under the 1931 Act because immediately before service of the notice to quit he was only a tenant from month to month.

[48] S. 13(1)(*b*), reducing the period of 30 years under s. 19(1)(*b*) of the 1931 Act; *Commrs. of Public Works* v. *Kavanagh* [1962] I.R. 216. The requirement that there should have been no purchase for valuable consideration during the period no longer exists. Also the right on the basis of a "short reversion" equity has been dropped from the 1980 Act, as recommended by the Landlord and Tenant Commission, 1967 Report (Pr. No. 9685), para. 174(s).

[49] S. 13(1)(*c*).

[50] Within the Rent Restrictions Act, 1946.

[51] S. 54. In *Mullane* v. *Brosman* [1974] I.R. 222, the Republic's Supreme Court held that s. 54 of the 1960 Act was confined to premises used entirely as business premises and a dwelling did not become decontrolled if part only was used for business purposes. S. 54 of the 1960 Act was repealed by the 1980 Act and re-enacted in substance by s. 14 of that Act.

[52] S. 13, replaced by s. 15 of the 1980 Act.

[53] S. 17, replacing 1931 Act, s. 21, *McEvoy* v. *Arnott* [1943] I.R. 214; *Tarlo* v. *Kenny* [1948] I.R. 28; *O'Connor* v. *Dinneen* [1964] Ir.Jur.Rep. 21; *Dunne* v. *Cogan* (1970) 104 I.L.T.R. 42. S 17(1)(*a*)(i) extends the exclusion in cases of termination for non-payment of rent, however the ejectment proceedings are framed (thus conforming with the new provisions relating to compensation for improvements, see para. 18.06, *ante*). S. 26 of the 1980 Act contains a new provision to the effect that, where, following the making of an order for a new tenancy, the existing tenancy is terminated in such manner that the tenant would be excluded under s. 17(1), then, if the new tenancy has not been granted, the obligation to grant it ceases and, if it has been granted, it is void.

[54] S. 17(2)(*a*)(v). *Gallagher* v. *Leitrim* [1948] Ir.Jur.Rep. 23; *Ryan* v. *Bradley* [1956] I.R. 31; *Lloyd* v. *Pembroke* (1955) 89 I.L.T.R. 40; *Dolan* v. *Corn Exchange Buildings* [1973] I.R. 269.

plan indicates objectives for its development or renewal as being an obsolete area.[55] However, in these cases, the tenant may be entitled to compensation for disturbance on quitting the tenement.[56]

18.10. The terms of a new tenancy, if the tenant is entitled, may be agreed between him and his landlord, otherwise they will be fixed by the circuit court. If the court fixes them, the Act lays down various provisions[57] relating to, *e.g.,* duration,[58] rent[59] and an allowance for improvements.[60] The new tenancy is deemed to be a continuance of the old one and, for all purposes, to be a graft upon it, so that the tenant's interest is subject to the same rights and equities.[61]

18.11. In the case of a tenement used wholly or partly for business purposes, a tenant who is not entitled to a new tenancy through no fault of his own, *e.g.,* owing to the landlord's reconstruction or development scheme, is entitled to compensation for disturbance instead.[62] This is measured according to his pecuniary loss, damage or expense sustained on quitting the tenement and which is the direct consequence of his quitting it.[63]

18.12. A claim for relief by a tenant under the 1980 Act must be preceded by service of a notice of intention to claim it,[64] though the court has power to

---

[55] S. 17, replacing s. 22 of the 1931 Act, with two modifications. First, under s. 17(2)(*a*)(i) and (ii), where the landlord opposes the grant of a new tenancy on the ground that he proposes to rebuild or that he has a scheme for development, he must have obtained planning permission for such work. Secondly, under s. 17(2)(*a*)(iv), a grant may be refused where the landlord is a local authority requiring possession, in circumstances where powers of compulsory acquisition apply, within five years after the existing tenancy terminates.

[56] S. 58.

[57] S. 23, replacing s. 29 of the 1931 Act with several modifications. Thus, under s. 23(7) and (8), when expenditure by the tenant on repairs is made a condition of the new tenancy, the court is empowered to require that the money be spent within a specified time and to declare that the tenant has forfeited his right to the new tenancy if he fails to comply. Also s. 23(9) provides that the new tenancy is to be subject to such covenants as may be agreed between the parties or, in default of agreement, as the court may determine.

[58] Under s. 23(2), the new tenancy is to be for 35 years unless the tenant nominates a shorter term. The various provisions in the 1931 Act (see ss.29(*b*) and 31-3) dealing with the case where the immediate landlord's reversion is shorter than the term of the new tenancy were not reenacted in the 1980 Act and instead s. 18(2) of that Act provides that as many superior landlords as are necessary should join in the grant of the new tenancy.

[59] Generally the difference between the gross rent (market rent less value of goodwill and scarcity element) and the allowance for improvements, *Tangney* v. *Carleton* [1937] Ir.Jur.Rep. 30; *Daly* v. *Love* (1945) 79 I.L.T.R. 71 *Farrell* v. *Caffrey* [1966] I.R. 170. The definition of "gross rent" is widened by s. 23(5) of the 1980 Act by permitting comparison with letting values of other tenements outside the vicinity of the tenement in question, provided those other tenements are in a comparable area. The court is no longer required to assume that the supply of similar tenements is sufficient to meet the demand – a provision described by one judge as an economic absurdity – or that competition therefor is normal. As was mentioned earlier (see para. 8.071, *ante*), the fixing of rent under the 1931 Act was discussed at length by the Republic's Supreme Court in *Byrne* v. *Loftus* [1978] I.R. 211; see also *Eamonn Andrews Productions Ltd.* v. *Gaiety Theatre (Dublin) Ltd.* (1976) Unrep. (H.C.,R.I.) (1976 No. 33); *McGovern* v. *Governors and Guardians of Jervis Street Hospital* [1981] I.L.R.M. 197. It was also pointed out that s. 24 of the 1980 Act (since replaced, with modifications, by s. 15 of the Landlord and Tenant (Amendment) Act, 1984) contained a new provision enabling an application to be made to the court for a review of the rent not less than five years after the new tenancy commences and thereafter at intervals of not less than five years.

[60] The proportion of the gross rent attributable to improvements in respect of which the tenant could claim compensation if Pt. II did not apply or no new tenancy was created, s. 23(6).

[61] S. 27. Cf. *Robinson* v. *Crosse and Blackwell, Ltd.* [1940] I.R. 56; *O'Donnell* v. *Grogan* [1941] I.R. 557.

[62] Ss. 17(2)(*b*) and 58(1). *Walsh* v. *Hendron Bros. (Dublin) Ltd.* (1948) 82 I.L.T.R. 64; *Ryan* v. *Bradley* [1956] I.R. 31; *Hardiman* v. *Galway C.C.* [1966] I.R. 124. Cf. *Herlihy* v. *Texaco (Ireland) Ltd.* [1971] I.R. 311.

[63] S. 58(2). In the case of houses or flats decontrolled by the Rent Restrictions Act, 1967, it may instead be, if greater, the sum the court thinks proper to enable the tenant to secure without hardship suitable alternative accommodation, being not less than 3 years' rent, including rates, s. 58(3).

[64] S. 20. S. 20 replaced s. 24 of the 1931 Act with some modifications recommended by the Landlord and Tenant Commission, 1967 Report (Pr. No. 9685), paras. 237 and 325. Under s. 24(2)(*b*) of the 1931 Act, a

extend the time for serving this,[65] and, where necessary, an application must be made to the court not less than one month after service.[66] The earlier provisions governing the court's discretion in section 45 of the 1931 Act have been replaced by section 83 of the 1980 Act, which makes it clear that, though the court still has a discretion to extend the time "on such terms as it thinks proper", it must extend the time ("unless satisfied that injustice would be caused") where it is shown that the failure to do the act or thing in time was occasioned "by disability, mistake, absence from the State, inability to obtain requisite information or any other reasonable cause." The extent of the discretion conferred by section 45 of the 1931 Act (especially how far a superior court could substitute its view for that of the Circuit Court judge who had first considered the matter) proved to be very controversial. The earlier authorities[67] seemed to establish two propositions: (1) that the Circuit Court judge should not exercise his discretion to extend the time unless there were "special circumstances" justifying themselves as reasonable;[68] (2) that the discretionary order of the Circuit Court judge should not be interfered with unless he had "erred in principle".[69] The first of these propositions was called into question by O'Higgins J. (as he then was) in *Linders Garage Ltd.* v. *Syme*,[70] where he emphasised that the "fundamental consideration is whether the interests of justice in the circumstances of this case require that the relief sought be granted...under such an Act when the Court is given powers to extend time provided by the Act for the service of statutory notice I think the Court should do so unless a clear injustice would be caused."[71] Section 82 of the 1980 Act now adopts this approach. The second proposition was called into question by Hamilton J. in *Grey Door Hotel Co. Ltd.* v. *Pembroke Trust Ltd.*[72] He held that, if the fundamental consideration was as laid down by O'Higgins J. in the *Linders* case, "I am entitled to consider the matter *de novo* and decide whether the circumstances of this particular case require the relief sought to be granted." The whole matter was then reviewed by the Supreme Court in *H. Wigoder & Co. Ltd.* v. *Moran*,[73] on a case stated by the High Court raising two questions: (1) on an appeal from the Circuit Court, was the High Court judge entitled to substitute his discretion for that of the

---

tenant could not serve a valid notice of claim later than 3 months before his tenancy terminated (in the case of fixed term tenancies, see *Linders Garage Ltd.* v. *Syme* [1975] I.R. 161, *Barton* v. *Boylan* (1978) 112 I.L.T.R. 6 and *Ryan* v. *Sheehan* (1978) 112 I.L.T.R. 65), but under s. 20(2)(*a*) a notice may be served in such cases at any time before termination of the tenancy or any time after the termination but before expiration of one month after service (not earlier than three months before termination of the tenancy) of a notice of termination. Under s. 24(2)(*c*) of the 1931 Act, in the case of a tenancy terminating by an uncertain event (*e.g.*, the dropping of a life) the tenant had to serve notice within one month of the event coming to his knowledge. Now under s. 20(2)(*b*) of the 1980 Act the tenant may claim relief up to one month after service by the landlord of a notice of the happening of the event.
[65] S.83. *O'Neill* v. *Carthy* [1937] I.R. 380; *Bridgeman* v. *Powell* [1973] I.R. 584; *Hayes* v. *Kilbride* [1963] I.R. 185.
[66] S. 21. *Nolan* v. *Waterford Corp.* (1933) 69 I.L.T.R. 184. S.21(2) now enables the landlord to bring the matter to court for resolution where the tenant has not done so within three months.
[67] *O'Neill* v. *Carthy* [1937] I.R. 380; *Bridgman* v. *Powell* [1937] I.R. 584; *Hayes* v. *Kilbride* [1963] I.R. 185.
[68] *Per* Johnson J. in the *Bridgeman* case, *supra*.
[69] *Per* Davitt P. in the *Hayes* case, *supra*.
[70] [1975] I.R. 161.
[71] *Ibid.*, pp. 166-7.
[72] (1976) Unrep. (H.C.,R.I.).
[73] [1977] I.R. 112.

judge below? (2) if it was found that the applicants for relief took all reasonable steps to protect their interests by giving proper instructions to their solicitor, but he failed to protect them due to a *bona fide* mistake of law, could the discretion be exercised in favour of the applicants? The Court (Henchy, Kenny and Parke JJ.) were unanimous in giving an affirmative answer to the first question and so held that the suggestions to the contrary in the earlier cases were clearly incorrect and no longer the law. As regards the basis upon which the court should exercise its discretion, Kenny J. stated:

> "It is impossible to state any general principle which court should apply in every case to decide the issue whether the time for service of notice of intention to claim relief should be extended, except that the court should make the order when justice requires that it should. I do not think that discussion is advanced in any way by saying that an applicant for extension of time must show the existence of special circumstances. Until one defines the sense in which the word 'special' is used, the sentence seems to me to be almost meaningless."[74]

He went on to hold that circumstances such as those posed by the second question in the case stated, being based on an error of law made by a solicitor, who got wrong advice from a barrister holding himself out to be an expert in the matter, justified an exercise of the discretion. On the other hand, Henchy J. was not so definite on this point, stating:

> "A mistake on the part of a legal adviser may be no impediment to the grant of an extension of time...but it should be treated otherwise if the grant of an extension of time would work an injustice on the other party; for instance, if the landlord has been misled into dealing with the property in the bona fide belief that the tenant's inactivity was not due to error, and if it would be unfair or oppressive to require him to undo what he has committed himself to as a result of the tenant's failure to serve the notice."[75]

And he went on to emphasise:

> "Each case must be decided on its own circumstances, and the improbability of any two cases failing under the same set of circumstances makes it unlikely that the decision in any one case will be anything more than a rough guide to the decision in another."[76]

Then, with respect to the second question posed for the opinion of the Supreme Court, he stated:

> "The question for the court in exercising that discretion is not simply whether the failure to serve the notice *was* excusable; in so far as the second question in the Case Stated before us postulates that test it is based on a wrong assumption. The failure to serve the statutory notice of intention to claim relief may be understandable and excusable in

---

[74] *Ibid.*, p.127.
[75] *Ibid.*, pp. 120-1.
[76] *Ibid.*, p. 121.

retrospect, but the question of extension of time must be decided in the light of the situation between the parties as it exists when the court has to give its decision."[77]

Later Henchy J. outlined the judge's duty in making that decision:

"When an application is made for an extension of the time for serving a notice of intention to claim relief, the judge must bring into review all the relevant circumstances including the reason put forward for not serving the notice in time, the conduct of the parties, the nature of the tenement, the respective purposes for which the tenant is seeking to get a new tenancy and for which the landlord wants to have vacant possession; the judge should then decide as a matter of fairness and justice whether time should be extended, having particular regard to the consequences of his decision to both parties. And it is for the tenant, as the person in breach of the statutory requirement of serving the notice in the prescribed time, to discharge the onus of satisfying the court that the judicial discretion should be exercised in his favour."[78]

Parke J. followed Henchy J. in taking the view that the second question posed could not be answered by "a simple affirmative or negative." In particular, he did not accept the view that a tenant was entitled to an extension merely because he gave appropriate instructions to his solicitor to enable him to serve a proper notice, again expressly adopting the principles stated by Henchy J.[79] The tenant is entitled to continue in occupation pending a final decision on his application.[80] Any contract directly or indirectly depriving the tenant of his right to relief under the Act is void.[81]

B. BUSINESS TENANCIES ACT (N.I.), 1964

18.13. This Act made permanent temporary legislation passed during the 1950s.[82] It relates only to tenancies of premises occupied wholly or partly for the purposes of a trade, profession or employment or any activity carried on by a corporate or unincorporate body of persons, whether or not for gain or reward.[83] Various tenancies are excluded, *e.g.,* tenancies for a 3 month term or less unless there has been more than 6 months' actual occupation for the

---

[77] *Ibid.*

[78] *Ibid.*, p. 122.

[79] *Ibid.*, p. 128.

[80] S. 28.

[81] S. 85. *Hardiman* v. *Galway C.C.* [1966] I.R. 124. S. 42 of the 1931 Act was replaced with different wording by s. 85 of the 1980 Act. In particular, s. 85 no longer uses the controversial word "indirectly," which was considered by the Supreme Court in *Gatien Motor Co. Ltd.* v. *Continental Oil Co. of Ireland Ltd.* [1979] I.R. 406 (see *A Casebook on Irish Land Law* (1984), p. 543). Kenny J. confessed in that case that he did not understand what the parliamentary draftsman had in mind, but he reserved a decision on the meaning of this "delphic phrase" for future consideration, as it was not required in that case (see paras. 17.009 and 18.08, *ante*).

[82] Beginning with the Business Tenancies (Temporary Provisions) Act (N.I.), 1952, see B.L.C. (1965) 16 N.I.L.Q. 33. *Cairns* v. *Prudential Assurance Co. Ltd.* [1956] N.I. 123; *Ulster Chemists Ltd.* v. *Hemsborough Investment Co. Ltd.* [1957] N.I. 185.

[83] S. 1. *Bryans* v. *McCormick* [1964] N.I. 59; *Crofts Inns Ltd.* v. *Scott* [1982] N.I. 95.

same business and "service" tenancies.[84] Like the Republic's 1980 Act, the 1964 Act gives the tenant a right to compensation for improvements on quitting the business premises and, in certain cases, a right to a new tenancy or, sometimes, compensation for disturbance.

1. Improvements

18.14. Under Part II of the 1964 Act the tenant is entitled to compensation for improvements which add to the letting value of the premises at the termination of the tenancy,[85] which, if necessary, is to be determined by the Lands Tribunal[86] established under the Lands Tribunal and Compensation Act (N.I.), 1964. Before making an improvement the tenant must serve on his landlord a "notice of improvement" and then the landlord has 3 months in which to serve either a "notice of objection" or a "notice of undertaking."[87] Objections may be referred to and dealt with by the Lands Tribunal.[88] These provisions are very much along the lines of the Republic's 1980 Act, except that the Lands Tribunal has jurisdiction rather than the county court, which is the nearest equivalent to the Republic's circuit court.

2. New Tenancies

18.15. Here Part I of the 1964 Act does differ more from the Republic's 1980 Act. The general principle is that business tenancies continue automatically for an indefinite period, i.e., until terminated by either party under the Act.[89] The landlord may determine the tenancy only by serving a "notice to determine" on the tenant, specifying a "date of termination" not more than 12 months nor less than 6 months after its service.[90] It must also require the tenant to notify the landlord within 2 months whether he is willing to give up possession and it must state whether, and on what ground listed in the Act, the landlord would oppose the granting of a new tenancy.[91] Alternatively, the tenant may, in certain cases, terminate his tenancy by requesting a new tenancy and the landlord has two months in which to notify the tenant of his objections and their grounds.[92]

18.16. On an application for a new tenancy to the Lands Tribunal,[93] the

---

[84] S. 2. In *Department of the Environment* v. *McCully* [1977] N.I. 85, Murray J. held that s. 2(1)(g) of the 1964 Act not only excluded premises acquired by a public authority for the purposes of carrying out its functions, but also premises where the authority's requirement of possession supervened at a date subsequent to that of its acquisition of the premises. In this respect he held that the N.I. Act gave much greater rights to public authorities and less security to private tenants than the English counterpart (s. 57 of the Landlord and Tenant Act, 1954). The query was also raised whether the 1964 Act binds the Crown, but since counsel for the Department did not rely upon the point, the judge preferred to decide the case on other points (*ibid.*, pp. 102-4)

[85] S. 30.

[86] S. 33(3) and (4).

[87] S. 34.

[88] S. 36.

[89] S. 3. They may still end by surrender, forfeiture and ejectment for non-payment of rent, s. 6(1), as amended by Business Tenancies (Amendment) Act (N.I.), 1968, s. 1.

[90] S. 4.

[91] S. 4(6).

[92] S. 5.

[93] S. 8. There is interim continuation of the old one pending determination of this, s. 9.

landlord may oppose the application on any of the grounds listed in section 10 (1), which include the tenant's failure to comply with repair and maintenance obligations, persistent delay in paying rent or other substantial breaches of obligations.[94] Other grounds include the landlord's offer and willingness to provide or secure suitable alternative accommodation, his intention to execute a demolition, rebuilding or substantial construction scheme or to occupy the premises for a reasonable period for his or his company's business, or as his residence.[95] If the landlord establishes any of these grounds to the satisfaction of the Tribunal, it must dismiss the application.[96] If he fails in this, the Tribunal must grant a new tenancy, which is deemed a graft on the old one.[97]

18.17. In the absence of agreement, the new tenancy is fixed for the period regarded by the Tribunal as reasonable in all the circumstances, but there is a maximum limit of 14 years.[98] The rent to be fixed, if necessary, by the Tribunal is the open market rent, having regard to factors such as goodwill established or improvements made by the tenant or his predecessors.[99]

18.18. Where the Tribunal dismisses the application on grounds not based on default by the tenant, the tenant is entitled to compensation for disturbance on quitting the premises.[1] The amount is the net annual value of the holding or, where the tenant or his predecessor has occupied the premises for business purposes for the last 14 years, twice that amount.[2]

Any agreement depriving a tenant of his rights under the 1964 Act is void.[3]

III. RESIDENTIAL AND OCCUPATIONAL TENANCIES

This category covers a very wide range of situations, from a minor periodic tenancy of a flat or part of a house to a long lease of a large detached house. There have been several legislative incursions into this field of law in both the Republic and Northern Ireland.

A. REPUBLIC OF IRELAND

1. Compensation and New Tenancies

18.19. We saw earlier that Parts II and IV of the Landlord and Tenant (Amendment) Act, 1980 cover other occupiers of tenements in addition to business tenants, and such persons may also seek the relief (discussed above)

---

[94] S. 10(1) (a)-(c).
[95] S. 10 (d), (f) and (g). Ground (e) covers a rearrangement of the letting of the entire property of which the premises form only a part.
[96] S. 11(1). Note the power to declare a later date for termination of the existing tenancy where the landlord can establish certain grounds only at such later date, s. 11(2).
[97] S. 12.
[98] S. 14.
[99] S. 15.
[1] S. 19(1).
[2] S. 19(2) and (3).
[3] Ss. 20 and 42.

in respect of compensation for improvements and a new tenancy on the basis
of a long occupation, or extensive improvement equity. Furthermore, tenants
of houses or self-contained flats decontrolled by the Rent Restrictions Act,
1967, now have similar rights.[4]

2. Reversionary Leases

18.20. Part V of the Landlord and Tenant Act, 1931 dealt with long term
"building" leases and sub-leases granted under them, referred to as
"proprietary" leases, by conferring on the lessees the right to claim a
"reversionary" lease upon the expiration of the building or proprietary lease.
Part V of the 1931 Act, as amended by the Landlord and Tenant
(Amendment) Act, 1943,[5] was then repealed and replaced by the Landlord
and Tenant (Reversionary Leases) Act, 1958.[6]

18.21. The 1958 Act, like the 1931 and 1943 Acts, was designed to protect
lessees who erect buildings on land or who acquire the beneficial interest in
such buildings by purchase of the lease or a sub-lease from the building lessee.
Under the common law, when the original lease expired the land reverted to
the lessor, or his successors, along with all buildings and fixtures attached to
the land, even though the lessee built and paid for these himself. This had
serious social and economic consequences in Ireland where so much urban
building development proceeded on the basis of leasehold conveyancing.[7]

18.22. The necessity for these provisions arose out of the way in which cities
and towns in Ireland developed in the nineteenth century. It was customary
for the landowner to make an agreement with the builder that he would grant
a lease when a house or number of houses had been built on the land agreed
to be let. When the builder had built the house or houses, he got a lease from
the landowner and then sold the house or houses by making sub-leases for
fines and at sub-rents which, added together, exceeded the head-rent. Thus
the ultimate purchaser, who had paid for the house by way of a fine (*i.e.,* a
capital sum), held nevertheless under a sub-lease only.

18.23. The 1958 Act contained detailed definitions of building and
proprietary leases. Essentially a *building* lease was a lease of land situated in
an urban area, or else demised for a term of at least 20 years, on which
permanent buildings, which were not merely ancillary and subsidiary
improvements as opposed to reconstructions, were erected by the lessee at
the time of erection or under an agreement for the grant of the lease on their
erection.[8] Several other leases were deemed to be building leases, *e.g.,* leases

---

[4] 1980 Act, s. 14.

[5] *Finn* v. *Barry* [1941] I.R. 450. Deale, *Landlord and Tenant Acts, 1931 and 1943* (1953); Kingsmill Moore
and Odell, *Landlord and Tenant Act, 1931* (1932).

[6] See *Report on Reversionary Leases under the Landlord and Tenant Acts* (1954, Pr.2532).

[7] The Settled Land Acts, 1882-90, are the source of many building leases, ch.8 *ante*.

[8] S.4. *McGrath* v. *Campbell* (1936) 70 I.L.T.R. 117; *Keating* v. *Carolin* [1968] I.R. 193; *Southern Health
Board* v. *Reeves-Smith* [1980] I.R. 26. Note the right of certain occupiers of land to apply to the circuit court for
a lease of ground for building purposes under s.60 of the 1931 Act. *Cf.* Harbours Act, 1946, s.169 (lease of
lands near a harbour) and Landlord and Tenant (Amendment) Act, 1971, ss.2-6 (sporting leases) and s.7
(application of 1958 Act to sporting leases).

granted to a builder's nominees,[9] "built-on" leases,[10] renewed leases,[11] reversionary leases granted after 1931[12] and "preserved" sub-leases.[13] A *proprietary* lease was basically a sub-lease, mediate or immediate, under a building lease, where the term of the former was either not less than 99 years or, if less, was equal to or greater than 20 years or, if this was the lesser period, two-thirds of the term of the building lease,[14] and which expired at the same time as, or not more than 15 years before, the expiration of the building lease. Payment of consideration for the sub-lease had to have been made to the sub-lessor by the sub-lessee.[15] The 1958 Act has now in turn been replaced by Part III of the Landlord and Tenant (Amendment) Act, 1980. The 1980 Act introduced some amendments recommended by the Landlord and Tenant Commission in the *Report on Certain Questions Arising under the Landlord and Tenant Acts, 1958 and 1967.*[16] In particular, it drops the references to building and proprietary leases and instead the right to a reversionary lease is now, in general, linked to the right to purchase the fee simple under the Landlord and Tenant (Ground Rents) (No.2) Act, 1978.[17]

18.24. Under section 30 of the 1980 Act a lessee entitled to acquire the fee simple under the Landlord and Tenant (Ground Rents) (No.2) Act, 1978, is entitled to a reversionary lease. This covers all the categories of persons previously coming within the 1958 legislation and adds some additional ones.[18] The provisions of section 2 (1) of the Landlord and Tenant (Ground Rents) Act, 1978,[19] restricting the right to create leases of dwellings do not apply where the lease is a reversionary lease.[20] There are provisions requiring the obtaining of certain consents (*e.g.,* of sub-lessees)[21] and relating to the parties to the reversionary lease and joining in, where necessary, superior lessors.[22] In the absence of agreement, the court fixes the terms of the reversionary lease according to the provisions of section 34, *i.e.,* for a term of 99 years at a rent not lower than the old rent, unless a new covenant or condition is included. Subject to that, the rent is one-eighth of the "gross" rent, *i.e.,* the open market rent for the land, excluding any scarcity element in this, with vacant possession and the lessee liable for rates, taxes and insurance. The court, which must have regard to other terms of the reversionary lease and letting values of similar land in the vicinity, or in a comparable area, must disregard the value of any goodwill, but have regard

[9] S.5.
[10] S. 6. *Baggott* v. *O'Doherty* [1945] I.R. 211.
[11] Landlord and Tenant (Amendment) Act, 1971, s. 8.
[12] S.19.
[13] S.20. *Irish Life Assurance Co.* v. *Weaklian* (1963) 97 I.L.T. 88.
[14] S.7.
[15] S.7(2)(d). *Foyle Shirt and Collar Factory Ltd.* v. *Gallagher* (1946) 80 I.L.T.R. 138.
[16] 1968 (Prl.59).
[17] See para.18.26, *post.*
[18] See 1978 Act, ss.9-12 and 14, as amended by ss.70-3 of 1980 Act.
[19] See para.1.74, *ante.*
[20] 1980 Act, s.30(3).
[21] S.31, which replaces ss.11 and 12 of the 1958 Act (as amended by s.25 of the Landlord and Tenant (Ground Rents) Act, 1967) with one amendment. The applicant for the reversionary lease is no longer required to obtain the consent of any underlessees who also have the right to a reversionary lease or, alternatively, to exclude the lands comprised in the underleases from his application.
[22] Ss.31 and 32.

to the condition of the premises.[23] In the absence of agreement, where the court fixes other terms, it must make the lessee liable for rates, taxes, insurance and repairs[24] and may even require him to execute repairs and authorise postponement of the execution of the reversionary lease until he does them.[25] The reversionary lease is deemed a graft on the previous lease.[26]

18.25. There is no right to a reversionary lease where the immediate lessor, or any superior lessor a necessary party to its granting, satisfies the court that his reversionary interest is a freehold estate or a term not less than 15 years and certain other conditions apply, *e.g.,* he has a reconstruction or development scheme.[27] In such cases, however, the lessee is entitled to compensation for disturbance based on the lessee's loss in not obtaining a reversionary lease and this is payable by the objecting lessor or lessors.[28]

3. Purchase of Fee Simple

18.26. The Landlord and Tenant (Ground Rents) Act, 1967, provided the ultimate solution to the problems of many occupational and building or proprietary lessees under the 1931, 1943 and 1958 Acts, namely, the right to acquire the fee simple in the land (enfranchisement).[29] Persons holding under building or proprietary leases, or entitled to reversionary leases under the 1958 Act, or occupying tenements within the 1931 Act for terms of not less than 99 years, with 25 years or more unexpired, or in occupation as yearly tenants for 25 years at a rent less than the land's rateable value, had the right to acquire the fee simple and any intermediate interests in the land.[30] The 1967 Act has been amended substantially by the Landlord and Tenant (Ground Rents) (No.2) Act, 1978, which in turn has been amended by the Landlord and Tenant (Amendment) Act, 1980. The main changes introduced by the 1978 Act are: (1) introduction of an optional purchase procedure to operate only in respect of dwellinghouses[31] for a period of five years from the commencement of the Act;[32] (2) consolidation of the provisions in earlier

---

[23] Ss.35 and 36, which introduce some amendments to the previous law in s.18(4) and (5) of the 1958 Act, as amended by s.26 of the Landlord and Tenant (Ground Rents) Act, 1967. For example, there is now a provision for abatement of the rent on foot of improvements carried out by the lessee (s.35(2)). Secondly, comparison with letting values may now include lands outside the vicinity, but in a comparable area (s.36(1)(b)). Similar rules apply to occupational tenancies (1980 Act, s.23(4) and (5)).

[24] S.34(6).

[25] S.38.

[26] S.39.

[27] S.33. Ss. 15 and 16 of the 1958 Act were reenacted by s.33 of the 1980 Act, but with some amendments. One is that a court will not refuse to grant a reversionary lease on the ground of landlord's rebuilding or development plans unless he has obtained planning permission for the work in question (s.33(1)(b)(i). Another is introduction of a new ground for refusal, namely, where a local authority landlord will require possession of premises used wholly or partly for business for any of the purposes for which it may acquire property compulsorily, within five years after termination of the existing lease. Lastly, s.33(5) provides that where a person does not within a reasonable time carry out any intention, agreement or purpose on account of which a reversionary lease was refused, the Circuit Court may now order him to pay punitive damages (s.15(3) of the 1958 Act instead made this an offence punishable by a fine up to £500).

[28] S.33(6).

[29] See *Report on Ground Rents* (1964, Pr.7783). Also *Report on Certain Questions Arising Under the Landlord and Tenant Acts, 1958 and 1967* (1968, Prl.59).

[30] S.3(1) and (2).

[31] S.19.

[32] S.18, see para 18.27, *infra*. This scheme, operated by the Land Registry, was extended for a further 12 months by the Landlord and Tenant (Grounds Rents)(Amendment) Act, 1983, and then for a further 3 years by the Landlord and Tenant (Ground Rents)(Amendment) Act, 1984 (see s.2).

legislation relating to entitlement to acquire the fee simple, together with introduction of new categories of tenants so entitled, as recommended by the Landlord and Tenant Commission in their 1968 Report.[33] The categories of lessees entitled to acquire the fee simple are now set out in detail in sections 9-15 of the 1978 Act, as amended by sections 70-3 of the Landlord and Tenant (Amendment) Act, 1980. These include the building and proprietary lessees who had the right under the 1967 Act and the Landlord and Tenant (Amendment) Act, 1971, but the 1978 Act adds various other categories, e.g., certain lessees with long leases at a low rent,[34] and relaxes the conditions which must be satisfied by some categories, e.g., yearly tenants.[35] Section 26 of the 1978 Act confers a new right of acquisition on lessees of local authorities. Section 70 of the 1980 Act confers a right of acquisition on lessees of dwellinghouses whose lessor is a State authority (e.g., the Commissioners of Public Works or the Irish Land Commission, or a body such as the Commissioners of Irish Lights or a harbour authority), unless it is certified that the acquisition is not in the public interest. Excluded are persons such as business tenants and tenants in buildings divided into not fewer than four separate and self-contained flats, with rent revision clauses in their leases, and lessees who have been declared not to be entitled to reversionary leases under the 1958 Act.[36]

18.27. Notice of intention to acquire the fee simple must be served on the immediate lessor, superior lessors and incumbrancers[37] and various consents are required from other lessees or sub-lessees.[38] Many of the lessees in question will be holding under complicated pyramid titles, so there are provisions for apportionment of the rent between the different parts of the land demised by the lease, along with the covenants and conditions contained in the lease.[39] As mentioned above, Part III of the 1978 Act introduces a new special purchase procedure, which is an alternative to the one prescribed by the 1967 Act. This new procedure will operate for a limited period only, namely, nine years from the commencement of the 1978 Act,[40] which was 1st August, 1978,[41] and applies only to dwellinghouses[42] and where the applicant has secured the consent of every person who would be a necessary party to a conveyance to him of the fee simple free from incumbrances,[43] though there are provisions dealing with cases where consent is not obtained.[44] The procedure involves an application to the Registrar of Titles for a "vesting certificate", which operates to convey the fee simple to the applicant on a

---

[33] Prl.59.
[34] Ss.10, 11 and 12.
[35] S.15.
[36] 1978 Act, s.16.
[37] 1967 Act, s.4. Note the special provisions if they are unknown or cannot be found or are under a disability, s.8; and for notices requiring information, s.7.
[38] S.5.
[39] Ss.12-16. See paras. 4.180-2, ante.
[40] S.18, as amended by the Landlord and Tenant (Ground Rents)(Amendment) Acts, 1983 and 1984.
[41] S.2, i.e., expiry date now is 31st July, 1987.
[42] S.19.
[43] S.20.
[44] S.21.

specified date.[45] If the consent of other parties is not obtained, the applicant must serve notice on his immediate lessor, or ask the Registrar to dispense with such service, and in either case the Registrar determines the application by arbitration.[46] No certificate will be issued unless the purchase price has been paid or deposited with the Registrar, the prescribed fees have been discharged and the rent has been paid up to date.[47] The fee for issue of a vesting certificate where the applicant is in occupation and lodges the necessary consents is £26 and, if an arbitration is necessary, £89.[48] In other cases, *e.g.,* where the applicant is not in occupation, the fees were prescribed by regulation, but this power to change the fees now applies to fees for all cases.[49]

18.28. The purchase price of the fee simple or other interest, if referred to arbitration under the Act,[50] is the open market value, *i.e.,* what a willing purchaser would give and a willing seller would accept, having regard to various factors such as the current rent, current interest yields on government securities, mortgages and charges and the price paid in any previous sales since 1964.[51] Recently a new price formula has had to be introduced to deal with problems which came to light in the Supreme Court decision in *Gilsenan* v. *Foundary House Investments Ltd. and Rathmines Properties Ltd.*[52] The Court held that the old formula was unworkable in certain cases, because it was linked to the rent that would be reserved by a reversionary lease granted for 99 years.[53] Since the evidence was clear that such a lease would have a rent revision provision, the Court held that it was impossible to determine inflationary trends over such a long term.[54] Under the new formula, in cases like that in *Gilsenan* the purchase price will normally be one-eighth of the current fee simple market value of the property subject to allowances and adjustments that are made in determining the rent of a reversionary lease.[55] Certain covenants, conditions or agreements, *e.g.,* enhancing or protecting amenities or relating to rights of way over the land or rights of drainage securing or assisting development of other land, continue, however, in full force and effect as against the acquired fee simple.[56]

Generally the applicant is liable for the costs and expenses of enfranchise-

---

[45] S.22.
[46] S.21.
[47] S.22(2).
[48] S.23(1), as amended by the Landlord and Tenant (Ground Rents)(Amendment) Acts, 1983 (s.2) and 1984 (s.3). Originally the fees were £5 and £17 respectively, raised to £15 and £51 by the 1983 Act and to the present figures by the 1984 Act.
[49] 1984 Act, s.3(2).
[50] To the county registrar, 1967 Act, s.17.
[51] S.7 of the Landlord and Tenant (Amendment) Act, 1984.
[52] (1980) Unrep. (Sup. Ct.,R.I.) (79/1980).
[53] See Landlord and Tenant (Reversionary Leases) Act, 1958, s.18; Landlord and Tenant (Ground Rents)(No.2) Act, 1978, s.17.
[54] The *Byrne* v. *Loftus* [1978] I.R. 223 approach (see para. 8.071, *ante*) was rejected for there the term was 21 years only.
[55] Landlord and Tenant (Amendment) Act, 1984, s.7(4). S.7 replaces s.17 of the Landlord and Tenant (Ground Rents)(No.2) Act, 1978.
[56] S.28 of the 1978 Act, replacing s.31 of the 1967 Act. S.28(1) now provides that all covenants other than those specified as continuing in force cease to have effect, provided the person acquiring the fee simple has an existing interest in the land. The subsection also provides that no new covenants are created in conveying the fee simple.

ment or apportionment of rent.[57] Any contractual provision varying, modifying or restricting rights under the Act is void.[58]

4. Rent Restriction Acts, 1960 and 1967
and Housing (Private Rented Dwellings) Acts 1982 and 1983

18.29. Rent restriction legislation was first introduced in Ireland, as in England, during the First World War to deal with what was then thought to be a temporary housing shortage, which was tempting landlords to exploit the gap between supply and demand for residential accommodation.[59] Alas, the problem has seemed to become a permanent one on both sides of the Irish Sea and so the legislation has become a permanent feature of our land law. After 1920 many Acts were passed over the years,[60] but these have all been replaced by the Rent Restrictions Act, 1960, as amended by the Rent Restrictions (Amendment) Act, 1967.[61] However, until recently neither part of Ireland had seen the British administrative developments on this subject, *i.e.*, the fixing of fair or reasonable rents by rent officers, rent assessment committees and rent tribunals.[62] In the Republic the position was changed radically when the Supreme Court in 1980 held Parts II and IV of the 1960 Act (which dealt with control of rents) unconstitutional.[63] After some legislative fumbling,[64] new provisions to control private rented dwellings came into force on 26th July, 1982.[65] These are to be found in the Housing (Private Rented Dwellings) Act, 1982.[66]

There are two main functions of this legislation: control of rents and giving security of tenure. These two functions are backed up by various provisions seeking to prevent landlords from defeating them by indirect means.

(i) Controlled Dwellings

18.30. The 1982 and 1983 Acts apply only to dwellings controlled previously by the 1960 and 1967 Acts, so that, though those earlier Acts were repealed by the 1982 Act, their provisions remain relevant when determining what property is subject to the 1982 and 1983 Acts. The Acts apply only to "dwellings," *i.e.*, houses or parts of houses let[67] as separate dwellings,

---

[57] Ss.9 and 15 of 1967 Act. *Cf.* costs of arbitration, liability for which is determined by the county registrar, s.19.

[58] S.33 of 1967 Act.

[59] See the Increase of Rent and Mortgage Interest (Restrictions) Acts, 1915-9, consolidated in the Act of 1920, all of which applied to Ireland, see s.18 (2) of the 1920 Act.

[60] See Coffey, *Digest of Cases under Rent Acts*, (1938); Coghlan, *Law of Rent Restriction in Ireland* (3rd ed., 1979); Walsh and Cosgrove, *Rent Restrictions Guide* (1943).

[61] In turn amended by the Landlord and Tenant (Amendment) Act, 1971, ss.10 and 11.

[62] See Rent Act, 1977 as amended by the Housing Act, 1980. Rent tribunals did operate in N.I., from 1941-60 but not successfully and the legislation has now lapsed, see Frazer and Wylie, "The Rent Restriction Law of Northern Ireland" (1971) 22 N.I.L.Q. 99 at 118-20.

[63] *Blake and Others* v. *Att.-Gen.* and *Madigan* v. *Att.-Gen.* [1982] I.R. 117 (see *A Casebook on Irish Land Law* (1984), p.55). See para. 1.71, *ante*.

[64] See *Re Reference under Article 26 of the Constitution of the Housing (Private Rented Dwellings) Bill, 1981* [1983] I.L.R.M. 246. See *ibid*.

[65] Housing (Private Rented Dwellings) Act, 1982 (Commencement) Order, 1982 (S.I. No.216 of 1982).

[66] Amended by the Housing (Private Rented Dwellings)(Amendment) Act, 1983. See De Blacam, *The Control of Private Rented Dwellings* (1984).

[67] *I.e.*, there must be a tenancy and not merely a licence, ch.20, *post. Keller* v. *O'Neill* (1926) 60 I.L.T.R. 83. See also *O'Neill* v. *Duncan* (1921) 55 I.L.T.R. 84. *Cf.* a tenancy at will, *Sisk* v. *Cronin* [1930] I.R. 98; *Delany* v. *Jones* [1938] I.R. 826; *Irish Sailors and Soldiers Land Trust* v. *Donnelly* [1944] I.R. 464.

whether or not the tenant shares accommodation, amenities or facilities with other persons.[68] Excluded are dwellings *above* certain rateable valuations.[69] These are, for the boroughs of Dublin and Dun Laoghaire, £40 (if a house), £30 (separate and self-contained flats) and £60 (other dwellings); elsewhere the limits are £30, £20 and £40 respectively.[70] Also excluded from control[71] are dwellings built since 1941, public housing (*i.e.*, dwellings let under the Labourers Acts and Housing Acts), furnished lettings,[72] owner-occupied residences,[73] separate and self-contained flats converted into such since 1960, or in the possession of the landlord after 1966,[74] dwellings let with land other than their sites[75] and houses, with a rateable value exceeding £10, where, after 1967, a bachelor or spinster over 21 and under 65 years of age has become tenant.[76] However, a dwelling is *not* excluded by reason only that part of it is used for the purpose of any business, trade or profession.[77]

(ii) Rent Control

18.31. Originally under the 1982 Act, in the absence of agreement between the landlord and tenant, the terms of a tenancy of a controlled dwelling were to be determined by the District Court.[78] Though the District Court still retains much of its jurisdiction under the 1982 Act,[79] the power to fix rents was transferred to the Rent Tribunal established by the 1983 Act.[80] Furthermore, under section 6 of the 1983 Act the Minister for the Environment was empowered to direct that all applications to fix rents of controlled dwellings should be made to housing authorities for determination by rent officers, with a right of appeal to the Rent Tribunal.[81] The rent to be fixed is the gross rent[82] which, in the opinion of the rent officer or tribunal,

---

[68] 1982 Act, s.2(1). See *White* v. *Freeman* [1947] I.R.55; *cf. Mason* v. *Leavy* [1952] I.R.40.

[69] 1960 Act, s.3(2)(*a*), as amended by 1967 Act, s.2(1). But the 1982 Act does not apply to previous controlled dwellings held under a contract of tenancy held for longer than from year to year, 1982 Act, s.8.

[70] Dwellings remain controlled despite increases in their rateable valuations above these limits, unless and until the landlord recovers possession, 1960 Act, s.3(4) and 1967 Act, s.2(1). Note also the decontrol on actual possession *within* the general valuation limits between 1960 and 1966, 1960 Act, s.3(2)(*f*) and (7), as amended by 1967 Act, s.2(2) and (5). *Donnelly* v. *O'Neill* [1935] I.R.286; *Logan* v. *Donohue* [1938] I.R. 427.

[71] 1960 Act, s.3(2), as amended by 1967 Act, s.2.

[72] *I.e.*, where the rent includes payments for board, attendance or use of furniture or supply of services (heat, hot water, fuel etc.), s.3(2)(*d*) *Kavanagh* v. *Whittle* [1926] I.R. 425; *Cotter* v. *Stenicka* [1926] I.R. 261; *Houlihan* v. *Nagle* (1937) 71 I.L.T.R. 161; *Tyson* v. *Munn* [1938] Ir.Jur.Rep. 77; *Parkinson* v. *O'Malley* [1940] I.R. 498; *Hanratty* v. *Hardy* [1947] Ir.Jur.Rep. 42; *Little* v. *Davies* [1949] Ir.Jur.Rep. 24; *Murphy* v. *Kenny* [1950] Ir.Jur.Rep. 1; *Fidbery* v. *Doyle* [1981] I.L.T.M. 370.

[73] 1960 Act, s.3(2)(*e*) and (6), as amended by 1967 Act, s.2(6).

[74] 1967 Act, s.2(3). See *McCann* v. *Cotter* (1925) 59 I.L.T.R. 113; *O'Sullivan* v. *Cullen* (1925) 59 I.L.T.R. 133; *Boyle* v. *Fitzsimons* [1926] I.R. 378; *Casserley* v. *Graham* (1929) 63 I.L.T.R. 162; *Garrett* v. *Filgate* [1949] Ir.Jur.Rep. 50; *Griffin* v. *Kennedy* (1965) 99 I.L.T.R. 199.

[75] See also 1960 Act, s.3(5). *Wills* v. *McGrane* (1931) 65 I.L.T.R. 86.

[76] 1967 Act, s.2(4). Dwellings decontrolled by the 1967 Act are now subject to Part II of the Landlord and Tenant (Amendment) Act, 1980, see s.15 of that Act.

[77] 1960 Act, s.4. *Burns* v. *Radcliffe* [1923] 2 I.R. 158; *Plunkett* v. *Lenehan* (1928) 62 I.L.T.R. 29; *Hardwick Ltd.* v. *Scott* [1937] Ir.Jur.Rep. 15; *Dineen* v. *McFarland* [1944] Ir.Jur.Rep. 68; *Walsh* v. *Coyne* [1958] I.R. 223.

[78] S.21. See *Dowd* v. *Pierce* [1984] I.L.R.M. 653 (fixing rent).

[79] *E.g.*, recovery of possession, see para.18.33, *post.*

[80] As regards its procedure, see the Housing (Rent Tribunal) Regulations, 1983 (1983 No.222 of 1983).

[81] S.11(1). At the time of writing this power had still not been exercised. Appeals on a point of law lie to the High Court, s.13. On "point of law", see *Rahill* v. *Brady* [1971] I.R. 69; *Quirke* v. *Folio Homes* (1985) Unrep. (H.C.,R.I.) (1984 No. 621 P).

[82] Less an allowance for improvements, 1982 Act, s.7(1). See *Ryan* v. *Phelan* [1940] Ir.Jur.Rep. 56; *Rabbitt* v. *Grant* [1940] I.R. 323. *Re* compensation for improvements on quitting a controlled tenancy, see s.15.

would be the just and proper rent having regard to the nature, character and location of the dwelling, other terms of the tenancy, the means of the landlord and tenant, the date the landlord purchased the premises and the purchase price, the length of the tenant's occupancy and the number and ages of the tenant's family residing there.[83]

18.32. A system for registration of rented accommodation with housing authorities has also been introduced[84] and landlords are required to provide rent books containing prescribed particulars.[85] There is also a system for payment of rent allowances to tenants of controlled dwellings who suffer hardship by reason of increases in rents.[86]

(iii) Security of Tenure

18.33. This is now provided under section 16 of the 1982 Act, whereby a landlord cannot recover possession of a controlled dwelling without a court order, which will not be made unless the court considers it reasonable[87] and one of the grounds listed in the section is established by the landlord.[88] These grounds are either cases of default, *e.g.,* breach of obligation by the tenant, nuisance or immoral or illegal user of the dwelling or waste, [89] or other matters such as the landlord needing the dwelling for his own residence[90] or his employee,[91] the financial stringency of the landlord, the interests of good estate management[92] or to enable the landlord to carry out a development scheme for which planning permission exists.[93] An order against the tenant does not prejudice the right of lawful sub-tenants to retain possession.[94]

18.34. These restrictions on recovery of possession do not apply to "service" or employment lettings nor to lettings *bona fide* for the temporary

---

[83] 1982 Act, s.13 and 1983 Act, s.9.

[84] See the Housing (Private Rented Dwellings) Regulations, 1982 (S.I. No.217 of 1982), implementing s.24 of the 1982 Act. See also s.26, relating to regulations prescribing standards for any class of rented dwelling and the Housing (Private Rented Dwellings) (Standards) Regulations, 1984 (S.I. No. 337 of 1984).

[85] See the 1982 Regulations, *supra*, implementing s.25 of the 1982 Act.

[86] 1982 Act, s.23 and Social Welfare (Rent Allowance) Regulations 1982 (S.I. No.220 of 1982) and 1983 (S.I. Nos. 186 and 352 of 1983).

[87] *Folan* v. *Lee* [1926] I.R. 87; *Noonan* v. *Reddy* (1925) 59 I.L.T.R. 131; *Westport Harbour Commrs.* v. *McBride* [1931] L.J.Ir. 50; *Fitzsimons* v. *Parker* [1949] Ir.Jur.Rep. 59; *Hardwicke Ltd.* v. *Murphy (No.2)* (1951) 85 I.L.T.R. 109.

[88] The Court is to have regard to the extent, if any, to which the landlord's conduct has contributed to the existence of these, s.16(2). *Merchant Banking Ltd.* v. *O'Beirne* [1964] I.R.370.

[89] *Patterson* v. *Culhane* (1916) 50 I.L.T.R. 116; *Folan* v. *Lee* [1926] I.R. 87; *Hall* v. *Nulty* (1937) 71 I.L.T.R. 198; *Brophy* v. *Robertson* [1937] Ir.Jur.Rep.16; *O'Connor* v. *Byrne* [1945] Ir.Jur.Rep. 30; *Hardwicke Ltd.* v. *Murphy* (No.2)(1951) I.L.T.R. 110.

[90] *Salmon* v. *Cawley* (1919) 53 I.L.T.R. 224; *Kieran* v. *Dunne* (1920) 54 I.L.T.R. 51; *G.N.R.* v. *Best* (1921) 55 I.L.T.R. 57; *Kavanagh* v. *Whittle* [1926] I.R. 425; *Rossiter* v. *Masterson* (1926) 60 I.L.T.R. 32; *Cooley* v. *Walsh* [1926] I.R. 239; *Lyons* v. *Lyons* [1935] Ir.Jur.Rep. 9; *McErlane* v. *McGowan* (1944) 78 I.L.T.R. 106; *Sheppard* v. *Collins (No.2)* [1942] Ir.Jur.Rep. 55; *O'Farrell* v. *Woods* [1957] Ir.Jur.Rep. 26; *Clinch* v. *MacKeogh* [1964] Ir.Jur.Rep. 37; *Dowling* v. *Hannon* [1964] I.R.19.

[91] *Cromer* v. *Murray* [1932] L.J.Ir. 101. See also *McArdle Moore & Co. Ltd.* v. *Kelly* (1960) 94 I.L.T.R. 48.

[92] Or the extension of business premises, provided in both cases the tenant is compensated. *Gallagher* v. *Earl of Leitrim* [1948] Ir.Jur.Rep.23; *Hardwicke Ltd.* v. *Byrne* [1963] I.R. 52; *Merchant Banking Ltd.* v. *O'Beirne* [1964] I.R. 370.

[93] S.16(4).

[94] S.30. *Hipps Ltd.* v. *Hughes* (1919) 53 I.L.T.R. 111; *Murphy* v. *Porter* (1919) 53 I.L.T.R. 151; *Walsh* v. *Byrne* [1940] Ir.Jur.Rep. 13; *Martin* v. *Mulligan* [1943] Ir.Jur.Rep. 43; *Lewis* v. *Shepperson* [1947] Ir.Jur.Rep. 47; *Wardron* v. *Burbage* (1957) 91 I.L.T.R. 30.

convenience or to meet a temporary necessity of the landlord or tenant,[95] or to recovery by a local authority for exercise of their statutory powers.[96]

18.35. Finally, a person who immediately prior to the operation of the 1982 Act was a tenant of a controlled dwelling is entitled to retain possession as the "original tenant" for his or her lifetime.[97] That tenant's spouse, if *bona fide* residing in the dwelling at the time of the tenant's death, has a similar right for life.[98] Also a member of the family so residing when the tenant or surviving spouse dies within 20 years from operation of the 1982 Act, can retain possession until expiration of the 20-year period.[99] For these purposes the original tenant includes a statutory tenant under the old legislation.[1] Under this legislation after determination of his contractual tenancy in the controlled dwelling, the tenant had the right to retain possession as "statutory" tenant[2] until the landlord obtained a court order for possession. Apart from former contractual tenants and lawful sub-tenants, the rights of a statutory tenant passed on death of a contractual or statutory tenant to his spouse or other member of his family *bona fide* residing with him at his death.[3] Certain assignees of statutory tenants could also retain possession on the same terms and conditions as their assignors.[4] Generally the terms and conditions of the original tenancy applied to the statutory tenancy, so far as they were consistent with the Acts.[5]

B. Northern Ireland

1. *Rent (N.I.) Order, 1978*

18.36. Until the 1978 order came into operation the Rent Restriction Acts (N.I.) were based on the original system introduced during the First World War and, as a result of decontrolling in the inter-War years and reintroduction of further control with the advent of the Second World War, a dual system of "old" and "new" control existed.[6] Some 11 major Acts on the subject were in force, dating from 1920 to 1967.[7] The rent restriction law of Northern Ireland was overhauled by the Rent (N.I.) Order, 1978, following

---

[95] 1982 Act, ss.9 and 16. *Kaye* v. *Kelly* [1948] I.R. 383; *Macbeth* v. *Bishopp* [1948] Ir.Jur.Rep. 4. *Murphy* v. *O'Connell* [1949] Ir.Jur.Rep. 1; *Stokes* v. *Moloney* [1959] Ir.Jur.Rep. 57. Nor do they apply to furnished lettings, see Rent Restriction Act, 1960, s.3(2)(*d*). See *Murphy* v. *Kenny* [1950] Ir.Jur.Rep. 1.

[96] See Housing Act, 1966, ss.62(6), 66(17) and 118(1). *Fitzsimons* v. *Menkin* [1938] I.R. 805; *Smyth* v. *Tyndall* [1957] Ir.Jur.Rep. 4.

[97] 1982 Act, s.9(1).

[98] S.9(2).

[99] S.9(3)-(7).

[1] S.7(1).

[2] See definition in s.2 of the 1960 Act.

[3] 1960 Act, s.31(3) and (4). See *Butler* v. *McCormack* (1929) 63 I.L.T.R. 176; *Graham* v. *Warren* [1937] Ir.Jur.Rep. 23; *O'Byrne* v. *O'Byrne* (1938) 72 I.L.T.R. 65; *Workingmen's Benefit Building Society* v. *Flanagan* [1939] IR.Jur.Rep. 90; *McCombe* v. *Sheehan* [1954] I.R. 183; *Reynolds* v. *McKane* (1958) 92 I.L.T.R. 86; *Jordan* v. *O'Brien* [1960] I.R. 363.

[4] 1960 Act, s.32(5). See also 1967 Act, s.10.

[5] 1960 Act, s.32, as amended by 1967 Act, s.10 and Landlord and Tenant (Amendment) Act, 1971, s.11.

[6] See Frazer and Wylie, "The Rent Restriction Law of Northern Ireland" (1971) 22 N.I.L.Q. 99. See also Getty, (1937) 1 N.I.L.Q. 86; Conaghan, (1944) 6 N.I.L.Q. 125; Fetherston, (1947) 7 N.I.L.Q. 103; Anon., (1951) 9 N.I.L.Q. 119.

[7] See the list in Frazer and Wylie, *op. cit.*, App.1.

the recommendations in the Department of Housing, Local Government and Planning (as it then was) *Report of the Committee on Rent Restriction Law of Northern Ireland* (1975). The 1978 Order repealed the earlier legislation and introduced new categories of protected, statutory, restricted and regulated tenancies.[8] Generally, protected tenancies are tenancies to which the earlier legislation applied,[9] tenancies of certain dwelling-houses let by a housing association[10] and new tenancies of dwelling-houses previously subject to protected tenancies, provided the net annual value does not exceed £140 and the dwelling-house is not *bona fide* let at a rent which includes payments in respect of board, attendance or the use of furniture.[11] A statutory tenancy arises on determination of a protected tenancy in favour of the protected tenant so long as he and his successors continue to occupy the dwelling-house as their residence.[12] A protected or statutory tenancy is a restricted tenancy if a restricted rent certificate has been served, or been deemed to have been served, by the district council, otherwise it is a regulated tenancy.[13]

(i) Controlled Dwellings

18.37. Under Article 8 of the 1978 Order the landlord or tenant of a dwelling-house subject to a protected tenancy had one year from the commencement of the Order (1st October 1978)[14] in which to apply to the district council to have the dwelling-house inspected with a view to ascertaining whether it met the "regulated tenancy standards".[15] If it did, the council were to issue a "regulated rent certificate" and, if it did not, a "restricted rent certificate". An appeal from the council's decision lay to the county court.[16] Upon subsequent application at any time by the landlord, the council may, after inspection, etc., issue a regulated rent certificate to convert a restricted tenancy into a regulated one.[17] The Order excludes various tenancies from its provisions, *e.g.,* tenancies where the rent includes payments in respect of board, attendance or the use of furniture,[18] public housing and housing owned by housing associations and industrial and provident societies.[19] Article 12 (1) provides that the mere fact that part of a dwelling-house is used as a shop or office or for business, trade or professional purposes is not to prevent the house from being let on a protected or statutory tenancy. Where it is possible to enter the residential part of the premises otherwise than through the non-residential part, the Order applies only to the residential part, otherwise it applies to the entire premises.[20]

[8] Pt.II.
[9] Art. 3(1).
[10] Art. 3(2).
[11] Art. 5.
[12] Art.84 and Sched.1.
[13] Arts. 7 and 8, see para. 18.37, *infra.*
[14] Rent (N.I.) Order (Commencement) Order 1978 (S.R. 1978 No.245).
[15] Set out in Sched.3 to the Order.
[16] Art. 11.
[17] Art. 9.
[18] Art. 5(3)-(6).
[19] Art. 5(7).
[20] Art. 12(3) and (4).

(ii) Rent Control

18.38. Under Part VI of the 1978 Order, rents of restricted tenancies are restricted to those payable at the commencement of the Order. Under Parts IV and V, rents of regulated tenancies are two-and-a-half times the net annual value of the dwelling-house, but are restricted to a maximum of £8 a week or £35 a month, until a rent assessment committee determines otherwise.[21] The Department of the Environment is required to prepare and keep up-to-date a register of rents payable under restricted and regulated tenancies, open to public inspection.[22] Upon being served with notice of the rent registered,[23] the landlord or tenant may apply within four weeks to a rent assessment committee to determine what he considers is the more appropriate rent.[24] The committee in making its assessment is to have regard to rents payable for comparable dwelling-houses let by the Housing Executive[25] and disregard any disrepair or defect attributable to a failure, or improvement made otherwise than under the tenancy agreement, by the tenant or any predecessor of his. A landlord intending to improve the dwelling-house can apply to a rent assessment committee for a certificate of future rent.[26] The Department of the Environment is also obliged to keep registered rents under review and vary them as appropriate.[27] Finally, Article 38 of the Order requires the landlord of a dwelling-house held under a private tenancy to provide the tenant with a rent book containing prescribed particulars and information.[28] Failure to do so, results in it being a criminal offence to demand or receive the rent.[29] For these purposes a private tenancy does not include a fee farm grant or tenancy for a term exceeding 99 years, unless terminable by notice before the end of the term.[30]

Part VIII of the Order prohibits the charging of premiums and loans on the grant or assignment of protected tenancies. For these purposes the requirement of the purchase of furniture at an excessive price, as a condition of the grant, renewal, continuance or assignment of such a tenancy is treated as a premium.[31] Part X empowered the Department of the Environment to institute a scheme (to be run by the Department of Finance) for granting rent allowances to private tenants in respect of their rents, based upon their needs and resources.[32]

(iii) Security of Tenure

18.39. Part III of the 1978 Order deals with the security of tenure conferred on protected and statutory tenants. The grounds for recovery of possession

---

[21] See Rent Assessment Committees Regulations, 1978 (S.R. 1978 No.259).
[22] Art. 25.
[23] Art. 26(4).
[24] Art. 27(1).
[25] Art. 27(2) and (3).
[26] Art. 32.
[27] Art. 33.
[28] See Rent Book Regulations 1978 (S.R. 1978 No.253).
[29] Art. 39.
[30] Art. 38(3).
[31] Art. 51.
[32] See Rent Allowance Scheme (Statutory Particulars) Regulations, 1978 (S.R. 1978 No.265).

are set out in Article 13 and Schedule 4. In essence, an order for possession is not to be made unless the court thinks it reasonable and either the court is satisfied that suitable alternative accommodation is available for the tenant or the circumstances specified in any of the cases set out in Part I of Schedule 4 exist (*e.g.*, default of the tenant in respect of rent, or use or treatment of the premises). However, in certain other cases set out in Part II of the Schedule the court *must* make an order for possession (e.g., owner-occupier residences and religious and employee premises). Article 14 now confers on the court an extended discretion to suspend enforcement of an order for possession or to postpone the date of possession. Article 17 enables a statutory tenancy to be changed by agreement, provided the landlord consents and no pecuniary consideration is required.[33] Succession to a statutory tenancy is dealt with by Schedule 1, which retains the rule allowing two successions.[34] Part IX of the Order now adopts the English measures giving protection against harassment and eviction without due process of law.[35]

2. Leasehold (Enlargement and Extension) Act (N.I.), 1971

18.40. This Act deals with the same problem as the Republic's Landlord and Tenant (Ground Rents) Act, 1967, and is designed to protect long lessees of residential property from losing their "equity" on determination of the lease.[36] The Act confers on "ground" lessees, with at least 5 years' occupation of the property[37] as the sole or principal residence, the right to enlarge the lease into a fee simple, by buying out all superior owners (including fee farm grantees) or, instead, to obtain a once-for-all extension of the lease for a further term of 50 years.[38] The purchase price for the fee simple, to be fixed, if necessary, by the Lands Tribunal, is based on its open market value, on the assumption largely that the lessee has an "equity" in the buildings and the ground is owned by the superior owners.[39] The fee simple is to be conveyed

---

[33] Art. 18.

[34] See also Art. 4. Note the English Court of Appeal decision in *Jessamine Investment Co.* v. *Schwartz* [1977] 2 W.L.R. 145, where it was held that transformation by adverse possession of a statutory tenant's interest in land into a possessory leasehold interest as against the intermediate landlord did not affect the continuance of the statutory tenancy as against the superior landlord (the freeholder). Protected sub-tenancies generally survive the granting of an order for possession in respect of the head-tenancy (Art. 19). As regards sub-tenants, see *Enniskillen U.D.C.* v. *Bartley* [1947] N.I. 177. In *McCullough* v. *Ministry of Commerce* [1960] N.I. 75 (see Calvert, (1964) 15 N.I.L.Q. 110), the Divisional Court held that a statutory tenant had a sufficient "estate or interest" in the land to be entitled to compensation on its compulsory purchase. *Cf. McKinty* v. *Belfast Corporation* [1973] N.I. 1. See also on statutory tenancies, *Martin Estates Co.* v. *Watt* [1925] N.I. 79; *McErlane* v. *McGowan* (1944) 78 I.L.T.R. 106. And *Drury* v. *Johnston* [1927] N.I. 25; *Apsley* v. *Barr* [1928] N.I. 183; *cf. Roddy* v. *O'Sullivan* (1927) 61 I.L.T.R. 66; *Deans* v. *Kelly* [1959] Ir.Jur.Rep. 22. Hand, "The Statutory Tenancy: An Unrecognised Proprietary Interest?" [1980] Conv. 351.

[35] See para.17.067, *ante.*

[36] See generally, Wylie, "Leasehold (Enlargement and Extensions) Act (N.I.) 1971 – A Critique" (1971) 22 N.I.L.Q. 389, which, *inter alia*, examines its operation in a typical urban pyramid title situation and its application to fee farm grants. See also (1972) 23 N.I.L.Q. 542-6, and *Report of the Committee on Long Leases* (1967, Cmd. 509).

[37] Only where the lease expires within 50 years; holders of longer leases can enfranchise immediately.

[38] S.1. Note, however, the grounds on which superior owners can resist enfranchisement, s.19.

[39] S.14. See also the Leasehold (Enlargement and Extension)(N.I.) Order, 1981. Suggestions that the English equivalent, the Leasehold Reform Act, 1967, might, in this regard, have been in breach of Art.1 of the First Protocol (1952) to the European Convention for the Protection of Human Rights and Fundamental Freedoms (1950)("no one shall be deprived of his possessions except in the public interest")(see, *e.g.*, Megarry and Wade, *The Law of Real Property* (5th ed., 1985), p.1128, fn.82) were rejected by the European Court of Human Rights in an application by trustees acting for the second Duke of Westminster's estate in respect of

generally "free from incumbrances,"[40] but, as under the Republic's 1967 Act, certain covenants and conditions retaining commercial value or enhancing amenities may continue to bind the land.[41] There are also provisions for apportionment of rents, covenants and conditions to deal with cases where the ground lessee holds under a pyramid title.[42]

18.41. Where the lessee opts instead for a 50 year extension of his lease, this is to be a graft on the old lease.[43] Where the Lands Tribunal has to fix its terms, the new ground rent is to be a "fair modern ground rent," which may be subject to revision after 25 years.[44]

18.42. The 1971 Act has not been a conspicuous success[45] and it is likely to be replaced by new comprehensive provisions dealing with ground rents generally.[46]

---

valuable properties in the centre of London, see *James and Others* v. *United Kingdom, The Times,* 22nd Feb., 1986. *Cf.* the attack on the jurisdiction to extinguish "impediments" under the Property (N.I.) Order, 1978, in *Scott* v. *United Kingdom,* which also failed, see para.19.46, *post.*

   [40] S. 3(1).
   [41] S. 28.
   [42] Ss. 8-13.
   [43] S. 18.
   [44] S. 18(3).
   [45] See the discussion of its defects in the Land Law Working Group's Discussion Document No. 1 (*Ground Rents and Other Periodic Rents*) (1980), ch. 8 and Interim Report (*Ground Rents and Other Period Rents*) (1983), ch. 4.
   [46] 1983 Interim Report, *supra,* p.45 *et seq.*

PART VIII

COVENANTS, LICENCES AND SIMILAR INTERESTS

CHAPTER 19

RESTRICTIVE COVENANTS

19.01. This is a subject which has become increasingly important in recent decades, despite the advent of public town and country planning control of the use of land.[1] A "covenant" is a promise under seal, *i.e.*, contained in a deed, and like all contractual obligations is enforceable between the parties according to the normal rules of contract law. What we are concerned with in this chapter, however, is to what extent certain covenants, *i.e.*, those restricting the use of land, do more than create purely contractual obligations by giving rise to interests in land in the sense that successors in title to the original parties and other persons can have rights and duties under them.[2]

19.02. In considering this subject a distinction has to be made between covenants affecting *leasehold* land and those affecting *freehold* land. It is usual for a lease to contain a number of covenants or agreements entered into by both the lessor and lessee, *e.g.*, to pay rent and do repairs.[3] A common form of covenant or agreement is one restricting the user the lessee can make of the demised premises, *e.g.*, confining its use to private residential purposes. Since most urban land in Ireland is held under leases, or fee farm grants creating the relationship of landlord and tenant,[4] the question of enforceability of such covenants against successors in title has to be determined by leasehold law.[5] However, this is not always the case, even in urban areas, and so we must also consider the position where the covenant relates to freehold land.

I. LEASEHOLD LAND

19.03. As we shall discuss further later in this chapter,[6] there is now little difficulty about the enforceability of restrictive covenants on leasehold land

---

[1] See Elphinstone, *Covenants Affecting Land* (1946); Preston and Newsom, *Restrictive Covenants Affecting Freehold Land* (7th ed., 1982). Garner, "Restrictive Covenants Restated" (1962) 26 Conv. 298; Mellows, "Planning and Restrictive Covenants" (1964) 28 Conv. 190; Robinson, "Restrictive Covenants" (1974) 38 Conv. 90; Strachan, "Restrictive Covenants Affecting Land" (1930) 46 L.Q.R. 159. Note also the recent controversy between Bell, "Tulk v. Moxhay Revisited" (1981) Conv. 55 and Griffith, "Tulk v. Moxhay Reclarified" [1983] Conv. 29.
[2] Wylie, "Contracts and Third Parties" (1966) 17 N.I.L.Q. 351.
[3] See, generally, ch. 17, *ante*.
[4] Ch. 4, *ante*.
[5] Bready, "Covenants Affecting Land" (1944) 6 N.I.L.Q. 48. *Dooner* v. *Odlum* [1914] 2 I.R. 411.
[6] Paras. 19.05 *et seq.*, *infra*.

by or against successors in title of the original lessor and lessee. The need for this was recognised at common law and later confirmed by statute.

19.04. Two aspects of enforceability must be considered. First, there is the question of how far the *benefit* of (*i.e.*, the right to sue on) a covenant passes to a successor in title of the lessor. Secondly, there is the question of how far the *burden* of (*i.e.*, the liability to be sued on) a covenant passes to a successor in title of the lessee. The following is a summary only of the position in Ireland, since the matter was discussed in an earlier chapter.

A. BENEFIT

19.05. At common law, the benefit of a covenant which "touched and concerned" the land[7] did not pass automatically with an assignment of the lessor's reversion.[8] This was not provided for in Ireland until the Statute of Reversions (Ir.), 1634.[9] Until 1860, the two conditions for enforceability were that the covenant should touch and concern the land, or have reference to the subject-matter of the lease,[10] and that the plaintiff was successor in title to the lessor, *i.e.*, an assignee.[11] Since 1860, the first condition probably no longer applies in most cases in Ireland because section 12 of Deasy's Act, 1860,[12] requires only that the covenant or agreement be contained or implied in the lease in order to pass to an assignee of the lessor.[13] If there is subletting for the whole term,[14] or a fee farm grant creating the relationship of landlord and tenant,[15] so that there is no reversion, the benefit of the covenant probably passes with the right to receive the rent. If the lessor's reversion is severed, *e.g.*, he assigns to a third person the reversion of half the land demised, the covenants run with the part assigned so far as they relate to it. If the covenant takes the form of a condition,[16] this is also apportioned between the respective parts of the land. In fact, conditions were not severable at common law,[17] but this rule was reversed by statute.[18]

19.06. If the reversion is extinguished by surrender to a superior owner or merger with a superior estate, *e.g.*, where a lessee surrenders his lease to the head-lessor and the question arises as to the enforceability of covenants in the sub-lease, the next vested estate, *e.g.*, the superior estate held by the head-lessor, is deemed the reversion on the sub-lease so as to allow the

---

[7] *Athol* v. *M. & G.W. Rly.* (1868) I.R. 3 C.L. 333.

[8] See *Spencer's Case* (1583) 5 Co.Rep. 16a. Also *Bishop of Raphoe* v. *Hawkesworth* (1829) 1 Hud. & Br. 606.

[9] 10 Chas. 1. sess. 2, c. 4. *Cf.* the English Grantees of Reversions Act, 1540. *Butler* v. *Archer* (1860) 12 I.C.L.R. 104.

[10] The phrase substituted by Conveyancing Act, 1881, ss. 10 and 11, but which has the same meaning, para. 17.071, *ante.*

[11] See *Dawson* v. *Baldwin* (1832) Hay. & Jon. 24.

[12] *Cf.* s. 13, which is confined to covenants or agreements "concerning the lands," para. 17.072, *ante.*

[13] *Lyle* v. *Smith* [1909] 2 I.R. 58. (see *A Casebook on Irish Land Law* (1984), p. 575). Para. 17.073, *ante.*

[14] Para. 17.006, *ante.*

[15] Ch. 4, *ante.*

[16] Para. 17.067, *ante.*

[17] *Dumpor's Case* (1603) 4 Co.Rep. 119b.

[18] Law of Property Amendment Act, 1859, s. 3; Conveyancing Act, 1881, s. 12. Note also the Notices to quit (Ir.) Act, 1876, s. 3, which permits a tenant of agricultural land, in certain circumstances, to treat a notice to quit part of a holding as a notice to quit the entire holding. See also *McFarlane* v. *Lawless* [1944] Ir.Jur.Rep. 23; *Survey of the Land Law of Northern Ireland* (1971), para. 301.

covenants in it to remain enforceable.[19]

19.07. An assignee of the reversion can recover damages for breach of covenant only in respect of breaches committed during the time when he was assignee, *i.e.*, owner of the estate assigned.[20] It has been suggested in England that the assignee, rather than the assignor, can sue for breaches of covenant committed *before* the assignment, even though the breaches were not of a continuing character.[21] This was said to be the effect of section 141 of the Law of Property Act, 1925, which provides generally that the benefit of covenants touching and concerning the land passes with the reversion. Section 141 of the 1925 Act replaced section 10 of the Conveyancing Act, 1881, which remains in force in Ireland.[22] However, section 14 of Deasy's Act, 1860, also in force in Ireland, seems to run contrary to this in providing that an assignee of a landlord has the benefit of breaches of covenant or agreement only in respect of breaches occurring or continuing subsequent to the assignment to him and while he continues to be such an assignee.

At common law a right of re-entry by way of forfeiture of a lease could not be assigned, but such a right is now enforceable by an assignee of the reversion unless it has been waived expressly or impliedly.[23]

B. BURDEN

19.08. At common law the burden of a lessee's covenants passed to his assignees, provided the covenants touched and concerned the land.[24] An assignment of the lease, as opposed to the granting of a sub-tenancy, creates privity of estate between the assignee and head-lessor or his successors in title.[25] This common law rule was confirmed by section 11 of the Conveyancing Act, 1881, the reference therein to the covenants having "reference to the subject-matter of the lease" being interpreted to mean the same as "touching and concerning the land."[26] The other statutory provision in Ireland, section 12 of Deasy's Act, however, does not so limit the running of the burden of a *tenant's* covenants or agreements with the lease or agreement, though section 13 does appear to do so with respect to the burden of the landlord's covenants or agreements for the benefit of the tenant or his assignees.[27]

19.09. Section 14 of Deasy's Act provides that an assignee ceases to enjoy

---

[19] Real Property Act, 1845, s. 9. *Craig* v. *Greer* [1899] 1 I.R. 258. (see *A Casebook on Irish Land Law* (1984), p. 616)

[20] *Doyle* v. *Hort* (1880) 4 L.R.Ir. 455 at 472. See also Deasy's Act, s. 14, *infra*.

[21] *Re King* [1963] Ch. 459 (Lord Denning M.R. *dissentiente*). See also *Arlesford Trading Co.* Ltd. v. *Servansingh* [1971] 3 All E.R. 113; *Warnford Investments Ltd.* v. *Duckworth* [1979] Ch. 127. Cf. *Re Smyth* [1965] I.R. 595. See also *Day* v. *Hales* (1858) 3 Ir.Jur. (N.S.) 367; *Maddock* v. *Mallet* (1860) 12 I.C.L.R. 173.

[22] Para. 17.071, *ante*.

[23] Conveyancing Act, 1911. s. 2. See further on waiver, para. 17.037, *ante*.

[24] *Spencer's Case* (1583) 5 Co.Rep. 16a.

[25] Para. 17.029, *ante*. A sub-tenant may, however, be liable on a restrictive covenant in the head-lease under the rule in *Tulk* v. *Moxhay*, discussed at paras. 19.25 *et seq., post*. See *Craig* v. *Greer* [1899] 1 I.R. 258 (see *A Casebook on Irish Land Law* (1984), p. 616).

[26] *Davis* v. *Town Properties Investment Co. Ltd.* [1903] 1 Ch. 797; *Breams Property Investment Co. Ltd.* v. *Stroulger* [1948] 2 K.B. 1.

[27] Para. 17.072, *ante*.

the benefit, or to be liable to the burden, of any covenant or agreement in a lease or tenancy agreement after he has assigned his interest to someone else, though he must give written notice of his assignment to the landlord to so discharge himself from liability.[28] However, under section 15 of the same Act, where the assignee gives notice of assignment in the interval between two "gale" days (*i.e.*, days when rent is due), he is not discharged immediately and remains liable up to and including the next gale day.[29]

19.10. Though the general rule is that only an assignee of the lease becomes subject to the burden of its covenants, other persons may in fact become liable. Thus it is established in Ireland that even a squatter on the demised land[30] may through his actions be estopped from denying that he has become bound by the covenants in the lease.[31] This was held to be the case in *Ashe* v. *Hogan,*[32] where the squatter took advantage of a provision in the lease for a reduction by half in the rent payable so long as the covenants were observed. As O'Connor M.R. put it, "a person taking advantage of a clause in a lease and deriving benefit under it must accept the burdens."[33]

C. STATUTORY MODIFICATION

19.11. In the Republic of Ireland there has been some statutory modification of covenants in leases restricting the user of the demised land, originally under the Landlord and Tenant Act, 1931, and the Landlord and Tenant (Ground Rents) Act, 1967, and now to be found in the Landlord and Tenant (Amendment) Act, 1980. These provisions were discussed in an earlier chapter.[34] As yet no equivalent provisions have been enacted in Northern Ireland.[35]

II. FREEHOLD

19.12. We now turn to the question of enforceability of covenants relating to freehold land.[36] It must be reiterated that such covenants have been comparatively rare in Ireland because most land was leasehold. However, this is no longer the case with agricultural land owing to the operation of the Land Purchase Acts,[37] and the recent enfranchisement legislation[38] in both parts of

---

[28] *Powell* v. *Adamson* [1895] 2 I.R. 41. S. 16 provides for discharge from liability of the original tenant on assignment with the consent of the landlord. Para. 17.030, *ante*.

[29] Para. 17.031, *ante*.

[30] Note, however, the controversy as to whether a squatter becomes an assignee through adverse possession, ch. 23, *post*.

[31] *O'Connor* v. *Foley* [1906] 1 I.R. 20 at 26 (*per* Fitzgibbon L.J.).

[32] [1920] 1 I.R. 159.

[33] *Ibid.*, p. 164.

[34] Para. 17.047, *ante*.

[35] See, however, the recommendations in the *Survey of the Land Law of Northern Ireland* (1971), paras. 392-5, to which effect was given by Pt. II of the Property (N.I.) Order, 1978, see para. 19.46, *post*.

[36] To be strictly accurate, the rules discussed in the rest of this chapter may also be invoked in leasehold situations, *e.g.*, where the occupier of the land is not an assignee of the lease and so there is no "privity of estate" between him and the head-lessor or his assignee. Thus a sub-tenant may nevertheless be liable on a restrictive covenant in the head-lease under the rule in *Tulk* v. *Moxhay* (para. 19.25, *post*.), see *Craig* v. *Greer* [1899] 1 I.R. 258 (see *A Casebook on Irish Land Law* (1984), p. 616).

[37] Ch. 18, *ante*.

[38] *Ibid.*

Ireland relating to urban land will also cause the question to be raised more often than in the past.

19.13. In considering the enforceability of freehold covenants, a distinction has to be drawn between the respective approaches of the common law and equity.

A. At Common Law

19.14. At common law there were considerable difficulties about the enforceability of covenants affecting freehold land, at least as regards the passing of the burden to successors in title.

1. *Original Parties*

19.15. The original covenantee can usually enforce the covenant against the original covenantor, unless the covenantee has assigned the benefit of the covenant to someone else.[39] However, if the benefit of the covenant relates to a particular piece of land owned by the covenantee at the time of entering into the covenant, and he has since conveyed that land to someone else, his action for breach of covenant will secure for him at most nominal damages only.

19.16. Usually the covenantee is one of the parties to the deed containing the covenant, though the covenantor may be expressed to covenant with other persons not parties to the deed. At common law this caused problems because it was a strict rule for a deed made *inter partes* that only a party to it could sue on it.[40] This rule, however, was modified by section 5 of the Real Property Act, 1845,[41] which provided:

> "Under an indenture executed after the first day of October one thousand eight hundred and forty-five an immediate estate or interest in any tenements or hereditaments, and the benefit of a condition or covenant respecting any tenements or hereditaments, may be taken, although the taker thereof be not named a party to the same indenture..."

It seems to be fairly clear that this was designed to get over the difficulties of the *inter partes* rule and for nothing else.[42] For example, if the purchaser of a piece of land covenants with the vendor "and also the owners for the time being" of certain specified adjacent plots, those owners can also enforce the covenant *as original covenantees*, despite not being executing parties to the deed.[43] Whether their successors in title can enforce the covenant is an

---

[39] Para. 19.28, *post*.

[40] *Lord Southampton* v. *Brown* (1827) 6 B. & C. 718. This was the rule for a deed poll, *i.e.*, executed by one party only as a unilateral act, *Chelsea & Waltham Green Building Soc.* v. *Armstrong* [1951] Ch. 853.

[41] Replacing s. 11 of Transfer of Property Act, 1844.

[42] See the discussion in *Beswick* v. *Beswick* [1968] A.C. 58 at 104-5 (*per* Lord Upjohn). Some Irish authorities suggest that it is confined to covenants "touching and concerning" the land, see *Lloyd* v. *Byrne* (1888) 22 L.R.Ir. 269; *Monroe* v. *Plunket* (1889) 23 I.L.T.R. 76, *cf. Forster* v. *Elvet Colliery Co. Ltd.* [1908] 1 K.B. 629, [1909] A.C. 98; *Grant* v. *Edmondson* [1931] 1 Ch. 1.

[43] See *Kelsey* v. *Dodd* (1881) 52 L.J.Ch. 34; *White* v. *Bijou Mansions Ltd.* [1937] Ch. 610; *Re Ecclesiastical Commrs.' Conveyance* [1936] Ch. 430. Wylie, "Contracts and Third Parties" (1966) 17 N.I.L.Q. 351 at 403-5.

entirely different matter, as we shall see.[44]

19.17. Section 5 of the 1845 Act was replaced in England by the somewhat wider wording of section 56(1) of the Law of Property Act, 1925, and the English judges have been arguing about its effect ever since.[45] Mercifully the legislators have so far spared the Irish judges a similar problem of interpretation.[46]

2. Successors in Title

19.18. Here two questions must be considered, namely, to what extent at common law the benefit of a covenant affecting freehold land can pass to a successor in title of the covenantee and to what extent the burden can pass to a successor in title of the covenantor.

(i) Benefit

19.19. Three conditions must be met for the benefit of a covenant to pass to the coventantee's successor in title. From the outset it should be noted that these conditions do *not* include two which are vital in equity, namely that the covenant should be *restrictive* or *negative* only[47] and that it should touch and concern the land of the *covenantor*.[48]

(a) Touch and Concern Covenantee's Land

While the covenant need not concern any land owned by the covenantor, it must touch and concern land of the covenantee which is to be benefited thereby.[49] It appears that "land" in this context includes an incorporeal hereditament, like an easement. In *Gaw* v. *C.I.E.*,[50] Dixon J. held that a covenant to repair a footpath ran with a right of way over the path and could be enforced by a successor in title to the original covenantee. It seems, however, that the benefit of a covenant to pay a rentcharge will not run with the rentcharge.[51]

(b) Legal Estate

19.20. The common law recognised legal estates only and so the successor

---

[44] Paras. 19.18 *et seq., infra.*

[45] See, *e.g., Smith* v. *River Douglas Catchment Board* [1949] 2 K.B. 500; *Stromdale & Ball Ltd.* v. *Burden* [1952] Ch. 223; *Drive Yourself Hire Co. (London) Ltd.* v. *Strutt* [1954] 1 Q.B. 250; *Beswick* v. *Beswick* [1968] A.C. 58; *Lyus* v. *Prowsa Developments Ltd.* [1982] 1 W.L.R. 1044. Andrews, "Section 56 Revisited" (1959) 23 Conv. 179; Ellinger, "Privity of Contract under Section 56 (1) of the Law of Property Act 1925" (1963) 26 M.L.R. 396; Elliott, "The Effect of Section 56 (1) of the Law of Property Act, 1925" (1956) 20 Conv. 43 and 114; Furmston, "Return to *Dunlop* v. *Selfridge*" (1960) 23 M.L.R. 373; Wylie, *op. cit.,* pp. 404-10.

[46] Note the recommendation in the *1971 Survey (N.I.)*, para. 170.

[47] *Sharp* v. *Waterhouse* (1857) 7 E. & B. 816. See also *Gaw* v. *C.I.E.* [1953] I.R. 232 (covenant to repair). Blease, "Positive Covenants and Third Parties" (1955) 19 Conv. 261; Pritchard, "Making Positive Covenants Run" (1973) 37 Conv. 194; Scamell, "Positive Covenants in Conveyances of the Fee Simple" (1954) 18 Conv. 546.

[48] *Smith* v. *River Douglas Catchment Board* [1949] 2 K.B. 500.

[49] *Rogers* v. *Hosegood* [1900] 2 Ch. 388; *Formby* v. *Barker* [1903] 2 Ch. 539; *Dyson* v. *Foster* [1909] A.C. 98.

[50] [1953] I.R. 232 (see *A Casebook on Irish Land Law* (1984), p. 622). Harrison, "Running of Covenants with Easements and Other Incorporeal Hereditaments" (1957) U.Q.L.J. 165.

[51] *Kennedy* v. *Stewart* (1836) 4 L.Rec. (N.S.) 160; *Grant* v. *Edmondson* [1931] 1 Ch. 1. Strachan, "Covenants to Pay Rentcharges" (1931) 47 L.Q.R. 380.

of the covenantee must show that he holds a legal estate in the land benefited by the covenant.[52]

(c) *Same Title*

The successor must, in addition, show that he has succeeded to the *same* legal estate in the land as was held by the original covenantee.[53] Thus, if the original covenantee held the fee simple in the land benefited by the covenant, a tenant of his cannot enforce the covenant. This remains the position under section 58(1) of the Conveyancing Act, 1881, which deems covenants "to be made with the covenantee, *his heirs and assigns,*"[54] so that they "shall have effect as if heirs and assigns were expressed." The traditional view was that this provision was a mere "word-saving" provision and was not intended to alter the common law rule.[55] "Heirs and assigns" were the appropriate words to use in 1881[56] to indicate that the benefit was intended to pass to successors in title. However, in England section 58 of the 1881 Act has been replaced by section 78 of the Law of Property Act, 1925, which uses the apparently wider phrase "successors in title *and the persons deriving title under him or them.*"[57] It has been suggested that this enables persons not succeeding to the same estate to enforce covenants.[58]

(ii) Burden

19.21. The general rule is that the burden of a freehold covenant does not run with the land at common law.[59] There are, however, ways round this rule, albeit somewhat indirect.

(a) *Indemnity Agreements*

19.22. If the original covenantor sells the land to which the covenant attaches, he remains liable on it by virtue of privity of contract with the covenantee, so he invariably insists on his purchaser undertaking to indemnify him against future breaches.[60] If the original covenantor is sued, he in turn may sue his purchaser on the indemnity agreement, or bring him into the action as a third party, and, in this way, the covenant is enforced indirectly against the current holder of the land. When that purchaser sells to

---

[52] *Webb* v. *Russell* (1789) 3 T.R. 393.

[53] *Gaw* v. *C.I.E.* [1953] I.R. 232 (see *A Casebook on Irish Land Law* (1984), p. 622).

[54] Italics added.

[55] *Westhoughton U.D.C.* v. *Wigan Coal & Iron Co. Ltd.* [1919] 1 Ch. 159.

[56] "Heirs," of course, is now misleading to the extent that the law of inheritance has been abolished in Ireland, ch. 15, *ante.*

[57] Italics added. In *Federated Homes Ltd.* v. *Mill Lodge Properties Ltd.* [1980] 1 All E.R.371, the English Court Appeal held that s.78 of the Law of Property Act, 1925, was *not* a mere word-saving provision, but had the effect of annexing the benefit of a restrictive covenant to the covenantee's land, so as to make it run with the land (see para. 19.33, *post*). See also s. 79, which replaces s. 59 of the 1881 Act.

[58] *Smith* v. *River Douglas Catchment Board* [1949] 2 K.B. 500. See Scamell, "Positive Covenants in Conveyances of the Fee Simple" (1954) 18 Conv. 546 at 553–6; *1971 Survey (N.I.),* para. 180.

[59] *Austerberry* v. *Oldham Corp.* (1885) 29 Ch.D. 750; *Smith* v. *Colbourne* [1914] 2 Ch. 533. See Pritchard, "Making Positive Covenants Run" (1973) 37 Conv. 194.

[60] See *De Vesci* v. *O'Connell* [1908] A.C. 298 (cross-indemnities in respect of fee farm rents).

another one, he too may insist upon an indemnity and so on indefinitely. The danger is, of course, that at some point the chain of indemnities may be broken by failure of one successor in title to insist upon an indemnity being entered into by his successor. Or one of the successors may disappear and thus prevent a chain reaction right down to the current holder of the land.

(b) Reciprocity Covenants

19.23. It seems to be settled now, at least in England, that a landowner may have the burden of covenants enforced against him because this is reasonable in view of the fact that he has a reciprocal right to enforce the benefit of related covenants.[61] For example, residents on a housing estate may have the right to use common facilities, *e.g.*, roads and playgrounds, provided they contribute towards the cost of repair and upkeep. It is reasonable that the benefit of the right of use should be matched by the burden of the liability to make such contribution so far as successors in title to the original residents are concerned. Such reciprocity may also be established by way of analogy with the doctrine of estoppel[62] and, as we shall see, may be achieved in housing estates through an estate scheme.[63]

(c) Enlarged or Converted Leases

19.24. It would seem that covenants normally enforceable in leases may continue to be enforceable to the same extent where a lease is converted into a fee farm grant, *e.g.*, under the Renewable Leasehold Conversion Act, 1849,[64] or enlarged into a fee simple, *e.g.*, under the Conveyancing Act, 1881.[65]

B. In Equity

19.25. Equity provided two major contributions to the law relating to enforceability of covenants. First, equity could provide what was in many cases a more effective remedy for breach of covenant, *i.e.*, an injunction to prevent further breaches as opposed to damages.[66] Secondly, it developed special rules relating to *restrictive* covenants, whereby the *burden* of such covenants could be enforced against successors in title.[67] This second

---

[61] Sometimes referred to as the rule in *Halsall* v. *Brizell* [1957] Ch. 169. Megarry, (1957) 73 L.Q.R. 154; Wade, (1957) 73 L.Q.R. 154; Wade, (1957) C.L.J. 35. See also the discussion by Megarry V.-C in *Tito* v. *Waddell (No. 2)* [1977] Ch. 106; Aughterson, "Enforcement of Positive Burdens – A New Viability" [1985] Conv. 12.

[62] See the discussion in *E.R. Investment Ltd.* v. *High* [1967] 2 Q.B. 379.

[63] Para. 19.34. *post*.

[64] Ss. 1, 7 and 10. See the discussion in *Re McNaul's Estate* [1902] 1 I.R. 114 (see *A Casebook on Irish Land Law* (1984), p. 41) and ch. 4, *ante*.

[65] S. 65 and see Conveyancing Act, 1882, s. 11. Taylor, "Enlargement of Leasehold to Freehold" (1958) 22 Conv. 101. Para. 17.108, *ante*. Note also the preservation of certain covenants under recent leasehold enfranchisement legislation, see Landlord and Tenant (Ground Rents) (No. 2) Act, 1978, s. 28 (R.I.) and Leasehold (Enlargement and Extension) Act (N.I.), 1971, s. 28. Ch. 18 *ante*.

[66] Ch. 3, *ante*. See Tettenborn, "Damages for Breach of Positive Covenants" (1978) Conv. 366.

[67] Garner, "Restrictive Covenants Restated" (1962) 26 Conv. 298; Hayton, "Restrictive Covenants as Property Interests" (1971) 87 L.Q.R. 539; Randall, "Covenants Running with Land" (1909) 25 L.Q.R. 380; Robinson, "Restrictive Covenants" (1974) 38 Conv. 90; Strachan, "Restrictive Covenants Affecting Land" (1930) 46 L.Q.R. 159. English Law Reform Committee, *Report of the Committee on Positive Obligations Relating to Land* (1965, Cmnd. 2719); *1971 Survey (N.I.)*, ch. 16.

contribution was largely a development of the nineteenth century and is usually referred to, after a leading case, as the rule in *Tulk* v. *Moxhay*.[68] In this case Lord Cottenham L.C. laid down the general principle of equity that the burden of a restrictive covenant will run with the land to which it relates so as to bind all successors in title of the original covenantor, *except* a *bona fide* purchaser of the land without notice of the covenant.

Before examining this equitable principle further, we must also consider the approach of equity to the question of the running of the benefit of such a covenant.

1. *Benefit*

19.26. Since the benefit of a covenant, positive or restrictive, was generally enforceable at common law both by the original covenantor and his successors in title, equity largely followed the law and adopted the same principles,[69] though, of course, it provided its own special remedy, the injunction. Thus equity adopted the principle that the covenant should touch and concern the covenantee's land.[70] However, when the law relating to the running of the burden of restrictive covenants developed, equity became even more precise in its requirements. The rule developed that a plaintiff seeking the aid of equity in enforcement of a restrictive covenant must establish that he is the current holder of the land to which the benefit relates and also that the benefit has passed to him. Thus in equity even the original covenantor would lose the benefit of such a covenant if he parts with the land benefited by it.[71]

19.27. The difficult matter, however, in many cases is to establish that the benefit has passed to a successor in title. The point is that the motive of a restrictive covenant, *e.g.*, prohibiting certain user of land, is often not an intention to benefit a piece of land, but to serve the interest or convenience of the covenantee personally, while a positive covenant, *e.g.*, to repair fences, usually is clearly for the benefit of the land. It seems that a plaintiff can establish that the benefit of a restrictive covenant has passed to him in equity in one of two main ways.[72]

(i) Express Assignment

19.28. The plaintiff can show that he owns some interest in the land benefited by the covenant and that the benefit has been expressly assigned to him, or at least that when he acquired the land it was agreed between him and the assignor that he was to have the benefit of the covenant.[73] There must be

---

[68] (1848) 2 Ph. 774. For earlier decisions, see *Whatman* v. *Gibson* (1838) 9 Sim. 196; *Mann* v. *Stephens* (1846) 15 Sim. 377. *Cf. Keppell* v. *Bailey* (1834) 2 My. & K. 517. Also *Tulk* v. *Metropolitan Board of Works* (1868) 16 W.R. 212.

[69] Paras. 3.047, *ante* and 19.19, *supra*.

[70] *Rogers* v. *Hosegood* [1900] 2 Ch. 388. Bailey "The Benefit of a Restrictive Covenant" (1938) C.L.J. 339.

[71] *Chambers* v. *Randall* [1923] 1 Ch. 149

[72] These are, perhaps, not the only ways, see *Re Dolphin's Conveyance* [1970] Ch. 654; *cf. Re Pinewood Estate Ltd.* [1958] Ch. 280.

[73] *Renals* v. *Cowlishaw* (1879) 11 Ch.D. 866; *Formby* v. *Barker* [1903] 2 Ch. 539.

something to indicate that the benefit has passed.

19.29. It seems that the position of an assignee may vary according to whether he is suing the original covenantor or an assignee from him. In the former case, it appears to be sufficient to prove that the benefit has been assigned like a chose in action, which need not occur as part of the same transaction as the transfer of the land benefited by the covenant. If, however, the original covenantor has parted with the land benefited, or even a part of it, the benefit of the covenant must be assigned along with it for the assignee to be able to sue successors of the covenantor in equity.[74] This rule seems to be based on the view that, as we shall see, equity enforces restrictive covenants on the ground that they are concerned with preserving the value of the neighbouring land, and so the benefit must go along with that land in cases where the aid of equity is required, as it is where a claim is made that the burden runs with the covenantor's land to bind his successors.[75]

19.30. It is also a moot point as to whether, once the benefit has been assigned along with the covenantee's land, it becomes "annexed" to the land so as to run automatically with the land without express assignment thereafter. It is arguable that such an assignment is a clear indication of intention that the benefit should run and there seems to be no reason why the benefit cannot be annexed to the land subsequent to the covenant being entered into.[76]

(ii) Annexation

19.31. The other way in which the plaintiff can establish his right to sue on the covenant in equity is to show that the benefit was "annexed" to the land and he has acquired that land. Once the benefit has been annexed to the land in question, it runs with it regardless of whether the subsequent owners have notice of it.[77] Conversely once the original covenantee has parted with all the land, he is no longer entitled to enforce it in equity.[78] Annexation may be established in one of three ways.

(a) *Expressly*

19.32. Express annexation may be indicated by the wording of the deed or covenant itself. It must, however, specify the land to be benefited and state that the benefit relates to it or that it is entered into with the covenantee as owner of that land.[79] It is *not* enough simply for the covenant to be made with the covenantee "his heirs and assigns,"[80] since this does not necessarily relate

---

[74] *Re Union of London & Smith's Bank Ltd.'s Conv.* [1933] Ch. 611 at 632 (*per* Romer L.J.)
[75] Para. 19.38, *post.*
[76] See *Rogers* v. *Hosegood* [1900] 2 Ch. 388 at 408; *Reid* v. *Bickerstaff* [1909] 2 Ch. 305 at 320. *Cf. Re Pinewood Estate* [1958] Ch. 280. Wade, (1957) C.L.J. 146.
[77] *Rogers* v. *Hosegood* [1900] 2 Ch. 388.
[78] *Chambers* v. *Randall* [1923] 1 Ch. 149 at 157-8.
[79] *Rogers* v. *Hosegood, op. cit.; Osborne* v. *Bradley* [1903] 2 Ch. 446.
[80] Which is implied anyway under s.58 of the Conveyancing Act, 1881, see para. 19.20, *ante*; but *cf.* the *Federated Homes* case, para. 19.33, *infra.*

to a particular piece of land.[81] To avoid difficulties over whether the covenant can reasonably benefit a very large piece of land, it is wise to annex it to the land "or any part" of it.[82]

(b) Impliedly

19.33. It seems to be settled now, at least in England, that annexation of the benefit to the land may be implied from the surrounding circumstances of the case, if they indicate with reasonable certainty that the covenant was taken for the benefit of that land.[83] It is not clear whether implied annexation may be imported into the conveyance by section 58 of the Conveyancing Act, 1881. In *Federated Homes Ltd.* v. *Mill Lodge Properties Ltd.*,[83a] the English Court of Appeal held that this was the effect of the English replacement of section 58, section 78 of the Law of Property Act, 1925 (thus following the view taken in *Smith* v. *River Douglas Catchment Board*[83b]). However, the English Court did emphasise that the wording of section 78 is "significantly different" from the wording of section 58. Brightman L.J. stated:

> "The distinction is underlined by sub-s (2) of s.78, which applies sub-s (1) only to covenants made after the commencement of the Act. Section 58(1) of the earlier Act did not include the covenantee's successors in title or persons deriving title under him or them, nor the owners or occupiers for the time being of the land of the covenantee intended to be benefited. The section was confined, in relation to realty, to the covenantee, his heirs and assigns, words which suggest a more limited scope of operation than is found in s.78.
>
> If, as the language of s.78 implies, a covenant relating to land which is restrictive of the user thereof is enforceable at the suit of (1) a successor in title of the covenantee, (2) a person deriving title under the covenant or under his successors in title, and (3) the owner or occupier of the land intended to be benefited by the covenant, it must, in my view, follow that the covenant runs with the land, because *ex hypothesi* every successor in title to the land, every derivative proprietor of the land and every other owner and occupier has a right by statute to the covenant. In other words, if the condition precedent of s.78 is satisfied, that is to say, there exists a covenant which touches and concerns the land of the covenantee, that covenant runs with the land for the benefit of his successors in title, persons deriving title under him or them and other owners and occupiers."[83c]

[81] *Renals* v. *Cowlishaw* (1879) 11 Ch.D. 866.

[82] *Cf. Re Ballard's Conveyance* [1937] Ch. 473 and *Marquess of Zetland* v. *Driver* [1939] Ch.1. See also *Stilwell* v. *Blackman* [1968] Ch.508. Again *cf.* the views of Brightman L.J. in the *Federated Homes* case, para. 19.33, *infra*.

[83] *Marten* v. *Flight Refuelling Ltd.* [1962] Ch.115. *Cf.* English *Report of the Committee on Positive Covenants Affecting Land* (1965, Cmnd. 2719), para. 17. See also *Newton Abbot Co-operative Society* v. *Williamson and Treadgold Ltd.* [1952] Ch. 286. Ryder, "Restrictive Covenants: The Problem of Implied Annexation" (1972) 36 Conv. 20.

[83a] [1980] 1 All E.R.371.

[83b] [1949] 2 All E.R.179.

[83c] *Op. cit.*, p.379. *Cf.* where the covenant itself requires the benefit to be assigned expressly, see *Roake* v. *Chadha* [1984] 1 W.L.R. 40.

Later, Brightman L.J. stated that "if the benefit of a covenant is, on a proper construction of a document, annexed to the land, *prima facie* it is annexed to every part thereof, unless the contrary clearly appears."[83d] Browne and Megaw L.JJ. agreed with Brightman L.J.'s judgment. It remains to be seen what the Irish courts' reaction to this case will be in relation to section 58 of the 1881 Act.[83e]

(c) *Estate Schemes*

19.34. One of the common situations for imposition of restrictive covenants is a housing estate consisting of many plots, where the value of each individual house and plot depends to some extent on the covenants restricting the use of their land by each of the other owners on the estate. To ensure enforceability all round of the mutual covenants, the building developer would, under the normal rules,[84] have to ensure, as he sells off each plot, that the purchaser covenants expressly with owners of lots previously sold,[85] as well as with the developer, and that the benefit is annexed to the land and any part of it retained by the developer, or that he expressly assigns it with each plot subsequently sold.[86]

19.35. Fortunately, these complexities can be avoided in the case of freehold land if the developer establishes a building or estate scheme, the rules as to which were enunciated in *Elliston* v. *Reacher*.[87] The underlying philosophy was stated in an earlier case by Lord MacNaghten: "Community of interest necessarily . . . requires and imports reciprocity of obligation."[88] Since each purchaser buys his plot on the same basis as all the other purchasers of plots on the same estate, each purchaser and his successors in title can sue and be sued by all or any of the other purchasers and their successors. If the requisites for an estate scheme are present, the courts will recognise this form of "local law" in the estate.[89] Thus the covenants entered into by one resident on the estate with his vendor are enforceable by any other resident on the same estate.

[83d] *Op. cit.*, p.381.

[83e] For the view that s.58 is even more likely to have been intended to assist annexation (by counteracting cases like *Renals* v. *Cowlishaw* (1878) 9 Ch.D. 125, (1879) 11 Ch.D. 866), see Megarry and Wade, *The Law of Real Property* (5th ed., 1984), p.786, fn. 6. *Cf.* Preston and Newsom, *Restrictive Covenants Affecting Freehold Land* (7th ed., 1982), p.17; Newsom, "Universal Annexation" (1981) 97 L.Q.R.32; Todd, "Annexation after Federated Homes" [1985] Conv.177.

[84] *I.e.*, relating to *freehold* land. Of course, these difficulties have been avoided in the past in Ireland by developers insisting on granting or assigning *leasehold* interests only to purchasers of plots from them.

[85] *I.e.*, to ensure that they can enforce the covenant, since the developer no longer retains their land for it to be benefited.

[86] *I.e.*, to ensure that subsequent purchasers of plots can enforce the covenant.

[87] [1908] 2 Ch.374 at 384 (*per* Parker J. aff'd at 665). For earlier recognition of this principle, see *Western* v. *MacDermot* (1866) L.R. 1 Eq. 499; *Renals* v. *Cowlishaw* (1878) 9 Ch.D. 125, 11 Ch.D. 866; *Spicer* v. *Martin* (1888) 14 App.Cas. 12. It was applied in Ireland in *Fitzpatrick* v. *Clancy* (1964) Unrep. (H.C.,R.I.) (1964 No. 1879 P.) (see *A Casebook on Irish Land Law* (1984), p. 642). The same principle may be applied in analogous situations, *e.g.*, a block of residential flats, *Hudson* v. *Cripps* [1896] 1 Ch.265; *Gedge* v. *Bartlett* (1900) 17 T.L.R. 43. *Cf. Kelly* v. *Battershell* [1949] 2 All ER. 830.

[88] *Spicer* v. *Martin*, *op. cit.*, p.25. *Cf.* the principle at common law, para. 19.23, *ante*.

[89] *Reid* v. *Bickerstaff* [1909] 2 Ch.305 at 319. See also the discussion in *Brunner* v. *Greenslade* [1971] Ch.993 and *Texaco Antilles Ltd.* v. *Kernochan* [1973] A.C. 609, both of which deal with application of the principle to sub-schemes.

19.36. The requisites for an estate scheme are: (1) the plaintiff and defendant in question must have derived title from a common vendor, *e.g.*, the building developer; (2) the common vendor must have originally laid out the estate in plots subject to common restrictions, either consistent only with some general scheme of development or intended to be enforceable under such a scheme;[90] (3) the common vendor must have intended the restrictions to be for the benefit of all plots sold; (4) the plaintiff and defendant must have purchased their plots on the basis that the restrictions would benefit the other plots; (5) the area covered by the scheme must be clearly defined.[91]

19.37. It avoids difficulties if the developer initially draws up a plan of the estate, with the restrictions endorsed on it, and negotiates sales of each plot by express reference to this. This makes it clear on all sides that a general scheme of development is in force. However, it is probably not necessary that the restrictions should be identical throughout the estate[92] and the common vendor may reserve a power to release all or part of the land from them.[93]

2. Burden

19.38. The particular contribution of equity to the law of freehold covenants has been the enforcement of the burden of certain covenants against successors in title of the original covenantor. The basis of the rule in *Tulk* v. *Moxhay* is the fact that the covenant in question concerns the preservation of the value of the covenantee's land[94] rather than, as was once thought,[95] the fact that the present owner of the covenantor's land acquired it with notice of the covenant. In this respect the law relating to restrictive covenants has similarities with the law of easements, *i.e.*, there must be a *dominant* and *servient* tenement, and this has led some to describe the law as an extension in equity of the doctrine of negative easements.[96] This must not be allowed, however, to obscure the fact that the law relating to restrictive covenants was really a new development in the nineteenth century, so that it is fair to say that equity created then a new interest in land.

We must consider now the conditions which must be satisfied if a successor in title of the original covenantor is to be bound by a covenant affecting freehold land in equity.

(i) Restrictive Covenant

19.39. It is settled that equity will enforce a covenant only if it is restrictive,

---

[90] See *Baxter* v. *Four Oaks Properties Ltd.* [1965] Ch.816.

[91] *Reid* v. *Bickerstaff, op. cit.*

[92] *Collins* v. *Castle* (1887) 36 Ch.D. 243 at 253-4.

[93] *Newman* v. *Real Estate Debenture Corp. Ltd.* [1940] 1 All E.R. 131.

[94] *L. & S.W. Rly.* v. *Gomm* (1882) 20 Ch.D.562 at 583 (*per* Jessel M.R.); *Formby* v. *Barker* [1903] 2 Ch.539.

[95] *Catt* v. *Tourle* (1869) 4 Ch.Ap, 654; *Luker* v. *Dennis* (1877) 7 Ch.D. 227. But see the recent academic controversy over the rule between Bell, "Tulk v. Moxhay Revisited" [1981] Conv. 55 and Griffith, "Tulk v. Moxhay Reclarified" [1983] Conv.29.

[96] *E.g.*, Jessel M.R. in the *Gomm* case, *op. cit.*, p.583. In *Re Tiltwood* [1978] Ch.269, Foster J. adopted the analogy with easements in holding that unity of seisin of the two pieces of land to which a restrictive covenant relates (the "dominant and servient tenements") extinguishes the covenant unless it is expressly revived in a subsequent sale by the common owner.

i.e., negative in nature.[97] The reason for this was that equity's contribution to the law of covenants stemmed from the availability of its special remedy, the injunction. This is a remedy which is more often used to restrain the commission or continuance of acts, which presents no particular difficulties of enforcement, than to require the doing of something positive, which may necessitate supervision. It is true that equity can grant mandatory injunctions and also decrees of specific performance, but we saw in an earlier chapter that these are not given as freely as a prohibitory injunction.[98]

19.40. Whether a covenant is negative or not is a matter of substance and cannot be disguised by the form of words used in the deed or covenant, *e.g.*, a covenant to refrain from building on Leicester Square Garden can be put in the form of a covenant to maintain it "in an open state, uncovered with any buildings."[99] The test usually adopted is whether compliance with the covenant requires expenditure of money. If it does, it is not negative in nature, *e.g.*, a covenant "not to let the premises fall into disrepair." If it does not, the covenant is more likely to be negative in nature,[1] but not necessarily so.

19.41. It has been recently held by the House of Lords that a covenant in the form that the covenantor is not to "cause or permit" certain types of user of land is *not* broken if the covenantor agrees to sell the land to a person who intends, with the full knowledge of the covenantor, to use it for such prohibited purposes.[2]

(ii) Benefit of Covenantee's Land

19.42. As mentioned above,[3] the basis of the rule in *Tulk* v. *Moxhay* is that the covenant is concerned with preserving the value of the land retained by the covenantee, *i.e.*, it is taken for its benefit. The general rule is, therefore, that the plaintiff must be the owner for the time being of the neighbouring land benefited by the covenant.[4] Thus the original covenantee cannot enforce the covenant in equity against a successor of the original covenantor if he has parted with all the "dominant" land.[5] There are, however, some exceptions to this general rule. Thus it has been held that a head-landlord, owning no neighbouring land, can sue under the doctrine of *Tulk* v. *Moxhay* a sublessee with whom he has neither privity of estate nor privity of contract.[6] We saw earlier that an estate scheme may avoid the difficulties of proving retention of neighbouring land.[7]

---

[97] *Haywood* v. *Brunswick Permanent Benefit Building Soc.* (1881) 8 Q.B.D. 403. There were earlier doubts on this, *Morland* v. *Cook* (1868) L.R. 6 Eq. 252; *Cooke* v. *Chilcott* (1876) 3 Ch.D. 694. *Cf.* the English recommendations in the *Report of the Committee on Positive Covenants Affecting Land* (1965, Cmnd. 2719) and Law Com. No.127, *Transfer of Land: The Law of Positive and Restrictive Covenants* (1984); and see *1971 Survey (N.I.)*, ch.16.   [98] Ch.3, *ante*.
[99] *Tulk* v. *Moxhay* (1848) 2 Ph. 774.
[1] *E.g.*, to use the premises for private residential purposes only, *German* v. *Chapman* (1877) 7 Ch.D. 271.
[2] *Tophams, Ltd.* v. *Sefton* [1967] 1 A.C. 50. *Cf. Leicester* v. *Wells U.D.C.* [1972] 3 All E.R. 77.
[3] Para. 19.38, *supra*.   [4] See *Kelly* v. *Barrett* [1924] 2 Ch. 379.   [5] *L.C.C.* v. *Allen* [1914] 3 K.B. 642.
[6] *Craig* v. *Greer* [1899] 1 I.R. 258 (see *A Casebook on Irish Land Law* (1984), p.616). See also *Regent Oil Co. Ltd.* v. *J.A. Gregory (Hatch End) Ltd.* [1965] 3 W.L.R. 1206.
[7] Para. 19.34, *ante*.

(iii) Intention to Run

19.43. There must be a clear indication that the burden of the covenant is intended to run with the covenantor's "servient" land.[8] If it is made by the covenantor on behalf of himself and his heirs and assigns, or his successors in title, *prima facie* the burden is intended to run.[9]

(iv) Equitable Interest

19.44. Since the enforceability of the burden against successors in title of the covenantor depends upon equity, the interest created by the covenant is equitable only. There are two important aspects of this principle. First, the remedy available to the plaintiff is an equitable one, the injunction since it is a negative covenant, and like all equitable remedies it is discretionary.[10] The court may in its discretion refuse to grant an injunction, *e.g.*, where the plaintiff has been guilty of *laches*.[11] If the character of the neighbourhood has changed since the covenant was first created, the covenant may have become almost worthless as a means of preserving the value of the dominant land and so the court may take the view that it is unreasonable to grant an injunction.[12] This may be a particularly significant factor where the covenant was imposed many years ago in relation to land on the outskirts of a town or city but now caught up in the middle of the urban "sprawl" so common in recent decades.

19.45. The second point about a restrictive covenant creating an equitable interest only is, of course, that it may lose priority if the servient land is transferred to a *bona fide* purchaser for value of the *legal* estate without notice of the covenant.[13] To this extent the question of notice is important in relation to the rule in *Tulk* v. *Moxhay*.[14] However, it is questionable whether this often happens in Ireland, because the existence of the Registry of Deeds system normally ensures that a purchaser discovers the existence of the deed containing the covenant, if not the covenant itself.[15] Since a Registry search is standard conveyancing practice on the purchase of unregistered land,[16] failure to make one will not usually absolve the purchaser. He will be fixed with constructive notice of matters he could have discovered had he made the normal search. If the title to the land is registered, the restrictive covenant must also be registered as a burden on the land so as to bind subsequent purchasers.[17]

---

[8] See *Power Supermarkets Ltd.* v. *Crumlin Investments Ltd.* (1981) Unrep. (H.C.,R.I.) (1978 No.4539P) (see *A Casebook on Irish Land Law* (1984), p.652). See also *Re Fawcett and Holmes' Contract* (1889) 42 Ch. 150.

[9] *Cf.* annexation of the benefit of a restrictive covenant, para. 19.32, *ante*.

[10] Para. 3.050, *ante*.

[11] Para. 3.066, *ante*.

[12] *Chatsworth Estates Co.* v. *Fewell* [1931] 1 Ch.224.

[13] Para. 3.074, *ante*. A restrictive covenant is enforceable against a squatter without notice, because he is not a "purchaser," *Re Nisbet and Potts' Contract* [1906] 1 Ch.386.

[14] Para. 19.38, *ante*.

[15] In England, since 1926 a restrictive covenant must be registered as a land charge under the Land Charges Act, 1925 (now replaced by the Land Charges Act, 1972). Rowley, "Registration of Restrictive Covenants" (1956) 20 Conv. 370.

[16] Ch. 22, *post*.

[17] Registration of Title Act, 1964, s.69(1)(*k*)(R.I.); Land Registration Act (N.I.), 1970, s.39 and Sched.6, Pt. I. para. 12. Ch. 21. *post*.

C. DISCHARGE AND MODIFICATION

19.46. One of the major problems of the present law in the Republic of Ireland relating to restrictive covenants is that there is no really effective method of dealing with freehold covenants which have become obsolete because of the change in the character of the neighbourhood since their original creation. At best, such covenants have a nuisance value as a flaw on the title to the property; at worst, they can impede development of property, including development for which public planning permission may be obtainable, and sometimes they are used to extract exorbitant sums for their release.[18] It is true that this was not as great a problem in Ireland as in England because there was little freehold land available for development, though more has been coming on the market as a result of leasehold enfranchisement.[19] The prohibition of the creation of new ground rents in respect of dwellings by the Landlord and Tenant (Ground Rents) Act, 1978, with the resultant switch to freehold conveyancing, has, of course, given impetus to this development. The time may be ripe for the legislators to consider introducing special legislation enabling the discharge or modification of restrictive covenants, which have become obsolete or are impeding reasonable development of land.[20] As we mentioned earlier, the Republic has already taken some steps in this direction in relation to leasehold covenants affecting unregistered land.[21] In Northern Ireland, Part II of the Property (N.I.) Order, 1978,[22] now contains comprehensive provisions dealing with identification and modification or extinguishment of certain "impediments" to the enjoyment of land, i.e., restrictions arising under covenants, conditions or agreements or a statutory provision of a local or personal character, obligations to execute works on land or pay or contribute to their costs, easements and profits.[23] The Lands Tribunal is given the power, on application by any person interested, to make orders declaring whether or not the land is or would be affected by an impediment, its nature and extent and whether it is enforceable and, if so, by whom.[24] It is also given power to modify or extinguish impediments on being satisfied that they "unreasonably" impede the enjoyment of the land or, if not modified or extinguished, would do so.[25] In determining whether to exercise this power, it is to take into account a number of listed matters, e.g., any change in the character of the

---

[18] See *1971 Survey (N.I.)*, paras. 392–5.

[19] And note the provisions in this legislation for preserving covenants enhancing amenities, etc., ch. 18, *ante*.

[20] Note, however, Housing (Ir.) Act, 1919, s.22 (conversion of single house into several tenements). *Cf.* the English provisions in the Law of Property Act, 1925, s.84, as amended by the Law of Property Act, 1969, s.28. Newsom, *Discharge and Modifications of Restrictive Covenants* (1957); Bodkin, "Discharge and Modification of Restrictive Covenants" (1942) 7 Conv. 17.

[21] Ch. 17, *ante*.

[22] Based on the recommendations in the *1971 Survey (N.I.)*, paras. 392–5. For a fuller discussion of these provisions in the Order, see Dawson, "Modification and Extinguishment of Land Obligations under the Property (N.I.) Order 1978" (1978) 29 N.I.L.Q. 223. The suggestion that these provisions were a violation of Art. 1 of the First Protocol of the European Convention for the Protection of Human Rights and Freedoms (see para. 18. 40, fn.39, *ante*) was rejected by the European Commission of Human Rights in 1984, see *Scott* v. *United Kingdom* (Applic. No.10741/84).

[23] Art. 3(1).

[24] Art. 4.

[25] Art. 5.

neighbourhood, any public interest (particularly as exemplified by any development plan adopted for the area) and any trend shown by planning permissions granted in the vicinity. But no application may be made (except with the permission of the Tribunal) in respect of an impediment arising under a lease until 21 years from the beginning of the term have elapsed. The Tribunal may require the payment of compensation in certain circumstances. The High Court or county court may refer such questions to the Lands Tribunal, where they arise in proceedings before them, or may exercise similar jurisdiction in certain cases.[26] Orders made under Articles 4 and 5 bind all persons interested in the impediment in question[27] and must be registered in the Land Registry or Registry of Deeds, according to whether the title to the land affected is registered or unregistered.[28]

19.47. So far as registered land is concerned, since 1892 the court has had power to modify or discharge a restrictive covenant registered on the folio on three grounds: (1) it does not run with the land; (2) it is incapable of being enforced against the land; (3) its modification or discharge will be "beneficial" to the persons "principally interested" in its enforcement.[29] There seems to be no reported case of this power being invoked, presumably owing, in part, to the rarity of covenants affecting freehold land. In the new registration legislation in both parts of Ireland, the Registrar can modify or discharge a restrictive covenant with the consent of *all* persons interested in its enforcement.[30] It is questionable whether the third ground mentioned above resolves the problem arising where the dominant owner uses his right to enforce the covenant to impede development or to force the developer to buy him out. In such cases, modification or discharge would be "beneficial" to one side only! It must also be remembered that the legislation applies only to covenants registered on the folio and this is a considerable restriction on the power to modify or discharge covenants in the Republic of Ireland, especially since the problems arise mainly in respect of urban land which is not generally registered land.

[26] Art. 6.
[27] Art. 7.
[28] Art. 8.
[29] Local Registration of Title (Ir.) Act, 1891, s. 45 (3).
[30] Registration of Title Act, 1964, s. 69 (3) (R.I.); Land Registration Act (N.I.), 1970, s. 48 (1) (*a*). S. 48 (1) of the Land Registration Act (N.I.), 1970 was amended by Sched. 1 to the Property (N.I.) Order, 1978, to confine the power to modify or discharge with consent to the Registrar and the court's powers to discharging on satisfaction that the covenant does not run with the land or is incapable of being enforced against the owner of the land.

CHAPTER 20

LICENCES AND SIMILAR INTERESTS

20.01. In this chapter we consider some other concepts which seem to involve recognition of interests in land which do not fall neatly into the well-established categories discussed in previous chapters. The first concept we discuss is that of a licence, a subject which has aroused much controversy in England in recent decades.[1] The paucity of authority in Ireland makes it difficult to estimate to what extent similar developments will occur here. However, apart from the subject of licences, we also discuss similar concepts which have been recognised for many years in Ireland.

I. LICENCES

20.02. So far as land is concerned, a licence is permission to do something in relation to the land which would otherwise be a trespass.[2] At common law, it seems to have been regarded as nothing more than that and certainly was not regarded as capable of creating an interest in land affecting third parties.[3] Usually it does not confer on the licensee any exclusive right to possession of land, as a lease or tenancy agreement does,[4] though there may be a limited right of occupation necessary to the enjoyment of the licence.[5] Thus rights to hire rooms for a whist drive and dance[6] and to moor and anchor eel tanks to an island[7] have been held to be mere licences. However, there is a danger of generalising in this area of law, because there are several different kinds of licences which may be created and they may have quite different characteristics.

A. BARE LICENCES

20.03. A bare licence is mere permission to do something, *i.e.*, not involving

---

[1] See now the first comprehensive textbook on the subject, Dawson and Pearce, *Licences Relating to the Occupation or Use of Land* (1979). See also Bandali, "Licence as an Interest in Land" (1973) 37 Conv. 402; Briggs, "Licences: Back to Basics" [1981] Conv. 212 and "Contractual Licences: A Reply" [1983] Conv. 185; Crane, "Licensees and Successors in Title of Licensor" (1952) 16 Conv. 323; Hanbury, "Licences, A Jonah's Gourd" (1954) C.L.J. 201 and (1955) C.L.J. 47; Hargreaves, "Licenced Possessors" (1953) 69 L.Q.R. 466; Marshall and Scamell, "Digesting the Licence" (1953) 31 C.B.R. 847; Mitchell, "Learner's Licence" (1954) 17 M.L.R. 211; Moriarty, "Licences and Land Law: Legal Principles and Public Bodies" (1984) 100 L.Q.R. 376; Robson and Watchman, "The Hidden Wealth of Licences" [1980] Conv. 27; Sheridan, "Licences to Live in Houses" (1953) 17 Conv. 440; Stoljar, "Licence, Interest and Contract" (1955) 33 C.B.R. 562; Todd, "Estoppel Licences and Third Party Rights" [1981] Conv. 347; Wade, "Licences and Third Parties" (1952) 68 L.Q.R. 337.

[2] See *Kelly* v. *Woolworth & Co. Ltd.* [1922] 2 I.R. 5; *MacGinley* v. *National Aid Committee* [1952] Ir.Jur.Rep. 43.

[3] *King* v. *David Allen and Sons Ltd.* [1915] 2 I.R. 448, on appeal [1916] 2 A.C. 54.

[4] See further, chs. 4 and 17, *ante.*

[5] See *Trappe* v. *Halpin* (1928) 62 I.L.T.R. 15; *Whyte* v. *Sheehan* [1943] Ir.Jur.Rep. 38.

[6] *Kelly* v. *Woolworth & Co. Ltd.* [1922] 2 I.R. 5.

[7] *Whipp* v. *Mackey* [1927] I.R. 372.

any contractual arrangement.[8] At common law such a licence is revocable at any time by the licensor and thereupon the licensee becomes a trespasser, provided he is given reasonable notice to leave. If he is not given such notice, it is now settled that he is entitled to a "packing-up" period, *i.e.*, he does not become a trespasser until a reasonable time for him to leave with his goods and belongings has elapsed.[9] It is questionable whether equity would restrain the licensor from revoking the licence too early, by granting the licensee an injunction, since the licensee is a volunteer. Apart from that, this would be limited protection only and, in itself, does not justify classification of such a licence as an interest in land. However, the presence of additional circumstances, such as factors giving rise to an estoppel, may change that.[10]

B. LICENCES COUPLED WITH AN INTEREST

20.04. Often a licence is included in a grant of a proprietary interest in land and, in this sense, it may acquire the characteristics of an interest in land.[11] Thus such a licence is irrevocable by the licensor so long as the proprietary interest lasts and may be assigned to a third party along with the interest in land. A common example of such a case is where a profit *à prendre* is granted, *e.g.*, shooting or fishing rights.[12] Such rights in respect of the land cannot be enjoyed unless accompanied by a licence to go on to the land to exercise them. The profit can be passed as an interest in land to successors in title of the grantee and it binds successors in title of the grantor, as does the licence necessarily attached to the profit.[13] As we shall see later in this chapter,[14] similar rights are frequently created in Ireland under conacre and agistment "lettings."

C. CONTRACTUAL LICENCES

20.05. There is much more doubt as to the position of a contractual licence, *i.e.*, one where the licensor's power of revocation is governed by a contract, but the licence is not coupled with a proprietary interest in land. So far as the common law was concerned, it seems that the licensor still had *power* to revoke the licence, even if his *right* to do so was restricted by contract.[15] If the revocation was contrary to the agreement, the licensee's remedy, if any, was

---

[8] See *Isitt* v. *Monoghan C.C.* (1905) 5 N.I.J.R. 118.

[9] *Winter Garden Theatre (London) Ltd.* v. *Millennium Productions Ltd.* [1948] A.C. 173. The *Winter Garden* case was applied by McWilliam J. in *Law* v. *Murphy* (1978) Unrep. (H.C.,R.I.) (1976 No. 4328P). And see *Devlin* v. *N.I. Housing Executive* [1982] N.I. 377. See also *Verrall* v. *Great Yarmouth Borough Council* [1980] Q.B. 202.

[10] See para. 20.07, *infra*.

[11] *Wood* v. *Manley* (1839) 112 A. & E. 34; *Wood* v. *Leadbitter* (1845) 13 M. & W. 838. *Cf. Smith* v. *Hogg* [1953–54] Ir.Jur.Rep. 58.

[12] Ch. 6, *ante*.

[13] Note that, in Ireland, such profits often form the subject-matter of a lease or tenancy agreement, *Bayley* v. *Conyngham* (1863) 15 I.C.L.R. 406 (see *A Casebook on Irish Land Law* (1984), p. 311).

[14] Para. 20.25, *infra*.

[15] See discussion in *Wood* v. *Leadbitter* (1845) 13 M. & W. 838; *Hurst* v. *Picture Theatres Ltd.* [1915] 1 K.B. 1; *Thompson* v. *Park* [1944] K.B. 408; *Winter Garden Theatre Ltd.* v. *Millennium Productions Ltd.* [1948] A.C. 173; *Hounslow London B.C.* v. *Twickenham Garden Developments Ltd.* [1971] Ch. 233. Also *King* v. *David Allen and Sons Ltd.* [1916] 2 A.C. 54.

for damages only. However, it seems that equity might intervene in certain circumstances by granting an injunction to restrain revocation contrary to agreement.[16]

20.06. The alleged extension of the law relating to contractual licences by the English Court of Appeal in *Errington* v. *Errington*,[17] in which the court decided that such licences may in equity bind successors in title of the licensor with notice, must now be regarded as doubtful for several reasons. First, there was little authority to support the view that a contractual licence could create by itself an interest in land[18] and much authority against it.[19] Secondly, much of the reasoning in the case was adopted around the same time in relation to the so-called "deserted wife's equity," which was later rejected by the House of Lords in *National Provincial Bank Ltd.* v. *Ainsworth*.[20] Thirdly, it is probable that the case can be explained on grounds more consistent with the authorities. One possibility is that the successor in title in *Errington* was also personal representative of the deceased licensor and might have been held bound by the deceased's contract on that basis, rather than as his devisee. Others have argued that the contract in the case was a specifically enforceable contract to convey land and, as such, would have bound any successor to the land with notice.[21] Finally, it is probable that, in the light of developments since the case was decided, it would be decided nowadays on the basis of estoppel.[22]

D. ESTOPPEL LICENCES

20.07. There is judicial authority in both Ireland[23] and England[24] that the

[16] *Cf. Cullen* v. *Cullen* [1962] I.R. 268 (injunction not appropriate to govern relations between fathers and sons) (see *A Casebook on Irish Land Law* (1984), p. 657). For a broad approach to equitable jurisdiction in such cases, see *Taylors Fashions Ltd.* v. *Liverpool Victoria Trustees Co. Ltd.* [1982] Q.B. 133. See also *Tanner* v. *Tanner* [1975] 1 W.L.R. 1346 (damages awarded since no longer practicable to enforce licence); *Horrocks* v. *Forray* [1976] 1 W.L.R. 230 (no contract); *Hardwick* v. *Johnson* [1978] 1 W.L.R. 683 (contractual licence irrevocable); *Chandler* v. *Kerley* [1978] 1 W.L.R. 693 (contractual licence held to be terminable on reasonable notice); *Verrall* v. *Great Yarmouth Borough Council* [1980] Q.B. 202 (specific performance of contractual licence). *Cf. McGill* v. *S.* [1979] I.R. 283 where Gannon J. held that the relationship between the parties did not give rise to a contractual licence (see also para. 25.15, *post*).
[17] [1952] 1 K.B. 290.
[18] Denning L.J.'s historical analysis of the cases is unconvincing, see Wylie, "Contracts and Third Parties" (1966) 17 N.I.L.Q. 351 at 364–5. But see the support in *Re Sharpe* [1980] 1 W.L.R. 219, where Browne-Wilkinson J. invoked the notion of a constructive trust in support, see para. 20.08, *post*. And see *Woods* v. *Donnelly* [1982] N.I. 257. See also *D.H.N. Food Distributors Ltd.* v. *Tower Hamlets L.B.C.* [1976] 1 W.L.R. 852.
[19] E.g., *King* v. *David Allen and Sons Ltd.* [1915] 2 I.R. 448, on appeal [1916] 2 A.C. 54; *Clore* v. *Theatrical Properties Ltd.* [1936] 3 All E.R. 483.
[20] [1965] A.C. 1175. See Wylie, (1965) 16 N.I.L.Q. 521 and (1966) 17 N.I.L.Q. 351 at 365–7. But see the English Matrimonial Homes Act, 1967.
[21] See Megarry and Wade, *Law of Real Property* (5th ed., 1984), p. 807.
[22] And see *Dodsworth* v. *Dodsworth* (1973) 228 Est.Gaz. 1115. But *cf.* Briggs, "Licences: Back to Basics" [1981] Conv. 212 and "Contractual Licences: A Reply" [1983] Conv. 285; Thompson, "Licences: Questioning the Basics" [1983] Conv. 50.
[23] *Cullen* v. *Cullen* [1962] I.R. 268 (see *A Casebook on Irish Land Law* (1984), p. 657). *Cf. Morrow* v. *Carty* [1957] N.I. 174. See Brady, "An English and Irish View of Proprietary Estoppel" (1970) Ir.Jur. (N.S.) 239. See also *Brownlee* v. *Duggan* (1976) 27 N.I.L.Q. 291.
[24] *Dillwyn* v. *Llewellyn* (1862) 4 De G.F. & J. 517; *Ramsden* v. *Dyson* (1865) L.R. 1 H.L. 129; *Plimmer* v. *Wellington Corp.* (1884) 9 App.Cas. 699; *Foster* v. *Robinson* [1951] 1 K.B. 149; *Inwards* v. *Baker* [1965] 2 Q.B. 29; *Ward* v. *Kirkland* [1967] Ch. 194; *E.R. Ives Investment Ltd.* v. *High* [1967] 2 Q.B. 279. *Cf.* the use of the concept of a "constructive trust" (para. 20.23, *post*) in *Binions* v. *Evans* [1972] Ch. 359. See Oughten, "Proprietary Estoppel: A Principled Remedy" (1979) 129 New L.J. 1193; People, "Promissory

licensor and his successors in title may in certain circumstances be estopped from revoking a licence relating to land, unless the successor is a *bona fide* purchaser of the legal estate without notice. The principle involved seems to be that, if the licensor induces the licensee into acting in relation to the land, *e.g.*, by building on it, on the basis that the licence will not be revoked, the licensor is estopped in equity from revoking it in a manner inconsistent with the understanding between the parties.[25] The rights of the licensee thus depend partly on the precise terms of his understanding or agreement with the licensor and partly on his being able to establish that it would be inequitable to allow the licensor to exercise his strict legal right to revoke the licence. And since the rights are dependent upon equitable principles, they will bind successors in title of the licensor only if such persons are not *bona fide* purchasers for value without notice of the licence.[26] In this respect, licences are like restrictive covenants.[27]

20.08. Sometimes the remedy sought by the licensee is an injunction to restrain the licensor or a person succeeding to his title to the land from revoking the licence. In other words, the doctrine of estoppel normally acts as a "shield" only and not as a "sword," though there have been suggestions in England that, in some cases, the licensee may be entitled to a lien on the land for the amount of any money he may have expended on it,[28] or to a declaration that he is entitled to the land[29] or that the licensor holds the land for him as constructive trustee.[30] What is not very clear is how far the licensee's rights extend, if this is not made clear in his arrangements with the licensor, *e.g.*, is it an indefinite right[31] or a right to remain on the land for the licensor's lifetime only?[32] Furthermore, can the licensor revoke the licence to remain on the condition that he pays compensation for its value to the

---

Estoppel in a New Context (1980) 130 New L.J. 373; Smith "Licences and Constructive Trusts" (1973) C.I.J. 123. See also *Dodsworth* v. *Dodsworth* (1973) 228 Est.Gaz. 1115.

[25] Thus to some extent the principle appears to be an application of the doctrine of promissory or equitable estoppel developed by Denning J. (as he then was) in *Central London Property Trusts Ltd.* v. *High Trees House Ltd.* [1947] K.B. 130; see also *Combe* v. *Combe* [1951] 2 K.B. 215; *Tool Metal Manufacturing Co. Ltd.* v. *Tungsten Electric Co. Ltd.* [1955] 1 W.L.R. 761; *D. & C. Builders Ltd.* v. *Rees* [1966] 2 W.L.R. 288. For recognition of the principle in Ireland, see *Revenue Commrs.* v. *Moroney* [1972] I.R. 372 (Kenny J.); *cf.* at 382 (Sup.Ct). See also *Woods* v. *Donnelly* [1982] N.I. 257; *Devlin* v. *N.I. Housing Executive* [1982] N.I. 377; *Smith* v. *Ireland* [1983] I.L.R.M. 300 (see *A Casebook on Equity and Trusts in Ireland* (1985), p. 80).

[26] Ch. 3, *ante*. As to the importance of the licensee's conduct in deciding whether to give him equitable relief, see *Williams* v. *Staite* [1978] 2 W.L.R. 825; *Re Sharpe* [1980] 1 W.L.R. 219. Since such licences are frequently informal arrangements it is unlikely that they will be contained in any document registered in the Registry of Deeds or that they will be noted on the register in the Land Registry, in the case of registered land, chs. 21 and 22, *post*.

[27] Ch. 19, *ante*. There are differences, however, see para. 20.11, *infra*.

[28] *Unity Joint Stock Mutual Banking Assoc.* v. *King* (1858) 25 Beav. 72. Cf. *Cullen* v. *Cullen* [1962] I.R. 268 at 282 (see *A Casebook on Irish Land Law* (1984), p. 657).

[29] *Dillwyn* v. *Llewellyn* (1862) 4 De G.F. and J. 517. *Cf. Cullen* v. *Cullen, op. cit.*, pp. 281–2.

[30] *Binions* v. *Evans* [1972] Ch. 359 *Cf. Lyus* v. *Prowsa Development Ltd.* [1982] 1 W.L.R. 1044. See also *Crabb* v. *Arun District Council* [1975] 3 W.L.R. 847. *Cf. Pascoe* v. *Turner* [1979] 1 W.L.R. 431. See also *Re Sharpe* [1980] 1 W.L.R. 219, where Browne-Wilkinson J. held that an irrevocable licence arose under a constructive trust so as to confer an equitable interest on the licensee taking priority over the trustee in bankruptcy of the licensor.

[31] *Plimmer* v. *Wellington Corp.* (1884) 9 App.Cas. 699; *Ward* v. *Kirkland* [1967] Ch. 194.

[32] *Inwards* v. *Baker* [1965] 2 Q.B. 29; *Binions* v. *Evans* [1972] Ch. 359. See also *Jones* v. *Jones* [1977] 1 W.L.R. 438; *Pascoe* v. *Turner* [1979] 1 W.L.R. 431.

licensee?[33] And lastly, there is the thorny question of whether the licensee can assign the benefit of his licence to a third party. The general view seems to be that he cannot and this is consistent with the approach of equity to questions of estoppel, *i.e.*, the equity raised is personal to the licensee and aims to protect or "shield" him from unfairness rather than to confer interests in property which he can sell or pass to others.[34]

20.09. Some of these difficulties may be illustrated by the Irish case of *Cullen* v. *Cullen*,[35] which involved a family business at Adamstown owned by the father, who gradually became mentally ill, until eventually paranoia was diagnosed. Previously his three sons had helped at various times to run the business, but there were several family quarrels owing to the father's erratic behaviour. The father resisted attempts to remove him to a mental hospital by "escaping" to another part of the country, from where he sent word to his wife informing her that, in return for transferring the business to her, which she was to carry on in her own name, he required a signed statement from his wife and sons that he was sane and withdrawal of any order for his committal to a mental hospital. His wife had won a portable house in a competition and had given this to one of her sons, M, who had offered it to his father, but the latter had refused it. When the father "escaped," the mother thought that M should erect the portable house on the land connected with the family business rather than on his own land. She sought her husband's permission and he sent another message that, as he was making the property at Adamstown over to her, she could erect what she liked. M then went ahead and erected the house on that land. Later the father sent letters to M and P, one of his other sons, requiring them to leave the house and to give up any connection with the business. The father then brought an action claiming (1) an injunction to restrain the defendants (his two sons) from interfering with the business and trespassing on the land (2) accounts and (3) damages for trespass. M counterclaimed that he was entitled to the house and its site. Kenny J. dismissed the claim for accounts and refused to grant the injunction for a variety of reasons, *e.g.*, such a remedy should not govern relations between fathers and sons and would make reconcilation between the various members of the family impossible. Anyway, the defendants had never attempted to exclude their father from control of his business and had stated in court that they did not intend to prevent him returning to or interfering in the business. If he did return, his wife might need somebody else in the house to protect her from her husband's hostility. Kenny J. did, however, award the father £50 damages against his two sons and, then, considered the position of the mother in relation to ownership of the business and M in relation to the

---

[33] *Beaufort* v. *Patrick* (1853) 17 Beav. 60. This raises the further question of how the compensation is to be calculated – *e.g.*, the licensee's outlay, or the current market value of his addition to the land or the cost of establishing him in the same position on other land? See *Dodsworth* v. *Dodsworth* (1973) 228 Est.Gaz. 1115.

[34] See *Cullen* v. *Cullen* [1962] I.R. 268 (see *A Casebook on Irish Land Law* (1984), p. 657). Cf. *Hopwood* v. *Brown* [1955] 1 W.L.R. 213; *E.R. Ives Investment Trust Ltd.* v. *High* [1967] 2 Q.B. 379.

[35] [1962] I.R. 268. See also *McMahon* v. *Kerry County Council* [1981] I.L.R.M. 419, discussed by Pearce, "The Mistaken Improver of Land" (1985) 79 Gaz. I.L.S.I. 179. *Cf. Thomas* v. *Thomas* [1956] N.Z.L.R. 785.

house erected on the land by him. He took the view that M could not require his father to execute a conveyance of the site of the house,[36] but the father was estopped by his conduct from asserting his title to it. The sons made the case that their mother was the owner of the business and that she wished them to stay. Kenny J. explained the operation of the principles in relation to the mother's claim to the business, upon which the sons relied, in this way.

"The equity... is a discretionary one and when I consider the circumstances in which the plaintiff made the statement that he was about to transfer the property at Adamstown to his wife and that he made it because he believed that it was the only way by which he could remain free, I have no doubt whatever that it would be grossly inequitable to regard Mrs. Cullen as being entitled to a transfer of the property at Adamstown or as having acquired any proprietary interest, legal or equitable, in the property as a result of what was said. The use by Mrs. Cullen of her own monies for the running of the business, particularly when she could have repaid this advance at any time, does not, in my opinion, create any claim in conscience or in equity which the court should enforce or give any ground for disregarding the general principle that equity will not aid an imperfect gift. As Mrs. Cullen has no proprietary interest in the property the defendants cannot shelter behind her permission to them or her employment of them in the business."[37]

20.10. Kenny J. felt that, to the extent that the principles involved were an application of the doctrine discussed in the *High Trees* case, the son who had built the house could invoke them only as a defence to his father's action, at least so far as existing authority stood at the time.[38] He was not entirely happy with the conclusion and ventured the suggestion, *obiter,* that, if the son remained in possession for the 12 year period of limitation, he could have his possessory title registered in the Land Registry.[39] However, there are difficulties about this, which simply illustrate further the uncertainties of this whole subject. Normally, possession for the period of limitation does not result in acquisition of title to land unless it is "adverse" possession, *i.e.,* actionable by the owner as a trespass, whereas protection of a licensee on the ground of estoppel is usually based on possession with permission, *i.e.,* normally negativing any adverse possession.[39a] On the other hand, once the licensor seeks to revoke the licence, it is arguable that the possession then becomes adverse and the licensee is trespasser. Thus Kenny J. awarded damages for trespass in the *Cullen* case. The question is whether the limited

---

[36] The question of the son having a lien was mentioned in the counterclaim, but not argued and so not dealt with.

[37] *Op. cit.,* p. 282. See Allen, "An Equity to Perfect a Gift" (1963) 79 L.Q.R. 238. Kenny J. also remarked that he was satisfied that M would have erected the house even if not given permission, *op. cit.,* p. 291.

[38] *Op. cit.,* pp. 291–2.

[39] Since the title to the land was registered. A similar view was expressed by Finlay P. in *McMahon* v. *Kerry County Council* [1981] I.L.R.M. 419. See Brady and Kerr, *The Limitation of Actions in the Republic of Ireland* (1984), pp. 105–6. See, generally, chs. 21 and 23, *post.*

[39a] See *Murphy* v. *Murphy* [1980] I.R. 183 (see *A Casebook on Irish Land Law* (1984), p. 696); *Bellew* v. *Bellew* [1982] I.R. 447, para. 23.05, *post.*

protection by equity of this technical "trespasser" stops the limitation period running in his favour. If it does not, as Kenny J. seems to suggest, many of the difficulties of licence cases may be resolved by the course of time. However, this does put the licensor in a very peculiar position. He has a trespasser on his land acquiring title under the Statute of Limitations and, yet, there appears to be nothing effective he can do to prevent this. Equity denies him the remedy necessary to remove the trespasser from possession of his land and thereby to prevent time running against him.

20.11. It is apparent, then, that the current of authority on both sides of the Irish Sea is running in favour of licences acquiring some proprietary characteristics. It seems to be accepted that, apart from the special case of licences coupled with an interest, these proprietary aspects are recognised in equity only. In that sense there is some similarity with the development in the nineteenth century of equitable rules as to the running of the burden of restrictive covenants.[40] This comparison must not, however, be taken too far. Even at common law, the benefit of a restrictive covenant could pass to a successor in title of the covenantee, yet the general view is that the benefit of a licence relating to land cannot be passed. Thus to the extent that such a licence does create an interest in land, it is an anomalous one, at least according to traditional concepts, *i.e.*, the burden runs, but the benefit does not. One further anomaly exists. The main basis of equity's enforcement of restrictive covenants is their *commercial* characteristics, *i.e.*, they relate to preservation of land values and do not depend on personal considerations of the particular landowners. Yet so many of the licence cases have involved *family* arrangements, which would not have been made were it not for the personal relationships involved. It is upon this basis that several judges have taken the view that the benefit of the licence must remain a personal privilege of the licensee only. So there appears to be something of a paradox here that licences involving such personal considerations should come to have commercial attributes.[41]

20.12. Finally, it must be emphasised that, perhaps, the most unsatisfactory feature of the present state of the law of licences relating to land is the difficulty it creates for conveyancers. Since so many of the arrangements in question are of an informal kind, it is unlikely that they will be revealed in a traditional investigation of title. Frequently no documentary evidence will exist and even if it does, it will probably not be registered in the Registry of Deeds, if the land is unregistered. If the land is registered, interests under licences are not registrable[42] and are burdens affecting land without

---

[40] Ch. 19, *ante. Cf.* Cheshire, "A New Equitable Interest in Land" (1953) 16 M.L.R. 1.

[41] Note that many of the earlier authorities confining licences to personal contractual, as opposed to proprietary, arrangements involved apparently "commercial" arrangements, *e.g.*, *King* v. *David Allen and Sons Ltd.* [1916] 2 A.C. 54; *Clore* v. *Theatrical Properties Ltd.* [1936] 3 All E.R. 483. *Cf.,* however, *E.R. Ives Investment Ltd.* v. *High* [1967] 2 Q.B. 379.

[42] *I.e.,* they are not listed in the Republic's Registration of Title Act, 1964, s. 69, nor in the Land Registration Act (N.I.), 1970, Sched. 6, Pt. I. Ch. 21, *post.*

registration.[43] Since, however, the licensee is often in possession of the land, a subsequent purchaser may nevertheless be fixed with constructive notice.[44] If the licensee is not in exclusive possession, it may be difficult to discover his existence and this makes his equitable interest an almost unavoidable trap for the conveyancer. Even a meticulous inspection of the land may not be a foolproof safeguard.[45]

II. RIGHTS OF RESIDENCE

20.13. It is extremely common in Ireland for wills and family settlements to confer rights of residence on, and to make provision for the maintenance and support of, members of the family.[46] Perhaps the most common example is that of a home-made farmer's will taking the form of a gift of the farm to his son "subject to the right of residence on the farm of my wife for her lifetime and subject to her being maintained in the manner in which she has been accustomed."[47]

20.14. From the outset it must be emphasised that the law on this subject is far from clear, despite recent legislation in both parts of Ireland.[48] The main reason is that these rights can take several forms and this has hindered the judges in deciding exactly what sort of interest in land, if any, is created. In particular, a distinction has to be drawn between two main categories, as Kennedy C.J. pointed out in *National Bank* v. *Keegan*[49]:

"The residential rights, which are so commonly given in farm holdings in this country, especially by way of testamentary provision for testators' widows, also frequently by the reservations to parents of rights in settlements made on the marriage of sons, are of two types, namely, the type which is a general right of residence charged on the holding usually coupled with a charge of maintenance; and the type which is a particular right of residence created by reserving or giving the right to the exclusive use during life of a specified room or rooms in the dwelling-house on the holding. The general right of residence charged on a holding is a right capable of being valued in moneys numbered at an annual sum, and of

---

[43] They presumably come within the category of "rights of every person in actual occupation of the land," see 1964 Act, s. 72 (1) (*j*) (R.I.); 1970 Act (N.I.) Sched. 5, Pt. I, para. 15. *Sed quaere*, see *National Provincial Bank Ltd.* v. *Ainsworth* [1965] A.C. 1175; *E.R. Ives Investment Ltd.* v. *High*, *op. cit.*

[44] *Hunt* v. *Luck* [1902] 1 Ch. 428.

[45] See Crane, (1967) 31 Conv. 341 and (1968) 32 Conv. 85.

[46] See Harvey, "Irish Rights of Residence – The Anatomy of a Hermaphrodite" (1970) 21 N.I.L.Q. 389; Peel, "Deserted Wife's Licence and Rights of Residence" (1964) 28 Conv. 253. The best judicial discussion is in *National Bank* v. *Keegan* [1931] I.R. 344 (see *A Casebook on Irish Land Law* (1984), p. 673). For earlier examples, see *Richardson* v. *McCausland* (1817) Beat. 457; *Ryan* v. *Ryan* (1848) 12 Ir.Eq.R. 226; *Gallagher* v. *Ferris* (1881) 7 L.R.Ir. 489; *Leonard* v. *Leonard* (1910) 44 I.L.T.R. 155; *Kelaghan* v. *Daly* [1913] 2 I.R. 328; *Re Shanahan* [1919] 1 I.R. 131; *Re Mooney* (1923) 57 I.L.T.R. 12; *Re Butler* (1925) 59 I.L.T.R. 166.

[47] See the precedent recommended in Harvey, *op. cit.*, pp. 423–4. It is important to note that the right often includes, in adition to a right of residence, provision for support and maintenance, including, *e.g.*, a specific bed and bedclothes (*Ryan* v. *Ryan*, *op. cit.*), clothing (*Leonard* v. *Leonard*, *op. cit.*, *Re Shanahan*, *op. cit.* and *Kelaghan* v. *Daly*, *op. cit.*) and fuel (*National Bank* v. *Keegan*, *op. cit.*).

[48] *Cf.* the Republic's Statute of Limitations, 1957, s. 40, and Registration of Title Act, 1964, ss. 69 (1) (*q*) and 81; Statute of Limitations (N.I.), 1958, s. 42, and Land Registration Act (N.I.), 1970, s. 47 and Sched. 6, Pt. I, para. 14.

[49] [1931] I.R. 344 (see *A Casebook on Irish Land Law* (1984), p. 673).

being represented by an annuity or money charge. It is clear that such is not the type of benefit given by the instrument before us. Here we have the second type of case in which the exclusive use during her life of a specified part of the holding comprising two rooms is given to the beneficiary. If this benefit were given to her by a deed or a will, I think that it is clear that she would hold an estate for life in the property, legal or equitable, according to the terms of the instrument."[50]

Bearing these remarks in mind we must consider the various possibilities as to the nature of such rights of residence.

A. LIFE ESTATE

20.15. There is considerable authority in Ireland for saying that, if the right of residence confers an *exclusive* right in the land or in some specified part of it, this creates a life estate. This was the view of the majority of the Republic's Supreme Court in *National Bank* v. *Keegan*.[51] The creation of a life estate is also often held to occur in English cases dealing with similar situations.[52]

20.16. The consequences of holding that a life estate is created in such cases are extremely serious. The grantee of the right of residence, *e.g.,* the farmer's widow, would have all the powers of a tenant for life under the Settled Land Acts, 1882-90.[53] She could, therefore, lease the land, or the part of it in which she has the exclusive right, to strangers or sell it outright over the heads of the other members of the family. In many cases, especially where the exclusive right relates to a part of the farm or land only, this would probably be quite contrary to the intention of the deceased farmer and so it is not surprising that the legislatures in both parts of Ireland have reconsidered the matter.

20.17. First, the Statutes of Limitations in both parts of Ireland[54] distinguish between a right in the nature of a lien for money's worth in or over land for a limited period not exceeding life, such as a right of support or a right of residence,[55] and an exclusive right of residence in a *specified part* of the land which they probably thought, in the light of *National Bank* v. *Keegan,* created a life interest like an exclusive right in the *whole* of the land.

20.18. The next legislative step was taken in respect of *registered* land. Section 81 of the Republic's Registration of Title Act, 1964 now states:

"A right of residence in or on registered land, whether a general right of residence on the land or an exclusive right of residence in or on part of the land, shall be deemed to be personal to the person beneficially entitled

---

[50] *Ibid.,* p. 354. *Cf.* at p. 346 (*per* Johnston J.) and at p. 356 (*per* Murnaghan J.).

[51] *Ibid.*

[52] *Re Carne's Settled Estate* [1899] 1 Ch. 324; *Re Baroness Llandover's Will Trusts* [1902] 2 Ch. 679; *Re Gibbons* [1920] 1 Ch. 372; *Bannister* v. *Bannister* [1948] 2 All E.R. 133; *Binions* v. *Evans* [1972] Ch. 359. See Hornby, "Tenancy for Life or Licence" (1977) 93 L.Q.R. 561; Martin, "Contractual Licensee or Tenant for Life" (1972) 36 Conv. 266.

[53] Ch. 8, *ante.*

[54] 1957, s. 40 (R.I.); 1958, s. 42 (N.I.).

[55] *I.e.,* a general right of residence, *Kelaghan* v. *Daly* [1913] 2 I.R. 328; *Re Shanahan* [1919] 1 I.R. 131; *National Bank* v. *Keegan* [1931] I.R. 344 (see *A Casebook on Irish Land Law* (1984), p. 673).

thereto and to be a right in the nature of a lien for money's worth in or over the land and shall not operate to create any equitable estate in the land."[56]

This clearly rules out for registered land (and remember that most farm land comes into this category[57]) the possibility of the grantee of the right of residence exercising the statutory powers of a tenant for life and thereby defeating the grantor's intention, except where the right is an *exclusive* right in respect of the *whole* land.

20.19. In Northern Ireland, section 47 of the Land Registration Act (N.I.), 1970[58] provides:

"Where—
  (a) a right of residence in or on any registered land, whether a general right of residence in or on that land or an exclusive right of residence in or on part of that land; or
  (b) a right to use a specified part of that land in conjunction with a right of residence referred to in paragraph(a);
  is granted by deed or by will, such right shall be deemed to be personal to the person beneficially entitled thereto and the grant made by such deed or will shall not operate to confer any right of ownership in relation to the land upon such person, but registration of any such right as a Schedule 6 burden shall make it binding upon the registered owner of the land and his successors in title."

This achieves the same general result as the Republic's Act, though it should be noted that it does make it clear that, while the right of residence is personal to the grantee, *i.e.,* the benefit does not run with the land, it binds successors in title of the owner of the land, *i.e.,* the burden does run.[59] This is not made explicit by the Republic's 1964 Act, though to the extent that the right creates a lien, this is an "incumbrance" within section 2 (vii) of the Conveyancing Act, 1881,[60] and presumably runs with the land.[61] Furthermore, rights of residence must be registered as burdens affecting the registered land; they are not burdens affecting such land without registration.[62]

B. LIEN

20.20. *Kelaghan* v. *Daly*[63] is usually taken to have established that a right of

---

[56] Such a right is now registrable as a burden on the land under s. 69 (1) (*q*).

[57] Ch. 18, *ante.*

[58] See *Report of the Committee on Registration of Title to Land in Northern Ireland* (1957, Cmd. 512), para. 97.

[59] *Cf.* licences, para. 20.11, *ante.*

[60] 1964 Act, s. 3 (1).

[61] See, however, Harvey, *op. cit.,* pp. 403–4 and 408–11. The difficulty of the question of running with the land, if, as is usual, it is freehold land, is that while the right of residence is passive and could be construed as negative in substance, any allied right to maintenance or support is positive and normally would not run with unregistered land, *if construed as a covenant,* ch. 19, *ante,* and see *Kelaghan* v. *Daly* [1913] 2 I.R. 328 at 330 (*per* Boyd J.) and *Colreavy* v. *Colreavy* [1940] I.R. 71 at 75 (*per* O'Byrne J.). Hence the reference to a lien, which usually does run with the land, *e.g.,* a vendor's lien for unpaid purchase money.

[62] See the list in the Republic's 1964 Act, s. 72; *cf.* 1970 Act (N.I.), Sched. 5. Pt. I and note the exclusion in para. 15 (*b*).

[63] [1913] 2 I.R. 328.

residence, unless capable of being constructed as a life estate, is a right "in the nature of a lien for money's worth,"[64] which binds successors in title taking with notice of it. The analogy was drawn with a vendor's lien for unpaid purchase money[65] and this view of the nature of the right has been recognised by the legislators in both parts of Ireland.[66] The Republic's Registration of Title Act, 1964, as we saw above, continues to use this terminology, whereas the Land Registration Act (N.I.), 1970, has dropped it.

20.21. There are, however, difficulties over the use of the concept of a lien. Usually a lien arises under a contract between the parties and is for a specific amount of money,[67] whereas rights of residence arise frequently under wills and are sometimes difficult to quantify in terms of money, especially when accompanied by vague provisions as to support or maintenance. Furthermore, it is not clear from the Irish cases how far the analogy with liens, *e.g.,* a vendor's lien, can be carried. Thus it is not clear whether, as is usual, the lien can be discharged by payment of money regardless of the wishes of the person entitled to it or, alternatively, whether the person entitled to it can realise it by, *e.g.,* requiring the land to be sold to discharge it.[68] Both these courses of action would seem to be inconsistent with the intention of many grantors in Ireland.

C. ANNUITY OR MONEY CHARGE

20.22. There is also authority for saying that a right of residence may be an "annuity or money charge." This was the view of Kennedy C.J., and Johnston J. at first instance, in *National Bank* v. *Keegan*[69] with respect to a *general* right of residence. Murnaghan J., who dissented from the Supreme Court decision in that case, regarded the right as "an equitable charge on the premises for residence and support"[70] and a similar view that it may create a charge was expressed in *Re Shanahan*.[71] The trouble about this analysis of the nature of the right is that an annuity charged on land, *e.g.,* a rentcharge, is usually for a definite sum of money.[72] Similarly, a charge on land is usually for a fixed capital sum and rights of residence, with allied rights of support or maintenance, are often not easily commutable into fixed sums.[73] Furthermore, the owner of land subject to an incumbrance, like a rentcharge, may sell the land free from the incumbrance, by getting permission from the court

---

[64] *Ibid.*, p. 330 (*per* Boyd J.). See also *Re Shanahan* [1919] 1 I.R. 131.
[65] See also Glover, *Registration of Ownership of Land in Ireland* (1933), p. 188; McAllister, *Registration of Title in Ireland* (1973), p. 201.
[66] Statute of Limitations, 1957, s. 40 (R.I.), and Statute of Limitations (N.I.), 1958, s. 42.
[67] *Mackreth* v. *Symmons* (1808) 15 Ves. 329 at 343 (*per* Lord Eldon L.C.).
[68] Para. 20.22, *infra.*
[69] [1931] I.R. 344 at 346 and 354 (see *A Casebook on Irish Land Law* (1984), p. 673). See also *Moynihan* v. *Moynihan* (1897) 31 I.L.T.R. 604.
[70] *Ibid.*, p. 356.
[71] [1919] 1 I.R. *Cf. Re McGuinness's Contract* (1901) 35 I.L.T.R. 65. *Cf. Re Hall* (1919) 53 I.L.T.R. 11.
[72] Ch. 6, *ante.*
[73] *Cf. National Bank* v. *Keegan* [1931] I.R. 344 (*per* Kennedy C.J.).

to lodge the amount necessary for discharge, plus interest, in court,[74] and a chargee can also have the land sold to pay off the charge.[75] That the farmer's son could do this to displace his mother without her consent would seem to be contrary to the wishes of most farmers who make this sort of family arrangement.

D. TRUST

20.23. Of course a right of residence may be included as part of an express trust arrangement, but there is a suggestion in some of the authorities that such a trust may be implied in favour of the grantee of the right of residence.[76] Thus in *Leonard* v. *Leonard,*[77] where an ante-nuptial settlement contained a covenant by M.L. to "support, maintain and clothe and keep in a suitable and proper manner in his house on the said farm [T.L.] and his wife and family they might have," Holmes L.J. stated:

> "The only question to be decided is whether or not we can find a trust in favour of the wife in the marriage settlement – that is, a trust attaching to the lands, and not merely a personal covenant to support and maintain her. I am satisfied from the whole document that such a trust exists."[78]

Later judges, however, do not seem to have been convinced by this formulation of the nature of the grantee's right and this is consistent with the courts' reluctance nowadays to establish "precatory" trusts.[79] Apart from that, the legislatures in both parts of Ireland have not adopted the concept of a trust with respect to registered land. Indeed, the Republic's Registration of Title Act, 1964, specifically states that a general right of residence in or on, or an exclusive right in or on part of, the land does not "operate to create any equitable estate in the land."[80] Similarly, the Land Registration Act (N.I.), 1970, states that such a right does not confer "any right of ownership in relation to the land" including, presumably, equitable ownership under a trust.[81]

E. LICENCE

20.24. It has been suggested that the most satisfactory theory is that a right of residence should be construed as a species of licence,[82] by analogy with recent developments in the law relating to estoppel licences.[83] It must be admitted, however, that there is little support for this view in the Irish authorities,[84]

---

[74] Conveyancing Act, 1881, s. 5. *Re McGuinness's Contract* (1901) 35 I.L.T.R. 65. Para. 6.145, *ante.*

[75] Ch. 13, *ante.*

[76] *Cf.* Lord Denning M.R.'s finding of a *constructive* trust in *Binions* v. *Evans* [1972] Ch. 359. Smith "Licences and Constructive Trusts" (1973) C.L.J. 123. On trusts, generally, see chs. 9 and 10, *ante.*

[77] (1910) 44 I.L.T.R. 155. See also *Gallagher* v. *Ferris* (1881) 7 L.R.Ir. 489; *Re Mooney* (1923) 57 I.L.T.R. 12; *Re Butler* (1925) 59 I.L.T.R. 166.

[78] *Ibid.*, p., 157. *Cf. Ryan* v. *Ryan* (1848) 12 Ir.Eq.R. 226 at 227 (*per* Brady L.C.).

[79] Para. 9.016, *post.*   [80] S. 81.   [81] S. 47.

[82] Harvey, (1970) 21 N.I.L.Q. 389 at 413–20. *Cf.* Peel, "Deserted Wife's Licence and Rights of Residence" (1964) 28 Conv. 253.

[83] Para. 20.07, *ante.*

[84] Note the interesting Canadian decision to this effect, *Moore* v. *Royal Trust Co* [1956] 5 D.L.R. 152. *Cf.* the Scottish case, *Wallace* v. *Simmers*, 1960 S.C. 255.

though it does seem to accord more with the real nature of the right intended by most grantors in Ireland.[85] The position adopted by both Irish legislatures with respect to registered land is very similar to that reached by the English and Irish courts with respect to estoppel licences, *i.e.,* the licence is personal to the licensee and does not confer an interest in the land capable of being passed to a successor in title, but the burden binds successors in title of the licensor.[86]

III. CONACRE AND AGISTMENT

20.25. Two other concepts familiar to Irish lawyers which seem to have some of the characteristics of licences are conacre and agistment "lettings" or "contracts." Conacre is the right to till land, sow crops in it and to harvest them in due course,[87] while agistment is the right to graze livestock on land.[88] It is clear from the authorities that such arrangements do not normally create tenancies,[89] for as Crampton J. explained in *Dease* v. *O'Reilly:*

"There is not, in fact, any exclusive right to the party in the conacre holding – from the time of the contract until the potato planting begins, the possession remains with the landlord; and from that time, although a special possession for a particular purpose is with the conacre holder, the general possession remains with the landlord. If this be a tenancy, it may be asked, when does it begin, and when does it end? It is said, it begins with the planting, and ends with the digging out of the potatoes. But if so, some part of each man's portion is held for one period, and some for another. For the potatoes are planted from time to time, and they are dug out in like manner and carried away according to the wants or convenience of the owner. It should seem to me that such a contract is not a demise of the land, but a sale of a profit to be derived from the land, a temporary easement, and not an estate in the land... the grantee has only a particular right in the land... not a tenancy, but being only a mode of farming the land."[90]

As Crampton J. said, this mode of farming, usually arranged on a seasonal basis[91] and often referred to as the "eleven month take," has obvious

---

[85] *Cf.* cases involving conditions attached to gifts, though these usually involve money payments rather than residence provisions, see *Re McMahon* [1901] 1 I.R. 489; *Duffy* v. *Duffy* [1920] 1 I.R. 132.

[86] Para. 20.11, *ante.*

[87] *Dease* v. *O'Reilly* (1845) 8 Ir.L.R. 52; *Booth* v. *McManus* (1861) 12 I.C.L.R. 418; *Evans* v. *Monagher* (1872) I.R. 6 C.L. 526; *I.L.C.* v. *Lawlor* [1944] Ir.Jur.Rep. 55.

[88] *Mulligan* v. *Adams* (1846) 8 Ir.L.R. 52; *Fletcher* v. *Hackett* (1906) 40 I.L.T.R. 37; *Re Moore's Estate* [1944] I.R. 295; *O'Connor* v. *Faul* (1957) 91 I.L.T.R. 7.

[89] Though, of course, the agreement in particular cases may create a tenancy, see *I.L.C.* v. *Andrews* [1941] I.R. 79. *Cf. Crane* v. *Naughten* [1912] 2 I.R. 318. See also *Collins* v. *O'Brien* [1981] I.L.R.M. 679 (see *A Casebook on Irish Land Law* (1984), p. 679).

[90] (1845) 8 Ir.L.R. 52 at 59–60 (see *A Casebook on Irish Land Law* (1984), p. 673). *Cf.* the views of Gibson J. in *Maurice E. Taylor (Merchants) Ltd.* v. *Commr. of Valuation* [1981] N.I. 236 (see *A Casebook on Irish Land Law* (1984), p. 680), para. 20.27, *infra.* See also *Shackleton* v. *O'Conaill* (1974) unrep. (H.C., R.I.).

[91] It is common, however, for the contract to cover several successive seasons, see *Re Moore's Estate* [1944] I.R. 295 (40 years' continuous agistment).

similarities with profits *à prendre, e.g.,* pasturage is a common profit.[92] There is one major difference and that is that easements and profits lie in grant, *i.e.,* must be created by deed, whereas conacre and agistment arrangements are created by "contract" in Ireland and, presumably, may be created orally, though written evidence may be required for enforcement.[93] Since the taker of conacre or agistment has at most only a "special" possession and the "general" possession remains with the owner of the land, such a "letting" does not infringe a covenant or agreement in a lease or tenancy agreement against subletting or otherwise parting with possession.[94]

20.26. Conacre and agistment arrangements also have similarities with certain licences, *e.g.,* licences coupled with a grant,[95] except, of course, that no "grant" in the technical sense is made. In *Booth* v. *McManus,* Pigot C.B. explained:

> "I have been in the habit of considering the dealing of con-acre to be one in which the owner of the land retains the occupation of the premises, the con-acre holder having a licence to till the land, and a right, connected with that licence, of egress and regress, for the purpose of so tilling. It is nothing more than a mode of tilling and farming the land... The dealing called con-acre in this country is a very peculiar one. The person who takes the con-acre has no absolute right to the crop. He has not a right to take the crop, with merely an obligation to pay for it as a debt. But the person who allows the land to be tilled retains the dominium over the crop, of holding it until the stipulated amount shall have been paid. He can prevent the con-acre holder from removing the crop from the ground before payment. Can he have the power of thus preventing the removal of the crop, if he has not possession of the ground? Does not the right to obstruct and prevent the removal of the crop involve the right to the possession of the soil on which the crop rests? It seems to me that it does."[96]

20.27. These characteristics account for the popularity of such arrangements in the rural areas of Ireland. They enable a small-holding farmer without much capital to extend his farming activities without contravening private restrictions against subletting or, more common nowadays as a result of the Land Purchase Acts, statutory restrictions on sub-division attaching to the freehold of the land.[97] However convenient the system is, there seems little doubt that its economic consequences can be disastrous. The following views of an experienced Northern solicitor were recently reported.

---

[92] Para. 6.113, *ante. Sed quaere* the analogy with easements, ch. 6, *ante.*

[93] In *Scully* v. *Corboy* [1950] I.R. 140, Gavan Duffy P. held that a "letting" of meadowing not evidenced in writing as required by s. 2 of the 1695 Statute of Frauds (Ir.) may constitute an enforceable sale of goods under the Sale of Goods Act, 1893. *Cf. McKenna* v. *Herlihy* (1920) 7 T.C. 620 (not cited in *Scully*). See also *Collins* v. *O'Brien* [1981] I.L.R.M. 679 (see *A Casebook on Irish Land Law* (1984), p. 679).

[94] *Booth* v. *McManus* (1861) 12 I.C.L.R. 418; *McKeowne* v. *Bradford* (1861) 7 Ir.Jur. (N.S.) 169; *Evans* v. *Monagher* (1872) I.R. 6 C.L. 526; *Allingham* v. *Atkinson* [1898] 1 I.R. 239. See also Deasy's Act, 1860, s. 18; Land Law (Ir.) Act, 1881, ss. 2 and 58.

[95] Para. 20.04, *ante.*

[96] (1861) 12 I.C.L.R. 418 at 435–6. See also *Foster* v. *Cunningham* [1956] N.I. 29; *Carson* v. *Jeffers* [1961] I.R. 44.

[97] Ch. 18, *ante.*

"Because he may not hold the land after the end of the season, the conacre tenant will take everything he can out of the land and put nothing in. Any manure which he applies is of short term effect such as nitrogen to boost a grass crop. He will not spend any money on repairs to fences and gates because he feels that he may lose the benefit at the end of the season. In the result, the state of the land let over a number of years deteriorates quite steadily and the yield falls off. One device to overcome the possibility of an unintended tenant right is the conacre agreement for one season with covenant to renew for a specified number of successive seasons. This is not widely used as its drafting is beyond the capacity of the average country Auctioneer who usually arranges these conacre lettings. I do not deny that conacre is of some value to the community as it enables the landless man without capital to get a start and I know of a few cases of a man starting with conacre takes who has been very successful. Far more numerous however are the cases where men, quite without resources, continue a kind of marginal farming on conacre land without ever bettering themselves and merely impoverishing the land they take."[98]

On the other hand, farming practices do change and recently the Northern Ireland Court of Appeal held that a commercial company, which had an 11-month conacre arrangement for growing seed potatoes on land, had exclusive occupation of the land, including buildings consisting of a dressing shed and store, sufficient to attract rating liability.[99] Gibson L.J., giving the main judgment of the Court, commented:

"The whole concept of conacre lettings has during the last 100 years undergone a radical change. No longer do the original considerations have any practical application, and with their disappearance have gone the early features which I have outlined. Nowadays it would be practically unknown for there to be a conacre letting of a small strip or area of ground having no obvious physical boundaries. The areas now correspond with the areas of fields or farms. The landowner no longer ploughs the land or provides the manure and he no longer reserves any right to exercise any control over or protection of the land, except in so far as the tenant may only grow one crop, is often obliged to fertilise the land and is required to vacate the land at the end of the term. The owner now merely has a claim in debt for the rent, and no longer has any lien or charge on the crop or right to prevent its removal. In perhaps most cases, as for example, where the farmer has retired or dies leaving a widow living in the house on the farm, the same land is let in conacre or agistment year after year, often to the same person, and in that case whether he vacates the land for a month is of little importance to the owner. In not a few cases, as, for example, where the owner is in America, the lettings are made for long periods, occasionally by

---

[98] *Survey of the Land Law of Northern Ireland* (1971), para. 287, wherein it was also reported that about 17 per cent. of agricultural land in Northern Ireland was so farmed. See the terms of the will considered in *Re Steele* [1976] N.I., 66.

[99] *Maurice E. Taylor (Merchants) Ltd.* v. *Commr. of Valuation* [1981] N.I. 236 (see *A Casebook on Irish Land Law* (1984), p. 680).

a single contract to the same tenant, and apart from any special covenants in the agreement no rights are reserved or exercised by or on behalf of the owner over the land during the period of the conacre or agistment agreements.

The terms on which the company takes the lands for the growing of potatoes in this case illustrate the modern practice in so far as it is expressly found as a fact that the conacre landlord is, under the agreements, not to enter upon the land nor to permit anyone else to do so during the period of the take, and not to undersow the potato crop, nor make any other use of the land.

Leaving aside for the moment the fact that the company has the right to be on the land for only 11 months, I am satisfied that the decisions of the Irish courts in the last century to the effect that a conacre tenant is not in occupation of the land for rating or other purposes have been overtaken both by the change in the nature of conacre lettings and also by the law.

The facts found by the Lands Tribunal establish that the company has exclusive occupation of the various plots for the purpose of growing and harvesting the potatoes. It also has the right to exclude all other persons, including the owners of the land, from the lands taken during the period of the take. Whereas, in earlier days, the landowner retained paramount occupation of the land, it is now clear that if there is any question of paramount occupation, which would only arise in the case of some rather exceptional contract, it now resides in the tenant.

Secondly, from the legal point of view the theory that a conacre agreement does not create a tenancy is so well established and embedded in our statute law that it cannot now be questioned. Yet the old notion that rateable occupation could only be found in the owner or lessee of the land has now disappeared from our law..."[1]

It should be noted that Gibson L.J. did acknowledge the fundamental principle that a conacre agreement does not create a tenancy,[2] but the question remains how far the courts in Northern Ireland will take this new view of conacre agreements. Presumably the point still holds that each agreement must be examined according to its own terms, so that it is dangerous to generalise. However, the Northern Ireland Court of Appeal has clearly shown a willingness to tackle this matter with an open mind and a determination not to be ruled by the authorities of the last century. Whether this will result in a fresh approach being adopted in the Republic remains to be seen.

---

[1] *Ibid.*, p. 238.
[2] See para. 20.25, *ante.*

PART IX

REGISTRATION

CHAPTER 21

REGISTRATION OF TITLE

21.01. Two main systems of registration in relation to land exist in Ireland. These are the registration of deeds system which was introduced in 1707[1] and the registration of title system which was first introduced by the Record of Title (Ireland) Act, 1865,[2] and firmly established by the Local Registration of Title (Ireland) Act, 1891.[3] It is crucial to recognise the distinction between the two systems which are generally mutually exclusive in relation to the *same estate* in the land.[4] The Registry of Deeds provides for the registration of *documents* dealing with land whereas the Land Registry provides for the registration of the *ownership* of land. Thus a search in the Registry of Deeds will disclose only whether documents have been executed dealing with the land in question. To discover the *effect* of those documents, in particular how they affect the ownership of the land, the documents themselves may still have to be examined.[5] A search in the Land Registry, however, reveals the details of the ownership of the land – it "mirrors" the details of the title, as it is sometimes said, and thereby greatly simplifies investigation of title for conveyancers. It must also be emphasised that what has just been said about the two systems is a statement of general principles and qualifications will become apparent in this and the next chapter. One further point should be made and that is that there are other registration systems relevant to land in Ireland, *e.g.,* those relating to judgments,[6] company charges,[7] planning matters[8] in the Republic of Ireland, and, in Northern Ireland, such matters and other statutory charges.[9]

21.02. The 1891 system was established at a time when the land purchase scheme[10] was getting into full swing and this background was reiterated by the

---

[1] Discussed in detail in ch. 22, *post.*

[2] Actually drafted by Sir Robert Torrens, who pioneered registration of title systems in the Antipodes. See *Report of the Royal Commission on Land Transfer and Registration* (1857, C. 2215); *Reports of the Commission on the Law Relating to Registration of Deeds in Ireland* (1879-81, Cc. 2243 and 2818). *Re Rooney's Estate* (1875) I.R. 9 Eq. 89; *Re Bayly's Estate* [1898] 1 I.R. 376.

[3] See Browning and Glover, *Local Registration of Title in Ireland* (2nd ed., 1912); Glover, *Registration of Ownership of Land in Ireland* (1933); Kelly, *Local Registration of Title Act, 1891* (1892) and *Registration Law* (1901). Also Hughes, *Select Cases in Registration of Title in Ireland.*

[4] See further, para. 21.07, *infra, Cf. Re a Solicitor* (1919) 53 I.L.T.R. 51.

[5] Of course, the "memorial" of the document registered in the Registry of Deeds should contain sufficient details to give some guidance as to the document's effect, see ch. 22, *post*

[6] See Judgments (Ir.) Act, 1844, Judgment Mortgage (Ir.) Act, 1850 and Judgments Registry (Ir.) Act, 1850 (R.I.); Judgments Enforcement (N.I.) Order, 1981, Pt IX.

[7] Companies Act 1963, ss. 99-108 (R.I.); Companies Act (N.I.), 1960, Pt. III and 1963, s. 1. See Rearden v. *Provincial Bank* [1896] 1 I.R. 532; *Re O'Carroll Kent Ltd.* (1955) 89 I.L.T.R. 72; *Re White & Shannon Ltd.* [1965] N.I. 15; *Re Interview Ltd.* [1975] I.R. 382; *Lombard & Ulster Banking (Ir.) Ltd.* v. *Amurec Ltd.* (1978) 112 I.L.T.R. 1.

[8] Local Government (Planning and Development) Act, 1963, s. 8 (R.I.). See *Irish Conveyancing Law* (1978), paras. 7.046-7.

[9] Land Registration Act (N.I.), 1970, Sched. 11, Para. 21.61. *infra.*   [10] Ch. 1, *ante.*

Attorney-General for Ireland who piloted the Act through Westminster, when he was later a judge.

> "That act was designed to relieve the smaller holders in fee from the ruinous expense of a system of Land Transfer and Registry of Assurances, developed under circumstances, and suitable to conditions, widely different from those of a peasant proprietary. But it was also intended to remedy a mischief of a different character. Public money, to a large and increasing extent, had been advanced on the security of holdings, and it became a matter of public and financial importance that the title to those holdings should be kept clear from doubt or complication."[11]

The result was, therefore, that all land bought out under the Land Purchase Acts was compulsorily registrable in the Land Registry and all subsequent dealings with the freehold title had to be and continue to be carried out under the registration system.[12] This has greatly simplified conveyancing of most agricultural land in both parts of Ireland and it is in relation to urban land only the Registry of Deeds plays a major part in conveyancing practice and complications continue to arise. The main aim of the system of registration of title is to make land transferable in the same way as shares in a public company. The analogy between the two systems is striking. There is a register of members kept by a company; there are folios kept in the Land Registry. The company issues a share certificate; the Registrar issues a land certificate. The company is not concerned with trusts affecting shares; no notice of any trust may be entered on any folio. The analogy with company law profoundly influenced the advocates of registration of title to land.

21.03. The 1891 Act, as amended,[13] was replaced in the Republic of Ireland by the Registration of Title Act, 1964.[14] Similar legislation to replace the 1891 system was passed in Northern Ireland, in the Land Registration Act (N.I.), 1970,[15] which is now in force.[16]

Before discussing the new schemes for both parts of Ireland, it may be useful to sketch an outline of the 1891 system which operated until recently in both parts of Ireland.

I. 1891 SYSTEM

21.04. The 1891 system provided for registration of the ownership of land at a

---

[11] *Re Keogh* [1896] 1 I.R. 285 at 294 (*per* Madden J.). See also Leech, *Registration of Title* v. *Registration of Assurances* (1891).

[12] However, leases of registered land were generally registered as "burdens" only, with no leasehold folio opened, so that subsequent dealing with the lease were registered in the Registry of Deeds.

[13] *E.g.*, by the Registration of Title Act, 1942.

[14] See the discussion by McAllister, *Registration of Title in Ireland* (1973). Note also the Land Registration Rules, 1972 (S.I. No. 230). The 1964 Act came into operation on Jan. 1, 1967.

[15] It was based on the recommendations in the Report entitled *Registration of Title to Land in Northern Ireland* (Cmd. 512, 1967). See Wylie, (1968) 19 N.I.L.Q. 89. Both Irish Acts have adopted features of the English system which is now based on the Land Registration Act, 1925. See Ruoff and Roper, *Law and Practice of Registered Conveyancing* (4th ed., 1979).

[16] See Wallace, *Land Registry Practice in Northern Ireland* (1981). See also Wallace, "The Untapped Potential of the Land Registration Act (N.I.) 1970" (1974) 25 N.I.L.Q. 1.

central registry in Dublin, and, after 1920, in Belfast for Northern Ireland.[17] Sometimes dealings were transmitted to the Central Office for registration by local county registries.[18] Four registers were kept under this system: for (1) Freeholders[19]; (2) Leaseholders[20]; (3) Proprietors[21]; (4) Subsidiary Interests.[22] Registered land could be subject to many kinds of burdens. Some affected the land only if registered as burdens[23]; others did so without registration.[24] Other interests were incapable of registration, *e.g.*, those held under a trust which were to be "kept off the title,"[25] though they could be protected by entries on the register known as "cautions" and "inhibitions."[26] The registered owner could raise loans on the security of the land by means of a registered charge,[27] or informally by deposit of his land or charge certificate.[28] Each registered owner was entitled to such a land certificate[29] or, in the case of a charge, a charge certificate.[30] Acquisition of title to registered land by mere "adverse possession"[31] was abolished, but the adverse possessor or squatter could get his title registered after the limitation period had run through a court order for rectification of the title as declared by the court.[32]

21.05. As already mentioned, *compulsory* registration of title was introduced for land whose freehold was bought out by tenant-farmers under the Land Purchase Acts.[33] Apart from this land and certain other land,[34] registration was *voluntary*, but the complications of "pyramid" titles in urban areas[35] often discouraged landowners from incurring the trouble and expense of a first registration. The new legislation in both parts of Ireland recognises that the ultimate benefits of fewer complications and cheaper conveyancing to be reaped when all land throughout the island is registered will come about

---

[17] Replacing the local registry for Co. Antrim.

[18] 1891 Act, Pt. I. See Glover, *Registration of Ownership of Land in Ireland* (1933), ch. XIV.

[19] With provision for registration of the applicant as "full" or "limited" owner (*i.e.*, as tenant for life under the Settled Land Acts, 1882–90). 1891 Act, ss. 4 (1) and 28. Glover, *op. cit.*, chs. III and IV.

[20] 1891 Act, s. 53, Glover, *op. cit.*, pp. 45-58.

[21] *I.e.*, of houses bought or built through an advance by a local authority under the Small Dwellings Acquisition Act, 1899, as later amended. Glover, *op cit.* p. 62.

[22] 1891 Act, s. 54. Glover, *op. cit.*, pp. 48-50.

[23] *E.g.*, judgment mortgages, easements, profits and restrictive covenants. 1891 Act, s. 45. Glover, *op cit.*, ch. VIII.

[24] *E.g.*, Crown and quit rents, tithe rentcharges, land purchase annuities and tenancies for terms not exceeding 31 years, provided there was occupation under such tenancies. 1891 Act, s. 47. Glover, *op. cit.*, ch. X.

[25] 1891 Act, s. 63. Glover, *op. cit.*, ch. X.

[26] 1891 Act, ss. 69 and 70.

[27] 1891 Act, ss. 40–3. Glover, *op. cit.*, ch. XII.

[28] 1891 Act, s. 81 (5). See ch. 12, *ante*.

[29] 1891 Act, s. 31.

[30] 1891 Act, s. 40.

[31] See, generally, ch. 23, *post*.

[32] 1891 Act, s. 52. Glover, *op. cit.*, ch. XIII.

[33] 1891 Act, s. 22. Note that the definition of "Land Purchase Acts" includes the Irish Church Act, 1869, para. 1.51, *ante*. See Marshall, "Compulsory Registration and the Irish Church Act, 1869" (1983) 77 Gaz. I.L.S.I. 5. As regards the special provisions in Pt. IV of the Act for devolution of such registered land, see para. 3.099, *ante*.

[34] *E.g.*, houses bought or built under the Small Dwellings Acquisition Act, 1899 (see s. 15), as amended, and land acquired by local authorities for labourers' plots under the Labourers (Ir.) Act, 1906 (see s. 21). This legislation has been replaced in the Republic by the Housing Act, 1966; see also Small Dwellings Acquisition Acts (N.I.), 1947 and 1948, and Housing (N.I.) Order, 1981.

[35] Paras. 4.179-82, *ante*.

only through extension of the compulsory system.

21.06. Once title to land was registered, the general principles of registered conveyancing under the 1891 system was that subsequent dealings with the title registered could be effected only by making appropriate alterations in the registers.[36] An insurance fund was established to compensate any persons suffering loss by any errors in operation of the system.[37]

21.07. The new legislation also deals with some of the recognised defects in the 1891 system. Perhaps one of the worst of these was the fact that most titles compulsorily registered as part of the land purchase scheme (and these make up the greatest proportion of all titles registered) were registered "subject to equities."[38] The policy of the Land Purchase Acts was to vest the fee simple in the person *ostensibly* the tenant working the farm in question[39] and to "graft" the fee simple on to the existing ownership of the tenancy, *i.e.,* to make it subject to burdens and equities held by third parties.[40] However, the Land Commission administering the land purchase scheme did not carry out an investigation of the "tenant's" title and so was in no position to register all these burdens and equities. Furthermore, it was a principle of the 1891 scheme that "trusts" were to be kept off the registered title.[41] So to protect third party rights the practice was adopted in most cases of registering the tenant's freehold title with a "note as to equities,"[42] which had the effect of preserving burdens and equities as if no registration had occurred. In effect, the registered title was subject to burdens affecting the land without registration and this continued to constitute a complication in the title which might have to be investigated in later transactions.[43] It is true that the freeholder could subsequently apply to have the equities note cancelled, but this was rarely done.[44] In effect, the applicant might have to trace the title back to and prove the original fee farm grant, lease or tenancy held by the tenant prior to his purchase of the freehold under the Land Purchase Acts.[45] However, in some cases evidence of title might be found in a "fair rent" order made under the Land Law Acts[46] and, more recently in the Republic, in purchase agreements entered into between the farmer and the Land Commission.

---

[36] 1891 Act, ss. 35-9. Glover, *op. cit.*, chs. VI and VII.

[37] 1891 Act, ss. 92 and 93. Glover, *op. cit.*, ch. XV.

[38] 1891 Act, s. 29 (3). Glover, *op. cit.*, ch. XI. *Re Smith* [1917] 1 I.R. 170 at 175-6 (*per* Madden J.), on appeal [1918] 1 I.R. 45. Wallace, (1974) 25 N.I.L.Q. 1 at 3–8.

[39] Who might be a tenant for life under a family settlement only, or the personal representative of a deceased tenant.

[40] *E.g.*, mortgages, charges, marriage settlements and restrictive covenants.

[41] 1891 Act, s. 63. Glover, *op. cit.*, ch. X.

[42] The tenant could, of course, insist on registration of registrable burdens provided he could establish the title to these.

[43] See *White* v. *Hague* [1921] 1 I.R. 138; *Honan* v. *O'Shea* [1935] Ir.Jur.Rep. 41; *McHugh* v. *O'Brien* (1974) unrep. (H.C., R.I. No. 61 Sp).

[44] See *Re Keelan* [1925] 1 I.R. 1; *Irwin* v. *McCabe* [1927] I.R. 361; *Re Irwin Estate* (1933) 67 I.L.T.R. 218; *Re Doran's Estate* (1934) 68 I.L.T.R. 145.

[45] 1891 Act, s. 29 (4). see *Re Hazlette* [1915] 1 I.R. 285; *Honan* v. *O'Shea* [1935] Ir.Jur.Rep. 41. In practice, the Registrar might dispense with full proof of the pre-registration title if a good "holding" title could be established.

[46] See para. 1.49, *ante*.

21.08. Another difficulty of the 1891 system was that the provisions seeking to ensure the mutual exclusiveness of the system and the Registry of Deeds system were not well-drafted.[47] Thus certain dispositions excluded from registration in the Registry of Deeds, *e.g.*, deeds dealing with fee farm rents and certain other burdens, did not seem to be adequately covered by the Land Registry either. The interests in question could be registered in the Subsidiary Register only.[48]

The new Acts also attempt to further the policy of giving the Registrar greater power to deal with many matters which had to be referred to the court under the 1891 scheme, *e.g.*, rectification of registers in cases of adverse possession and modification or discharge of restrictive covenants.

II. 1964 AND 1970 SYSTEMS

A. LAND REGISTRY

1. *Central and Local Offices*

21.09. The Republic's 1964 Act preserves the system of a central office in Dublin and local offices in each county,[49] but makes the crucial change that the central office is now responsible for registration of *all* land in the State.[50] The local offices now perform largely advisory functions to aid local practitioners,[51] though they do keep and maintain duplicates of the freehold and leasehold registers.[52] Similar provisions are contained in the Land Registration Act (N.I.), 1970,[53] with respect to the central office in Belfast and local county offices.

21.10. The central offices in Dublin and Belfast are under the management and control of the respective Registrars of Titles[54] and, subject to their overall direction, local offices are run by local registrars.[55] The Registrars have powers to summon witnesses, to require production of documents and to examine persons on oath.[56]

21.11. Persons aggrieved by orders or decisions of the Registrar have a right of appeal to the High Court or, in the Republic, the circuit court, or, in Northern Ireland, the county court.[57] The Registrar may also refer doubtful questions of fact or law to the court.[58]

---

[47] 1891 Act, s. 19. Glover, *op. cit.*, pp. 63-7.

[48] 1891 Act, s. 54. Note the Republic's Land Registration Rules 1959, r. 222.

[49] S. 7 (1). Collectively the central and local offices are known as the "Land Registry," s. 7 (4).

[50] S. 7 (2).

[51] Their precise functions are prescribed by regulations made under s. 7 (3), see Land Registration Rules, 1972, r. 13. Applications for registration may be delivered to a local office for transmission to the central office, r. 59.

[52] 1972 Rules, r. 12.

[53] S. 1.

[54] 1964 Act, s. 9 (1); 1970 Act (N.I.), s. 1 (4). For details as to their appointment, etc., see 1964 Act, s. 9 (2)-(8); 1970 Act (N.I.)., Sched. 1, paras. 1-6.

[55] 1964 Act, s. 10 (1) (county registrars); 1970 Act (N.I.), s. 1 (5) (clerks of the Crown and Peace). See further 1964 Act, s. 10 (2) and (3); 1970 Act (N.I.), Sched. 1, paras. 7 and 8.

[56] 1964 Act, s. 16; 1970 Act (N.I.), s. 2.

[57] 1964 Act, ss. 18 and 19 (1); 1970 Act (N.I.), ss. 4 and 6 (1).   [58] 1964 Act, s. 19 (2); 1970 Act (N.I.), s. 6 (2).

2. Registers

21.12. The new Acts provide for maintenance of three registers covering (1) freehold land (2) leasehold land and (3) incorporeal hereditaments held *in gross* and other rights.[59] These are essentially the same registers, of freeholders, leaseholders and subsidiary interests, as were kept under the 1891 system.

21.13. The basic principle is retained that these registers are "conclusive evidence" of the title of the owner to the land as appearing on the register.[60] However, both Acts now add that the registers are also conclusive evidence of "any right, privilege, appurtenance or burden" appearing on them.[61] This removes the doubt cast on this matter by the Northern Ireland Court of Appeal in *Miscampbell* v. *McAllister*.[62] The title of any person shown on the register is not affected by his having notice of any deed, document or matter relating to or affecting the title shown, unless there is actual fraud on his part. This in effect abrogates the doctrine of notice with respect to registered land,[63] at least to the extent that a purchaser for value who becomes registered as new owner of the land is not affected by notice of anything not appearing on the register,[64] unless it is a burden affecting registered land without registration.[65] It must be emphasised, however, that, while the register is conclusive as to the matters appearing on it, it is *not* conclusive evidence of the entire title to the land and the continued existence within the system of concepts such as burdens affecting the land without registration necessarily weakens the system.[66] The nature of land law makes a compromise necessary. To attempt to enter on the register every minor right and interest relating to every piece of land would be a huge administrative task and would cause long delays on first registrations, not to mention the expense involved.[67] If compulsory registration is going to be extended to much urban land in the foreseeable future, this compromise has to be made.

21.14. The court may order rectification of the register on the grounds of fraud or mistake,[68] and also where errors originating in the Land Registry[69]

[59] 1964 Act, s. 8; 1970 Act (N.I.), s. 10.

[60] 1964 Act, s. 31 (1); 1970 Act (N.I.), s. 11 (1).

[61] *Ibid. Cf.* 1891 Act, s. 34 (1).

[62] [1930] N.I. 174. See the controversy over the decision between Glover and Montrose in (1938) 2 N.I.L.Q. 38, 63 and 142; (1939) 3 N.I.L.Q. 34 and 68.

[63] *Cf.* the Registry of Deeds, para. 3.086, *ante* and ch. 22, *post.*

[64] *Re Walsh* [1916] 1 I.R. 40 at 44-5 (*per* Madden J.); *Re Mulhern* [1931] I.R. 700; *Re Mackin* [1938] I.R. 1. See also Glover, *op. cit.*, p. 14.

[65] Para. 21.36. *post.*

[66] *Devoy* v. *Hanlon* [1929] I.R. 246; *McPartland* v. *Conlon* [1930] N.I. 138; *Duff* v. *Bousfield* [1939] I.R. 160; *Lalor* v. *Prunty* [1939] I.R. 618; *Re Strong* [1940] I.R. 382. *Cf.* the English concept of "overriding interests." See Crane, "Conveyancing with Registered Land" (1937) 2 Conv. 42, 106, 241 and 342 and (1940) 4 Conv. 189; Dworkin, "Registered Land Reform" (1961) 24 M.L.R. 135; Jackson, "Registration of Land Interests – The English Version" (1972) 88 L.Q.R. 93 and "Security of Title in Registered Land" (1978) 94 L.Q.R. 239; Potter, "Covenants for Title and Overriding Interests" (1942) 58 L.Q.R. 356; Ruoff, "Conclusiveness of Registered Titles" (1953) 17 Conv. 39; Smith, "The Priority of Competing Minor Interests in Registered Land" (1977) 93 L.Q.R. 541.

[67] There is also the problem of manpower, for skilled title searchers and mappers have been in short supply for years. See Lowry Report (N.I.) (Cmnd. 512, 1967), para. 137.

[68] 1964 Act, s. 32 (1); 1970 Act (N.I.), s. 69 (4). *Re Mulhern's Estate* [1931] I.R. 700; *Duffy* v. *Duffy* [1947] Ir.Jur.Rep. 49; *Gregg* v. *Kidd* [1956] I.R. 183.

[69] See *Re Cooke's Application* [1948] I.R. 318.

occur in registration, provided this can be done without injustice to any person.[70] In the Northern Ireland 1970 Act, it is made clear that this includes a person claiming for valuable consideration and in good faith through the registered owner, e.g., where the latter contributed to the error or acted in bad faith.[71]

3. Maps and Boundaries

21.15. The latest available Ordnance Survey maps are now kept in the central offices and registry maps based on these are used for marking or defining land the title of which is registered.[72] Registered land is described in the appropriate register by the names of denominations on the Ordnance Survey map, or as the Registrar considers best calculated to secure accuracy, with a cross-reference to the registry map relating to the land.[73] However, the description of land in the register or on the maps is not conclusive as to the boundaries or extent of the land,[74] but this provision may give protection against minor errors only.[75] Registered owners of adjoining lands, or a registered owner and an owner of adjoining unregistered land, can apply to have the boundaries entered on the register as conclusive as between themselves and their respective successors in title, but this does not confirm title to the lands in question.[76] The Registrar may also enter boundaries as conclusive, where part of the registered land only is transferred, between the part transferred and part retained,[77] and may settle any question as to the boundaries or extent of registered land when it is being transferred.[78] Also kept in the Central Office is a names index for each county, which complements the official maps. Thus a folio can be traced either through the identity of the land or the name of the registered owner.

4. Folios

21.16. Under the 1891 system the register consisted of a series of folios

---

[70] 1964 Act, s. 32; 1970 Act (N.I.), s. 69. See the discussion by Murray J. of the authorities on the question of rectification of errors in Re Skelton [1976] N.I. 132. See also Re Leonard's Estate [1912] 1 I.R. 212 at 226 (per Holmes L.J.) and 295 (per Cherry L.J.); Re Walsh [1916] 1 I.R. 40 at 49 (per Madden J.); Dooley v. Hough [1931] I.R. 197; Re Trainor [1936] N.I. 197; Re Ryan's Application [1945] I.R. 359; Moley's Case [1957] N.I. 130. McAllister, Registration of Title in Ireland (1973), pp. 285-92.

[71] S. 69(3).

[72] 1964 Act, s. 84; 1970 Act (N.I.), s. 62.

[73] 1964 Act, s. 85; 1970 Act (N.I.), s. 63.

[74] 1964 Act, s. 85; 1970 Act (N.I.) s. 64(1). Hickey v. Broderick [1931] L.J.Ir. 136.

[75] Gillespie v. Hogg [1947] Ir.Jur.Rep. 51. See also McManus v. Kiernan [1939] I.R. 297. Note the comments in the Gillespie case on the effect of the registration system on "pretenced titles" coming within the Maintenance and Embracery Act (Ir.) 1634. See on these titles, Robb v. Dorrian (1877) I.R. 11 C.L. 292. See also the discussion of the Maintenance and Embracery Act (Ir.) 1634, in Browne v. Fahy (1975) Unrep. (H.C.,R.I.), wherein Kenny J. queried why the whole of section 2 (which was relied upon in the case) was not repealed by the Republic's Statute Law Revision (Pre-Union Irish Statutes) Act, 1962, "when it is so totally inappropriate to modern conditions." The whole of the 1634 Act was repealed in Northern Ireland by the Criminal Justice (Miscellaneous Provisions) Act (N.I.), 1968, s. 16 and Sched. 4.

[76] 1964 Act, s. 87; 1970 Act (N.I.), s. 64 (2) and (3). Note also s. 86 of the 1964 Act (conclusive entry of boundaries where defined, e.g., in an Incumbered or Landed Estates Court conveyance or Land Commission vesting order).

[77] 1964 Act, s. 88 (1); 1970 Act (N.I.), s. 64 (4).

[78] 1964 Act, s. 88 (2); 1970 Act (N.I.), s. 64 (5).

relating to each registered title. The first page of each folio usually described the land registered and the first registered owner and then there followed pages of entries of subsequent dealings with the land and cancellations of entries. The result was often that the folio became a "jumble of entries" which could take almost as much time to read and disentangle as the title deeds if the land had remained unregistered.[79] However in both parts of Ireland the folio is now divided into three parts.[80] The first describes the land whose ownership is registered, with a cross-reference to the plan on the registry map, and includes notes relating to easements, mines and minerals, boundaries, Land Commission reference numbers, issue of the land certificate and, possibly, copy maps. The second contains entries of the name, description and address of the owner and relating to such matters as the classes of owners and titles, devolution of the land, cautions and inhibitions restricting the registration of dispositions. The third contains entries relating to such matters as registered burdens, charges and sub-charges, cautions and inhibitions against dealings with registered burdens and this part of the folio may have a plan attached to it.[81]

5. Searches

21.17. The practice since 1891 of making the registers open to public inspection is now confirmed expressly by statute.[82] Also instituted for the first time under the new legislation is the concept of official searches and the issue of a search certificate by the Registrar of the result of such a search.[83] Where the Registrar is satisfied that such a certificate is issued to a person who is prospective purchaser, lessee or chargee of the land in question, he may, at that person's request, make a "priority" entry on the register.[84] This will secure priority for an application for registration of the document completing the transaction in question, provided the application is in order and is delivered at the central office within 14 days of issue of the certificate.[85]

6. Compensation and Indemnity

21.18. Any person suffering loss by reason of official errors[86] in registration or entries obtained by fraud or forgery[87] is entitled to compensation, so that, to this extent, a registered title is guaranteed.[88] In the Republic, there is no

---

[79] See *Report of the Committee on Registration of Title to Land in Northern Ireland* (Cmd. 512, 1967), para. 103.

[80] 1972 Rules (R.I.), r. 3, replacing provisions in the 1966 Rules, which in turn replaced provisions in the 1937 and 1959 Rules. For N.I., see Land Registration Rules (N.I.) 1977, r. 5.

[81] These changes were recommended by the 1967 Report (fn. 79, *supra*), para. 103.

[82] 1964 Act, s. 107 (1); 1970 Act (N.I.), s. 81 (1). Note the limits on inspection and making copies of registers and other documents in the Republic's 1972 Rules, r. 188 (see also r. 198). See also *Re Fitzgerald* [1925] 1 I.R. 39; *Re Fairbairn* (1940) 74 I.L.T.R. 4; *Re Nolan* (1941) 75 I.L.T.R. 56.

[83] 1964 Act, s. 107 (2); 1970 Act (N.I.), s. 81 (2).   [84] 1964 Act, s. 108 (1); 1970 Act (N.I.), s. 81 (3).

[85] 1964 Act, s. 108 (2); 1970 Act (N.I.), s. 81 (4).

[86] *Dooley* v. *Hough* [1931] I.R. 197; *Re Cooke's Application* [1948] I.R. 318.

[87] Note the penalties for fraud, etc. 1964 Act, s. 119; 1970 Act (N.I.), s. 82.

[88] 1964 Act, s. 120; 1970 Act (N.I.) s. 71. *Re Patterson* (1903) 3 N.I.J.R. 90; *Re Keelan* [1925] 1 I.R. 1; *Re Serridge* [1926] I.R. 169; *Re Ryan's Application* [1945] I.R. 359; *Re Wicklow C.C.'s Application* (1958) 92 I.L.T.R. 110.

longer an Insurance Fund and compensation is paid by the State.[89] In Northern Ireland, the Insurance Fund established by the 1891 Act remains in force under the 1970 Act and continues to be supported by a proportion of the Registry fees, with the Department of the Environment meeting any deficiencies.[90]

21.19. An indemnity is provided for the Registrar and other Registry officials, and persons acting under their authority, in respect of all matters *bona fide* done or omitted in the exercise or supposed exercise of their duties.[91]

B. Registration of Ownership

1. *Voluntary and Compulsory*

21.20. One of the main policies of the new legislation in both parts of Ireland is the furtherance of an extension of compulsory registration of title, *i.e.,* in addition to the existing areas of compulsion.[92] As we have mentioned before, such compulsion is the only effective method of bringing about any major extension of registration of title to urban areas in Ireland where titles can be so complicated.[93]

21.21. Both Acts adopt the same two main methods of extension. One is that all freehold and leasehold land compulsorily acquired by a statutory authority, including local or public authorities and semi-state bodies in the Republic, becomes subject to compulsory registration.[94] The other is that an order may be made designating any county or county borough as a compulsory registration area.[95] Thereupon registration is compulsory, if not already so, on the first conveyance on sale[96] of the freehold thereafter or grant or assignment on sale of a leasehold interest in the land exceeding 21 years.[97] The sanction is that the grantee or assignee does not acquire the estate or interest in question unless he registers it within 6 months in the Republic,[98] and in Northern Ireland the conveyance or grant becomes void after 3 months from execution unless an application is made for registration within that time.[99]

---

[89] 1964 Act, s. 120 (4).

[90] 1970 Act (N.I.), s. 70 and Departments (N.I.) Order, 1982, Art. 5 and Sched. 1, Pt.II. *Re Trainor* [1936] N.I. 197; *Re Irwin* [1938] I.R. 818.

[91] 1964 Act, s. 118; 1970 Act (N.I.), s. 3.

[92] 1964 Act, s. 23 (1) (*a*); 1970 Act (N.I.), s. 24 (1) and Sched. 2, Pt. I, para. 1.

[93] Para. 4.182, *ante*.

[94] 1964 Act, s. 23 (1) (*b*) and (2) (*a*); 1970 Act (N.I.), Sched. 2. Pt. I, para. 3.

[95] 1964 Act, s. 23 (1) (*c*) and (2) (*b*) and 24 (1); 1970 Act (N.I.), s. 25 and Sched. 2, Pt. I. para. 2. In the Republic, Counties Carlow, Laoighis and Meath were designated compulsory areas from January 1, 1970, see S.I. 1969 No. 87. In these counties new ordnance surveys have been completed and new maps published.

[96] *I.e.*, a sale for money or money's worth, including by way of exchange, 1964 Act, s. 24 (3); 1970 Act (N.I.), Sched. 2, Pt. III. See *Colreavy* v. *Colreavy* [1940] I.R. 71.

[97] 1964 Act, s. 24 (2); 1970 Act (N.I.), Sched. 2, Pt. I, para. 2. After first registration, certain other burdens will have to be registered to continue to affect the registered land, *e.g.*, leases for lives or for terms exceeding 21 years, and perpetual rentcharges or other fee farm rents. 1964 Act, s. 69; 1970 Act (N.I.), Sched. 2, Pt. I, paras. 4-6 and Sched. 6, Pt. I.

[98] 1964 Act, s. 25.

[99] 1970 Act (N.I.), Sched. 2, Pt. I, para. 2.

21.22. Apart from situations where registration is compulsory, the owner of land may still make a voluntary application for registration. This is usually done now by developers who are about to build an industrial or housing estate. It remains to be seen whether voluntary registration will have to be suspended outside compulsory areas to concentrate efforts on extension of compulsory registration, as has happened in England.[1]

2. Classes of Owners

21.23. In the case of freehold land, the owner may be registered either as *full* owner, *i.e.*, as tenant in fee simple, or *limited* owner of a settled estate, *i.e.*, tenant in tail, for life or as having the powers of a tenant for life under the Settled Land Acts.[2] The same applies to leasehold land, *i.e.*, the owner is registered either as full owner of the leasehold interest in possession or limited owner of a settled leasehold estate.[3] On registration the owner is entitled to delivery of a land certificate of his title to the land.[4] This is the same scheme as operated under the 1891 system.

3. Classes of Title

An innovation in the new Acts is the additional classes of title which may be registered on first registration.

(i) Freehold Land

21.24. In the Republic, a freehold owner may be registered with an absolute, qualified or possessory title.[5] In Northern Ireland, the 1970 Act includes a fourth class, a good fee farm grant title.[6]

(a) *Absolute Title*

This indicates that the registered owner has the full or limited freehold estate in the land, subject only to the registered burdens and burdens affecting land without registration.[7] If, however, the registered owner is a trustee, he is still subject to his duties and liabilities as a trustee.[8]

(b) *Qualified Title*

21.25. If the title cannot be established as absolute to the satisfaction of the Registrar, *e.g.*, it can be established for a limited period only or subject to qualifications, it may be registered as a qualified title. This has the same effect

---

[1] Land Registration Act, 1966, s. 1 (2).
[2] 1964 Act, s. 27 (*a*) and (*b*); 1970 Act (N.I.), s. 12 (*a*) and (*b*). Note the amendment to the wording of s. 12 (*b*) of the 1970 Act (N.I.) made by Sched. 1, para. 1 to the Property (N.I.) Order, 1978.
[3] 1964 Act, s. 27(*c*) and (*d*); 1970 Act (N.I.), s. 12 (*c*) and (*d*).
[4] 1964 Act, s. 28; 1970 Act (N.I.), s. 79 (1). See *Re Associated Banks* [1944] Ir.Jur.Rep. 29.
[5] 1964 Act, s. 33.
[6] 1970 Act, s. 13 (1). See the discussion in the Lowry Report (Cmd. 512, 1967), paras 113-22.
[7] 1964 Act, s. 37; 1970 Act (N.I.), s. 15.
[8] 1964 Act, s. 37 (3) 1970 Act (N.I.) s. 15 (4). Trusts are kept off the title, para. 21.34, *post*.

as an absolute title except that it is subject to the estates or rights included in the qualification noted on the register.[9]

(c) *Possessory Title*

21.26. This is the sort of title which will usually be registered where the applicant cannot produce documentary evidence of title, *e.g.,* a squatter,[10] and can show only actual occupation of the land or receipt of rents and profits. Such a registered title does not affect or prejudice the enforcement of any right adverse to or in derogation of the applicant's title and subsisting or capable of arising at the time of registration.[11] "Right" here includes any right or equity existing by reason of the applicant's interest being deemed a graft on his previous interest in the land.[12]

(d) *Good Fee Farm Grant Title*

21.27. Provision of this class is an attempt by the Northern legislators to alleviate the complications that will arise on a first registration of land held under a pyramid title in Belfast or other urban areas.[13] The 1970 Act provides that such a registered title is not to prejudice or affect any estate arising by virtue of any grant superior to the fee farm grant under which the applicant holds the land.[14] In other words, the applicant in such a case need not prove to the Registrar that he has declared all superior rights and interests so as to be entitled to be registered with an absolute title, subject to those rights and interests being specified on the register. It is important to note that this provision simply facilitates speedier first registration of a fee farm grant pyramid title. It does nothing to solve the underlying conveyancing difficulties of such a title, *i.e.,* that all kinds of superior estates and interests may exist affecting the land. Such superior estates and interests will remain hidden in the pyramid where a good fee farm grant title is registered under the 1970 Act and, where necessary, will have to be investigated on subsequent dealings with the land.[15] This is also the position in the Republic, though the problem of first registration of pyramid titles has been tackled in a different way, by providing that perpetual yearly rents and covenants and conditions contained in superior deeds are burdens affecting land without registration.[16]

(ii) Leasehold Land

21.28. In both parts of Ireland, four classes of title are provided for leasehold land, absolute, qualified, possessory and good leasehold.[17] The first

---

[9] 1964 Act, s. 39; 1970 Act (N.I.), s. 18.
[10] *Re Richardson* (1935) 69 I.L.T.R. 252. See ch. 23, *post.*
[11] 1964 Act, s. 38 (1); 1970 Act (N.I.), s. 17 (1) and (2).
[12] 1964 Act, s. 38 (2); 1970 Act (N.I.), s. 17 (3), See also 1964 Act, s. 35.
[13] Para. 4.182, *ante.*
[14] S. 16 (2).
[15] *Cf.* the English 1925 system, under which superior burdens must be disclosed, see Ruoff and Roper, *Law and Practice of Registered Conveyancing* (4th ed., 1979), pp. 198-9.
[16] 1964 Act, s. 72 (1) (*l*) and (*m*), replacing Registration of Title Act, 1942, s. 16.
[17] 1964 Act, s. 40; 1970 Act (N.I.), s. 19.

three have the same general effect as regards the leasehold title as they have in the case of freehold land.[18] A good leasehold title does not affect or prejudice the enforcement of any right adverse to or in derogation of the title of the lessor to grant the lease.[19] In other words, superior leasehold interests are protected and this facilitates first registration where the pyramid title consists, as is often the case, especially in Dublin, of leases and sub-leases rather than fee farm and sub-fee farm grants. Once again, however, the underlying conveyancing problems of such titles remain, until enfranchisement by the "ground" lessees eventually gets rid of them.[20]

(iii) Conversion or Reclassification of Titles

21.29. Where titles other than absolute ones have been registered, the Registrar may, either on his own initiative or on application of the registered owner or other person entitled, convert or reclassify the titles into one of the better classes, *i.e.*, convert qualified or possessory titles into absolute or good fee farm grant or leasehold titles. Leasehold titles may be converted into absolute titles. Generally this may be done because the lapse or efflux of time justifies this or on production of new evidence.

21.30. In the Republic of Ireland, the Registrar has a general power to convert inferior titles into absolute or good leasehold titles, if he is satisfied as to the title, either on his own initiative or on application of the registered owner or other person interested.[21] Apart from this general discretion, in the case of possessory or qualified titles, other than those relating to land bought out under the Land Purchase Acts, any application for registration of a transfer for valuable consideration must be accompanied by all relevant documents to enable the Registrar to decide whether to convert the title.[22] In the case of land purchase land, the title was registered under the 1891 Act subject to a note as to equities and is deemed to be possessory.[23] When land is vested by the Land Commission after January 1, 1967, it is registered by them with a possessory title.[24] Where the possessory title has been registered for 30 years, it may be converted to absolute on registration of any disposition or transmission on death, and in practice the Registry does this without application.[25] If the possessory title has been registered for 15 years, it may be converted to absolute, if freehold, or good leasehold, if leasehold.[26] Conversion of land purchase possessory titles may also be made on registration of a transfer for valuable consideration, where there has been such a registered transfer more than 12 years previously. In this way the problems created by the equities note will gradually disappear.

---

[18] 1964 Act, ss. 44, 46 and 47; 1970 Act (N.I.), ss. 20, 22 and 23.
[19] 1964 Act, s. 45; 1970 Act (N.I.), s. 21 (2).
[20] Ch. 18, *ante*.
[21] 1964 Act, s. 50 (1). *Re Smith* [1918] 1 I.R. 45.
[22] S. 50 (2) (*a*) and (*b*).
[23] S. 35.
[24] S. 26.
[25] S. 50 (3) (*a*).
[26] S. 50 (2) (*c*).

21.31. Similar provisions are contained in the Northern 1970 Act, though there are considerable differences in detail. In the case of land purchase land registered subject to equities, which is deemed to be registered subject to a possessory title,[27] the Registrar may reclassify the title as absolute, on application of the registered owner.[28] There is *no* prerequisite of an efflux of time nor a transfer for value, perhaps due to the fact that the land purchase scheme was wound up in 1935 in Northern Ireland and such titles have been registered at least since then.[29] In other cases of a possessory title, the Registrar may reclassify the title as absolute or good fee farm grant or, with leasehold land, a good leasehold title. Here, however, there must be an application to register a transfer for valuable consideration and the possessory title must have been registered at least 15 years previously.[30] In addition to these special cases, the Registrar is given a general discretion to reclassify inferior titles after due examination, so as to reclassify a good fee farm grant or good leasehold title as absolute, and possessory or qualified titles as absolute, good fee farm grant or good leasehold, as the case requires.[31]

4. *Special Cases*

Within the framework of the general system for registration of ownership described above, there are many special cases dealt with by the new legislation.

(i) Co-Ownership

21.32. The owner of an undivided share in land may have his share indicated by an appropriate entry on the register.[32] Where two or more persons are registered as owners of the same land, they are deemed to be joint tenants unless there is an entry to the effect that they are tenants in common.[33] The Land Commission normally vested land bought out under the Land Purchase Acts in co-purchasers as joint tenants, but it has been held that registration of purchasers as joint tenants with no entry as to their tenancy in common, but subject to a notice as to equities, does not terminate their beneficial interests as tenants in common.[34]

(ii) Appurtenant Rights

21.33. A new provision has now been introduced to enable the Registrar to make an entry noting the existence of rights, privileges and appurtenances on the folio relating to the *dominant* land, *i.e.*, the land benefited by them.[35] Prior to the new legislation such rights could be entered only as burdens on the folio relating to the *servient* land.

---

[27] Sched. 13, Pt. i, para. 2.
[28] Sched. 3, para. 1.
[29] Thus the "equities note" problem may disappear even more quickly in Northern Ireland.
[30] Sched. 3, para. 2.
[31] Sched. 3, para. 3.
[32] 1964 Act, s. 91 (1); 1970 Act (N.I.), s. 55 (1).
[33] 1964 Act, s. 91 (2); 1970 Act (N.I.), s. 55 (2). See ch. 7, *ante*.
[34] *Wellwood* v. *Wellwood* (1903) 3 N.I.J.R. 149; *Cahill* v. *Ledwith* [1934] I.R. 258. See also *Flynn* v. *Flynn* [1930] I.R. 337. *Cf. Beck* v. *Beck* (1916) 50 I.L.T.R. 135.
[35] 1964 Act, s. 82; 1970 Act (N.I.), s. 51, See ch. 6, *ante*.

(iii) Trusts

21.34. Generally trusts, whether express, implied or constructive, may not be entered in the register and a purchaser for value of the registered land need not enquire as to whether the land is subject to a trust.[36] However, beneficiaries can protect themselves against fraudulent dealings by the trustees, who, of course, will be the registered owners,[37] by lodging "cautions" or "inhibitions."[38]

(iv) Settled Land

21.35. Registration of a person as a limited owner of settled land does not confer any greater powers on him than he had under the Settled Land Acts, 1882–90, and the names of the trustees of the settlement (if any) may be entered on the register.[39] Where the land is held under a trust for sale, but deemed settled land under section 63 of the Settled Land Act, 1882, the provisions of the Acts in relation to registration of limited owners do not apply unless the settlement gives the limited owner the power conferred by the Settled Land Acts on the tenant for life, or he gets a court order under the Settled Land Act, 1884.[40] The effect of this is that the trustees are registered as full owners.

(v) Burdens

21.36. Two main types of burden may affect registered land, as under the 1891 Act.[41] One class may be registered as burdens, and the other class affects registered land without registration.[42] Burdens which may be registered include such matters as: fee farm rents or other perpetual rentcharges[43]; a vendor's lien for unpaid purchase money[44]; a lease for life or lives or for a term exceeding 21 years[45]; judgment mortgages in the Republic[46]; easements and profits *à prendre*[47]; restrictive covenants[48]; certain rights of residence.[49] If an application is made for registration of one of these burdens without the concurrence of the registered owner, a court order is needed before the registration can be made.[50] In certain cases, *e.g.*, leases exceeding 21 years, ownership of the burden itself may also be registered, *i.e.*, in addition to entry

---

[36] 1964 Act, s. 92; 1970 Act (N.I.), s. 54. See ch. 9, *ante*.

[37] Note 1970 Act (N.I.), s. 56 (2) and Sched. 8, Pt ii (charitable trustees). See Lowry Report (N.I.) (Cmd. 512, 1967), para. 98.

[38] 1964 Act, ss. 96–8; 1970 Act (N.I.), Pt. vii. Para. 21.51, *infra*.

[39] 1964 Act, s. 99; 1970 Act (N.I.), s. 56 (1) and Sched. 8, Pt. i. see ch. 18, *ante*.

[40] 1964 Act, s. 99 (6); 1970 Act (N.I.), Sched. 8, Pt. i, para. 6.

[41] Ss. 45 and 47.

[42] 1964 Act, ss. 69 and 72; 1970 Act (N.I.), ss. 38 and 39, Scheds. 5 and 6.

[43] But not including such matters as tithe rentcharges, Crown or quit rents or land purchase annuities, 1964 Act, s. 69 (1) (c); 1970 Act (N.I.), Sched. 6, Pt. i, para. 2. see chs. 4 and 6, *ante*.

[44] 1964 Act, s. 69 (1) (f); 1970 Act (N.I.), Sched. 6 Pt. i, para. 5. Ch. 9, *ante*.

[45] 1964 Act, s. 69 (1) (g); 1970 Act (N.I.), Sched. 6 Pt. i, para. 6. Ch. 4., *ante*,

[46] 1964 Act, s. 69 (1) (i); *cf.* 1970 Act (N.I.), Sched. 6, Pt. i, para. 7. Ch. 13, *ante*.

[47] 1964 Act, s. 69 (1) (j); 1970 Act (N.I.), Sched. 6, Pt. i, para. 11. Ch. 6 *ante*.

[48] 1964 Act, s. 69 (1) (k); 1970 Act (N.I.), Sched. 6, Pt. i, para. 12. ch. 19, *ante*.

[49] 1964 Act, s. 69 (1) (q); 1970 Act (N.I.), Sched. 6, Pt. i, para. 14. Ch. 20, *ante*.

[50] 1964 Act, s. 69 (2); 1970 Act (N.I.), Sched. 6, Pt. ii, Para. 3. In practice, the Registry in Dublin does not require this for a judgment mortgage.

as a burden on the "servient" owner's folio.[51] Registered burdens, which, if unregistered, would rank in priority according to the date of their creation, rank according to the order of their entry on the register instead, unless there is an entry to the contrary.[52]

21.37. In the case of restrictive covenants registered as burdens, the court may, as under the 1891 Act,[53] modify or discharge the covenant on the ground that it does not run with the land, it is incapable of being enforced against the landowner or the modification or discharge will be beneficial to the persons principally interested in enforcement.[54] The Registrar is also given power now to modify or discharge such a covenant with the consent of all persons interested in its enforcement.[55] Other burdens may be modified or cancelled by the Registrar.[56]

21.38. Burdens which affect registered land without registration include such matters as: Crown or quit rents and tithe rentcharges[57]; land purchase annuities[58]; public rights and franchises[59]; tenancies for terms not exceeding 21 years, where there is occupation under the tenancies[60]; rights acquired, or in the course of being acquired, under the Statute of Limitations[61]; the rights of every person in actual occupation of the land or in receipt of the rents and profits, unless such rights are not revealed when enquiry is made to such persons.[62] If it can be established that the registered land is not in fact subject to certain of the burdens, e.g., tithe rentcharges or land purchase annuities, the Registrar may enter on the register a notice of this fact.[63] He may also enter a notice of such burden's existence, with the consent of the registered owner or an applicant for registration or in pursuance of an order of the court.[64]

(vi) Adverse Possession

21.39. As under the 1891 Act,[65] the statutes of limitations apply to registered land as they apply to unregistered land,[66] and the adverse possessor

---

[51] 1964 Act, s. 70; 1970 Act (N.I.), Sched. 6, Pt.II, para. 1. In *Nolan* v. *Driscoll* (1978) Unrep. (H.C.,R.I.) (1977) No. 1820 P), McWilliam J. held that a lease for a term exceeding 21 years need not be registered on a leasehold folio under s. 70 unless it has been registered as a burden on the freehold under s. 69 (1) (g) of the 1964 Act. It is not compulsory to register it as a burden and, unless it is in fact so registered, it is not compulsory to register it on a leasehold folio.

[52] 1964 Act, s. 74; 1970 Act (N.I.), s. 40. This does not affect the priority of burdens which affect registered land *without* registration, *ibid*.   [53] S. 45 (3).

[54] 1964 Act, s. 69 (3); 1970 Act (N.I.), s. 48 (1) (b). See ch. 20, *ante*.

[55] 1964 Act, s. 69 (3); 1970 Act (N.I.), s. 48 (1) (a).

[56] 1964 Act, s. 69 (4); 1970 Act (N.I.), s. 48 (2). *Re Hall* (1919) 53 I.L.T.R. 11.

[57] 1964 Act, s. 72 (1) (a); 1970 Act (N.I.), Sched. 5, Pt. I, para. 2. Ch. 6, *ante*.

[58] 1964 Act, s. 72 (1) (c); 1970 Act (N.I.), Sched. 5, Pt. I, para. 3.

[59] 1964 Act, s. 72 (1) (f) and (g); 1970 Act (N.I.) Sched. 5, Pt. I, paras. 7 and 8. Ch. 6 *ante*.

[60] 1964 Act, s. 72 (1) (i); 1970 Act (N.I.), Sched. 5, Pt. I, para. 12.

[61] 1964 Act, s. 72 (1) (p); 1970 Act (N.I.), Sched. 5, Pt. I, para. 14.

[62] 1964 Act, s. 72 (1) (f); 1970 Act (N.I.), Sched. 5, Pt. I, para. 15. See the discussion of the English equivalent (s. 70 (1) (g) of the Land Registration Act, 1925) in *Williams and Glyn's Bank Ltd.* v. *Boland* [1981] A.C. 487, considered by Murray J. In *Ulster Bank Ltd.* v. *Shanks and Others* [1982] N.I. 143. See also Wallace, *Land Registry Practice in Northern Ireland* (1981), pp. 12–15.

[63] 1964 Act, s. 72 (2); 1970 Act (N.I.), Sched. 5, Pt. II, para. 1.

[64] 1964 Act, s. 72 (3); 1970 Act (N.I.), s. 38 (1).

[65] S. 52. See *Re Skelton* [1976] N.I. 132 (para. 23.21, *post*).

[66] This whole subject is discussed in detail in ch. 23, *post*.

can apply to be registered as owner after he has acquired title so as to extinguish the title of the previous registered owner.[67] The one difference is that under the new legislation an order of the court for rectification is no longer necessary, though the Registrar may refer the matter to the court if he is doubtful.[68]

(vii) Rights of Residence

This matter was discussed in an earlier chapter.[69]

(viii) Disabilities

21.40. An infant or minor registered owner is described as such on the register,[70] and he may be represented for the purposes of the legislation by such person as is prescribed by the rules[71] or appointed by the court.[72] In the case of a lunatic or person of unsound mind, he may be represented by the committee of his estate or guardian appointed by the court.[73] A person of weak mind temporarily incapable of managing his affairs may be represented by his guardian appointed under the Lunacy Regulation (Ireland) Act, 1871, or appointed by the court.[74]

(ix) Bankruptcy

21.41. The provisions in the 1891 Act[75] relating to bankruptcy of the registered owner have been tightened up in the new legislation. In the Republic, the registrar of the bankruptcy court must now give notice to the Registrar of Titles of every petition of bankruptcy or for arrangement and the latter must then check to see if the debtor is a registered owner of land.[76] If the debtor is a registered owner, the Registrar must now, instead of merely noting the presentation of the petition on the register, enter an inhibition[77] against further dealings with the land for a period of three months, *i.e.,* effectively until the bankruptcy proceedings are completed.[78] This entry may be cancelled on notice from the bankruptcy registrar of the ending of the bankruptcy proceedings.[79] Under the Northern 1970 Act, the bankruptcy registrar is still obliged to give notice only of petitions relating to owners of registered land and so the onus remains on him to determine this initial question with respect to each debtor.[80] Furthermore, a notice of the

---

[67] 1964 Act, s. 49; 1970 Act (N.I.), s. 53.

[68] 1964 Act, s. 19 (2); 1970 Act (N.I.), s. 53 (3) (which also provides that he *must* refer it if requested to do so by the applicant or any other person lodging an objection).

[69] Ch. 20, *ante.*

[70] 1964 Act, s. 101; 1970 Act (N.I.), s. 60.

[71] 1972 Rules (R.I.), rr. 177–8.

[72] *E.g.,* under Settled Land Act, 1882, s. 60.

[73] 1964 Act, s. 102 (1) and (2); 1970 Act (N.I.), s. 61 (1). *Rattigan* v. *Regan* [1929] I.R. 342.

[74] 1964 Act, s. 102 (3); 1970 Act (N.I.), s. 61 (2). Ch. 25, *post.*

[75] S. 76.

[76] 1964 Act, s. 103 (1). Note, however, that these provisions are described as "singularly inept" in *McAllister,* pp. 121-2.

[77] Para. 21.51, *post.*

[78] *Ibid.*

[79] S. 103 (3). See *Re Reilly* [1942] I.R. 416; *Re Gibbons* [1960] Ir.Jur.Rep. 60.

[80] S. 59 (1).

presentation of the petition only is entered on the register, but it is now provided that no further dealing with the registered land may be entered without the leave of the High Court, unless and until the entry is cancelled.[81]

(x) Foreshore

21.42. In the Republic, no registration of land which appears to comprise the foreshore[82] may be made without sending prior notice in writing to the Minister for Transport and Power.[83] In Northern Ireland, one month's notice in writing must be given to the Crown Estate Commissioners.[84]

C. DEALINGS

21.43. The new legislation contains a number of provisions governing dealings with registered land, *i.e.*, after the ownership of the land has been registered as discussed above. The general principle is that the registered owner alone is entitled to deal with the land by a registered disposition.[85] However, a person entitled to registered land, *e.g.*, on the death of the registered owner or by virtue of a transfer, but not yet registered as the new owner, may now deal with the land by transferring or charging it.[86] Such dispositions will be subject to burdens which would have been entered had he been registered as owner and to the priority to be accorded to prior registered dispositions for value.[87]

1. *Transfers*

21.44. The registered owner may, subject to statutory restrictions,[88] transfer the registered land by using the prescribed form[89] or such other form as appears to the Registrar to be sufficient to convey the land.[90] Such a transfer does not itself vest the land in the transferee; at most he has an "equity" to be registered. He must complete the transfer by having himself entered on the register as the new owner.[91] Once registered, the transferee is entitled to delivery of a land certificate.[92] If part only of the land is transferred, the Registrar may either allow the transferor to retain his certificate with an entry in it as to the part transferred, or deliver to him a new certificate as to the part retained.[93]

21.45. Generally such a transfer operates as a conveyance by deed within

---

[81] S. 59 (3) and (4).
[82] Vested in the State, see the Foreshore Act, 1933, ch. 6, *ante.*
[83] 1964 Act, s. 125.
[84] 1970 Act (N.I.), s. 78.
[85] 1964 Act, s. 68 (1); 1976 Act (N.I.), s. 32 (1).
[86] 1964 Act, s. 90; 1970 Act (N.I.), s. 33. See *McGirr* v. *Devine* [1925] N.I. 94.
[87] Para. 21.13, *ante.*
[88] *E.g.*, under the Settled Land Acts, 1882-90, in the case of settled land.
[89] See 1972 Rules (R.I.), r. 69 and Sched. of Forms; 1977 Rules (N.I.), Sched. of Forms.
[90] 1964 Act, s. 51; 1970 Act (N.I.), s. 34. *Re Gallagher* (1911) 45 I.L.T.R. 269; *Maguire* v. *Conway* [1950] I.R. 44; *Re Foley's Application* (1951) 85 I.L.T.R. 61; *Gardiner* v. I.L.C. (1976) 110 I.L.T.R. 21.
[91] 1964 Act, s. 51 (2); 1970 Act (N.I.), s. 34 (3). *Re Furlong and Bogan's Contract* (1892) 31 L.R.Ir. 191; *Re Mitchell and McElhinney's Contract* [1902] 1 I.R. 83.
[92] 1964 Act, s. 51 (3); 1970 Act (N.I.), s. 79.
[93] 1964 Act, s. 51 (4); *cf.* 1970 Act (N.I.), s. 79.

the Conveyancing Acts and the transferee is registered with the appropriate title subject to express or implied rights, privileges and appurtenances, and registered burdens or burdens affecting land without registration.[94] If, however, the transfer is not for value, the voluntary transferee is registered subject also to all *unregistered* rights subject to which the transferor held the land and these bind all persons claiming through the transferee otherwise than for valuable consideration.[95] Such unregistered rights may be protected by cautions or inhibitions.[96]

21.46. As discussed in an earlier chapter, an instrument of transfer of freehold registered land will pass the fee simple, or the whole interest which the transferor had power to transfer, without words of limitation unless a contrary intention appears.[97] Furthermore, a resulting use or trust is not implied merely by omitting an expression that the land is transferred "to the use or benefit" of the transferee.[98]

2. Defeasance

21.47. Where the ownership of registered land passes to a person by defeasance rather than transfer, *e.g.*, under a power of sale in a mortgage or under a power of appointment, that person may be registered as owner on production of the appropriate evidence.[99] If the application for registration is not made with the existing registered owner's or his personal representative's concurrence, or he is not the full owner, the Registrar must give notice to these persons and may decline to register the person in question without a court order.[1]

3. Transmission on Death

21.48. On death of a sole full registered owner or the survivor of joint tenants registered as full owner, the Registrar is to recognise the deceased's personal representatives as alone having any rights in the land and registered dispositions by them have the same effect as if they were the registered owners.[2] The person entitled to the deceased's registered land may be registered as full or limited owner, provided an assent in his favour from the personal representatives is produced.[3] In the Republic the Registrar does not have to examine the will to see that its terms have been complied with, nor

---

[94] 1964 Act, s. 52 (1) (see also ss. 53-8); 1970 Act (N.I.), s. 34 (4) (see also subss. (6) and (7)).
[95] 1964 Act, s. 52 (2); 1970 Act (N.I.), s. 34 (5). See *Pim* v. *Coyle* [1929] I.R. 246; *Rattigan* v. *Regan* [1929] I.R. 342; *Quinn* v. *McCool* [1929] I.R. 620; *Re Murphy and McCormack* [1930] I.R. 322; *McManus* v. *Kiernan* [1939] I.R. 297; *Colreavy* v. *Colreavy* [1940] I.R. 71.
[96] *Devoy* v. *Hanlon* [1929] I.R. 246; *McParland* v. *Conlon* [1930] N.I. 138; *Re Strong* [1940] I.R. 382.
[97] Ch. 4, *ante*.
[98] Ch. 3, *ante*.
[99] 1964 Act, s. 60 (1); 1970 Act (N.I.), s. 36(1).
[1] 1964 Act, s. 60 (2); 1970 Act (N.I.), s. 36 (2).
[2] 1964 Act, s. 61 (2); 1970 Act (N.I.), Sched. 4, para. 1.
[3] 1964 Act, s. 61 (3) (*a*) (as substituted by s. 54 (2) of the Succession Act, 1965); 1970 Act N.I.), Sched. 4, para. 4. *Re Sheridan* [1946] I.R. 400. The person entitled under the settlement on death of a limited owner may also be registered, 1964 Act, s. 61 (1); 1970 Act (N.I.), Sched. 4, para. 6.

determine that the rules of intestate succession have been met.[4] In this respect the Registrar is in a similar position to that of a purchaser from the personal representatives.[5] If the personal representative is himself the deceased's successor in title, no assent need, of course, be produced since the title is vested in him automatically and the Registrar may register him as owner.[6] A personal representative need not be registered as owner in his capacity as representative, though a note may be entered on the register setting out the fact of the registered owner's death and the names of his personal representatives.[7]

21.49. Where the court makes a vesting order in relation to registered land,[8] it may also order that the person in whose favour the order is made be registered as owner.[9] Furthermore, on the application of a person claiming to be successor to a deceased full owner of registered land, the court may dispense with the necessity of raising representation or giving notice to the personal representatives, if it is satisfied that at least six years have elapsed since the deceased owner's death and the personal representatives are dead or out of the jurisdiction.[10] This covers the common situation in the rural parts of Ireland where the registered owner of a farm dies, leaving the farm to his eldest son and appointing his widow executrix, but she dies without ever transferring the land to the son.[11]

4. *Charges*

21.50. Detailed provisions are included in the new legislation governing the creation of charges on registered land and their transfer, transmission and discharge.[12] In addition to permitting the creation of formal charges of this kind, the informal creation of security for loans which is so popular in Ireland is preserved, *i.e.*, by deposit of the land or charge certificate.[13] This whole subject was discussed in detail in an earlier chapter.[14]

5. *Cautions and Inhibitions*

21.51. The new legislation preserves the right under the 1891 system of persons holding *unregistered* interests in *registered* land to protect them by lodging "cautions" or "inhibitions." Indeed, a caution may even be lodged by the owner of an interest in *unregistered* land, entitling him to notice of any application for the land's registration, unless the owner's interest is already

---

[4] 1964 Act, s. 61 (3) (*b*); *cf*, 1970 Act (N.I.), Sched. 4, para. 4. The Land Registry in N.I. continues to take responsibility for the accuracy of assents lodged for registration, and so the terms of the relevant will or the position on intestacy are examined in detail. See the Land Registration Rules (N.I.), 1977, rr. 55–7.
[5] Para. 16.46, *ante*.
[6] Ch. 16, *ante*.
[7] 1964 Act, s. 61 (6); 1970 Act (N.I.), Sched. 4, paras. 2 and 3. *Cf. Lynch* v. *Harper* [1909] 2 I.R. 53.
[8] Succession Act, 1965, s. 52 (4) (R.I.); Administration of Estates Act (N.I.), 1955, s. 34 (3).
[9] 1964 Act, s. 61 (5); 1970 Act (N.I.), Sched. 4, para. 5 (*a*).
[10] 1964 Act, s. 61 (7); 1970 Act (N.I.), Sched. 4, Para. 5 (*b*).
[11] See further, ch. 23, *post*.
[12] 1964 Act, ss. 62-7; 1970 Act (N.I.), ss. 41-6.
[13] 1964 Act, s. 105 (5); 1970 Act (N.I.), s. 50.
[14] Ch. 12, *ante*.

protected by registration of an instrument in the Registry of Deeds.[15] The owner of an unregistered interest in registered land, *e.g.*, a prospective purchaser's rights under a contract for the sale of the land, may also protect his interest by lodging a caution.[16] This prevents any dealings by the registered owner (vendor) until notice is served on the cautioner. Thus the registered owner cannot sell to someone else, so as to enable him to complete the purchase and obtain priority over the cautioner by registering his title. A caution is, therefore, essentially of a temporary nature, to protect the cautioner until his own unregistered interest can be secured by registration, and is designed to bring the dealings in question to the notice of the cautioner. It also generally restricts the activities of the registered owner only. An inhibition, on the other hand, may restrict dealings by any person able to deal with the registered land, *e.g.*, on defeasance of the registered owners' interest.[17] It may be used to protect interests which can never be secured by registration, *e.g.*, the interests of beneficiaries under a trust.[18] An inhibition, which may be ordered by the court or entered by the Registrar, may prevent dealings with the registered land or charge for a specified time or until the occurrence of a specified event, or except with the consent of or after notice to some specified person, or generally until further order or entry.[19] The Registrar may also enter an inhibition to prevent dealings with the registered land until an error in registration he has discovered is corrected.[20]

D. MISCELLANEOUS MATTERS

A few other miscellaneous matters concerning registered land may be mentioned.

1. *Jurisdiction of Courts*

21.52. There is a general right of appeal against orders or decisions of the Registrar to the High Court or, in the Republic, the circuit court or, in Northern Ireland, the county court.[21] The Registrar may refer any doubtful questions of law or fact relating to registration to the court.[22] In an action for specific performance of a contract relating to registered land or a registered charge, the court may make an order binding on all interested parties, if necessary by causing them to appear in the action and show cause why the

[15] 1964 Act, s. 96; 1970 Act (N.I.), s. 65.

[16] 1964 Act, s. 97; 1970 Act (N.I.), s. 66. *Northern Banking Co.* v. *Devlin* [1924] 1 I.R. 90.

[17] Para. 21.47, *ante.* Under section 12 of the Republic's Family Home Protection Act, 1976, a notice, stating that he or she is married to the owner of the registered land, may be registered by a spouse and no fee is payable in respect of such notice. S. 13 of the 1976 Act provides that s. 59 (2) of the Registration of Title Act, 1964 (which requires the Registrar to note on the register statutory restrictions on alienation, etc.), does not apply to the provisions of the 1976 Act. See further on the 1976 Act, *Irish Conveyancing Law* (1978), ch. 6, espec. para. 6.40.

[18] Para. 21.34, *ante.*

[19] 1964 Act, s. 98; 1970 Act (N.I.), s. 67. *Re Kelleher* (1936) 70 I.L.T.R. 201. Inhibitions cannot restrict the powers of a tenant for life under the Settled Land Acts, 1882-90, 1964 Act, s. 98 (4) (*a*); 1970 Act (N.I.), s. 67 (3).

[20] 1964 Act, s. 121; 1970 Act (N.I.), s. 68.

[21] 1964 Act, s. 19 (1); 1970 Act (N.I.), s. 6 (1). See *Gardiner* v. *I.L.C.* (1976) 110 I.L.T.R. 21.

[22] 1964 Act, s. 19 (2); 1970 Act (N.I.), s. 6 (2). *Re Congested Districts Board* [1919] 1 I.R. 146; *Re Neely* [1936] I.R. 381.

order should not be made.[23] Generally the Registrar must obey court orders, though he may apply to the court for a variation in the original order or for directions as to how it is to be obeyed.[24] This does not, however, give the court power to review its own order.[25]

2. *Discovery of Instruments and Facts*

21.53. The Registrar may require affidavits to the effect that all title deeds and facts material to the title have been disclosed before he registers land in respect of which an examination of title is required.[26] He can refuse to proceed until the further evidence he requires is produced.[27]

3. *Production of Deeds*

21.54. The Registrar may require any person, who has in his possession or custody any deeds, wills or instruments affecting title, which he has occasion to investigate, to produce them or show cause why he should not produce them within a specified time.[28] The Registrar may also require production of deeds to have them endorsed, stamped or marked with notice of registration, so as to prevent the concealment of this fact from subsequent purchasers or other persons dealing with the land.[29] If a person disobeys an order of the Registrar, the latter may certify the disobedience to the High Court and thereby have the order enforced as if it were an order of the court.[30]

4. *Fraud*

21.55. It is a criminal offence with intent to conceal a title or claim, to substantiate a false claim or to suppress any document or fact in any proceedings before the Registrar or court.[31] It is also an offence to procure fraudulently any entry, erasure or alteration in the register or to make wilfully a false statement in any affidavit required by the Registrar.[32]

5. *Exemption from Registry of Deeds*

21.56. The general rule is that the two systems of registration of title and of deeds are mutually exclusive in relation to the *same estate* in the land because of their different functions.[33] Thus it is provided that registration of the ownership of a particular estate or interest in land exempts that estate or interest from the Registry of Deeds system, so that any deed or other document concerning the registered estate or interest need not be registered

---

[23] 1964 Act, s. 22; 1970 Act (N.I.), s. 5.
[24] 1964 Act, s. 21; 1970 Act (N.I.), s. 9.
[25] See *O'Leary* v. *O'Dea* [1922] 1 I.R. 8.
[26] 1964 Act, s. 93; 1970 Act (N.I.), s. 29.
[27] 1964 Act, s. 93 (2); 1970 Act (N.I.), s. 29 (3).
[28] 1964 Act, s. 94; 1970 Act (N I.), s. 30.
[29] 1964 Act, s. 95; 1970 Act (N.I.), s. 31.
[30] 1964 Act, s. 20; 1970 Act (N.I.), s. 8. *Re Kellaghan* (1936) 70 I.L.T.R. 193.
[31] 1964 Act, s. 119 (1) (*a*); 1970 Act (N.I.), s. 82 (1) (*a*).
[32] 1964 Act, s. 119 (1) (*b*) and (*c*); 1970 Act (N.I.), s. 82 (1) (*b*). *Re Mulhern* [1931] I.R. 700.
[33] Para. 21.01, *ante*. *Cf. Re a Solicitor* (1919) 53 I.L.T.R. 51.

in the Registry of Deeds.[34] It is important to note that this exemption relates only to the particular estate or interest whose ownership is registered in the Land Registry. It does *not* cover deeds or documents relating to the title of any *other* estate or interest in the same land.[35] This exemption also applies in the case of registered burdens.[36]

III. STATUTORY CHARGES REGISTER (N.I.)

21.57. Under the Statutory Charges Register Act (N.I.), 1951,[37] a special register of that name was established in the central office of the Land Registry in Belfast. The provisions of the 1951 Act were replaced by Part X of the Land Registration Act (N.I.), 1970, and this part of the 1970 Act was brought into force in 1971.[38]

21.58. The object of this legislation is to provide prospective purchasers with an easy method of checking the existence of certain encumbrances on land which could not be easily discovered otherwise. As the name implies, it is primarily concerned with charges on land which arise under statutory provisions rather than by acts of parties and is generally confined to charges which are not registrable burdens under the registration of title system[39] nor created by a deed relating to unregistered land and registered in the Registry of Deeds. Furthermore these charges, which for the most part are created by or in favour of government departments or local authorities, are not easily discoverable by an inspection of the land.

21.59. There is no such separate register in the Republic of Ireland, but it should be noted that one of the categories of burdens which may be registered as affecting registered land is "a burden created by statute or under a statutory power,"[40] unless it is a burden affecting registered land without registration.[41]

A. REGISTER

21.60. It is crucial to remember that, though the register is maintained at the central office of the Land Registry, under the control of the Registrar,[42] it relates to both registered and unregistered land.[43] The register and indexes are open to public inspection and any person may make searches and apply to receive copies of, or extracts from, the register.[44] Official searches may also be made and certificates issued of their results.[45]

---

[34] 1964 Act, s. 116 (1); 1970 Act (N.I.), s. 72 (1).

[35] 1964 Act, s. 116 (1); 1970 Act (N.I.), s. 72 (2).

[36] 1964 Act, s. 117; 1970 Act (N.I.), s. 73. In the Republic, if a lease is registered as a burden only, the lease itself is exempt but not documents subsequently dealing with the lessee's interest (*e.g.*, assignments), 1964 Act, s. 117 (1); *cf.* 1970 Act (N.I.), s. 73.

[37] See Murray, "Statutory Charges Register Act (N.I.), 1951" (1951) 9 N.I.L.Q. 90. See also on the Statutory Charges Register, *Irish Conveyancing Law* (1978), paras. 7.097-125.

[38] S.R. & O. (N.I.) 1971 No. 176.

[39] 1970 Act (N.I.), s. 87 (3).

[40] 1964 Act, s. 69 (1) (*r*).

[41] 1964 Act, s. 72.

[42] 1970 Act (N.I.), s. 86 (1).

[43] See ss. 86 (2) and 87 (1).

[44] S. 86 (3).

[45] S. 86 (4).

B. MATTERS REGISTRABLE

21.61. A considerable number of different types of statutory charges on land are now registrable.[46] Included are charges acquired by local authorities under town improvement and public health legislation[47]; clearance orders and resolutions declaring redevelopment areas[48]; notices, demands and charges relating to private streets.[49] Government department charges include turbary regulations[50] and preservation orders.[51] Other miscellaneous charges are notices under the Rights of Light Act (N.I.), 1961,[52] agreements or covenants under the Amenity Lands Act (N.I.), 1965,[53] and conditions attached to land under the Land Development Values (Compensation) Act (N.I.), 1965.[54]

21.62. Registration in the Statutory Charges Register does not render a statutory charge valid if it is not otherwise so nor render land subject to the charge if it was not already subject to it.[55]

Whenever a statutory charge is discharged, becomes unenforceable, ceases to affect the land or is declared invalid by a court, it is the duty of the chargeant to apply for cancellation.[56] Apart from that, the Registrar may himself cancel registration, after giving at least one week's notice to all interested parties,[57] and may make such other modification of entries as he decides, from time to time, to be necessary.[58]

C. PRIORITIES

21.63. Apart from simplifying investigation of title, the Statutory Charges Register governs priorities. The general rule is that a statutory charge is void as against a purchaser of any state in the land affected by the charge, unless the chargeant is protected in one of the ways specified.[51] In this context, "purchaser" means any person who has entered into an enforceable contract to acquire the estate for money or money's worth.[60] A statutory charge remains valid against volunteers, *e.g.*, persons taking under a will or on intestacy, and persons taking in consideration of marriage. The method of protection varies according to the circumstances of the case.

1. *Registered Land*

21.64. To be protected, the charge may be registered before the purchaser is registered in the Land Registry as owner of the estate purchased.[61]

---

[46] See Sched. 11 of the 1970 Act, which lists 21 categories. See further on the matters registrable, *Irish Conveyancing Law* (1978), paras. 7.098-121.
[47] Sched. 11, para. 1.
[48] Sched. 11, paras. 5 and 13.
[49] Sched. 11, para. 18.
[50] Sched. 11, para. 3.
[51] Sched. 11, para. 4.
[52] Sched. 11, para. 16. Ch. 6, *ante*.
[53] Sched. 11, para. 19.
[54] Sched. 11, para. 20.
[55] 1970 Act, s. 88 (8).
[56] S. 91 (1).
[57] S. 91 (3).
[58] S. 91 (5).
[59] S. 88 (1).
[60] S. 88 (2).
[61] S. 88 (1) (a).

2. *Unregistered Land*

21.65. The Charge may be proteced by registration in the Registry of Deeds before registration there of the document whereby the estate purchased is assured to the purchaser.[62]

3. *Priority Notice*

21.66. The charge may be protected by registration of a "priority notice" in the Statutory Charges Register before the purchaser registers his title in the Land Registry or his conveyance in Registry of Deeds, as the case may be.[63] A priority notice may be registered by a person intending to register a contemplated statutory charge before it is actually created.[64] If an application for registration of the charge itself is then made within three months, the registration of the charge is deemed to have been made when the charge was created.[65]

4. *Actual Notice*

21.67. If the purchaser has received *actual* notice of the statutory charge before he registers in the Land Registry or Registry of Deeds, he does not get priority by his registration, even though the charge was created or arose after he entered into his enforceable contract for purchase.[66]

---

[62] S. 88 (1) (*b*).
[63] S. 88 (1) (*c*).
[64] S. 89 (1).
[65] S. 89 (2).
[66] s. 88 (1) (*d*). *Cf.* the provisions as to notice in the Registration of Deeds Act (N.I.), 1970, para. 3.089, *ante*.

CHAPTER 22

REGISTRATION OF DEEDS

22.01. In Ireland, conveyancing of unregistered land, *i.e.,* land the *title* to which is not registered in the Land Registry,[1] is governed by the registration of *deeds* system which was introduced by the Registration of Deeds Act (Ireland), 1707.[2] It is essential to note that the 1707 Act, as amended, [3] introduced a system which extended throughout Ireland[4] and this will remain in force until eventually all land in both parts of Ireland becomes subject to compulsory registration of title and all titles are eventually registered. In Northern Ireland, the 1707 Act, as amended by later Acts, has been repealed and the legislation has been consolidated in the Registration of Deeds Act (N.I.), 1970. Since April 1, 1923, a separate Registry for Northern Ireland has operated in Belfast,[5] but searches with respect to documents referring to dealings in the Province before then still have to be made in the Dublin Registry.

I. FUNCTION

22.02. As we discussed in earlier chapters,[6] the primary function of the Registry of Deeds is to govern priorities between documents dealing with the same piece of land. This is done, as the preamble to the 1707 Act said:

> "For securing purchasers, preventing forgeries and fraudulent gifts and conveyances of lands, tenements and hereditaments, which have been frequently practised in this kingdom. . . ."[7]

Fraud and the like is prevented by an indirect means. There is no compulsion to register, but failure to do so may result in a loss of priority,[8] so that it is standard conveyancing practice in Ireland to register deeds or other documents dealing with unregistered land.[9] Registration does not achieve

---

[1] See ch. 21, *ante.*

[2] The leading work is Madden, *Registration of Deeds, Conveyances and Judgment Mortgages* (2nd ed., 1901). See also Maguire, *Registration of Deeds, Wills and Judgment Mortgages* (1912); Molesworth, *Essay on Registration of Deeds and Conveyances in Ireland* (1838); Irwin, "Registry of Deeds for Northern Ireland" (1971) 22 N.I.L.Q. 140; *Reports on the Office for Registration of Deeds in Ireland* (1861); *Reports of the Royal Commission on the Law Relating to Registration of Deeds* (1879-81, Cc. 2443 and 2818); *Report of the Committee on the Registry of Deeds Office, Dublin* (1887).

[3] See Registration of Deeds (Amendment) Acts (Ir.), 1709, 1721 and 1785; Registry of Deeds (Amendment) (Ir.) Acts, 1822, 1832 and 1864; Land Transfer (Ir.) Act, 1848; Judgment-Mortgage (Ir.) Acts, 1850 and 1858. Most of these Acts remain in force in R.I. For N.I., note the amendments made by Registration of Deeds (Amendment) Acts (N.I.), 1957 and 1967. See Wylie, (1968) 19 N.I.L.Q. 228.

[4] *Cf.* the Scottish Registry of Sasines, see *Report on Registration of Title to Land in Scotland* (1963, Cmnd. 2032), chs. II and III. Also the (now defunct) *local* registries in Middlesex (Middlesex Registry Act, 1708) and Yorkshire (Yorkshire Registry Acts, 1703-34), Land Registration Act, 1936, s. 2; Middlesex Deeds Act, 1940; Law of Property Act, 1969, Pt. II.

[5] Irish Free State (Consequential Provisions) Act, 1922.

[6] Chs. 3 and 13, *ante.*

[7] As a sign of the times (!), the preamble ran on: "especially by Papists, to the great prejudice of the Protestant interest thereof."   [8] Para. 22.19. *post.*   [9] See further, para. 22.05, *infra.*

anything other than priority over unregistered registrable documents and documents registered later[10] and this limitation must be kept in mind. Registration does not guarantee the title to the land dealt with by those documents (in this respect it must be distinguished from the registration of title system) nor, indeed, the validity of the document itself.[11] It clearly modifies the operation of the doctrine of notice, but it does not displace it.[12] Finally, a "memorial"[13] of a lost deed is secondary evidence of the contents of the deed which appear, as required by statute, in the memorial.[14] It may also be accepted as admissible evidence in respect of statements in it against those who executed it and all claiming under them, but not generally against those who did not execute it.[15]

II. DOCUMENTS REGISTRABLE

22.03. Deeds and other conveyances affecting unregistered land may be registered in the Registry of Deeds.[16] However, even documents not under seal, *e.g.,* an unsealed memorandum accompanying a mortgage by deposit of title deeds,[17] are registrable and should be registered. Apart from deeds of transfer, settlement and mortgage which may be registered, some documents must be registered: judgment mortgages,[18] bankruptcy vesting certificates of adjudication[19] and drainage and improvement charging orders.[20] Also registrable are judgments, decrees and orders of court. Pending actions affecting unregistered land may be registered, though these are more usually registered as *lites pendentes* in the Central Office of the High Court, or Judgments Office.[21]

22.04. Wills affecting land were registrable under the 1707 Act,[22] but for some reason were excluded from the section governing priorities between registered and unregistered documents.[23] This, of course, nullified the main function of the Registry in relation to wills and so in practice they were rarely registered. Not surprisingly, then, the provisions relating to registration of wills have been repealed in both parts of Ireland.[24] However, assents by

[10] Ch. 13, *ante*.
[11] There is no requirement of prior registration before the document can be produced in evidence, as in some countries, *e.g.*, parts of Nigeria.   [12] Ch. 3, *ante*.   [13] Para. 22.05, *infra*.
[14] Registry of Deeds (Ir.) Act, 1832, s. 32; 1970 Act (N.I.), s. 6. *Re Ward's Estate* (1909) 43 I.L.T.R. 113; *Chism* v. *Lipsett* [1905] 1 I.R.; *Re J.P.R.* (1940) 74 I.L.T.R. 11.
[15] Note, however, that the requirement of execution of memorials has been abolished in N.I., para. 22.06, *infra*.
[16] 1707 Act (Ir.), ss. 1 and 3; 1970 Act (N.I.), s. 1.
[17] Para. 12.46, *ante*. It is settled in Ireland that a *contract* for the sale of land is registrable, see *Irish Conveyancing Law* (1978), para. 9.065, cited with approval by Costello J. in *O'Connor* v. *McCarthy* [1982] I.R. 161 at 171 (see *A Casebook on Irish Land Law* (1984), p. 106). *Cf.* in England in respect of the, now defunct, Yorkshire Registry of Deeds, *Rodger* v. *Harrison* [1893] 1 Q.B. 161.
[18] Only in R.I. now, Judgment-Mortgage (Ir.) Act, 1850, ss. 6-8. For N.I., orders charging land must be registered, Judgments (Enforcement) (N.I.) Order, 1981, Art. 46 (3). See ch. 13, *ante*.
[19] Irish Bankrupt and Insolvent Act, 1857, s. 269.
[20] Landed Property (Improvement) (Ir.) Act, 1847, ss. 21 and 51-2.
[21] Judgments (Ir.) Acts, 1844 and 1849; Judgments Registry (Ir.) Act, 1850; 1970 Act (N.I.), ss. 2 (3) and 3 (see also Judgments Enforcement (N.I.) Order, 1981, Art. 117).
[22] S. 3.
[23] Ss. 4 and 5 were confined to "deeds and conveyances."
[24] Succession Act, 1965, s. 8 and 2nd Sched., Pt II (R.I.); Registration of Deeds (Amendment) Act (N.I.), 1967, s. 2.

personal representatives[25] to the vesting of unregistered land in the persons entitled under the deceased's will or on intestacy are deemed conveyances for the purposes of registration of deeds and operate subject to the provisions as to priorities.[26]

Finally, leases for a term not exceeding 21 years, where actual possession goes with the lease, are not registrable.[27]

III. REGISTRATION

There are several provisions governing registration of documents in the Registry of Deeds. The original provisions, which remain in force in the Republic, were somewhat technical and complex and have been simplified recently in Northern Ireland.[28]

A. EXECUTION OF DOCUMENTS AND MEMORIALS

22.05. Section 6 of the 1707 Act provided that (1) the deed or conveyance affecting the land had to be properly executed; (2) a "memorial" (*i.e.*, a summary of the deed or conveyance),[29] which is what is registered, had to be presented, signed and sealed by *one* of the grantors or grantees; (3) the execution of memorial had to be attested by *two* witnesses, one of whom had to be a witness to the execution of the deed or conveyance; (4) the latter "double" witness had to swear an affidavit proving the signing and sealing of the memorial, the execution of the deed or conveyance and the day and time of delivery of the memorial to the Registrar.[30] In several decisions, which have been much criticised,[31] the Irish courts held that section 6 required that proof of execution by the *grantor* had to be attested by the witness swearing the affidavit and that attestation of execution by the *grantee,* or any other person, made the registration void.[32]

22.06. Section 6 remains in force in the Republic of Ireland, but it has been replaced and modified in Northern Ireland. First, the fear of loss of priority due to defective proof of execution of a document was removed in 1967 as to documents already registered or lodged for registration during the next six months.[33] As to the future, however, it is clearly provided that the document lodged for registration must have its execution by a *grantor* attested by two

---

[25] Para. 16.44, *ante.* Note that assents need not be deeds and may be in writing only, Succession Act, 1965, s. 53 (1) (*a*); Administration of Estates Act (N.I.), 1955, s. 35 (1) (*a*).

[26] 1965 Act, s. 53 (1) (*c*) and (*d*); 1955 Act (N.I.), s. 35 (1) (*c*) and (*d*).

[27] 1707 Act s. 14; 1970 Act (N.I.), s. 5 (*c*). *Fury* v. *Smith* (1829) 1 Hud. & Br. 735; *Fleming* v. *Neville* (1830) Hayes 23.

[28] By the 1967 Act, which is now replaced by the 1970 Act.

[29] See further, para. 22.07, *infra.*

[30] See the discussion in Madden, *op. cit.*, pp. 59–69.

[31] *Report of the Royal Commission on the Law Relating to Registration of Deeds* (1879), 30; Madden, *op. cit.*, pp. 59-67, where it was pointed out that many deeds have, in fact, been registered without attestation by the grantor.

[32] *Rennick* v. *Armstrong* (1819) 1 Hud. & Br. 727; *Re Stephens* (1875) I.R. 10 Eq. 282; *Re Hurley* [1894] 1 I.R. 488. *Cf. R.* v. *Register of Deeds for County Middlesex* (1881) 21 Q.B.D. 555.

[33] 1967 Act (N.I.), s. 4, which provided that proof of execution by a witness to execution by a *grantee* was, and was to be deemed always to have been, as valid as if the witness had been a witness to execution by a *grantor.*

witnesses, who subscribe their names and addresses and occupations or descriptions to the document.[34] If this is done, there is no further need for proof by affidavit.[35] Secondly, it is no longer necessary for memorials to be signed, sealed or attested in Northern Ireland; they need be in writing only,[36] provided they contain the requisite information.[37]

22.07. Memorials of documents must contain the information which is required by statute,[38] *i.e.*, (1) date of the document and when it was perfected[39]; (2) names, addresses and occupations or descriptions of all parties and witnesses to the document, as stated in the document[40]; (3) the land affected by the document and details of its description in the document.[41] As regards the description of the lands, section 29 of the Registry of Deeds (Ireland) Act, 1832,[42] requires the memorial to specify the county and barony, or town or county of a city, and the parish, or the town and parish where the land is stated to be situated by the document. If the land lies in two or more counties, baronies, parishes or streets, or partly in one and partly in another, this must be stated in the memorial. This provision has been substituted in Northern Ireland by one requiring,[43] where the land is wholly or partly in a county borough, the name of the county borough and every street in question only to be stated. Where land is situated elsewhere, the memorial should specify the name of every county, barony and townland and, where situated in any town or village, the name of every town, village and street.[44] In Northern Ireland every memorial brought into the Registry of Deeds for registration must be endorsed with the name and address of the solicitor or party bringing it in or causing it to be brought in.[45]

22.08. The Registrar is obliged to check that the execution of documents lodged for registration has been properly witnessed and must compare the memorial with that document, checking that the statutory particulars are present.[46] In practice, many memorials contain considerably more information than is strictly necessary for registration purposes, though it may be helpful or useful in later conveyances of the land.[47]

[34] 1967 Act (N.I.), s. 3 (1); see now 1970 Act (N.I.), s. 2 (1). Two or more persons signing a document executed by a corporation and present at the affixing of the corporation seal are valid witnesses of the execution, 1970 Act, (N.I.), s. 2 (2).

[35] Judgments, decrees and court orders may be registered by lodgment of two copies, one of them being a certified one, 1970 Act (N.I.), s. 2 (3); *cf.* Judgment-Mortgage (Ir.) Act, 1850, s. 6, para. 13.168, *ante*.

[36] 1967 Act (N.I.), s. 5 and 15 (2); see now 1970 Act (N.I.), s. 1 (2).

[37] Para. 22.07, *infra*.

[38] 1707 Act, s. 7 and 1832 Act, s. 29 (R.I.); 1970 Act (N.I.), s. 1 (2) and Sched. 1. *Harding* v. *Carry* (1859) 10 I.C.L.R. 140; *Rochard* v. *Fulton* (1844) 7 Ir.Eq.R. 131.

[39] *Re Monsell* (1855) 5 Ir.Ch.R. 529.

[40] *Re Jennings* (1858) 8 Ir.Ch.R. 421.

[41] *Gardiner* v. *Blesington* (1850) 1 Ir.Ch.R. 79; *Stephenson* v. *Royce* (1856) 5 Ir.Ch.R. 401; *Re Butler's Estate* (1890) 25 L.R.Ir. 230.

[42] See also 1707 Act, ss. 7 and 15.

[43] 1970 Act (N.I.), Sched. 1, para. 1 (*c*). See now Local Govt. (Boundaries) Act (N.I.), 1971.

[44] If two or more documents effect the transaction, a memorial of one with the requisite information is enough description of the land, provided the memorials of the others cross-refer to it and give particulars of its registration, 1707 Act, s. 15; 1970 Act (N.I.), Sched. 1, para. 2.

[45] 1970 Act (N.I.), Sched. 1, para. 3; *cf.* 1832 Act, s. 29.

[46] 1832 Act, s. 29; 1970 Act (N.I.), s. 1 (3) and (4).

[47] *Cf.* the two examples given by the Belfast Registrar, (1971) 22 N.I.L.Q. 140 at 145-6.

B. CERTIFICATES AND SERIAL NUMBERS

22.09. In the Republic of Ireland, it remains the duty of the Registrar or his deputy to endorse on every document lodged a signed certificate stating the day and time of registration of the memorial and indicating in what book and at what page and number it is entered.[48] In Northern Ireland, the certificate need state the serial number allocated[49] and the date of allocation only.[50] In other words, priority of documents is now determined by the serial numbers rather than, as in the Republic, the actual time of registration of the memorial.[51] This change was made largely for administrative simplicity and usually will make no difference to priority, *i.e.,* except in cases where several documents dealing with the same land are handed in at the same time and get out of order when actually registered.

In both parts of Ireland, the certificate of registration is evidence of registration in any court of record.[52]

C. FILING AND BOOKS

22.10. All memorials of registered documents must be kept in files or books in the Registry, and must be filed in the order in which they are received.[53] Furthermore, abstracts or abridgements, *i.e.,* "brief chronicles," must be made of memorials and these are entered in the "Abstract Book,"[54] which is really a series of books. The Registry of Deeds (Ireland) Act, 1832, also required the keeping of a "Day Book,"[55] and the entering of transcripts of memorials in a "Transcript Book."[56] The need to keep these last two books and for transcripts was abolished in Northern Ireland in 1957.[57]

D. INDEXES

22.11. The key to use of the Registry of Deeds is the "Index of Names."[58] This is a series of books in which are entered in alphabetical order the names of all grantors specified in registered documents.[59] An "Index of Lands" was also formerly kept,[60] but in recent decades it had not been kept up to date in either part of Ireland. However, there was no statutory authority for not

---

[48] 1707 Act, s. 7.
[49] Since the 1967 Act (N.I.), s. 6, which provided for serial numbers for the first time, see now 1970 Act (N.I.), s. 8.
[50] 1970 Act (N.I.), s. 1 (5).
[51] See 1707 Act, s. 4; 1970 (N.I.), s. 4 (1).
[52] 1707 Act, s. 7; 1970 Act (N.I.), s. 1 (6).
[53] 1707 Act, s. 7 and 1832 Act, ss. 9 and 10; 1970 Act (N.I.), s. 9 (1) (see also S.R. & O. (N.I.) 1968 No. 92, regs. 3 and 4).
[54] 1832 Act, s. 12; 1970 Act (N.I.), s. 9 (2). See the example of an entry in the Abstract Book in (1971) 22 N.I.L.Q. 140 at 147.
[55] S. 11.
[56] S. 13.
[57] Registration of Deeds (Amendment) Act (N.I.), 1957, ss. 5 and 8 (2).
[58] 1832 Act, ss. 14-6 and Land Transfer (Ir.) Act, 1848, s. 7; 1970 Act (N.I.), s. 10 (see also S.R. & O. (N.I.) 1968 No. 92, reg. 6).
[59] See the example of an extract from the Index in (1971) 22 N.I.L.Q. 140 at 148.
[60] 1832 Act, ss. 17 and 18; 1848 Act, s. 7.

maintaining this Index and the Registry in Dublin began in the late sixties to bring it up to date with respect to land in Dublin. The Index may prove convenient in certain cases, *e.g.,* where the searcher does not have a name to search in the Index of Names.[61] In Northern Ireland, however, it is now provided by statute that the Index of Lands is deemed to have been closed on December 31, 1944.[62]

IV. SEARCHES

22.12. Because of the provisions relating to priorities as between registered and unregistered documents relating to unregistered land in Ireland, searches in the Registry of Deeds are essential in conveyancing throughout in Ireland.

A. HAND SEARCHES

22.13. Members of the general public have a right to make a search in the books and indexes kept in the Registry, upon paying the appropriate fees.[63] Such "hand" searches may involve the making of extracts from, or the taking of short notes of, the various records and documents in the Registry. More often, however, hand searches are made by professional law searchers.

B. COMMON AND NEGATIVE SEARCHES

22.14. Instead of making a hand search, a requisition may be made to the Registry for a "common" or "negative" search to be made by a Registry official.[64] A common search is a search made by one official, which is initialled by the Registrar but not warranted. A negative search is made by two officials and a certificate is issued, signed by the Registrar, which certifies that no memorial is registered which comes within the terms of the requisition and is not abstracted in the certificate. Errors or omissions from such certificates are evidence of a breach of duty imposed on the Registry officials by the legislation, for which they or, in Northern Ireland, the Department of the Environment may be liable in damages for loss.[65] Furthermore, since 1957 it has been the duty of the Registrar in Northern Ireland to record and index the particulars of every negative search issued or prepared for issue, so as to facilitate the subsequent issue of "duplicate" negative searches.[66] Duplicate negative searches must be certified as correct by the Registrar or his assistant and, if this is done, they have the same force and effect as the original, to the same extent and in the same terms.[67]

---

[61] Apart from this sort of case, it is questionable how useful it is in view of the notorious inaccuracy of descriptions of land in many title documents. *Cf. Report of the Committee on Registration of Title to Land in Northern Ireland* (1967, Cmd. 512), para. 11; (1913) 47 I.L.T.S.J. 169.

[62] 1967 Act (N.I.), s. 1 (1).

[63] 1832 Act, s. 7; 1970 Act (N.I.), s. 15. See further on searches, *Irish Conveyancing Law* (1978), paras. 14.60-1.

[64] 1707 Act, s. 10 and 1832 Act, ss. 8 and 21-5 and Sched. C; 1970 Act (N.I.), s. 13 (see also S.R. & O. (N.I.) 1968 No. 92, regs. 7-9 and S.R. & O. (N.I.) 1971 No. 152).

[65] 1707 Act, s. 12 and 1832 Act, s. 26; 1970 Act (N.I.), ss. 13 (6) and 17.

[66] 1957 Act (N.I.), s. 6.

[67] 1970 Act (N.I.), s. 14 (2).

C. PERSONS SEARCHED AND PERIOD OF SEARCH

22.15. The search in the Registry of Deeds is made against the persóns specified in the requisition for the search, for the periods stated in it and against any lands described. Each person appearing on the title should be searched against from the date of the *accrual* of his title to the date of registration of a conveyance by him, which makes all subsequent deeds or documents by him ineffectual. These basic principles may be illustrated by the following example of the searches which should be made.

22.16. The title shown consists of: (1) a *lease,* dated January 1, 1946, of a house for 150 years granted by A to B, which was registered on January 30, 1946; (2) an *assignment* by B to C of April 1, 1956, which was registered on July 1, 1956; (3) an *assignment* by C to D of April 10, 1966, which was not registered; (4) the *death* of D on January 10, 1984, having made a will by which he appointed E and F to be his executors and by which he left all his property to his wife, G; (5) *probate* of the will was granted to E and F on December 20, 1984. If the executors are now selling the property, the necessary searches in the Registry of Deeds are: (i) against A from January 1, 1946 (date of the lease) to January 30, 1946 (date of the lease's registration); (ii) against B from January 1, 1946 (the date of the accrual of his interest) to July 1, 1956 (date of registration of the assignment by him); (iii) against C from April 1, 1956 (date of accrual of his interest) to the present day (because the assignment by him was *not* registered); (iv) against D from April 10, 1966 (date of accrual of his interest) to the present day (because no deed disposing of his interest has been registered); (v) against E and F from January 10, 1984 (date of death of D, because probate relates back to that date) to the present day.

22.17. Some conveyancers maintain that it is necessary to search against G from the date of the death of D, because she might have charged her prospective interest in the estate and she has an equitable interest from the date of death. However, she does not acquire any legal interest in the land until the executors have assented to the bequest of the lease to her.

22.18. It is essential that the description of the land in the requisition should include all descriptions by which the land is known at any time. Failure to do this in a recent case in the Republic led to a purchaser acquiring land without notice of a judgment mortgage to which the land was subject.[68]

V. PRIORITIES

22.19. The subject of priorities under the registration of deeds system[69] was discussed in detail in earlier chapters and need not be repeated here.[70] Suffice

---

[68] *Dardis and Dunns Seeds Ltd.* v. *Hickey* (1972) unrep. (No. 1165 Sp.).
[69] 1707 Act, ss. 4 and 5; 1970 Act (N.I.), s. 4.
[70] Chs. 3 and 13, *ante.*

it to reiterate that the position arrived at by the Irish courts in interpreting the provisions of the original 1707 Act relating to priorities has been given statutory recognition recently in Northern Ireland.[71]

[71] 1967 Act, s. 7, and see now 1970 Act (N.I.), s. 4 (3) and (4).

PART X

EXTINGUISHMENT OF INTERESTS

CHAPTER 23

ADVERSE POSSESSION

23.01. One of the main ways in which an estate or interest in land may be extinguished is under the doctrine of "adverse possession," as it operates under modern Statutes of Limitations.[1] This doctrine, however, has become one of the most controversial features of modern land law.

I. BASIS OF DOCTRINE

23.02. The modern doctrine of adverse possession finds expression in the Statute of Limitations[2] as it applies to land. This Statute governs the extinguishment of "stale"claims generally, *i.e.*, rights of action are limited in point of time and are lost if not brought within that limit.[3] In its application to land the Statute may have the effect of extinguishing the title of one person to the land and thereby leave some other person with "rights" to the land. One of the central points of controversy is the linking of these two aspects of its application to land.

23.03. The underlying philosophy of the doctrine remains that of "quieting men's titles," for as Lord St. Leonards (formerly Sir Edward Sugden), who was successively Lord Chancellor of Ireland and Great Britain, remarked:

> "All statutes of limitation have for their object the prevention of the rearing up of claims at great distances of time when evidences are lost; and in all well-regulated countries the quieting of possession is held an important point of policy."[4]

The doctrine thus operates as much to confirm long-held titles which can no longer be proved by documentary evidence as to sanction the activities of squatters deliberately setting out to dispossess the true owner of the land. In Ireland, the doctrine has played a vital role in regularising informal transfers

---

[1] See Brady and Kerr, *The Limitation of Actions in the Republic of Ireland* (1984), espec. chs. 4-6. See also Darby and Bosanquet, *Statutes of Limitations in England and Ireland* (2nd ed., 1893, Supp. 1899). Also Beytagh, *Statute of Limitations* (1846); Franks, *Limitation of Actions* (1959); Lightwood, *Possession of Land* (1894), *Time Limit on Actions* (1909); Pollock and Wright, *Possession in the Common Law* (1888); Preston and Newsom, *Limitation of Actions* (1953); *Prichard, Squatting* (1981). Goodman, "Adverse Possession of Land – Morality and Crime" (1970) 33 M.L.R. 281; Prichard, "Squatters – The Law and the Mythology" (1976) 40 Conv. 255.

[2] *I.e.*, Statute of Limitations, 1957 (R.I.); Statute of Limitations (N.I.), 1958. See Delany (1961) 63 J.I.B.I. 126. See also Limitation Act (N.I.), 1964, *Stewart* v. *Mersey Insulation Co. Ltd.* [1971] N.I. 1,

[3] *Cf.* the equitable doctrine of *laches,* para. 3,066, *ante.* Also the common law doctrine of prescription, as extended by statute, ch. 6, *ante.* Note that prescription is essentially a positive concept, *i.e.* the conferment of rights through a presumed grant, and is confined to minor interests in land, *i.e.*, easements and profits.

[4] *Dundee Harbour Trustees* v. *Dougall* (1852) 1 Macq. 317 at 321.

934

of ownership, *e.g.*, where a farmer dies, but no representation is taken out of his estate and subsequent disputes arise between the beneficiaries under his will or between those entitled to distributive shares on his intestacy.[5]

A. ADVERSE POSSESSION

23.04. Prior to the Real Property Limitation Act, 1833, "adverse possession" had a technical meaning.[6] Before 1833 there were several cases where a person could be in possession of land without any title to it and yet this possession was not regarded as "adverse." Thus possession by a younger brother was deemed to be possession by the heir to land[7]; possession by one co-owner was deemed to be possession by all the co-owners (whether joint tenants or tenants in common), unless an intention to claim the whole was expressed[8]; a tenant for years holding over after termination of his lease was deemed to hold possession for the lessor.[9] The 1833 Act, however, established the modern concept of fixed periods of limitation running from the time when a right of action accrues. The period fixed by the Act for actions in relation to land was generally 20 years.[10] This was reduced to 12 years by the Real Property Limitation Act, 1874,[11] and this remains the general period under the latest Statutes of Limitations in both parts of Ireland.[12]

23.05. Since 1833, "adverse possession" means simply possession of land which is inconsistent with the title of the true owner, *i.e.*, possession giving rise to a right of action in the owner which will be barred after lapse of the limitation period from the date of the right of action's accrual. As Lord St., Leonards said in another case:

> "It is perfectly settled that adverse possession is no longer necessary in the sense in which it was formerly used, but that mere possession may be and is sufficient under many circumstances to give a title adversely."[13]

What these circumstances are we discuss later in this chapter, but the modern Statutes now adopt this meaning of adverse possession expressly:

> "No right of action to recover land shall be deemed to accrue unless the land is in the posession (in this section referred to as adverse possession) of some person in whose favour the period of limitation can run."[14]

---

[5] Paras. 23.40 *et seq., infra.*

[6] See Lightwood, *op. cit.,* pp. 159 *et. seq. Howard* v. *Sherwood* (1832) Alc. & Nap. 217; *Brownrigg* v. *Cruikshank* (1849) 1 Ir.Jur.(o.s.) 212; *Davies* v. *D'Arcy* (1853) 3 I.C.L.R. 617.

[7] *Cf.* para. 23.37, *infra.*

[8] *Cf.* para. 23.36, *infra.*

[9] *Cf.* para. 23.31, *infra.*

[10] S. 2.

[11] S. 1.

[12] 1957 Act, s. 13 (2) (*a*); 1958 Act (N.I.), s. 17 (3).

[13] *Dean of Ely* v. *Bliss* (1852) 2 De G.M. & G. 459 at 476-7.

[14] 1957 Act. s. 18 (1); 1958 Act (N.I.), s. 22 (1). See the discussion by Kenny J. in *Browne* v. *Fahy* (1975) Unrep. (H.C.,R.I.) and the Republic's Supreme Court in *Murphy* v. *Murphy* [1980] I.R. 183 (see *A Casebook on Irish Land Law* (1984), p. 696), para. 23.21, *post.*

B. EXTINGUISHMENT

23.06. The effect of adverse possession for the limitation period is expressed in the following form:

> ". . . at the expiration of the period fixed by this Act for any person to bring an action to recover land, the *title* of that person to the land shall be extinguished."[15]

This provision emphasises that the key concepts in relation to the operation of the Statutes of Limitations are those of "title" and "extinguishment."

1. *Title*

23.07. Prior to 1833, possession for the limitation period barred the dispossessed owner's *right of action* only and left his *title* intact. The practical significance of this was that, if he subsequently came into lawful possession again, his title could be invoked against the dispossessor.[16] The modern system established since 1833, however, extinguishes the dispossessed's owner's title as well as his right of action, so that, if he subsequently re-enters without permission, he is a trespasser.[17] This highlights what is, perhaps, the central feature of ownership of land nowadays, namely the relativity of title.[18]

   23.08. Where a squatter bars the right of action and title of the dispossessed owner of land, he acquires a title good against anyone other than a person with a better title to the land. Unless such a person interferes with him, the squatter is free to defend his possession against trespass by another, who may not impugn the squatter's title by pleading a *jus tertii, i.e.*, that a superior title lies in some third party. The question remains, however, as to how far such a superior title may affect the squatter. This is really another way of asking the basic question: what sort of title does the squatter obtain by adverse possession? Or, to put it yet another way, what do the Irish Statutes of Limitations mean when they say that the dispossessed owner's title to the land is "extinguished"?[19]

2. *Parliamentary Conveyance*

23.09. Determination of the precise title obtained by a squatter under the Statute of Limitations has centred on the issue of whether or not the Statute effects a "parliamentary conveyance" or "statutory transfer" of the dispossessed owner's title to the squatter. No less an authority than Parke B. took the view that "the effect of the Act [Real Property Limitation Act, 1833] is to make a parliamentary conveyance of the land to the person in possession after

---

[15] 1957 Act, s. 24; 1958 Act (N.I.) s. 28 (italics added).
[16] Lightwood, *Possession of Land* (1894), p. 153.
[17] See *Incorporated Society* v. *Richards* (1841) 1 Dr. & War. 258.
[18] See Rudden, "Terminology of Title" (1964) 80 L.Q.R. 63.
[19] See Omotola, "Nature of Interest Acquired by Adverse Possession of Land under the Limitation Act, 1939" (1973) 37 Conv. 85; Sweet, "Title by Possession" (1906) 18 Jud.Rev. 415.

the period has elapsed."[20] Sir Edward Sugden (later Lord St. Leonards) held the same view and expressed it both while he was on the Bench in Ireland and England[21] and in his legal writings.[22] His view was accepted as the correct one by the Irish Queen's Bench Division in *Rankin* v. *McMurtry*,[23] where Holmes J. stated:

> "Whatever the mode of transfer, I am of opinion that the estate and interest the right to which is extinguished, so far as the original owner is concerned, became vested in the person whose possession has caused such extinction. The opposite conclusion would seriously affect leasehold tenancies in this country; and it is satisfactory to know that Lord St. Leonards seems to have had no doubt that the view I have expressed is the correct one."[24]

The court approved a passage from the leading treatise of the period which stated:

> "Though the title extinguished . . . is not directly transferred by the statute to the wrongdoer who has been in possession, yet the title gained by such possession, being limited by rights yet remaining unextinguished, is clearly commensurate with the interest which the rightful owners have lost by operation of the statute, and must, therefore, it is apprehended, have the same legal character, and be freehold, leasehold or copyhold accordingly."[25]

It is important to note that *Rankin* v. *McMurtry* concerned leasehold land, which, of course, was the predominant tenure in the rural parts of Ireland at the time and remains so today in urban areas. Furthermore, the existence of so many long leases in Ireland, *e.g.*, 999 or 10,000 years, makes it crucial to determine the precise nature of the title obtained by the squatter and it is, perhaps, not surprising that the court held that the squatter took over the lease.

23.10. The next development was the English decision in *Tichborne* v. *Weir*,[26] where the English Court of Appeal rejected the concept of a parliamentary conveyance. Lord Esher M.R. took the view that "the effect of

[20] *Doe d. Jukes* v. *Sumner* (1845) 14 M. & W. 39 at 42.
[21] *Incorporated Society for Protestant Schools* v. *Richards* (1841) 1 Dr. & War. 258 at 289; *Scott* v. *Nixon* (1843) 3 Dr. & War. 388 at 405-8; *Tuthill* v. *Rogers* (1844) 1 Jo. & Lat. 36 at 72; *Burroughs* v. *McCreight* (1844) 1 Jo. & Lat. 290 at 303; *Trustees of Dundee Harbour* v. *Dougall* (1852) 1 Macq. 317 at 321.
[22] Sugden, *Law of Vendors and Purchasers* (14th ed., 1862), p. 476. See Meredith, "A Paradox of Sugden's" (1918) 34 L.Q.R. 253.
[23] (1889) 24 L.R.Ir. 290. See also *Kennedy* v. *Woods* (1868) I.R. 2 C.L. 436; *McCormack* v. *Courtney* [1895] 2 I.R. 97; *Re Hayden* [1904] 1 I.R. 1. And see *Re Field* [1918] 1 I.R. 140.
[24] *Ibid.*, p. 301. *Cf.* Gibson J. at p. 303: "If the statute has barred the right of the representative of the original lessee, in whom is the term now vested? I think it must be taken that the defendants, assuming the statutory bar has arisen, have in some way, whether by statutory estoppel, transfer, or otherwise, become owners of the lease."
[25] Darby and Bosanquet, *Statutes of Limitations in England and Ireland* (1st ed., 1867), p. 390. Contrary views in Dart, *Vendors and Purchasers* (6th ed.), vol. 1, p. 463 and Hayes, *Conveyancing* (5th ed.), vol. 1, p. 269 drew the following comment by Holmes J.: "I dare say some speculation on the subject has been indulged in by textwriters whose contributions to legal learning consist in expressing doubts without venturing to offer a solution to them."
[26] (1892) 67 L.T. 735, followed in *Taylor* v. *Twinberrow* [1930] 2 K.B. 16.

the statute is not that the right of one person is conveyed to another, but that the right is extinguished and destroyed,"[27] and Bowen L.J. similarly refused to accept the "fiction of a transfer of title."[28] The views of Lord St. Leonards[29] in the Irish cases were cited to the court, but were considered to be confined to cases of adverse possession relating to freehold land only.[30] The authority of *Tichborne* v. *Weir* in Ireland was discussed by the Court of Appeal in *O'Connor* v. *Foley*,[31] where the majority[32] seem to have accepted it as a correct statement of the law. Thus Fitzgibbon L.J. said:

> "I do not question the authority of *Tichborne* v. *Weir*. It is the decision of three eminent Judges of Appeal; it appears never to have been questioned in any text-book or subsequent case, and I respectfully say that it seems to me to be right."[33]

Holmes L.J. dissented vigorously and felt unable to resist, despite *Tichborne* v. *Weir*, "the steady current of Irish decisions."[34] He commented:

> "I should think every circuit-going Judge has taken the law as laid down in the cases I have mentioned. The title of the occupier who pays the rent for small agricultural holdings in this country is generally dependent on the Statute of Limitations, for personal representations in such cases are rarely raised, and even where the holding is transferred *inter vivos*, there is often no writing. A fair rent under the Irish Land Acts can only be fixed on the application of a tenant in occupation, and yet the cases in which the only title of the applicants to the tenancy is such as I have described may be counted by the hundreds."[35]

Nevertheless, later Irish judges still tended to adopt the view of the majority and to accept the authority of *Tichborne* v. *Weir*, though usually *obiter*.[36]

23.11. Then the position under English law was reviewed by the House of Lords in *Fairweather* v. *St. Marylebone Property Co. Ltd.*,[37] which involved the acquisition of squatter's rights over part of a garden shed straddling the boundary line between adjoining properties, both held under 99-year leases. The dispossessed lessee purported to surrender his "lease" to the lessor, who claimed the right to eject the squatter immediately, *i.e.*, without having to await the expiration of the remainder of the 99-year term of the lease. The

---

[27] *Ibid.*, p. 737.
[28] *Ibid.*, p. 737.
[29] Recognised by Lord Esher as "a very great real property lawyer."
[30] *Ibid.*, p. 737 (*per* Bowen L.J.).
[31] [1906] 1 I.R. 20. This discussion was *obiter*, since the court distinguished *Tichborne* on the ground that the squatter had become a tenant by estoppel, para. 23.14, *infra*.
[32] Fitzgibbon and Walker L.JJ.
[33] *Ibid.*, p. 26. Fitzgibbon L.J. also explained Lord St. Leonard's views as being applicable to freehold land only, *ibid.*
[34] Fn. 23, *supra*.
[35] *Ibid.*, p. 39.
[36] *Ashe* v. *Hogan* [1920] 1 I.R. 159, espec. at 169 (*per* O'Connor M.R.); *Clibborn* v. *Horan* [1921] 1 I.R. 93 at 101 (O'Connor M.R.); *R.C.B.* v. *Dublin Board of Assistance* [1948] I.R. 287 at 293-4 (Dixon J.); *Re Ryan's Estate* [1960] I.R. 174 at 179 (Dixon J.). Cf. *Bank of Ireland* v. *Domvile* [1956] I.R. 37 at 58 (Dixon J.).
[37] [1963] A.C. 510.

law lords unanimously confirmed the authority of *Tichborne* v. *Weir* and the majority[38] held that, in the case of leasehold land, the title of the dispossessed lessee is extinguished as against the squatter only and not as against the lessor. Thus the majority held that the lease remained on foot as between the dispossessed lessee and lessor, so that the lessee could surrender it to the lessor. The consequences for the leasehold squatter were disastrous, for the majority then held that the effect of such a surrender was to remove the restriction created by the lease on the lessor's paramount right to possession of the land, so that he could immediately invoke that right.[39] The principle *nemo dat quod non habet* was held not to apply, *i.e.*, that the dispossessed lessee could surrender his lease only on the footing that it was subject to the squatter's right to possession for the remainder of the term of the lease.[40] In a subsequent case it was held that the lessor could forfeit the lease for non-payment of rent by the dispossessed lessee and the squatter had no right to claim relief against forfeiture.[41]

23.12. The implications of the *Fairweather* decision were that a squatter on leasehold land was in an extremely precarious position. The dispossessed lessee and lessor could indulge in collusion to "squeeze" him out, through a surrender of the lease, ejectment by the lessor, followed, if the parties wished, by a regrant to the dispossessed lessee.[42] If the dispossessed lessee ceased to comply with the terms of his lease, the landlord might forfeit it and again eject the squatter. The risk to the squatter's title could have enormous significance in terms of policy in cases where a very long lease of land might be involved, as would often happen in Ireland. The title to such land could be in doubt for centuries rather than "quieted" as the doctrine of adverse possession was supposed to achieve.[43] Despite some Irish judges' apparent acceptance of the principle in *Tichborne* v. *Weir*, which was the foundation of the House of Lords decision in *Fairweather*, one factor did, however, make it possible that the decision might not have such serious consequences in Ireland. This factor was the readiness with which the Irish judges have held that the squatter on leasehold land may be estopped from denying that he has become an assignee of the lease.

23.13. In *O'Connor* v. *Foley*[44] the Court of Appeal held that a squatter, who applied to have a fair rent fixed under the Irish Land Acts, [45] was estopped from denying that he had become an assignee of the lease, so as to be bound

---

[38] Lord Morris *dissentiente*. See the criticism in Wade, "Landlord, Tenant and Squatter" (1962) 78 L.Q.R. 541.

[39] [1963] A.C. 510 at 537 and 539 (*per* Lord Radcliffe) and at 543-5 (*per* Lord Denning).

[40] As Lord Morris thought, *ibid.*, p. 550. *Walter* v. *Yalden* [1902] 2 K.B. 304 supported him, as did Wade, *op. cit.*

[41] *Tickner* v. *Buzzacott* [1965] Ch. 426.

[42] Lord Denning recognised this, [1963] A.C. 510 at 547. See also Lord Morris at p. 554.

[43] See, generally, Wallace, "Adverse Possession of Leaseholds – The Case for Reform" (1975) 10 Jur.(N.S.) 74; Wylie, "Adverse Possession: An Ailing Concept?" (1965) 16 N.I.L.Q. 467.

[44] [1906] 1 I.R. 20. See also *Rankin* v. *McMurtry* (1889) 24 L.R.Ir. 290. *Cf. Cullen* v. *Cullen* [1962] I.R. 268 (para. 20.10, *ante.*).

[45] Para. 1.49, *ante.*

by its covenants. Similarly in *Ashe* v. *Hogan*[46] it was held that a squatter, who took advantage of a proviso in the lease, whereby the rent was halved so long as the covenants were performed, and paid the reduced rent, which was accepted by the landlord, was bound by the covenants in the lease. As O'Connor M.R. said, "a person taking advantage of a clause in a lease and deriving benefit under it must accept the burdens."[47] The implication seems to have been that in such cases the landlord would similarly be estopped from denying the tenancy of the squatter by his acceptance of the rent and performance by the squatter of other obligations of the tenancy agreement.

23.14. It seems to have been partly on this basis that the practice has been adopted in the Land Registries in both parts of Ireland of treating the squatter as if he had become a transferee of the registered land.[48] Section 52 of the Local Registration of Title (Ireland) Act, 1891, preserved the operation of the doctrine of adverse possession, by providing that the squatter could apply to the court for an order declaring the title to the land he would have acquired if it had been unregistered land, and for an order for rectification of the register accordingly.[49] In practice, section 52 orders have directed rectification by registration of the squatter in the *same* folio as the dispossessed owner, *i.e.*, as if the squatter were a transferee of the same title. Yet if the *Tichborne* and *Fairweather* principle of there being no statutory transfer had been adopted, in strict theory a new folio should have been opened to deal with the new title acquired by the squatter. The problem would then have arisen, however, of determining what title the squatter should have been registered with and, in the case of leasehold land, it would have been difficult to answer this question, unless a tenancy by estoppel arose. According to the *Fairweather* case, he had neither the freehold nor the leasehold interest in the land. It is apparent, then, that the practice adopted by the Land Registries was extremely convenient, even though it might not have accorded with strict theory. For this reason it was recommended in Northern Ireland that the "parliamentary conveyance" theory should be expressly adopted by the legislation for both registered and unregistered land.[50]

23.15. Since then, the whole matter has been reviewed by the Republic's Supreme Court in *Perry* v. *Woodfarm Homes Ltd.*,[51] which concerned a small plot of ground at the back of a house held under a 999-year lease granted in 1947. The plaintiff had been in exclusive possession of the plot since 1955 and clearly had extinguished the lessee's title by 12 years' adverse possession. In 1970 the defendants took an assignment of the 1947 lease and then, a month

---

[46] [1920] 1 I.R. 159.

[47] *Ibid.*, p. 164. *Cf. Tichborne* v. *Weir, op. cit.*, and *Tickner* v. *Buzzacott* [1965] Ch. 426. where it was held that mere payment of rent is *not* sufficient to raise an estoppel.

[48] See *Survey of the Land Law of Northern Ireland* (1971), para. 413.

[49] On s. 52, see *Re Skelton* [1976] N.I. 132. The new registration legislation adopts the same provision, except that an application to the court is no longer necessary, Registration of Title Act, 1964, s. 49 (R.I.); Land Registration Act (N.I.), 1970, s. 53. Para. 23.43. *post.*

[50] *1971 Survey (N.I.)*, paras. 411-3.

[51] [1975] I.R. 104 (see *A Casebook on Irish Land Law* (1984), p. 685) (Walsh and Griffin JJ., Henchy J. *dissentiente*).

later, an assignment of the fee simple reversion. Their title to the freehold was registered in the Land Registry later the following month. The defendants argued that, on the basis of the *Fairweather* case, the plaintiff's title was good against the lessee's interest only and that had merged in their fee simple,[52] so as to give them an immediate right to possession, *i.e.*, the merger had the same effect as the surrender in the *Fairweather* case. The defendants indicated that they intended to take over the plot for building purposes and the plaintiff applied for an interlocutory injunction[53] to restrain them. On the parties agreeing to have the application treated as the hearing of the action, O'Keefe P. granted a perpetual injunction.[54] On appeal to the Supreme Court, the majority upheld this decision.

23.16. Walsh J. took the view that the majority in *Fairweather* misconstrued the meaning of modern Statutes of Limitations in providing that the "title" to the land is "extinguished." He seemed to agree with much of the majority's analysis, but not with their conclusions. He agreed that the Statute did not destroy the lease itself, so that it remained an encumbrance preventing the freeholder from entering into immediate possession. He thought it "well established" that in relation to unregistered land "there is not a statutory conveyance or assignment of the estate to the squatter." Where he differed from the law lords was in his view that:

"... a person who has lost all his title to a leasehold estate is not in a position to effectively deal with it at all and therefore he has nothing to surrender and nothing to assign. A person who takes from him a purported assignment or a surrender of the leasehold estate cannot be in any stronger position or have any better title than the person making the purported assignment or surrender."

In other words, Walsh J. accepted the view of Lord Morris, who dissented in *Fairweather*, that the principle *nemo dat quod non habet* applied. He also accepted that the implication of saying the lease remained on foot as between the lessor and lessee was that the "squatter may be indirectly forced to carry out the covenants to preserve his possession from ejectment by forfeiture for non-observance of the covenants." Yet he did take the view, albeit *obiter*, that the position as regards a statutory transfer of title was different in the case of registered land. He commented on the effect of section 49 of the Registration of Title Act, 1964:

"This would appear to permit in the case of a squatter who has dispossessed a registered leaseholder where registered land is concerned to have himself registered as the owner of the leasehold."[55]

Griffin J. agreed with Walsh J. in accepting the view of Lord Morris as to the

---

[52] Ch. 24, *post.*
[53] Para. 3.133, *ante.*
[54] Para. 3.132, *ante.*
[55] This seems to anticipate the view taken of the English Land Registry system in *Spectrum Investment Co.* v. *Holmes* [1981] 1 W.L.R. 221. Neither Griffin J. nor Henchy J. dealt with this point.

effect of a purported surrender or merger of the lease.

23.17. He also reviewed the Irish and English cases on the question of a parliamentary conveyance and concluded:

> ". . . though there is no statutory transfer or conveyance to the squatter, what the squatter . . . has gained is the right to possession of the premises in dispute as against the fee simple owner . . . for the unexpired portion of the term, subject to the risk and the possibility of a forfeiture. During the currency of the term limited by a lease, the lessor has no right to possession of the demised property unless the lessee has incurred a forfeiture for breach of one or more of the covenants in the lease . . . The ousted lessee continues to be contractually liable to the lessor upon the covenants in the lease."

Since no forfeiture had occurred in this case, the squatter remained protected for the unexpired term of the 999-year lease.

23.18. Henchy J., who dissented, also took the view that the Irish and English authorities had now established that no parliamentary conveyance took place. He, however, preferred the view that a merger took place between the fee simple and the lease so as to give the freeholders an immediate right to possession against the squatter.

> "It seems to me to be inequitable and contrary to first principles that as a result of the merger of the leasehold in the fee simple the rights of the freeholder should be reduced and those of the squatter who had displaced the lessee should be enlarged."

23.19. In the light of the *Fairweather* and *Perry* cases, it seems to be established now in both parts of Ireland[56] that the Statutes of Limitations have a negative effect only, at least as regards unregistered land. With respect to Walsh J., it is by no means clear that the position is different with respect to registered land and this point should be settled beyond doubt by appropriate legislation.[57] It should also be emphasised that the majority view in *Perry* gives the squatter on leasehold land limited protection only. He is still subject to the risk of forfeiture brought about by a default of the dispossessed lessee and to this extent there remains the failure of the doctrine of adverse possession to "quiet" the title. If the *Tickner* case is correct, [58] he may not even be able to apply for relief against the forfeiture by offering to take over the lease, though he may protect himself if he induces the landlord into co-operative acts sufficient to raise an estoppel. The ultimate conclusion must remain, therefore, that the recommendation in Northern Ireland for introduction of the parliamentary conveyance theory should still be consi-

---

[56] Since the *Fairweather* decision was not an appeal from Northern Ireland, it is just possible that the courts there might still follow the earlier Irish decisions, but in view of the unanimous rejection by the Republic's Supreme Court in *Perry* the possibility is extremely remote.
[57] See further para. 23.43, *infra*. Also Wylie, (1968) 19 N.I.L.Q. 89 at 96-102.
[58] Para. 23.11, *ante*.

dered by the legislators for both parts of Ireland.[59]

II. OPERATION OF DOCTRINE

Having considered the underlying theory of the doctrine of adverse possession, we must consider in some more detail its operation with respect to land.

A. LIMITATION PERIODS

23.20. As mentioned above, the main limitation period for land is 12 years,[60] but other periods exist in certain special cases. The period is 30 years for recovery of land by a State authority in the Republic and the Crown in Northern Ireland,[61] and 60 years for recovery of foreshore.[62] In the case of arrears of rentcharges or conventional rents the period is 6 years.[63]

B. RUNNING OF TIME

23.21. The general rule is that time does not begin to run against the owner of land until a right of action accrues to him. Thus there must be both a dispossession of the true owner, or discontinuance of possession by him, and adverse possession by some other person. Mere abandonment or leaving land vacant is not enough, because, until someone else goes into adverse possession, the owner has no right of action against anyone. In *Browne* v. *Fahy*,[64] Kenny J. held that there was no adverse possession because the acts relied upon were not inconsistent with the enjoyment of the land in question by the owners. He stated:

> "The cattle were on the lands because of permission given by [the owners' predecessors] and the [owners] had no cattle. The planting of trees was to give shelter for the cattle which were on the lands. The erection of fences on the boundary with the public road was to keep the cattle in so that they would not stray while the erection of a fence between the lands and the avenue was intended to prevent the cattle from getting on to the avenue

---

[59] *1971 Survey (N.I.)*, paras, 411-3. See also the Land Law Working Group's Discussion Document No. 4 (*Conveyancing and Miscellaneous Matters*)(1983), Ch. 6.

[60] 1957 Act, s. 13 (2) (*a*); 1958 Act (N.I.), s. 17 (3).

[61] 1957 Act, s. 13 (1) (*a*); 1958 Act (N.I.), s. 17 (1).

[62] Or 40 years (30 years in N.I.) from the date when the land has ceased to be foreshore, but remains State or Crown property, 1957, s. 13 (1) (*b*) and (*c*); 1958, s. 17 (2). Note also the Public Authorities Protection Act, 1893, repealed in the Republic by the Public Authorities (Judicial Proceedings) Act, 1954, s. 2, and in Northern Ireland by the Law Reform (Misc.Prov.) Act (N.I.), 1954, ss. 3, 9 (2) and Sched. See *Carroll* v. *Kildare C.C.* [1950] I.R. 258; *Donovan* v. *Minister for Justice* (1951) 85 I.L.T.R. 134; *McDowell* v. *Lynch* [1952] I.R. 264.

[63] 1957 Act, ss. 27 and 28; 1958 Act (N.I.), ss. 31 and 32. *Re Bryan's Estate* [1941] I.R. 446.

[64] (1975) Unrep. (H.C.,R.I.). In *Murphy* v. *Murphy* [1980] I.R. 183 (see *A Casebook on Irish Land Law* (1984), p. 696) the Republic's Supreme Court emphasised that the question whether or not the person in possession of land was in *adverse* possession is ultimately a question of fact (see also para. 23.22, *infra*.). In that case the claimant had farmed his mother's land for many years and had mortgaged them to a bank. (See also *Re Skelton* [1976] N.I. 132). The issue of what acts amount to adverse possession has also given rise to some dispute amongst English judges recently, see *Wallis's Cayton Bay Holiday Camp Ltd.* v. *Shell-Mex and B.P. Ltd.* [1975] Q.B. 94; *Treloar* v. *Nute* [1976] 1 W.L.R. 1295. See also the criticisms of some aspects of these decisions by the English Law Reform Committee, 21st Report, paras. 3.49-52 and now for England, Limitation Act, 1980, Sched. 1, para. 8 (4) (replacing s. 4 of the Limitation Amendment Act, 1980) and, for N.I., Art. 7 of the Limitation Amendment (N.I.) Order, 1982. See also *McDonnell* v. *McKinty* (1847) 10 Ir.L.R. 514.

and from there on to the road. The draining and manuring of the land was consistent with a licence to use the lands for grazing and the collection of money from the campers was what would be expected when a person had the grazing of the lands and lived near them. Any person seeking permission to camp would naturally assume that the person whose cattle were on the lands was the owner. The property was of little value and the only way that [the owners] could use the lands was by walking on them and I accept the evidence that [one of the owners] walked over the lands on a number of occasions."

Since the squatter has a title based on his possession which is good against everyone except the dispossessed owner, he can pass this title to others. Thus a squatter in the process of barring the true owner by adverse possession, *e.g.*, 10 years' possession, can pass his interest in the land to someone else who can add the 10 years' possession to his own, *i.e.*, after another 2 years' possession he completes the acquisition of ownership by adverse possession.[65]

23.22. It is also established that the adverse possession may take place without either party being aware of it.[66] Generally there is no relief for mistake and, indeed, the doctrine is often used to settle boundary disputes arising from some earlier mistake in the true line of the boundary between adjoining properties, which comes to light later only when a conveyance of one of them is being made.[67]

There may be special circumstances present, however, which will affect the running of the limitation period.

1. *Postponement of Period*

The date from which the limitation period begins to run may be postponed because of the existence of a disability, fraud or mistake.

(i) **Disability**

23.23. In the case of a person under a disability,[68] *e.g.*, an infant[69] or person of unsound mind,[70] the limitation period may be extended to 6 years after that person ceases to be under the disability or dies, whichever happens first, even though the normal period has expired.[71] However, in the case of land there is a limit of 30 years from the date the action accrued.[72]

---

[65] *Asher* v. *Whitlock* (1865) L.R. 1 Q.B. 1; *Wallis* v. *Howe* [1893] 2 Ch. 545.

[66] *Murphy* v. *Murphy* [1980] I.R. 183 (see *A Casebook on Irish Land Law* (1984), p. 696). See Brady, "Adverse Possession in Particular Circumstances" (1982) 4 D.U.L.J. (N.S.) 79.

[67] *Re Vernon's Estate* [1901] 1 I.R. 1. See also *Cartledge* v. *Jopling & Sons Ltd.* [1963] A.C.758. See further, para. 23.25, *infra*.

[68] 1957 Act, s. 48; 1958 Act (N.I.) s. 49.

[69] *Lambert* v. *Browne* (1871) I.R. 5 C.L. 218; *Jennings* v. *Coughlan* (1927) 61 I.L.T.R. 122; *Currie* v. *Fairy Hill Ltd.* [1968] I.R. 232.

[70] *Re P.M.K.* [1944] I.R. 107; *Re R.* [1941] Ir.Jur.Rep. 67; *Re J.S.* [1941] I.R. 378; *Re Waters* [1945] I.R. 484; *Re Noblett* [1946] I.R. 155; *Re Nixon* [1949] Ir.Jur.Rep. 37; *Re Dowd* [1960] Ir.Jur.Rep. 64; *Re Gill* [1964] I.R. 143.

[71] 1957 Act, s. 49 (1) (*a*); 1958 Act (N.I.), s. 50 (1).

[72] 1957 Act, s. 49 (1) (*d*); 1958 Act (N.I.), s. 50 (4).

(ii) Fraud

23.24. The general rule is that, if the action is based on the defendant's or his agent's fraud or if any fact relevant to the plaintiff's right of action has been deliberately concealed from him by the defendant or his agent, time does not begin to run until the plaintiff discovers the fraud or could with reasonable diligence discover it.[73] However, a plea of fraud will not postpone the running of time where the property has been purchased for valuable consideration, by a person who was not a party to the fraud and did not at the time of the purchase know or have reason to believe that any fraud had been committed.[74]

(iii) Mistake

23.25. As mentioned above, the general rule is that mistake does *not* stop time running [75] and squatter's rights are often acquired by such means, *e.g.*, where neighbouring landowners make a mistake as to where the boundary lies between their adjoining lands. However, where the action in question is for relief from the consequences of mistake, time does not run until the plaintiff discovers the mistake, or could have done so with reasonable diligence.[76] In the case of land, relief for mistake usually involves an application for *equitable* relief, *i.e.*, rescission[77] or rectification,[78] and as such is not subject to the Statute of Limitations anyway. Like all equitable relief, on the other hand, it is subject to the doctrine of *laches*.[79]

2. *Fresh Accrual*

In certain cases time may start running afresh.

(i) Acknowledgment

23.26. Time may start afresh and run from the date of a written and signed acknowledgment by or on behalf of the defendant of the plaintiff's title.[80] No particular form of acknowledgment, however, is laid down and it may be inferred from the actions of the party concerned.[81]

(ii) Part Payment

23.27. Time may also begin to run afresh where payment of part of the

---

[73] 1957 Act, s. 71 (1); 1958 Act (N.I.), s. 70 (1). See the discussion of fraudulent concealment by Carroll J. in *Morgan* v. *Park Developments Ltd.* [1983] I.L.R.M. 156. Brady and Kerr, *The Limitation of Actions in the Republic of Ireland* (1984), pp. 50-2 and 108.

[74] 1957 Act, s. 71 (2); 1958 Act (N.I.), s. 70 (2).

[75] *Re Jones's Estate* [1914] 1 I.R. 188.

[76] 1957 Act, s. 72 (1); 1958 Act (N.I.), s. 71 (1).

[77] Para. 3.157, *ante*.

[78] Para. 3.162, *ante*.

[79] Para. 3.066, *ante*.

[80] 1957 Act, ss. 50-60; 1958 Act (N.I.), ss. 51-60. *Johnston* v. *Smith [1896] 2 I.R. 82; Re Mathew's Estate* (1904) 38 I.L.T.R. 246; *Howard* v. *Hennessy* [1947] I.R. 336.

[81] *Hobson* v. *Burns* (1850) 13 Ir.L.R. 286; *Re Deeney* [1933] N.I. 80; *Re Mitchell's Estate* [1943] I.R. 74; *Hart* v. *Carswell* [1973] N.I. 15.

principal or interest due in respect of a debt is made to or for the account of the person whose title is being barred.[82]

It is important to note, however, that, once the full limitation period has run in respect of land, no acknowledgment or part payment can revive any action to recover the land. This was the change first introduced by the Real Property Limitation Act, 1833,[83] namely that not only is the remedy to recover the land barred but the title to it is also barred.[84] The opposite position remains with respect to other actions, *e.g.*, for debts. Thus an acknowledgment or part payment by a mortgagor in favour of his mortgagee, after time has run, revives the mortgagor's liability on his personal covenant for the debt, but does not revive the mortgagee's security on the mortgagor's land.[85]

C. PARTICULAR CASES

We must now examine the operation of the doctrine of adverse possession in particular cases involving land, both unregistered and registered.

1. *Unregistered Land*

In the case of unregistered land the following are the situations most likely to arise.

(i) Freehold in Possession

23.28. This is the straightforward case where the only problem is the basic question of whether or not the squatter on such land obtains a transfer of the freeholder or leaseholder's title. This matter we discussed at length earlier in the chapter.

(ii) Leases

23.29. The position of a squatter on leasehold land was also discussed earlier. Time does not run against the freehold reversioner until the lease ends, *e.g.*, by expiry or forfeiture by the reversioner.[86]

23.30. As between a tenant and his landlord, there can be no adverse possession by the tenant during the currency of the tenancy. He is estopped from denying his landlord's title.[87] Any "encroachment" by the tenant on another person's land generally enures for the landlord's benefit, unless the conduct of the landlord or tenant indicates a contrary intention.[88] Non-

---

[82] 1957 Act, ss. 61-70; 1958 Act (N.I.), ss. 61-9. *McAuliffe* v. *Fitzsimons* (1889) 26 L.R.Ir. 29; *Beamish* v. *Whiting* [1909] 1 I.R. 360; *Re Irwin's Estate* [1907] 1 I.R. 357; *Addiscott* v. *Fagan* [1946] I.R. 194.

[83] Para. 23.04, *ante*.

[84] 1957 Act, s. 24; 1958 Act (N.I.), s. 28. See *Re Field* [1918] 1 I.R. 140.

[85] *Re Conlon's Estate* (1892) 29 L.R.Ir. 199; *Beamish* v. *Whiting* [1909] 1 I.R. 360; *Re Lloyd* [1911] 1 I.R. 153; *Re Lohan* [1936] I.R. 621.

[86] 1957 Act, s. 15 (1); 1958 Act (N.I.) s. 19 (1).

[87] *Cf.* licensees or other occupiers, *e.g.*, caretakers or "service tenants," *Ellis* v. *Crawford* (1842) Long. & Town. 664; *Moore* v. *Doherty* (1842) 5 Ir.L.R. 449; *Musgrave* v. *McAvey* (1907) 41 I.L.T.R. 230.

[88] *Meares* v. *Collis* [1927] I.R. 397. See also *Kingsmill* v. *Millard* (1855) 11 Exch. 313; *Att.-Gen.* v. *Tomline* (1880) 15 Ch.D. 150; *King* v. *Smith* [1950] 1 All E.R. 553.

payment of rent for six years merely bars the landlord's right to the rent[89] and does not destroy his title to the land. Similarly, failure to exercise a right of re-entry under a forfeiture clause bars the right after 12 years,[90] but the landlord's title remains and he can still claim possession on expiration of the lease. However, if the tenant holding under a lease, reserving of rent of at least £1, pays the rent to a person wrongfully claiming to be the immediate reversioner, this is equivalent to adverse possession against the true reversioner and his title is barred after 12 years.[91]

23.31. In the case of a tenancy at will, time runs against the landlord in favour of the tenant after one year, or earlier determination of the tenancy,[92] unless rent is paid or a written acknowledgment is made.[93] Time runs against the landlord from the beginning of a "tenancy" at sufferance, since this is really adverse possession without the landlord's consent.[94] Yearly or other periodic tenancies are in a similar position to tenancies at will, provided there is no lease, i.e., the tenancy is deemed to determine after the first year or other period of the tenancy.[95] However, if rent is subsequently received, time runs from the date of the last receipt.[96]

(iii) Future Interests

23.32. The general rule is that in the case of a future interest, whether in reversion or remainder, time runs from the date on which the future interest falls into possession by determination of the preceding estate.[97] However, if the previous owner[98] has been dispossessed, the reversioner or remainderman must sue within 12 years from the adverse possession or 6 years from his own interest vesting in possession, [99] whichever is the longer.[1] This alternative 6 year period is not available to a reversioner or remainderman entitled upon determination of an entail in possession, whose estate or interest might have been barred by the tenant in tail.[2]

---

[89] 1957 Act, s. 28; 1958 Act (N.I.), s. 32.

[90] 1957 Act, s. 16; 1958 Act (N.I.), s. 20.

[91] 1957 Act, s. 17 (3); 1958 Act (N.I.), s. 21 (5).

[92] 1957 Act, s. 17 (1); 1958 Act (N.I.), s. 21 (1). See the discussion by the Republic's Supreme Court in *Bellew* v. *Bellew* [1982] I.R. 447. See also *Woodhouse* v. *Hooney* [1915] 1 I.R. 296; *Trappe* v. *Halpin* (1928) 62 I.L.T.R. 15; *McAuliffe* v. *Irish Sailors and Soldiers Land Trust* [1959] I.R. 78. No mortgagor or beneficiary is to be deemed a tenant at will to his mortgagee or trustee, 1957 Act, s. 17 (1) (c); 1958 Act (N.I.), s. 21 (2). *Cf.* guests, *Peakin* v. *Peakin* [1895] 2 I.R. 359; *Jennings* v. *Coughlan* (1927) 61 I.L.T.R. 122.

[93] Para. 23.26, *ante*.

[94] Para. 4.012, *ante*.

[95] 1957 Act, s. 17 (2) (a); 1958 Act (N.I.), s. 21 (3). In *Jessamine Investment Co.* v. *Schwartz* [1978] Q.B. 264, the English Court of Appeal held that a weekly tenancy was a "tenancy from year to year or other period" and time continued to run against the reversioner even though that contractual tenancy was transformed into a statutory tenancy under the Rent Acts.

[96] 1957 Act, s. 17 (2) (b); 1958 Act (N.I.), s. 21 (4).

[97] 1957 Act, s. 15 (1); 1958 Act (N.I.), s. 19 (1). *Barcroft* v. *Murphy* [1896] 1 I.R. 590; *Blake* v. *Bracken* (1901) 1 N.I.J.R. 246.

[98] Unless he holds a "term of years absolute" (R.I.) or "leasehold estate or interest" (N.I.).

[99] 30 and 12 years respectively where the State or Crown is the reversioner or remainderman, 1957 Act, s. 15 (2) (b); 1958 Act (N.I.), s. 19 (3).

[1] 1957 Act, s. 15 (2) (a); 1958 Act (N.I.), s. 19 (2). *Re Keone's Estate* (1905) 5 N.I.J.R. 145.

[2] 1957 Act, s. 15 (3); 1958 Act (N.I.), s. 19 (4).

(iv) Mortgages

23.33. A mortgagor's right to redeem is barred if the mortgagee has been in possession for 12 years, without acknowledgment of the mortgagor's title or receiving part payment on account of principal or interest.[3] Where a mortgagee takes possession (which is rare), it is a temporary measure to ensure payment of interest or preservation of the value of his security and he is liable to account strictly to the mortgagor.[4] Thus in this case there is an exception to the rule that time does not run unless there is "adverse" possession[5] and, if there is a mortgage by demise, an exception to the rule that a lessee cannot bar his lessor's title.[6]

23.34. So far as the mortgagee's rights to enforce his security are concerned, his right of action for sale of the land or to sue for possession is barred after 12 years from the date where repayment became due and his title is extinguished.[7] His right to sue for recovery of principal is also barred after 12 years and thereafter his right to recover principal or interest is extinguished.[8] The period is 6 years in respect of arrears of interest.[9] If an action is brought to realise the amount due on a mortgage by a sale of the property, other mortgagees may prove their claims in the action, as it is regarded as being for the benefit of all incumbrancers. Since it is so regarded, the order for sale normally stops the Statute of Limitations running against all persons who could prove in the action and, in this sense, the order might enure for the benefit of all incumbrancers.[10] However, it seems that the action enures for the benefit only of those mortgagees who prove their claims in the action. The Statute continues to run against those who do not do so.

23.35. It has also been held that, where a third party is in adverse possession against the mortgagor when the mortgage is created, title so acquired against the mortgagor is also valid against the mortgagee, notwithstanding an action by him in respect of principal or interest within the limitation period.[11]

---

[3] 1957 Act, ss. 33, 34 (1) (*a*), 54 and 64; 1958 Act (N.I.), ss. 36 (1), 37, 54 and 63. *Re Huddleston's Estate* [1920] 1 I.R. 29. Where under a Welsh mortgage (ch. 13, *ante*) the rents and profits received by the mortgagee in possession are to be applied in reduction of principal and interest, the mortgagor is barred 12 years after he knows the principal and interest have been satisfied, 1957 Act, s. 34 (2); 1958 Act (N.I.), s. 36 (2). *Shields* v. *Shields* (1904) 38 I.L.T.R. 188; *Johnston* v. *Moore* (1904) 4 N.I.J.R. 218; *Fenton* v. *Walsh* (1909) 43 I.L.T.R. 54; *Re Cronin* [1914] 1 I.R. 23.
[4] Ch. 13, *ante*. See *Forster* v. *Forster* [1918] 1 I.R. 95.
[5] Para. 23.05, *supra*. See also *1971 Survey (N.I.)*, para. 416.
[6] Para. 23.30, *supra*.
[7] 1957 Act, ss. 32 and 33; 1958 Act (N.I.), ss. 34 and 35. Once again the period is 30 years in the case of the State or Crown, *ibid.*, but 12 years is the period for rights of residence (ch. 20, *ante*), 1957 Act, ss. 40 and 41; 1958 Act (N.I.), ss. 42 and 43.
[8] 1957 Act, ss. 36 and 39; 1958 Act (N.I.), ss. 38 and 41. The period is 30 years for certain mortgages, *e.g.*, those payable into the Church Temporalities Fund (ch.6, *ante*), 1957 Act, s. 36 (1) (*b*); 1958 Act (N.I.), s. 38 (2).
[9] 1957 Act, s. 37; 1958 Act (N.I.), s. 39. *Re Howlin's Estate* (1906) 40 I.L.T.R. 207; *Re Finnegan's Estate* [1906] 1 I.R. 370; *Harpur* v. *Buchanan* [1919] 1 I.R. 1; *Re Huggard's Estate* [1930] I.R. 532.
[10] *Bennett* v. *Bernard* (1849) 12 Ir.Eq.R. 229; *Harpur* v. *Buchanan* [1919] 1 I.R. 1; *Royal Bank of Ireland* v. *Sproule* [1940] Ir.Jur.Rep. 33.
[11] *Eyre* v. *Walsh* (1859) 10 I.C.L.R. 346; *Munster and Leinster Bank Ltd.* v. *Croker* [1940] I.R. 185. *Cf. Halpin* v. *Cremin* [1954] I.R. 19 (adverse possession before "crystallisation" of floating debenture charge).

(v) Co-Ownership

23.36. The pre-1833 rule that possession by one co-owner, *i.e.*, joint tenant, tenant in common or co-parcener, was deemed to be possession of them all, so that there could be no adverse possession unless there was some additional "ouster,"[12] no longer applies.[13]

(vi) Younger Brother

23.37. The pre-1833 rule that possession by a younger brother or other relation was deemed to be possession by the heir to any land has also been abolished,[14] though it should be noted that the law of inheritance no longer applies (except to a fee tail) in either part of Ireland.

(vii) Trusts

23.38. The general rule is that the 12-year period of limitation applies to equitable estates in land,[15] including interests in the proceeds of the sale of land under a trust for sale, in the same manner as it applies to legal estates in land.[16] However, a stranger in adverse possession of trust property does not bar the trustees' legal title until *all* the beneficiaries' equitable interests are barred.[17]

As a general rule trustees cannot bar their own beneficiaries' rights to the trust property, though there is a 6-year period of limitation laid down for actions to recover trust property, or for any breach of trust, where no other period is prescribed.[18] But this does not apply to claims against trustees founded on fraud or fraudulent breach of trust or to recover trust property or its proceeds still retained by the trustees or previously received by them and converted to their own use.[19] In these cases the trustee can never bar the beneficiaries' rights.

23.39. So far as adverse possession by a beneficiary is concerned, it is provided that time does not run in favour of a beneficiary in possession of settled land, or land held on trust for sale, as against the trustees or other beneficiaries.[20] However, adverse possession can occur where the beneficiary

---

[12] *O'Sullivan* v. *McSweeny* (1840) 2 Ir.L.R. 89, (1841) Long. & Town. 111; *Scott* v. *Knox* (1841) 4 Ir.Eq.R. 397.

[13] See now 1957 Act, s. 21; 1958 Act (N.I.), s. 25. *Re Dane's Estate* (1871) I.R. 5 Eq. 498; *Hawkesworth* v. *Ryan* (1902) 36 I.L.T.R. 238; *Broome* v. *Lundy* (1906) 40 I.L.T.R. 88, Battersby, "Adverse Possession and Concurrent Owners of Land" (1971) 35 Conv. 6. See also *Re McCann* (1966) 17 N.I.L.Q. 292; *Fagan* v. *McParland* (1977) 28 N.I.L.Q. 201.

[14] See now 1957 Act, s. 22; 1958 Act (N.I.), s. 26.

[15] 1957 Act, s. 25 (1); 1958 Act (N.I.), s. 29 (1).

[16] See definition of "land" in 1957 Act, s. 2 (1); 1958 Act, s. 74 (1).

[17] 1957 Act, s. 25 (2); 1958 Act (N.I.), s. 29 (2).

[18] 1957 Act, s. 43; 1958 Act (N.I.), s. 44. As regards personal representatives who may also be trustees, see ch. 16, *ante*.

[19] 1957 Act, s. 44; 1958 Act (N.I.), s. 45. *Clarke* v. *Crowley* (1930) 64 I.L.T.R. 1.

[20] 1957 Act, s. 25 (4); 1958 Act (N.I.), s. 29 (4). *Commrs. of Charitable Donations and Bequests* v. *Wybrants* (1845) 7 Ir.Eq.R. 580; *Re Drake's Estate* [1909] 1 I.R. 136; *McAuliffe* v. *Irish Sailors and Soldiers Land Trust* [1959] I.R. 78; *Fagan* v. *McParland* (1977) 28 N.I.L.Q. 201. Goodman, "Adverse Possession by a Cestui Que Trust – A Renewed Plea" (1965) 29 Conv. 356.

in possession is solely and absolutely entitled to the property, *e.g.*, where a purchaser under an uncompleted contract for the sale of land[21] takes possession.[22] Presumably the usual 12-year period of limitation applies in such cases.[23]

(viii) Deceased Persons' Estates

23.40. This is a subject upon which there has been much litigation in Ireland, partly due to the emigration of younger people from rural areas. It is very common on the death of a farmer[24] for his will to remain unproved or for no letters of administration of his estate to be taken out, and for his widow and one of his sons to continue living on the farm regardless of the rights of absent beneficiaries or next-of-kin entitled to distributive shares on intestacy. In these situations the rights of the various parties often can be determined only by the doctrine of adverse possession. Until recently in both parts of Ireland, the limitation period in respect of estates of deceased persons was 12 years, with 6 years for recovery of arrears of interest on a legacy,[25] excluding actions against personal representatives for fraud.[26] This remains the case in Northern Ireland, but in the Republic these periods have been reduced to 6 years and 3 years respectively and the exclusion for fraud actions repealed.[27]

23.41. Until recently, there were difficulties about the position of personal representatives, if they, as is often the case, are left in possession of the land. Generally personal representatives are trustees for the beneficiaries entitled under the deceased's will or his intestate successors, as the case may be.[28] For some time the Irish courts held that a personal representative entering into possession could not, as express trustee, bar the claims of beneficiaries or intestate successors.[29] Then the Northern Ireland Court of Appeal in *McNeill* v. *McNeill*[30] and the Republic's Supreme Court in *Vaughan* v. *Cottingham*[31] held that, despite their position as trustees under the law of devolution, personal representatives could bar the claims of beneficiaries or intestate successors by adverse possession. This view has now been confirmed by legislation in both parts of Ireland, which provides that a personal representative *in his capacity as personal representative* is not a trustee for the purposes of the Statute of Limitations.[32] In the Republic, legislation has also

---

[21] For whom the vendor is a constructive trustee, ch. 9, *ante*.

[22] See *Bridges* v. *Mees* [1957] Ch. 475.

[23] See *Re Cussons Ltd.* (1904) 73 L.J.Ch. 296.

[24] So that in most cases the land is registered land. Ch. 21, *ante*.

[25] 1957 Act, s. 45; 1958 Act (N.I.), s. 46.

[26] 1957 Act, s. 46; 1958 Act (N.I.), s. 47.

[27] Succession Act, 1965, s. 126 (substituting a new s. 45 in the 1957 Act) and ss.8 and 9, 2nd Sched., Pt. IV. See *J.H.* v. *W.J.H.* (1979) Unrep. (H.C.,R.I.) (1977 No. 5831 P); *Drohan* v. *Drohan* [1981] I.L.R.M. 473.

[28] Succession Act, 1965, s. 10 (3); Administration of Estates Act (N.I.), s. 2 (3). And under the Trustee Act, 1893, s. 50 and Trustee Act (N.I.), 1958, s. 67, "trust" generally includes the duties of personal representatives for the purposes of those Acts.

[29] *Nugent* v. *Nugent* (1884) 15 L.R.Ir. 321; *Re Laughlin's Application* (1941) 75 I.L.T.R. 24; *Re Loughlin* [1942] I.R. 15. *Cf. Toates* v. *Toates* [1926] 2 K.B. 30. Also *Re McCausland's Trusts* [1908] 1 I.R. 327; *Owens* v. *McGarry* [1948] I.R. 226. And *Molony* v. *Molony* [1894] 2 I.R. 1.

[30] [1957] N.I. 10, followed in *Re Hughes* [1974] N.I. 83. See also *Fagan* v. *McParland* (1977) 28 N.I.L.Q. 201.

[31] [1961] I.R. 184. See also *Ruddy* v. *Gannon* [1965] I.R. 283 at 292 (*per* O'Dálaigh (C.J.).

[32] 1957 Act, s. 2 (2) (*d*) (as substituted by s. 123 of Succession Act, 1965); 1958 Act (N.I.), s. 47 (1).

overruled the line of Irish authority applying the maxim "once a bailiff always a bailiff" to persons entering into possession of a deceased person's estate.[33] Section 124 of the Succession Act, 1965, now provides that, notwithstanding any rule of law, "trustee" in the Statute of Limitations, 1957, does not include a person whose fiduciary relationship arises merely because he is in possession of a deceased person's property in the capacity of bailiff for another person. This resolves the difficulty of proving a change in the character of the possession to being adverse to the claimant, *e.g.*, where the widow of an intestate runs the farm and her children, who are entitled to distributive shares on the intestacy, never live there.[34] Bailiffship is usually presumed in cases involving land to which an infant[35] or lunatic[36] is entitled. A similar distinction between adverse and non-adverse possession has been drawn as between husband and wife, *e.g.*, on their separation or the husband's desertion leaving the wife in possession.[37]

23.42. A next-of-kin entitled to a share in an intestate's estate may bar the rights of other next-of-kin by adverse possession. Once again this is common in the rural areas of Ireland, where one of a deceased farmer's sons is left to run the farm and the others emigrate or leave home. The Irish courts have generally taken the view, though they have not always been consistent, that next-of-kin in adverse possession acquire title as tenants in common in respect of their own shares, but as joint tenants of the shares of the barred next-of-kin.[38] This rule has now been reversed in the Republic by section 125(1) of the Succession Act, 1965, which provides:

"Where each of two or more persons is entitled to any shares in land comprised in the estate of a deceased person, whether such shares are equal or unequal, and any or all of them enter into possession of the land, then, notwithstanding any rule of law to the contrary, those who enter shall (as between themselves and as between themselves and those (if any) who do not enter) be deemed, for the purposes of the Statute of Limitations, 1957, to have entered and to acquire title by possession as joint tenants (and not as tenants in common) as regards their own respective shares and also as regards the respective shares of those (if any) who do not enter."

This new rule applies whether or not the person entered into possession as

---

[33] *McMahon* v. *Hastings* [1913] 1 I.R. 395; *Rice* v. *Begley* [1920] 1 I.R. 243; *Leonard* v. *Walsh* [1941] I.R. 25. See also *Moloney* v. *Moloney* (1924) 58 I.L.T.R. 81.

[34] See *Re Maguire and McClelland's Contract* [1907] 1 I.R. 393.

[35] *Graham* v. *Chambers* (1902) 2 N.I.J.R. 194; *Re Codd and Pettitt* (1910) 44 I.L.T.R. 193; *McMahon* v. *Hastings* [1913] 1 I.R. 395; *Mallon* v. *McAlea* [1923] 1 I.R. 30; *Ruddy* v. *Gannon* [1965] I.R. 283. *Cf. Re McGee* [1964] Ir.Jur.Rep. 26.

[36] *Smyth* v. *Byrne* [1914] 1 I.R. 53; *Leonard* v. *Walsh* [1941] I.R. 25.

[37] See *McArdle* v. *Gaughran* [1903] 1 I.R. 106; *Keelan* v. *Garvey* [1925] 1 I.R. 1; *Re Daily* [1944] N.I. 1; *Re Downey* (1946) 80 I.L.T.R. 44; *Re McCann* (1966) 17 N.I.L.Q. 292. See also *Murland* v. *Despard* [1956] I.R. 170; *O'Shea* v. *O'Shea* (1966) 100 I.L.T.R. 16.

[38] *Coyle* v. *McFadden* [1901] 1 I.R. 298; *Martin* v. *Kearney* (1902) 36 I.L.T.R. 117; *Morteshed* v. *Morteshed* (1902) 36 I.L.T.R. 142; *Smith* v. *Savage* [1906] 1 I.R. 469; *Tobin* v. *Brett* (1906) 40 I.L.T.R. 249; *Re Christie* [1917] 1 I.R. 17; *cf. Ward* v. *Ward* (1871) 6 Ch. App. 789.

personal representative of the deceased,[39] or, having entered, was subsequently granted representation of the deceased's estate.[40]

Once the limitation period has run, subsequent taking out of representation of the deceased's estate generally does not affect the title acquired by the adverse possession.[41]

2. Registered Land

23.43. In view of the numerous applications of the doctrine of adverse possession to farm land in Ireland, it is hardly suprising that the Local Registration of Title (Ireland) Act, 1891, preserved the doctrine in relation to registered land, which agricultural land has become.[42] Section 52 provided that, once the title to the land was registered,[43] the right to be registered as owner in derogation of the registered owner's title could not be acquired by "mere possession," but the possessor was given the right to apply for a court order declaring his title and for rectification of the register accordingly. The court could make such an order only "if satisfied that such title would have been acquired but for the provisions of this [1891] Act." The problem about this condition was that it appeared to import the rules relating to unregistered land and, in particular, the rule, recently confirmed by the House of Lords and the Republic's Supreme Court, that there is no parliamentary conveyance of the previous owner's title to the squatter.[44] Yet the Irish judges have adopted the practice, which has had to be followed by the Land Registries in Dublin and Belfast, of directing that the squatter's title be registered in the *same* folio as the dispossessed owner's title, *i.e.*, as if in effect there had been a conveyance or transfer of title. The predicament of the judges and Registrars was clear, if one considered leasehold land. If the dispossessed lessee's title was not "extinguished" as regards the lessor, how could his registered title be cancelled in the register? If the squatter did not become the new owner of the leasehold title, with what title could he be registered as owner? Fortunately this conundrum was usually solved in respect of leasehold land by regarding the squatter as estopped from denying that he had become an assignee of the lease, and, presumably, his landlord from denying the tenancy.[45]

23.44. It is questionable how far the new registration legislation in both parts of Ireland changes the position, apart from enabling the respective Registrars to deal with applications for rectification of the registers, without the need for reference to the court except in cases of doubt or opposition by

---

[39] *Cf. Re Ryan's Estate* [1960] I.R. 174; *Ruddy* v. *Gannon* [1965] I.R. 283.

[40] S. 125 (2).

[41] *Re McClure and Garrett's Contract* [1899] 1 I.R. 225; *Re Deeny* [1933] N.I. 80; *Brennan* v. *Brennan* [1948] Ir.Jur.Rep. 3; *Re Fallon* (1949) 83 I.L.T.R. 77. *Cf. Duffy* v. *Duffy* [1906] 1 I.R. 205.

[42] Land sold under the Land Purchase Acts was compulsorily registrable, 1891 Act, s. 23.

[43] See *Re Healy* [1947] Ir.Jur.Rep. 24; *Re Greaney* [1956] I.R. 226; *Fagan* v. *McParland* (1977) 28 N.I.L.Q. 201; *Re Skelton* [1976] N.I. 132. *Cf. O'Regan* v. *White* [1919] 2 I.R. 339.

[44] Paras. 23.11-9, *supra.*

[45] Para. 23.13, *supra.* In these cases, the courts and Registries also seem to have resolved the doubts whether s. 52 of the 1891 Act applied to leasehold land at all (see also s. 53), see Wylie, (1965) 16 N.I.L.Q. 467 at 484-5, (1968) 19 N.I.L.Q. 89 at 97-8; *cf.* McAllister, *Registration of Title in Ireland* (1973), p. 95.

one party. Section 49(1) of the Republic's Registration of Title Act, 1964, indeed, introduces the replacement for section 52 of the 1891 Act by providing that, subject to the rest of the section, the Statute of Limitations, 1957 "shall apply to registered land as it applies to unregistered land." This would seem to import the unregistered law laid down by the House of Lords and the Republic's Supreme Court. Subsection (2) then provides that the applicant may be registered "*as owner of the land* with an absolute, good leasehold, possessory or qualified title, as the case may require, but without prejudice to any right not *extinguished* by such possession." Subsection (3) concludes by providing that, on such registration "the title of the person whose right of action to recover the land has expired shall be *extinguished*." The difficulty is to reconcile the words italicised, bearing in mind the general principle enunciated in subsection (1).

23.45. On the one hand, it is arguable that subsection (2) means that the squatter must be registered as the new "owner" of the land, *i.e.*, it effects a parliamentary conveyance which the Statute of Limitations does not do. This seems to have been the view of Walsh J. in the *Perry* case,[46] but, unfortunately, he appears to have been the only Supreme Court judge to have adverted to the point. This is certainly in line with the Dublin Registry's practice under the 1891 Act and seems to have been the view adopted in drafting the rules made under the 1964 Act.[47] The doubt remains, however, about the use in subsections (2) and (3) of the key word in the Statute of Limitations, *i.e.*, "extinguished," which, taken with subsection (1), still seems to import the rules of unregistered land. And the last clause of subsection (2) seems to be a precise description of the lessor's right of forfeiture for breach of covenant *by the dispossessed lessee*, which the Supreme Court held in *Perry* was a risk which would continue to affect the squatter's interest for the remainder of the term of the lease. One cannot help concluding that this matter would have been better settled if the word "cancelled" had been substituted for "extinguished" in subsection (3).[48]

23.46. It is arguable that section 53 of the Land Registration Act (N.I.), 1970, leaves the same lingering doubt. Subsection (1) enunciates the same general principle that the Statute of Limitations (N.I.), 1958 applies to registered land as it applies to unregistered land. Subsection (2), however, does not use the word "extinguished" and, instead, speaks of a "defeasance of an estate in any registered land" and of a person claiming to have acquired a "right by possession to be registered as owner of an estate in that land." Such a person may apply for registration of "the title to that estate." This seems to contemplate a transfer of title, but, then, subsection (4) introduces

---

[46] Para. 23.16, *supra*. But see now on the English Land Registry system, *Spectrum Investment Co.* v. *Holmes* [1981] 1 W.L.R. 221.

[47] See 1972, rr. 17 and 46 and Sched. Form 5, which requires a declaration from the applicant that he is "entitled for [his] own benefit to the fee simple interest in the property (*or, otherwise as the case may be*) and [he is] not aware of any contract or agreement for sale, or of any mortgage, charge, lease, agreement for lease, restrictive covenant, or incumbrance . . . affecting the property." In the *Perry* case, the leasehold squatter was held to be subject to the lease remaining on foot as between the dispossessed lessee and lessor.

[48] *Cf.* s. 32 (rectification of errors, issue of new land certificate and cancellation of old certificate).

the doubt by providing that the registration is not "to prejudice any estate of any other person in the land to which the application relates, being an estate which is not *extinguished* by operation of the said Statute."[49]

[49] See Wallace, *Land Registry Practice in Northern Ireland* (1981), pp. 54-6. See also *McLean and Another* v. *McErlean* [1983] N.I. 258.

CHAPTER 24

MERGER

24.01. The second main way in which estates in land are extinguished is by merger.[1] This occurs when a greater estate in land comes into the hands of the holder of a lesser estate in the same piece of land, because then the lesser estate merges into the greater estate and is destroyed by operation of law.[2] Where the lesser interest in the land is not an estate but is an interest or incumbrance only, such as a mortgage or charge, the doctrine is often referred to as extinguishment rather than merger,[3] though the latter term is also used sometimes to cover estates *and* interests in land.[4]

24.02. Another distinction which is sometimes drawn is that between merger and surrender of estates in land. The modern view seems to be that surrender occurs where the holder of the greater estate acquires a lesser estate in the same land, *e.g.,* where the landlord buys in the lease on his own property.[5] Merger occurs where the holder of the lesser estate acquires the greater one or where some third party acquires both the greater and lesser estates.[6] At common law this distinction was based on the view that merger occurred by operation of law, regardless of the intention of the parties, whereas surrender was regarded as an act of the parties and to that extent based on their intentions. However, since, as we shall see, merger in equity has always been based on the intention of the parties and this view now applies to legal estates as well, the distinction between merger and surrender may have little practical significance.[7] In both cases, the lesser estate or interest is extinguished.

24.03. The present law of merger must be considered in the light of the different approaches of the common law and equity to the subject. This point was well-summarised by Andrews L.J. in *McIlvenny* v. *McKeever*[8]–

---

[1] See Mayhew, *Merger* (1861); Challis, *Law of Real Property* (3rd ed., 1911) ch. X, *Irish Supp.*, (1956), A 5-6. Also the discussion in *Re Toppin's Estate* [1915] 1 I.R. 330 (see *A Casebook on Irish Land Law* (1984), p. 703); *McIlvenny* v. *McKeever* [1931] N.I. 161; *Re Sergie* [1954] N.I. 1. And para. 17.105, *ante*. Robinson, "Merger and Systems of Title of Land by Registration" (1973) 37 Conv. 342. Note also the operation of the doctrine of merger in relation to conveyancing contracts, see *Irish Conveyancing Law* (1978), ch. 19.

[2] *Lemon* v. *Mark* [1899] 1 I.R. 416.

[3] Challis, *op.cit.*, p. 88. *Dixon* v. *Rowan* (1859) 9 Ir.Ch.R. 365; *Re Toppin's Estate* [1915] 1 I.R. 330 (see *A Casebook on Irish Land Law* (1984), p. 703).

[4] See, *e.g., Re Bury's Estate* [1898] 1 I.R. 379 (mortgages); *Re Lloyd's Estate* [1903] 1 I.R. 144 (charges); *Re Alexander's Estate* [1938] I.R. 23 (charges).

[5] Para. 17.084, *ante*.

[6] This distinction was recognised in *Hartnett* v. *Power* (1836) 2 Jones 145.

[7] Note, however, the distinction in operation mentioned in Challis, *op.cit.*, p. 88 (see also *Coke upon Littleton* (19th ed., 1832), 183a) in the following situation. If X and Y are joint tenants in fee simple of Blackacre, holding subject to Z's life estate in Blackacre, and Z *surrenders* his life estate to X only, the life estate will be destroyed and leave X and Y as joint tenants in fee simple in possession. If, instead, Z *grants* or *assigns* his life estate to X, it seems that only one moiety of it will merge in X's moiety of the fee simple, leaving X holding the other moiety as an estate *pur autre vie* with the reversion in Y, *i.e.,* the merger effects a severance of the joint tenancy in the fee simple.

[8] [1931] N.I. 161.

"At law when two estates—a greater and a lesser—become vested in the same person and in the same right without any intervening estate between them, the lesser estate merged as a necessary consequence in the greater, wholly irrespective of any question of intention. But equity has long since relaxed the rigour of the law and has looked to the intent, either actual or presumed, of the person in whom the interests have become united."[9]

I. COMMON LAW

The attitude of the common law was a purely formal or technical one. Provided the requisite conditions were satisfied, a merger occurred regardless of the intention of the parties concerned. The first question to arise, therefore, is what these conditions were.

A. CONDITIONS

The following were the main conditions for merger required at common law.

1. *Unity of Possession*

24.04. The first condition was that the two estates in the same land had to come into the ownership or possession of the same person.[10] There would be no merger if there was a *vested* intervening estate between the two estates in question.[11] For example, if land was settled on X for life, remainder to Y for life, remainder to Z in fee simple, there would be no merger at common law if X purchased Z's remainder. Y's vested intervening life estate prevented such a merger. On the other hand, if the intervening estate was not vested, but was contingent only,[12] this did not prevent merger at common law.[13] If the two vested estates came into the same hands at the same time as the creation of the intervening contingent estate, *e.g.,* under the terms of the original settlement, the merger was not permanent. It remained liable to open again to let in the intervening estate when and if it became vested.[14]

2. *Same Right*

24.05. The second condition for merger at common law was that the two estates must come into the same person's possession in the same right or capacity. There was no merger if he possessed one estate in his own right and the other in another capacity, *e.g.,* personal representative of another person.[15]

[9] *Ibid.*, p. 176. See also *Craig* v. *Greer* [1899] 1 I.R. 258 at 272 (*per* Chatterton V.-C.) (see *A Casebook on Irish Land Law* (1984), p. 616).
[10] *Cf. Hurley* v. *Hurley* [1910] 1 I.R. 86 at 90 (*per* Holmes L.J.) (see *A Casebook on Irish Land Law* (1984), p. 701).
[11] *Dixon* v. *Rowan* (1859) 9 Ir.Ch.R. 365.
[12] Ch. 5, *ante.*
[13] *Lemon* v. *Mark* [1899] 1 I.R. 416. See also *Bower* v. *Eccles* (1823) Rowe 466.
[14] *Lemon* v. *Mark, op. cit.*, p. 445 (*per* Walker L.J.).
[15] *Hurley* v. *Hurley* [1910] 1 I.R. 86 (see *A Casebook on Irish Land Law* (1984), p. 701). See also *Chambers* v. *Kingham* (1878) 10 Ch.D. 743.

3. *Both Legal*

24.06. It would appear that the two estates to be merged had to be both legal estates. No merger took place where one was legal and one was equitable.[16] In *Re Sergie*,[17] the Northern Ireland Court of Appeal held that a legal lease for a term of 10,000 years did not merge in an equitable fee simple.[18]

B. EXAMPLES

The following are examples of situations where merger was held to occur at common law.

1. *Greater and Lesser Freeholds*

24.07. A lesser freehold estate such as a life estate merged in a greater freehold estate, *i.e.*, a fee simple or fee tail.[19] In *Hartnett* v. *Power*,[20] it was held that a lease for lives renewable for ever merged in a base fee.

2. *Fees Tail*

24.08. At common law, a fee tail estate did not merge in a fee simple reversion or remainder.[21] This was regarded as being contrary to the policy of *De Donis*, 1285,[22] since it would mean that the owner of a fee tail could defeat the issue in tail by acquiring the fee simple.[23] However, section 37 of the Fines and Recoveries (Ireland) Act, 1834, provided that, where the holder of a base fee acquires the fee simple reversion or remainder,[24] though no merger occurs, the base fee is enlarged into as large an estate as a tenant in tail, with the consent of the protector, might have created by a disposition under the 1834 Act, if such remainder had been vested in any other person, *i.e.*, the fee simple absolute free from any incumbrances on the reversion or remainder.[25]

3. *Leaseholds*

24.09. The general rule at common law was that a leasehold estate merged in a freehold estate.[26] It was also the rule at common law that merger of a

---

[16] *Stoney* v. *Saunders* (1833) Hay. & Jon. 519 (*equitable* fee tail and *legal* fee simple).

[17] [1954] N.I. 1 (see *A Casebook on Irish Land Law* (1984), p. 70).

[18] See Curran L.J. at p. 24 and Black L.J. at pp. 24-5; *cf.* Lord MacDermott L.C.J. (at first instance), who considered merger occurred, on his view that both estates were legal, pp. 5 and 8.

[19] See *Lemon* v. *Mark* [1899] 1 I.R. 416; *Re Toppin's Estate* [1915] 1 I.R. 330 (see *A Casebook on Irish Land Law* (1984), p. 703).

[20] (1836) 2 Jones 145.

[21] *Stoney* v. *Saunders* (1833) Hay. & Jon. 519.

[22] Ch. 4, *ante*.

[23] *Wiscot's Case* (1599) 2 Co.Rep. 60b, 61a.

[24] *E.g.*, in a case of a settlement on A for life, remainder to B in fee tail, remainder to C in fee simple, where B executes a disentailing assurance in favour of X without A's consent (ch.4, *ante*) and X subsequently acquires C's fee simple remainder.

[25] Paras. 4.123 *et seq.*, *ante*.

[26] *Smith* v. *Chichester* (1848) 12 Ir.Eq.R. 519; *Williams* v. *Morris* (1849) 13 Ir.Eq.R. 147; *cf.* *Hurley* v. *Hurley* [1910] 1 I.R. 86 (see *A Casebook on Irish Land Law* (1984), p. 701). *Cf.* *McIlvenny* v. *McKeever* [1931] N.I. 161. Note, however, the Irish practice of granting a lease for life combined with a concurrent or reversionary term of years to the same person, ch. 4, *ante*.

head-lease in the head-reversion destroyed covenants contained in any sub-lease supported by the extinguished head-lease.[27] This position was, however, reversed by section 9 of the Real Property Act, 1845, which provided that, where the reversion on a lease is destroyed by surrender or merger, the next vested interest in the land is to be deemed the reversion for the purpose of preserving the incidents and obligations of the reversion destroyed.[28] For example, if L, the fee simple owner, leased land to R for 99 years and R sub-leased the land to S for 21 years, and subsequently P purchased both L and R's interests, so that they merged, P's fee simple is to be treated as the reversion of S's sub-lease so as to make the covenants entered into between R and S enforceable as between P and S.[29] In other words, the merger or surrender of a head-lease operates in effect as an assignment of the reversion on the sub-lease.[30]

4. Equal Estates

24.10. There is some authority for saying that merger at common law is confined to cases where the estates or interests in question are different or of unequal value.[31] In *Creagh* v. *Blood*[32] it was held that a present estate *pur autre vie* did not merge in an estate in remainder for the same *vie*. On the other hand, in *Re Bruen's Estate*,[33] it was held that an assignment of the first life estate to the holder of the second life estate under the same settlement caused a merger so as to confer on the second tenant for life the powers under the Settled Land Acts.

II. EQUITY

24.11. Equity took quite a different approach to the subject of merger and adopted the principle that the matter should be governed by the intention of the parties, in particular the intention of the person acquiring both estates or interests. Thus, in cases where a merger would occur automatically at law, equity would give effect to an intention that the lesser estate or other interest should be kept alive.[34] This intention could either be expressly declared by the person acquiring both estates or interests[35] or could be presumed from his subsequent dealing with the property.[36] In the absence of any clear intention, equity would take the view that the parties intended the result which was the

---

[27] See *Craig* v. *Greer* [1899] 1 I.R. 258 (see *A Casebook on Irish Land Law* (1984), p. 616). Also *Webb* v. *Russell* (1789) 3 Term Rep. 393.

[28] *Per* Chatterton V.-C., *ibid.*, p. 272.

[29] Alternatively, it may be held that no merger takes place in equity since it is against the interest of P to destroy covenants enforceable against S, *per* Chatterton V.-C., *ibid.*

[30] *Survey of the Land Law of Northern Ireland* (1971), para. 297.

[31] See Andrews L.J. in *McIlvenny* v. *McKeever* [1931] N.I. 161 at 176 (para. 24.03, *supra*) ("greater and lesser" estates) and Lord MacDermott L.C.J. in *Re Sergie* [1954] N.I. 1 at 5 ("different" estates or interests).

[32] (1845) 8 Ir.Eq.R. 688.

[33] [1911] 1 I.R. 76.

[34] *Smith* v. *Chichester* (1848) 12 Ir.Eq.R. 519; *Williams* v. *Morris* (1849) 13 Ir.Eq.R. 147.

[35] See *Re Lloyd's Estate* [1903] 1 I.R. 144; *Re Wallace's Estate* [1907] 1 I.R. 91.

[36] *Smith* v. *Smith* (1887) 19 L.R.Ir. 514; *Craig* v. *Greer* [1899] 1 I.R. 258 (see *A Casebook on Irish Land Law* (1984), p. 616); *McIlvenny* v. *McKeever* [1931] N.I. 161. *Cf. Re Lloyd's Estate, op. cit.*; *Re Butlin's Estate* [1907] 1 I.R. 159.

more beneficial to the party acquiring the two estates or interests.[37] Indeed, it seems that equity would presume an intention against merger even if it was a matter of indifference to the party in question whether or not merger occurred, at least in cases of estates in land.[38] There is, however, authority in Ireland for saying that where there is a question of merger destroying incumbranches, *e.g.*, mortgages or charges, merger will still occur so as to extinguish the incumbrances, where it is a matter of indifference to the party whether or not the charges are kept alive.[39]

III. MODERN LAW

24.12. The division between the approaches of the common law and equity has now been dealt with by the Judicature (Ireland) Act, 1877, section 28 (4) of which provides that there shall "not be any merger by operation of law only of any estate, the beneficial interest in which would not be deemed to be merged or extinguished in equity." In Northern Ireland, section 28 (4) of the Judicature (Ireland) Act, 1877, has been replaced by section 89 of the Judicature (Northern Ireland) Act, 1978, which reads: "There is no merger by operation of law only of any estate the beneficial interest in which would not be deemed to be merged or extinguished in equity." The practical effect of these provisions is that nowadays there will still be no merger in any of the situations where the conditions for merger at common law are not met[40] and, even more important, no merger in cases where those conditions are met if there is a contrary intention.

24.13. The modern law may be illustrated by a series of Irish cases dealing with the situation where the same person acquires both an estate in land and a mortgage or charge on that estate. The question arises whether the mortgage or charge is extinguished or merged in the estate and, as mentioned above, the Irish courts have taken the view that the general rule is that the charge is extinguished or merged unless there is a contrary intention.[41] Such a contrary intention may be found in acts of the party in question which are inconsistent with the charge's extinguishment or in express statements.[42] The Irish courts have also held that the circumstances of the case may raise a presumption of an intention to keep the charge alive, *e.g.*, where there are other charges on the estate and merger of the charge paid off by the estate owner might cause him inconvenience by advancing those other charges in priority.[43] It would appear that this presumption of intention to keep the first charge alive will still be raised even though the value of the land is quite sufficient to cover the

---

[37] *Smith* v. *Chichester* (1848) 12 Ir.Eq.R. 519; *Keogh* v. *Keogh* (1874) I.R. 8 Eq. 449.

[38] *Craig* v. *Greer* [1899] 1 I.R. 258.

[39] *Re Bury's Estate* [1898] 1 I.R. 379; *Re Toppin's Estate* [1915] 1 I.R. 330 (see *A Casebook on Irish Land Law* (1984), p. 703).

[40] Paras. 24.04-6, *supra*.

[41] *Smith* v. *Smith* (1887) 19 L.R.Ir. 514; *Re Lloyd's Estate* [1903] 1 I.R. 144; *Re Butlin's Estate* [1907] 1 I.R. 159; *Re Alexander's Estate* [1938] I.R. 23.

[42] *Cf. Re Wallace's Estate* [1907] 1 I.R. 91 with *Re Butlin's Estate, op. cit.*

[43] *Keogh* v. *Keogh* (1874) I.R. 8 Eq. 449; *Re Bury's Estate* [1898] 1 I.R. 379; *Re Burke's Estate* (1904) 38 I.L.T.R. 174.

other charges.[44] On the other hand, if it can be shown that it is a matter of indifference to the party in question whether the charge is kept alive, it will be regarded as being merged or extinguished.[45]

24.14. Another question which has arisen recently relates to pyramid titles so common in Dublin and Belfast, whereby a ground or occupation lessee is a sub- or sub-sub-lessee holding under the same title as his neighbours.[46] The problem has arisen because of the right of enfranchisement given to such a lessee recently in both parts of Ireland.[47] If the ground lessee exercises this right, the higher he proceeds up the pyramid the larger usually the plot of land concerned with the estate at each tier of the pyramid. This was recognised in the recent legislation in both parts of Ireland, hence the provisions for apportionment of rents and covenants between the part of the original plot occupied by the ground lessee and the other parts occupied by his neighbours, who may not wish to enfranchise. Thus, while the ground lessee's interest no doubt merges in the intermediate interest next above him in the pyramid, when he enfranchises, there are difficulties about holding that, as the ground lessee enfranchises further up to the ultimate fee simple, merger occurs between the intermediate interests and the ultimate fee simple. It is arguable that these intermediate interests must survive at least in respect of the other land held under them, including the enfranchising ground lessee's neighbours' lands. Indeed, it is questionable whether merger could occur at common law, since often the area of land held under the respective interests will vary, and it is arguable that it is in the interests of the parties to keep the intermediate interests alive in respect of the other land held under them,[48] though this presumption might be rebutted by an express declaration of merger.[49] In *Craig* v. *Greer*,[50] where a lease for 100 years was made to X, then a sub-lease to Y and then X purchased the fee simple reversion, it was held by the Irish Court of Appeal that there was no merger in equity so as to destroy the sub-lease, since this would deprive X of his right to enforce restrictive covenants contained in the sub-lease against Y. Unfortunately, neither enfranchisement statute in Ireland states clearly what the position is about merger of intermediate and superior interests when the ground lessee "enlarges" his interest into a fee simple.[51]

24.15. An example may make the problem clearer. In 1910 A, the freehold owner, granted to B a lease of 2 acres of land, at a rent of £50 per annum. B subsequently granted three sub-leases of different parts of the land leased in 1910, at rents of £25 in each sub-lease. C, now entitled to one of these sub-leases, serves notice to purchase the interests of A and B in the land

---

[44] See *Re Bayly's Estate* (*No. 2*) [1898] 1 I.R. 383.

[45] *Re Bury's Estate* [1898] 1 I.R. 379; *Re Toppin's Estate* [1915] 1 I.R. 330.

[46] See the illustration given in an earlier chapter, paras. 4.179 *et seq., ante.*

[47] Ch. 18, *ante.*

[48] *Cf.* Real Property Act, 1845, s. 9, para. 24.09, *supra.*

[49] Though if there could be no merger at common law, there will not usually be one in equity.

[50] [1899] 1 I.R. 258.

[51] There is no reference to merger in, *e.g.*, s. 29 of the Republic's Landlord and Tenant (Ground Rents) (No. 2) Act, 1978, nor ss. 1 and 3 of the Leasehold (Enlargement and Extension) Act (N.I.), 1971.

contained in his sub-lease. If he acquires the freehold and the interest in the lease is regarded as merging in the freehold, some strange consequences follow. Since C becomes the freeholder, he cannot be successfully sued, or indeed, sue on, covenants in the lease or sub-leases and so the whole scheme of protection for the entire 2 acres of land originally devised in 1910, which was most likely contained in those covenants, disappears.[52] If, however, the lease is not regarded as merging in the freehold, covenants designed to be enforceable as between the three parts of the original 2 acres will remain enforceable and cross-indemnity agreements backing them up can still be invoked.

---

[52] See further on covenants, ch. 19, *ante*.

PART XI

DISABILITIES

CHAPTER 25

DISABILITIES

25.01. We must now consider the various persons who, under our law, are subject to disabilities in relation to land. To the extent that these persons are still subject to disabilities, they are usually restricted in their powers of holding or making dispositions of the land.

I. INFANTS

25.02. A person remains an infant until he reaches his age of majority.[1] Until recently this point was reached at the first moment of the day *preceding* the twenty-first anniversary of his birth,[2] for the common law did not take account of part of a day and treated any part as a whole day, including the day during which the infant was born.[3] In both parts of Ireland, however, the age of majority has recently been reduced for most purposes to 18 years of age by provisions which give effect to the more common belief that the "time at which a person attains a particular age expressed in years shall . . . be the commencement of the relevant anniversary of the date of his birth."[4] It may also be noted that it is provided that "a person who is not of full age *may* be described as a minor instead of as an infant."[5] The English Latey Committee, which reported on this subject in 1967, considered that it was "quite ludicrous that legally speaking a married man with three children can be referred to as an 'infant'."[6]

A. OWNERSHIP OF LAND

25.03. In both parts of Ireland an infant can hold both legal and equitable

---

[1] See P.R.T., "Infants" (1947) 7 Ir.Jur. 51, "Infants and Children" (1957) 23 Ir.Jur. 40.

[2] The age of 21 years seems to have been adopted by the common law during the middle ages, see the English *Report of the Committee on the Age of Majority* (1967, Cmnd. 3342). The Report resulted in Pt I of the Family Law Reform Act, 1969. See also *Sir Robert Howard's Case* (1700) 2 Salk. 625; *Re Shurey* [1918] 1 Ch. 263.

[3] See *Re Shurey* [1918] 1 Ch. 263.

[4] Age of Majority Act, 1985, ss. 2 (1) and 4 (1) (R.I.); Age of Majority Act (N.I.), 1969, ss. 1 (1) and 5 (1). See Newark, "Age of Majority Act (N.I.) 1969" (1970) 21 N.I.L.Q. 357. The Republic's Law Reform Commission originally proposed reduction of the age of majority to 18 in Working Paper No. 2 (1977), *The Law Relating to the Age of Majority, the Age for Marriage and Some Connected Matters* (reviewed by Duncan, (1979) 30 N.I.L.Q. 89). See also Clarke, "The Contractual Liability of Infants in Irish Law: A Response to the Law Reform Commission" (1978) 72 Gaz. I.L.S.I. 207. The Commission's final recommendations were contained in its *Report on the Law Relating to the Age of Majority, the Age for Marriage and Some Connected Subjects* (L.R.C. 5–1983).

[5] Italics added, 1985 Act, s. 3 (R.I.); 1969 Act (N.I.), s. 7.

[6] *Report of the Committee on the Age of Majority* (1967, Cmnd. 3342). Yet there can still be a seventeen-year-old with triplets!

962

estates and interests in land.[7] However, this has little practical significance because, as we have seen,[8] land to which an infant is entitled in possession, even if absolutely, is declared to be settled land and the infant to be deemed to be tenant for life thereof.[9] Furthermore, the powers of dealing with the land conferred on the tenant for life by the Settled Land Acts, 1882-90, are exercisable on the infant's behalf by the trustees of the settlement and not by the infant himself.[10]

25.04. Because an infant can still technically hold a legal estate in land, he can in both parts of Ireland be appointed, for example, a trustee of the land for another person, but, as this is hardly advisable, it is rarely, if ever, done. It has been held often by the courts that an infant may lack capacity to act as a trustee in terms of judgment and discretion,[11] and this may be a ground for applying to the court for his removal from office.[12] An infant cannot, however, act as personal representative until he reaches his age of majority and obtains a grant from the court empowering him to act. It is provided in both parts of Ireland that, until then, probate of a will will not be granted to an infant who is sole executor of a will and, in the meantime, administration with the will annexed will be granted to his guardian.[13] Until the court grants him probate under this provision, any appointment by a testator of an infant to be an executor does not operate to transfer any interest in the property of the deceased to the infant or constitute him a personal representative for any purpose.[14]

25.05. There appears to be nothing to prevent an infant taking a mortgage of land as security for a loan in Ireland, since he can hold a legal estate.[15] Frequently, however, such a transaction would be of questionable commercial value to the borrower since the infant is in general free to set aside the transaction on attaining his majority.[16]

B. DISPOSITIONS

25.06. The general position with respect to land is that dispositions of an infant's land must be made on his behalf by the trustees of the settlement

[7] *Davis* v. *Cotter* (1837) S. & Sc. 685; *Re Murray* (1842) 5 Ir.Eq.R. 266; *Edgeworth* v. *Edgeworth* (1848) 12 Ir.Eq.R. 81; *Re Porter* (1853) 5 Ir.Jur.(O.S.) 204. *Cf.* the English Law of Property Act, 1925, s. 1 (6). *Survey of the Land Law of Northern Ireland* (1971), paras. 82 and 101-2.
[8] Ch. 8, *ante.*
[9] Settled Land Act, 1882, s. 59.
[10] *Ibid.*, s. 60. *Re Brabason's Estate* [1909] 1 I.R. 209; *Re Locke's Estate* (1913) 47 I.L.T.R. 147; *Re Scally* (1952) 86 I.L.T.R. 171. See discussion in ch. 8, *ante.*
[11] *Hearle* v. *Greenbank* (1749) 3 Atk. 695. *Cf. Re Barry* (1844) 2 Jo. & Lat. 1; *Jones* v. *Ham* (1837) 2 Ir.Eq.R. 65; *Goddard* v. *Macauley* (1844) 6 Ir.Eq.R. 221; *Moore* v. *Grogan* (1846) 9 Ir.Eq.R. 472.
[12] *Re Shelmerdine* (1864) 33 L.J.Ch. 474; *Re Tallatire* [1885] W.N. 191. Infancy is not a specific ground for removal under either s. 10 (1) of the Trustee Act, 1893 or s. 35 (1) of the Trustee Act (N.I.), 1958, para. 10.013, *ante. Cf.* the English Law of Property Act, 1925, s. 20.
[13] Succession Act, 1965, s. 32 (1) (R.I.); Administration of Estates Act (N.I.), 1955, s. 24 (1). *In b. Magrath* [1896] 1 I.R. 203; *Re Thompson and McWilliam's Contract* [1896] 1 I.R. 362; *In b. Gordon* (1898) 32 I.L.T.R. 134; *In b. Wilson* (1902) 36 I.L.T.R. 52.
[14] 1965 Act, s. 32 (2); 1955 Act (N.I.), s. 24 (2). Ch. 16, *ante.*
[15] *Jones* v. *Ham* (1837) 3 Ir.Eq.R. 65; *Hutton* v. *Mayne* (1846) 9 Ir.Eq.R. 343. *Cf.* the English Law of Property Act, 1925, s. 19 (6). See also *National Bank* v. *Gourley* (1886) 17 L.R.Ir. 357; *Re Hurst* (1891) 29 L.R.Ir. 219.
[16] *Blake* v. *Concannon* (1870) I.R. 4 C.L. 323 (see *A Casebook on Irish Land Law* (1984), p. 709).

exercising the powers of a tenant for life under the Settled Land Acts, 1882-90.[17] In this way a binding transaction can be entered into with respect to his land. Apart from this, the infant himself cannot in general make a binding disposition of his land. The rule at common law is that any disposition he makes is *voidable* at his option[18] when he attains his majority,[19] or within a reasonable time thereafter.[20] If he dies before reaching his majority, the disposition is avoidable by his personal representatives.[21] On the other hand, since the disposition is voidable only and not void, it will become binding on the former infant if he fails to repudiate it within a reasonable time after attaining his majority.[22] The courts tend to regard what may appear to be slight acts, *e.g.*, receipt of rent under a tenancy agreement,[23] as ratification of the transaction by the infant so as to make it binding on him.[24]

Apart from these general principles, the following special cases should be noted.

1. *Marriage Settlements*

25.07. The Infant Settlements Act, 1855,[25] enabled an irrevocable marriage settlement[26] to be made with the leave of the court by a male infant of 20 years or more and a female infant of 17 years or more.[27] The 1855 Act has been repealed in both parts of Ireland, where the age of majority has been reduced to 18 years.[28]

2. *Wills*

25.08. In the Republic of Ireland, a will may be made by a person who has attained the age of 18 years or is or has been married.[29] Apart from that a will cannot be made by an infant.

In Northern Ireland, a person who has attained the age of 18 years may now make a will.[30] If he is under that age, the will is valid only if the will is made by

---

[17] Ch. 8, *ante.*

[18] But *not* by his grantee, *Zouch d. Abbot* v. *Parsons* (1765) 3 Burr. 1784.

[19] *Blake* v. *Concannon* (1870) I.R. 4 C.L. 323; *Re Paget's Estate* (1884) 11 L.R.Ir. 26. See also *Ashfield* v. *Ashfield* (1628) W.Jo. 157.

[20] *Carnell* v. *Harrison* [1916] 1 Ch. 328. See also *Re McLoughlin* [1944] I.R. 520 (jurisdiction of court to make orders after infant's majority); *cf. Re Walsh* [1944] I.R. 22 (lease by guardian). Note the special provison in s. 10 of the Republic's Family Law Act, 1981, dealing with consents by minor spouses required under the Family Home Protection Act, a point to which attention was drawn in *Irish Conveyancing Law* (1978), para. 6.45.

[21] *North Western Rly Co.* v. *McMichael* (1950) 5 Ex. 114 at 123.

[22] *Edwards* v. *Carter* [1893] A.C. 360. See also *Stapleton* v. *Prudential Assurance Co. Ltd.* (1928) 62 I.L.T.R. 56.

[23] *Slator* v. *Brady* (1863) 14 I.C.L.R. 61. *Cf.* the courts' attitude to mere payment or receipt of rent in relation to establishment of a tenancy by estoppel, *O'Connor* v. *Foley* [1906] 1 I.R. 20; *Ashe* v. *Hogan* [1920] 1 I.R. 159. See also *Tickner* v. *Buzzacott* [1965] 1 W.L.R. 154.

[24] *Kelly* v. *Coote* (1857) 2 Ir.Jur.(N.S.) 195; *Slator* v. *Trimble* (1862) 7 Ir.Jur.(N.S.) 255. See also *Milliken* v. *Milliken* (1845) 8 Ir.Eq.R. 16; *Lindsay* v. *Yelverton* (1873) 7 I.L.T.R. 2.

[25] See also the Infant Marriage Act, 1860. *Re Armit's Trusts* (1871) I.R. 5 Eq. 352.

[26] Ante-nuptial or post-nuptial, *Re Sampson and Wall* (1884) 25 Ch.D. 482. *Cf.* where the court has sanctioned the barring of an entail and then the infant dies under age, *Re Scott* [1891] 1 Ch. 298.

[27] *Re Armit's Trusts* (1871) I.R. 5 Eq. 352. It was held in *Re Leigh* (1888) 40 Ch.D. 290 that the court has no power to compel such a settlement to be made.

[28] Age of Majority Act, 1985, s. 8 (R.I.); Age of Majority Act (N.I.), 1969, s. 6.

[29] Succession Act, 1965, s. 77 (1) (*a*).

[30] Age of Majority Act (N.I.), 1969, s. 2.

a soldier in actual military service or a mariner or seaman being at sea.[31] Apart from those cases, there is no provision enabling a married infant to make a will.[32]

II. MARRIED WOMEN

25.09. The position of a married woman has been radically altered in recent decades, so that she is now in general under no disability with respect to holding and disposing of property.[33] It may still be useful to recall briefly the background to the current position.

A. COMMON LAW

25.10. At common law the general rule was that a married woman could not dispose of her own property unless her husband joined in the disposition. An *inter vivos* conveyance of the fee simple was achieved by the cumbersome process of levying a fine,[34] later by execution of a deed under the Fines and Recoveries (Ireland) Act, 1834,[35] in which the husband concurred[36] and which the wife acknowledged "upon examination" to ascertain that she really did agree to the transaction.[37] A married woman had no power to dispose of her freehold property by will, even if her husband concurred.[38] Her husband could dispose of her leasehold property without her concurrence during his lifetime,[39] and her personal property both during his lifetime and on his death.[40]

B. EQUITY

25.11. Equity began to temper the strictness of the common law, from the eighteenth century onwards, by development of the concept of the wife's "separate property."[41] It became established in equity that property conveyed to trustees or the wife's husband for her "separate use" could be dealt with by her as if she were unmarried.[42]

---

[31] Wills Act, 1837, s. 11; Wills (Soldiers and Sailors) Act, 1918. Para. 14.05, *ante*. These provisions have been repealed by the Republic's Succession Act, 1965, s. 8 and 2nd Sched., Pt. III.

[32] One has been recommended, *Survey of the Land Law of Northern Ireland* (1971), para. 352.

[33] Married Women's Status Act, 1957 (R.I.); Law Reform (Husband and Wife) Act (N.I.), 1964; Delany, "The Legal Status of Married Women" (1956) 22 Ir.Jur. 49; Wylie, "Law Reform (Husband and Wife) Act (N.I.), 1964" (1966) 17 N.I.L.Q. 535; (1962) 96 I.L.S.J. 303.

[34] Ch. 4, *ante. Miller* v. *Wheatley* (1891) 28 L.R.Ir. 144.

[35] Para. 4.123, *ante. Lightburne* v. *McEvoy* (1852) 4 Ir.Jur.(o.s.) 179; *Re Smallman's Estate* (1873) I.R. 8 Eq. 249; *Cahill* v. *Cahill* (1883) 8 App. Cas. 420; *Re McIntyre's Trustees' Estate* (1887) 21 L.R.Ir. 421.

[36] The court could dispense with the husband's concurrence if, *e.g.*, he was a lunatic or person of unsound mind, 1834 Act, s. 81.

[37] See Challis, *Law of Real Property* (3rd ed., 1911), pp. 395-6. Also *Darcy* v. *Maddock* (1854) 4 Ir.Ch.R. 40; *Newcomen* v. *Hassard* (1854) 4 Ir.Ch.R. 268; *Adams* v. *Gamble* (1862) 12 Ir.Ch.R. 102; *Bestall* v. *Bunbury* (1862) 13 Ir.Ch.R. 549; *Re Grierson* (1870) I.R. 4 C.L. 232; *Re Lynch* (1880) 4 L.R.Ir. 210; *Re P.* (1898) 32 I.L.T.R. 96.

[38] The Statute of Wills (Ir.), 1634, s. 16, expressly so disabled married women.

[39] *Copinger* v. *Quirk* (1855) 4 I.C.L.R. 444; *Pollok* v. *Kelly* (1856) 6 I.C.L.R. 367; *Donegan* v. *Hibson* (1869) I.R. 3 Eq. 441. The wife's rights revived on his death, *Re Bellamy* (1883) 25 Ch.D. 620.

[40] See the discussion in *Willock* v. *Noble* (1875) L.R. 7 H.L. 580. Also *Box* v. *Box* (1843) 6 Ir.Eq.R. 174.

[41] *Rollfe* v. *Budder* (1724) Bunb. 187; *Bennet* v. *Davis* (1725) 2 P. Wms. 316. Also *Hackett* v. *Farrell* (1842) 4 Ir.Eq.R. 515; *Archer* v. *Rorke* (1845) 7 Ir.Eq.R. 478. See Keeton and Sheridan, *Equity* (1969), ch. xv.

[42] *Burke* v. *Tuite* (1860) Ir.Ch.R. 467; *Re Jenning's Estate* (1868) 2 I.L.T.R. 316; *Hartford* v. *Power* (1869) I.R. 3 Eq. 602; *Redington* v. *O'Connor* (1880) 14 I.L.T.R. 39.

C. Married Women's Property Acts

25.12. The Married Women's Property Act, 1882,[43] extended the equitable concept of a married woman's separate estate by providing that in law a married woman was entitled, from January 1, 1883, to hold and dispose of, as if she were unmarried, all real and personal property belonging to her at the time of her marriage or acquired by her afterwards.[44] This far-reaching provision did not put a married woman entirely in the position of a *feme sole,* for it was held that her liabilities in debt could still be enforced against her to the extent of her separate estate only.[45] Furthermore, an express exception was made to her freedom of disposition where a restraint upon anticipation was imposed by a settlement.[46]

D. Restraints Upon Anticipation

25.13. Having developed the concept of separate property, equity then set about protecting married women from what were regarded as the dangers of their new-found freedom of disposition, *e.g.,* the influence of her husband or her own improvidence. The concept devised by equity was known as a "restraint upon anticipation," which was essentially a restriction on alienation inserted in a conveyance of property to her separate use.[47] Such a restraint, which could operate during coverture only,[48] prevented the married woman from alienating or charging the capital of her estate or future income.[49]

25.14. Subsequently, the courts were given power to remove such restraints and to authorise dispositions of the property, provided the married woman concurred and it was for her benefit.[50] The final step was taken when restraints upon anticipation were abolished altogether in Ireland and their future creation prohibited.[51] The concept of a married woman's "separate" property has also disappeared now and the most recent legislation simply

---

[43] As extended retrospectively by s. 1 of the Married Women's Property Act, 1907. Note also the earlier legislation, *e.g.*, Married Women's Property Act, 1870; and see the Married Women's Property Act, 1893. *Lowry* v. *Derham* [1895] 2 I.R. 123; *Robb* v. *Watson* [1910] 1 I.R. 243.

[44] Ss. 1 and 2. *Re Evan's Estate* [1910] 1 I.R. 95; *O'Malley* v. *O'Malley* (1951) 85 I.L.T.R. 213.

[45] *Scott* v. *Morley* (1887) 20 Q.B.D. 120, applied in *The State (Kingston)* v. *Circuit Court Judge of Cork* [1943] I.R. 611.

[46] 1882, Act, s. 19. See *Re Lumley* [1896] 2 Ch. 690.

[47] Lord Thurlow L.C. played a major part in its development, see *Pybus* v. *Smith* (1791) 3 Bro.C.C. 340 at 344, n. 1; *Parkes* v. *White* (1805) 11 Ves. 209 at 221-2; *Jackson* v. *Hobhouse* (1817) 2 Mer. 483 at 487.

[48] *Re Chrimes* [1917] 1 Ch. 30.

[49] *Doolan* v. *Blake* (1853) 3 Ir.Ch.R. 340.

[50] Originally a restraint upon anticipation could operate against a married woman's property in equity only, but the Married Women's Property Acts enabled it to attach to her "statutory" property owned at law, see Married Women's Property Act, 1882, s. 19; Conveyancing Act, 1911, s. 7. *Lowry* v. *Derham* [1895] 2 I.R. 123. See also Conveyancing Act, 1881, s. 39; Married Women's Property Act, 1893, s. 2. *Re Flood's Trusts* (1883) 11 L.R.Ir. 355; *Re Miller* (1890) 25 L.R.Ir. 107; *Re Tennant's Estate* (1890) 25 L.R.Ir. 522; *Re Sawyer's Trusts* [1896] 1 I.R. 40; *Re Lavender's Policy* [1898] 1 I.R. 175; *Bolster* v. *Bolster* [1916] 1 L.R. 57. Note also the Bankruptcy Act (N.I.), 1929, s. 18, to which there is no equivalent in the Republic.

[51] In the Republic by the Married Women's Status Act, 1957, s. 6. In Northern Ireland the abolition and prohibition occurred, as in England, in two stages, see Law Reform (Miscellaneous Provisions) Act (N.I.), 1937, ss. 9-13 (see O'Neill (1944-6) 6 N.I.L.Q. 131 and 301; (1946-8) 7 N.I.L.Q. 215; (1948-50) 8 N.I.L.Q. 99); Married Women (Restraint upon Anticipation) Act (N.I.), 1952. *Cf.* the English Law Reform (Married Women and Tortfeasors) Act, 1935, and Married Women (Restraint upon Anticipation) Act, 1949.

refers to her "property" which she is free to hold and dispose of as if she were a *feme sole*.[52] If any restriction on her freedom of disposition is to be imposed nowadays, it must be done through a device equally applicable to an unmarried woman or, for that matter, a man, *e.g.,* by a discretionary or protective trust.[53]

E. PROPERTY DISPUTES BETWEEN SPOUSES

25.15. Section 17 of the Married Women's Property Act, 1882, provided a special summary method for determination of property disputes between husband and wife. It enabled either party to a marriage to make a summary application to the county court or High Court for determination of any dispute affecting title to or possession of property and the court could make such order as it thought fit.[54] This provision is now contained in the Republic's Married Women's Status Act, 1957,[55] and has been extended in Northern Ireland by section 3 (3) of the Law Reform (Husband and Wife) Act (N.I.), 1964, to enable the court in such cases to make a money judgment.[56] There has been much controversy in England in recent decades as to the scope of the courts' discretion under section 17, especially concerning how far it enables the courts to vary substantive legal or equitable rights to matrimonial property in accordance with what the courts consider "fair and just" or to confer, for example, an equal right to matrimonial property on a spouse who has not contributed financially to its acquisition, or at least only indirectly, and who would not be entitled under the usual doctrines of property law, such as the presumptions of a resulting trust or advancement.[57] Some English judges took the view that section 17 conferred a very wide-ranging discretion on the courts and appeared to be developing a

---

[52] Married Women's Status Act, 1957; Law Reform (Husband and Wife) Act (N.I.), 1964.

[53] Paras. 9.081 and 9.083, *ante*. Freedom of disposition has been curtailed in the Republic in respect of the family home by the Family Home Protection Act, 1976, as to which see *Irish Conveyancing Law* (1978) paras. 6.31-60. See also Shatter, *Family Law in the Republic of Ireland* (2nd ed., 1981), ch. 15.

[54] *Gaynor* v. *Gaynor* [1901] 1 I.R. 217.

[55] S. 12, extended to engaged couples who break off their engagement by s. 5 of the Family Law Act, 1981.

[56] Previously it was held that the court could not do so on the ground that s. 17 of the 1882 Act was confined to questions relating to "title to or possession of property." See the English *Report of the Royal Commission on Marriage and Divorce* (1956, Cmd. 9678), paras. 601 and 705; also *Tunstall* v. *Tunstall* [1953] 1 W.L.R. 770. Note that in Northern Ireland s. 17 of the 1882 Act has been further extended by Art. 55 of the Matrimonial Causes (N.I.) Order, 1978, to permit applications by either of the parties to a void marriage (whether or not it has been annulled), a voidable marriage (which has been annulled) or a dissolved marriage. Such an application cannot be made, however, more than 3 years after the dissolution or annulment or, in the case of a void marriage which has not been annulled, more than 3 years after the parties have ceased to live with each other in the same household.

[57] See ch. 9, *ante*. Cooney, "Wives, Mistresses and Beneficial Ownership" (1979) 14 Ir.Jur. (N.S.) 1; Palley, "Wives, Creditors and the Matrimonial Home" (1969) 20 N.I.L.Q. 132. In *Re Barnes* (1979) 30 N.I.L.Q. 249, Lowry L.C.J. held that the wife's contributions to purchase of a previous home and the spouses' present one were indirect and unaccompanied by any agreement or arrangement that she should acquire a beneficial interest in either home. See also Gibson, "A Wife's Rights in the Matrimonial Home" (1976) 27 N.I.L.Q. 333; Zuckerman "Ownership of the Matrimonial Home – Common Sense and Reformist Nonsense" (1978) 94 L.Q.R. 26 *Cf.* the positon of a mistress, *Eves* v. *Eves* [1975] 1 W.L.R. 1338; *Tanner* v. *Tanner* [1975] 1 W.L.R. 1346. See also Richards, "The Mistress and the Family Home" (1976) 40 Conv. 351.

concept of "family assets,"[58] whereby, in the event of a dispute between the parties to a marriage, in relation to the family home (even when in the sole name of the husband), its contents and any bank or building society account to which both made lodgments, the only fair and just settlement in many cases would be on the basis of "equality is equity," so that each was owner of a half share.[59] Other judges castigated this as "palm-tree justice" and the House of Lords finally took the view that a more restrictive view had to be taken of the discretion conferred by section 17 of the 1882 Act.[60] The same subject has recently been considered by the Court of Appeal of Northern Ireland in *McFarlane* v. *McFarlane*[61] and, after a review of the English authorities, Lord MacDermott L.C.J. stated that in his view the House of Lords had overruled the notion of "family assets" and the practice of "palm-tree justice."[62] The court held that section 17 of the 1882 Act was procedural only and could not operate to confer on a spouse a beneficial interest he or she did not otherwise have. There must have been a mutual intention on the part of the spouses to create such interest in favour of either of them, *i.e.*, it must arise by virtue of an agreement between them or through a presumption recognised by the law or equity, such as that of a resulting trust.

25.16. *McFarlane* v. *McFarlane* was recently considered in the Republic of Ireland in *Heavey* v. *Heavey,* where Kenny J. stated:

"It seems to me that it is unreal to approach the question of the ownership of or claims for shares in or reimbursement of expenditure on property as between husband and wife when each has made contributions to its purchase or improvement by trying to ascertain what the agreement between them was or what agreement can be implied from their behaviour. Husband and wife do not contemplate dispute or break up of their marriage when they are getting married or when they are living happily together and the arrangements about domestic expenditure and their dealings in property are very informal and are not the result of negotiations between them which result in legal agreements . . . When there is an express agreement the courts must give effect to it, but in the absence of a proved contract I think that the question whether a husband has a claim for improvements carried out to his wife's property should be solved by the application of the flexible concept of a resulting trust

---

[58] See, *e.g.*, the view expressed, especially by Lord Denning in *Re Rogers' Question* [1948] 1 All E.R. 328; *Bendall* v. *McWhirter* [1952] 2 Q.B. 466; *Rimmer* v. *Rimmer* [1953] 1 Q.B. 63; *Cobb* v. *Cobb* [1955] 1 W.L.R. 731; *Short* v. *Short* [1960] 1 W.L.R. 833; *Hine* v. *Hine* [1962] 1 W.L.R. 1124; *Wilson* v. *Wilson* [1963] 2 All E.R. 442; *Rawlings* v. *Rawlings* [1964] P. 398; *Appleton* v. *Appleton* [1965] 1 W.L.R. 25. See also *Toner* v. *Toner* (1972) 23 N.I.L.Q. 208. Miller, "Family Assets" (1970) 86 L.Q.R. 98.

[59] Para. 9.048. *ante.*

[60] *Pettitt* v. *Pettitt* [1970] A.C. 777; *Gissing* v. *Gissing* [1971] A.C. 886. See also *National Provincial Bank Ltd.* v. *Ainsworth* [1965] A.C. 1175. *Cf.* the recent strictures of the English Court of Appeal in *Burns* v. *Burns* [1984] 2 W.L.R. 582. Note, however, the provisions now contained in the English Matrimonial Proceedings and Property Act, 1970, ss. 37-41, *Davis* v. *Vale* [1971] 2 All E.R. 1021; *Kowalczuk* v. *Kowalczuk* [1973] 2 All E.R. 1043; *Griffiths* v. *Griffiths* [1974] 1 All E.R. 932; *Re Nicholson* [1974] 2 All E.R. 386.

[61] [1972] N.I. 59.

[62] *Ibid.*, pp. 66-7. Lord MacDermott followed the principles he enunciated in the *McFarlane* case in *McKeown* v. *McKeown* [1975] N.I. 139. See also Murray J. in *Watters* v. *Watters* (1979) 30 N.I.L.Q. 251.

or constructive trust."[63]

The Supreme Court has recently sounded a strong note of caution against finding a beneficial interest in such cases without clear evidence of an agreement to this affect by the parties or of their intention that such an interest should arise.[64]

III. PERSONS SUFFERING FROM MENTAL DISORDER

25.17. By statutes of the fourteenth century, *De Prerogativa Regis*,[65] custody and management of the lands of "idiots" and "lunatics" lay with the Crown. This jurisdiction came to be exercised by the Lord Chancellor of Ireland[66] and detailed provisions relating to his jurisdiction over the property of persons of unsound mind,[67] as they came to be called, were contained in the Lunacy Regulation (Ir.) Act, 1871.[68] Today this jurisdiction is vested in the President of the High Court of the Republic of Ireland[69] and in the High Court of Northern Ireland.[70]

25.18. The 1871 Act gives the President of the High Court and the Northern Ireland High Court powers to effect sales, leases, mortgages and other dealings with the property of a person of unsound mind for the purposes of paying his debts, maintaining him and similar purposes.[71] In *O'Connell* v. *Harrison*,[72] Kennedy C.J. laid down the general policy and practice followed in the case of such persons' property as follows:

"It is the long-settled policy and practice of the court in administering lunatics' estates to preserve the character of their property as far as possible, and to avoid disturbing the succession to such property. But the policy and practice is always subject to the paramount obligation and duty upon the court to provide for the maintenance and care of the patient out

[63] (1977) III I.L.T.R. 1 at (see *A Casebook on Irish Land Law* (1984), p. 714). The principles enunciated in the *Heavey* case have since been followed in a series of cases decided by the High Court in the Republic, see *C.* v. *C.* [1976] I.R. 254; *B* v. *B.* (1978) Unrep. (H.C.,R.I.) (1977 No. 500 Sp); *M.* v. *M.* (1978) Unrep. (H.C.,R.I.) (1978 No. 155 Sp); *K.* v. *K.* (1978) Unrep. (H.C.,R.I.) (1978 No. 330 Sp); *R.* v. *R.* (1979) Unrep. (H.C.,R.I.) (1978 No. 243 Sp); *McGill* v. *S.* [1979] I.R. 283; *F.G.* v. *F.G.* [1982] I.L.R.M. 155; *N.A.D.* v. *T.D.* [1985] I.L.R.M. 153; *Cf.* the statement of the principles of law by Finlay P. in *W.* v. *W.* [1981] I.L.R.M. 202.

[64] *McC.* v. *McC.* (1984) Unrep. (Sup. Ct., R.I.) (1982/32), thus echoing the approach of the English Court of Appeal in *Burns* v. *Burns* [1984] 2 W.L.R. 582.

[65] Concerning prerogatives of the Crown, which are of uncertain date but were printed as 17 Edw. 2, St. 1, cc. 9 and 10 in Ruffhead's *Statutes* (ed. Runnington 1786).

[66] *Re Earl of Lanesborough* (1826) Beat. 638; *Re McDermott* (1843) 3 Dr. & War. 480; *Re Singleton* (1858) 8 Ir.Ch.R. 263.

[67] In the Republic of Ireland, such persons may now be described as wards of court in certain forms, see Courts (Supplemental Provisions) Act, 1961, s. 9 (4). *Re Dowd* [1960] Ir.Jur.Rep. 64. See also Mental Treatment Act, 1945; Health Act, 1953; Mental Treatment Act, 1961. In Northern Ireland they are described as " patients " under the Mental Health Act (N.I.), 1961. See especially ss. 73-5 of the 1961 Act (N.I.) for the duties of welfare authorities in relation to patients' property. Donaghty, (1965) 16 N.I.L.Q. 426.

[68] See also Lunacy (Ir.) Act, 1901. *Re A.* [1939] N.I. 42; *Re Stuart* [1940] N.I. 30; *Re J.S.* (1941) 75 I.L.T.R. 192; *Re S.* [1943] Ir.Jur.Rep. 76; *Re R.W.T.* [1953–54] Ir.Jur.Rep. 48.

[69] Courts of Justice Act, 1936, s. 9. See also Courts (Supplemental Provisions) Act, 1961, s. 9 (3).

[70] S. 28 (1) of the Judicature (N.I.) Act, 1978, replacing the jurisdiction vested in the Lord Chief Justice by the Irish Free State (Consequential Provisions) Act, 1922, s. 2 and 2nd Sched., Pt. II; S.R. & O. 1921, No. 1802, Art. 2 (3). S. 29 of the 1978 Act provides for the making of rules co-ordinating exercise of the jurisdiction in relation to persons under a disability.

[71] Ss. 60-85. Note also as regards N.I., Mental Health Act, 1959, s. 120 and Sched. 4 (U.K.).

[72] [1927] I.R. 330. See also *Batteste* v. *Maunsell* (1876) I.R. 10 Eq. 314; *Latham* v. *Travers* [1912] 1 I.R. 306; *Kiernan* v. *McGauran* [1922] 1 I.R. 1.

of his means, and to manage and administer his property in his interest and for his benefit."[73]

Where a person of unsound mind is "so found" after judicial "inquisition" under the 1871 Act,[74] he is committed to the care of a "committee," who has general control over his person and property,[75] subject to the overriding supervision of the President or the High Court.[76] The committee can exercise the powers of a tenant for life under the Settled Land Acts, 1882-90.[77] Any attempt to deal with the property under the control of a committee, or under the direct control of a court receiver, without his concurrence is ineffective and the purported transaction is void *ab initio*.[78] Apart from this, the person subject to the mental disorder may become a mental patient admitted to a mental hospital or institution for care and treatment.[79] In Northern Ireland such a person may alternatively be subjected to guardianship.[80]

IV. TRAITORS AND FELONS

25.19. As we saw in an earlier chapter,[81] under the feudal system of tenure introduced into Ireland by the Normans, a person guilty of treason forfeited his land to the Crown[82] and, if guilty of felony, his land escheated to his immediate feudal lord.[83] Attainder of treason was to remain a common method of forfeiture of Irish land to the English Crown for centuries.[84] Then the Forfeiture Act, 1870, abolished forfeiture and escheat of property on conviction or attainder for treason or felony.[85] However, the 1870 Act did provide that a "convict" could not make any disposition of his property during the period of his sentence.[86] Under the 1870 Act, the convict's property vested in an administrator who had general powers to dispose of it.[87] However, in the Republic, since 1922 only interim curators over the property

---

[73] *Ibid.*, p. 338. *Cf.* Bushe C.J. in *Smith* v. *Creagh* (1826) Batty 384 at 408-12.

[74] Ss. 11-48. *Re J.G.M.* (1928) 62 I.L.T.R. 105; *Re M.J.* [1929] I.R. 509; *Re H.M.* [1933] I.R. 383; *Re H.* [1936] Ir.Jur.Rep. 71; *Re Nixon* [1949]Ir.Jur.Rep. 37.

[75] Committees had long had this jurisdiction, see *Re Earl of Lanesborough* (1826) Beat. 638; *Newcombe* v. *Newcombe* (1841) 3 Ir.Eq.R. 414; *Re Crosbie* (1860) 5 Ir.Jur.(N.S.) 257. As regards the 1871 Act, see *Re Lahiff* [1904] 1 I.R. 147; *Latham* v. *Travers* [1912] 1 I.R. 306.

[76] Note, *e.g.*, his duty to report to the President or the High Court on the death of a person of unsound mind, 1871, ss. 51-5.

[77] Settled Land Act, 1882, s. 62, ch. 8, *ante*. *Re Bradbury* (1901) 1 N.I.J.R. 187; *Re D.* [1917] 1 I.R. 344. See also Settled Estates Act, 1877, s. 49 and Leases for Schools (Ir.) Act, 1881, s. 3.

[78] *Re R.* [1941] Ir.Jur.Rep. 67.

[79] See the Republic's Mental Treatment Acts, 1945, ss. 102-3 and 1961, ss. 2-3; Mental Health Act (N.I.), 1961, ss. 12-20 and 24-36 (see also s. 73 concerning duty of welfare authorities in relation to patients' property).

[80] Mental Health Act (N.I.), 1961, ss. 21-3. Note the power of the court to order hospital admission or guardianship, ss. 48-53.

[81] Ch. 2, *ante*.

[82] See also the Treason Act, 1351, 25 Edw. 3, stat. 5, c. 2; Crown of Ireland Act, 1542, s. 2, 33 Hen. 8, c. 1 (Ir.). *Marquis of Ormonde* v. *Bishop of Cashel* (1848) 10 Ir.L.R. 577.

[83] Para. 2.24, *ante*.

[84] Para. 1.30, *ante*. R. v. *Tandy* (1810) Rowe 472; *Grace* v. *Bishop of Ossory* (1848) 12 Ir.L.R. 128.

[85] S. 1. See also Criminal Law Act (N.I.), 1967, ss. 7 (7), 15 and Sched. 2, Pt. II.

[86] S. 8.

[87] Ss. 9, 10 and 12. See also ss. 21-6 relating to appointment of an interim curator pending appointment of an administrator. *Woods* v. *Att.-Gen.* (1974) unrep. (H.C., R.I.).

of convicts have been appointed by district courts and the practice of appointing an administrator has become obsolete. These disabilities for convicts remain in force in the Republic of Ireland,[88] but they have been swept away in Northern Ireland, where a convict is now free to deal with his property in the normal way, using agents where necessary.[89]

V. ALIENS

25.20. At common law an alien could not hold land and any attempt to convey land to one resulted in forfeiture to the Crown.[90] Various minor exceptions to this rule were allowed[91] until the Naturalisation Act, 1870, provided that an alien could hold, acquire and dispose of real and personal property just as a natural-born subject could.[92] The 1870 Act was later replaced by the Status of Aliens Act, 1914, which still governs the matter in Northern Ireland.[93] In the Republic of Ireland the matter is now governed by the Aliens Act, 1935.[94]

VI. CORPORATIONS

25.21. The extent to which a corporation can hold and dispose of land is governed in general by its articles and memorandum of association.[95] In the case of corporations established by statute or charter the matter is governed by the terms of the statute or charter.[96] The Ecclesiastical Lands Act (Ireland) 1634,[97] restricted the dispositions of land which can be made by ecclesiastical persons and governors of colleges and hospitals.[98]

Until quite recent times gifts of land to corporations could be caught by the "mortmain" restrictions, unless the particular corporation was excepted by statute or Crown licence.[99] The mortmain restrictions have now been repealed in both parts of Ireland,[1] and corporations are no longer under such a disability.

---

[88] See, *e.g.*, Statute of Limitations, 1957, s. 48 (1) (*c*).

[89] Criminal Justice Act, 1953, ss. 9 (1), 10, 29 and Sched. 3.

[90] *Coke upon Littleton* (19th ed., 1832), 2b and 117a. *Dumoncel* v. *Dumoncel* (1848) 13 Ir.Eq.R. 92; *cf. In b. Chateauvillard* (1863) 8 Ir.Jur.(N.S.) 197.

[91] *E.g.*, Aliens Act, 1844, s. 5 (friendly aliens holding short leases).

[92] S. 2.

[93] S. 17. See also the British Nationality Act, 1948, s. 34 and Sched. 4, Pt. II.

[94] S. 2. See also the Irish Nationality and Citizenship Act, 1956.

[95] See also Companies Act, 1963, ss. 11-16 and 37-41 (R.I.); Companies Act (N.I.), 1960, ss. 6-11 and 32-6.

[96] *Page* v. *R.* (1792) 2 Ridgw.P.C. 445; *Att.-Gen.* v. *Corporation of Cashel* (1843) 3 Dr. & War. 294; *Att.-Gen.* v. *College of Physicians in Ireland* (1863) 9 Ir.Jur.(N.S.) 362; *Industrial Development Authority* v. *Moran* [1976] I.R. 159 (see *A Casebook on Irish Land Law* (1984), p. 419) (also para. 11.33, *ante*). See also Municipal Corporations (Ir.) Acts, 1840, ss. 140–2; 1843, ss. 7 and 8; 1860, ss. 3–5 and 9. *Att.-Gen.* v. *Corporation of Dublin* (1849) 12 Ir.Eq.R. 465; *Att.-Gen* v. *Belfast Corporation* (1855) 4 Ir.Ch.R. 119; *Att.-Gen* v. *Ball* (1846) 10 Ir.Eq.R. 146; *Att.-Gen* v. *Marrett* (1846) 10 Ir.Eq.R. 167; *Keyland* v. *Corporation of Belfast* (1857) 6 Ir.Ch.R. 161; *Steeven's Hospital* v. *Dyas* (1864) 15 Ir.Ch.R. 405.

[97] 10 & 11 Chas. 1, c. 3 (Ir.). *Att.-Gen.* v. *Flood* (1816) Hayes 611. This statute was recommended for repeal in Northern Ireland, *Survey of the Land Law of Northern Ireland* (1971), see Property Bill (N.I.), 5th Sched., App. B., and was repealed by the Property (N.I.) Order, 1978, Art. 16 (2) and Sched. 2.

[98] *Cf.* Irish Universities Act, 1908, s. 9. See also University Education (Agriculture and Dairy Science) Act, 1926, ss. 8 and 14-15 (R.I.); New Universities (Acquisition of Land) Act (N.I.), 1966.

[99] Ch. 2, *ante*. *Incorporated Society for Protestant Schools in Ireland* v. *Richards* (1841) 1 Dr. & War. 258.

[1] Mortmain (Repeal of Enactments) Act, 1954 (R.I.); Mortmain (Repeals) Act (N.I.), 1960.

VII. CHARITIES

25.22. The general position of charities in our law was considered in an earlier chapter and little need be added here.[2] The restriction on "death-bed" dispositions of land to charities contained in section 16 of the Charitable Donations and Bequests (Ireland) Act, 1844, has been repealed in both parts of Ireland.[3] With respect to land held by charities in Ireland, various dispositions may be authorised by, in the Republic, the Commissioners of Charitable Donations and Bequests,[4] or, in Northern Ireland, the Department of Finance,[5] or, in either part of Ireland, the court.[6] By section 2 of the Inalienable Lands Act (N.I.), 1966, this power of the Department of Finance now extends to charity land rendered inalienable by any public or local or private statute.[7] In the Republic of Ireland, the Commissioners have recently been given further powers to frame schemes in relation to charity property where, by reason of the statute or charter establishing or regulating the charity in question, the powers given by such scheme would not otherwise be within those exercisable in relation to that property.[8]

---

[2] Ch. 9, *ante.*
[3] Charities Act, 1961, s. 4 and Sched. (R.I.); Charities Act (N.I.), 1964, s. 37 and Sched.
[4] Charities Act, 1961, s. 34, as substituted by s. 11 of the Charities Act, 1973.
[5] Charities Act (N.I.), 1964, s. 18. See *Re Steele* [1976] N.I. 66.
[6] 1961 Act, s. 51; 1964 Act, s. 29.
[7] Excluding land held inalienably by the National Trust for Places of Historic Interest or Natural Beauty.
[8] Charities Act, 1973, s. 4. Note also s. 6 relating to cases where the reversioner of a lease made under the Leases for Schools (Ir.) Act, 1881, or other lease for a charitable purpose, is unknown or cannot be found.

INDEX

[*N.B.* References in this Index are to *paragraph* numbers.]